FOOTBALL
YEARBOOK
2003-4 DAVID GOLDBLATT

THE COMPLETE GUIDE TO THE WORLD GAME

LONDON, NEW YORK, MUNICH, MELBOURNE, DELHI

Dorling Kindersley

Project Designer Purple Carol

Project Editors Sam Atkinson, Margaret Hynes

Digital Cartography and Graphics
Peter Winfield

Editorial and Design Assistance
Victoria Clark, Michelle Crane, Louise Dick,
Wim Jenkins, Simon Mumford, Julie Turner

Systems Co-ordinator Philip Rowles

Production Louise Daly

Jacket Designer Nicola Powling

Jacket Copywriter Beth Apple

Project Manager David Roberts

Senior Managing Art Editor Philip Lord

Editorial Director Andrew Heritage

Art Director Bryn Walls

Produced for Dorling Kindersley by designsection

Caxton Road, Frome, Somerset, BA11 1DY

Project Editors Julian Flanders
Louise Cassell

Senior Designer Kathie Wilson

Editorial and Design Assistance
Helen Burge, Nick Heal, Sue Lee,
Sandra Morgan, Craig Stevens

www.designsection.com

Index by Indexing Specialists (UK) Ltd

Digital Cartography and Graphics
Encompass Graphics Limited
Tom Coulson, Martin Darlison
www.encompass-graphics.co.uk

First published in Great Britain as the *World Football Yearbook 2002-3*
by Dorling Kindersley Ltd, 80 Strand, London WC2R 0RL
A Penguin Company

2 4 6 8 10 9 7 5 3

A CIP catalogue record for this book is available from the British Library.

ISBN: 0-4043-0053-1

Printed and bound in the UK by Butler & Tanner Limited, Frome and London

See our complete catalogue at
www.dk.com

Contents

Foreword

'There is absolutely no question… that the world turns around a spinning ball.'
Eduardo Galeano

AND SO IT DOES. WHAT OTHER CULTURAL PHENOMENON has demanded the world's attention so insistently? The fifth Harry Potter novel, the fastest-selling book in history, sold nearly two million copies in a week, yet European football alone sells more seats each weekend and offers the audience considerably less than the novel's nearly 800 pages of magical adventure. Does any film star, musician or artist command the attention of the world's press like David Beckham?

But football does not have its own way all the time. The gravitational pull of the world remains inescapable. War and conflict have shaped the schedules of Western Asia and the Middle East. Disease and epidemic has cast its shadow over the Far East as summer tours and the Champions Cup have been cancelled. Economic decline has squeezed the clubs of South America and Eastern Europe to breaking point; while Western European football has tried to cope with the demands of excess. To map the contours of world football, to record its sporting feats and to tell its stories remains a brilliant window on the shape of the world.

Welcome to the Football Yearbook 2003–4, now in its second year of publication. While readers of last year's edition will find much that is familiar, we are pleased to announce that there is also much that has changed and much that is new in this year's updated and revised edition. Almost every single page in the book has been revisited in some way or another. Any errors of judgement and (occasionally) fact from last year have been adjusted and all data has been updated to take account of another global season. Additional details have been added to many of the football city maps. So, for example, for those of you who missed and wanted to see Benfica's early stadiums before they settled at the Estadio da Luz in Lisbon in 1954, your wish has now been granted.

We have added 32 new pages to this year's edition. For England, we have added 16 pages that cover the whole of the 2002–03 English football season, including the top four divisions, the fortunes of the national team, as well as the cup competitions in more detail. You will also find much greater coverage of the seasons in France, Germany, Italy and Spain as well as more extensive coverage of the European Champions League. There is also additional coverage and overviews of the seasons in Asia, CONCACAF and South America. Finally, we have added a new football city spread covering the North East of England.

In last year's book I apologised in advance for crass errors and asked readers to send us corrections and concerns. I am delighted to say that many of you did so and have saved our blushes. Many, many thanks to you all. Please keep them coming.

David Goldblatt

Introduction

IN DECEMBER 2002, REAL MADRID signed off its centenary year by winning its third World Club Cup. They beat Copa Libertadores champions, Olimpia of Paraguay, 2-0 in the Yokohama World Cup stadium. Champions of Europe and now champions of the world, Real Madrid has dominated this season.

Construction magnate and Real president Florentine Perez continued Real's strategy of buying the best and most marketable players on the planet by luring Ronaldo from Internazionale for £30 million at the end of the season. Although the team struggled in the first half of the Spanish season, it won the world's most competitive league on the final day. In the Champion's League, Real was beaten by Juventus in the semi-finals but played, without doubt, the most scintillating, expressive, attacking football on the planet. As the merchandise sales and prize money rolled in Real Madrid became the richest club in the world, overhauling Manchester United.

Finally, as the season closed, Perez revealed the new balance of power and glamour by capturing Manchester United's David Beckham for a mere £25 million. Not content with that spectacular raid on Manchester, he went back for Carlos Queiroz, Sir Alex Ferguson's number two, who will start the 2003–04 season as Real's coach. Whether Beckham was the best player in the world not already at Real is a moot point; he is, unquestionably, the most marketable, especially in Asia where Real's appeal has, so far, been limited. With nine out of ten Japanese knowing Beckham's name and the Castrol Oil company signing him up for a huge Asian promotional tour, the transfer made clear the already implicit strategy at Madrid; that Real Madrid must be the best and the biggest football club – not merely in its Spanish-speaking strongholds, but globally. But for the less well placed – and that means 99 per cent of global football – it was a year of financial constraints, diminished transfer markets and occasional bankruptcies.

It was, by contrast, a quiet year for FIFA. Bidding opened for the right to host the 2010 World Cup, and a clear indication was given that the 2014 tournament will go to South America. It is transparent that no one has the facilities or money in South America to contemplate a realistic bid except Brazil. But in

Africa the contest will be between favourites South Africa and four North African states – Morocco, Tunisia, Libya and Egypt. Nigeria's last minute bid has already been effectively dismissed.

After retaining his FIFA presidency in a bitter election last year, Sepp Blatter has kept a relatively low profile. Opponents have departed from FIFA HQ and Blatter has announced that he will go in 2006. South American attempts to expand the number of teams at the 2006 World Cup have been deflected and no one needs to lose any sleep over whether the Germans will be ready to host the tournament; they are, in fact, ahead of schedule.

Above: Florentino Perez, President of Real Madrid, and multi-millionaire construction magnate. Perez's business acumen has guided Real's transfer strategy and global branding, helping turn it into the world's richest club this year.

Below: The race for 2010. With Africa guaranteed the World Cup in 2010, national bids started rolling in. South Africa are the favourites over Morocco, Libya, Tunisia, Egypt and Nigeria. Here the head of the South African bidding committee, Danny Jordan (left) and South African FA President and Vice President Molefi Oliphant (centre) and Irvine Khoza (right) get serious.

Top, left: *Real Madrid celebrates its victory in the World Club Cup 2002 and the culmination of its centenary year.*

Top, right: *Real's Zinedine Zidane and Olimpia's Julio Cesar Caceres fight for the ball as the two sides contest the 2002 World Club Cup in Yokohama, Tokyo.*

Left: *You won't be seeing this again. David Beckham in his final season for Manchester United. The alice band in his hair makes sure everyone can see the cut from Ferguson's flying boot – one among many issues that saw Beckham transferred to Real Madrid. Although Barcelona offered £30 million, United had to accept the player's wishes and take £25 million from Real. It may yet be the bargain of the decade.*

Above: *The power and the glory in world football, lining up for a World Cup 2006 press conference. Back row, the power, from left to right: Franz Beckenbauer, Eugenio Figueredo (CONMEBOL Vice President), Pele, Sepp Blatter (President of FIFA) and Lennart Johansson (President of UEFA). Front row, the glory, from left to right: the Copa Libertadores, the UEFA Cup, the European Cup, the World Cup and the Copa América.*

**WORLD CLUB CUP
2002 FINAL**

December 3 – Yokohama, Japan
Real **2-0** Olimpia
Madrid   (Paraguay)
(Spain)
(Ronaldo 14,
Guti 84)

h/t : 1-0 **Att:** 66,070
Ref: Carlos Simon (Brazil)

England

SEASON OVERVIEW

IF THE 2001–02 SEASON had laid bare the economic fragility and irresponsibility of English football, 2002–03 let us in on the precise balance of political power in the game. In a move of breathtaking political astuteness and narrowness of vision the Premiership chairman and his allies within the FA eased Adam Crozier, the FA's chief executive, out of his job and left the post effectively unfilled for six months. Crozier was unquestionably the most competent, focused administrator to walk into the FA since C.W. Alcock. He was just too good at his job and too busy representing the interests of the national team and the wider game; which is, of course, his official remit.

Stern warning

The England team proved to be multi-faceted. In friendlies the team were sharp against Portugal, laughably uncompetitive against Australia and tired but superior in South Africa. In the Euro 2004 qualifying campaign they dug in against a hostile and often racist crowd to win in Slovakia, but looked nervier and more disorganised against the less challenging Macedonia when they dropped vital points. A laborious 2-0 victory over Liechtenstein was achieved with few problems but in the key game of the year against Turkey at Sunderland, they produced by far their best performance. However, the recent history of trouble between English and Turkish fans during European games provided sufficient pretext for a display of threats and intimidation by a couple of hundred people outside the stadium, and extensive arrests followed. A pitch invasion to celebrate Darius Vassell's 75th-minute goal saw UEFA issue their sternest warnings in a long time to the FA over fans' conduct and the future participation of England in the competition.

England's trip to South Africa saw David Beckham break a wrist bone and retire from the pitch to attend to his moving plans. In his absence a late Joe Cole strike saw England beat Serbia in a friendly. But a lamentable first-half performance against Slovakia left them 1-0 down. In a copy of their earlier encounter in the Euro 2004 qualifying campaign, England won 2-1. Michael Owen's guile won a penalty and his cool head drove Steven Gerard's pinpoint cross home to give England the winner. Automatic qualification remains in England and its fans' hands.

ENGLAND FRIENDLIES

Sept 7, 2002 – Villa Park, Birmingham
England 1-1 Portugal
(Smith 39)   (Costinha 79)
h/t : 1-0 Att: 40,058
Ref: Ovrebo (Norway)

Feb 12, 2003 – Upton Park, London
England 1-3 Australia
(Jeffers 69)   (Popovic 11,
    Kewell 41,
    Emerton 85)
h/t : 0-2 Att: 34,590
Ref: Menjuto Gonzalez (Spain)

May 22, 2003 – Durban, South Africa
South Africa 1-2 England
(McCarthy 18 pen)   (Southgate 1,
    Heskey 64)
h/t : 1-1 Att: 52,000
Ref: Lim Kee Chong (Mauritius)

June 3, 2003, Walker's Bowl, Leicester
England 2-1 Serbia &
(Gerrard 35,   Montenegro
J. Cole 82)   (Jestrovic 45)
h/t : 1-1 Att: 30,000
Ref: Paul Allaerts (Belgium)

Too good at his job. The FA's Chief Executive Adam Crozier leaves his job after being sacked by the Premiership. Football's loss is the Royal Mail's gain.

In 2002–03 Sven Goran Eriksson discovered the nasty underbelly of the English press.

From Devon to Rio they're celebrating Yeovil Town's dominance of the Conference and its elevation to the Football League.

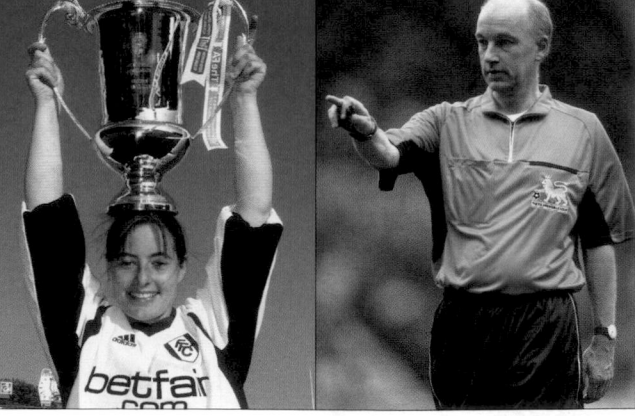

Above, left: Kim Jerray-Silver raises the Women's Premier League Cup after Fulham beat Arsenal in the Final. The team's joy was short-lived as the FA's plans for a professional women's league collapsed again.

Above, right: The housemaster bows out. David Elleray retired from top-flight refereeing after Newcastle beat Birmingham in April. His record: 1,708 games, 2,064 cautions and 246 dismissals. Birmingham City's Matthew Upson was his last sending off.

EURO 2004 QUALIFYING ROUND GROUP STAGE

Oct 12, 2002 – Bratislava, Slovakia
Slovakia **1-2** England
(Nemeth 24)   *(Beckham 65,*
                    Owen 82)

h/t : 1-0 **Att:** 30,000
Ref: Messina (Italy)

Oct 16, 2002 – St Mary's, Southampton
England **2-2** Macedonia
(Beckham 14,   *(Sakiri 11,*
Gerrard 36)   *Trajanov 24)*

h/t : 2-2 **Att:** 32,095
Ref: Dauden Ibanez (Spain)

Mar 29, 2003 – Rheinpark Stadium,
Vaduz, Liechtenstein
Liechtenstein **0-2** England
                    (Owen 28,
                    Beckham 53)

h/t : 1-0 **Att:** 3,548
Ref: Kasnaferis (Greece)

April 2, 2003 – Stadium of Light,
Sunderland
England **2-0** Turkey
(Vassell 75,
Beckham
90 pen)

h/t : 0-0 **Att:** 47,667
Ref: Meier (Switzerland)

June 11, 2003 – Riverside,
Middlesbrough
England **2-1** Slovakia
(Owen 62 pen,   *(Janocko 31)*
73)

h/t : 0-1 **Att:** 35,000
Ref: Wolfgang Stark (Germany)

GROUP 7

CLUB	P	W	D	L	F	A	Pts	
Turkey	6	5	0	1	14	5	**15**	Qualification position
England	5	4	1	0	10	4	**13**	Play-off position
Slovakia	6	2	0	4	8	8	**6**	
Macedonia	6	1	2	3	9	11	**5**	
Liechtenstein	5	0	1	4	2	15	**1**	

Top team qualifies automatically, second-placed team goes into a play-off.

Below: After the pitch invasion when England played Turkey in April, UEFA issued its sternest warning yet to the FA over crowd behaviour and England's continued participation in Euro 2004.

Bottom: Wayne Rooney cuts the Turkish midfield apart. The 17-year-old striker showed what he is capable of at the highest level with his pace, urgency and directness.

The Premier League

SEASON REVIEW

IN ANOTHER YEAR in which Premiership football has tried to defy the economic logic of capitalism by running unsustainable wage bills and stacking up unbelievable levels of debt, sporting logic was also under attack. Arsène Wenger argued that the best team did not win the league. On its day Arsenal was sublime, Thierry Henry graced the nation with a display of balletic movement and insouciant brilliance. But there were just not enough of those days, and hardly any in the final quarter of the season. Manchester United ground Arsenal's eight-point lead into the dust, of which Ruud van Nistelrooy's relentless, charging goalscoring run was emblematic. Sporting logic, at least, retains a precarious place in the league and Newcastle, Chelsea and Liverpool duly secured European places, as did Blackburn, lifted by the management of Graeme Souness and the running of Damien Duff.

Limited logic

But there are limits to logic. Everton, Manchester City and Southampton all performed above themselves; while Tottenham, Middlesbrough and Charlton did not. Fulham's indolence and Birmingham's grit, leavened by the style of Christoph Dugarry, made the two teams inseparable. Aston Villa wouldn't spend money, lost its manager and ended up in the bottom six; Leeds spent too much money, lost another manager, and ended up in the bottom six. Bolton and West Ham duelled for the final safe spot for the last four months of the season. West Ham's Glenn Roeder succumbed to the heart condition his touchline demeanour had been promising all season, and a late rally under Trevor Brooking could not save them. At least West Bromwich and Sunderland settled their fates early. The former was predictably gallant and predictably outclassed, while Sunderland, pinned to the bottom, played without heart, hope or plan and recorded a dismal 19 points. The logic of this was plain to all except the bemused Howard Wilkinson.

Final Premier League Table 2002–03

CLUB	P	W	D	L	F	A	Pts	
Manchester United	38	25	8	5	74	34	**83**	Champions League
Arsenal	38	23	9	6	85	44	**78**	Champions League
Newcastle United	38	21	6	11	63	48	**69**	Champions League
Chelsea	38	19	10	9	68	38	**67**	Champions League
Liverpool	38	18	10	10	61	41	**64**	UEFA Cup
Blackburn Rovers	38	16	12	10	52	43	**60**	UEFA Cup
Everton	38	17	8	13	48	49	**59**	
Southampton	38	13	13	12	43	46	**52**	UEFA Cup
Manchester City	38	15	6	17	47	54	**51**	UEFA Cup (Fair Play)
Tottenham Hotspur	38	14	8	16	51	62	**50**	
Middlesbrough	38	13	10	15	48	44	**49**	
Charlton Athletic	38	14	7	17	35	49	**49**	
Birmingham City	38	13	9	16	41	49	**48**	
Fulham	38	13	9	16	41	50	**48**	
Leeds United	38	14	5	19	58	57	**47**	
Aston Villa	38	12	9	17	42	47	**45**	
Bolton Wanderers	38	10	14	14	42	51	**44**	
West Ham United	38	10	12	16	42	59	**42**	Relegated
West Bromwich Albion	38	6	8	24	29	65	**26**	Relegated
Sunderland	38	4	7	27	21	65	**19**	Relegated

Promoted clubs: Portsmouth, Leicester City, Wolverhampton Wanderers.

Top Goalscorers 2002–03

PLAYER	CLUB	NATIONALITY	GOALS
Ruud van Nistelrooy	Manchester United	Dutch	25
Thierry Henry	Arsenal	French	24
James Beattie	Southampton	English	23

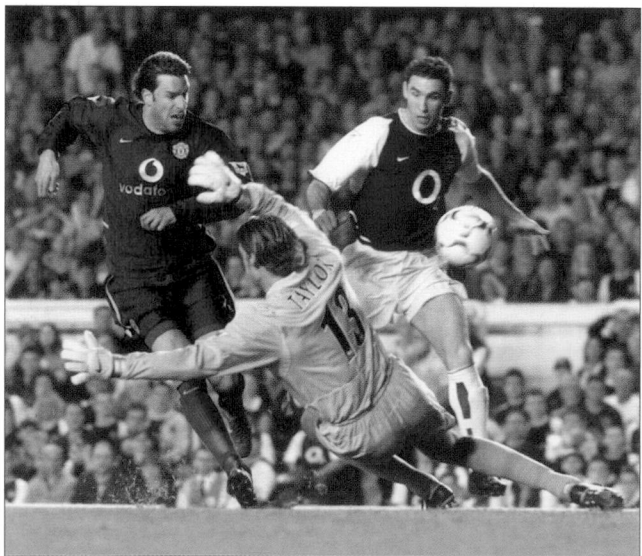

Ruud van Nistelrooy slots the ball past Arsenal's Stuart Taylor in a thrilling 2-2 draw at Highbury in April, which earned United a psychological advantage against Arsène Wenger's men.

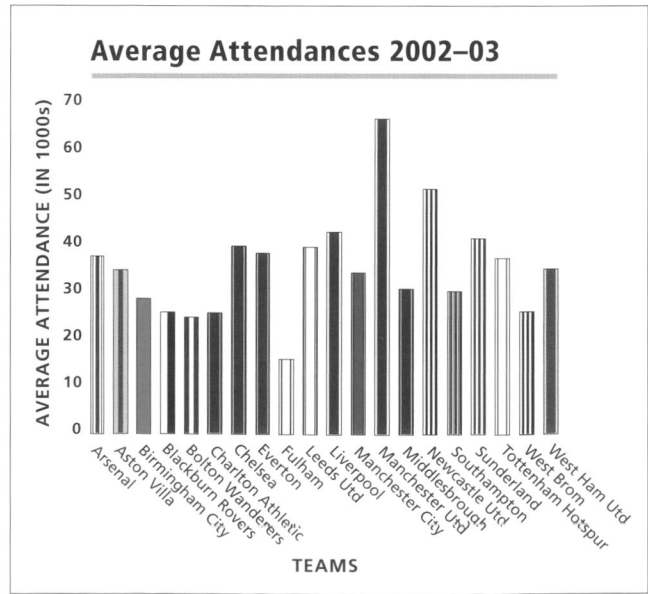

Average Attendances 2002–03

AVERAGE ATTENDANCE (IN 1000s)

TEAMS

Arsenal, Aston Villa, Birmingham City, Blackburn Rovers, Bolton Wanderers, Charlton Athletic, Chelsea, Everton, Fulham, Leeds Utd, Liverpool, Manchester Utd, Manchester City, Middlesbrough, Newcastle Utd, Southampton, Sunderland, Tottenham Hotspur, West Brom, West Ham Utd

ENGLAND

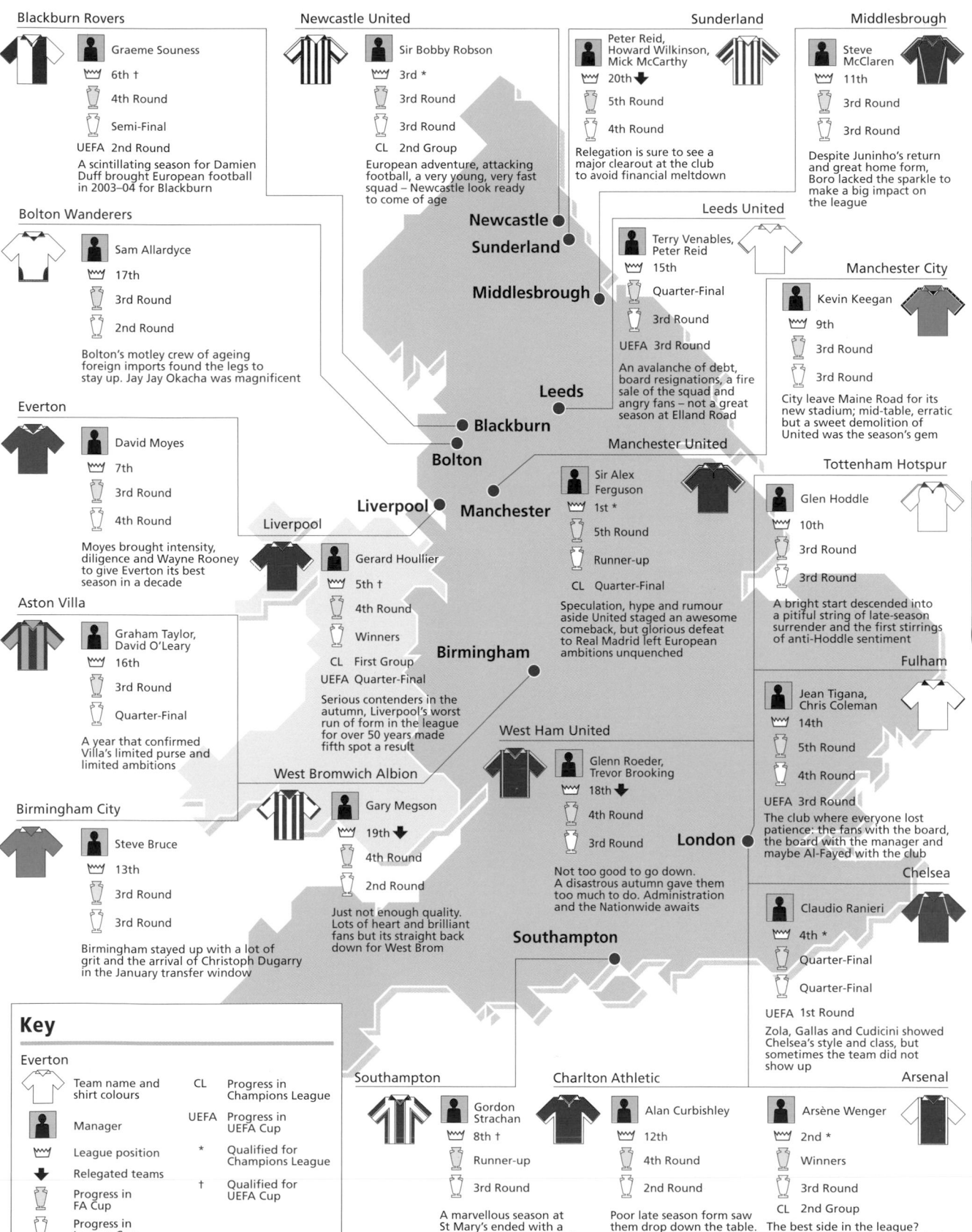

Blackburn Rovers

Graeme Souness
6th †
4th Round
Semi-Final
UEFA 2nd Round

A scintillating season for Damien Duff brought European football in 2003–04 for Blackburn

Newcastle United

Sir Bobby Robson
3rd *
3rd Round
3rd Round
CL 2nd Group

European adventure, attacking football, a very young, very fast squad – Newcastle look ready to come of age

Sunderland

Peter Reid, Howard Wilkinson, Mick McCarthy
20th ↓
5th Round
4th Round

Relegation is sure to see a major clearout at the club to avoid financial meltdown

Middlesbrough

Steve McClaren
11th
3rd Round
3rd Round

Despite Juninho's return and great home form, Boro lacked the sparkle to make a big impact on the league

Bolton Wanderers

Sam Allardyce
17th
3rd Round
2nd Round

Bolton's motley crew of ageing foreign imports found the legs to stay up. Jay Jay Okacha was magnificent

Leeds United

Terry Venables, Peter Reid
15th
Quarter-Final
3rd Round
UEFA 3rd Round

An avalanche of debt, board resignations, a fire sale of the squad and angry fans – not a great season at Elland Road

Manchester City

Kevin Keegan
9th
3rd Round
3rd Round

City leave Maine Road for its new stadium; mid-table, erratic but a sweet demolition of United was the season's gem

Everton

David Moyes
7th
3rd Round
4th Round

Moyes brought intensity, diligence and Wayne Rooney to give Everton its best season in a decade

Manchester United

Sir Alex Ferguson
1st *
5th Round
Runner-up
CL Quarter-Final

Speculation, hype and rumour aside United staged an awesome comeback, but glorious defeat to Real Madrid left European ambitions unquenched

Tottenham Hotspur

Glen Hoddle
10th
3rd Round
3rd Round

A bright start descended into a pitiful string of late-season surrender and the first stirrings of anti-Hoddle sentiment

Aston Villa

Graham Taylor, David O'Leary
16th
3rd Round
Quarter-Final

A year that confirmed Villa's limited purse and limited ambitions

Liverpool

Gerard Houllier
5th †
4th Round
Winners
CL First Group
UEFA Quarter-Final

Serious contenders in the autumn, Liverpool's worst run of form in the league for over 50 years made fifth spot a result

Fulham

Jean Tigana, Chris Coleman
14th
5th Round
4th Round
UEFA 3rd Round

The club where everyone lost patience: the fans with the board, the board with the manager and maybe Al-Fayed with the club

Birmingham City

Steve Bruce
13th
3rd Round
3rd Round

Birmingham stayed up with a lot of grit and the arrival of Christoph Dugarry in the January transfer window

West Bromwich Albion

Gary Megson
19th ↓
4th Round
2nd Round

Just not enough quality. Lots of heart and brilliant fans but its straight back down for West Brom

West Ham United

Glenn Roeder, Trevor Brooking
18th ↓
4th Round
3rd Round

Not too good to go down. A disastrous autumn gave them too much to do. Administration and the Nationwide awaits

Chelsea

Claudio Ranieri
4th *
Quarter-Final
Quarter-Final
UEFA 1st Round

Zola, Gallas and Cudicini showed Chelsea's style and class, but sometimes the team did not show up

Southampton

Gordon Strachan
8th †
Runner-up
3rd Round

A marvellous season at St Mary's ended with a place in the FA Cup Final

Charlton Athletic

Alan Curbishley
12th
4th Round
2nd Round

Poor late season form saw them drop down the table. Scott Parker remains the heart of a tireless squad

Arsenal

Arsène Wenger
2nd *
Winners
3rd Round
CL 2nd Group

The best side in the league? Sublime attack let down by a leaky defence and unparalleled hubris

Map labels: Newcastle, Sunderland, Middlesbrough, Leeds, Blackburn, Bolton, Liverpool, Manchester, Birmingham, London, Southampton

ENGLAND

Key

Everton

Team name and shirt colours

Manager

League position

Relegated teams

Progress in FA Cup

Progress in League Cup

CL Progress in Champions League

UEFA Progress in UEFA Cup

* Qualified for Champions League

† Qualified for UEFA Cup

Division One

SEASON REVIEW

THE FIRST DIVISION PROVIDED some clear parallels with the Premiership this season, at a fraction of the cost. The championship was always a two-horse race between Portsmouth and Leicester. The race for play-offs went to the likely contenders at the halfway stage. Two clubs looked doomed all year – Sheffield Wednesday and Grimsby – while two clubs making a late surge fought it out to the final day. Stoke escaped and Brighton was back down to the Second Division after a just a year in the First.

Smart move

At Portsmouth, chairman Milan Mandaric has achieved his promise of four years ago to take the club into the Premiership – the club's first season in the top flight for 15 years. Perhaps his smartest move was to lure Harry Redknapp from his south coast mansion where he had retreated after his surprise departure from West Ham. Redknapp made his usual visit to the transfer market and fashioned a side around the ageing but undimmed talents of Paul Merson, Svetoslav Todorov, Steve Stone and Gianlucca Festa. Leicester nearly went out of business as it failed to cope with relegation from the Premiership. The club went into administration only to emerge with settled debts, new owners, a new ground and new manager – Micky Adams – and played reliable if unadventurous winning football. Both clubs know that was the easy bit. The bearpit awaits.

Sheffield United confirmed its status as comeback experts, when, in the second leg of its semi-final play-off, it went two goals behind, then scored four. Wolves just had too much for Reading and in the end too much for Sheffield. A goal in the sixth minute of the Final steadied the nerves, and two more followed. Sheffield pressed to the end, but a missed penalty and a goal lost to a handball on the line summed up the team's day.

Portsmouth manager Harry Redknapp, more relieved than elated, shakes hands with Burnley boss Stan Ternent as Portsmouth secures promotion to the Premiership. The more ebullient Jim Smith (behind) gives praise and thanks.

Final Division One Table 2002–03

CLUB	P	W	D	L	F	A	Pts	
Portsmouth	46	29	11	6	97	45	**98**	Champions – promoted
Leicester City	46	26	14	6	73	40	**92**	Runners-up – promoted
Sheffield United	46	23	11	12	72	52	**80**	Play-offs
Reading	46	25	4	17	61	46	**79**	Play-offs
Wolverhampton Wanderers	46	20	16	10	81	44	**76**	Play-offs – promoted
Nottingham Forest	46	20	14	12	82	50	**74**	Play-offs
Ipswich Town	46	19	13	14	80	64	**70**	
Norwich City	46	19	12	15	60	49	**69**	
Millwall	46	19	9	18	59	69	**66**	
Wimbledon	46	18	11	17	76	73	**65**	
Gillingham	46	16	14	16	56	65	**62**	
Preston North End	46	16	13	17	68	70	**61**	
Watford	46	17	9	20	54	70	**60**	
Crystal Palace	46	14	17	15	59	52	**59**	
Rotherham United	46	15	14	17	62	62	**59**	
Burnley	46	15	10	21	65	89	**55**	
Walsall	46	15	9	22	57	69	**54**	
Derby County	46	15	7	24	55	74	**52**	
Bradford City	46	14	10	22	51	73	**52**	
Coventry City	46	12	14	20	46	62	**50**	
Stoke City	46	12	14	20	45	69	**50**	
Sheffield Wednesday	46	10	16	20	56	73	**46**	Relegated
Brighton & Hove Alb	46	11	12	23	49	67	**45**	Relegated
Grimsby Town	46	9	12	25	48	85	**39**	Relegated

Promoted clubs: Wigan Athletic, Crewe Alexandra, Cardiff City.

Promotion Play-off Matches

SEMI-FINALS
Nottingham Forest **1-1, 3-4** (aet)(2 legs) Sheffield United
Sheffield United won 5-4 on aggregate
Wolverhampton Wanderers **2-1, 1-0** (2 legs) Reading
Wolverhampton Wanderers won 3-1 on aggregate

FINAL
Wolverhampton Wanderers **3-0** Sheffield United

Top Goalscorers 2002–03

PLAYER	CLUB	NATIONALITY	GOALS
Svetoslav Todorov	Portsmouth	Bulgarian	26
David Johnson	Nottingham Forest	English	25
David Connolly	Wimbledon	Irish	24

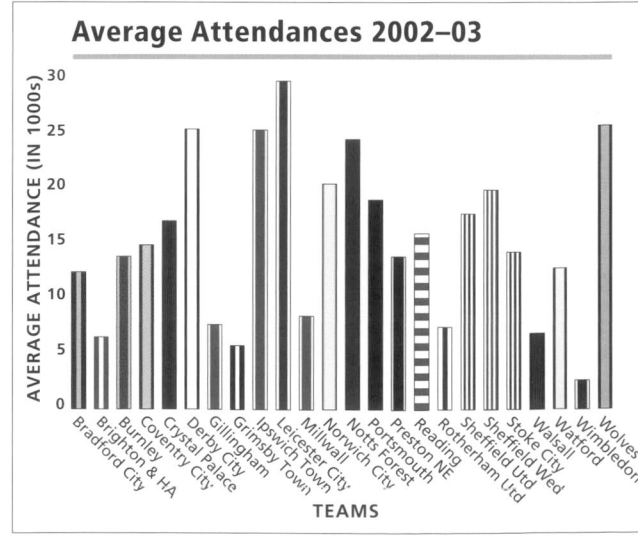

Average Attendances 2002–03

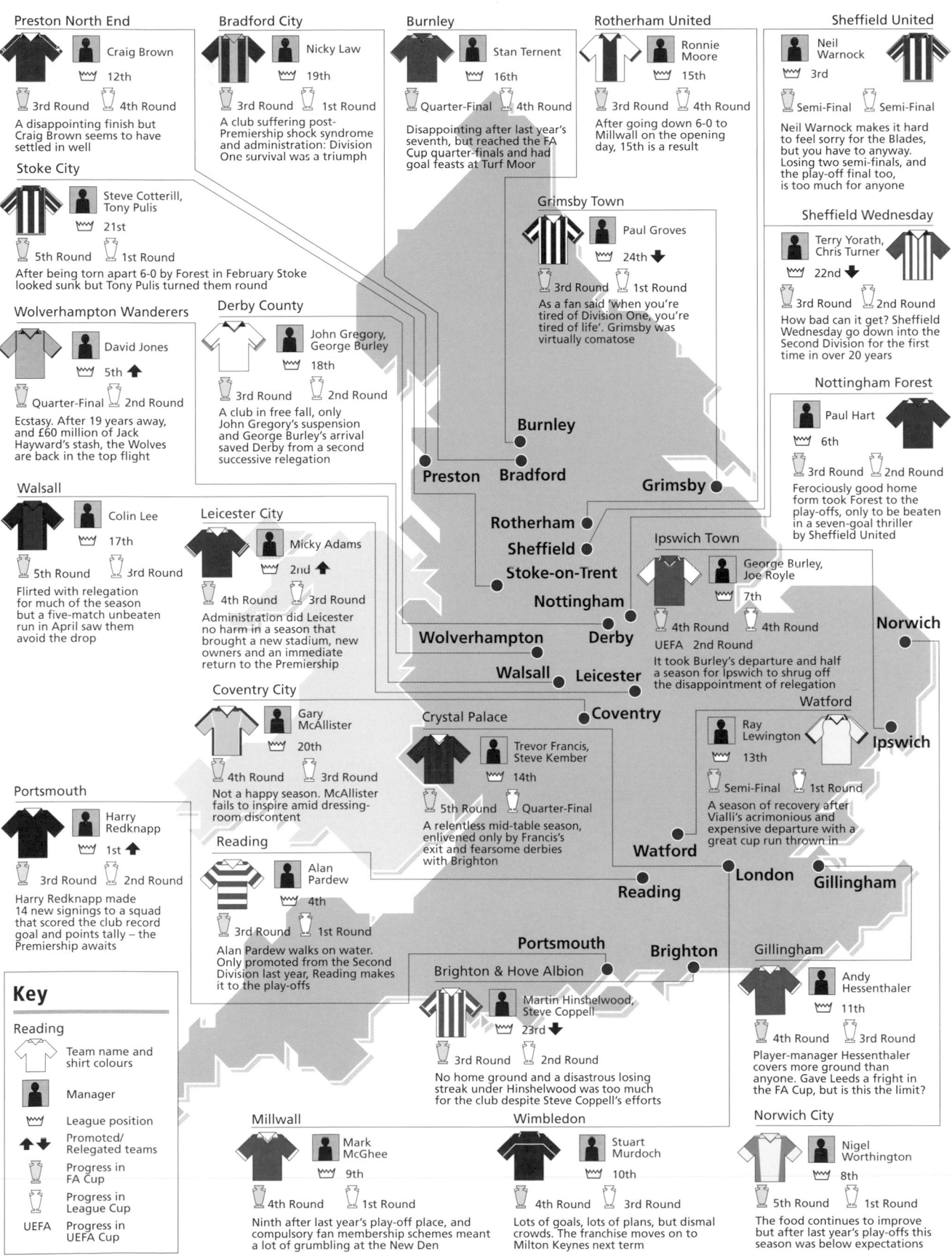

Preston North End
Craig Brown
12th
3rd Round | 4th Round
A disappointing finish but Craig Brown seems to have settled in well

Stoke City
Steve Cotterill, Tony Pulis
21st
5th Round | 1st Round
After being torn apart 6-0 by Forest in February Stoke looked sunk but Tony Pulis turned them round

Wolverhampton Wanderers
David Jones
5th ▲
Quarter-Final | 2nd Round
Ecstasy. After 19 years away, and £60 million of Jack Hayward's stash, the Wolves are back in the top flight

Walsall
Colin Lee
17th
5th Round | 3rd Round
Flirted with relegation for much of the season but a five-match unbeaten run in April saw them avoid the drop

Portsmouth
Harry Redknapp
1st ▲
3rd Round | 2nd Round
Harry Redknapp made 14 new signings to a squad that scored the club record goal and points tally – the Premiership awaits

Bradford City
Nicky Law
19th
3rd Round | 1st Round
A club suffering post-Premiership shock syndrome and administration: Division One survival was a triumph

Derby County
John Gregory, George Burley
18th
3rd Round | 2nd Round
A club in free fall, only John Gregory's suspension and George Burley's arrival saved Derby from a second successive relegation

Leicester City
Micky Adams
2nd ▲
4th Round | 3rd Round
Administration did Leicester no harm in a season that brought a new stadium, new owners and an immediate return to the Premiership

Coventry City
Gary McAllister
20th
4th Round | 3rd Round
Not a happy season. McAllister fails to inspire amid dressing-room discontent

Reading
Alan Pardew
4th
3rd Round | 1st Round
Alan Pardew walks on water. Only promoted from the Second Division last year, Reading makes it to the play-offs

Burnley
Stan Ternent
16th
Quarter-Final | 4th Round
Disappointing after last year's seventh, but reached the FA Cup quarter-finals and had goal feasts at Turf Moor

Grimsby Town
Paul Groves
24th ▼
3rd Round | 1st Round
As a fan said 'when you're tired of Division One, you're tired of life'. Grimsby was virtually comatose

Crystal Palace
Trevor Francis, Steve Kember
14th
5th Round | Quarter-Final
A relentless mid-table season, enlivened only by Francis's exit and fearsome derbies with Brighton

Brighton & Hove Albion
Martin Hinshelwood, Steve Coppell
23rd ▼
3rd Round | 2nd Round
No home ground and a disastrous losing streak under Hinshelwood was too much for the club despite Steve Coppell's efforts

Rotherham United
Ronnie Moore
15th
3rd Round | 4th Round
After going down 6-0 to Millwall on the opening day, 15th is a result

Ipswich Town
George Burley, Joe Royle
7th
UEFA 2nd Round | 4th Round | 4th Round
It took Burley's departure and half a season for Ipswich to shrug off the disappointment of relegation

Watford
Ray Lewington
13th
Semi-Final | 1st Round
A season of recovery after Vialli's acrimonious and expensive departure with a great cup run thrown in

Gillingham
Andy Hessenthaler
11th
4th Round | 3rd Round
Player-manager Hessenthaler covers more ground than anyone. Gave Leeds a fright in the FA Cup, but is this the limit?

Norwich City
Nigel Worthington
8th
5th Round | 1st Round
The food continues to improve but after last year's play-offs this season was below expectations

Sheffield United
Neil Warnock
3rd
Semi-Final | Semi-Final
Neil Warnock makes it hard to feel sorry for the Blades, but you have to anyway. Losing two semi-finals, and the play-off final too, is too much for anyone

Sheffield Wednesday
Terry Yorath, Chris Turner
22nd ▼
3rd Round | 2nd Round
How bad can it get? Sheffield Wednesday go down into the Second Division for the first time in over 20 years

Nottingham Forest
Paul Hart
6th
3rd Round | 2nd Round
Ferociously good home form took Forest to the play-offs, only to be beaten in a seven-goal thriller by Sheffield United

ENGLAND

Burnley
Preston
Bradford
Grimsby
Rotherham
Sheffield
Stoke-on-Trent
Nottingham
Wolverhampton
Derby
Walsall
Leicester
Coventry
Norwich
Watford
Ipswich
London
Gillingham
Reading
Portsmouth
Brighton
Gillingham

Key

Reading
Team name and shirt colours
Manager
League position
Promoted/ Relegated teams
Progress in FA Cup
Progress in League Cup
UEFA Progress in UEFA Cup

Millwall
Mark McGhee
9th
4th Round | 1st Round
Ninth after last year's play-off place, and compulsory fan membership schemes meant a lot of grumbling at the New Den

Wimbledon
Stuart Murdoch
10th
4th Round | 3rd Round
Lots of goals, lots of plans, but dismal crowds. The franchise moves on to Milton Keynes next term

Division Two

SEASON REVIEW

THERE WAS REALLY NEVER ANY DOUBT that Paul Jewell's Wigan would win Division Two and the team did it in some style: 100 points, a 14-point gap, and though Wigan didn't score as freely as some, its defence was the best by a massive margin. Decisive as its victory was, one might wonder quite what Wigan chairman Dave Whelan was on when he said, 'We are now not that far from the Premiership and you can rest assured we will give it a go'. The club must be saving every penny it can to fund this vaulting ambition, which perhaps explains its shoddy championship celebration: a Showaddywaddy tribute band miming to the PA in the pouring Lancashire rain. Close-up photos reveal they didn't even bother to put leads in the guitars.

Trailing in Wigan's wake all season were Crewe, Cardiff, Bristol City and Oldham. Crewe, despite some last-minute wobbles at Swindon and Bristol, grabbed the second spot with Rob Hulse leading the line. Dario Gradi takes his latest batch of youngsters for another crack at the First Division on a budget. The other three sides all made the play-offs. QPR took the final spot, indeed it scrambled back to fourth place after an appalling mid-season wobble.

The semi-finals of the play-offs proved tense affairs as the two best supported clubs in the division – Cardiff and QPR – squeezed into the Final. A complete sell-out at the Millennium Stadium watched a very tense 0-0 draw over 90 minutes with a single agonising goal giving Cardiff promotion.

Below the play-off scramble, the division proved to be incredibly close with only 10 points regularly separating 7th and 24th position. Peterborough crawled its way out of danger while Northampton, under Terry Fenwick, crumbled in its almost headlong dive for bottom spot.

Top Goalscorers 2002–03

PLAYER	CLUB	NATIONALITY	GOALS
Robert Earnshaw	Cardiff City	Welsh	31
Luke Beckett	Stockport County	English	27
Sammy Parkin	Swindon Town	English	25

Not just a rugby league town: Wigan manager Paul Jewell and captain Jason De Vos lift the Second Division trophy.

Final Division Two Table 2002–03

CLUB	P	W	D	L	F	A	Pts	
Wigan Athletic	46	29	13	4	68	25	100	Champions – promoted
Crewe Alexandra	46	25	11	10	76	40	86	Runners-up – promoted
Bristol City	46	24	11	11	79	48	83	Play-offs
Queens Park Rangers	46	24	11	11	69	45	83	Play-offs
Oldham Athletic	46	22	16	8	68	38	82	Play-offs
Cardiff City	46	23	12	11	68	43	81	Play-offs – promoted
Tranmere Rovers	46	23	11	12	66	57	80	
Plymouth Argyle	46	17	14	15	63	52	65	
Luton Town	46	17	14	15	67	62	65	
Swindon Town	46	16	12	18	59	63	60	
Peterborough United	46	14	16	16	51	54	58	
Colchester United	46	14	16	16	52	56	58	
Blackpool	46	15	13	18	56	64	58	
Stockport County	46	15	10	21	65	70	55	
Notts County	46	13	16	17	62	70	55	
Brentford	46	14	12	20	47	56	54	
Port Vale	46	14	11	21	54	70	53	
Wycombe Wanderers	46	13	13	20	59	66	52	
Barnsley	46	13	13	20	51	64	52	
Chesterfield	46	14	8	24	43	73	50	
Cheltenham Town	46	10	18	18	53	68	48	Relegated
Huddersfield Town	46	11	12	23	39	61	45	Relegated
Mansfield Town	46	12	8	26	66	97	44	Relegated
Northampton Town	46	10	9	27	40	79	39	Relegated

Promoted clubs: Rushden & Diamonds, Hartlepool United, Wrexham, Bournemouth.

Promotion Play-off Matches

SEMI-FINALS

Cardiff City **0-0, 1-0** (2 legs) Bristol City

Cardiff City won 1-0 on aggregate

Oldham Athletic **1-1, 0-1** (2 legs) QPR

QPR won 2-1 on aggregate

FINAL

Cardiff City **1-0** QPR

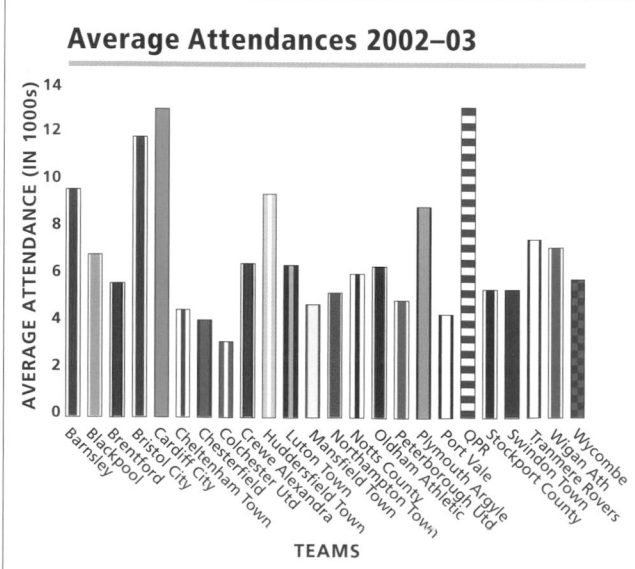

Average Attendances 2002–03

(Bar chart: AVERAGE ATTENDANCE (IN 1000s) vs TEAMS — Barnsley, Blackpool, Brentford, Bristol City, Cardiff City, Cheltenham Town, Chesterfield, Colchester Utd, Crewe Alexandra, Huddersfield Town, Luton Town, Mansfield Town, Northampton Town, Notts County, Oldham Athletic, Peterborough, Plymouth Argyle, Port Vale, QPR, Stockport County, Swindon Town, Tranmere Rovers, Wigan Ath, Wycombe Wanderers)

ENGLAND

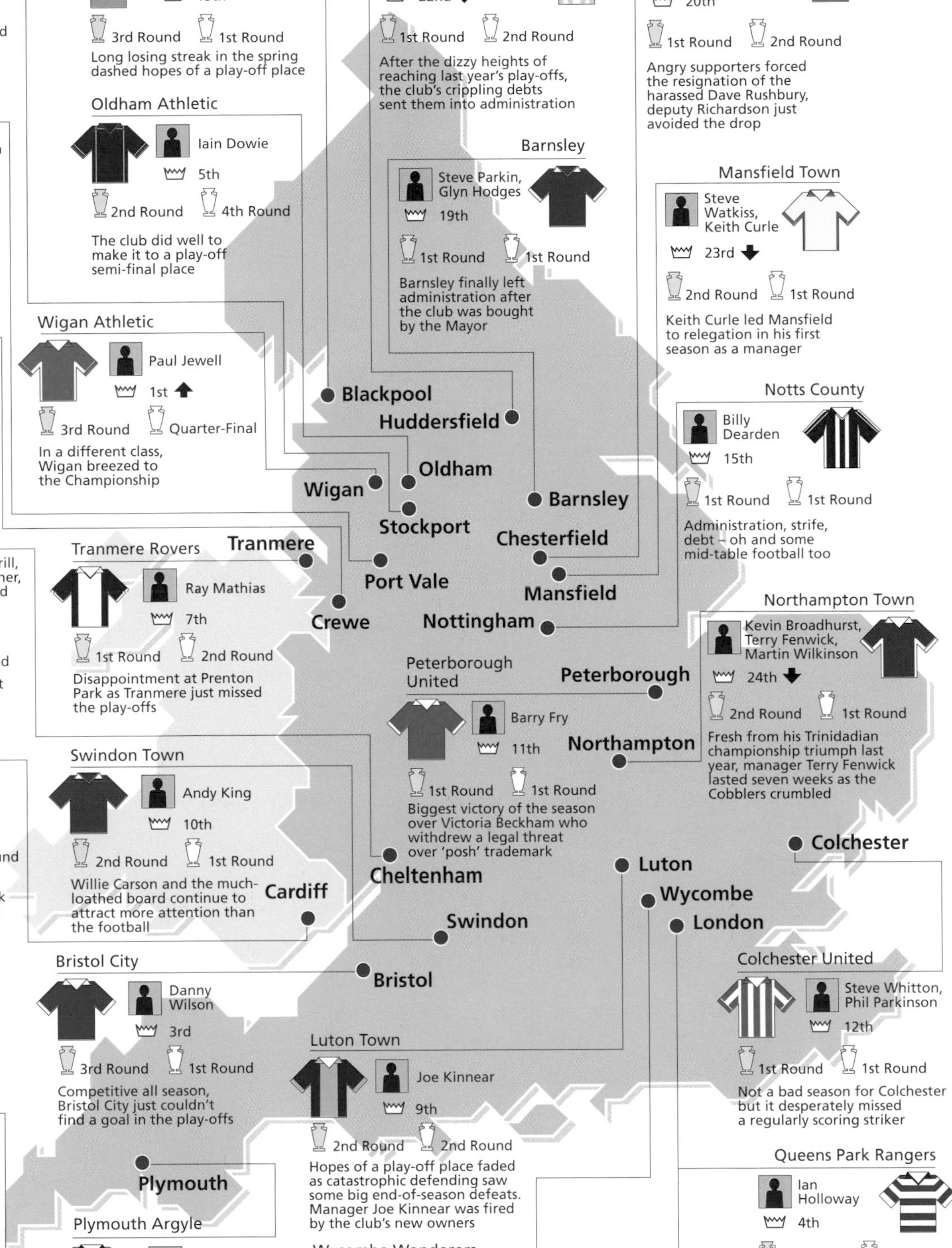

ENGLAND

Stockport County
Carlton Palmer
14th
2nd Round | 2nd Round
End mediocre season announcing merger with rugby union club Sale Sharks

Port Vale
Brian Horton
17th
1st Round | 1st Round
Vale finally escaped administration as the club was sold to supporters trust Valiant 2001

Crewe Alexandra
Dario Gradi
2nd ⬆
3rd Round | 2nd Round
Consistency rewarded, Gradi takes Crewe and his latest crop of youngsters back up to Division One

Cheltenham Town
Steve Cotterill, Graham Allner, Bobby Gould
21st ⬇
3rd Round | 2nd Round
Bobby Gould stopped the rot but was unable to prevent the drop

Cardiff City
Lennie Lawrence
6th ⬆
3rd Round | 2nd Round
Sam Hamman's £10 million gamble pays off. Cardiff back in the top half of the league for the first time in over 20 years

Blackpool
Steve McMahon
13th
3rd Round | 1st Round
Long losing streak in the spring dashed hopes of a play-off place

Oldham Athletic
Iain Dowie
5th
2nd Round | 4th Round
The club did well to make it to a play-off semi-final place

Wigan Athletic
Paul Jewell
1st ⬆
3rd Round | Quarter-Final
In a different class, Wigan breezed to the Championship

Tranmere Rovers
Ray Mathias
7th
1st Round | 2nd Round
Disappointment at Prenton Park as Tranmere just missed the play-offs

Swindon Town
Andy King
10th
2nd Round | 1st Round
Willie Carson and the much-loathed board continue to attract more attention than the football

Bristol City
Danny Wilson
3rd
3rd Round | 1st Round
Competitive all season, Bristol City just couldn't find a goal in the play-offs

Plymouth Argyle
Paul Sturrock
8th
3rd Round | 1st Round
Would have taken 8th in the league at the start of the season, but finished a long way off the play-off places. Best moment – watching rivals Exeter depart the Football League

Huddersfield Town
Mick Wadsworth, Mel Machin
22nd ⬇
1st Round | 2nd Round
After the dizzy heights of reaching last year's play-offs, the club's crippling debts sent them into administration

Barnsley
Steve Parkin, Glyn Hodges
19th
1st Round | 1st Round
Barnsley finally left administration after the club was bought by the Mayor

Peterborough United
Barry Fry
11th
1st Round | 1st Round
Biggest victory of the season over Victoria Beckham who withdrew a legal threat over 'posh' trademark

Luton Town
Joe Kinnear
9th
2nd Round | 2nd Round
Hopes of a play-off place faded as catastrophic defending saw some big end-of-season defeats. Manager Joe Kinnear was fired by the club's new owners

Wycombe Wanderers
Lawrie Sanchez
18th
1st Round | 2nd Round
After a great cup run and finishing 11th last season this was a disappointing campaign for Wycombe

Chesterfield
Dave Rushbury, Lee Richardson, Dave Thompson
20th
1st Round | 2nd Round
Angry supporters forced the resignation of the harassed Dave Rushbury, deputy Richardson just avoided the drop

Mansfield Town
Steve Watkiss, Keith Curle
23rd ⬇
2nd Round | 1st Round
Keith Curle led Mansfield to relegation in his first season as a manager

Notts County
Billy Dearden
15th
1st Round | 1st Round
Administration, strife, debt – oh and some mid-table football too

Northampton Town
Kevin Broadhurst, Terry Fenwick, Martin Wilkinson
24th ⬇
2nd Round | 1st Round
Fresh from his Trinidadian championship triumph last year, manager Terry Fenwick lasted seven weeks as the Cobblers crumbled

Colchester United
Steve Whitton, Phil Parkinson
12th
1st Round | 1st Round
Not a bad season for Colchester but it desperately missed a regularly scoring striker

Queens Park Rangers
Ian Holloway
4th
1st Round | 1st Round
A mid-season collapse was followed by a brilliant final run in, but it ended in tears

Brentford
Wally Downes
16th
4th Round | 2nd Round
Ron Noades finally bowed out, selling the club to the supporters' organization Bees United

Map labels: Blackpool, Huddersfield, Oldham, Wigan, Barnsley, Stockport, Chesterfield, Port Vale, Mansfield, Crewe, Nottingham, Peterborough, Northampton, Cheltenham, Swindon, Cardiff, Bristol, Plymouth, Luton, Wycombe, London, Colchester

Key
Barnsley — Team name and shirt colours
Manager
League position
⬆⬇ Promoted/Relegated teams
Progress in FA Cup
Progress in League Cup

15

Division Three

SEASON REVIEW

AMID THE FINANCIAL WRECKAGE, Division Three gave us a long and fiercely competitive season. Hartlepool was the form team in the first half of the season, taking the lead and holding on to it till Christmas. Rushden & Diamonds, suffering from the disappointment of last year's play-offs, languished up to 14 points behind Hartlepool at one point, before beginning a steady ascent up the table. By the turn of the year the team was a point off the leaders. In the New Year it took the lead and kept it before a 1-1 draw with its close rivals in May sealed its triumph.

Any of another ten teams looked possible candidates for the third automatic promotion place and the play-offs. Cambridge, Oxford and Hull all fell away in the spring, while Wrexham began to climb and with a nine-game winning run at the end, grabbed the final spot. The play-off places went to Bournemouth, Scunthorpe, Bury and late arrivals at the party – Lincoln. In a clash of fan-owned clubs in the final at Cardiff, open football and goals were the order of the day: Bournemouth deservedly beat Lincoln 5-2.

Down in the depths, it looked for a long time as if Bristol Rovers and Swansea City would be enjoying Conference football next year. But both pulled themselves off the bottom while Exeter and Shrewsbury did them the favour of losing it in the spring. Neither Uri Geller nor giant-killing cup runs could save them.

Top Goalscorers 2002–03

PLAYER	CLUB	NATIONALITY	GOALS
Andy Morrell	Wrexham	English	35
Martin Carruthers	Scunthorpe United	English	20
Dave Kitson	Cambridge United	English	20
Bo Henricksen	Kidderminster Harriers	Danish	20

Final Third Division Table 2002–03

CLUB	P	W	D	L	F	A	Pts	
Rushden & Diamonds	46	24	15	7	73	47	**87**	Champions – promoted
Hartlepool United	46	24	13	9	71	51	**85**	Runners-up – promoted
Wrexham	46	23	15	8	84	50	**84**	Promoted
AFC Bournemouth	46	20	14	12	60	48	**74**	Play-offs – promoted
Scunthorpe United	46	19	15	12	68	49	**72**	Play-offs
Lincoln City	46	18	16	12	46	37	**70**	Play-offs
Bury	46	18	16	12	57	56	**70**	Play-offs
Oxford United	46	19	12	15	57	47	**69**	
Torquay United	46	16	18	12	71	71	**66**	
York City	46	17	15	14	52	53	**66**	
Kidderminster Harriers	46	16	15	15	62	63	**63**	
Cambridge United	46	16	13	17	67	70	**61**	
Hull City	46	14	17	15	58	53	**59**	
Darlington	46	12	18	16	58	59	**54**	
Boston United*	46	15	13	18	55	56	**54**	
Macclesfield Town	46	14	12	20	57	63	**54**	
Southend United	46	17	3	26	47	59	**54**	
Leyton Orient	46	14	11	21	51	61	**53**	
Rochdale	46	12	16	18	63	70	**52**	
Bristol Rovers	46	12	15	19	50	57	**51**	
Swansea City	46	12	13	21	48	65	**49**	
Carlisle United	46	13	10	23	52	78	**49**	
Exeter City	46	11	15	20	50	64	**48**	Relegated
Shrewsbury Town	46	9	14	23	62	92	**41**	Relegated

* Boston United deducted 4 points for financial irregularities.
Promoted clubs: Yeovil Town, Doncaster Rovers.

Promotion Play-off Matches

SEMI-FINALS
Bury **0-0, 1-3** (2 legs) Bournemouth
Bournemouth won 3-1 on aggregate

Lincoln City **5-3, 1-0** (2 legs) Scunthorpe United
Lincoln City won 6-3 on aggregate

FINAL
Bournemouth **5-2** Lincoln City

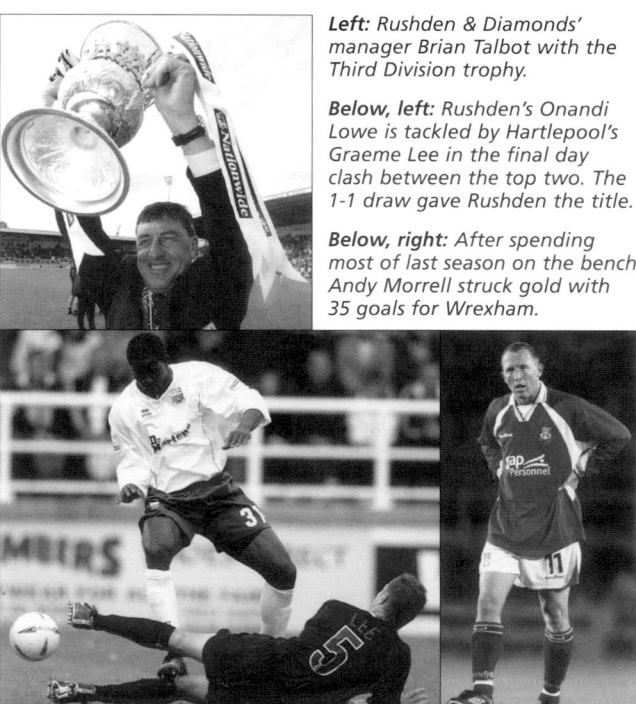

*Left: Rushden & Diamonds'
manager Brian Talbot with the
Third Division trophy.*

*Below, left: Rushden's Onandi
Lowe is tackled by Hartlepool's
Graeme Lee in the final day
clash between the top two. The
1-1 draw gave Rushden the title.*

*Below, right: After spending
most of last season on the bench
Andy Morrell struck gold with
35 goals for Wrexham.*

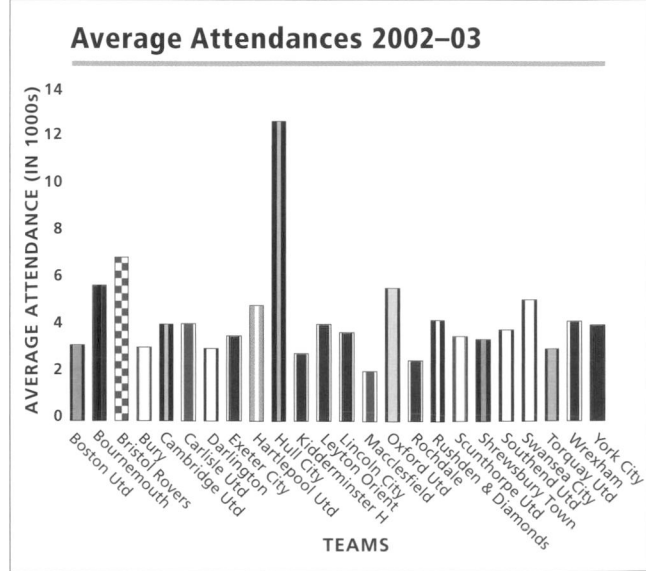

Average Attendances 2002–03

AVERAGE ATTENDANCE (IN 1000s)

TEAMS

ENGLAND

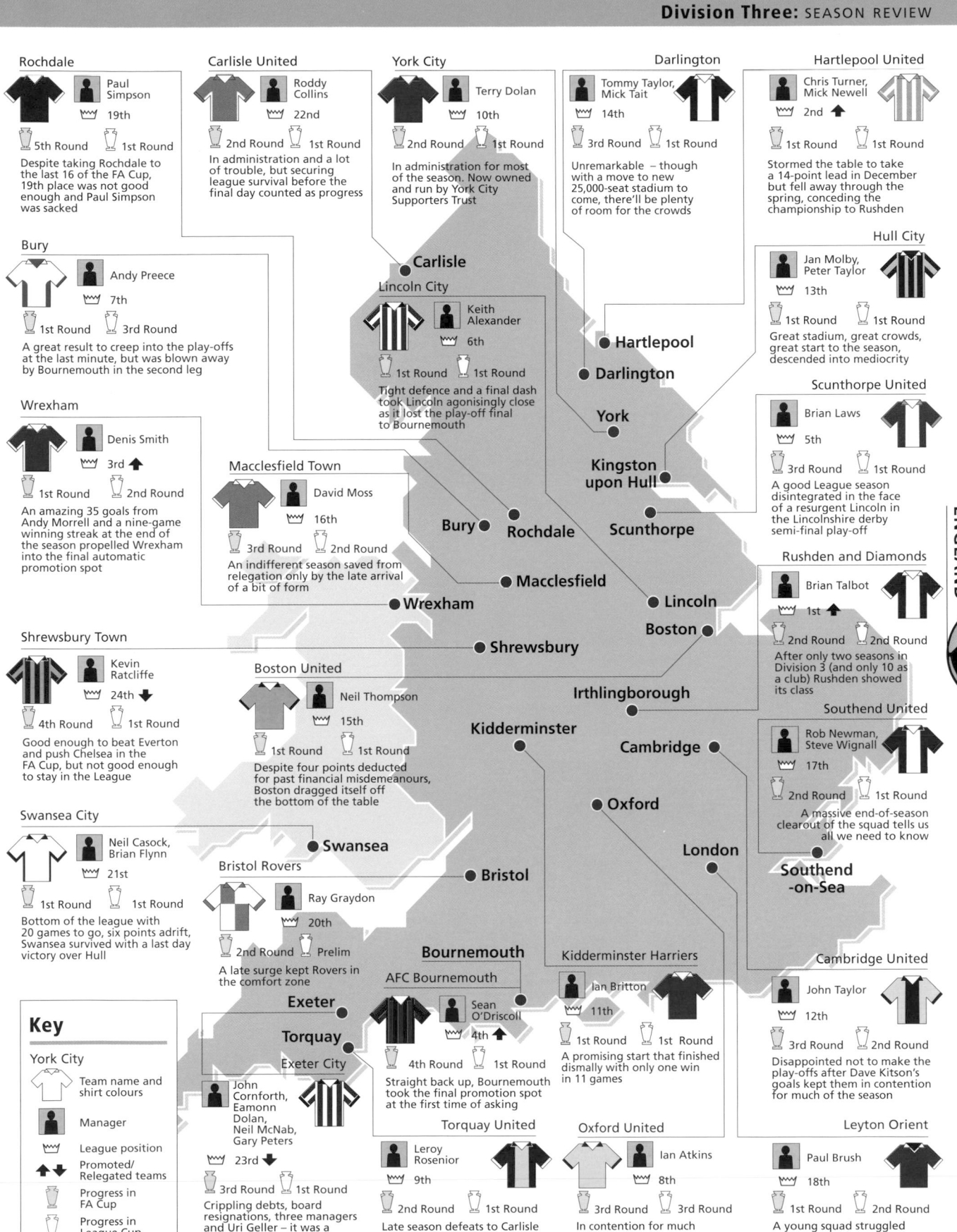

ENGLAND

Rochdale
Paul Simpson
19th
5th Round | 1st Round
Despite taking Rochdale to the last 16 of the FA Cup, 19th place was not good enough and Paul Simpson was sacked

Carlisle United
Roddy Collins
22nd
2nd Round | 1st Round
In administration and a lot of trouble, but securing league survival before the final day counted as progress

York City
Terry Dolan
10th
2nd Round | 1st Round
In administration for most of the season. Now owned and run by York City Supporters Trust

Darlington
Tommy Taylor, Mick Tait
14th
3rd Round | 1st Round
Unremarkable – though with a move to new 25,000-seat stadium to come, there'll be plenty of room for the crowds

Hartlepool United
Chris Turner, Mick Newell
2nd ▲
1st Round | 1st Round
Stormed the table to take a 14-point lead in December but fell away through the spring, conceding the championship to Rushden

Bury
Andy Preece
7th
1st Round | 3rd Round
A great result to creep into the play-offs at the last minute, but was blown away by Bournemouth in the second leg

Hull City
Jan Molby, Peter Taylor
13th
1st Round | 1st Round
Great stadium, great crowds, great start to the season, descended into mediocrity

Lincoln City
Keith Alexander
6th
1st Round | 1st Round
Tight defence and a final dash took Lincoln agonisingly close as it lost the play-off final to Bournemouth

Wrexham
Denis Smith
3rd ▲
1st Round | 2nd Round
An amazing 35 goals from Andy Morrell and a nine-game winning streak at the end of the season propelled Wrexham into the final automatic promotion spot

Macclesfield Town
David Moss
16th
3rd Round | 2nd Round
An indifferent season saved from relegation only by the late arrival of a bit of form

Scunthorpe United
Brian Laws
5th
3rd Round | 1st Round
A good League season disintegrated in the face of a resurgent Lincoln in the Lincolnshire derby semi-final play-off

Rushden and Diamonds
Brian Talbot
1st ▲
2nd Round | 2nd Round
After only two seasons in Division 3 (and only 10 as a club) Rushden showed its class

Shrewsbury Town
Kevin Ratcliffe
24th ▼
4th Round | 1st Round
Good enough to beat Everton and push Chelsea in the FA Cup, but not good enough to stay in the League

Boston United
Neil Thompson
15th
1st Round | 1st Round
Despite four points deducted for past financial misdemeanours, Boston dragged itself off the bottom of the table

Southend United
Rob Newman, Steve Wignall
17th
2nd Round | 1st Round
A massive end-of-season clearout of the squad tells us all we need to know

Swansea City
Neil Cusack, Brian Flynn
21st
1st Round | 1st Round
Bottom of the league with 20 games to go, six points adrift, Swansea survived with a last day victory over Hull

Bristol Rovers
Ray Graydon
20th
2nd Round | Prelim
A late surge kept Rovers in the comfort zone

AFC Bournemouth
Sean O'Driscoll
4th ▲
4th Round | 1st Round
Straight back up, Bournemouth took the final promotion spot at the first time of asking

Kidderminster Harriers
Ian Britton
11th
1st Round | 1st Round
A promising start that finished dismally with only one win in 11 games

Cambridge United
John Taylor
12th
3rd Round | 2nd Round
Disappointed not to make the play-offs after Dave Kitson's goals kept them in contention for much of the season

Exeter City
John Cornforth, Eamonn Dolan, Neil McNab, Gary Peters
23rd ▼
3rd Round | 1st Round
Crippling debts, board resignations, three managers and Uri Geller – it was a miracle the team didn't go down until the final day

Torquay United
Leroy Rosenior
9th
2nd Round | 1st Round
Late season defeats to Carlisle and Southend kept Torquay out of the play-offs

Oxford United
Ian Atkins
8th
3rd Round | 3rd Round
In contention for much of the season, but just missed the play-offs

Leyton Orient
Paul Brush
18th
1st Round | 2nd Round
A young squad struggled to keep out of the danger zone but did so

Map labels
Carlisle
Hartlepool
Darlington
York
Kingston upon Hull
Scunthorpe
Lincoln
Boston
Irthlingborough
Cambridge
Oxford
London
Southend-on-Sea
Bury
Rochdale
Macclesfield
Wrexham
Shrewsbury
Kidderminster
Bristol
Swansea
Exeter
Torquay

Key
York City
- Team name and shirt colours
- Manager
- League position
- ▲▼ Promoted/Relegated teams
- Progress in FA Cup
- Progress in League Cup

The League Cup

TOURNAMENT REVIEW

AFTER YEARS OF INSIGNIFICANCE, the Worthington Cup finally acquired a leading role in the season's narrative. Manchester United finally deigned to take it seriously, seeing off Burnley, Chelsea and Blackburn with some passion. Liverpool, reeling from a precipitous winter decline which had seen them tumble from the top of the Premiership, go out of the Champions League and depart the FA Cup, hung on by the skin of their teeth. Ipswich took them to penalties and a goal fest at Villa saw them come through 4-3. But Michael Owen's extra time goal in the flinty semi-final with Sheffield United hinted at revival.

In the Final itself, early United pressure was absorbed by Liverpool who counter-attacked. Jerzy Dudek, whose form reached rock bottom after Manchester United had crushed Liverpool at Anfield in December, was reborn, making vital saves from Scholes and van Nistelrooy. Those chances aside, United's mental and physical lethargy was punished by Gerrard's free strike in the first half, and Owen's *coup de grace* in the last five minutes.

United's element of greatness

Gerard Houllier's evident pleasure in taking the trophy was unlikely to be matched by Ferguson's disappointment at losing it. Far more perturbing, Manchester United were forced to watch Arsenal take an eight-point Premiership lead over the Final weekend. An element of greatness is response to victory and defeat: Liverpool left Cardiff only to exit the UEFA Cup and falter in the race for a Champions League spot, while United began a run of scintillating domestic victories that would take them to the championship. In a display of predictable petulance, Ferguson passed on the post-match press conference. It's a shame, as he must have been saving up something great to say.

The highlight of a dismal season? Sunderland beat Arsenal 3-2 at Highbury. Defeat to Sheffield United in the next round saw normal service resumed.

Another Premiership turnover: Carl Asaba of Sheffield United cuts through the Leeds' defence in their torrid Third Round Yorkshire derby.

SECOND ROUND

Ipswich Town **3-1** Brighton	Tottenham **1-0** Cardiff City Hotspur
Brentford **1-4** Middlesbrough	Wrexham **0-3** Everton
Cambridge **0-7** Sunderland United	Aston Villa **3-0** Luton Town
Charlton **0-0** Oxford Athletic United Oxford won 6-5 on pens	Bolton **0-1** Bury Wanderers
Chesterfield **1-1** West Ham United West Ham won 5-4 on pens	Coventry City **8-0** Rushden & Diamonds
Huddersfield **0-1** Burnley	Crystal Palace **7-0** Cheltenham Town
Macclesfield **1-2** Preston North End	Derby County **1-2** Oldham Athletic
Manchester **3-2** Crewe City Alexandra	Leyton Orient **2-3** Birmingham City
Portsmouth **1-3** Wimbledon	Nottingham **1-2** Walsall Forest
Rotherham **4-4** Wolverhampton United Wanderers Rotherham won 4-2 on pens	Sheffield **1-2** Leicester City Wednesday
Sheffield **4-1** Wycombe United Wanderers	Southampton **6-1** Tranmere Rovers
Stockport **1-2** Gillingham County	Wigan Athletic **3-1** West Bromwich Albion

THIRD ROUND

Birmingham **0-2** Preston City North End	Crystal Palace **3-0** Coventry City
Manchester **2-0** Leicester City United	Fulham **3-1** Bury
Wigan Athletic **1-0** Manchester City	Ipswich Town **3-1** Middlesbrough
Wimbledon **1-3** Rotherham	Liverpool **3-1** Southampton
Arsenal **2-3** Sunderland	Newcastle **3-3** Everton United Everton won 3-2 on pens
Blackburn **2-2** Walsall Rovers Blackburn won 5-4 on pens	Oxford United **0-3** Aston Villa
Burnley **2-1** Tottenham Hotspur	Sheffield **2-1** Leeds United United
Chelsea **2-1** Gillingham	West Ham **0-1** Oldham United Athletic

FOURTH ROUND

Burnley **0-2** Manchester United	Blackburn **4-0** Rotherham Rovers
Crystal Palace **2-0** Oldham Athletic	Chelsea **4-1** Everton
Sheffield **2-0** Sunderland United	Liverpool **1-1** Ipswich Town Liverpool won 5-4 on pens
Aston Villa **5-0** Preston North End	Wigan Athletic **2-1** Fulham

Left: Michael Owen of Liverpool watches his extra-time winner sail into Sheffield United's net.

Below left: Diego Forlan's best moment of the season was arguably scoring United's winner against Chelsea in the quarter-final.

Below: Gerard Houllier shows off the season's first silverware to the Liverpool fans at the Millennium Stadium after the team's unexpected victory against Manchester United.

Bottom: Manchester United had no answer to goals from Steven Gerrard and Michael Owen.

Top: Robbie Blake scored for Burnley in the memorable Third Round victory over Spurs.

Above: Sheffield United's smiling but abrasive Neil Warnock contemplates his post-match wind-ups.

QUARTER-FINALS

Wigan Athletic **0-2** Blackburn Rovers

Sheffield **3-1** Crystal Palace
United

Manchester **1-0** Chelsea
United

Aston Villa **3-4** Liverpool

SEMI-FINALS (2 legs)

Manchester **1-1** Blackburn
United   Rovers
(Scholes 58)   (Thompson 61)

Blackburn **1-3** Manchester
Rovers   United
(Cole 12)   (Scholes 30, 42,
              van Nistelrooy
              77 pen)
Manchester United won 4-2
on aggregate

Sheffield **2-1** Liverpool
United   (Mellor 36)
(Tonge 76, 81)

Liverpool **2-0** Sheffield
(Diouf 9,   United
Owen 107)
After extra time
Liverpool won 3-2 on aggregate

2003 FINAL

Mar 2 – Millennium Stadium, Cardiff
Liverpool **2-0** Manchester
(Gerrard 39,   United
Owen 86)
h/t: 1-0   **Att:** 74,500
Ref: P. Durkin

The FA Cup

TOURNAMENT REVIEW

THESE ARE DIFFICULT TIMES for the world's oldest football tournament. Despite extensive sponsorship and TV coverage, it is desperate to convince that its glamour and unpredictability remain untouched. However, in reality the leading teams would trade the cup for even a slot in the qualifying rounds of the Champions League. Of course, it still offers up its usual pleasures.

The appearance of non-league teams and part-time players provides a strangely parochial exoticism to the early rounds – Harrogate Railway, Vauxhall Motors, Margate, Stevenage and Barrow had their moments in the Second Round. Dagenham & Redbridge and Farnborough Town both skirted the arrival of the top flight in the Third Round to make the Fourth, before succumbing to Norwich and Arsenal respectively.

If financial pressures are distorting the meaning of the cup at the top of the game, things are no different at the bottom. Harrogate imploded into vicious arguments over TV money and bonuses. Given a Fourth Round home tie with Arsenal, Farnborough shamelessly passed on the pressure and the edge the draw had given them for an altogether larger payday at Highbury. Real giant killing was rarer, with the top sides knocking each other out in a war of attrition. Crystal Palace dispensed with Liverpool, while Gillingham and Millwall took Leeds and Southampton to replays, but for a real disparity, Shrewsbury's last-minute victory over Everton at an icy Gay Meadow was the neutral's favourite.

The Fifth Round saw the Premiership contingent reduced to four as Arsenal decisively beat Manchester United 2-0, Burnley took Fulham back to Turf Moor and won 3-0 and Sunderland capitulated to Watford. But the weekend will be remembered for the flying boot incident. The trajectory of the boot and even its ownership remain secret, but its take-off and landing seem sure. As Ferguson excoriated his squad in the dressing room he lashed out at the footwear and it ended up on David Beckham's forehead. And just in case any of us should be left wondering as to the contact, Becks sported a revealing Alice band and sticking plaster for the next few weeks.

Sing when you're winning. Shrewsbury Town celebrates a brilliant last-minute victory over Premiership team Everton in the Third Round.

SECOND ROUND

Morecambe **3-2** Chester City

Shrewsbury **3-1** Barrow Town

Darlington **4-1** Stevenage Borough

Oldham **1-2** Cheltenham Athletic Town

Macclesfield **2-0** Vauxhall Motors

Cambridge **2-2** Northampton United Town
Replay
Northampton **0-1** Cambridge Town United

Exeter City **3-1** Rushden & Diamonds

Southport **0-3** Farnborough Town

Bristol Rovers **1-1** Rochdale
Replay
Rochdale **3-2** Bristol Rovers

Crawley **1-2** Dagenham & Redbridge

Wigan Athletic **3-0** Luton Town

Stockport **0-3** Plymouth County Argyle

Southend **1-1** Bournemouth United
Replay
Bournemouth **3-2** Southend United

York City **1-2** Brentford

Margate **0-3** Cardiff City

Scunthorpe **0-0** Carlisle United
Replay
Carlisle United **0-1** Scunthorpe

Blackpool **3-1** Torquay United

Crewe **3-0** Mansfield Alexandra Town

Harrogate **1-3** Bristol Railway City

Oxford United **1-0** Swindon Town

THIRD ROUND

Arsenal **2-0** Oxford United

Aston Villa **1-4** Blackburn Rovers

Blackpool **1-2** Crystal Palace

Bolton **1-1** Sunderland Wanderers
Replay
Sunderland **2-0** Bolton Wanderers

Bournemouth **0-0** Crewe Alexandra
Replay
Crewe **2-2** Bournemouth Alexandra
Bournemouth won 3-1 on pens

Brentford **1-0** Derby County

Cambridge **1-1** Millwall United
Replay
Millwall **3-2** Cambridge United

Cardiff City **2-2** Coventry City
Replay
Coventry City **3-0** Cardiff City

Charlton **3-1** Exeter City Athletic

Chelsea **1-0** Middlesbrough

Darlington **2-3** Farnborough Town

Grimsby Town **2-2** Burnley
Replay
Burnley **4-0** Grimsby Town

Ipswich Town **4-0** Morecambe

Leicester City **2-0** Bristol City

Macclesfield **0-2** Watford

Manchester **4-1** Portsmouth United

Plymouth **2-2** Dagenham Argyle & Redbridge
Replay
Dagenham **2-0** Plymouth & Redbridge Argyle

Preston **1-2** Rochdale North End

Rotherham **0-3** Wimbledon United

Scunthorpe **0-2** Leeds United

Sheffield **4-0** Cheltenham United Town

Shrewsbury **2-1** Everton Town

Southampton **4-0** Tottenham Hotspur

Stoke City **3-0** Wigan Athletic

Walsall **0-0** Reading
Replay
Reading **1-1** Walsall
Wallsall won 4-1 on pens

West Bromwich **3-1** Bradford City Albion

West Ham **3-2** Nottingham United Forest

Fulham **3-1** Birmingham City

Manchester **0-1** Liverpool City

Wolverhampton **3-2** Newcastle Wanderers United

Gillingham **4-1** Sheffield Wednesday

Norwich City **3-1** Brighton & Hove Albion

Above right: Rocky Baptiste grabs a consolation goal for Farnborough as the team go down 5-1 to Arsenal at Highbury.

Right: Peter Ndlovu, Tommy Mooney, Michael Brown, Stuart McCall and Steve Kabba celebrate Sheffield United's winner against Walsall in Fifth Round.

ENGLAND

FOURTH ROUND

Blackburn **3-3** Sunderland Rovers

Sunderland **2-2** Blackburn Rovers

Sunderland won 3-0 on pens

Brentford **0-3** Burnley

Farnborough **1-5** Arsenal Town

Played at Highbury

Gillingham **1-1** Leeds United

Replay
Leeds United **2-1** Gillingham

Norwich City **1-0** Dagenham & Redbridge

Rochdale **2-0** Coventry City

Sheffield **4-3** Ipswich Town United

Southampton **1-1** Millwall

Replay
Millwall **1-2** Southampton

Walsall **1-0** Wimbledon

Watford **1-0** West Bromwich Albion

Wolverhampton **4-1** Leicester City Wanderers

Crystal Palace **0-0** Liverpool

Replay
Liverpool **0-2** Crystal Palace

Fulham **3-0** Charlton Athletic

Manchester **6-0** West Ham United United

Shrewsbury **0-4** Chelsea Town

Stoke City **3-0** Bournemouth

FIFTH ROUND

Manchester **0-2** Arsenal United

Sheffield **2-0** Walsall United

Southampton **2-0** Norwich City

Sunderland **0-1** Watford

Crystal Palace **1-2** Leeds United

Fulham **1-1** Burnley

Replay
Burnley **3-0** Fulham

Stoke City **0-2** Chelsea

Wolverhampton **3-1** Rochdale Wanderers

Gillingham's Nicky Southall and Leeds United's Mark Viduka slug it out in a tense 1-1 draw in the Fourth Round. Leeds won the replay, but only just.

Watford's Tommy Smith coolly slots his penalty past the Sunderland keeper to give his side a place in the semi-finals.

ENGLAND

THE QUARTER-FINALS

For the first time in 50 years, the top flight had only four teams in the last eight of the FA Cup. Watford got past Burnley comfortably. Sheffield United made it two from the Nationwide with victory over a Leeds side in financial and footballing freefall. Southampton showed the team's growing composure with two late goals taking them past Wolves. But the pick of the ties was Arsenal v Chelsea. The first match was graced by the goal of the tournament from Thierry Henry but Arsenal let Chelsea back into the game. After gifting Arsenal an own goal after 25 minutes in the replay, Chelsea went out.

March 8 – Highbury, London
Attendance 38,104

ARSENAL 2-2 **CHELSEA**
h/t: 2-1

Scorers	
Jeffers 37, Henry 45	Terry 3, Lampard 84

March 25 – Stamford Bridge, London
Attendance 41,456
REPLAY

CHELSEA 1-3 **ARSENAL**
h/t: 0-2

Scorers	
Terry 79	Terry 25 o.g., Wiltord 33, Lauren 82

March 9 – Bramall Lane, Sheffield
Attendance 24,633

SHEFFIELD UNITED 1-0 **LEEDS UNITED**
h/t: 0-0

Scorers	
Kabba 78	

March 9 – Vicarage Road, Watford
Attendance 31,715

WATFORD 2-0 **BURNLEY**
h/t: 0-0

Scorers	
Marsden 56, Butler 81 o.g.	

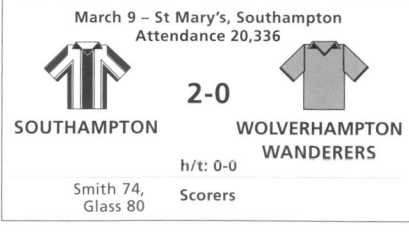

March 9 – St Mary's, Southampton
Attendance 20,336

SOUTHAMPTON 2-0 **WOLVERHAMPTON WANDERERS**
h/t: 0-0

Scorers	
Smith 74, Glass 80	

THE SEMI-FINALS

The semi-finals were short on upsets and long on scrappy play and sour words. Watford arrived on the back of a 7-4 league victory at Burnley and started with gusto but failed to capitalize on its pressure. Southampton kept its shape and Brett Ormerod's first goal for 23 games gave them a lead not to be relinquished.

A controversial goal from Freddie Ljungberg separated Arsenal and Sheffield United. Sol Campbell's tackle had left Sheffield's Wayne Allison on the floor. Referee Graham Poll not only let play continue but collided with Michael Tonge as he moved in to tackle Patrick Vieira. Sheffield manager Neil Warnock described Poll as Arsenal's 'best midfield player'. Arsenal was mediocre, but for a single David Seaman save. Paul Peschisolido's shot, six minutes from the end, seemed a certain goal as Seaman's outstretched hand cupped the cusp of the spinning ball and flicked it away – on the day of his 1000th club game David Seaman earned his trip to Cardiff.

April 13 – Old Trafford, Manchester
Attendance 59,170
Ref: Graham Poll

SHEFFIELD UNITED 0-1 **ARSENAL**
h/t: 0-1

Scorers	
	Ljungberg 34

April 13 – Villa Park, Birmingham
Attendance 42,603
Ref: Mike Riley

SOUTHAMPTON 2-1 **WATFORD**
h/t: 1-0

Scorers	
Ormerod 43, Robinson 80 o.g.	Gayle 88

Goal of the tournament: *Thierry Henry gives Arsenal the lead in the team's first quarter-final game against Chelsea.*

THE FINAL

In the last decade only one FA Cup winner has come from outside the Premiership's top six – Everton in 1995. In the previous 20 years there were 13 lower-placed winners. The relentless concentration of power at the top of the game was confirmed as an understrength Arsenal beat Southampton at Cardiff by the narrowest of margins – Robert Pires's 37th-minute goal, scrambled under the body of the diving Niemi.

Thierry Henry's lightning strike into the Southampton area 30 seconds into the game saw him brush off Lundekvam's blatant shirt pull, and shoot wide. It promised an afternoon of dash, but though Henry's running and Bergkamp's passing panicked the Southampton defence, the game barely rose to the occasion. Southampton, no doubt scalded by their 6-1 destruction by Arsenal in the league rehearsal the previous week, played safe and looked to set pieces and long balls for its break. A late flurry bought a Seaman save from Brett Ormerod's shot while Ashley Cole cleared Beattie's stoppage-time header. The break never came.

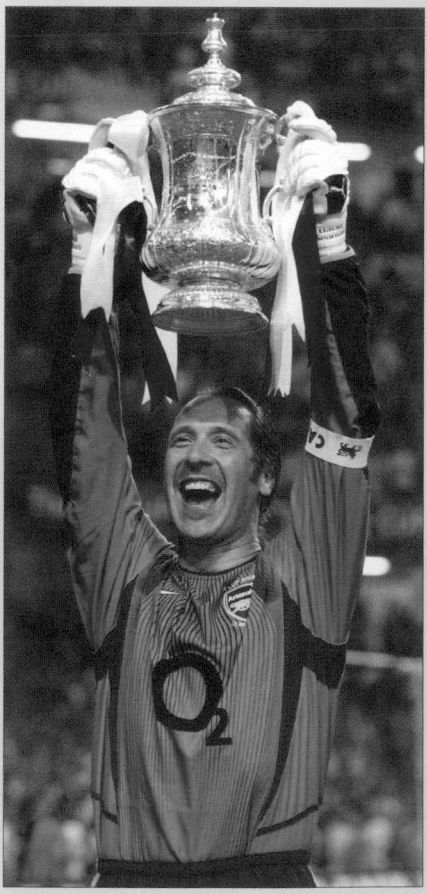

The Starting Line-Up

May 17 – Millennium Stadium, Cardiff
Attendance 73,726

ARSENAL	Referee	SOUTHAMPTON
Formation: 4-4-2	Graham Barber	**Formation: 4-4-2**
Manager		**Manager**
Arsène Wenger		Gordon Strachan

Substitutes		Substitutes	
Kanu	25	Jones	1
Toure	28	Tessem	21
Wiltord	11	Higginbotham	15
Taylor	13	Williams	6
van Bronckhorst	16	Fernandes	29

Left: Going out on a high? David Seaman, Arsenal's captain for the day, celebrates. His saves from Chris Baird and Brett Ormerod kept Arsenal on top. But as his 40th birthday approached he decided on a short-term move to Manchester City.

Below: Will it, won't it? Southampton's last and best chance. James Beattie headed the ball towards the inside of the post, but Ashley Cole cleared with an outstretched thigh.

Highlights of the Game

KEY

Player booked ▯   ↪ Substitution
Goal ⚽

ARSENAL   ▼ KICK OFF 0 mins   **SOUTHAMPTON**

1 min: Henry breaks into the Southampton penalty area

10 min: 50 metre Bergkamp pass sends Henry through. Baird clears the shot off the line

19 min: Baird forces sprawling save from Seaman

22 min: Southampton win first corner

30 min: Keown booked ▯

▯ **31 min:** Beattie booked

37 min: Pires's goal ⚽

45 mins + 1 min injury time

HALF-TIME: 1-0

52 min: Bergkamp shoots

▯ **60 min:** Telfer booked

66 min: Henry booked ▯

↪ **65 min:** Niemi off, Jo Tessem on

77 min: Bergkamp off, Wiltord on ↪

75 min: A. Svensson off, Jo Tessem on

▯ **77 min:** Marsden booked

83 min: Reflex save from Seaman keeps Brett Ormerod's shot out

↪ **86 min:** Baird off, Fernandes on

87 min: Extended period of exclusive Arsenal possession begins

▯ **90 min:** M. Svensson booked

90 mins + 4 mins injury time

▯ **92 min:** Beattie's header cleared off the line by Cole

FULL-TIME: 1-0

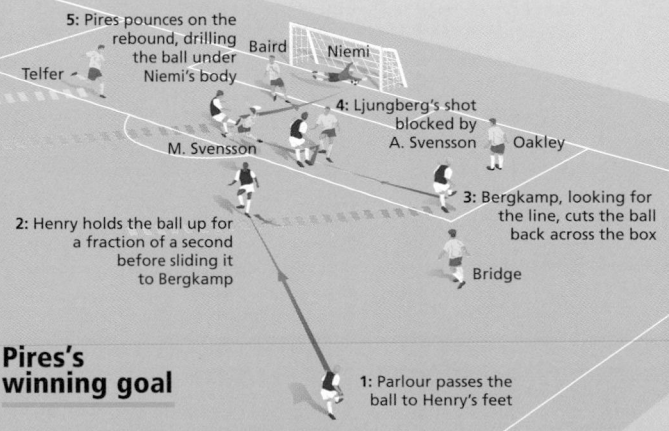

5: Pires pounces on the rebound, drilling the ball under Niemi's body

4: Ljungberg's shot blocked by A. Svensson

3: Bergkamp, looking for the line, cuts the ball back across the box

2: Henry holds the ball up for a fraction of a second before sliding it to Bergkamp

1: Parlour passes the ball to Henry's feet

Pires's winning goal

The Origins of Football

THE IRRESISTIBLE URGE of children to kick things, and the general availability of round objects in the world, suggest that people have been playing some version of football since the beginning of history. Chinese archeologists have found stone balls from the Neolithic era (around 10,000 BC), and have claimed China to be the home of the global game. Reports from South America suggest that access to rubber in the Amazonian rainforest gave the region its head start in ball skills and control. Certainly there is evidence of various ball and kicking games among the indigenous Indian civilizations of Patagonia and the Andes.

Stronger records exist for a game called Tsu Chu played under the Han Empire of China (206 BC–221 AD), which spread into Japan and Korea with local variations and names. A stuffed animal-skin ball was kicked between large bamboo posts; some accounts suggest that it formed part of festivities, others that it was an element of military training. Frescoes from the era clearly indicate women playing the game.

Li Yu, a Chinese writer (c. 50–130 AD), wrote a eulogy to the game, which was intended to be hung on the goalposts:

A round ball and a square goal
Suggest the shape of the Yin and the Yang.
The ball is like the full moon,
And the two teams stand opposed:
Captains are appointed and take their place.
In the game make no allowance for relationship
And let there be no partiality.
Determination and coolness are essential
And there must not be the slightest irritation for failure.
Such is the game. Let its principles apply to life.

Folk football in Europe

Evidence of folk football in Europe dates from around the beginning of the second millennium. A variety of ball games were played by the Celtic periphery of Europe, such as Knappan in Wales and the game of Ba' in the Orkney Islands. First-hand reports from the 11th and 12th centuries mention a game called *La Soule*, popular among the peasantry of medieval Brittany and northern France, while a distinctive rule-bound game called *Calcio* was played by the ruling elites of Florence from the 16th century. But it is in England that the most regular and systematic reports of football come in the medieval period. William Fitzstephen, living in London between 1170 and 1183, wrote:

'After dinner all the youth of the city goes out into the fields for the very popular game of ball. The elders, the fathers and the men of wealth come on horseback to view the contests of their juniors.'

What the game of 'ball' seems to have consisted of was a very tough, often violent, unstructured brawling game in which two ill-defined and often ill-matched mobs moved a ball

Calcio, or Giuoco del calcio Fiorentino, was played in Florence and other parts of Northern Italy from the 16th century. This fresco by Giovanni Stradano, painted in 1555, shows a game in progress in the city's Piazza Santa Maria Novella.

The Origins of Football

ENGLAND
Mob or folk football
(1100)

Location
Early form of football
Approximate date

WALES
Knappan
(1000)

ORKNEY ISLANDS
Ba'
(1000)

ENGLAND
Mob or folk football
(1100)

FRANCE
(Brittany)
Soule (1100)

ITALY
Giuoco del calcio Fiorentino (1500)
Harpastum (200 BC)

GREECE
Episkyros
(200 BC)

NORTH AMERICA
Passuckquakkohowog
(17th century)

MEXICO
Pok-ta-pok
(800 BC)

CHILE
Pilimatum
(1500 BC)

PATAGONIA
Tchoekah

Passuckquakkohowog. This Native American word literally translates as 'those who gather to play football'. The earliest written reports of the game in North America come from 17th century English pilgrims.

Although a rudimentary form of football called Episkyros could be found in Classical Greece, it was of low status – the domain of women and children. No ball game was allowed into the prestigious ancient Olympic Games.

This ring is found on the wall of the Ball Court at the Mayan temple at Chichen-Itza in Mexico. Pok-ta-pok was just one of many games played by American Indians before the European conquest, along with Pilimatum in Chile and Tchoekah in Patagonia.

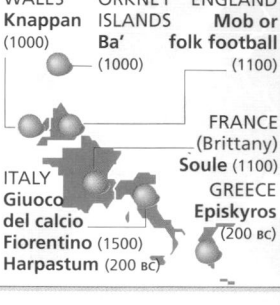

Though no codified forms of African football have been recorded, the San people of southern Africa played a vertical kickabout game. Modern football spread like wildfire during the colonization of the continent in the late 19th and early 20th centuries. This batik shows a game in contemporary Uganda.

A 19th-century engraving of mob or folk football, England.

to some specified location by almost any means, and any limb, available. Reports abound of serious injuries and accidental stabbings, even deaths, during these games. More worrying for local elites, these games often led to, or turned into, acts of major social disturbance and riot. Not surprisingly, Edward II, King of England, issued a proclamation in 1314 banning the game, claiming that there was 'great uproar in the city through certain tumults arising from great footballs in the fields of the public, from which many evils may arise'. The ban was repeated in 1331 and 1365 in the hope of encouraging more archery, but without success.

Derby day

Shrove Tuesday was a particularly popular day for rural football matches – the game played in Derby between the parishes of St. Peter and All Saints was notorious for its unrestrained ferocity, and gave birth to the term for fiercely fought local contests – derbies. In the cities, football often accompanied rites of passage for journeymen and apprentices. An observer in 18th-century London wrote:

> *I spy the furies of the football war*
> *The Prentice quits his shop,*
> *To join the crew,*
> *Increasing crowds the flying*
> *Game pursue...*

These Chinese characters mean 'to kick with the foot' and 'a ball made of leather ... to allow it to be kicked around for recreation'.

JAPAN
Kemari
(400)

CHINA
Cuju or Tsu Chu
(200 BC)

Kemari, a Japanese variant of a Chinese ball game, was played from around the 5th century AD.

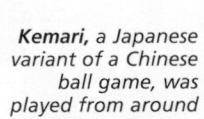

A fierce game called La Soule was popular in Normandy and Brittany in France during the 11th and 12th centuries.

Yet despite ruling class disapproval of folk football, it had begun to find a home in the schools and universities of England. Reports of football at Oxford and Cambridge date from the 16th century.

By the beginning of the 19th century, team sports had been enthusiastically adopted by England's elite public schools as an essential element of the practical and moral education of the ruling class. Football in a variety of forms and with a variety of rules was the predominant sport. Simultaneously, folk and mob football were in decline as the congested spaces and stricter policing of modern industrial cities made the game increasingly difficult to play. It would eventually disappear altogether, to be replaced by a game with fixed rules derived from the public school game (see pages 26–27).

The Global Game

CODIFICATION AND SPREAD

IN 19TH-CENTURY ENGLAND, there was no shortage of rules for the game of football. The elite public schools had embraced team sports as an essential component of ruling-class character formation, and each had created rules that suited their environment. Harrow's heavy ball favoured dribbling, while Winchester's narrow pitch suited kick and rush, and Westminster's cloisters the short pass. These rules collided when old boys played each other at university, so common football rules were drafted in 1846 at Cambridge University. A revised version of these rules formed the basis of the rules drawn up in 1863 by the newly created Football Association and representatives of 12 London clubs. The only dissenters from the rules were Blackheath, who opted to retain handling and hacking; they went on to play the newly codified game of rugby union in 1871.

In the English-speaking world local variations produced codified rules for American, Australian, Canadian and Gaelic football. Armed with the FA rules, an empire and the world's biggest trading network, Britons of every social class carried the game to Europe and the Americas. Sailors played in the ports of Chile and Germany, textile workers in the Netherlands, public schoolboy merchants in Rio and Barcelona. In Britain's formal Empire, in Asia and Africa, the colonial power was more reticent to spread the game, fearing the anti-colonial social organization that might emerge from football.

Caged into the tighter spaces of an urban environment, rural folk football acquired the rudiments of organized play, such as goals and duration, but violence and injury remained regular features of the game.

The Evolution of Football

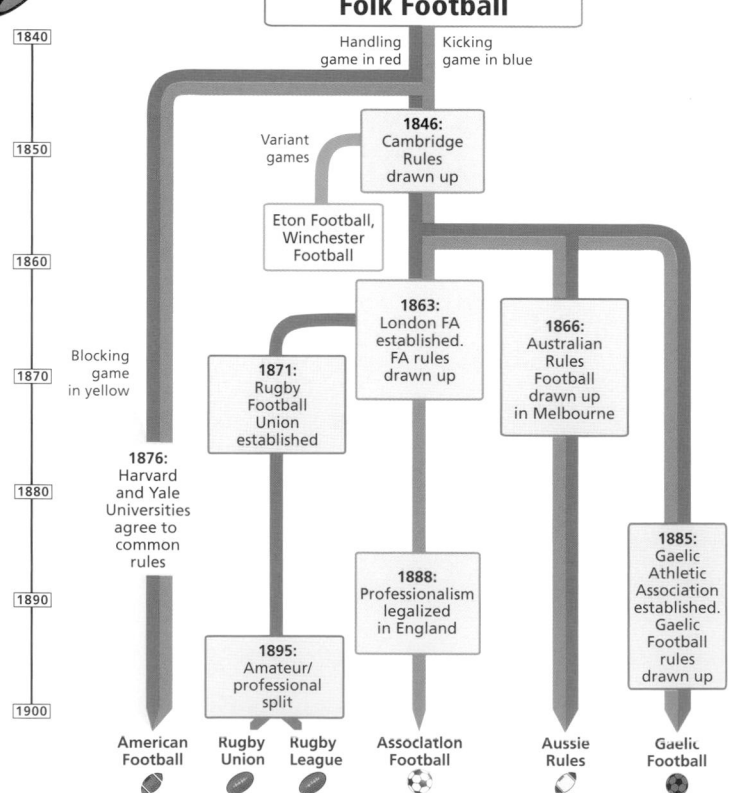

The global spread of football 1850–1930

THE GLOBAL GAME

Codification of the Rules

Shrewsbury
● Birmingham
● Rugby

Cambridge
Cambridge Rules drawn up in 1846 and revised in 1863

E N G L A N D

Oxford ●

● Harrow

Eton
Westminster

Marlborough

London
FA founded and rules drawn up in 1863

Charterhouse

Winchester

A competing set of rules was established by Sheffield FC, founded in 1857. The Sheffield FA, innovators in the use of free kicks and corner kicks, brought its rules into line with the FA in 1877.

Key

Cambridge University

Public school represented at the rewriting of the Cambridge Rules in 1863

Other public school

School with own rules

Rugby rules

Clubs involved in the formation of FA in 1863

Barnes
Blackheath (later withdrew)
Blackheath School
Charterhouse
Crusaders
Crystal Palace
Forest
Kensington School
No Names of Kilburn
Percival House
Surbiton
The War Office

Harrow School Football XI 1867.
Harrow's poorly drained fields required a heavy leather ball and encouraged dribbling rather than hoofing the ball up the pitch.

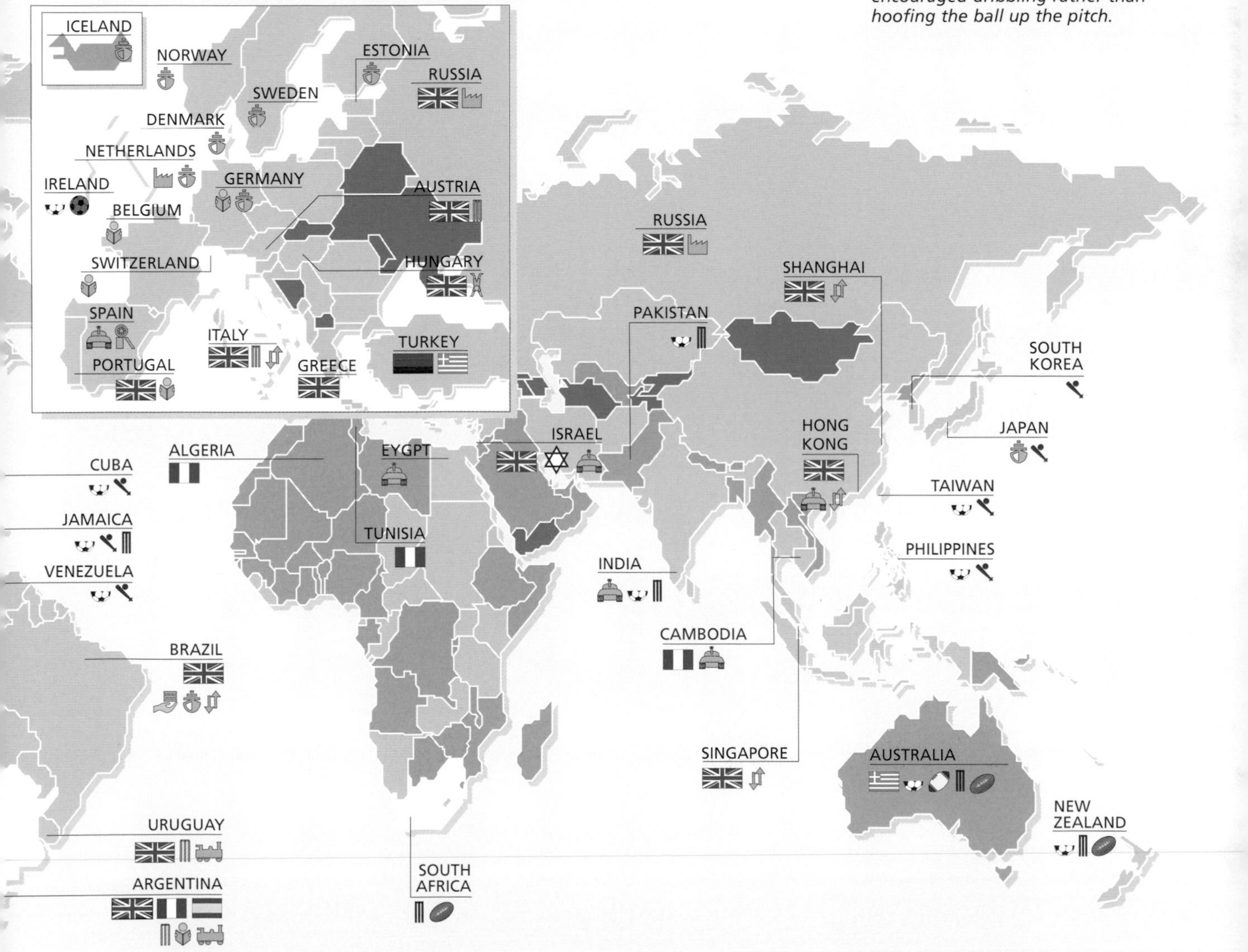

ICELAND
NORWAY
ESTONIA
RUSSIA
SWEDEN
DENMARK
NETHERLANDS
GERMANY
AUSTRIA
IRELAND
BELGIUM
HUNGARY
SWITZERLAND
SPAIN
ITALY
PORTUGAL
GREECE
TURKEY

RUSSIA
SHANGHAI
PAKISTAN
SOUTH KOREA
HONG KONG
JAPAN
ISRAEL
TAIWAN
PHILIPPINES

CUBA
ALGERIA
EYGPT
JAMAICA
TUNISIA
VENEZUELA
INDIA
CAMBODIA

BRAZIL

SINGAPORE
AUSTRALIA

URUGUAY
NEW ZEALAND

ARGENTINA
SOUTH AFRICA

The Laws of the Game

THE LAWS OF THE GAME

LAW I: FIELD OF PLAY

The field of play must be a rectangle of specific size (see diagram for length). The field must have clear lines marked on it: touchlines, goal lines, halfway line, centre circle, goal areas, goal area lines, goals, penalty areas, penalty spots, corner arcs and flagposts.

LAW II: BALL

The ball must be made of an approved material. At the start of the match the ball must be 68–70 cm in diameter, 410–450 grams in weight, and have an internal pressure of 0.6–1.1 atmospheres at sea level. It can only be changed by the referee. If the ball bursts during a game, play stops and restarts with a drop ball.

LAW III: PLAYERS

A match consists of two teams of not more than 11 players each including a goalkeeper. Any outfield player may change places with the goalkeeper during a stoppage. Teams need at least seven players to begin a game.

LAW V: REFEREE

The referee is the final arbiter on the interpretation and enforcement of the laws. They decide whether a game can be played and the duration of play. They can suspend and abandon a match, stop play to allow treatment of injured players, caution players (yellow card) for a range of misconduct and fouls or send off a player (red card) for serious foul play, violent conduct, offensive language and for two cautions. Referees make sure all equipment meets the relevant specifications and keeps a record of the match. They have a duty to allow play to flow and refrain from punishing insignificant or non-deliberate infringements.

LAW VI: ASSISTANT REFEREES

Formerly called the linesmen, the assistant referees help the referee primarily by signalling corner kicks, goal kicks, throw-ins and offsides. However, the referee's word is final.

LAW VIII: START & RESTART OF PLAY

Before the start of play a coin is tossed. The winning team chooses ends for the first half and the losing team takes the kick-off. This is reversed in the second half. Play begins after the referee has signalled. The kick-off is taken from the centre spot and the ball must move into the opposition's half of the field. All players must be in their half of the field and opposition players must be at least ten yards from the ball. The ball must be touched by another player before the kicker can touch it again.

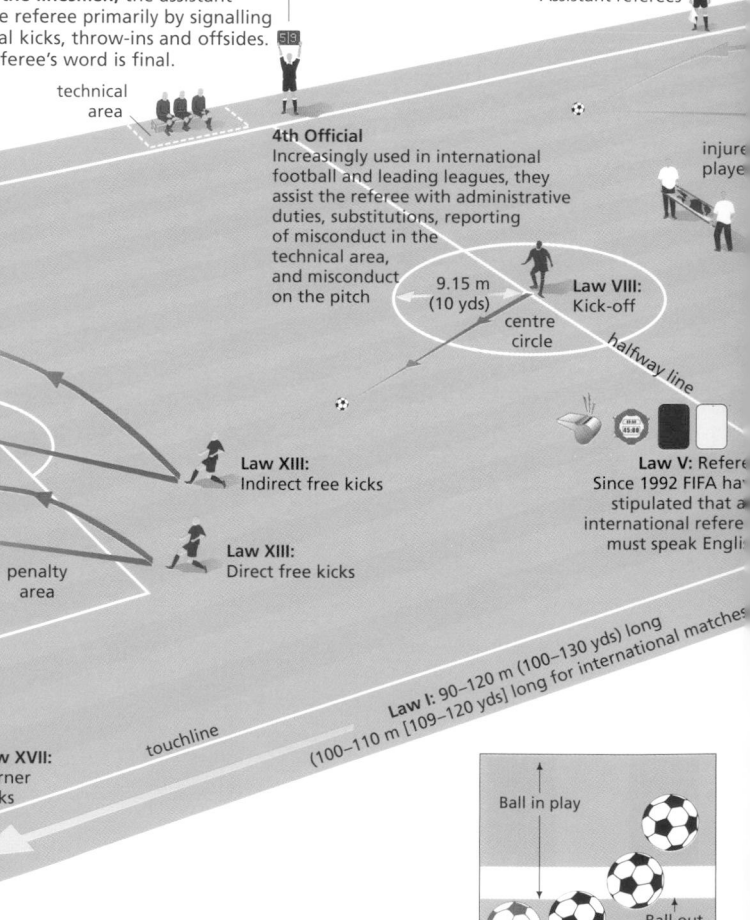

Law VI:
Assistant referees

technical area

4th Official
Increasingly used in international football and leading leagues, they assist the referee with administrative duties, substitutions, reporting of misconduct in the technical area, and misconduct on the pitch

injured player

9.15 m (10 yds)

Law VIII: Kick-off

centre circle

halfway line

16.5 m (18 yds)

goal line

Law I: 45–90 m (50–100 yds) wide (64–75 m [70–82 yds] wide for international matches)

goal area

5.5 m (6 yds)

5.5 m (6 yds)

10.5 m (11.5 yds)

penalty area

Law XIII: Indirect free kicks

Law XIII: Direct free kicks

Law V: Referee Since 1992 FIFA have stipulated that all international referees must speak English

Law XVII: Corner kicks

touchline

Law I: 90–120 m (100–130 yds) long for international matches (100–110 m [109–120 yds] long)

International FA Board
Founded in 1886 by the FAs of England, Scotland, Wales and Northern Ireland, the International FA Board governs the Laws of the Game. It meets annually and now includes four additional FIFA members and its decisions are binding on national FAs.

Substitutes
The number of substitutes is governed by FIFA and confederation rules, not the International FA Board. Normally three substitutions from seven are allowed. They can only enter the field at the halfway line during a stoppage after another player has left.

Ball in play

Ball out of play

LAW IV: PLAYERS' EQUIPMENT

Compulsory equipment for players are a shirt, shorts, socks, shin-guards and football boots. Goalkeepers must wear kit that distinguishes them from outfield players and officials.

LAW VII: DURATION OF PLAY

There are two equal periods of 45 minutes. Additional time may be added at the discretion of the referee for injuries, time-wasting and substitutions. Time can also be added to allow a penalty to be taken after the end of normal play.

LAW IX: IN & OUT OF PLAY

The game is in play when the ball is inside the field of play and the referee has not stopped play. The ball is out of play when the whole ball, whether in the air or on the ground, has crossed either touchlines or goal lines.

LAW X: SCORING

A goal has been scored when the whole of the ball has crossed the goal line between the goalposts and under the crossbar, provided no other infringements have taken place. The team with the most goals wins.

LAW XI: OFFSIDE

Offside is an illegal playing position taken up by a player relative to the ball, the field of play and opposition players at the moment when the ball is played by an attacking teammate. A player is offside when **a)** they are in the opposition's half of the field, **b)** they are closer to the opponent's goal line than the ball and **c)** there are fewer than two defenders, including the goalkeeper, who are closer to the goal line than the attacking player. A player will be penalized for being offside if they are interfering with play or with an opponent and they can gain some advantage from being in that position.

The Offside Rule

Onside: Attacking player is level with defending players

Onside: Attacking player is further from the opposition's goal line than defending players

Offside: Attacking player is closer to the opposition's goal line than defending players

Extra Time

Determined by the rules of the competition, but usually two periods of 15 minutes play after normal time where the scores are level. If the score remains level this often extends to a penalty shootout. In some competitions the 'golden goal' rule is applied to extra time. This means that during the period of extra time, the team which scores the first goal is declared the winner.

00:00 45:00

Law XVI: Goal kicks

Law XIV: Penalty kicks First introduced in 1891

penalty area

goalpost 2.44 m (2.67 yds)

penalty spot

Crossbar 7.32 m (8 yds) A cross tape was originally introduced between the posts by the FA in 1886.

corner arc → corner flag

Law VI: Assistant referees First introduced as linesmen in 1891

Law XV: Throw-ins

LAW XIII: FREE KICKS

Free kicks restart play after the game has been stopped for a foul or another act of misconduct. The referee will award the team which did not commit the offence with a direct free kick (from which a goal can be scored) or an indirect free kick (where the ball must touch another player before a goal can be scored). A free kick is usually taken from the point at which the offence was committed.

LAW XIV: PENALTY KICKS

A penalty is awarded for a foul by a defending player inside their own penalty area. A penalty kick is taken from the penalty spot. All other players, apart from the goalkeeper and penalty taker, must be at least ten yards from the spot and on the field of play. The ball is in play as soon as it is kicked. The penalty taker may touch the ball if it rebounds from the goalkeeper but not if it rebounds from the post or crossbar. Other players may touch the ball in that situation. The goalkeeper must face the penalty taker and stand on the goal line.

LAW XV: THROW-INS

A throw-in is awarded to a team when the ball has crossed the touchline and an opposition player was the last to touch it. The throw-in is taken from the point where the ball crossed the touchline. The taker must have both feet on the ground, use two hands, throw the ball from behind and over the head and be facing the field of play.

LAW XVI: GOAL KICKS

A goal kick is awarded to the defending team when the ball crosses its goal line, a goal has not been scored, and the last player to touch the ball was from the attacking team. Any player may take the goal kick by placing it within the team's own penalty area. The kick must go outside the penalty area or be retaken. The taker must not touch the ball again until another player has touched it. Opposition players must remain outside the penalty area while the kick is taken. A goal may be scored directly from a goal kick.

LAW XVII: CORNER KICKS

A corner kick is awarded to the attacking team when the ball was last touched by a member of the defending team and crosses its goal line without a goal being scored. A corner kick is also awarded if the ball enters the goal from a throw-in or an indirect free kick. The attacking team restarts the game with the ball placed in the corner arc nearest to where the ball crossed the goal line. Defending players must be at least 10 yards from the ball when it is kicked. The corner taker may not touch the ball after the corner kick until another player has touched it.

LAW XII: FOULS AND MISCONDUCT

A foul is committed if a player **(1)** trips, kicks, pushes, recklessly charges or uses excessive force against another player; **(2)** strikes, attempts to strike, or spits at an opponent; **(3)** makes a tackle but connects with their opponent before the ball; **(4)** deliberately handles the ball (except for goalkeepers inside their penalty area); **(5, 6)** obstructs an opponent or prevents the goalkeeper from releasing the ball. Goalkeepers commit a foul if they: fail to release the ball within six seconds of picking it up; release the ball into play and then handle it; handle a backpass or a throw-in from a teammate; or are guilty of time-wasting. An indirect free kick is awarded for the above.

FIFA and the Confederations

FIFA

Fédération Internationale de Football Association

Founded: 1904
Headquarters: Zurich, Switzerland
President: Joseph Sepp Blatter (Switzerland)
General Secretary: Situation
now vacant
Members: 204
Competitions: World Cup
Women's World Cup
Under-17 World Championship
World Youth Championship
Club World Championship
Confederation's Cup
Awards: FIFA World Player of the Year
FIFA World Team of the Year
FIFA Fair Play Award

NORTH & CENTRAL AMERICA
DOM REP DOMINICAN REPUBLIC
NETH ANT NETHERLANDS ANTILLES

CONCACAF

Founded: 1961
Headquarters: New York, USA
President: Jack Austin Warner (Trinidad & Tobago)
General Secretary: Chuck Blazer (USA)
Members: 35
Competitions: CONCACAF Gold Cup
CONCACAF Women's Gold Cup
CONCACAF Champions Cup

FIFA (FÉDÉRATION INTERNATIONALE DE FOOTBALL ASSOCIATION) is the global governing body of football. From its headquarters in Switzerland it organizes and promotes the World Cup, the Women's World Cup and a range of other tournaments and prizes, as well as setting the legal and institutional framework for global football. Founded in 1904 by representatives of seven European nations, FIFA's early years were marked by struggles with both the British footballing associations and other competing international football groupings. The British nations in particular were slow to join, reflecting both insecurity and indifference. They were also quick to leave after the First World War when the admission of Germany to FIFA was agreed. Similarly, the British Home Countries remained individually represented on the international rule-making Association Football Board, while FIFA represented the rest of the world. Once the British had left and the French visionary Jules Rimet had assumed the presidency, FIFA's growth began. With the successful creation of the World Cup in 1930, FIFA's control of the global game was secured.

The confederations that make up FIFA vary widely: from the fearsomely powerful UEFA to the marginal OFC (Oceanic Football Confederation). All nations get a single vote at FIFA's biennial conferences, but as usual, in the real corridors of power, money and contacts talk.

Daniel Woolfall (1906–18)
Arthur Drewry (1956–61)
Sir Stanley Rous (1961–74)
Rodolfe Seeldrayers (1954–55)
Jules Rimet (1921–54)
Robert Guerin (1904–06)
Joseph Sepp Blatter (1998–)

Dr Joao Havelange (1974–98)

SOUTH AMERICA
VENEZ VENEZUELA

CONMEBOL

Confederación Sudamericana de Fútbol

Founded: 1916
Headquarters: Asunción, Paraguay
President: Dr Nicolas Leóz (Paraguay)
General Secretary: Eduardo Deluca (Argentina)
Members: 10
Competitions: Copa América
Copa Libertadores
Copa Sudamericana

UEFA

Union of European Football Associations

Founded: 1954
Headquarters: Nyon, Switzerland
President: Lennart Johansson (Sweden)
General Secretary: Gerhard Aigner (Germany)
Members: 51
Competitions: European Championships
European Champions League
UEFA Cup
Intertoto Cup
European Super Cup
European Women's Championships

EUROPE

ARM	ARMENIA
AUS	AUSTRIA
AZER	AZERBAIJAN
BEL	BELGIUM
B-H	BOSNIA-HERZEGOVINA
CZ REP	CZECH REPUBLIC
ISR	ISRAEL
LIECH	LIECHTENSTEIN
LUX	LUXEMBOURG
NETH	NETHERLANDS
REP OF IRELAND	REPUBLIC OF IRELAND
SWITZ	SWITZERLAND
YUG	YUGOSLAVIA

FIFA and the Confederations

☆ FIFA presidents
☐ FIFA headquarters
■ Confederation headquarters
◎ Associate members
○ Non-members

Date of joining FIFA

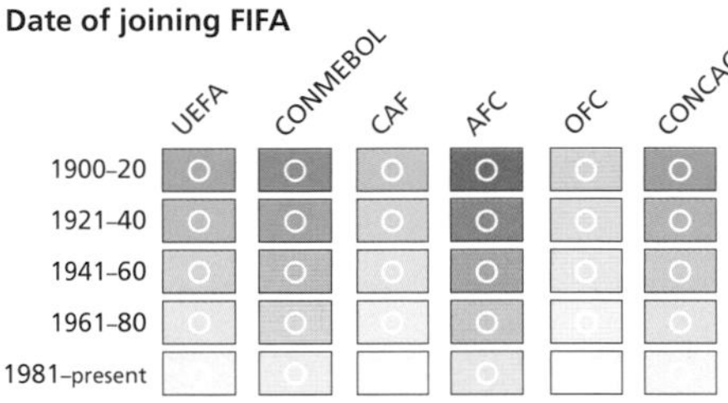

	UEFA	CONMEBOL	CAF	AFC	OFC	CONCACAF
1900–20	○	○	○	○	○	○
1921–40	○	○	○	○	○	○
1941–60	○	○	○	○	○	○
1961–80	○	○	○	○	○	○
1981–present						

AFC

Asian Football Confederation

Founded: 1954
Headquarters: Kuala Lumpur, Malaysia
President: Mohammed Bin Hamman (Qatar)
General Secretary: Dato' Peter Velappan (Malaysia)
Members: 45
Competitions: Asian Cup
Asian Games
Asian Champions League
Asian Women's Championship

ASIA

AFGHAN	AFGHANISTAN
JOR	JORDAN
LEB	LEBANON
PAL	PALESTINE
TAJ	TAJIKISTAN
TURK	TURKMENISTAN
UZBEK	UZBEKISTAN

AFRICA

BF	BURKINA FASO
CI	CÔTE D'IVOIRE

CAF

Confédération Africaine de Football

Founded: 1957
Headquarters: Cairo, Eygpt
President: Issa Hayatou (Cameroon)
General Secretary: Mustapha Fahmy (Egypt)
Members: 52
Associate Members: 1
Competitions: African Cup of Nations
CAF Cup
African Champions League
African Cup-Winners' Cup
CAF Super Cup

OFC

Oceania Football Confederation

Founded: 1966
Headquarters: Auckland, New Zealand
President: Basil Scarsella (Australia)
General Secretary: Josephine King (New Zealand)
Members: 11
Associate Members: 1 (+1 Provisional)
Competitions: Oceania Nations Cup
OFC Club Championship
Oceania Women's Tournament

Seats on FIFA Executive

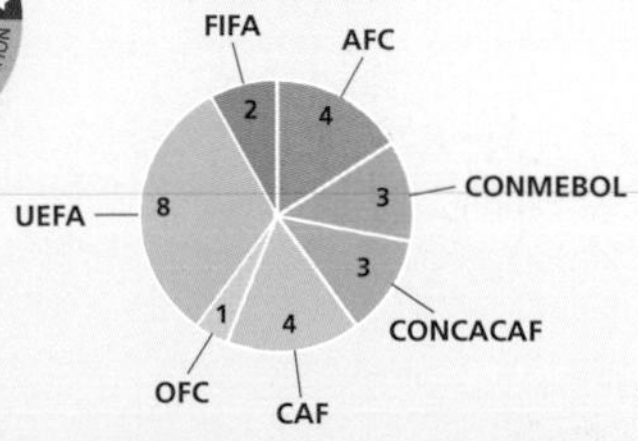

FIFA 2
AFC 4
CONMEBOL 3
CONCACAF 3
CAF 4
OFC 1
UEFA 8

Map labels: RUSSIA, UKRAINE, MOLDOVA, TURKEY, KAZAKHSTAN, MONGOLIA, GEORGIA, AZER, ARM, UZBEK, KYRGYZSTAN, TURK, TAJ, AFGHAN, ASIA, CHINA, NORTH KOREA, JAPAN, SOUTH KOREA, LEB, CYPRUS, ISR, SYRIA, IRAN, PAL, IRAQ, JOR, KUWAIT, PAKISTAN, NEPAL, BHUTAN, BANGLADESH, HONG KONG, TAIWAN, Cairo, EGYPT, BAHRAIN, QATAR, UAE, SAUDI ARABIA, OMAN, INDIA, BURMA, LAOS, VIETNAM, MACAO, CHAD, SUDAN, YEMEN, DJIBOUTI, THAILAND, CAMBODIA, GUAM, CENTRAL AFRICAN REPUBLIC, ETHIOPIA, ERITREA, SRI LANKA, Kuala Lumpur, BRUNEI, MALAYSIA, PHILIPPINES, PACIFIC OCEAN, UGANDA, KENYA, SOMALIA, SINGAPORE, RWANDA, BURUNDI, MALDIVES, INDONESIA, NORTHERN MARIANA ISLANDS, TANZANIA, DEMOCRATIC REPUBLIC OF CONGO (Zaïre), PAPUA NEW GUINEA, SOLOMON ISLANDS, MALAWI, INDIAN OCEAN, ZAMBIA, MOZAMBIQUE, MADAGASCAR, MAURITIUS, REUNION (Associate), SEYCHELLES, VANUATU, WESTERN SAMOA, AMERICAN SAMOA, TAHITI, SWAZILAND, LESOTHO, SOUTH AFRICA, OCEANIA, AUSTRALIA, NEW CALEDONIA (Provisional Associate), FIJI, TONGA, COOK ISLANDS, Auckland, NEW ZEALAND

The World Cup

TOURNAMENT OVERVIEW

ALTHOUGH FIFA had given itself the right to organize a global football competition when created in 1904, it did not do so for some 25 years. Prior to this the tournament at the Olympics had functioned as the *de facto* world championships. However, as professionalism took hold in major footballing nations, the amateur ethos of the Olympic Games became a block on the appearance of the world's best players and teams. At the FIFA conference in Barcelona in 1929, Jules Rimet, the French general secretary of FIFA, proposed that an international championship be held within the next 12 months. Almost unanimous agreement saw the tournament established and destined for Uruguay, where on 13 July 1930, the very first World Cup fixture was played between France and Mexico.

The development of the competition parallels the global development of football. From only 13 entrants in 1930, all from Latin America or Europe, it now has over 200 from every corner of the globe in its qualifying stages. Since 1998, the finals have expanded to include 32 participants in a month-long event. The early domination of Europe and Latin America culminated in 1966 when FIFA allocated one place to Africa, Asia and Central America combined, prompting a widespread boycott. The steady shift in the balance of global football power saw 13 finalists from these confederations in 1998. From 2006, Oceania will be guaranteed a place at the finals and the champions will be forced to qualify. Most importantly, the finals are now one of the most significant televisual and media events in the calendar, as evidenced by the huge increase in the cost of acquiring TV broadcast rights and the astronomical viewing figures it achieves.

THE WORLD CUP

World Cup Finals (1930–2002)

YEAR	WINNERS	SCORE	RUNNERS-UP
1930	Uruguay	4-2	Argentina
1934	Italy	2-1 (aet)	Czechoslovakia
1938	Italy	4-2	Hungary
1950	Uruguay	2-1	Brazil
1954	West Germany	3-2	Hungary
1958	Brazil	5-2	Sweden
1962	Brazil	3-1	Czechoslovakia
1966	England	4-2 (aet)	West Germany
1970	Brazil	4-1	Italy
1974	West Germany	2-1	Netherlands
1978	Argentina	3-1 (aet)	Netherlands
1982	Italy	3-1	West Germany
1986	Argentina	3-2	West Germany
1990	West Germany	1-0	Argentina
1994	Brazil	0-0 (3-2 pens)	Italy
1998	France	3-0	Brazil
2002	Brazil	2-0	Germany

World Cup Football

Number of appearances at tournament 1930–98	
▓	12+ times
▓	8–11 times
▓	5–7 times
░	2–4 times
░	1 time
□	0 times

World Cup

👕 Winners

🏆 **1954,** Winners in bold
66 Runners-up in italic

〔1999〕 Host country and year

● Rome Location of Final

REP OF IRELAND
WALES
PORTUG.
CANADA
UNITED STATES OF AMERICA 〔1994〕
Pasadena ●
MEXICO 〔1970, 86〕 Mexico City
HAITI
CUBA
JAMAICA
EL SALVADOR
HONDURAS
COSTA RICA
COLOMBIA
PERU
BOLIVIA
PARAGUAY
CHILE 〔1962〕 Montevideo
Buenos Aires
Santiago
ARGENTINA 〔1978〕
🏆 1930, 78, 86, *90*

The World Cup
Top Goalscorers (1930–2002)

YEAR	SCORER	NATIONALITY	GOALS
1930	Stabile	Argentina	8
1934	Nejedly	Czechoslovakia	5
1938	Leonidas	Brazil	8
1950	Ademir	Brazil	9
1954	Kocsis	Hungary	8
1958	Fontaine	France	13
1962	Ivanov	Soviet Union	4
	Sancjez	Chile	
	Garrincha	Brazil	
	Vava	Brazil	
	Albert	Hungary	
	Jerkovic	Yugoslavia	
1966	Eusebio	Portugal	9
1970	Müller	W. Germany	10
1974	Lato	Poland	7
1978	Kempes	Argentina	6
1982	Rossi	Italy	6
1986	Lineker	England	6
1990	Schillachi	Italy	6
1994	Salenko	Russia	6
	Stoichkov	Bulgaria	
1998	Suker	Croatia	6
2002	Ronaldo	Brazil	7

World Cup finals: number and origins of participants

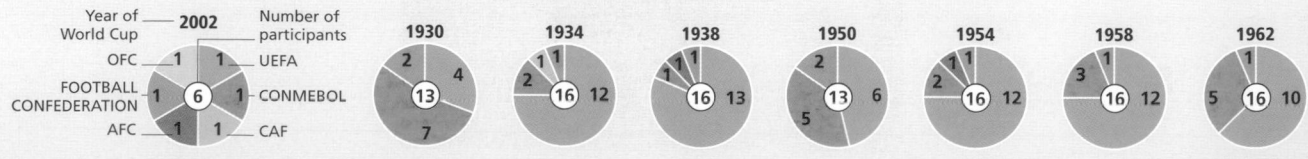

Year of World Cup — 2002 — Number of participants
OFC 1 | 1 UEFA
FOOTBALL CONFEDERATION 1 | 6 | 1 CONMEBOL
AFC 1 | 1 CAF

1930 — 13
1934 — 16
1938 — 16
1950 — 13
1954 — 16
1958 — 16
1962 — 16

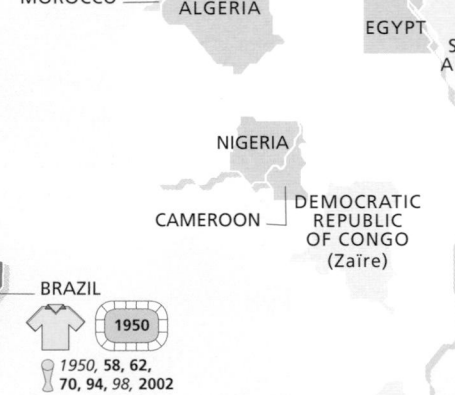

NORWAY
NORTHERN IRELAND
SWEDEN
1958
1958
SCOTLAND
DENMARK
NGLAND
ENGLAND
1966
● Stockholm
RUSSIA
GERMANY
1974
1954, 66, 74, 82, 86, **90**, 2002
1966
NETH
1974, 78
POLAND
ondon
London
Munich
BELGIUM
CZECH REP
1934, 62
FRANCE
Paris
Bern
AUSTRIA
HUNGARY
1938, 54
1938, 98
CROATIA
ROMANIA
YUGOSLAVIA
BULGARIA
RUSSIA
● Rome
1998
SWITZ
1954
GREECE
TURKEY
Madrid
1982
SPAIN
ITALY
1934, 90
1934, 38, 70, 82, 94
ISRAEL
TUNISIA
IRAQ
IRAN
KUWAIT
MOROCCO
ALGERIA
EGYPT
SAUDI ARABIA
UAE

NORTH KOREA
SOUTH KOREA
2002*
*Co-hosts
JAPAN
2002*

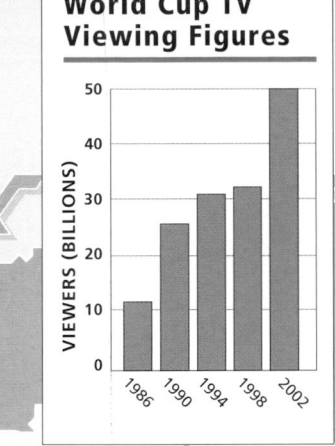

World Cup TV Viewing Figures

VIEWERS (BILLIONS)

50	
40	
30	
20	
10	
0	

1986 · 1990 · 1994 · 1998 · 2002

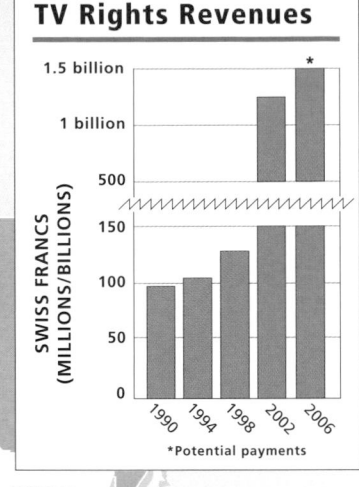

TV Rights Revenues

SWISS FRANCS (MILLIONS/BILLIONS)

1.5 billion *
1 billion
500
150
100
50
0

1990 · 1994 · 1998 · 2002 · 2006

*Potential payments

NIGERIA
CAMEROON
DEMOCRATIC REPUBLIC OF CONGO (Zaïre)

INDONESIA

BRAZIL
1950
1950, 58, 62, 70, 94, *98*, 2002

Rio de Janiero

AUSTRALIA

URUGUAY
1930
1930, 50

SOUTH AFRICA

NEW ZEALAND

The Coupe Jules Rimet was made by French sculptor Abel Lafleur and presented to Brazil on its third World Cup victory in 1970. It was stolen and recovered in England in 1966 and stolen again in Rio in 1983. It is believed to have been melted down.

The second World Cup trophy was made by Italian sculptor Silvio Gazzangia and is solid gold on a base of malachite. Copies are given to the victors but FIFA keeps the real thing.

THE WORLD CUP

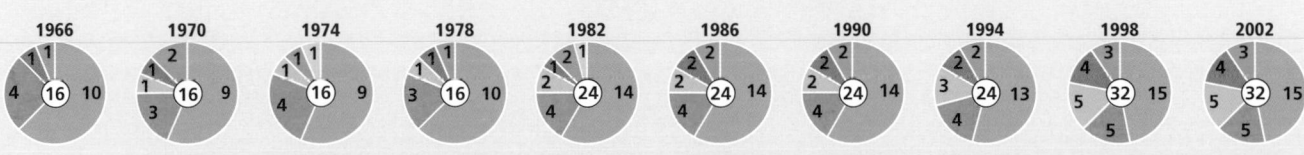

1966	1970	1974	1978	1982	1986	1990	1994	1998	2002
1 / 1 / 4 (16) 10	2 / 1 / 1 / 3 (16) 9	1 / 1 / 4 (16) 9	1 / 1 / 3 (16) 10	2 / 1 / 2 / 4 (24) 14	2 / 2 / 2 / 4 (24) 14	2 / 2 / 2 / 4 (24) 14	2 / 2 / 3 / 4 (24) 13	3 / 4 / 5 (32) 15	3 / 4 / 5 / 5 (32) 15

WORLD CUP FINALS (1930–98)

The World Cup has invariably laid bare the distribution of power in world football. Only seven nations have won the tournament, three from Latin America (Argentina, Brazil and Uruguay) and four from Europe (England, France, Germany and Italy), and only four others have appeared in a Final, again all from Europe (Czechoslovakia, Hungary, Sweden, the Netherlands). Only the USA in 1930 has broken the presence of Latin Americans and Europeans in the semi-finals. Similarly, prior to 2002 no country outside of Europe

and the Americas has hosted the games. Home advantage has often proved decisive. Only Brazil has won a World Cup on a continent not their own (Sweden 1958) while home victories have been scored by Uruguay (1930), Italy (1934), England (1966), West Germany (1974), Argentina (1978) and France (1998).

A few World Cup Finals have ultimately disappointed. The fantastic play at Italia '90 was crowned with a bad-tempered and rather ugly game between West Germany and Argentina (including two

sending-offs for the Argentines). A tense, goalless 120 minutes between Brazil and Italy in the 1994 Final in Los Angeles was ultimately decided by the cruel lottery of a penalty shootout. On the other hand, most Finals have been exhilarating displays of football. The World Cup has delivered the pulsating 1986 Final between Argentina and West Germany in Mexico City, the drama of England's two extra-time goals in the 1966 Final, and the sublime majesty of Brazil's 1970 triumph against Italy, again in Mexico City.

1930: Pedro Cea of Uruguay makes it 2-2 in the 57th minute of the first-ever World Cup Final. The Uruguayans scored twice more to take the trophy.

1934: Italy's squad give the Fascist salute to Il Duce in the VIP box at the Flaminio Stadium, Rome. Italy went on to beat the Czechs 2-1 in extra time.

1938: Italy celebrates its second World Cup title after beating Hungary 4-2. Azzurri coach, Vittorio Pozzo (suited on the left), embraces his players.

1950: The Uruguayans pose before the final pool match against Brazil. In front of nearly 200,000 Brazilian fans, the Uruguayans found the strength to beat their hosts 2-1.

1954: Hidejkuti of Hungary shoots, watched by West Germany's Horst Eckel. The Germans won 3-2 in the Final, the only match the Magical Magyars lost between 1950 and 56.

1958: Just Fontaine celebrates 13 goals in the World Cup, a record that still stands. But France was decisively beaten in the semi-final against Brazil by 5-2.

1962: The battle of Santiago. The first round match between Italy and Chile descended into foul play and violence. The Italian David argues before being sent off.

1966: Wolfgang Weber equalizes for Germany in the dying seconds of normal time in the Final against England. Gordon Banks stretches to no avail.

1970: Pele's World Cup. In the 18th minute of the Final, Pele opens the scoring against Italy. He made two more goals as the Brazilians won 4-1.

1974: Captain Franz Beckenbauer (left) and manager Helmut Schön (right) exchange an embrace as West Germany wins its second World Cup title.

1978: Daniel Pasarella, Argentina's captain and defensive lynchpin, grasps the World Cup. Argentina beat the Netherlands 3-1 after extra time.

1982: Paulo Rossi opens the scoring for Italy in the 56th minute of the Final against West Germany. Harold Schumacher, the German goalkeeper, watches the ball in.

1986: Diego Maradona sets off on the electrifying run through the England midfield and defence for his second goal in Argentina's 2-1 victory in the quarter-finals.

1990: Roger Milla celebrates another Cameroon goal at Italia '90. In 1994, he became the oldest player to play and score during a World Cup finals tournament.

1994: Roberto Baggio (Italy) contemplates his missed penalty in the Final shootout. The Brazilians celebrate their fourth World Cup victory.

1998: Zinedine Zidane rises above the Brazilian defence to head the opening goal in the Final. France won 3-0 against a team fatally weakened by a clearly under par Ronaldo. The Brazilian centre-forward had been withdrawn from the team sheet after he was taken ill at the team's hotel; a mixture of stress, stomach upset and allergy. But he arrived in the dressing room at the Stade de France and was reinstated minutes before the kick-off.

THE WORLD CUP

Japan/Korea 2002

TOURNAMENT REVIEW

THE 17th WORLD CUP FINALS, the first to be played outside of Europe and the Americas, were bound to herald some change in the balance of global football power. Japan/Korea 2002 will be remembered for the giant-killing of the early rounds, the colourful runs of Senegal, Turkey and South Korea and the reassertion of the old order in the Final.

The tournament opened with the sensational defeat of reigning champions France by Senegal in the country's first World Cup finals game. France looked tired, and without Zidane lacked the zest to compete with a skillful and committed Senegalese side. South Korea and the USA meted out a similar fate to the Portuguese. England and Sweden saw off the mighty Argentinians and Nigeria in the Group of Death. South Korea would do the same to Italy and Spain in the following rounds.

But in a tournament where teamwork, fitness and pressure seemed to have the upper hand, Brazil progressed imperiously to the Final where its unparalleled talent in attack was too much for a German defence that had conceded only a single goal on the way to Yokohama.

THE GROUP STAGES

The *ancien régime* appears to crumble as France, Argentina, Portugal, Russia and Cameroon all go out and Italy almost joins them. Brazil looks in a different league to everyone else. Sweden, Senegal, the USA, England, Ireland, Japan and South Korea all play above expectations. Only Saudi Arabia and China look out of their depth.

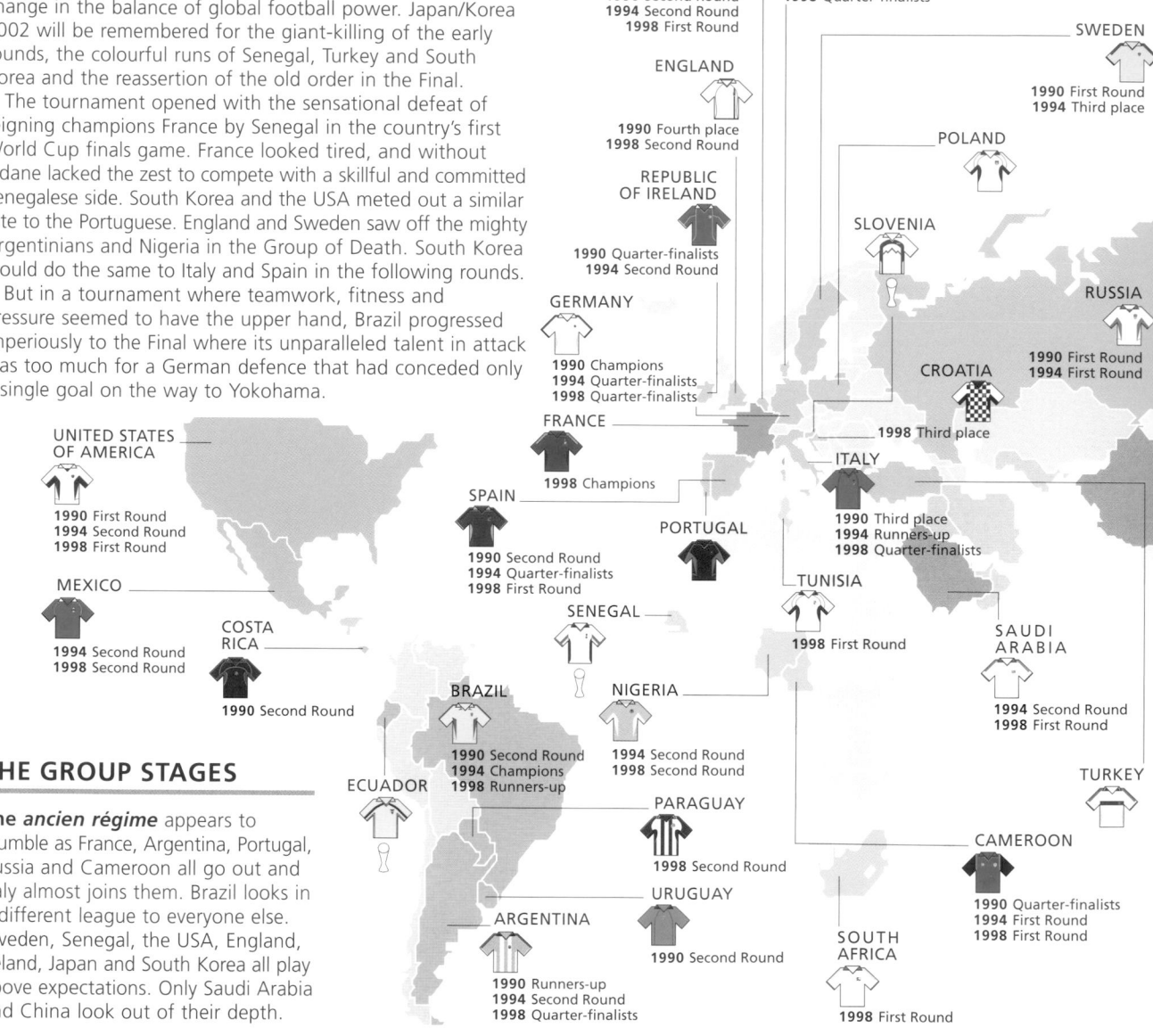

BELGIUM
1990 Second Round
1994 Second Round
1998 First Round

DENMARK
1998 Quarter-finalists

SWEDEN
1990 First Round
1994 Third place

ENGLAND
1990 Fourth place
1998 First Round

POLAND

REPUBLIC OF IRELAND
1990 Quarter-finalists
1994 Second Round

SLOVENIA

RUSSIA
1990 First Round
1994 First Round

GERMANY
1990 Champions
1994 Quarter-finalists
1998 Quarter-finalists

CROATIA
1998 Third place

FRANCE
1998 Champions

ITALY
1990 Third place
1994 Runners-up
1998 Quarter-finalists

SPAIN
1990 Second Round
1994 Quarter-finalists
1998 First Round

PORTUGAL

TUNISIA
1998 First Round

SAUDI ARABIA
1994 Second Round
1998 First Round

UNITED STATES OF AMERICA
1990 First Round
1994 Second Round
1998 First Round

SENEGAL

MEXICO
1994 Second Round
1998 Second Round

COSTA RICA
1990 Second Round

NIGERIA
1994 Second Round
1998 Second Round

TURKEY

BRAZIL
1990 Second Round
1994 Champions
1998 Runners-up

PARAGUAY
1998 Second Round

CAMEROON
1990 Quarter-finalists
1994 First Round
1998 First Round

ECUADOR

URUGUAY
1990 Second Round

ARGENTINA
1990 Runners-up
1994 Second Round
1998 Quarter-finalists

SOUTH AFRICA
1998 First Round

GROUP A							
Senegal **1-0** France							
Denmark **2-1** Uruguay							
Denmark **1-1** Senegal							
France **0-0** Uruguay							
Denmark **2-0** France							
Senegal **3-3** Uruguay							
	P	W	D	L	F	A	Pts
Denmark	3	2	1	0	5	2	7
Senegal	3	1	2	0	5	4	5
Uruguay	3	0	2	1	4	5	2
France	3	0	1	2	0	3	1

GROUP B							
Paraguay **2-2** South Africa							
Spain **3-1** Slovenia							
Spain **3-1** Paraguay							
South Africa **1-0** Slovenia							
Spain **3-2** South Africa							
Paraguay **3-1** Slovenia							
	P	W	D	L	F	A	Pts
Spain	3	3	0	0	9	4	9
Paraguay	3	1	1	1	6	6	4
South Africa	3	1	1	1	5	5	4
Slovenia	3	0	0	3	2	7	0

GROUP C							
Brazil **2-1** Turkey							
Costa Rica **2-0** China							
Brazil **4-0** China							
Costa Rica **1-1** Turkey							
Brazil **5-2** Costa Rica							
Turkey **3-0** China							
	P	W	D	L	F	A	Pts
Brazil	3	3	0	0	11	3	9
Turkey	3	1	1	1	5	3	4
Costa Rica	3	1	1	1	5	6	4
China	3	0	0	3	0	9	0

GROUP D							
South Korea **2-0** Poland							
USA **3-2** Portugal							
South Korea **1-1** USA							
Portugal **4-0** Poland							
South Korea **1-0** Portugal							
Poland **3-1** USA							
	P	W	D	L	F	A	Pts
South Korea	3	2	1	0	4	1	7
USA	3	1	1	1	5	6	4
Portugal	3	1	0	2	6	4	3
Poland	3	1	0	2	3	7	3

Japan/Korea 2002 Qualification

FRANCE	Team name
(shirt)	Team shirt
1998 Champions	Performance in last 3 World Cups

- ☐ Hosts
- 🏆 First-time qualifiers
- ☐ Reigning champions
- ☐ Final Round Non-qualifiers

Qualified teams		Qualification Final Round
☐	UEFA	☐
☐	CONMEBOL	☐
☐	CAF	☐
☐	AFC	☐
☐	OFC	☐
☐	FOOTBALL CONFEDERATION	☐

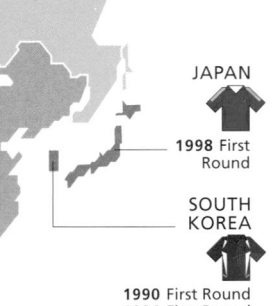

JAPAN
- 1998 First Round

SOUTH KOREA
- 1990 First Round
- 1994 First Round
- 1998 First Round

CHINA

World Cup 2002: The Venues

43,138 — SUWON WORLD CUP STADIUM

49,000 — Tournament stadium with capacity and name / MIYAGI STADIUM

• Miyagi — Location of stadium

50,256 — INCHEON MUNHAK STADIUM

64,640 — SEOUL WORLD CUP STADIUM

70,140 — DAEGU WORLD CUP STADIUM

41,024 — DAEJEON WORLD CUP STADIUM

42,477 — JEONJU WORLD CUP STADIUM

42,900 — GWANGJU WORLD CUP STADIUM

42,526 — JEJU WORLD CUP STADIUM

55,000 — BUSAN STADIUM

43,000 — OITA STADIUM BIG EYE

43,512 — ULSAN MUNSU FOOTBALL STADIUM

42,000 — KOBE WING STADIUM

50,000 — NAGAI STADIUM

51,349 — SHIZUOKA STADIUM ECOPA

42,585 — SAPPORO DOME

49,133 — MIYAGI STADIUM

42,300 — NIIGATA STADIUM BIG SWAN

41,800 — IBARAKI PREFECTURAL KASHIMA SOCCER STADIUM

63,700 — SAITAMA STADIUM 2002

72,370 — INTERNATIONAL STADIUM YOKOHAMA

SOUTH KOREA: Seoul, Incheon, Suwon, Daejeon, Daegu, Jeonju, Gwangju, Ulsan, Busan, Seogwipo

JAPAN: Sapporo, Miyagi, Niigata, Ibaraki, Saitama, Yokohama, Shizuoka, Kobe, Osaka, Oita

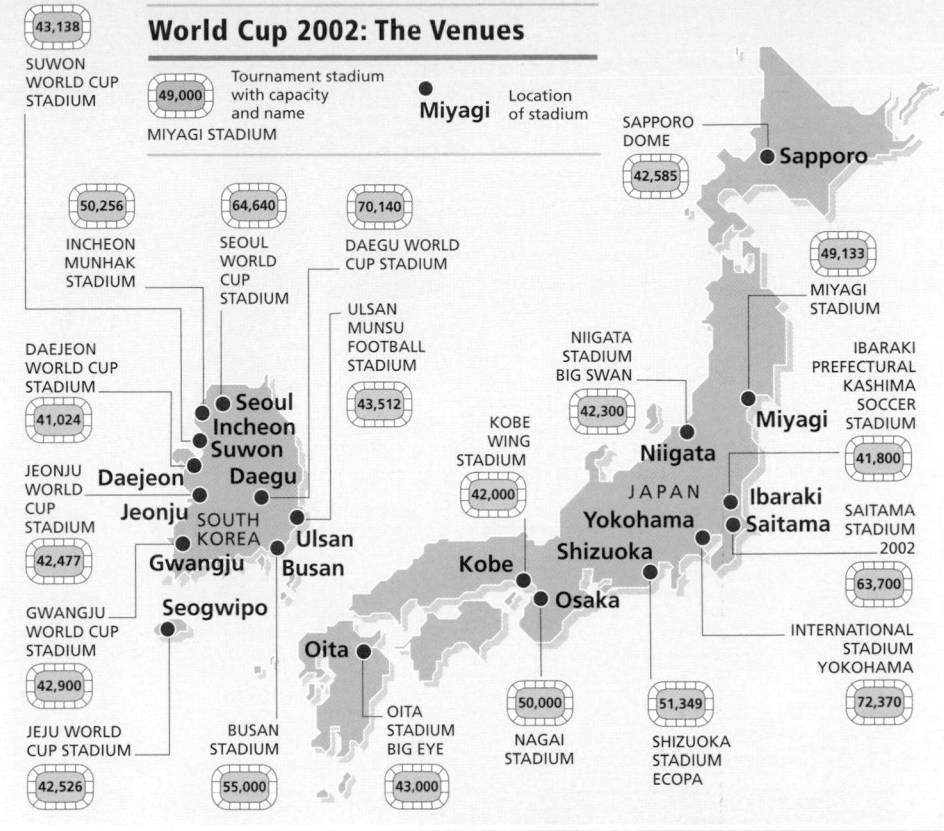

Qualification by Confederation

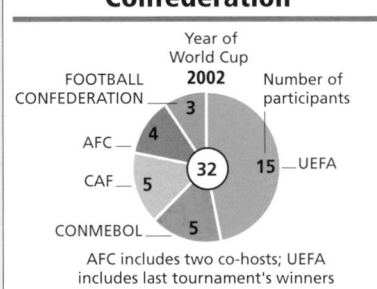

Year of World Cup **2002** — Number of participants

FOOTBALL CONFEDERATION	3
AFC	4
CAF	5
CONMEBOL	5
UEFA	15
Total	32

AFC includes two co-hosts; UEFA includes last tournament's winners

Football is politics. Japan qualifies for the Second Round. The country's leading newspaper writes, 'Finally we understand how important the initiatives and imagination of the individual are to the group.'

GROUP E
Rep. of Ireland **1-1** Cameroon
Germany **8-0** Saudi Arabia
Germany **1-1** Rep. of Ireland
Cameroon **1-0** Saudi Arabia
Germany **2-0** Cameroon
Rep. of Ireland **3-0** Saudi Arabia

	P	W	D	L	F	A	Pts
Germany	3	2	1	0	11	1	7
Ireland	3	1	2	0	5	2	5
Cameroon	3	1	1	1	2	3	4
Saudi Arabia	3	0	0	3	0	10	0

GROUP F
Argentina **1-0** Nigeria
England **1-1** Sweden
Sweden **2-1** Nigeria
England **1-0** Argentina
Sweden **1-1** Argentina
Nigeria **0-0** England

	P	W	D	L	F	A	Pts
Sweden	3	1	2	0	4	3	5
England	3	1	2	0	2	1	5
Argentina	3	1	1	1	2	2	4
Nigeria	3	0	1	2	1	3	1

GROUP G
Mexico **1-0** Croatia
Italy **2-0** Ecuador
Croatia **2-1** Italy
Mexico **2-1** Ecuador
Mexico **1-1** Italy
Ecuador **1-0** Croatia

	P	W	D	L	F	A	Pts
Mexico	3	2	1	0	4	2	7
Italy	3	1	1	1	4	3	4
Croatia	3	1	0	2	2	3	3
Ecuador	3	1	0	2	2	4	3

GROUP H
Japan **2-2** Belgium
Russia **2-0** Tunisia
Japan **1-0** Russia
Tunisia **1-1** Belgium
Japan **2-0** Tunisia
Belgium **3-2** Russia

	P	W	D	L	F	A	Pts
Japan	3	2	1	0	5	2	7
Belgium	3	1	2	0	6	5	5
Russia	3	1	0	2	4	4	3
Tunisia	3	0	1	2	1	5	1

THE WORLD CUP

THE SECOND ROUND

More favourites fall, as South Korea beat Italy with a golden goal that provokes the biggest outburst of sour grapes in the tournament's history. Ireland ran Spain to penalties in the round's best match. The USA beat Mexico in a bad-tempered game. Brazil was held for 70 minutes by the Belgians before scoring twice and Germany scraped past Paraguay. It was goodbye to Sweden, Denmark and Japan as Senegal, England and Turkey went through.

June 15 – Seogwipo
Attendance 25,176
1-0
h/t: 0-0
GERMANY — PARAGUAY

June 15 – Niigata
Attendance 40,582
0-3
h/t: 0-3
DENMARK — ENGLAND

June 16 – Oita
Attendance 39,747
1-2
(Senegal won on golden goal)
h/t: 1-1, f/t: 1-1
SWEDEN — SENEGAL

June 16 – Suwon
Attendance 38,926
1-1
(Spain won 3-2 on pens)
h/t: 1-0
SPAIN — IRELAND

June 17 – Jeonju
Attendance 36,380
0-2
h/t: 0-1
MEXICO — USA

June 17 – Kobe
Attendance 40,440
2-0
h/t: 0-0
BRAZIL — BELGIUM

June 18 – Miyagi
Attendance 45,666
0-1
h/t: 0-1
JAPAN — TURKEY

June 18 – Daejeon
Attendance 38,588
2-1
(South Korea won on golden goal)
h/t: 0-1, f/t: 1-1
SOUTH KOREA — ITALY

THE QUARTER-FINALS

Brazil showed grit as well as flair to come back from one down and kill the game with England when down to ten men. Germany rode its luck against a rampant American team and survived a handball on the line. Turkey and Senegal played end-to-end football separated only by a single strike. South Korea took another Mediterranean scalp, after even more controversial refereeing, beating Spain on penalties.

June 21 – Shizuoka
Attendance 47,436
1-2
h/t: 1-1
ENGLAND — BRAZIL

June 21 – Ulsan
Attendance 37,337
1-0
h/t: 1-0
GERMANY — USA

June 22 – Gwangju
Attendance 42,114
0-0
(South Korea won 5-3 on pens)
h/t: 0-0, f/t: 0-0
SPAIN — SOUTH KOREA

June 22 – Osaka
Attendance 44,233
0-1
(Turkey won on golden goal)
h/t: 0-0, f/t: 0-0
SENEGAL — TURKEY

THE SEMI-FINALS

In the end the old order held with Brazil and Germany seeing off the outsiders. A moment of genius from the outside of Ronaldo's boot was enough to take Brazil past a tenacious and technically superb Turkish team. South Korea ran and ran, but Michael Ballack, booked and out of the Final, found the composure to collect a rebound and slot in Germany's winner.

June 25 – Seoul
Attendance 65,625
1-0
h/t: 0-0
GERMANY — SOUTH KOREA

June 26 – Saitama
Attendance 61,058
1-0
h/t: 0-0
BRAZIL — TURKEY

THE THIRD PLACE PLAY-OFF

Hakan Sukur, Turkey's captain, finally found his form, scoring the World Cup's fastest-ever goal in the first minute. Korea equalized from a free kick, but two more goals for Turkey in the next half an hour left them chasing the game. Even the super-fit Koreans didn't quite have enough after that despite a late strike.

June 29 – Daegu
Attendance 64,483
2-3
h/t: 1-3
SOUTH KOREA — TURKEY

THE FINAL

Although they had won seven World Cups between them, Brazil and Germany had never met in a World Cup Final. Germany's pressing game gave them the best of possession and the marking closed down Brazil's flanks, but it was Ronaldo's moment of redemption for France 98, and three chances in the first half became two goals in the second.

Brazil's first goal was Ronaldo's seventh of the tournament. It meant that he equalled his compatriot Jairzinho's record of scoring in every round of the World Cup finals on the way to victory, a record set in Mexico in 1970.

Ronaldo's second goal

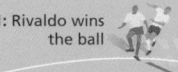

1: Rivaldo wins the ball

The Starting Line-Up

June 30 – Yokohama
Attendance 69,029

BRAZIL — Referee — **GERMANY**

Formation: 3-5-2	⊙ Pierluigi Collina (Italy)	Formation: 3-5-2
Manager		**Manager**
Luiz Felipe Scolari		Rudi Völler
Substitutes		**Substitutes**
Juninho ⑲		⑳ Bierhoff
Denilson ⑰		㉑ Asamoah
		⑥ Ziege

Highlights of the Game

KEY

Player booked — ▯ ↪ — Substitution

Goal — ⚽

BRAZIL ▼ KICK OFF 0 mins **GERMANY**

6 min: Roque Junior after clash with Neuville

9 min: Klose for an elbow on Edmilson

14 min: German pressure ends when Bode fails to reach Metzelder's pass

18 min: First clear chance, Ronaldo pokes the ball past Kahn's left post

28 min: Bode fails to reach Schneider's pass

44 min: Kleberson's shot beats Kahn but rockets off the crossbar

41 min: Jeremies shoots over the bar

45 min: Ronaldo shoots from 6 metres but Kahn's legs are in the way

45 mins

HALF-TIME: **0-0**

49 min: Germany's best chance: Neuville's 35-metre free kick is tipped round the right post by Marcos

67 min: Kahn spills Rivaldo's shot and Ronaldo pounces on the ball to score ⚽

79 min: Kleberson crosses into the box, Rivaldo steps over, Ronaldo curls the ball past Kahn ⚽

73 min: Bierhoff for Klose

78 min: Asamoah for Jeremies

85 min: Juninho for Ronaldinho

83 min: Bierhoff swivels and shoots in the box but Marcos saves at the post

90 min: Denilson for Ronaldo

84 min: Ziege for Linke

90 mins

+ 3 mins injury time

FULL-TIME: **2-0**

4: Ronaldo takes one touch to control and then fires low past Kahn

Asamoah

Kahn

Linke

Ramelow

Cafu

3: Rivaldo steps over Kleberson's pass

Metzelder

2: Kleberson runs then plays a square pass

Kleberson

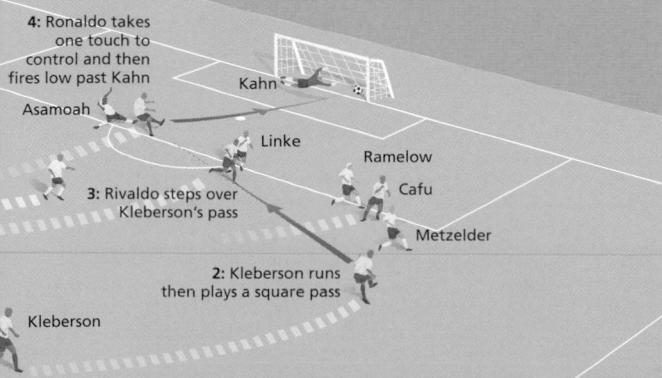

BRAZIL 2-0 GERMANY

Team			Match Statistics	Team		
First Half	Second Half	Full Time		First Half	Second Half	Full Time
45	48	46.5	Possession	55	52	53.5
–	–	9(7)	Attempts (on target)	–	–	12(4)
–	–	9	Successful tackles	–	–	12
–	–	7	Fouls conceded	–	–	4
2	1	3	Corners won	8	5	13
0	0	0	Offside	1	0	1

The World Cup

THE IDEA OF THE WORLD CUP began with the establishment of FIFA in 1904, but for the first three decades of the century the football tournament at the Olympic Games served as the *de facto* football world championships. With the advent of professionalism in many European countries in the 1920s (and the resultant limit to participation in the amateur Olympic football tournament) the World Cup came into being.

The first tournament was held in Uruguay in 1930 as the Uruguayans were the current Olympic champions and promised to pay everybody's expenses. Despite this, only three European countries made the trip to a tournament dominated by South Americans. In Italy in 1934 and France in 1938, the early group rounds were dispensed with and the tournament became a knockout competition from the beginning. This format was tough on the Americans, Brazilians and Argentinians who often crossed an ocean for a single game.

After the Second World War, the World Cup settled into a 16-team final tournament, with a group phase followed by knockout stages. There were two exceptions: the 1950 tournament in Brazil had a league format for the final placing, and the 1954 competition in Switzerland saw 16 teams divided into four groups, with two teams in each group seeded. The two seeded teams didn't play each other in the group rounds.

The increasing financial attraction of the World Cup, and the increasing strength and numbers of footballing nations outside of Europe and Latin America, has led to a steady expansion of the tournament. There were 24 teams in 1982 (with four second round mini-leagues producing four semi-finalists); and 32 teams in 1998 and 2002 (reverting to opening groups and then knockout stages for the last 16).

1930 URUGUAY

POOL 1

France 4-1 Mexico
Argentina 1-0 France
Chile 3-0 Mexico
Chile 1-0 France
Argentina 6-3 Mexico
Argentina 3-1 Chile

	P	W	D	L	F	A	Pts
Argentina	3	3	0	0	10	4	6
Chile	3	2	0	1	5	3	4
France	3	1	0	2	4	3	2
Mexico	3	0	0	3	4	13	0

POOL 2

Yugoslavia 2-1 Brazil
Yugoslavia 4-0 Bolivia
Brazil 4-0 Bolivia

	P	W	D	L	F	A	Pts
Yugoslavia	2	2	0	0	6	1	4
Brazil	2	1	0	1	5	2	2
Bolivia	2	0	0	2	0	8	0

POOL 3

Romania 3-1 Peru
Uruguay 1-0 Peru
Uruguay 4-0 Romania

	P	W	D	L	F	A	Pts
Uruguay	2	2	0	0	5	0	4
Romania	2	1	0	1	3	5	2
Peru	2	0	0	2	1	4	0

POOL 4

USA 3-0 Belgium
USA 3-0 Paraguay
Paraguay 1-0 Belgium

	P	W	D	L	F	A	Pts
USA	2	2	0	0	6	0	4
Paraguay	2	1	0	1	1	3	2
Belgium	2	0	0	2	0	4	0

SEMI-FINALS

Argentina 6-1 USA
(Monti 20, (Brown 88)
Scopello 56,
Stabile 69, 87,
Peucelle 80, 85)

Uruguay 6-1 Yugoslavia
(Cea 18, 67, 72, (Sekulic 4)
Anselmo 20, 31,
Iriarte 60)

THIRD PLACE PLAY-OFF

not held

FINAL

July 30 – Centenario, Montevideo
Uruguay 4-2 Argentina
(Dorado 12, (Peucelle 20,
Cea 58, Stabile 37)
Iriarte 68,
Castro 89)

h/t: 1-2 **Att:** 93,000
Ref: Langenus (Belgium)

1934 ITALY

FIRST ROUND

Italy 7-1 USA
Czechoslovakia 2-1 Romania
Germany 5-2 Belgium
Austria 3-2 France
(after extra time)
Spain 3-1 Brazil
Switzerland 3-2 Netherlands
Sweden 3-2 Argentina
Hungary 4-2 Egypt

SECOND ROUND

Germany 2-1 Sweden
Austria 2-1 Hungary
Italy 1-1 Spain
(after extra time)
Replay
Italy 1-0 Spain
Czechoslovakia 3-2 Switzerland

SEMI-FINALS

Czechoslovakia 3-1 Germany
(Nejedly 19, 81, (Noack 62)
Krcil 71)

Italy 1-0 Austria
(Guaita 19)

THIRD PLACE PLAY-OFF

Germany 3-2 Austria
(Lehner 1, 42, (Horvath 28,
Conen 27) Sesta 54)

FINAL

June 10 – Flaminio, Rome
Italy 2-1 Czechoslovakia
(Orsi 81, (Puc 71)
Schiavio 95)
(after extra time)
h/t: 0-0 **90 mins:** 1-1
Att: 55,000 **Ref:** Eklind (Sweden)

1938 FRANCE

FIRST ROUND

Switzerland 1-1 Germany
(after extra time)
Replay
Switzerland 4-2 Germany
Cuba 3-3 Romania
(after extra time)
Replay
Cuba 2-1 Romania
Hungary 6-0 Dutch East Indies
Sweden w/o Austria
France 3-1 Belgium
Czechoslovakia 3-0 Netherlands
(after extra time)
Brazil 6-5 Poland
(after extra time)
Italy 2-1 Norway
(after extra time)

w/o denotes walk over

QUARTER-FINALS

Sweden 8-0 Cuba
Hungary 2-0 Switzerland
Italy 3-1 France
Brazil 1-1 Czechoslovakia
(after extra time)
Replay
Brazil 2-1 Czechoslovakia

SEMI-FINALS

Italy 2-1 Brazil
(Colaussi 55, (Romeo 87)
Meazza 60)

Hungary 5-1 Sweden
(Zsengeller (Nyberg 1)
18, 38, 86,
Titkos 26,
Sarosi 61)

THIRD PLACE PLAY-OFF

Brazil 4-2 Sweden
(Romeo 43, (Jonasson 18,
Leonidas 63, 73, Nyberg 38)
Peracio 80)

FINAL

June 19 – Stade Colombes, Paris
Italy 4-2 Hungary
(Colaussi 5, 35, (Titkos 7,
Piola 16, 82) Sarosi 70)
h/t: 3-1 **Att:** 55,000
Ref: Capdeville (France)

1950 BRAZIL

POOL 1

Brazil 4-0 Mexico
Yugoslavia 3-0 Switzerland
Yugoslavia 4-1 Mexico
Brazil 2-2 Switzerland
Brazil 2-0 Yugoslavia
Switzerland 2-1 Mexico

	P	W	D	L	F	A	Pts
Brazil	3	2	1	0	8	2	5
Yugoslavia	3	2	0	1	7	3	4
Switzerland	3	1	1	1	4	6	3
Mexico	3	0	0	3	2	10	0

POOL 2

Spain 3-1 USA
England 2-0 Chile
USA 1-0 England
Spain 2-0 Chile
Spain 1-0 England
Chile 5-2 USA

	P	W	D	L	F	A	Pts
Spain	3	3	0	0	6	1	6
England	3	1	0	2	2	2	2
Chile	3	1	0	2	5	6	2
USA	3	1	0	2	4	8	2

POOL 3

Sweden 3-2 Italy
Sweden 2-2 Paraguay
Italy 2-0 Paraguay

	P	W	D	L	F	A	Pts
Sweden	2	1	1	0	5	4	3
Italy	2	1	0	1	4	3	2
Paraguay	2	0	1	1	2	4	1

POOL 4

Uruguay 8-0 Bolivia

	P	W	D	L	F	A	Pts
Uruguay	1	1	0	0	8	0	2
Bolivia	1	0	0	1	0	8	0

FINAL POOL

Uruguay 2-2 Spain
Brazil 7-1 Sweden
Uruguay 3-2 Sweden

World Cup Winners

Uruguay
1930, 50

Italy
1934, 38, 82

West Germany
1954, 74, 90

Brazil
1958, 62, 70, 94, 2002

England
1966

Argentina
1978, 86

France
1998

Brazil **6-1** Spain
Sweden **3-1** Spain
Uruguay **2-1** Brazil

	P	W	D	L	F	A	Pts
Uruguay	3	2	1	0	7	5	5
Brazil	3	2	0	1	14	4	4
Sweden	3	1	0	2	6	11	2
Spain	3	0	1	2	4	11	1

THIRD PLACE
Sweden

FINAL
July 16 – Maracana, Rio de Janeiro
Uruguay 2-1 Brazil
(Schiaffino 66,   (Friaca 48)
Ghiggia 79)
h/t: 0-0 **Att:** 199,854
Ref: Reader (England)

1954 SWITZERLAND
POOL 1
Yugoslavia **1-0** France
Brazil **5-0** Mexico
France **3-2** Mexico
Brazil **1-1** Yugoslavia

	P	W	D	L	F	A	Pts
Brazil	2	1	1	0	6	1	3
Yugoslavia	2	1	1	0	2	1	3
France	2	1	0	1	3	3	2
Mexico	2	0	0	2	2	8	0

POOL 2
Hungary **9-0** South Korea
West Germany **4-1** Turkey
Hungary **8-3** West Germany
Turkey **7-0** South Korea

	P	W	D	L	F	A	Pts
Hungary	2	2	0	0	17	3	4
West Germany	2	1	0	1	7	9	2
Turkey	2	1	0	1	8	4	2
South Korea	2	0	0	2	0	16	0

PLAY-OFF
West Germany **7-2** Turkey

POOL 3
Austria **1-0** Scotland
Uruguay **2-0** Czechoslovakia
Austria **5-0** Czechoslovakia
Uruguay **7-0** Scotland

	P	W	D	L	F	A	Pts
Uruguay	2	2	0	0	9	0	4
Austria	2	2	0	0	6	0	4
Czechoslovakia	2	0	0	2	0	7	0
Scotland	2	0	0	2	0	8	0

POOL 4
England **4-4** Belgium
England **2-0** Switzerland
Switzerland **2-1** Italy
Italy **4-1** Belgium

	P	W	D	L	F	A	Pts
England	2	1	1	0	6	4	3
Italy	2	1	0	1	5	3	2
Switzerland	2	1	0	1	2	3	2
Belgium	2	0	1	1	5	8	1

PLAY-OFF
Switzerland **4-1** Italy

QUARTER-FINALS
West Germany **2-0** Yugoslavia
Hungary **4-2** Brazil
Austria **7-5** Switzerland
Uruguay **4-2** England

SEMI-FINALS
West Germany **6-1** Austria
(Schäfer 30,   (Probst 51)
Morlock 49,
F. Walter 54, 65,
O. Walter 60, 89)

Hungary **4-2** Uruguay
(Czibor 13,   (Hohberg 75, 86)
Hidegkuti 47,
Kocsis 111, 116)
(after extra time)

THIRD PLACE PLAY-OFF
Austria **3-1** Uruguay
(Stojaspal 16,   (Hohberg 21)
Cruz o.g. 59,
Ocwirk 79)

FINAL
July 4 – Wankdorf, Berne
West Germany 3-2 Hungary
(Morlock 11,   (Puskas 6,
Rahn 16, 83)   Czibor 8)
h/t: 2-2 **Att:** 60,000
Ref: Ling (England)

1958 SWEDEN
POOL 1
West Germany **3-1** Argentina
N. Ireland **1-0** Czechoslovakia
West Germany **2-2** Czechoslovakia
Argentina **3-1** N. Ireland
West Germany **2-2** N. Ireland
Czechoslovakia **6-1** Argentina

	P	W	D	L	F	A	Pts
West Germany	3	1	2	0	7	5	4
Czechoslovakia	3	1	1	1	8	4	3
N. Ireland	3	1	1	1	4	5	3
Argentina	3	1	0	2	5	10	2

PLAY-OFF
N. Ireland **2-1** Czechoslovakia

POOL 2
France **7-3** Paraguay
Yugoslavia **1-1** Scotland
Yugoslavia **3-2** France
Paraguay **3-2** Scotland
France **2-1** Scotland
Yugoslavia **3-3** Paraguay

	P	W	D	L	F	A	Pts
France	3	2	0	1	11	7	4
Yugoslavia	3	1	2	0	7	6	4
Paraguay	3	1	1	1	9	12	3
Scotland	3	0	1	2	4	6	1

POOL 3
Sweden **3-0** Mexico
Hungary **1-1** Wales
Wales **1-1** Mexico
Sweden **2-1** Hungary
Sweden **0-0** Wales
Hungary **4-0** Mexico

	P	W	D	L	F	A	Pts
Sweden	3	2	1	0	5	1	5
Hungary	3	1	1	1	6	3	3
Wales	3	0	3	0	2	2	3
Mexico	3	0	1	2	1	8	1

PLAY-OFF
Wales **2-1** Hungary

POOL 4
England **2-2** Soviet Union
Brazil **3-0** Austria
England **0-0** Brazil
Soviet Union **2-0** Austria
Brazil **2-0** Soviet Union
England **2-2** Austria

	P	W	D	L	F	A	Pts
Brazil	3	2	1	0	5	0	5
England	3	0	3	0	4	4	3
Soviet Union	3	1	1	1	4	4	3
Austria	3	0	1	2	2	7	1

PLAY-OFF
Soviet Union **1-0** England

QUARTER-FINALS
France **4-0** N. Ireland
West Germany **1-0** Yugoslavia
Sweden **2-0** Soviet Union
Brazil **1-0** Wales

SEMI-FINALS
Brazil **5-2** France
(Vava 2,   (Fontaine 8,
Didi 38,   Piantoni 83)
Pele 53, 64, 76)

Sweden **3-1** West Germany
(Skoglund 30,   (Schäfer 21)
Gren 81,
Hamrin 88)

THIRD PLACE PLAY-OFF
France **6-3** West Germany
(Fontaine   (Cieslarczyk 18,
16, 36, 78, 89,   Rahn 52,
Kopa 27,   Schäfer 83)
Douis 50)

FINAL
June 29 – Rasunda, Stockholm
Brazil 5-2 Sweden
(Vava 9, 32,   (Liedholm 4,
Pele 55, 89,   Simonsson 80)
Zagallo 68)
h/t: 2-1 **Att:** 49,737
Ref: Guigue (France)

1962 CHILE
GROUP 1
Uruguay **2-1** Colombia
Soviet Union **2-0** Yugoslavia
Yugoslavia **3-1** Uruguay
Soviet Union **4-4** Colombia
Soviet Union **2-1** Uruguay
Yugoslavia **5-0** Colombia

	P	W	D	L	F	A	Pts
Soviet Union	3	2	1	0	8	5	5
Yugoslavia	3	2	0	1	8	3	4
Uruguay	3	1	0	2	4	6	2
Colombia	3	0	1	2	5	11	1

GROUP 2
Chile **3-1** Switzerland
West Germany **0-0** Italy
Chile **2-0** Italy
West Germany **2-1** Switzerland
West Germany **2-0** Chile
Italy **3-0** Switzerland

	P	W	D	L	F	A	Pts
West Germany	3	2	1	0	4	1	5
Chile	3	2	0	1	5	3	4
Italy	3	1	1	1	3	2	3
Switzerland	3	0	0	3	2	8	0

GROUP 3
Brazil **2-0** Mexico
Czechoslovakia **1-0** Spain
Brazil **0-0** Czechoslovakia
Spain **1-0** Mexico
Brazil **2-1** Spain
Mexico **3-1** Czechoslovakia

	P	W	D	L	F	A	Pts
Brazil	3	2	1	0	4	1	5
Czechoslovakia	3	1	1	1	2	3	3
Mexico	3	1	0	2	3	4	2
Spain	3	1	0	2	2	3	2

GROUP 4
Argentina **1-0** Bulgaria
Hungary **2-1** England
England **3-1** Argentina
Hungary **6-1** Bulgaria
Argentina **0-0** Hungary
England **0-0** Bulgaria

	P	W	D	L	F	A	Pts
Hungary	3	2	1	0	8	2	5
England	3	1	1	1	4	3	3
Argentina	3	1	1	1	2	3	3
Bulgaria	3	0	1	2	1	7	1

QUARTER-FINALS
Yugoslavia **1-0** West Germany
Brazil **3-1** England
Chile **2-1** Soviet Union
Czechoslovakia **1-0** Hungary

SEMI-FINALS
Brazil **4-2** Chile
(Garrincha 9, 31,   (Toro 41,
Vava 49, 77)   L. Sanchez 61)

Czechoslovakia **3-1** Yugoslavia
(Kadraba 49,   (Jerkovic 69)
Scherer 80, 86)

THIRD PLACE PLAY-OFF
Chile **1-0** Yugoslavia
(Rojas 89)

FINAL
June 17 – Nacional, Santiago
Brazil 3-1 Czechoslovakia
(Amarildo 18,   (Masopust 16)
Zito 69,
Vava 77)
h/t: 1-1 **Att:** 68,679
Ref: Latishev (Soviet Union)

THE WORLD CUP

1966 ENGLAND

GROUP 1

England 0-0 Uruguay
France 1-1 Mexico
Uruguay 2-1 France
England 2-0 Mexico
Uruguay 0-0 Mexico
England 2-0 France

	P	W	D	L	F	A	Pts
England	3	2	1	0	4	0	5
Uruguay	3	1	2	0	2	1	4
Mexico	3	0	2	1	1	3	2
France	3	0	1	2	2	5	1

GROUP 2

West Germany 5-0 Switzerland
Argentina 2-1 Spain
Spain 2-1 Switzerland
Argentina 0-0 West Germany
Argentina 2-0 Switzerland
West Germany 2-1 Spain

	P	W	D	L	F	A	Pts
West Germany	3	2	1	0	7	1	5
Argentina	3	2	1	0	4	1	5
Spain	3	1	0	2	4	5	2
Switzerland	3	0	0	3	1	9	0

GROUP 3

Brazil 2-0 Bulgaria
Portugal 3-1 Hungary
Hungary 3-1 Brazil
Portugal 3-0 Bulgaria
Portugal 3-1 Brazil
Hungary 3-1 Bulgaria

	P	W	D	L	F	A	Pts
Portugal	3	3	0	0	9	2	6
Hungary	3	2	0	1	7	5	4
Brazil	3	1	0	2	4	6	2
Bulgaria	3	0	0	3	1	8	0

GROUP 4

Soviet Union 3-0 North Korea
Italy 2-0 Chile
Chile 1-1 North Korea
Soviet Union 1-0 Italy
North Korea 1-0 Italy
Soviet Union 2-1 Chile

	P	W	D	L	F	A	Pts
Soviet Union	3	3	0	0	6	1	6
North Korea	3	1	1	1	2	4	3
Italy	3	1	0	2	2	2	2
Chile	3	0	1	2	2	5	1

QUARTER-FINALS

England 1-0 Argentina
West Germany 4-0 Uruguay
Portugal 5-3 North Korea
Soviet Union 2-1 Hungary

SEMI-FINALS

West Germany 2-1 Soviet Union
*(Haller 44,   (Porkuyan 88)
Beckenbauer 68)*

England 2-1 Portugal
*(R. Charlton   (Eusebio 82)
30, 79)*

THIRD PLACE PLAY-OFF

Portugal 2-1 Soviet Union
*(Eusebio 12,   (Metreveli 43)
Torres 88)*

FINAL

July 30 – Wembley Stadium, London
England 4-2 West Germany
*(Hurst   (Haller 13,
19, 100, 119,   Weber 89)
Peters 77)*

(after extra time)

h/t: 1-1 **90 mins:** 2-2
Att: 96,924 **Ref:** Dienst (Switzerland)

1970 MEXICO

GROUP 1

Mexico 0-0 Soviet Union
Belgium 3-0 El Salvador
Soviet Union 4-1 Belgium
Mexico 4-0 El Salvador
Soviet Union 2-0 El Salvador
Mexico 1-0 Belgium

	P	W	D	L	F	A	Pts
Soviet Union	3	2	1	0	6	1	5
Mexico	3	2	1	0	5	0	5
Belgium	3	1	0	2	4	5	2
El Salvador	3	0	0	3	0	9	0

GROUP 2

Uruguay 2-0 Israel
Italy 1-0 Sweden
Uruguay 0-0 Italy
Sweden 1-1 Israel
Sweden 1-0 Uruguay
Italy 0-0 Israel

	P	W	D	L	F	A	Pts
Italy	3	1	2	0	1	0	4
Uruguay	3	1	1	1	2	1	3
Sweden	3	1	1	1	2	2	3
Israel	3	0	2	1	1	3	2

GROUP 3

England 1-0 Romania
Brazil 4-1 Czechoslovakia
Romania 2-1 Czechoslovakia
Brazil 1-0 England
Brazil 3-2 Romania
England 1-0 Czechoslovakia

	P	W	D	L	F	A	Pts
Brazil	3	3	0	0	8	3	6
England	3	2	0	1	2	1	4
Romania	3	1	0	2	4	5	2
Czechoslovakia	3	0	0	3	2	7	0

GROUP 4

Peru 3-2 Bulgaria
West Germany 2-1 Morocco
Peru 3-0 Morocco
West Germany 5-2 Bulgaria
West Germany 3-1 Peru
Morocco 1-1 Bulgaria

	P	W	D	L	F	A	Pts
West Germany	3	3	0	0	10	4	6
Peru	3	2	0	1	7	5	4
Bulgaria	3	0	1	2	5	9	1
Morocco	3	0	1	2	2	6	1

QUARTER-FINALS

West Germany 3-2 England
(after extra time)
Brazil 4-2 Peru
Italy 4-1 Mexico
Uruguay 1-0 Soviet Union

SEMI-FINALS

Italy 4-3 West Germany
*(Boninsegna 7,   (Schellinger 90,
Burgnich 99,   G. Müller 95, 110)
Riva 104,
Rivera 111)*

(after extra time)

Brazil 3-1 Uruguay
*(Clodoaldo 45,   (Cubilla 19)
Jairzinho 76,
Rivelino 88)*

THIRD PLACE PLAY-OFF

West Germany 1-0 Uruguay
(Overath 26)

FINAL

June 21 – Azteca, Mexico City
Brazil 4-1 Italy
*(Pele 18,   (Boninsegna 37)
Gerson 66,
Jairzinho 71,
Carlos Alberto 86)*

h/t: 1-1 **Att:** 107,000
Ref: Glockner (East Germany)

1974 WEST GERMANY

GROUP 1

West Germany 1-0 Chile
East Germany 2-0 Australia
West Germany 3-0 Australia
East Germany 1-1 Chile
Australia 0-0 Chile
East Germany 1-0 West Germany

	P	W	D	L	F	A	Pts
East Germany	3	2	1	0	4	1	5
West Germany	3	2	0	1	4	1	4
Chile	3	0	2	1	1	2	2
Australia	3	0	1	2	0	5	1

GROUP 2

Brazil 0-0 Yugoslavia
Scotland 2-0 Zaire
Brazil 0-0 Scotland
Yugoslavia 9-0 Zaire
Yugoslavia 1-1 Scotland
Brazil 3-0 Zaire

	P	W	D	L	F	A	Pts
Yugoslavia	3	1	2	0	10	1	4
Brazil	3	1	2	0	3	0	4
Scotland	3	1	2	0	3	1	4
Zaïre	3	0	0	3	0	14	0

GROUP 3

Netherlands 2-0 Uruguay
Bulgaria 0-0 Sweden
Netherlands 0-0 Sweden
Bulgaria 1-1 Uruguay
Netherlands 4-1 Bulgaria
Sweden 3-0 Uruguay

	P	W	D	L	F	A	Pts
Netherlands	3	2	1	0	6	1	5
Sweden	3	1	2	0	3	0	4
Bulgaria	3	0	2	1	2	5	2
Uruguay	3	0	1	2	1	6	1

GROUP 4

Italy 3-1 Haiti
Poland 3-2 Argentina
Argentina 1-1 Italy
Poland 7-0 Haiti
Argentina 4-1 Haiti
Poland 2-1 Italy

	P	W	D	L	F	A	Pts
Poland	3	3	0	0	12	3	6
Argentina	3	1	1	1	7	5	3
Italy	3	1	1	1	5	4	3
Haiti	3	0	0	3	2	14	0

SECOND ROUND - GROUP A

Brazil 1-0 East Germany
Netherlands 4-0 Argentina
Netherlands 2-0 East Germany
Brazil 2-1 Argentina
East Germany 1-1 Argentina
Netherlands 2-0 Brazil

	P	W	D	L	F	A	Pts
Netherlands	3	3	0	0	8	0	6
Brazil	3	2	0	1	3	3	4
East Germany	3	0	1	2	1	4	1
Argentina	3	0	1	2	2	7	1

SECOND ROUND - GROUP B

Poland 1-0 Sweden
West Germany 2-0 Yugoslavia
Poland 2-1 Yugoslavia
West Germany 4-2 Sweden
Sweden 2-1 Yugoslavia
West Germany 1-0 Poland

	P	W	D	L	F	A	Pts
West Germany	3	3	0	0	7	2	6
Poland	3	2	0	1	3	2	4
Sweden	3	1	0	2	4	6	2
Yugoslavia	3	0	0	3	2	6	0

THIRD PLACE PLAY-OFF

Poland 1-0 Brazil
(Lato 76)

FINAL

July 7 – Olympiastadion, Munich
West Germany 2-1 Netherlands
*(Breitner 25 pen,   (Neeskens 2 pen)
G. Müller 43)*

h/t: 2-1 **Att:** 77,833
Ref: Taylor (England)

1978 ARGENTINA

GROUP 1

Argentina 2-1 Hungary
Italy 2-1 France
Argentina 2-1 France
Italy 3-1 Hungary
Italy 1-0 Argentina
France 3-1 Hungary

	P	W	D	L	F	A	Pts
Italy	3	3	0	0	6	2	6
Argentina	3	2	0	1	4	3	4
France	3	1	0	2	5	5	2
Hungary	3	0	0	3	3	8	0

GROUP 2

West Germany 0-0 Poland
Tunisia 3-1 Mexico
Poland 1-0 Tunisia
West Germany 6-0 Mexico
Poland 3-1 Mexico
West Germany 0-0 Tunisia

	P	W	D	L	F	A	Pts
Poland	3	2	1	0	4	1	5
West Germany	3	1	2	0	6	0	4
Tunisia	3	1	1	1	3	2	3
Mexico	3	0	0	3	2	12	0

GROUP 3

Austria **2-1** Spain
Sweden **1-1** Brazil
Austria **1-0** Sweden
Brazil **0-0** Spain
Spain **1-0** Sweden
Brazil **1-0** Austria

	P	W	D	L	F	A	Pts
Austria	3	2	0	1	3	2	4
Brazil	3	1	2	0	2	1	4
Spain	3	1	1	1	2	2	3
Sweden	3	0	1	2	1	3	1

GROUP 4

Peru **3-1** Scotland
Netherlands **3-0** Iran
Scotland **1-1** Iran
Netherlands **0-0** Peru
Peru **4-1** Iran
Scotland **3-2** Netherlands

	P	W	D	L	F	A	Pts
Peru	3	2	1	0	7	2	5
Netherlands	3	1	1	1	5	3	3
Scotland	3	1	1	1	5	6	3
Iran	3	0	1	2	2	8	1

SECOND ROUND - GROUP A

Italy **0-0** West Germany
Netherlands **5-1** Austria
Italy **1-0** Austria
Austria **3-2** West Germany
Netherlands **2-1** Italy
Netherlands **2-2** West Germany

	P	W	D	L	F	A	Pts
Netherlands	3	2	1	0	9	4	5
Italy	3	1	1	1	2	2	3
West Germany	3	0	2	1	4	5	2
Austria	3	1	0	2	4	8	2

SECOND ROUND - GROUP B

Argentina **2-0** Poland
Brazil **3-0** Peru
Argentina **0-0** Brazil
Poland **1-0** Peru
Brazil **3-1** Poland
Argentina **6-0** Peru

	P	W	D	L	F	A	Pts
Argentina	3	2	1	0	8	0	5
Brazil	3	2	1	0	6	1	5
Poland	3	1	0	2	2	5	2
Peru	3	0	0	3	0	10	0

THIRD PLACE PLAY-OFF

Brazil **2-1** Italy
(Nelinho 64,   (Causio 38)
Dirceu 71)

FINAL

June 25 – Monumental, Buenos Aires
Argentina **3-1** Netherlands
(Kempes 37, 104,   (Nanninga 81)
Bertoni 114)
(after extra time)
h/t: 1-0 **90 mins:** 1-1 **Att:** 77,260
Ref: Gonella (Italy)

1982 SPAIN

GROUP 1

Italy **0-0** Poland
Peru **0-0** Cameroon
Italy **1-1** Peru
Poland **0-0** Cameroon
Poland **5-1** Peru
Italy **1-1** Cameroon

	P	W	D	L	F	A	Pts
Poland	3	1	2	0	5	1	4
Italy	3	0	3	0	2	2	3
Cameroon	3	0	3	0	1	1	3
Peru	3	0	2	1	2	6	2

GROUP 2

Algeria **2-1** West Germany
Austria **1-0** Chile
West Germany **4-1** Chile
Austria **2-0** Algeria
Algeria **3-2** Chile
West Germany **1-0** Austria

	P	W	D	L	F	A	Pts
West Germany	3	2	0	1	6	3	4
Austria	3	2	0	1	3	1	4
Algeria	3	2	0	1	5	5	4
Chile	3	0	0	3	3	8	0

GROUP 3

Belgium **1-0** Argentina
Hungary **10-1** El Salvador
Argentina **4-1** Hungary
Belgium **1-0** El Salvador
Belgium **1-1** Hungary
Argentina **2-0** El Salvador

	P	W	D	L	F	A	Pts
Belgium	3	2	1	0	3	1	5
Argentina	3	2	0	1	6	2	4
Hungary	3	1	1	1	12	6	3
El Salvador	3	0	0	3	1	13	0

GROUP 4

England **3-1** France
Czechoslovakia **1-1** Kuwait
England **2-0** Czechoslovakia
France **4-1** Kuwait
France **1-1** Czechoslovakia
England **1-0** Kuwait

	P	W	D	L	F	A	Pts
England	3	3	0	0	6	1	6
France	3	1	1	1	6	5	3
Czechoslovakia	3	0	2	1	2	4	2
Kuwait	3	0	1	2	2	6	1

GROUP 5

Spain **1-1** Honduras
N. Ireland **0-0** Yugoslavia
Spain **2-1** Yugoslavia
N. Ireland **1-1** Honduras
Yugoslavia **1-0** Honduras
N. Ireland **1-0** Spain

	P	W	D	L	F	A	Pts
N. Ireland	3	1	2	0	2	1	4
Spain	3	1	1	1	3	3	3
Yugoslavia	3	1	1	1	2	2	3
Honduras	3	0	2	1	2	3	2

GROUP 6

Brazil **2-1** Soviet Union
Scotland **5-2** New Zealand
Brazil **4-1** Scotland
Soviet Union **3-0** New Zealand
Scotland **2-2** Soviet Union
Brazil **4-0** New Zealand

	P	W	D	L	F	A	Pts
Brazil	3	3	0	0	10	2	6
Soviet Union	3	1	1	1	6	4	3
Scotland	3	1	1	1	8	8	3
New Zealand	3	0	0	3	2	12	0

SECOND ROUND - GROUP A

Poland **3-0** Belgium
Soviet Union **1-0** Belgium
Soviet Union **0-0** Poland

	P	W	D	L	F	A	Pts
Poland	2	1	1	0	3	0	3
Soviet Union	2	1	1	0	1	0	3
Belgium	2	0	0	2	0	4	0

SECOND ROUND - GROUP B

West Germany **0-0** England
West Germany **2-1** Spain
England **0-0** Spain

	P	W	D	L	F	A	Pts
West Germany	2	1	1	0	2	1	3
England	2	0	2	0	0	0	2
Spain	2	0	1	1	1	2	1

SECOND ROUND - GROUP C

Italy **2-1** Argentina
Brazil **3-1** Argentina
Italy **3-2** Brazil

	P	W	D	L	F	A	Pts
Italy	2	2	0	0	5	3	4
Brazil	2	1	0	1	5	4	2
Argentina	2	0	0	2	2	5	0

SECOND ROUND - GROUP D

France **1-0** Austria
N. Ireland **2-2** Austria
France **4-1** N. Ireland

	P	W	D	L	F	A	Pts
France	2	2	0	0	5	1	4
Austria	2	0	1	1	2	3	1
N. Ireland	2	0	1	1	3	6	1

SEMI-FINALS

Italy **2-0** Poland
(Rossi 22, 73)
West Germany **3-3** France
(Littbarski 18,   (Platini 27,
Rummenigge 102,   Tresor 93,
Fischer 107)   Giresse 97)
(after extra time)
West Germany won 5-4 on pens

THIRD PLACE PLAY-OFF

Poland **3-2** France
(Szarmach 41,   (Girard 14,
Majewski 44,   Couriol 75)
Kupcewicz 47)

FINAL

July 11 – Estadio Santiago Bernabeu, Madrid
Italy **3-1** West Germany
(Rossi 56,   (Breitner 82)
Tardelli 69,
Altobelli 80)
h/t: 0-0 **Att:** 90,080
Ref: Coelho (Brazil)

1986 MEXICO

GROUP A

Bulgaria **1-1** Italy
Argentina **3-1** South Korea
Italy **1-1** Argentina
Bulgaria **1-1** South Korea
Argentina **2-0** Bulgaria
Italy **3-2** South Korea

	P	W	D	L	F	A	Pts
Argentina	3	2	1	0	6	2	5
Italy	3	1	2	0	5	4	4
Bulgaria	3	0	2	1	2	4	2
South Korea	3	0	1	2	4	7	1

GROUP B

Mexico **2-1** Belgium
Paraguay **1-0** Iraq
Mexico **1-1** Paraguay
Belgium **2-1** Iraq
Paraguay **2-2** Belgium
Mexico **1-0** Iraq

	P	W	D	L	F	A	Pts
Mexico	3	2	1	0	4	2	5
Paraguay	3	1	2	0	4	3	4
Belgium	3	1	1	1	5	5	4
Iraq	3	0	0	3	1	4	0

GROUP C

Soviet Union **6-0** Hungary
France **1-0** Canada
Soviet Union **1-1** France
Hungary **2-0** Canada
France **3-0** Hungary
Soviet Union **2-0** Canada

	P	W	D	L	F	A	Pts
Soviet Union	3	2	1	0	9	1	5
France	3	2	1	0	5	1	5
Hungary	3	1	0	2	2	9	2
Canada	3	0	0	3	0	5	0

GROUP D

Brazil **1-0** Spain
N. Ireland **1-1** Algeria
Spain **2-1** N. Ireland
Brazil **1-0** Algeria
Spain **3-0** Algeria
Brazil **3-0** N. Ireland

	P	W	D	L	F	A	Pts
Brazil	3	3	0	0	5	0	6
Spain	3	2	0	1	5	2	4
N. Ireland	3	0	1	2	2	6	1
Algeria	3	0	1	2	1	5	1

GROUP E

West Germany **1-1** Uruguay
Denmark **1-0** Scotland
Denmark **6-1** Scotland
West Germany **2-1** Scotland
Scotland **0-0** Uruguay
Denmark **2-0** West Germany

	P	W	D	L	F	A	Pts
Denmark	3	3	0	0	9	1	6
West Germany	3	1	1	1	3	4	3
Uruguay	3	0	2	1	2	7	2
Scotland	3	0	1	2	1	3	1

GROUP F

Morocco **0-0** Poland
Portugal **1-0** England
England **0-0** Morocco
Poland **1-0** Portugal
England **3-0** Poland
Morocco **3-1** Portugal

	P	W	D	L	F	A	Pts
Morocco	3	1	2	0	3	1	4
England	3	1	1	1	3	1	3
Poland	3	1	1	1	1	3	3
Portugal	3	1	0	2	2	4	2

SECOND ROUND

Mexico **2-0** Bulgaria
Belgium **4-3** Soviet Union
(after extra time)
Brazil **4-0** Poland
Argentina **1-0** Uruguay
France **2-0** Italy
West Germany **1-0** Morocco
England **3-0** Paraguay
Spain **5-1** Denmark

THE WORLD CUP

QUARTER-FINALS

France **1-1** Brazil
(after extra time)
France won 4-3 on pens
West Germany **0-0** Mexico
(after extra time)
West Germany won 4-1 on pens
Argentina **2-1** England
Belgium **1-1** Spain
(after extra time)
Belgium won 5-4 on pens

SEMI-FINALS

Argentina **2-0** Belgium
*(Maradona
51, 62)*
West Germany **2-0** France
*(Brehme 9,
Völler 90)*

THIRD PLACE PLAY-OFF

France **4-2** Belgium
*(Ferreri 27,   (Ceulemans 10,
Papin 42,   Claesen 73)
Genghini 103,
Amoros 108)*

FINAL

June 29 – Azteca, Mexico City
Argentina **3-2** West Germany
*(Brown 22,   (Rummenigge 73,
Valdano 56,   Völler 82)
Burruchaga 84)*
h/t: 1-0 **Att:** 114,590
Ref: Filho (Brazil)

1990 ITALY

GROUP A

Italy **1-0** Austria
Czechoslovakia **5-1** USA
Italy **1-0** USA
Czechoslovakia **1-0** Austria
Italy **2-0** Czechoslovakia
Austria **2-1** USA

	P	W	D	L	F	A	Pts
Italy	3	3	0	0	4	0	6
Czechoslovakia	3	2	0	1	6	3	4
Austria	3	1	0	2	2	3	2
USA	3	0	0	3	2	8	0

GROUP B

Cameroon **1-0** Argentina
Romania **2-0** Soviet Union
Argentina **2-0** Soviet Union
Cameroon **2-1** Romania
Argentina **1-1** Romania
Soviet Union **4-0** Cameroon

	P	W	D	L	F	A	Pts
Cameroon	3	2	0	1	3	5	4
Romania	3	1	1	1	4	3	3
Argentina	3	1	1	1	3	2	3
Soviet Union	3	1	0	2	4	4	2

GROUP C

Brazil **2-1** Sweden
Costa Rica **1-0** Scotland
Brazil **1-0** Costa Rica
Scotland **2-1** Sweden
Brazil **1-0** Scotland
Costa Rica **2-1** Sweden

	P	W	D	L	F	A	Pts
Brazil	3	3	0	0	4	1	6
Costa Rica	3	2	0	1	3	2	4
Scotland	3	1	0	2	2	3	2
Sweden	3	0	0	3	3	6	0

GROUP D

Colombia **2-0** UAE
West Germany **4-1** Yugoslavia
Yugoslavia **1-0** Colombia
West Germany **5-1** UAE
West Germany **1-1** Colombia
Yugoslavia **4-1** UAE

	P	W	D	L	F	A	Pts
West Germany	3	2	1	0	10	3	5
Yugoslavia	3	2	0	1	6	5	4
Colombia	3	1	1	1	3	2	3
UAE	3	0	0	3	2	11	0

GROUP E

Belgium **2-0** South Korea
Uruguay **0-0** Spain
Belgium **3-1** Uruguay
Spain **3-1** South Korea
Spain **2-1** Belgium
Uruguay **1-0** South Korea

	P	W	D	L	F	A	Pts
Spain	3	2	1	0	5	2	5
Belgium	3	2	0	1	6	3	4
Uruguay	3	1	1	1	2	3	3
South Korea	3	0	0	3	1	6	0

GROUP F

England **1-1** Rep. of Ireland
Netherlands **1-1** Egypt
England **0-0** Netherlands
Egypt **0-0** Rep. of Ireland
England **1-0** Egypt
Netherlands **1-1** Rep. of Ireland

	P	W	D	L	F	A	Pts
England	3	1	2	0	2	1	4
Netherlands	3	0	3	0	2	2	3
Rep. of Ireland	3	0	3	0	2	2	3
Egypt	3	0	2	1	1	2	2

SECOND ROUND

Cameroon **2-1** Colombia
(after extra time)
Czechoslovakia **4-1** Costa Rica
Argentina **1-0** Brazil
West Germany **2-1** Netherlands
Rep. of Ireland **0-0** Romania
(after extra time)
Rep. of Ireland won 5-4 on pens
Italy **2-0** Uruguay
Yugoslavia **2-1** Spain
(after extra time)
England **1-0** Belgium
(after extra time)

QUARTER-FINALS

Argentina **0-0** Yugoslavia
(after extra time)
Argentina won 3-2 on pens
Italy **1-0** Rep. of Ireland
West Germany **1-0** Czechoslovakia
England **3-2** Cameroon
(after extra time)

SEMI-FINALS

Argentina **1-1** Italy
(Caniggia 67)   (Schillaci 17)
(after extra time)
Argentina won 4-3 on pens
West Germany **1-1** England
(Brehme 59)   (Lineker 80)
(after extra time)
West Germany won 4-3 on pens

THIRD PLACE PLAY-OFF

Italy **2-1** England
*(R. Baggio 71,   (Platt 80)
Schillaci 84)*

FINAL

July 8 – Olimpico, Rome
West Germany **1-0** Argentina
(Brehme 84 pen)
h/t: 0-0 **Att:** 73,603
Ref: Codesal (Mexico)

1994 UNITED STATES

GROUP A

USA **1-1** Switzerland
Romania **3-1** Colombia
USA **2-1** Colombia
Switzerland **4-1** Romania
Romania **1-0** USA
Colombia **2-0** Switzerland

	P	W	D	L	F	A	Pts
Romania	3	2	0	1	5	5	6
Switzerland	3	1	1	1	5	4	4
USA	3	1	1	1	3	3	4
Colombia	3	1	0	2	4	5	3

GROUP B

Cameroon **2-2** Sweden
Brazil **2-0** Russia
Brazil **3-0** Cameroon
Sweden **3-1** Russia
Russia **6-1** Cameroon
Brazil **1-1** Sweden

	P	W	D	L	F	A	Pts
Brazil	3	2	1	0	6	1	7
Sweden	3	1	2	0	6	4	5
Russia	3	1	0	2	7	6	3
Cameroon	3	0	1	2	3	11	1

GROUP C

Germany **1-0** Bolivia
Spain **2-2** South Korea
Germany **1-1** Spain
South Korea **0-0** Bolivia
Spain **3-1** Bolivia
Germany **3-2** South Korea

	P	W	D	L	F	A	Pts
Germany	3	2	1	0	5	3	7
Spain	3	1	2	0	6	4	5
South Korea	3	0	2	1	4	5	2
Bolivia	3	0	1	2	1	4	1

GROUP D

Argentina **4-0** Greece
Nigeria **3-0** Bulgaria
Argentina **2-1** Nigeria
Bulgaria **4-0** Greece
Nigeria **2-0** Greece
Bulgaria **2-0** Argentina

	P	W	D	L	F	A	Pts
Nigeria	3	2	0	1	6	2	6
Bulgaria	3	2	0	1	6	3	6
Argentina	3	2	0	1	6	3	6
Greece	3	0	0	3	0	10	0

GROUP E

Rep. of Ireland **1-0** Italy
Norway **1-0** Mexico
Italy **1-0** Norway
Mexico **2-1** Rep. of Ireland
Rep. of Ireland **0-0** Norway
Italy **1-1** Mexico

	P	W	D	L	F	A	Pts
Mexico	3	1	1	1	3	3	4
Rep. of Ireland	3	1	1	1	2	2	4
Italy	3	1	1	1	2	2	4
Norway	3	1	1	1	1	1	4

GROUP F

Belgium **1-0** Morocco
Netherlands **2-1** Saudi Arabia
Belgium **1-0** Netherlands
Saudi Arabia **2-1** Morocco
Netherlands **2-1** Morocco
Saudi Arabia **1-0** Belgium

	P	W	D	L	F	A	Pts
Netherlands	3	2	0	1	4	3	6
Saudi Arabia	3	2	0	1	4	3	6
Belgium	3	2	0	1	2	1	6
Morocco	3	0	0	3	2	5	0

SECOND ROUND

Germany **3-2** Belgium
Spain **3-0** Switzerland
Sweden **3-1** Saudi Arabia
Romania **3-2** Argentina
Netherlands **2-0** Rep. of Ireland
Brazil **1-0** USA
Italy **2-1** Nigeria
(after extra time)
Bulgaria **1-1** Mexico
(after extra time)
Bulgaria won 3-1 on pens

QUARTER-FINALS

Italy **2-1** Spain
Brazil **3-2** Netherlands
Bulgaria **2-1** Germany
Sweden **2-2** Romania
(after extra time)
Sweden won 5-4 on pens

SEMI-FINALS

Brazil **1-0** Sweden
(Romario 80)
Italy **2-1** Bulgaria
(R. Baggio 21, 26)   (Stoichkov 44 pen)

THIRD PLACE PLAY-OFF

Sweden **4-0** Bulgaria
*(Brolin 8,
Mild 30,
H. Larsson 37,
K. Andersson 39)*

FINAL

July 17 – Rose Bowl, Pasadena
Brazil **0-0** Italy
(after extra time)
Brazil won 3-2 on pens
h/t: 0-0 **90 mins:** 0-0 **Att:** 94,000
Ref: Puhl (Hungary)

1998 FRANCE

GROUP A

Brazil **2-1** Scotland
Morocco **2-2** Norway
Brazil **3-0** Morocco
Scotland **1-1** Norway
Norway **2-1** Brazil
Morocco **3-0** Scotland

	P	W	D	L	F	A	Pts
Brazil	3	2	0	1	6	3	6
Norway	3	1	2	0	5	4	5
Morocco	3	1	1	1	5	5	4
Scotland	3	0	1	2	2	6	1

GROUP B

Italy **2-2** Chile
Austria **1-1** Cameroon
Chile **1-1** Austria
Italy **3-0** Cameroon
Chile **1-1** Cameroon
Italy **2-1** Austria

	P	W	D	L	F	A	Pts
Italy	3	2	1	0	7	3	7
Chile	3	0	3	0	4	4	3
Austria	3	0	2	1	3	4	2
Cameroon	3	0	2	1	2	5	2

GROUP C

Denmark **1-0** Saudi Arabia
France **3-0** South Africa
France **4-0** Saudi Arabia
South Africa **1-1** Denmark
France **2-1** Denmark
South Africa **2-2** Saudi Arabia

	P	W	D	L	F	A	Pts
France	3	3	0	0	9	1	9
Denmark	3	1	1	1	3	3	4
South Africa	3	0	2	1	3	6	2
Saudi Arabia	3	0	1	2	2	7	1

GROUP D

Paraguay **0-0** Bulgaria
Nigeria **3-2** Spain
Nigeria **1-0** Bulgaria
Spain **0-0** Paraguay
Paraguay **3-1** Nigeria
Spain **6-1** Bulgaria

	P	W	D	L	F	A	Pts
Nigeria	3	2	0	1	5	5	6
Paraguay	3	1	2	0	3	1	5
Spain	3	1	1	1	8	4	4
Bulgaria	3	0	1	2	1	7	1

GROUP E

Mexico **3-1** South Korea
Netherlands **0-0** Belgium
Belgium **2-2** Mexico
Netherlands **5-0** South Korea
Belgium **1-1** South Korea
Netherlands **2-2** Mexico

	P	W	D	L	F	A	Pts
Netherlands	3	1	2	0	7	2	5
Mexico	3	1	2	0	7	5	5
Belgium	3	0	3	0	3	3	3
South Korea	3	0	1	2	2	9	1

GROUP F

Germany **2-0** USA
Yugoslavia **1-0** Iran
Germany **2-2** Yugoslavia
Iran **2-1** USA
Germany **2-0** Iran
Yugoslavia **1-0** USA

	P	W	D	L	F	A	Pts
Germany	3	2	1	0	6	2	7
Yugoslavia	3	2	1	0	4	2	7
Iran	3	1	0	2	2	4	3
USA	3	0	0	3	1	5	0

GROUP G

England **2-0** Tunisia
Romania **1-0** Colombia
Colombia **1-0** Tunisia
Romania **2-1** England
Romania **1-1** Tunisia
England **2-0** Colombia

	P	W	D	L	F	A	Pts
Romania	3	2	1	0	4	2	7
England	3	2	0	1	5	2	6
Colombia	3	1	0	2	1	3	3
Tunisia	3	0	1	2	1	4	1

GROUP H

Argentina **1-0** Japan
Croatia **3-1** Jamaica
Croatia **1-0** Japan
Argentina **5-0** Jamaica
Argentina **1-0** Croatia
Jamaica **2-1** Japan

	P	W	D	L	F	A	Pts
Argentina	3	3	0	0	7	0	9
Croatia	3	2	0	1	4	2	6
Jamaica	3	1	0	2	3	9	3
Japan	3	0	0	3	1	4	0

SECOND ROUND

Italy **1-0** Norway
Brazil **4-1** Chile
France **1-0** Paraguay
(after extra time)
Denmark **4-1** Nigeria
Germany **2-1** Mexico
Netherlands **2-1** Yugoslavia
Croatia **1-0** Romania
Argentina **2-2** England
(after extra time)
Argentina won 4-3 on pens

QUARTER-FINALS

France **0-0** Italy
(after extra time)
France won 4-3 on pens
Brazil **3-2** Denmark
Netherlands **2-1** Argentina
Croatia **3-0** Germany

SEMI-FINALS

Brazil **1-1** Netherlands
(Ronaldo 46)   *(Kluivert 87)*
(after extra time)
Brazil won 4-2 on pens
France **2-1** Croatia
(Thuram 47, 70)   *(Suker 46)*

THIRD PLACE PLAY-OFF

Croatia **2-1** Netherlands
(Prosinecki 13,   *(Zenden 21)*
Suker 36)

FINAL

July 12 – Stade St France, Paris
France **3-0** Brazil
(Zidane 27, 45,
Petit 90)
h/t: 2-0 **Att:** 75,000
Ref: Belqola (Morocco)

2002 JAPAN/KOREA

GROUP A

Senegal **1-0** France
Denmark **2-1** Uruguay
Denmark **1-1** Senegal
France **0-0** Uruguay
Denmark **2-0** France
Senegal **3-3** Uruguay

	P	W	D	L	F	A	Pts
Denmark	3	2	1	0	5	2	7
Senegal	3	1	2	0	5	4	5
Uruguay	3	0	2	1	4	5	2
France	3	0	1	2	0	3	1

GROUP B

Paraguay **2-2** South Africa
Spain **3-1** Slovenia
Spain **3-1** Paraguay
South Africa **1-0** Slovenia
Spain **3-2** South Africa
Paraguay **3-1** Slovenia

	P	W	D	L	F	A	Pts
Spain	3	3	0	0	9	4	9
Paraguay	3	1	1	1	6	6	4
South Africa	3	1	1	1	5	5	4
Slovenia	3	0	0	3	2	7	0

GROUP C

Brazil **2-1** Turkey
Costa Rica **2-0** China
Brazil **4-0** China
Costa Rica **1-1** Turkey
Brazil **5-2** Costa Rica
Turkey **3-0** China

	P	W	D	L	F	A	Pts
Brazil	3	3	0	0	11	3	9
Turkey	3	1	1	1	5	3	4
Costa Rica	3	1	1	1	5	6	4
China	3	0	0	3	0	9	0

GROUP D

South Korea **2-0** Poland
USA **3-2** Portugal
South Korea **1-1** USA
Portugal **4-0** Poland
South Korea **1-0** Portugal
Poland **3-1** USA

	P	W	D	L	F	A	Pts
South Korea	3	2	1	0	4	1	7
USA	3	1	1	1	5	6	4
Portugal	3	1	0	2	6	4	3
Poland	3	1	0	2	3	7	3

GROUP E

Rep. of Ireland **1-1** Cameroon
Germany **8-0** Saudi Arabia
Germany **1-1** Rep. of Ireland
Cameroon **1-0** Saudi Arabia
Germany **2-0** Cameroon
Rep. of Ireland **3-0** Saudi Arabia

	P	W	D	L	F	A	Pts
Germany	3	2	1	0	11	1	7
Rep. of Ireland	3	1	2	0	5	2	5
Cameroon	3	1	1	1	2	3	4
Saudi Arabia	3	0	0	3	0	12	0

GROUP F

England **1-1** Sweden
Argentina **1-0** Nigeria
Sweden **2-1** Nigeria
England **1-0** Argentina
Sweden **1-1** Argentina
England **0-0** Nigeria

	P	W	D	L	F	A	Pts
Sweden	3	1	2	0	4	3	5
England	3	1	2	0	2	1	5
Argentina	3	1	1	1	2	2	4
Nigeria	3	0	1	2	1	3	1

GROUP G

Mexico **1-0** Croatia
Italy **2-0** Ecuador
Croatia **2-1** Italy
Mexico **2-1** Ecuador
Italy **1-1** Mexico
Ecuador **1-0** Croatia

	P	W	D	L	F	A	Pts
Mexico	3	2	1	0	4	2	7
Italy	3	1	1	1	4	3	4
Croatia	3	1	0	2	2	3	3
Ecuador	3	1	0	2	2	4	3

GROUP H

Japan **2-2** Belgium
Russia **2-0** Tunisia
Japan **1-0** Russia
Tunisia **1-1** Belgium
Japan **2-0** Tunisia
Belgium **3-2** Russia

	P	W	D	L	F	A	Pts
Japan	3	2	1	0	5	2	7
Belgium	3	1	2	0	6	5	5
Russisa	3	1	0	2	4	4	3
Tunisia	3	0	1	2	1	5	1

SECOND ROUND

Germany **1-0** Paraguay
England **3-0** Denmark
Senegal **2-1** Sweden
(golden goal in extra time)
Spain **1-1** Rep. of Ireland
(after extra time)
Spain won 3-2 on pens
USA **2-0** Mexico
Brazil **2-0** Belgium
Turkey **1-0** Japan
South Korea **2-1** Italy
(golden goal in extra time)

QUARTER-FINALS

Brazil **2-1** England
Germany **1-0** USA
Spain **0-0** South Korea
(extra time)
South Korea won 5-3 on pens
Turkey **1-0** Senegal
(golden goal in extra time)

SEMI-FINALS

Germany **1-0** South Korea
(Ballack 78)
Brazil **1-0** Turkey
(Ronaldo 49)

THIRD PLACE PLAY-OFF

Turkey **3-2** South Korea
(Sukur 1,   *(Lee Eul-yong 9,*
Mansiz 13, 32)   *Song Chong-guk 93)*

FINAL

June 30 – Yokohama, Japan
Brazil **2-0** Germany
(Ronaldo 67, 79)
h/t: 0-0 **Att:** 69,029
Ref: Collina (Italy)

Brazilian players celebrate by doing the samba after beating Germany in Japan 2002.

The Olympic Games

TOURNAMENT OVERVIEW

THE FOOTBALL TOURNAMENT at the Olympic Games has changed its status as a global tournament four or five times over its existence. As with all Olympic events, it began as a competition for national teams of amateurs only. As football became a professional sport all over the world, it inevitably collided with the Olympic amateur ethos. As football has acquired its own ruling body – FIFA – and its own global tournament – the World Cup – its relationship with the Olympics has become more complex.

At the earliest Olympics football was played as an exhibition sport. At the first modern Olympics in Athens in 1896, a tournament was played between a Danish XI, an Athenian XI and an Izmir XI (then a Greek area of Asian Turkey), but the records have been lost. In Paris in 1900 Upton Park FC (of east London) took on a French XI, while 1906 saw a rematch of the 1900 Games with the addition of a Thessaloniki XI (whose fixture with Athens descended into violence).

Football becomes official

Football became an official Olympic sport at the 1908 Games in London; it was in effect the first world championship. With the exception of Egypt, who played at the 1920 games, this was an exclusively European affair until 1924. Great Britain and Denmark set the early pace contesting two Finals (1908 and 1912). The 1924 games in Paris saw the arrival of South American teams for the first time and a new global football power was revealed. The dazzling Uruguayans took the title with ease, while 1928 saw them triumph again, beating an equally fearsome Argentinian team in a replayed Final.

The 1932 Olympics in Los Angeles showed that the global spread of football had stopped at Ellis Island; there was no football tournament. By the time football returned to the Olympics in Berlin in 1936, professionalism had been legalized in most of the key footballing nations (England, Scotland, France, Uruguay, Argentina, Brazil, Italy and Spain) and two World Cups had been held; the status of Olympic football plummeted. For the next 30 years the tournament was effectively contested by the enduring amateur teams of Scandinavia and the state-sponsored amateurs of Eastern Europe; teams from these regions contested every Final from 1948 to 1980. This pattern was broken by FIFA's ban on players who had taken part in World Cup qualifiers from appearing at the Olympics – though this, of course, excluded some genuine amateurs.

The Africans are coming

The low to which the tournament had sunk has been redeemed by three changes. First, football's developing nations in Asia and Africa have taken an increasing interest and pride in Olympic performances and the global coverage it provides. Crowds for Olympic football at Seoul and Los Angeles were enormous and FIFA finally squared the amateurism circle by making the Olympic tournament an under-23 competition open to all players. Gold medals for Nigeria (1996) and Cameroon (2000) have kept global interest in the tournament alive.

In 1928 in Amsterdam the Uruguayans returned to the Olympics as holders. They were triumphant once again, beating the Netherlands 2-0, Germany 4-1 (pictured here, Uruguay in white), and Italy 3-2 on the way to the Final. There the team met its fellow South Americans from Argentina and triumphed 2-1 in a replay for which 250,000 people applied for tickets. This signalled a shift in the balance of power in world football from Europe to Latin America.

The Olympic Games Football Tournament

Number of appearances at Olympic Games

▨	10+ times
▨	7–9 times
▨	4–6 times
▨	1–3 times
☐	none

Olympic medals and date

- 🥇 Gold
- 🥈 Silver
- 🥉 Bronze

VI* Games
1916* cancelled

XIX Host city and Olympiad number

● **Sydney** 2000 Location and year of Games

Montreal 1976 — XXI
XXVI
Los Angeles 1932, 84 — X, XXIII
Atlanta 1996
Mexico City 1968 — XIX
GHANA 🥉 1992
BRAZIL 🥈 1984, 88 🥉 1996
CHILE 🥉 2000
URUGUAY 🥇 1924, 28
ARGENTINA 🥈 1928, 96

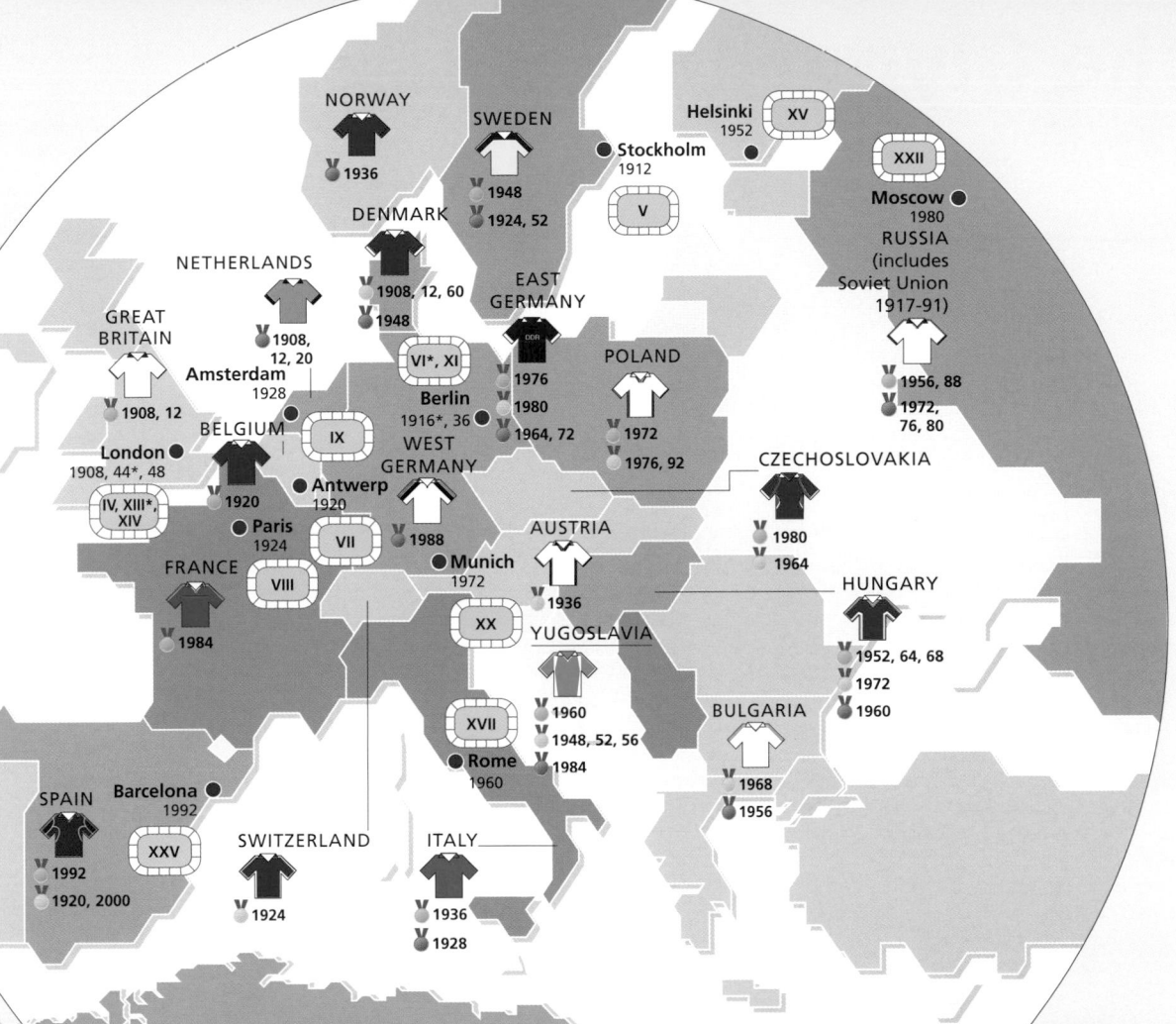

NORWAY
1936

SWEDEN
1948
1924, 52

Helsinki
1852
XV

Stockholm
1912
V

XXII

Moscow
1980
RUSSIA
(includes
Soviet Union
1917-91)
1956, 88
1972, 76, 80

DENMARK
1908, 12, 60
1948

NETHERLANDS
1908, 20

GREAT
BRITAIN
1908, 12

Amsterdam
1928

EAST
GERMANY
DDR
1976
1980
1964, 72

POLAND
1972
1976, 92

CZECHOSLOVAKIA
1980
1964

VI*, XI
Berlin
1916*, 36
WEST
GERMANY

London
1908, 44*, 48
IV, XIII*, XIV

BELGIUM
1920

IX

Antwerp
1920
1988

VII

AUSTRIA
1936

HUNGARY
1952, 64, 68
1972
1960

Paris
1924

FRANCE
1984

VIII

Munich
1972
XX

YUGOSLAVIA
1960
1948, 52, 56
1984

BULGARIA
1968
1956

XVII

Rome
1960

SPAIN
1992
1920, 2000

Barcelona
1992
XXV

SWITZERLAND
1924

ITALY
1936
1928

Seoul
1988

XII*, XVIII
Tokyo
1940*, 64

JAPAN
XXIV
1968

NIGERIA
1996

CAMEROON
2000

Melbourne
1956
XVI

Sydney
2000
XXVII

YEAR	WINNERS	SCORE	RUNNERS-UP
1908	Great Britain	**2-0**	Denmark
1912	Great Britain	**4-2**	Denmark
1916		*cancelled*	
1920	Belgium	**2-0**	Czechoslovakia*
1924	Uruguay	**3-0**	Switzerland
1928	Uruguay	**1-1, 2-1**	Argentina
1932		*no tournament*	
1936	Italy	**2-1**	Austria
1940		*cancelled*	
1944		*cancelled*	
1948	Sweden	**3-1**	Yugoslavia
1952	Hungary	**2-0**	Yugoslavia
1956	Soviet Union	**1-0**	Yugoslavia
1960	Yugoslavia	**3-1**	Denmark
1964	Hungary	**2-1**	Czechoslovakia
1968	Hungary	**4-1**	Bulgaria
1972	Poland	**2-1**	Hungary
1976	East Germany	**3-1**	Poland
1980	Czechoslovakia	**1-0**	East Germany
1984	France	**2-0**	Brazil
1988	Soviet Union	**2-1**	Brazil
1992	Spain	**3-2**	Poland
1996	Nigeria	**3-2**	Argentina
2000	Cameroon	**2-2 (5-3 pens)**	Spain

* In 1920 the silver medal was awarded to Spain after Czechoslovakia
was disqualified. Please see over for further details.

The Olympic Games

AT THE FIRST THREE OLYMPIADS, between 1896 and 1904, the format for the football tournament was eclectic to say the least, and included exhibition games and mini-leagues with selected XIs and local clubs. For example, at the 1900 Games in France, Club Français of Paris represented the hosts against Upton Park FC from Great Britain and a Belgian Student XI; and at St. Louis in 1904 two local teams, St. Rose Kickers FC and Christian Brothers College, lost to the Canadian side Galt FC. A more formal knockout competition was played between eight teams at the 1908 games, though only after the rest of the Olympics had finished.

In 1912 a consolation tournament for first round losers was also played so that teams that crossed the world would get more than a single game. Sixteen teams, including Egypt – the first team to represent Africa in the Olympic football tournament – played in 1920 at Antwerp. This format was maintained, with the addition of various preliminary rounds to even out the numbers, until the 1956 Melbourne games in Australia.

The Melbourne Olympic tournament was preceded by a qualifying tournament, and this was formalized for the 1960 Olympics with places being allocated to each FIFA football confederation. However, the greater willingness of developing nations to compete at the Olympics saw Africa and Asia gain more places than they did in the World Cup.

Under FIFA regulations the tournament has become an Under-23's World competition since 1992, though a number of over-age players may be included in squads.

1908 LONDON
SEMI-FINALS
England **4-0** Netherlands
Denmark **17-1** France A
THIRD PLACE PLAY-OFF
Netherlands **2-0** Sweden
France A refused to play
FINAL
October 24 – White City
England **2-0** Denmark
(Chapman 20,
Woodward 46)
h/t: 1-0 **Att:** 15,000
Ref: Lewis (Great Britain)

1912 STOCKHOLM
SEMI-FINALS
England **4-0** Finland
Denmark **4-1** Netherlands
THIRD PLACE PLAY-OFF
Netherlands **9-0** Finland
FINAL
July 4 – Olympic Stadium
England **4-2** Denmark
(Walden 10,   (Olsen 27, 81)
Hoare 22, 41,
Berry 43)
h/t: 4-1 **Att:** 25,000
Ref: Groothoof (Netherlands)

1920 ANTWERP
SEMI-FINALS
Belgium **3-0** Netherlands
Czechoslovakia **4-1** France
SECOND PLACE PLAY-OFF*
Spain **3-1** Netherlands
FINAL
September 5 – Olympisch
Belgium **2-0** Czechoslovakia**
(Coppee 6 pen,
Larnoe 30)
h/t: n/a **Att:** 35,000
Ref: Lewis (Great Britain)

* Spain won the silver medal after a
special mini tournament.
** Match abandoned after 39 minutes.
Czechoslovakia left the pitch
complaining of biased refereeing
and were disqualified.

1924 PARIS
SEMI-FINALS
Uruguay **2-1** Netherlands
Switzerland **2-1** Sweden
THIRD PLACE PLAY-OFF
Sweden **3-1** Netherlands
FINAL
June 9 – Colombes
Uruguay **3-0** Switzerland
(Petrone 27,
Cea 63,
Romano 81)
h/t: 1-0 **Att:** 41,000
Ref: Slawick (France)

1928 AMSTERDAM
SEMI-FINALS
Uruguay **3-2** Italy
Argentina **6-0** Egypt
THIRD PLACE PLAY-OFF
Italy **11-3** Egypt
FINAL
June 10 – Olympic Stadium
Uruguay **1-1** Argentina
(Ferreira)   (Petrone)
(after extra time)
h/t: n/a **Att:** n/a
Ref: Lewis (Great Britain)
REPLAY
June 13 – Olympic Stadium
Uruguay **2-1** Argentina
(Figueroa,   (Monti)
H. Scarone)
h/t: n/a **Att:** n/a
Ref: Mutter (Netherlands)

1932 LOS ANGELES
no football tournament

1936 BERLIN
SEMI-FINALS
Italy **2-1** Norway
Austria **3-1** Poland
THIRD PLACE PLAY-OFF
Norway **3-2** Poland
FINAL
August 16 – Olympia Stadion
Italy **2-1** Austria
(Frossi 70, 92)   (Kainberger 80)
(after extra time)
h/t: 0-0 **90 mins:** 1-1 **Att:** 90,000
Ref: Bauwens (Germany)

1948 LONDON
SEMI-FINALS
Sweden **4-2** Denmark
Yugoslavia **3-1** Great Britain
THIRD PLACE PLAY-OFF
Denmark **5-3** Great Britain
FINAL
August 13 – Wembley Stadium
Sweden **3-1** Yugoslavia
(Gren 24, 67   (Bobek 42)
G. Nordahl 48)
h/t: 1-1 **Att:** 60,000
Ref: Ling (Great Britain)

1952 HELSINKI
SEMI-FINALS
Hungary **6-0** Sweden
Yugoslavia **3-1** West Germany
THIRD PLACE PLAY-OFF
Sweden **2-0** West Germany
FINAL
August 2 – Olympiastadion
Hungary **2-0** Yugoslavia
(Puskas 25,
Czibor 88)
h/t: 1-0 **Att:** 60,000
Ref: Ellis (Great Britain)

1956 MELBOURNE
SEMI-FINALS
Yugoslavia **4-1** India
Soviet Union **2-1** Bulgaria
THIRD PLACE PLAY-OFF
Bulgaria **3-0** India
FINAL
August 12 – Olympic Park
Soviet Union **1-0** Yugoslavia
(Ilyin 48)
h/t: 0-0 **Att:** 120,000
Ref: Wright (Australia)

1960 ROME
SEMI-FINALS
Yugoslavia **1-1** Italy
Yugoslavia won by drawing lots
Denmark **2-0** Hungary
THIRD PLACE PLAY-OFF
Hungary **2-1** Italy
FINAL
September 10 – Flaminio Stadium
Yugoslavia **3-1** Denmark
(Galic,   (F. Nielsen)
Matous,
Kostic)
h/t: n/a **Att:** 40,000
Ref: Lo Bello (Italy)

1964 TOKYO
SEMI-FINALS
Czechoslovakia **2-1** East Germany
Hungary **6-0** United Arab
Republic
THIRD PLACE PLAY-OFF
East Germany **3-1** United Arab
Republic
FINAL
October 23 – National Stadium
Hungary **2-1** Czechoslovakia
(Weiss o.g. 47,   (Brumousky 80)
Bene 59)
h/t: 1-0 **Att:** 75,000
Ref: Ashkenazi (Israel)

1968 MEXICO CITY
SEMI-FINALS
Hungary **5-0** Japan
Bulgaria **3-2** Mexico
THIRD PLACE PLAY-OFF
Japan **2-0** Mexico
FINAL
October 26 – Azteca Stadium
Hungary **4-1** Bulgaria
(Menczel 22,   (Dimitrov 40)
A. Dunai 41, 49,
Juhasz 62)
h/t: 2-1 **Att:** 75,000
Ref: Le de Diego (Mexico)

Olympic Games Winners

 England 1908, 12

 **Belgium** 1920

 **Uruguay** 1924, 28

 **Italy** 1936

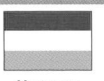 **Sweden** 1948

Hungary 1952, 64, 68

Soviet Union 1956, 88

 **Yugoslavia** 1960

 Poland 1972

 **East Germany** 1976

 Czechoslovakia 1980

France 1984

 **Spain** 1992

 Nigeria 1996

Cameroon 2000

1972 MUNICH

SECOND ROUND – GROUP A

Poland **2-1** Soviet Union
Poland **1-1** Denmark
Poland **5-0** Morocco
Soviet Union **4-0** Denmark
Soviet Union **3-0** Morocco
Denmark **3-1** Morocco

SECOND ROUND – GROUP B

Hungary **2-0** East Germany
Hungary **4-1** West Germany
Hungary **2-0** Mexico
East Germany **3-2** West Germany
East Germany **7-0** Mexico
West Germany **1-1** Mexico

THIRD PLACE PLAY-OFF

Soviet Union **2-2** East Germany
Bronze medal was shared

FINAL

September 10 – Olympic Stadium
Poland **2-1** Hungary
(Deyna 47, 68)   (Varadi 42)
h/t: 0-1 **Att:** 50,000
Ref: Tschenscher (West Germany)

1976 MONTREAL

SEMI-FINALS

East Germany **2-1** Soviet Union
Poland **2-0** Brazil A

THIRD PLACE PLAY-OFF

Soviet Union **2-0** Brazil A

FINAL

July 31 – Olympic Stadium
East Germany **3-1** Poland
(Schade 7,   (Lato 59)
Hoffmann 14,
Hofner 79)
h/t: 2-0 **Att:** 71,000
Ref: Barreto (Uruguay)

1980 MOSCOW

SEMI-FINALS

East Germany **1-0** Soviet Union
Czechoslovakia **2-0** Yugoslavia

THIRD PLACE PLAY-OFF

Soviet Union **2-0** Yugoslavia

FINAL

August 2 – Luzhniki Stadium
Czechoslovakia **1-0** East Germany
(Svoboda 77)
h/t: 0-0 **Att:** 70,000
Ref: Zade (Soviet Union)

1984 LOS ANGELES

SEMI-FINALS

France **4-2** Yugoslavia
Brazil **2-1** Italy

THIRD PLACE PLAY-OFF

Yugoslavia **2-1** Italy

FINAL

August 11 – Rose Bowl, Pasadena
France **2-0** Brazil
(Brisson 55,
Xuereb 62)
h/t: 0-0 **Att:** 101,000
Ref: Keizer (Netherlands)

1988 SEOUL

SEMI-FINALS

Soviet Union **3-2** Italy
Brazil **1-1** West Germany
Brazil won 3-2 on pens

THIRD PLACE PLAY-OFF

West Germany **3-0** Italy

FINAL

October 1 – Olympic Stadium
Soviet Union **2-1** Brazil
(Dobrovolski 61,   (Romario 30)
Savichev 103)
(after extra time)
h/t: 0-1 **90 mins:** 1-1 **Att:** 73,000
Ref: Bignet (France)

1992 BARCELONA

SEMI-FINALS

Poland **6-1** Australia
Spain **2-0** Ghana

THIRD PLACE PLAY-OFF

Ghana **1-0** Australia

FINAL

August 8 – Nou Camp
Spain **3-2** Poland
(Abelardo 65,   (Kowalczyk 44,
Quico 72, 90)   Staniek 76)
h/t: 0-1 **Att:** 95,000
Ref: Torres (Colombia)

1996 ATLANTA

SEMI-FINALS

Argentina **2-0** Portugal
Nigeria **4-3** Brazil

THIRD PLACE PLAY-OFF

Brazil **5-0** Portugal

FINAL

August 3 – Sanford Stadium
Nigeria **3-2** Argentina
(Babayaro 27,   (C. Lopez 3,
Amokachi 74,   Crespo pen 50)
Amunike 89)
h/t: 1-1 **Att:** 86,000
Ref: Collina (Italy)

2000 SYDNEY

SEMI-FINALS

Spain **3-1** USA
Cameroon **2-1** Chile

THIRD PLACE PLAY-OFF

Chile **2-0** USA

FINAL

September 30 – Olympic Stadium
Cameroon **2-2** Spain
(Amaya o.g. 53,   (Xavi 2,
Eto'o 58)   Gabri 45)
h/t: 0-2 **Att:** n/a
Ref: Rizo (Mexico)
Cameroon won 5-3 on pens

The victorious Nigerian team proudly shows off its gold medals after winning the Olympic football tournament at the 1996 Games in Atlanta in the United States. It beat a powerful Argentinian team 3-2 in the Final having already beaten Brazil 4-3 in the semi-final.

The World Club Cup

TOURNAMENT OVERVIEW

THE WORLD CLUB CUP was originally known as the Copa Internacional in Latin America and the Intercontinental Cup in Europe. Henri Delaunay, the then general secretary of UEFA, originally proposed it in 1958 as an annual contest between the champions of the two major footballing continents. With the advent of the Copa Libertadores in Latin America in 1960, following the creation of the European Cup in 1956, an intercontinental championship was finally possible, and the first contest, between Real Madrid and Peñarol, was held in 1960 over two legs, Real winning 5-1 in Madrid after a 0-0 draw in Uruguay.

In the late 1960s and early 1970s, the World Club Cup began to acquire a reputation for on-field violence, particularly matches featuring the Argentinian team Estudiantes. As a consequence a number of European champions refused to take their place, which was then taken up by the European Cup runners-up – this included Panathinaikos instead of Ajax in 1971, Juventus over Ajax in 72, Atlético Madrid over Bayern München in 74, Borussia Mönchengladbach over Liverpool in 77 and Malmö rather than Nottingham Forest in 1979.

The potential demise of the fixture was halted by making it a single match, with extra time and penalties, played in Japan with the acquisition of Toyota as sponsors. Despite a poor run of performances in the 1990s Latin American clubs have accorded the game greater significance than their opponents. But with Real Madrid's victory in its centenary year attracting wide coverage, Europeans are acquiring a taste for the cup too.

The World Club Cup

CONMEBOL	UEFA	
		Winners
		Runners-up
		Members
		Non-members

Team details

ARGENTINA — Country
● **Buenos Aires** — City of origin
River Plate — Team name

— Team colours

1986, *96* — Winners in bold / Runners-up in italics

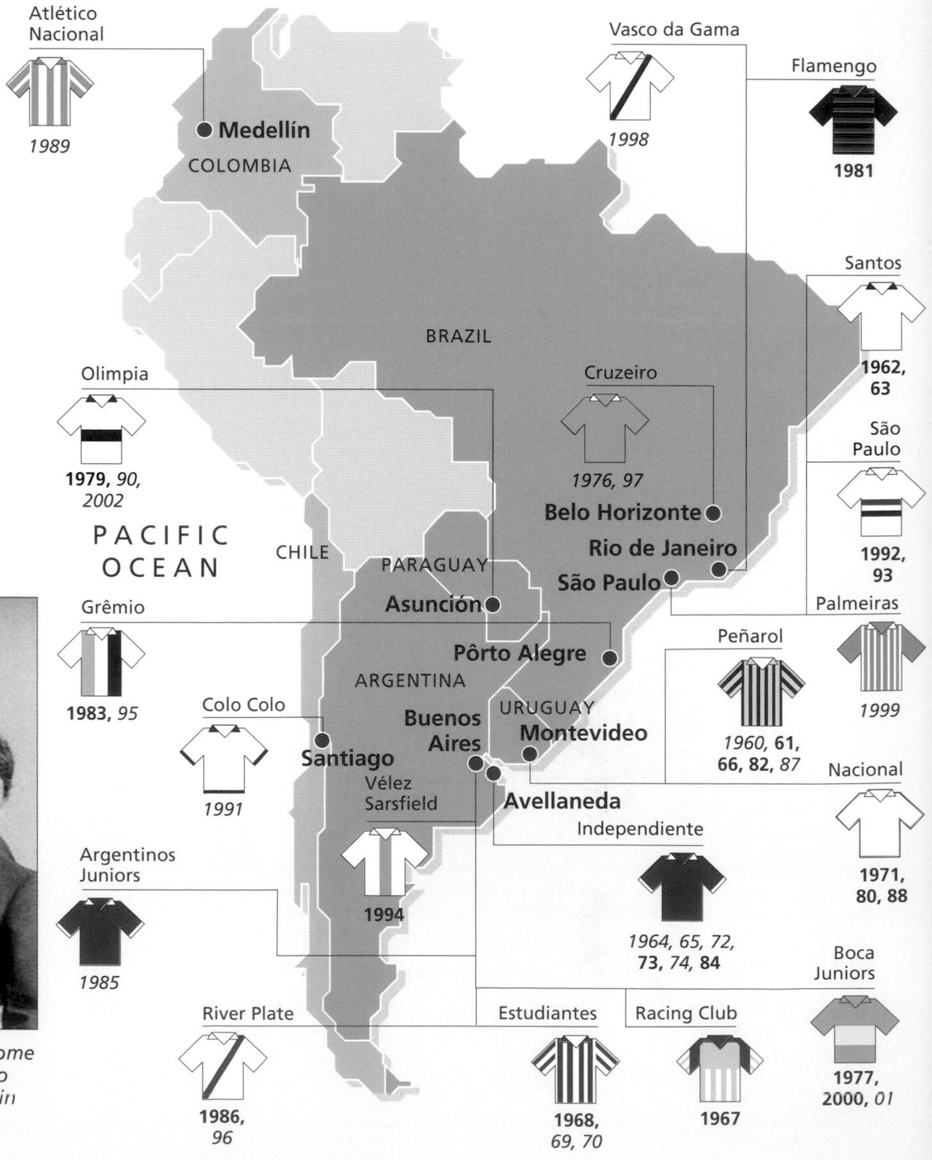

Members of the victorious Milan team, some showing signs of battle, on their return to Italy after their Final against Estudiantes in 1969, a match famous for its violence.

Atlético Nacional
1989
● **Medellín**
COLOMBIA

Vasco da Gama
1998

Flamengo
1981

Santos
1962, 63

São Paulo
1992, 93

Olimpia
1979, *90,* **2002**

Cruzeiro
1976, 97
Belo Horizonte
Rio de Janeiro
São Paulo

BRAZIL

PACIFIC OCEAN

CHILE
PARAGUAY
Asunción ●

Palmeiras
1999

Peñarol
1960, **61,** **66, 82,** *87*

Nacional
1971, *80,* **88**

Grêmio
1983, *95*

Pôrto Alegre
ARGENTINA

Colo Colo
1991
Santiago
Buenos Aires
Vélez Sarsfield
1994

URUGUAY
Montevideo

Avellaneda
Independiente
1964, 65, **72, 73, 74,** *84*

Argentinos Juniors
1985

River Plate
1986, *96*

Estudiantes
1968, *69, 70*

Racing Club
1967

Boca Juniors
1977, 2000, *01*

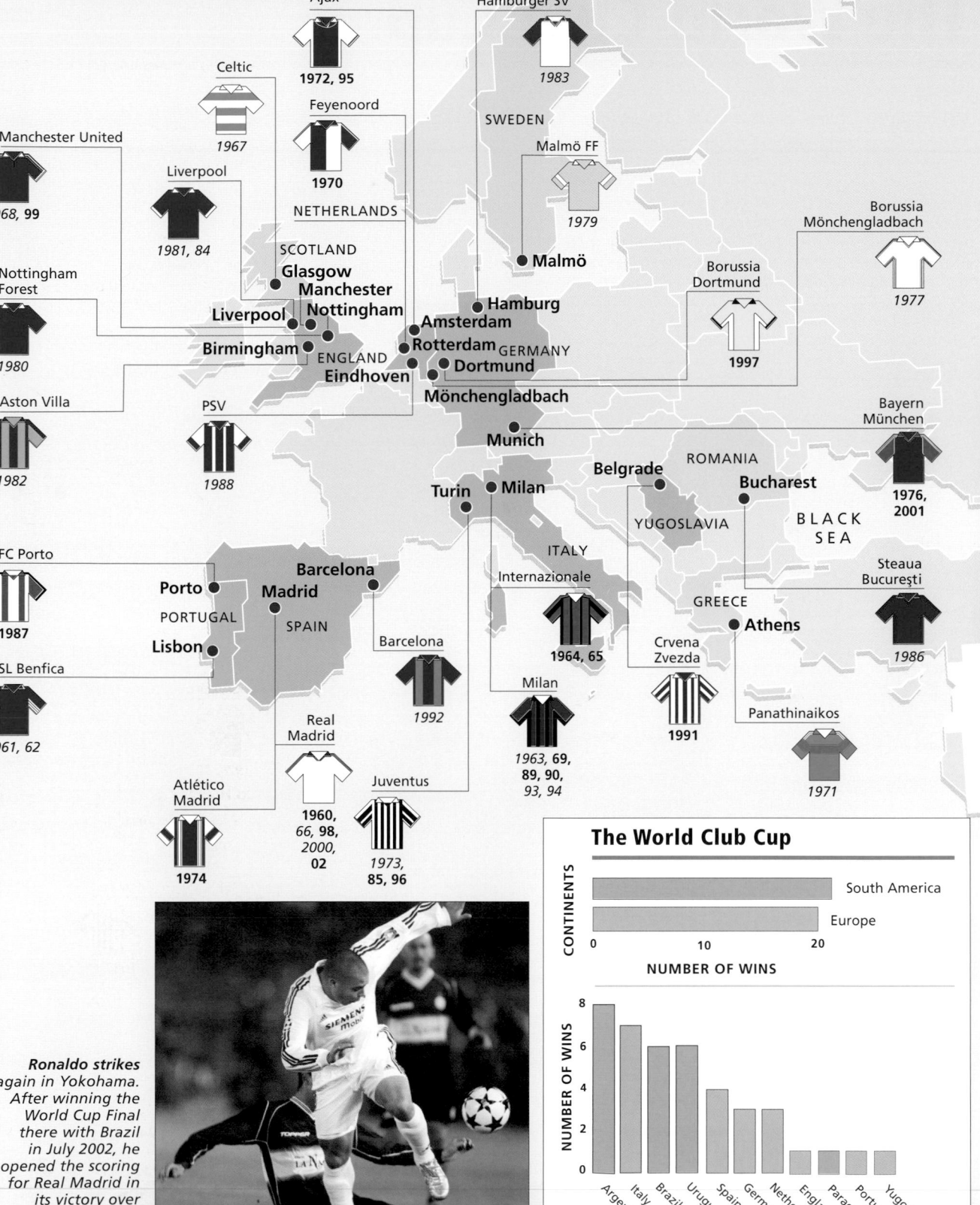

THE WORLD CLUB CUP

Ajax
1972, 95

Hamburger SV
1983

Celtic
1967

Feyenoord
1970

NETHERLANDS

SWEDEN

Malmö FF
1979

Borussia
Mönchengladbach
1977

Manchester United
1968, **99**

Liverpool
1981, 84

SCOTLAND
Glasgow
Manchester
Liverpool **Nottingham**
Birmingham
ENGLAND

● **Malmö**

Borussia
Dortmund
1997

Nottingham
Forest
1980

● **Hamburg**
● **Amsterdam**
● **Rotterdam** GERMANY
● **Dortmund**
● **Mönchengladbach**

Aston Villa
1982

PSV
1988

Eindhoven

● **Munich**

Bayern
München
**1976,
2001**

FC Porto
1987

Porto ●

Barcelona
Madrid
PORTUGAL
SPAIN

Turin ● **Milan**

● **Belgrade**
ROMANIA
● **Bucharest**

BLACK
SEA

SL Benfica
1961, 62

Lisbon ●

Barcelona
1992

Internazionale
1964, 65

ITALY

YUGOSLAVIA

GREECE
● **Athens**

Steaua
Bucureşti
1986

Atlético
Madrid
1974

Real
Madrid
**1960,
66, 98,
2000,
02**

Juventus
*1973,
85, 96*

Milan
*1963, 69,
89, 90,
93, 94*

Crvena
Zvezda
1991

Panathinaikos
1971

The World Club Cup

CONTINENTS

South America

Europe

0   10   20

NUMBER OF WINS

NUMBER OF WINS

8

6

4

2

0

Argentina
Italy
Brazil
Uruguay
Spain
Germany
Netherlands
England
Paraguay
Portugal
Yugoslavia

COUNTRIES

*Ronaldo strikes
again in Yokohama.
After winning the
World Cup Final
there with Brazil
in July 2002, he
opened the scoring
for Real Madrid in
its victory over
Olimpia of
Paraguay in the
World Club Cup
in December.*

The World Club Cup

THE FORMAT OF THE WORLD CLUB CUP and its earlier incarnation the Intercontinental Cup has been changed on a number of occasions since 1960. However, in the event of a draw, the annual play-off between the European Champions League winners (formerly the European Cup) and the Copa Libertadores has always been decided by extra time or penalties. The Cup began as a two-leg affair at the two finalists' home grounds. If both sides had won one match, irrespective of aggregate scores, then a replay was deemed necessary to decide the winners (see 1961, 63, 64 and 67). The fixture acquired a well-deserved reputation for aggressive, even violent play, beginning with the Milan v Santos games in 1963 and peaking in the finals contested by Estudiantes of Argentina between 1968 and 1970.

Between 1969 and 1979 the two-leg format was retained, but aggregate scores determined the winner. However, this change of format couldn't help an ailing fixture that European champions refused to contest.

In 1980, with a new Japanese sponsor, the format shifted to a single match played at the national stadium in Tokyo. With the creation of the more global Club World Championship, the future of this competition looked uncertain, but the demise of the disappointing FIFA tournament has left it with no rival.

1960 FINAL (2 legs)
July 3 – Centenario, Montevideo
Peñarol 0-0 Real Madrid
(Uruguay)   (Spain)

September 4 – Santiago Bernabeu, Madrid
Real Madrid 5-1 Peñarol
(Puskas 3, 9,   (Borges 69)
di Stefano 4,
Herrera 44,
Gento 54)

Real Madrid won 5-1 on aggregate

1961 FINAL (2 legs)
September 17 – Estadio da Luz, Lisbon
SL Benfica 1-0 Peñarol
(Portugal)   (Uruguay)
(Coluna 60)

September 17 – Centenario, Montevideo
Peñarol 5-0 SL Benfica
(Sasia 10,
Joya 18, 28,
Spencer 42, 60)

PLAY-OFF
September 19 – Centenario, Montevideo
Peñarol 2-1 SL Benfica
(Sasia 6, 41)   (Eusebio 35)

1962 FINAL (2 legs)
September 19 – Maracana, Rio de Janeiro
Santos 3-2 SL Benfica
(Brazil)   (Portugal)
(Pele 31, 86,   (Santana 58, 87)
Coutinho 64)

October 11 – Estadio da Luz, Lisbon
SL Benfica 2-5 Santos
(Eusebio 87,   (Pele 17, 28, 64,
Santana 89)   Coutinho 49,
          Pepe 77)

Santos won 8-4 on aggregate

1963 FINAL (2 legs)
October 16 – San Siro, Milan
Milan 4-2 Santos
(Italy)   (Brazil)
(Trappattoni 4,   (Pele 59, 87)
Amarildo 15, 65,
Mora 80)

November 14 – Maracana, Rio de Janeiro
Santos 4-2 Milan
(Pepe 50, 67,   (Altafini 12,
Almir 60,   Mora 17)
Lima 63)

PLAY-OFF
November 16 – Maracana, Rio de Janeiro
Santos 1-0 Milan
(Dalmo 26)

1964 FINAL (2 legs)
September 9 – Cordero, Avellaneda
Independiente 1-0 Internazionale
(Argentina)   (Italy)
(Rodriguez 60)

September 23 – San Siro, Milan
Internazionale 2-0 Independiente
(Mazzola 8,
Corso 39)

PLAY-OFF
September 26 – Santiago Bernabeu, Madrid
Internazionale 1-0 Independiente
(Corso 120)
(after extra time)

1965 FINAL (2 legs)
September 8 – San Siro, Milan
Internazionale 3-0 Independiente
(Italy)   (Argentina)
(Peiro 3,
Mazzola 23, 61)

September 15 – Cordero, Avellaneda
Independiente 0-0 Internazionale

Internazionale won 3-0 on aggregate

1966 FINAL (2 legs)
October 12 – Centenario, Montevideo
Peñarol 2-0 Real Madrid
(Uruguay)   (Spain)
(Spencer 39, 82)

October 26 – Santiago Bernabeu, Madrid
Real Madrid 0-2 Peñarol
(Rocha 28,
Spencer 37)

Peñarol won 4-0 on aggregate

1967 FINAL (2 legs)
October 18 – Hampden Park, Glasgow
Celtic 1-0 Racing Club
(Scotland)   (Argentina)
(McNeill 67)

November 1 – Mozart y Cuyo, Avellaneda
Racing Club 2-1 Celtic
(Raffo 32,   (Gemmell 20)
Cardenas 48)

PLAY-OFF
November 4 – Centenario, Montevideo
Racing Club 1-0 Celtic
(Cardenas 55)

1968 FINAL (2 legs)
September 25 –
Bombonera, Buenos Aires
**Estudiantes 1-0 Manchester
de la Plata   United**
(Argentina)   (England)
(Conigliaro 28)

October 16 – Old Trafford, Manchester
**Manchester 1-1 Estudiantes
United   de la Plata**
(Morgan 8)   (Veron 5)

Estudiantes de la Plata won 2-1
on aggregate

1969 FINAL (2 legs)
October 8 – San Siro, Milan
**Milan 3-0 Estudiantes
(Italy)   de la Plata**
(Sormani 8, 73,   (Argentina)
Combin 44)

October 22 – Bombonera, Buenos Aires
**Estudiantes 2-1 Milan
de la Plata   (Rivera 30)**
(Conigliaro 43,
Aguirre
Suarez 44)

Milan won 4-2 on aggregate

1970 FINAL (2 legs)
August 26 – Bombonera, Buenos Aires
**Estudiantes 2-2 Feyenoord
de la Plata   (Netherlands)**
(Argentina)   (Kindvall 21,
(Echecopar 6,   Van Hanegem 65)
Veron 10)

September 9 –
Feyenoord Stadium, Rotterdam
**Feyenoord 1-0 Estudiantes
(Van Daele 65)   de la Plata**

Feyenoord won 3-2 on aggregate

1971 FINAL (2 legs)
December 15 – Karaiskakis, Piraeus
**Panathinaikos 1-1 Nacional
(Greece)   Montevideo
(Filakouris 48)   (Uruguay)
          (Artime 50)**

December 29 – Centenario, Montevideo
**Nacional 2-1 Panathinaikos
Montevideo   (Filakouris 89)**
(Artime 34, 75)

Nacional Montevideo won 3-2
on aggregate

1972 FINAL (2 legs)
September 6 – Mozart y Cuyo, Avellaneda
**Independiente 1-1 Ajax
(Argentina)   (Netherlands)
(Sa 82)   (Cruyff 6)**

September 28 –
Olympish Stadion, Amsterdam
Ajax 3-0 Independiente
(Neeskens 12,
Rep 16, 78)

Ajax won 4-1 on aggregate

1973 FINAL
November 28 – Stadio Olimpico, Rome
Independiente 1-0 Juventus
(Argentina)   (Italy)
(Bochini 40)

1974 FINAL (2 legs)
March 12 – Mozart y Cuyo, Avellaneda
**Independiente 1-0 Atlético
(Argentina)   Madrid**
(Balbuena 33)   (Spain)

April 10 – Vicente Calderon, Madrid
**Atlético 2-0 Independiente
Madrid**
(Irureta 21,
Ayala 86)

Atlético Madrid won 2-1 on aggregate

1975 FINAL
**Bayern v Independiente
München   (Argentina)**
(West Germany)
not contested

1976 FINAL (2 legs)
November 23 – Olympiastadion, Munich
**Bayern 2-0 Cruzeiro
München   (Brazil)**
(West Germany)
(Müller 80,
Kappellmann 83)

December 21 – Mineirao, Belo Horizonte
**Cruzeiro 0-0 Bayern
          München**

Bayern München won 2-0 on aggregate

1977 FINAL (2 legs)
March 22 – Bombonera, Buenos Aires
**Boca Juniors 2-2 Borussia
(Argentina)   Mönchen-
(Mastrangelo 16,   gladbach
Ribolzi 51)   (West Germany)
          (Hannes 24,
          Bonhof 29)**

March 26 – Wildpark Stadion, Karlsruhe
Borussia 0-3 Boca
Mönchen-   Juniors
gladbach   *(Zanabria 2,*
                Mastrangelo 33,
                Salinas 35)

Boca Juniors won 5-2 on aggregate

1978 FINAL
Liverpool v Boca Juniors
(England)   (Argentina)
not contested

1979 FINAL (2 legs)
November 18 – Malmö Stadion, Malmö
Malmö FF 0-1 Olimpia
(Sweden)   (Paraguay)
               (Isasi 41)

March 3 – Manuel Ferreira, Asunción
Olimpia 2-1 Malmö FF
(Solalinde 40 pen,   (Earlandsson 48)
Michelagnoli 71)

Olimpia won 3-1 on aggregate

1980 FINAL
February 11 – National Stadium, Tokyo
Nacional 1-0 Nottingham
(Uruguay)   Forest
(Victorino 10)   (England)

1981 FINAL
December 13 – National Stadium, Tokyo
Flamengo 3-0 Liverpool
(Brazil)   (England)
(Nunes 13, 41,
Adilio 34)

1982 FINAL
December 12 – National Stadium, Tokyo
Peñarol 2-0 Aston Villa
(Uruguay)   (England)
(Jair 27,
Charrua 68)

1983 FINAL
December 11 – National Stadium, Tokyo
Grêmio 2-1 Hamburger SV
(Brazil)   (West Germany)
(Renato 37, 93)   *(Schröder 85)*

1984 FINAL
December 9 – National Stadium, Tokyo
Independiente 1-0 Liverpool
(Argentina)   (England)
(Percudiani 6)

1985 FINAL
December 8 – National Stadium, Tokyo
Juventus 2-2 Argentinos
(Italy)   Juniors
(Platini 63,   (Argentina)
M. Laudrup 82)   *(Ereros 55,*
                   Castro 75)

Juventus won 4-2 on pens

1986 FINAL
December 14 – National Stadium, Tokyo
River Plate 1-0 Steaua
(Argentina)   Bucureşti
(Alzamendi 28) (Romania)

1987 FINAL
December 13 – National Stadium, Tokyo
FC Porto 2-1 Peñarol
(Portugal)   (Uruguay)
(Gomes 41,   *(Viera 80)*
Madjer 108)

(after extra time)

1988 FINAL
December 11 – National Stadium, Tokyo
Nacional 2-2 PSV
(Uruguay)   (Netherlands)
(Ostolaza 7, 119) *(Romario 75,*
                     R. Koeman 109)

(after extra time)

Nacional won 7-6 on pens

1989 FINAL
December 17 – National Stadium, Tokyo
Milan 1-0 Atlético
(Italy)   Nacional
(Evani 118)   (Colombia)

1990 FINAL
December 9 – National Stadium, Tokyo
Milan 3-0 Olimpia
(Italy)   (Paraguay)
(Rijkaard 43, 65,
Stroppa 62)

1991 FINAL
December 8 – National Stadium, Tokyo
Crvena Zvezda 3-0 Colo Colo
(Yugoslavia)   (Chile)
(Jugovic 19, 58,
Pancev 72)

1992 FINAL
December 13 – National Stadium, Tokyo
São Paulo 2-1 Barcelona
(Brazil)   (Spain)
(Rai 26, 79)   *(Stoichkov 13)*

1993 FINAL
December 12 – National Stadium, Tokyo
São Paulo 3-2 Milan
(Brazil)   (Italy)
(Palinha 20,   *(Massaro 48,*
Cerezo 59,   *Papin 82)*
Müller 86)

1994 FINAL
December 1 – National Stadium, Tokyo
Vélez Sarsfield 2-0 Milan
(Argentina)   (Italy)
(Trotta 50 pen,
Asad 57)

1995 FINAL
November 28 – National Stadium, Tokyo
Ajax 0-0 Grêmio
(Netherlands)   (Brazil)

(after extra time)

Ajax won 4-3 on pens

1996 FINAL
November 26 – National Stadium, Tokyo
Juventus 1-0 River Plate
(Italy)   (Argentina)
(Del Piero 82)

1997 FINAL
December 2 – National Stadium, Tokyo
Borussia 2-0 Cruzeiro
Dortmund   (Brazil)
(Germany)
(Zorc 34,
Herrlich 85)

1998 FINAL
December 1 – National Stadium, Tokyo
Real Madrid 2-1 Vasco da Gama
(Spain)   (Brazil)
(Nasa o.g. 26, *(Juninho 56)*
Raúl 82)

1999 FINAL
November 30 – National Stadium, Tokyo
Manchester 1-0 Palmeiras
United   (Brazil)
(England)
(Keane 35)

2000 FINAL
November 28 – National Stadium, Tokyo
Boca Juniors 2-1 Real Madrid
(Argentina)   (Spain)
(Palermo 2, 5) *(Roberto Carlos 11)*

2001 FINAL
November 27 – National Stadium, Tokyo
Bayern 1-0 Boca Juniors
München   (Argentina)
(Germany)
(Kuffour 109)

(after extra time)

2002 FINAL
December 3 – Yokohama, Japan
Real 2-0 Olimpia
Madrid   (Paraguay)
(Spain)
(Ronaldo 14,
Guti 84)

THE WORLD CLUB CUP

Real Madrid's Roberto Carlos (left, white shirt) shoots past Oscar Cordoba, the Boca Juniors goalkeeper, in the 11th minute of the 2000 *World Club Cup Final. However, Boca, for whom Martin Palermo scored twice in the first five minutes, held on to win 2-1.*

Women's Football

WORLD CUP AND OLYMPIC FOOTBALL

WOMEN'S FOOTBALL

PICTURES FROM CHINA during the Han Dynasty (206 BC–221 AD) clearly show women playing rudimentary forms of football, but other evidence of early participation in the game is rare. The male predominance at English public schools gave the boys a 30-year head start when the new codified rules were drawn up in 1863. The catch up began with the first recorded women's football match under FA rules played on 23 March 1895, at Crouch End in North London, when South of England beat North of England 7-1. However, the backlash soon arrived in the shape of systematic opposition to women's football from the male football establishment all over Europe.

In 1896, the Dutch football authority, KNVB, banned a women's match between a Sparta Rotterdam XI and an England XI and followed this up with a ban on women's games at any stadium of a club affiliated to it. Similar policies of exclusion were pursued by the English FA and by the German FA, the DFB, who banned women from affiliated stadiums in the 1950s. Medical, social and footballing commentators claimed that football was detrimental to the moral and physical health of women.

Despite all this, women's football grew in popularity and with the massive flow of European women into industrial employment during the First World War, players and teams multiplied. In fact, so great was the growth of women's football that the English FA moved to a stadium ban for women's teams in 1920, and the sport was forced into the world of exhibition matches and charity events. Dick Kerr's Ladies, a Preston-based factory team, played to large audiences in the 1920s, while Manchester Corinthians was the leading women's club in England in the 1940s and 50s.

The tide turns

Independent attempts to organize international women's football began with the creation of the International Ladies Football Association in 1957 and a Women's European Championship won by Manchester Corinthians. The Italian-based CIEFF was formed in 1969 and held informal women's world cups, the Mundialato, in Italy in 1970 and Mexico in 1971. Driven by fear of losing control and by some dim recognition that women's football was a significant sporting force, FIFA and UEFA acted. UEFA called for all member nation's FAs to incorporate women's football into the mainstream of the game (though in England this took until 1993).

In terms of participation and sporting success women's football has three strongholds: North America, China and Northern Europe. In America and China, the relative weakness of men's football has created the space in which women's football could grow. In northern Europe, the egalitarianism and social engineering of social democratic governments has helped promote women's football. Not surprisingly then these regions have hosted the official FIFA Women's World Cup and contested its Finals (as well as the Olympic Finals). China will be hosting the finals in 2003 for the second time. As the women's game grows, professional leagues are beginning to emerge. The first, in Japan in 1993, has been joined by leagues in the USA, England and other countries.

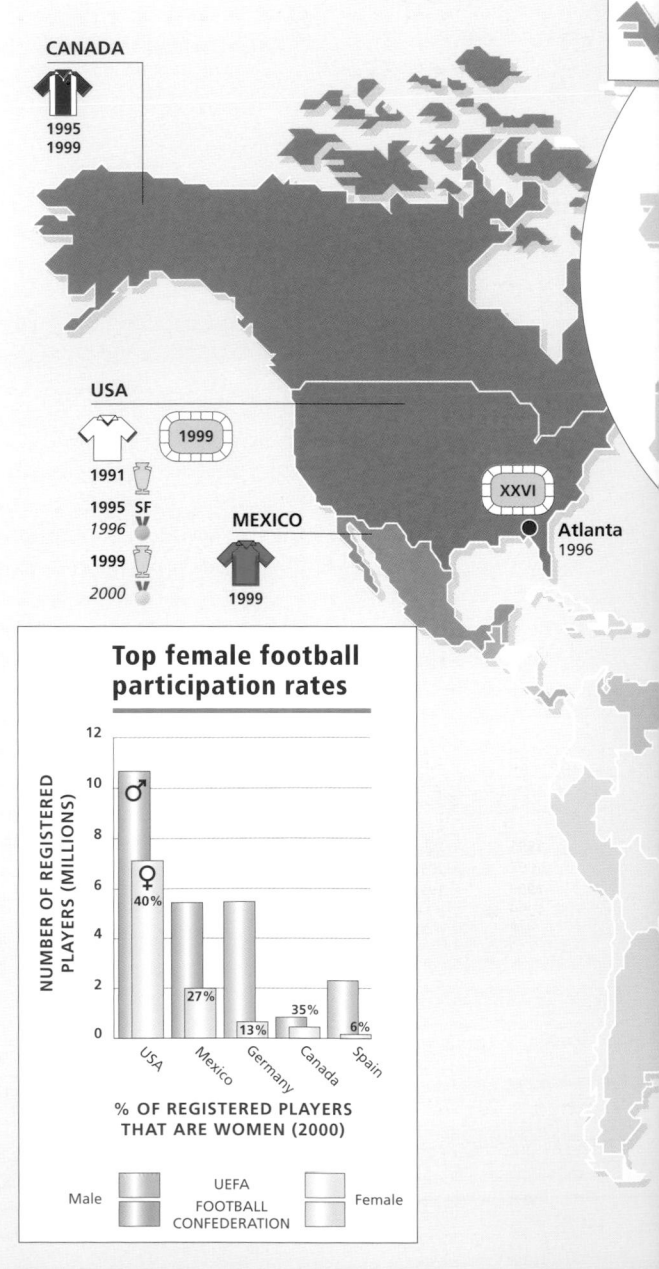

Women's World Cup and Olympic Games

Percentage of registered players that are women

- 30+%
- 20–30%
- 10–20%
- 3–10%
- 1–3%
- less than 1%
- zero
- no data

World Cup
- Winners
- RU Runners-up
- SF Semi-finalist
- 1999 Participant

Olympic medals
- Gold
- Silver
- Bronze
- 2000 Participant

1999 Host country and year

XVI Host city and Olympiad number

Sydney 2000 Location and year of Games

CANADA
1995
1999

USA
1999
1991
1995 SF
1996
1999
2000

MEXICO
1999

XXVI Atlanta 1996

Top female football participation rates

NUMBER OF REGISTERED PLAYERS (MILLIONS)

♂
♀ 40%

USA — 27%
Mexico — 13%
Germany — 35%
Canada — 6%
Spain

% OF REGISTERED PLAYERS THAT ARE WOMEN (2000)

Male — Female
UEFA FOOTBALL CONFEDERATION

The Preston Ladies football team prepares for a European tour at Bedford in 1939. Though women's football was confined to exhibition matches and charity events during the 1930s and 40s, it remained hugely popular with players and spectators, and tours such as this were regular events.

The second WUSA Founders Cup in 2002 saw Carolina Courage (in blue) defeat the Washington Freedom 3-2 at Herndon Stadium, Atlanta. The match, which features the top two teams in the women's professional league as decided by regular season and play-offs, was watched by over 15,000 spectators.

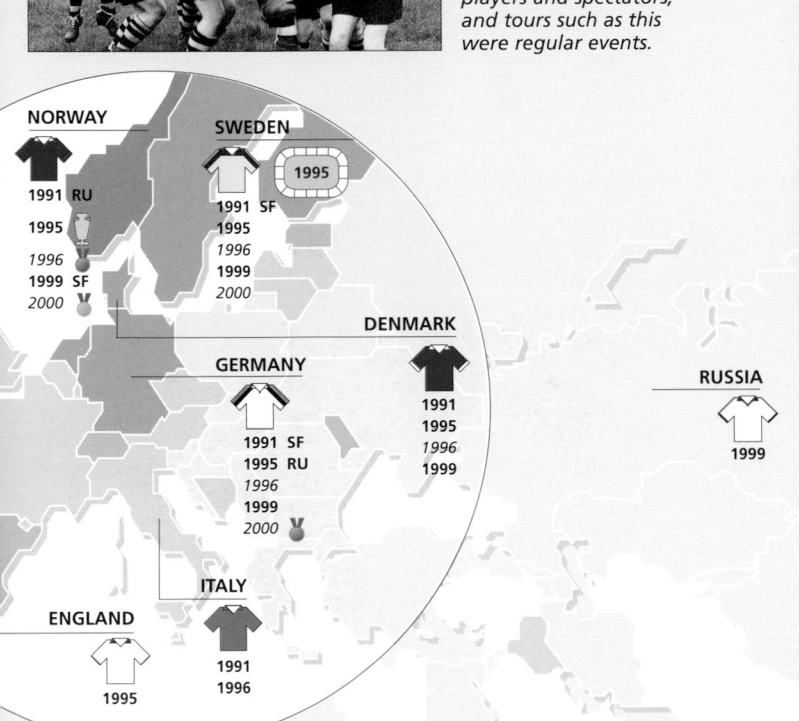

NORWAY
1991 RU
1995
1996
1999 SF
2000

SWEDEN
1995
1991 SF
1995
1996
1999
2000

DENMARK
1991
1995
1996
1999

GERMANY
1991 SF
1995 RU
1996
1999
2000

ITALY
1991
1996

ENGLAND
1995

RUSSIA
1999

NORTH KOREA
1999

JAPAN
1991
1995
1996
1999

TAIWAN
1991

GHANA
1999

BRAZIL
1991
1995
1996
1999 SF
2000

NIGERIA
1991
1995
1999
2000

CHINA
1991, 2003
1991
1995 SF
1996
1999 RU
2000

AUSTRALIA
1995
1999
2000

Sydney
2000
XXVII

NEW ZEALAND
1991

Women's World Cup Finals (1991–99)

YEAR	WINNERS	SCORE	RUNNERS-UP
1991	USA	2-1	Norway
1995	Norway	5-2	Germany
1999	USA	0-0 (5-4 pens)	China

Women's Olympic Finals (1996–2000)

YEAR	WINNERS	SCORE	RUNNERS-UP
1996	USA	2-1	China
2000	Norway	3-2	USA

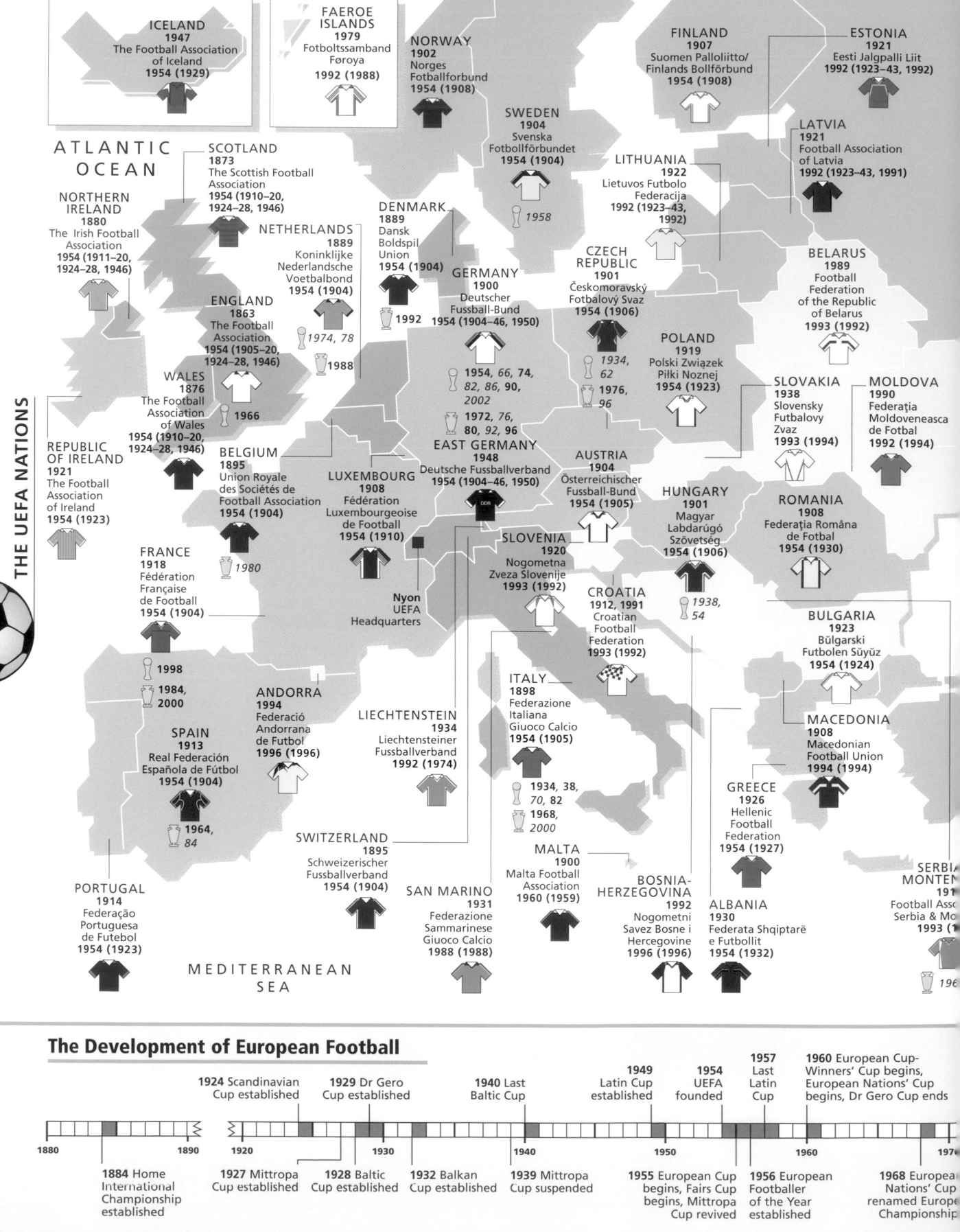

ICELAND
1947
The Football Association
of Iceland
1954 (1929)

FAEROE ISLANDS
1979
Fotboltssamband
Føroya
1992 (1988)

NORWAY
1902
Norges
Fotballforbund
1954 (1908)

FINLAND
1907
Suomen Palloliitto/
Finlands Bollförbund
1954 (1908)

ESTONIA
1921
Eesti Jalgpalli Liit
1992 (1923–43, 1992)

SWEDEN
1904
Svenska
Fotbollförbundet
1954 (1904)

1958

LITHUANIA
1922
Lietuvos Futbolo
Federacija
1992 (1923–43, 1992)

LATVIA
1921
Football Association
of Latvia
1992 (1923–43, 1991)

ATLANTIC
OCEAN

SCOTLAND
1873
The Scottish Football
Association
1954 (1910–20,
1924–28, 1946)

DENMARK
1889
Dansk
Boldspil
Union
1954 (1904)

CZECH REPUBLIC
1901
Českomoravský
Fotbalový Svaz
1954 (1906)

BELARUS
1989
Football
Federation
of the Republic
of Belarus
1993 (1992)

NORTHERN IRELAND
1880
The Irish Football
Association
1954 (1911–20,
1924–28, 1946)

NETHERLANDS
1889
Koninklijke
Nederlandsche
Voetbalbond
1954 (1904)

1992

GERMANY
1900
Deutscher
Fussball-Bund
1954 (1904–46, 1950)

POLAND
1919
Polski Związek
Piłki Nożnej
1954 (1923)

ENGLAND
1863
The Football
Association
1954 (1905–20,
1924–28, 1946)

1974, 78

1988

1954, 66, 74,
82, 86, 90,
2002

1972, 76,
80, 92, 96

1934,
62

1976,
96

SLOVAKIA
1938
Slovensky
Futbalovy
Zvaz
1993 (1994)

MOLDOVA
1990
Federaţia
Moldoveneasca
de Fotbal
1992 (1994)

WALES
1876
The Football
Association
of Wales
1954 (1910–20,
1924–28, 1946)

1966

EAST GERMANY
1948
Deutsche Fussballverband
1954 (1904–46, 1950)

AUSTRIA
1904
Österreichischer
Fussball-Bund
1954 (1905)

HUNGARY
1901
Magyar
Labdarúgó
Szövetség
1954 (1906)

ROMANIA
1909
Federaţia Română
de Fotbal
1954 (1930)

REPUBLIC OF IRELAND
1921
The Football
Association
of Ireland
1954 (1923)

BELGIUM
1895
Union Royale
des Sociétés de
Football Association
1954 (1904)

LUXEMBOURG
1908
Fédération
Luxembourgeoise
de Football
1954 (1910)

Nyon
UEFA
Headquarters

SLOVENIA
1920
Nogometna
Zveza Slovenije
1993 (1992)

1938,
54

CROATIA
1912, 1991
Croatian
Football
Federation
1993 (1992)

BULGARIA
1923
Bŭlgarski
Futbolen Sŭyŭz
1954 (1924)

FRANCE
1918
Fédération
Française
de Football
1954 (1904)

1980

1998

1984,
2000

ANDORRA
1994
Federació
Andorrana
de Futbol
1996 (1996)

LIECHTENSTEIN
1934
Liechtensteiner
Fussballverband
1992 (1974)

ITALY
1898
Federazione
Italiana
Giuoco Calcio
1954 (1905)

MACEDONIA
1908
Macedonian
Football Union
1994 (1994)

SPAIN
1913
Real Federación
Española de Fútbol
1954 (1904)

1964,
84

1934, 38,
70, 82

1968,
2000

GREECE
1926
Hellenic
Football
Federation
1954 (1927)

PORTUGAL
1914
Federação
Portuguesa
de Futebol
1954 (1923)

SWITZERLAND
1895
Schweizerischer
Fussballverband
1954 (1904)

SAN MARINO
1931
Federazione
Sammarinese
Giuoco Calcio
1988 (1988)

MALTA
1900
Malta Football
Association
1960 (1959)

BOSNIA-HERZEGOVINA
1992
Nogometni
Savez Bosne i
Hercegovine
1996 (1996)

ALBANIA
1930
Federata Shqiptarë
e Futbollit
1954 (1932)

SERBIA MONTEN
1919
Football Asso
Serbia & Mo
1993 (1

196

MEDITERRANEAN
SEA

The Development of European Football

1884 Home
International
Championship
established

1924 Scandinavian
Cup established

1927 Mittropa
Cup established

1928 Baltic
Cup established

1929 Dr Gero
Cup established

1932 Balkan
Cup established

1939 Mittropa
Cup suspended

1940 Last
Baltic Cup

1949
Latin Cup
established

1954
UEFA
founded

1955 European Cup
begins, Fairs Cup
begins, Mittropa
Cup revived

1956 European
Footballer
of the Year
established

1957
Last
Latin
Cup

1960 European Cup-
Winners' Cup begins,
European Nations'
Cup begins, Dr Gero
Cup ends

1968 Europea
Nations' Cu
renamed Europe
Championship

1880   1890   1920   1930   1940   1950   1960   1970

The UEFA Nations

Date of formation of the national Football Association		
■ Before 1899		
■ 1900–39		
■ 1940–79		
■ After 1980		

Formation of national FA — **COUNTRY**
1916
Date of affiliation to UEFA — **1916 (1912)** — Date of affiliation to FIFA

Name of Football Association

Team colours

World Cup — 🏆 **1990** — Winners in bold
European Championship — 🏆 *1990* — Runners-up in italic

UEFA

European Tournaments and Cup Competitions:
European Championships
European Champions League
UEFA Cup
Intertoto Cup
European Super Cup
European Women's Championships

UKRAINE
1991
Football Federation of Ukraine
1992 (1992)

RUSSIA
1912, 1991
Rossiyskiy Futbol'nyy Soyuz
1954 (1912, 1992)

🏆 1960, *64, 72, 88*

BLACK SEA

CASPIAN SEA

GEORGIA
1990
Georgian Football Federation
1992 (1992)

TURKEY
1923
Türkiye Futbol Federasyonu
1962 (1923)

AZERBAIJAN
1992
Association of Football Federations of Azerbaijan
1994 (1994)

CYPRUS
1934
Kipriaki Omospondia Podosferu
1962 (1948)

ARMENIA
1992
Football Federation of Armenia
1993 (1992)

ISRAEL
1928
Israel Football Association
1992 (1929)

1978 European Under-21 Championships established

1984 Last Home International Championship

1991 Last Baltic Cup

1999 Last European Cup-Winners' Cup

1980   1990   2000

1972 UEFA establishes Women's Football Committee

1982 First European Championship for Women

1992 European Cup becomes European Champions League

The UEFA Nations

IN 1954, ALMOST 50 YEARS after the foundation of FIFA, and 38 years after the formation of CONMEBOL in South America, Europe acquired its own football federation in the form of UEFA: the Union of European Football Associations, based in Nyon, Switzerland. Football may have spread to every corner of the continent, but it took two world wars to overcome the Continent's divisions in order to reach agreement on the organization of football. UEFA had 35 founding members, and with the break-up of the Soviet Union and Yugoslavia it has grown to 51. Israel has transferred in from the Asian and Oceanic confederations as UEFA's contribution to global peacekeeping.

With the arrival of UEFA, the older international competitions, like the Scandinavian Cup organized by national FAs and ad hoc committees, were replaced by the European Nations' Championship. UEFA also spurred the development of European club competition in the 1950s and early 1960s, replacing the Latin Cup and Mittel Europa Cup with the European Cup. In the 1990s, UEFA had to fight to retain its political weight within world football, as FIFA, the European Community and the biggest European clubs have challenged its authority. At the turn of the century, its place was no more secure.

Lennart Johannsson, the Swedish-born President of UEFA, was re-elected to the post in January 2002 as the sole nominee and will serve a further four years in the hot seat.

Calendar of Events

Club Tournaments	European Champions League 2003–04
	UEFA Cup 2003–04
	Intertoto Cup 2004
	European Super Cup 2004
International Tournaments	European Championships 2004
	Qualifying Tournament for Olympic Games 2004 (Under–23s)

Europe

THE SEASONS IN REVIEW 2002, 2002–03

WAS THIS EUROPE'S LONGEST SEASON EVER? With the opening rounds of the Intertoto Cup beginning after the 2002 World Cup in July, play continued to the very end of June. The long-suffering French and Turkish squads played out the Confederations Cup in France and the Copa del Rey Final brought an end to the long season in Spain. But with most big clubs embarking on lucrative foreign tours in the USA and Asia, end is a relative concept. The Champions League, the UEFA Cup, international friendlies and the qualifying rounds for the Euro 2004 championships ensured there was barely a let up for anyone.

If last season saw the bubble of TV rights values burst, then this season was all about living with the consequences, but not before another TV collapse in Greece – Alpha Digital – brought football to a halt there for over month. National Football associations, player's unions and journalists announced at regular intervals the huge extent of accumulated debt at all levels of European football. In any other line of business the administration and insolvency offices would be overwhelmed with work, but football is not a normal business. Nonetheless, bankruptcies, demotions and the withdrawal of playing licenses were scattered across the top leagues of the continent. The transfer market was the quietest it has been in a decade, with few clubs buying and a lot selling. The new January transfer window was virtually empty across Europe.

The spectre of organized and disorganized violence in football continued to haunt the continent: Turkey, Greece and Italy saw extensive trouble all season, and fans following the Turkish national team have been regularly throwing objects at their opponents. More worrying is the persistent racial abuse on and off the field in European club and international matches.

The division in European football was as stark as ever in the major tournaments. Only one team east of Berlin made the last stage of the Champions League – Spartak Moscow – and the region's clubs made little impact in the UEFA Cup. With Austria and Switzerland winning the right to host the 2008 European Championships, it will be over 30 years since an Eastern European country has hosted the tournament. Within Western Europe the divide is equally harsh. The Champions League quarter-finals were dominated by Spain and Italy with Ajax and Manchester United making up the final eight. The UEFA Cup provided more space for the second rank European nations and a thrilling final was fought out between Portugal's Porto and Scotland's Celtic.

UEFA Leagues

COUNTRY	CHAMPIONS	CUP WINNERS
Albania	SK Tirana	Dinamo Tiranë
Andorra	Santa Coloma	*no cup*
Armenia	Pyunik Yerevan	Pyunik Yerevan
Austria	FK Austria Wien	FK Austria Wien
Azerbaijan	Şämkir	*no cup*
Belarus	FC BATE Borisov	Dinamo Minsk
Belgium	Club Brugge KV	La Louviére
Bosnia-Herzegovina	FK Leotar	Željeznicar Sarajevo
Bulgaria	CSKA Sofia	FC Levski
Croatia	Dinamo Zagreb	Hajduk Split
Cyprus	Omonia	Anorthosis Famagusta
Czech Republic	Sparta Praha	FK Teplice
Denmark	FC København	Brøndby
England	Manchester United	Arsenal
Estonia	FC Flora Tallinn	FC Levadia Tallinn
Faeroe Islands	HB	NSÍ
Finland	HJK Helsinki	Haka Valkeakoski
France	Olympique Lyonnais	AJ Auxerre
Georgia	Dinamo Tbilisi	Dinamo Tbilisi
Germany	Bayern München	Bayern München
Greece	Olympiakos	PAOK
Netherlands	PSV	Utrecht
Hungary	MTK	Ferencváros
Iceland	KR	Fylkir
Israel	Maccabi Tel-Aviv	Hapoel Ramat Gan
Italy	Juventus	Milan
Khazakhstan	Irtysh Pavlodar	Zhenis Astana
Latvia	Skonto Riga	Skonto Riga
Liechtenstein	*no league*	FC Vaduz
Lithuania	FBK Kaunas	Atlantas Klaipėda
Luxembourg	F91 Dudelange	CS Grevenmacher
Macedonia	Vardar Skopje	Cemenetarnica Skopje
Malta	Sliema Wanderers	Birkirkara
Moldova	Sherif Tiraspl	Zimbru Chişinău
Northern Ireland	Glentoran	Coleraine
Norway	Rosenborg BK	Vålerenga
Poland	Wisła Kraków	Wisła Kraków
Portugal	FC Porto	FC Porto
Republic of Ireland	Bohemians	Derry City
Romania	Rapid Bucureşti	Dinamo Bucureşti
Russia	Lokomotiv Moskva	CSKA Moskva
San Marino	Domagnano	*no cup*
Scotland	Rangers	Rangers
Serbia & Montenegro	Partizan Beograd	Sartid Smederevo
Slovakia	MSK Žilina	Matidor Púchov
Slovenia	NK Maribor	Olimpija Lubljana
Spain	Real Madrid	RCD Mallorca
Sweden	Djurgårdens IF	Djurgårdens IF
Switzerland	Grasshopper-Club	FC Basel
Turkey	Beşiktaş	Trabzonspor K
Ukraine	Dynamo Kyiv	Dynamo Kyiv
Wales	Barry Town	Barry Town

The World Cup is coming to Germany, and Munich will be acquiring a new stadium – the Allianz Arena – that will also be used by Munich's club teams. Here, the Bayern München team dons protective headgear as it awaits another blast of invective from club president Franz Beckenbauer.

European Super Cup

2002 FINAL

August 30 – Stade Louis II, Monaco
Real Madrid 3-1 Feyenoord
(Spain) (Netherlands)
*(Paauwe o.g. 15, (van
Roberto Carlos 21, Hooijdonk 56)
Guti 60)*
h/t : 2-0 **Att**: 15,000
Ref: Hugh Dallas (Scotland)

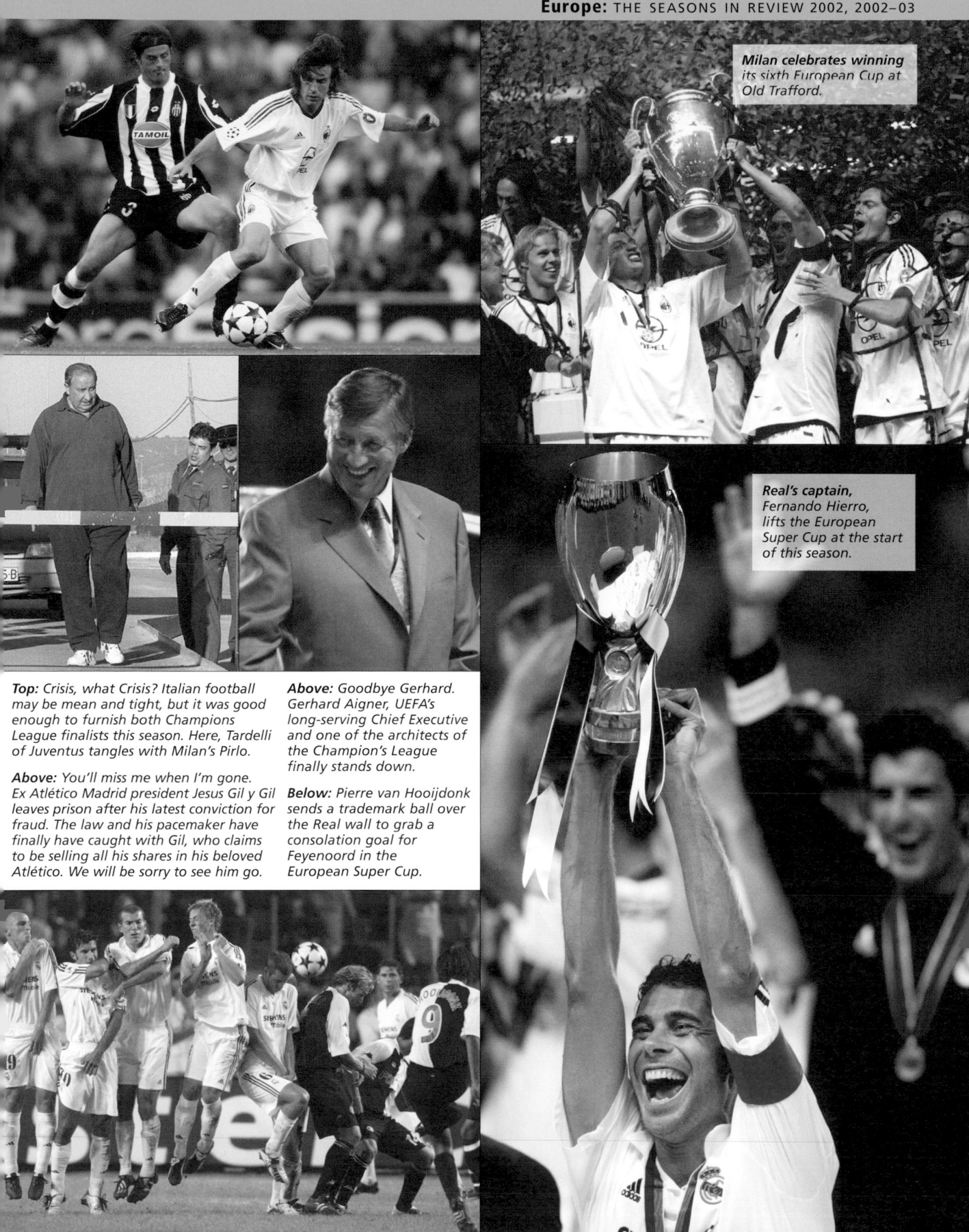

Milan celebrates winning its sixth European Cup at Old Trafford.

Real's captain, Fernando Hierro, lifts the European Super Cup at the start of this season.

Top: Crisis, what Crisis? Italian football may be mean and tight, but it was good enough to furnish both Champions League finalists this season. Here, Tardelli of Juventus tangles with Milan's Pirlo.

Above: You'll miss me when I'm gone. Ex Atlético Madrid president Jesus Gil y Gil leaves prison after his latest conviction for fraud. The law and his pacemaker have finally have caught with Gil, who claims to be selling all his shares in his beloved Atlético. We will be sorry to see him go.

Above: Goodbye Gerhard. Gerhard Aigner, UEFA's long-serving Chief Executive and one of the architects of the Champion's League finally stands down.

Below: Pierre van Hooijdonk sends a trademark ball over the Real wall to grab a consolation goal for Feyenoord in the European Super Cup.

The European Championships

TOURNAMENT OVERVIEW

HENRI DELAUNAY, head of the French FA, proposed the idea of a European nations tournament as early as 1927, but in the absence of a European football federation it failed to materialize. With the foundation of UEFA in 1954 Delaunay revived the idea. After much internal politics and the usual scepticism, UEFA announced that the first finals would be held in 1960. Though Delaunay died in 1955, he was honoured when the trophy was named the Henri Delaunay Cup. The format of the early tournaments was a series of two-leg qualifying rounds played home and away, producing four finalists who would contest semi-finals and a Final over a week in a single location.

The first finals, held in France, are best remembered for the controversial quarter-final between Spain and the USSR. Franco's love of football was more than matched by his hatred of Communism and he refused the Soviet team entry into Spain. UEFA awarded the tie to the Soviets. Under the inspirational Lev Yashin, the USSR won the Final beating Yugoslavia 2-1 in extra time. In 1964 Spain hosted the tournament and, having allowed the Soviets in this time, beat them 2-1 in the Final. In 1968, Italy was host and beat Yugoslavia in a replayed Final.

Penalties and golden goals

In 1972, the Nations Cup was renamed the European Championships and West Germany thrashed the USSR 3-0 in a warm-up for their 1974 World Cup victory. But in Yugoslavia in 1976, Eastern Europe struck back when the Czechs beat the Germans in a tense penalty shootout. In 1980, the tournament was expanded to eight teams and in 1996 to 16, including group games to determine the finalists.

The 1980s saw two truly great teams take the trophy. In 1984, Platini's France swept to victory, while in 1988, the Dutch, with Gullit, van Basten and Rijkaard, triumphed. In 1992, Denmark, a late entrant in place of Yugoslavia (then embroiled in a civil war), made it to the Final and beat the favourites Germany 2-0. But the Germans were back four years later, defeating the English hosts in an excruciating penalty shootout before a rematch of the 1976 Final saw them beating the Czechs with a golden goal by Oliver Bierhoff – the first time an 'official' golden goal had decided the Final of a major competition. In 2000, France confirmed its then status as the world's No.1 team by beating Italy 2-1, with a last-minute equalizer and a golden goal in extra time.

The European Championships (1960–2000)

YEAR	WINNERS	SCORE	RUNNERS-UP
1960	USSR	2-1	Yugoslavia
1964	Spain	2-1	USSR
1968	Italy	1-1, (replay) 2-0 (aet)	Yugoslavia
1972	West Germany	3-0	USSR
1976	Czechoslovakia	2-2 (5-3 pens)	West Germany
1980	West Germany	2-1	Belgium
1984	France	2-0	Spain
1988	Netherlands	2-0	USSR
1992	Denmark	2-0	Germany
1996	Germany	2-1 (golden goal)	Czech Republic
2000	France	2-1 (golden goal)	Italy

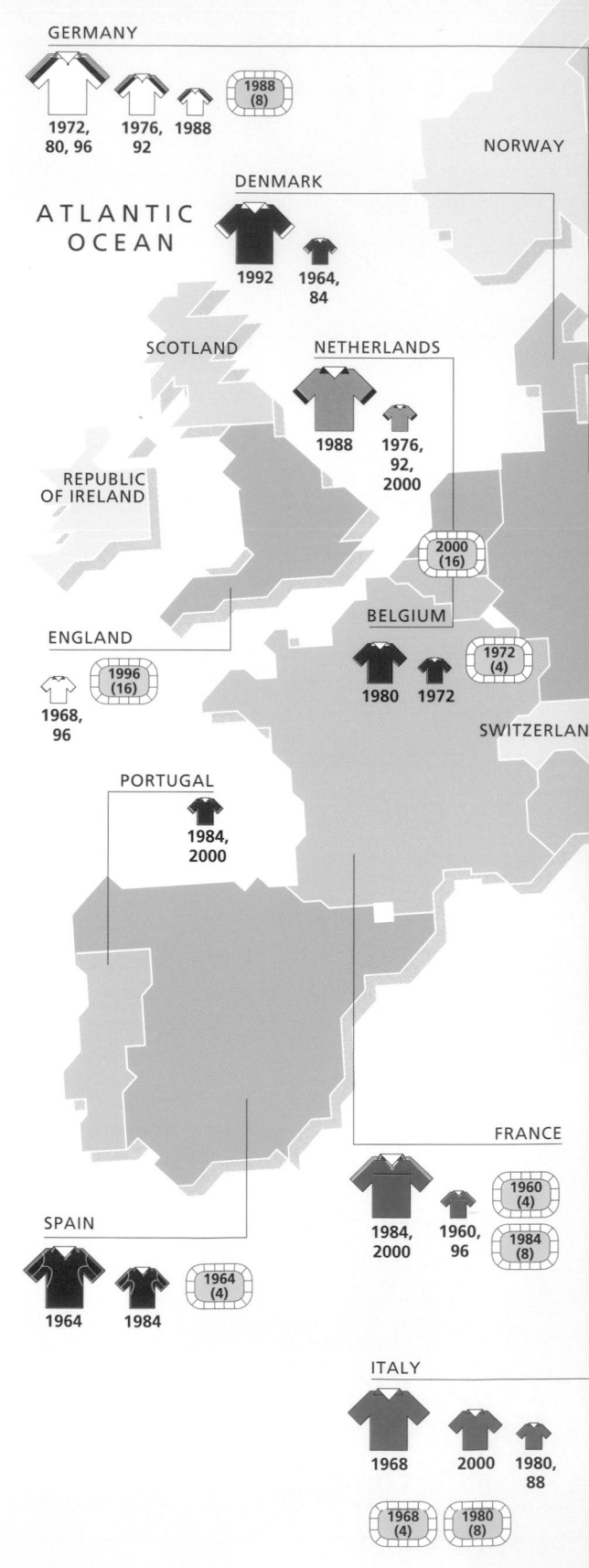

THE EUROPEAN CHAMPIONSHIPS

The European Championships

Participation in the European Championships

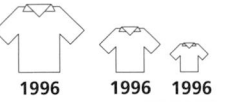

- 6+ times
- 3–5 times
- 2 times
- 1 time
- 0 times

Winners, runners-up and semi-finalists with date

1996 1996 1996

Host country, with date in stadium and number of participants in brackets

ENGLAND   1996 (16)

SWEDEN
1992
1992 (8)

RUSSIA (includes USSR 1917–91)

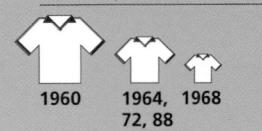

1960 1964, 72, 88 1968

CZECH REPUBLIC

1976 1996 1960, 80

YUGOSLAVIA

1960, 68 1976 1976 (4)

HUNGARY

1964, 72

SLOVENIA

CROATIA

ROMANIA

SLOVENIA

BULGARIA

BLACK SEA

GREECE

TURKEY

MEDITERRANEAN SEA

Czechoslovakia's Antonin Panenka chips his penalty over Sepp Maier in the German goal to win the 1976 tournament in Belgrade, Yugoslavia.

Germany's revenge against the Czech Republic for defeat in 1976 came at Wembley in 1996 when Oliver Bierhoff (in white) scored a precious golden goal winner in extra time.

The European Championships Top Goalscorers

YEAR	SCORER	NATIONALITY	GOALS
1960	Ivanov Jerkovic	Russian Yugoslavian	2
1964	Pereda Novak	Spanish Hungarian	2
1968	Drazij	Yugoslavian	2
1972	G. Müller	W. German	4
1976	D. Müller	W. German	4
1980	Allofs	W. German	3
1984	Platini	French	8
1988	van Basten	Dutch	5
1992	Bergkamp Brolin Larsen Riedle	Dutch Swedish Danish German	3
1996	Shearer	English	5
2000	Kluivert Milosevic	Dutch Yugoslavian	6

The European Championships

THE EUROPEAN CHAMPIONSHIPS are the most prestigious European national competition. Established in 1957, the first competition was held in 1960, and since then the Henri Delaunay Cup has been contested every four years, as with the World Cup. The Championship is open to the senior national representative teams of all UEFA's member associations, and the qualifying competition and final round are staged over the two-year period following every FIFA World Cup. The first tournaments comprised only semi-finals and Finals. In 1976 quarter-finals were added, and in 1980 eight teams competed in two mini-leagues before the semi-finals. Expansion in 1996 saw 16 teams compete in four leagues to produce eight quarter-finalists.

1960 FRANCE

SEMI-FINALS
Yugoslavia **5-4** France
(Galic 11,   (Vincent 12,
Zanetic 55,   Heutte 43, 62,
Knez 75,   Wisnieski 52)
Jerkovic 77, 79)

Soviet Union **3-0** Czechoslovakia
(V. Ivanov 34, 56,
Ponedelnik 65)

THIRD PLACE PLAY-OFF
Czechoslovakia **2-0** France
(Bubernik 58,
Pavlovic 88)

FINAL
July 10 – Parc des Princes, Paris
Soviet Union **2-1** Yugoslavia
(Metreveli 49,   (Galic 41)
Ponedelnik 113)
(after extra time)
h/t: 0-1 **90 mins:** 1-1
Att: 17,966 **Ref:** Ellis (England)

1964 SPAIN

SEMI-FINALS
Spain **2-1** Hungary
(Pereda 35,   (Bene 85)
Amancio 115)
(after extra time)
Soviet Union **3-0** Denmark
(Voronin 19,
Ponedelnik 40,
V. Ivanov 87)

THIRD PLACE PLAY-OFF
Hungary **3-1** Denmark
(Bene 11,   (Bertelsen 81)
Novák
107 pen, 110)
(after extra time)

FINAL
June 21 – Santiago Bernabeu, Madrid
Spain **2-1** Soviet Union
(Pereda 6,   (Khusainov 8)
Marcelino 84)
h/t: 1-1 **Att:** 105,000
Ref: Holland (England)

1968 ITALY

SEMI-FINALS
Yugoslavia **1-0** England
(Dzajic 86)

Italy **0-0** Soviet Union
(after extra time)
Italy won on toss of coin

THIRD PLACE PLAY-OFF
England **2-0** Soviet Union
(R. Charlton 39,
Hurst 63)

FINAL
June 8 – Stadio Olimpico, Rome
Italy **1-1** Yugoslavia
(Domenghini 80)   (Dzajic 38)
(after extra time)
h/t: 0-1 **90 mins:** 1-1
Att: 85,000 **Ref:** Dienst (Switzerland)

REPLAY
June 10 – Stadio Olimpico, Rome
Italy **2-0** Yugoslavia
(Riva 11,
Anastasai 32)
h/t: 2-0 **Att:** 50,000
Ref: Ortiz (Spain)

1972 BELGIUM

SEMI-FINALS
Soviet Union **1-0** Hungary
(Konkov 53)

West Germany **2-1** Belgium
(G. Müller 24, 71)   (Polleunis 83)

THIRD PLACE PLAY-OFF
Belgium **2-1** Hungary
(Lambert 24,   (Kü 53 pen)
Van Himst 28)

FINAL
June 18 – Stade Heysel, Brussels
West Germany **3-0** Soviet Union
(G. Müller 27, 58,
Wimmer 52)
h/t: 1-0 **Att:** 50,000
Ref: Marschall (Austria)

1976 YUGOSLAVIA

SEMI-FINALS
Czechoslovakia **3-1** Netherlands
(Ondrus 20,   (Ondrus o.g. 74)
Nehoda 115,
F. Vesely 118)
(after extra time)

West Germany **4-2** Yugoslavia
(Flohe 65,   (Popivoda 20,
D. Müller 82,   Dzajic 30)
114, 119)
(after extra time)

THIRD PLACE PLAY-OFF
Netherlands **3-2** Yugoslavia
(Geels 27, 107,   (Katalinski 43,
Van de Kerkhof 39)   Dzajic 82)
(after extra time)

FINAL
June 20 – Crvena Zvezda, Belgrade
Czechoslovakia **2-2** West Germany
(Svehlík 8,   (D. Müller 28,
Dobiás 25)   Hölzenbein 89)
(after extra time)
h/t: 2-1 **90 mins:** 2-2
Att: 33,000 **Ref:** Gonella (Italy)
Czechoslovakia won 5-3 on pens

1980 ITALY

GROUP 1
West Germany **1-0** Czechoslovakia
Netherlands **1-0** Greece
West Germany **3-2** Netherlands
Czechoslovakia **3-1** Greece
Czechoslovakia **1-1** Netherlands
West Germany **0-0** Greece

	P	W	D	L	F	A	Pts
West Germany	3	2	1	0	4	2	5
Czechoslovakia	3	1	1	1	4	3	3
Netherlands	3	1	1	1	4	4	3
Greece	3	0	1	2	1	4	1

GROUP 2
England **1-1** Belgium
Italy **0-0** Spain
Belgium **2-1** Spain
Italy **1-0** England
England **2-1** Spain
Italy **0-0** Belgium

	P	W	D	L	F	A	Pts
Belgium	3	1	2	0	3	2	4
Italy	3	1	2	0	1	0	4
England	3	1	1	1	3	3	3
Spain	3	0	1	2	2	4	1

THIRD PLACE PLAY-OFF
Czechoslovakia **1-1** Italy
(Jurkemik 48)   (Graziani 74)
(after extra time)
Czechoslovakia won 9-8 on pens

FINAL
June 22 – Stadio Olimpico, Rome
West Germany **2-1** Belgium
(Hrubesch 10, 88)   (Vandereycken 72 pen)
h/t: 1-0 **Att:** 48,000
Ref: Rainea (Romania)

1984 FRANCE

GROUP 1
France **1-0** Denmark
Belgium **2-0** Yugoslavia
France **5-0** Belgium
Denmark **5-0** Yugoslavia
France **3-2** Yugoslavia
Denmark **3-2** Belgium

	P	W	D	L	F	A	Pts
France	3	3	0	0	9	2	6
Denmark	3	2	0	1	8	3	4
Belgium	3	1	0	2	4	8	2
Yugoslavia	3	0	0	3	2	10	0

GROUP 2
West Germany **0-0** Portugal
Spain **1-1** Romania
West Germany **2-1** Romania
Portugal **1-1** Spain
Spain **1-0** West Germany
Portugal **1-0** Romania

	P	W	D	L	F	A	Pts
Spain	3	1	2	0	3	2	4
Portugal	3	1	2	0	2	1	4
West Germany	3	1	1	1	2	2	3
Romania	3	0	1	2	2	4	1

SEMI-FINALS
France **3-2** Portugal
(Domergue   (Jordão 73, 97)
24, 114,
Platini 119)
(after extra time)

Spain **1-1** Denmark
(Maceda 66)   (Lerby 6)
(after extra time)
Spain won 5-4 on pens

FINAL
June 27 – Parc des Princes, Paris
France **2-0** Spain
(Platini 56,
Bellone 90)
h/t: 0-0 **Att:** 47,000
Ref: Christov (Czechoslovakia)

1988 WEST GERMANY

GROUP 1
West Germany **1-1** Italy
Spain **3-2** Denmark
West Germany **2-0** Denmark
Italy **1-0** Spain
West Germany **2-0** Spain
Italy **2-0** Denmark

	P	W	D	L	F	A	Pts
West Germany	3	2	1	0	5	1	5
Italy	3	2	1	0	4	1	5
Spain	3	1	0	2	3	5	2
Denmark	3	0	0	3	2	7	0

GROUP 2
Rep. of Ireland **1-0** England
Soviet Union **1-0** Netherlands
Netherlands **3-1** England
Soviet Union **1-1** Rep. of Ireland
Soviet Union **3-1** England
Netherlands **1-0** Rep. of Ireland

	P	W	D	L	F	A	Pts
Soviet Union	3	2	1	0	5	2	5
Netherlands	3	2	0	1	4	2	4
Rep. of Ireland	3	1	1	1	2	2	3
England	3	0	0	3	2	7	0

European Championship Winners

 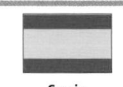       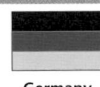

Soviet Union 1960	Spain 1964	Italy 1968	West Germany 1972, 80	Czechoslovakia 1976	France 1984, 2000	Netherlands 1988	Denmark 1992	Germany 1996

SEMI-FINALS

Netherlands **2-1** West Germany
(R. Koeman *(Matthäus*
74 pen, *55 pen)*
van Basten 89)

Soviet Union **2-0** Italy
(Litovchenko 60,
Protasov 62)

FINAL

June 25 – Olympiastadion, Munich
Netherlands **2-0** Soviet Union
(Gullit 33,
van Basten 54)

h/t: 1-0 **Att:** 72,300
Ref: Vautrot (France)

1992 SWEDEN

GROUP A

Sweden **1-1** France
Denmark **0-0** England
France **0-0** England
Sweden **1-0** Denmark
Denmark **2-1** France
Sweden **2-1** England

	P	W	D	L	F	A	Pts
Sweden	3	2	1	0	4	2	5
Denmark	3	1	1	1	2	2	3
France	3	0	2	1	2	3	2
England	3	0	2	1	1	2	2

GROUP B

Netherlands **1-0** Scotland
Germany **1-1** CIS
Germany **2-0** Scotland
Netherlands **0-0** CIS
Netherlands **3-1** Germany
Scotland **3-0** CIS

	P	W	D	L	F	A	Pts
Netherlands	3	2	1	0	4	1	5
Germany	3	1	1	1	4	4	3
Scotland	3	1	0	2	3	3	2
CIS	3	0	2	1	1	4	2

SEMI-FINALS

Germany **3-2** Sweden
(Hässler 11, *(Brolin 64,*
Riedle 59, 88) *Andersson 89)*

Denmark **2-2** Netherlands
(H. Larsen 5, 32) *(Bergkamp 23,*
Rijkaard 85)

(after extra time)
Denmark won 5-4 on pens

FINAL

June 26 – Nya Ullevi, Gothenburg
Denmark **2-0** Germany
(Jensen 18,
Vilfort 78)

h/t: 1-0 **Att:** 37,000
Ref: Galler (Switzerland)

1996 ENGLAND

GROUP A

England **1-1** Switzerland
Netherlands **0-0** Scotland
Netherlands **2-0** Switzerland
England **2-0** Scotland
Scotland **1-0** Switzerland
England **4-1** Netherlands

	P	W	D	L	F	A	Pts
England	3	2	1	0	7	2	7
Netherlands	3	1	1	1	3	4	4
Scotland	3	1	1	1	1	2	4
Switzerland	3	0	1	2	1	4	1

GROUP B

Spain **1-1** Bulgaria
France **1-0** Romania
Bulgaria **1-0** Romania
France **1-1** Spain
France **3-1** Bulgaria
Spain **2-1** Romania

	P	W	D	L	F	A	Pts
France	3	2	1	0	5	2	7
Spain	3	1	2	0	4	3	5
Bulgaria	3	1	1	1	3	4	4
Romania	3	0	0	3	1	4	0

GROUP C

Germany **2-0** Czech Rep.
Italy **2-1** Russia
Czech Rep. **2-1** Italy
Germany **3-0** Russia
Italy **0-0** Germany
Czech Rep. **3-3** Russia

	P	W	D	L	F	A	Pts
Germany	3	2	1	0	5	0	7
Czech Rep.	3	1	1	1	5	6	4
Italy	3	1	1	1	3	3	4
Russia	3	0	1	2	4	8	1

GROUP D

Denmark **1-1** Portugal
Croatia **1-0** Turkey
Portugal **1-0** Turkey
Croatia **3-0** Denmark
Portugal **3-0** Croatia
Denmark **3-0** Turkey

	P	W	D	L	F	A	Pts
Portugal	3	2	1	0	5	1	7
Croatia	3	2	0	1	4	3	6
Denmark	3	1	1	1	4	4	4
Turkey	3	0	0	3	0	5	0

QUARTER-FINALS

England **0-0** Spain
(after extra time)
England won 4-2 on pens

France **0-0** Netherlands
(after extra time)
France won 5-4 on pens

Germany **2-1** Croatia
(Klinsmann *(Suker 51)*
21 pen,
Sammer 59)

Czech Rep. **1-0** Portugal
(Poborsky 53)

SEMI-FINALS

Czech Rep. **0-0** France
(after extra time)
Czech Rep. won 6-5 on pens

Germany **1-1** England
(Kuntz 16) *(Shearer 3)*
(after extra time)
Germany won 6-5 on pens

FINAL

June 30 – Wembley, London
Germany **2-1** Czech Rep.
(Bierhoff 73, 94) *(Berger 58 pen)*
h/t: 0-0 **90 mins:** 1-1
Att: 76,000 **Ref:** Pairetto (Italy)
Germany won on golden goal
in extra time

2000 BELGIUM AND THE NETHERLANDS

GROUP A

Germany **1-1** Romania
Portugal **3-2** England
Portugal **1-0** Romania
England **1-0** Germany
Romania **3-2** England
Portugal **3-0** Germany

	P	W	D	L	F	A	Pts
Portugal	3	3	0	0	7	2	9
Romania	3	1	1	1	4	4	4
England	3	1	0	2	5	6	3
Germany	3	0	1	2	1	5	1

GROUP B

Belgium **2-1** Sweden
Italy **2-1** Turkey
Italy **2-0** Belgium
Sweden **0-0** Turkey
Turkey **2-0** Belgium
Italy **2-1** Sweden

	P	W	D	L	F	A	Pts
Italy	3	3	0	0	6	2	9
Turkey	3	1	1	1	3	2	4
Belgium	3	1	0	2	2	5	3
Sweden	3	0	1	2	2	4	1

GROUP C

Norway **1-0** Spain
Yugoslavia **3-3** Slovenia
Spain **2-1** Slovenia
Yugoslavia **1-0** Norway
Spain **4-3** Yugoslavia
Slovenia **0-0** Norway

	P	W	D	L	F	A	Pts
Spain	3	2	0	1	6	5	6
Yugoslavia	3	1	1	1	7	7	4
Norway	3	1	1	1	1	1	4
Slovenia	3	0	2	1	4	5	2

GROUP D

France **3-0** Denmark
Netherlands **1-0** Czech Rep.
France **2-1** Czech Rep.
Netherlands **3-0** Denmark
Netherlands **3-2** France
Czech Rep. **2-0** Denmark

	P	W	D	L	F	A	Pts
Netherlands	3	3	0	0	7	2	9
France	3	2	0	1	7	4	6
Czech Rep.	3	1	0	2	3	3	3
Denmark	3	0	0	3	0	8	0

QUARTER-FINALS

Portugal **2-0** Turkey
(Nuno Gomes
44, 56)

Italy **2-0** Romania
(Totti 33,
Inzaghi 43)

Netherlands **6-1** Yugoslavia
(Kluivert *Milosevic 90)*
24, 38, 54,
Govedarica
o.g. 51,
Overmars 78, 90)

France **2-1** Spain
(Zidane 33, *(Mendieta*
Djorkaeff 44) *38 pen)*

SEMI-FINALS

France **2-1** Portugal
(Henry 51, *(Nuno Gomes 19)*
Zidane 117 pen)
France won on golden goal
in extra time

Italy **0-0** Netherlands
(after extra time)
Italy won 3-1 on pens

FINAL

July 2 – De Kuip, Rotterdam
France **2-1** Italy
(Wiltord 90, *(Delvecchio 55)*
Trezeguet 103)

France won on golden goal
in extra time
h/t: 0-0 **90 mins:** 1-1
Att: 55,000 **Ref:** Frisk (Sweden)

Dutch striker Marco van Basten scores against England to give the Netherlands a 3-1 victory in the team's group game in the 1988 European Championships. The Dutch went on to win the tournament.

The European Champions League

TOURNAMENT REVIEW 2002–03

ALTHOUGH THIS WAS THE last year in which the Champions League will have two group stages and next year will see a slimmed down second round, there can be no doubt that the shadow of the tournament over European football was longer and more powerful than ever. As the value of TV rights has shrunk across Europe and the economic reckoning for years of excess and insanity creeps up on every club, the enormous prize money the tournament yields has become central to the budgeting plans of every major team on the continent.

The power of money

However, as with all industrial sectors, the power of money includes some and excludes others; the rich get richer and the poor get poorer. The first group stage of the tournament has an increasingly familiar feel about it. Only 14 nations were represented in the 32 teams that kicked off in eight groups in September 2002. Take out the outsiders – like Maccabi Haifa, FC Basel, Rosenborg, and Dynamo Kyiv – and that's 28 teams from just ten countries – including four each from Spain, England and Italy. More worryingly, not a single nation between Germany and the Ukraine was represented as the best of the Czechs, Yugoslavs, Poles and other Central Europeans fell in the qualifying rounds. The regular absence of the region from even the early stages of the tournament has led to talk of an alternative Central European tournament.

Roy Keane and Juan Sebastian Veron combine to deny Zalaegerszeg's Kenesei in their third qualifying round meeting. United won 5-1 over two legs.

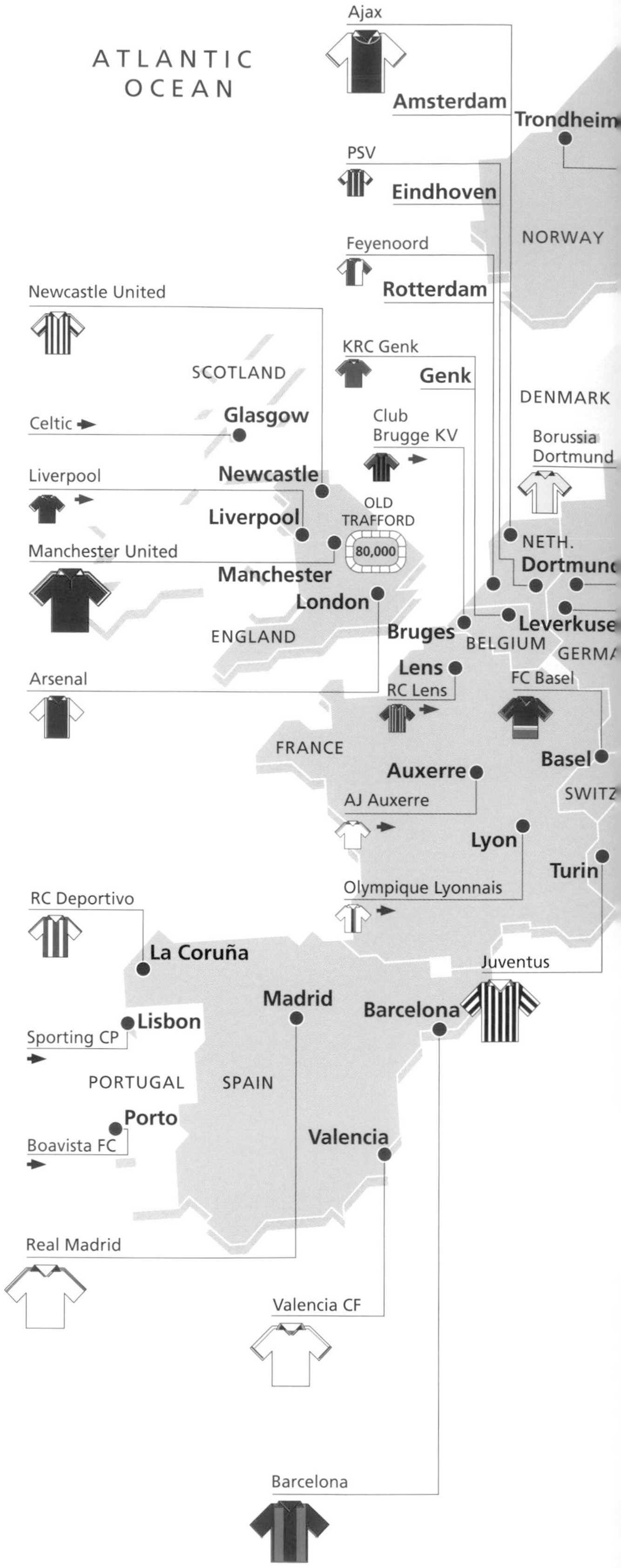

ATLANTIC OCEAN

Ajax
Amsterdam
Trondheim

PSV
Eindhoven

NORWAY

Feyenoord
Rotterdam

Newcastle United

KRC Genk
Genk

DENMARK

SCOTLAND

Celtic
Glasgow

Club Brugge KV

Borussia Dortmund

Liverpool
Newcastle

NETH.
Dortmund

Liverpool
OLD TRAFFORD
80,000

Manchester United
Manchester
London

Leverkusen

ENGLAND

Bruges
BELGIUM
GERMA

Lens
RC Lens

FC Basel

Arsenal

Basel

FRANCE

Auxerre
AJ Auxerre

SWITZ

Lyon

RC Deportivo

Olympique Lyonnais
Turin

La Coruña

Juventus

Madrid
Barcelona

Lisbon
Sporting CP

PORTUGAL   SPAIN

Porto
Boavista FC

Valencia

Real Madrid

Valencia CF

Barcelona

Qualifying Round 1

Zhenis Astana	Kazakhstan
B36	Faeroe Islands
Barry Town	Wales
F'91 Dudelange	Luxembourg
ÍA	Iceland
FBK Kaunas	Lithuania
Portadown	Northern Ireland
Shelbourne	Rep. of Ireland
FC Flora Tallinn	Estonia
Tampere United	Finland

Qualifying Round 2

Belshyna Babruisk	Belorussia
Dinamo Bucuresti	Romania
Hammarby If	Sweden
Hibernians	Malta
Torpedo Kutaisi	Georgia
Lillestrøm SK	Norway
NK Maribor	Slovenia
Skonto Riga	Latvia
Vardar Skopje	Macedonia
Dinamo Tirana	Albania
Serif Tiraspol	Moldova
Pyunik Yerevan	Armenia
Zagreb	Croatia
MSK Zilina	Slovakia

Map labels:

Rosenborg BK
Brøndby IF
Copenhagen
Bayer 04 Leverkusen
Bayern München
POLAND
Warsaw — Legia Warszawa
Slovan Liberec
Liberec — Sparta Praha
Prague
CZECH REPUBLIC
Munich
AUSTRIA
SK Sturm Graz
Graz
Grazer AK
Zalaegerszeg
Zalaegerszeg
HUNGARY
ROMANIA
Milan
Roma
Rome
ITALY
Internazionale
Milan
MEDITERRANEAN SEA
Moscow
Lokomotiv Moskva
Spartak Moskva
Kiev
Dynamo Kyiv
UKRAINE
Shakhtar Donetsk
Donetsk
BOSNIA HERZEGOVINA
Sarajevo
Zeljeznicar Sarajevo
SERBIA & MONTENEGO
Partizan Beograd
Belgrade
BULGARIA
Sofia
Levski Sofia
BLACK SEA
GREECE
Athens
AEK Athens
Olympiakos
Istanbul
Fenerbahçe
TURKEY
Galatasaray SK
Nicosia
CYPRUS
APOEL
Maccabi Haifa
ISRAEL
Haifa

The European Champions League 2002–03

Milan	Team name
	Teams into Final Stages
	Teams knocked out in Group Stage 2
	Teams knocked out in Group Stage 1
➤	Teams into UEFA Cup First Round
➤	Teams into UEFA Cup Third Round
	Stadium for Final

Champions League Top Goalscorers 2002–03

PLAYER	CLUB	NATIONALITY	GOALS
Ruud van Nistelrooy	Manchester United	Dutch	12
Filippo Inzaghi	Milan	Italian	10
Hernan Crespo	Lazio	Argentinian	9
Roy Makaay	Deportivo La Coruña	Dutch	9
Raúl González	Real Madrid	Spanish	9
Jurgen Koller	Borussia Dortmund	Czech	8

THE EUROPEAN CHAMPIONS LEAGUE

Group Stage 1

Beyond the first stage, smaller clubs and countries were even thinner on the ground with only FC Basel playing above itself to find a place in the last 16 at the expense of Liverpool and Spartak Moskva. That said, the first round did deliver a pleasing shock as a fractious and under par Bayern München crashed out of Group G, beaten home and away by both Milan and Deportivo La Coruña. Only Spartak Moskva's failure to rack up a single point in Group B was worse.

Newcastle United performed a minor miracle by qualifying, at the expense of Dynamo Kyiv and Feyenoord, despite losing its first three matches. As usual there wasn't much joy for the Belgians, Olympiakos and Galatasaray. No French teams progressed to the second group stage, but Olympique Lyonnais' defeat of Inter, Auxerre's victory over Arsenal at Highbury and Lens' 2-1 home defeat of Milan suggested that they were not completely outclassed. They were, however, outspent and understaffed in comparison to the Spanish, Italian and English clubs. Though even here, the strain of fighting on two fronts simultaneously saw Barcelona and Manchester United struggle domestically while they sailed through to Group Stage 2 of the Champions League.

Above: Barcelona's Luis Enrique celebrates another goal in Barca's awesome Champions League progress – the only team to win all six of its opening games. Its domestic form was diametrically opposed as it dropped into the lower half of La Liga.

Below: Rui Costa looks on as Oliver Kahn fails to stop another Milan goal. Milan did the double over Bayern, beating them 2-1 home and away.

GROUP STAGE 1

GROUP A
AJ Auxerre **0-0** PSV
Arsenal **2-0** Borussia Dortmund
PSV **0-4** Arsenal
Borussia **2-1** AJ Auxerre Dortmund
PSV **1-3** Borussia Dortmund
AJ Auxerre **0-1** Arsenal
Borussia **1-1** PSV Dortmund
Arsenal **1-2** AJ Auxerre
PSV **3-0** AJ Auxerre
Borussia **2-1** Arsenal Dortmund
Arsenal **0-0** PSV
AJ Auxerre **1-0** Borussia Dortmund

GROUP B
Valencia **2-0** Liverpool
FC Basel **2-0** Spartak Moskva
Liverpool **1-1** FC Basel
Spartak Moskva **0-3** Valencia
Liverpool **5-0** Spartak Moskva
Valencia **6-2** FC Basel
Spartak Moskva **1-3** Liverpool
FC Basel **2-2** Valencia
Liverpool **0-1** Valencia
Spartak Moskva **0-2** FC Basel
FC Basel **3-3** Liverpool
Valencia **3-0** Spartak Moskva

GROUP C
KRC Genk **0-0** AEK
Roma **0-3** Real Madrid
AEK **0-0** Roma
Real Madrid **6-0** KRC Genk
AEK **3-3** Real Madrid
KRC Genk **0-1** Roma
Real Madrid **2-2** AEK
Roma **0-0** KRC Genk
AEK **1-1** KRC Genk
Real Madrid **0-1** Roma
Roma **1-1** AEK
KRC Genk **1-1** Real Madrid

GROUP D
Rosenborg BK **2-2** Internazionale
Ajax **2-1** Olym. Lyonnais
Internazionale **1-0** Ajax
Olym. Lyonnais **5-0** Rosenborg BK
Internazionale **1-2** Olym. Lyonnais
Rosenborg BK **0-0** Ajax
Olym. Lyonnais **3-3** Internazionale
Ajax **1-1** Rosenborg BK
Internazionale **3-0** Rosenborg BK
Olym. Lyonnais **0-2** Ajax
Ajax **1-2** Internazionale
Rosenborg BK **1-1** Olym. Lyonnais

GROUP E
Feyenoord **1-1** Juventus
Dynamo Kyiv **2-0** Newcastle Utd
Juventus **5-0** Dynamo Kyiv
Newcastle Utd **0-1** Feyenoord
Juventus **2-0** Newcastle Utd
Feyenoord **0-0** Dynamo Kyiv
Newcastle Utd **1-0** Juventus
Dynamo Kyiv **2-0** Feyenoord
Juventus **2-0** Feyenoord
Newcastle Utd **2-1** Dynamo Kyiv
Dynamo Kyiv **1-2** Juventus
Feyenoord **2-3** Newcastle Utd

GROUP F
Manchester Utd **5-2** Maccabi Haifa
Olympiakos **6-2** Bayer Leverkusen
Maccabi Haifa **3-0** Olympiakos
Bayer Leverkusen **1-2** Manchester Utd
Maccabi Haifa **0-2** Bayer Leverkusen
Manchester Utd **4-0** Olympiakos
Bayer Leverkusen **2-1** Maccabi Haifa
Olympiakos **2-3** Manchester Utd
Maccabi Haifa **3-0** Manchester Utd
Bayer Leverkusen **2-0** Olympiakos
Olympiakos **3-3** Maccabi Haifa
Manchester Utd **2-0** Bayer Leverkusen

GROUP G
Bayern München **2-3** RC Deportivo
Milan **2-1** RC Lens
RC Deportivo **0-4** Milan
RC Lens **1-1** Bayern München
RC Deportivo **3-1** RC Lens
Bayern München **1-2** Milan
RC Lens **3-1** RC Deportivo
Milan **2-1** Bayern München
RC Deportivo **2-1** Bayern München
RC Lens **2-1** Milan
Milan **1-2** RC Deportivo
Bayern München **3-3** RC Lens

GROUP H
Lokomotiv **0-2** Galatasaray Moskva
FC Barcelona **3-2** Club Brugge KV
Galatasaray **0-2** FC Barcelona
Club Brugge KV **0-0** Lokomotiv Moskva
Galatasaray **0-0** Club Brugge KV
Lokomotiv **1-3** FC Barcelona Moskva
Club Brugge KV **3-1** Galatasaray
FC Barcelona **1-0** Lokomotiv Moskva
Galatasaray **1-2** Lokomotiv Moskva
Club Brugge KV **0-1** FC Barcelona
FC Barcelona **3-1** Galatasaray
Lokomotiv **2-0** Club Brugge KV Moskva

GROUP A						
CLUB	P	W	D	L	F	A	Pts
Arsenal (England)	6	3	1	2	9	4	**10**	Group Stage 2
Borussia Dortmund (Germany)	6	3	1	2	8	7	**10**	Group Stage 2
AJ Auxerre (France)	6	2	1	3	4	7	**7**	UEFA Cup
PSV (Netherlands)	6	1	3	2	5	8	**6**	

GROUP B						
CLUB	P	W	D	L	F	A	Pts
Valencia (Spain)	6	5	1	0	17	4	**16**	Group Stage 2
FC Basel (Switzerland)	6	2	3	1	12	12	**9**	Group Stage 2
Liverpool (England)	6	2	2	2	12	8	**8**	UEFA Cup
Spartak Moskva (Russia)	6	0	0	6	1	18	**0**	

GROUP C						
CLUB	P	W	D	L	F	A	Pts
Real Madrid (Spain)	6	2	3	1	15	7	**9**	Group Stage 2
Roma (Italy)	6	2	3	1	3	4	**9**	Group Stage 2
AEK (Greece)	6	0	6	0	7	7	**6**	UEFA Cup
KRC Genk (Belgium)	6	0	4	2	2	9	**4**	

GROUP D						
CLUB	P	W	D	L	F	A	Pts
Internazionale (Italy)	6	3	2	1	12	8	**11**	Group Stage 2
Ajax (Netherlands)	6	2	2	2	6	5	**8**	Group Stage 2
Olympique Lyonnais (France)	6	2	2	2	12	9	**8**	UEFA Cup
Rosenborg BK (Norway)	6	0	4	2	4	12	**4**	

GROUP E						
CLUB	P	W	D	L	F	A	Pts
Juventus (Italy)	6	4	1	1	12	3	**13**	Group Stage 2
Newcastle United (England)	6	3	0	3	6	8	**9**	Group Stage 2
Dynamo Kyiv (Russia)	6	2	1	3	6	9	**7**	UEFA Cup
Feyenoord (Netherlands)	6	1	2	3	4	8	**5**	

GROUP F						
CLUB	P	W	D	L	F	A	Pts
Manchester United (England)	6	5	0	1	16	8	**15**	Group Stage 2
Bayer Leverkusen (Germany)	6	3	0	3	9	11	**9**	Group Stage 2
Maccabi Haifa (Israel)	6	2	1	3	12	12	**7**	UEFA Cup
Olympiakos (Greece)	6	1	1	4	11	17	**4**	

GROUP G						
CLUB	P	W	D	L	F	A	Pts
Milan (Italy)	6	4	0	2	12	7	**12**	Group Stage 2
RC Deportivo (Spain)	6	4	0	2	11	12	**12**	Group Stage 2
RC Lens (France)	6	2	2	2	11	11	**8**	UEFA Cup
Bayern München (Germany)	6	0	2	4	9	13	**2**	

GROUP H						
CLUB	P	W	D	L	F	A	Pts
FC Barcelona (Spain)	6	6	0	0	13	4	**18**	Group Stage 2
Lokomotiv Moskva (Russia)	6	2	1	3	5	7	**7**	Group Stage 2
Club Brugge KV (Belgium)	6	1	2	3	5	7	**5**	UEFA Cup
Galatasaray SK (Turkey)	6	1	1	4	5	10	**4**	

Top: *Bayern players contemplate their undignified departure from the first stage of the Champions League without even a ticket to the UEFA Cup to console them. The team didn't deserve it and Lens took the spot after beating both Milan and Deportivo.*

Above: *Maccabi Haifa beat Manchester United 3-0 in a hastily rearranged game in Cyprus. United had already qualified and virtually sent the reserves.*

Below, left: *FC Basel players celebrate their progress into Group Stage 2 – a brilliant achievement for a club from a small footballing country.*

Below: *Juninho of Olympique Lyonnais takes on Ajax's Victor Sikora, but a 2-0 victory for the Dutchmen saw them through on goal difference.*

THE EUROPEAN CHAMPIONS LEAGUE

Group Stage 2

In Group A, Barcelona carried on where it had left off, with only a goalless draw at Inter blemishing its winning record in the competition. The second spot was taken by Inter, although Newcastle threatened another last-minute triumph. Back-to-back wins against Leverkusen, including Alan Shearer's first European hat-trick, put them in with a shout, but a 2-2 draw at the San Siro was not enough. Group B was the tightest and the draws kept piling up as four teams playing below and within themselves ground it out to the last game. Ajax qualified with its fifth draw, while Valencia finally got the better of Arsenal at the Mestalla.

Group C was a three-way race as Lokomotiv Moskva suffered from playing during the break in the Russian season. Dortmund gave its best performances of a disappointing season, but the team was not enough to pass Real Madrid and Milan. In Group D, Manchester United looked a cut above the rest with two successive victories over Juventus. Basel continued to defy expectation, beating Deportivo and Juventus; but the goals amassed in its 4-0 drubbing of the Swiss team allowed the Italians to scrape through on goal difference.

The quarter-finals

'It's a fix' was Alex Ferguson response to the draw for the quarter-finals, which kept all the Spanish and Italian teams apart, and pitted Manchester United against Real Madrid. All three ties with an Italian interest were very tense and occasionally bad-tempered affairs. Inter beat Valencia by the narrowest of margins on away goals. Christian Vieri grabbed the lead for the Milanese early in both legs and Inter hung on for grim death. Valencia coach Benitez raged that 'Inter was the death of football'. Juve showed an altogether more composed steeliness and resolve to take Barca, playing for its life in the competition, to two 1-1 draws, before Zalayeta's golden goal won it for Juve in the Nou Camp. Milan ground out a 0-0 draw at Ajax and then played more freely at home, twice taking the lead as twice Ajax managed to come back on level terms – in the end only John Dahl Tomasson's last-minute strike separated them. Madrid v Manchester was an altogether different prospect. At the Bernabeu, Real was unstoppable – inventive and commanding in attack as United's defence failed to control Raul. But, true to form, United refused to crumble and a goal from van Nistlerooy kept them in the hunt. In the return game at Old Trafford, unquestionably the match of the tournament, Ronaldo produced a hat-trick of the highest standards to seemingly put the game beyond United. But the relentless charging runs of van Nistlerooy and two goals from Beckham, who only came on as a late substitute, gave United hope and victory on the night.

GROUP STAGE 2

GROUP A
Bayer Leverkusen **1-2** FC Barcelona
Newcastle Utd **1-4** Internazionale
Internazionale **3-2** Bayer Leverkusen
FC Barcelona **3-1** Newcastle Utd
FC Barcelona **3-0** Internazionale
Bayer Leverkusen **1-3** Newcastle Utd
Internazionale **0-0** FC Barcelona
Newcastle Utd **3-1** Bayer Leverkusen
FC Barcelona **2-0** Bayer Leverkusen
Internazionale **2-2** Newcastle Utd
Bayer Leverkusen **0-2** Internazionale
Newcastle Utd **0-2** FC Barcelona

GROUP B
Roma **1-3** Arsenal
Valencia **1-1** Ajax
Ajax **2-1** Roma
Arsenal **0-0** Valencia
Arsenal **1-1** Ajax
Roma **0-1** Valencia
Ajax **0-0** Arsenal
Valencia **0-3** Roma
Arsenal **1-1** Roma
Ajax **1-1** Valencia
Roma **1-1** Ajax
Valencia **2-1** Arsenal

GROUP C
Milan **1-0** Real Madrid
Lokomotiv **1-2** Borussia
Moskva   Dortmund
Borussia **0-1** Milan
Dortmund
Real Madrid **2-2** Lokomotiv
                Moskva
Real Madrid **2-1** Borussia
                Dortmund
Milan **1-0** Lokomotiv
            Moskva
Borussia **1-1** Real Madrid
Dortmund
Lokomotiv **0-1** Milan
Moskva
Real Madrid **3-1** Milan
Borussia **3-0** Lokomotiv
Dortmund   Moskva
Milan **0-1** Borussia
            Dortmund
Lokomotiv **0-1** Real Madrid
Moskva

GROUP D
FC Basel **1-3** Manchester Utd
RC Deportivo **2-2** Juventus
Juventus **4-0** FC Basel
Manchester Utd **2-0** RC Deportivo
Manchester Utd **2-1** Juventus
FC Basel **1-0** RC Deportivo
Juventus **0-3** Manchester Utd
RC Deportivo **1-0** FC Basel
Manchester Utd **1-1** FC Basel
Juventus **3-2** RC Deportivo
FC Basel **2-1** Juventus
RC Deportivo **2-0** Manchester Utd

Below, left: Sylvain Wiltord tries to escape the clutches of the Ajax defence. Two draws against the Dutch side cost Arsenal a quarter-final berth.

GROUP A								
CLUB	P	W	D	L	F	A	Pts	
FC Barcelona	6	5	1	0	12	2	**16**	Quarter-Finals
Internazionale	6	3	2	1	11	8	**11**	Quarter-Finals
Newcastle United	6	2	1	3	10	13	**7**	
Bayer Leverkusen	6	0	0	6	5	15	**0**	

GROUP B								
CLUB	P	W	D	L	F	A	Pts	
Valencia	6	2	3	1	5	6	**9**	Quarter-Finals
Ajax	6	1	5	0	6	5	**8**	Quarter-Finals
Arsenal	6	1	4	1	6	5	**7**	
Roma	6	1	2	3	7	8	**5**	

GROUP C								
CLUB	P	W	D	L	F	A	Pts	
Milan	6	4	0	2	5	4	**12**	Quarter-Finals
Real Madrid	6	3	2	1	9	6	**11**	Quarter-Finals
Borussia Dortmund	6	3	1	2	8	5	**10**	
Lokomotiv Moskva	6	0	1	5	3	10	**1**	

GROUP D								
CLUB	P	W	D	L	F	A	Pts	
Manchester United	6	4	1	1	11	5	**13**	Quarter-Finals
Juventus	6	2	1	3	11	11	**7**	Quarter-Finals
FC Basel	6	2	1	3	5	10	**7**	
RC Deportivo	6	2	1	3	7	8	**7**	

Andrei Shevchenko holds off Real Madrid's Pavon as Milan beat the champions 1-0 at the San Siro.

Left: *Norberto Solano and Alan Shearer make it 2-2 at Inter. On an intimidating evening in Milan, Newcastle kept its hopes of a quarter-final place alive.*

Below: *Alan Shearer watches his second goal fly through a demoralised Leverkusen defence. He later made it three to score his first European hat-trick.*

Above: *Pavel Nedved scores Juve's first goal in the quarter-final clash with Barcelona. Nedved's drive and vision took Juve to the Final from which he was suspended.*

Right, top: *How good is that? Steve McManaman roars his approval of Ronaldo's brilliant quarter-final hat-trick at Old Trafford.*

Right, below: *The cavalry arrives. David Beckham came on late as substitute against Real at Old Trafford. This goal from a free kick was soon followed by a second but in the end it was not enough.*

THE EUROPEAN CHAMPIONS LEAGUE

The semi-finals

The semi-finals included the first Milan Derby in the history of the tournament and, in the seething intensity of the San Siro, Milan and Inter went through 135 minutes of hard-fought chess before Shevchenko scored a priceless away goal for Milan. With Vieri injured and Crespo and Recoba misfiring, Cuper threw the young Congolese Martins on and his strike six minutes from time raised Inter for a final fling. But a team of uncompromising defence and midfield caution just could not rise to the challenge. Juve, against the odds, kept itself in the tie by restricting Real Madrid to just two goals at home. In the return, Pavel Nedved played his game of the season, combining fearsome midfield tackling with surging runs and inventive passing. Real, utterly shaken, could find no response until Zidane's virtually solo attempt to retrieve the situation in the final minute.

A test of Italian football

In a Champions League season that had seen the resurrection of Italy's strongest teams it was inevitable that the Final would be seen as a test of the character and mettle of their nation's game; and if it did not surprise, it did not disappoint. Two hours of 0-0 does not do justice to the taut complexity and technical precision of this tightly contested game. If Shevchenko's tenth-minute goal had not been ruled offside, or if Inzaghi's short, sharp header had eluded Buffon's flexed forearm, the game would have assumed another dynamic. But in the absence of an early goal the first half saw inventive Milan pressure from Rui Costa and Shevchenko yield them a range of corners, free kicks and shots, but in every case Juventus had the answer. Extra time came and went and although Milan was effectively down to ten men after Roque Junior pulled up, Juventus, desperately short of invention in the absence of the suspended Nedved, had neither the nerve nor the moves to fashion a serious chance. Of course, it came down to penalties and although the odds seemed stacked Juve's way, shooting first, in front of its own fans with Buffon's awesome penalty saving record to calm them – it was Milan's players who looked right as they walked up for their turn. Weak shots and indecision let Dida save three in a row from Juventus and, despite two Buffon saves, it was in Shevchenko's hands. His eyes flicked manically from referee to ball, but as he stepped up there was no doubt it was going in.

QUARTER-FINALS (2 legs)
April 8, Bernabéu, Madrid
Real Madrid 3-1 Manchester
(Figo 12, **United**
Raúl 28, 49) (van Nistelrooy 52)
Att: 74,700
Ref: Frisk (Sweden)
April 23, Old Trafford, Manchester
Manchester 4-3 Real Madrid
United (Ronaldo 12, 50 59)
(van Nistelrooy 43,
Helguera o.g. 52,
Beckham 71, 85)
Att: 66,708
Ref: Collina (Italy)
Real Madrid won 6-5 on aggregate
April 9, San Siro, Milan
Internazionale 1-0 Valencia
(Vieri 14)
Att: 52,623
Ref: Merk (Germany)
April 22, Mestalla, Valencia
Valencia 2-1 Internazionale
(Aimar 7, (Vieri 5)
Baraja 51)
Att: 52,000
Ref: Nielsen (Denmark)
Internazionale won on away goals rule
April 8, Arena, Amsterdam
Ajax 0-0 Milan
Att: 50.976
Ref: Hauge (Norway)
April 23, San Siro, Milan
Milan 3-2 Ajax
(Inzaghi 30, (Litmanen 63,
Shevchenko 65, Pienaar 78)
Tomasson 90)
Att: 76,079
Ref: Mejuto Gonzalez (Spain)
Milan won 3-2 on aggregate
April 9, Stadio delle Alpi, Turin
Juventus 1-1 FC Barcelona
(Montero 16) (Saviola 78)
Att: 48,738
Ref: Michel (Slovakia)
April 22, Nou Camp, Barcelona
FC Barcelona 1-2 Juventus
(Xavi 66) (Nedved 53,
Zalayeta 114)
Att: 98,000
Ref: Poll (England)
golden goal after extra time
Juventus won 3-2 on aggregate

SEMI-FINALS (2 legs)
May 6, Bernabeu, Madrid
Real Madrid 2-1 Juventus
(Ronaldo 23, (Trezuguet 45)
Roberto Carlos 73)
Att: 75,000
Ref: Hauge (Norway)
May 13, Delle Alpi, Turin
Juventus 3-1 Real Madrid
(Trezuguet 12, (Zidane 89)
Del Piero 43,
Nedved 73)
Att: 60,253
Ref: Meier (Switzerland)
Juventus won 4-3 on aggregate
May 7, San Siro, Milan
Milan 0-0 Internazionale
Att: 78,175
Ref: Ivanov (Russia)
May 14 San Siro, Milan
Internazionale 1-1 Milan
(Martins 84) (Shevchenko 45)
Att: 76,854
Ref: Veissiere (France)
Milan won on away goals rule

Just like dad. *Paolo Maldini, Milan's captain, lifts the club's sixth European Cup aloft. His father Cesare captained Milan to the team's second win in 1969.*

The narrowest of margins. *Shevchenko slips the ball over Inter's Toldo to give Milan the away goal edge in the Milanese semi-final. Inter's Cordoba looks on.*

Milan's Gattuso and Juve's Del Pierro *clash in the Final. Gattuso's boundless running and controlled aggression helped blunt Juve's attacking edge.*

Highlights of the Game

KEY

Player booked ——▮◀▶▮—— Substitution

JUVENTUS | KICK OFF 0 mins | **MILAN**

1 min: Trezeguet runs to the edge of the Milan box but is disposessed

10 min: Shevchenko shoots past Buffon, but Rui Costa is ruled offside

12 min: Ferrara's brilliant tackle in the box keeps Shevchenko out again

17 min: Buffon makes a brilliant one-handed save from Inzaghi's header

18 min: Costacurta booked

32 min: Already Milan's 7th corner but Juventus effortlessly clear again

36 min: Del Piero is off for treatment after a clash of heads with Nesta

39 min: Rui Costa nutmegs Tacchinardi on the edge of the box but shoots wide

45 mins + 3 min injury time

HALF-TIME: 0-0

46 min: Conte off, Camoranesi on

45 min: Nesta heads away Del Piero's perfect cross

47 min: Conte's diving header flashes off the Milan crossbar

57 min: Inzaghi and Gattuso both receive treatment

62 min: Kaladze's smart interception breaks up Juve attack

65 min: Davids off, Zalayeta on

66 min: Costacurta off, Roque Junior on

67 min: Zalayeta heads Del Piero free kick wide

71 min: Pirlo off, Serginho on

72 min: Buffon saves Serginho's shot

76 min: Inzaghi header goes wide

80 min: Juventus break comes to nothing

87 min: Rui Costa off, Ambrosini on

90 min: Buffon saves a low shot from Seedorf

90 mins + 1 min injury time

FULL-TIME: 0-0

EXTRA TIME
0 mins

5 min: Roque Junior pulls up. Milan effectively down to 10 men

11 min: Shots from Conte and Del Piero go high

14 min: Buffon catches Maldini header

15 mins

HALF-TIME: 0-0

21 min: Del Piero booked

27 min: Del Piero shoots high again

30 min: Seedorf's cross is brilliantly headed clear by Thuram

30 mins + 1 min injury time

FULL TIME: 0-0

AC Milan won 3-2 on pens

The Starting Line-Up

May 28 – Old Trafford, Manchester
Attendance 63,215

Thuram 21, Tacchinardi 3, Shevchenko 7, Costacurta 19
Montero 4, Trezeguet 17, Gattuso 8, Nesta 13
Buffon 1, Camoranesi 16, Rui Costa 10, Pirlo 21, Dida 12
Tudor 5, Davids 26, Del Piero 10, Maldini 3
Ferrara 2, Zambrotta 19, Inzaghi 9, Seedorf 20, Kaladze 4

JUVENTUS	Referee	MILAN
Formation: 4-4-2	Markus Merk (Germany)	Formation: 4-3-1-2
Manager		Manager
Marcello Lippi		Carlo Ancelotti
Substitutes		Substitutes

Substitutes

Chimenti 12, Iuliano 13
Pessotto 7, Birindelli 15
Conte 8, Di Vaio 18
Zalayeta 25

Abbiata 18, Laursen 24
Rivaldo 11, Serginho 27
Ambrosini 23, Brocchi 32
Roque Junior 25

Penalties

KEY: ⬤ Score ⬤ No score

	Juventus				Milan	
Comment	Scored	Penalty Taker	SCORE	Penalty Taker	Scored	Comment
Low but close to the centre, Trezeguet made it easy for Dida	⬤	Trezeguet	0-1	Serginho	⬤	Simple, focussed, easy
Relief for Juve as Birindelli scores	⬤	Birindelli	1-1	Seedorf	⬤	Did Seedorf really fancy this? It didn't look like it
Another weak shot is saved by Dida	⬤	Zalayeta	1-1	Kaladze	⬤	Another Buffon save kept Juve level
Dida, a metre off his line, blocked Montero's weak shot	⬤	Montero	1-2	Nesta	⬤	At last someone looked prepared. Nesta finds the top right corner
Del Piero looked calm as he walked up and slid the ball home	⬤	Del Piero	2-3	Shevchenko	⬤	Shevchenko's eyes flicked manically from referee to the spot, but scored easily

Above, right: The final strike. Shevchenko's penalty sends Buffon the wrong way and the Milan end at Old Trafford prepares to erupt.

THE EUROPEAN CHAMPIONS LEAGUE

The European Champions League

TOURNAMENT OVERVIEW

ORGANIZED EUROPEAN CLUB COMPETITIONS began in 1927 with the Mittel Europa Cup, contested by the leading teams in Austria, Hungary, Italy and Czechoslovakia. Although it was revived after the Second World War, Cold War divisions made the logistics difficult. Moreover, the power base of club football had shifted west and the Latin Cup was established in 1949 among the champions of France, Italy, Spain and Portugal. Based on this model of two aggregate legs and a single-match Final, Gabriel Hunot, editor of French sports paper *L'Equipe*, proposed the creation of a European Cup, contested by its national champions in 1955. Formally sanctioned by FIFA, the cup was first contested in 1956. But Chelsea, the English champions at the time, was not allowed to compete by the FA.

Real win five in a row

Thus the European Cup began as a small affair with no sponsors, and barely any television coverage. The first Final was won by Real Madrid beating Stade de Reims 4-3 in Paris. The following year, against the wishes of the English FA, Manchester United entered the tournament. On the flight home from a successful quarter-final second-leg match against Red Star Belgrade the core of the squad was killed in an air crash in Munich. Fatally weakened, United was put out in the semi-finals by Real Madrid who went on to win the Final against Fiorentina. Madrid won a further three consecutive titles, culminating in their extraordinary 7-3 demolition of Eintracht Frankfurt in the 1960 Final at Hampden Park in Glasgow, thought by many who saw it to have been the finest match ever seen.

With Real on the slide, the next five cups fell two apiece to Benfica and Internazionale, with a win for Milan in between, before a sixth Real victory in 1966. A shift of footballing power northward soon followed with British victories in 1967 and 1968 (Celtic and Manchester United). Four Dutch victories, three for Ajax, began the 1970s followed by three victories for Bayern München. Liverpool's triumph in 1977 began a series of six consecutive English victories. Liverpool's last Final, in 1985, was the occasion of the Heysel Stadium disaster after which English clubs were banned from European competition for six years. In their absence, the cup went east for the first time to Steaua Bucureşti of Romania.

Birth of the Champions League

Under considerable pressure from big clubs and TV companies the tournament was steadily expanded and reformatted during the late 1990s as the European Champions League, with winning teams playing at least 16 matches to get to the Final and more clubs from the bigger leagues getting into the tournament. The huge sums of TV and sponsorship money the Champions League generates has made it the biggest footballing event outside the World Cup.

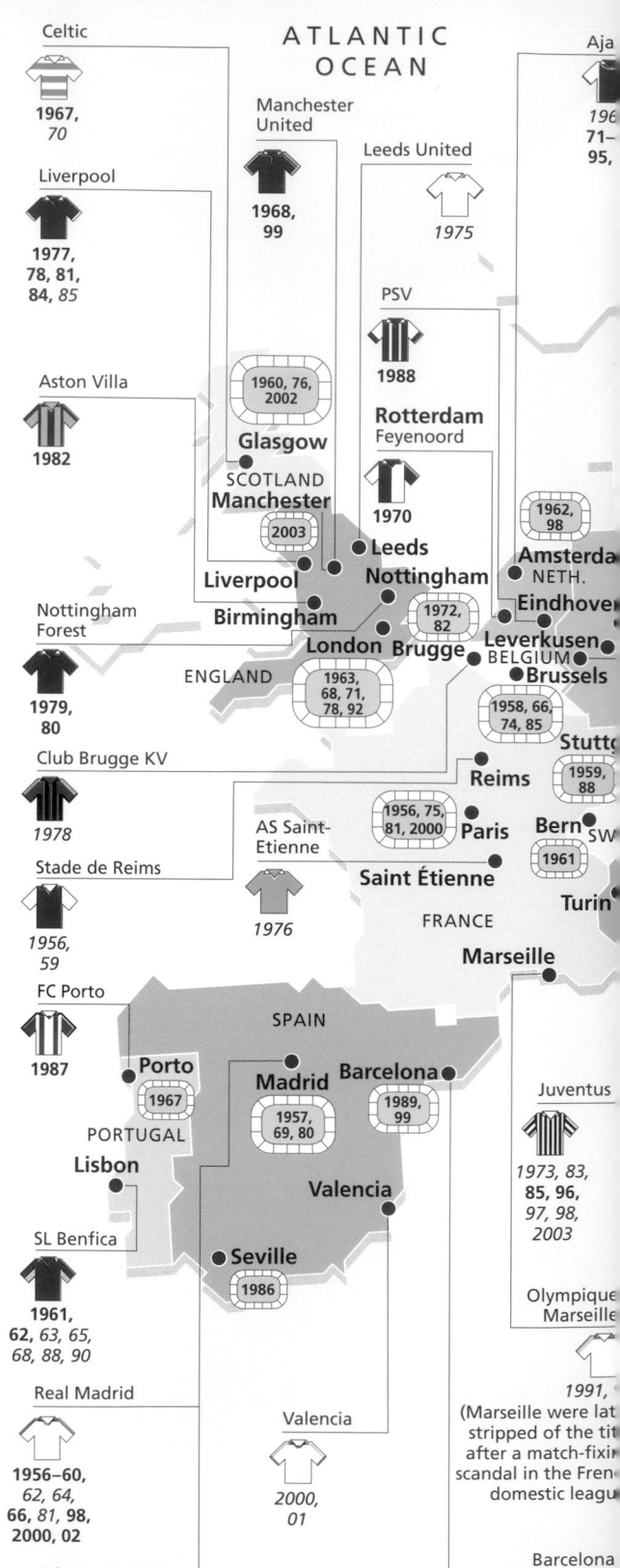

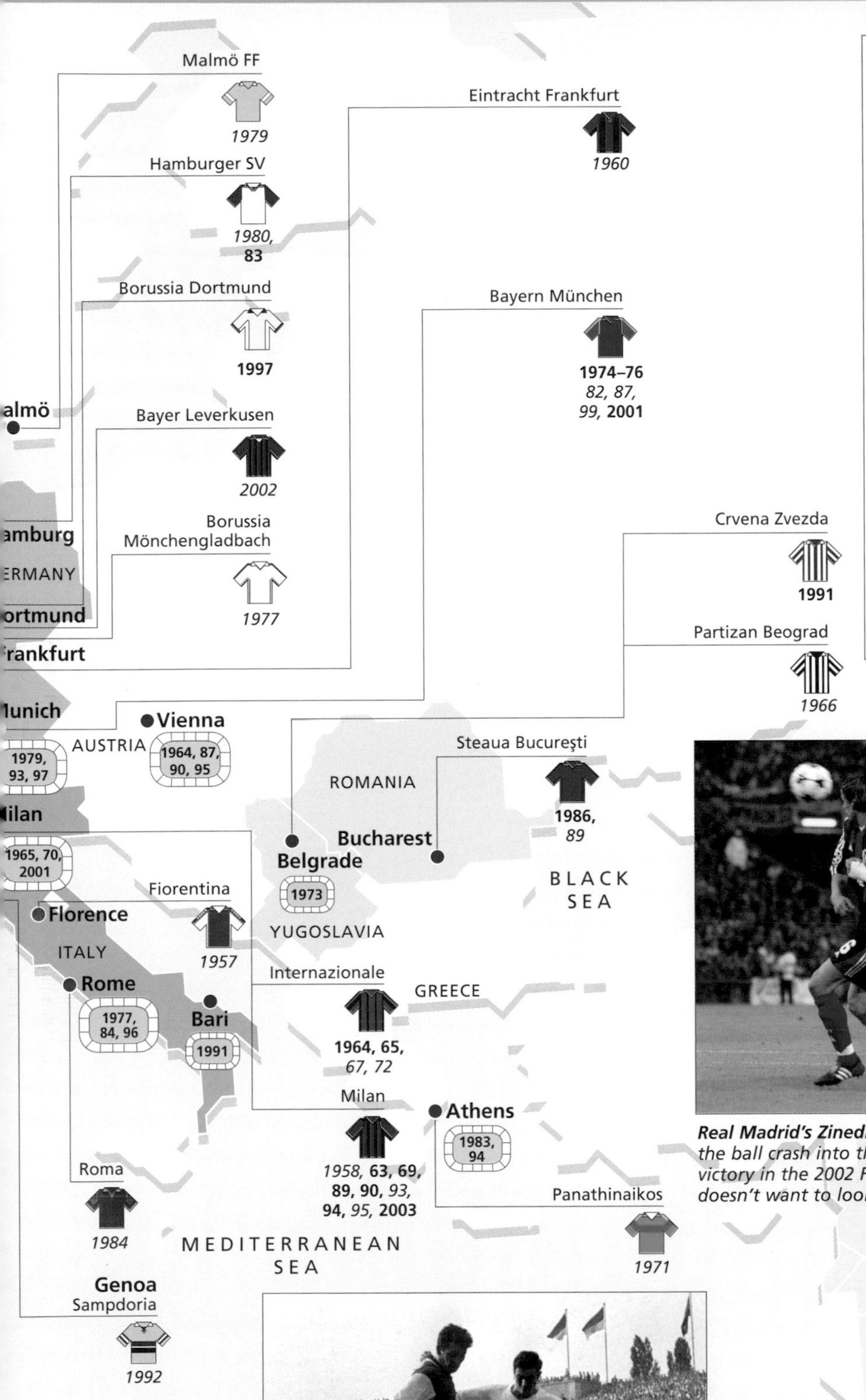

Malmö FF
1979

Eintracht Frankfurt
1960

Hamburger SV
1980, **83**

Borussia Dortmund
1997

Bayern München
1974–76
82, 87,
99, **2001**

Bayer Leverkusen
2002

Borussia Mönchengladbach
1977

Crvena Zvezda
1991

Partizan Beograd
1966

almö

amburg

ERMANY

ortmund

rankfurt

Munich

●**Vienna**
AUSTRIA
1964, 87, 90, 95

1979, 93, 97

Milan

1965, 70, 2001

Steaua Bucureşti
1986, *89*

ROMANIA

Bucharest
Belgrade
1973

BLACK SEA

YUGOSLAVIA

Fiorentina
1957

●**Florence**
ITALY

●**Rome**
1977, 84, 96

Bari
1991

Internazionale
1964, 65, *67, 72*

GREECE

Milan
1958, **63, 69,** *89,* **90,** *93,* **94, 95, 2003**

●**Athens**
1983, 94

Panathinaikos
1971

Roma
1984

MEDITERRANEAN SEA

Genoa
Sampdoria
1992

The European Champions League

Number of wins in the European Champions League (by country)

- 8+ times
- 5–7 times
- 2–4 times
- 1 time
- 0 times

Team details
PORTUGAL — Country
● **Lisbon** — City of origin
Benfica — Team name
— Team colours
1961, 62 *63, 65, 68,* **88,** *90* — Winners in bold / Runners-up in italic
● **Belgrade**
1973 — Host city of Final and year

Real Madrid's Zinedine Zidane swivels, volleys and watches the ball crash into the roof of the net to seal the team's victory in the 2002 Final. Bayer Leverkusen's Michael Ballack doesn't want to look.

Just Fontaine of Stade de Reims (dark shirt) challenges Real Madrid's Domingues during the 1959 Final in Stuttgart – Real's fourth victory in the first four years of the competition.

The European Champions League 1956–2003

COUNTRY	WINNERS	RUNNERS-UP
Italy	10	13
Spain	10	9
England	9	2
Germany	6	7
Netherlands	6	2
Portugal	3	5
France	1	4
Romania	1	1
Scotland	1	1
Yugoslavia	1	1
Belgium	0	1
Greece	0	1
Sweden	0	1

The European Champions League

THE EUROPEAN CUP was established in 1955 after a meeting called by Gabriel Hunot, then editor of the French sports newspaper *L'Equipe*. Although the initial tournament had an eclectic mix of national champions and other big clubs, it was soon codified and run by UEFA with entry restricted to national champions and the previous year's winner. Two-leg matches in each round were played with a single final match at a neutral venue. In 1992, mini-leagues were played to produce the finalists. In 1995, there was a shift back to two-leg quarter- and semi-finals, but the really big change in the competition's format came in 1996. Under pressure from the big clubs for more games and more money, UEFA created qualifying rounds for smaller countries and a first round of four mini-leagues of four to produce eight quarter-finalists.

In 2000 the tournament was expanded even further, with two places guaranteed to the strongest leagues in Europe and extra routes in for clubs via a longer qualifying round. The first round now consists of eight groups of four clubs with 16 progressing into the second round. Third-place teams qualify for the later rounds of the UEFA Cup, while teams defeated in the preliminary stages are entered for the first round of the UEFA Cup. The final 16 play in four groups of four to produce eight quarter-finalists. Two-legged matches determine the finalists, who still play a single match at a neutral venue. As a consequence teams may have needed to play more than 20 matches to win the tournament. However, with UEFA worried by fatigue amongst TV audiences and fixture congestion the second group phase will end in 2003. In 2004 it will be replaced with two-leg knockout second round matches.

1955–56 FINAL
June 13 – Parc des Princes, Paris
Real Madrid 4-3 Stade de Reims
(Spain) (France)
(di Stefano 15, (Leblond 6,
Rial 30, 79, Templin 10,
Marquitos 71) Hidalgo 62)
h/t: 2-2 **Att:** 38,239
Ref: Ellis (England)

1956–57 FINAL
May 30 – Santiago Bernabeu, Madrid
Real Madrid 2-0 Fiorentina
(Spain) (Italy)
(di Stefano
70 pen,
Gento 76)
h/t: 0-0 **Att:** 120,000
Ref: Horn (Netherlands)

1957–58 FINAL
May 29 – Heysel, Brussels
Real Madrid 3-2 Milan
(Spain) (Italy)
(di Stefano 74, (Schiaffino 69,
Rial 79, Grillo 78)
Gento 107)
(after extra time)
h/t: 0-0 **90 mins:** 2-2
Att: 70,000 **Ref:** Alsteen (Belgium)

1958–59 FINAL
June 3 – Neckar, Stuttgart
Real Madrid 2-0 Stade de Reims
(Spain) (France)
(Mateos 2,
di Stefano 47)
h/t: 1-0 **Att:** 72,000
Ref: Dusch (France)

1959–60 FINAL
May 18 – Hampden Park, Glasgow
Real Madrid 7-3 Eintracht
(Spain) **Frankfurt**
(di Stefano (West Germany)
26, 29, 74, (Kress 18,
Puskas 44, 56, Stein 72, 76)
60 pen, 71)
h/t: 3-1 **Att:** 127,621
Ref: Mowat (Scotland)

1960–61 FINAL
May 31 – Wankdorf, Bern
SL Benfica 3-2 Barcelona
(Portugal) (Spain)
(Aguas 30, (Kocsis 20,
Ramallets o.g. 31, Czibor 75)
Coluna 54)
h/t: 2-1 **Att:** 33,000
Ref: Dienst (Switzerland)

1961–62 FINAL
May 2 – Olympic, Amsterdam
SL Benfica 5-3 Real Madrid
(Portugal) (Spain)
(Aguas 25, (Puskas
Cavem 34, 17, 23, 38)
Coluna 61,
Eusebio
68 pen, 78)
h/t: 2-3 **Att:** 68,000
Ref: Horn (Netherlands)

1962–63 FINAL
May 22 – Wembley, London
Milan 2-1 SL Benfica
(Italy) (Portugal)
(Altafini 58, 66) (Eusebio 18)
h/t: 0-1 **Att:** 45,000
Ref: Holland (England)

1963–64 FINAL
May 27 – Prater, Vienna
Internazionale 3-1 Real Madrid
(Italy) (Spain)
(Mazzola 43, 76, (Felo 69)
Milani 62)
h/t: 1-0 **Att:** 72,000
Ref: Stoll (Austria)

1964–65 FINAL
May 27 – San Siro, Milan
Internazionale 1-0 SL Benfica
(Italy) (Portugal)
(Jair 42)
h/t: 1-0 **Att:** 80,000
Ref: Dienst (Switzerland)

1965–66 FINAL
May 11 – Heysel, Brussels
Real Madrid 2-1 Partizan
(Spain) **Beograd**
(Amancio 70, (Yugoslavia)
Serena 76) (Vasovic 55)
h/t: 0-0 **Att:** 55,000
Ref: Kreitlein (West Germany)

1966–67 FINAL
May 25 – Estadio da Luz, Lisbon
Celtic 2-1 Internazionale
(Scotland) (Italy)
(Gemmell 62, (Mazzola 6 pen)
Chalmers 83)
h/t: 0-1 **Att:** 55,000
Ref: Tschenscher (West Germany)

1967–68 FINAL
May 29 – Wembley, London
Manchester 4-1 SL Benfica
United (Portugal)
(England) *(Jaime Graca 78)*
(Charlton 54, 98,
Best 92, Kidd 95)
(after extra time)
h/t: 0-0 **90 mins:** 1-1
Att: 100,000 **Ref:** Lo Bello (Italy)

1968–69 FINAL
May 28 – Santiago Bernabeu, Madrid
Milan 4-1 Ajax
(Italy) (Netherlands)
(Prati 7, 39, 74, (Vasovic 61 pen)
Sormani 66)
h/t: 2-0 **Att:** 50,000
Ref: Ortiz (Spain)

1969–70 FINAL
May 6 – San Siro, Milan
Feyenoord 2-1 Celtic
(Netherlands) (Scotland)
(Israel 29, (Gemmell 31)
Kindvall 116)
(after extra time)
h/t: 1-1 **90 mins:** 1-1
Att: 53,187 **Ref:** Lo Bello (Italy)

1970–71 FINAL
June 2 – Wembley, London
Ajax 2-0 Panathinaikos
(Netherlands) (Greece)
(Van Dijk 5,
Haan 87)
h/t: 1-0 **Att:** 90,000
Ref: Taylor (England)

1971–72 FINAL
May 31 – De Kuip, Rotterdam
Ajax 2-0 Internazionale
(Netherlands) (Italy)
(Cruyff 48, 77)
h/t: 0-0 **Att:** 61,000
Ref: Helies (France)

1972–73 FINAL
May 30 – Crvena Zvezda, Belgrade
Ajax 1-0 Juventus
(Netherlands) (Italy)
(Rep 4)
h/t: 1-0 **Att:** 93,000
Ref: Gugulovic (Yugoslavia)

1973–74 FINAL
May 15 – Heysel, Brussels
Bayern 1-1 Atlético
München **Madrid**
(West Germany) (Spain)
(Schwarzenbeck (Luis Aragones
120) 113)
(after extra time)
h/t: 0-0 **90 mins:** 0-0
Att: 65,000 **Ref:** Loraux (Belgium)

REPLAY
May 17 – Heysel, Brussels
Bayern 4-0 Atlético
München **Madrid**
(Hoeness 28, 81,
Müller 57, 70)
h/t: 1-0 **Att:** 23,000
Ref: Delcourt (Belgium)

1974–75 FINAL
May 28 – Parc des Princes, Paris
Bayern 2-0 Leeds
München **United**
(West Germany) (England)
(Roth 71,
Müller 81)
h/t: 0-0 **Att:** 48,000
Ref: Kitabdjian (France)

1975–76 FINAL
May 12 – Hampden Park, Glasgow
Bayern 1-0 AS Saint-
München **Etienne**
(West Germany) (France)
(Roth 57)
h/t: 0-0 **Att:** 54,684
Ref: Palotai (Hungary)

THE EUROPEAN CHAMPIONS LEAGUE

1976–77 FINAL

May 25 – Olimpico, Rome
Liverpool 3-1 Borussia
(England) **Mönchen-**
(McDermott 27, **gladbach**
Smith 65, (West Germany)
Neal 82 pen) *(Simonsen 51)*
h/t: 1-0 **Att:** 57,000
Ref: Wurtz (France)

1977–78 FINAL

May 10 – Wembley, London
Liverpool 1-0 Club Brugge KV
(England) (Belgium)
(Dalglish 64)
h/t: 0-0 **Att:** 92,000
Ref: Corver (Netherlands)

1978–79 FINAL

May 30 – Olympiastadion, Munich
Nottingham 1-0 Malmö FF
Forest (Sweden)
(England)
(Francis 44)
h/t: 1-0 **Att:** 57,500
Ref: Linemayr (Austria)

1979–80 FINAL

May 28 – Santiago Bernabeu, Madrid
Nottingham 1-0 Hamburger SV
Forest (West Germany)
(England)
(Robertson 19)
h/t: 1-0 **Att:** 51,000
Ref: Garrido (Portugal)

1980–81 FINAL

May 27 – Parc des Princes, Paris
Liverpool 1-0 Real Madrid
(England) (Spain)
(A. Kennedy 82)
h/t: 0-0 **Att:** 48,360
Ref: Palotai (Hungary)

1981–82 FINAL

May 26 – De Kuip, Rotterdam
Aston Villa 1-0 Bayern
(England) **München**
(Withe 67) (West Germany)
h/t: 0-0 **Att:** 45,000
Ref: Konrath (France)

1982–83 FINAL

May 25 – Olympic, Athens
Hamburger SV 1-0 Juventus
(West Germany) (Italy)
(Magath 9)
h/t: 1-0 **Att:** 73,500
Ref: Rainea (Romania)

1983–84 FINAL

May 30 – Olimpico, Rome
Liverpool 1-1 Roma
(England) (Italy)
(Neal 15) *(Pruzzo 38)*
(after extra time)
h/t: 1-1 **90 mins:** 1-1
Att: 69,693 **Ref:** Fredriksson (Sweden)
Liverpool won 4-2 on pens

1984–85 FINAL

May 29 – Heysel, Brussels
Juventus 1-0 Liverpool
(Italy) (England)
(Platini 57 pen)
h/t: 0-0 **Att:** 60,000
Ref: Daina (Switzerland)

1985–86 FINAL

May 7 – Sanchez Pizjuan, Seville
Steaua 0-0 Barcelona
Bucureşti (Spain)
(Romania)
(after extra time)
h/t: 0-0 **90 mins:** 0-0
Att: 75,000 **Ref:** Vautrot (France)
Steaua Bucureşti won 2-0 on pens

1986–87 FINAL

May 27 – Prater, Vienna
FC Porto 2-1 Bayern
(Portugal) **München**
(Madjer 77, (West Germany)
Juary 81) *(Kogl 25)*
h/t: 0-1 **Att:** 62,000
Ref: Ponnet (Belgium)

1987–88 FINAL

May 25 – Neckar, Stuttgart
PSV 0-0 SL Benfica
(Netherlands) (Portugal)
(after extra time)
h/t: 0-0 **90 mins:** 0-0
Att: 68,000 **Ref:** Agnolin (Italy)
PSV won 6-5 on pens

1988–89 FINAL

May 24 – Nou Camp, Barcelona
Milan 4-0 Steaua
(Italy) **Bucureşti**
(Gullit 18, 38, (Romania)
van Basten 27, 46)
h/t: 3-0 **Att:** 100,000
Ref: Tritschler (West Germany)

1989–90 FINAL

May 23 – Prater, Vienna
Milan 1-0 SL Benfica
(Italy) (Portugal)
(Rijkaard 67)
h/t: 0-0 **Att:** 58,000
Ref: Kohl (Austria)

1990–91 FINAL

May 29 – San Nicola, Bari
Crvena Zvezda 0-0 Olympique
(Yugoslavia) **Marseille**
(France)
(after extra time)
h/t: 0-0 **90 mins:** 0-0
Att: 58,000 **Ref:** Lanese (Italy)
Crvena Zvezda won 5-3 on pens

1991–92 FINAL

May 20 – Wembley, London
Barcelona 1-0 Sampdoria
(Spain) (Italy)
(Koemann 111)
(after extra time)
h/t: 0-0 **90 mins:** 0-0 **Att:** 70,827
Ref: Schmidhuber (Germany)

1992–93 FINAL

May 26 – Olympiastadion, Munich
Olympique 1-0 Milan
Marseille (Italy)
(France)
(Boli 43)
h/t: 1-0 **Att:** 64,400
Ref: Rothlisberger (Switzerland)
Marseille later stripped of title

1993–94 FINAL

May 18 – Olympic, Athens
Milan 4-0 Barcelona
(Italy) (Spain)
(Massaro 22, 45,
Savicevic 47,
Desailly 59)
h/t: 2-0 **Att:** 70,000
Ref: Don (England)

1994–95 FINAL

May 24 – Ernst-Happel Stadion, Vienna
Ajax 1-0 Milan
(Netherlands) (Italy)
(Kluivert 83)
h/t: 0-0 **Att:** 49,500
Ref: Craciunescu (Romania)

1995–96 FINAL

May 22 – Olimpico, Rome
Juventus 1-1 Ajax
(Italy) (Netherlands)
(Ravanelli 12) *(Litmanen 40)*
(after extra time)
h/t: 1-1 **90 mins:** 1-1
Att: 70,000 **Ref:** Diaz Vega (Spain)
Juventus won 4-2 on pens

1996–97 FINAL

May 28 – Olympiastadion, Munich
Borussia 3-1 Juventus
Dortmund (Italy)
(Germany) *(Del Piero 64)*
(Riedle 29, 34,
Ricken 71)
h/t: 2-0 **Att:** 65,000
Ref: Puhl (Hungary)

1997–98 FINAL

May 20 – Arena, Amsterdam
Real Madrid 1-0 Juventus
(Spain) (Italy)
(Mijatovic 66)
h/t: 0-0 **Att:** 50,000
Ref: Krug (Germany)

1998–99 FINAL

May 26 – Nou Camp, Barcelona
Manchester 2-1 Bayern
United **München**
(England) (Germany)
(Sheringham 89, *(Basler 6)*
Solskjaer 90)
h/t: 0-1 **Att:** 90,000
Ref: Collina (Italy)

1999–2000 FINAL

May 24 – Stade St Denis, Paris
Real Madrid 3-0 Valencia
(Spain) (Spain)
(Morientes 39,
McManaman 67,
Raúl 75)
h/t: 1-0 **Att:** 78,000
Ref: Braschi (Italy)

2000–01 FINAL

May 23 – San Siro, Milan
Bayern 1-1 Valencia
München (Spain)
(Germany) *(Mendieta 3 pen)*
(Effenberg
51 pen)
(after sudden death extra time)
h/t: 0-1 **90 mins:** 1-1 **Att:** 74,000
Ref: Jol (Netherlands)
Bayern München won 5-4 on pens

2001–02 FINAL

May 15 – Hampden Park, Glasgow
Real Madrid 2-1 Bayer
(Spain) **Leverkusen**
(Raúl 8, (Germany)
Zidane 45) *(Lucio 14)*
h/t: 2-1 **Att:** 52,000
Ref: Meier (Switzerland)

2002–03 FINAL

May 28 – Old Trafford, Manchester
Milan 0-0 Juventus
(Italy) (Italy)
(after extra time)
h/t: 0-0 **90 mins:** 0-0
Att: 68,000 **Ref:** Markus (Germany)
Milan won 3-2 on pens

Experts seldom agree on much, but many pundits concur that the 1959–60 European Cup Final between Real Madrid and Eintracht Frankfurt at Hampden Park was the finest match ever seen. Here, Ferenc Puskas makes it 5-1 from the penalty spot on the hour. Real went on to win 7-3.

The UEFA Cup

TOURNAMENT REVIEW 2002–03

THE UEFA CUP MAY BE Europe's second competition, but in Porto and Celtic it acquired finalists hungry for glory. Porto last took a European trophy in 1987; Celtic had not made a European final since 1970. Indeed, so fervent were the Celtic fans, that they were barely out of the quarter-finals before accommodation in Seville – venue for the Final – was being booked up. Of course, the tricky matter of the semi-finals remained, but both Porto and Celtic showed themselves worthy finalists.

Despite going behind to an early goal at home against Lazio, Porto surged back to demolish the Italians 4-1 with a display of scintillating attacking football. Celtic, who had arrived in the semi-final against Boavista via some very tough fixtures against Stuttgart and Liverpool, squeezed home with another spirited away leg in Portugal. The fever was palpable; Glasgow sold out of replica strips and green sombreros. While Porto brought 15,000 to the game, Celtic must have had 50,000.

In the hot Andalucian evening, Porto twice took the lead with goals from Derlei and Alentichev. The Portuguese looked more comfortable on the ball and in playmaker Deco possessed the best player on the field. But Celtic, roused by the irrepressible Martin O'Neill and the singing of 30,000 voices, came back on level terms each time inevitably from the head of Henrik Larsson – scoring his 200th goal for the club. But in extra time Celtic's Bobo Balde was sent off for a second yellow card and the heart of the Celtic defence was lost. The balance of power tipped Porto's way and Derlei put them ahead with five minutes to go. The game disintegrated as Porto's excessive goal celebrations ate time and although five minutes extra were allowed, they were consumed by the laughable play-acting of Porto goalkeeper Vítor Baía. On the final whistle the delirium of the Porto end was dimmed by the agony in the Celtic stands.

THIRD ROUND (2 legs)

Wisla Kraków **1-1** Schalke 04
(Poland)   (Germany)
Schalke 04 **1-4** Wisla Kraków
Wisla Kraków won 5-2 on aggregate

SK Sturm Graz **1-3** Lazio
(Austria)   (Italy)
Lazio **0-1** SK Sturm Graz
Lazio won 3-2 on aggregate

Real Betis **1-0** AJ Auxerre
(Spain)   (France)
AJ Auxerre **2-0** Real Betis
Auxerre won 2-1 on aggregate

Beşiktaş **3-1** Dynamo Kyiv
(Turkey)   (Ukraine)
Dynamo Kyiv **0-0** Beşiktaş
Beşiktaş won 3-1 on aggregate

Paris Saint- **2-1** Boavista FC
Germain   (Portugal)
(France)
Boavista FC **1-0** Paris Saint-
Germain
Boavista won on away goals rule

Club Brugge KV **1-2** VfB Stuttgart
(Belgium)   (Germany)
VfB Stuttgart **1-0** Club Brugge KV
VfB Stuttgart won 3-1 on aggregate

Vitesse Arnhem **0-1** Liverpool
(Netherlands)   (England)
Liverpool **1-0** Vitesse Arnhem
Liverpool won 2-0 on aggregate

FC Slovan **2-2** Panathinaikos
Liberec   (Greece)
(Czech Republic)
Panathinaikos **1-0** FC Slovan
Liberec
Panathinaikos won 3-2 on aggregate

Denizlispor **0-0** Olympique
(Turkey)   Lyonnais
(France)
Olympique **0-1** Denizlispor
Lyonnais
Denizlispor won 1-0 on aggregate

Girondins **0-2** RSC Anderlecht
de Bordeaux   (Belgium)
(France)
RSC Anderlecht **2-2** Girondins
de Bordeaux
Anderlecht won 4-2 on aggregate

Málaga CF **0-0** Leeds United
(Spain)   (England)
Leeds United **1-2** Málaga CF
Málaga won 2-1 on aggregate

PAOK **1-0** SK Slavia Praha
(Greece)   (Czech Republic)
SK Slavia Praha **4-0** PAOK
Slavia Praha won 4-1 on aggregate

Hertha Berlin **2-1** Fulham
(Germany)   (England)
Fulham **0-0** Hertha Berlin
Hertha Berlin won 2-1 on aggregate

AEK **4-0** Maccabi Haifa
(Greece)   (Israel)
Maccabi Haifa **1-4** AEK
AEK won 8-1 on aggregate

FC Porto **3-0** RC Lens
(Portugal)   (France)
RC Lens **1-0** FC Porto
FC Porto won 3-1 on aggregate

Celtic **1-0** RC Celta
(Scotland)   (Spain)
RC Celta **2-1** Celtic
Celtic won on away goals rule

FOURTH ROUND (2 legs)

SK Slavia Praha **1-0** Beşiktaş
Beşiktaş **4-2** SK Slavia Praha
Beşiktaş won 4-3 on aggregate

Hertha Berlin **3-2** Boavista FC
Boavista FC **1-0** Hertha Berlin
Boavista won on away goals rule

Málaga CF **0-0** AEK
AEK **0-1** Málaga CF
Málaga won 1-0 on aggregate

Lazio **3-3** Wisla Kraków
Wisla Kraków **1-2** Lazio
Lazio won 5-4 on aggregate

Panathinaikos **3-0** RSC Anderlecht
RSC Anderlecht **2-0** Panathinaikos
Panathinaikos won 3-2 on aggregate

Celtic **3-1** VfB Stuttgart
VfB Stuttgart **3-2** Celtic
Celtic won 5-4 on aggregate

FC Porto **6-1** Denizlispor
Denizlispor **2-2** FC Porto
Porto won 8-3 on aggregate

AJ Auxerre **0-1** Liverpool
Liverpool **2-0** AJ Auxerre
Liverpool won 3-0 on aggregate

Above: John Hartson scores Celtic's second goal against Liverpool at Anfield, sending the Glasgow giants into the semi-finals.

Right: Coach Benny Lennartson celebrates as Viking FK from Stavanger in Norway put Chelsea out of the competition in the First Round.

QUARTER-FINALS (2 legs)

Málaga CF **1-0** Boavista FC
Boavista FC **1-0** Málaga CF

Boavista won 4-1 on pens

Lazio **1-0** Beşiktaş
Beşiktaş **1-2** Lazio

Lazio won 3-1 on aggregate

FC Porto **0-1** Panathinaikos
Panathinaikos **0-2** FC Porto

FC Porto won 2-1 on aggregate

Celtic **1-1** Liverpool
Liverpool **0-2** Celtic

Celtic won 3-1 on aggregate

SEMI-FINALS (2 legs)

April 10 – Celtic Park, Glasgow
Celtic 1-1 Boavista FC
(Larsson 50)   (Valgaereno
                          o.g. 48)

April 24 – Do Bessa, Porto
Boavista FC 0-1 Celtic
                     (Larsson 79)

Celtic won 2-1 on aggregate

April 10 – Das Antas, Porto
FC Porto 4-1 Lazio
(Maniche 10,   (Claudio López 6)
Derlei 28,50
Hélder Postiga 56)

April 24 – Olimpico, Rome
Lazio 0-0 FC Porto

FC Porto won 4-1 on aggregate

2003 FINAL

May 21 – Olimpico, Seville
Celtic 2-3 FC Porto
(Larsson 47, 56)   (Derlei 45, 115,
                            Alenitchev 54)
h/t : 0-1 Att: 52,972
Ref: Lubos Michel (Slovakia)

(after extra time)

Below: Vítor Baía (99) celebrates Porto's victory; next stop the Oscars.

Left: Celtic's Johan Mjallby challenges Boavista's Duda in the home leg of their semi-final clash.

Below, left: Panathinaikos fans protest the Cyprus issue during its UEFA Cup clash with Fenerbahçe. Fighting, arrests and damage to the centre of Istanbul followed.

Below: Alan Thompson is inconsolable as Celtic contemplates another 31 years without a European final.

Bottom: Derlei, Porto's striker, shoots past Rab Douglas in the Celtic goal to win the UEFA Cup and break the hearts of the Scottish fans in Seville.

The UEFA Cup

TOURNAMENT OVERVIEW

IN 1950, THE SWISS VICE-PRESIDENT of FIFA, Ernst Thommen, proposed a competition between select XIs from European cities with industrial fairs. Bizarre as the concept may seem it was strongly supported by Sir Stanley Rous, president of FIFA. Representatives from 12 cities met in Basle to draw up rules for the competition with matches planned to coincide with the industrial fairs. As a consequence, the first edition of the Fairs Cup took nearly three years to complete (1955–58) and was won by Barcelona who beat a London XI over two legs.

Fixture congestion forced the tournament into a single season alongside the European Cup in 1960–61 and Barcelona found itself competing in both. The team went out in the quarter-finals leaving the way for Roma to take the trophy. The rest of the 1960s saw Spanish dominance, initially maintained by Valencia and Real Zaragoza, before giving way to four successive English victories (1968–71).

In 1971, UEFA finally took the competition over, renamed it the UEFA Cup, and awarded places systematically to the highest-placed league clubs not entering other competitions. In the mid-1990s, the disintegration of the Soviet Union saw the competition contested by over 100 clubs with additional places available via UEFA Fair Play awards and the Intertoto Cup.

The 1970s were dominated by English (five winners), German (two) and Dutch (two) teams. The 1980s saw clubs from smaller leagues doing well: RSC Anderlecht from Belgium won it once and IFK Göteborg from Sweden won it twice.

In the 1990s, however, it was the Italian sides who dominated. Between 1989 and 99, Italian clubs took the title eight times, including four all-Italian finals. However, new challengers have risen: 2000 saw Galatasaray win Turkey's first European victory, 2001 saw the return of Liverpool to winning ways and in 2002 Feyenoord won its first European trophy for 18 years.

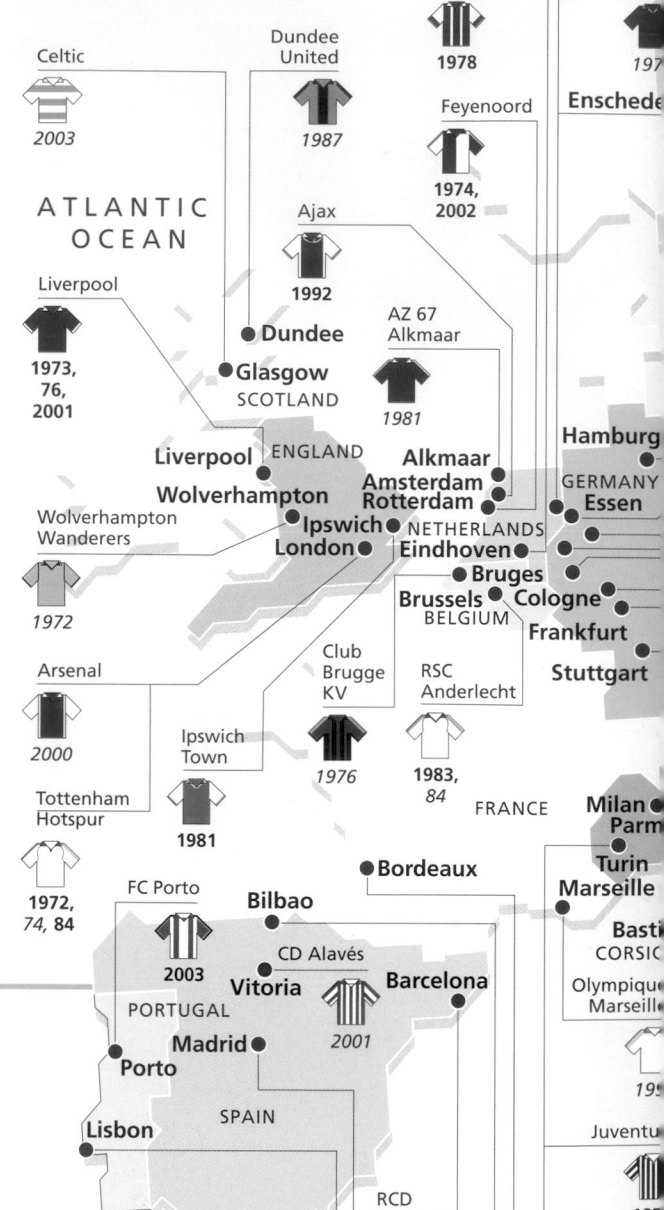

The UEFA Cup

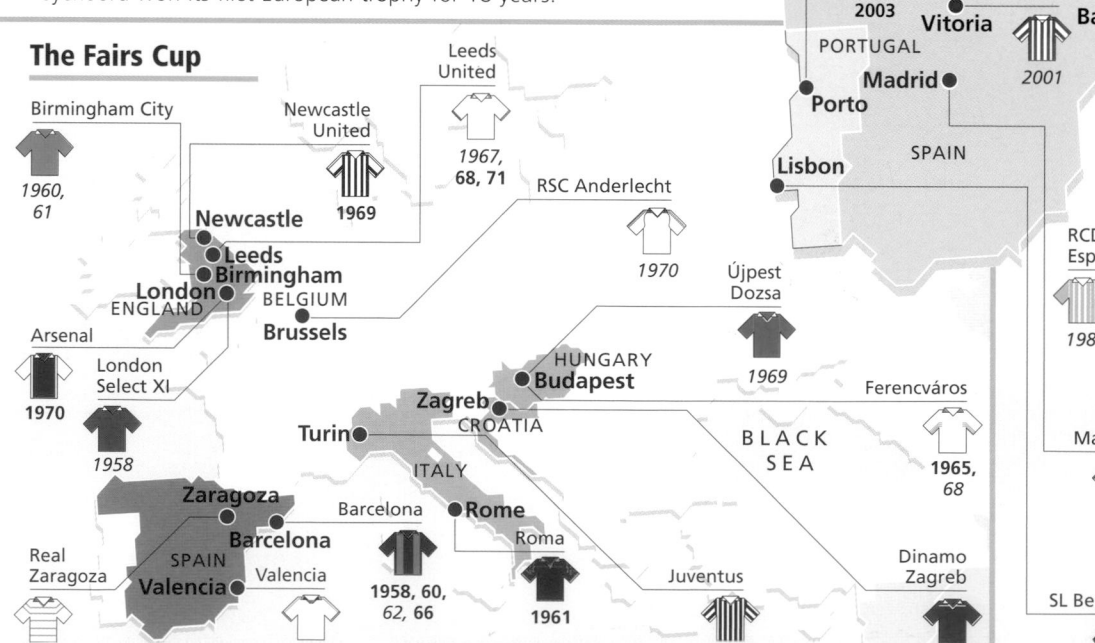

The Fairs Cup

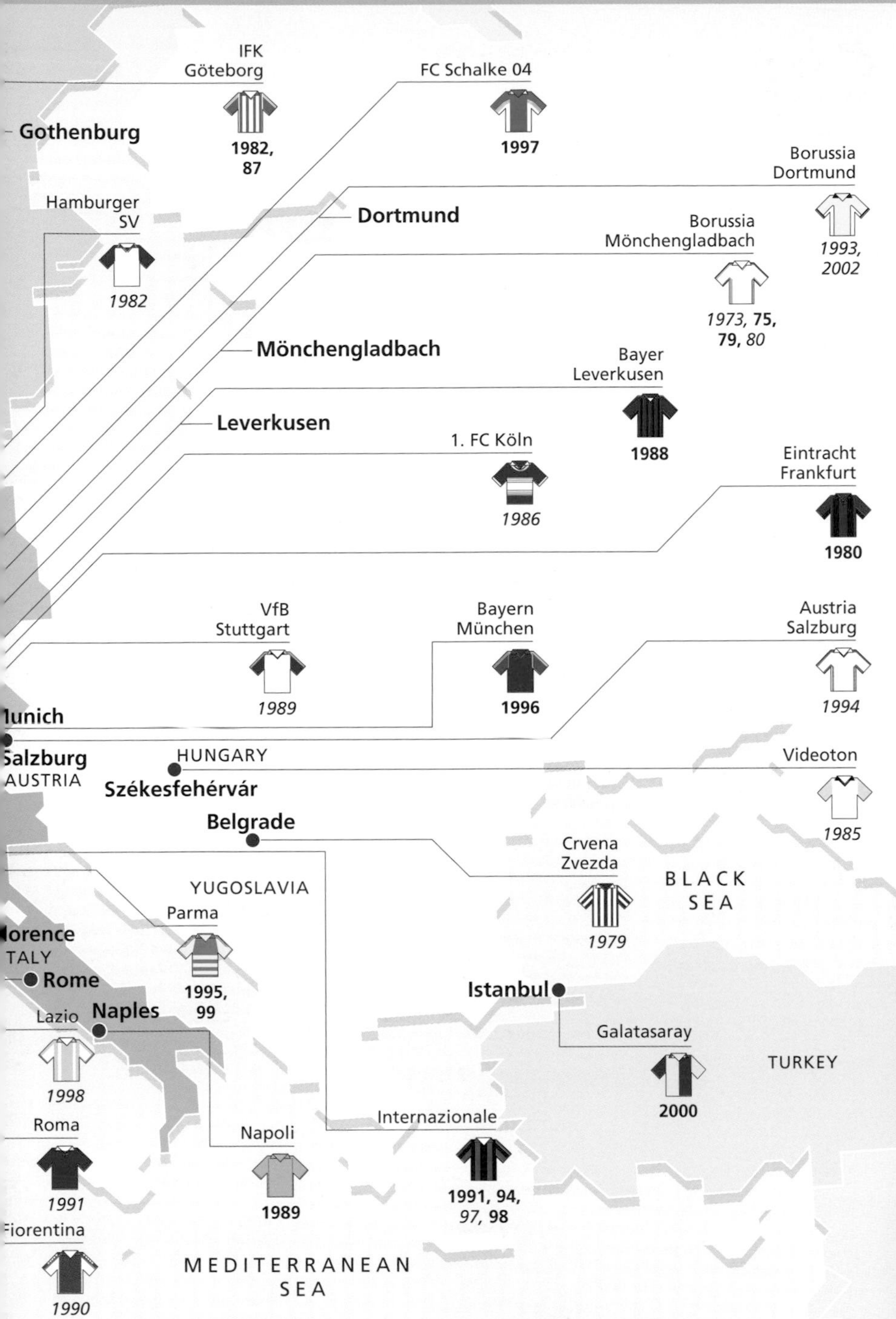

IFK
Göteborg
**1982,
87**

FC Schalke 04
1997

Borussia
Dortmund

Gothenburg

Hamburger
SV
1982

Dortmund

Borussia
Mönchengladbach
*1993,
2002*

Borussia
Mönchengladbach
**1973, 75,
79,** *80*

Mönchengladbach

Bayer
Leverkusen
1988

Leverkusen

1. FC Köln
1986

Eintracht
Frankfurt
1980

VfB
Stuttgart
1989

Bayern
München
1996

Austria
Salzburg
1994

Munich

Salzburg
AUSTRIA

HUNGARY
Székesfehérvár

Videoton
1985

Belgrade

Crvena
Zvezda
1979

**BLACK
SEA**

YUGOSLAVIA
Parma
**1995,
99**

Florence
ITALY
Rome

Lazio
1998

Naples

Roma
1991

Napoli
1989

Istanbul

Galatasaray
2000

TURKEY

Internazionale
**1991, 94,
97, 98**

Fiorentina
1990

MEDITERRANEAN
SEA

The Fairs Cup and the UEFA Cup

Number of wins (by country)

The Fairs Cup		The UEFA Cup	
	5+ times		9+ times
	2–4 times		6–8 times
	1 time		2–5 times
	0 times		1 time
			0 times

Team details

HUNGARY — Country
● Budapest — City of origin
Ferencváros — Team name

— Team colours

1965, *68* — Winners in bold / Runners-up in italic

The UEFA Cup 1958–2003

COUNTRY	WINNERS	RUNNERS-UP
Italy	9	6
Germany	6	7
England	6	3
Netherlands	4	2
Spain	2	3
Sweden	2	0
Belgium	1	2
Portugal	1	1
Turkey	1	0
France	0	3
Scotland	0	2
Austria	0	1
Hungary	0	1
Yugoslavia	0	1

Pierre van Hooijdonk viciously curves the ball over the Borussia Dortmund wall for his and Feyenoord's second goal in 2002's frantic, entertaining Final .

Consecutive participation

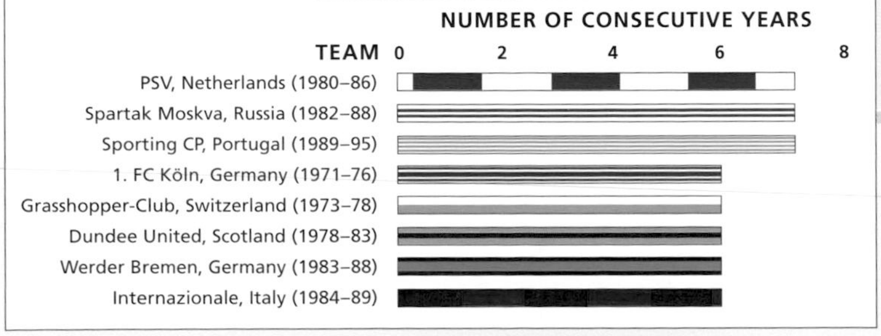

NUMBER OF CONSECUTIVE YEARS

TEAM	0	2	4	6	8

PSV, Netherlands (1980–86)
Spartak Moskva, Russia (1982–88)
Sporting CP, Portugal (1989–95)
1. FC Köln, Germany (1971–76)
Grasshopper-Club, Switzerland (1973–78)
Dundee United, Scotland (1978–83)
Werder Bremen, Germany (1983–88)
Internazionale, Italy (1984–89)

The UEFA Cup

ERNST THOMMEN'S International Industrial Fairs Inter City Cup was open to teams from cities that had hosted international trade fairs. The first tournament, in 1955, had ten entrants from ten cities. Two-leg, home and away rounds were played over three years to produce the first winner of the (now abbreviated) Fairs Cup. The away goals rule was first introduced into the tournament in 1967, and, in 1971, penalties replaced the toss of a coin for drawn matches. In 1972 it became the UEFA Cup. In 1998 the two-leg final was replaced by a single match at a neutral venue.

From 1961 the tournament spread its net, with three places allocated to each UEFA nation. Places are now allocated on a nation's past performance in European competition, though national associations can allocate those places as they choose. With the merger of the Cup-Winners' Cup into an expanded UEFA Cup in 2000, national cup winners are generally awarded a place and preliminary rounds have been added. Defeated teams from the preliminary round of the Champions League now enter the first round, and third-place teams from the Champions League first-round mini-leagues enter the third round.

1955–58 FINAL (2 legs)

March 5 – Stamford Bridge, London
London 2-2 Barcelona
Select XI   (Spain)
(England)   (Tejada 7,
(Greaves 10,   Martinez 35)
Langley 88 pen)

May 1 – Nou Camp, Barcelona
Barcelona 6-0 London
(Suarez 6, 8,   Select XI
Evaristo 52, 75,
Martinez 43,
Verges 63)

Barcelona won 8-2 on aggregate

1958–60 FINAL (2 legs)

March 29 – St. Andrew's, Birmingham
Birmingham 0-0 Barcelona
City   (Spain)
(England)

May 4 – Nou Camp, Barcelona
Barcelona 4-1 Birmingham
(Czibor 6, 48,   City
Martinez 43,   (Hooper 82)
Coll 78)

Barcelona won 4-1 on aggregate

1960–61 FINAL (2 legs)

September 27 – St. Andrew's, Birmingham
Birmingham 2-2 Roma
City   (Italy)
(England)   (Manfredini
(Hellawell 78,   30, 56)
Orritt 85)

October 11 – Stadio Olimpico, Rome
Roma 2-0 Birmingham
(Farmer o.g. 56,   City
Pestrin 90)

Roma won 4-2 on aggregate

1961–62 FINAL (2 legs)

August 9 – Luis Casanova, Valencia
Valencia 6-2 Barcelona
(Spain)   (Spain)
(Yosu 14, 42,   (Kocsis 4, 20)
Guillot 35, 54, 67,
Nunez 74)

September 9 – Nou Camp, Barcelona
Barcelona 1-1 Valencia
(Kocsis 46)   (Guillot 87)

Valencia won 7-3 on aggregate

1962–63 FINAL (2 legs)

June 12 – Dinamo Stadion, Zagreb
Dinamo Zagreb 1-2 Valencia
(Yugoslavia)   (Spain)
(Zambata 13)   (Waldo 64,
                    Urtiaga 67)

June 25 – Mestalla, Valencia
Valencia 2-0 Dinamo Zagreb
(Manio 68,
Nunez 78)

Valencia won 4-1 on aggregate

1963–64 FINAL

June 25 – Nou Camp, Barcelona
Real Zaragoza 2-1 Valencia
(Spain)   (Spain)
(Villa 40,   (Urtiaga 41)
Marcelino 83)

1964–65 FINAL

June 23 – Communale, Turin
Ferencváros 1-0 Juventus
(Hungary)   (Italy)
(Fenyvesi 74)

1965–66 FINAL (2 legs)

September 14 – Nou Camp, Barcelona
Barcelona 0-1 Real Zaragoza
(Spain)   (Spain)
                  (Canario 30)

September 21 – La Romareda, Zaragoza
Real Zaragoza 2-4 Barcelona
(Marcelino   (Pujol 3, 86, 119,
24, 87)   Zaballa 89)

(after extra time)

Barcelona won 4-3 on aggregate

1966–67 FINAL (2 legs)

August 30 – Dinamo Stadion, Zagreb
Dinamo Zagreb 2-0 Leeds United
(Yugoslavia)   (England)
(Cercek 39, 59)

September 6 – Elland Road, Leeds
Leeds United 0-0 Dinamo Zagreb

Dinamo Zagreb won 2-0 on aggregate

1967–68 FINAL (2 legs)

September 7 – Elland Road, Leeds
Leeds United 1-0 Ferencváros
(England)   (Hungary)
(Jones 41)

September 11 – Nep, Budapest
Ferencváros 0-0 Leeds United

Leeds United won 1-0 on aggregate

1968–69 FINAL (2 legs)

May 29 – St. James' Park, Newcastle
Newcastle 3-0 Újpest Dozsa
United   (Hungary)
(England)
(Moncur 63, 72,
Scott 83)

June 11 – Nep, Budapest
Újpest Dozsa 2-3 Newcastle
(Bene 31,   United
Gorocs 44)   (Moncur 46,
                    Arentoft 50,
                    Foggon 74)

Newcastle United won 6-2 on aggregate

1969–70 FINAL (2 legs)

April 22 – Parc Astrid, Brussels
RSC Anderlecht 3-1 Arsenal
(Belgium)   (England)
(Devrindt 25,   (Kennedy 82)
Mulder 30, 74)

April 28 – Highbury, London
Arsenal 3-0 RSC Anderlecht
(Kelly 25,
Radford 75,
Sammels 76)

Arsenal won 4-3 on aggregate

1970–71 FINAL (2 legs)

May 26 – Communale, Turin
Juventus 0-0 Leeds United
(Italy)   (England)

Match abandoned after 51 mins
due to waterlogged pitch

REPLAY

May 28 – Communale, Turin
Juventus 2-2 Leeds United
(Bettega 27,   (Madeley 48,
Capello 55)   Bates 77)

June 3 – Communale, Turin
Leeds United 1-1 Juventus
(Clarke 12)   (Anastasi 20)

Leeds United won on away goals rule

1971–72 FINAL (2 legs)

May 3 – Molineux, Wolverhampton
Wolverhampton 1-2 Tottenham
Wanderers   Hotspur
(England)   (England)
(McCalliog 72)   (Chivers 57, 87)

May 17 – White Hart Lane, London
Tottenham 1-1 Wolverhampton
Hotspur   Wanderers
(Mullery 30)   (Wagstaffe 41)

Tottenham Hotspur won 3-2
on aggregate

1972–73 FINAL (2 legs)

May 9 – Anfield, Liverpool
Liverpool 0-0 Borussia
(England)   Mönchen-
                    gladbach
                    (West Germany)

Match abandoned after 27 mins
due to waterlogged pitch

REPLAY

May 10 – Anfield, Liverpool
Liverpool 3-0 Borussia
(Keegan 21, 32,   Mönchen-
Lloyd 61)   gladbach

May 23 – Bokelberg, Mönchengladbach
Borussia 2-0 Liverpool
Mönchen-
gladbach
(Heynckes 29, 40)

Liverpool won 3-2 on aggregate

1973–74 FINAL (2 legs)

May 21 – White Hart Lane, London
Tottenham 2-2 Feyenoord
Hotspur   (Netherlands)
(England)   (Van Hanegem 43,
(England 39,   De Jong 85)
Van Daele o.g. 64)

May 28 – Feyenoord, Rotterdam
Feyenoord 2-0 Tottenham
(Rijsbergen 43,   Hotspur
Ressel 84)

Feyenoord won 4-2 on aggregate

1974–75 FINAL (2 legs)

May 7 – Rheinstadion, Düsseldorf
Borussia 0-0 FC Twente
Mönchen-   (Netherlands)
gladbach
(West Germany)

September 11 – Arke, Enschede
FC Twente 1-5 Borussia
(Drost 76)   Mönchen-
                    gladbach
                    (Simonsen 2, 86,
                    Heynckes
                    9, 50, 60)

Borussia Mönchengladbach won 5-1
on aggregate

1975–76 FINAL (2 legs)

April 28 – Anfield, Liverpool
Liverpool 3-2 Club Brugge KV
(England)   (Belgium)
(Kennedy 59,   (Lambert 5,
Case 61,   Cools 15)
Keegan 65)

May 19 – Olympiastadion, Bruges
Club Brugge KV 1-1 Liverpool
(Lambert 11)   (Keegan 15)

Liverpool won 4-3 on aggregate

1976–77 FINAL (2 legs)

May 4 – Communale, Turin
Juventus 1-0 Athletic Bilbao
(Italy)   (Spain)
(Tardelli 15)

May 18 – San Mames, Bilbao
Athletic Bilbao 2-1 Juventus
(Churruca 11,   (Bettega 7)
Carlos 78)

Juventus won on away goals rule

1977–78 FINAL (2 legs)

April 26 – Furiani, Bastia
SC Bastia 0-0 PSV
(France)   (Netherlands)

May 9 – Philips, Eindhoven
PSV 3-0 SC Bastia
(W. Van der Kerkhof 24, Deijkers 67, Van der Kuijlen 69)

PSV Eindhoven won 3-0 on aggregate

1978–79 FINAL (2 legs)

May 9 – Crvena Zvezda, Belgrade
Crvena Zvezda 1-1 Borussia
(Yugoslavia)   Mönchen-
(Sestic 21)   gladbach
                (West Germany)
                (Jurisic o.g. 60)

May 23 – Rheinstadion, Düsseldorf
Borussia 1-0 Crvena Zvezda
Mönchen-
gladbach
(Simonsen 15)

Borussia Mönchengladbach won 2-1 on aggregate

1979–80 FINAL (2 legs)

May 7 – Bokelberg, Mönchengladbach
Borussia 3-2 Eintracht
Mönchen-   Frankfurt
gladbach   (West Germany)
(West Germany)   *(Karger 37,*
(Kulik 44, 88,   Hlzenbein 71)
Matthäus 76)*

May 21 – Waldstadion, Frankfurt
Eintracht 1-0 Borussia
Frankfurt   Mönchen-
(Schaub 81)   gladbach

Eintracht Frankfurt won on away goals rule

1980–81 FINAL (2 legs)

May 6 – Portman Road, Ipswich
Ipswich Town 3-0 AZ 67 Alkmaar
(England)   (Netherlands)
*(Wark 28,
Thijssen 46,
Mariner 56)*

May 20 – Alkmaarderhout, Alkmaar
AZ 67 Alkmaar 4-2 Ipswich Town
*(Welzl 7,   (Thijssen 4,
Metgod 25,   Wark 32)*
Tol 40, Jonker 74)*

Ipswich Town won 5-4 on aggregate

1981–82 FINAL (2 legs)

May 5 – Nya Ullevi, Gothenburg
IFK Göteborg 1-0 Hamburger SV
(Sweden)   (West Germany)
*(Tord Holmgren
87)*

May 19 – Volksparkstadion, Hamburg
Hamburger SV 0-3 IFK Göteborg
*(Nilsson 6,
Corneliusson 26,
Fredriksson 63)*

IFK Göteborg won 4-0 on aggregate

1982–83 FINAL (2 legs)

May 4 – Heysel, Brussels
RSC Anderlecht 1-0 Benfica
(Belgium)   (Portugal)
(Brylle 29)

May 18 – Estadio da Luz, Lisbon
Benfica 1-1 RSC Anderlecht
(Sheu 36)   *(Lozana 38)*

RSC Anderlecht won 2-1 on aggregate

1983–84 FINAL (2 legs)

May 9 – Parc Astrid, Brussels
RSC Anderlecht 1-1 Tottenham
(Belgium)   Hotspur
(Olsen 85)   (England)
                (Miller 57)

May 23 – White Hart Lane, London
Tottenham 1-1 RSC Anderlecht
Hotspur   *(Czerniatynski 60)*
(Roberts 84)
(after extra time)

Tottenham Hotspur won 4-3 on pens

1984–85 FINAL (2 legs)

May 8 – Sostol, Székesfehérvár
Videoton 0-3 Real Madrid
(Hungary)   (Spain)
                *(Michel 31,
                Santillana 77,
                Valdano 89)*

May 22 – Santiago Bernabeu, Madrid
Real Madrid 0-1 Videoton
                (Majer 86)

Real Madrid won 3-1 on aggregate

1985–86 FINAL (2 legs)

April 30 – Santiago Bernabeu, Madrid
Real Madrid 5-1 1. FC Köln
(Spain)   (West Germany)
(Sanchez 38,   (Allofs 29)
Gordillo 42,
Valdano 51, 84,
Santillana 89)*

May 6 – Olympiastadion, Berlin
1. FC Köln 2-0 Real Madrid
*(Bein 22,
Geilenkirchen 72)*

Real Madrid won 5-3 on aggregate

1986–87 FINAL (2 legs)

May 6 – Nya Ullevi, Gothenburg
IFK Göteborg 1-0 Dundee
(Sweden)   United
(Pettersson 38)   (Scotland)

May 20 – Tannadice Park, Dundee
Dundee 1-1 IFK Göteborg
United   *(Nilsson 22)*
(Clark 60)

IFK Göteborg won 2-1 on aggregate

1987–88 FINAL (2 legs)

May 4 – Sarria, Barcelona
RCD Español 3-0 Bayer
(Spain)   Leverkusen
*(Losada 45, 56,   (West Germany)
Soler 49)*

May 18 – Haberland Stadion, Leverkusen
Bayer 3-0 RCD Español
Leverkusen
*(Tita 57,
Götz 63,
Cha Bumkun 81)*
(after extra time)

Bayer Leverkusen won 3-2 on pens

1988–89 FINAL (2 legs)

May 3 – San Paolo, Naples
Napoli 2-1 VfB Stuttgart
(Italy)   (West Germany)
(Maradona 68,   (Gaudino 17)
Careca 87)*

May 17 – Neckarstadion, Stuttgart
VfB Stuttgart 3-3 Napoli
*(Klinsmann 27,   (Alemo 18,
De Napoli o.g. 70,   Ferrara 39,
Schmäler 89)*   Careca 62)*

Napoli won 5-4 on aggregate

1989–90 FINAL (2 legs)

May 2 – Stadio Communale, Turin
Juventus 3-1 Fiorentina
(Italy)   (Italy)
(Galia 3,   (Buso 10)
Casiraghi 59,
De Agostini 73)*

May 16 – Partenio, Avellino
Fiorentina 0-0 Juventus

Juventus won 3-1 on aggregate

1990–91 FINAL (2 legs)

May 8 – Guiseppe Meazza, Milan
Internazionale 2-0 Roma
(Italy)   (Italy)
*(Mätthaus 55,
Berti 67)*

May 22 – Stadio Olimpico, Rome
Roma 1-0 Internazionale
(Rizzitelli 81)

Internazionale won 2-1 on aggregate

1991–92 FINAL (2 legs)

April 29 – Stadio Delle Alpi, Turin
Torino 2-2 Ajax
(Italy)   (Netherlands)
*(Casagrande   (Jonk 17,
65, 82)*   Pettersson 73)*

May 13 – Olympisch Stadion, Amsterdam
Ajax 0-0 Torino

Ajax won on away goals rule

1992–93 FINAL (2 legs)

May 5 – Westfalenstadion, Dortmund
Borussia 1-3 Juventus
Dortmund   (Italy)
(Germany)   *(D. Baggio 27,
(M. Rummenigge 2)*   R. Baggio 31, 74)*

May 19 – Delle Alpi, Turin
Juventus 3-0 Borussia
*(D. Baggio 5, 40,   Dortmund
Möller 65)*

Juventus won 6-1 on aggregate

1993–94 FINAL (2 legs)

April 26 – Ernst-Happel-Stadion, Vienna
Austria 0-1 Internazionale
Salzburg   (Italy)
(Austria)   *(Berti 35)*

May 11 – Guiseppe Meazza, Milan
Internazionale 1-0 Austria
(Jonk 63)   Salzburg

Internazionale won 2-0 on aggregate

1994–95 FINAL (2 legs)

May 3 – Tardini, Parma
Parma 1-0 Juventus
(Italy)   (Italy)
(D. Baggio 5)

May 17 – Guiseppe Meazza, Milan
Juventus 1-1 Parma
(Vialli 33)   *(D. Baggio 54)*

Parma won 2-1 on aggregate

1995–96 FINAL (2 legs)

May 1 – Olympia, Munich
Bayern 2-0 Girondins de
München   Bordeaux
(Germany)   (France)
*(Helmer 35,
Scholl 60)*

May 15 – Bordeaux
Girondins de 1-3 Bayern
Bordeaux   München
(Dutuel)   *(Scholl 53,
                Kostadinov 65,
                Klinsmann 79)*

Bayern München won 5-1 on aggregate

1996–97 FINAL (2 legs)

May 7 – Parkstadion, Gelsenkirchen
FC Schalke 04 1-0 Internazionale
(Germany)   (Italy)
(Wilmots 70)

May 21 – Giuseppe Meazza, Milan
Internazionale 1-0 FC Schalke 04
(Zamorano 84)
(after extra time)

FC Schalke 04 won 4-1 on pens

1997–98 FINAL

May 6 – Parc des Princes, Paris
Lazio 0-3 Internazionale
(Italy)   (Italy)
                *(Zamorano 5,
                Zanetti 60,
                Ronaldo 70)*

1998–99 FINAL

May 12 – Luzhniki, Moscow
Parma 3-0 Olympique
(Italy)   Marseille
*(Crespo 26,   (France)
Vanoli 36,
Chiesa 55)*

1999–2000 FINAL

May 17 – Parken, Copenhagen
Galatasaray 0-0 Arsenal
(Turkey)   (England)
(after extra time)

Galatasaray won 4-1 on pens

2000–01 FINAL

May 16 – Westfalenstadion, Dortmund
Liverpool 5-4 CD Alavés
(England)   (Spain)
*(Babbel 4,   (Alonzo 27,
Gerrard 16,   Moreno 48, 51,
McAllister 41 pen,   Cruyff 89)*
Fowler 73,
Gelí o.g. 116)*
(after extra time)

2001–02 FINAL

May 8 – De Kuip, Rotterdam
Feyenoord 3-2 Borussia
(Netherlands)   Dortmund
*(van Hooijdonk   (Germany)
33 pen, 40,   (Amoroso 47 pen,
Tomasson 50)*   Koller 58)*

2002–03 FINAL

May 21 – Olimpico, Seville
Celtic 2-3 FC Porto
(Scotland)   (Portugal)
(Larsson 47, 56)   (Derlei 45, 115,
                Alenitchev 54)*

THE UEFA CUP

The European Cup-Winners' Cup

TOURNAMENT OVERVIEW

WITH THE SUCCESS OF THE EUROPEAN CUP clear to all, and entry to the Fairs Cup initially restricted to certain cities, pressure built up for a further European club competition. The European Cup-Winners' Cup was officially set up in February 1960 at a meeting in Vienna, and was originated by the organizing committee of the now tiring Mittel Europa Cup. Based on the same format as the European Cup, the tournament was open to the winners of national knockout competitions (or losing finalists, if the winners were going to compete in the European Cup). Of course, not all European nations possessed a domestic cup, but with the establishment of the tournament, they all soon acquired one. Only ten teams entered the first tournament, which was won by Fiorentina, beating Glasgow Rangers 4-1 on aggregate – Italy's first European club triumph. The tournament was taken over and expanded by UEFA for the 1961–62 competition and that final saw Atlético Madrid beat champions Fiorentina 3-0 in a replay. In 1963, Atlético Madrid lost 5-1 to Tottenham Hotspur in a single match Final in Rotterdam.

Over the next ten years British clubs won the cup four times, German clubs twice, with Slovan Bratislava's victory over Barcelona in 1969 the first win for an Eastern European club in the competition. The rest of the 1970s saw further Eastern European success (1. FC Magdeburg, Dinamo Kiev) and RSC Anderlecht's run of three consecutive finals 1976–78 (of which the team won the first and last).

The late 1980s and 90s saw a much wider spread of teams getting to the Final, with some smaller clubs securing victory: Belgium's KV Mechelen beat Ajax in 1988, with Sampdoria beating RSC Anderlecht in 1990. Barcelona, winners in 1997, chose to enter the newly expanded Champions League the following year. This was perhaps the death knell for the tournament, whose significance appeared to be slipping. The final tournament was held in 1999 and won by Lazio before the whole show was wrapped up into the newly-expanded UEFA Cup.

West Ham captain *Bobby Moore shakes hands with TSV 1860 München's Rudi Brunnenmeier before the start of the 1965 European Cup-Winners' Cup Final at Wembley. West Ham won the cup with two goals in two minutes from Alan Sealey.*

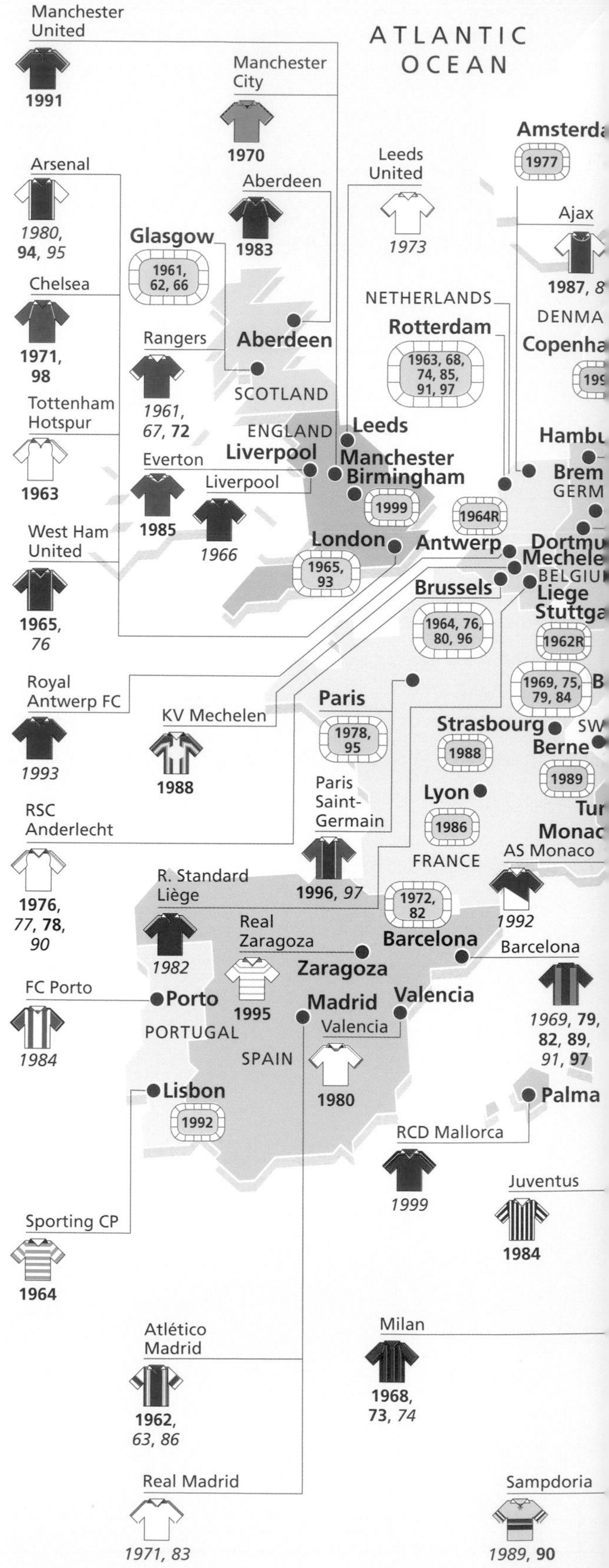

Manchester United
1991

Manchester City
1970

ATLANTIC OCEAN

Aberdeen
1983

Leeds United
1973

Amsterdam
1977

Arsenal
1980, 94, 95

Glasgow
1961, 62, 66

Ajax
1987, 8

NETHERLANDS

Chelsea
1971, 98

Rangers
1961, 67, 72

Aberdeen

Rotterdam
1963, 68, 74, 85, 91, 97

DENMARK
Copenhagen
199

SCOTLAND

Tottenham Hotspur
1963

ENGLAND
Liverpool

Leeds
Manchester
Birmingham

Hambu

Everton
1985

Liverpool
1966

1999

1964R

Brem
GERM

West Ham United
1965, 76

London
1965, 93

Antwerp

Dortmu
Mechele
BELGIU
Liege
Stuttga

Royal Antwerp FC
1993

KV Mechelen
1988

Paris
1978, 95

Brussels
1964, 76, 80, 96

1962R

1969, 75, 79, 84
B

RSC Anderlecht
1976, 77, 78, 90

Paris Saint-Germain
1996, *97*

Strasbourg
1988

SW

Berne
1989

R. Standard Liège
1982

Lyon
1986

Tur
Monac
AS Monaco
1992

FRANCE

FC Porto
1984

Real Zaragoza
1995

1972, 82

Barcelona

Barcelona
1969, 79, 82, 89, 91, **97**

Porto
PORTUGAL

Zaragoza

Madrid

Valencia

SPAIN

Valencia
1980

Lisbon
1992

RCD Mallorca
1999

Palma

Juventus
1984

Sporting CP
1964

Milan
1968, *73, 74*

Atlético Madrid
1962, *63, 86*

Sampdoria
1989, 90

Real Madrid
1971, 83

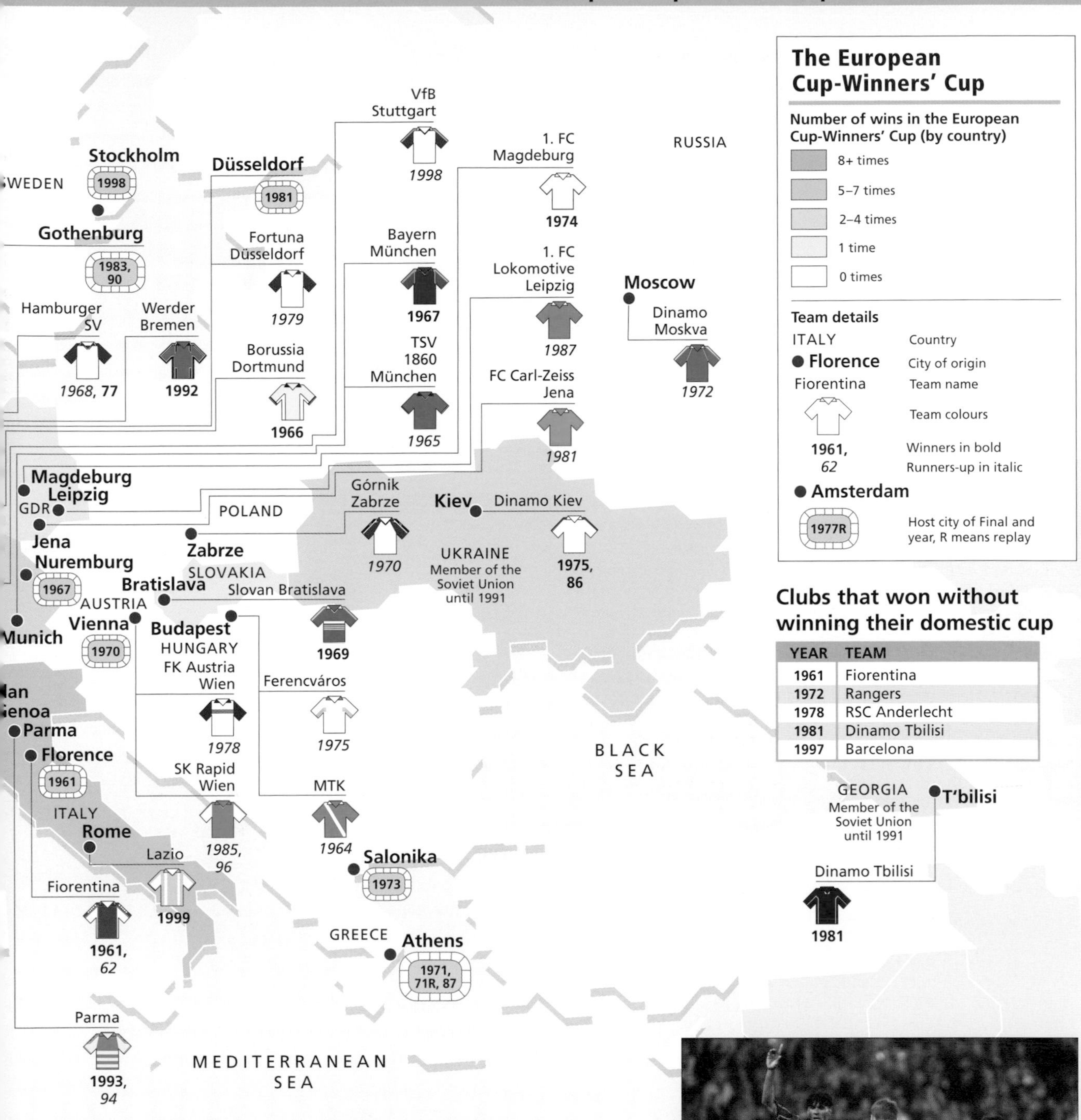

SWEDEN

Stockholm
1998

Gothenburg
1983, 90

Hamburger SV
1968, 77

Werder Bremen
1992

Düsseldorf
1981

Fortuna Düsseldorf
1979

Borussia Dortmund
1966

VfB Stuttgart
1998

Bayern München
1967

TSV 1860 München
1965

1. FC Magdeburg
1974

1. FC Lokomotive Leipzig
1987

FC Carl-Zeiss Jena
1981

RUSSIA

Moscow

Dinamo Moskva
1972

Magdeburg Leipzig
GDR

Jena Nuremburg
1967

AUSTRIA

Munich
1970

Vienna
1970

Budapest
HUNGARY
FK Austria Wien
1978

SK Rapid Wien
1985, 96

Ferencváros
1975

MTK
1964

POLAND

Zabrze

SLOVAKIA

Bratislava
Slovan Bratislava
1969

Górnik Zabrze
1970

Kiev   Dinamo Kiev
1975, 86

UKRAINE
Member of the Soviet Union until 1991

Salonika
1973

GREECE   **Athens**
1971, 71R, 87

BLACK SEA

Man Genoa

Parma

Florence
1961

ITALY

Rome
Lazio
1999

Fiorentina
1961, 62

Parma
1993, 94

MEDITERRANEAN SEA

The European Cup-Winners' Cup

Number of wins in the European Cup-Winners' Cup (by country)

	8+ times
	5–7 times
	2–4 times
	1 time
	0 times

Team details

ITALY	Country
● **Florence**	City of origin
Fiorentina	Team name
	Team colours
1961, *62*	Winners in bold / Runners-up in italic
● **Amsterdam**	
1977R	Host city of Final and year, R means replay

Clubs that won without winning their domestic cup

YEAR	TEAM
1961	Fiorentina
1972	Rangers
1978	RSC Anderlecht
1981	Dinamo Tbilisi
1997	Barcelona

GEORGIA
Member of the Soviet Union until 1991

● **T'bilisi**

Dinamo Tbilisi
1981

Consecutive participation

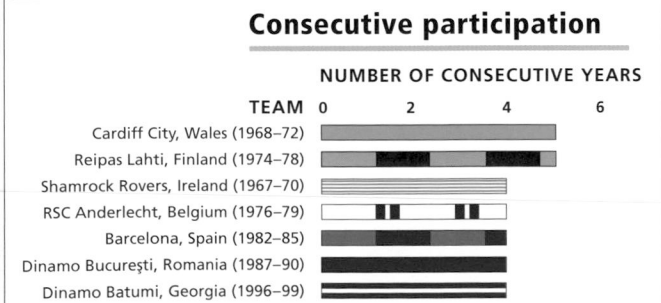

NUMBER OF CONSECUTIVE YEARS

TEAM   0   2   4   6

Cardiff City, Wales (1968–72)
Reipas Lahti, Finland (1974–78)
Shamrock Rovers, Ireland (1967–70)
RSC Anderlecht, Belgium (1976–79)
Barcelona, Spain (1982–85)
Dinamo Bucureşti, Romania (1987–90)
Dinamo Batumi, Georgia (1996–99)

Pavel Nedved *of Lazio strikes home the winning goal against Mallorca in the 81st minute of the last-ever Cup-Winners' Cup Final at Villa Park in Birmingham, England, in May 1999.*

The European Cup-Winners' Cup

THE CUP-WINNERS' CUP was the last of the major European tournaments to be established, and the first to be completely abandoned. It was first organized by UEFA in 1960–61, and ran for 39 years. The competition was open to the previous year's winners and the winners of national cup competitions. Throughout the whole of the tournament's history the same format was used: two-leg home and away rounds, with away goals counting double, and penalties to decide drawn matches. The final has always been a single match played at a neutral venue.

When the tournament was first created, many UEFA nations had no national cup competition, and if nothing else, the Cup-Winners' Cup ensured that knockout-format cup football would spread right across the continent. In its final years, preliminary rounds were introduced to produce 17 entrants from among the weaker footballing nations for a 32-club first round. Fourteen places were reserved for the strongest national leagues and one for the previous year's winner. The last Final was played in 1999. The cup has been effectively merged with the expanded UEFA cup, as national cup winners now enter that competition.

1960–61 FINAL (2 legs)
May 17 – Ibrox, Glasgow
Rangers **0-2** Fiorentina
(Scotland)   (Italy)
                    (Milani 12, 88)
h/t: 0-1 **Att:** 80,000
Ref: Steiner (Austria)

May 27 – Communale, Florence
Fiorentina **2-1** Rangers
(Milani 12,   Scott 60)
Hamrin 88)
h/t: 1-0 **Att:** 50,000
Ref: Hernadi (Hungary)

Fiorentina won 4-1 on aggregate

1961–62 FINAL
May 10 – Hampden Park, Glasgow
Atlético **1-1** Fiorentina
Madrid   (Italy)
(Spain)   (Hamrin 27)
(Peiro 11)
h/t: 1-1 **Att:** 27,000
Ref: Wharton (Scotland)

REPLAY
September 5 –
Neckarstadion, Stuttgart
Atlético **3-0** Fiorentina
Madrid
(Jones 8,
Mendoca 27,
Peiro 59)
h/t: 2-0 **Att:** 38,000
Ref: Tschenscher (West Germany)

1962–63 FINAL
May 15 – De Kuip, Rotterdam
Tottenham **5-1** Atlético
Hotspur   Madrid
(England)   (Spain)
(Greaves 16, 80,   Collar 47)
White 35,
Dyson 67, 85)
h/t: 2-0 **Att:** 49,000
Ref: Van Leuwen (Netherlands)

1963–64 FINAL
May 13 – Heysel, Brussels
Sporting CP **3-3** MTK
(Portugal)   (Hungary)
(Mascarenhas 40,   Sandor 18, 75,
Figueiredo 45, 80) Kuti 73)
(after extra time)
h/t: 2-1 **Att:** 30,000
Ref: Van Nuffel (Belgium)

REPLAY
May 15 – Bosuilstadion, Antwerp
Sporting CP **1-0** MTK
(Morais 19)
h/t: 1-0 **Att:** 19,000
Ref: Versyp (Belgium)

1964–65 FINAL
May 19 – Wembley, London
West Ham **2-0** TSV 1860
United   München
(England)   (West Germany)
(Sealey 70, 72)
h/t: 0-0 **Att:** 100,000
Ref: Zsolt (Hungary)

1965–66 FINAL
May 5 – Hampden Park, Glasgow
Borussia **2-1** Liverpool
Dortmund   (England)
(West Germany)   (Hunt 68)
(Held 62,
Libuda 109)
(after extra time)
h/t: 0-0 **90 mins:** 1-1
Att: 41,000 **Ref:** Schwinte (France)

1966–67 FINAL
May 31 – Frankenstadion, Nüremberg
Bayern **1-0** Rangers
München   (Scotland)
(West Germany)
(Roth 108)
(after extra time)
h/t: 0-0 **90 mins:** 0-0
Att: 69,000 **Ref:** Lo Bello (Italy)

1967–68 FINAL
May 23 – De Kuip, Rotterdam
Milan **2-0** Hamburger SV
(Italy)   (West Germany)
(Hamrin 3, 19)
h/t: 2-0 **Att:** 53,000
Ref: Ortiz (Spain)

1968–69 FINAL
May 21 – St Jakob, Basle
Slovan **3-2** Barcelona
Bratislava   (Spain)
(Czechoslovakia)   (Zaldua 16,
(Cvetler 2,   Rexach 52)
Hrivnak 30,
Jan Capkovic 42)
h/t: 3-1 **Att:** 19,000
Ref: Van Raven (Netherlands)

1969–70 FINAL
May 29 – Prater, Vienna
Manchester **2-1** Górnik
City   Zabrze
(England)   (Poland)
(Young 11,   (Oslizlo 70)
Lee 43)
h/t: 2-0 **Att:** 10,000
Ref: Schiller (Austria)

1970–71 FINAL
May 19 – Karaiskakis, Piraeus
Chelsea **1-1** Real Madrid
(England)   (Spain)
(Osgood 55)   (Zoco 30)
h/t: 0-0 **90 mins:** 1-1 **Att:** 42,000
Ref: Scheurer (Switzerland)

REPLAY
May 21 – Karaiskakis, Piraeus
Chelsea **2-1** Real Madrid
(Dempsey 31,   Fleitas 75)
Osgood 39)
h/t: 2-0 **Att:** 19,917
Ref: Bucheli (Switzerland)

1971–72 FINAL
May 24 – Nou Camp, Barcelona
Rangers **3-2** Dinamo
(Scotland)   Moskva
(Stein 23,   (Soviet Union)
Johnston 40, 49)   (Estrekov 60,
                   Makovikov 87)
h/t: 2-0 **Att:** 24,000
Ref: Ortiz (Spain)

1972–73 FINAL
May 16 – Kaftantzoglio, Salonica
Milan **1-0** Leeds United
(Italy)   (England)
(Chiarugi 5)
h/t: 1-0 **Att:** 45,000
Ref: Michas (Greece)

1973–74 FINAL
May 8 – De Kuip, Rotterdam
1. FC **2-0** Milan
Magdeburg   (Italy)
(East Germany)
(Lanzi o.g. 40,
Seguin 74)
h/t: 1-0 **Att:** 4,000
Ref: Van Gemert (Netherlands)

1974–75 FINAL
May 14 – St Jakob, Basle
Dinamo Kiev **3-0** Ferencváros
(Soviet Union)   (Hungary)
(Onischenko
18, 39,
Blokhin 67)
h/t: 2-0 **Att:** 10,000
Ref: Davidson (Scotland)

1975–76 FINAL
May 5 – Heysel, Brussels
RSC Anderlecht **4-2** West Ham
(Belgium)   United
(Rensenbrink   (England)
42, 73,   (Holland 28,
Van der Elst   Robson 68)
48, 87)
h/t: 1-1 **Att:** 58,000
Ref: Wurtz (France)

1976–77 FINAL
May 11 – Olympisch, Amsterdam
Hamburger SV **2-0** RSC Anderlecht
(West Germany)   (Belgium)
(Volkert 78,
Magath 88)
h/t: 0-0 **Att:** 66,000
Ref: Partridge (England)

1977–78 FINAL
May 3 – Parc des Princes, Paris
RSC Anderlecht **4-0** FK Austria
(Belgium)   Wien
(Rensenbrink   (Austria)
13, 41,
Van Binst 45, 80)
h/t: 2-1 **Att:** 48,000
Ref: Alginder (West Germany)

1978–79 FINAL
May 16 – St Jakob, Basle
Barcelona **4-3** Fortuna
(Spain)   Düsseldorf
(Sanchez 5,   (West Germany)
Asensi 34,   (K. Allofs 8,
Rexach 104,   Seel 41, 114)
Krankl 111)
(after extra time)
h/t: 2-2 **90 mins:** 2-2
Att: 58,000 **Ref:** Palotai (Hungary)

1979–80 FINAL

May 15 – Heysel, Brussels
Valencia 0-0 Arsenal
(Spain)   (England)
(after extra time)
h/t: 0-0 **90 mins:** 0-0
Att: 36,000
Ref: Christov (Czechoslovakia)
Valencia won 5-4 on pens

1980–81 FINAL

May 13 – Rheinstadion, Düsseldorf
Dinamo 2-1 FC Carl-Zeiss
Tbilisi   Jena
(Soviet Union)   (East Germany)
(Gutsayev 67,   (Hoppe 63)
Daraselia 86)
h/t: 0-0 **Att:** 9,000
Ref: Lattanzi (Italy)

1981–82 FINAL

May 12 – Nou Camp, Barcelona
Barcelona 2-1 R. Standard
(Spain)   **Liège**
(Simonsen 44,   (Belgium)
Quini 63)   (Vandersmissen 7)
h/t: 1-1 **Att:** 100,000
Ref: Eschweller (West Germany)

1982–83 FINAL

May 11 – Nya Ullevi, Gothenburg
Aberdeen 2-1 Real Madrid
(Scotland)   (Spain)
(Black 4,   (Juanito 15)
Hewitt 112)
(after extra time)
h/t: 1-1 **90 mins:** 1-1
Att: 17,000 **Ref:** Menegali (Italy)

1983–84 FINAL

May 16 – St Jakob, Basle
Juventus 2-1 FC Porto
(Italy)   (Portugal)
(Vignola 12,   (Sousa 29)
Boniek 41)
h/t: 2-1 **Att:** 60,000
Ref: Galler (Switzerland)

1984–85 FINAL

May 15 – De Kuip, Rotterdam
Everton 3-1 SK Rapid Wien
(England)   (Austria)
(Gray 57,   (Krankl 85)
Steven 72,
Sheedy 85)
h/t: 0-0 **Att:** 50,000
Ref: Casarin (Italy)

1985–86 FINAL

May 2 – Gerland, Lyon
Dinamo Kiev 3-0 Atlético
(Soviet Union)   **Madrid**
(Zavarov 4,   (Spain)
Blokhin 85,
Yevtushenko 87)
h/t: 1-0 **Att:** 50,000
Ref: Wohrer (Austria)

1986–87 FINAL

May 13 – Olympic, Athens
Ajax 1-0 1. FC
(Netherlands)   **Lokomotive**
(van Basten 21)   **Leipzig**
(East Germany)
h/t: 1-0 **Att:** 35,000
Ref: Agnolin (Italy)

1987–88 FINAL

May 11 – Meinau, Strasbourg
KV Mechelen 1-0 Ajax
(Belgium)   (Netherlands)
(Den Boer 53)
h/t: 0-0 **Att:** 40,000
Ref: Pauly (West Germany)

1988–89 FINAL

May 10 – Wankdorf, Berne
Barcelona 2-0 Sampdoria
(Spain)   (Italy)
(Salinas 4,
Rekarte 79)
h/t: 1-0 **Att:** 45,000
Ref: Courtney (England)

1989–90 FINAL

May 9 – Nya Ullevi, Gothenburg
Sampdoria 2-0 RSC Anderlecht
(Italy)   (Belgium)
(Vialli 105, 107)
(after extra time)
h/t: 0-0 **90 mins:** 0-0
Att: 20,000 **Ref:** Galler (Switzerland)

1990–91 FINAL

May 15 – De Kuip, Rotterdam
Manchester 2-1 Barcelona
United   (Spain)
(England)   (Koeman 79)
(Bruce 67,
Hughes 74)
h/t: 0-0 **Att:** 48,000
Ref: Karlsson (Sweden)

1991–92 FINAL

May 6 – Estadio da Luz, Lisbon
Werder Bremen 2-0 AS Monaco
(Germany)   (France)
(K. Allofs 41,
Rufer 54)
h/t: 1-0 **Att:** 15,000
Ref: D'Elia (Italy)

1992–93 FINAL

May 12 – Wembley, London
Parma 3-1 Royal
(Italy)   **Antwerp FC**
(Minotti 9,   (Belgium)
Melli 30,   (Severeyns 11)
Cuoghi 83)
h/t: 2-1 **Att:** 37,000
Ref: Assenmacher (Germany)

1993–94 FINAL

May 4 – Park Stadion, Copenhagen
Arsenal 1-0 Parma
(England)   (Italy)
(Smith 19)
h/t: 1-0 **Att:** 33,765
Ref: Krondl (Czechoslovakia)

1994–95 FINAL

May 10 – Parc des Princes, Paris
Real Zaragoza 2-1 Arsenal
(Spain)   (England)
(Esnaider 68,   (Hartson 77)
Nayim 119)
(after extra time)
h/t: 0-0 **90 mins:** 1-1
Att: 42,424 **Ref:** Ceccarini (Italy)

1995–96 FINAL

May 8 – King Baudoui, Brussels
Paris Saint- 1-0 SK Rapid
Germain   Wien
(France)   (Austria)
(N'Gotty 28)
h/t: 1-0 **Att:** 37,500
Ref: Pairetto (Italy)

1996–97 FINAL

May 14 – De Kuip, Rotterdam
Barcelona 1-0 Paris Saint-
(Spain)   **Germain**
(Ronaldo 37 pen)   (France)
h/t: 1-0 **Att:** 50,000
Ref: Merk (Germany)

1997–98 FINAL

May 13 – Rasunda, Stockholm
Chelsea 1-0 VfB Stuttgart
(England)   (Germany)
(Zola 71)
h/t: 0-0 **Att:** 30,216
Ref: Braschi (Italy)

1998–99 FINAL

May 19 – Villa Park, Birmingham
Lazio 2-1 RCD Mallorca
(Italy)   (Spain)
(Vieri 7,   (Dani 11)
Nedved 81)
h/t: 1-1 **Att:** 33,000
Ref: Benko (Austria)

The 1982–83 European Cup-Winners' Cup Final was played in Gothenburg, Sweden, in appalling weather conditions. Both Real Madrid and Aberdeen scored in the first 15 minutes, but the match was level after 90. In the 112th minute, Aberdeen's substitute John Hewitt dived forward to head the ball past the Real keeper and clinch the cup for the only time in the Scottish club's history.

England

THE SEASON IN REVIEW 2002–03

WHILE IT WAS A YEAR IN WHICH the quality of play and the intensity of competition at the top of English football were gratifying, it was not a year of surprises. As ever the opening weeks threw up a rogue leader and, astonishingly enough, this year it was Tottenham who held the lead for four weeks before beginning its inevitable slide into mid-table mediocrity. Spurs has finished every one of the last 12 seasons outside the top six and the bottom six and this year was no different. The lead passed first to Arsenal, who were playing by far the best football in the league. In fact, the team was so good that manager Arsène Wenger began to speculate as to whether it might go the entire season unbeaten. But despite breaking the club's record for runs of unbeaten and scoring games, Arsenal finally succumbed at Everton when, a week before his 17th birthday, Wayne Rooney stepped up with a fantastic long-range shot to beat them 2-1. It was a game that demonstrated the huge strides Everton have taken under David Moyes.

Liverpool go up and down again

As Arsenal faltered in early November, Liverpool beat West Ham 2-0 and moved seven points clear at the top. The team would not win another game in the league until late January, by which time it had departed the FA Cup, the Champions League and abandoned all hope of the title. Michael Owen hit a barren stretch, the team looked disjointed, and its lack of width exposed a paucity of attacking options. Worse, Manchester United's 2-1 victory at Anfield in December announced its steady rise up the table after an uncharacteristically poor autumn, and demonstrated the poor form of Liverpool's troubled keeper Jerzy Dudek.

Final Premier League Table 2002–03

CLUB	P	W	D	L	F	A	Pts	
Manchester United	38	25	8	5	74	34	**83**	Champions League
Arsenal	38	23	9	6	85	44	**78**	Champions League
Newcastle United	38	21	6	11	63	48	**69**	Champions League
Chelsea	38	19	10	9	68	38	**67**	Champions League
Liverpool	38	18	10	10	61	41	**64**	UEFA Cup
Blackburn Rovers	38	16	12	10	52	43	**60**	UEFA Cup
Everton	38	17	8	13	48	49	**59**	
Southampton	38	13	13	12	43	46	**52**	UEFA Cup
Manchester City	38	15	6	17	47	54	**51**	UEFA Cup (Fair Play)
Tottenham Hotspur	38	14	8	16	51	62	**50**	
Middlesbrough	38	13	10	15	48	44	**49**	
Charlton Athletic	38	14	7	17	35	49	**49**	
Birmingham City	38	13	9	16	41	49	**48**	
Fulham	38	13	9	16	41	50	**48**	
Leeds United	38	14	5	19	58	57	**47**	
Aston Villa	38	12	9	17	42	47	**45**	
Bolton Wanderers	38	10	14	14	42	51	**44**	
West Ham United	38	10	12	16	42	59	**42**	Relegated
West Bromwich Albion	38	6	8	24	29	65	**26**	Relegated
Sunderland	38	4	7	27	21	65	**19**	Relegated

Promoted clubs: Portsmouth, Leicester City, Wolverhampton Wanderers.

Why did I take this job? Terry Venables feels for his wallet as Leeds' season disintegrates around him.

Steve Cotterill checks it's really happening: Sunderland scrapes a point with a 0-0 draw against Liverpool. Howard Wilkinson tries to take it all in.

Damien Duff brought confident and direct running to Blackburn's excellent season and plenty of gossip to the transfer market. Here he leaves United's Phil Neville sprawling.

Above: Gianfranco Zola, deservedly voted best foreign player in the first decade of the Premiership, showed magnificent form for Chelsea throughout the season with invention, intelligence and grace on the ball.

Above, right: Shaun Goater made Manchester City fans' dreams come true with the winner against United at Maine Road in November.

Below: The Mersey derby gets nasty. Steven Gerrard's season was as varied as Liverpool's with raking long-range passes, searing shots and two-footed studs-up challenges. Gary Naysmith feels the impact of the latter.

Below, right: Gordon Strachan reminds Southampton where the opposition's goal is. Strachan brought the best out of the Saints, but without James Beattie's goals the team was dangerously short of attacking options.

Wayne Rooney and the whole of Goodison Park celebrate. Rooney's curling shot and goal for Everton ended Arsenal's record unbeaten run and announced the arrival of a singular new talent.

Liverpool was not the only side to have a bad autumn. Leeds, under Terry Venables, lost five out of six league games, departed the UEFA Cup and began its long and torrid flirtation with relegation. Although the club would avoid the drop, neither Venables nor chairman Peter Risdale survived the dismantling of the squad, angry fans and very disappointed shareholders. To prove the point that it's not just about money, Aston Villa, under Graham Taylor, plodded through the season and achieved the same number of points spending nothing. One wonders what will happen now that David O'Leary, responsible for spending all that money at Leeds, has taken over at Villa Park.

A familiar look

After Christmas, the table assumed a familiar look: Arsenal led by five points from Chelsea and Manchester United. Newcastle, Everton and Liverpool all looked to be in the hunt for a Champions League spot. In mid-table were all the usual suspects: Blackburn, Southampton, Spurs, Middlesbrough, Charlton and Manchester City. Of the newly promoted sides Keegan's City had always looked the most likely to stay up and its derby day defeat of Manchester United proved its worth. Birmingham, by contrast, had looked less likely survivors. But at the halfway stage the team was above the bottom four and Steve Bruce shrewdly reinforced the squad – Christoph Dugarry, among others, arriving from Bordeaux. It was money well spent and Birmingham finished higher than rivals Aston Villa for the first time in years.

West Ham began the new year at the bottom of the table. Bolton, Sunderland and West Brom were keeping them very close company. Over the spring, it became clear that Sunderland, despite three coaching changes, was going down, and did so with a record low number of Premiership points. West Brom, though more spirited, fared little better, but both Bolton and West Ham staged recoveries, duelling for the final safe spot until the very last day of the season. West Ham's penultimate match saw them beat Chelsea 1-0 to give themselves a chance, but Bolton, inspired by the mercurial Jay-Jay Okocha, won its final game at home to Middlesbrough and West Ham was down with a record points score for a relegated team.

ENGLAND

Left: Everyone wondered if he really had the heart for a lower table slog, but Christoph Dugarry won the hearts of Birmingham fans and helped keep them safely up.

Right: Ivan Campo and his hair settled in the Bolton defence. A rare shot on goal flies past Liverpool's Dudek to give Bolton three precious points.

Below: Craig Bellamy gave real depth to Newcastle's already strong attacking options. But his temperament, discipline and extra-curricular activities did not.

Race for the Championship

'Arsenal must still be considered the best team in the country.'
Arsène Wenger

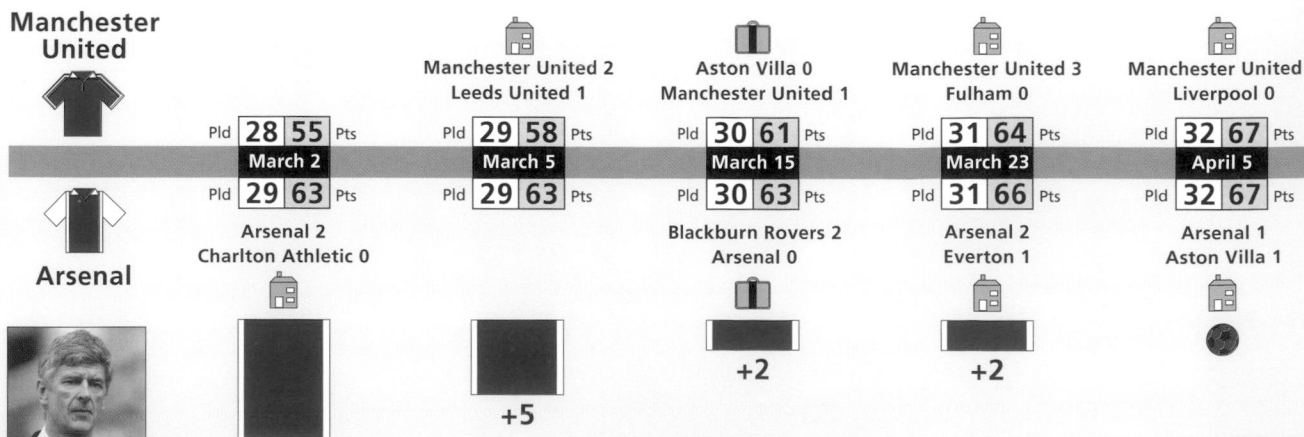

Manchester United

	Manchester United 2 Leeds United 1	Aston Villa 0 Manchester United 1	Manchester United 3 Fulham 0	Manchester United 4 Liverpool 0
Pld **28** **55** Pts **March 2**	Pld **29** **58** Pts **March 5**	Pld **30** **61** Pts **March 15**	Pld **31** **64** Pts **March 23**	Pld **32** **67** Pts **April 5**
Pld **29** **63** Pts	Pld **29** **63** Pts	Pld **30** **63** Pts	Pld **31** **66** Pts	Pld **32** **67** Pts
Arsenal 2 Charlton Athletic 0		Blackburn Rovers 2 Arsenal 0	Arsenal 2 Everton 1	Arsenal 1 Aston Villa 1

Arsenal

+8   +5   +2   +2

Above: Arsenal at its best: Patrick Vieira led this merciless demolition of Manchester City, but the team's edge seemed to desert them right at the end of the season.

Far left: Glenn Roeder squints as West Ham struggle. The pressure finally got to him when with three games to go he was incapacitated by a stroke.

Left, middle: Business as usual. David Elleray's last season in the Premiership included the fractious Birmingham Derby, in which he indulged in several bookings and a number of sendings-off.

Left: Still going strong at 70. Manager Bobby Robson declared that his Newcastle squad is the strongest he has ever coached.

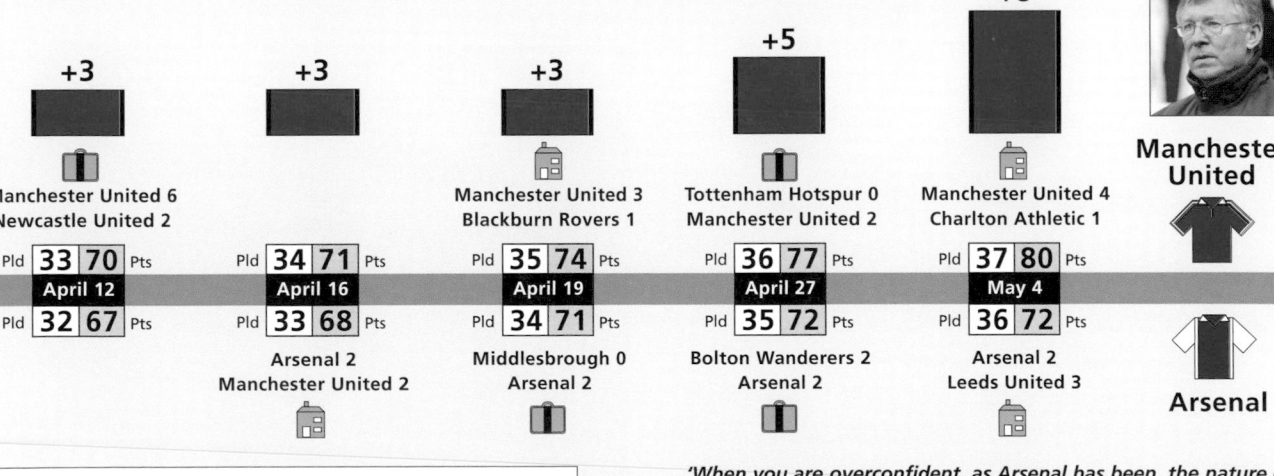

+3	**+3**	**+3**	**+5**	**+8**

Manchester United

Manchester United 6 Newcastle United 2	Manchester United 3 Blackburn Rovers 1	Tottenham Hotspur 0 Manchester United 2	Manchester United 4 Charlton Athletic 1

Pld **33** **70** Pts	Pld **34** **71** Pts	Pld **35** **74** Pts	Pld **36** **77** Pts	Pld **37** **80** Pts
April 12	**April 16**	**April 19**	**April 27**	**May 4**
Pld **32** **67** Pts	Pld **33** **68** Pts	Pld **34** **71** Pts	Pld **35** **72** Pts	Pld **36** **72** Pts

Arsenal 2 Manchester United 2	Middlesbrough 0 Arsenal 2	Bolton Wanderers 2 Arsenal 2	Arsenal 2 Leeds United 3

Arsenal

Key

🏠 Home   💼 Away   ⚽ Ahead on goal difference   **+2** Points clear

'When you are overconfident, as Arsenal has been, the nature of football is that it will come back and kick you in the teeth... the bottom line is that Arsenal has not won the Premiership yet.'
Alex Ferguson

ENGLAND

Last minute charge fails to materialize

In the final run-in, there were whispers of a last-minute charge by the constantly improving Newcastle United under Bobby Robson. With Alan Shearer, Craig Bellamy and Shola Ameobi all scoring, and an exciting midfield including Hugo Viana (when fit), Kieron Dyer and Jermaine Jenas, Newcastle deserved its third place. But a crushing defeat by Manchester United in April put paid to any lingering title hopes. Chelsea never even hinted at a title run, although undoubtedly possessing the class to trouble the leaders and with Zola in extraordinary form, the team still flattered to deceive. Inconsistency and lack of concentration bedevilled them. Inevitably it came down to a two-horse race. On the weekend of the League Cup Final when Liverpool beat Manchester United 2-0, Arsenal beat Charlton by the same scoreline and took an eight-point lead at the top of the table. But if United's task seemed hopeless, European form gave a clue to the future. Arsenal was squeezed out of the Champions League second group stage with a series of insipid home draws, while United progressed easily to the quarter-finals only to meet its nemesis Real Madrid in the tie of the tournament. United went out, but the team's attacking brio and spirit was unmistakable.

Finally, in a relentless two-month charge, the pendulum swung Manchester United's way. By the time the team met Arsenal in April, United had stolen a three-point lead as Arsenal threw points away at Blackburn and Villa. Although Arsenal had a game in hand and held United in a pulsating 2-2 draw at Highbury, it had conceded the advantage. United pressed it home as a seemingly incapacitated Arsenal squad surrendered the lead at Bolton and capitulated at home to Leeds in early May. United, eight points ahead and a game to go, won its eighth title in 11 years. Arsenal's victory over Southampton in the FA Cup Final was cold comfort for a club with such high expectations.

Above, top: And that's another one. Ruud van Nistelrooy's 25 goals topped the Premiership scoring list.

Above: Jermaine Jenas's fabulous shot against Manchester United tries to break the net. Newcastle's Jenas was voted PFA Young Player of the Season.

League Cup

2002–03 FINAL
March 2 – Millennium Stadium, Cardiff
Liverpool 2-0 Manchester
(Gerrard 39, United
Owen 86)
h/t: 1-0 **Att:** 74,500
Ref: P. Durkin

FA Cup

2002–03 FINAL
May 17 – Millennium Stadium, Cardiff
Arsenal 1-0 Southampton
(Pires 38)
h/t: 1-0 **Att:** 73,726
Ref: G. Barber

International Club Performances 2002–03

CLUB	COMPETITION	PROGRESS
Arsenal	Champions League	Group Phase 2
Liverpool	Champions League	Group Phase 1
	UEFA Cup	Quarter-finals
Manchester United	Champions League	Quarter-finals
Newcastle United	Champions League	Group Phase 2
Blackburn Rovers	UEFA Cup	2nd Round
Chelsea	UEFA Cup	1st Round
Fulham	UEFA Cup	3rd Round
Ipswich Town	UEFA Cup	2nd Round
Leeds United	UEFA Cup	3rd Round

Top Goalscorers 2002–03

PLAYER	CLUB	NATIONALITY	GOALS
Ruud van Nistelrooy	Manchester United	Dutch	25
Thierry Henry	Arsenal	French	24
James Beattie	Southampton	English	23
Mark Viduka	Leeds United	Australian	20
Michael Owen	Liverpool	English	19

Wenger admits defeat – shake hands and make up? Arsenal and United draw with six games to go. It's really hard to know what Wenger and Ferguson have to talk about.

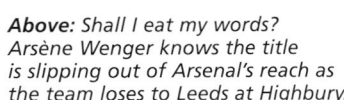

The £10 million goal. Jesper Gronkjaer runs the length of the pitch as his goal seals Chelsea's last day win over Liverpool and a place in the Champions League.

Above: Shall I eat my words? Arsène Wenger knows the title is slipping out of Arsenal's reach as the team loses to Leeds at Highbury.

Below: The mercurial Paolo Di Canio was injured or sidelined for much of the season at West Ham. It all ended in tears.

Below, left: Jay Jay Okocha brought a little magic to Bolton's hard-running scrapping game – it was enough to keep them up.

Below, bottom: Robert Pires slots the ball away for the only goal of the FA Cup Final.

Thierry Henry shows poise and balance on the ball as he scores in Arsenal's 2-2 draw with United at Highbury.

Here we go again. It's now eight out of 11 Premiership titles for Manchester United.

2002   2003

ENGLAND

Association Football in England

1846: Cambridge Rules drawn up — 1845

1850

1863: Formation of FA. First game under new rules played 19 December, Richmond v Barnes, drawn 0-0 — 1855 / 1860

1865

 **1870:** First unofficial international, v Scotland, drawn 1-1, venue: London — 1870

1872: First FA Cup Final First official international, v Scotland, drawn 0-0, venue: Partick — 1875

1880

1885: Professionalism legalized — 1885

1888: First league championship — 1890

1892: Second Division established — 1895

1900

1905: Affiliation to FIFA — 1905

1910

1923: Wembley Stadium opened and hosts its first FA Cup Final — 1915

1924: Reaffiliation to FIFA — 1925

1928: Resigned from FIFA — 1930

1935

1946: Reaffiliation to FIFA — 1940

1949: Burnden Park, Bolton, 33 die and 500 injured in terrace crush — 1945

1954: Affiliation to UEFA — 1950 / 1955

1961: League Cup first played — 1960

1969: Women's Football Association formed — 1965

1970: FA ban on women's teams lifted — 1970

1975

1989: Hillsborough disaster, 95 killed by crushing. Taylor report calls for all-seater stadiums — 1980 / 1985

1991: Ban on English clubs in Europe lifted — 1990

1992: Premier League breaks away from FA — 1995

1993: WFA dissolved. Women's football incorporated into FA — 2000

2005

English football's finest hour – Bobby Moore holds up the 1966 World Cup.

Key

 International football

⚽ Affiliation to FIFA

⚽ Affiliation to UEFA

♀ Women's football

War

Disaster

1916–19: Seasons cancelled for war

1920: Resigned from FIFA. Third Division established

1921: English Ladies' FA founded. FA bans women's teams from FA member grounds. Fourth Division added, bottom division renamed Third Division North and South

1940–46: Football reduced to regional leagues for duration of war

1953: England beaten 6-3 at Wembley by Hungary

1958: Third Division North and South became Third and Fourth Divisions

1966: England hosts and wins World Cup

1972: First women's international, v Scotland, won 3-2, venue: Greenock

1983: WFA affiliated to FA

1985: Bradford fire, 56 killed. Heysel disaster, 39 killed after crowd disturbances, Liverpool v Juventus, European Cup Final. Beginning of five-year ban on English clubs in European football

2002: Demolition of Wembley Stadium begins

England: The main clubs

Arsenal 1886 — Team name with year of formation

● Club formed before 1912

★ Founder members of League (1888)

Champions (1888–1915)

Champions (1920–39)

Originated from a military institution

Originated from a cricket club

Originated from a school or college

Teachers' Association

Originated from a hockey club

Singers Cycle factory

Railway workers

Salter's Spring Works

Thames Ironworks

† Originated from a church

Originated from a rugby club

★ **Blackburn Rovers** 1875

★ **Bolton Wanderers** 1874
Christ Church (1874–77)

★ **Preston North End** 1881

Blackpool 1881
Formed after the break-up of Blackpool St. John's club Combined with South Shore (1899)

Blackpool ●

Liverpool 1892

Tranmere Rovers 1884
Belmont AFC (1884–85)

★ **Everton** 1878
St Domingo (1878–79)

Liverpool ◎

Crewe Alexan... 18...

Manchester City 1887
Ardwick FC (1887–94) Amalgamation of West Gorton and Gorton Athletic

Manchester United 1878
Newton Heath LYR (1878–80), Newton Heath (1880–1902)

Stockport County 1883
Heaton Norris Rovers (1883–88), Heaton Norris (1888–90)

★ **Stoke City** 1863
Stoke Ramblers (1868–70), Stoke (1870–1925)

★ **Derby County** 1884

★ **Wolverhampton Wanderers** 1879
Merger of St Lukes (1877) and Wanderers Cricket Club

★ **West Bromwich Albion** 1879
West Bromwich Strollers (1878–81)

E N G L A N D

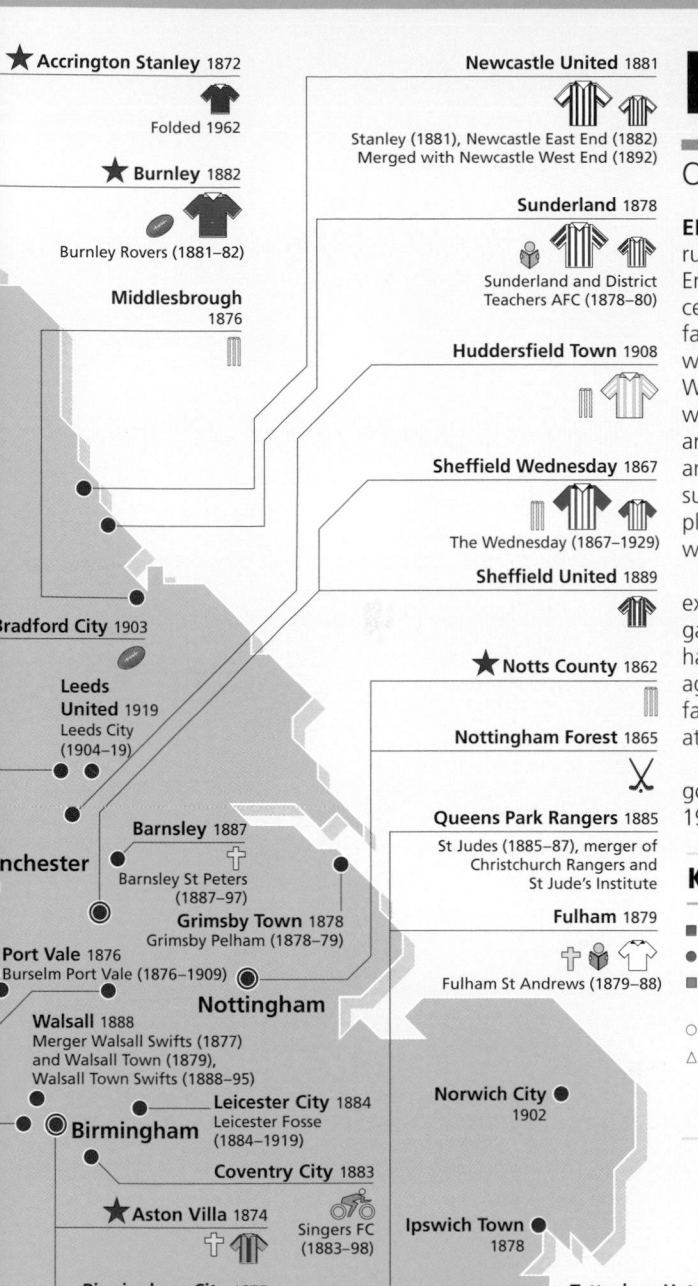

★ **Accrington Stanley** 1872

Folded 1962

★ **Burnley** 1882

Burnley Rovers (1881–82)

Middlesbrough 1876

Bradford City 1903

Leeds United 1919
Leeds City (1904–19)

Barnsley 1887
Barnsley St Peters (1887–97)

anchester

Grimsby Town 1878
Grimsby Pelham (1878–79)

Port Vale 1876
Burselm Port Vale (1876–1909)

Nottingham

Walsall 1888
Merger Walsall Swifts (1877) and Walsall Town (1879), Walsall Town Swifts (1888–95)

Leicester City 1884
Leicester Fosse (1884–1919)

Birmingham

Coventry City 1883

★ **Aston Villa** 1874

Singers FC (1883–98)

Birmingham City 1875

Small Heath Alliance (1875), Small Heath (1888), Birmingham (1905–45)

windon Town 1881

Watford 1881
Watford Rovers (1881–93), West Herts (1893–98), 1898 absorbed Watford St Mary's

Southampton 1885
Southampton St Mary's (1885–97)

Portsmouth 1898

West Ham United 1895

Thames Ironworks (1895–1900)

London

Newcastle United 1881

Stanley (1881), Newcastle East End (1882) Merged with Newcastle West End (1892)

Sunderland 1878

Sunderland and District Teachers AFC (1878–80)

Huddersfield Town 1908

Sheffield Wednesday 1867

The Wednesday (1867–1929)

Sheffield United 1889

★ **Notts County** 1862

Nottingham Forest 1865

Queens Park Rangers 1885

St Judes (1885–87), merger of Christchurch Rangers and St Jude's Institute

Fulham 1879

Fulham St Andrews (1879–88)

Norwich City 1902

Ipswich Town 1878

Tottenham Hotspur 1882

Hotspurs FC (1882–84)

Arsenal 1886

Dial Square (1886), Royal Arsenal (1886–91), Woolwich Arsenal (1891–1914)

Wimbledon 1889

Wimbledon Old Centrals (1899–1905)

Crystal Palace 1905

Charlton Athletic 1905

Chelsea 1905

England

ORIGINS AND GROWTH OF FOOTBALL

ENGLISH FOOTBALL EMERGED from the coincidence of a rural folk football tradition and the sporting enthusiasm of England's upper-class public schools. Team games became a central part of the culture of these schools and football was the favourite sport. The wide variety of rules of the game at the time were settled with the formation of the world's first FA (1863). While many of the earliest clubs grew out of these schools, they were soon joined by clubs founded by works' teams, churches and boys' clubs from the industrial cities of the West Midlands and Lancashire. The amateur traditions of the south were surpassed in the 1880s by the alliance of working-class fans and players and middle-class directors leading to the creation of the world's first professional league in 1888.

Before the First World War all of today's leading clubs were in existence. However, the security of a hugely popular domestic game left England uninterested in international football. England had reluctantly joined FIFA in 1905 but withdrew in 1920 and again in 1928. The illusion of English dominance was crushed by failure at the 1950 World Cup and a 6-3 thrashing by Hungary at Wembley in 1953.

Pride was partly restored by World Cup victory in 1966 and a good record in Europe for English clubs in the 1970s and early 1980s. But the process of catch up seems to continue unabated.

ENGLAND

Key

- ■ World Cup host
- ● World Cup winner
- ■ European Championships host
- ○ Competition winner
- △ Competition runner-up

Villa – Aston Villa
B'ham – Birmingham City

Ipswich – Ipswich Town
Leeds – Leeds United
Lon XI – London Select XI
L'pool – Liverpool
Man C – Manchester City
Man U – Manchester United
N'castle – Newcastle United
Notts F – Nottingham Forest
Spurs – Tottenham Hotspur
West H – West Ham United
Wolves – Wolverhampton Wanderers

International Competitions

	European Cup	UEFA Cup	European Cup-Winners' Cup
1958:		△ Lon XI	
1960:		△ B'ham	
1961:		△ B'ham	
1963:			○ Spurs
1965:			○ West H
1966: ● ■			
1967:		△ Leeds	△ L'pool
1968:	○ Man U	△ Leeds	
1969:		○ N'castle	
1970:		○ Arsenal	○ Man C
1971:		○ Leeds	○ Chelsea
1972:		○ Spurs	△ Wolves
1973:		○ L'pool	△ Spurs
1974:			
1975:		△ Leeds	△ Leeds
1976:		○ L'pool	
1977:	○ L'pool		△ West H
1978:	○ L'pool		
1979:	○ Notts F		
1980:	○ Notts F		△ Arsenal
1981:	○ L'pool	○ Ipswich	
1982:	○ Villa		
1984:	○ L'pool	○ Spurs	
1985:		△ L'pool	○ Everton
1991:			○ Man U
1994:			○ Arsenal
1995:			△ Arsenal
1996: ■			
1998:			○ Chelsea
1999:	○ Man U		
2000:		△ Arsenal	
2001:		○ L'pool	

ENGLAND

Port Vale (1950–)
VALE PARK
22,546
A53

HANLEY
Birthplace of Stanley Matthews

VICTORIA GROUND

STOKE-ON-TRENT

BRITANNIA STADIUM
24,050

Stoke City (1878–1997)

Stoke City (1997–)

A34

A50

RECREATION GROUND

Port Vale (1913–1950)

Sir Stanley Matthews was born in Hanley, Stoke-on-Trent on 1 February 1915. He retired 50 years later. He is rightly regarded as the first great footballer of the modern era.

A518

The Midlands

22,350 — Capacity of stadium

Stadium no longer in use for top-flight football

Cricket ground

Team colours

M8 — Motorway

A82 — Major road

1900 — Champions

2000 — Runners-up

DERBY COUNTY 1884

League	*1896*, **1930**, *36*, **72**, **75**
FA Cup	*1898, 99, 1903*, **46**

Derby County (1997–)

THE BASEBALL GROUND

PRIDE PARK
33,597

Derby County (1895–1997)

DERBY

THE RACECOURSE GROUND

Derby County (1884–95)
Venue for the first FA Cup Final replay in 1886 between Blackburn Rovers and West Bromwich Albion

Burton Wanderers

BURTON UPON TRENT

DERBY TURN

PEEL CROFT

Members of the Football League 1894–97

FA NATIONAL TRAINING CENTRE
Currently under construction

Burton Swifts

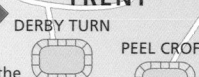

Members of the Football League 1892–1901

Burton United

Members of the Football League 1901–07. Merger of Burton Swifts and Burton Wanderers

STOKE CITY 1863

League Cup	*1964*, **72**

ASTON VILLA 1874

League	**1889**, **94**, **96**, **97**, *99*, **1900**, *03*, **08**, **10**, *11*, **13**, **14**, **31**, *33*, **81**, *90*, *93*
FA Cup	**1887**, *92*, **95**, **97**, **1905**, **13**, **20**, **24**, *57*, **2000**
League Cup	**1961**, *63*, **71**, **75**, **77**, **94**, *96*
European Cup	**1982**
World Club Cup	*1982*

BIRMINGHAM CITY 1875

FA Cup	*1931, 56*
League Cup	**1963**, *2001*
Fairs Cup	*1960, 61*

A51

WOLVERHAMPTON WANDERERS 1879

League	*1938, 39, 50*, **54**, **55**, **58**, **59**, **60**
FA Cup	**1889**, **93**, **96**, *1908, 21, 39*, **49**, **60**
League Cup	**1974**, **80**
UEFA Cup	*1972*

A5

Wolverhampton Wanderers

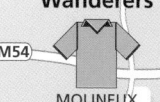

M54

MOLINEUX
28,525

WOLVERHAMPTON

M6

Walsall

BESCOT STADIUM
9,400

WALSALL

Aston Villa

VILLA PARK
39,217

WEST BROMWICH

SALTER'S SPRING WORKS
West Bromwich Albion started as the works' team here. Originally called West Bromwich Strollers

THE HAWTHORNS
25,400

M5

A458

DUDLEY

West Bromwich Albion

VILLA PARK

39,217	**Club:** Aston Villa
	Built: 1897
	Rebuilt: 1971, 1994
	Record Attendance: 76,588 Aston Villa v Derby County, FA Cup Sixth Round, 2 Feb 1946
	Significant Matches: 1966 World Cup: two matches; 1996 European Championships: three matches; European Cup-Winners' Cup Final: 1999

M6

BIRMINGHAM

ST. ANDREWS
30,200

Birmingham City

SOLIHULL

M42

A452

Coventry City

SINGER'S BICYCLE FACTORY
Coventry City was founded as a works team here called Singers FC

M6

HIGHFIELD ROAD
23,611

COVENTRY

COVENTRY CITY 1883

FA Cup	**1987**

WEST BROMWICH ALBION 1879

League	**1920**, *25*, **54**
FA Cup	*1886, 87*, **88**, **92**, **95**, *1912*, **31**, *35*, **54**, **68**
League Cup	**1966**, *67*, *70*

The Midlands

FOOTBALL CITIES

THE CLUSTER OF CITIES that make up the English Midlands are home to some of the oldest professional clubs in England; six were founder members of the Football League in 1888 (Stoke City, West Bromwich Albion, Aston Villa, Notts County, Derby County and Wolverhampton Wanderers). By the turn of the century, Leicester Fosse (later Leicester City), Nottingham Forest, Small Heath (later Birmingham City) and Loughborough had joined them. Although Loughborough was unable to cut it in the professional leagues, and became defunct in 1900, Coventry's entry into the Second Division in 1919 kept the Midlands' numbers up. The industrial economy of the region provided both works' teams and a large number of spectators. Coventry City was founded as a works' team at the Singer's bicycle factory, West Bromwich at a spring factory in Smethwick, while Birmingham, Aston Villa, Wolves and Derby emerged out of cricket clubs.

Villa dominant

Across the last 120 years Aston Villa has been the dominant team in the region. In the first 12 years of English professional football, Villa won five league championships and three FA Cups, including the double in 1897. Villa remained a force in the First Division for three decades before its first relegation in 1936, after which followed a spiral of decline, culminating in relegation to the Third Division in 1970. But revival came in the shape of manager Ron Saunders who led the team to the title in 1981 and the European Cup in 1982. Wolves (in the 1950s), Derby and Nottingham Forest in the 1970s have all risen to the top of the English game, and under the unique direction of Brian Clough, Forest took the European Cup back-to-back in 1979 and 1980. But the 1990s and beyond have been harder times for the region's clubs. Under the Doug Ellis regime of recent years, Villa has remained on the fringe of the title race despite considerable spending, but it remains the only Midlands' club whose place in the Premiership looks at all secure.

NOTTS COUNTY 1862	
FA Cup	*1891, 94*

NOTTINGHAM FOREST 1865	
League	*1967,* **78,** *79*
FA Cup	**1898, 1959,** *91*
League Cup	**1978,** *79, 80,* **89, 90, 92**
European Cup	**1979, 80**
World Club Cup	*1980*

Notts County (1910–)

MEADOW LANE

21,300

TRENT BRIDGE

NOTTINGHAM

CITY GROUND

30,602

Notts County (1883–1910)

Nottingham Forest (1898–)

Nottingham Forest (1880–82)

A60

M1

A6

Brian Clough (left) and Peter Taylor steered Nottingham Forest to back-to-back European Cup victories in 1979 and 1980.

LOUGHBOROUGH

THE ATHLETIC GROUND

Loughborough Athletic

The record-winning score in a football league match was Arsenal's 12-0 win over Loughborough 12 March 1900. Arsenal's biggest defeat was against Loughborough when it lost 8-0 12 December 1896.

Members of the Football League 1895–1900

LEICESTER CITY 1884	
League	*1929*
FA Cup	*1949, 61, 63, 69*
League Cup	**1964,** *65,* **97,** *99,* **2000**

LEICESTER

M1

FILBERT STREET

WALKERS BOWL

32,000

Leicester City (1891–2002)

Leicester City (2002–)

M69

West Bromwich Albion began life as West Bromwich Strollers – the works' team of Salter's Spring Works in the Smethwick area of the city.

ENGLAND

EST.D 1760
GEO SALTER & CO. LTD
SPRINGS
SPRING BALANCES

London

FOOTBALL CITY

ENGLAND

AS FOOTBALL EMERGED out of the public school and university system in England in the 1850s, old boy and graduate networks created teams all over Victorian London, where their players were busy staffing the hub of the British Empire. When the FA was founded in 1863 in Central London, the representatives of the clubs all came from the city. Replays aside, London has hosted all but eight of the FA Cup Finals since the first was played at Kennington Oval in 1872. For a moment in the late 19th century it looked as if London might be displaced as the football capital of the country. The newly professional Football League was a distinctly northern institution, with its headquarters in Lancashire, and not a single London team appeared in the First Division until Woolwich Arsenal in 1904. However, the size, wealth and power of London has steadily brought more clubs into contention: Chelsea made its debut in 1907, Tottenham in 1909, West Ham in 1922. London's place was sealed with the opening of the national stadium – Wembley – in 1923 (see Wembley box overleaf). More recently, the breakaway Premier League has based itself in London alongside the other key institutions in modern English football – the stock market in the City of London and the headquarters of the major television stations.

Despite great strength in depth (with half a dozen London teams in the Premiership at any one time) London's footballing strength has been concentrated for most of the 20th century in the north London rivals Arsenal and Tottenham (see North London box overleaf). Beyond this, constant success has been thin on the ground. South of the river, economic survival and even migration are the preoccupations of groundless Wimbledon and financially crippled Crystal Palace. In the east, West Ham has ridden the modern wave of football money well, but has yet to replicate its cup successes of the mid-1960s. In the west, Chelsea, buoyed up on the combined fortunes and machinations of Ken Bates and Matthew Harding, has turned on the style to take domestic and European cups in the 1990s, but has yet to mount a serious challenge for the league. Its neighbour Fulham is on the rise, care of Mohamed Al Fayed, while QPR remains mired in lower division debt.

WATFORD
VICARAGE ROAD
22,000
Watford
(1922–)

Formed in 1898,
merger of Watford
St Mary's and West Herts

WATFORD 1881	
League	*1983*
FA Cup	*1984*

HARROW

HARROW
SCHOOL
Football played
under a variety of
rules at Harrow
in the early
19th century

KENTON

RUISLIP

WEMBLEY

UXBRIDGE

A40

SOUTHALL   EALING   A406

GRIFFIN
PARK
12,750
Brentford

HOUNSLOW

RICHMOND

QUEENS PARK RANGERS 1885	
League	*1976*
FA Cup	*1982*
League Cup	**1967**, *86*

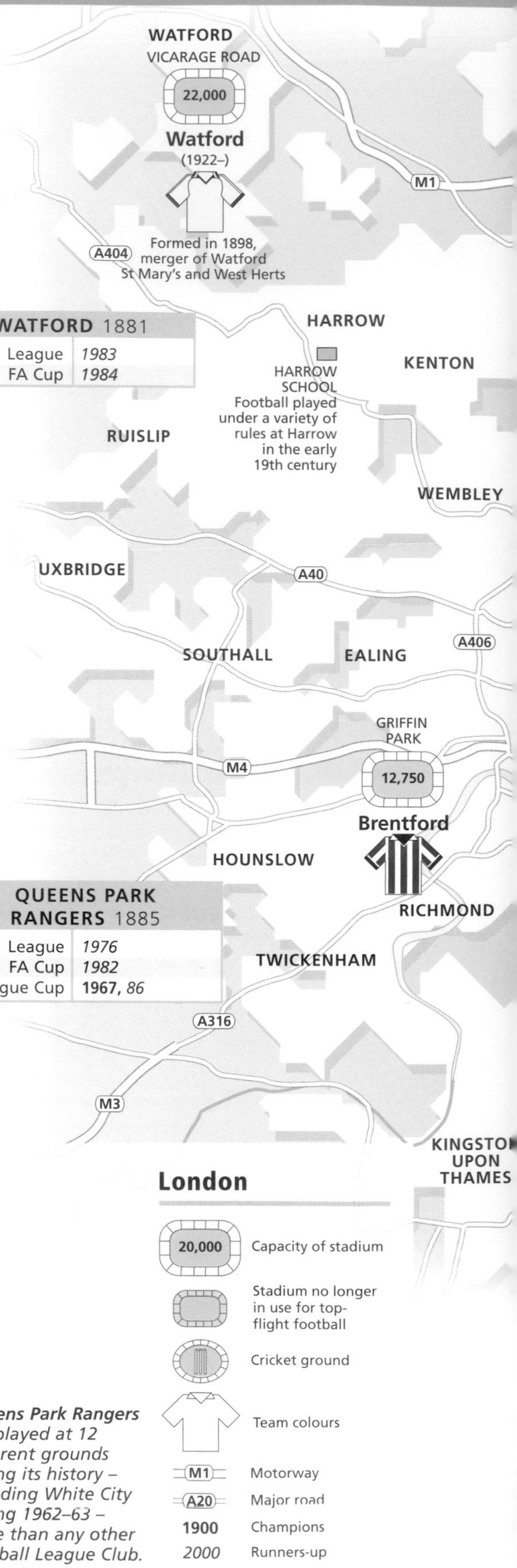

TWICKENHAM

A316

M3

KINGSTON
UPON
THAMES

London

20,000	Capacity of stadium
	Stadium no longer in use for top-flight football
	Cricket ground
	Team colours
M1	Motorway
A20	Major road
1900	Champions
2000	Runners-up

Queens Park Rangers has played at 12 different grounds during its history – including White City during 1962–63 – more than any other Football League Club.

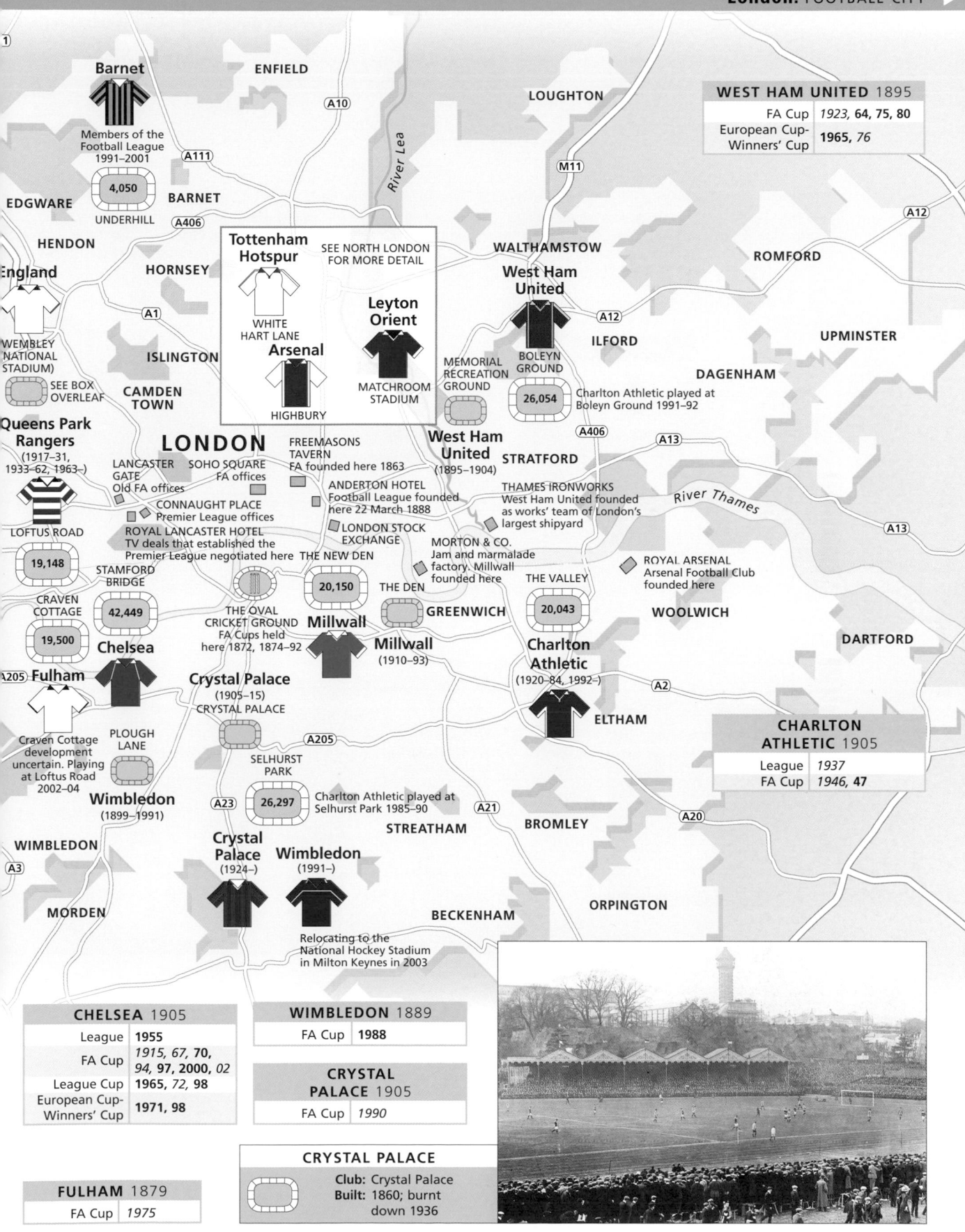

Barnet

Members of the Football League 1991–2001

4,050

UNDERHILL

ENFIELD

LOUGHTON

A10

River Lea

M11

WEST HAM UNITED 1895	
FA Cup	*1923*, **64, 75, 80**
European Cup-Winners' Cup	**1965**, *76*

BARNET

A111

A406

A12

EDGWARE

HENDON

England

WEMBLEY NATIONAL STADIUM)

SEE BOX OVERLEAF

Queens Park Rangers
(1917–31, 1933–62, 1963–)

LOFTUS ROAD

19,148

HORNSEY

A1

ISLINGTON

CAMDEN TOWN

Tottenham Hotspur

SEE NORTH LONDON FOR MORE DETAIL

WHITE HART LANE

Arsenal

HIGHBURY

Leyton Orient

MATCHROOM STADIUM

WALTHAMSTOW

West Ham United

BOLEYN GROUND

26,054

Charlton Athletic played at Boleyn Ground 1991–92

A12

ILFORD

UPMINSTER

DAGENHAM

A13

A13

River Thames

LONDON

LANCASTER GATE
Old FA offices

SOHO SQUARE
FA offices

FREEMASONS TAVERN
FA founded here 1863

ANDERTON HOTEL
Football League founded here 22 March 1888

LONDON STOCK EXCHANGE

West Ham United
(1895–1904)

STRATFORD

A406

THAMES IRONWORKS
West Ham United founded as works' team of London's largest shipyard

CONNAUGHT PLACE
Premier League offices

ROYAL LANCASTER HOTEL
TV deals that established the Premier League negotiated here

THE NEW DEN

20,150

MORTON & CO.
Jam and marmalade factory. Millwall founded here

ROYAL ARSENAL
Arsenal Football Club founded here

STAMFORD BRIDGE

42,449

Chelsea

CRAVEN COTTAGE

19,500

Fulham

A205

THE OVAL CRICKET GROUND
FA Cups held here 1872, 1874–92

THE DEN

Millwall

Millwall
(1910–93)

GREENWICH

THE VALLEY

20,043

Charlton Athletic
(1920–84, 1992–)

WOOLWICH

DARTFORD

A2

ELTHAM

CHARLTON ATHLETIC 1905	
League	*1937*
FA Cup	*1946*, **47**

Craven Cottage development uncertain. Playing at Loftus Road 2002–04

PLOUGH LANE

Crystal Palace
(1905–15)
CRYSTAL PALACE

A205

SELHURST PARK

26,297

Charlton Athletic played at Selhurst Park 1985–90

A23

A21

STREATHAM

BROMLEY

A20

ORPINGTON

Wimbledon
(1899–1991)

WIMBLEDON

A3

Crystal Palace
(1924–)

Wimbledon
(1991–)

MORDEN

Relocating to the National Hockey Stadium in Milton Keynes in 2003

BECKENHAM

CHELSEA 1905	
League	**1955**
FA Cup	*1915, 67, 70, 94*, **97, 2000**, *02*
League Cup	**1965**, *72*, **98**
European Cup-Winners' Cup	**1971, 98**

WIMBLEDON 1889	
FA Cup	**1988**

CRYSTAL PALACE 1905	
FA Cup	*1990*

CRYSTAL PALACE	
	Club: Crystal Palace
	Built: 1860; burnt down 1936

FULHAM 1879	
FA Cup	*1975*

NORTH LONDON

London's footballing power has been gathered in north London for almost a century. To the east of both clubs are the great stretches of Hackney Marshes where amateur football flourishes on a Sunday, but on Saturdays attention turns west. Local schoolboys founded Tottenham Hotspur in 1882. The club first played at Northumberland Park, close to the ancestral home of Henry Percy (nicknamed Harry Hotspur by Shakespeare) before settling at White Hart Lane in 1899. Arsenal began life south of the river in 1886 as Dial Square FC, a works' team from the Royal Arsenal in Woolwich. The team soon turned professional, changing its name to Royal Arsenal in 1891 before migrating

north to settle at Highbury in 1913. Tottenham was the first to win a major trophy, but it was Arsenal in the early 1930s under Herbert Chapman that first won the league and, for a time, dominated English football. Tottenham has regularly achieved cup success at home and abroad, as well as winning the first double of the 20th century in 1961, but it is Arsenal that has pulled ahead in its consistent capacity to challenge for the title (winning the double in 1971, 98 and 2002). Tottenham is often cast as London's Jewish team, and the area is certainly one of the strongholds of English Jewry, but in reality Arsenal's fans and board of directors seem to draw on London's Jews in equal number.

ENGLAND

North London

13,842	Capacity of stadium
60,000	Site of proposed new stadium
	Stadium no longer in use for top-flight football
	Team colours
A10	Motorway
	Major road
1900	Champions
2000	Runners-up

THE LOCAL DERBY

ARSENAL **SPURS**

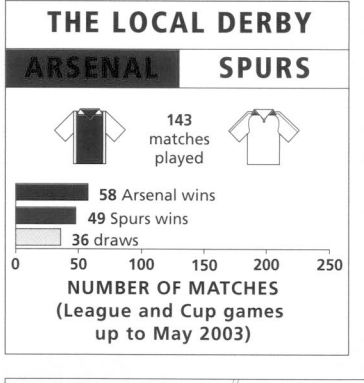

143 matches played

58 Arsenal wins
49 Spurs wins
36 draws

0   50   100   150   200   250

NUMBER OF MATCHES
(League and Cup games
up to May 2003)

WHITE HART LANE

36,236	**Club:** Tottenham Hotspur
	Built: 1899
	Rebuilt: 1909, 1934, 1980, 1991–94
	Record Attendance: 75,038 Spurs v Sunderland, 5 March 1938

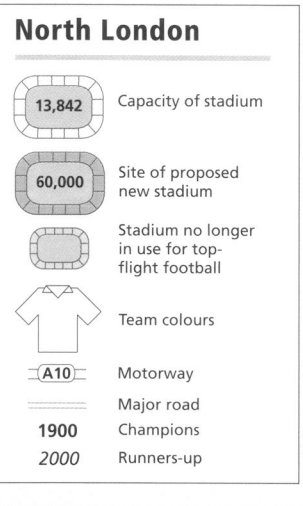

HIGHBURY

38,500	**Club:** Arsenal
	Built: 1913
	Rebuilt: 1932–36, 1991
	Record Attendance: 73,295 Arsenal v Sunderland, 9 March 1931

TOTTENHAM HOTSPUR 1882

League	*1922,* **51, 52,** *57,* **61,** *63*
FA Cup	**1901, 21, 61, 62, 67, 81, 82,** *87,* **91**
League Cup	**1971, 73,** *82,* **99,** *2002*
European Cup-Winners' Cup	**1963**
UEFA Cup	**1972,** *74,* **84**

ARSENAL 1886

League	*1926,* **31, 32,** *33–35,* **38, 48, 53, 71,** *73,* **89, 91, 98,** *99–2001,* **02, 03**
FA Cup	*1927,* **30,** *32,* **36, 50,** *52,* **71, 72,** *78,* **79, 80, 93, 98, 2001,** *02,* **03**
League Cup	**1968,** *69,* **87,** *88,* **93**
European Cup-Winners' Cup	**1980,** *94,* **95**
Fairs Cup	**1970**
UEFA Cup	*2000*

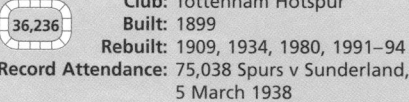

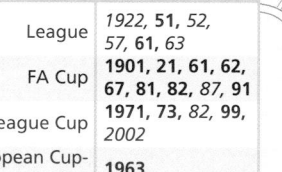

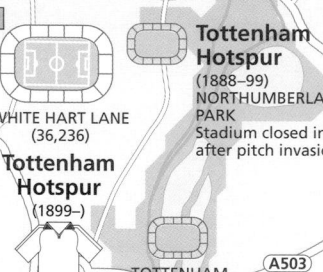

A10

PERCY HOUSE
Historical home of
the Percy family

Tottenham Hotspur
(1888–99)
NORTHUMBERLAND PARK
Stadium closed in 1899 after pitch invasion

WHITE HART LANE
(36,236)

Tottenham Hotspur
(1899–)

A503

TOTTENHAM MARSHES

WALTHAMSTOW

From 1882–86 the Hotspur FC committee met under a gaslight on Tottenham High Road

Tottenham Hotspur
(1882–88)

reservoirs

Leyton Orient
(1930–37)

Leyton Orient
(1937–)

TOTTENHAM **A503**

Finsbury Park

FINSBURY PARK
Scene of 1998 and 2002 double celebrations

**N O R T H
L O N D O N**

LEA BRIDGE ROAD

MATCHROOM STADIUM

13,842

MILLFIELDS ROAD

Hackney Marshes

HIGHBURY
(38,500)

Arsenal

STOKE NEWINGTON

Leyton Orient
(1900–30)

Hackney Marshes, home of Sunday morning football

ARSENAL UNDERGROUND STATION

60,000

A10

ISLINGTON

HACKNEY

A12

STRATFORD

Arsenal
ASHBURTON GROVE

A12

Victoria Park

River Lea

CAMDEN TOWN

A1

SHOREDITCH **A10**

BOW

	WEMBLEY	
Closed	**Club:**	None; national stadium
	Built:	1923
	Original	
	Capacity:	100,000 approx
	Rebuilt:	1948, 1963, 1990
	Record Attendance:	Approx 200,000, Bolton v West Ham, FA Cup Final, 1923
	Significant Matches:	1966 World Cup: nine matches including semi-final, 3rd place play-off, Final; 1996 European Championships: six matches, including semi-final, Final; European Cup Final: 1963, 68, 71, 78, 92; European Cup-Winners' Cup Final: 1965, 93

PC Scorey and his legendary horse Billy organize the huge crowd at Wembley in April 1923. The first-ever FA Cup Final at the new stadium, between West Ham and Bolton, attracted some 250,000 spectators – and only the self-discipline of the fans and the police, led by the white horse, averted a possible disaster.

WEMBLEY STADIUM

Designed by Sir John Simpson and Maxwell Ayrton, Wembley, opened in 1923, was originally the centrepiece of the British Empire Exhibition. It took a mere 300 days to build, cost £750,000 and staged its first football match – the 'White Horse' FA Cup – in April that year. But internationals and the FA Cup Final were not enough to sustain the vast stadium, and it was only saved by the investment of Arthur Elvin, who brought greyhound racing and speedway to Wembley. In its lifetime, Wembley also hosted the 1948 Olympic Games, and sports such as boxing, American football, and rugby league, as well as music concerts.

But it is for football that Wembley is best known: 77 FA Cup Finals, innumerable internationals, as well as the finals of the 1966 World Cup, the 1996 European Championships and numerous European Cup Finals. Nostalgia aside, the stadium's facilities, sightlines and atmosphere have been in steady decline, and the decision to rebuild Wembley with a mixture of government, lottery and private money saw it stage its last match in 2000. However, the enormous cost of the proposed rebuild, including the demolition of the iconic twin towers, has foundered in cost overruns and hubris. After innumerable financial reassessments and the abandonment of plans for hotels and offices, the redevelopment plan was rescued by the intervention of a German bank. The financial future of Wembley Stadium hinges on the successful sale of a considerable number of premium priced seats. While this may secure the balance sheet its impact on the atmosphere inside the stadium on a matchday remains to be seen.

February 2003: the most iconic buildings in world football are summarily torn down. The demolition and rebuilding of the stadium has proved so controversial that no one, including the architects, are allowed on to the demolition site.

Merseyside

FOOTBALL CITY

AT THE CENTRE of the Merseyside region is the city of Liverpool, and close to its heart is Stanley Park, site of the stadiums of the city's eternal rivals, Everton and Liverpool. In their great shadow, smaller teams (like Bootle and South Liverpool) have withered, and only Tranmere Rovers on the Wirral peninsula across the Mersey has survived. In the city's hinterland, football has been abandoned and rugby league has grown up in the available sporting spaces. Everton was founded in 1878 out of a church team playing as St. Domingo's. Immediate popularity made the club a founder member of the Football League in 1888. In 1892 the club split, with John Houlding, owner of the Anfield ground at which they played, forming Liverpool, while the rest of the club headed to the other side of the park to play at Goodison Park.

Fierce and bitter rivalry

Both teams have garnered fanatical support across the city, and although Houlding was an active member of the Protestant Orange order, no sectarian (Catholic-Protestant) division between the clubs has ever emerged. Nonetheless, rivalry is fierce and bitter. Everton was the stronger side for the first half of the 20th century, its peak coming when it won the 1928 league title courtesy of a record-breaking 60 goals from its centre-forward Dixie Dean. But in the modern era, it is Liverpool that has been dominant. With Bill Shankly's arrival in 1959, successive dynasties of players and managers were created, and style and success were intertwined at Anfield. As the city declined through grim years of de-industrialization and unemployment, the team surged, winning ten league titles and four European Cups between 1976 and 1990. But the Heysel and Hillsborough disasters seemed to bring an end to that glorious era. Over a decade on from Hillsborough, Liverpool has risen again, Everton has rediscovered its form under David Moyes and both clubs are looking to build new stadiums.

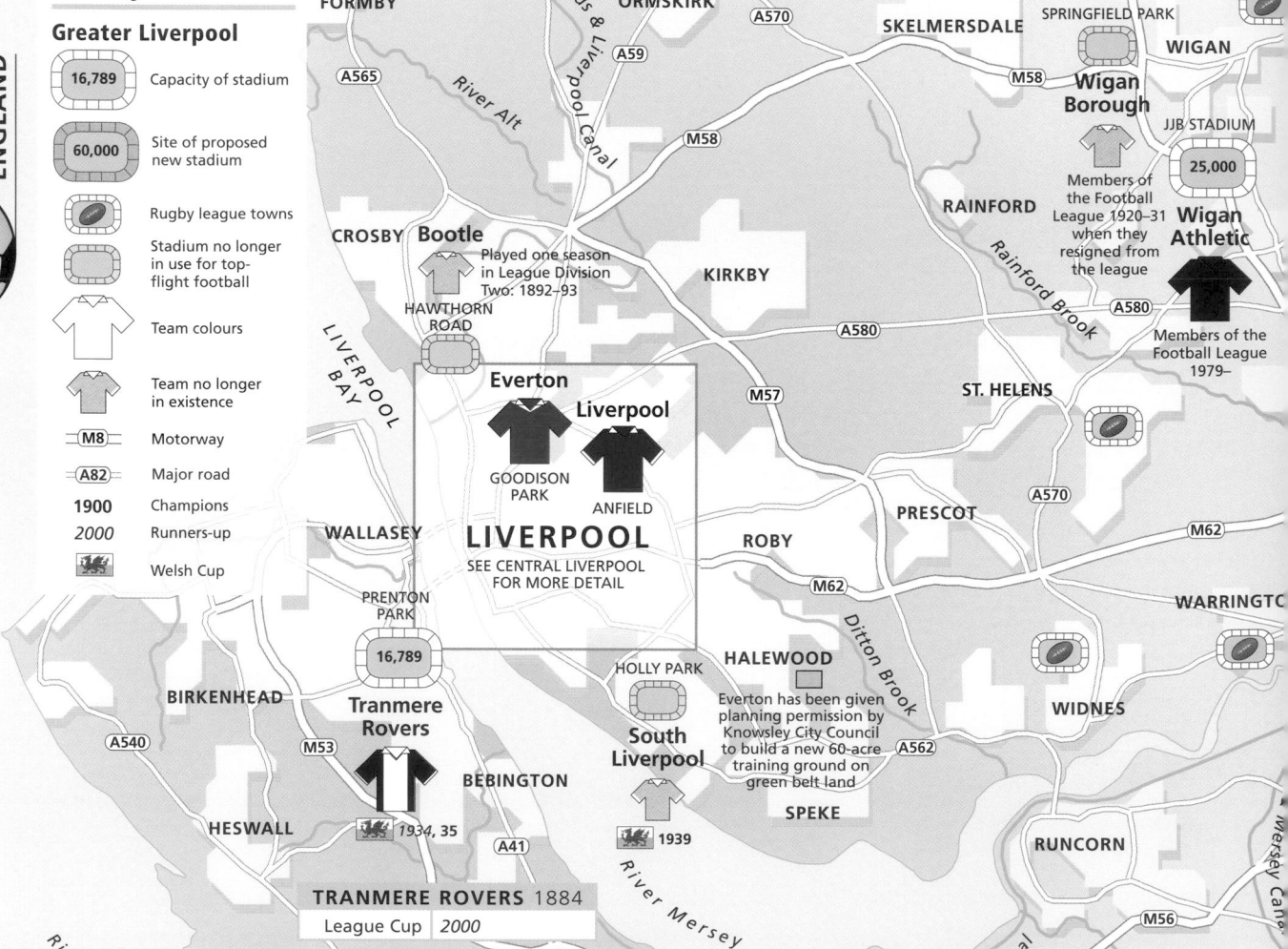

ENGLAND

Merseyside

Greater Liverpool

16,789	Capacity of stadium
60,000	Site of proposed new stadium
	Rugby league towns
	Stadium no longer in use for top-flight football
	Team colours
	Team no longer in existence
M8	Motorway
A82	Major road
1900	Champions
2000	Runners-up
	Welsh Cup

FORMBY · ORMSKIRK · SKELMERSDALE · SPRINGFIELD PARK · WIGAN · M6

A565 · River Alt · A59 · M58 · M58 · Wigan Borough · JJB STADIUM · 25,000 · Wigan Athletic

CROSBY · Bootle · KIRKBY · RAINFORD · Rainford Brook · A580

Played one season in League Division Two: 1892–93

HAWTHORN ROAD

LIVERPOOL BAY

Members of the Football League 1920–31 when they resigned from the league

Members of the Football League 1979–

Everton · Liverpool · ST. HELENS · M57

GOODISON PARK · ANFIELD

LIVERPOOL

SEE CENTRAL LIVERPOOL FOR MORE DETAIL

A580 · A570 · PRESCOT · M62

WALLASEY · ROBY · M62 · WARRINGTON

PRENTON PARK · HALEWOOD · Ditton Brook · A562 · WIDNES

16,789 · HOLLY PARK

Everton has been given planning permission by Knowsley City Council to build a new 60-acre training ground on green belt land

BIRKENHEAD · Tranmere Rovers · South Liverpool · SPEKE

M53 · BEBINGTON · RUNCORN · Mersey Canal

HESWALL · 1934, 35 · A41 · 1939 · River Mersey · FRODSHAM · River Weaver

TRANMERE ROVERS 1884	
League Cup	2000

River Dee · M53 · M56

NESTON · A540 · A41 · Manchester Ship Canal · M56

ELLESMERE PORT

GOODISON PARK

40,260

Club: Everton
Built: 1892
Original
Capacity: 11,000
Rebuilt: 1906–9, 1926, 1938, 1994
Record Attendance: 78,299 Everton v Liverpool, 18 Sept 1948. Record for women's match: 53,000 for Dick Kerr's Ladies v St Helens, 26 Dec 1920
Significant Matches: 1966 World Cup: three matches including semi-final

Policemen help a fan out of the Anfield Kop before a league match in 1966 – when full during those years, the Kop had a capacity of 28,000 people, all standing.

ENGLAND

EVERTON 1878	
League	*1890,* **91,** *95, 1902, 05, 09, 12,* **15, 28, 32, 39, 63, 70, 85,** *86,* **87**
FA Cup	*1893, 97,* **1906,** *07, 33, 66, 68,* **84,** *85, 86, 89,* **95**
League Cup	*1977, 84*
European Cup-Winners' Cup	**1985**

ANFIELD

45,362

Club: Liverpool
Built: 1884
Original
Capacity: Approximately 10,000
Rebuilt: 1906 (the Kop), 1963, 1990–98
Record Attendance: 61,905 Liverpool v Wolverhampton Wanderers, FA Cup 4th Round, 2 Feb 1952
Significant Matches: 1996 European Championships: three matches

THE LOCAL DERBY

EVERTON   LIVERPOOL

170 matches played

■ 55 Everton wins
■ 62 Liverpool wins
□ 53 draws

0   50   100   150   200   250
NUMBER OF MATCHES
(League only up to May 2003)

BOOTLE   Everton   **WALTON**   A580

LITTLEWOODS POOLS
Owned by the Moores family, major shareholders at Liverpool, Littlewoods have made a fortune from the Pools, a football betting system

GOODISON PARK (40,260)   **Liverpool**

NEW ANFIELD 60,000   *Stanley Park*

KIRKDALE

NORRIS GREEN

MELWOOD Liverpool training ground

In a post-Hillsborough display of solidarity, a chain of football scarves was hung between the two stadiums

SANDON HOTEL
In 1892 Everton and Liverpool split into two clubs at a meeting in this hotel

ST. DOMINGO'S METHODIST HALL
Everton began life here as St. Domingo's

ANFIELD (45,362)   **Liverpool**
Everton at Anfield 1884–92

EVERTON

CENTRAL LIVERPOOL

BELLEFIELD
Everton training ground. Due to close in 2006 when new training ground opens in Halewood

STONEYCROFT   A57

Town Hall and St George's Hall are both sites of the clubs' victory celebrations

EVERTON BROW
The tower on Everton's badge is based on the single tower prison built on Everton Brow in 1787

TOWN HALL   **ST. GEORGE'S HALL**   METROPOLITAN CATHEDRAL (Catholic)

Memorial plaques to the Hillsborough victims were laid in both cathedrals

River Mersey

55,000

Everton   LIVERPOOL CATHEDRAL (Anglican)   A562

KING'S DOCK
Future of development remains uncertain due to financial difficulties

TOXTETH

BIRKENHEAD

LIVERPOOL 1892		
League		*1899,* **1901, 06,** *10,* **22, 23, 47, 64, 66,** *69,* **73,** *74, 75,* **76, 77,** *78, 79, 80,* **82–84,** *85,* **86, 87, 88,** *89,* **90, 91, 2002**
FA Cup		*1914, 50,* **65,** *71,* **74,** *77,* **86, 88, 89, 92, 96, 2001**
League Cup		**1978,** *81–84,* **87,** *95,* **2001,** *03*
European Cup		**1977, 78, 81, 84,** *85*
European Cup-Winners' Cup		*1966*
UEFA Cup		**1973,** *76,* **2001**
World Club Cup		*1981, 84*

Manchester

FOOTBALL CITY

ALTHOUGH FOOTBALL WAS FIRST DEVELOPED and codified in the public schools and universities of southern England, its transformation into a professional mass-spectator sport was centred on Lancashire – and on the periphery of Manchester and a little further north are many of the country's first professional teams. Some of the key meetings that preceded the Football League's creation took place in Manchester, as did the formation of the Professional Footballers' Association.

The heart and soul of the city

Within Manchester itself, the game took longer to mature. Manchester United began life as a railway works' team in Newton Heath to the north-east of the city centre, while Manchester City was formed from the merger of small teams in the Ardwick area

to the south-east. The rivalry between the two has taken on a religious dimension, with United inclined towards the Catholic community and regularly fielding Scottish and Irish players and City towards the Protestant community. But those sectarian undertones have been lost in what has become a conflict for the soul of the city. United, the richest and most famous club in the world, garners support from every continent, its stands filled with out-of-towners. City, Manchester's own authentic, local team, has stands filled by the Moss Side faithful, where resilience in the face of disaster on and off the pitch is worn as a badge of honour.

Although City has had moments of ascendancy – between the wars, and in the early 1970s when it sent United down with a Denis Law backheel – United has cast an awesome shadow over its rival, with two league titles before the First World War, three in the 1950s before the Munich air disaster, two in the 60s, Sir Matt Busby's European Cup triumph in 1968, and, under Alex Ferguson, seven league titles and the European Cup as one third of a treble in 1999. Nonetheless, City appears to be on its way back, with more stable finances, an unflinching fan base and a move to the City of Manchester Stadium in August 2003.

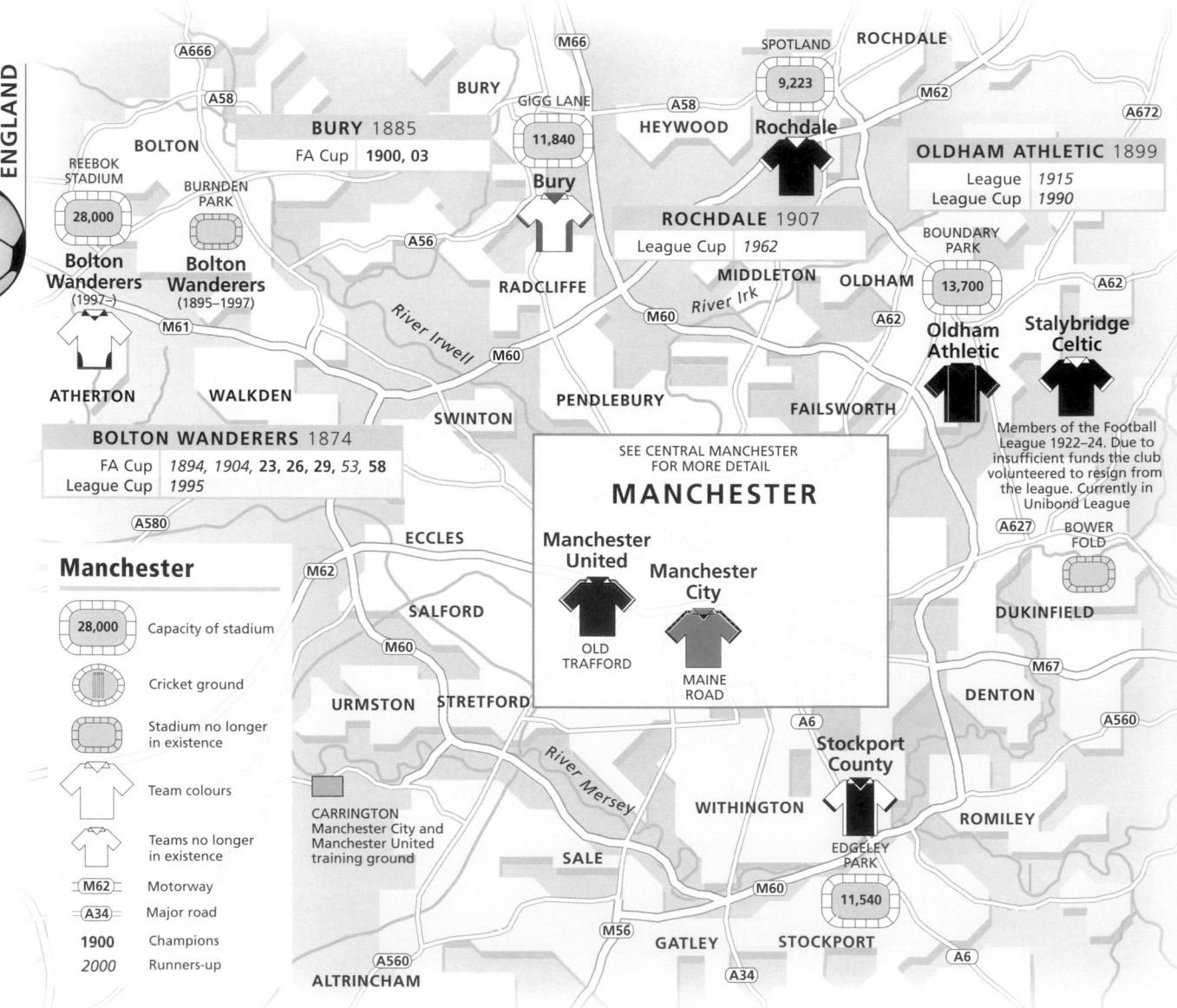

ENGLAND

BURY 1885

| FA Cup | **1900, 03** |

GIGG LANE — 11,840 — **Bury**

SPOTLAND — 9,223 — **Rochdale**

ROCHDALE

ROCHDALE 1907

| League Cup | *1962* |

OLDHAM ATHLETIC 1899

| League | *1915* |
| League Cup | *1990* |

BOUNDARY PARK — 13,700 — **Oldham Athletic**

Stalybridge Celtic

Members of the Football League 1922–24. Due to insufficient funds the club volunteered to resign from the league. Currently in Unibond League

REEBOK STADIUM — 28,000 — **Bolton Wanderers** (1997–)

BURNDEN PARK — **Bolton Wanderers** (1895–1997)

BOLTON WANDERERS 1874

| FA Cup | *1894, 1904,* **23, 26, 29,** *53,* **58** |
| League Cup | *1995* |

Manchester

28,000	Capacity of stadium
	Cricket ground
	Stadium no longer in existence
	Team colours
	Teams no longer in existence
M62	Motorway
A34	Major road
1900	Champions
2000	Runners-up

CARRINGTON Manchester City and Manchester United training ground

SEE CENTRAL MANCHESTER FOR MORE DETAIL

MANCHESTER

Manchester United
OLD TRAFFORD

Manchester City
MAINE ROAD

Stockport County

EDGELEY PARK — 11,540 — STOCKPORT

ATHERTON · WALKDEN · SWINTON · RADCLIFFE · PENDLEBURY · FAILSWORTH · BOLTON · BURY · HEYWOOD · MIDDLETON · OLDHAM · DUKINFIELD · BOWER FOLD · DENTON · ROMILEY · ECCLES · SALFORD · URMSTON · STRETFORD · SALE · WITHINGTON · GATLEY · ALTRINCHAM

River Irwell · River Irk · River Mersey

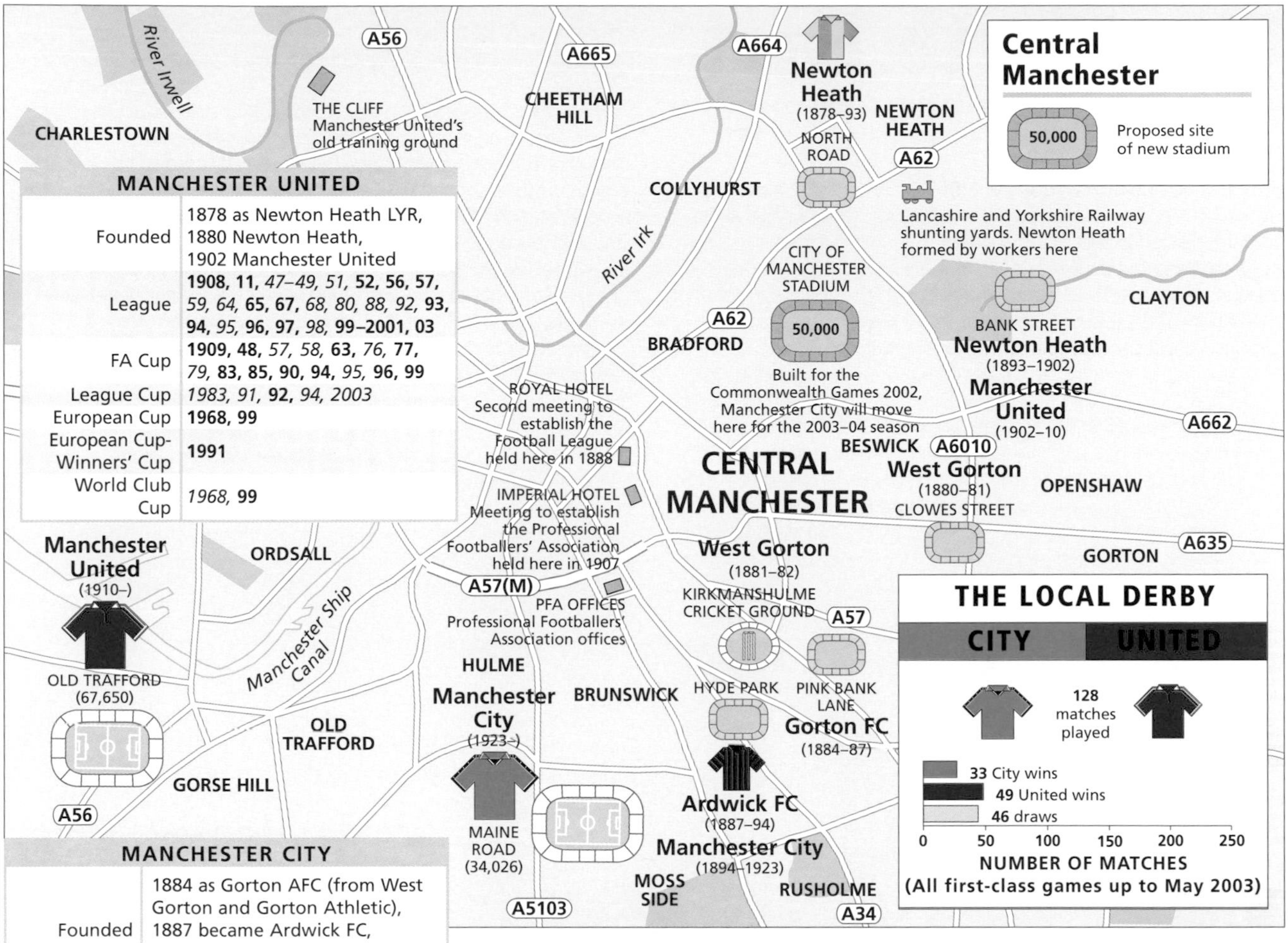

Central Manchester

| 50,000 | Proposed site of new stadium |

CHARLESTOWN

River Irwell

A56

THE CLIFF
Manchester United's
old training ground

CHEETHAM HILL

A665

A664

Newton Heath
(1878–93) **NEWTON HEATH**
NORTH ROAD

A62

Lancashire and Yorkshire Railway
shunting yards. Newton Heath
formed by workers here

COLLYHURST

River Irk

CITY OF MANCHESTER STADIUM

A62 | 50,000 |

Built for the
Commonwealth Games 2002,
Manchester City will move
here for the 2003–04 season

BRADFORD

BANK STREET

Newton Heath
(1893–1902)

CLAYTON

Manchester United
(1902–10)

A662

MANCHESTER UNITED

Founded	1878 as Newton Heath LYR, 1880 Newton Heath, 1902 Manchester United
League	**1908, 11,** *47–49,* 51, **52, 56, 57,** *59, 64,* **65, 67,** *68,* **80, 88, 92, 93,** **94, 95, 96, 97, 98, 99–2001,** *03*
FA Cup	**1909,** *48,* **57, 58,** *63,* **76, 77,** *79,* **83,** *85,* **90,** *94,* **95, 96, 99**
League Cup	*1983,* **91, 92,** *94,* **2003**
European Cup	**1968, 99**
European Cup- Winners' Cup	**1991**
World Club Cup	*1968, 99*

ROYAL HOTEL
Second meeting to
establish the
Football League
held here in 1888

BESWICK A6010

West Gorton
(1880–81)
CLOWES STREET

OPENSHAW

CENTRAL MANCHESTER

IMPERIAL HOTEL
Meeting to establish
the Professional
Footballers' Association
held here in 1907

West Gorton
(1881–82)

GORTON

A635

Manchester
United
(1910–)

ORDSALL

Manchester Ship Canal

A57(M)

KIRKMANSHULME
CRICKET GROUND A57

PFA OFFICES
Professional Footballers'
Association offices

THE LOCAL DERBY

CITY	UNITED

128 matches played

33 City wins
49 United wins
46 draws

0 50 100 150 200 250
NUMBER OF MATCHES
(All first-class games up to May 2003)

OLD TRAFFORD
(67,650)

HULME

Manchester
City
(1923–)

BRUNSWICK

HYDE PARK

PINK BANK LANE

Gorton FC
(1884–87)

OLD TRAFFORD

GORSE HILL

A56

MAINE ROAD
(34,026)

Ardwick FC
(1887–94)

Manchester City
(1894–1923)

MOSS SIDE

RUSHOLME

A5103

A34

MANCHESTER CITY

Founded	1884 as Gorton AFC (from West Gorton and Gorton Athletic), 1887 became Ardwick FC, 1894 changed its name to Manchester City
League	*1904, 21,* **37, 68,** *77*
FA Cup	**1904,** *26, 33,* **34,** *55,* **56, 69,** *81*
League Cup	**1970,** *74,* **76**
European Cup- Winners' Cup	**1970**

MAINE ROAD

| 34,026 | **Club:** Manchester City |
| **Built:** 1923 |
| **Original
Capacity:** 80–90,000 estimate |
| **Record Attendance:** 84,569 Manchester City v
Stoke City, FA Cup Sixth
Round, 3 February 1934 |
| **Significant Matches:** England internationals: 1946,
48, 49; League Cup Final
replay: 1984 |

*On 11 March 1941 Old Trafford was
badly damaged by German bombs.
United played home games at Maine
Road until repairs were complete.*

OLD TRAFFORD

| 67,650 | **Club:** Manchester United |
| **Built:** 1910 |
| **Original
Capacity:** 80,000 |
| **Rebuilt:** Bombed 1940–41, rebuilt
1948–49; rebuilt with
Europe's first executive
boxes, mid-1966; fully
covered 1973; 1992–2000
constant rebuilding |
| **Record Attendance:** 76,962 Wolves v Grimsby FA
Cup semi-final, 25 Mar 1939 |
| **Significant Matches:** FA Cup Final: 1915; FA Cup
Final replays: 1911, 1970; 1966 World Cup:
three group matches; 1996 European
Championships: three group matches,
quarter-final and semi-final; England
internationals: 1926, 97, 2001 |

The North East

FOOTBALL CITIES

Although professional football arrived in the North East slightly later than its Lancastrian and Midlands heartlands, the region soon made up for lost time. Sunderland was founded by students at a teacher training college in 1879, but soon opened its doors to everyone and entered the Football League in 1890. The 'team of all talents' as it was known won three titles in four years and saw off the threat of the splinter club, Sunderland Albion, who played in the league for a year before folding.

Newcastle and the wider Tyneside region threw up a number of clubs in the 1880s before the fusion of Newcastle East End (previously Stanley) – who had fans and players but no ground – and Newcastle West End who just had the lease of what is now St. James' Park. The two teams fused to create Newcastle United in 1882, joined the league the following year and won its first title in 1905. Sunderland took the title in the 1930s and Newcastle peaked with its 1950s FA Cup wins and triumph in the Fairs Cup. But league titles eluded it and all the region's clubs have spent long periods in the lower divisions.

Economic boom of the 1990s

The advent of the economic boom in football in the 1990s has allowed the region's big clubs to capitalize on the massive and fervent support that sets it apart. With the personal fortune of Sir John Hall at Newcastle combined with massive sponsorship, merchandise and TV money, St. James' Park has been transformed almost out of recognition. Both the Riverside in Middlesbrough and the Stadium of Light in Sunderland have architecturally announced the erosion of the region's industrial heritage.

Beyond the professional game, the North East boasts among the strongest semi-professional and amateur leagues in the country which have helped nurture a steady flow of nationally recognized talent: Jackie Milburn and his nephews the Charlton brothers and Paul Gascoigne among others. Non-league Blythe Spartans, formed in 1899, almost reached the sixth round of the FA Cup in 1978 after its Fifth Round tie with Wrexham went to a replay at St. James' Park. Over 42,000 people saw them lose 2-1. How many other regions can even begin to imagine that level of support for such a club?

ENGLAND

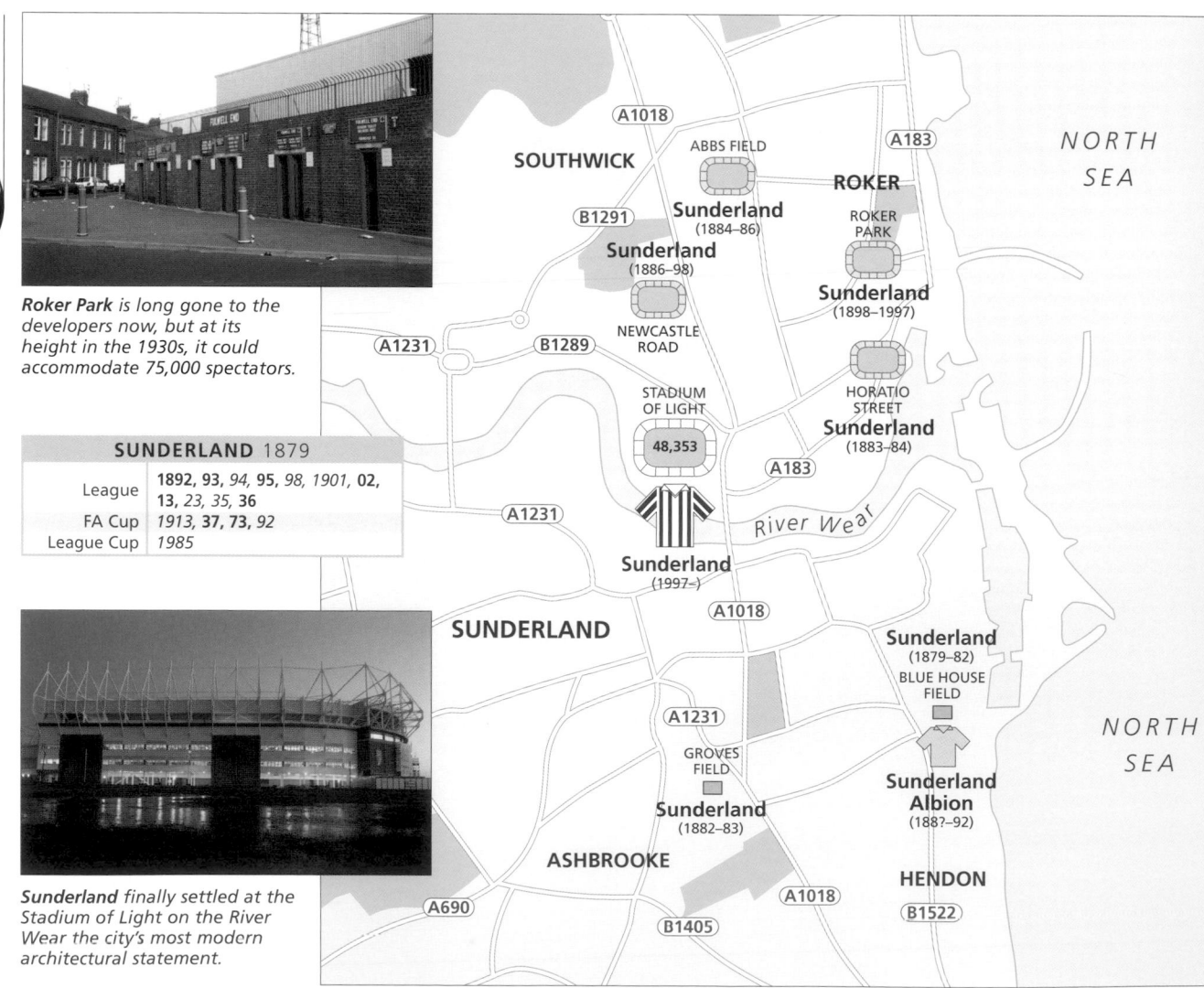

Roker Park is long gone to the developers now, but at its height in the 1930s, it could accommodate 75,000 spectators.

SUNDERLAND 1879	
League	**1892, 93,** *94,* **95,** *98, 1901,* **02,** **13,** *23,* **35, 36**
FA Cup	*1913,* **37, 73, 92**
League Cup	*1985*

Sunderland finally settled at the Stadium of Light on the River Wear the city's most modern architectural statement.

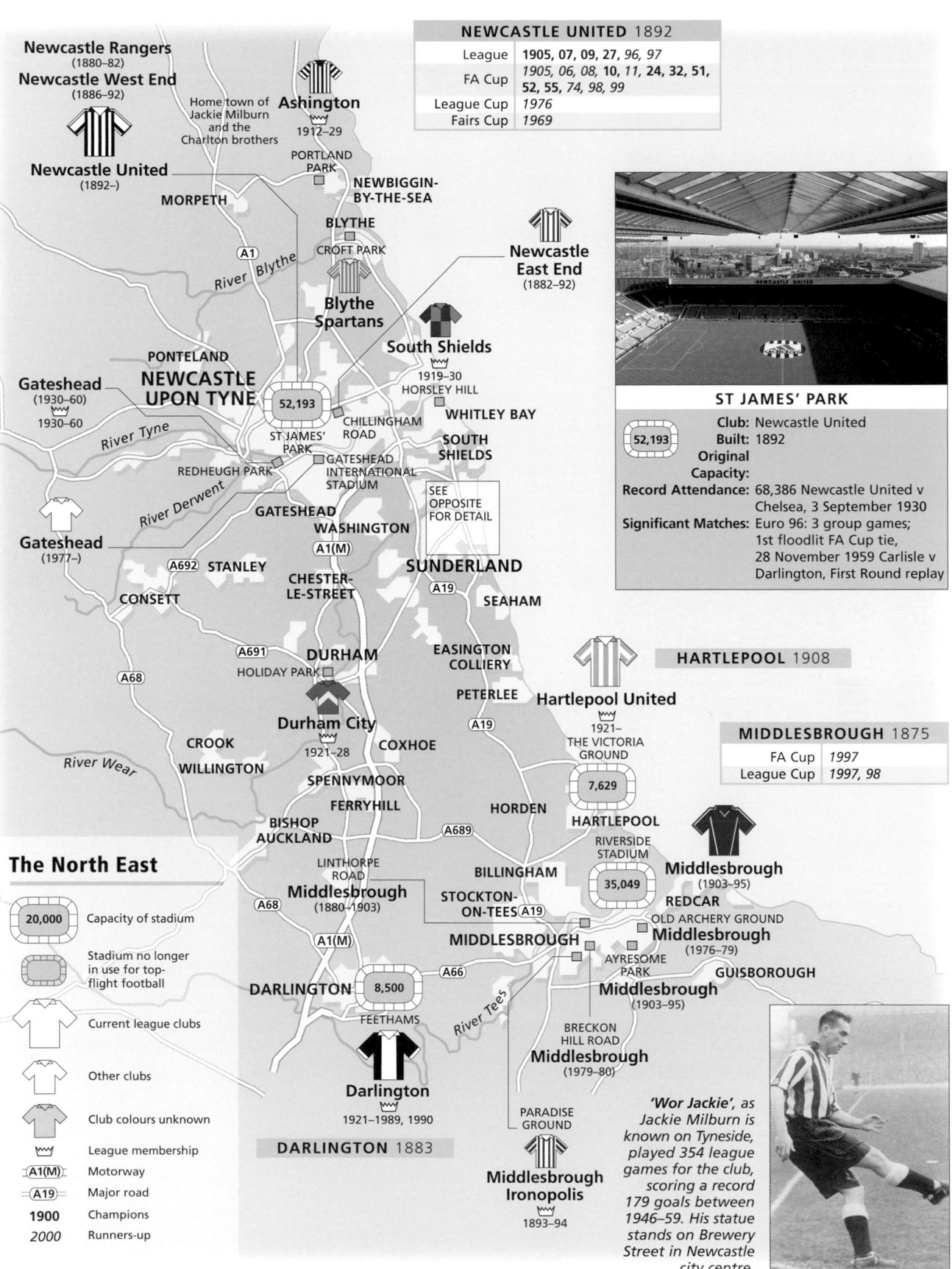

Newcastle Rangers
(1880–82)

Newcastle West End
(1886–92)

Newcastle United
(1892–)

NEWCASTLE UNITED 1892	
League	**1905, 07, 09, 27,** *96, 97*
FA Cup	*1905, 06, 08,* **10, 11, 24, 32, 51, 52, 55,** *74, 98, 99*
League Cup	*1976*
Fairs Cup	*1969*

Home town of Jackie Milburn and the Charlton brothers

Ashington
1912–29

PORTLAND PARK

NEWBIGGIN-BY-THE-SEA

MORPETH

BLYTHE

A1

River Blythe

CROFT PARK

Blythe Spartans

Newcastle East End
(1882–92)

South Shields
1919–30
HORSLEY HILL

PONTELAND

Gateshead
(1930–60)
1930–60

NEWCASTLE UPON TYNE

52,193

ST JAMES' PARK

CHILLINGHAM ROAD

WHITLEY BAY

SOUTH SHIELDS

River Tyne

REDHEUGH PARK

River Derwent

GATESHEAD INTERNATIONAL STADIUM

GATESHEAD

WASHINGTON

A1(M)

SEE OPPOSITE FOR DETAIL

ST JAMES' PARK

52,193	**Club:** Newcastle United
	Built: 1892
	Original Capacity:
	Record Attendance: 68,386 Newcastle United v Chelsea, 3 September 1930
	Significant Matches: Euro 96: 3 group games; 1st floodlit FA Cup tie, 28 November 1959 Carlisle v Darlington, First Round replay

Gateshead
(1977–)

A692 STANLEY

CHESTER-LE-STREET

SUNDERLAND

A19

SEAHAM

CONSETT

A691 DURHAM

HOLIDAY PARK

EASINGTON COLLIERY

PETERLEE

A19

HARTLEPOOL 1908

A68

Durham City
1921–28

CROOK

WILLINGTON

COXHOE

Hartlepool United
1921–
THE VICTORIA GROUND

MIDDLESBROUGH 1875

FA Cup	*1997*	
League Cup	*1997, 98*	

River Wear

SPENNYMOOR

FERRYHILL

HORDEN

7,629

HARTLEPOOL

BISHOP AUCKLAND

A689

RIVERSIDE STADIUM

LINTHORPE ROAD

BILLINGHAM

Middlesbrough
(1903–95)

Middlesbrough
(1880–1903)

A68

STOCKTON-ON-TEES

A19

35,049

REDCAR

OLD ARCHERY GROUND

Middlesbrough
(1976–79)

A1(M)

MIDDLESBROUGH

A66

AYRESOME PARK

GUISBOROUGH

DARLINGTON

8,500

River Tees

Middlesbrough
(1903–95)

FEETHAMS

BRECKON HILL ROAD

Middlesbrough
(1979–80)

Darlington
1921–1989, 1990

PARADISE GROUND

DARLINGTON 1883

Middlesbrough Ironopolis
1893–94

The North East

20,000	Capacity of stadium
	Stadium no longer in use for top-flight football
	Current league clubs
	Other clubs
	Club colours unknown
♛	League membership
A1(M)	Motorway
A19	Major road
1900	Champions
2000	Runners-up

'Wor Jackie', as Jackie Milburn is known on Tyneside, played 354 league games for the club, scoring a record 179 goals between 1946–59. His statue stands on Brewery Street in Newcastle city centre.

England

FANS AND OWNERS

SINCE THE FORMATION of the Premiership, patterns of club ownership in English football have changed. A core of top clubs continue to be owned privately by rich individuals, either directly (the Moores at Liverpool) or indirectly through trusts and offshore arrangements (Ken Bates at Chelsea, Al Fayed at Fulham). Others have floated as public companies on one of the British stock exchanges. Finance companies and media companies (Granada, BSkyB and NTL) have taken the lead in buying stakes in clubs. However, since the collapse of ITV Digital and the global transfer market, share prices have plummeted and there are few takers for shares in most clubs.

Numbers up, volume down

Whoever the fans are, there are more of them. Gates in all divisions, but especially the Premiership, have steadily risen since the lows of the early 1980s. Since then, all-seater stadiums have become compulsory, private boxes and corporate hospitality have become integral features of club incomes, and crowd trouble has all but been eliminated within the grounds (although it has been partially displaced to outside the ground, to the lower division clubs and to the national team's following). The concern remains that these changes have come at a price, as the noise and passion of the crowd has been sanitized.

Old fans, new fans

Inside the stands, the traditional long-term football fans remain but they have been joined by a wave of new fans. These are, on average, wealthier than the older fans and include significantly more women. The enormous number of domestic and foreign black players is not, however, mirrored on the terraces. Unsurprisingly, fans from the north of England tend to be lower earners than fans from the south, and are much more likely to have been born locally to the club. Manchester United is the exception, drawing significant support country-wide.

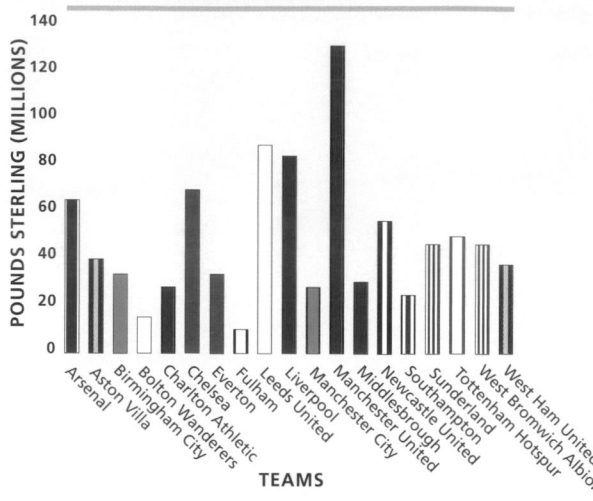

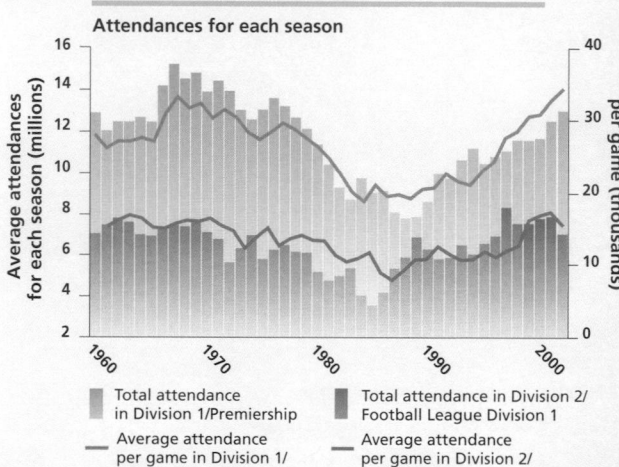

Fans Income

% of season ticket holders earning over £50,000 PA

40% 30% 20% 10% 0%

TEAMS
Arsenal
Aston Villa
Chelsea
Everton
Leeds United
Liverpool
Manchester United
Middlesbrough
Newcastle United
Southampton
Sunderland
Tottenham Hotspur
West Ham United

Fans Origins

% of season ticket holders who were born locally

40% 45% 50% 55% 60% 65% 70% 75% 80% 85%

Details from season 2002–03

The Toon Army on tour: Newcastle's devoted following are unique in their capacity to brave the cold. They are a truly home grown audience with 85 per cent of their season ticket holders born locally.

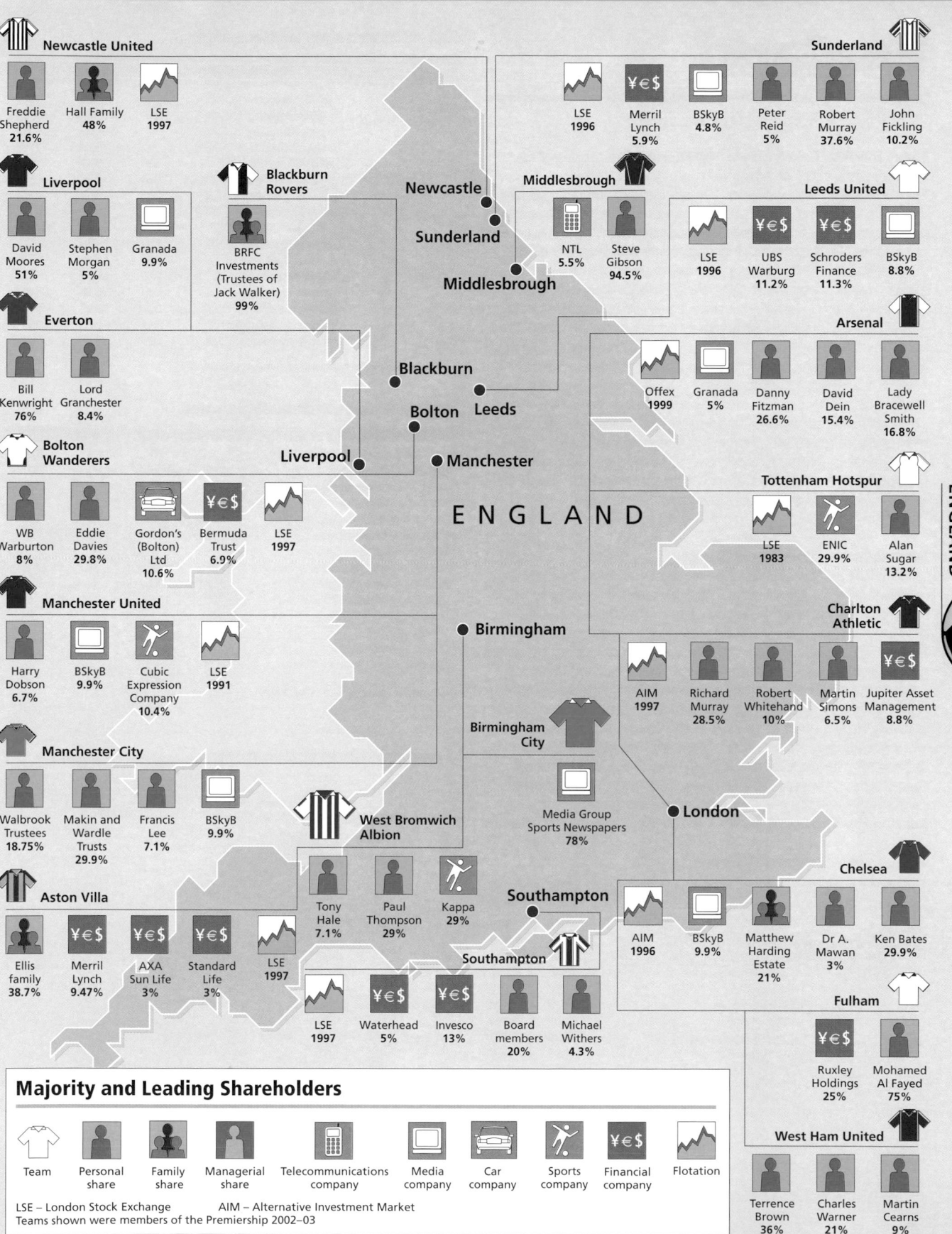

Newcastle United

Freddie Shepherd 21.6%	Hall Family 48%	LSE 1997

Liverpool

David Moores 51%	Stephen Morgan 5%	Granada 9.9%

Blackburn Rovers

BRFC Investments (Trustees of Jack Walker) 99%

Everton

Bill Kenwright 76%	Lord Granchester 8.4%

Bolton Wanderers

WB Warburton 8%	Eddie Davies 29.8%	Gordon's (Bolton) Ltd 10.6%	Bermuda Trust 6.9%	LSE 1997

Manchester United

Harry Dobson 6.7%	BSkyB 9.9%	Cubic Expression Company 10.4%	LSE 1991

Manchester City

Walbrook Trustees 18.75%	Makin and Wardle Trusts 29.9%	Francis Lee 7.1%	BSkyB 9.9%

Aston Villa

Ellis family 38.7%	Merril Lynch 9.47%	AXA Sun Life 3%	Standard Life 3%	LSE 1997

Sunderland

LSE 1996	Merril Lynch 5.9%	BSkyB 4.8%	Peter Reid 5%	Robert Murray 37.6%	John Fickling 10.2%

Middlesbrough

NTL 5.5%	Steve Gibson 94.5%

Leeds United

LSE 1996	UBS Warburg 11.2%	Schroders Finance 11.3%	BSkyB 8.8%

Arsenal

Offex 1999	Granada 5%	Danny Fitzman 26.6%	David Dein 15.4%	Lady Bracewell Smith 16.8%

Tottenham Hotspur

LSE 1983	ENIC 29.9%	Alan Sugar 13.2%

Charlton Athletic

AIM 1997	Richard Murray 28.5%	Robert Whitehand 10%	Martin Simons 6.5%	Jupiter Asset Management 8.8%

Birmingham City

Media Group Sports Newspapers 78%

West Bromwich Albion

Tony Hale 7.1%	Paul Thompson 29%	Kappa 29%

Southampton

LSE 1997	Waterhead 5%	Invesco 13%	Board members 20%	Michael Withers 4.3%

Chelsea

AIM 1996	BSkyB 9.9%	Matthew Harding Estate 21%	Dr A. Mawan 3%	Ken Bates 29.9%

Fulham

Ruxley Holdings 25%	Mohamed Al Fayed 75%

West Ham United

Terrence Brown 36%	Charles Warner 21%	Martin Cearns 9%

Map labels: Newcastle, Sunderland, Middlesbrough, Blackburn, Bolton, Leeds, Liverpool, Manchester, Birmingham, London, Southampton, ENGLAND

ENGLAND

Majority and Leading Shareholders

Team	Personal share	Family share	Managerial share	Telecommunications company	Media company	Car company	Sports company	Financial company	Flotation

LSE – London Stock Exchange   AIM – Alternative Investment Market
Teams shown were members of the Premiership 2002–03

England

PLAYERS AND MANAGERS

THE CULTURE OF ENGLISH PROFESSIONAL football has changed over the last hundred years, particularly since professionalism was legalized. Before that it had been solidly working class, simultaneously tough and impassioned on the pitch and apparently deferential to authority off it. It was only in the 1960s that money began to move into the game, the maximum wage for players was abolished and contractual freedom was obtained. In the shape of Bobby Moore, Geoff Hurst and Bobby Charlton, a new generation of talent emerged.

But, to the surprise and horror of many of the foreign players that arrived in England in the early 1990s, little else has changed. Heart and lungs are still often valued over technique and training. Scientific analysis, nutritional care and tactical preparation have been disdained in favour of rough and ready measures, fried breakfasts and just getting 'stuck into them'. Above all, the drinking and nightlife culture of professional footballers has not gone away; if anything, the riches of the Premiership have intensified it. For every clean-cut dedicated Michael Owen there seems to be an unruly Stan Collymore, the wasted talent of Paul Gascoigne or the headlining antics of Jonathan Woodgate.

Motivation over technique

The limit of the motivation over technique school of English management was reached with the demise of Kevin Keegan as England manager and his replacement with the national team's first foreign manager, Sven-Göran Eriksson. Although Glenn Hoddle and Bobby Robson continue to thrive as leading managers, the bulk of the Premiership's top teams are coached by Scots (Alex Ferguson at Manchester United, David Moyes at Everton and Graeme Souness at Blackburn), Frenchmen (Gérard Houllier at Liverpool, Arsène Wenger at Arsenal) or Italians (Claudio Ranieri at Chelsea). The influx of foreign players appears to have peaked as the current financial crisis limits clubs' wage bills. However, more leading foreign players are coming to the Premiership earlier in their careers – Juan Sebastian Veron and Ruud van Nistelrooy at Manchester United are leading examples of this.

Top 20 International Caps

PLAYER	CAPS	GOALS	FIRST MATCH	LAST MATCH
Peter Shilton	125	0	1970	1990
Bobby Moore	108	2	1962	1973
Bobby Charlton	106	49	1958	1970
Billy Wright	105	3	1946	1959
Bryan Robson	90	26	1980	1991
Kenny Sansom	86	1	1979	1988
Ray Wilkins	84	3	1976	1986
Gary Lineker	80	48	1984	1992
John Barnes	79	11	1983	1995
Stuart Pearce	78	5	1987	1999
Terry Butcher	77	3	1980	1990
Tom Finney	76	30	1946	1958
David Seaman*	75	0	1988	2003
Alan Ball	72	8	1965	1975
Gordon Banks	72	0	1963	1972
Martin Peters	67	20	1966	1974
Tony Adams	66	5	1987	2000
Dave Watson	65	4	1974	1982
Kevin Keegan	63	21	1972	1982
Alan Shearer*	63	30	1991	2000

Top 16 International Goalscorers

PLAYER	GOALS	CAPS	FIRST MATCH	LAST MATCH
Bobby Charlton	49	106	1958	1970
Gary Lineker	48	80	1984	1992
Jimmy Greaves	43	57	1959	1967
Nat Lofthouse	30	33	1950	1958
Alan Shearer*	30	63	1991	2000
Tom Finney	30	76	1946	1958
Vivian Woodward	29	23	1903	1911
Stephen Bloomer	28	23	1895	1907
David Platt	27	62	1989	1996
Bryan Robson	26	90	1980	1991
Geoff Hurst	24	49	1966	1972
Stan Mortensen	23	25	1947	1953
Tommy Lawton	22	23	1938	1948
Michael Owen*	22	50	1998	2003
Mick Channon	21	46	1972	1977
Kevin Keegan	21	63	1972	1982

* Indicates players still playing at least at club level.

English International Managers

DATES	NAME	GAMES	WON	DRAWN	LOST
1946–62	Walter Winterbottom	139	78	33	28
1963–74	Alf Ramsey	113	69	27	17
1974	Joe Mercer	7	3	3	1
1974–77	Don Revie	29	14	8	7
1977–82	Ron Greenwood	55	33	12	10
1982–90	Bobby Robson	95	47	30	18
1990–93	Graham Taylor	38	18	13	7
1994–96	Terry Venables	23	11	11	1
1996–99	Glenn Hoddle	28	17	6	5
1999	Howard Wilkinson	2	0	1	1
1999–2000	Kevin Keegan	18	7	7	4
2000	Peter Taylor	1	0	0	1
2000–	Sven Goran Eriksson	29	16	9	4

All figures correct as of 11 June 2003.

Foreign Players in England (in top division squads)

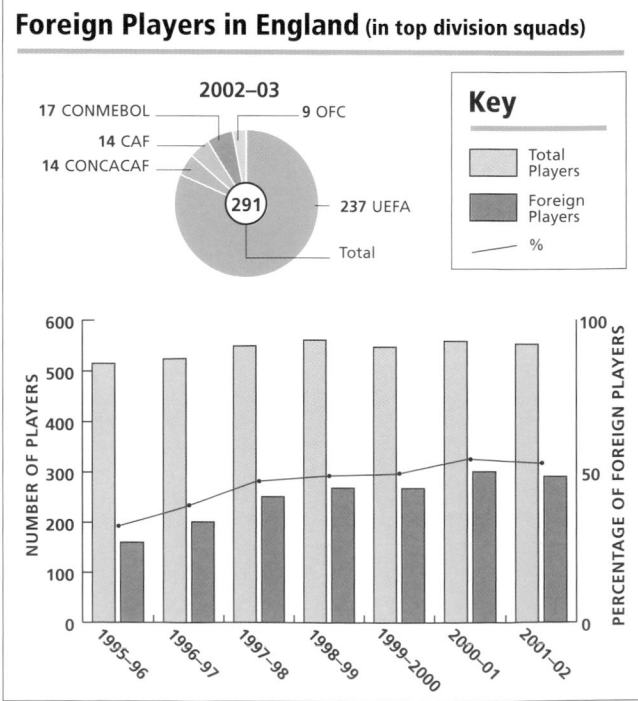

2002–03

17 CONMEBOL
14 CAF
14 CONCACAF
9 OFC
291
237 UEFA
Total

Key
Total Players
Foreign Players
%

ENGLAND

Player of the Year

YEAR	PLAYER	CLUB
1948	Matthews	Blackpool
1949	Carey	Manchester United
1950	Mercer	Arsenal
1951	Johnston	Blackpool
1952	Wright	Wolverhampton W
1953	Lofthouse	Bolton Wanderers
1954	Finney	Preston North End
1955	Revie	Manchester City
1956	Trautmann	Manchester City
1957	Finney	Preston North End
1958	Blanchflower	Tottenham Hotspur
1959	Owen	Luton Town
1960	Slater	Wolverhampton W
1961	Blanchflower	Tottenham Hotspur
1962	Adamson	Burnley
1963	Matthews	Stoke City
1964	Moore	West Ham United
1965	Collins	Leeds United
1966	R. Charlton	Manchester United
1967	J. Charlton	Leeds United
1968	Best	Manchester United
1969	Mackay	Derby County
1969	Book	Manchester City
1970	Bremner	Leeds United
1971	McLintock	Arsenal
1972	Banks	Stoke City
1973	Jennings	Tottenham Hotspur
1974	Callaghan	Liverpool
1975	Mullery	Fulham
1976	Keegan	Liverpool

Player of the Year (*continued*)

YEAR	PLAYER	CLUB
1977	Hughes	Liverpool
1978	Burns	Nottingham Forest
1979	Dalglish	Liverpool
1980	McDermott	Liverpool
1981	Thijssen	Ipswich Town
1982	Perryman	Tottenham Hotspur
1983	Dalglish	Liverpool
1984	Rush	Liverpool
1985	Southall	Everton
1986	Lineker	Everton
1987	Allen	Tottenham Hotspur
1988	Barnes	Liverpool
1989	Nicol	Liverpool
1990	Barnes	Liverpool
1991	Strachan	Leeds United
1992	Lineker	Tottenham Hotspur
1993	Waddle	Sheffield Wednesday
1994	Shearer	Blackburn Rovers
1995	Klinsmann	Tottenham Hotspur
1996	Cantona	Manchester United
1997	Zola	Chelsea
1998	Bergkamp	Arsenal
1999	Ginola	Tottenham Hotspur
2000	Keane	Manchester United
2001	Owen	Liverpool
2002	Pires	Arsenal
2003	Henry	Arsenal

Awarded by the English Football Writers' Association.

The legendary Dixie Dean presents the Player of the Year trophy to Liverpool's Kevin Keegan in 1976.

The late Walter Winterbottom, England's first international manager, remained in charge of the team from 1946 to 1962.

Top Goalscorers by Season 1947–2003

SEASON	PLAYER	CLUB	GOALS
1947–48	Rooke	Arsenal	33
1948–49	Moir	Bolton W	25
1949–50	Davies	Sunderland	25
1950–51	Mortensen	Blackpool	30
1951–52	Robledo	Newcastle Utd	33
1952–53	Wayman	Preston NE	24
1953–54	Glazzard	Huddersfield T	29
1954–55	Allen	WBA	27
1955–56	Lofthouse	Bolton W	33
1956–57	Charles	Leeds United	38
1957–58	Smith	Spurs	36
1958–59	Greaves	Chelsea	33
1959–60	Viollet	Manchester U	32
1960–61	Greaves	Chelsea	41
1961–62	Crawford	Ipswich Town	33
1961–62	Kevan	WBA	33
1962–63	Greaves	Spurs	37
1963–64	Greaves	Spurs	35
1964–65	Greaves	Spurs	29
1964–65	McEvoy	Blackburn R	29
1965–66	Irvine	Burnley	29
1966–67	Davies	Southampton	37
1967–68	Best	Manchester U	28
1967–68	Davies	Southampton	28
1968–69	Greaves	Spurs	27
1969–70	Astle	WBA	25
1970–71	Brown	WBA	28
1971–72	Lee	Manchester C	33
1972–73	Robson	West Ham U	28
1973–74	Channon	Southampton	21
1974–75	Macdonald	Newcastle Utd	21
1975–76	MacDougall	Norwich City	23
1976–77	Macdonald	Newcastle Utd	25
1976–77	Gray	Aston Villa	25
1977–78	Latchford	Everton	30
1978–79	Worthington	Bolton W	24
1979–80	Boyer	Southampton	23

SEASON	PLAYER	CLUB	GOALS
1980–81	Withe	Aston Villa	20
1980–81	Archibald	Spurs	20
1981–82	Keegan	Southampton	26
1982–83	Blisset	Watford	27
1983–84	Rush	Liverpool	32
1984–85	Dixon	Chelsea	24
1984–85	Lineker	Leicester City	24
1985–86	Lineker	Everton	30
1986–87	Allen	Spurs	33
1987–88	Aldridge	Liverpool	26
1988–89	Smith	Arsenal	23
1989–90	Lineker	Spurs	24
1990–91	Chapman	Leeds United	31
1991–92	Wright	Crystal Palace/ Arsenal	29
1992–93	Sheringham	Nottingham F/ Spurs	22
1993–94	Cole	Newcastle Utd	34
1994–95	Shearer	Blackburn R	35
1995–96	Shearer	Blackburn R	31
1996–97	Shearer	Newcastle Utd	25
1997–98	Owen	Liverpool	18
1997–98	Sutton	Blackburn R	18
1997–98	Dublin	Coventry City	18
1998–99	Yorke	Manchester U	18
1998–99	Owen	Liverpool	18
1998–99	Hasselbaink	Leeds United	18
1999–2000	Phillips	Sunderland	30
2000–01	Hasselbaink	Chelsea	23
2001–02	Henry	Arsenal	24
2001–02	Shearer	Newcastle	24
2002–03	van Nistelrooy	Manchester United	25

*With **49 goals** in 106 appearances, Bobby Charlton (right) is one of England's greatest players. His brother Jack (left) also played 35 times for England, and both were members of the 1966 World Cup-winning team.*

ENGLAND

England

THE PREMIERSHIP 1992–2002

IN 1992, THE ENGLISH PREMIER LEAGUE was established by the country's 22 leading clubs, breaking away from the control of the English FA and the Football League. Correctly anticipating an enormous increase in TV income for football, the Premier League was primarily a device for keeping that income at the top and excluding both non-league and lower division football from the goldrush; to that extent it has succeeded. The most recent TV deal (2001–2004) has brought in nearly £1.6 billion over three years. Combined with rising gate income, sponsorship deals and intensive merchandising, the English Premier League is the richest in global football.

Where does the money go?
Yet as fast as the money comes in, it goes out, drained by the explosive rise in player's wages and the increasingly large transfer budgets of Premiership clubs. Most of the latter have been spent overseas. Clubs have brought players from all over Europe, as well as South America, the Caribbean and Africa. The increasing financial muscle of the Premiership can be seen in the gradual acquisition of players from the strongest European leagues (Italy, Germany and the Netherlands) – and not just players coming to the end of their career (Klinsmann, Gullit, Vialli) but players in their prime (van Nistelrooy, Veron, Viera).

Below the Premiership, the English lower divisions have seen transfer income steadily diminish while wage bills rise, a situation exacerbated by the ITV Digital disaster, which may well see clubs close down. The enormous foreign presence in the Premiership (both among players and, increasingly, managers as well) has raised the technical and tactical sophistication of the game immeasurably, but it remains to be seen what the consequence of this will be for the development of indigenous English talent.

Unite and rule
Financial and sporting success has become increasingly concentrated at the top end of the Premiership. In nine seasons, Alex Ferguson's Manchester United has taken seven championships; in 2000–01 it won at a canter. Ferguson has built a series of teams at United based on an attacking and aggressive 4-4-2 play. Passing, moving and possessed of an unquenchable confidence, his team persistently dominated the weaker teams when its challengers have shown inconsistency. United has shown the capacity to come back from behind, raise its game at the crucial moments of the season and score more goals than anyone else. Only Blackburn Rovers, fuelled by Jack Walker's personal fortune (1995) and Alan Shearer's best year, and Arsenal, under the cerebral Arsène Wenger (1998), have broken the Mancunian monopoly. In both seasons, United still came in a close second. Challenges from Leeds, Liverpool, Chelsea and Kevin Keegan's Newcastle were all seen off.

Life at the bottom
Financial imbalances have created a whole category of clubs that are too strong for Division One but too weak to sustain their place in the Premiership. Manchester City, Bolton, Crystal Palace and others have been condemned to a cycle of relegation and promotion. Excluded from significant TV income while in the First Division, a single year in the Premiership does not deliver enough money to sufficiently strengthen the team. Outspending resources in a gamble to stay up can see clubs left deep in debt. Others constantly teeter on the edge of the relegation precipice, like Everton, Southampton and, in the case of Coventry, eventually fall over it. Even clubs with bigger resources, such as Tottenham and Aston Villa, have been reduced to mid-table scrapping and the fight for a place in the UEFA Cup.

Above: *The shift of power begins: Arsenal players celebrate the double after beating Manchester United 1-0 at Old Trafford in May 2002.*

Above right: *Going for broke: under chairman Peter Ridsdale Leeds United broke the bank in pursuit of Premiership and Champions League glory. After two disappointing seasons in 2000–01 and 2001–02, Terry Venables was called in to pick up the pieces – he lasted eight months, Ridsdale soon followed.*

Player Salaries 1995–2000

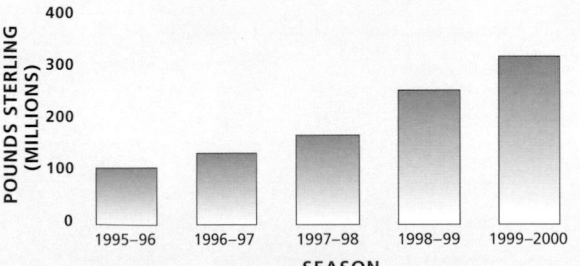

Total wage bill of Premiership clubs

Annual TV Rights Income

YEAR	POUNDS STERLING (MILLIONS)
1983	(2.6 BBC/ITV)
1984	(2.6 BBC/ITV)
1985	(1.3 BBC/ITV)
1986	(3.1 BBC/ITV)
1987	(3.1 BBC/ITV)
1988	(11 ITV)
1989	(11 ITV)
1990	(11 ITV)
1991	(11 ITV)
1992	(38.3 BskyB)
1993	(38.3 BskyB)
1994	(38.3 BskyB)
1995	(38.3 BskyB)
1996	(38.3 BskyB)
1997	(168 BskyB)
1998	(168 BskyB)
1999	(168 BskyB)
2000	(168 BskyB)
2001	(367 BskyB)
2002	(367 BskyB)
2003	(367 BskyB)

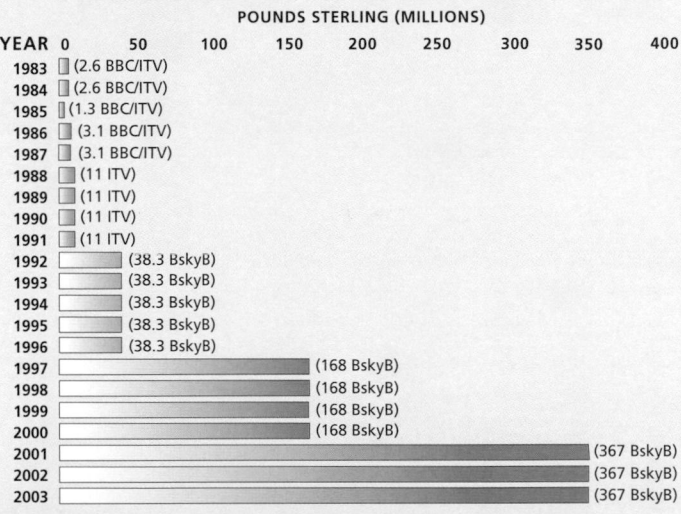

Financial and sporting success has become increasingly concentrated at the top end of the Premiership. In nine seasons, Alex Ferguson's Manchester United (below) took seven championships.

ENGLAND

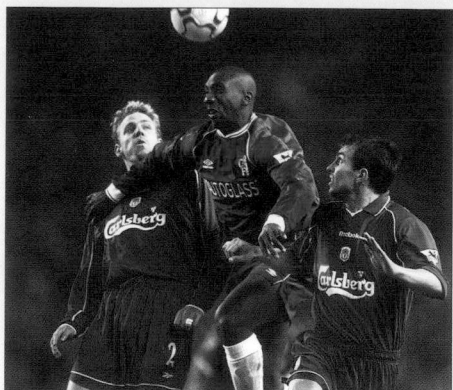

The new look Liverpool under Gérard Houllier has crept back into contention for the Premiership title since the beginning of the Millennium but, like fellow challenger Chelsea, it has yet to deliver the prize.

Key to League Positions Table

- League champions
- Season of promotion to league
- Season of relegation from league
- Other teams playing in league
- **5** Final position in league

English League Positions 1992–2002

TEAM	1992–93	1993–94	1994–95	1995–96	1996–97	1997–98	1998–99	1999–2000	2000–01	2001–02
Arsenal	10	4	12	5	3	1	2	2	2	1
Aston Villa	2	10	18	4	5	7	6	6	8	8
Barnsley						19				
Birmingham City										
Blackburn Rovers	4	2	1	7	13	6	19			10
Bolton Wanderers			20		18					16
Bradford City								17	20	
Charlton Athletic							18		9	14
Chelsea	11	14	11	11	6	4	3	5	6	6
Coventry City	15	11	16	16	17	11	15	14	19	
Crystal Palace	20		19			20				
Derby County					12	9	8	16	17	19
Everton	13	17	15	6	15	17	14	13	16	15
Fulham										13
Ipswich Town	16	19	22						5	18
Leeds United	17	5	5	13	11	5	4	3	4	5
Leicester City		21		9	10	10	8	13	20	
Liverpool	6	8	4	3	4	3	7	4	3	2
Manchester City	9	16	17	18					18	
Manchester United	1	1	2	1	1	2	1	1	1	3
Middlesbrough	21		12	19		9	12	14	12	
Newcastle United		3	6	2	2	13	13	11	11	4
Norwich City	3	12	20							
Nottingham Forest	22		3	9	20		20			
Oldham Athletic	19	21								
Queens Park Rangers	5	9	8	19						
Sheffield United	14	20								
Sheffield Wednesday	7	7	13	15	7	16	12	19		
Southampton	18	18	10	17	16	12	17	15	10	11
Sunderland					18			7	7	17
Swindon Town		22								
Tottenham Hotspur	8	15	7	8	10	14	11	10	12	9
Watford								20		
West Bromwich Albion										
West Ham United		13	14	10	14	8	5	9	15	7
Wimbledon	12	6	9	14	8	15	16	18		

Champions' Winning Margin 1992–2002

CHAMPIONS' WINNING MARGIN (POINTS)

y-axis: 68, 70, 72, 74, 76, 78, 80, 82, 84, 86, 88, 90, 92

x-axis (SEASON): 1992–93, 1993–94, 1994–95, 1995–96, 1996–97, 1997–98, 1998–99, 1999–2000, 2000–01, 2001–02

42	42	38	38	38	38	38	38	38	38

Total games played by each team (3 points awarded for a win)

- Arsenal
- Aston Villa
- Blackburn Rovers
- Liverpool
- Manchester United
- Newcastle United

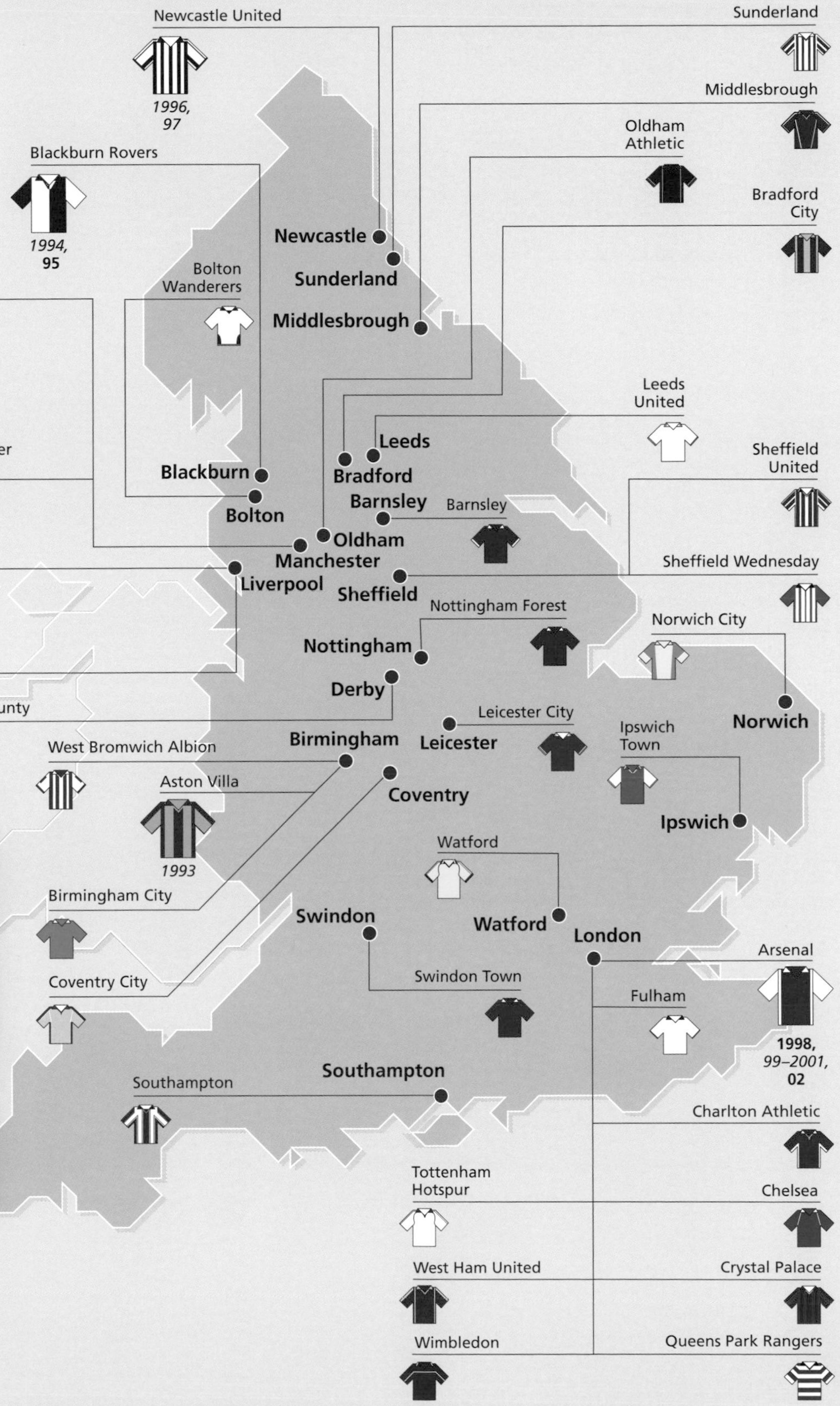

ENGLAND

The Premiership

Arsenal — Team name

League champions/runners-up

1998, *99* — Champions in bold / Runners-up in italics

Other teams in the Premiership

● **London** — City of origin

Newcastle United
1996,
97

Sunderland

Middlesbrough

Oldham Athletic

Bradford City

Blackburn Rovers
1994,
95

Bolton Wanderers

● **Newcastle**

● **Sunderland**

● **Middlesbrough**

Leeds United

Sheffield United

Manchester United
1993, 94,
95, **96, 97,**
98, 99–2001

Manchester City

● **Blackburn**

● **Leeds**

● **Bradford**
● **Barnsley** Barnsley

Sheffield Wednesday

Liverpool
2002

Everton

● **Bolton**

● **Oldham**
● **Manchester**
● **Liverpool** ● **Sheffield**

Nottingham Forest

Norwich City

Derby County

● **Nottingham**

● **Derby**

Leicester City

● **Norwich**

West Bromwich Albion

Aston Villa
1993

● **Birmingham**

● **Leicester** Leicester

Ipswich Town

● **Coventry**

● **Ipswich**

Birmingham City

Watford

Coventry City

● **Swindon**

● **Watford**

● **London**

Arsenal
1998,
99–2001,
02

Swindon Town

Fulham

Charlton Athletic

● **Southampton**

Southampton

Tottenham Hotspur

Chelsea

West Ham United

Crystal Palace

Wimbledon

Queens Park Rangers

In 1995, Blackburn Rovers took the Premiership, stalling Manchester United's run for a title hat trick. The victory was due, in part, to its generous chairman Jack Walker (above) who granted Kenny Dalglish an unprecedented budget to buy the calibre of players it needed to win.

 # England

The Football Association
Founded: 1863
Joined FIFA: 1905–20, 1924–28, 1946
Joined UEFA: 1954

IN ENGLAND, UNLIKE MOST NATIONS, national football competitions began with the cup rather than the league. The Football Association Challenge Cup, or FA Cup as it is usually known, began in 1872, and is the oldest formal footballing tournament in the world. It was open to amateur clubs and, after legalization in 1885, to professional teams as well. The Final found a permanent home at Wembley in 1923, but moved to the Millennium Stadium in Cardiff in 2001. Currently, over 500 non-league teams compete in preliminary rounds before the bottom two league divisions join in the first round, and the First Division and Premiership teams join in the third round. Each year the competition takes ten months to complete.

A separate League Cup, not open to amateur teams, was created in 1961. For the first six years, the Final was decided over two legs, home and away, before finding a new home at Wembley in 1967. Despite rather low attendances, often gruelling two-leg rounds, and endless changes of name and sponsor, the lure of a UEFA Cup place for the winners has retained interest in the competition.

The Football League was established in 1888 by a core of 12 professional clubs from the Midlands and the north of England. A second division was added in 1892, a third in 1920 and a fourth in 1921, when the lower division was divided into Third Division North and South. These were amalgamated to create a Third and Fourth Division in 1950. The national leagues were replaced by regional competitions for most of the First and Second World Wars. The FA Cup competition was suspended between 1916 and 1919, and again between 1940 and 1945, though a War Cup, with a Final at Wembley, was hastily organized in 1941 and contested for the next few years.

In 1992, the top 22 clubs broke away from the FA's control to create an independently administered Premiership. Three teams are relegated from the now 20-team league, and three come up from Division One (two automatically and one by play-off).

English League Record 1889–2003

SEASON	CHAMPIONS	RUNNERS-UP
1889	Preston North End	Aston Villa
1890	Preston North End	Everton
1891	Everton	Preston North End
1892	Sunderland	Preston North End
1893	Sunderland	Preston North End
1894	Aston Villa	Sunderland
1895	Sunderland	Everton
1896	Aston Villa	Derby County
1897	Aston Villa	Sheffield United
1898	Sheffield United	Sunderland
1899	Aston Villa	Liverpool
1900	Aston Villa	Sheffield United
1901	Liverpool	Sunderland
1902	Sunderland	Everton
1903	Sheffield Wednesday	Aston Villa
1904	Sheffield Wednesday	Manchester City
1905	Newcastle United	Everton
1906	Liverpool	Preston North End
1907	Newcastle United	Bristol City

English League Record (*continued*)

SEASON	CHAMPIONS	RUNNERS-UP
1908	Manchester United	Aston Villa
1909	Newcastle United	Everton
1910	Aston Villa	Liverpool
1911	Manchester United	Aston Villa
1912	Blackburn Rovers	Everton
1913	Sunderland	Aston Villa
1914	Blackburn Rovers	Aston Villa
1915	Everton	Oldham Athletic
1916–19	*no championship*	
1920	West Bromwich Albion	Burnley
1921	Burnley	Manchester City
1922	Liverpool	Tottenham Hotspur
1923	Liverpool	Sunderland
1924	Huddersfield Town	Cardiff City
1925	Huddersfield Town	West Bromwich Albion
1926	Huddersfield Town	Arsenal
1927	Newcastle United	Huddersfield Town
1928	Everton	Huddersfield Town
1929	Sheffield Wednesday	Leicester City
1930	Sheffield Wednesday	Derby County
1931	Arsenal	Aston Villa
1932	Everton	Arsenal
1933	Arsenal	Aston Villa
1934	Arsenal	Huddersfield Town
1935	Arsenal	Sunderland
1936	Sunderland	Derby County
1937	Manchester City	Charlton Athletic
1938	Arsenal	Wolverhampton Wanderers
1939	Everton	Wolverhampton Wanderers
1940–46	*no championship*	
1947	Liverpool	Manchester United
1948	Arsenal	Manchester United
1949	Portsmouth	Manchester United
1950	Portsmouth	Wolverhampton Wanderers
1951	Tottenham Hotspur	Manchester United
1952	Manchester United	Tottenham Hotspur
1953	Arsenal	Preston North End
1954	Wolverhampton Wanderers	West Bromwich Albion
1955	Chelsea	Wolverhampton Wanderers
1956	Manchester United	Blackpool
1957	Manchester United	Tottenham Hotspur
1958	Wolverhampton Wanderers	Preston North End
1959	Wolverhampton Wanderers	Manchester United
1960	Burnley	Wolverhampton Wanderers
1961	Tottenham Hotspur	Sheffield Wednesday
1962	Ipswich Town	Burnley
1963	Everton	Tottenham Hotspur
1964	Liverpool	Manchester United
1965	Manchester United	Leeds United
1966	Liverpool	Leeds United
1967	Manchester United	Nottingham Forest
1968	Manchester City	Manchester United
1969	Leeds United	Liverpool
1970	Everton	Leeds United
1971	Arsenal	Leeds United
1972	Derby County	Leeds United
1973	Liverpool	Arsenal
1974	Leeds United	Liverpool
1975	Derby County	Liverpool
1976	Liverpool	Queens Park Rangers
1977	Liverpool	Manchester City
1978	Nottingham Forest	Liverpool

ENGLAND

English League Record (*continued*)

SEASON	CHAMPIONS	RUNNERS-UP
1979	Liverpool	Nottingham Forest
1980	Liverpool	Manchester United
1981	Aston Villa	Ipswich Town
1982	Liverpool	Ipswich Town
1983	Liverpool	Watford
1984	Liverpool	Southampton
1985	Everton	Liverpool
1986	Liverpool	Everton
1987	Everton	Liverpool
1988	Liverpool	Manchester United
1989	Arsenal	Liverpool
1990	Liverpool	Aston Villa
1991	Arsenal	Liverpool
1992	Leeds United	Manchester United
1993	Manchester United	Aston Villa
1994	Manchester United	Blackburn Rovers
1995	Blackburn Rovers	Manchester United
1996	Manchester United	Newcastle United
1997	Manchester United	Newcastle United
1998	Arsenal	Manchester United
1999	Manchester United	Arsenal
2000	Manchester United	Arsenal
2001	Manchester United	Arsenal
2002	Arsenal	Liverpool
2003	Manchester United	Arsenal

English League Summary

TEAM	TOTALS	CHAMPIONS & RUNNERS-UP (BOLD) (*ITALICS*)
Liverpool	**18**, *11*	*1899*, **1901, 06, 10, 22, 23, 47, 64, 66,** *69*, **73,** *74, 75,* **76, 77, 78, 79, 80, 82–84,** *85,* **86, 87, 88, 89, 90,** *91,* **2002**
Manchester United	**15**, *12*	**1908,** *11, 47–49, 51,* **52,** *56,* **57,** *59, 64,* **65,** *67,* **68,** *80,* **88,** *92,* **93, 94,** *95,* **96, 97,** *98,* **99–2001,** *03*
Arsenal	**12**, *7*	*1926,* **31,** *32,* **33–35,** *38,* **48,** *53,* **71,** *73,* **89,** *91,* **98,** *99–2001,* **02,** *03*
Everton	**9**, *7*	*1890,* **91,** *95,* **1902,** *05,* **09,** *12,* **15,** *28,* **32, 39,** *63,* **70,** *85,* **86, 87**
Aston Villa	**7**, *10*	**1889,** *94, 96, 97, 99,* **1900,** *03,* **08,** *10, 11, 13, 14,* **31,** *33,* **81,** *90, 93*
Sunderland	**6**, *5*	**1892,** *93,* **94, 95,** *98,* **1901,** *02,* **13,** *23,* **35,** *36*
Newcastle United	**4**, *2*	**1905, 07, 09, 27,** *96, 97*
Sheffield Wednesday	**4**, *1*	**1903, 04, 29, 30,** *61*
Leeds United	**3**, *5*	*1965, 66,* **69,** *70–72,* **74,** *92*
Wolverhampton Wanderers	**3**, *5*	*1938, 39, 50,* **54, 55,** *58, 59,* **60**
Huddersfield Town	**3**, *3*	**1924–26,** *27, 28,* **34**
Blackburn Rovers	**3**, *1*	**1912, 14,** *94,* **95**
Preston North End	**2**, *6*	**1889, 90,** *91–93, 1906, 53, 58*
Tottenham Hotspur	**2**, *4*	*1922,* **51,** *52, 57,* **61,** *63*
Derby County	**2**, *3*	*1896, 1930, 36,* **72,** *75*
Manchester City	**2**, *3*	*1904, 21,* **37,** *68, 77*
Burnley	**2**, *2*	*1920,* **21,** *60,* **62**
Portsmouth	**2**, *0*	**1949, 50**
Ipswich Town	**1**, *2*	**1962,** *81, 82*
Nottingham Forest	**1**, *2*	*1967,* **78,** *79*
Sheffield United	**1**, *2*	*1897,* **98,** *1900*
West Bromwich Albion	**1**, *2*	**1920,** *25, 54*
Chelsea	**1**, *0*	**1955**
Blackpool	**0**, *1*	*1956*
Bristol City	**0**, *1*	*1907*
Cardiff City	**0**, *1*	*1924*
Charlton Athletic	**0**, *1*	*1937*
Leicester City	**0**, *1*	*1929*

English League Summary (*continued*)

TEAM	TOTALS	CHAMPIONS & RUNNERS-UP (BOLD) (*ITALICS*)
Oldham Athletic	**0**, *1*	*1915*
Queens Park Rangers	**0**, *1*	*1976*
Southampton	**0**, *1*	*1984*
Watford	**0**, *1*	*1983*

English FA Cup Record 1872–2003

YEAR	WINNERS	SCORE	RUNNERS-UP
1872	Wanderers	1-0	Royal Engineers
1873	Wanderers	2-0	Oxford University
1874	Oxford University	2-0	Royal Engineers
1875	Royal Engineers	1-1 (aet), (replay) **2-0**	Old Etonians
1876	Wanderers	1-1 (aet), (replay) **3-0**	Old Etonians
1877	Wanderers	2-1 (aet)	Oxford University
1878	Wanderers	3-1	Royal Engineers
1879	Old Etonians	1-0	Clapham Rovers
1880	Clapham Rovers	1-0	Oxford University
1881	Old Carthusians	3-0	Old Etonians
1882	Old Etonians	1-0	Blackburn Rovers
1883	Blackburn Olympic	2-1 (aet)	Old Etonians
1884	Blackburn Rovers	2-1	Queen's Park
1885	Blackburn Rovers	2-0	Queen's Park
1886	Blackburn Rovers	0-0, (replay) **2-0**	West Bromwich Albion
1887	Aston Villa	2-0	West Bromwich Albion
1888	West Bromwich Albion	2-1	Preston North End
1889	Preston North End	3-0	Wolverhampton Wanderers
1890	Blackburn Rovers	6-1	Sheffield Wednesday
1891	Blackburn Rovers	3-1	Notts County
1892	West Bromwich Albion	3-0	Aston Villa
1893	Wolverhampton Wanderers	1-0	Everton
1894	Notts County	4-1	Bolton Wanderers
1895	Aston Villa	1-0	West Bromwich Albion
1896	Sheffield Wednesday	2-1	Wolverhampton Wanderers
1897	Aston Villa	3-2	Everton
1898	Nottingham Forest	3-1	Derby County
1899	Sheffield United	4-1	Derby County
1900	Bury	4-0	Southampton
1901	Tottenham Hotspur	2-2, (replay) **3-1**	Sheffield United
1902	Sheffield United	1-1, (replay) **2-1**	Southampton
1903	Bury	6-0	Derby County
1904	Manchester City	1-0	Bolton Wanderers
1905	Aston Villa	2-0	Newcastle United
1906	Everton	1-0	Newcastle United
1907	Sheffield Wednesday	2-1	Everton
1908	Wolverhampton Wanderers	3-1	Newcastle United
1909	Manchester United	1-0	Bristol City
1910	Newcastle United	1-1, (replay) **2-0**	Barnsley
1911	Bradford City	0-0, (replay) **1-0**	Newcastle United
1912	Barnsley	0-0, (replay) **1-0 (aet)**	West Bromwich Albion
1913	Aston Villa	1-0	Sunderland
1914	Burnley	1-0	Liverpool
1915	Sheffield United	3-0	Chelsea
1916–19		*no competition*	

ENGLAND

ENGLAND

English FA Cup Record (*continued*)

YEAR	WINNERS	SCORE	RUNNERS-UP
1920	Aston Villa	1-0 (aet)	Huddersfield Town
1921	Tottenham Hotspur	1-0	Wolverhampton Wanderers
1922	Huddersfield Town	1-0	Preston North End
1923	Bolton Wanderers	2-0	West Ham United
1924	Newcastle United	2-0	Aston Villa
1925	Sheffield United	1-0	Cardiff City
1926	Bolton Wanderers	1-0	Manchester City
1927	Cardiff City	1-0	Arsenal
1928	Blackburn Rovers	3-1	Huddersfield Town
1929	Bolton Wanderers	2-0	Portsmouth
1930	Arsenal	2-0	Huddersfield Town
1931	West Bromwich Albion	2-1	Birmingham City
1932	Newcastle United	2-1	Arsenal
1933	Everton	3-0	Manchester City
1934	Manchester City	2-1	Portsmouth
1935	Sheffield Wednesday	4-2	West Bromwich Albion
1936	Arsenal	1-0	Sheffield United
1937	Sunderland	3-1	Preston North End
1938	Preston North End	1-0 (aet)	Huddersfield Town
1939	Portsmouth	4-1	Wolverhampton Wanderers
1940–45	*no competition*		
1946	Derby County	4-1 (aet)	Charlton Athletic
1947	Charlton Athletic	1-0 (aet)	Burnley
1948	Manchester United	4-2	Blackpool
1949	Wolverhampton Wanderers	3-1	Leicester City
1950	Arsenal	2-0	Liverpool
1951	Newcastle United	2-0	Blackpool
1952	Newcastle United	1-0	Arsenal
1953	Blackpool	4-3	Bolton Wanderers
1954	West Bromwich Albion	3-2	Preston North End
1955	Newcastle United	3-1	Manchester City
1956	Manchester City	3-1	Birmingham City
1957	Aston Villa	2-1	Manchester United
1958	Bolton Wanderers	2-0	Manchester United
1959	Nottingham Forest	2-1	Luton Town
1960	Wolverhampton Wanderers	3-0	Blackburn Rovers
1961	Tottenham Hotspur	2-0	Leicester City
1962	Tottenham Hotspur	3-1	Burnley
1963	Manchester United	3-1	Leicester City
1964	West Ham United	3-2	Preston North End
1965	Liverpool	2-1 (aet)	Leeds United
1966	Everton	3-2	Sheffield Wednesday
1967	Tottenham Hotspur	2-1	Chelsea
1968	West Bromwich Albion	1-0 (aet)	Everton
1969	Manchester City	1-0	Leicester City
1970	Chelsea	2-2 (aet), (replay) 2-1 (aet)	Leeds United
1971	Arsenal	2-1 (aet)	Liverpool
1972	Leeds United	1-0	Arsenal
1973	Sunderland	1-0	Leeds United
1974	Liverpool	3-0	Newcastle United
1975	West Ham United	2-0	Fulham
1976	Southampton	1-0	Manchester United
1977	Manchester United	2-1	Liverpool
1978	Ipswich Town	1-0	Arsenal
1979	Arsenal	3-2	Manchester United

English FA Cup Record (*continued*)

YEAR	WINNERS	SCORE	RUNNERS-UP
1980	West Ham United	1-0	Arsenal
1981	Tottenham Hotspur	1-1 (aet), (replay) 3-2	Manchester City
1982	Tottenham Hotspur	1-1 (aet), (replay) 1-0	Queens Park Rangers
1983	Manchester United	2-2 (aet), (replay) 4-0	Brighton & Hove Albion
1984	Everton	2-0	Watford
1985	Manchester United	1-0 (aet)	Everton
1986	Liverpool	3-1	Everton
1987	Coventry City	3-2 (aet)	Tottenham Hotspur
1988	Wimbledon	1-0	Liverpool
1989	Liverpool	3-2 (aet)	Everton
1990	Manchester United	3-3 (aet), (replay) 1-0	Crystal Palace
1991	Tottenham Hotspur	2-1 (aet)	Nottingham Forest
1992	Liverpool	2-0	Sunderland
1993	Arsenal	1-1 (aet), (replay) 2-1 (aet)	Sheffield Wednesday
1994	Manchester United	4-0	Chelsea
1995	Everton	1-0	Manchester United
1996	Manchester United	1-0	Liverpool
1997	Chelsea	2-0	Middlesbrough
1998	Arsenal	2-0	Newcastle United
1999	Manchester United	2-0	Newcastle United
2000	Chelsea	1-0	Aston Villa
2001	Liverpool	2-1	Arsenal
2002	Arsenal	2-0	Chelsea
2003	Arsenal	1-0	Southampton

English FA Cup Summary

TEAM	TOTALS	WINNERS & RUNNERS-UP (**BOLD**) (*ITALICS*)
Manchester United	10, 5	**1909**, *48, 57, 58*, **63**, *76*, **77**, *79, 83, 85*, **90**, *94*, **95, 96, 99**
Arsenal	9, 7	*1927*, **30**, *32*, **36**, *50, 52*, **71**, *72, 78, 79, 80*, **93**, *98*, **2001**, *02*, **03**
Tottenham Hotspur	8, 1	**1901, 21, 61, 62, 67, 81, 82, 87**, *91*
Aston Villa	7, 3	**1887**, *92*, **95, 97, 1905**, *13*, **20**, *24*, **57**, *2000*
Newcastle United	6, 7	*1905, 06, 08*, **10, 11**, *24*, **32**, *51, 52*, **55**, *74, 98, 99*
Liverpool	6, 6	*1914, 50*, **65**, *71*, **74**, *77*, **86**, *88*, **89, 92**, *96*, **2001**
Blackburn Rovers	6, 2	*1882*, **84–86, 90, 91, 1928**, *60*
Everton	5, 7	*1893, 97*, **1906**, *07, 33*, **66**, *68*, **84**, *85, 86*, **89**, *95*
West Bromwich Albion	5, 5	*1886, 87*, **88**, *92, 95, 1912*, **31**, *35*, **54, 68**
Wanderers	5, 0	**1872, 73, 76–78**
Manchester City	4, 4	**1904**, *26, 33*, **34**, *55, 56*, **69**, *81*
Wolverhampton Wanderers	4, 4	*1889, 93, 96*, **1908**, *21*, **39**, *49*, **60**
Bolton Wanderers	4, 3	*1894*, **1904**, *23*, **26, 29**, *53*, **58**
Sheffield United	4, 2	**1899, 1901, 02**, *15*, **25**, *36*
Chelsea	3, 4	*1915, 67*, **70**, *94*, **97, 2000**, *02*
Sheffield Wednesday	3, 3	*1890, 96*, **1907**, *35*, **66**, *93*
West Ham United	3, 1	*1923*, **64, 75, 80**
Preston North End	2, 5	*1888*, **89**, *22, 37*, **38**, *54, 64*
Old Etonians	2, 4	*1875*, **76**, *79, 81*, **82**, *83*
Sunderland	2, 2	*1913*, **37**, *73*, **92**
Nottingham Forest	2, 1	**1898, 1959**, *91*

English FA Cup Summary (*continued*)

TEAM	TOTALS	WINNERS & RUNNERS-UP (BOLD) (*ITALICS*)
Bury	2, 0	**1900, 03**
Huddersfield Town	1, 4	*1920,* **22,** *28, 30, 38*
Derby County	1, 3	*1898, 99, 1903,* **46**
Leeds United	1, 3	*1965, 70,* **72,** *73*
Oxford University	1, 3	*1873,* **74,** *77, 80*
Royal Engineers	1, 3	*1872,* **74,** *75, 78*
Southampton	1, 3	*1900, 02,* **76,** *03*
Blackpool	1, 2	*1948, 51,* **53**
Burnley	1, 2	**1914,** *47, 62*
Portsmouth	1, 2	*1929, 34,* **39**
Barnsley	1, 1	*1910,* **12**
Cardiff City	1, 1	*1925,* **27**
Charlton Athletic	1, 1	*1946,* **47**
Clapham Rovers	1, 1	*1879,* **80**
Notts County	1, 1	*1891,* **94**
Blackburn Olympic	1, 0	**1883**
Bradford City	1, 0	**1911**
Coventry City	1, 0	**1987**
Ipswich Town	1, 0	**1978**
Old Carthusians	1, 0	**1881**
Wimbledon	1, 0	**1988**
Leicester City	0, 4	*1949, 61, 63, 69*
Birmingham City	0, 2	*1931, 56*
Queen's Park	0, 2	*1884, 85*
Brighton & Hove Albion	0, 1	*1983*
Bristol City	0, 1	*1909*
Crystal Palace	0, 1	*1990*
Fulham	0, 1	*1975*
Luton Town	0, 1	*1959*
Middlesbrough	0, 1	*1997*
Queens Park Rangers	0, 1	*1982*
Watford	0, 1	*1984*

English League Cup Record 1961–2003

YEAR	WINNERS	SCORE	RUNNERS-UP
1961	Aston Villa	0-2, 3-0 (aet) (2 legs)	Rotherham United
1962	Norwich City	3-0, 1-0 (2 legs)	Rochdale
1963	Birmingham City	3-1, 0-0 (2 legs)	Aston Villa
1964	Leicester City	1-1, 3-2 (2 legs)	Stoke City
1965	Chelsea	3-2, 0-0 (2 legs)	Leicester City
1966	West Bromwich Albion	1-2, 4-1 (2 legs)	West Ham United
1967	Queens Park Rangers	3-2	West Bromwich Albion
1968	Leeds United	1-0	Arsenal
1969	Swindon Town	3-1 (aet)	Arsenal
1970	Manchester City	2-1 (aet)	West Bromwich Albion
1971	Tottenham Hotspur	2-0	Aston Villa
1972	Stoke City	2-1	Chelsea
1973	Tottenham Hotspur	1-0	Norwich City
1974	Wolverhampton Wanderers	2-1	Manchester City
1975	Aston Villa	1-0	Norwich City
1976	Manchester City	2-1	Newcastle United
1977	Aston Villa	0-0, (replay) 1-1 (aet), (replay) 3-2 (aet)	Everton
1978	Nottingham Forest	0-0 (aet), (replay) 1-0	Liverpool
1979	Nottingham Forest	3-2	Southampton
1980	Wolverhampton Wanderers	1-0	Nottingham Forest
1981	Liverpool	1-1 (aet), (replay) 2-1	West Ham United

English League Cup Record (*continued*)

YEAR	WINNERS	SCORE	RUNNERS-UP
1982	Liverpool	3-1 (aet)	Tottenham Hotspur
1983	Liverpool	2-1 (aet)	Manchester United
1984	Liverpool	0-0 (aet), (replay) 1-0	Everton
1985	Norwich City	1-0	Sunderland
1986	Oxford United	3-0	Queens Park Rangers
1987	Arsenal	2-1	Liverpool
1988	Luton Town	3-2	Arsenal
1989	Nottingham Forest	3-1	Luton Town
1990	Nottingham Forest	1-0	Oldham Athletic
1991	Sheffield Wednesday	1-0	Manchester United
1992	Manchester United	1-0	Nottingham Forest
1993	Arsenal	2-1	Sheffield Wednesday
1994	Aston Villa	3-1	Manchester United
1995	Liverpool	2-1	Bolton Wanderers
1996	Aston Villa	3-0	Leeds United
1997	Leicester City	1-1 (aet), (replay) 1-0 (aet)	Middlesbrough
1998	Chelsea	2-0 (aet)	Middlesbrough
1999	Tottenham Hotspur	1-0	Leicester City
2000	Leicester City	2-1	Tranmere Rovers
2001	Liverpool	1-1 (aet)(5-4 pens)	Birmingham City
2002	Blackburn Rovers	2-1	Tottenham Hotspur
2003	Liverpool	2-0	Manchester United

English League Cup Summary

TEAM	TOTALS	WINNERS & RUNNERS-UP (BOLD) (*ITALICS*)
Liverpool	7, 2	*1978,* **81–84, 87, 95, 2001, 03**
Aston Villa	5, 2	**1961,** *63,* **71, 75, 77,** *94,* **96**
Nottingham Forest	4, 2	**1978, 79, 80,** *89,* **90,** *92*
Leicester City	3, 2	**1964,** *65,* **97,** *99,* **2000**
Tottenham Hotspur	3, 2	**1971, 73, 82,** *99, 2002*
Arsenal	2, 3	*1968, 69,* **87,** *88,* **93**
Norwich City	2, 2	**1962,** *73,* **75,** *85*
Chelsea	2, 1	**1965,** *72,* **98**
Manchester City	2, 1	**1970,** *74,* **76**
Wolverhampton Wanderers	2, 0	**1974, 80**
Manchester United	1, 4	*1983, 91,* **92,** *94, 2003*
West Bromwich Albion	1, 2	**1966,** *67, 70*
Birmingham City	1, 1	**1963,** *2001*
Leeds United	1, 1	**1968,** *96*
Luton Town	1, 1	**1988,** *89*
Queens Park Rangers	1, 1	**1967,** *86*
Sheffield Wednesday	1, 1	**1991,** *93*
Stoke City	1, 1	**1964,** *72*
Blackburn Rovers	1, 0	**2002**
Oxford United	1, 0	**1986**
Swindon Town	1, 0	**1969**
Everton	0, 2	*1977, 84*
Middlesbrough	0, 2	*1997, 98*
Bolton Wanderers	0, 1	*1995*
Newcastle United	0, 1	*1976*
Oldham Athletic	0, 1	*1990*
Rochdale	0, 1	*1962*
Rotherham United	0, 1	*1961*
Southampton	0, 1	*1979*
Sunderland	0, 1	*1985*
Tranmere Rovers	0, 1	*2000*

Scotland

THE SEASON IN REVIEW 2002–03

THE GAP IS SO BIG IN SCOTTISH FOOTBALL that Hearts, in third place in the SPL this year, was 25 points behind second-placed Celtic. At the top the margin is so narrow that Rangers and Celtic began their last games of the season level on points and goal difference. Rangers held the top spot by virtue of having scored a single additional goal. Motherwell, the only team to beat both the old firm clubs this season, should have been relegated, but between the SPL and the First Division is another vast gap. Falkirk, First Division champions, cannot meet the SPL's stadium requirements and so Motherwell stayed up.

Nail-biting drama

On the final day of the League season Rangers, already crowned League Cup winners and looking forward to playing Dundee in the Scottish FA Cup Final, was at home to Dunfermline. Celtic, trying to raise itself after its morale-sapping defeat in the UEFA Cup Final in Seville just four day beforehand, was away to Kilmarnock. It was an afternoon of nail-biting turning points, communicated back and forth between the crowds at Ibrox and Rugby Road on radios in the stands. Rangers took the advantage when a quick Michael Mols goal put them one up. Though Dunfermline pulled one back, Rangers scored again. But when Celtic took the lead through a Sutton goal, the Old Firm were back on level terms.

Early in the second half, Celtic actually took the lead in the title race as another Sutton goal and an Alan Thompson penalty put them 3-0 ahead with a better goal average. For nine minutes an almost silent Ibrox fretted and panicked as chances went astray. But a De Boer header made it 4-1 and Thompson strike made it 5-1, Ibrox erupted. Although Celtic had another goal with a late penalty, the title was Rangers'. Like his Celtic counterpart Martin O'Neill, Alex McLeish took his side to a treble in the first year of asking, as a single Amoroso goal was enough for Rangers to beat Dundee in the Cup Final. If this signals a shift of power at the apex of Scottish football, rest assured the rest of the landscape will look pretty identical next season.

Scottish League Cup

2003 FINAL

March 16 – Hampden Park, Glasgow
Rangers 2-1 Celtic
(Canniggia 23,   (Larsson 57)
Lovenkrands 35)
h/t: 2-0 **Att:** 52,000
Ref: Clark

Scottish FA Cup

2003 FINAL

May 31 – Hampden Park, Glasgow
Rangers 1-0 Dundee
(Amoruso 66)
h/t: 0-0 **Att:** 47,136
Ref: Clark

Top Goalscorers 2002–03

PLAYER	CLUB	NATIONALITY	GOALS
Henrik Larsson	Celtic	Swedish	28
John Hartson	Celtic	Welsh	18
Steve Crawford	Dunfermline	Scottish	18

International Club Performances 2002–03

CLUB	COMPETITION	PROGRESS
Celtic	Champions League	3rd Qualifying Round
	UEFA Cup	Runners-up
Aberdeen	UEFA Cup	1st Round
Livingston	UEFA Cup	1st Round
Rangers	UEFA Cup	1st Round

Scottish Premier League Table 2002–03

CLUB	P	W	D	L	F	A	Pts	
Rangers	38	31	4	3	101	28	**97**	Champions League
Celtic	38	31	4	3	98	26	**97**	UEFA Cup
Hearts	38	18	9	11	57	51	**63**	UEFA Cup
Kilmarnock	38	16	9	13	47	56	**57**	
Dunfermline	38	13	7	18	54	71	**46**	
Dundee	38	10	14	14	50	60	**44**	UEFA Cup (cup finalists)
Hibernian	38	15	6	17	56	64	**51**	
Aberdeen	38	13	10	15	41	54	**49**	
Livingston	38	9	8	21	48	62	**35**	
Partick Thistle	38	8	11	19	37	58	**35**	
Dundee United	38	7	11	20	35	68	**32**	
Motherwell	38	7	7	24	45	71	**28**	

No promotion this season as the stadium of Division One Champions Falkirk, does not meet SPL standards.

Above: You can feel it slipping away. Celtic fans at Rugby Road on the final day of the season react to the news of another Rangers goal at Ibrox.

Below: How close can it get? Martin O'Neill and Alex McLeish take it in turns to do the treble, sharing the same tailor and body language.

SCOTLAND

Left: *After looking like runaway winners of the League, Rangers are pegged back. John Hartson's goal helps Celtic win 2-1 at Ibrox in April and reopen the race for the championship.*

Below: *Terry Butcher wonders how his Motherwell squad can beat both Old Firm clubs this season and still finish bottom of the league.*

Below, left: *That makes it three. Captain for the day, Lorenzo Amoroso bows out of Rangers with the goal that wins the Scottish FA Cup and the treble.*

Below, second left: *Mark de Vries is Hearts' leading scorer, but even in a good year Hearts can barely manage half of Rangers and Celtic's points totals.*

Below, far left: *Henrik Larsson, top scorer in the SPL again, chases down the ball.*

Ibrox prepares to explode: *Steve Thompson toe pokes the ball past the Dunfermline defence to make 5-1 on the last day of the season.*

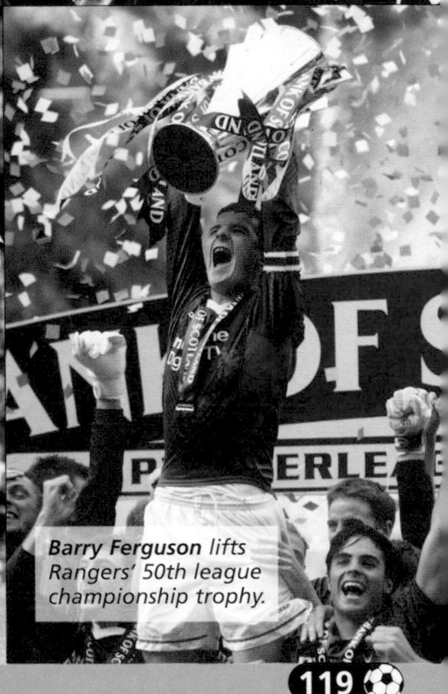

Barry Ferguson *lifts Rangers' 50th league championship trophy.*

SCOTLAND

Association Football in Scotland

1867: Queen's Park FC, Scotland's oldest club founded — 1865

1870

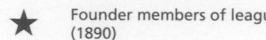 **1872:** First official international, v England, drawn 0-0, venue: Glasgow — 1875

1873: Formation of Scottish FA — 1880

1874: First Scottish Cup Final — 1885

1891: First league championship — 1890

1893: Professionalism adopted, Scottish Second Division created — 1895

1900

1902: Ibrox disaster. Stand collapses at Scotland v England match, 29 killed, 500 injured — 1905

1910: Affiliation to FIFA — 1910

1915

1920: Withdrew from FIFA — 1920

1924: Reaffiliated to FIFA — 1925

1928: Withdrew from FIFA — 1930

1929: Scotland play first foreign international, beating Norway 7-3 in Oslo — 1935

1940–46: League abandoned during war — 1940

1946: Reaffiliated to FIFA — 1945

1947: First Scottish League Cup Final — 1950

1954: Affiliation to UEFA — 1955

1968: First women's league formed — 1960

1971: Ibrox disaster. Crush during Rangers v Celtic match, 66 killed — 1965

1972: Scottish Women's Football Association founded. First international, v England, lost 2-3, venue: Greenock — 1970

1975: Scottish league reorganization, creating ten-team Premier League, First and Second Divisions — 1975

1994: Two lower leagues turned into three with addition of two new clubs from the Highlands — 1980 / 1985

1997: Scottish Premier League separates from Scottish FA — 1990

1999: Scottish Women's FA affiliates to SFA — 1995

2002: Ten non-Old Firm clubs resign from SPL and threaten to establish breakaway league — 2000 / 2005

In March 1878, the annual Scotland v England match ended in a convincing 7-2 victory for the Scots at Queen's Park, Glasgow.

Key

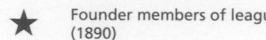 International football		○	Competition winner
Affiliation to FIFA		△	Competition runner-up
Affiliation to UEFA		Dons	– Aberdeen
Women's football		Dun U	– Dundee United
Disaster		Gers	– Rangers
War			

International Competitions

	European Cup	UEFA Cup	European Cup-Winners' Cup
1961:			△ Gers
1967:	○ Celtic		△ Gers
1970:	△ Celtic		
1972:			○ Gers
1983:			○ Dons
1987:		△ Dun U	
2003:		△ Celtic	

Scotland: The main clubs

Clyde 1878 — Team name with year of formation

● Club formed before 1912
● Club formed 1912–25
● Club formed 1925–50
○ Club formed after 1950

★ Founder members of league (1890)

 Pre-1914 champions

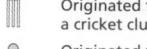 English origins

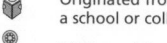 Originated from a military institution

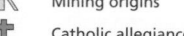 Originated from a cricket club

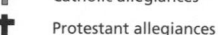 Originated from a school or college

Mining origins

✝ Catholic allegiances

✝ Protestant allegiances

▼ YMCA

★ **Third Lanark** 1872
Founded by members of Third Lanark Rifle Volunteers, changed name to Third Lanark (1878). Dissolved 1966

Renton 1872
Left league 1898

Hamilton Academical 1874

★ **Cambuslang** 1875
Left league 1892

★ **Cowlairs** 1876
Left league 1891

Queen's Park 1867

Clydebank 1965
Played one year (1964–65) as ES Clydebank, merger with East Stirlingshire

Partick Thistle 1876

★ **Rangers** 1873 ✝

★ **Celtic** 1888 ✝

★ **Clydebank** 1914
Dissolved 1931

★ **Abercorn** 1870s
Left league 1915

★ **St. Mirren** 1877

Founded in 1867, Queen's Park is Scotland's oldest club. The team is shown here in action during a friendly match with the English club Corinthians in 1901.

Scotland

ORIGINS AND GROWTH OF FOOTBALL

SCOTTISH FOOTBALL FOLLOWED RAPIDLY on the heels of its English counterpart. Its first club, Queen's Park, was formed in Glasgow in 1867 by members of the YMCA and went on to compete in the English FA Cups of the era. Along with the other home countries Scotland is a political region that has nation status in international football, and in 1872 the first-ever international, against England, was played in Glasgow. The following year saw the establishment of the Scottish FA in Glasgow and the first Scottish Cup competition. In the following decade football swept through the working-class communities of Scotland's central belt. Clubs and followings were often established around Protestant and Irish immigrant/Catholic neighbourhoods and identities, especially in the cities of Glasgow, Edinburgh and Dundee.

The price of success

The world's second oldest national league began in 1890 and professionalism arrived in 1893. But more significant was the fact that Scottish football provided much of the manpower for the early English professional league, also exporting players, missionaries and coaches of the game to Europe and Latin America. They pioneered the passing game – a style at odds with the dreary solo dribbling and long balls of the emerging English game – where players moved the ball on the ground in structured passing and running moves.

But the explosive growth of Scottish football came at a cost. In 1902, 29 people died and over 500 were injured when a new stand at Rangers' Ibrox stadium collapsed during a Scotland v England international match. In 1909, a Celtic v Rangers fixture at Hampden Park descended into football's first full-scale stadium riot.

The economics of failure

Like England, Scotland's international performance during the early World Cups was limited by the SFA's disinterest or active opposition to FIFA. It has yet to recover. In the postwar era, the economic and footballing dominance of Celtic and Rangers has increased, their domestic strength bringing European success in the late 1960s and early 1970s. However, the economics of football in a small country since then has meant that both clubs have failed to repeat those successes.

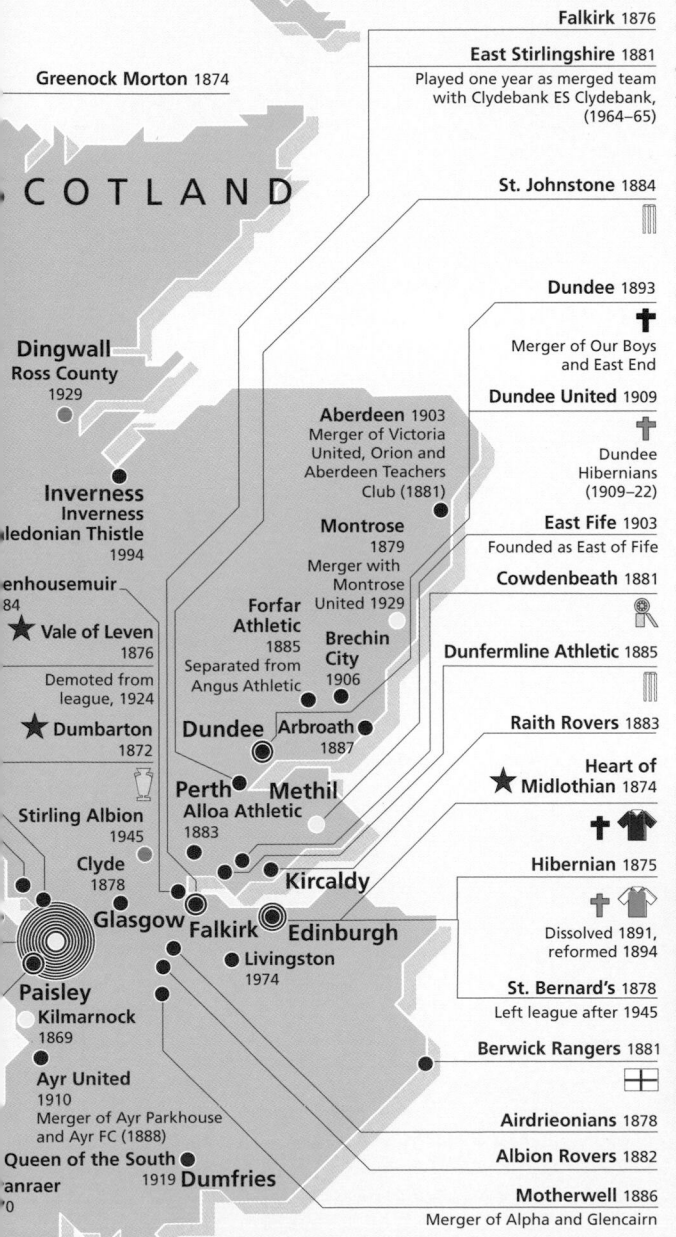

Greenock Morton 1874

C O T L A N D

Dingwall
Ross County
1929

Inverness
Inverness
ledonian Thistle
1994

enhousemuir
84
★ Vale of Leven
1876
Demoted from
league, 1924
★ Dumbarton
1872

Stirling Albion
1945
Clyde
1878
Glasgow
Paisley
Kilmarnock
1869
Ayr United
1910
Merger of Ayr Parkhouse
and Ayr FC (1888)
Queen of the South
anraer
'0 1919 **Dumfries**

Aberdeen 1903
Merger of Victoria
United, Orion and
Aberdeen Teachers
Club (1881)

Montrose
1879
Merger with
Montrose
United 1929

Forfar
Athletic
1885
Separated from
Angus Athletic

Brechin
City
1906

Dundee Arbroath
1887
Perth Methil
Alloa Athletic
1883
Kircaldy
Falkirk Edinburgh
Livingston
1974

Falkirk 1876

East Stirlingshire 1881
Played one year as merged team
with Clydebank ES Clydebank,
(1964–65)

St. Johnstone 1884

Dundee 1893
Merger of Our Boys
and East End

Dundee United 1909
Dundee
Hibernians
(1909–22)

East Fife 1903
Founded as East of Fife

Cowdenbeath 1881

Dunfermline Athletic 1885

Raith Rovers 1883

Heart of
★ Midlothian 1874

Hibernian 1875
Dissolved 1891,
reformed 1894

St. Bernard's 1878
Left league after 1945

Berwick Rangers 1881

Airdrieonians 1878

Albion Rovers 1882

Motherwell 1886
Merger of Alpha and Glencairn

In 1902, at a friendly match between Scotland and England at Ibrox Park, seven rows of wooden planking on the newly-built eastern terrace collapsed under the weight of spectators. Hundreds plunged 40 feet to the ground below, resulting in 29 deaths.

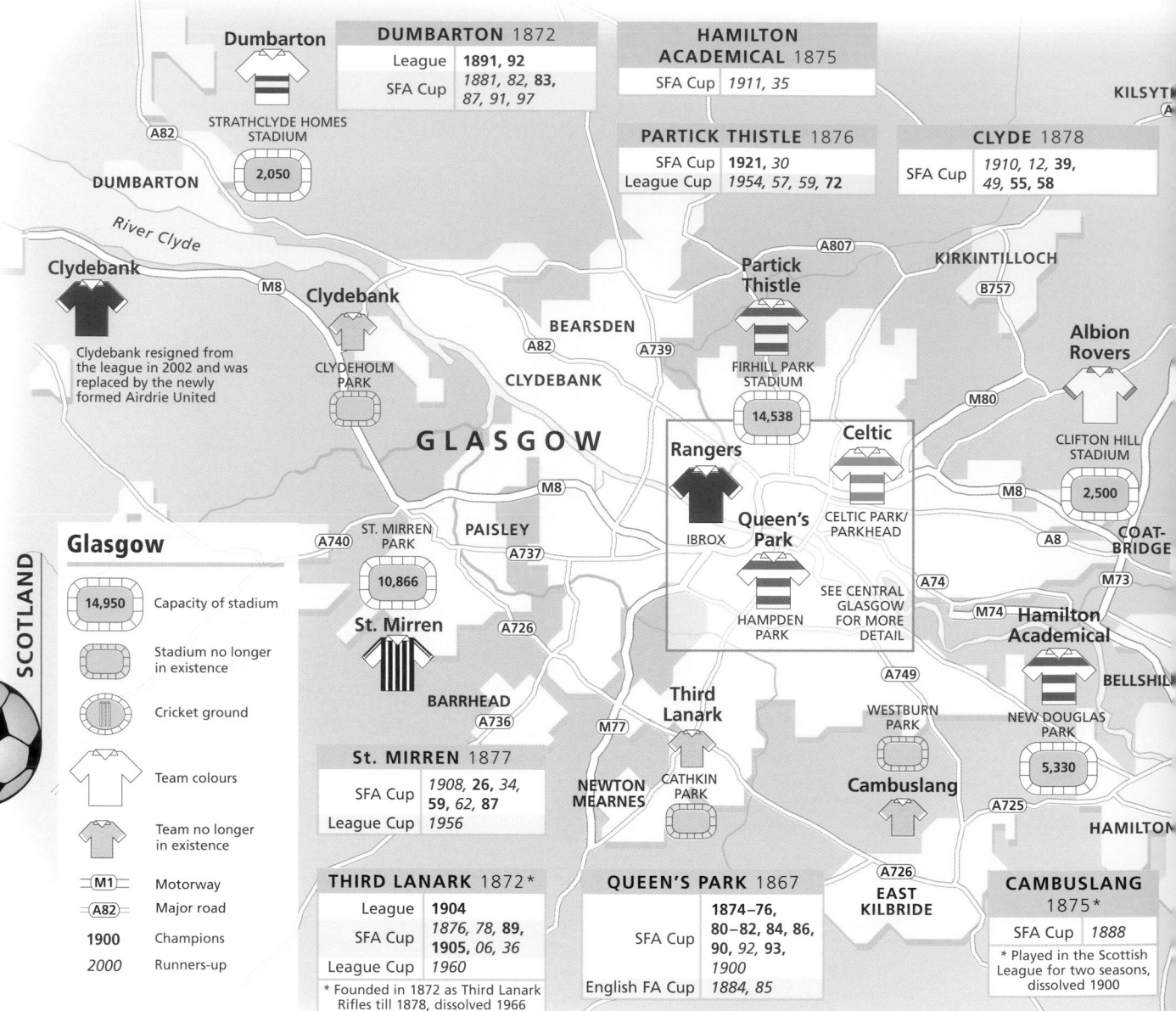

SCOTLAND

Dumbarton

STRATHCLYDE HOMES STADIUM

2,050

DUMBARTON

River Clyde

DUMBARTON 1872	
League	**1891, 92**
SFA Cup	*1881, 82, 83,* 87, 91, 97

HAMILTON ACADEMICAL 1875	
SFA Cup	*1911, 35*

KILSYT

A82

Clydebank

Clydebank resigned from the league in 2002 and was replaced by the newly formed Airdrie United

M8

Clydebank

CLYDEHOLM PARK

BEARSDEN

A82   A739

CLYDEBANK

GLASGOW

PARTICK THISTLE 1876	
SFA Cup	**1921,** *30*
League Cup	*1954, 57, 59, 72*

CLYDE 1878	
SFA Cup	*1910, 12, 39,* 49, **55, 58**

A807

KIRKINTILLOCH

B757

Partick Thistle

FIRHILL PARK STADIUM

14,538

Albion Rovers

M80

CLIFTON HILL STADIUM

2,500

Rangers

IBROX

Celtic

CELTIC PARK/ PARKHEAD

Queen's Park

HAMPDEN PARK

SEE CENTRAL GLASGOW FOR MORE DETAIL

M8

A8

COAT-BRIDGE

A74

M73

M74

Hamilton Academical

BELLSHIL

NEW DOUGLAS PARK

5,330

A725

HAMILTON

Glasgow

14,950 — Capacity of stadium

— Stadium no longer in existence

— Cricket ground

— Team colours

— Team no longer in existence

M1 — Motorway

A82 — Major road

1900 — Champions

2000 — Runners-up

ST. MIRREN PARK

A740

PAISLEY

A737

10,866

St. Mirren

A726

BARRHEAD

A736

M77

NEWTON MEARNES

Third Lanark

CATHKIN PARK

A749

WESTBURN PARK

Cambuslang

A726

EAST KILBRIDE

St. MIRREN 1877	
SFA Cup	*1908,* **26,** *34,* 59, 62, **87**
League Cup	*1956*

THIRD LANARK 1872*	
League	**1904**
SFA Cup	*1876, 78,* **89,** **1905,** *06, 36*
League Cup	*1960*

* Founded in 1872 as Third Lanark Rifles till 1878, dissolved 1966

QUEEN'S PARK 1867	
SFA Cup	*1874–76,* 80–82, 84, 86, 90, 92, 93, 1900
English FA Cup	*1884, 85*

CAMBUSLANG 1875*	
SFA Cup	*1888*

* Played in the Scottish League for two seasons, dissolved 1900

Glasgow

FOOTBALL CITY

GLASGOW MAY NOT BE the political capital of Scotland, but there was no question that the Scottish FA would be located anywhere but in the country's footballing capital. Scotland's first club, Queen's Park, was founded in the south of the city in 1867. Glasgow saw the world's first international, played in Partick in 1872, the world's first penalty in 1891; the world's first stadium collapse in 1902; and the first stadium riot in 1909.

In the late 19th century, Glasgow's booming heavy industries drew heavily on rural Scottish Protestant and Irish Catholic immigrants. In the following two decades, football clubs sprang up all over greater Glasgow as this divided working class embraced Scottish football. However, the centre of the city was dominated by the rivalry between Celtic and Rangers – the 'Old Firm'.

The origins of the Old Firm

Celtic was founded in 1888 by Brother Walfrid of the Marist Order as both a football club and a social service for Catholic boys. The club's affiliations have remained clear: a shamrock emblem and the flying of the Irish tricolor at the stadium. Rangers was formed over a decade earlier out of a rowing club north of the River Clyde, but soon settled among the docks and Protestant dockworkers of the Govan area. Rangers' affiliation to Unionism and Protestantism, always present, grew with the emergence of Celtic as sporting and cultural rivals. By 1910, Rangers would no longer sign Catholic players, and its strip, predominantly blue, had acquired red and white trimmings. Persistent conflict on and off the pitch has been tempered in recent years by the geographical dispersal of the old religious ghettoes and concerted official efforts to challenge sectarianism, including Rangers' signing of the Catholic Mo Johnston in 1989. But, like the issue of sectarianism in wider Scottish society, it remains largely unexamined and intact.

Airdrieonians went into liquidation in 2002. The remnants of the club have been reborn as Airdrie United

Clyde   Airdrieonians

BROADWOOD STADIUM   **CUMBERNAULD**

| 8,200 |

AIRDRIEONIANS
1878

| | League | *1923–26* |
| | SFA Cup | **1924,** *75,* **92, 95** |

| A73 |

NEW BROOMFIELD

| 10,000 |

Airdrie United

AIRDRIE

MOTHERWELL 1886

	League	*1927, 30,* **32,** *33, 34,* **95**
	SFA Cup	**1931,** *33,* **39,** *51,* **52,** *91*
	League Cup	**1951,** *55*

| A721 |

MOTHERWELL

FIR PARK STADIUM

| M74 | | 13,742 |

River Clyde

Motherwell

LARKHALL

HAMPDEN PARK

| 52,000 |

Clubs: Scotland, Queen's Park
Built: 1903
Rebuilt: 1992–94, 96–98
Record Attendance: 149,415 Scotland v England, 24 April 1937

IBROX STADIUM (previously Ibrox Park)

| 50,467 |

Club: Rangers
Built: 1899
Rebuilt: 1971–81, 94
Record Attendance: 118,567 Rangers v Celtic, 2 January 1939

RANGERS 1873

	League	*1891,* **93,** *96,* **98, 99–1902,** *05,* **11–13,** *14, 16,* **18, 19, 20, 21, 22, 23–25,** *27–31, 32,* **33–35,** *36,* **37,** *39, 47,* **48,** *49,* **50,** *51, 52,* **53, 56,** *57, 58,* **59, 61,** *62,* **63, 64,** *66–70, 73,* **75, 76, 77, 78, 79,** *87,* **89–97,** *98,* **99, 2000,** *01,* **02,** *03*
	SFA Cup	*1877, 79,* **94,** *97, 98, 99,* **1903,** *04, 05, 21, 22,* **28,** *29,* **30, 32, 34–36,** *48–50,* **53,** *60,* **62–64,** *66,* **69,** *71,* **73,** *76, 77,* **78, 79,** *80,* **81,** *82, 83,* **89, 92, 93, 94, 96, 98, 99, 2000, 02, 03**
	League Cup	*1947,* **49,** *52,* **58, 61,** *62,* **64,** *65,* **66,** *67,* **71,** *76,* **78,** *79, 82, 83, 84, 85,* **87–89,** *90,* **91,** *93, 94,* **97,** *99,* **2002, 03**
	European Cup-Winners' Cup	*1961,* **67, 72**

CELTIC 1888

	League	*1892,* **93, 94, 95, 96, 98,** *1900–02,* **05–10,** *12, 13,* **14–17,** *18,* **19,** *20, 21,* **22, 26,** *28,* **29,** *31,* **35, 36,** *38,* **39, 54, 55,** *66–74,* **76, 77, 79,** *80,* **81, 82,** *83–85,* **86, 87, 88,** *96,* **97, 98,** *99,* **2000,** *01,* **02,** *03*
	SFA Cup	*1889,* **92, 93, 94,** *99,* **1900,** *01,* **02,** *04,* **07, 08,** *11,* **12,** *14,* **23,** *25, 26,* **27,** *28,* **31, 33, 37,** *51,* **54,** *55,* **56,** *61,* **63, 65, 66, 67, 69,** *70,* **71,** *72,* **73,** *74,* **75,** *77,* **80,** *84,* **85, 88, 89, 90,** *95,* **99, 2001,** *02*
	League Cup	**1957,** *58,* **65,** *66–70,* **71–74,** *75, 76–78,* **83, 84,** *87,* **91,** *95,* **98,** *2000,* **01,** *03*
	European Cup	**1967,** *70*
	UEFA Cup	*2003*
	World Club Cup	*1967*

CELTIC PARK/PARKHEAD

| 60,506 |

Club: Celtic
Built: 1892
Rebuilt: 1995
Record Attendance: 92,000 Celtic v Rangers, 1 January 1938

PARTICKHILL   **DUMBARTON ROAD**

WOODSIDE

WEST OF SCOTLAND CRICKET GROUND
The first international ever was played here. Scotland v England, 30 Nov 1872, score 0–0

SCOTTISH FOOTBALL ASSOCIATION

THE LOCAL DERBY

| CELTIC | RANGERS |

566 matches played

188 Celtic wins
241 Rangers wins
137 draws

0   100   200   300   400   500

**NUMBER OF MATCHES
(All first-class games up to July 2003)**

Rangers
IBROX (50,467)

| A814 |

GOVAN

CENTRAL GLASGOW

| A8 |
| A761 |
| M8 |
| M77 |

POLLOCKSHIELDS
Area of Protestant support at the turn of the 20th century

Area of Catholic support at the turn of the 20th century

CARLTON

BRIGTON

| A74 |
| A77 |

GORBALS

CELTIC PARK/ PARKHEAD (60,506)

River Clyde

PARKHEAD

| A749 |
| A730 |

Celtic

RUTHERGLEN

Scotland   **Queen's Park**
HAMPDEN PARK (52,000)

| A728 |

At the 1980 Scottish FA Cup Final between Celtic and Rangers, a lap of victory by the Celtic team triggered a pitch invasion and a full-scale riot between fans and police. The incident led to the banning of alcohol from Scottish grounds

Scotland

PLAYERS AND MANAGERS

ALMOST INEVITABLY SCOTTISH football has been a great exporter of talent. Among the earliest players of the game and the earliest professionals, Scottish players and managers have constantly found themselves outgrowing their small and economically limited leagues. In the late 19th century, Scots were central to the spread of the game in Latin America and continental Europe, while Scottish teams pioneered the short passing game as it was known, displacing the kick and rush that was dominant south of the border. Scots took their talents and their style to Germany, Central Europe and, above all, to England, for it is the old enemy that has most consistently provided the better wages and the bigger stage that Scottish football talent has demanded. It is the same logic that has seen a steady influx of foreign talent not only to the big two Glasgow teams, but also to the smallest Premier Division sides.

Working-class politics

The great Scottish managers of the modern era – Sir Matt Busby, Sir Alex Ferguson and Bill Shankly – have all really made their mark south of the border, not only winning trophies but building teams and clubs that lasted. Only Jock Stein (a disastrous month at Leeds United aside) built his career in Scotland at Celtic and as national team manager. The working-class and often political roots of these men has provided a context in which their special kind of leadership and management talent could be awakened. Similarly, among the greatest players of the modern era it has often been an English club that has provided the home in which their talent could fully mature: Denis Law at Manchester United, and Kenny Dalglish, Alan Hansen and Graeme Souness at Liverpool.

In the early years of the football league Preston North End redefined the style of professional football in a team stuffed with Scots. Sunderland, another dominant team of the era, also drew heavily on Scottish players. The same logic of labour migration has transformed contemporary Scottish football. In the last decade, a flood of foreign players has gone to Scotland.

It is arguable that the decline of the national team in recent years can be attributed to the squeezing out of domestic talent, a situation made starker by the appointment of the German coach Berti Vogts as national team manager.

Top 16 International Caps

PLAYER	CAPS	GOALS	FIRST MATCH	LAST MATCH
Kenny Dalglish	102	30	1972	1987
Jim Leighton	91	0	1983	1999
Alex McLeish	77	1	1980	1993
Paul McStay	76	9	1984	1997
Tommy Boyd*	73	1	1991	2001
Willie Miller	65	1	1975	1990
Danny McGrain	62	0	1973	1982
Richard Gough	61	6	1983	1993
Ally McCoist	61	19	1986	1998
John Collins*	58	12	1988	2000
Roy Aitken	57	1	1980	1992
Gary McAllister*	57	5	1990	1999
Denis Law	55	30	1959	1974
Maurice Malpas	55	0	1984	1993
Billy Bremner	54	3	1965	1976
Graeme Souness	54	4	1975	1986

Top 10 International Goalscorers

PLAYER	GOALS	CAPS	FIRST MATCH	LAST MATCH
Denis Law	30	55	1959	1974
Kenny Dalglish	30	102	1972	1987
Hugh Gallacher	23	53	1924	1935
Lawrie Reilly	22	38	1949	1957
Ally McCoist	19	61	1986	1998
Robert Cumming Hamilton	14	11	1899	1911
Mo Johnston	14	38	1984	1992
John Smith	13	10	1877	1884
Andrew Nesbit Wilson	13	12	1920	1923
Robert Smyth McColl	13	13	1896	1908

* Indicates players still playing at least at club level.

Scottish International Managers

DATES	NAME	GAMES	WON	DRAWN	LOST
1954	Andy Beattie	6	2	1	3
1958	Matt Busby	2	1	1	0
1959–60	Andy Beattie	12	3	3	6
1960–65	Ian McColl	28	17	3	8
1965	Jock Stein	7	3	1	3
1966	John Prentice	4	0	1	3
1966	Malcolm McDonald	2	1	1	0
1967–71	Bobby Brown	28	9	8	11
1971–72	Tommy Docherty	12	7	2	3
1973–77	Willie Ormond	38	18	8	12
1977–78	Ally McLeod	17	7	5	5
1978–85	Jock Stein	61	26	12	23
1985–86	Alex Ferguson	10	3	4	3
1986–93	Andy Roxburgh	61	23	19	19
1993–2001	Craig Brown	70	32	18	20
2002–	Berti Vogts	16	4	3	9

All figures correct as of 7 June 2003.

Foreign Players in Scotland (in top division squads)

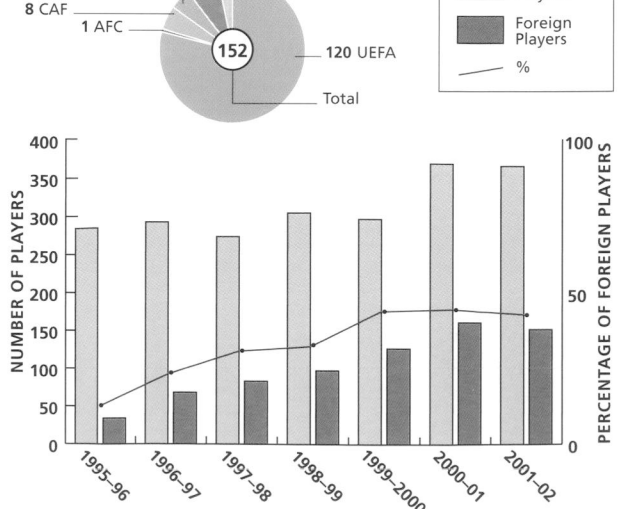

2002–03

11 CONMEBOL
5 OFC
7 CONCACAF
8 CAF
1 AFC
152 — 120 UEFA
Total

Key

Total Players
Foreign Players
%

SCOTLAND

Player of the Year

YEAR	PLAYER	CLUB
1965	McNeill	Celtic
1966	Greig	Rangers
1967	Simpson	Celtic
1968	Wallace	Raith Rovers
1969	Murdoch	Celtic
1970	Stanton	Hibernian
1971	Buchan	Aberdeen
1972	Smith	Rangers
1973	Connelly	Celtic
1974	Scotland World Cup Squad	
1975	Jardine	Rangers
1976	Greig	Rangers
1977	McGrain	Celtic
1978	Johnstone	Rangers
1979	Ritchie	Morton
1980	Strachan	Aberdeen
1981	Rough	Partick Thistle
1982	Sturrock	Dundee United
1983	Nicholas	Celtic
1984	Miller	Aberdeen
1985	McAlpine	Dundee United
1986	Jardine	Heart of Midlothian
1987	McClair	Celtic
1988	McStay	Celtic
1989	Gough	Rangers
1990	McLeish	Aberdeen
1991	Malpas	Dundee United
1992	McCoist	Rangers
1993	Goram	Rangers
1994	Hateley	Rangers
1995	Laudrup	Rangers
1996	Gascoigne	Rangers
1997	Laudrup	Rangers
1998	Burley	Celtic
1999	Larsson	Celtic
2000	B. Ferguson	Rangers
2001	Larsson	Celtic
2002	Lambert	Celtic
2003	B. Ferguson	Rangers

Awarded by the Scottish Football Writers' Association.

Manager of the Year

YEAR	MANAGER	CLUB
1987	Jim McLean	Dundee United
1988	Billy McNeill	Celtic
1989	Graeme Souness	Rangers
1990	Andy Roxburgh	Scotland
1991	Alex Totten	St. Johnstone
1992	Walter Smith	Rangers
1993	Walter Smith	Rangers
1994	Walter Smith	Rangers
1995	Jimmy Nichol	Raith Rovers
1996	Walter Smith	Rangers
1997	Walter Smith	Rangers
1998	Wim Jansen	Celtic
1999	Dick Advocaat	Rangers
2000	Dick Advocaat	Rangers
2001	Martin O'Neill	Celtic
2002	John Lambie	Partick Thistle
2003	Alex McLeish	Rangers

Awarded by Tennents.

Celtic's Billy McNeill is held up by his teammates after their victory in the 1965 Scottish Cup Final against Dunfermline. McNeill's efforts that season earned him the Scottish Player of the Year award.

Top Goalscorers by Season 1965–2003

SEASON	PLAYER	CLUB	GOALS
1965–66	McBride	Celtic	31
1965–66	A. Ferguson	Dunfermline Athletic	31
1966–67	Chalmers	Celtic	21
1967–68	Lennox	Celtic	32
1968–69	Cameron	Dundee United	26
1969–70	Stein	Rangers	24
1970–71	Hood	Celtic	22
1971–72	Harper	Aberdeen	33
1972–73	Gordon	Hibernian	27
1973–74	Deans	Celtic	26
1974–75	Gray	Dundee United	20
1974–75	Pettigrew	Motherwell	20
1975–76	Dalglish	Celtic	24
1976–77	Pettigrew	Motherwell	21
1977–78	Johnstone	Rangers	25
1978–79	Ritchie	Morton	22
1979–80	Somner	St. Mirren	25
1980–81	McGarvey	Celtic	23
1981–82	McCluskey	Celtic	21
1982–83	Nicholas	Celtic	29
1983–84	McClair	Celtic	23
1984–85	McDougall	Dundee	22
1985–86	McCoist	Rangers	24
1986–87	McClair	Celtic	35
1987–88	Coyne	Dundee	33
1988–89	McGhee	Celtic	16
1988–89	Nicholas	Aberdeen	16
1989–90	Robertson	Heart of Midlothian	17
1990–91	Coyne	Celtic	18
1991–92	McCoist	Rangers	34
1992–93	McCoist	Rangers	34
1993–94	Hateley	Rangers	22
1994–95	Coyne	Motherwell	16

SEASON	PLAYER	CLUB	GOALS
1995–96	Hooijdonk	Celtic	26
1996–97	Cadete	Celtic	25
1997–98	Negri	Rangers	32
1998–99	Larsson	Celtic	29
1999–2000	Viduka	Celtic	25
2000–01	Larsson	Celtic	35
2001–02	Larsson	Celtic	29
2002–03	Larsson	Celtic	28

Despite limited resources, Craig Brown presided over one of the most successful periods of Scottish footballing history between 1993 and 2001: with a record of 32 wins, 18 draws and 20 defeats in 70 matches he is also Scotland's longest-serving manager.

Scotland

SCOTLAND

SCOTTISH PREMIER LEAGUE 1975–2002

IN THE LAST 25 YEARS the Scottish League has been through three reorganizations (two under the auspices of the Scottish FA in 1975 and 1994, and then again in 1997 with the establishment of the Scottish Premier League). Each time the issue has been the same – how to create a competitive, financially viable league when two clubs are so much bigger than the others. In spring 2002, a fourth shift looks likely, as all the other Premier League teams have resigned, leaving Celtic and Rangers and their ever-greater demands for TV income out in the cold; the situation remains unresolved.

Rangers revolution, Celtic dominance

The era began with the usual Glasgow monopoly on the title, including Jock Stein's last championship with Celtic. Post-Stein, Billy McNeill's team continued to win, but Rangers went into a decade of decline. Into the vacuum stepped Alex Ferguson's Aberdeen and, for a glorious season in 1983, Dundee United. But with the arrival of businessman David Murray at Rangers, the vacuum was filled again. Money was spent on the squad, first in England and then in Europe and, shortly after the appointment of Graeme Souness as manager, the sectarian ban on signing Catholic players was ended.

Under Souness, Walter Smith and Dick Advocaat, Rangers then won 11 out of 12 titles (1989–2000) – a sequence broken by a revived Celtic under Wim Jansen and then by Martin O'Neill's team in 2000, Celtic's best squad for two decades. Beyond these two, only Hearts, Aberdeen and Motherwell have been regular members of the Premier League but none of them have mounted a sustained challenge to the Old Firm's dominance on the field. It may require the entire league to do so off the field.

Scottish League Positions 1975–2002

SEASON

TEAM	1975-76	1976-77	1977-78	1978-79	1979-80	1980-81	1981-82	1982-83	1983-84	1984-85	1985-86	1986-87	1987-88	1988-89	1989-90	1990-91	1991-92	1992-93	1993-94	1994-95	1995-96	1996-97	1997-98	1998-99	1999-2000	2000-01	2001-02
Aberdeen	7	3	2	4	1	2	2	3	1	1	4	4	4	2	2	2	6	2	2	9	3	6	6	8	10	7	4
Airdrieonians						7	10										7	12									
Ayr United	6	8	9																								
Celtic	2	1	5	1	2	1	1	2	2	2	1	2	1	3	5	3	3	3	4	4	2	2	1	2	2	1	1
Clydebank		10							10	11																	
Dumbarton								9																			
Dundee	9						8	6	8	6	6	6	7	8	10			10	12				5	7	6		9
Dundee United	8	4	3	3	4	5	4	1	3	3	3	3	5	4	4	4	4	6	10			3	7	9	8	11	8
Dunfermline Athletic													11		8	8	12					5	8	10		9	6
Falkirk											10	10					9	11			5	10					
Hamilton Academical												12		10													
Heart of Midlothian	5	9		9		10				5	7	2	6	3	5	2	5	7	4	6	4	4	3	6	3	5	5
Hibernian	3	6	4	5	10		6	7	7	8	9	6	5	7	9	5	7	5	3	5	9	10			6	3	10
Kilmarnock		10		8	9	10														8	7	7	4	4	9	4	7
Livingston																											3
Morton					7	6	8	7	9		10		12														
Motherwell	4	7	6	10			8	10			9	8	8	9	6	6	10	9	3	2	8	8	9	7	4	8	11
Partick Thistle		5	7	8	7	6	9										8	9	8	9							
Raith Rovers																			11		6	10					
Rangers	1	2	1	2	5	3	3	4	4	4	5	1	3	1	1	1	1	1	1	1	1	1	2	1	1	2	2
St. Johnstone	10				9			9									7	8	6	10			5	3	5	10	12
St. Mirren		8	6	3	4	5	5	6	5	7	7	9	7	9	7	9	10	11									12

Rangers turns the screw in 1990: another goal, another Old Firm derby, another Rangers championship. Mo Johnston, Ally McCoist and Ian Ferguson celebrate.

Manager Alex Ferguson and trainer Archie Knox celebrate as Aberdeen win the 1983 European Cup-Winners' Cup. The two moved on to fame and fortune at Manchester United.

SCOTLAND

Key to League Positions Table

- League champions
- Season of promotion to league
- Season of relegation from league
- Other teams playing in league
- 5   Final position in league

SCOTLAND

Aberdeen
1978, **80** *81, 82,* **84,** **85,** 89–91, 93, 94

Dunfermline Athletic

St. Johnstone

Aberdeen

Dundee

Falkirk

Dundee

Perth

Dundee United
1983

Dunfermline

Kircaldy

Raith Rovers

Falkirk

Edinburgh

Heart of Midlothian

Livingston

Morton

Dumbarton

Dumbarton
Glasgow

Airdrie

Hibernian
1986, *88, 92*

Clydebank

Kilmarnock

Livingston

Hamilton Academical

Ayr

Airdrieonians

Motherwell
1995

Partick Thistle

Ayr United

St. Mirren

Rangers
1976, *77,* **78,** *79,* **87,** 89–97, **98,** **99,** **2000,** **01, 02**

Celtic
1976, **77,** **79,** **80,** **81,** **82,** 83–85, **86,** *87,* **88,** 96, 97, **98,** *99,* **2000,** **01, 02**

Kilmarnock

Premier League

Hibernian	Team name
	League champions/runners-up
1982, *83*	Champions in bold Runners-up in italics
	Other teams in the Premier League
● Perth	City of origin

Scotland

The Scottish Football Association
Founded: 1873
Joined FIFA: 1910–20, 1924–28, 1946
Joined UEFA: 1954

SCOTLAND'S FOOTBALL INSTITUTIONS are the second oldest in the world. Even before the establishment of the Scottish FA in 1873, Glasgow club Queen's Park was competing in the English FA Cup. With the creation of the SFA came the Scottish Cup, first played in 1874. A national league was created in 1890, rapidly followed by the arrival of professionalism in 1893 and the creation of a second division for the 1893–94 season.

Both these tournaments and the Scottish League Cup, first played in 1947, have been dominated by the Glasgow 'Old Firm' – Celtic and Rangers. There has been an occasional look in for Aberdeen, the two Dundee sides and the two Edinburgh teams – Hibernian and Heart of Midlothian.

During the Second World War, national championships were abandoned and teams played in smaller regional leagues. The continued dominance of the Old Firm led to a reorganization of the league structure for the 1975–76 season. A ten-team Premiership was created, with the big teams playing each other four times a year. Two lower divisions of 14 teams were also created. In 1994–95 the lower divisions were reorganized again, the two being expanded into three, with the addition of two teams from the Highland League. In 1997 the Scottish top flight followed the lead of the English first division, creating a separate and independent Premiership.

However, none of these structural changes can mask the basic problem that the two big Glasgow teams are economically and sportingly in a different class from the rest of the country. The Scottish Premiership continues, but the Old Firm has explored the possibility of forming an Atlantic league with other small European nations (an idea which has been blocked by UEFA) and has continued to pursue the preferred option of joining the English Premiership.

The Old Firm derby between Celtic and Rangers is one of the most keenly contested fixtures in the world.

Scottish League Record 1891–2003

SEASON	CHAMPIONS	RUNNERS-UP
1891	Dumbarton/Rangers*	
1892	Dumbarton	Celtic
1893	Celtic	Rangers
1894	Celtic	Heart of Midlothian
1895	Heart of Midlothian	Celtic
1896	Celtic	Rangers
1897	Heart of Midlothian	Hibernian
1898	Celtic	Rangers
1899	Rangers	Heart of Midlothian
1900	Rangers	Celtic
1901	Rangers	Celtic
1902	Rangers	Celtic
1903	Hibernian	Dundee
1904	Third Lanark	Heart of Midlothian
1905	Celtic	Rangers
1906	Celtic	Heart of Midlothian
1907	Celtic	Dundee
1908	Celtic	Falkirk
1909	Celtic	Dundee
1910	Celtic	Falkirk
1911	Rangers	Aberdeen
1912	Rangers	Celtic
1913	Rangers	Celtic
1914	Celtic	Rangers
1915	Celtic	Heart of Midlothian
1916	Celtic	Rangers
1917	Celtic	Morton
1918	Rangers	Celtic
1919	Celtic	Rangers
1920	Rangers	Celtic
1921	Rangers	Celtic
1922	Celtic	Rangers
1923	Rangers	Airdrieonians
1924	Rangers	Airdrieonians
1925	Rangers	Airdrieonians
1926	Celtic	Airdrieonians
1927	Rangers	Motherwell
1928	Rangers	Celtic
1929	Rangers	Celtic
1930	Rangers	Motherwell
1931	Rangers	Celtic
1932	Motherwell	Rangers
1933	Rangers	Motherwell
1934	Rangers	Motherwell
1935	Rangers	Celtic
1936	Celtic	Rangers
1937	Rangers	Aberdeen
1938	Celtic	Heart of Midlothian
1939	Rangers	Celtic
1940–46	*no championship*	
1947	Rangers	Hibernian
1948	Hibernian	Rangers
1949	Rangers	Dundee
1950	Rangers	Hibernian
1951	Hibernian	Rangers
1952	Hibernian	Rangers
1953	Rangers	Hibernian
1954	Celtic	Heart of Midlothian
1955	Aberdeen	Celtic
1956	Rangers	Aberdeen
1957	Rangers	Heart of Midlothian
1958	Heart of Midlothian	Rangers

SCOTLAND

Scottish League Record (*continued*)

SEASON	CHAMPIONS	RUNNERS-UP
1959	Rangers	Heart of Midlothian
1960	Heart of Midlothian	Kilmarnock
1961	Rangers	Kilmarnock
1962	Dundee	Rangers
1963	Rangers	Kilmarnock
1964	Rangers	Kilmarnock
1965	Kilmarnock	Heart of Midlothian
1966	Celtic	Rangers
1967	Celtic	Rangers
1968	Celtic	Rangers
1969	Celtic	Rangers
1970	Celtic	Rangers
1971	Celtic	Aberdeen
1972	Celtic	Aberdeen
1973	Celtic	Rangers
1974	Celtic	Hibernian
1975	Rangers	Hibernian
1976	Rangers	Celtic
1977	Celtic	Rangers
1978	Rangers	Aberdeen
1979	Celtic	Rangers
1980	Aberdeen	Celtic
1981	Celtic	Aberdeen
1982	Celtic	Aberdeen
1983	Dundee United	Celtic
1984	Aberdeen	Celtic
1985	Aberdeen	Celtic
1986	Celtic	Heart of Midlothian
1987	Rangers	Celtic
1988	Celtic	Heart of Midlothian
1989	Rangers	Aberdeen
1990	Rangers	Aberdeen
1991	Rangers	Aberdeen
1992	Rangers	Heart of Midlothian
1993	Rangers	Aberdeen
1994	Rangers	Aberdeen
1995	Rangers	Motherwell
1996	Rangers	Celtic
1997	Rangers	Celtic
1998	Celtic	Rangers
1999	Rangers	Celtic
2000	Rangers	Celtic
2001	Celtic	Rangers
2002	Celtic	Rangers
2003	Rangers	Celtic

* Both teams had equal points, and the title was held jointly.

Scottish League Summary

TEAM	TOTALS	CHAMPIONS & RUNNERS-UP (BOLD) (ITALICS)
Rangers	50, 26	**1891**, *93, 96, 98,* **1899–1902,** *05,* **11–13,** *14,* **16,** *18, 19,* **20, 21, 22, 23–25,** *27–31,* **32,** *33–35,* **36, 37, 39, 47, 48, 49,** **50, 51, 52, 53, 56, 57, 58, 59, 61, 62,** **63, 64,** *65–70, 73,* **75, 76, 77, 78,** *79,* **87, 89–97,** *98,* **99, 2000,** *01, 02,* **03**
Celtic	38, 27	*1892,* **93, 94, 95, 96, 98,** *1900–02,* **05–10,** *12, 13,* **14–17,** *18,* **19,** *20, 21,* **22,** *26,* **28, 29,** *31,* **35, 36, 38, 39, 54,** *55,* **66–74,** *76,* **77,** *79,* **80,** *81,* **82,** *83–85,* **86,** *87,* **88,** *96, 97,* **98,** *99,* **2000, 01, 02, 03**
Aberdeen	4, 13	*1911, 37,* **55,** *56, 71, 72, 78,* **80,** *81,* **82,** *84,* **85,** *89–91, 93, 94*
Heart of Midlothian	4, 13	*1894,* **95,** *97, 99, 1904, 06, 15,* **38,** *54, 57,* **58,** *59,* **60,** *65, 86, 88, 92*
Hibernian	4, 6	*1897,* **1903,** *47, 48,* **50, 51, 52, 53,** *74, 75*
Dumbarton	2, 0	**1891, 92**
Motherwell	1, 5	*1927,* **30,** *32,* **33,** *34, 95*

Scottish League Summary (*continued*)

TEAM	TOTALS	CHAMPIONS & RUNNERS-UP (BOLD) (ITALICS)
Dundee	1, 4	*1903, 07, 09, 49,* **62**
Kilmarnock	1, 4	*1960, 61, 63, 64,* **65**
Dundee United	1, 0	**1983**
Third Lanark	1, 0	**1904**
Airdrieonians	0, 4	*1923–26*
Falkirk	0, 2	*1908, 10*
Morton	0, 1	*1917*

Scottish Cup Record 1874–2003

YEAR	WINNERS	SCORE	RUNNERS-UP
1874	Queen's Park	2-0	Clydesdale
1875	Queen's Park	3-0	Renton
1876	Queen's Park	1-1, (replay) 2-0	Third Lanark
1877	Vale of Leven	0-0, (replay) 1-1, (replay) 3-2	Rangers
1878	Vale of Leven	1-0	Third Lanark
1879	Vale of Leven	1-1, (replay) w/o	Rangers
1880	Queen's Park	3-0	Thornley Bank
1881	Queen's Park	3-1*	Dumbarton
1882	Queen's Park	2-2, (replay) 4-1	Dumbarton
1883	Dumbarton	2-2, (replay) 2-1	Vale of Leven
1884	Queen's Park	w/o	Vale of Leven
1885	Renton	0-0, (replay) 3-1	Vale of Leven
1886	Queen's Park	3-1	Renton
1887	Hibernian	2-1	Dumbarton
1888	Renton	6-1	Cambuslang
1889	Third Lanark	2-1**	Celtic
1890	Queen's Park	1-1, (replay) 2-2	Vale of Levan
1891	Heart of Midlothian	1-0	Dumbarton
1892	Celtic	5-1	Queen's Park
1893	Queen's Park	2-1	Celtic
1894	Rangers	3-1	Celtic
1895	St. Bernard's	2-1	Renton
1896	Heart of Midlothian	3-1	Hibernian
1897	Rangers	5-1	Dumbarton
1898	Rangers	2-0	Kilmarnock
1899	Celtic	2-0	Rangers
1900	Celtic	4-3	Queen's Park
1901	Heart of Midlothian	4-3	Celtic
1902	Hibernian	1-0	Celtic
1903	Rangers	1-1, (replay) 0-0, (replay) 2-0	Heart of Midlothian
1904	Celtic	3-2	Rangers
1905	Third Lanark	0-0, (replay) 3-1	Rangers
1906	Heart of Midlothian	1-0	Third Lanark
1907	Celtic	3-0	Heart of Midlothian
1908	Celtic	5-1	St. Mirren
1909	*cup withheld †*	2-2, (replay) 1-1	Celtic v Rangers
1910	Dundee	0-0, (replay) 2-2, (replay) 2-1	Clyde
1911	Celtic	0-0, (replay) 2-0	Hamilton Academical
1912	Celtic	2-0	Clyde
1913	Falkirk	2-0	Raith Rovers
1914	Celtic	0-0, (replay) 4-1	Hibernian
1915–19	*no competition*		
1920	Kilmarnock	3-2	Albion Rovers
1921	Partick Thistle	1-0	Rangers
1922	Morton	1-0	Rangers
1923	Celtic	1-0	Hibernian
1924	Airdrieonians	2-0	Hibernian
1925	Celtic	2-1	Dundee
1926	St. Mirren	2-0	Celtic
1927	Celtic	3-1	East Fife
1928	Rangers	4-0	Celtic
1929	Kilmarnock	2-0	Rangers
1930	Rangers	0-0, (replay) 2-1	Partick Thistle
1931	Celtic	2-2, (replay) 4-2	Motherwell

SCOTLAND

SCOTLAND

Scottish Cup Record (*continued*)

YEAR	WINNERS	SCORE	RUNNERS-UP
1932	Rangers	1-1, (replay) 3-0	Kilmarnock
1933	Celtic	1-0	Motherwell
1934	Rangers	5-0	St. Mirren
1935	Rangers	2-1	Hamilton Academical
1936	Rangers	1-0	Third Lanark
1937	Celtic	2-1	Aberdeen
1938	East Fife	1-1, (replay) 4-2 (aet)	Kilmarnock
1939	Clyde	4-0	Motherwell
1940–46		*no competition*	
1947	Aberdeen	2-1	Hibernian
1948	Rangers	1-1, (replay) 1-0 (aet)	Morton
1949	Rangers	4-1	Clyde
1950	Rangers	3-0	East Fife
1951	Celtic	1-0	Motherwell
1952	Motherwell	4-0	Dundee
1953	Rangers	1-1, (replay) 1-0	Aberdeen
1954	Celtic	2-1	Aberdeen
1955	Clyde	1-1, (replay) 1-0	Celtic
1956	Heart of Midlothian	3-1	Celtic
1957	Falkirk	1-1, (replay) 2-1 (aet)	Kilmarnock
1958	Clyde	1-0	Hibernian
1959	St. Mirren	3-1	Aberdeen
1960	Rangers	2-0	Kilmarnock
1961	Dunfermline Athletic	0-0, (replay) 2-0	Celtic
1962	Rangers	2-0	St. Mirren
1963	Rangers	1-1, (replay) 3-0	Celtic
1964	Rangers	3-1	Dundee
1965	Celtic	3-2	Dunfermline Athletic
1966	Rangers	0-0, (replay) 1-0	Celtic
1967	Celtic	2-0	Aberdeen
1968	Dunfermline Athletic	3-1	Heart of Midlothian
1969	Celtic	4-0	Rangers
1970	Aberdeen	3-1	Celtic
1971	Celtic	1-1, (replay) 2-1	Rangers
1972	Celtic	6-1	Hibernian
1973	Rangers	3-2	Celtic
1974	Celtic	3-0	Dundee United
1975	Celtic	3-1	Airdrieonians
1976	Rangers	3-1	Heart of Midlothian
1977	Celtic	1-0	Rangers
1978	Rangers	2-1	Aberdeen
1979	Rangers	0-0, (replay) 0-0, (replay) 3-2 (aet)	Hibernian
1980	Celtic	1-0 (aet)	Rangers

Scottish Cup Record (*continued*)

YEAR	WINNERS	SCORE	RUNNERS-UP
1981	Rangers	0-0, (replay) 4-1	Dundee United
1982	Aberdeen	4-1 (aet)	Rangers
1983	Aberdeen	1-0 (aet)	Rangers
1984	Aberdeen	2-1	Celtic
1985	Celtic	2-1 (aet)	Dundee United
1986	Aberdeen	3-0	Heart of Midlothian
1987	St. Mirren	1-0 (aet)	Dundee United
1988	Celtic	2-1	Dundee United
1989	Celtic	1-0	Rangers
1990	Aberdeen	0-0 (9-8 pens)	Celtic
1991	Motherwell	4-3 (aet)	Dundee United
1992	Rangers	2-1	Airdrieonians
1993	Rangers	2-1	Aberdeen
1994	Dundee United	1-0	Rangers
1995	Celtic	1-0	Airdrieonians
1996	Rangers	5-1	Heart of Midlothian
1997	Kilmarnock	1-0	Falkirk
1998	Heart of Midlothian	2-1	Rangers
1999	Rangers	1-0	Celtic
2000	Rangers	4-0	Aberdeen
2001	Celtic	3-0	Hibernian
2002	Rangers	3-2	Celtic
2003	Rangers	1-0	Dundee

w/o denotes walk over
 * Dumbarton protested result of first game.
 ** SFA ordered replay due to playing conditions.
 † Cup withheld due to riots.

Scottish Cup Summary

TEAM	TOTALS	WINNERS & RUNNERS-UP
		(BOLD) (*ITALICS*)
Celtic	31, 18	*1889*, **92, 93, 94, 99, 1900**, *01, 02, 04, 07, 08, 11, 12, 14, 23, 25, 26, 27, 28, 31, 33, 37*, **51, 54, 55, 56, 61, 63, 65, 66, 67, 69, 70, 71, 72, 73, 74, 75, 77, 80,** *84*, **85, 88, 89, 90,** *95, 99,* **2001,** *02*
Rangers	31, 17	**1877,** *79,* **94, 97, 98, 99, 1903,** *04, 05, 21, 22,* **28,** *29,* **30,** *32, 34–36,* **48–50, 53, 60, 62–64, 66, 69, 71, 73, 76, 77, 78,** *79,* **80, 81, 82, 83, 89, 92, 93, 94, 96,** *98,* **99, 2000,** *02,* **03**
Queen's Park	10, 2	**1874–76,** *80–82,* **84, 86, 90, 92, 93,** *1900*
Aberdeen	7, 8	*1937,* **47,** *53, 54, 59, 67,* **70,** *78,* **82–84, 86, 90,** *93, 2000*
Heart of Midlothian	6, 6	**1891, 96, 1901,** *03,* **06,** *07,* **56,** *68,* **76,** *86, 96,* **98**
Kilmarnock	3, 5	*1898,* **1920,** *29, 32, 38, 57, 60,* **97**
Vale of Leven	3, 4	**1877–79,** *83–85,* **90**
Clyde	3, 3	*1910, 12,* **39,** *49,* **55, 58**
St. Mirren	3, 3	*1908,* **26,** *34,* **59,** *62,* **87**
Hibernian	2, 9	**1887,** *96,* **1902,** *14, 23, 24, 47, 58, 72, 79, 2001*
Motherwell	2, 4	*1931, 33, 39,* **51,** *52,* **91**
Third Lanark	2, 4	**1876,** *78,* **89,** *1905, 06, 36*
Renton	2, 3	*1875,* **85,** *86,* **88,** *95*
Dunfermline Athletic	2, 1	**1961,** *65,* **68**
Falkirk	2, 1	**1913, 57,** *97*
Dundee United	1, 6	*1974, 81, 85, 87, 88, 91,* **94**
Dumbarton	1, 5	*1881, 82,* **83,** *87, 91, 97*
Dundee	1, 4	**1910,** *25, 52, 64, 2003*
Airdrieonians	1, 3	**1924,** *75, 92, 95*
East Fife	1, 2	*1927,* **38,** *50*
Morton	1, 1	**1922,** *48*
Partick Thistle	1, 1	**1921,** *30*
St. Bernard's	1, 0	**1895**
Hamilton Academical	0, 2	*1911, 35*

Though both Celtic and Rangers have superb modern stadiums Scottish football also incorporates smaller clubs like Falkirk whose Brockville Park is deemed unsuitable for Premier League football.

Scottish Cup Summary (*continued*)

TEAM	TOTALS	WINNERS & RUNNERS-UP (BOLD) (*ITALICS*)
Albion Rovers	**0,** *1*	*1920*
Cambuslang	**0,** *1*	*1888*
Clydesdale	**0,** *1*	*1874*
Raith Rovers	**0,** *1*	*1913*
Thornley Bank	**0,** *1*	*1880*

Scottish League Cup Summary

TEAM	TOTALS	WINNERS & RUNNERS-UP (BOLD) (*ITALICS*)
Rangers	**23,** *6*	**1947, 49,** *52, 58,* **61, 62, 64, 65,** *66, 67,* **71, 76, 78, 79, 82,** *83,* **84, 85, 87–89,** *90,* **91, 93, 94, 97,** *99,* **2002, 03**
Celtic	**11,** *13*	*1957, 58,* **65,** *66–70,* **71–74,** *75,* **76–78,** *83,* **84,** *87,* **91,** *95,* **98, 2000, 01,** *03*
Aberdeen	**5,** *7*	*1947,* **56,** *77,* **79,** *80,* **86,** *88,* **89, 90,** *93,* **96,** *2000*
Heart of Midlothian	**4,** *2*	**1955, 59, 60,** *62, 63,* **97**
Dundee	**3,** *3*	**1952,** *68,* **74,** *81, 96*
East Fife	**3,** *0*	**1948, 50, 54**
Hibernian	**2,** *5*	*1951, 69, 73, 75, 86,* **92,** *94*
Dundee United	**2,** *3*	**1980, 81,** *82, 85,* **98**
Partick Thistle	**1,** *3*	*1954, 57, 59,* **72**
Motherwell	**1,** *1*	**1951,** *55*
Raith Rovers	**1,** *1*	*1949,* **95**
Kilmarnock	**0,** *4*	*1953, 61, 63, 2001*
Dunfermline Athletic	**0,** *2*	*1950, 92*
St. Johnstone	**0,** *2*	*1970, 99*
Ayr United	**0,** *1*	*2002*
Falkirk	**0,** *1*	*1948*
Morton	**0,** *1*	*1964*
St. Mirren	**0,** *1*	*1956*
Third Lanark	**0,** *1*	*1960*

Scottish League Cup Record 1947–2003

YEAR	WINNERS	SCORE	RUNNERS-UP
1947	Rangers	4-0	Aberdeen
1948	East Fife	0-0, (replay) 4-1	Falkirk
1949	Rangers	2-0	Raith Rovers
1950	East Fife	3-0	Dunfermline Athletic
1951	Motherwell	3-0	Hibernian
1952	Dundee	3-2	Rangers
1953	Dundee	2-0	Kilmarnock
1954	East Fife	3-2	Partick Thistle
1955	Heart of Midlothian	4-2	Motherwell
1956	Aberdeen	2-1	St. Mirren
1957	Celtic	3-0	Partick Thistle
1958	Celtic	7-1	Rangers
1959	Heart of Midlothian	5-1	Partick Thistle
1960	Heart of Midlothian	2-1	Third Lanark
1961	Rangers	2-0	Kilmarnock
1962	Rangers	1-1, (replay) 3-1	Heart of Midlothian
1963	Heart of Midlothian	1-0	Kilmarnock
1964	Rangers	5-0	Morton
1965	Rangers	2-1	Celtic
1966	Celtic	2-1	Rangers
1967	Celtic	1-0	Rangers
1968	Celtic	5-3	Dundee
1969	Celtic	6-2	Hibernian
1970	Celtic	1-0	St. Johnstone
1971	Rangers	1-0	Celtic
1972	Partick Thistle	4-1	Celtic
1973	Hibernian	2-1	Celtic
1974	Dundee	1-0	Celtic
1975	Celtic	6-3	Hibernian
1976	Rangers	1-0	Celtic
1977	Aberdeen	2-1 (aet)	Celtic
1978	Rangers	2-1 (aet)	Celtic
1979	Rangers	2-1	Aberdeen
1980	Dundee United	0-0, (replay) 3-0	Aberdeen
1981	Dundee United	3-0	Dundee
1982	Rangers	2-1	Dundee United
1983	Celtic	2-1	Rangers
1984	Rangers	3-2 (aet)	Celtic
1985	Rangers	1-0	Dundee United
1986	Aberdeen	3-0	Hibernian
1987	Rangers	2-1	Celtic
1988	Rangers	3-3 (aet)(5-3 pens)	Aberdeen
1989	Rangers	3-2	Aberdeen
1990	Aberdeen	2-1 (aet)	Rangers
1991	Rangers	2-1 (aet)	Celtic
1992	Hibernian	2-0	Dunfermline Athletic
1993	Rangers	2-1	Aberdeen
1994	Rangers	2-1	Hibernian
1995	Raith Rovers	2-2 (aet)(6-5 pens)	Celtic
1996	Aberdeen	2-0	Dundee
1997	Rangers	4-3	Heart of Midlothian
1998	Celtic	3-0	Dundee United
1999	Rangers	2-1	St. Johnstone
2000	Celtic	2-0	Aberdeen
2001	Celtic	3-0	Kilmarnock
2002	Rangers	4-0	Ayr United
2003	Rangers	2-1	Celtic

SCOTLAND

It's not often that a major Scottish trophy is won by anyone outside the 'Old Firm'. When it is, it's a major cause for celebration, as Aberdeen's Stewart McKimmie shows as he lifts the Scottish League Cup after the team's victory over Dundee in 1996.

Ireland
(Republic of)

The Football Association of Ireland
Founded: 1921
Joined FIFA: 1923
Joined UEFA: 1954

PRIOR TO PARTITION AND INDEPENDENCE in 1921, few clubs from the south of Ireland had made much impression in national competitions. With independence and the creation of a separate league and cup competition in 1922, domestic football improved, but Ireland has never been able to sustain a professional league as money, fans and players cross the Irish Sea to England and Scotland.

Ireland League Record 1922–2003

SEASON	CHAMPIONS	SEASON	CHAMPIONS
1922	St. James' Gate	1964	Shamrock Rovers
1923	Shamrock Rovers	1965	Drumcondra
1924	Bohemians	1966	Waterford
1925	Shamrock Rovers	1967	Dundalk
1926	Shelbourne	1968	Waterford
1927	Shamrock Rovers	1969	Waterford
1928	Bohemians	1970	Waterford
1929	Shelbourne	1971	Cork Hibernians
1930	Bohemians	1972	Waterford
1931	Shelbourne	1973	Waterford
1932	Shamrock Rovers	1974	Cork Celtic
1933	Dundalk	1975	Bohemians
1934	Bohemians	1976	Dundalk
1935	Dolphin	1977	Sligo Rovers
1936	Bohemians	1978	Bohemians
1937	Sligo Rovers	1979	Dundalk
1938	Shamrock Rovers	1980	Limerick United
1939	Shamrock Rovers	1981	Athlone Town
1940	St. James' Gate	1982	Dundalk
1941	Cork United	1983	Athlone Town
1942	Cork United	1984	Shamrock Rovers
1943	Cork United	1985	Shamrock Rovers
1944	Shelbourne	1986	Shamrock Rovers
1945	Cork United	1987	Shamrock Rovers
1946	Cork United	1988	Dundalk
1947	Shelbourne	1989	Derry City
1948	Drumcondra	1990	St. Patrick's Athletic
1949	Drumcondra	1991	Dundalk
1950	Cork Athletic	1992	Shelbourne
1951	Cork Athletic	1993	Cork City
1952	St. Patrick's Athletic	1994	Shamrock Rovers
1953	Shelbourne	1995	Dundalk
1954	Shamrock Rovers	1996	St. Patrick's Athletic
1955	St. Patrick's Athletic	1997	Derry City
1956	St. Patrick's Athletic	1998	St. Patrick's Athletic
1957	Shamrock Rovers	1999	St. Patrick's Athletic
1958	Drumcondra	2000	Shelbourne
1959	Shamrock Rovers	2001	Bohemians
1960	Limerick	2002	Shelbourne
1961	Drumcondra	2003	Bohemians
1962	Shelbourne		
1963	Dundalk		

Ireland Cup Record 1922–2003

YEAR	WINNERS	YEAR	WINNERS
1922	St. James' Gate	1926	Fordsons
1923	Alton United	1927	Drumcondra
1924	Athlone Town	1928	Bohemians
1925	Shamrock Rovers	1929	Shamrock Rovers

Ireland Cup Record (*continued*)

YEAR	WINNERS	YEAR	WINNERS
1930	Shamrock Rovers	1968	Shamrock Rovers
1931	Shamrock Rovers	1969	Shamrock Rovers
1932	Shamrock Rovers	1970	Bohemians
1933	Shamrock Rovers	1971	Limerick
1934	Cork	1972	Cork Hibernians
1935	Bohemians	1973	Cork Hibernians
1936	Shamrock Rovers	1974	Finn Harps
1937	Waterford	1975	Home Farm
1938	St. James' Gate	1976	Bohemians
1939	Shelbourne	1977	Dundalk
1940	Shamrock Rovers	1978	Shamrock Rovers
1941	Cork United	1979	Dundalk
1942	Dundalk	1980	Waterford
1943	Drumcondra	1981	Dundalk
1944	Shamrock Rovers	1982	Limerick United
1945	Shamrock Rovers	1983	Sligo Rovers
1946	Drumcondra	1984	UCD
1947	Cork United	1985	Shamrock Rovers
1948	Shamrock Rovers	1986	Shamrock Rovers
1949	Dundalk	1987	Shamrock Rovers
1950	Transport	1988	Dundalk
1951	Cork Athletic	1989	Derry City
1952	Dundalk	1990	Bray Wanderers
1953	Cork Athletic	1991	Galway United
1954	Drumcondra	1992	Bohemians
1955	Shamrock Rovers	1993	Shelbourne
1956	Shamrock Rovers	1994	Sligo Rovers
1957	Drumcondra	1995	Derry City
1958	Dundalk	1996	Shelbourne
1959	St. Patrick's Athletic	1997	Shelbourne
1960	Shelbourne	1998	Cork City
1961	St. Patrick's Athletic	1999	Bray Wanderers
1962	Shamrock Rovers	2000	Shelbourne
1963	Shelbourne	2001	Bohemians
1964	Shamrock Rovers	2002	Dundalk
1965	Shamrock Rovers	2003	Derry City
1966	Shamrock Rovers		
1967	Shamrock Rovers		

Northern Ireland

The Irish Football Association
Founded: 1880
Joined FIFA: 1911–20, 1924–28, 1946
Joined UEFA: 1954

NORTHERN IRELAND'S league and cup competitions are the third oldest in the world. The cup dates from 1881 and the league from 1890. These all-Ireland competitions organized from Belfast became purely Northern Irish in 1921 after the partition of the island. Derry City, a team based in Catholic Londonderry, withdrew from both competitions in 1972 and joined the FA south of the border.

Northern Ireland League Record 1891–2003

SEASON	CHAMPIONS	SEASON	CHAMPIONS
1891	Linfield	1898	Linfield
1892	Linfield	1899	Distillery
1893	Linfield	1900	Celtic
1894	Glentoran	1901	Distillery
1895	Linfield	1902	Linfield
1896	Distillery	1903	Distillery
1897	Glentoran	1904	Linfield

REPUBLIC OF IRELAND, NORTHERN IRELAND

Northern Ireland League Record (*continued*)

SEASON	CHAMPIONS	SEASON	CHAMPIONS
1905	Glentoran	1960	Glenavon
1906	Cliftonville	1961	Linfield
1907	Linfield	1962	Linfield
1908	Linfield	1963	Distillery
1909	Linfield	1964	Glentoran
1910	Cliftonville	1965	Derry City
1911	Linfield	1966	Linfield
1912	Glentoran	1967	Glentoran
1913	Glentoran	1968	Glentoran
1914	Linfield	1969	Linfield
1915	Celtic	1970	Glentoran
1916–19	*no championship*	1971	Linfield
1920	Celtic	1972	Glentoran
1921	Glentoran	1973	Crusaders
1922	Linfield	1974	Coleraine
1923	Linfield	1975	Linfield
1924	Queen's Island	1976	Crusaders
1925	Glentoran	1977	Glentoran
1926	Celtic	1978	Linfield
1927	Celtic	1979	Linfield
1928	Celtic	1980	Linfield
1929	Celtic	1981	Glentoran
1930	Linfield	1982	Linfield
1931	Glentoran	1983	Linfield
1932	Linfield	1984	Linfield
1933	Celtic	1985	Linfield
1934	Linfield	1986	Linfield
1935	Linfield	1987	Linfield
1936	Celtic	1988	Glentoran
1937	Celtic	1989	Linfield
1938	Celtic	1990	Portadown
1939	Celtic	1991	Portadown
1940	Celtic	1992	Glentoran
1941–47	*no championship*	1993	Linfield
1948	Celtic	1994	Linfield
1949	Linfield	1995	Crusaders
1950	Linfield	1996	Portadown
1951	Glentoran	1997	Crusaders
1952	Glentoran	1998	Cliftonville
1953	Glentoran	1999	Glentoran
1954	Linfield	2000	Linfield
1955	Linfield	2001	Linfield
1956	Linfield	2002	Portadown
1957	Glenavon	2003	Glentoran
1958	Ards		
1959	Linfield		

Northern Ireland Cup Record 1881–2003

YEAR	WINNERS	YEAR	WINNERS
1881	Moyola Park	1903	Distillery
1882	Queen's Island	1904	Linfield
1883	Cliftonville	1905	Distillery
1884	Distillery	1906	Shelbourne
1885	Distillery	1907	Cliftonville
1886	Distillery	1908	Bohemians
1887	Ulster	1909	Cliftonville
1888	Cliftonville	1910	Distillery
1889	Distillery	1911	Shelbourne
1890	Gordon Highlanders	1912	Linfield
1891	Linfield	1913	Linfield
1892	Linfield	1914	Glentoran
1893	Linfield	1915	Linfield
1894	Distillery	1916	Linfield
1895	Linfield	1917	Glentoran
1896	Distillery	1918	Celtic
1897	Cliftonville	1919	Linfield
1898	Linfield	1920	Shelbourne
1899	Linfield	1921	Glentoran
1900	Cliftonville	1922	Linfield
1901	Cliftonville	1923	Linfield
1902	Linfield	1924	Queen's Island

Northern Ireland Cup Record (*continued*)

YEAR	WINNERS	YEAR	WINNERS
1925	Distillery	1966	Glentoran
1926	Celtic	1967	Crusaders
1927	Ards	1968	Crusaders
1928	Willowfield	1969	Ards
1929	Ballymena United	1970	Linfield
1930	Linfield	1971	Distillery
1931	Linfield	1972	Coleraine
1932	Glentoran	1973	Glentoran
1933	Glentoran	1974	Ards
1934	Linfield	1975	Coleraine
1935	Glentoran	1976	Carrick Rangers
1936	Linfield	1977	Coleraine
1937	Celtic	1978	Linfield
1938	Celtic	1979	Cliftonville
1939	Linfield	1980	Linfield
1940	Ballymena United	1981	Ballymena United
1941	Celtic	1982	Linfield
1942	Linfield	1983	Glentoran
1943	Celtic	1984	Ballymena United
1944	Celtic	1985	Glentoran
1945	Linfield	1986	Glentoran
1946	Linfield	1987	Glentoran
1947	Celtic	1988	Glentoran
1948	Linfield	1989	Ballymena United
1949	Derry City	1990	Glentoran
1950	Linfield	1991	Portadown
1951	Glentoran	1992	Glenavon
1952	Ards	1993	Bangor
1953	Linfield	1994	Linfield
1954	Derry City	1995	Linfield
1955	Dundela	1996	Glentoran
1956	Distillery	1997	Glenavon
1957	Glenavon	1998	Glentoran
1958	Ballymena United	1999	Portadown
1959	Glenavon	2000	Glentoran
1960	Linfield	2001	Glentoran
1961	Glenavon	2002	Linfield
1962	Linfield	2003	Coleraine
1963	Linfield		
1964	Derry City		
1965	Coleraine		

Wales

The Football Association of Wales
Founded: 1876
Joined FIFA: 1910–20, 1924–28, 1946
Joined UEFA: 1954

In Wales, the strength of rugby and the allure of the English game have seen a weak and often fragmented football culture. The largest clubs (Swansea, Cardiff and Wrexham) play their league football in England, though the Welsh Cup has provided a convenient route for the holders into European football via the Cup-Winners' Cup and now the UEFA Cup. In 1992 a unified semi-professional league was established.

SEASON	LEAGUE CHAMPIONS
1999	Bangor Town
2000	Total Network Solutions
2001	Barry Town
2002	Barry Town
2003	Barry Town

YEAR	CUP WINNERS
1999	ICT Cardiff
2000	Bangor City
2001	Barry Town
2002	Barry Town
2003	Barry Town

YEAR	LEAGUE CUP WINNERS
1999	ICT Cardiff
2000	Bangor City
2001	Caersws
2002	Caersws
2003	Wrexham

Scandinavia

THE SEASONS IN REVIEW 2002, 2002–03

WITH GATES UP ALMOST THIRTY PER CENT and no clubs going bankrupt, Danish football is on a more even keel this season. There was certainly no change at the top, where the season eventually came down to a two-horse race between last year's champions Brøndby and runners-up FC København, where as last year Brøndby was the early leader, FC København began much the stronger and went in at the winter break nine points clear. As little as seven points separated the other 11 clubs.

FC København was held together by the defensive play of Martin Albrechtsen and the midfield work of Thomas Roll Larsen. Brøndby began the season under new coach and national hero Michael Laudrup. He announced his attentions by dismissing seven members of the squad, including long-standing club favourites. Laudrup introduced a raft of younger players into the squad and set about developing a much more attacking and short passing game at the club. Occasionally brilliant, they were fatally inconsistent.

However, in the new year, FC København began to fall away as up to nine members of the first-team squad were injured and Norwegian midfielder Erik Mykland was peeled off a Copenhagen pavement after a nocturnal visit to the city centre. Brøndby steadily closed the gap, won the cup and took the lead in the final weeks of the season. It came down to the penultimate game of the year, FCK away at Brøndby, and Brøndby blew it. A nervous performance from the home side saw them play out for the draw only to be beaten by a goal in the third minute of injury time.

In Norway, normal service looked like it might be interrupted when Lyn and Molde reached the halfway stage at the top of the table. But, inevitably, Rosenborg began to find its form, and won its 11th consecutive national title in coach Nils Arne Eggen's final season. In Sweden, the smallest of Stockholm's three clubs, Djurgårdens, won the double, while HJK Helsinki made it 20 Finnish League titles with room to spare. It was not a happy season outside Scandinavia. Only Rosenborg made the Champions League group stage, and though it held Internazionale to a draw in a heroic home game, it made no further progress. No Scandinavian club made it past the second round of the UEFA Cup.

Leading Danish referee *Kim Milton Nielsson studies a pitch side TV replay during the FC København-Brøndby clash. This is the first use of the technology in Denmark.*

Danish League Table 2002–03

CLUB	P	W	D	L	F	A	Pts	
FC København	33	17	10	6	51	32	**61**	Champions League
Brøndby IF	33	15	11	7	61	35	**56**	UEFA Cup
Farum BK	33	16	3	14	50	58	**51**	UEFA Cup
OB Odense	33	12	12	9	55	50	**48**	
Esbjerg fB	33	12	11	10	65	57	**47**	
AaB Aalborg	33	14	4	15	42	45	**46**	
FC Midtjylland	33	11	11	11	49	45	**44**	
Viborg FF	33	11	10	12	58	55	**43**	
AB	33	10	12	11	44	49	**42**	
AGF Aarhus	33	10	10	13	49	59	**40**	
Silkeborg IF	33	9	9	15	52	54	**36**	Relegated
Køge BK	33	8	3	22	45	82	**27**	Relegated

Promoted clubs: Herfølge BK, BK Frem.

Finnish League Table 2002

CLUB	P	W	D	L	F	A	Pts	
HJK Helsinki	29	20	5	4	51	21	**65**	Champions League
MyPa Anjalankoski	29	17	9	3	57	25	**60**	UEFA Cup
Haka Valkeakoski	29	15	7	7	51	30	**52**	UEFA Cup (cup winners)
Allianssi Vantaa	29	12	5	12	39	44	**41**	
United Tampere	29	8	15	6	31	24	**39**	
Inter Turku	29	9	9	11	33	29	**36**	
Jaro Pietarsaari	29	10	6	13	34	46	**36**	
FC Lahti	29	9	6	14	25	44	**33**	

The Finnish Premier League has 12 teams. In a Preliminary Stage teams play each other twice. The top eight go into a Championship Group (above), the bottom four join the top four teams from the Second Division and play each other once to determine relegation and promotion. Promoted teams: TSP Turku, Jokerit Helsinki, KooTeePee Kotka. Relegated team: VPS Vaasa

Norwegian League Table 2002

CLUB	P	W	D	L	F	A	Pts	
Rosenborg BK	26	17	5	4	57	30	**56**	Champions League
Molde FK	26	15	5	6	48	26	**50**	UEFA Cup
SFK Lyn	26	14	5	7	36	29	**47**	UEFA Cup
Viking FK	26	11	11	4	44	31	**44**	
Stabaek Fotball	26	12	6	8	48	34	**42**	
Odd Grenland	26	12	5	9	36	30	**41**	
Lillestrøm SK	26	10	6	10	37	30	**36**	
Vålerenga IF	26	7	12	7	38	31	**33**	UEFA Cup (cup winners)
Bryne IL	26	8	7	11	38	39	**31**	
Bodø/Glimt	26	9	4	13	38	41	**31**	
Sogndal IL	26	8	6	12	37	51	**30**	
SK Brann	26	8	3	15	35	52	**27**	
Moss FK	26	6	6	14	32	49	**24**	Relegated
IK Start	26	2	5	19	21	72	**11**	Relegated

Promoted clubs: Tromsø IL, Aalesund.

Swedish League Table 2002

CLUB	P	W	D	L	F	A	Pts	
Djurgårdens IF	26	16	4	6	51	33	**52**	Champions League
Malmö FF	26	14	4	8	52	32	**46**	UEFA Cup
Örgryte IS	26	12	8	6	49	38	**44**	
Helsingborgs IF	26	10	8	8	38	38	**38**	
AIK	26	9	10	7	35	38	**37**	UEFA Cup (cup finalists)
Halmstads BK	26	8	12	6	35	28	**36**	
Örebro SK	26	9	8	9	32	39	**35**	
GIF Sundsvall	26	8	9	9	29	35	**33**	
Hammarby IF	26	8	8	10	43	42	**32**	
Elfsborg IF	26	8	8	10	25	31	**32**	
Landskrona BoIS	26	8	6	12	41	39	**30**	
IFK Göteborg	26	8	4	14	25	39	**28**	
IFK Norrköpping	26	6	9	11	37	40	**27**	Relegated
Kalmar FF	26	6	6	14	20	40	**24**	Relegated

Promoted clubs: Östers IF, Enköpings SK.

SCANDINAVIA

Top Goalscorers 2002, 2002–03

COUNTRY	PLAYER	CLUB	GOALS
Denmark	Søren Frederiksen	Viborg	18
Finland	Mika Kottila	HJK Helsinki	18
Norway	Harald Brattbakk	Rosenborg BK	17
Sweden	Peter Ljeh	Malmö FF	24

International Club Performances 2002–03

CLUB	COMPETITION	PROGRESS
Brøndby IF (Den)	Champions League	3rd Qualifying Stage
	UEFA Cup	1st Round
Hammarby IF (Swe)	Champions League	2nd Qualifying Stage
Rosenborg BK (Nor)	Champions League	1st Group Stage
United Tampere (Fin)	Champions League	1st Qualifying Stage
AIK (Swe)	UEFA Cup	1st Round
SK Brann (Nor)	UEFA Cup	Qualifying Round
Djurgårdens IF (Swe)	UEFA Cup	2nd Round
IFK Göteborg (Swe)	UEFA Cup	Qualifying Round
HJK Helsinki (Fin)	UEFA Cup	Qualifying Round
FC København (Den)	UEFA Cup	1st Round
Lillestrom (Nor)	UEFA Cup	2nd Qualifying Stage
FC Midtjylland (Den)	UEFA Cup	2nd Round
MyPa Anjalankoski (Fin)	UEFA Cup	Qualifying Round
OB Odense (Den)	UEFA Cup	1st Round
Stabaek Fotball (Nor)	UEFA Cup	1st Round
Viking FK (Nor)	UEFA Cup	2nd Round

National Cup Finals 2002, 2002–03

COUNTRY	WINNERS	SCORE	RUNNERS-UP
*Denmark	Brøndby IF	3-0	FC Midtjylland
Finland	Haka Valkeakoski	4-1	FC Lahti
Norway	Vålerenga IF	1-0	Odd Grenland
Sweden	Djurgårdens IF	1-0 (aet)	AIK

* Denotes 2002–03 winners.

Above, right: *Jonas Kamper of Brøndby gets a grip on FC København's Peter Nielsen – an intimacy that was reflected in their season-long battle for the top spot in Denmark.*

Right: *Norwegian cup-winners and champions clash; Rosenborg's Orjan Berg takes on the Vålerenga defence.*

Below: *HJK Helsinki's Jukka Santala (left) shoots for goal as he is closed down by FF Jaro's Roope Heilala.*

The double for Djurgårdens. Kim Kallstrom and Johan Elmander celebrate the club's league championship after beating Elfsborg.

Association Football in Sweden

SWEDEN

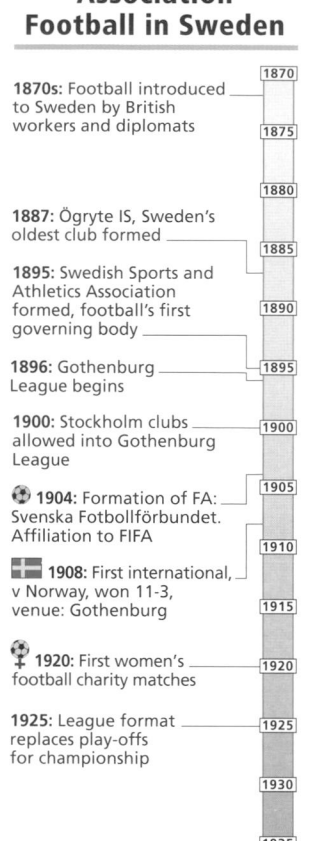

1870s: Football introduced to Sweden by British workers and diplomats

1870
1875
1880

1887: Ögryte IS, Sweden's oldest club formed

1885

1895: Swedish Sports and Athletics Association formed, football's first governing body

1890

1896: Gothenburg League begins

1895

1900: Stockholm clubs allowed into Gothenburg League

1900

1905

1904: Formation of FA: Svenska Fotbollförbundet. Affiliation to FIFA

1910

1908: First international, v Norway, won 11-3, venue: Gothenburg

1915

1920: First women's football charity matches

1920

1925: League format replaces play-offs for championship

1925

1930

1935

1941: First Swedish Cup Final

1940

1945

1948: Sweden wins gold medal at London Olympics

1950

1954: Affiliation to UEFA

1955

1958: Professionals allowed to play for national team

1960

1965

1973: First women's international, v Finland, drawn 0-0

1970

1975

1978: National FA incorporates women's football

1980

1982: League decided by final play-off

1985

1990: League reverts to simple format

1990

1995
2000
2005

Gunnar Nordahl moved from IFK Norrköping to Milan in 1949 to become part of an all-Swedish forward line with Gunnar Gren and Nils Liedholm.

Key

🇸🇪 International football

⚽ Affiliation to FIFA

⚽ Affiliation to UEFA

⚥ Women's football

■ World Cup host

▲ World Cup runner-up

■ European Championships host

○ Competition winner

△ Competition runner-up

IFK – IFK Göteborg
Mal – Malmö FF

International Competitions

	European Cup	UEFA Cup	European Cup-Winners' Cup
1958: ▲ ■			
1979:	△ Mal		
1982:		○ IFK	
1987:		○ IFK	
1992: ■			

Sweden: The main clubs

IFK Elfsborg 1905 Team name with year of formation

● Club formed before 1912

● Club formed 1912–25

● Club formed 1925–50

○ Club formed after 1950

★ Founder members of League (1925)

Pre-1925 champions

Champions (1925–55)

● Colours and date unknown

★ **Örgryte IS** 1887

★ **IFK Göteborg** 1904

Gunnilse

Västra Frölunda 1930

★ **GAIS** 1894

Göteborg IF

BK Häcken 1940

Fässbergs IF 1916

★ **Helsingborgs IF** 1907

Råå IF Helsingborg 1921

★ **Landskrona** 1915

★ **IFK Malmö** 1899

Malmö FF 1887

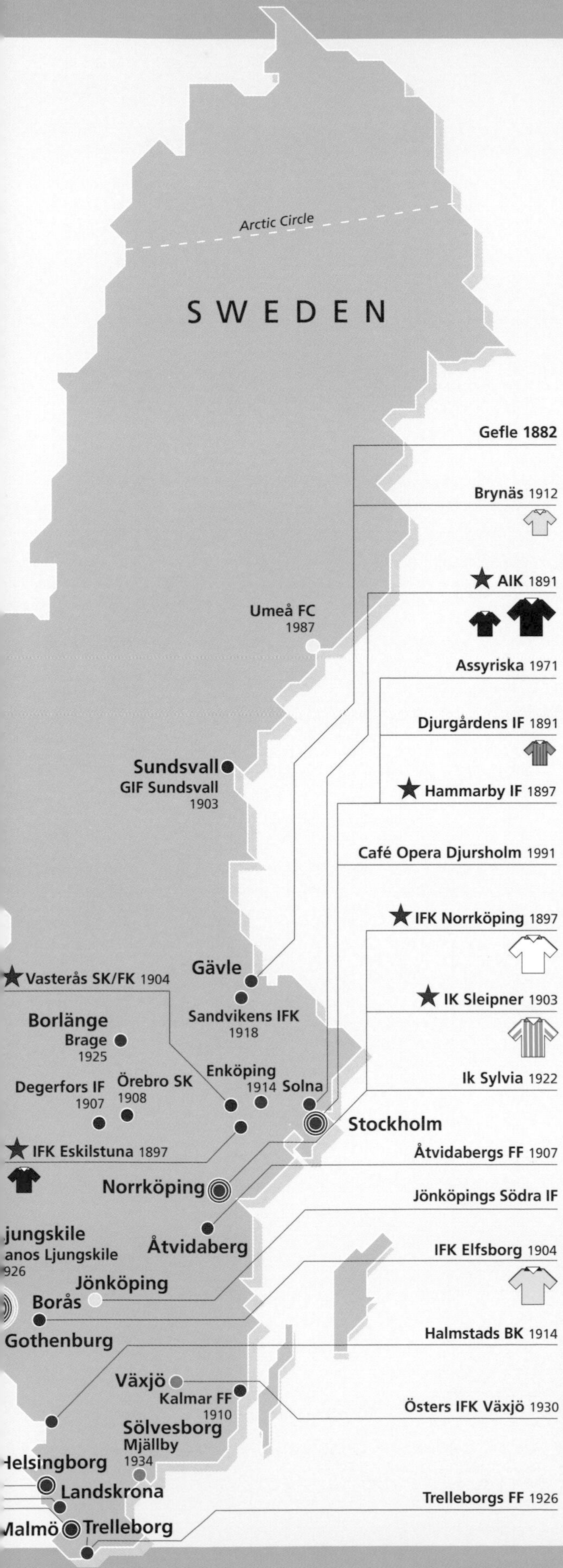

Sweden

ORIGINS AND GROWTH OF FOOTBALL

FOOTBALL ARRIVED IN SWEDEN IN THE 1870s by a variety of routes: Scottish riveters and English sailors in Gothenburg, British engineers and railway workers, as well as British embassy staff in the parks of Stockholm. Swedish football's centre of gravity was quickly established in Gothenburg with the formation of Ögryte (1887) and GAIS Gothenburg (1894). In 1895 a Gothenburg-based tournament was set up. Stockholm clubs joined in 1900 and a national league was created in 1925. Sweden absorbed footballing influences from Britain and Continental Europe, both providing coaches and managers to leading club sides and the national teams prior to the Second World War.

Swedes in Milan

The development of Swedish football has obvious parallels with wider Swedish society, most clearly an active international presence out of all proportion with the strength of its domestic football. Sweden was a founder member of FIFA, won the gold medal at the 1948 Olympics, has been third or fourth at three World Cups (1938, 1950, 1994) and was runner-up and host at the 1958 World Cup. Domestically, the persistence of amateurism saw the best players migrate south, most famously the forward line of Gren, Nordahl and Liedholm to Milan in 1949. This move was met by the exclusion of professionals from the national team until 1958. Limited economic resources combined with a continuing exodus of talent left Swedish clubs weak in postwar European competitions until the de facto arrival of professionalism at the bigger clubs and the UEFA Cup triumphs of IFK Gothenburg in the 1980s.

Women on top

The egalitarian and anti-commercial ethos of much of Swedish society may have been barriers to the success of Swedish men's football but it has certainly encouraged the relatively early adoption and active promotion of women's football in Sweden. The Swedish women's team won the inaugural Women's European Championships in 1984 and was runner-up in the first Women's World Cup in 1988.

The Swedish Women's team won the first-ever Women's European Championships in 1984 beating England in the Final.

SWEDEN

Map labels

Arctic Circle

S W E D E N

Gefle 1882

Brynäs 1912

AIK 1891

Umeå FC 1987

Assyriska 1971

Djurgårdens IF 1891

Sundsvall
GIF Sundsvall 1903

Hammarby IF 1897

Café Opera Djursholm 1991

IFK Norrköping 1897

Vasterås SK/FK 1904

Gävle

IK Sleipner 1903

Borlänge
Brage 1925

Sandvikens IFK 1918

Degerfors IF 1907

Örebro SK 1908

Enköping 1914

Solna

Ik Sylvia 1922

IFK Eskilstuna 1897

Stockholm

Norrköping

Åtvidabergs FF 1907

jungskile
anos Ljungskile 926

Åtvidaberg

Jönköpings Södra IF

Jönköping

IFK Elfsborg 1904

Borås

Halmstads BK 1914

Gothenburg

Växjö
Kalmar FF 1910

Östers IFK Växjö 1930

Sölvesborg
Mjällby 1934

Helsingborg

Landskrona

Trelleborgs FF 1926

Malmö   Trelleborg

Sweden

Svenska Fotbollförbundet
Founded: 1904
Joined FIFA: 1904
Joined UEFA: 1954

THE FIRST SWEDISH league championship was played in 1896 and was restricted to clubs from Gothenburg. In 1900, the league was expanded to include teams from Stockholm and the final rounds were played as a knockout competition until 1925, when a normal league format was adopted (this accounts for the two championships awarded that year).

The Swedish Cup was established in 1941, and ran fitfully over the next couple of decades until European qualification for the winners made it a more pressing engagement. Despite this, Finals have attracted crowds of less than 2,000.

Swedish League Record 1896–2002

SEASON	CHAMPIONS	RUNNERS-UP
1896	Örgryte IS	IV Göteborg
1897	Örgryte IS	Örgryte II
1898	Örgryte IS	AIK
1899	Örgryte IS	Göteborg FF
1900	AIK	Örgryte IS
1901	AIK	Örgryte II
1902	Örgryte IS	Jönköpings AIF
1903	Göteborg IF	Göteborg FF
1904	Örgryte IS	Djurgårdens IF
1905	Örgryte IS	IFK Stockholm
1906	Örgryte IS	Djurgårdens IF
1907	Örgryte IS	IFK Uppsala
1908	IFK Göteborg	IFK Uppsala
1909	Örgryte IS	Djurgårdens IF
1910	IFK Göteborg	Djurgårdens IF
1911	AIK	IFK Uppsala
1912	Djurgårdens IF	Örgryte IS
1913	Örgryte IS	Djurgårdens IF
1914	AIK	Helsingborgs IF
1915	Djurgårdens IF	AIK
1916	AIK	Djurgårdens IF
1917	Djurgårdens IF	AIK
1918	IFK Göteborg	Helsingborgs IF
1919	GAIS	Djurgårdens IF
1920	Djurgårdens IF	IK Sleipner
1921	IFK Eskilstuna	IK Sleipner
1922	GAIS	Hammarby IF
1923	AIK	IFK Eskilstuna
1924	Fassbergs IF	Sirius Uppsala
1925	Brynas IF Gävle	Derby BK Linköping
1925	GAIS	IFK Göteborg
1926	Örgryte IS	GAIS
1927	GAIS	IFK Göteborg
1928	Örgryte IS	Helsingborgs IF
1929	Helsingborgs IF	Örgryte IS
1930	Helsingborgs IF	IFK Göteborg
1931	GAIS	AIK
1932	AIK	Örgryte IS
1933	Helsingborgs IF	GAIS
1934	Helsingborgs IF	GAIS
1935	IFK Göteborg	AIK
1936	IF Elfsborg	AIK
1937	AIK	IK Sleipner
1938	IK Sleipner	Helsingborgs IF
1939	IF Elfsborg	AIK
1940	IF Elfsborg	IFK Göteborg
1941	Helsingborgs IF	Degerfors IF
1942	IFK Göteborg	GAIS
1943	IFK Norrköping	IF Elfsborg

Swedish League Record (*continued*)

SEASON	CHAMPIONS	RUNNERS-UP
1944	Malmö FF	IF Elfsborg
1945	IFK Norrköping	IF Elfsborg
1946	IFK Norrköping	Malmö FF
1947	IFK Norrköping	AIK
1948	IFK Norrköping	Malmö FF
1949	Malmö FF	Helsingborgs IF
1950	Malmö FF	Jonköpings Södra
1951	Malmö FF	Råå IF Helsingborg
1952	IFK Norrköping	Malmö FF
1953	Malmö FF	IFK Norrköping
1954	GAIS	Helsingborgs IF
1955	Djurgårdens IF	Halmstads BK
1956	IFK Norrköping	Malmö FF
1957	IFK Norrköping	Malmö FF
1958	IFK Göteborg	IFK Norrköping
1959	Djurgårdens IF	IFK Norrköping
1960	IFK Norrköping	IFK Malmö
1961	IF Elfsborg	IFK Norrköping
1962	IFK Norrköping	Djurgårdens IF
1963	IFK Norrköping	Degerfors IF
1964	Djurgårdens IF	Malmö FF
1965	Malmö FF	IF Elfsborg
1966	Djurgårdens IF	IFK Norrköping
1967	Malmö FF	Djurgårdens IF
1968	Östers IF Växjö	Malmö FF
1969	IFK Göteborg	Malmö FF
1970	Malmö FF	Åtvidabergs FF
1971	Malmö FF	Åtvidabergs FF
1972	Åtvidabergs FF	AIK
1973	Åtvidabergs FF	Östers IF Växjö
1974	Malmö FF	AIK
1975	Malmö FF	Östers IF Växjö
1976	Halmstads BK	Malmö FF
1977	Malmö FF	IF Elfsborg
1978	Östers IF Växjö	Malmö FF
1979	Halmstads BK	Malmö FF
1980	Östers IF Växjö	Malmö FF
1981	Östers IF Växjö	IFK Göteborg
1982	IFK Göteborg	Hammarby IF
1983	IFK Göteborg	Östers IF Växjö
1984	IFK Göteborg	IFK Norrköping
1985	Örgryte IS	IFK Göteborg
1986	Malmö FF	AIK
1987	IFK Göteborg	Malmö FF
1988	Malmö FF	Djurgårdens IF
1989	IFK Norrköping	Malmö FF
1990	IFK Göteborg	IFK Norrköping
1991	IFK Göteborg	IFK Norrköping
1992	AIK	IFK Norrköping
1993	IFK Göteborg	IFK Norrköping
1994	IFK Göteborg	Örebro SK
1995	IFK Göteborg	Helsingborgs IF
1996	IFK Göteborg	Malmö FF
1997	Halmstads BK	IFK Göteborg
1998	AIK	Helsingborgs IF
1999	Helsingborgs IF	AIK
2000	Halmstads BK	Helsingborgs IF
2001	Hammarby IF	Djurgårdens IF
2002	Djurgårdens IF	Malmö FF

Swedish League Summary

TEAM	TOTALS	CHAMPIONS & RUNNERS-UP (BOLD) (*ITALICS*)
IFK Göteborg	17, 7	**1908, 10, 18,** *25, 27, 30, 35,* *40,* **42, 58, 69,** *81,* **82–84,** *85,* **87, 90, 91, 93–96,** *97*
Malmö FF	14, 16	*1944, 46, 48,* **49–51,** *52,* **53,** *56, 57, 64,* **65, 67, 68, 69, 70, 71, 74, 75,** *76,* *77, 78–80,* **86,** *87,* **88,** *89, 96,* **2002**
Örgryte IS	14, 4	**1896–99, 1900,** *02,* **04–07, 09,** *12,* **13,** *26,* **28,** *29, 32,* **85**
IFK Norrköping	12, 10	**1943,** *45–48,* **52,** *53,* **56, 57, 58, 59,** **60,** *61,* **62, 63,** *66, 84,* **89,** *90–93*
AIK	10, 12	*1898,* **1900,** *01,* **11, 14,** *15,* **16,** *17,* *23, 31,* **32,** *35,* **36,** *37,* **39,** *47, 72,* *74, 86,* **92,** *98,* **99**
Djurgårdens IF	9, 11	*1904, 06,* **09, 10,** *12,* **13,** *15,* **16,** *17,* **19,** **20,** *55,* **59,** *62,* **64,** *66,* **67,** *88,* **2001,** *02*
Helsingborgs IF	6, 9	*1914, 18,* **28,** *29,* **30,** *33, 34,* **38,** *41,* **49,** *54, 95, 98,* **99,** *2000*
GAIS	6, 4	**1919, 22,** *25,* **26,** *27,* **31,** *33,* *34, 42,* **54**
IF Elfsborg	4, 5	**1936, 39, 40,** *43–45,* **61,** *65,* **77**
Östers IF Växjö	4, 3	**1968,** *73,* **75,** *78, 80, 81,* **83**
Halmstads BK	4, 1	*1955,* **76, 79, 97, 2000**
Åtvidabergs FF	2, 2	*1970, 71,* **72, 73**
IK Sleipner	1, 3	*1920, 21, 37,* **38**
Hammarby IF	1, 2	*1922, 82,* **2001**
IFK Eskilstuna	1, 1	**1921,** *23*
Brynas IF Gävle	1, 0	**1925**
Fassbergs IF	1, 0	**1924**
Göteborg IF	1, 0	**1903**
IFK Uppsala	0, 3	*1907, 08, 11*
Degerfors	0, 2	*1941, 63*
Göteborg FF	0, 2	*1899, 1903*
Örgryte II	0, 2	*1897, 1901*
Derby BK Linköping	0, 1	*1925*
IFK Malmö	0, 1	*1960*
IFK Stockholm	0, 1	*1905*
IV Göteborg	0, 1	*1896*
Jönköpings Södra	0, 1	*1950*
Jönköpings AIF	0, 1	*1902*
Örebro SK	0, 1	*1994*
Råå IF Helsingborg	0, 1	*1951*
Sirius Uppsala	0, 1	*1924*

Swedish Cup Record 1941–2002

YEAR	WINNERS	SCORE	RUNNERS-UP
1941	Helsingborgs IF	3-1	IK Sleipner
1942	GAIS	2-1	IK Elfsborg
1943	IFK Norrköping	0-0, (replay) 5-2	AIK
1944	Malmö FF	4-3 (aet)	IFK Norrköping
1945	IFK Norrköping	4-1	Malmö FF
1946	Malmö FF	3-0	Åtvidabergs FF
1947	Malmö FF	3-2	AIK
1948	Råå IF Helsingborg	6-0	BK Kenty Linköping
1949	AIK	1-0	Landskrona BoIS
1950	AIK	3-2	Helsingborgs IF
1951	Malmö FF	2-1	Djurgårdens IF
1952	*no competition*		
1953	Malmö FF	3-2	IFK Norrköping
1954–66	*no competition*		
1967	Malmö FF	2-0	IFK Norrköping
1968	*no competition*		
1969	IFK Norrköping	1-0	AIK
1970	Åtvidabergs FF	2-0	Sandvikens IF
1971	Åtvidabergs FF	3-2	Malmö FF
1972	Landskrona BoIS	0-0, (replay) 3-2 (aet)	IFK Norrköping
1973	Malmö FF	7-0	Åtvidabergs FF

Swedish Cup Record (*continued*)

YEAR	WINNERS	SCORE	RUNNERS-UP
1974	Malmö FF	2-0	Östers IF Växjö
1975	Malmö FF	1-0	Djurgårdens IF
1976	AIK	1-1, (replay) 3-0	Landskrona BoIS
1977	Östers IF Växjö	1-0	Hammarby IF
1978	Malmö FF	2-0 (aet)	Kalmar FF
1979	IFK Göteborg	6-1	Åtvidabergs FF
1980	Malmö FF	3-3 (aet)(4-3 pens)	IK Brage
1981	Kalmar FF	4-0	IF Elfsborg
1982	IFK Göteborg	3-2	Östers IF Växjö
1983	IFK Göteborg	1-0 (aet)	Hammarby IF
1984	Malmö FF	1-0	Landskrona BoIS
1985	AIK	1-1 (aet)(3-2 pens)	Östers IF Växjö
1986	Malmö FF	2-1	IFK Göteborg
1987	Kalmar FF	2-0	GAIS
1988	IFK Norrköping	3-1	Örebro SK
1989	Malmö FF	3-0	Djurgårdens IF
1990	Djurgårdens IF	2-0	Hacken BK Göteborg
1991	IFK Norrköping	4-1	Östers IF Växjö
1992	IFK Göteborg	3-2 (aet)	AIK
1993	Degerfors IF	3-0	Landskrona BoIS
1994	IFK Norrköping	4-3 (gg)	Helsingborgs IF
1995	Halmstads BK	3-1	AIK
1996	AIK	1-0 (gg)	Malmö FF
1997	AIK	2-1	IF Elfsborg
1998	Helsingborgs IF	1-1, 1-1 (aet) (3-0 pens)(2 legs)	Örgryte IS
1999	AIK	1-0, 0-0 (2 legs)	IFK Göteborg
2000	Örgryte IS	2-0, 0-1 (2 legs)	AIK
2001	IF Elfsborg	1-1 (aet)(9-8 pens)	AIK
2002	Djurgårdens IF	1-0 (aet)	AIK

(gg)   denotes victory on golden goal

Swedish Cup Summary

TEAM	TOTALS	WINNERS & RUNNERS-UP (BOLD) (*ITALICS*)
Malmö FF	14, 3	**1944,** *45,* **46, 47, 51, 53, 67, 71,** **73–75, 78, 80, 84, 86, 89,** *96*
AIK	7, 8	*1943, 47,* **49, 50,** *69,* **76, 85,** *92,* *95,* **96, 97,** *99,* **2000–02**
IFK Norrköping	6, 4	**1943,** *44,* **45,** *53,* **57,** *69,* **72,** **88,** *91,* **94**
IFK Göteborg	4, 2	**1979,** *82,* **83,** *86,* **92,** *99*
Åtvidabergs FF	2, 3	*1946,* **70, 71,** *73,* **79**
Djurgårdens IF	2, 3	*1951, 75, 89,* **90, 2002**
Helsingborgs IF	2, 2	**1941,** *50, 94,* **98**
Kalmar FF	2, 1	*1978,* **81, 87**
Landskrona BoIS	1, 4	*1949,* **72,** *76, 84, 93*
Östers IF Växjö	1, 4	*1974,* **77,** *82, 85, 91*
IF Elfsborg	1, 2	*1981, 97,* **2001**
GAIS	1, 1	**1942,** *87*
Örgryte IS	1, 1	*1998,* **2000**
Degerfors IF	1, 0	**1993**
Halmstads BK	1, 0	**1995**
Råå IF Helsingborg	1, 0	**1948**
Hammarby IF	0, 2	*1977, 83*
BK Kenty Linköping	0, 1	*1948*
Hacken BK Göteborg	0, 1	*1990*
IK Brage	0, 1	*1980*
IK Elfsborg	0, 1	*1942*
IK Sleipner	0, 1	*1941*
Örebro SK	0, 1	*1988*
Sandvikens IF	0, 1	*1970*

DENMARK

Association Football in Denmark

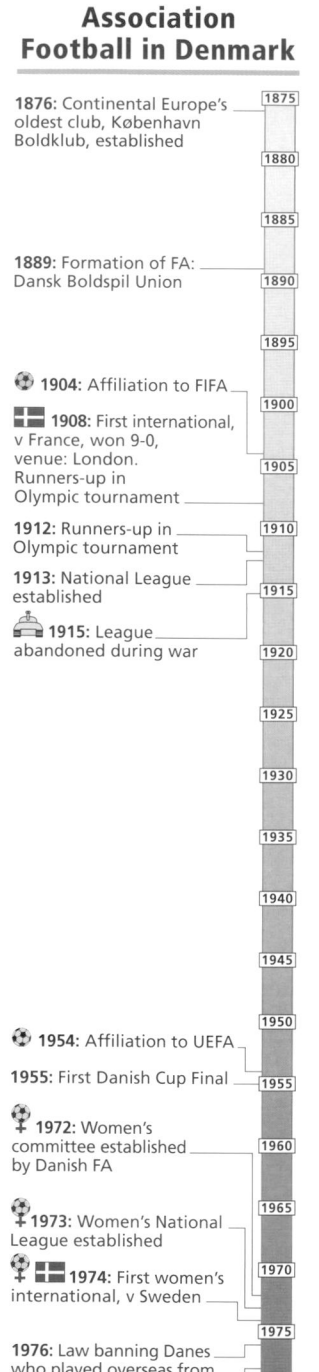

1876: Continental Europe's oldest club, København Boldklub, established · 1875

· 1880

· 1885

1889: Formation of FA: Dansk Boldspil Union · 1890

· 1895

1904: Affiliation to FIFA · 1900

1908: First international, v France, won 9-0, venue: London. Runners-up in Olympic tournament · 1905

1912: Runners-up in Olympic tournament · 1910

1913: National League established · 1915

1915: League abandoned during war · 1920

· 1925

· 1930

· 1935

· 1940

· 1945

1954: Affiliation to UEFA · 1950

1955: First Danish Cup Final · 1955

1972: Women's committee established by Danish FA · 1960

1973: Women's National League established · 1965

1974: First women's international, v Sweden · 1970

1976: Law banning Danes who played overseas from the national side ended · 1975

1978: Professionalism introduced · 1980

1991: Professional Premier League, the Superliga, formed · 1985

1992: Victory over Germany made Denmark European Champions · 1990

· 1995

1995: Superliga expanded to 12 clubs · 2000

· 2005

Nils Bohr, *the first Dane to win the Nobel Prize for Physics, was also reserve goalkeeper for AB, one of the teams from Copenhagen.*

Jan Molby was transferred *from Molding to Liverpool in 1984. His success in England paved the way for a generation of other Danish exports.*

Key

⬛	International football
⚽	Affiliation to FIFA
⚽	Affiliation to UEFA
♀	Women's football
●	European Championships winner
⌂	War

International Competitions

	European Cup	UEFA Cup	European Cup-Winners' Cup
1992: ●			

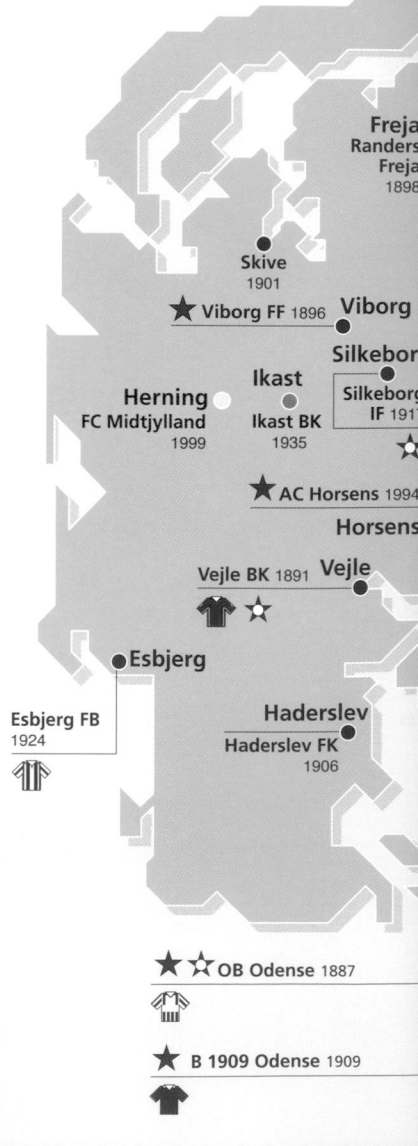

Freja Randers Freja 1898

Skive 1901

★ **Viborg FF** 1896 · **Viborg**

Silkebor

Ikast · **Silkeborg** IF 1917

Herning FC Midtjylland 1999 · Ikast BK 1935 · ☆

★ **AC Horsens** 1994

Horsens

Vejle BK 1891 · **Vejle**

👕 ☆

● **Esbjerg**

Esbjerg FB 1924

Haderslev Haderslev FK 1906

★ ☆ **OB Odense** 1887

👕

★ **B 1909 Odense** 1909

👕

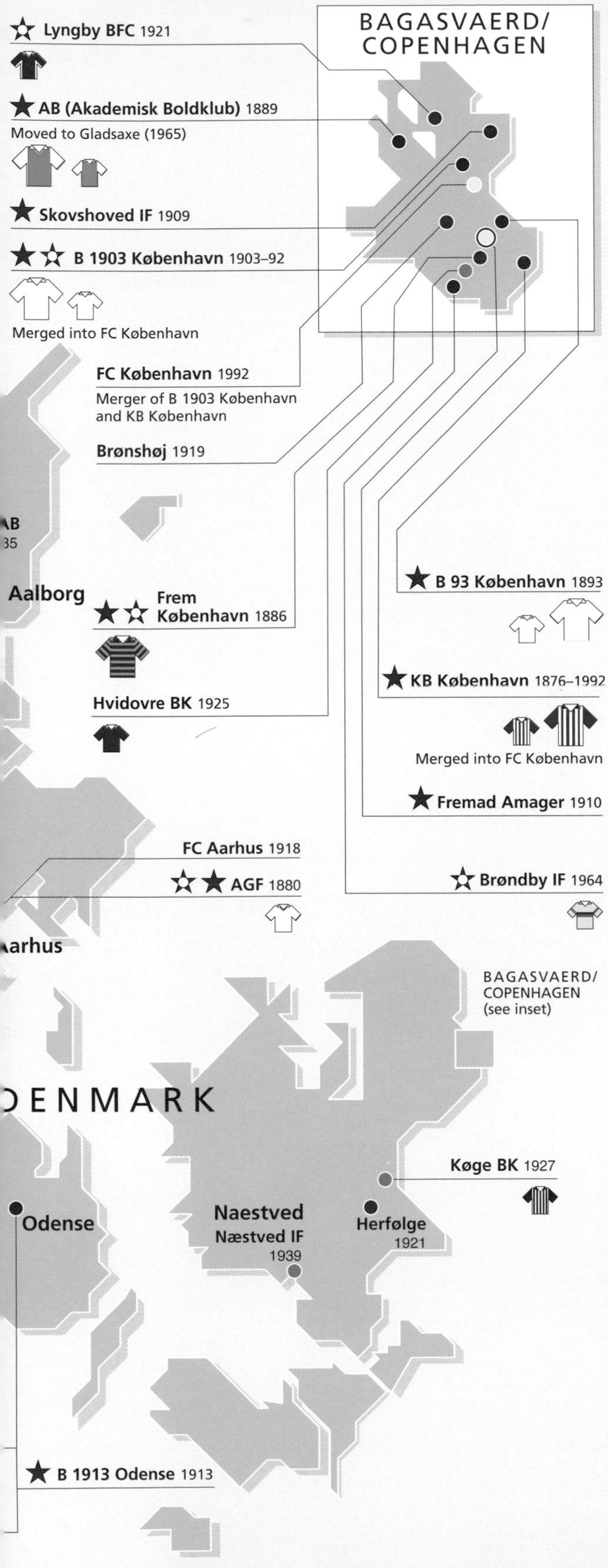

☆ **Lyngby BFC** 1921

BAGASVAERD/ COPENHAGEN

★ **AB (Akademisk Boldklub)** 1889
Moved to Gladsaxe (1965)

★ **Skovshoved IF** 1909

★ ☆ **B 1903 København** 1903–92

Merged into FC København

FC København 1992
Merger of B 1903 København
and KB København

Brønshøj 1919

AB
35

Aalborg

★ ☆ **Frem København** 1886

Hvidovre BK 1925

FC Aarhus 1918

☆ ★ **AGF** 1880

Aarhus

★ **B 93 København** 1893

★ **KB København** 1876–1992

Merged into FC København

★ **Fremad Amager** 1910

☆ **Brøndby IF** 1964

BAGASVAERD/
COPENHAGEN
(see inset)

DENMARK

● **Odense**

Køge BK 1927

Naestved
Næstved IF
1939

Herfølge
1921

★ **B 1913 Odense** 1913

Denmark

ORIGINS AND GROWTH OF FOOTBALL

PERHAPS IT WAS JUST PROXIMITY and the regular flow of British sailors and ships through Danish ports that explains Denmark's early enthusiasm for football. The dockside games recorded in the 1860s were soon followed by the foundation of Europe's oldest continental football club, København Boldklub, in 1876. KB was soon joined by Copenhagen teams Akademisk, Frem and B93, who played together as Staevnet against touring top British club sides. A national FA was formed in 1889 and four clubs were founded in provincial cities: AGF Aarhus in 1880, AAB in Aalborg in 1885, OB Odense in 1887 and Viborg FF in 1896. Denmark was also a founder member of FIFA in 1904.

Early enthusiasm and organization brought international success as Denmark took the silver medal at the Olympic tournaments in 1908 and 1912 (losing both Finals to Great Britain, 2-0 and 4-2). Despite this the game remained unequivocally amateur in Denmark. In the wake of this success a league was established in 1913 which has run ever since, but for a single season in 1915.

Ups and downs

However, it was not a professional league and the standard of Danish football steadily fell relative to the rest of Europe and Latin America. Each crop of promising players (including the Olympic squads of 1948 and 1960) were spirited away to foreign clubs as the Danish FA insisted on banning foreign-based professionals from the national side. Change came in the 1970s as a new generation of Danes, like Allan Simonsen at Barcelona and Jan Molby at Liverpool, played at the highest level in Europe. The national team ban was lifted and Denmark qualified for its first World Cup in 1986. In 1992, as late entrants to the European Championships, it took the title, beating Germany in the Final.

This success helped encourage a transformation of the domestic scene, and in 1991, a professional Premier League was finally established. Since then, a wave of mergers and club reorganizations have attempted to modernise Danish football but the recent financial crisis has seen many top clubs teeter on the verge of bankruptcy.

DENMARK

John Jensen is buried *underneath a pile of his teammates after giving Denmark the lead in the 1992 European Championships Final against Germany in Gothenburg. Denmark won the match 2-0.*

Denmark

Dansk Boldspil Union
Founded: 1889
Joined FIFA: 1904
Joined UEFA: 1954

FOOTBALL ARRIVED EARLY IN DENMARK, making its way into Scandinavia through the ports. KB København, the first Danish club, was founded in 1876, considerably in advance of most English and Scottish clubs. Despite this early enthusiasm, the formation of a national football association in 1889, and becoming a founder member of FIFA, organized domestic competition lagged behind. Nonetheless, Denmark made it to the Finals of the first two Olympic Games with a football competition (1908 and 1912). Future international successes were limited by the DBU's fierce amateurism, as Danes playing professionally overseas were excluded from the national team. In 1913 a national league was established and it has run uninterrupted since 1916. The championship was won by Copenhagen clubs until the 1950s, when Køge, Aarhus and Vejle broke the capital's stronghold.

A Danish Cup competition was created in 1955 and professionalism arrived in 1978. In 1976 the DBU allowed players playing outside Denmark to play for the national teams for the first time which, combined with the advent of professionalism, led to the beginnings of an exodus of Danish talent. In response to this, and the uneven quality of Danish football clubs, the Danish league was reorganized in 1991 with the creation of an eight-team, wholly professional, Superliga, with clubs playing each other four times a year. In 1992, these changes seemed to have borne fruit, as Denmark were crowned unexpected winners of the European Championship. In 1995 the Superliga was expanded to 12 teams playing each other three times a season. There is a standard two-up/two-down promotion/relegation system between the Superliga and the second division.

Danish League Record 1913–2003

SEASON	CHAMPIONS	RUNNERS-UP
1913	KB København	B93 København
1914	KB København	B93 København
1915	*no championship*	
1916	B93 København	KB København
1917	KB København	Akademisk
1918	KB København	Frem København
1919	Akademisk	B93 København
1920	B1903 København	KB København
1921	Akademisk	B1903 København
1922	KB København	Frem København
1923	Frem København	B93 København
1924	B1903 København	KB København
1925	KB København	Akademisk
1926	B1903 København	B93 København
1927	B93 København	B1903 København
1928	B93 København	Frem København
1929	B93 København	KB København
1930	B93 København	Frem København
1931	Frem København	KB København
1932	KB København	Akademisk
1933	Frem København	B1903 København
1934	B93 København	B1903 København
1935	B93 København	Frem København
1936	Frem København	Akademisk
1937	Akademisk	Frem København
1938	B1903 København	Frem København

Danish League Record (*continued*)

SEASON	CHAMPIONS	RUNNERS-UP
1939	B93 København	KB København
1940	KB København	Fremad Amager
1941	Frem København	Fremad Amager
1942	B93 København	Akademisk
1943	Akademisk	KB København
1944	Frem København	Akademisk
1945	Akademisk	AGF Aarhus
1946	B93 København	KB København
1947	Akademisk	KB København
1948	KB København	Frem København
1949	KB København	Akademisk
1950	KB København	Akademisk
1951	Akademisk	OB Odense
1952	Akademisk	Køge BK
1953	KB København	Skovshoved IF
1954	Køge BK	KB København
1955	AGF Aarhus	Akademisk
1956	AGF Aarhus	Esbjerg FB
1957	AGF Aarhus	Akademisk
1958	Vejle BK	Frem København
1959	B1909 Odense	KB København
1960	AGF Aarhus	KB København
1961	Esbjerg FB	KB København
1962	Esbjerg FB	B1913 Odense
1963	Esbjerg FB	B1913 Odense
1964	B1909 Odense	AGF Aarhus
1965	Esbjerg FB	Vejle BK
1966	Hvidovre BK	Frem København
1967	Akademisk	Frem København
1968	KB København	Esbjerg FB
1969	B1903 København	KB København
1970	B1903 København	Akademisk
1971	Vejle BK	Hvidovre BK
1972	Vejle BK	B1903 København
1973	Hvidovre BK	Randers Freja
1974	KB København	Vejle BK
1975	Køge BK	Holbaek BK
1976	B1903 København	Frem København
1977	OB Odense	B1903 København
1978	Vejle BK	Esbjerg FB
1979	Esbjerg FB	KB København
1980	KB København	Naestved IF
1981	Hvidovre BK	Lyngby FC
1982	OB Odense	AGF Aarhus
1983	Lyngby FC	OB Odense
1984	Vejle BK	AGF Aarhus
1985	Brøndby IF	Lyngby FC
1986	AGF Aarhus	Brøndby IF
1987	Brøndby IF	Ikast BK
1988	Brøndby IF	Naestved IF
1989	OB Odense	Brøndby IF
1990	Brøndby IF	B1903 København
1991	Brøndby IF	Lyngby FC
1992	Lyngby FC	B1903 København
1993	FC København	OB Odense
1994	Silkeborg IF	FC København
1995	AaB Aalborg	Brøndby IF
1996	Brøndby IF	AGF Aarhus
1997	Brøndby IF	Vejle BK
1998	Brøndby IF	Silkeborg IF
1999	AaB Aalborg	Brøndby IF
2000	Herfølge	Brøndby IF

DENMARK

Danish League Record (*continued*)

SEASON	CHAMPIONS	RUNNERS-UP
2001	FC København	Brøndby IF
2002	Brøndby IF	FC København
2003	FC København	Brøndby IF

Danish League Summary

TEAM	TOTALS	CHAMPIONS & RUNNERS-UP (BOLD) (ITALICS)
KB København	15, 15	**1913**, *14*, **16**, **17**, **18**, *20*, **22**, *24*, **25**, *29*, *31*, **32**, *39*, **40**, *43*, **46**, **47**, **48–50**, *53*, *54*, *59–61*, **68**, **69**, **74**, *79*, **80**
B93 København	10, 5	*1913*, *14*, **16**, **19**, **23**, **26**, **27–30**, **34**, **35**, **39**, **42**, **46**
Akademisk	9, 11	*1917*, **19**, **21**, *25*, **32**, **36**, **37**, *42*, **43**, *44*, *45*, *47*, *49*, *50*, **51**, **52**, *55*, *57*, **67**, *70*
Brøndby IF	9, 7	**1985**, *86*, **87**, **88**, *89*, **90**, **91**, *95*, **96–98**, *1999–2001*, **02**, *03*
B1903 København	7, 8	**1920**, *21*, **24**, **26**, *27*, *33*, *34*, **38**, *69*, **70**, *72*, **76**, *77*, *90*, *92*
Frem København	6, 12	*1918*, *22*, **23**, *28*, *30*, **31**, *33*, *35*, **36**, *37*, *38*, **41**, *44*, *48*, *58*, *66*, *67*, *76*
AGF Aarhus	5, 5	*1945*, **55–57**, *60*, **64**, *82*, **84**, **86**, *96*
Esbjerg FB	5, 3	*1956*, **61–63**, **65**, *68*, *78*, **79**
Vejle BK	5, 3	*1958*, **65**, *71*, *72*, **74**, **78**, **84**, *97*
OB Odense	3, 3	*1951*, **77**, *82*, **83**, **89**, *93*
FC København*	3, 2	**1993**, *94*, **2001**, *02*, *03*
Hvidovre BK	3, 1	**1966**, *71*, **73**, **81**
Lyngby FC	2, 3	*1981*, **83**, *85*, *91*, **92**
Køge BK	2, 1	*1952*, **54**, **75**
AaB Aalborg	2, 0	**1995**, **99**
B1909 Odense	2, 0	**1959**, **64**
Silkeborg IF	1, 1	**1994**, *98*
Herfølge	1, 0	**2000**
B1913 Odense	0, 2	*1962*, *63*
Naestved IF	0, 2	*1980*, *88*
Fremad Amager	0, 2	*1940*, *41*
Randers Freja	0, 1	*1973*
Ikast BK	0, 1	*1987*
Holbaek BK	0, 1	*1975*
Shovshoved IF	0, 1	*1953*

* Formed in 1993 after a merger of KB København and B1903 København.

Danish Cup Record 1955–2003

YEAR	WINNERS	SCORE	RUNNERS-UP
1955	AGF Aarhus	4-0	Aalborg Chang
1956	Frem København	1-0	Akademisk
1957	AGF Aarhus	2-0	Esbjerg FB
1958	Vejle BK	3-2	AGF Aarhus
1959	Vejle BK	1-1 (aet), (replay) 2-0	AGF Aarhus
1960	AGF Aarhus	2-0	Frem Sakskøbing
1961	AGF Aarhus	2-0	KB København
1962	B1909 Odense	1-0	Esbjerg FB
1963	B1913 Odense	2-1	Køge BK
1964	Esbjerg FB	2-1	Odense KFUM
1965	AGF Aarhus	1-0	KB København
1966	AaB Aalborg	3-1 (aet)	KB København
1967	Randers Freja	1-0	AaB Aalborg
1968	Randers Freja	3-1	Vejle BK
1969	KB København	3-0	Frem København
1970	AaB Aalborg	2-1	Lyngby FC
1971	B1909 Odense	1-0	Frem København
1972	Vejle BK	2-0	Fremad Amager
1973	Randers Freja	2-0	B1901 Nykøbing
1974	Vanlose BK	5-2	OB Odense
1975	Vejle BK	1-0	Holbaek BK

Danish Cup Record (*continued*)

YEAR	WINNERS	SCORE	RUNNERS-UP
1976	Esbjerg FB	2-1	Holbaek BK
1977	Vejle BK	2-1	B1909 Odense
1978	Frem København	1-1 (aet), (replay) 1-1 (aet) (6-5 pens)	Esbjerg FB
1979	B1903 København	1-0	Køge BK
1980	Hvidovre BK	5-3	Lyngby FC
1981	Vejle BK	2-1	Frem København
1982	B93 København	3-3 (aet), (replay) 1-0	B1903 København
1983	OB Odense	3-0	B1901 Nykøbing
1984	Lyngby FC	2-1	KB København
1985	Lyngby FC	3-2	Esbjerg FB
1986	B1903 København	2-1	Ikast BK
1987	AGF Aarhus	3-0	AaB Aalborg
1988	AGF Aarhus	2-1 (aet)	Brøndby IF
1989	Brøndby IF	6-3 (aet)	Ikast BK
1990	Lyngby FC	0-0 (aet), (replay) 6-1	AGF Aarhus
1991	OB Odense	0-0 (aet), (replay) 0-0 (aet) (4-3 pens)	AaB Aalborg
1992	AGF Aarhus	3-0	B1903 København
1993	OB Odense	2-0	AaB Aalborg
1994	Brøndby IF	0-0 (aet)(4-3 pens)	Naestved IF
1995	FC København	5-0	Akademisk
1996	AGF Aarhus	2-0	Brøndby IF
1997	FC København	2-0	Ikast BK
1998	Brøndby IF	4-1	FC København
1999	Akademisk	2-1	AaB Aalborg
2000	Viborg FF	1-0	AaB Aalborg
2001	Silkeborg IF	4-1	Akademisk
2002	OB Odense	2-1	FC København
2003	Brøndby IF	3-0	FC Midtjylland

Danish Cup Summary

TEAM	TOTALS	WINNERS & RUNNERS-UP (BOLD) (ITALICS)
AGF Aarhus	9, 3	**1955**, **57**, *58*, **59**, **60**, **61**, **65**, **87**, *88*, *90*, **92**, *96*
Vejle BK	6, 1	**1958**, **59**, **68**, **72**, **75**, **77**, *81*
Brøndby IF	4, 2	**1988**, **89**, **94**, *96*, **98**, **2003**
OB Odense	4, 1	*1974*, **83**, **91**, **93**, **2002**
Lyngby FC	3, 2	*1970*, *80*, **84**, **85**, **90**
Randers Freja	3, 0	**1967**, **68**, **73**
AaB Aalborg	2, 6	**1966**, *67*, **70**, *87*, *91*, *93*, *99*, *2000*
Esbjerg FB	2, 4	*1957*, *62*, **64**, *76*, *78*, **85**
Frem København	2, 3	**1956**, *69*, *71*, **78**, *81*
B1903 København	2, 2	**1979**, *82*, **86**, *92*
FC København	2, 2	**1995**, *98*, **97**, *2002*
B1909 Odense	2, 1	**1962**, **71**, *77*
KB København	1, 4	*1961*, *65*, *66*, **69**, *84*
Akademisk	1, 3	*1956*, *95*, **99**, *2001*
B1913 Odense	1, 0	**1963**
Vanlose BK	1, 0	**1974**
Viborg FF	1, 0	**2000**
Hvidovre BK	1, 0	**1980**
Silkeborg IF	1, 0	**2001**
Ikast BK	0, 3	*1986*, *89*, *97*
B1901 Nykøbing	0, 2	*1973*, *83*
Holbaek BK	0, 2	*1975*, *76*
Køge BK	0, 2	*1963*, *79*
Aalborg Chang	0, 1	*1955*
Frem Sakskøbing	0, 1	*1960*
Fremad Amager	0, 1	*1972*
FC Midtjylland	0, 1	*2003*
Naestved IF	0, 1	*1994*
Odense KFUM	0, 1	*1964*

Association Football in Norway

NORWAY

1892: Kongsvinger IL formed, Norway's oldest club

1902: Formation of FA: Norges Fotballforbund. First Norwegian Cup Final

1905: Independence from Sweden

 **1908:** Affiliation to FIFA. First international, v Sweden, lost 11-3, venue: Gothenburg

1938: First national championship

 **1940–45:** Norwegian sport strike against German occupation. Cup abandoned 1941–44

1954: Affiliation to UEFA

1962: National championship reorganized as full league

1975: National FA incorporates women's football

1978: First women's international, v Sweden

1991: Women's World Cup runners-up. Premier League formed

1995: Women's World Cup winners

1997: Rosenborg reach quarter-finals of the Champions League – the best performance ever by a Norwegian team in European competition

2000: Women's team win Olympic gold medal

1890
1895
1900
1905
1910
1915
1920
1925
1930
1935
1940
1945
1950
1955
1960
1965
1970
1975
1980
1985
1990
1995
2000
2005

Key

 International football

⚽ Affiliation to FIFA

⚽ Affiliation to UEFA

Women's football

War

Extreme weather presents a considerable problem for regular football in Norway. Alfheim Stadium (above), home of Tromsø IL, is above the Arctic Circle.

Since the advent of the Premier League in 1991, teams like Rosenborg BK from Trondheim (in white, playing against Feyenoord from the Netherlands) have appeared regularly in the Champions League.

Norway: The main clubs

Moss FK
1906
Team name with year of formation

● Club formed before 1912

● Club formed 1912–25

● Club formed 1925–50

Club formed after 1950

★ Founder members of Premier League (1991)

 Leading clubs in 1938 national championship

 Colours unknown

Steinkjer IFK 1919

Rosenborg BK 1917

Fyllingen 1946

SK Brann Bergen 1908

Steinkjer

Trondheim

Molde

Molde FK 1911

★ **Gjøvik Lyn** 1902

Sogndal IL 1926

Bergen

Drammen

IF Strømsgodset 1907

Kongsvinger

Lillestrøm

FK Haugesund 1993

Moss

Stavanger

Horten

Skien

★ **Viking FK Stavanger** 1899

Larvik

★ **IK Start** 1892

Kristiansand

★ **Odd Grenland** 1894

Formerly Odd SK Skien

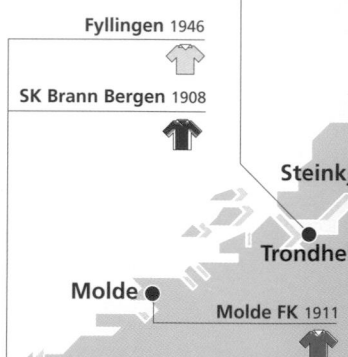

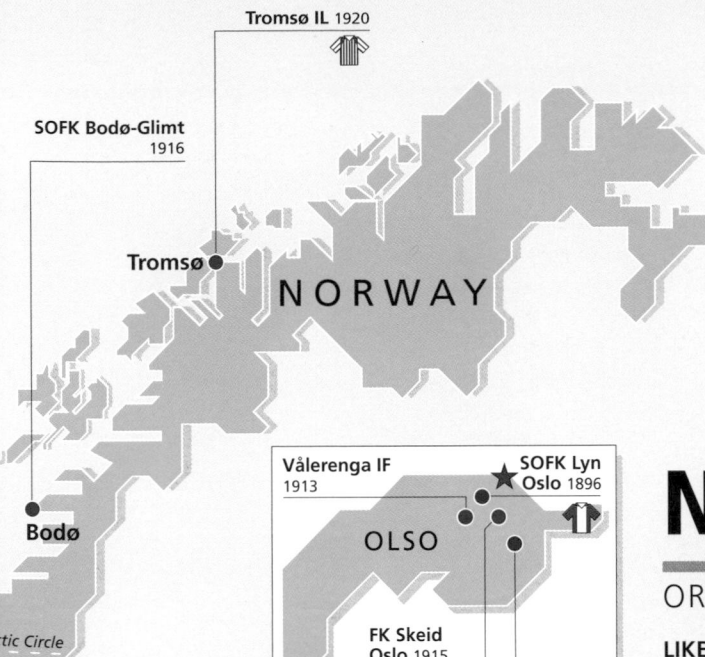

Tromsø IL 1920

SOFK Bodø-Glimt 1916

Tromsø

N O R W A Y

Bodø

Arctic Circle

Vålerenga IF 1913

SOFK Lyn Oslo 1896

OLSO

FK Skeid Oslo 1915

Frigg SK Oslo 1904

Stabaek 1912

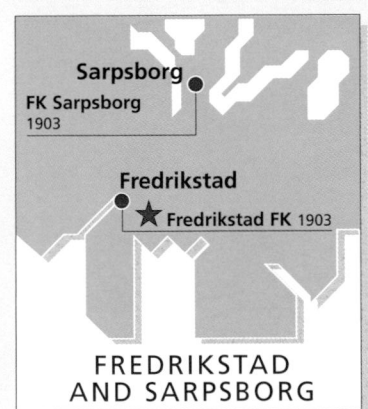

Sarpsborg

FK Sarpsborg 1903

Fredrikstad

Fredrikstad FK 1903

FREDRIKSTAD AND SARPSBORG

Kongsvinger IL 1892

Lillestrøm SK 1917

OSLO
(see inset)

Moss FK 1906

FREDRIKSTAD AND SARPSBORG
(see inset)

Mjøndalen IF 1910

Orn FK Horten 1904

IF Fram 1894

Larvik Turn IF 1906

The Norwegian national women's team is one of the strongest in the world. It is shown here sporting its Olympic gold medals from Sydney 2000. The team beat the USA 3-2 in a memorable Final.

Norway

ORIGINS AND GROWTH OF FOOTBALL

LIKE ITS SCANDINAVIAN NEIGHBOURS Norway was exposed to football in the late 19th century, and proved an early and enthusiastic adopter of the game. Clubs emerged all over the country in the years up to and including the First World War, some of the earliest being Kongsvinger IL (1892), Odd SK Skien (1894), SOFK Lyn Oslo (1896) and Viking FK Stavanger (1899).

The cost of amateurism

A national FA was set up in 1902, joining FIFA in 1908. However, the development of the sport was always constrained by weather and sentiment. The extremes of cold and snow present a considerable problem for regular football, and make the competing attractions of winter sports and games compelling. This aside, the prevailing amateurism of Norwegian football has ensured that little money or development could take place in the game relative to the international competition. A national league was not actually created until 1937 and it was decided by play-offs until 1961 when a more conventional league was created. Despite all of this, Oslo, the capital city, has yet to produce a consistently powerful team and leading clubs and players continue to come from small towns and rural Norway.

Norwegian football's finest hour was during the Second World War. After the German invasion and occupation in 1940, Quislings (or collaborators) were placed in charge of every Norwegian club and sports association. Players refused to play, fans refused to attend and the national league effectively collapsed. Tournaments organized by the Norwegian resistance were played in secret deep in the countryside.

Powerful women

In the 1990s Norwegian football began to change with the arrival of significant government support for elite sports, the installation of the tough-minded Egil Olsen as national team manager and an increasing place for professional footballers in the leading clubs. A national premier league has been created, and at European level Rosenborg and SK Brann have performed creditably. By contrast to the men's game, Norwegian women's football is a strong force on the global stage, with the national team winning the inaugural FIFA Women's World Cup in China in 1988 and the Olympic gold in Sydney 2000.

Egil Olsen (professor of economics and national team manager 1990–98) brought a new tactical awareness.

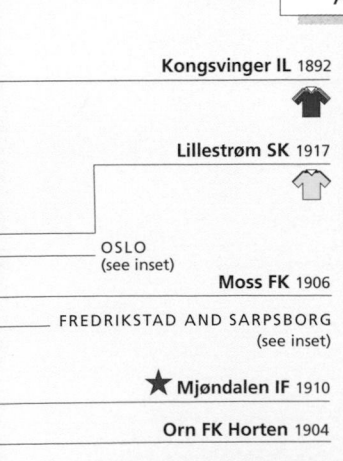

Norway

Norges Fotballforbund
Founded: 1902
Joined FIFA: 1908
Joined UEFA: 1954

NORWEGIAN DOMESTIC FOOTBALL began with the establishment of the Norges Fotballforbund in 1902 when a national cup competition was set up; this has run every year since, only stopping between 1941 and 1944 in the midst of the Second World War. However, antiquity does not guarantee popularity, and attendances at some Finals have dipped below the 2,000 mark. A national league arrived later, and the first championships took place in 1938. Until 1961, the title was decided by a knockout phase, but since 1962 it has kept a simplified league format.

Norwegian League Record 1938–2002

SEASON	CHAMPIONS	RUNNERS-UP
1938	Fredrikstad FK	SOFK Lyn Oslo
1939	Fredrikstad FK	FK Skeid Oslo
1940–47	*no championship*	
1948	Freidig SK	Sparta Sarpsborg
1949	Fredrikstad FK	Vålerenga IF
1950	Fram Larvik	Fredrikstad FK
1951	Fredrikstad FK	Odd SK Skien
1952	Fredrikstad FK	SK Brann Bergen
1953	Larvik Turn IF	FK Skeid Oslo
1954	Fredrikstad FK	FK Skeid Oslo
1955	Larvik Turn IF	Fredrikstad FK
1956	Larvik Turn IF	Fredrikstad FK
1957	Fredrikstad FK	Odd SK Skien
1958	Viking FK Stavanger	FK Skeid Oslo
1959	Lillestrøm SK	Fredrikstad FK
1960	Fredrikstad FK	Lillestrøm SK
1961	Fredrikstad FK	IF Eik
1962	SK Brann Bergen	Steinkjer IFK
1963	SK Brann Bergen	SOFK Lyn Oslo
1964	SOFK Lyn Oslo	Fredrikstad FK
1965	Vålerenga IF	SOFK Lyn Oslo
1966	FK Skeid Oslo	Fredrikstad FK
1967	Rosenborg BK	FK Skeid Oslo
1968	SOFK Lyn Oslo	Rosenborg BK
1969	Rosenborg BK	Fredrikstad FK
1970	IF Strømgodset	Rosenborg BK
1971	Rosenborg BK	SOFK Lyn Oslo
1972	Viking FK Stavanger	Fredrikstad FK
1973	Viking FK Stavanger	Rosenborg BK
1974	Viking FK Stavanger	Molde FK
1975	Viking FK Stavanger	SK Brann Bergen
1976	Lillestrøm SK	Mjøndalen IF
1977	Lillestrøm SK	SOFK Bodø-Glimt
1978	Start Kristiansand	Lillestrøm SK
1979	Viking FK Stavanger	Moss FK
1980	Start Kristiansand	Bryne FK
1981	Vålerenga IF	Viking FK Stavanger
1982	Viking FK Stavanger	Bryne FK
1983	Vålerenga IF	Lillestrøm SK
1984	Vålerenga IF	Viking FK Stavanger
1985	Rosenborg BK	Lillestrøm SK
1986	Lillestrøm SK	Mjøndalen IF
1987	Moss FK	Molde FK
1988	Rosenborg BK	Lillestrøm SK
1989	Lillestrøm SK	Rosenborg BK
1990	Rosenborg BK	Tromsø IL
1991	Viking FK Stavanger	Rosenborg BK
1992	Rosenborg BK	Viking FK Stavanger
1993	Rosenborg BK	SOFK Bodø-Glimt

Norwegian League Record (*continued*)

SEASON	CHAMPIONS	RUNNERS-UP
1994	Rosenborg BK	Lillestrøm SK
1995	Rosenborg BK	Molde FK
1996	Rosenborg BK	Lillestrøm SK
1997	Rosenborg BK	SK Brann Bergen
1998	Rosenborg BK	Molde FK
1999	Rosenborg BK	Molde FK
2000	Rosenborg BK	SK Brann Bergen
2001	Rosenborg BK	Lillestrøm SK
2002	Rosenborg BK	Molde FK

Norwegian League Summary

TEAM	TOTALS	CHAMPIONS & RUNNERS-UP (BOLD) (*ITALICS*)
Rosenborg BK	17, 5	**1967**, *68, 69, 70,* **71**, *73,* **85, 88, 89, 90, 91, 1992–2002**
Fredrikstad FK	9, 8	**1938, 39, 49,** *50,* **51, 52, 54,** *55, 56, 57, 59,* **60,** *61,* **64,** *66,* **69,** *72*
Viking FK Stavanger	8, 3	**1958,** *72–75,* **79,** *81,* **82,** *84,* **91,** *92*
Lillestrøm SK	5, 8	*59, 60,* **76, 77,** *78, 83, 85,* **86,** *88,* **89,** *94, 96,* **2001**
Vålerenga IF	4, 1	*1949,* **65, 81, 83, 84**
Larvik Turn IF	3, 0	**1953, 55, 56**
SK Brann Bergen	2, 4	*1952,* **62, 63,** *75, 97,* **2000**
SOFK Lyn Oslo	2, 4	*1938, 63,* **64,** *65,* **68,** *71*
Start Kristiansand	2, 0	**1978, 80**
FK Skeid Oslo	1, 5	*1939, 53, 54, 58,* **66,** *67*
Moss FK	1, 1	*1979,* **87**
Fram Larvik	1, 0	**1950**
Freidig SK	1, 0	**1948**
IF Strømgodset	1, 0	**1970**
Molde FK	0, 6	*1974, 87, 95, 98, 99, 2002*
Bryne FK	0, 2	*1980, 82*
Mjøndalen IF	0, 2	*1976, 86*
Odd Grenland (includes Odd Sk Skien)	0, 2	*1951, 57*
SOFK Bodø-Glimt	0, 2	*1977, 93*
IF Eik	0, 1	*1961*
Sparta Sarpsborg	0, 1	*1948*
Steinkjer IFK	0, 1	*1962*
Tromsø IL	0, 1	*1990*

Norwegian Cup Record 1902–2002

YEAR	WINNERS	SCORE	RUNNERS-UP
1902	Grand Nordstrand	2-0	Odd SK Skien
1903	Odd SK Skien	1-0	Grand Nordstrand
1904	Odd SK Skien	4-0	IF Uraed
1905	Odd SK Skien	2-1	Akademisk FK Oslo
1906	Odd SK Skien	1-0	FK Sarpsborg
1907	Mercantile	3-0	FK Sarpsborg
1908	SOFK Lyn Oslo	3-2	Odd SK Skien
1909	SOFK Lyn Oslo	4-3	Odd SK Skien
1910	SOFK Lyn Oslo	4-2	Odd SK Skien
1911	SOFK Lyn Oslo	5-2	IF Uraed

NORWAY

Norwegian Cup Record (*continued*)

YEAR	WINNERS	SCORE	RUNNERS-UP
1912	Mercantile	6-0	Fram Larvik
1913	Odd SK Skien	2-1	Mercantile
1914	Frigg SK Oslo	4-0	Gjøvik Lyn
1915	Odd SK Skien	2-1	Kvik Halden
1916	Frigg SK Oslo	2-0	Orn FK Horten
1917	FK Sarpsborg	4-1	SK Brann Bergen
1918	Kvik Halden	4-0	SK Brann Bergen
1919	Odd SK Skien	1-0	Frigg SK Oslo
1920	Orn FK Horten	1-0	Frigg SK Oslo
1921	Frigg SK Oslo	2-0	Odd SK Skien
1922	Odd SK Skien	5-1	Kvik Halden
1923	SK Brann Bergen	2-1	SOFK Lyn Oslo
1924	Odd SK Skien	3-0	Mjøndalen IF
1925	SK Brann Bergen	3-0	FK Sarpsborg
1926	Odd SK Skien	3-0	Orn FK Horten
1927	Orn FK Horten	4-0	Drafn SK
1928	Orn FK Horten	2-1	SOFK Lyn Oslo
1929	FK Sarpsborg	2-1	Orn FK Horten
1930	Orn FK Horten	4-2	Drammens BK
1931	Odd SK Skien	3-1	Mjøndalen IF
1932	Fredrikstad FK	6-1	Orn FK Horten
1933	Mjøndalen IF	3-1	Viking FK Stavanger
1934	Mjøndalen IF	2-1	FK Sarpsborg
1935	Fredrikstad FK	4-0	FK Sarpsborg
1936	Fredrikstad FK	2-0	Mjøndalen IF
1937	Mjøndalen IF	4-2	Odd SK Skien
1938	Fredrikstad FK	3-2	Mjøndalen IF
1939	FK Sarpsborg	2-1	FK Skeid Oslo
1940	Fredrikstad FK	3-0	FK Skeid Oslo
1941–44		*no competition*	
1945	SOFK Lyn Oslo	1-1, (replay) 1-1, (replay) 4-0	Fredrikstad FK
1946	SOFK Lyn Oslo	3-2	Fredrikstad FK
1947	FK Skeid Oslo	2-0	Viking FK Stavanger
1948	FK Sarpsborg	1-0	Fredrikstad FK
1949	FK Sarpsborg	3-1	FK Skeid Oslo
1950	Fredrikstad FK	3-0	SK Brann Bergen
1951	FK Sarpsborg	3-2	Asker
1952	Sparta Sarpsborg	3-2	Solberg
1953	Viking FK Stavanger	2-1	Lillestrøm SK
1954	FK Skeid Oslo	3-0	Fredrikstad FK
1955	FK Skeid Oslo	5-0	Lillestrøm SK
1956	FK Skeid Oslo	2-1	Larvik Turn IF
1957	Fredrikstad FK	4-0	Sandefjord BK
1958	FK Skeid Oslo	1-0	Lillestrøm SK
1959	Viking FK Stavanger	2-1	Sandefjord BK
1960	Rosenborg BK	3-3, (replay) 3-2	Odd SK Skien
1961	Fredrikstad FK	7-0	SK Hauger
1962	Gjøvik Lyn	2-0	SK Vard Haugesund
1963	FK Skeid Oslo	2-1	Fredrikstad FK
1964	Rosenborg BK	2-1	FK Sarpsborg
1965	FK Skeid Oslo	2-2, (replay) 1-1, (replay) 2-1	Frigg SK Oslo
1966	Fredrikstad FK	3-2	SOFK Lyn Oslo
1967	SOFK Lyn Oslo	4-1	Rosenborg BK
1968	SOFK Lyn Oslo	3-0	Mjøndalen IF
1969	IF Strømgodset	2-2, (replay) 5-3	Fredrikstad FK
1970	IF Strømgodset	4-2	SOFK Lyn Oslo
1971	Rosenborg BK	4-1	Fredrikstad FK
1972	SK Brann Bergen	1-0	Rosenborg BK
1973	IF Strømgodset	1-0	Rosenborg BK
1974	FK Skeid Oslo	3-1	Viking FK Stavanger
1975	SOFK Bodø-Glimt	2-0	SK Vard Haugesund
1976	SK Brann Bergen	2-1	Sogndal IL
1977	Lillestrøm SK	1-0	SOFK Bodø-Glimt
1978	Lillestrøm SK	2-1	SK Brann Bergen
1979	Viking FK Stavanger	2-1	SK Hauger
1980	Vålerenga IF	4-1	Lillestrøm SK
1981	Lillestrøm SK	3-1	Moss FK
1982	SK Brann Bergen	3-2	Molde FK
1983	Moss FK	2-0	Vålerenga IF
1984	Fredrikstad FK	3-3, (replay) 3-2	Viking FK Stavanger
1985	Lillestrøm SK	4-1	Vålerenga IF

Norwegian Cup Record (*continued*)

YEAR	WINNERS	SCORE	RUNNERS-UP
1986	Tromsø IL	4-1	Lillestrøm SK
1987	Bryne FK	1-0	SK Brann Bergen
1988	Rosenborg BK	2-2, (replay) 2-0	SK Brann Bergen
1989	Viking FK Stavanger	2-2, (replay) 2-1	Molde FK
1990	Rosenborg BK	5-1	Fyllingen
1991	IF Strømgodset	3-2	Rosenborg BK
1992	Rosenborg BK	3-2	Lillestrøm SK
1993	SOFK Bodø-Glimt	2-0	IF Strømgodset
1994	Molde FK	3-2	Lyn
1995	Rosenborg BK	1-1, (replay) 3-1	SK Brann Bergen
1996	Tromsø IL	2-1	SOFK Bodø-Glimt
1997	Vålerenga IF	4-2	IF Strømgodset
1998	Stabaek	3-1	Rosenborg BK
1999	Rosenborg BK	2-0	SK Brann Bergen
2000	Odd Grenland	2-1	Viking FK Stavanger
2001	Viking FK Stavanger	3-0	Bryne FK
2002	Vålerenga IF	1-0	Odd Grenland

Norwegian Cup Summary

TEAM	TOTALS	WINNERS & RUNNERS-UP (BOLD) (ITALICS)
Odd Grenland (includes Odd Sk Skien)	12, 8	**1902, 03–06,** *08–10,* **13, 15, 19, 21, 22, 24, 26, 31,** *37, 60,* **2000,** *02*
Fredrikstad FK	10, 7	**1932, 35, 36, 38, 40,** *45, 46, 48,* **50,** *54, 57,* **61,** *63,* **66,** *69,* **71,** *84*
Rosenborg BK	8, 5	**1960, 64,** *67,* **71, 72, 73, 88, 90,** *91,* **92, 95, 98, 99**
SOFK Lyn Oslo	8, 4	**1908–11,** *23, 28,* **45, 46,** *66,* **67, 68,** *70*
FK Skeid Oslo	8, 3	**1939, 40, 47, 49,** *54–56,* **58,** *63,* **65, 74**
FK Sarpsborg	6, 6	*1906, 07,* **17,** *25,* **29,** *34, 35,* **39,** *48,* **49, 51,** *64*
SK Brann Bergen	5, 8	*1917, 18,* **23, 25,** *50,* **72,** *76, 78,* **82,** *87, 88,* **95,** *99*
Viking FK Stavanger	5, 5	*1933, 47,* **53,** *59,* **74,** *79, 84, 89,* **2000, 01**
Lillestrøm SK	4, 6	*1953, 55, 58,* **77,** *78,* **80, 81,** *85, 86, 92*
Orn FK Horten	4, 4	**1916,** *20,* **26, 27, 28,** *29,* **30,** *32*
IF Strømgodset	4, 2	**1969, 70, 73, 91,** *93,* **97**
Mjøndalen IF	3, 5	*1924, 31,* **33, 34,** *36,* **37,** *38, 68*
Frigg SK Oslo	3, 3	**1914, 16,** *19, 20,* **21,** *65*
Vålerenga IF	3, 2	**1980,** *83, 85,* **97, 2002**
SOFK Bodø-Glimt	2, 2	**1975,** *77,* **93,** *96*
Mercantile	2, 1	**1907, 12,** *13*
Tromsø IL	2, 0	**1986, 96**
Kvik Halden	1, 2	*1915,* **18,** *22*
Molde FK	1, 2	*1982, 89,* **94**
Bryne FK	1, 1	**1987,** *2001*
Gjøvik Lyn	1, 1	**1914,** *62*
Grand Nordstrand	1, 1	**1902,** *03*
Moss FK	1, 1	*1981,* **83**
Sparta Sarpsborg	1, 0	**1952**
Stabaek	1, 0	**1998**
IF Uraed	0, 2	*1904, 11*
Sandefjord	0, 2	*1957, 59*
SK Hauger	0, 2	*1961, 79*
SK Vard Haugesund	0, 2	*1962, 75*
Akademisk FK Oslo	0, 1	*1905*
Asker	0, 1	*1951*
Drafn SK	0, 1	*1927*
Drammens BK	0, 1	*1930*
Fram Larvik	0, 1	*1912*
Fyllingen	0, 1	*1990*
Larvik Turn IF	0, 1	*1956*
Lyn	0, 1	*1994*
Sogndal IL	0, 1	*1976*
Solberg	0, 1	*1952*

Finland

Suomen Palloliitto/Finlands Bollförbund
Founded: 1907
Joined FIFA: 1908
Joined UEFA: 1954

FINLAND'S OLDEST CLUB – Reipas Lahti – was founded in 1891, and its association was founded in 1907. A regular league, based in Helsinki, started almost immediately, and gradually spread to include the rest of the country. Until 1929, the title was decided via a play-off, after which a league format was adopted. A national cup competition was established in 1955.

Finnish League Record 1908–2002

SEASON	CHAMPIONS	RUNNERS-UP
1908	Unitas Helsinki	PUS Helsinki
1909	PUS Helsinki	HIFK Helsinki
1910	ÅIFK Turku	Reipas Viipuri
1911	HJK Helsinki	HIFK Helsinki
1912	HJK Helsinki	HIFK Helsinki
1913	KIF Helsinki	ÅIFK Helsinki
1914	*no championship*	
1915	KIF Helsinki	ÅIFK Turku
1916	KIF Helsinki	ÅIFK Turku
1917	HJK Helsinki	ÅIFK Turku
1918	HJK Helsinki	Reipas Viipuri
1919	HJK Helsinki	Reipas Viipuri
1920	ÅIFK Turku	HPS Helsinki
1921	HPS Helsinki	HJK Helsinki
1922	HPS Helsinki	Reipas Viipuri
1923	HJK Helsinki	TPS Turku
1924	ÅIFK Turku	HPS Helsinki
1925	HJK Helsinki	TPS Turku
1926	HPS Helsinki	TPS Turku
1927	HPS Helsinki	Reipas Viipuri
1928	TPS Turku	HIFK Helsinki
1929	HPS Helsinki	HIFK Helsinki
1930	HIFK Helsinki	TPS Turku
1931	HIFK Helsinki	HPS Helsinki
1932	HPS Helsinki	VPS Vaasa
1933	HIFK Helsinki	HJK Helsinki
1934	HPS Helsinki	HIFK Helsinki
1935	HPS Helsinki	HIFK Helsinki
1936	HJK Helsinki	HPS Helsinki
1937	HIFK Helsinki	HJK Helsinki
1938	HJK Helsinki	TPS Turku
1939	TPS Turku	HJK Helsinki
1940	Sudet Viipuri	TPS Turku
1941	TPS Turku	VPS Vaasa
1942	HT Helsinki	Sudet Viipuri
1943	*no championship*	
1944	VIFK Vaasa	TPS Turku
1945	VPS Vaasa	HPS Helsinki
1946	VIFK Vaasa	TPV Tampere
1947	HIFK Helsinki	TuTo Turku
1948	VPS Vaasa	TPS Turku
1949	TPS Turku	VPS Vaasa
1950	Ikissat Tampere	KuPS Kuopio
1951	KTP Kotka	VIFK Vaasa
1952	KTP Kotka	VIFK Vaasa
1953	VIFK Vaasa	Jäntevä Kotka
1954	Pyrkivä Turku	KuPS Kuopio
1955	KIF Helsinki	Haka Valkeakoski
1956	KuPS Kuopio	HJK Helsinki
1957	HPS Helsinki	Haka Valkeakoski
1958	KuPS Kuopio	HPS Helsinki
1959	HIFK Helsinki	RU-38 Pori
1960	Haka Valkeakoski	TPS Turku
1961	HIFK Helsinki	KIF Helsinki

Finnish League Record (*continued*)

SEASON	CHAMPIONS	RUNNERS-UP
1962	Haka Valkeakoski	Reipas Lahti
1963	Reipas Lahti	Haka Valkeakoski
1964	HJK Helsinki	KuPS Kuopio
1965	Haka Valkeakoski	KuPS Kuopio
1966	KuPS Kuopio	HJK Helsinki
1967	Reipas Lahti	KuPS Kuopio
1968	TPS Turku	Reipas Lahti
1969	KPV Kokkola	KuPS Kuopio
1970	Reipas Lahti	MP Mikkeli
1971	TPS Turku	HIFK Helsinki
1972	TPS Turku	MP Mikkeli
1973	HJK Helsinki	KPV Kokkola
1974	KuPS Kuopio	Reipas Lahti
1975	TPS Turku	KuPS Kuopio
1976	KuPS Kuopio	Haka Valkeakoski
1977	Haka Valkeakoski	KuPS Kuopio
1978	HJK Helsinki	KPT Kuopio
1979	OPS Oulu	KuPS Kuopio
1980	OPS Oulu	Haka Valkeakoski
1981	HJK Helsinki	KPT Kuopio
1982	Kuusysi Lahti	HJK Helsinki
1983	Ilves Tampere	HJK Helsinki
1984	Kuusysi Lahti	TPS Turku
1985	HJK Helsinki	Ilves Tampere
1986	Kuusysi Lahti	TPS Turku
1987	HJK Helsinki	Kuusysi Lahti
1988	HJK Helsinki	Kuusysi Lahti
1989	Kuusysi Lahti	TPS Turku
1990	HJK Helsinki	Kuusysi Lahti
1991	Kuusysi Lahti	MP Mikkeli
1992	HJK Helsinki	Kuusysi Lahti
1993	Jazz Pori	MyPa Anjalankoski
1994	TPV Tampere	MyPa Anjalankoski
1995	Haka Valkeakoski	MyPa Anjalankoski
1996	Jazz Pori	MyPa Anjalankoski
1997	HJK Helsinki	VPS Vaasa
1998	Haka Valkeakoski	VPS Vaasa
1999	Haka Valkeakoski	HJK Helsinki
2000	Haka Valkeakoski	Jokerit Helsinki
2001	Tampere United	HJK Helsinki
2002	HJK Helsinki	MyPa Anjalankoski

Finnish League Summary

TEAM	TOTALS	CHAMPIONS & RUNNERS-UP (BOLD) (*ITALICS*)
HJK Helsinki	20, 10	**1911, 12, 17–19**, *21*, **23**, *25*, **33**, *36*, **37, 38, 39, 56**, *64*, **66**, *73*, **78, 81**, *82, 83*, **85, 87, 88, 90, 92, 97**, *99*, **2001, 2002**
HPS Helsinki	9, 6	*1920*, **21, 22**, *24*, **26, 27, 29, 31, 32, 34, 35**, *36*, **45**, *57, 58*
TPS Turku	8, 12	*1923, 25, 26*, **28**, *30, 38, 39*, **40, 41**, *44, 48*, **49**, *60, 68, 71, 72, 75, 84, 86, 89*
Haka Valkeakoski	8, 5	*1955, 57*, **60**, *62, 63*, **65**, *76*, **77**, *80*, **95**, *98, 99*, **2000**
HIFK Helsinki	7, 8	*1909, 11, 12, 28, 29*, **30, 31, 33**, *34, 35*, **37**, *47*, **59, 61**, *71*
KuPS Kuopio	5, 9	*1950, 54*, **56**, *58*, **64**, *65*, **66**, *67, 69, 74, 75, 76, 77, 79*
Kuusysi Lahti	5, 4	**1982**, *84*, **86**, *87, 88*, **89**, *90*, **91**, *92*
KIF Helsinki	4, 1	**1913, 15, 16, 55**, *61*
ÅIFK Turku	3, 3	**1910**, *15, 16, 17*, **20, 24**
Reipas Lahti	3, 3	*1962*, **63, 67**, *68*, **70**, *74*
VIFK Vaasa	3, 2	**1944, 46**, *51, 52*, **53**
VPS Vaasa	2, 5	*1932, 41*, **45, 48**, *49, 97, 98*

Finnish League Summary (*continued*)

TEAM	TOTALS	CHAMPIONS & RUNNERS-UP (BOLD) (*ITALICS*)
Tampere United (includes Ikissat Tampere, Ilves Tampere)	3, 1	**1950, 83,** *85,* **2001**
Jazz Pori	2, 0	**1993, 96**
KTP Kotka	2, 0	**1951, 52**
OPS Oulu	2, 0	**1979, 80**
KPV Kokkola	1, 1	**1969,** *73*
PUS Helsinki	1, 1	*1908,* **09**
Sudet Viipuri	1, 1	**1940,** *42*
TPV Tampere	1, 1	*1946,* **94**
HT Helsinki	1, 0	**1942**
Pyrkivä Turku	1, 0	**1954**
Unitas Helsinki	1, 0	**1908**

This summary only features clubs that have won the Finnish League. For a full list of league champions and runners-up please see the League Record opposite.

Finnish Cup Record 1955–2002

YEAR	WINNERS	SCORE	RUNNERS-UP
1955	Haka Valkeakoski	5-1	HPS Helsinki
1956	PPojat Helsinki	2-1	TKT Tampere
1957	Drott Pietarsaari	2-1 (aet)	KPT Kuopio
1958	KTP Kotka	4-1	KIF Helsinki
1959	Haka Valkeakoski	2-1	HIFK Helsinki
1960	Haka Valkeakoski	3-1 (aet)	RU-38 Pori
1961	KTP Kotka	5-2	PPojat Helsinki
1962	HPS Helsinki	5-0	RoPS Rovaniemi
1963	Haka Valkeakoski	1-0	Reipas Lahti
1964	Reipas Lahti	1-0	LaPa Lappeenranta
1965	ÅIFK Turku	1-0	TPS Turku
1966	HJK Helsinki	6-1	KTP Kotka
1967	KTP Kotka	2-0	Reipas Lahti
1968	KuPS Kuopio	2-1	KTP Kotka
1969	Haka Valkeakoski	2-0	Honka Espoo
1970	MP Mikkeli	4-1 (aet)	Reipas Lahti
1971	MP Mikkeli	4-1	Sport Vaasa
1972	Reipas Lahti	2-0	VPS Vaasa
1973	Reipas Lahti	1-0	SePS Seinäjoki
1974	Reipas Lahti	1-0	OTP Oulu
1975	Reipas Lahti	6-2 (aet)	HJK Helsinki
1976	Reipas Lahti	2-0	Ilves Tampere
1977	Haka Valkeakoski	3-1	SePS Seinäjoki
1978	Reipas Lahti	3-1, 1-1 (2 legs)	KPT Kuopio
1979	Ilves Tampere	2-0	TPS Turku
1980	KTP Kotka	3-2	Haka Valkeakoski
1981	HJK Helsinki	4-0	Kuusysi Lahti
1982	Haka Valkeakoski	3-2	KPV Kokkola
1983	Kuusysi Lahti	2-0	Haka Valkeakoski
1984	HJK Helsinki	2-1	Kuusysi Lahti
1985	Haka Valkeakoski	2-2 (aet)(2-1 pens)	HJK Helsinki
1986	RoPS Rovaniemi	2-0	KePS Kemi
1987	Kuusysi Lahti	5-4	OTP Oulu
1988	Haka Valkeakoski	1-0	OTP Oulu
1989	KuPS Kuopio	3-2	Haka Valkeakoski
1990	Ilves Tampere	2-1	HJK Helsinki
1991	TPS Turku	0-0 (aet)(5-3 pens)	Kuusysi Lahti
1992	MyPa Anjalankoski	2-0	Jaro Pietarsaari
1993	HJK Helsinki	2-0	RoPS Rovaniemi
1994	TPS Turku	2-1	HJK Helsinki
1995	MyPa Anjalankoski	1-0	Jazz Pori
1996	HJK Helsinki	0-0 (aet)(4-3 pens)	TPS Turku
1997	Haka Valkeakoski	2-1 (aet)	TPS Turku
1998	HJK Helsinki	3-2	PK-35 Helsinki
1999	Jokerit Helsinki	2-1	Jaro Pietarsaari
2000	HJK Helsinki	1-0	KTP Kotka
2001	Atlantis Helsinki	1-0	Tampere United
2002	Haka Valkeakoski	4-1	FC Lahti

Finnish Cup Summary

TEAM	TOTALS	WINNERS & RUNNERS-UP (BOLD) (*ITALICS*)
Haka Valkeakoski	11, 3	**1955, 59, 60, 63, 69, 77,** *80,* **82, 83, 85, 88,** *89,* **97, 2002**
HJK Helsinki	7, 4	**1966,** *75,* **81, 84,** *85,* **90, 93,** *94,* **96, 98, 2000**
Reipas Lahti	7, 3	*1963,* **64, 67, 70,** *72–76,* **78**
KTP Kotka	4, 3	**1958,** *61,* **66, 67,** *68,* **80,** *2000*
FC Lahti (includes Kuusysi Lahti)	2, 4	*1981,* **83, 84,** *87,* **91,** *2002*
TPS Turku	2, 4	*1965,* **79,** *91,* **94,** *96, 97*
Tampere United (includes Ilves Tampere)	2, 2	*1976,* **79, 90,** *2001*
KuPS Kuopio	2, 0	**1968, 89**
MP Mikkeli	2, 0	**1970, 71**
MyPa Anjalankoski	2, 0	**1992, 95**
Jaro Pietarsaari (includes Drott Pietarsaari)	1, 2	**1957,** *92, 99*
RoPS Rovaniemi	1, 2	*1962,* **86,** *93*
FC Jokerit (includes PK-35 Helsinki and Jokerit Helsinki)	1, 1	*1998,* **99**
HPS Helsinki	1, 1	*1955,* **62**
PPojat Helsinki	1, 1	**1956,** *61*
ÅIFK Turku	1, 0	**1965**
Atlantis Helsinki	1, 0	**2001**

This summary only features clubs that have won the Finnish Cup. For a full list of cup winners and runners-up please see the Cup Record left.

Faeroe Islands

Fotboltssamband Føroya
Founded: 1979
Joined FIFA: 1988
Joined UEFA: 1992

The tiny Faeroe Islands have played regular league football since 1942. The national team played their first competitive international in 1990, beating a lacklustre and complacent Austrian side. In 2002 they famously drew with Scotland.

SEASON	LEAGUE CHAMPIONS
1998	HB
1999	KÍ
2000	VB
2001	GÍ
2002	HB

YEAR	CUP WINNERS
1998	HB
1999	KÍ
2000	GÍ
2001	B36
2002	NSi

Iceland

The Football Association of Iceland
Founded: 1947
Joined FIFA: 1929
Joined UEFA: 1954

The first Icelandic football club, KR of Reykjavík, was set up in 1899. Football formalized in Iceland in 1912 with the creation of a Reykjavik league, though the national football association was not formed until 1947. A cup was established in 1960, ensuring a berth in the Cup-Winners' Cup for the victors.

SEASON	LEAGUE CHAMPIONS
1998	ÍBV
1999	KR
2000	KR
2001	ÍA
2002	KR

YEAR	CUP WINNERS
1998	ÍBV
1999	KR
2000	ÍA
2001	Fylkir
2002	Fylkir

FINLAND, FAEROE ISLANDS, ICELAND

Association Football in the Netherlands

Association Football in Belgium

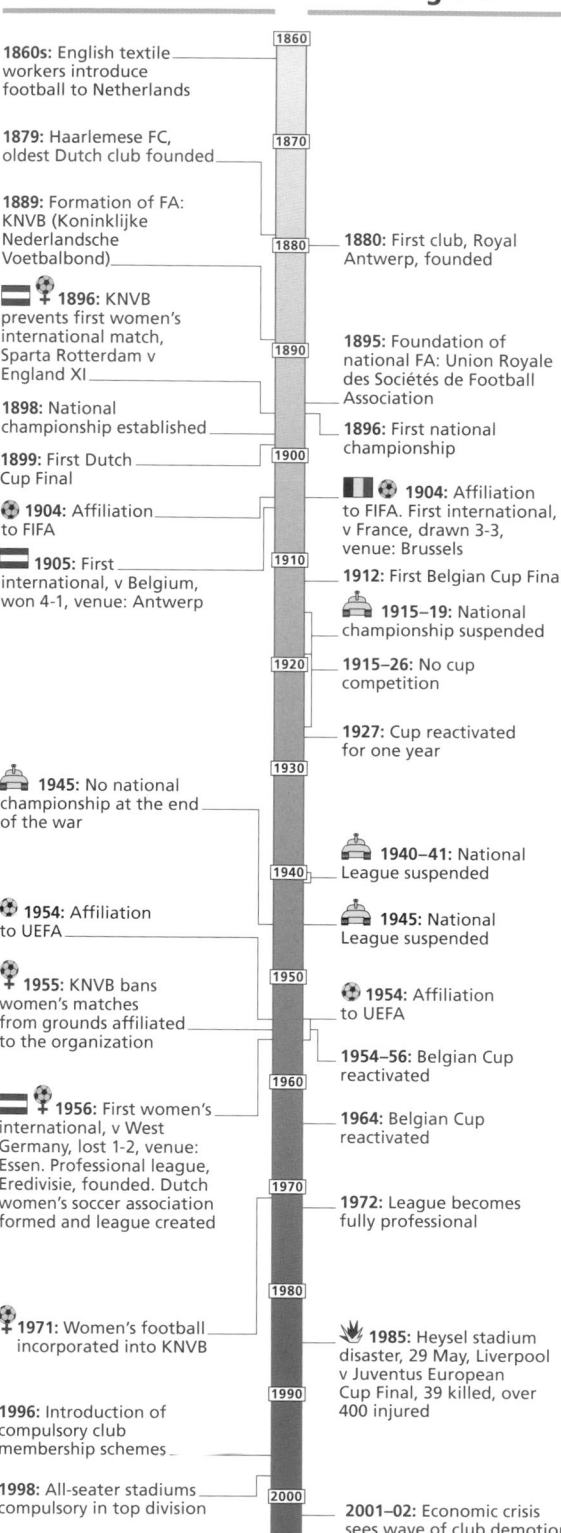

1860s: English textile workers introduce football to Netherlands

1879: Haarlemese FC, oldest Dutch club founded

1889: Formation of FA: KNVB (Koninklijke Nederlandsche Voetbalbond)

1896: KNVB prevents first women's international match, Sparta Rotterdam v England XI

1898: National championship established

1899: First Dutch Cup Final

1904: Affiliation to FIFA

1905: First international, v Belgium, won 4-1, venue: Antwerp

1945: No national championship at the end of the war

1954: Affiliation to UEFA

1955: KNVB bans women's matches from grounds affiliated to the organization

1956: First women's international, v West Germany, lost 1-2, venue: Essen. Professional league, Eredivisie, founded. Dutch women's soccer association formed and league created

1971: Women's football incorporated into KNVB

1996: Introduction of compulsory club membership schemes

1998: All-seater stadiums compulsory in top division

1860
1870
1880
1890
1900
1910
1920
1930
1940
1950
1960
1970
1980
1990
2000
2010

1880: First club, Royal Antwerp, founded

1895: Foundation of national FA: Union Royale des Sociétés de Football Association

1896: First national championship

 1904: Affiliation to FIFA. First international, v France, drawn 3-3, venue: Brussels

1912: First Belgian Cup Final

1915–19: National championship suspended

1915–26: No cup competition

1927: Cup reactivated for one year

1940–41: National League suspended

1945: National League suspended

 1954: Affiliation to UEFA

1954–56: Belgian Cup reactivated

1964: Belgian Cup reactivated

1972: League becomes fully professional

1985: Heysel stadium disaster, 29 May, Liverpool v Juventus European Cup Final, 39 killed, over 400 injured

2001–02: Economic crisis sees wave of club demotions, relegations and mergers

Low Countries: The main clubs

Ajax 1900 — Team name with year of formation
● Club formed before 1912
● Club formed 1912–25
● Club formed 1925–50
○ Club formed after 1950

Winners of Amateur Championship

Runners-up in Amateur Championship

Colours and formation date unknown

HBS Den Haag 1893

HVV Den Haag 1885

Quick Den Haag 1896

ADO Den Haag 1971
Merger of ADO Den Hagg (1905) and Holland Sport (1954) in 1971 as FC Den Haag new name 1996

Sparta Rotterdam 1888

Excelsior 1902
Feyenoord 1908

Dordrecht 90 1904

DFC Dodrecht (1904–74). Merged with SVV Schiedamse Voetbal Vvereniging (1904) in 1991

Club Brugge KV 1899
Cercle Brugge 1899
NAC Breda 1912

K Lierse SK 1908

Royal Antwerp FC 1880
KV Oostende 1981
Merger of AS Oostende and KVG Oostende
Beerschot VAV 1899–1999

Germinal Beerschot Antwerpen 1999

KRC Harlebeke 1930
AA Gent 1896
SK Beveren 1935
K. ST Niklase SK 1920

FC Germinal Ekiren 1942–99
KV Kortrijk 1971
Merger of Kortrijk Sport (1901) and Stade Kortrijk
KSC Eendracht Aalst 1919
Merger of Amical and Standard

Berchem Sport 1906

KSV Waregem 1946
Merger of Red Star Waregem and Sportif
R Excelsior Mouscron 1964
Merger of ARA Mouscronnois and R. Stade Mouscron
KSC Lokeren 1970
Merger of Racing Lokeren and Standard Lokeren

RC Jet Wavre 1970
Merger of Racing Stade de Bruxelles and RC Jette. Racing Jet de Bruxelles (1970–88)
Union FC d'Ixelles 1896
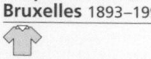 (Folded)
Daring Club Brussels 1895–1973

White Star FC 1910–63

RSC Anderlecht 1908

Merged with Brussels D' 71 in 1994
Leopold Club de Bruxelles 1893–1990
Racing Club Brussels 1891–1963

RWD Molenbeek 1973
Merger of Racing White Brussels (1963) and Daring CB (1895)
Union St Gilloise 1899

Ajax 1900

De Volewijckers 1920

Merged with DWS and Blauwit in 1972 to form FC Amsterdam, demerge in 1983
RAP Amsterdam 1887
 (Folded)
BVC Amsterdam 1954
 (Folded)
Haarlem 1889
Telstar 1
Ijmuide

Haarlem
Haarlemese FC 1879
RCH Haarlem

The Hag
Rotterdam

Breda
RBS Roosendaal 1912
Antwerp
Bruges
Ostend
Lier
Waregem
Mechelen
Aalst
Kortrijk
Mouscron
Brussels
Royal Charleroi FC 1904
Charleroi
KSC Lokeren

LOW COUNTRIES

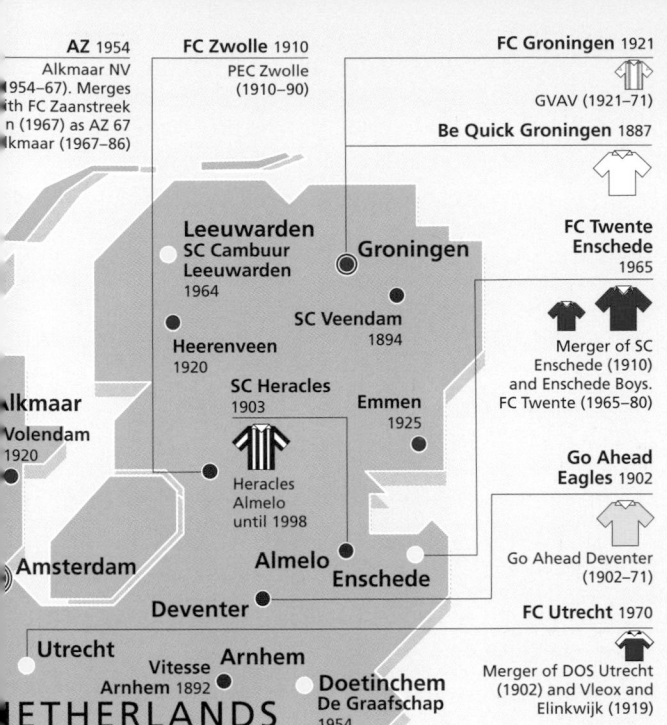

AZ 1954
Alkmaar NV
(1954–67). Merges
with FC Zaanstreek
in (1967) as AZ 67
Alkmaar (1967–86)

FC Zwolle 1910
PEC Zwolle
(1910–90)

FC Groningen 1921
GVAV (1921–71)
Be Quick Groningen 1887

Leeuwarden
SC Cambuur
Leeuwarden
1964

Groningen

FC Twente
Enschede
1965

SC Veendam
1894

Merger of SC
Enschede (1910)
and Enschede Boys.
FC Twente (1965–80)

Heerenveen
1920

SC Heracles
1903

Emmen
1925

Heracles
Almelo
until 1998

Go Ahead
Eagles 1902

lkmaar
Volendam
1920

Almelo
Enschede

Go Ahead Deventer
(1902–71)

Amsterdam

Deventer

FC Utrecht 1970

Utrecht
Vitesse
Arnhem 1892
Arnhem

Merger of DOS
Utrecht (1902) and Vleox and
Elinkwijk (1919)

NETHERLANDS

Doetinchem
De Graafschap
1954

NEC Nijmegen
1900

KC
Waalwijk
1940

Oss TOP Oss 1928
Top until 1994

Willem II Tilburg 1896

's-Hertogen-
bosch

FC Den Bosch 1906

Tilburg Helmond

Helmond Sport 1967
Splits from Helmondia 55

ndhoven
C Verbr.
el 1924
Lommel

BVV Den Bosch
(1906–67) merges
with Willhelmia (1967)

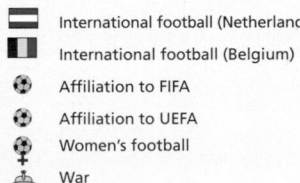

VVV Venlo 1920

Geel
Beringen
Royal Beringen FC

PSV 1913

VC
esterlo
64

Heerlen

Maastricht Geleen

Eindhoven 1909

Hasselt

1902

MVV

Racing
Club
Mechelen
1904

Liège

Roda JC Kerkrade 1914

KV
Mechelen
1904

KSK
Tongeren
1969
Merger of
Tongerse
SV Cercle
and K. Patria
FC Tongeren

Roda Sport merged with
Rapid JC (1954) in 1962

Fortuna Sittard 1968

BELGIUM

Merger of Fortuna 54 Geleen
and Sittardia (1950) in 1968.
FSC (1968–79)

K. Waterschei SV
Thor Genk
1925–88

RFC Seresien

FC Winterslag
1923–88

R. Standard Liège 1898

SC Hasselt 1964
Merger of Excelsior Hasselt
and K. Hasselt VV

RFC Liège 1892

Racing Club Genk 1988
Merger of FC Winterslag
and Waterschei Thor

RFC Leiegois (1892–1989)

Low Countries

ORIGINS AND GROWTH OF FOOTBALL

THE TRAJECTORIES OF football in Belgium and the Netherlands have clear parallels – early arrival through British influences, the establishment of national FAs and leagues before the end of the 19th century, followed by decades of weak domestic football due to the persistence of amateurism. In Belgium, English colleges in Brussels and Bruges and English workers in Antwerp were the main points of arrival. In the Netherlands, English textile workers in Enschede were playing football in the late 1860s. Pim Mulier, an English-educated journalist, established the country's first club, Haarlemese FC, in 1879.

Professionalism came to the Netherlands in 1956, while in Belgium semi-professionalism began in the late 1950s and full professionalism in 1972. In both countries there has been a massive concentration of football strength into a few big clubs, followed by waves of small club mergers in an attempt to keep up. In Belgium the balance of power has shifted to Brussels, Anderlecht and French-speaking Belgium and away from Flemish-speaking areas in the North. In the Netherlands the big three, Ajax, Feyenoord and PSV, have been dominant.

LOW COUNTRIES

Key

- International football (Netherlands)
- International football (Belgium)
- Affiliation to FIFA
- Affiliation to UEFA
- Women's football
- War
- Disaster
- ▲ World Cup runner-up
- ■ European Championships host

- ● European Championships winner
- ▲ European Championships runner-up
- ○ Netherlands competition winner
- △ Netherlands competition runner-up
- ● Belgian competition winner
- ▲ Belgian competition runner-up

Alk – AZ Alkmaar
And – Anderlecht
Ant – Royal Antwerp FC
Brug – Club Brugge
Feyn – Feyenoord
Liege – Standard Liège
Mech – KV Mechelen
Twen – FC Twente

International Competitions

Year	European Cup	UEFA Cup	European Cup-Winners' Cup
	△ Ajax		
1969:			
1970:	○ Feyn	△ And	
1971:	○ Ajax		
1972:	■ ○ Ajax		
1973:	○ Ajax		
1974:	▲	○ Feyn	
1975:		△ Twen	
1976:		△ Brug	
1977:			○ And
1978:	▲ △ Brug	○ PSV	○ And △ And
1980:	▲		
1981:	▲	△ Alk	
1982:			△ Liege
1983:		○ And	
1984:		△ And	
1987:	●		○ Ajax
1988:	◉ ○ PSV		○ Mech △ Ajax
1990:			△ And
1992:		○ Ajax	△ And
1993:			△ Ant
1995:	○ Ajax		
1996:	△ Ajax		
2000:	■		
2002:		○ Feyn	

Belgium

THE SEASON IN REVIEW 2002–03

WITH ATTENDANCE FIGURES UP this season, access to improved stadiums since Euro 2000 refurbishments and a decent run for the national team to the second round of the 2002 World Cup, Belgian football strides onwards and upwards. The only question is, will enough teams survive financially to make a top-flight division possible? In 2002, RWD Molenbeek and Eendracht Aalst went under, this year it was the turn of Mechelen and Lommel. Lommel looked like a candidate for liquidation from very early on and the side only managed to continue playing with players on loan from some of the big clubs who continued to pay their wages. Lommel's disintegration was so complete that its results were removed from the final league standings. Discussions on the possibility of a Dutch-Belgian league continue as the few potentially solvent teams, perhaps as few as five, plan their escape.

Trond Sollied hits the jackpot

On the pitch it was a fabulous season for Club Brugge. After finishing runners-up for four seasons, it finally found the consistency and ruthlessness that victory requires. Under Norwegian coach Trond Sollied, Brugge hit the front by the New Year and just pulled away from the rest. Over 70 goals in the season outclassed everyone else. While most clubs were relying on a single prolific striker – like Wesley Sonck at Genk whose six goals in a 9-0 demolition of Mechelen equalled the league's scoring record in a single game – Club Brugge was getting goals from all over the park.

One club scrabbling for the European places was Anderlecht, who recovered from a terrible start to go on a late-season run. This included a 5-1 thrashing of Brugge that gave the team a shot at the Champions League – virtually the only thing worth winning in Belgian football if you want to survive financially. Last season's champion, Genk, was as dismal as its Champions League campaign that yielded four draws and two goals. More entertaining were two unfancied small clubs, Lokeren and Lierse. Lokeren fielded a side with at least nine or ten regulars coming from Africa or Iceland, and was good enough to take third spot and a crack at the UEFA Cup. Lierse had one of the tightest defences in the league and only the lack of goals kept it out of fourth spot, which went to St. Truidense. Most surprising of all, La Louvière, a team that flirted with relegation for most of the season, beat St. Truidense 3-1 in the cup final.

Jupiler League Table 2002–03

CLUB	P	W	D	L	F	A	Pts	
Club Brugge KV	32	25	4	3	96	33	79	Champions League
RSC Anderlecht	32	23	2	7	72	31	71	UEFA Cup
KSC Lokeren	32	18	6	8	69	51	60	UEFA Cup
St. Truidense	32	16	8	8	63	44	56	
K Lierse SK	32	16	8	8	51	41	56	
KRC Genk	32	16	7	9	73	52	55	
Standard Liège	32	14	8	10	53	39	50	
KAA Gent	32	15	2	15	49	55	47	
RAEC Mons	32	13	4	15	45	45	43	
KVC Westerlo	32	12	4	16	39	46	40	
KSK Beveren	32	12	2	18	50	69	38	
Royal Antwerp	32	9	7	16	44	44	34	
R Excelsior Mouscron	32	9	5	18	42	72	32	
G Beerschot Antwerpen	32	8	7	17	49	57	31	
La Louvière	32	7	9	16	34	44	30	UEFA Cup (cup winners)
RSC Charleroi	32	6	9	17	39	66	27	
KV Mechelen*	32	4	6	22	18	86	18	Relegated
KFC Lommel†	0	0	0	0	0	0	0	Relegated

Promoted clubs: KSV Cercle Brugge, K Heusden-Zolder.

* Went into liquidation. Will play in third level next season as Geel Red KV; will start the season with a 9-point penalty.

† Went into liquidation with 8 matches left to play; all previous results were annuled.

La Louvière players celebrate their cup semi-final victory. They had already beaten last year's champions Genk in the previous round and then they went on to beat St. Truidense in the Final.

Top Goalscorers 2002–03

PLAYER	CLUB	NATIONALITY	GOALS
Wesley Sonck	KRC Genk	Belgian	24
Cedric Roussel	RAEC Mons	Belgian	22
Ole Martin Aarst	Standard Liège	Norwegian	21
Nenad Jestrovic	RSC Anderlecht	Serbian	20
Paul Kpaka	G Beerschot Antwerpen	Sierra Leonean	20

International Club Performances 2002–03

CLUB	COMPETITION	PROGRESS
Club Brugge KV	Champions League	1st Group Stage
	UEFA Cup	3rd Round
KRC Genk	Champions League	1st Group Stage
RSC Anderlecht	UEFA Cup	4th Round
R Excelsior Mouscron	UEFA Cup	1st Round

Belgian Cup

2003 FINAL

June 1 – King Boudewin, Brussels
La Louvière 3-1 St. Truidense
(Ishiaku 27, 72,   (Buvens 84)
Arts 32)
h/t: 2-0 **Att:** 32,000
Ref: Verbist

Right: Robert Waseige, who took the national team to the second round of last year's World Cup, went to Standard Liège this season only to be sacked after a very poor start.

BELGIUM

Above, left: *KV Mechelen's Alen Mrzlecki (right) runs at Antwerp's Gideon Imagbudu (left).*

Above: *Antwerp's Hussain Abdulrahma (left) battles for the ball with Anderlecht's Walter Baseggio.*

Left: *The surprise team of the year, Lokeren got itself into the UEFA Cup with the most multi-national team in the country.*

Below, left: *At last. After being runners-up for the last four seasons, Club Brugge celebrates its league championship after playing St. Truidense.*

Below: *Norwegian Trond Sollied in characteristically expansive mood has done his homework and taken Club Brugge to the title and the Champions League.*

Belgium

THE JUPILER LEAGUE 1982–2002

THE LAST 20 YEARS of Belgian football have been dominated by three teams: Standard Liège, who opened the 1980s with a couple of titles; Club Brugge KV, who has consistently challenged for the title and took a string of them in the late 1980s under former player Jan Ceulemans; and the biggest club of all, Anderlecht. Beyond these teams only three minnows have taken the title: Lierse, Beveren and Mechelen.

Anderlecht has risen to the top under the control of Constant Vanden Stock. Previously a player with the club and national team manager, he made an enormous fortune in the brewing industry. Under his control the club won three titles in a row in the mid-1980s, built the first executive boxes in a European stadium and brought the leading Belgian player of the era – Enzo Schifo – to the club. In the mid-1990s, the championship-winning team was built around Luc Nilis and Marc Degryse.

Competition has consistently come from the likes of Gent, Antwerpen and Charleroi, but most clubs are struggling to survive, and the league has seen a wave of mergers forced on the smaller sides, while older established clubs, like Cercle Brugge, have disappeared from view. In 2002, two top-flight clubs are to be relegated on financial rather than sporting grounds as Eendracht Aalst failed to pay its players and RWD Molenbeek collapsed under its debts.

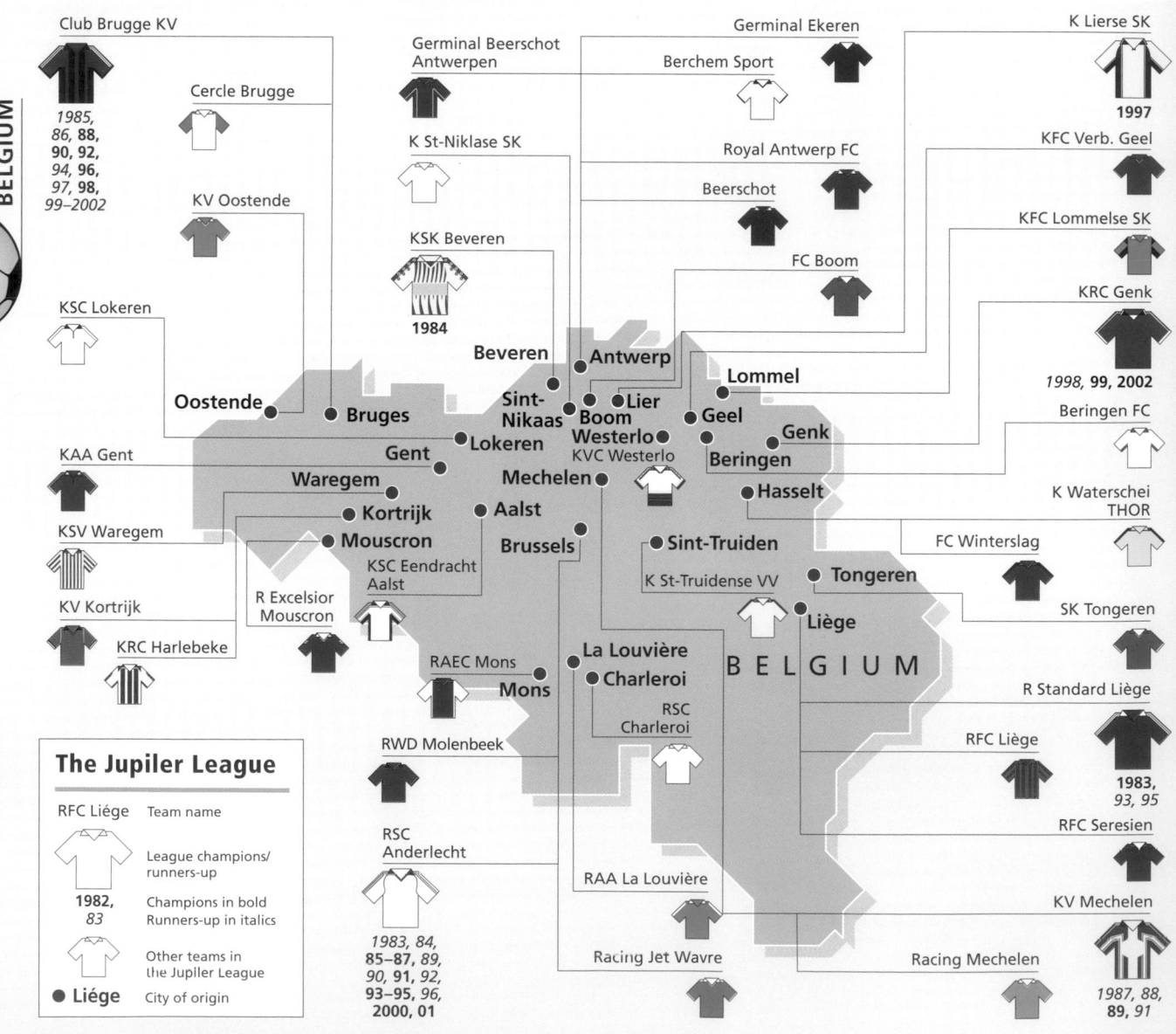

BELGIUM

The Jupiler League

RFC Liége — Team name

League champions/runners-up

1982, 83 — Champions in bold / Runners-up in italics

Other teams in the Jupiler League

● Liége — City of origin

Key to League Positions Table

- League champions
- Other team playing in league
- Season promoted to league
- Season of relegation from league
- 5 — Final positition in league
- Merger between teams

FC Winterslag and K Waterschei THOR merged to form KRC Genk for the 1988–99 season

R Standard Liège and RFC Seresien merged to form R Standard Liège for the 1996–97 season

Germinal Ekeren and Beerschot merged to form Germinal Beerschot Antwerpen for the 1999–2000 season

***Former RSC Anderlecht** president Constant Vanden Stock looks benignly down on his son and current supremo, Roger.*

***Enzo Schifo,** the most gifted Belgian player ever and an inspiration for RSC Anderlecht.*

Belgian League Positions 1982–2002

TEAM	1982–83	1983–84	1984–85	1985–86	1986–87	1987–88	1988–89	1989–90	1990–91	1991–92	1992–93	1993–94	1994–95	1995–96	1996–97	1997–98	1998–99	1999–2000	2000–01	2001–02
KSC Eendracht Aalst										18			4	10	15	15	13	12	16	17
RSC Anderlecht	2	2	1	1	1	4	2	2	1	2	1	1	1	2	4	4	3	1	1	3
Royal Antwerp FC	3	8	7	9	14	3	5	4	7	5	5	5	16	13	6	18			12	16
Germinal Beerschot Antwerpen																		7	6	9
Beerschot	15	16	16	7	9	13	16	8	18											
Berchem Sport					18															
Beringen FC		18																		
KSK Beveren	6	1	5	5	5	14	12	17		12	8	9	10	17		16	15	15	14	18*
FC Boom											18									
Cercle Brugge	12	11	11	10	11	7	15	9	16	9	13	12	15	8	18					
Club Brugge KV	5	3	2	2	3	1	4	1	4	1	6	2	3	1	2	1	2	2	2	2
RSC Charleroi				12	7	8	11	14	8	13	7	4	13	7	13	13	14	16	9	12
Germinal Ekeren								13	5	8	14	10	6	3	10	3	10			
KRC Genk							18		14	16	15	18			8	2	1	8	11	1
KFC Verb. Geel																		17		
KAA Gent	4	15	6	4	16	17		6	3	6	9	15	14	14	14	8	8	3	5	4
KRC Harlebeke														12	9	5	11	14	17	
KV Kortrijk	11	12	13	15	15	9	8	7	15	17							17			
RFC Liège	9	13	3	6	6	5	3	12	10	15	12	13	18							
R Standard Liège	1	4	8	3	10	10	6	5	6	3	2	6	2	6	7	9	6	5	3	5
K Lierse SK	14	14	15	18			10	10	11	7	10	14	5	5	1	7	7	9	10	15
KSC Lokeren	8	10	10	14	4	16	14	11	9	14	17				12	6	5	10	4	7
KFC Lommelse SK											16	11	7	9	5	11	16	18		13
RAA La Louvière																			15	11
KV Mechelen		6	12	11	2	2	1	3	2	4	3	8	11	11	17			11	18	
Racing Mechelen							13	18												
RWD Molenbeek	10	17		13	13	12	17		12	11	11	16	12	4	16	17				10*
RAEC Mons																				
R Excelsior Mouscron															3	10	4	4	7	6
KV Oostende												7	17				18			
K St-Niklase SK			17																	
K St-Truidense VV						11	7	15	17				8	15	11	14	9	13	13	8
RFC Seresien	13	5	14	16	17							3	9	16						
SK Tongeren	17																			
KSV Waregem	16	7	4	8	8	6	9	16	13	10	4	17		18						
K Waterschei THOR	7	9	9	17																
Racing Jet Wavre			18		12	18														
KVC Westerlo																12	12	6	8	14
FC Winterslag	18					15														

*Despite finishing bottom, Beveren were spared relegation as RWD Molenbeek were relegated for financial reasons.

BELGIUM

Belgium

Union Royale des Sociétés de Football Association
Founded: 1895
Joined FIFA: 1904
Joined UEFA: 1954

BELGIUM

BELGIUM SHARES WITH Sweden the honour of having Europe's oldest football league outside the British Isles. Established in 1895 across both French- and Flemish-speaking Belgium, the league has run for over 100 years, breaking only for the First World War and the beginning and the end of the Second World War. Power in the league has shifted from the early dominance of Brussels-based teams such as Union St. Gilloise and Racing CB, to include the clubs of Antwerp, Bruges and Liège. By contrast, the Belgian Cup has been a sporadic and low-key affair and was played only once between 1915 and 1954. Interest has risen since the early 1960s when the winners were awarded a place in European competitions. The current league has 18 teams with two relegated each year and two promoted from the lower league in a complex series of play-offs.

Belgian League Record 1896–2003

SEASON	CHAMPIONS	RUNNERS-UP
1896	RFC Liège	Royal Antwerp FC
1897	Racing CB	RFC Liège
1898	RFC Liège	Racing CB
1899	RFC Liège	Racing CB
1900	Racing CB	Royal Antwerp FC
1901	Racing CB	Beerschot
1902	Racing CB	Leopold CB
1903	Racing CB	Union St. Gilloise
1904	Union St. Gilloise	Racing CB
1905	Union St. Gilloise	Racing CB
1906	Union St. Gilloise	Club Brugge KV
1907	Union St. Gilloise	Racing CB
1908	Racing CB	Union St. Gilloise
1909	Union St. Gilloise	Daring CB
1910	Union St. Gilloise	Club Brugge KV
1911	Cercle Brugge	Club Brugge KV
1912	Daring CB	Union St. Gilloise
1913	Union St. Gilloise	Daring CB
1914	Daring CB	Union St. Gilloise
1915–19	*no championship*	
1920	Club Brugge KV	Union St. Gilloise
1921	Daring CB	Union St. Gilloise
1922	Beerschot	Union St. Gilloise
1923	Union St. Gilloise	Beerschot
1924	Beerschot	Union St. Gilloise
1925	Beerschot	Royal Antwerp FC
1926	Beerschot	R Standard Liège
1927	Cercle Brugge	Beerschot
1928	Beerschot	R Standard Liège
1929	Royal Antwerp FC	Beerschot
1930	Cercle Brugge	Royal Antwerp FC
1931	Royal Antwerp FC	KV Mechelen
1932	K Lierse SK	Royal Antwerp FC
1933	Union St. Gilloise	Royal Antwerp FC
1934	Union St. Gilloise	Daring CB
1935	Union St. Gilloise	K Lierse SK
1936	Daring CB	R Standard Liège
1937	Daring CB	Beerschot
1938	Beerschot	Daring CB
1939	Beerschot	K Lierse SK
1940–41	*no championship*	
1942	K Lierse SK	Beerschot
1943	KV Mechelen	Beerschot

Belgian League Record (*continued*)

SEASON	CHAMPIONS	RUNNERS-UP
1944	Royal Antwerp FC	RSC Anderlecht
1945	*no championship*	
1946	KV Mechelen	Royal Antwerp FC
1947	RSC Anderlecht	Olympic Charleroi
1948	KV Mechelen	RSC Anderlecht
1949	RSC Anderlecht	Berchem Sport
1950	RSC Anderlecht	Berchem Sport
1951	RSC Anderlecht	Berchem Sport
1952	RFC Liège	Racing Mechelen
1953	RFC Liège	RSC Anderlecht
1954	RSC Anderlecht	KV Mechelen
1955	RSC Anderlecht	AA Gent
1956	RSC Anderlecht	Royal Antwerp FC
1957	Royal Antwerp FC	RSC Anderlecht
1958	R Standard Liège	Royal Antwerp FC
1959	RSC Anderlecht	RFC Liège
1960	K Lierse SK	RSC Anderlecht
1961	R Standard Liège	RFC Liège
1962	RSC Anderlecht	R Standard Liège
1963	R Standard Liège	Royal Antwerp FC
1964	RSC Anderlecht	FC Beringen
1965	RSC Anderlecht	R Standard Liège
1966	RSC Anderlecht	St. Truidense
1967	RSC Anderlecht	Club Brugge KV
1968	RSC Anderlecht	Club Brugge KV
1969	R Standard Liège	RSC Charleroi
1970	R Standard Liège	Club Brugge KV
1971	R Standard Liège	Club Brugge KV
1972	RSC Anderlecht	Club Brugge KV
1973	Club Brugge KV	R Standard Liège
1974	RSC Anderlecht	Royal Antwerp FC
1975	RWD Molenbeek	Royal Antwerp FC
1976	Club Brugge KV	RSC Anderlecht
1977	Club Brugge KV	RSC Anderlecht
1978	Club Brugge KV	RSC Anderlecht
1979	KSK Beveren	RSC Anderlecht
1980	Club Brugge KV	R Standard Liège
1981	RSC Anderlecht	KSC Lokeren
1982	R Standard Liège	RSC Anderlecht
1983	R Standard Liège	RSC Anderlecht
1984	KSK Beveren	RSC Anderlecht
1985	RSC Anderlecht	Club Brugge KV
1986	RSC Anderlecht	Club Brugge KV
1987	RSC Anderlecht	KV Mechelen
1988	Club Brugge KV	KV Mechelen
1989	KV Mechelen	RSC Anderlecht
1990	Club Brugge KV	RSC Anderlecht
1991	RSC Anderlecht	KV Mechelen
1992	Club Brugge KV	RSC Anderlecht
1993	RSC Anderlecht	Standard Liège
1994	RSC Anderlecht	Club Brugge KV
1995	RSC Anderlecht	Standard Liège
1996	Club Brugge KV	RSC Anderlecht
1997	K Lierse SK	Club Brugge KV
1998	Club Brugge KV	KRC Genk
1999	KRC Genk	Club Brugge KV
2000	RSC Anderlecht	Club Brugge KV
2001	RSC Anderlecht	Club Brugge KV
2002	KRC Genk	Club Brugge KV
2003	Club Brugge KV	RSC Anderlecht

Belgian League Summary

TEAM	TOTALS	CHAMPIONS & RUNNERS-UP (BOLD) (ITALICS)
RSC Anderlecht	26, 17	*1944,* **47, 48, 49–51, 53, 54–56, 57,** *59, 60,* **62, 64–68, 72, 74,** *76–79, 81, 82–84, 85–87,* **89, 90, 91, 92, 93–95,** *96,* **2000, 01,** *03*
Club Brugge KV	12, 16	*1906, 10, 11,* **20,** *67, 68, 70–72,* **73,** *76–78,* **80,** *85, 86,* **88,** *90,* **92,** *94, 96, 97, 98, 99–2002,* **03**
Union St. Gilloise	11, 8	*1903,* **04–07,** *08,* **09, 10,** *12,* **13, 14,** *20–22,* **23,** *24,* **33–35**
R Standard Liège	8, 9	*1926,* **28,** *36,* **58, 61, 62, 63,** *65,* **69–71,** *73,* **80,** *82, 83,* **93,** *95*
Beerschot	7, 7	*1901,* **22,** *23,* **24–26,** *27,* **28,** *29,* **37,** *38, 39, 42, 43*
Racing CB	6, 5	**1897, 98, 99, 1900–03,** *04,* **05,** *07,* **08**
Daring CB	5, 4	*1909,* **12, 13,** *14,* **21,** *34,* **36, 37,** *38*
RFC Liège	5, 3	**1896, 97, 98, 99, 1952,** *53,* **59,** *61*
Royal Antwerp FC	4, 12	*1896,* **1900,** *25,* **29,** *30,* **31,** *32, 33,* **44,** *46,* **56,** *57, 58, 63, 74, 75*
KV Mechelen	4, 5	*1931, 43,* **46,** *48,* **54,** *87,* **88, 89,** *91*
K Lierse SK	4, 2	**1932,** *35,* **39,** *42,* **60, 97**
Cercle Brugge	3, 0	**1911, 27, 30**
KRC Genk	2, 1	*1998,* **99, 2002**
KSK Beveren	2, 0	**1979, 84**
RWD Molenbeek	1, 0	**1975**

This summary only features clubs that have won the Belgian League. For a full list of league champions and runners-up please see the League Record opposite.

Belgian Cup Record 1912–2003

YEAR	WINNERS	SCORE	RUNNERS-UP
1912	Racing CB	1-0	Racing Gent
1913	Union St. Gilloise	3-2	Cercle Brugge
1914	Union St. Gilloise	4-1	Club Brugge KV
1915–26		no competition	
1927	Cercle Brugge	2-1	Tubantia Borgerhout
1928–53		no competition	
1954	R Standard Liège	3-1	Racing Mechelen
1955	Royal Antwerp FC	4-0	Waterschei THOR
1956	Racing Tournai	2-1	CS Verviers
1957–63		no competition	
1964	KAA Gent	4-2	FC Diest
1965	RSC Anderlecht	3-2 (aet)	R Standard Liège
1966	R Standard Liège	1-0	RSC Anderlecht
1967	R Standard Liège	3-1 (aet)	KV Mechelen
1968	Club Brugge KV	1-1, (replay) 4-4 (4-2 pens)	Beerschot
1969	K Lierse SK	2-0	Racing White
1970	Club Brugge KV	6-1	Daring CB
1971	Beerschot	2-1	St. Truidense
1972	RSC Anderlecht	1-0	R Standard Liège
1973	RSC Anderlecht	2-1	R Standard Liège
1974	KSV Waregem	4-1	SK Tongeren
1975	RSC Anderlecht	1-0	Royal Antwerp FC
1976	RSC Anderlecht	4-0	K Lierse SK
1977	Club Brugge KV	4-3	RSC Anderlecht
1978	KSK Beveren	2-0	RSC Charleroi
1979	Beerschot	1-0	Club Brugge KV
1980	Waterschei THOR	2-1	KSK Beveren
1981	R Standard Liège	4-0	KSC Lokeren
1982	Waterschei THOR	2-0	KSV Wagerem
1983	KSK Beveren	3-1	Club Brugge KV
1984	KAA Gent	2-0	R Standard Liège
1985	Cercle Brugge	1-1 (aet)(5-4 pens)	KSK Beveren
1986	Club Brugge KV	3-0	Cercle Brugge
1987	KV Mechelen	1-0	RFC Liège
1988	RSC Anderlecht	2-0	R Standard Liège
1989	RSC Anderlecht	2-0	R Standard Liège
1990	RFC Liège	2-1	Germinal Ekeren

Belgian Cup Record (continued)

YEAR	WINNERS	SCORE	RUNNERS-UP
1991	Club Brugge KV	3-1	KV Mechelen
1992	Royal Antwerp FC	2-2 (aet)(9-8 pens)	KV Mechelen
1993	R Standard Liège	2-0	RSC Charleroi
1994	RSC Anderlecht	2-0	Club Brugge KV
1995	Club Brugge KV	3-1	Germinal Ekeren
1996	Club Brugge KV	2-1	Cercle Brugge
1997	Germinal Ekeren	4-2 (aet)	RSC Anderlecht
1998	Racing Genk	4-0	Club Brugge KV
1999	K Lierse SK	3-1	R Standard Liège
2000	Racing Genk	4-1	R Standard Liège
2001	KVC Westerlo	1-0	Lommel
2002	Club Brugge KV	3-1	Excelsior Mouscron
2003	La Louvière	3-1	St. Truidense

Belgian Cup Summary

TEAM	TOTALS	WINNERS & RUNNERS-UP (BOLD) (ITALICS)
Club Brugge KV	8, 5	*1914,* **68, 70, 77,** *79,* **83, 86, 91, 94, 95, 96, 98, 2002**
RSC Anderlecht	8, 3	**1965,** *66,* **72, 73, 75, 76,** *77,* **88, 89, 94,** *97*
R Standard Liège	5, 8	**1954,** *65,* **66, 67,** *72, 73,* **81,** *84, 88, 89,* **93,** *99, 2000*
Cercle Brugge	2, 3	*1913,* **27,** *85,* **86,** *96*
KSK Beveren	2, 2	**1978,** *80,* **83,** *85*
Beerschot	2, 1	*1968,* **71, 79**
K Lierse SK	2, 1	**1969,** *76,* **99**
Racing Genk	2, 1	*1912,* **98, 2000**
Royal Antwerp FC	2, 1	**1955,** *75,* **92**
Waterschei THOR	2, 1	*1955,* **80, 82**
KAA Gent	2, 0	**1964, 84**
Union St. Gilloise	2, 0	**1913, 14**
KV Mechelen	1, 3	*1967,* **87,** *91, 92*
Germinal Ekeren	1, 2	*1990, 95,* **97**
KSV Waregem	1, 1	**1974,** *82*
RFC Liège	1, 1	*1987,* **90**
La Louvière	1, 0	**2003**
KVC Westerlo	1, 0	**2001**
Racing CB	1, 0	**1912**
Racing Tournai	1, 0	**1956**

This summary only features clubs that have won the Belgian Cup. For a full list of cup winners and runners-up please see the Cup Record left.

Luxembourg

Fédération Luxembourgeoise de Football
Founded: 1908
Joined FIFA: 1910
Joined UEFA: 1954

SEASON	LEAGUE CHAMPIONS
1999	Jeunesse Esch
2000	F91 Dudelange
2001	F91 Dudelange
2002	F91 Dudelange
2003	CS Grevenmacher

YEAR	CUP WINNERS
1999	Jeunesse Esch
2000	Jeunesse Esch
2001	Etzella Ettelbruck
2002	Avenir Beggen
2003	CS Grevenmacher

Football in Luxembourg is almost as old as in Belgium, with a league established in 1910 and a cup in 1922.

A new system of play-offs for the top four teams was introduced in 1999–2000 to decide the championship with the remaining teams involved in relegation play-offs.

Netherlands

THE SEASON IN REVIEW 2002–03

STRAIGHT TALKING is meant to be a Dutch characteristic, and the season began with some very straight and deeply unpleasant talking among Dutch fans. Guus Hiddink, new coach of PSV, and Bert van Marwijk, coach at Feyenoord, both received death threats – they were sent anonymous letters with bullets enclosed.

The football itself was worryingly predictable as PSV and Ajax duelled for the top spot throughout the autumn and winter. Only Feyenoord's poor form was a surprise. The dismal performances of PSV and Feyenoord in the Champions League saw both exit at the first group stage while Ajax eventually made it to the quarter-finals where only a last-minute goal by Milan's Jon Dahl Tomasson kept the team out of the semis. Unencumbered by European distractions, PSV seemed to have the edge in the domestic league and took the top spot from Ajax just before Christmas, with a 4-2 win in Amsterdam.

Down in the depths of the division, Excelsior was rooted in the bottom three and relegation was inevitable after a disastrous spring in which not a single victory was registered between Christmas and mid-April.

Clubs get out the begging bowl

It was just as well that Ajax did manage a Champions League run as it announced record levels of loss and debt this season, and promptly sold a number of the overseas clubs in which it had stakes. Ajax, of course, had the luxury of doing so; for many other Eredivisie clubs the begging bowl was the only option. Debts, unpaid players, unpaid tax bills and disappearing investors were the norm outside the top three. Twente looked like it was going bankrupt when the Dutch tax authorities issued insolvency proceedings and Vitesse, Utrecht and NAC Breda all faced similar dilemmas. In every case, the local council came to their club's rescue, orchestrating complex buyouts of the clubs' stadiums, as well as more conventional loans.

PSV hit top form

While things were reasonably tight at the top in the New Year, PSV showed a fantastic run of form through the early spring, culminating in a 2-0 victory over Ajax in late March. With two goals, inevitably, from Mateja Kezman, PSV were ten points ahead with only nine games to go. However, as Ajax recovered

Eredivisie Table 2002–03

CLUB	P	W	D	L	F	A	Pts	
PSV	34	26	6	2	87	20	**84**	Champions League
Ajax	34	26	5	3	96	32	**83**	Champions League
Feyenoord	34	25	5	4	89	39	**80**	UEFA Cup
NAC Breda	34	13	13	8	42	31	**52**	UEFA Cup
NEC	34	14	9	11	41	40	**51**	UEFA Cup
Roda JC	34	14	8	12	58	54	**50**	
Heerenveen	34	13	8	13	61	55	**47**	
FC Utrecht	34	12	11	11	49	49	**47**	UEFA Cup (cup winners)
RKC Waalwijk	34	14	4	16	44	51	**46**	
AZ Alkmaar	34	12	8	14	50	69	**44**	
Willem II	34	11	9	14	48	51	**42**	
FC Twente	34	10	11	13	36	45	**41**	
RBC Roosendaal	34	10	6	18	33	54	**36**	
Vitesse Arnhem	34	8	9	17	37	51	**33**	
Groningen	34	7	11	16	28	44	**32**	
FC Zwolle	34	8	8	18	31	62	**32**	
Excelsior	34	5	8	21	38	72	**23**	Relegated
De Graafschap	34	6	5	23	35	84	**23**	Relegated

Promoted clubs: ADO Den Haag, FC Volendam.

Above: Mateja Kezman's amazingly prolific goalscoring was the key to PSV's league triumph this season.

Far left: Mike Snoei, the bright, breezy young coach at Vitesse, was one of four managerial casualties in the Eredivisie this year.

Left: Bert van Marwijk, Feyenoord coach, stays cool despite death threats and a woefully underperforming squad.

Key

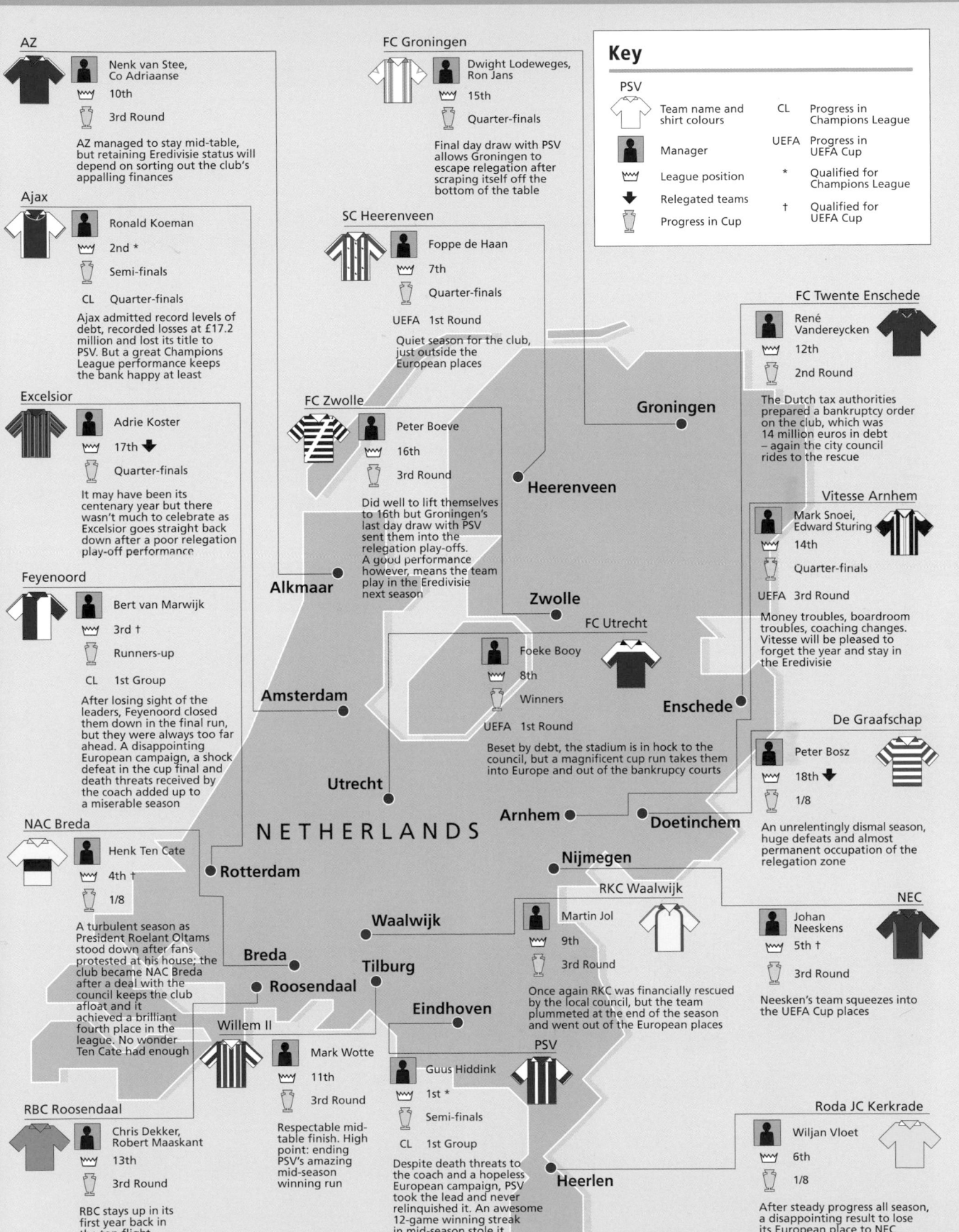

PSV — Team name and shirt colours

Manager

League position

Relegated teams

Progress in Cup

CL — Progress in Champions League

UEFA — Progress in UEFA Cup

* — Qualified for Champions League

† — Qualified for UEFA Cup

AZ
Nenk van Stee, Co Adriaanse
10th
3rd Round

AZ managed to stay mid-table, but retaining Eredivisie status will depend on sorting out the club's appalling finances

Ajax
Ronald Koeman
2nd *
Semi-finals
CL — Quarter-finals

Ajax admitted record levels of debt, recorded losses at £17.2 million and lost its title to PSV. But a great Champions League performance keeps the bank happy at least

Excelsior
Adrie Koster
17th ↓
Quarter-finals

It may have been its centenary year but there wasn't much to celebrate as Excelsior goes straight back down after a poor relegation play-off performance

Feyenoord
Bert van Marwijk
3rd †
Runners-up
CL — 1st Group

After losing sight of the leaders, Feyenoord closed them down in the final run, but they were always too far ahead. A disappointing European campaign, a shock defeat in the cup final and death threats received by the coach added up to a miserable season

NAC Breda
Henk Ten Cate
4th †
1/8

A turbulent season as President Roelant Oltams stood down after fans protested at his house; the club became NAC Breda after a deal with the council keeps the club afloat and it achieved a brilliant fourth place in the league. No wonder Ten Cate had enough

RBC Roosendaal
Chris Dekker, Robert Maaskant
13th
3rd Round

RBC stays up in its first year back in the top flight

FC Groningen
Dwight Lodeweges, Ron Jans
15th
Quarter-finals

Final day draw with PSV allows Groningen to escape relegation after scraping itself off the bottom of the table

SC Heerenveen
Foppe de Haan
7th
Quarter-finals
UEFA — 1st Round

Quiet season for the club, just outside the European places

FC Zwolle
Peter Boeve
16th
3rd Round

Did well to lift themselves to 16th but Groningen's last day draw with PSV sent them into the relegation play-offs. A good performance however, means the team play in the Eredivisie next season

FC Utrecht
Foeke Booy
8th
Winners
UEFA — 1st Round

Beset by debt, the stadium is in hock to the council, but a magnificent cup run takes them into Europe and out of the bankrupcy courts

Willem II
Mark Wotte
11th
3rd Round

Respectable mid-table finish. High point: ending PSV's amazing mid-season winning run

PSV
Guus Hiddink
1st *
Semi-finals
CL — 1st Group

Despite death threats to the coach and a hopeless European campaign, PSV took the lead and never relinquished it. An awesome 12-game winning streak in mid-season stole it

FC Twente Enschede
René Vandereycken
12th
2nd Round

The Dutch tax authorities prepared a bankruptcy order on the club, which was 14 million euros in debt – again the city council rides to the rescue

Vitesse Arnhem
Mark Snoei, Edward Sturing
14th
Quarter-finals
UEFA — 3rd Round

Money troubles, boardroom troubles, coaching changes. Vitesse will be pleased to forget the year and stay in the Eredivisie

De Graafschap
Peter Bosz
18th ↓
1/8

An unrelentingly dismal season, huge defeats and almost permanent occupation of the relegation zone

RKC Waalwijk
Martin Jol
9th
3rd Round

Once again RKC was financially rescued by the local council, but the team plummeted at the end of the season and went out of the European places

NEC
Johan Neeskens
5th †
3rd Round

Neesken's team squeezes into the UEFA Cup places

Roda JC Kerkrade
Wiljan Vloet
6th
1/8

After steady progress all season, a disappointing result to lose its European place to NEC

NETHERLANDS

Groningen
Heerenveen
Zwolle
Alkmaar
Amsterdam
Enschede
Utrecht
Arnhem
Doetinchem
Nijmegen
Rotterdam
Waalwijk
Breda
Roosendaal
Tilburg
Eindhoven
Heerlen

NETHERLANDS

its form and PSV dropped points to lowly opponents, the gap steadily closed and Feyenoord came back into the frame as well. The pressure on the top two seemed to be telling when both went out of the semi-finals of the Dutch Cup, Ajax to Feyenoord and PSV to Utrecht. Utrecht then went on to win the tournament 4-1 over its Rotterdam opponents.

On the final day of the season, with the lead cut to three points, PSV still needed a point to take the championship, and its opponents, Groningen, also needed a point to keep out of the relegation play-offs. A 0-0 draw was duly served up, with the second half reduced to a display of ball rolling and jogging. For the neutral it was hard to see it as anything other than an act of collusion. Peter Boeve, coach at Zwolle, who subsequently went into the relegation play-offs, sourly remarked, 'For a team like PSV, who scored in almost every match this season, to end with a goalless draw against the 14th-placed side [sic] is a disgrace'. But it was enough for PSV who took its 17th league title.

International Club Performances 2002–03

CLUB	COMPETITION	PROGRESS
Ajax	Champions League	Quarter-finals
Feyenoord	Champions League	1st Group Stage
PSV	Champions League	1st Group Stage
Vitesse Arnhem	UEFA Cup	3rd Round
Heerenveen	UEFA Cup	1st Round
FC Utrecht	UEFA Cup	1st Round

Top Goalscorers 2002–03

PLAYER	CLUB	NATIONALITY	GOALS
Mateja Kezman	PSV	Serbian	35
Pierre van Hooijdonk	Feyenoord	Dutch	28
Dirk Kuyt	Utrecht	Dutch	20
Rafael van der Vaart	Ajax	Dutch	18
Thomas Buffel	Feyenoord	Dutch	18

Dutch Cup

2003 FINAL

June 1 – De Kuip, Rotterdam
FC Utrecht **4-1** Feyenoord
(de Jong 39,   (Kalou 72)
Gluscevic 49, 57,
Kuyt 81)
h/t: 1-0 **Att:** 45,000
Ref: Bossen

Right: The Swiftian character of Dutch football revealed. Ajax giant Zlatan crashes through NAC Breda's Lilliputian defence.

Ajax's van Dammart rises above the PSV melee.

It may be broke but Utrecht was the surprise winner of the Dutch cup, securing a place in the UEFA Cup after thrashing a below-par Feyenoord in the Final.

Top: Rene Vandereycken, coach of FC Twente, absorbs the meaning of the Dutch tax authorities' bankruptcy order on the club.

Above, left: Ronald Koeman, Ajax coach, traded the championship for European success this year.

Above, right: Guus Hiddink made a triumphant return to Dutch football after his South Korean adventure, coaching PSV to the title.

Left: Harpo Marx lives. Mateja Kezman (right) and Mark van Bommel lift the Eredivisie championship trophy on the final day of the season.

Below: PSV fans celebrate in central Eindhoven; replica championship plate sellers have a field day.

Amsterdam

FOOTBALL CITY

FOR THE MOST PART, Amsterdam is a city of footballing ghosts. RAP Amsterdam won the city's first league title in 1898 and the double a year later, but has left no mark. In 1972, a new professional club was formed – FC Amsterdam (from the fusion of three amateur clubs: Blauwit, De Volewijckers and DWS) – only to return to obscurity in 1982. The Olympic Stadium that housed the team sits empty. De Meer, the site of Ajax's greatest years, has gone. The old Jewish areas which provided a significant share of Ajax's support and players have shrunk. Jordaan, home to Surinamese immigrants and their families (including Ruud Gullit), has been gentrified.

Only on the south-eastern edge of the city at the Amsterdam Arena does football have its single, gigantic material expression. And even here Ajax must share it with a weekly roster of concerts and commercial events. Formed in 1900, Ajax has gradually migrated from its first playing field in Amsterdam Noord, down to the south-eastern edge of the city, settling at De Meer in the 1930s. A rash of league titles followed, but the club remained small and intensely local in its connections; a relationship so close that a special area has been set aside in the Westtergaarde Cemetery and laid with De Meer turf, where ashes can continue to be scattered long after the pitch has gone.

The total football revolution

What transformed Amsterdam and Ajax were the 1960s, Johan Cruyff and Rinus Michels. An outburst of political situationism and light anarchic protest erupted in the mid-1960s, bringing first inept police violence and then the elite acceptance that made Amsterdam a bohemian paradise. Out of this peculiar Dutch brew of playful anti-authoritarianism and liberation, Cruyff on the field and Michels off it added technical virtuosity and iron discipline to create the unstable but unstoppable 'total football'. In less than a decade, Ajax had gone from near relegation to triple European champions. Cruyff left in 1972 and the club eventually imploded, though its awesome youth training system (now a global phenomenon) created the team under Louis van Gaal who won the 1995 European Cup. However, the iron laws of post-Bosman economics saw the squad scattered to the richest clubs in Europe.

In its curiously rural setting, the De Meer had ivy-covered cottages in three of its corners which housed the stadium staff.

OLYMPISCH STADIUM

22,500

Club: Previously Ajax, FC Amsterdam
Built: 1928
Original Capacity: 24,700
Rebuilt: 2000
Significant Matches: 1928 Amsterdam Olympics; Ajax European matches; European Cup Final 1962; European Cup-Winners' Cup Final 1977

The old Jewish areas of Amsterdam have shrunk, but many Ajax supporters identify themselves and the club with Amsterdam's Jewish legacy, and have taken the Star of David as their symbol.

AMSTERDAM ARENA

51,324

Club: Ajax
Built: 1996
Significant Matches: 2000 European Championships: four matches including quarter-final and semi-final; European Cup Final: 1998

SPIERINGHORN

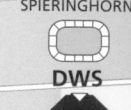

DWS

OSDORP

WESTTERGAARDE CEMETERY

Ringvaart

A9

BADHOEVEDOR

A4

Haarlemmermeer

NETHERLANDS

NETHERLANDS

ZAANSTAD

LANDSMEER

Noordhollands Kanaal

A10

TUINDORP
OOSTZAAN

Het IJ

A10

BUIKSLOTER-
BANNE

AMSTERDAM
NOORD

De Volewijckers

Ajax
(1900–07)

Het IJ

IJmeer

AMSTERDAM STOCK EXCHANGE
Ajax partially floated on Amsterdam
Stock Exchange in 1998

JORDAAN

THE HEART OF OLD
JEWISH AMSTERDAM
Amsterdam's substantial
Jewish community
was decimated by
German deportations
during the Second
World War

LEIDSEPLEIN
Traditional location for Ajax victory
celebration and site of surreal
'happenings' in 1960s

CAFE OOST INDIË
Ajax founded here
in Kalverstraat,
18 March 1900

FC Amsterdam
(1972–83)

A M S T E R D A M

HET HOUTEN
STADION

A1

LOTERVAART

JEWISH BUTCHERS
In the late 1960s and early 70s Ajax
players ritually ate Kosher salami
before home games from a Jewish
butchers in Beethovenstraat

DE MEER

Ajax
(1907–34)

ORTPARK
LOTEN

OLYMPISCH
STADION

DIEMEN

auwit

22,500

Ajax
(1934–96)

OUDE STADION
The Netherlands' first-purpose built
stadium was situated here and opened
in 1914. It was demolished in 1928 to
make way for the Olympish Stadion

BUITENVELDERT

Amstel

AMSTERDAM
ARENA

AMSTERDAM
ZUIDOOST

AMSTELVEEN

51,324

DE TOEKOMST
Ajax's youth academy

Ajax
(1996–)

OUDERKERK
AAN DE AMSTEL

A2

A9

Amstel

Amsterdam

51,324	Capacity of stadium
	Amateur club stadium
	Stadium no longer in use for top-flight football
	Team colours
	Amateur teams
M8	Motorway
A82	Major road
1900	Champions
2000	Runners-up

THE NATIONAL DERBY
'De Klassieker'

AJAX	FEYENOORD

Feyenoord play
in Rotterdam

148
matches
played

62 Ajax wins
50 Feyenoord wins
36 draws

0   50   100   150   200   250

NUMBER OF MATCHES
(All first-class games
up to August 2003)

AJAX 1900	
League	**1918, 19,** *28, 30,* **31, 32, 34,** *36,* **37, 39,** *46,* **47, 57, 60,** *61, 63,* **66–68,** *69,* **70, 71, 72, 73, 77,** *78,* **79, 80,** *81,* **82, 83, 85,** *86–89,* **90,** *91, 92,* **94–96, 98, 2002,** *03*
Cup	*1900, 17,* **43,** *61,* **67,** *68,* **70–72,** *78,* **79, 80, 81, 83, 86, 87, 93, 98, 99, 2002**
European Cup	*1969,* **71–73, 95,** *96*
European Cup-Winners' Cup	**1987,** *88*
UEFA Cup	**1992**
World Club Cup	**1972, 95**

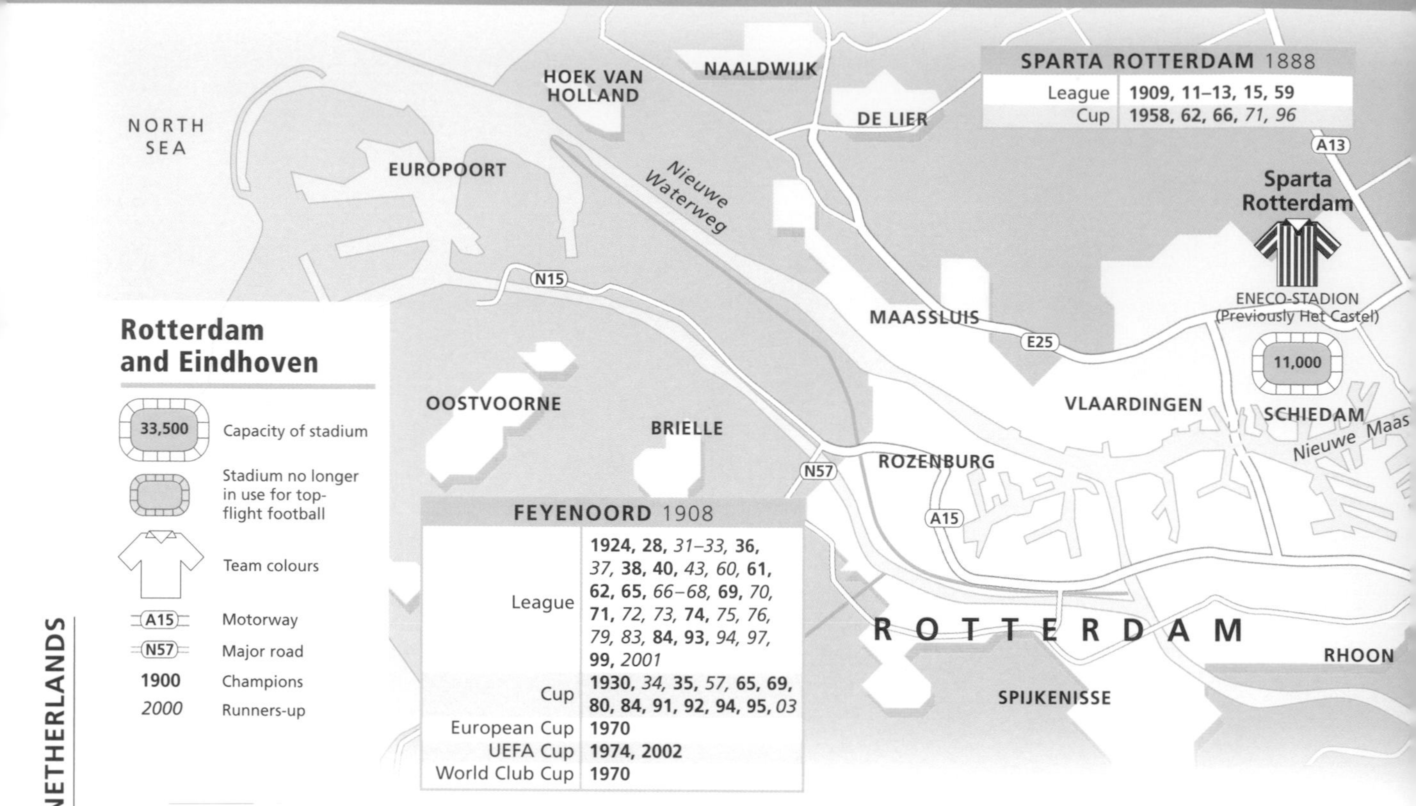

NETHERLANDS

HOEK VAN HOLLAND

NAALDWIJK

NORTH SEA

EUROPOORT

DE LIER

Nieuwe Waterweg

N15

A13

Sparta Rotterdam

MAASSLUIS

E25

ENECO-STADION
(Previously Het Castel)

11,000

Rotterdam and Eindhoven

33,500	Capacity of stadium
	Stadium no longer in use for top-flight football
	Team colours
A15	Motorway
N57	Major road
1900	Champions
2000	Runners-up

OOSTVOORNE

BRIELLE

VLAARDINGEN

SCHIEDAM

Nieuwe Maas

N57

ROZENBURG

A15

FEYENOORD 1908

League	**1924, 28,** *31–33,* **36, 37, 38, 40,** *43, 60,* **61, 62, 65,** *66–68,* **69, 70, 71,** *72,* **73, 74,** *75,* **76,** *79, 83,* **84, 93, 94, 97, 99,** *2001*
Cup	**1930,** *34,* **35,** *57,* **65, 69, 80, 84, 91, 92, 94, 95,** *03*
European Cup	**1970**
UEFA Cup	**1974, 2002**
World Club Cup	**1970**

R O T T E R D A M

RHOON

SPIJKENISSE

Rotterdam and Eindhoven

FOOTBALL CITIES

IF THE DUTCH are the Brazilians of European football, then Rotterdam is São Paulo – hard working, industrial, no-nonsense, perpetually comparing itself to bohemian glamorous Amsterdam. In footballing terms, the same comparison is made between Feyenoord and Ajax, a fact well demonstrated by the bitterness of their derby matches. Although Feyenoord can claim championships in every decade since the 1960s, and a European Cup in 1970, the team has always remained in Ajax's shadow.

Feyenoord was founded in 1908 in the heart of the old docks area, and there the club remains. Its stadium, De Kuip, was opened in 1937, surviving the carpet bombing of the docks during the Second World War only to disintegrate through neglect before renovation turned it into a venue for the 2000 European Championships.

Bitterness erupts
Feyenoord fans don't all come from Rotterdam, but from right across the Brabant and Zeeland regions as well. In the 1990s a hooligan element emerged; Ajax v Feyenoord matches were often seen as an excuse for organized violence, and fans fought street battles with the police after the Rotterdam club's 1999 championship victory.

The city's second club, Sparta, has scraped along in the top division for most of the century, apart from two golden eras of success in the years before the First World War and in the late 1950s. The city's third team, Excelsior, is as much Feyenoord's nursery club as anything else.

Southeast of Rotterdam, Eindhoven is a prosperous company town. The electronics giant Philips is headquartered there, employing 20 per cent of the population; it founded PSV in 1913 after a company sports event held to celebrate Holland's independence. Considerable sponsorship has seen PSV rise to the top of Dutch football. Across town, tiny Eindhoven ekes out an existence in the lower divisions.

***Feyenoord was founded** in 1908 in the old docks area of Rotterdam close to where its stadium, De Kuip, stands today.*

LEGERSBERG
Y COUNCIL
ditional site of
otball celebrations.
e of riots after
yenoord's league
tory in 1999
Excelsior
STAD ROTTERDAM
VERZEKERINGEN
3,500
CAPELLE
E25
Hollandsch
KRIMPEN
Noord
KROMME
ANDWEG
Sparta
otterdam
1895–1904)
DE KUIP
51,180
Feyenoord founded as Wilhelmina 08 by youths who played on the square in front of Wilhelmina Church on Oranjeboomstraat
E19
RIDDERKERK
RIKAANDER
PLEIN
Feyenoord
(1937–)
yenoord
(1908–17)
BARENDRECHT
A29
A16
PAPENDRECHT
ude Maas

stadion feyenoord

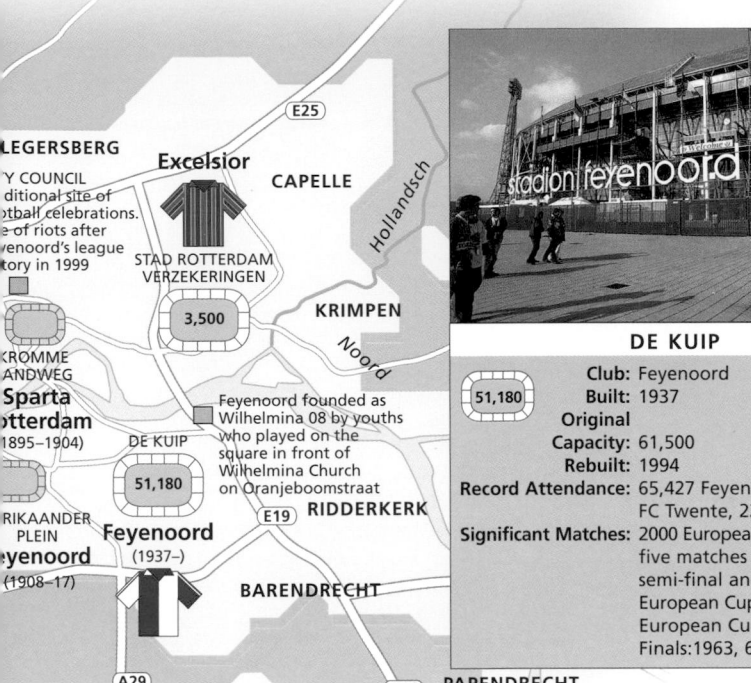

DE KUIP

51,180 **Club:**	Feyenoord
Built:	1937
Original Capacity:	61,500
Rebuilt:	1994
Record Attendance:	65,427 Feyenoord v FC Twente, 22 Dec 1968
Significant Matches:	2000 European Championships: five matches including semi-final and Final; European Cup Finals: 1972, 82; European Cup-Winners' Cup Finals:1963, 68, 74, 85, 91, 97

EMMELOORD
GROET
FEYENOOR

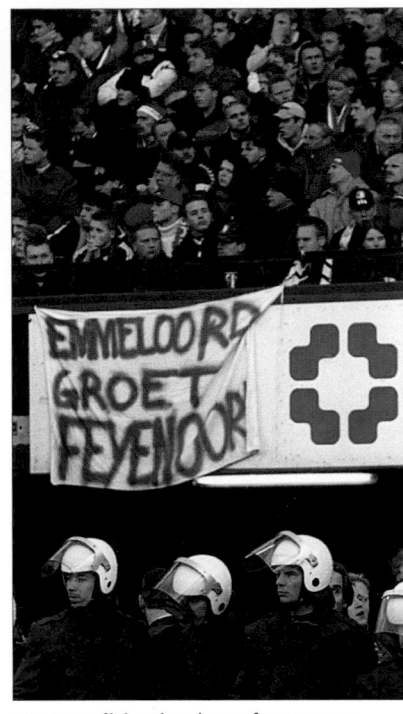

Heavy policing *has been frequent at De Kuip stadium since the rise of hooligan activity among Feyenoord fans in the 1990s.*

NETHERLANDS

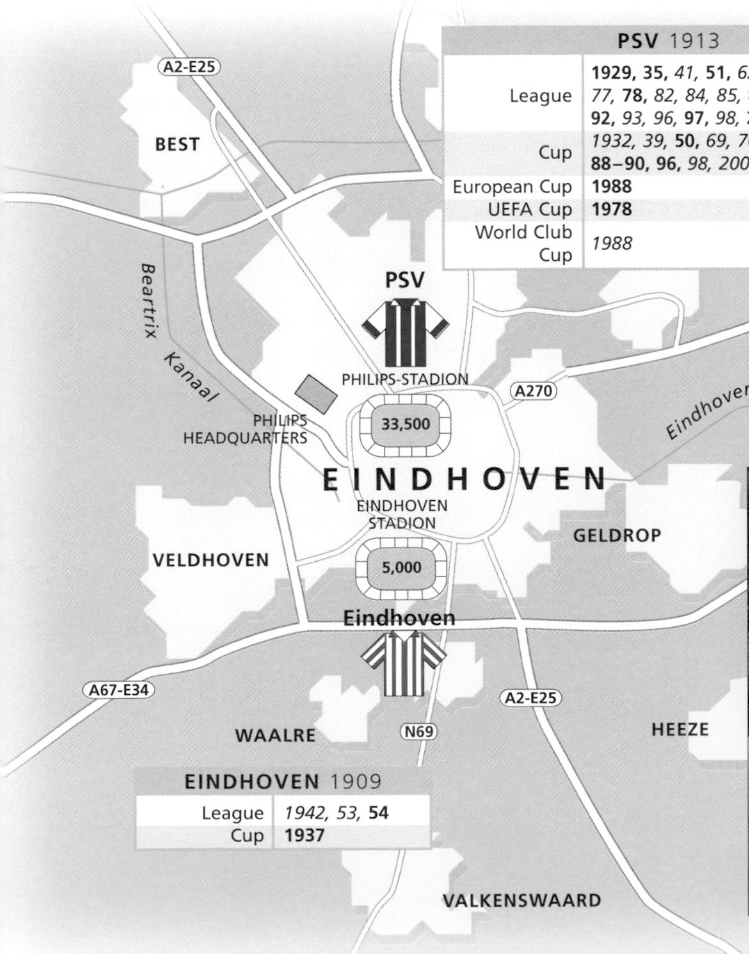

A2-E25
BEST
DE BRAAK
4,000
HELMOND
Helmond Sport
N270
Beartrix Kanaal
PSV
PHILIPS-STADION
33,500
PHILIPS HEADQUARTERS
A270
Eindhovensch Kanaal
N270
EINDHOVEN
EINDHOVEN STADION
5,000
Eindhoven
GELDROP
VELDHOVEN
A67-E34
ASTEN
A67-E34
A2-E25
WAALRE
N69
HEEZE
Zuid-Willemsvaart
VALKENSWAARD

PSV 1913	
League	**1929, 35,** *41,* **51,** *62,* **63,** *64,* **75, 76,** *77,* **78,** *82, 84, 85,* **86–89,** *90,* **91, 92,** *93, 96,* **97,** *98,* **2000, 01,** *02,* **03**
Cup	*1932, 39,* **50,** *69, 70,* **74, 76, 88–90, 96,** *98, 2001*
European Cup	**1988**
UEFA Cup	**1978**
World Club Cup	*1988*

EINDHOVEN 1909	
League	*1942, 53,* **54**
Cup	**1937**

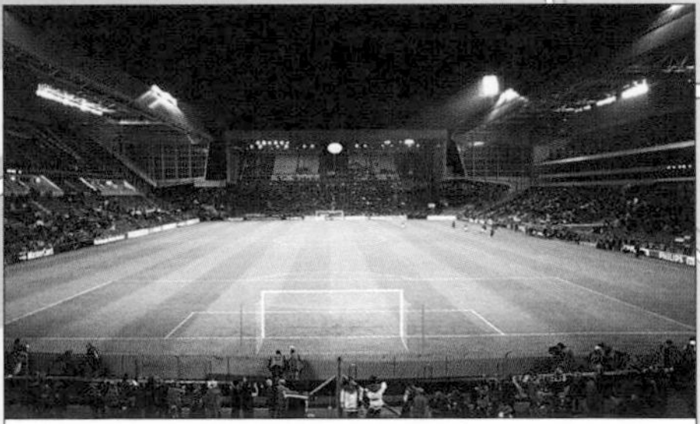

PHILIPS-STADION

33,500 **Club:**	PSV
Built:	1913
Rebuilt:	1999
Significant Matches:	2000 European Championships: three first-round matches

Netherlands

FANS AND OWNERS

PROFESSIONALISM AND COMMERCIALISM arrived late in Dutch football (1956 was the first professional season) and the ownership of Dutch clubs still reflects the amateur and social club character of the past. While many clubs continue as small membership associations, private investors have begun to take more significant shares in some clubs. PSV remains the property of the electronics giant Philips. Only Ajax has so far explored a further option – partial flotation. In 1997, Ajax was allowed to separate out its membership association and commercial activities. The club retained 70 per cent of the Ajax NV and the rest was sold on the stock market.

These four clubs are in a different league of income and attendances from the rest of the league, though they remain small by European standards. Dutch TV income is particularly small compared to the big leagues. The current economic crisis in Dutch football has plunged many clubs into debt and several city councils have been forced to act as lenders of last resort to keep the clubs in operation.

The not-so-jolly orange ranks

Dutch fan culture has many sides: from the newly-fashionable executive boxes of the Ajax Arena to the tiny, windswept stands of the small provincial clubs; from the absurdly jolly, mass-orange ranks that follow the national team; to the organized and violent *ultras* of Feyenoord and Ajax. An early occurrence of violence in Dutch football first appeared in the 1970s, when Tottenham fans started fighting at a UEFA Cup tie with Feyenoord. Since then, violence has been concentrated among Ajax, Feyenoord and Den Haag supporters. The peak of trouble was the mid-1980s, and led to intensive and complex policing measures and hefty bans from the courts. The problem has continued to simmer. In March 1997, Feyenoord and Ajax fans fought on an area of wasteland, resulting in one death. In 1999, Feyenoord fans celebrating the club's victory in the league began rioting and fighting with the police in the city streets. Euro 2000 saw a further development of Dutch policing methods, including highly visible preventative work, which was rewarded with the absence of trouble during the tournament.

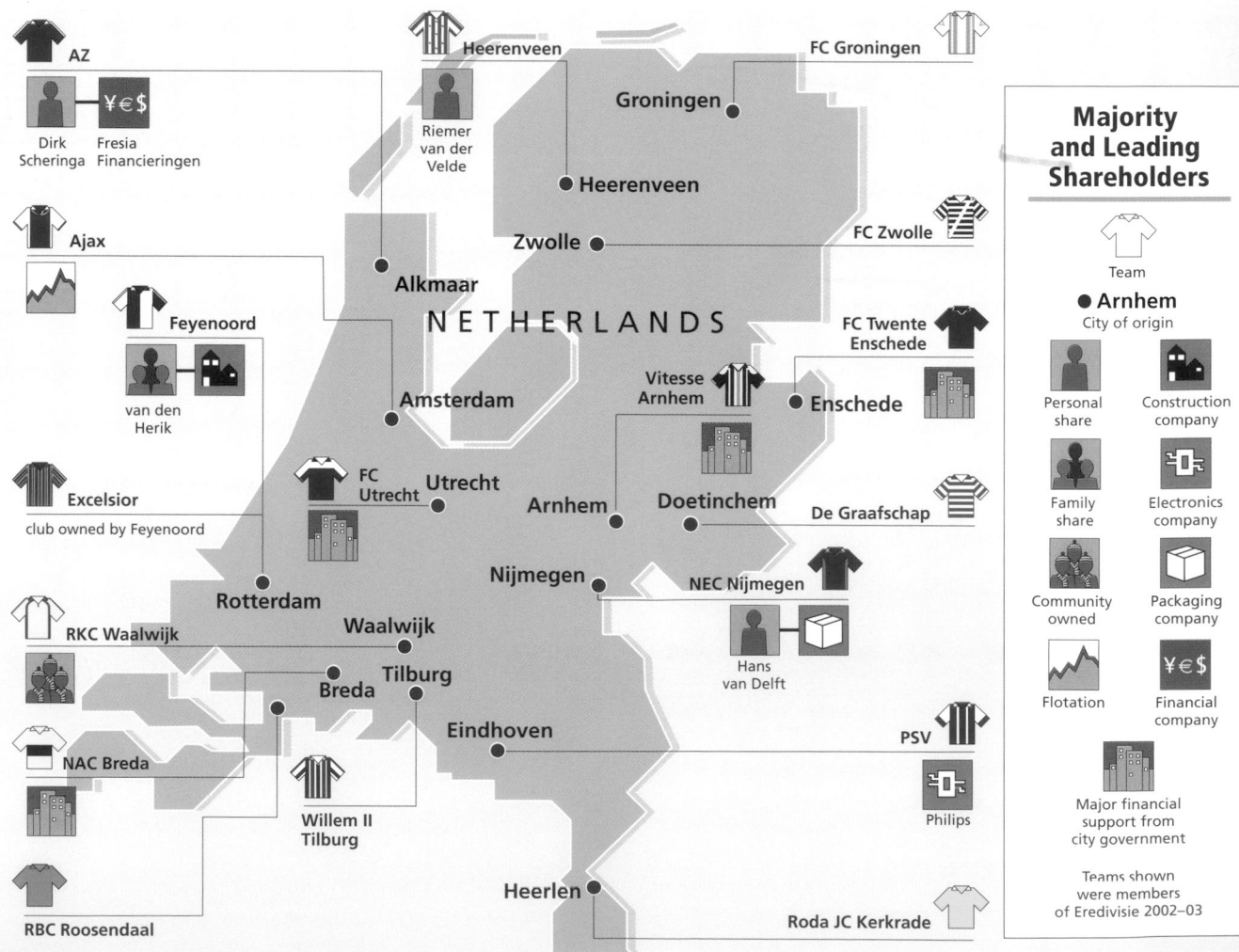

Club Budgets 1999–2000, 2000–01

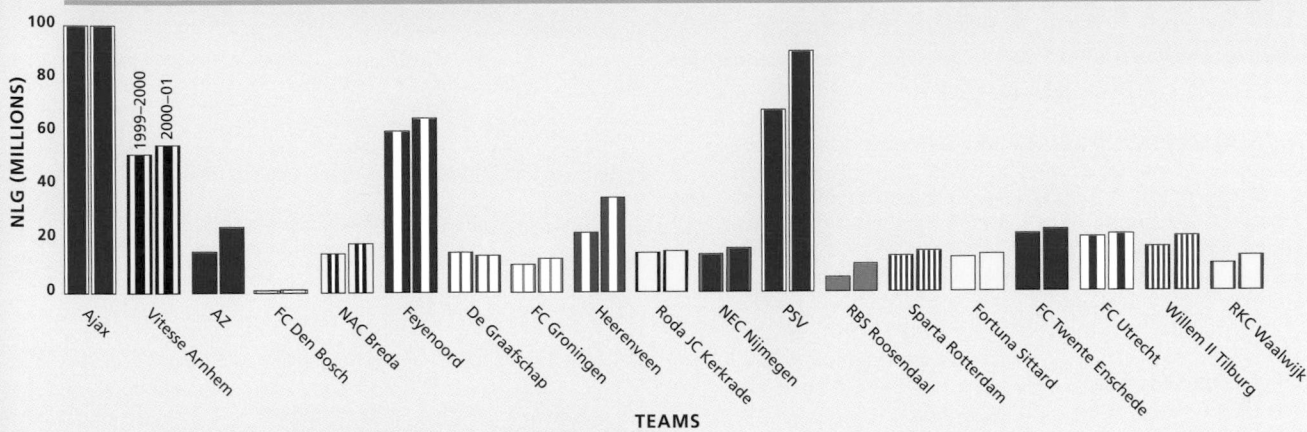

NLG (MILLIONS)

100
80
60
40
20
0

1999–2000
2000–01

Ajax, Vitesse Arnhem, AZ, FC Den Bosch, NAC Breda, Feyenoord, De Graafschap, FC Groningen, Heerenveen, Roda JC Kerkrade, NEC Nijmegen, PSV, RBS Roosendaal, Sparta Rotterdam, Fortuna Sittard, FC Twente Enschede, FC Utrecht, Willem II Tilburg, RKC Waalwijk

TEAMS

Rotterdam police arrest a fan after trouble at Feyenoord. In 2002 there has been a resurgence of trouble at Ajax as well, with the club threatening to lock fans out of the Amsterdam Arena.

Dutch Attendances

Attendances for each season

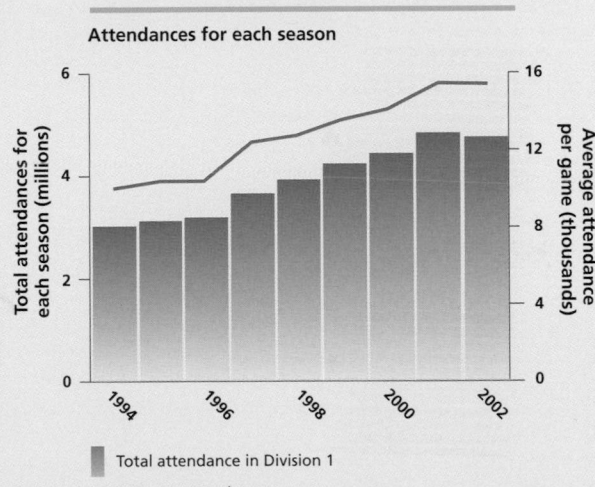

Total attendances for each season (millions)

Average attendance per game (thousands)

1994 1996 1998 2000 2002

Total attendance in Division 1

Average attendance per game in Division 1

NETHERLANDS

Average Attendance

Average attendance for season 2002–03 (thousands)

40 35 30 25 20 15 10 5 0

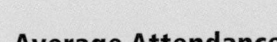

Capacity

Attendance as a percentage of capacity for season 2002–03 (capacity in brackets)

40% 50% 60% 70% 80% 90% 100%

TEAMS	
Ajax	(51,324)
Vitesse Arnhem	(29,000)
AZ	(8,320)
FC Den Bosch	(6,000)
NAC Breda	(16,400)
Excelsior	(3,600)
Feyenoord	(51,180)
De Graafschap	(11,000)
FC Groningen	(13,000)
Heerenveen	(14,300)
Roda JC Kerkrade	(19,500)
NEC Nijmegen	(12,500)
PSV	(33,500)
RBC Roosendaal	(4,995)
FC Twente Enschede	(13,350)
FC Utrecht	(14,220)
Willem II Tilburg	(14,700)
RKC Waalwijk	(7,500)

Riemer van der Velde, president of Heerenveen, has seen attractive small-town football pull almost sell-out crowds at home.

Netherlands

PLAYERS AND MANAGERS

ALTHOUGH FOOTBALL ARRIVED EARLY in the Netherlands, the game did not go professional until 1956, and the only truly great players of this long era were the suitably named Kick Smit and the Italian-suited Faas Wilkes, the dribble-king, whose departure to Valencia triggered the start of professionalism. In their wake, Dutch football was transformed by the social and sporting innovations of the 1960s. From the Ajax crucible of total football and the anti-authoritarian politics of the time a new kind of Dutch footballer was born. Exemplified by Johan Cruyff, Dutch footballers have come to prize technique and tactics above all else. Individual artistry, speed of thought, movement and accurate perception of space have become the hallmark of two generations of Dutch players since the amateur era. Along with Cruyff in the first wave of total footballers were Ruud Krol, Johan Neeskens and Johnny Rep. But self-possession, self-belief and ardent individualism among Dutch players has also been nurtured, and this has made for loose and fragmented teams.

More players overseas

In the 1980s, players of Surinamese origin, like Ruud Gullit and Frank Rijkaard, began to take their place in the Dutch team, and in the 1990s the ethnic divisions within the Dutch national squad boiled over into open conflict. With the advent of Cruyff, Dutch players started playing abroad in significant numbers and today their leading players are more likely to play overseas than those of any other leading European football nation: Edgar Davids, Dennis Bergkamp, Patrick Kluivert, Marc Overmars and the de Boer brothers have all played the bulk of their careers in Spain, Italy and Britain. Ruud van Nistelrooy, now of Manchester United, is just the latest in a long line of homegrown players whose exceptional performances in the Netherlands have seen them transfer overseas. Sadly for a country whose players possess so much talent, the national team has become the biggest underachiever in Europe.

Dutch coaches have proved almost as cosmopolitan as their players – Dick Advocaat coached Glasgow Rangers, Johan Cruyff coached Barcelona, Guus Hiddink won tremendous praise for his coaching of the South Korean national team at the 2002 World Cup, while Leo Beenhakker has recently made his way to Mexico's biggest club, América.

Top 15 International Goalscorers

PLAYER	GOALS	CAPS	FIRST MATCH	LAST MATCH
Patrick Kluivert*	38	69	1994	2003
Dennis Bergkamp*	37	79	1990	2000
Faas Wilkes	35	38	1946	1961
Johan Cruyff	33	47	1966	1977
Abe Lenstra	33	48	1940	1959
Bep Bakhuys	28	23	1928	1937
Kick Smit	26	29	1934	1946
Marco van Basten	24	58	1983	1992
Leen Vente	19	21	1933	1940
Mannus Franken	17	22	1906	1914
Tommy van der Linden	17	24	1957	1963
John Bosman	17	30	1986	1997
Wim Tap	17	33	1925	1931
Johan Neeskens	17	49	1970	1981
Ruud Gullit	17	66	1981	1994

* Indicates players still playing at least at club level.

Dutch International Managers

DATES	NAME	GAMES	WON	DRAWN	LOST
1973	Frantisek Fadrhonc	5	3	2	0
1974	Rinus Michels	10	6	3	1
1974–76	Georg Knobel	15	9	1	5
1976–77	Jan Zwartkruis	5	4	1	0
1977–78	Ernst Happel and Jan Zwartkruis	13	8	3	2
1978–81	Jan Zwartkruis	22	8	6	8
1981	Rob Baan	3	3	0	0
1981–84	Kees Rijvers	19	9	3	7
1984–85	Rinus Michels	34	19	8	7
1985–86	Leo Beenhakker	7	4	1	2
1986–88	Rinus Michels	20	12	5	3
1988–90	Thijs Lijbregts	13	6	4	3
1990	Leo Beenhakker	6	1	3	2
1990–92	Rinus Michels	19	11	4	4
1992–95	Dick Advocaat	26	15	5	6
1995–98	Guus Hiddink	37	22	7	8
1998–2000	Frank Rijkaard	22	11	8	3
2000–02	Louis van Gaal	14	8	4	2
2002–	Dick Advocaat	12	9	3	0

All figures correct as of 12 June 2003.

Top 16 International Caps

PLAYER	CAPS	GOALS	FIRST MATCH	LAST MATCH
Frank de Boer*	103	12	1990	2003
Aron Winter	84	6	1987	2000
Ruud Krol	83	4	1969	1983
Dennis Bergkamp*	79	37	1990	2000
Ronald Koeman	78	14	1983	1994
Marc Overmars*	74	16	1993	2003
Hans van Breukelen	73	0	1980	1992
Frank Rijkaard	73	10	1981	1994
Edwin van der Saar*	72	0	1995	2003
Jan Wouters	70	4	1982	1994
Patrick Kluivert*	69	38	1994	2003
Phillip Cocu*	68	6	1996	2003
Ronald de Boer*	67	13	1993	2003
Ruud Gullit	66	17	1981	1994
Wim Jansen	65	1	1967	1980
Clarence Seedorf*	65	11	1994	2003

Foreign Players in the Netherlands
(in top division squads)

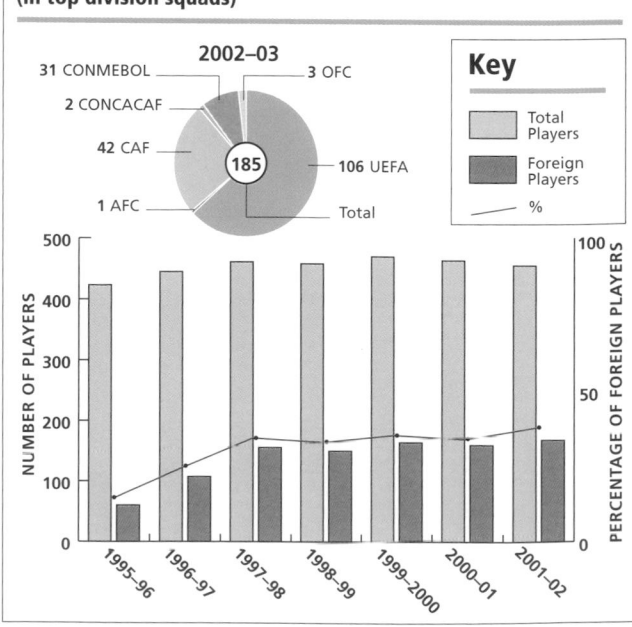

2002–03

31 CONMEBOL
2 CONCACAF
42 CAF
1 AFC
3 OFC
106 UEFA
185 Total

Key
Total Players
Foreign Players
%

NETHERLANDS

The Dutch national team has had little success during the last 30 years despite the amount of talent available. The most successful team was this one that won the European Championships in 1988 and which included (back row, left to right) van Basten, R. Koeman, Rijkaard, E. Koeman, Gullit, van Breukelen; (front row) van Tiggelen, Muhren, van Aerle, Wouters, Vaneburg.

Johnny Rep, a mercurial striker for both Ajax and the national team during the golden age of Dutch football in the 1970s, followed in the footsteps of Faas Wilkes when he left Holland to join Valencia in 1976.

NETHERLANDS

Player of the Year

YEAR	PLAYER	CLUB
1984	Gullit	Feyenoord
1985	van Basten	Ajax
1986	Gullit	PSV
1987	R. Koeman	PSV
1988	R. Koeman	PSV
1989	Romario	PSV
1990	Wouters	Ajax
1991	Bergkamp	Ajax
1992	Bergkamp	Ajax
1993	Litmanen	Ajax
1994	R. de Boer	Ajax
1995	Nilis	PSV
1996	R. de Boer	Ajax
1997	Stam	PSV
1998–99	van Nistelrooy	PSV
1999–2000	van Nistelrooy	PSV
2000–01	van Bommel	PSV
2001–02	van Hooijdonk	Feyenoord
2002–03	Kezman	PSV

Manager of the Year

YEAR	MANAGER	CLUB
1996	Louis van Gaal	Ajax
1997	Foppe de Haan	Heerenveen
1998–99	Leo Beenhakker	Feyenoord
1999–2000	Foppe de Haan	Heerenveen
2000–01	Martin Jol	RKC Wallwijk
2001–02	Bert van Marwijk	Feyenoord
2002–03	Ronald Koeman	Ajax

Awarded by the Dutch Professional Footballers' Association.

Top Goalscorers by Season 1956–2003

SEASON	PLAYER	CLUB	GOALS	SEASON	PLAYER	CLUB	GOALS
1956–57	Dillen	PSV	43	1980–81	Geels	Sparta R	22
1957–58	Canjels	NAC Breda	32	1981–82	Kieft	Ajax	32
1958–59	Canjels	NAC Breda	34	1982–83	Houtman	Feyenoord	30
1959–60	Henk Groot	Ajax	38	1983–84	van Basten	Ajax	28
1960–61	Henk Groot	Ajax	41	1984–85	van Basten	Ajax	22
1961–62	Tol	Volendam	27	1985–86	van Basten	Ajax	37
1962–63	Kerkhoffs	PSV	22	1986–87	van Basten	Ajax	31
1963–64	Guertsen	DWS	28	1987–88	Kieft	PSV	29
1964–65	Guertsen	DWS	23	1988–89	Romario	PSV	19
1965–66	van der Kuijlen	PSV	23	1989–90	Romario	PSV	23
1965–66	Kruiver	Feyenoord	23	1990–91	Romario	PSV	25
1966–67	Cruyff	Ajax	33	1991–92	Bergkamp	Ajax	24
1967–68	Kindvall	Feyenoord	28	1992–93	Bergkamp	Ajax	26
1968–69	van Dijk	FC Twente	30	1993–94	Litmanen	Ajax	26
1969–70	van der Kuijlen	PSV	26	1994–95	Ronaldo	PSV	30
1970–71	Kindvall	Feyenoord	24	1995–96	Nilis	PSV	21
1971–72	Cruyff	Ajax	25	1996–97	Nilis	PSV	21
1972–73	Janssens	NEC	18	1997–98	Machlas	Vitesse Arnhem	34
1972–73	Brokamp	MVV	18	1998–99	van Nistelrooy	PSV	31
1973–74	van der Kuijlen	PSV	27	1999–2000	van Nistelrooy	PSV	29
1974–75	Geels	Ajax	30	2000–01	Kezman	PSV	24
1975–76	Geels	Ajax	29	2001–02	van Hooijdonk	Feyenoord	24
1976–77	Geels	Ajax	34	2002–03	Kezman	PSV	35
1977–78	Geels	Ajax	30				
1978–79	Kist	AZ 67 Alkmaar	34				
1979–80	Kist	AZ 67 Alkmaar	27				

Netherlands

EREDIVISIE 1982–2002

IN 1981, THE SMALL PROVINCIAL CLUB AZ Alkmaar finally broke the stranglehold of the big three – Ajax, Feyenoord and PSV – by taking the Dutch league title. It was not to last, however, and the next 20 seasons have all gone to one of the big three. Ajax was the first to revive when Johan Cruyff came home from his foreign travels and took the club to two consecutive titles, including a league and cup double in 1983. Alongside Cruyff, the next generation of Dutch internationals was maturing, including the gangly 17-year-old Marco van Basten, Frank Rijkaard, Dennis Bergkamp and Aron Winter. Cruyff left Ajax in 1984, to manage its old rival Feyenoord. There he joined the young Ruud Gullit in a magical display of intelligent and zestful football. But financial decline and poor attendances followed, and the club was close to bankruptcy before being rejuvenated in the early 1990s by the money of building magnate Jorein van den Herik.

The rise of PSV

A further title for Ajax in 1985 was a prelude to the dominance of PSV. A top three spot for the team in the previous five seasons was finally converted into a title in 1986. PSV would go on to win another five titles in six years; only Ajax in 1990 under Leo Beenhakker could stop them. PSV was initially led by Hans Kraay, who systematically bought the leading players of the other top clubs in the country: Ruud Gullit came in from Feyenoord, Ronald Koeman from Ajax; two titles and a European Cup in 1987 followed. New manager Guus Hiddink added the goalscoring Wim Kieft and Dutch international goalkeeper Hans van Breukelen, and the titles kept coming. Gullit was eventually sold to Milan and with the proceeds PSV bought Brazilian striker Romario. He delivered over 100 goals in five seasons before leaving for Barcelona.

Ajax before Bosman

The rejuvenated Feyenoord under manager Wim Jansen took a surprise title in 1993. Then the new Ajax of Louis van Gaal, previously the club's youth coach, burst on the scene. Drawing on the legendary youth scouting and coaching system at the club, van Gaal nurtured and drilled a new generation of young Dutch internationals: Davids, Seedorf, Overmars, Bogarde, the De Boer brothers and Patrick Kluivert. Fast passing, awesome team play and deadly striking brought three titles and a European Cup. But with the Bosman ruling on transfers coming into force and the perennial pressures of money on the club, the squad was quickly scattered across Europe's biggest clubs. In the late 1990s, with no single dominant club, titles were split between PSV, Ajax and Feyenoord. The lack of competition

In 1984 the Feyenoord team featured Johan Cruyff, in his final playing year, and the rising star Ruud Gullit. The team took an unexpected and unforgettable title. This picture shows Ruud Gullit in action for Feyenoord against Fortuna Sittard.

Key to Champions' Winning Margin

Ajax	Feyenoord	SC Heerenveen
PSV	Roda JC	Willem II

lower down the league, and the meagre income from gates and television compared to the bigger European leagues, has left the big three looking for an alternative league to play in: Ajax and PSV have been leading forces in campaigning for the creation of either an Atlantic League (with the biggest clubs from western Europe's smaller nations) or a joint league with Belgium.

Ruud's roots

Among the challengers, the tiny SC Heerenveen has been the most surprising. Under a new president and coach in the early 1990s, Riemer van der Velde and Foppe de Haan respectively, the club has seen regular European competition. Clever buys from smaller footballing nations like Denmark, Finland and Romania were combined with nurturing and selling its own talent: Ruud van Nistlerooy being the greatest success. Vitesse Arnhem, under chairman Karel Aalbers, avoided bankruptcy in 1991, built the new Gelredrome stadium, but has yet to do better than third. Regular Eredivisie members include the solidly supported but limited charms of FC Twente Enschede, Roda JC Kerkrade, AZ from Alkmaar and FC Utrecht. While down at the bottom, a range of clubs come up and down the divisions and contemplate mergers and reorganizations in an effort to stay afloat.

Ruud van Nistelrooy's career typifies the dilemmas of Dutch football. A ruthless striker, he has migrated from tiny SC Heerenveen to PSV and on to Manchester United. He is one of many great players lost by a Dutch domestic game which cannot currently pay them enough.

Champions' Winning Margin 1992–2002

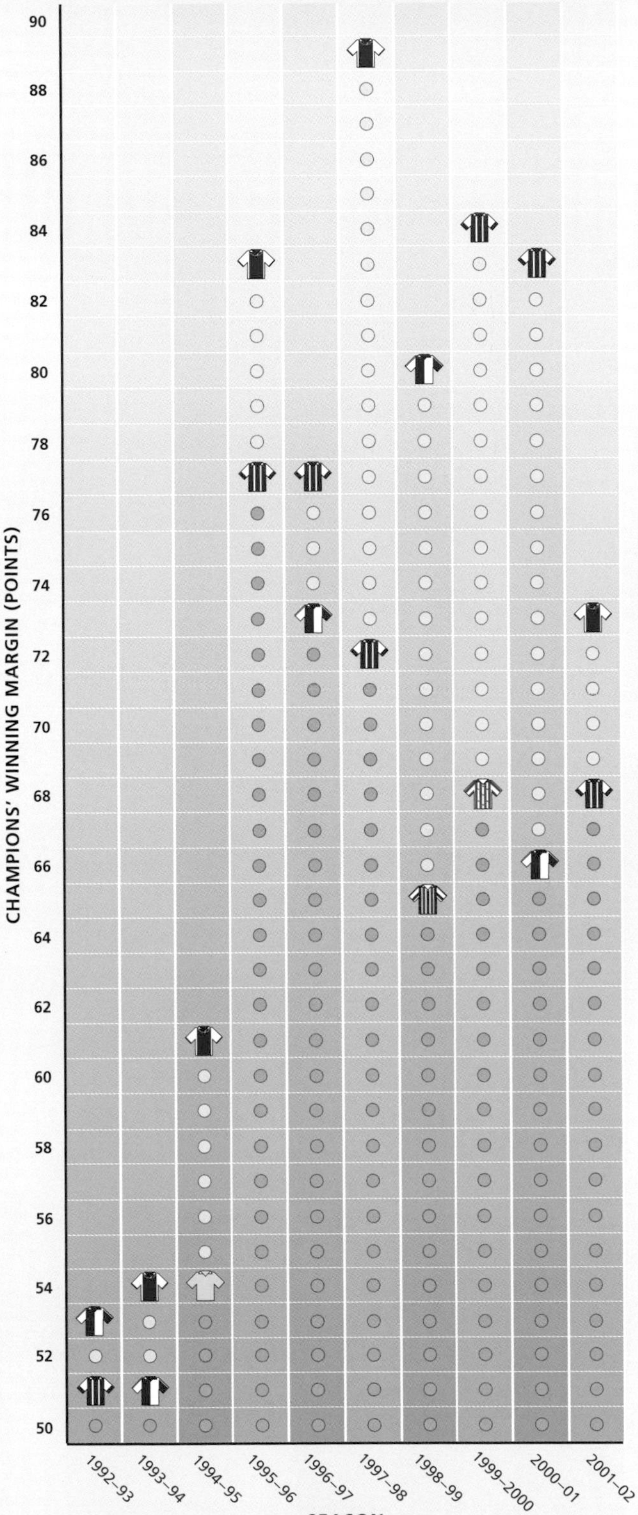

CHAMPIONS' WINNING MARGIN (POINTS) — y-axis from 50 to 90.

SEASON — x-axis: 1992–93, 1993–94, 1994–95, 1995–96, 1996–97, 1997–98, 1998–99, 1999–2000, 2000–01, 2001–02.

34	34	34	34	34	34	34	34	34	34

Total games played by each team
(2 points awarded for a win until 1996, when 3 points awarded)

NETHERLANDS

The strongest side in the Netherlands in the late 1990s, PSV is the model of a medium-sized modern club: it has corporate backing; it is careful in its transfer dealings; it has had huge domestic success, but has a poor record in Europe.

NETHERLANDS

Louis van Gaal, whose great young Ajax squads of the mid-1990s climbed the peaks of Dutch and European football, only to be dismembered in the transfer market, with van Gaal himself moving to Barcelona.

Ronald Koeman made a mid-season switch in 2001–02 from Vitesse Arnhem to Ajax and took the club from a mid-table wobble to a league and cup double.

Key to League Positions Table

- League champions
- Season of promotion to league
- Season of relegation from league
- Other teams playing in league
- **5** Final position in league

Dutch League Positions 1982–2002

TEAM	1982-83	1983-84	1984-85	1985-86	1986-87	1987-88	1988-89	1989-90	1990-91	1991-92	1992-93	1993-94	1994-95	1995-96	1996-97	1997-98	1998-99	1999-2000	2000-01	2001-02
Ajax	1	3	1	2	2	2	2	1	2	2	3	1	1	1	4	1	6	5	3	1
Vitesse Arnhem								4	5	4	4	6	4	6	5	5	3	4	6	5
AZ	11	5	13	9	15	16										18	9	7	13	10
FC Den Bosch		10	6	6	10	7	7	17			17							18		16
NAC Breda	17		17									7	10	8	9	12	18		9	6
Dordrecht '90									16	15	18		18							
DS '79		18					18													
Excelsior	9	13	12	15	18															
Feyenoord	2	1	3	3	3	6	4	11	8	3	1	2	4	3	2	4	1	3	2	3
Go Ahead Eagles	12	12	15	10	16						15	12	17	18						
De Graafschap											17			14	8	11	13	14	15	14
FC Groningen	5	7	5	4	13	11	6	9	3	5	12	15	13	9	10	17			14	15
ADO Den Haag			14	17				10	14	16										
Haarlem	7	4	9	11	12	9	10	18												
SC Heerenveen											17	13	9	7	7	6	7	2	10	4
Helmond Sport	15	16																		
SC Heracles						18														
Roda JC Kerkrade	6	9	11	5	4	15	5	5	10	9	11	6	2	4	6	14	5	8	4	13
SC Cambuur Leeuwarden												14	18				15	17		
MVV			14	16			14	15	15	7	7	10	16				15	14	16	
NEC	18		17						16	18			15	17	17	8	11	15	12	9
PSV	3	2	2	1	1	1	1	2	1	1	2	3	3	2	1	2	3	1	1	2
RBC Roosendaal																			18	
Sparta Rotterdam	4	6	4	7	8	12	12	12	13	8	13	9	14	6	13	13	17	13	17	17
Fortuna Sittard	8	11	7	8	9	8	8	7	12	14	16			13	11	7	10	12	16	18
FC Twente Enschede	16		8	14	7	3	3	3	6	6	5	5	5	10	3	9	8	6	11	12
FC Utrecht	10	8	10	12	6	10	13	14	4	11	8	14	12	15	12	10	12	10	5	7
BV Veendam					17		18													
VVV Venlo			13	5	5	17				18		17								
FC Volendam		15	16				14	9	6	9	13	6	11	11	16	14	18			
RKC Waalwijk							11	8	7	10	9	16	8	11	16	16	16	11	7	8
Willem II	14	17				4	15	13	11	12	10	8	7	12	15	5	2	9	8	11
FC Zwolle	13	14	18			11	13	16												

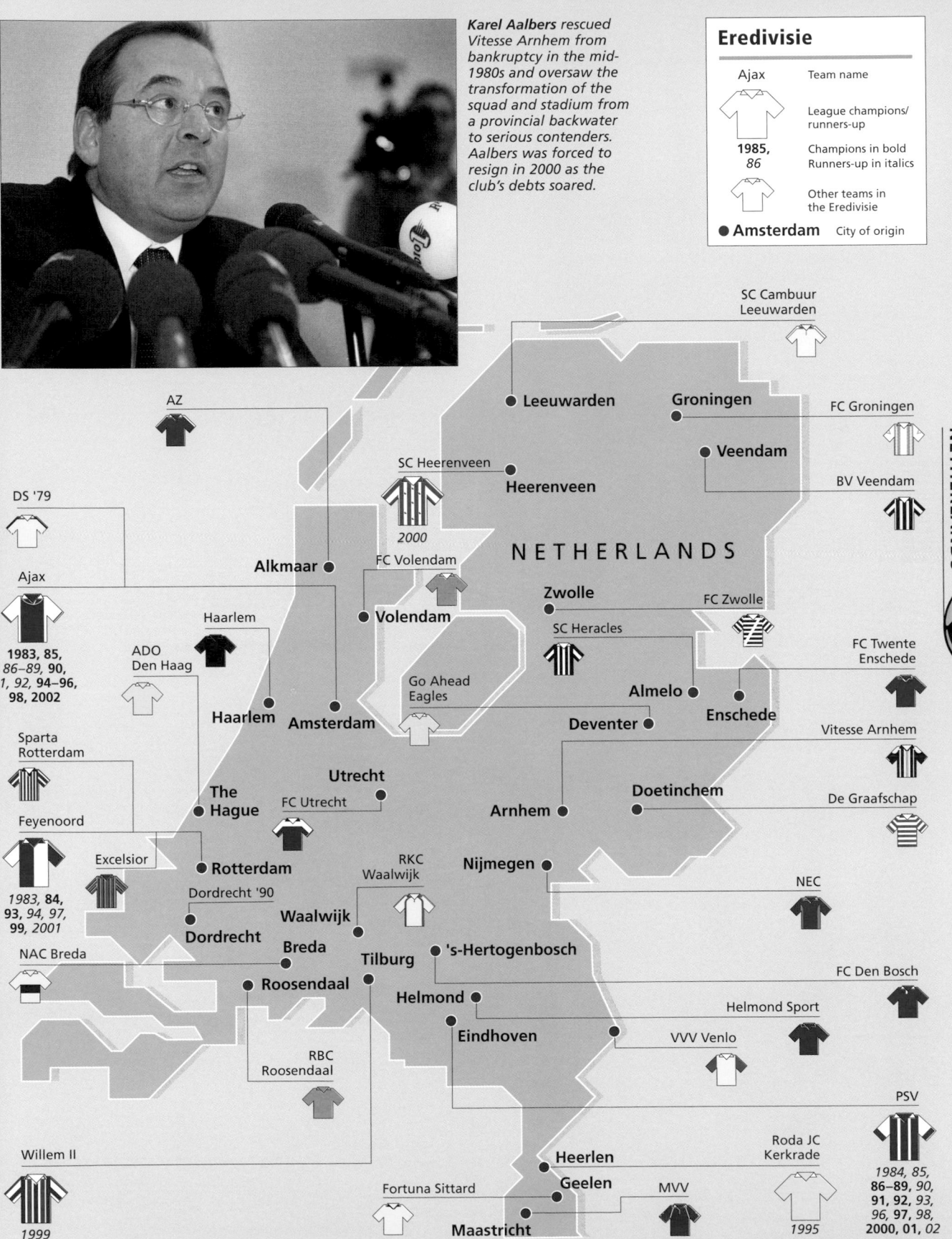

Karel Aalbers rescued Vitesse Arnhem from bankruptcy in the mid-1980s and oversaw the transformation of the squad and stadium from a provincial backwater to serious contenders. Aalbers was forced to resign in 2000 as the club's debts soared.

Eredivisie

Ajax — Team name

League champions/runners-up

1985, 86 — Champions in bold Runners-up in italics

Other teams in the Eredivisie

● Amsterdam — City of origin

NETHERLANDS

SC Cambuur Leeuwarden

● Leeuwarden

● Groningen

FC Groningen

● Veendam

BV Veendam

AZ

SC Heerenveen
2000

● Heerenveen

DS '79

NETHERLANDS

FC Volendam

Alkmaar ●

Zwolle ●

FC Zwolle

● Volendam

Ajax
1983, 85, 86–89, 90, 91, 92, 94–96, 98, 2002

SC Heracles

FC Twente Enschede

Haarlem

ADO Den Haag

Go Ahead Eagles

Almelo ●

● Deventer

● Enschede

Vitesse Arnhem

● Haarlem

● Amsterdam

Sparta Rotterdam

Utrecht ●

● Doetinchem

De Graafschap

Feyenoord
1983, 84, 93, 94, 97, 99, 2001

The Hague ●

FC Utrecht

Arnhem ●

Excelsior

● Rotterdam

RKC Waalwijk

● Nijmegen

NEC

Dordrecht '90

Waalwijk ●

NAC Breda

● Dordrecht

Breda ●

's-Hertogenbosch ●

● Roosendaal

Tilburg ●

FC Den Bosch

● Helmond

Helmond Sport

RBC Roosendaal

● Eindhoven

VVV Venlo

PSV

Willem II

● Heerlen

Roda JC Kerkrade

● Geelen

MVV

1999

Fortuna Sittard

1995

1984, 85, 86–89, 90, 91, 92, 93, 96, 97, 98, 2000, 01, 02

Maastricht

Netherlands

Koninklijke Nederlandsche Voetbalbond
Founded: 1889
Joined FIFA: 1904
Joined UEFA: 1954

FOOTBALL ARRIVED EARLY in the Netherlands with the first clubs being set up in the late 1870s. But somehow it took until 1956 for a fully-fledged national league to develop. The amateur era in Dutch football ran from the first national competition in 1898 until the legalization of professionalism in 1956.

It is truly extraordinary that despite being enveloped by two world wars the Netherlands has only lost one league season (1945) to social and political chaos.

Dutch Amateur League Record 1898–1956

SEASON	CHAMPIONS	RUNNERS-UP
1898	RAP Amsterdam	Vitesse Arnhem
1899	RAP Amsterdam	PW Enschede
1900	HVV Den Haag	Victoria Wageningen
1901	HVV Den Haag	Victoria Wageningen
1902	HVV Den Haag	Victoria Wageningen
1903	HVV Den Haag	Vitesse Arnhem
1904	HBS Den Haag	Velocitas Breda
1905	HVV Den Haag	PW Enschede
1906	HBS Den Haag	PW Enschede
1907	HVV Den Haag	PW Enschede
1908	Quick Den Haag	UD
1909	Sparta Rotterdam	Wilhelmina
1910	HVV Den Haag	Quick Nijmegen
1911	Sparta Rotterdam	GVC
1912	Sparta Rotterdam	GVC
1913	Sparta Rotterdam	Vitesse Arnhem
1914	HVV Den Haag	Vitesse Arnhem
1915	Sparta Rotterdam	Vitesse Arnhem
1916	Willem II	Go Ahead Deventer
1917	Go Ahead Deventer	UVV
1918	Ajax	Go Ahead Deventer
1919	Ajax	Go Ahead Deventer
1920	Be Quick Groningen	VOC Rotterdam
1921	NAC Breda	Be Quick Groningen
1922	Go Ahead Deventer	Blauw-Wit Amsterdam
1923	RCH Haarlem	Be Quick Groningen
1924	Feyenoord	Stormvogels Velsen
1925	HBS Den Haag	NAC Breda
1926	SC Enschede	MVV Maastricht
1927	Heracles Almelo	NAC Breda
1928	Feyenoord	Ajax
1929	PSV	Go Ahead Deventer
1930	Go Ahead Deventer	Ajax
1931	Ajax	Feyenoord
1932	Ajax	Feyenoord
1933	Go Ahead Deventer	Feyenoord
1934	Ajax	KFC Alkmaar
1935	PSV	Go Ahead Deventer
1936	Feyenoord	Ajax
1937	Ajax	Feyenoord
1938	Feyenoord	Heracles Almelo
1939	Ajax	DWS Amsterdam
1940	Feyenoord	Blauw-Wit Amsterdam
1941	Heracles Almelo	PSV
1942	ADO Den Haag	Eindhoven
1943	ADO Den Haag	Feyenoord
1944	De Volewijckers	VUC Den Haag
1945	*no championship*	
1946	Haarlem	Ajax
1947	Ajax	SC Heerenveen
1948	BVV Hertogenbosch	SC Heerenveen

Dutch Amateur League Record (*continued*)

SEASON	CHAMPIONS	RUNNERS-UP
1949	SVV Schiedam	BVV Hertogenbosch
1950	Limburg Brunssue	Blauw-Wit Amsterdam
1951	PSV	DWS Amsterdam
1952	Willem II	Hermes Schiedam
1953	RCH Haarlem	Eindhoven
1954	Eindhoven	DOS Utrecht
1955	Willem II	NAC Breda
1956	Rapid JC Heerlen	NAC Breda

Dutch Professional League Record 1957–2003

SEASON	CHAMPIONS	RUNNERS-UP
1957	Ajax	Fortuna '54 Geleen
1958	DOS Utrecht	SC Enschede
1959	Sparta Rotterdam	Rapid JC Heerlen
1960	Ajax	Feyenoord
1961	Feyenoord	Ajax
1962	Feyenoord	PSV
1963	PSV	Ajax
1964	DWS Amsterdam	PSV
1965	Feyenoord	DWS Amsterdam
1966	Ajax	Feyenoord
1967	Ajax	Feyenoord
1968	Ajax	Feyenoord
1969	Feyenoord	Ajax
1970	Ajax	Feyenoord
1971	Feyenoord	Ajax
1972	Ajax	Feyenoord
1973	Ajax	Feyenoord
1974	Feyenoord	FC Twente
1975	PSV	Feyenoord
1976	PSV	Feyenoord
1977	Ajax	PSV
1978	PSV	Ajax
1979	Ajax	Feyenoord
1980	Ajax	AZ 67 Alkmaar
1981	AZ 67 Alkmaar	Ajax
1982	Ajax	PSV
1983	Ajax	Feyenoord
1984	Feyenoord	PSV
1985	Ajax	PSV
1986	PSV	Ajax
1987	PSV	Ajax
1988	PSV	Ajax
1989	PSV	Ajax
1990	Ajax	PSV
1991	PSV	Ajax
1992	PSV	Ajax
1993	Feyenoord	PSV
1994	Ajax	Feyenoord
1995	Ajax	Roda JC
1996	Ajax	PSV
1997	PSV	Feyenoord
1998	Ajax	PSV
1999	Feyenoord	Willem II
2000	PSV	SC Heerenveen
2001	PSV	Feyenoord
2002	Ajax	PSV
2003	PSV	Ajax

NETHERLANDS

Dutch League Summary

TEAM	TOTALS	CHAMPIONS & RUNNERS-UP (BOLD) (*ITALICS*)
Ajax	28, *17*	**1918, 19,** *28,* **30,** *31, 32,* **34,** *36,* **37,** *39,* **46,** *47,* **57, 60, 61,** *63,* **66–68, 69, 70, 71,** *72,* **73, 77,** *78,* **79, 80, 81, 82, 83, 85,** *86–89,* **90, 91, 92,** *94–96,* **98,** *2002, 03*
PSV	17, *12*	**1929,** *35,* **41,** *51,* **62,** *63,* **64,** *75,* **76, 77,** *78,* **82,** *84,* **85,** *86–89,* **90,** *91,* **92,** *93,* **96,** *97, 98,* **2000,** *01,* **02,** *03*
Feyenoord	14, *19*	**1924,** *28, 31–33,* **36,** *37,* **38,** *40,* **43,** *60,* **61,** *62,* **65,** *66–68,* **69,** *70, 71, 72, 73,* **74,** *75, 76, 79,* **83, 84,** *93, 94,* **97,** *99, 2001*
HVV Den Haag	8, *0*	**1900–03, 05, 07, 10, 14**
Sparta Rotterdam	6, *0*	**1909, 11–13, 15, 59**
Go Ahead Deventer	4, *5*	*1916,* **17,** *18, 19,* **22,** *29, 30, 33,* **35**
Willem II	3, *1*	**1916,** *52,* **55,** *99*
HBS Den Haag	3, *0*	**1904, 06, 25**

This summary only features clubs that have won the Dutch League three times or more. For a full list of league champions and runners-up please see the League Records opposite.

Dutch Cup Record 1899–2003

YEAR	WINNERS	SCORE	RUNNERS-UP
1899	RAP Amsterdam	1-0 (aet)	HVV Den Haag
1900	Velocitas Breda	3-1	Ajax
1901	HBS Den Haag	4-3	RAP Amsterdam
1902	Haarlem	2-1	HBS Den Haag
1903	HVV Den Haag	6-1	HBS Den Haag
1904	HFC Haarlem	3-1	HVV Den Haag
1905	VOC Rotterdam	3-0	HBS Den Haag
1906	Concordia	3-2	Volharding
1907	VOC Rotterdam	4-3 (aet)	Voolwaarts
1908	HBS Den Haag	3-1	VOC Rotterdam
1909	Quick Den Haag	2-0	VOC Rotterdam
1910	Quick Den Haag	2-0	HVV Den Haag
1911	Quick Den Haag	1-0	Haarlem
1912	Haarlem	2-0	Vitesse Arnhem
1913	HFC Haarlem	4-1	DFC Dordrecht
1914	DFC Dordrecht	3-2	Haarlem
1915	HFC Haarlem	1-0	HBS Den Haag
1916	Quick Den Haag	2-1 (aet)	HBS Den Haag
1917	Ajax	5-0	VSV Velsen
1918	RCH Haarlem	2-1	VVA
1919		*no competition*	
1920	CVV	2-1	VUC Den Haag
1921	Schoten	2-1	RFC
1922–24		*no competition*	
1925	ZFC	5-1	Xerxes
1926	LONGA Lichtenvoorde	5-2	De Spartan
1927	VUC Den Haag	3-1	Vitesse Arnhem
1928	RCH Haarlem	2-0	PEC Zwolle
1929		*no competition*	
1930	Feyenoord	1-0	Excelsior
1931		*no competition*	
1932	DFC Dordrecht	5-4 (aet)	PSV
1933		*no competition*	
1934	Velocitas Groningen	3-2 (aet)	Feyenoord
1935	Feyenoord	5-2	Helmondia
1936	Roermond	4-2	KFC Alkmaar
1937	Eindhoven	1-0	De Spartan
1938	VSV Velsen	4-1	AGOVV
1939	Wageningen	2-1 (aet)	PSV
1940–42		*no competition*	
1943	Ajax	3-2	DFC Dordrecht
1944	Willem II	9-2	Groene Star
1945–47		*no competition*	
1948	Wageningen	0-0 (aet)(2-1 pens)	DWV
1949	Quick Nijmegen	1-1 (aet)(2-1 pens)	Helmondia
1950	PSV	4-3	Haarlem
1951–56		*no competition*	

Dutch Cup Record (*continued*)

YEAR	WINNERS	SCORE	RUNNERS-UP
1957	Fortuna '54 Geelen	4-2	Feyenoord
1958	Sparta Rotterdam	4-3	Volendam
1959	VVV Venlo	4-1	ADO Den Haag
1960		*no competition*	
1961	Ajax	3-0	NAC Breda
1962	Sparta Rotterdam	1-0	DHC
1963	Willem II	3-0	ADO Den Haag
1964	Fortuna '54 Geelen	0-0 (aet)(4-3 pens)	ADO Den Haag
1965	Feyenoord	1-0	Go Ahead Deventer
1966	Sparta Rotterdam	1-0	ADO Den Haag
1967	Ajax	2-1 (aet)	NAC Breda
1968	ADO Den Haag	2-1	Ajax
1969	Feyenoord	1-1 (aet), (replay) 2-0	PSV
1970	Ajax	2-0	PSV
1971	Ajax	2-2 (aet), (replay) 2-1	Sparta Rotterdam
1972	Ajax	3-2	FC Den Haag
1973	NAC Breda	2-0	NEC Nijmegen
1974	PSV	6-0	NAC Breda
1975	FC Den Haag	1-0	FC Twente
1976	PSV	1-0 (aet)	Roda JC Kerkrade
1977	FC Twente	3-0 (aet)	PEC Zwolle
1978	AZ 67 Alkmaar	1-0	Ajax
1979	Ajax	1-1 (aet), (replay) 3-0	FC Twente
1980	Feyenoord	3-1	Ajax
1981	AZ 67 Alkmaar	3-1	Ajax
1982	AZ 67 Alkmaar	5-1, 0-1 (2 legs)	FC Utrecht
1983	Ajax	3-1, 3-1 (2 legs)	NEC Nijmegen
1984	Feyenoord	1-0	Fortuna Sittard
1985	FC Utrecht	1-0	Helmond Sport
1986	Ajax	3-0	RBC Roosendaal
1987	Ajax	4-2	FC Den Haag
1988	PSV	3-2	Roda JC Kerkrade
1989	PSV	4-1	FC Groningen
1990	PSV	1-0	Vitesse Arnhem
1991	Feyenoord	1-0	BVV Den Bosch
1992	Feyenoord	3-0	Roda JC Kerkrade
1993	Ajax	6-2	SC Heerenveen
1994	Feyenoord	2-1	NEC Nijmegen
1995	Feyenoord	2-1	Volendam
1996	PSV	5-2	Sparta Rotterdam
1997	Roda JC Kerkrade	4-2	SC Heerenveen
1998	Ajax	5-0	PSV
1999	Ajax	2-0	Fortuna Sittard
2000	Roda JC Kerkrade	2-0	NEC Nijmegen
2001	FC Twente	0-0 (aet)(4-3 pens)	PSV
2002	Ajax	3-2 (aet)	FC Utrecht
2003	FC Utrecht	4-1	Feyenoord

Dutch Cup Summary

TEAM	TOTALS	WINNERS & RUNNERS-UP (BOLD) (*ITALICS*)
Ajax	15, *5*	*1900,* **17,** *43,* **61,** *67,* **68,** *70–72,* **78,** *79, 80, 81,* **83, 86, 87, 93, 98, 99, 2002**
Feyenoord	10, *3*	**1930,** *34,* **35,** *57,* **65, 69, 80, 84, 91, 92, 94, 95,** *2003*
PSV	7, *6*	*1932, 39,* **50,** *69, 70,* **74, 76,** *88-90* **96,** *98,* **2001**
Quick Den Haag	4, *0*	**1909–11, 16**
Sparta Rotterdam	3, *2*	**1958,** *62,* **66,** *71,* **96**
AZ 67 Alkmaar	3, *0*	**1978, 81, 82**
HFC Haarlem	3, *0*	**1904, 13, 15**

This summary only features clubs that have won the Dutch Cup three times or more. For a full list of cup winners and runners-up please see the Cup Record above.

Germany

THE SEASON IN REVIEW 2002–03

ALTHOUGH THE KIRCH MEDIA EMPIRE has long been reduced to dust and shredded balance sheets, the lingering effect of the collapsing value of TV rights remains poised to strike German football down. The German Football League (DFL) announced that revenues for the two top leagues would be slashed by 180 million Euros. More worryingly, the level of accumulated debt had risen to 600 million Euros. Even Bayern München was forced to think about reducing its expenses this season, as it crashed out of the first group stage of the Champions League and kissed goodbye to at least another 10 million Euros.

If that wasn't enough to upset Franz Beckenbauer – a very active member of the Bayern board – he had to contend with the demand from certain quarters within FIFA that the 2006 World Cup in Germany should be expanded yet again to an enormous 36 teams. Aside from smoothing the fevered brows of the South American football confederation, quite how nine groups of four can be made to yield 16 second-round teams without impossibly unfair runner-up places is anyone's guess.

Bayern's shock exit from the Champions League was not the only disappointment for Germany in Europe. Neither Leverkusen nor Dortmund ever looked like they would make it out of the second group, while Stuttgart and Hertha's stuttering progress in the UEFA Cup meant that the quarter-finals of both European cups were without a German representative.

Internal fighting, domestic dominance

Released from European obligations, Bayern was able to indulge in its favourite pastimes – internal fighting and domestic dominance. Scenting blood, the German press closed in on a number of Bayern stories. Goalkeeper Oliver Kahn was seen on a regular basis investigating the pleasures of Munich nightlife, indeed he claimed that he could write a guide to the city's hot spots. Coverage was quadrupled when he was snapped with a barmaid unknown to his pregnant wife. Coach Hitzfeld fared no better as old affairs and future contracts were a constant source of speculation. Frustration boiled over regularly on the training pitch as fines and reprimands were handed out like confetti: Bixente Lizarazu hit Niko Kovac, Michael Ballack fell out with Hitzfeld over tactics and Sammy Kuffour lost it with everyone.

However, while everyone enjoyed the show, Bayern remembered that it was a football club as well as a niche player in the gossip and glamour business. Relentless Bayern racked up the victories, taking a six-point lead by Christmas, one it never looked like relinquishing. Indeed, from the spring onwards, despite the odd upset, they never looked like anything other than champions. The class of Elber and Pizarro up front and Ballack and Scholl in midfield made it unassailable.

Bayern win again

As the footballing drama was reduced to a fight for the Champions League spots, Bayern kept things interesting. An ongoing and ugly conflict with former captain Lothar Matthäus was amusing, but was a sideshow to the newspaper revelations that Bayern had negotiated and banked a secret 20 million Euro bung from Kirch Media during the last sales of Bundesliga rights. Despite this additional payment being completely in breach of

Bundesliga Table 2002–03

CLUB	P	W	D	L	F	A	Pts	
Bayern München	34	23	6	5	70	25	75	Champions League
VfB Stuttgart	34	17	8	9	53	39	59	Champions League
Borussia Dortmund	34	15	13	6	51	27	58	Champions League
Hamburger SV	34	15	11	8	46	36	56	UEFA Cup
Hertha Berlin	34	16	6	12	52	43	54	UEFA Cup
Werder Bremen	34	16	4	14	51	50	52	
FC Schalke 04	34	12	13	9	46	40	49	
VfL Wolfsburg	34	13	7	14	39	42	46	
VfL Bochum	34	12	9	13	55	56	45	
TSV 1860 München	34	12	9	13	44	52	45	
Hannover 96	34	12	7	15	47	57	43	
Borussia Mönchengladbach	34	11	9	14	43	45	42	
Hansa Rostock	34	11	8	15	35	41	41	
Kaiserslautern	34	10	10	14	40	42	40	UEFA Cup (cup finalists)
Bayer Leverkusen	34	11	7	16	47	56	40	
Arminia Bielefeld	34	8	12	14	35	46	36	Relegated
FC Nürnberg	34	8	6	20	33	60	30	Relegated
Energie Cottbus	34	7	9	18	34	64	30	Relegated

Promoted clubs: SC Freiburg, 1.FC Köln, Eintracht Frankfurt.

Top: Stefan Effenberg, newly signed to Wolfsburg this season, signs his name for a fan. An average season in the field has been boosted by the publication of his warts and all biography.

Below: Klaus Toppmöller express his exasperation as Bayer Leverkusen plummet down the table.

Key

VfB Stuttgart

Team name and shirt colours	CL	Progress in Champions League
Manager	UEFA	Progress in UEFA Cup
League position	*	Qualified for Champions League
Relegated teams	†	Qualified for UEFA Cup
Progress in Cup		

Hamburger SV

Kurt Jara
4th †
3rd Round

A big improvement for Hamburg who can look forward to European football next season

Werder Bremen

Thomas Schaff
6th
Semi-finals
UEFA 2nd Round

When he turned up Ailton gave Werder a real edge, but after a real shot at a Champions League spot the team fell away in the second half of the season

FC Hansa Rostock

Armin Veh
13th
3rd Round

Is the club doomed to the lower reaches of the Bundesliga forever?

VfL Wolfsburg

Wolfgang Wolf, Jurgen Rober
8th
2nd Round

Volkswagen, Wolfsburg's ambitious owners, fired the surely perfect Wolfgang Wolf. Tobias Rau and the erratic Stefan Effenberg helped take them up to 8th

Hertha BSC Berlin

Huub Stevens
5th †
1st Round
UEFA 4th Round

Still not quite there. But Hertha got stronger as the season went on

Borussia Dortmund

Matthias Sammer
3rd *
2nd Round
CL 2nd Group Stage

After last year's championship, third was a real disappointment

Hannover 96

Ralf Rangnick
11th
2nd Round

Hannover received massive support for their return to the Bundesliga

FC Schalke 04

Frank Neubarth, Marc Wilmots
7th
3rd Round
UEFA 3rd Round

Five games without a win saw Neubarth lose the confidence of a cabal of senior players. Marc Wilmots took over the squabbling squad as a useful prelude to his career in Belgian politics

Arminia Bielefeld

Benno Mohlmann
16th
2nd Round

It's straight back down for Bielefeld

Energie Cottbus

Eduard Geyer
18th
2nd Round

Rooted to the bottom of the table at the halfway stage, a New Year streak of form was not enough to save them

VfL Bochum

Peter Neururer
9th
Quarter-finals

Despite some very barren patches, the best start of the promoted sides saw Bochum safely home

1. FC Nürnberg

Klaus Augenthaler, Wolfgang Wolf
17th
3rd Round

With just one win before the New Year it's amazing the team and Augenthaler lasted so long

Borussia Mönchengladbach

Hans Meyer, Ewald Lienen
12th
2nd Round

A quiet season for Mönchengladbach. The change of coaches barely disturbed the team

VfB Stuttgart

Felix Magath
2nd *
2nd Round
UEFA 4th Round

Magath's no-nonsense style and the goals of Kevin Kuranyi turned Stuttgart into serious contenders

TSV 1860 München

Peter Pacult, Falko Gotz
10th
Quarter-finals

A 6-0 thrashing at Hertha saw Pacult out the door, but it was mid-table for TSV again

Bayer Leverkusen

Klaus Toppmöller, Thomas Horster, Klaus Augenthaler
15th
Semi-finals
CL 2nd Group Stage

Fate is a cruel master. Last year's nearly men imploded under the pressure of injury and expectation. Disastrous league form was only rescued on the final day

1. FC Kaiserslautern

Andreas Brehme, Eric Gerets
14th
Runners-up

Only Bayern gave better entertainment value off the pitch. Brehme was fired after a disastrous start. Points were docked for next season, the team were 30 million Euros in debt and the stadium put in hock. Under the stern Gerets 7th and a cup final is the performance of the season

Bayern München

Ottmar Hitzfeld
1st *
Winners
CL 1st Group Stage

Training ground fights, secret TV deals, threats to leave the league and Bayern still found time to dominate the Bundesliga

Hamburg
Bremen
Rostock
Berlin
Hannover
Bielefeld
Braunschweig
Dortmund
Essen
Mönchengladbach
Leverkusen
Cottbus
Kaiserslautern
Nürnberg
GERMANY
Stuttgart
Munich

DFL rules, Bayern toughed it out. As the DFL threatened a points deduction, Bayern threatened to leave the Bundesliga altogether. Beckenbauer and general manager Uli Hoeness both suggested Bayern might take itself south of the alps and join Serie A. Bayern fans were seen holding banners at home games saying 'Milan, Lazio, Juve'. Whatever the political realities of the argument, the DFL caved in, accepting a pathetic 2.5 million Euro repayment and a small donation by Bayern to charity.

Back to the football

Back in the real world, the Bundesliga was divided between a handful of clubs chasing European places and the rest struggling to keep out of trouble most of the season. Among the chasing pack the strongest proved to be Borussia Dortmund and VfB Stuttgart. Dortmund proved organized and muscular and equal to Bayern in its head-to-head encounters, but inconsistency over the season cost it dearly. While last year's champions clearly underpeformed, Stuttgart, under Felix Magath, raised its game. Strapped for cash with a very young and untested side, but with regular goals from Kevin Kuranyi, Stuttgart dragged itself up the table and secured a priceless automatic spot for next season's Champions League.

Further down the table, the best sport was at crisis-ridden Kaiserslautern and Bayer Leverkusen. Kaiserslautern spent lavishly on upgrading its stadium in pursuit of a role in hosting the 2006 World Cup, and found that the cupboard was not merely bare but in hock to the bank to the tune of 30 million Euros. Worse, the DFL announced it would be deduct three points next season – if Kaiserslautern could get itself into sufficient financial shape to get that far – for financial irregularity. With dissolution threatening, the club sold prize striker Miroslav Klose's transfer rights and sold its stadium to a local consortium of government and business, renting it back from them. No wonder Andreas Brehme found the club a hard place to manage and, after a disastrous opening streak of form, he was fired and replaced by the tough Belgian Eric Gerets. Gerets dragged them up to seventh place – one of the stories of the season.

Below, left: Late season 0-0 draws are rarely a cause for celebration, but for Kaiserslautern coach Eric Gerets this one meant Bundesliga survival was assured.

Below, middle: The ball is round. Matthias Sammer, Dortmund coach, goes back to basics with his squad.

GERMANY

Above: Bundesliga president Werner Hackmann looks evasive as he tries to pick his way through the Bayern München TV rights scandal.

Below: Borussia Mönchengladbach hauled itself up the table and out of trouble with the goals of on-loan striker Mikael Forsell.

Bottom: The struggle for second place. Giant Czech striker Jan Koller rises above the defence in this clash between Stuttgart and Borussia Dortmund, who duelled for second and third place for the second half of the season.

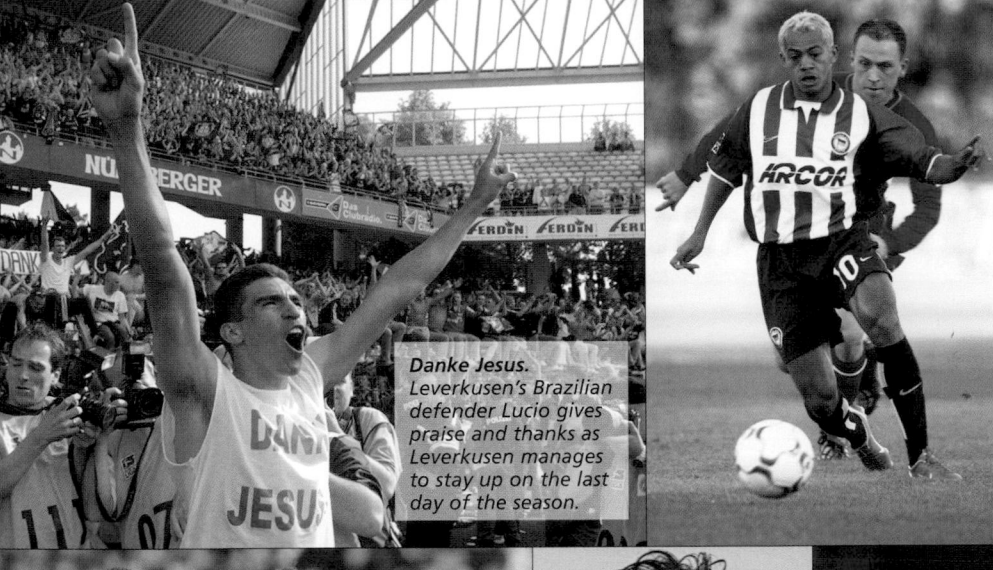

Danke Jesus. Leverkusen's Brazilian defender Lucio gives praise and thanks as Leverkusen manages to stay up on the last day of the season.

Left: Hertha Berlin's mercurial Marcelinho on the ball, pursued by Energie Cottbus's Timo Rost.

Below, left: Out of the frying pan into the fire. Schalke captain and coach Marc Wilmots announced his retirement from football and his entrance into Belgian politics…

Below, middle: … and the man who replaced him, new Schalke coach Frank Neubarth, smiling despite losing the confidence of the dressing room.

Below: Felix Magath brings old-time style and old-time values to Stuttgart. A Champions League spot followed.

Werder Bremen's Brazilian striker Ailton chases down the ball.

Race for the Championship

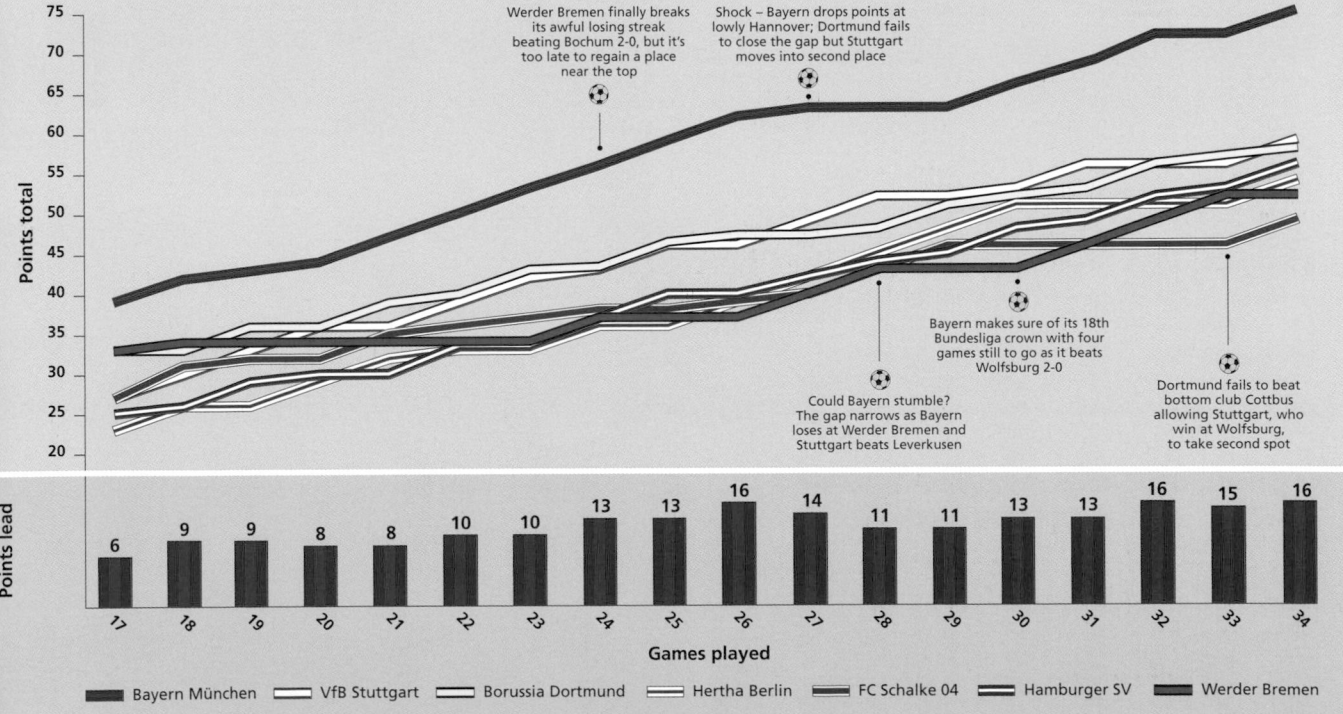

Werder Bremen finally breaks its awful losing streak beating Bochum 2-0, but it's too late to regain a place near the top

Shock – Bayern drops points at lowly Hannover; Dortmund fails to close the gap but Stuttgart moves into second place

Bayern makes sure of its 18th Bundesliga crown with four games still to go as it beats Wolfsburg 2-0

Could Bayern stumble? The gap narrows as Bayern loses at Werder Bremen and Stuttgart beats Leverkusen

Dortmund fails to beat bottom club Cottbus allowing Stuttgart, who win at Wolfsburg, to take second spot

Points total

Points lead

6 · 9 · 9 · 8 · 8 · 10 · 10 · 13 · 13 · 16 · 14 · 11 · 11 · 13 · 13 · 16 · 15 · 16

17 · 18 · 19 · 20 · 21 · 22 · 23 · 24 · 25 · 26 · 27 · 28 · 29 · 30 · 31 · 32 · 33 · 34

Games played

▬ Bayern München ▭ VfB Stuttgart ▭ Borussia Dortmund ▭ Hertha Berlin ▬ FC Schalke 04 ▬ Hamburger SV ▬ Werder Bremen

GERMANY

Leverkusen saves itself

Bayer Leverkusen, who had finished runners-up in both domestic competitions last season as well as the Champions League, knew that repeating last year's spectacular progress would be hard: the loss of Ballack and Ze Roberto to Bayern München would make it harder. But no one was ready for the calamities that were in store. Tired and disorganized, Leverkusen opened the season in disarray. There was no shortage of goals, but the defence was a sieve, injuries rapidly mounted, and worst of all, captain Jens Nowotny was sidelined for the first half of the season. But perennial optimists hungered for the end of the winter break, the return of Nowotny and the chance for revival. In the opening game Leverkusen went down 3-0 to bottom-placed Cottbus, and Nowotny snapped his ligaments all over again. Toppmöller's days were numbered and his place reluctantly taken by his deputy Horster. But the defeats kept coming. Bayer Leverkusen's director of football, Jurgen Kohler, began to panic and considered replacing Horster with Udo Lattek – the ex-Bayern coach – but £1.3 million for six weeks seemed a little excessive even for performing the impossible. In the end the club took on Klaus Augenthaler, who had recently been dismissed by the even more desperate Nürnberg. With the prospect of being the first manager to take two teams down from the Bundesliga in a single season facing him, Augenthaler confounded his critics and a mini late-season rally, including victories over TSV and Nürnberg on the last day, saw the desperate Leverkusen survive.

Bayern do the double

The last act of the season was the Cup Final between Bayern and Kaiserslautern at the Olympiastadion in Berlin, and inevitably it was Bayern who carried the day. Two goals from Michael Ballack in the opening ten minutes gave Bayern their usual lead, and Claudio Pizarro scored another early in the second half. Miroslav Klose got one back ten minutes from time, but it was too little, too late. However, a place in the UEFA Cup was a good return for Geret's efforts in the hot seat at Kaiserslautern.

Top, right: Franz Beckenbauer seems pleased with himself. Despite crossing swords with FIFA, the DFB, the Bundesliga and the players of his own club, Bayern's Kaiser has kept Germany's World Cup show on the road.

Claudio Pizarro heads home for Bayern against Hertha. Together he and Giovane Elber scored 37 goals – over half of Bayern's total.

Facing the music: Karl-Heinz Rummenigge, Bayern Munich's general manager, tries to explain Bayern's appalling form in the Champions League and the team's financially punitive exit from the competition's first stage.

German Cup

2003 FINAL

May 31 – Olympiastadion, Berlin
Bayern 3-1 Kaiserslautern
München   (Klose 80)
(Ballack 3, 10 pen,
Pizarro 50)
h/t: 2-0 **Att:** 70,490
Ref: Friehlich

Bundesliga Top Goalscorers 2002–03

PLAYER	CLUB	NATIONALITY	GOALS
Thomas Christiansen	VfL Bochum	German	21
Giovane Elber	Bayern München	Brazilian	21
Ailton	Werder Bremen	Brazilian	16
Kevin Kuranyi	VfB Stuttgart	German	15
Claudio Pizarro	Bayern München	Peruvian	15

International Club Performances 2002–03

CLUB	COMPETITION	PROGRESS
Borussia Dortmund	Champions League	2nd Group Stage
Bayer Leverkusen	Champions League	2nd Group Stage
Bayern München	Champions League	1st Group Stage
Hertha BSC Berlin	UEFA Cup	4th Round
Werder Bremen	UEFA Cup	2nd Round
FC Schalke 04	UEFA Cup	3rd Round
VfB Stuttgart	UEFA Cup	4th Round

Far left: Ottmar Hitzfeld, Bayern coach, feels the strain: the Bundesliga aside, an early exit from the Champions League and tabloid revelations about his personal life made it a very hot seat at Bayern this season.

Left: Here we go again. After last year's embarrassing absence of city-centre football celebrations, Bayern's fans are back. Celebrations break out in front of the city hall in the Marienplatz, Munich, as Bayern claim its latest Bundesliga crown.

Below: Michael Ballack and Oliver Kahn lift the Bundesliga trophy after Bayern's match with Stuttgart.

Below, bottom: Big hands, big cup. Bayern's captain Oliver Kahn lifts the German cup as Bayern do the double. Kahn announced this season that he knew Munich nightlife so well he could write a guidebook. Maybe he could take the cup on a pub-crawl.

Michael Ballack finishes off a good season for himself by heading the opening goal in Bayern's Cup Final victory over Kaiserslautern.

Association Football in Germany

GERMANY

1887: First football only club created – SC Germania Hamburg

1898: First regional leagues – Southern Germany and Berlin

1900: Formation of FA: Deutscher Fussball-Bund

1902: First national championships

1904: Affiliation to FIFA. First international, v Switzerland, won 1-0, venue: Stuttgart

1930: Schalke 04 banned by DFB for professionalism

1933: German government ban Jews from football club membership

1938: Anschluss with Austria, Austrian teams played in German championships until 1944

1944: German Cup abandoned

1952: East German FA readmitted to FIFA

1953: East German Cup abandoned due to Berlin uprising. West German Cup re-established

1954: East and West German affiliation to UEFA

1955: DFB bans affiliated clubs from letting women use their grounds. West German Women's Football Association founded in Essen

1956: First women's international, v Netherlands, won 2-1, venue: Essen

1961: East German Cup and League abandoned. Berlin wall erected

1963: West German Bundesliga established

1970: DFB ban on women at affiliated clubs lifted

1990: East German FA dissolved into all German FA, two Bundesliga places only for eastern teams

1997: Borussia Dortmund become first German club partially floated on stock exchange

2002: Kirch Media collapses causing financial crisis. Germany awarded 2006 World Cup finals

1935: German Cup established

1945–48: No national championships

1946: Expelled from FIFA

1948: East German FA created, national championships begin in East and West

1950: West German FA readmitted to FIFA

Timeline years: 1885, 1890, 1895, 1900, 1905, 1910, 1915, 1920, 1925, 1930, 1935, 1940, 1945, 1950, 1955, 1960, 1965, 1970, 1975, 1980, 1985, 1990, 1995, 2000, 2005

Key

International football

Affiliation to FIFA

Affiliation to UEFA

Women's football

War

■ World Cup host
● World Cup winner
▲ World Cup runner-up
■ European Championships host
● European Championships winner
▲ European Championships runner-up
○ Competition winner
△ Competition runner-up

BayL – Bayer Leverkusen
BayM – Bayern München
BorD – Borussia Dortmund
BorM – Borussia Mönchengladbach
Carl – Carl Zeiss Jena
Ein – Eintracht Frankfurt
For – Fortuna Düsseldorf
Ham – Hamburger SV
Köln – 1.FC Köln
Loko – Lokomotive Leipzig
Mag – FC Magdeburg
Schl – FC Schalke 04
Stutt – VfB Stuttgart
TSV – TSV 1860 München
Wer – Werder Bremen

International Competitions

Year	International Competitions	European Cup	UEFA Cup	European Cup-Winners' Cup
1954:	●			
1960:		△ Ein		
1965:	▲			△ TSV
1966:				○ BorD
1967:				○ BayM
1968:				△ Ham
1972:	●		△ BorM	
1973:				
1974:	● ■	○ BayM		○ Mag
1975:	■	○ BayM	○ BorM	
1976:	●	○ BayM		
1977:		△ BorM		○ Ham
1979:		△ Ham	○ BorM	△ For
1980:	●		△ Ein △ BorM	
1981:				△ Carl
1982:	▲	△ BayM	△ Ham	
1983:		○ Ham		
1986:	▲		△ Köln	
1987:		△ BayM		△ Loko
1988:	■		○ BayL	
1989:			△ Stutt	
1990:	●			
1992:	▲			○ Wer
1993:			△ BorD	
1996:	●		○ BayM	
1997:		○ BorD	△ Schl	
1998:				
1999:		△ BayM		△ Stutt
2001:		○ BayM		
2002:	▲	△ BayM	○ BorD	

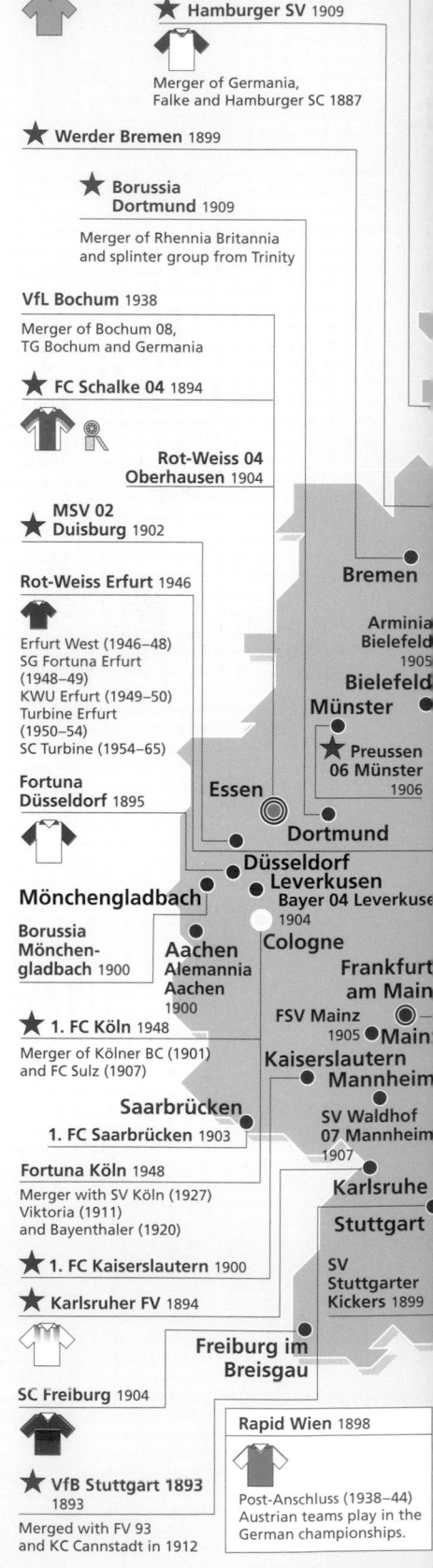

Holstein Kiel 1900

Hamburger SV 1909
Merger of Germania, Falke and Hamburger SC 1887

Werder Bremen 1899

Borussia Dortmund 1909
Merger of Rhennia Britannia and splinter group from Trinity

VfL Bochum 1938
Merger of Bochum 08, TG Bochum and Germania

FC Schalke 04 1894

Rot-Weiss 04 Oberhausen 1904

MSV 02 Duisburg 1902

Rot-Weiss Erfurt 1946
Erfurt West (1946–48)
SG Fortuna Erfurt (1948–49)
KWU Erfurt (1949–50)
Turbine Erfurt (1950–54)
SC Turbine (1954–65)

Fortuna Düsseldorf 1895

Mönchengladbach
Borussia Mönchen-gladbach 1900

1. FC Köln 1948
Merger of Kölner BC (1901) and FC Sulz (1907)

Fortuna Köln 1948
Merger with SV Köln (1927) Viktoria (1911) and Bayenthaler (1920)

1. FC Kaiserslautern 1900

Karlsruher FV 1894

SC Freiburg 1904

VfB Stuttgart 1893 1893
Merged with FV 93 and KC Cannstadt in 1912

Bremen

Arminia Bielefeld 1905

Bielefeld

Münster

Preussen 06 Münster 1906

Essen

Dortmund

Düsseldorf

Leverkusen
Bayer 04 Leverkusen 1904

Aachen
Alemannia Aachen 1900

Cologne

Frankfurt am Main

FSV Mainz 1905

Mainz

Kaiserslautern

Mannheim

Saarbrücken
1. FC Saarbrücken 1903

SV Waldhof 07 Mannheim 1907

Karlsruhe

Stuttgart
SV Stuttgarter Kickers 1899

Freiburg im Breisgau

Rapid Wien 1898
Post-Anschluss (1938–44) Austrian teams play in the German championships.

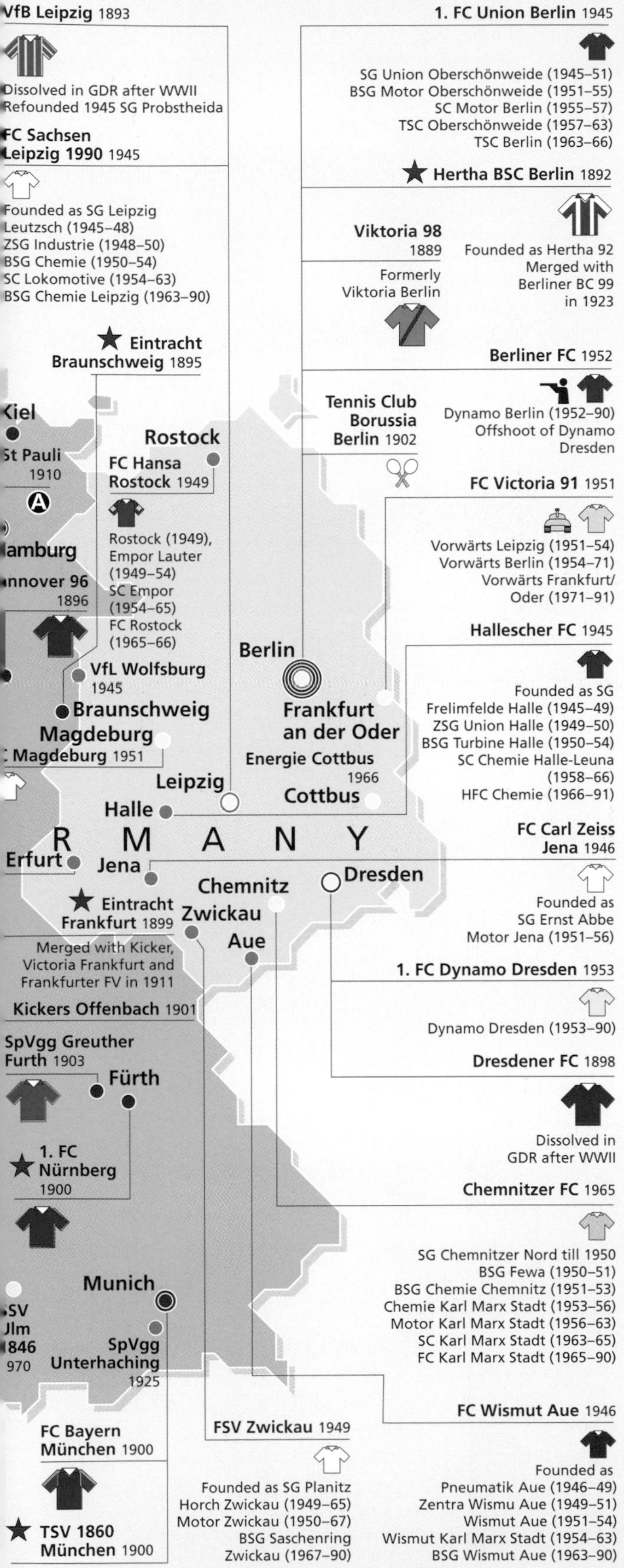

VfB Leipzig 1893

Dissolved in GDR after WWII
Refounded 1945 SG Probstheida

FC Sachsen Leipzig 1990 1945

Founded as SG Leipzig
Leutzsch (1945–48)
ZSG Industrie (1948–50)
BSG Chemie (1950–54)
SC Lokomotive (1954–63)
BSG Chemie Leipzig (1963–90)

★ **Eintracht Braunschweig** 1895

Kiel

St Pauli 1910 Ⓐ

Rostock

FC Hansa Rostock 1949

Rostock (1949),
Empor Lauter
(1949–54)
SC Empor
(1954–65)
FC Rostock
(1965–66)

Hamburg

Hannover 96 1896

VfL Wolfsburg 1945

Braunschweig

Magdeburg

Magdeburg 1951

Berlin

Leipzig

Halle

Frankfurt an der Oder

Energie Cottbus 1966

Cottbus

G E R M A N Y

Erfurt   **Jena**

★ **Eintracht Frankfurt** 1899

Merged with Kicker,
Victoria Frankfurt and
Frankfurter FV in 1911

Chemnitz
Zwickau
Aue

Dresden

Kickers Offenbach 1901

SpVgg Greuther Fürth 1903

Fürth

★ **1. FC Nürnberg** 1900

Munich

SV Ulm 1846 1970

SpVgg Unterhaching 1925

FC Bayern München 1900

FSV Zwickau 1949

Founded as SG Planitz
Horch Zwickau (1949–65)
Motor Zwickau (1950–67)
BSG Sachsenring
Zwickau (1967–90)

★ **TSV 1860 München** 1900

---

1. FC Union Berlin 1945

SG Union Oberschöneweide (1945–51)
BSG Motor Oberschöneweide (1951–55)
SC Motor Berlin (1955–57)
TSC Oberschöneweide (1957–63)
TSC Berlin (1963–66)

★ **Hertha BSC Berlin** 1892

Viktoria 98 1889

Formerly
Viktoria Berlin

Founded as Hertha 92
Merged with
Berliner BC 99
in 1923

Berliner FC 1952

Dynamo Berlin (1952–90)
Offshoot of Dynamo
Dresden

Tennis Club Borussia Berlin 1902

FC Victoria 91 1951

Vorwärts Leipzig (1951–54)
Vorwärts Berlin (1954–71)
Vorwärts Frankfurt/
Oder (1971–91)

Hallescher FC 1945

Founded as SG
Frelimfelde Halle (1945–49)
ZSG Union Halle (1949–50)
BSG Turbine Halle (1950–54)
SC Chemie Halle-Leuna
(1958–66)
HFC Chemie (1966–91)

FC Carl Zeiss Jena 1946

Founded as
SG Ernst Abbe
Motor Jena (1951–56)

1. FC Dynamo Dresden 1953

Dynamo Dresden (1953–90)

Dresdener FC 1898

Dissolved in
GDR after WWII

Chemnitzer FC 1965

SG Chemnitzer Nord till 1950
BSG Fewa (1950–51)
BSG Chemie Chemnitz (1951–53)
Chemie Karl Marx Stadt (1953–56)
Motor Karl Marx Stadt (1956–63)
SC Karl Marx Stadt (1963–65)
FC Karl Marx Stadt (1965–90)

FC Wismut Aue 1946

Founded as
Pneumatik Aue (1946–49)
Zentra Wismu Aue (1949–51)
Wismut Aue (1951–54)
Wismut Karl Marx Stadt (1954–63)
BSG Wismut Aue (1963–90)

Germany

ORIGINS AND GROWTH OF FOOTBALL

DESPITE AN EARLY START, football was a late developer in Germany. In the early 1870s, English students and traders played the game in Berlin and the northern ports. Oxford University toured in 1875 and the country's first club, SC Germania Hamburg, was founded in 1887. However, football faced considerable athletic and political opposition. It was viewed by German nationalists as a foreign import and a threat to *Turnen*, the Prussian tradition of individual athleticism. It was excluded from Prussian schools and the armed forces and was socially frowned upon by both Protestant and Catholic church leaders.

White-collar success

Despite the foundation of a national FA in 1900, football remained a predominantly lower middle class amateur game. However, it found favour with the white-collar workers of Germany's new cities. For them it was a perfect vehicle for social mixing. By 1911, the army lifted its ban on the game and it became a huge element of life in the armed forces during the First World War. In the postwar era crowds and players became progressively more working class. This phenomenon culminated in 1934, when a miners' team from the Ruhr – Schalke 04 – won the championship.

The Nazi takeover saw the collapse of semi-professionalism and a dismal performance on the international stage. After the war, in 1946, Germany was excluded from FIFA. Partition followed and both West and East Germany rejoined FIFA separately in 1950 and 1952. In East Germany, football remained a relatively minor sport carved up among state agencies, but West German football bloomed. An extraordinary victory in the 1954 World Cup against the unbeatable Hungarians encouraged the gradual introduction of professionalism and the eventual establishment of a national league – the Bundesliga – in 1963.

The world stage

Since then, Germany at all levels has remained a major player on the world football scene, with regular victories at both club and international level. Reunification in 1991 saw a merger of East and West German football, but East German teams were only given two places in the top division.

Despite some poor performances by the national team in the late 1990s Germany reached the 2002 World Cup Final and was chosen as host for the 2006 finals. It remains one of the world's most powerful footballing nations.

Germany: The main clubs

St Pauli 1910	Team name with year of formation
●	Club formed before 1912
●	Club formed 1912–25
●	Club formed 1925–50
○	Club formed after 1950
	Former East Germany
	Former West Germany
★	Founder members of Bundesliga (1963)
	Pre-war champions
	East German champions
	Originated from East German army
Ⓐ	Associated with anarchists
	Associated with the Stasi
	Mining origins
	Originated from a tennis club

GERMANY

The Ruhr

FOOTBALL CITIES

GERMANY

GERMAN INDUSTRIALIZATION and German football were both late developers which rose to world-class status towards the end of the 20th century. The heartland of both is the Ruhr valley in the north-west of the country. The connections are intimate: FC Schalke grew out of a mining community with Polish immigrant roots; Borussia Dortmund remains actively involved in the struggles of the region's steelworkers; Bayer Leverkusen has been owned and run by the chemical giant Bayer since its foundation in 1904. A hundred years later, the post-industrial economy of the Ruhr is churning out vast new stadiums and arenas all over the area.

Changing balance of power

The region's earliest footballing power lay in the north: in Essen, Bochum, Duisburg and Dortmund. Strong traditions were given a practical boost with the fusion in 1924 of two small teams, FC Westfalia 04 and TV 1877 Schalke, to create FC Schalke 04. The footballing authority's strict insistence on amateur regulations were used to exclude Schalke and its squad (made up of miners) from competition, but the team forced its way into the national championships, winning six titles in the 1930s and 40s. The postwar era was altogether harder for the club, and it was only in the 1990s that Schalke started to fill the Parkstadion and challenge for the country's major honours.

Borussia Dortmund was formed from the fusion in 1909 of three clubs: Trinity, Rhenania and Britannia. It remained in the shadow of Schalke until its first national championship in 1956. However, no dynasty was established, and only the shock of a relegation play-off in 1986 raised the club from its torpor. A decade of commercial growth peaked in 1997 when Ottmar Hitzfeld's team took the European Cup. A public flotation soon followed and success eventually returned with a Bundesliga title in 2002.

To the south of the region, Mönchengladbach, a small industrial town, produced the surprise package of the 1970s, when Borussia became a force both at home and in Europe. Cologne's teams were born from the bombed-out wreckage of the city in the 1940s, when small teams were amalgamated to create two sustainable clubs: 1. FC Köln was formed from KBC and Sülz 07, while its poorer neighbour Fortuna Köln was raised from the ashes of Bayernthaler and SV Köln.

ARENA AUFSCHALKE

| 60,215 | **Club:** FC Schalke 04 |
| | **Built:** 2001 |

MSV DUISBURG 1902	
German Championship 1903–44	*1913*
Bundesliga 1964–2003	*1964*
Cup	*1966, 75, 98*

The Ruhr

35,000	Capacity of stadium
	Stadium no longer in use for top-flight football
	Team colours
A43	Motorway
7	Major road
1900	Champions
2000	Runners-up

WESEL

Rhein

58

DINSLAKE

A57

MOERS

9

A40

KFC Uerdingen

9

GROTENBURG

35,000

KREFELD

A44

MÖNCHEN-GLADBACH

A61

NEU

BÖKELBERG

34,500

During its European heyday in the 1970s Mönchengladbach often switched home games to Rheinstadion in Düsseldo

Borussia Mönchengladbach

Erft

A46

BORUSSIA MÖNCHENGLADBACH 1900	
Bundesliga 1964–2003	**1970, 71,** *74,* **75–77,** *78*
Cup	**1960, 73,** *84, 92, 95*
European Cup	*1977*
UEFA Cup	*1973,* **75, 79,** *80*
World Club Cup	*1977*

FORTUNA KÖLN 1948	
Cup	*1983*

The Bayer Chemical Works: the German Parliament passed a special law, the 'Lex Leverkusen', allowing Bayer to retain 100 per cent ownership of Bayer Leverkusen.

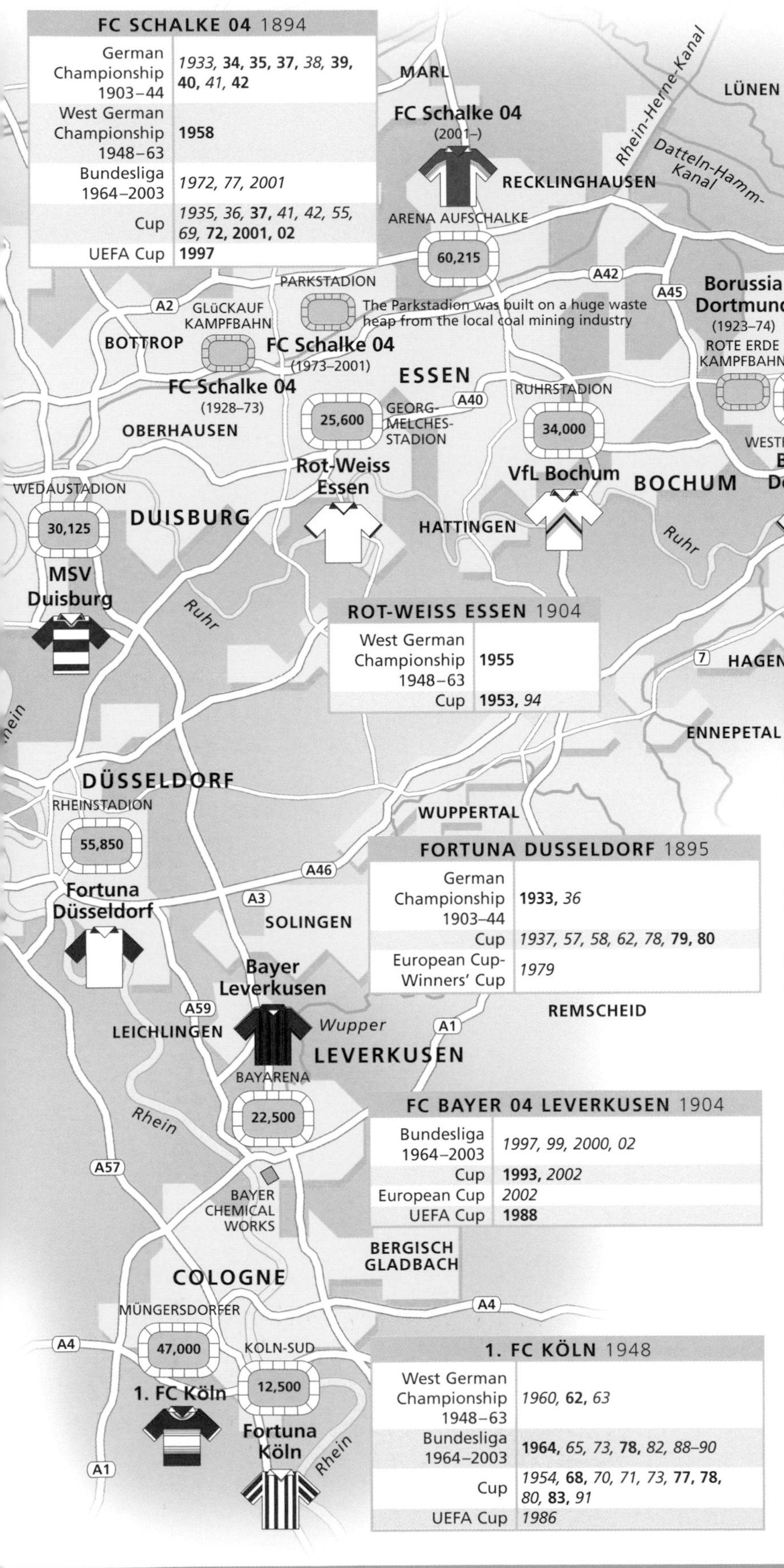

GERMANY

FC SCHALKE 04 1894

German Championship 1903–44	*1933,* **34, 35, 37,** *38,* **39, 40, 41, 42**
West German Championship 1948–63	**1958**
Bundesliga 1964–2003	*1972, 77, 2001*
Cup	*1935, 36,* **37,** *41, 42, 55, 69,* **72, 2001, 02**
UEFA Cup	**1997**

BORUSSIA DORTMUND 1909

West German Championship 1948–63	*1949,* **56, 57,** *61,* **63**
Bundesliga 1964–2003	*1966,* **92,** *95, 96,* **2002**
Cup	*1963,* **65,** *89*
European Cup	**1997**
European Cup-Winners' Cup	**1966**
UEFA Cup	*1993, 2002*
World Club Cup	**1997**

MARL

LÜNEN

Rhein-Herne-Kanal

Datteln-Hamm-Kanal

FC Schalke 04
(2001–)

RECKLINGHAUSEN

ARENA AUFSCHALKE

60,215

A42

A45

PARKSTADION

The Parkstadion was built on a huge waste heap from the local coal mining industry

A2

GLÜCKAUF KAMPFBAHN

BOTTROP

FC Schalke 04
(1973–2001)

FC Schalke 04
(1928–73)

OBERHAUSEN

ESSEN

GEORG-MELCHES-STADION

25,600

RUHRSTADION

A40

34,000

Borussia Dortmund
(1923–74)

ROTE ERDE KAMPFBAHN

DORTMUND

1

A44

Ruhr

68,600

WESTFALENSTADION

Uniquely among major European stadiums, the Westfalenstadion retains terracing which can be replaced by seats to comply with UEFA regulations

Rot-Weiss Essen

VfL Bochum

BOCHUM

Borussia Dortmund

MENDEN

ISERLOHN

WEDAUSTADION

30,125

DUISBURG

MSV Duisburg

Ruhr

HATTINGEN

Ruhr

Lenne

7

VFL BOCHUM 1938

Cup	*1968, 88*

ROT-WEISS ESSEN 1904

West German Championship 1948–63	**1955**
Cup	**1953,** *94*

7 HAGEN

A45

ENNEPETAL

Rhein

DÜSSELDORF

RHEINSTADION

55,850

Fortuna Düsseldorf

A3

A46

SOLINGEN

WUPPERTAL

FORTUNA DÜSSELDORF 1895

German Championship 1903–44	**1933,** *36*
Cup	*1937, 57, 58, 62, 78,* **79, 80**
European Cup-Winners' Cup	*1979*

WESTFALENSTADION

	Club: Borussia Dortmund
68,600	**Built:** 1974
	Rebuilt: 1996–98
Significant Matches:	1974 World Cup: three group matches and one second-round match

Bayer Leverkusen

A59

LEICHLINGEN

Wupper

A1

REMSCHEID

LEVERKUSEN

BAYARENA

22,500

FC BAYER 04 LEVERKUSEN 1904

Bundesliga 1964–2003	*1997, 99, 2000, 02*
Cup	**1993,** *2002*
European Cup	*2002*
UEFA Cup	**1988**

Rhein

A57

BAYER CHEMICAL WORKS

BERGISCH GLADBACH

COLOGNE

MÜNGERSDORFER

A4

47,000

KÖLN-SÜD

12,500

1. FC Köln

A4

Fortuna Köln

Rhein

A1

1. FC KÖLN 1948

West German Championship 1948–63	*1960,* **62,** *63*
Bundesliga 1964–2003	**1964,** *65, 73,* **78,** *82,* **88–90**
Cup	*1954,* **68,** *70, 71, 73,* **77, 78,** *80,* **83,** *91*
UEFA Cup	*1986*

MÜNGERSDORFER

	Club: 1. FC Köln
47,000	**Built:** 1923
	Rebuilt: 1975, 2003–04 for 2006 World Cup (capacity 50,000)

Munich

FOOTBALL CITY

IN THE EARLY 20TH CENTURY, Bavaria was a German byword for inept conservatism and peasant values, and Munich was its antiquated capital. In the 21st century, the city has become the new hub of German industrial and commercial success, and in Bayern München, it has the team that has dominated German football for a quarter of a century. Bayern was born in the working-class Schwabing district of the city in 1900, and was bold enough to win a national championship title in 1932. But its provincial obscurity was such that when the professional Bundesliga was formed in 1963, the club chosen to represent Munich was its rival TSV 1860 München. TSV was founded in the south of the city as a gymnastics club that later took up football. Its early inclusion in professional football seemed justified when it won the cup in 1964 and then the league two years later, but a steady decline saw the team lose its licence in 1981 and it only returned to the top flight a decade later. Even further down the footballing ladder is SpVgg Unterhaching on the southern edge of the city – this relative newcomer made it to the Bundesliga in 1999.

Bayern rise to the top

Despite the snub from the Bundesliga, Bayern went professional anyway and gained quick promotion, successive cup victories and then the 1967 European Cup-Winners' Cup. The team now emerging around Sepp Maier, Franz Beckenbauer and Gerd Müller would eventually win three European Cups and sustain a decade of unbroken dominance in German football. In the 1990s, under Beckenbauer, Trapattoni and Hitzfield, Bayern has returned to the very top of European football. In 1972 Bayern moved to the Olympiastadion and TSV joined the team, having abandoned its old Grunwalderstrasse stadium on its return to the top flight. While Bayern fills the stadium with fans from all across Germany, TSV's defiantly local supporters leave it almost two-thirds empty. Both are due to move to the new Allianz Arena in the city's northern suburbs, which will open in time to host the World Cup Finals tournament in 2006.

OLYMPIASTADION

69,000

Clubs: Bayern München, TSV 1860 München
Built: 1972
Significant Matches: 1974 World Cup: five matches including 3rd place play-off, Final; 1972 Munich Olympics: Final; 1988 European Championships: Final; European Cup Final: 1979, 93

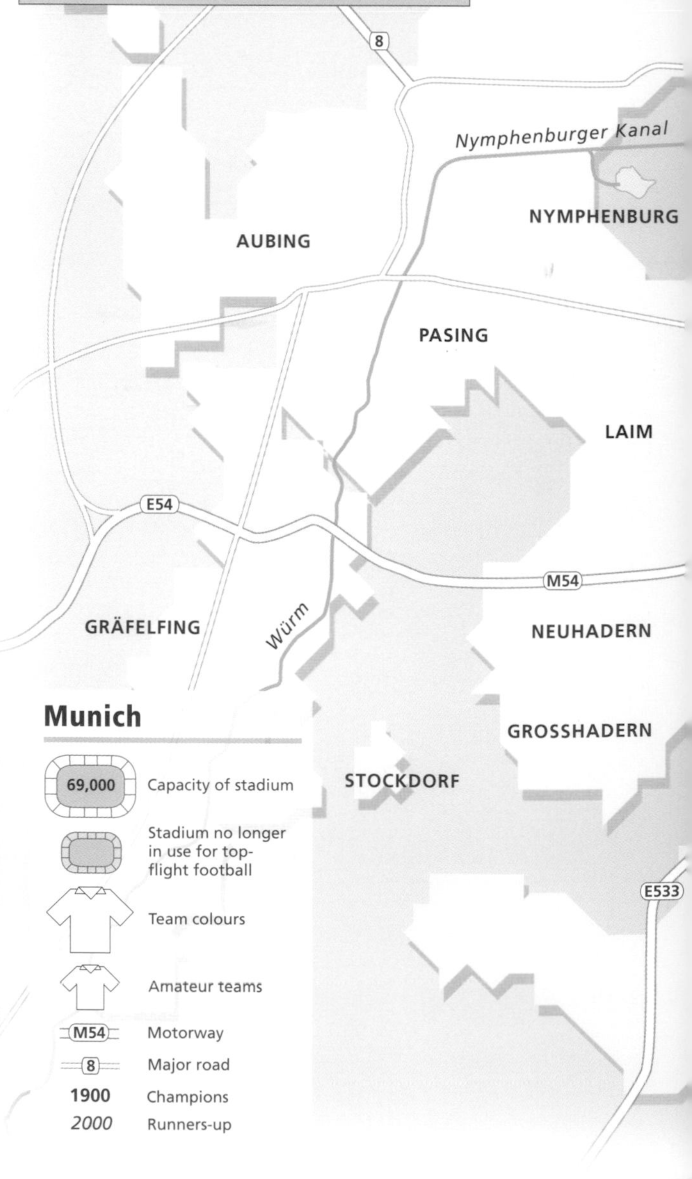

The Grunwalder Strasse is the old and now empty heart of football in Munich. A classic rectangular stadium with open teraces behind the goals, the stadium hosted both TSV and Bayern's debut matches in the Bundesliga. Many TSV fans would prefer to return to this cosy venue where their smaller crowds could actually fill the place.

KARLSFELD

ALLACH

UNTERMENZING

Nymphenburger Kanal

NYMPHENBURG

AUBING

PASING

LAIM

GRÄFELFING

Würm

NEUHADERN

GROSSHADERN

STOCKDORF

Munich

69,000 Capacity of stadium

Stadium no longer in use for top-flight football

Team colours

Amateur teams

M54 Motorway

8 Major road

1900 Champions

2000 Runners-up

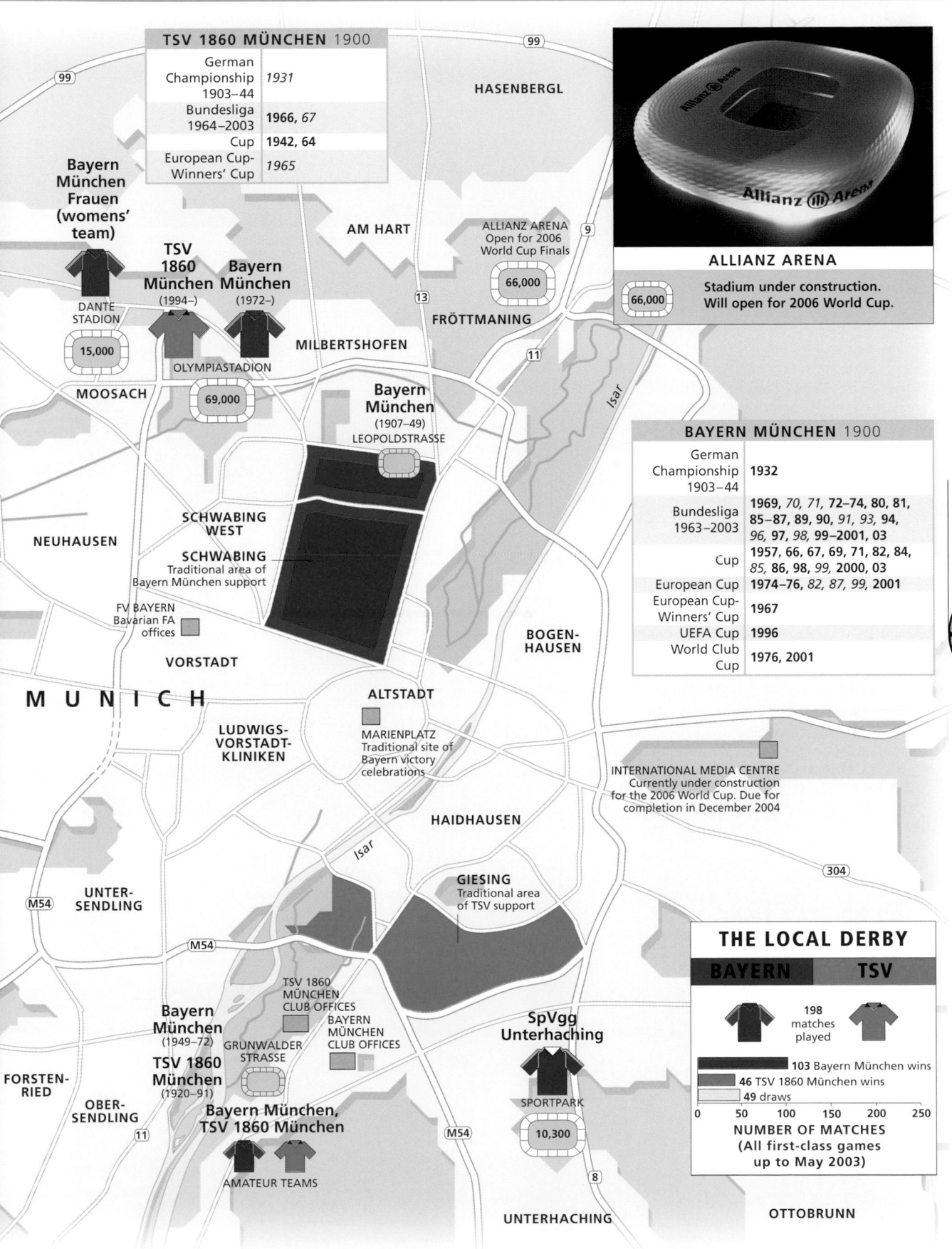

TSV 1860 MÜNCHEN 1900

German Championship 1903–44	*1931*
Bundesliga 1964–2003	**1966,** *67*
Cup	**1942,** **64**
European Cup-Winners' Cup	*1965*

99

HASENBERGL

ALLIANZ ARENA
Open for 2006
World Cup Finals
66,000

9

13

FRÖTTMANING

11

AM HART

MILBERTSHOFEN

Bayern München Frauen (womens' team)

DANTE STADION
15,000

TSV 1860 München (1994–)

Bayern München (1972–)

OLYMPIASTADION
69,000

MOOSACH

Bayern München (1907–49)
LEOPOLDSTRASSE

Isar

ALLIANZ ARENA

66,000

Stadium under construction.
Will open for 2006 World Cup.

GERMANY

BAYERN MÜNCHEN 1900

German Championship 1903–44	**1932**
Bundesliga 1963–2003	**1969,** *70, 71, 72–74,* **80, 81, 85–87, 89, 90,** *91, 93,* **94,** *96,* **97,** *98,* **99–2001,** *03*
Cup	**1957,** *66, 67, 69, 71,* **82, 84, 85, 86, 98,** *99,* **2000, 03**
European Cup	**1974–76,** *82, 87, 99,* **2001**
European Cup-Winners' Cup	**1967**
UEFA Cup	**1996**
World Club Cup	**1976, 2001**

NEUHAUSEN

SCHWABING WEST

SCHWABING
Traditional area of
Bayern München support

FV BAYERN
Bavarian FA
offices

VORSTADT

M U N I C H

LUDWIGS-VORSTADT-KLINIKEN

ALTSTADT

MARIENPLATZ
Traditional site of
Bayern victory
celebrations

BOGEN-HAUSEN

INTERNATIONAL MEDIA CENTRE
Currently under construction
for the 2006 World Cup. Due for
completion in December 2004

304

HAIDHAUSEN

Isar

M54

UNTER-SENDLING

M54

GIESING
Traditional area
of TSV support

THE LOCAL DERBY

BAYERN	TSV

198
matches
played

103 Bayern München wins

46 TSV 1860 München wins

49 draws

0   50   100   150   200   250

NUMBER OF MATCHES
(All first-class games
up to May 2003)

Bayern München (1949–72)

TSV 1860
MÜNCHEN
CLUB OFFICES

BAYERN
MÜNCHEN
CLUB OFFICES

GRUNWALDER STRASSE

TSV 1860 München (1920–91)

Bayern München, TSV 1860 München

AMATEUR TEAMS

SpVgg Unterhaching

SPORTPARK
10,300

FORSTEN-RIED

OBER-SENDLING

11

M54

8

UNTERHACHING

OTTOBRUNN

Berlin

FOOTBALL CITY

BERLIN TOOK TO FOOTBALL more quickly than much of Germany, and produced early national champions like Viktoria Berlin (which still survives as amateur outfit Viktoria 98). But the city did not create a team of sufficient size and working-class popularity until Hertha 92 and Berliner BC 99 combined in 1923 to create Hertha Berlin. Runners-up for four consecutive years in the national championships, Hertha finally took the prize in 1930 and 31. But the winning streak was soon over and the club languished throughout the Nazi era and in the divided, isolated West Berlin of the postwar era. With the erection of the Berlin Wall in 1961, the club was severed from its supporters in the East and the move to the Olympiastadion saw its old fans in Wedding drift away. Berlin's post-unification boom has seen money and sponsors flow in, but fans and trophies are thinner on the ground. West Berlin's other teams to have made the Bundesliga have all fared poorly, though the city's new immigrant communities are making their mark in the lower leagues with clubs like Croatia Berlin and Türkiyemspor Berlin.

Decline in the East

In the East, Vorwärts Berlin, the East German army club, moved into the city from Leipzig, where the immediate postwar team had played. But in the internal struggles of the East German state, Vorwärts and the army lost out. The team was expelled to Frankfurt-an-der-Oder in 1971, where it has declined and now plays in amateur leagues. In its place, and in its now empty stadium, rose Dynamo Berlin, a team staffed, supported and funded by the *Stasi* – the East German secret police. Two decades of bizarre and biased decisions and questionable triumphs followed. As for the rest of the East Berlin teams, 1. FC Union was the people's team of choice and its loyal fan base has seen it survive the post-unification collapse of East German institutions, especially in a glorious Cup run in 2001. Dynamo by contrast has, like its masters, changed its name to Berliner FC, and sunk into grim suburban, lower-league obscurity at the bleak Sportpark Forum.

OLYMPIASTADION

76,243

Clubs:	Blau-Weiss 90, Hertha BSC Berlin, Tasmania Berlin
Built:	1936
Rebuilt:	1974
Record Attendance:	88,075 Hertha BSC Berlin v 1. FC Köln, Bundesliga, 26 Sep 1969
Significant Matches:	1936 Berlin Olympics; 1974 World Cup: three group matches; German Cup Final 1992–2001

HERTHA BSC BERLIN 1892

German Championship 1903–44	*1926–29*, **30, 31**
Bundesliga 1964–2003	*1975*
Cup	*1977, 79, 93*

The building of the Berlin Wall in 1961 separated Hertha Berlin from many of its fans. Legend has it that many of them assembled by the wall on match days to hear the roar of the crowd.

GERMANY

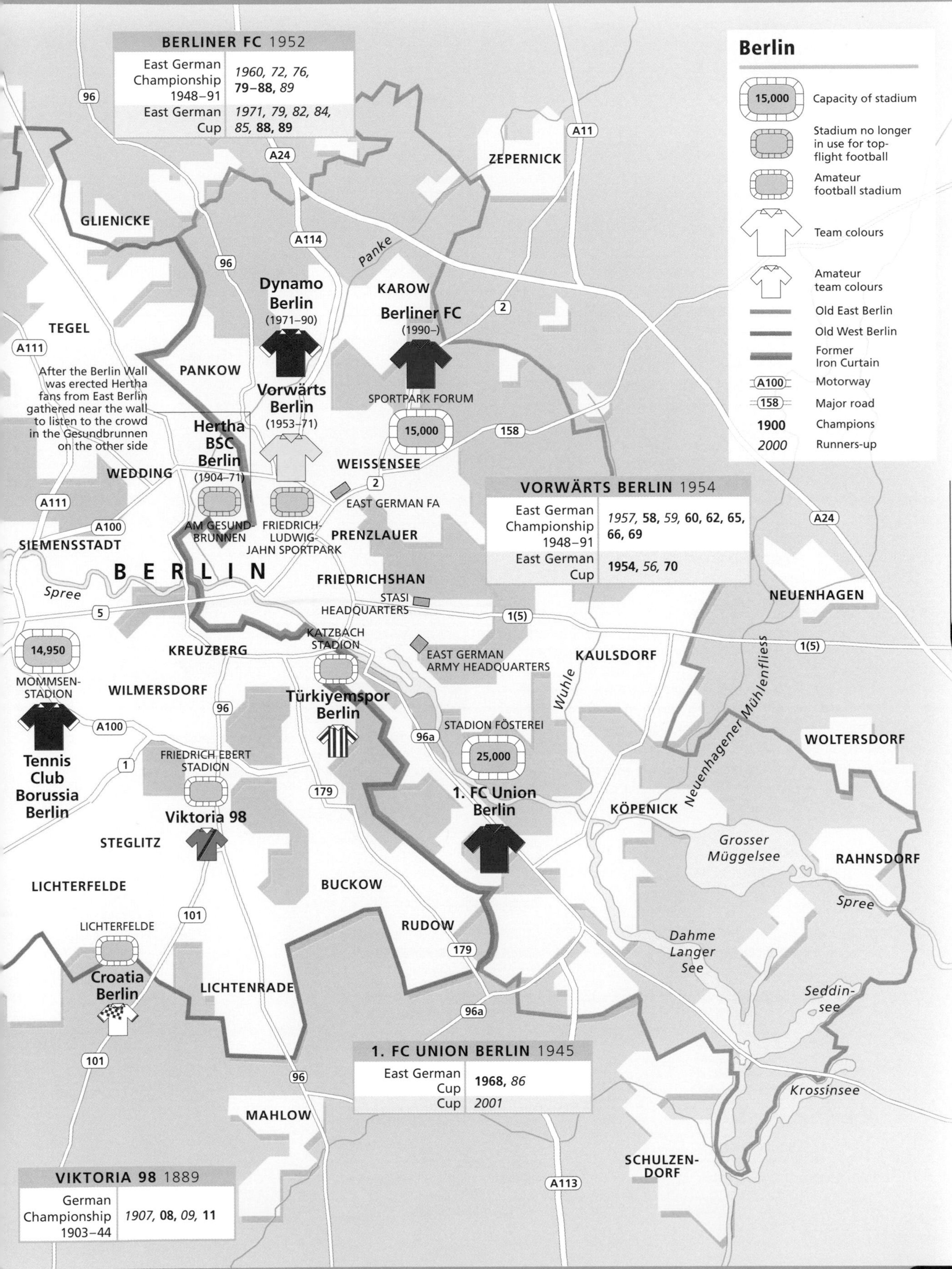

GERMANY

BERLINER FC 1952

East German Championship 1948–91	*1960, 72, 76,* **79–88,** *89*
East German Cup	*1971, 79, 82, 84,* 85, **88, 89**

Berlin

15,000	Capacity of stadium
	Stadium no longer in use for top-flight football
	Amateur football stadium
	Team colours
	Amateur team colours
	Old East Berlin
	Old West Berlin
	Former Iron Curtain
A100	Motorway
158	Major road
1900	Champions
2000	Runners-up

96

A11

ZEPERNICK

A24

GLIENICKE

A114

Panke

96

Dynamo Berlin
(1971–90)

KAROW
Berliner FC
(1990–)

2

TEGEL

A111

Vorwärts Berlin
(1953–71)

SPORTPARK FORUM

15,000

158

PANKOW

After the Berlin Wall was erected Hertha fans from East Berlin gathered near the wall to listen to the crowd in the Gesundbrunnen on the other side

Hertha BSC Berlin
(1904–71)

WEISSENSEE

2

EAST GERMAN FA

VORWÄRTS BERLIN 1954

East German Championship 1948–91	*1957,* **58,** *59,* **60, 62, 65, 66, 69**
East German Cup	**1954,** *56,* **70**

WEDDING

A111

AM GESUND-BRUNNEN

FRIEDRICH-LUDWIG-JAHN SPORTPARK

PRENZLAUER

A24

A100

SIEMENSSTADT

B E R L I N

Spree

FRIEDRICHSHAN

STASI HEADQUARTERS

1(5)

NEUENHAGEN

5

14,950

MOMMSEN-STADION

KATZBACH STADION

EAST GERMAN ARMY HEADQUARTERS

KAULSDORF

1(5)

Tennis Club Borussia Berlin

A100

1

KREUZBERG

Türkiyemspor Berlin

Wuhle

96a

STADION FÖSTEREI

25,000

WOLTERSDORF

WILMERSDORF

96

FRIEDRICH EBERT STADION

179

1. FC Union Berlin

KÖPENICK

RAHNSDORF

Viktoria 98

STEGLITZ

LICHTERFELDE

101

BUCKOW

RUDOW

Grosser Müggelsee

Spree

LICHTERFELDE

179

Dahme Langer See

Seddin-see

Croatia Berlin

LICHTENRADE

96a

Krossinsee

101

96

1. FC UNION BERLIN 1945

East German Cup	**1968,** *86*
Cup	*2001*

MAHLOW

SCHULZEN-DORF

VIKTORIA 98 1889

German Championship 1903–44	*1907,* **08,** *09,* **11**

A113

Germany

FANS AND OWNERS

GERMANY

THE LEGAL STRUCTURE OF GERMAN CLUBS has been very tightly regulated, leaving control with the elected boards of sports and social clubs. Although German sides have appeared to prosper on smaller turnovers than the giants of Italy, Spain and England, the economic limits of this kind of structure have seen the government allow clubs to either float on the stock exchange or to spin off their professional football activities into a separate public company. That is, as long as the social club continues to holds 51 per cent of the equity. Borussia Dortmund was the first to convert, partially floating the club. Bayer 04 Leverkusen became a plc in 1999, but under a special regulation, the 'Lex Leverkusen', the club is 100 per cent owned by Bayer AG, the chemical company that has run the club for nearly 100 years. Borussia Mönchenglabdach, FC Schalke 04 and Hertha BSC Berlin have all considered floating but have so far declined. More likely, they will follow the path of 1. FC Köln, TSV 1860 München and FC Bayern München, which have opted to take Aktien Gesellschaft status, in which the commercial and amateur sporting components of the club are separated, the latter holding a majority stake in the former, but with the option of external private investment taking the rest. In Bayern's case, Adidas took a 10 per cent stake in 2001, valuing the club at the time at £475 million.

Alternative fans

There are recognizable tribes of German fans. The mainstream combines an older and younger generation, boisterous and noisy but very peaceful. A handful of clubs can claim a following beyond their immediate locality: Bayern München, Dortmund, Schalke and FC Hansa Rostock in particular. Many of the smaller teams, like Berlin's smaller clubs and St. Pauli in Hamburg, attract the alternative scene in Germany: punks, anarchists, Greens and hippies. In the east, skinhead gangs have clustered around some old East German clubs, and have made a speciality of following the national team, causing extensive trouble at France 98, where a policeman was seriously injured in an encounter with German fans. In response, policing has been tightened and, with a characteristic German mixture of incorporation and social reasonability, clubs have set up *fanprojekts*. These bring autonomous supporters' groups, local authority youth projects and the clubs together in a range of activities, including a chance for fans to meet and quiz clubs' directors.

Warning: football can damage your health. Reiner Calmund, general manager of Bayer Leverkusen, watches his team disintegrate on and off the pitch during a turbulent season at the club.

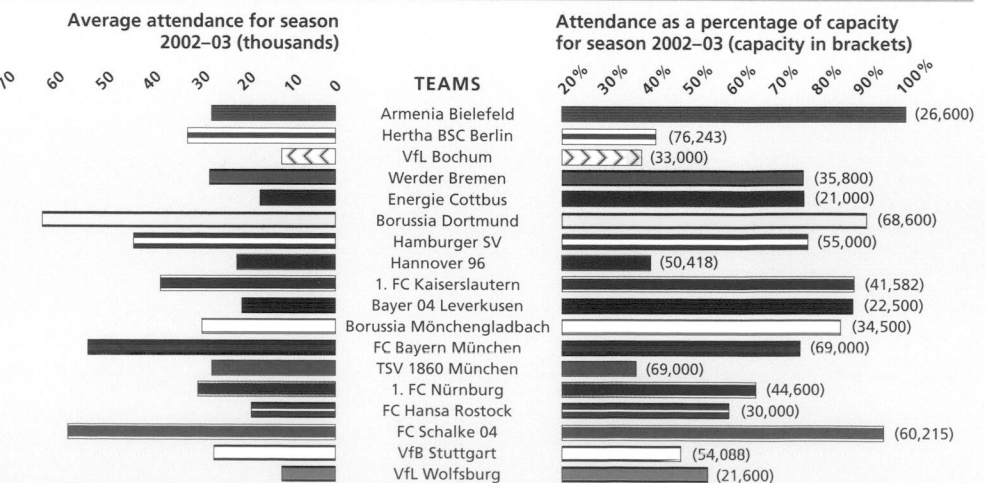

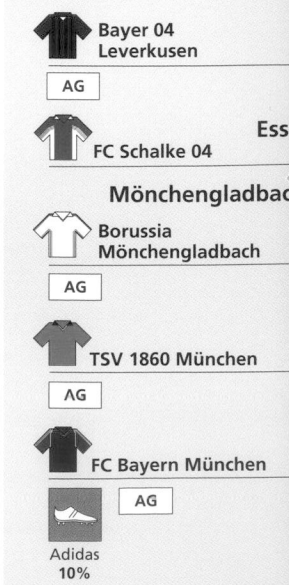

Bayer 04 Leverkusen — AG

FC Schalke 04 — Esse

Mönchengladbach — Borussia Mönchengladbach — AG

TSV 1860 München — AG

FC Bayern München — AG

Adidas 10%

Average Attendance

Average attendance for season 2002–03 (thousands)

70 60 50 40 30 20 10 0

Capacity

Attendance as a percentage of capacity for season 2002–03 (capacity in brackets)

20% 30% 40% 50% 60% 70% 80% 90% 100%

TEAMS	Capacity
Armenia Bielefeld	(26,600)
Hertha BSC Berlin	(76,243)
VfL Bochum	(33,000)
Werder Bremen	(35,800)
Energie Cottbus	(21,000)
Borussia Dortmund	(68,600)
Hamburger SV	(55,000)
Hannover 96	(50,418)
1. FC Kaiserslautern	(41,582)
Bayer 04 Leverkusen	(22,500)
Borussia Mönchengladbach	(34,500)
FC Bayern München	(69,000)
TSV 1860 München	(69,000)
1. FC Nürnburg	(44,600)
FC Hansa Rostock	(30,000)
FC Schalke 04	(60,215)
VfB Stuttgart	(54,088)
VfL Wolfsburg	(21,600)

Club Budgets 2000–01, 2001–02

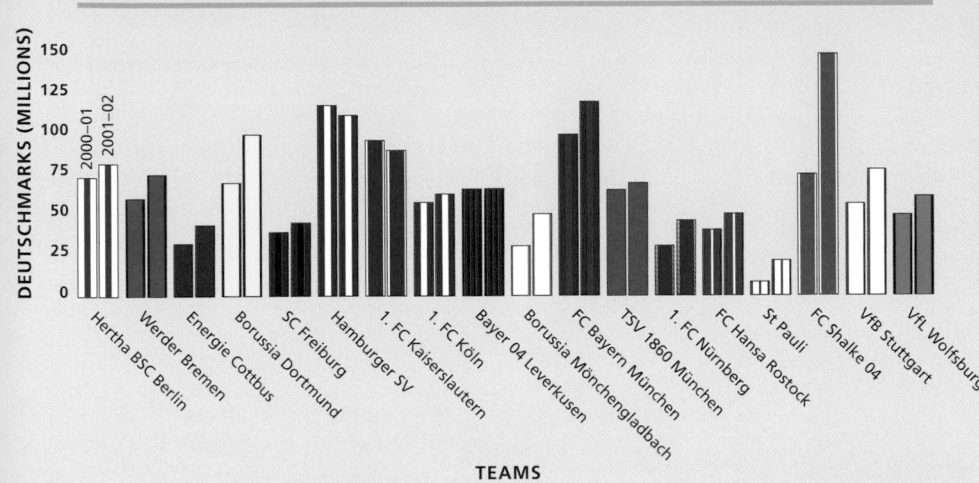

DEUTSCHMARKS (MILLIONS)

2000–01
2001–02

TEAMS

Teams: Hertha BSC Berlin, Werder Bremen, Energie Cottbus, Borussia Dortmund, SC Freiburg, Hamburger SV, 1. FC Kaiserslautern, 1. FC Köln, Bayer 04 Leverkusen, Borussia Mönchengladbach, FC Bayern München, TSV 1860 München, 1. FC Nürnberg, FC Hansa Rostock, St Pauli, FC Schalke 04, VfB Stuttgart, VfL Wolfsburg

Leo Kirch created a media empire that paid enormous sums for the Bundesliga's TV rights. The collapse of the Kirch group in 2002 with debts of £10 billion is likely to see budgets in the Bundesliga slashed.

Majority and Leading Shareholders

Team

● Berlin — City of origin

Sportswear company

AG — Aktien Gesellschaft

Partial flotation

Teams shown were members of Bundesliga 2002–03

Borussia Dortmund

FC Hansa Rostock

Hamburg   Rostock

Hamburger SV

Bremen

Werder Bremen

VfL Wolfsburg

AG

Hannover   Wolfsburg

Hertha BSC Berlin

Berlin

Bielefeld

Dortmund

Hannover 96   Cottbus

Energie Cottbus

Leverkusen

G E R M A N Y

Armenia Bielefeld

ochum

Nürnberg

1. FC Nürnburg

aiserslautern

1. FC Kaiserslautern

AG

Stuttgart   VfB Stuttgart

Munich

Income from Sponsorship 2001–02

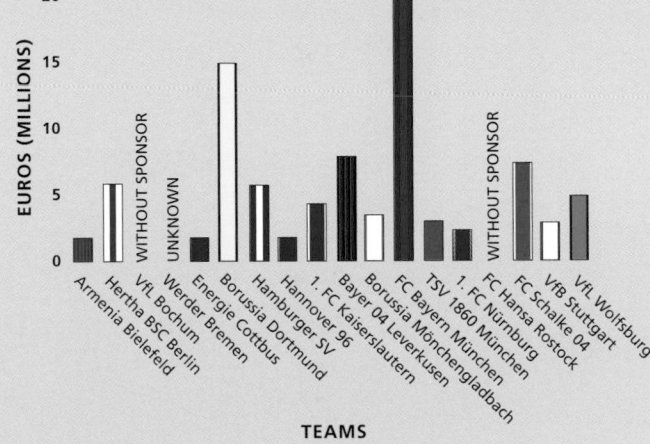

EUROS (MILLIONS)

WITHOUT SPONSOR
UNKNOWN
WITHOUT SPONSOR

Teams: Armenia Bielefeld, Hertha BSC Berlin, VfL Bochum, Werder Bremen, Energie Cottbus, Borussia Dortmund, Hamburger SV, Hannover 96, 1. FC Kaiserslautern, Bayer 04 Leverkusen, Borussia Mönchengladbach, FC Bayern München, TSV 1860 München, 1. FC Nürnberg, FC Hansa Rostock, FC Schalke 04, VfB Stuttgart, VfL Wolfsburg

TEAMS

German Attendances

Attendances for each season

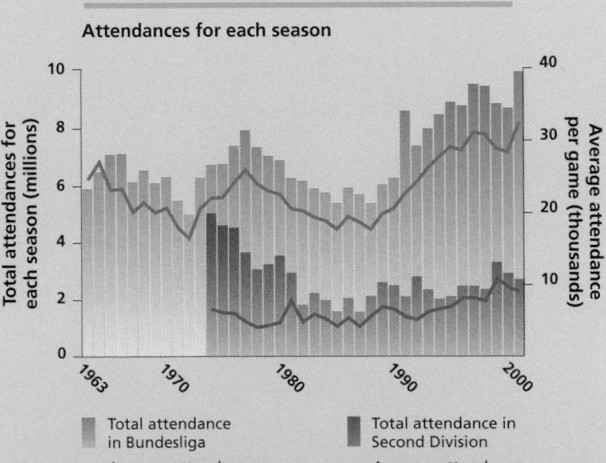

Total attendances for each season (millions)

Average attendance per game (thousands)

1963   1970   1980   1990   2000

Total attendance in Bundesliga

Total attendance in Second Division

Average attendance per game in Bundesliga

Average attendance per game in Second Division

Germany

PLAYERS AND MANAGERS

GERMAN FOOTBALL BEGAN LATER than in many European countries, and remained an amateur and regional affair for longer than in any other leading footballing nation. Originally a middle-class sport, it took two generations to reach the huge German urban working-class and to begin to significantly draw on its pool of talent. From the pre-Second World War generation two names stand out: Fritz Walter and Uwe Seeler. Walter captained the 1954 World Cup-winning side; Seeler the side that lost in 1966. Both played for a single club their whole career: Kaiserslautern and Hamburger SV respectively.

Arrival of the Bundesliga

But Germany's greatest players emerged from the new national professional league – the Bundesliga – formed in 1963. These players would win the 1974 World Cup, and those at Bayern München would come to dominate the national and European game in the mid-1970s: Gerd Müller, whose goalscoring record is almost unsurpassable; Paul Brietner, Bayern's midfield intellectual and bearded radical; and the Kaiser himself, Franz Beckenbauer, Germany's greatest player, manager and football politician.

In the 1990s, German players spread their wings and began to play abroad; Kohler, Klinsmann and Matthäus – the spine of the 1990 World Cup side – have all played in Italy, and displayed consistency, quiet intelligence and longevity. Matthias Sammer, one of the few East Germans to make it to the highest level after unification, picked up Beckenbauer's mantle as sweeper. Simultaneously, the growing wealth of the Bundesliga has seen a steady expansion in its overseas players, with strong African and Eastern European contingents. However, the current crisis in German football finances, and its relative weakness compared to Europe's other big leagues, means that the biggest talents from Africa and Latin America go elsewhere.

German football is also remarkable for the degree of stability and longevity in the coaching of the national squad. From Otto Nerz's appointment in 1926 to Rudi Völler's in 2000, there have been only eight coaches in over 70 years; a point worth pondering when you're trying to work out just why the national team has been so phenomenally successful despite the weaknesses of the domestic league.

Top 20 International Caps

PLAYER	CAPS	GOALS	FIRST MATCH	LAST MATCH
Lothar Matthäus	150	23	1980	2000
Jürgen Klinsmann	108	47	1987	1998
Jürgen Kohler*	105	2	1986	1998
Franz Beckenbauer	103	14	1965	1977
Thomas Hässler*	101	11	1988	2000
Hans-Hubert Vogts	96	1	1967	1978
Sepp Maier	95	0	1966	1979
Karl-Heinz Rummenigge	95	45	1976	1986
Rudi Völler	90	47	1982	1994
Andreas Brehme	86	8	1984	1994
Andreas Möller*	85	30	1988	1999
Karl Heinz Forster	81	2	1978	1986
Wolfgang Overath	81	17	1963	1974
Guido Buchwald	76	4	1984	1994
Harald Schumacher	76	0	1979	1986
Pierre Littbarski	73	18	1981	1990
Hans Peter Briegel	72	4	1979	1986
Uwe Seeler	72	43	1954	1970
Paul Janes	71	7	1932	1942
Manfred Kaltz	69	8	1975	1983

Top 10 International Goalscorers

PLAYER	GOALS	CAPS	FIRST MATCH	LAST MATCH
Gerd Müller	68	62	1966	1974
Rudi Völler	47	90	1982	1994
Jürgen Klinsmann	47	108	1987	1998
Karl-Heinz Rummenigge	45	95	1976	1986
Uwe Seeler	43	72	1954	1970
Fritz Walter	33	61	1940	1958
Klaus Fischer	32	45	1977	1982
Oliver Bierhoff*	32	60	1996	2002
Ernst Lehner	30	65	1933	1942
Andreas Möller*	30	85	1988	1999

* Indicates players still playing at least at club level.

German International Managers

DATES	NAME	GAMES	WON	DRAWN	LOST
1926–36	Otto Nerz	70	42	10	18
1936–63	Sepp Herberger	162	92	26	44
1963–78	Helmut Schön	139	87	30	22
1978–84	Jupp Derwall	67	45	11	11
1984–90	Franz Beckenbauer	66	36	17	13
1990–98	Berti Vogts	102	67	23	12
1998–2000	Erich Ribbeck	24	10	6	8
2000–	Rudi Völler	40	24	8	8

All figures correct as of 11 June 2003.

Foreign Players in Germany (in top division squads)

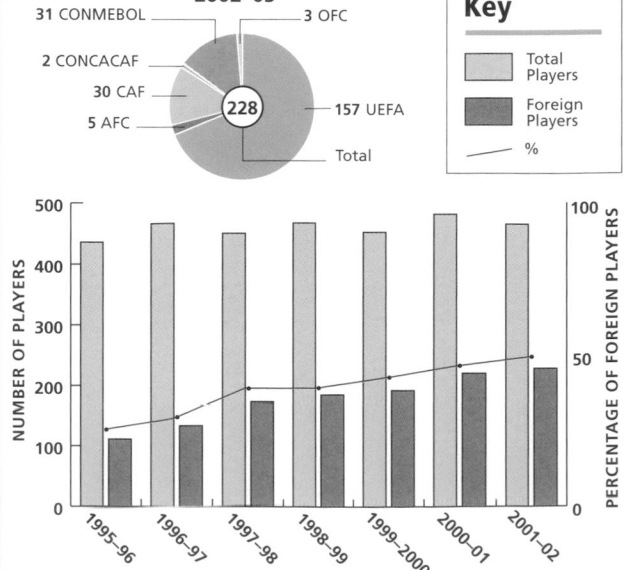

2002–03

31 CONMEBOL
3 OFC
2 CONCACAF
30 CAF
5 AFC
228
157 UEFA
Total

Key
- Total Players
- Foreign Players
- %

GERMANY

Places in the Top 20 International Caps and Top 10 International Goalscorers tables (left) make Rudi Völler the perfect choice as manager of the German national team. The wisdom of the appointment was confirmed when Völler took an unfancied German team to the Final of the 2002 World Cup.

Player of the Year

YEAR	PLAYER	CLUB
1963	Schäfer	1. FC Köln
1964	Seeler	Hamburger SV
1965	Tilkowski	Borussia Dortmund
1966	Beckenbauer	Bayern München
1967	G. Müller	Bayern München
1968	Beckenbauer	Bayern München
1969	G. Müller	Bayern München
1970	Seeler	Hamburger SV
1971	Vogts	Borussia Mönchengladbach
1972	Netzer	Borussia Mönchengladbach
1973	Netzer	Borussia Mönchengladbach
1974	Beckenbauer	Bayern München
1975	Maier	Bayern München
1976	Beckenbauer	Bayern München
1977	Maier	Bayern München
1978	Maier	Bayern München

YEAR	PLAYER	CLUB
1979	Vogts	Borussia Mönchengladbach
1980	Rummenigge	Bayern München
1981	Breitner	Bayern München
1982	Förster	VfB Stuttgart
1983	Völler	Werder Bremen
1984	Schumacher	1. FC Köln
1985	Briegel	Hellas Verona [Ita]
1986	Schumacher	1. FC Köln
1987	Rahn	Borussia Mönchengladbach
1988	Klinsmann	VfB Stuttgart
1989	Hässler	1. FC Köln
1990	Matthäus	Internazionale [Ita]
1991	Kuntz	1. FC Kaiserslautern
1992	Hässler	Roma [Ita]
1993	Köpke	1. FC Nürnberg
1994	Klinsmann	Tottenham Hotspur [Eng]
1995	Sammer	Borussia Dortmund
1996	Sammer	Borussia Dortmund
1997	Kohler	Borussia Dortmund
1998	Bierhoff	Udinese/Milan [Ita]
1999	Matthäus	Bayern München
2000	Kahn	Bayern München
2001	Kahn	Bayern München
2002	Ballack	Bayer Leverkusen

Awarded by *Kicker* magazine.

Top Goalscorers by Season 1963–2003

SEASON	PLAYER	CLUB	GOALS
1963–64	Seeler	Hamburger SV	30
1964–65	Brunnenmeier	TSV 1860 München	24
1965–66	Emmerich	Borussia Dortmund	31
1966–67	G. Müller	Bayern München	28
1966–67	Emmerich	Borussia Dortmund	28
1967–68	Lohr	1. FC Köln	27
1968–69	G. Müller	Bayern München	30
1969–70	G. Müller	Bayern München	38
1970–71	Kobluhn	Rot-Weiss Oberhausen	24
1971–72	G. Müller	Bayern München	40
1972–73	G. Müller	Bayern München	36
1973–74	G. Müller	Bayern München	30
1973–74	Heynckes	Borussia M'gladbach	30
1974–75	Heynckes	Borussia M'gladbach	29
1975–76	Fischer	FC Schalke 04	29
1976–77	D. Müller	1. FC Köln	34
1977–78	D. Müller	1. FC Köln	24
1977–78	G. Müller	Bayern München	24
1978–79	K. Allofs	Fortuna Dusseldorf	22
1979–80	Rummenigge	Bayern München	26
1980–81	Rummenigge	Bayern München	29
1981–82	Hrubesch	Hamburger SV	27
1982–83	Völler	Werder Bremen	23
1983–84	Rummenigge	Bayern München	26
1984–85	K. Allofs	1. FC Köln	26
1985–86	Kuntz	VfL Bochum	22
1986–87	Rahn	Borussia M'gladbach	24

SEASON	PLAYER	CLUB	GOALS
1987–88	Klinsmann	VfB Stuttgart	18
1988–89	T. Allofs	1. FC Köln	17
1988–89	Wohlfahrth	Bayern München	17
1989–90	Andersen	Eintracht Frankfurt	18
1990–91	Wohlfahrth	Bayern München	21
1991–92	Walter	VfB Stuttgart	22
1992–93	Kirsten	Bayer Leverkusen	20
1992–93	Yeboah	Eintracht Frankfurt	20
1993–94	Kuntz	1. FC Kaiserslautern	18
1993–94	Yeboah	Eintracht Frankfurt	18
1994–95	Bassler	Werder Bremen	20
1994–95	Herrlich	Borussia M'gladbach	20
1995–96	Bobic	VfB Stuttgart	17
1996–97	Kirsten	Bayer Leverkusen	22
1997–98	Kirsten	Bayer Leverkusen	22
1998–99	Preetz	Hertha Berlin	23
1999–2000	Max	TSV 1860 München	19
2000–01	Barbarez	Hamburger SV	22
2000–01	Sand	FC Schalke 04	22
2001–02	Amoroso	Borussia Dortmund	18
2001–02	Max	TSV 1860 München	18
2002–03	Christiansen	VfL Bochum	21
2002–03	Elber	Bayern München	21

One of Germany's first exports was naturally one of its finest players. Jürgen Klinsmann left VfB Stuttgart to join Italian giants Internazionale in 1989. He had three successful years in Milan before moving to AS Monaco of France in 1992.

GERMANY

Germany

BUNDESLIGA 1981–2002

IN THE 1970s, GERMAN FOOTBALL was dominated by Bayern München and an unlikely small-town team from the Ruhr called Borussia Mönchengladbach. However, by the beginning of the 1980s, Hamburger SV was the power in the land. Even without the departed Kevin Keegan (European Footballer of the Year in 1978 and 79) the team from Hamburg was formidable: the side was managed by Austrian warhorse Ernst Happel, Horst Hrubesch led the line and sweeper Manni Kaltz kept it tidy at the back. Hamburger took back-to-back titles (1982 and 83) and was pipped for a third by a revived Stuttgart in 1984.

The rest of the decade saw a reversion to old form as a newly constructed Bayern München, under manager Otto Latek and captain Lothar Mätthaus, took five of the next six championships. The only constant challenge came from Werder Bremen under Otto Rehhagel (who stayed a record 14 years at the club). With very little income Werder fielded a compact, clever and hardworking team, and nurtured future German internationals like Rudi Völler and Karlheinz Riedle. The team became famed for its *Wesermiracles*, as it consistently demonstrated its ability to come back from behind at its home, Weserstadion. Together, the mix allowed Bremen to take two championships (1988 and 93), as well as finding European success.

Formation of the modern Bundesliga

As the Berlin Wall was dismantled in 1991, and East Germany was effectively liquidated by the Federal Republic, the Bundesliga of the newly unified Germany dutifully offered two places to the top East German league sides, Hansa Rostock and Dynamo Dresden. Leipzig came up a year later only to go straight back down, and Dresden lasted only four seasons before relegation. Hansa was immediately relegated only to return in the mid-1990s. With a couple of sixth place finishes, Hansa Rostock is easily the most successful team from the East. Geographically Eastern, but politically and economically from West Berlin, Hertha BSC has made a comeback in the last five years. Buoyed by the money flooding into the new Berlin, it has made the top six regularly. Similarly strong challenges have come from two teams from the Ruhr with substantial crowds and financial support: FC Schalke and Bayer Leverkusen.

Bayern went off the boil in the years immediately after reunification and the title was more evenly spread with Borussia Dortmund, Kaiserslautern, Stuttgart and Bremen all winning the top prize. Dortmund, under inspirational president Gerd Niebaum and manager Ottmar Hitzfeld, was the most consistent team. With a massive programme of redevelopment and commercialization (culminating in partial flotation on the German stock exchange), Hitzfeld brought in the Brazilian César from under the noses of Bayern, and a number of German internationals who had been playing abroad, like Andy Möller and Jurgen Kohler; together they won two Bundesliga titles and the European Cup. But with Hitzfeld moving upstairs the side began to creak and break up. Kaiserslautern, under Otto

Rehhagel, won the title on the last day of the 1998 season by beating Borussia Mönchengladbach 3-2.

Despite fearsome competition and perennial feuding between its leading players, Bayern still managed two titles in the mid-1990s. In 1998, Beckenbauer, now president of the club, recalled manager Trapattoni for his second spell in charge, and the first of three titles duly came back to the Olympiastadion. Two more followed with Ottmar Hitzfeld at the helm. Hitzfeld's Bayern has included leading German internationals (like Steffan Effenberg, Oliver Khan, Jens Jeremies and Mehmet Schol) as well as clever buys in the foreign transfer market (the Brazilian Giovane Elber and French defender Bixente Lizarazu) and one of the strictest wage policies in European football.

The collapse of Kirch

While sponsorship and attendance money has been rising in the Bundesliga, the strict controls on the commercialization of German clubs have left them heavily dependent on TV income. TV money has poured into the Bundesliga in the last decade, but a reality check may be in store. The Kirch group – holder of the Bundesliga TV rights – went spectacularly bankrupt in 2002. With some clubs at the bottom end of the table dependent for 60 per cent of their income on this money, their prospects look bleak; so bleak that the German government has been considering a very expensive safety net for the clubs and their players.

Out with the old, in with the new. Giovanni Trapattoni (left) of Bayern München and Ottmar Hitzfeld of Borussia Dortmund in 1997. A year later, Hitzfeld replaced Trapattoni at the helm of Germany's most famous club.

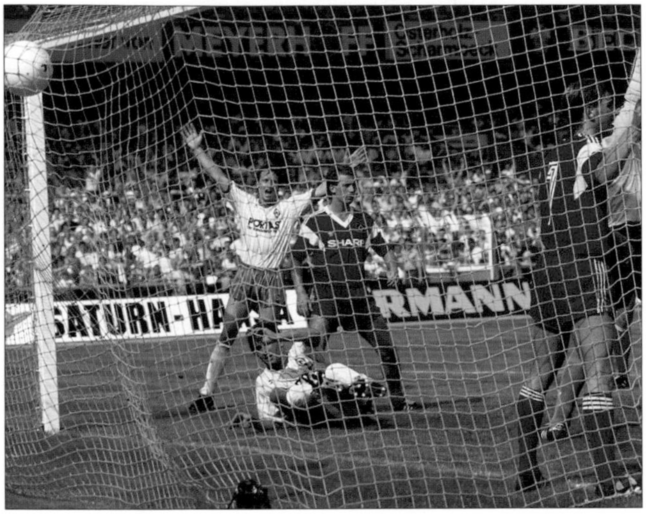

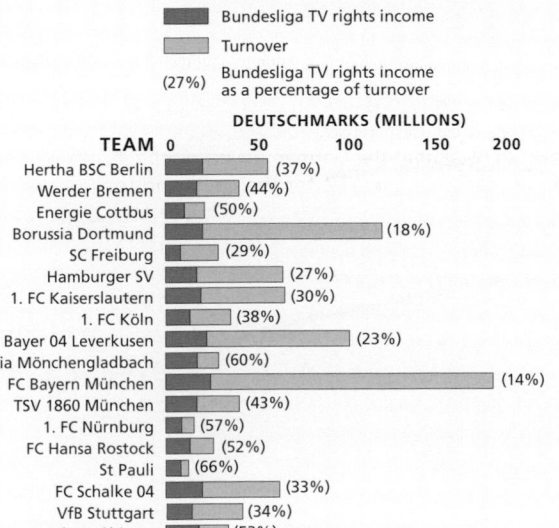

Karlheinz Riedle (on ground) *scores for Werder Bremen, performing one of its* Wesermiracles, *at home to Hamburger SV in 1988.*

TV Rights Income 2001

- ▣ Bundesliga TV rights income
- ▣ Turnover
- (27%) Bundesliga TV rights income as a percentage of turnover

DEUTSCHMARKS (MILLIONS)

TEAM	0	50	100	150	200
Hertha BSC Berlin	(37%)				
Werder Bremen	(44%)				
Energie Cottbus	(50%)				
Borussia Dortmund			(18%)		
SC Freiburg	(29%)				
Hamburger SV	(27%)				
1. FC Kaiserslautern	(30%)				
1. FC Köln	(38%)				
Bayer 04 Leverkusen		(23%)			
Borussia Mönchengladbach	(60%)				
FC Bayern München				(14%)	
TSV 1860 München	(43%)				
1. FC Nürnburg	(57%)				
FC Hansa Rostock	(52%)				
St Pauli	(66%)				
FC Schalke 04	(33%)				
VfB Stuttgart	(34%)				
VfL Wolfsburg	(53%)				

Players' Salaries 1990–2001

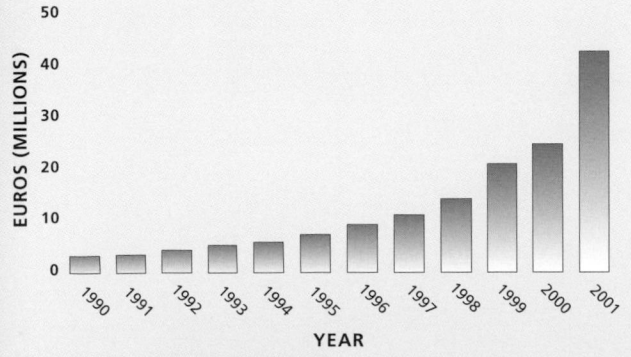

YEAR

EUROS (MILLIONS)

Total wage bill of Bundesliga clubs

Champions' Winning Margin 1992–2002

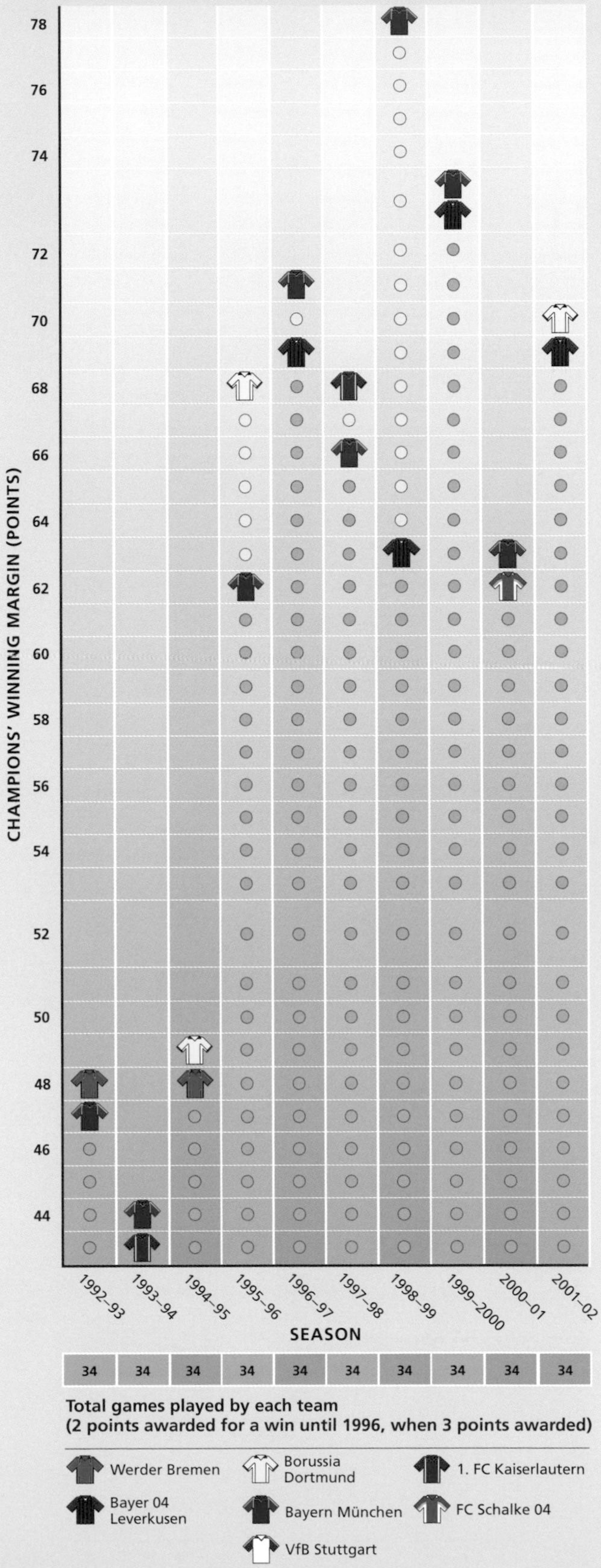

CHAMPIONS' WINNING MARGIN (POINTS)

(y-axis values: 44, 46, 48, 50, 52, 54, 56, 58, 60, 62, 64, 66, 68, 70, 72, 74, 76, 78)

SEASON

1992–93	1993–94	1994–95	1995–96	1996–97	1997–98	1998–99	1999–2000	2000–01	2001–02
34	34	34	34	34	34	34	34	34	34

Total games played by each team
(2 points awarded for a win until 1996, when 3 points awarded)

- Werder Bremen
- Bayer 04 Leverkusen
- Borussia Dortmund
- Bayern München
- VfB Stuttgart
- 1. FC Kaiserslautern
- FC Schalke 04

GERMANY

GERMANY

Key to League Positions Table

- League champions
- Season of promotion to league
- Season of relegation from league
- Other teams playing in league
- 5   Final position in league

Since retiring from playing, Franz Beckenbauer has coached both the national team and Bayern München, and become president of both Bayern and Germany's World Cup bidding committees.

Klaus Toppmöller, the Bayer Leverkusen coach, saw his team lose three major competitions in 2001–02. The club, cruelly named 'Neverkusen', sacked him in 2003 after a disastrous six months.

German League Positions 1981–2002

SEASON

TEAM	1981-82	1982-83	1983-84	1984-85	1985-86	1986-87	1987-88	1988-89	1989-90	1990-91	1991-92	1992-93	1993-94	1994-95	1995-96	1996-97	1997-98	1998-99	1999-2000	2000-01	2001-02
Blau-Weiss 90 Berlin						18															
Hertha BSC Berlin		18							18									11	3	6	5	4
Arminia Bielefeld	12	8	8	16												15	18		17		
VfL Bochum	10	13	15	8	9	12	12	15	16	14	15	16		16		5	12	17	18		
Eintracht Braunschweig	11	15	9	18																	
Werder Bremen	5	2	5	2	2	4	1	3	7	3	9	1	9	2	9	8	7	14	9	7	6
Energie Cottbus																				14	13
Darmstadt 98	17																				
Borussia Dortmund	6	7	13	14	16	5	14	7	4	10	2	4	3	1	1	3	10	4	11	3	1
1. FC Dynamo Dresden										14	15	12	18								
MSV Duisburg	18									19		8	17		9	8	8	18			
Fortuna Düsseldorf	15	9	14	15	14	17			9	12	20			13	16						
Eintracht Frankfurt	8	10	16	12	15	15	10	16	3	5	3	3	5	9	17			15	14	17	
SC Freiburg													15	3	11	17		11	12	6	16
Hamburger SV	1	1	2	5	7	2	6	4	11	4	12	11	13	13	5	13	9	7	3	13	11
Hannover 96					18		11	18													
FC Homburg						16	17		18												
1. FC Kaiserslautern	4	6	12	11	11	7	15	9	13	1	5	8	2	4	16		1	5	5	8	7
Karlsruher SC	14	17		17				13	11	10	13	8	6	6	7	6	16				
1. FC Köln	2	5	6	3	13	10	3	2	2	7	4	12	11	10	12	10	17			10	17
VfB Leipzig													18								
Bayer 04 Leverkusen	16	11	7	13	6	6	8	8	5	8	4	5	4	7	15	2	3	2	2	4	2
SV Waldhof Mannheim			11	6	8	14	16	12	17												
Borussia Mönchengladbach	7	12	3	4	4	3	7	6	15	9	13	9	10	6	4	11	15	18			12
Bayern München	3	4	4	1	1	1	2	1	1	2	10	2	1	5	2	1	2	1	1	1	3
TSV 1860 München														14	8	7	13	10	4	11	9
1. FC Nürnberg	13	14	18		12	9	5	14	8	15	7	14	16				16				15
Kickers Offenbach		17																			
FC Hansa Rostock											18				6	14	6	13	15	12	14
1. FC Saarbrücken					17							18									
St Pauli								10	12	16					14	18					18
FC Schalke 04		16		9	10	13	18				11	10	14	11	3	12	5	9	13	2	5
VfB Stuttgart	9	3	1	10	5	4	5	1	7	7	12	10	4	4	12	8	15	8			
Stuttgarter Kickers								17			17										
KFC Uerdingen		10	7	3	8	9	13	14	17		17		15	18							
SV Ulm																			16		
SpVgg Unterhaching																			10	16	
Wattenscheid 09										11	16	13	17								
VfL Wolfsburg																	14	6	7	9	10

Coach Otto Rehhagel *celebrates as newly-promoted club 1. FC Kaiserslautern wins the Bundesliga in 1998. It was the first and only time a newly-promoted side had won the championship.*

Otmar Hitzfeld *claims Bayern München's third consecutive Bundesliga title in 2001. Victory in the European Cup Final followed soon afterwards.*

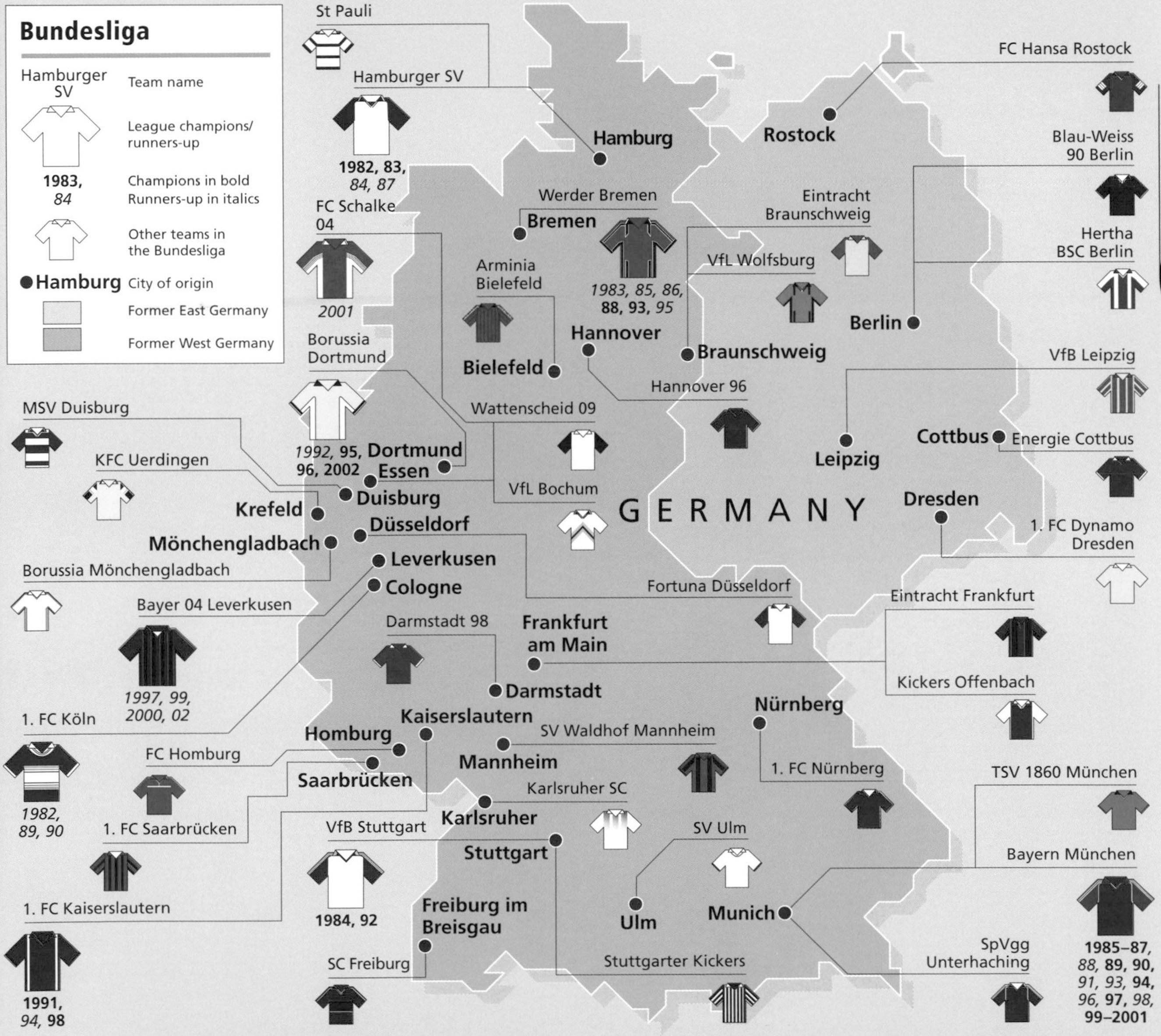

Bundesliga

Hamburger SV	Team name
	League champions/ runners-up
1983, *84*	Champions in bold Runners-up in italics
	Other teams in the Bundesliga
● **Hamburg**	City of origin
	Former East Germany
	Former West Germany

GERMANY

St Pauli

Hamburger SV
1982, 83, *84, 87*

FC Schalke 04
2001

Borussia Dortmund
1992, 95, 96, 2002

MSV Duisburg

KFC Uerdingen
Krefeld

Mönchengladbach
Borussia Mönchengladbach

Bayer 04 Leverkusen
1997, 99, 2000, 02

1. FC Köln
1982, 89, 90

FC Homburg

1. FC Saarbrücken

1. FC Kaiserslautern
1991, *94, 98*

● **Hamburg**

Werder Bremen
Bremen
1983, 85, 86, **88, 93,** *95*

Arminia Bielefeld
Bielefeld

Dortmund
Essen
Duisburg
Düsseldorf

Wattenscheid 09

VfL Bochum

Leverkusen
Cologne

Darmstadt 98
Frankfurt am Main
● **Darmstadt**

Homburg
Kaiserslautern
Saarbrücken

Mannheim
SV Waldhof Mannheim
Karlsruher SC

VfB Stuttgart
Karlsruher
Stuttgart
1984, 92

Freiburg im Breisgau
SC Freiburg

● **Hamburg**
● **Rostock**

Eintracht Braunschweig
VfL Wolfsburg
Hannover
● **Braunschweig**

Hannover 96

Leipzig

G E R M A N Y

Fortuna Düsseldorf

● **Nürnberg**
1. FC Nürnberg

Stuttgart
SV Ulm
● **Ulm**

Stuttgarter Kickers

FC Hansa Rostock

Blau-Weiss 90 Berlin

Hertha BSC Berlin
● **Berlin**

VfB Leipzig

● **Cottbus** Energie Cottbus

● **Dresden**
1. FC Dynamo Dresden

Eintracht Frankfurt

Kickers Offenbach

TSV 1860 München

Bayern München
1985–87, **88,** *89, 90, 91, 93,* **94,** *96,* **97,** *98,* **99–2001**

SpVgg Unterhaching

● **Munich**

Germany (including former East and West Germany)

Deutscher Fussball-Bund
Founded: 1900
Joined FIFA: 1904–46, 1950
Joined UEFA: 1954

LOCAL, CITY AND INTER-CITY LEAGUE matches were being played all across Germany in the late 19th century. In 1898 the first national championship was awarded after a play-off between the winners of the two strongest regional leagues: Southern Germany and Berlin. With the formation of the Deutscher Fussball-Bund in 1900 a more systematic play-off system was introduced between the winners of all the regional leagues in 1902. The format remained the same while the German state grew and shrank. Between 1938 and 1944 Austrian teams were included, and after 1948, when the format was recreated, East Germany and its teams had been separated off.

East Germany retained the format until 1949, before moving to a conventional national league format. In 1963–64 the old championship was abandoned and a national professional league – the Bundesliga – was established. Its format has remained broadly the same since, with two teams from the former East Germany being awarded a place after German unification in 1991. There are now two national leagues of 18 teams, with a standard three up, three down promotion system.

The German Cup was set up in 1935 and it too has seen Austrians join and East Germans depart and return.

German National Championship Record 1903–44

SEASON	CHAMPIONS	SEASON	CHAMPIONS
1903	VfB Leipzig	1926	SpVgg Furth
1904	*	1927	1. FC Nürnberg
1905	Union 92 Berlin	1928	Hamburger SV
1906	VfB Leipzig	1929	SpVgg Furth
1907	SC Freiburg	1930	Hertha BSC Berlin
1908	Viktoria Berlin	1931	Hertha BSC Berlin
1909	Phoenix Karlsruhe	1932	Bayern München
1910	Karlsruher FV	1933	Fortuna Düsseldorf
1911	Viktoria Berlin	1934	FC Schalke 04
1912	Holstein Keil	1935	FC Schalke 04
1913	VfB Leipzig	1936	1. FC Nürnberg
1914	SpVgg Furth	1937	FC Schalke 04
1915–19	no championship	1938	Hannover 96
1920	1. FC Nürnberg	1939	FC Schalke 04
1921	1. FC Nürnberg	1940	FC Schalke 04
1922	**	1941	Rapid Wien
1923	Hamburger SV	1942	FC Schalke 04
1924	1. FC Nürnberg	1943	Dresdener FC
1925	1. FC Nürnberg	1944	Dresdener FC

* Final not played after a dispute over semi-final venues.

** Hamburger SV awarded championship but declined it following an appeal by FC Nürnberg.

West German League Record 1948–63

SEASON	CHAMPIONS	SEASON	CHAMPIONS
1948	1. FC Nürnberg	1956	Borussia Dortmund
1949	VfR Mannheim	1957	Borussia Dortmund
1950	VfB Stuttgart	1958	FC Schalke 04
1951	1. FC Kaiserslautern	1959	Eintracht Frankfurt
1952	VfB Stuttgart	1960	Hamburger SV
1953	1. FC Kaiserslautern	1961	1. FC Nürnberg
1954	Hannover 96	1962	1. FC Köln
1955	Rot-Weiss Essen	1963	Borussia Dortmund

East German League Record 1948–91

SEASON	CHAMPIONS	SEASON	CHAMPIONS
1948	SG Planitz	1970	Carl-Zeiss Jena
1949	ZGS Halle	1971	Dynamo Dresden
1950	Horch Zwickau	1972	1. FC Magdeberg
1951	Chemie Leipzig	1973	Dynamo Dresden
1952	Turbine Halle	1974	1. FC Magdeberg
1953	Dynamo Dresden	1975	1. FC Magdeberg
1954	Turbine Erfurt	1976	Dynamo Dresden
1955	Turbine Erfurt	1977	Dynamo Dresden
1956	Wismut KMS	1978	Dynamo Dresden
1957	Wismut KMS	1979	Dynamo Berlin
1958	Vorwärts Berlin	1980	Dynamo Berlin
1959	Wismut KMS	1981	Dynamo Berlin
1960	Vorwärts Berlin	1982	Dynamo Berlin
1961	no championship	1983	Dynamo Berlin
1962	Vorwärts Berlin	1984	Dynamo Berlin
1963	Motor Jena	1985	Dynamo Berlin
1964	Chemie Leipzig	1986	Dynamo Berlin
1965	Vorwärts Berlin	1987	Dynamo Berlin
1966	Vorwärts Berlin	1988	Dynamo Berlin
1967	FC Karl-Marx-Stadt	1989	Dynamo Dresden
1968	Carl-Zeiss Jena	1990	Dynamo Dresden
1969	Vorwärts Berlin	1991	Hansa Rostock

East German Cup Record 1949–91

YEAR	WINNERS	YEAR	WINNERS
1949	BSG Waggonbau Dessau	1971	SG Dynamo Dresden
1950	BSG EHW Thale	1972	FC Carl-Zeiss Jena
1951	no competition	1973	1. FC Magdeburg
1952	SG Volkspolizei Dresden	1974	FC Carl-Zeiss Jena
1953	no competition	1975	BSG Sachsenring Zwickau
1954	Vorwärts Berlin	1976	1. FC Lokomotive Leipzig
1955	no competition	1977	SG Dynamo Dresden
1956	SC Chemie Halle	1978	1. FC Magdeburg
1957	SC Lokomotive Leipzig	1979	1. FC Magdeburg
1958	SC Einheit Dresden	1980	FC Carl-Zeiss Jena
1959	SC Dynamo Berlin	1981	1. FC Lokomotive Leipzig
1960	SC Motor Jena	1982	SG Dynamo Dresden
1961	no competition	1983	1. FC Magdeburg
1962	SC Chemie Halle	1984	SG Dynamo Dresden
1963	BSC Motor Zwickau	1985	SG Dynamo Dresden
1964	SC Aufbau Magdeburg	1986	1. FC Lokomotive Leipzig
1965	SC Aufbau Magdeburg	1987	1. FC Lokomotive Leipzig
1966	BSG Motor Leipzig	1988	Berliner FC Dynamo
1967	BSC Motor Zwickau	1989	Berliner FC Dynamo
1968	1. FC Union Berlin	1990	SG Dynamo Dresden
1969	1. FC Magdeburg	1991	FC Hansa Rostock
1970	Vorwärts Berlin		

Bundesliga Record 1964–2003

SEASON	CHAMPIONS	RUNNERS-UP
1964	1. FC Köln	MSV Duisburg
1965	Werder Bremen	1. FC Köln
1966	TSV 1860 München	Borussia Dortmund
1967	Eintracht Braunschweig	TSV 1860 München
1968	1. FC Nürnberg	Werder Bremen
1969	Bayern München	Alemania Aachen
1970	Borussia Mönchengladbach	Bayern München
1971	Borussia Mönchengladbach	Bayern München
1972	Bayern München	FC Schalke 04
1973	Bayern München	1. FC Köln
1974	Bayern München	Borussia Mönchengladbach
1975	Borussia Mönchengladbach	Hertha BSC Berlin
1976	Borussia Mönchengladbach	Hamburger SV
1977	Borussia Mönchengladbach	FC Schalke 04

GERMANY

Bundesliga Record (*continued*)

SEASON	CHAMPIONS	RUNNERS-UP
1978	1. FC Köln	Borussia Mönchengladbach
1979	Hamburger SV	VfB Stuttgart
1980	Bayern München	Hamburger SV
1981	Bayern München	Hamburger SV
1982	Hamburger SV	1. FC Köln
1983	Hamburger SV	Werder Bremen
1984	VfB Stuttgart	Hamburger SV
1985	Bayern München	Werder Bremen
1986	Bayern München	Werder Bremen
1987	Bayern München	Hamburger SV
1988	Werder Bremen	Bayern München
1989	Bayern München	1. FC Köln
1990	Bayern München	1. FC Köln
1991	1. FC Kaiserslautern	Bayern München
1992	VfB Stuttgart	Borussia Dortmund
1993	Werder Bremen	Bayern München
1994	Bayern München	1. FC Kaiserslautern
1995	Borussia Dortmund	Werder Bremen
1996	Borussia Dortmund	Bayern München
1997	Bayern München	Bayer Leverkusen
1998	1. FC Kaiserslautern	Bayern München
1999	Bayern München	Bayer Leverkusen
2000	Bayern München	Bayer Leverkusen
2001	Bayern München	FC Schalke 04
2002	Borussia Dortmund	Bayer Leverkusen
2003	Bayern München	VfB Stuttgart

Bundesliga Summary

TEAM	TOTALS	CHAMPIONS & RUNNERS-UP (BOLD) (*ITALICS*)
Bayern München	17, 6	**1969**, *70, 71, 72–74*, **80, 81, 85–87, 89, 90**, *91, 93,* **94**, *96,* **97**, *98, 99–2001,* **03**
Borussia Mönchengladbach	5, 2	**1970, 71**, *74,* **75–77**, *78*
Hamburger SV	3, 5	*1976, 79, 80, 81,* **82, 83**, *84, 87*
Werder Bremen	3, 5	**1965**, *68, 83, 85, 86,* **88, 93**, *95*
Borussia Dortmund	3, 2	*1966, 92,* **95, 96**, *2002*
1. FC Köln	2, 6	**1964**, *65, 73,* **78**, *82, 88–90*
VfB Stuttgart	2, 2	*1979,* **84, 92**, *2003*
1. FC Kaiserslautern	2, 1	**1991**, *94,* **98**
TSV 1860 München	1, 1	**1966**, *67*
1. FC Nürnberg	1, 0	**1968**
Eintracht Braunschweig	1, 0	**1967**
Bayer Leverkusen	0, 4	*1997, 99, 2000, 02*
FC Schalke 04	0, 3	*1972, 77, 2001*
Alemania Aachen	0, 1	*1969*
Hertha BSC Berlin	0, 1	*1975*
MSV Duisberg	0, 1	*1964*

German Cup Record 1935–2003

YEAR	WINNERS	SCORE	RUNNERS-UP
1935	1. FC Nürnberg	2-0	FC Schalke 04
1936	VfB Leipzig	2-1	FC Schalke 04
1937	FC Schalke 04	2-1	Fortuna Düsseldorf
1938	SK Rapid Wien	3-1	FSV Frankfurt
1939	1. FC Nürnberg	2-0	SV Waldhof Mannheim
1940	Dresdener SC	2-1 (aet)	1. FC Nürnberg
1941	Dresdener SC	2-1	FC Schalke 04
1942	TSV 1860 München	2-0	FC Schalke 04
1943	First Vienna FC	3-2 (aet)	Hamburger SV
1944–52		no competition	
1953	Rot-Weiss Essen	2-1	Alemania Aachen
1954	VfB Stuttgart	1-0 (aet)	1. FC Köln
1955	Karlsruher SC	3-2	FC Schalke 04

German Cup Record (*continued*)

YEAR	WINNERS	SCORE	RUNNERS-UP
1956	Karlsruher SC	3-1	Hamburger SV
1957	Bayern München	1-0	Fortuna Düsseldorf
1958	VfB Stuttgart	4-3	Fortuna Düsseldorf
1959	Schwarz Weiss Essen	5-2	Borussia Neunkirchen
1960	Borussia Mönchengladbach	3-2	Karlsruher FC
1961	Werder Bremen	2-0	1. FC Kaiserslautern
1962	1. FC Nurnberg	2-1 (aet)	Fortuna Düsseldorf
1963	Hamburger SV	3-0	Borussia Dortmund
1964	TSV 1860 München	2-0	Eintracht Frankfurt
1965	Borussia Dortmund	2-0	Alemania Aachen
1966	Bayern München	4-2	MSV Duisburg
1967	Bayern München	4-0	Hamburger SV
1968	1. FC Köln	4-1	VfL Bochum
1969	Bayern München	2-1	FC Schalke 04
1970	Kickers Offenbach	2-1	1. FC Köln
1971	Bayern München	2-1 (aet)	1. FC Köln
1972	FC Schlake 04	5-0	1. FC Kaiserslautern
1973	Borussia Mönchengladbach	2-1 (aet)	1. FC Köln
1974	Eintracht Frankfurt	3-1 (aet)	Hamburger SV
1975	Eintracht Frankfurt	1-0	MSV Duisburg
1976	Hamburger SV	2-0	1. FC Kaiserslautern
1977	1. FC Köln	1-1 (aet), (replay) 1-0	Hertha BSC Berlin
1978	1. FC Köln	2-0	Fortuna Düsseldorf
1979	Fortuna Düsseldorf	1-0 (aet)	Hertha BSC Berlin
1980	Fortuna Düsseldorf	2-1	1. FC Köln
1981	Eintracht Frankfurt	3-1	1. FC Kaiserslautern
1982	Bayern München	4-2	1. FC Nürnberg
1983	1. FC Köln	1-0	Fortuna Köln
1984	Bayern München	1-1 (aet)(7-6 pens)	Borussia Mönchengladbach
1985	Bayer Uerdingen	2-1	Bayern München
1986	Bayern München	5-2	VfB Stuttgart
1987	Hamburger SV	3-1	Stuttgarter Kickers
1988	Eintracht Frankfurt	1-0	VfL Bochum
1989	Borussia Dortmund	4-1	Werder Bremen
1990	1. FC Kaiserslautern	3-2	Werder Bremen
1991	Werder Bremen	1-1 (aet)(4-3 pens)	1. FC Köln
1992	Hannover 96	0-0 (aet)(4-3 pens)	Borussia Mönchengladbach
1993	Bayer 04 Leverkusen	1-0	Hertha BSC Berlin
1994	Werder Bremen	3-1	Rot-Weiss Essen
1995	Borussia Mönchengladbach	3-0	Wolfsburg
1996	1. FC Kaiserslautern	1-0	Karlsruher FC
1997	VfB Stuttgart	2-0	Energie Cottbus
1998	Bayern München	2-1	MSV Duisburg
1999	Werder Bremen	1-1 (aet)(5-4 pens)	Bayern München
2000	Bayern München	3-0	Werder Bremen
2001	FC Schalke 04	2-0	1. FC Union Berlin
2002	FC Schalke 04	4-2	Bayer Leverkusen
2003	Bayern München	3-1	1. FC Kaiserslautern

German Cup Summary

TEAM	TOTAL	WINNERS & RUNNERS-UP (BOLD) (*ITALICS*)
Bayern München	11, 2	**1957, 66, 67, 69, 71, 82, 84**, *85,* **86, 98, 99, 2000, 03**
1. FC Köln	4, 6	*1954,* **68**, *70, 71, 73,* **77, 78**, *80, 83, 91*
FC Schalke 04	4, 6	*1935, 36,* **37**, *41, 42, 55, 69,* **72, 2001, 02**
Werder Bremen	4, 3	**1961**, *89, 90,* **91, 94, 99**, *2000*
Eintracht Frankfurt	4, 1	*1964,* **74, 75, 81**, *88*

This summary only features clubs that have won the German Cup four times or more. For a full list of cup winners and runners-up please see the Cup Record above.

GERMANY

France

THE SEASON IN REVIEW 2002–03

UNLIKE THE OTHER BIG LEAGUES in Europe, nine different clubs have won France's Championnat in the last decade. No club had managed to retain the championship since Marseilles in the early 1990s. The price of such variety is that no club or small group of clubs has been able to consolidate its financial and sporting success sufficiently to challenge the Spanish, Italian and English giants. This year was no different; all three French teams – Lyon, Lens and Auxerre – went out of the Champions League at the first time of asking. Things were little better in the UEFA Cup. But, while the Italian, English and German championships descended into three, two and one horse races respectively, Le Championnat had six or seven teams in with a real chance almost to the end.

Unexpected early pacesetters

The pacesetters in the league came from the most unexpected quarters. First off the mark was the tiny En Avant Guingamp, whose uninhibited start to the season saw them take the lead. Guingamp, with only 9,000 residents, is by far the smallest town to ever hold the lead of the top flight in France. Next up was Nice, a club with a distinguished record but who were only narrowly promoted to the first division last season after endless wrangling over the state of their finances and bankability. With a hastily assembled squad of journeymen and cast-offs, Gernot Rohr took his side to the top of the table until early in the New Year.

Below the top three, Auxerre was a regular feature, but Guy Roux's side found goals hard to come by and never looked like disturbing them. Bordeaux took its time to get going and the loss of Christophe Dugarry to Birmingham during the winter transfer window looked like it might knock them off balance.

Everson Da Silva – one of Nice's gems – keeps his eye on the ball. A motley collection of cut-price but big-hearted players at Nice this season saw the surprise team of the year lead the table from bigger and richer clubs through the winter.

Le Championnat League Table 2002–03

CLUB	P	W	D	L	F	A	Pts	
Olympique Lyonnais	38	19	11	8	63	41	68	Champions League
AS Monaco*	38	19	10	9	66	33	67	Champions League*
Olympique Marseille	38	19	8	11	41	36	65	Champions League
Bordeaux	38	18	10	10	57	36	64	UEFA Cup
FC Sochaux	38	17	13	8	46	31	64	UEFA Cup
AJ Auxerre	38	18	10	10	38	29	64	UEFA Cup (cup winners)
Guingamp	38	19	5	14	59	46	62	
RC Lens	38	14	15	9	43	31	57	UEFA Cup (Fair Play)
FC Nantes	38	16	8	14	37	39	56	
Nice	38	13	16	9	39	31	55	
Paris SG	38	14	12	12	47	36	54	
SC Bastia	38	12	11	15	40	48	47	
RC Strasbourg	38	11	12	15	40	54	45	
Lille OSC	38	10	12	16	29	44	42	
Stade Rennais	38	10	10	18	35	45	40	
Montpellier HSC	38	10	10	18	37	54	40	
AC Ajaccio	38	9	12	17	29	49	39	
Le Havre	38	10	8	20	27	47	38	Relegated
CS Sedan	38	9	9	20	41	59	36	Relegated
A Troyes AC	38	7	10	21	23	48	31	Relegated

Promoted clubs: Le Mans UC 72, FC Metz, Toulouse FC.

* AS Monaco were forcibly relegated to 2nd level due to financial problems; the club have appealed.

Marseille's Manuel dos Santos goes past PSG's Fabrice Fiorese in their league clash at Paris in front of a very bad-tempered crowd.

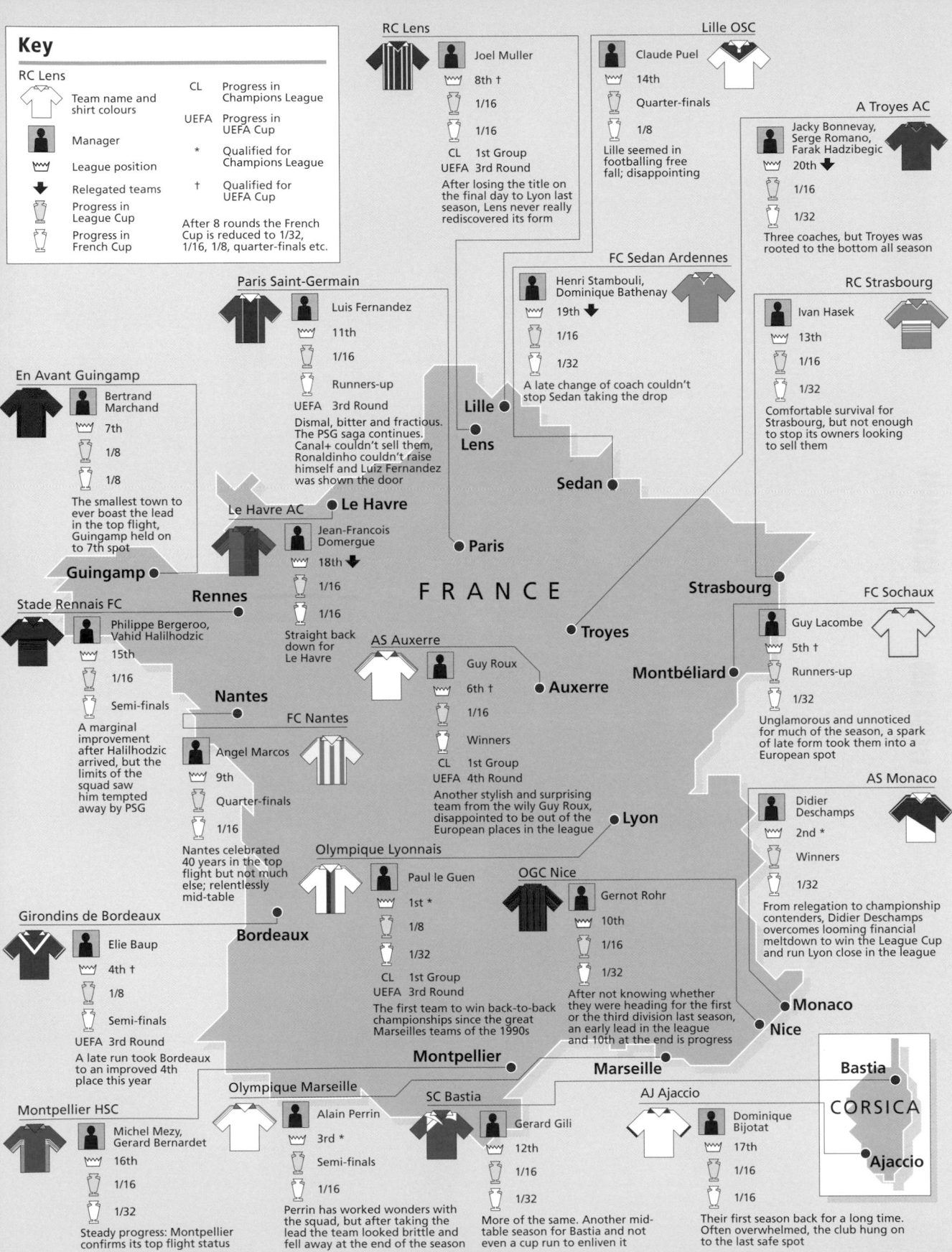

Key

RC Lens

Team name and shirt colours

Manager

League position

Relegated teams

Progress in League Cup

Progress in French Cup

CL — Progress in Champions League

UEFA — Progress in UEFA Cup

* — Qualified for Champions League

† — Qualified for UEFA Cup

After 8 rounds the French Cup is reduced to 1/32, 1/16, 1/8, quarter-finals etc.

RC Lens
Joel Muller
8th †
1/16
1/16
CL — 1st Group
UEFA — 3rd Round

After losing the title on the final day to Lyon last season, Lens never really rediscovered its form

Lille OSC
Claude Puel
14th
Quarter-finals
1/8

Lille seemed in footballing free fall; disappointing

A Troyes AC
Jacky Bonnevay, Serge Romano, Farak Hadzibegic
20th ↓
1/16
1/32

Three coaches, but Troyes was rooted to the bottom all season

RC Strasbourg
Ivan Hasek
13th
1/16
1/32

Comfortable survival for Strasbourg, but not enough to stop its owners looking to sell them

Paris Saint-Germain
Luis Fernandez
11th
1/16
Runners-up
UEFA — 3rd Round

Dismal, bitter and fractious. The PSG saga continues. Canal+ couldn't sell them, Ronaldinho couldn't raise himself and Luiz Fernandez was shown the door

FC Sedan Ardennes
Henri Stambouli, Dominique Bathenay
19th ↓
1/16
1/32

A late change of coach couldn't stop Sedan taking the drop

En Avant Guingamp
Bertrand Marchand
7th
1/8
1/8

The smallest town to ever boast the lead in the top flight, Guingamp held on to 7th spot

Le Havre AC
Jean-Francois Domergue
18th ↓
1/16
1/16

Straight back down for Le Havre

Stade Rennais FC
Philippe Bergeroo, Vahid Halilhodzic
15th
1/16
Semi-finals

A marginal improvement after Halilhodzic arrived, but the limits of the squad saw him tempted away by PSG

AS Auxerre
Guy Roux
6th †
1/16
Winners
CL — 1st Group
UEFA — 4th Round

Another stylish and surprising team from the wily Guy Roux, disappointed to be out of the European places in the league

FC Sochaux
Guy Lacombe
5th †
Runners-up
1/32

Unglamorous and unnoticed for much of the season, a spark of late form took them into a European spot

FC Nantes
Angel Marcos
9th
Quarter-finals
1/16

Nantes celebrated 40 years in the top flight but not much else; relentlessly mid-table

AS Monaco
Didier Deschamps
2nd *
Winners
1/32

From relegation to championship contenders, Didier Deschamps overcomes looming financial meltdown to win the League Cup and run Lyon close in the league

Olympique Lyonnais
Paul le Guen
1st *
1/8
1/32
CL — 1st Group
UEFA — 3rd Round

The first team to win back-to-back championships since the great Marseilles teams of the 1990s

OGC Nice
Gernot Rohr
10th
1/16
1/32

After not knowing whether they were heading for the first or the third division last season, an early lead in the league and 10th at the end is progress

Girondins de Bordeaux
Elie Baup
4th †
1/8
Semi-finals
UEFA — 3rd Round

A late run took Bordeaux to an improved 4th place this year

Montpellier HSC
Michel Mezy, Gerard Bernardet
16th
1/16
1/32

Steady progress: Montpellier confirms its top flight status

Olympique Marseille
Alain Perrin
3rd *
Semi-finals
1/16

Perrin has worked wonders with the squad, but after taking the lead the team looked brittle and fell away at the end of the season

SC Bastia
Gerard Gili
12th
1/16
1/32

More of the same. Another mid-table season for Bastia and not even a cup run to enliven it

AJ Ajaccio
Dominique Bijotat
17th
1/16
1/16

Their first season back for a long time. Often overwhelmed, the club hung on to the last safe spot

F R A N C E

Lille

Lens

Sedan

Paris

Le Havre

Guingamp

Rennes

Strasbourg

Troyes

Nantes

Montbéliard

Auxerre

Lyon

Bordeaux

Monaco

Nice

Montpellier

Marseille

Bastia

CORSICA

Ajaccio

But, in his absence, the strike force of Darcheville and French Player of the Year Pauleta came good and Bordeaux deserved its fourth spot.

PSG provided an amusing subplot to the season. Canal Plus and its masters Vivendi appear to have lost patience with the club's expensive habits and poor performances and were looking for a new owner all season. They eventually had to look for a new manager too, as Luis Fernandez failed to get the best from his expensively assembled squad. PSG roused itself in the over-hyped TV spectaculars of the season against Marseilles in the cup and the league, beating them three times. But woeful inconsistency saw them throw points away all season. Things reached rock bottom when a 2-0 lead over Guingamp turned into a 3-2 defeat. Fans booed the team from the pitch and a minority stoned the team bus. Eleventh was about where it deserved to be.

Down at the bottom Rennes was propping up the table for most of the early part of the season. Philippe Bergeroo was hastily replaced by Vahid Halilhodzic who dragged them out of trouble. Montpellier, another club in the brink of bankruptcy, did well to keep out of trouble, though the same cannot be said of its president Louis Nicollin, who was convicted in the

Above: The French cups produced a whole host of giant killings and upsets this season. Here the amateurs of Schiltigheim celebrate their victory over Toulouse and a place in the French Cup quarter-finals.

Below: Marseille's Frank Leboeuf rises to head the ball clear in its clash with Lyon. Despite holding the lead, Marseille's under par performances and ill discipline in the final run saw the title slip away.

FRANCE

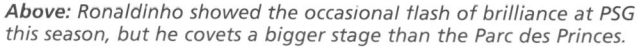

Above: Ronaldinho showed the occasional flash of brilliance at PSG this season, but he covets a bigger stage than the Parc des Princes.

Right: A cup triumph and a European place, but Guy Roux will probably be selling the best of the Auxerre squad over the summer.

Far right: Nice's wily coach Gernot Rohr welded together a team good enough to hold the lead at mid-season on a tiny budget.

Far left: Khalilou Fadiga had a brilliant World Cup for Senegal and continued his good form for Auxerre during the league season.

Left: Bordeaux's Pedro Pauleta stretches for the ball as Auxerre's Grichting looks on. Pauleta's goals kept Bordeaux in the hunt for a European spot but the team could never quite crack a top three place.

Lyon's Sonny Anderson roars past the Monaco defence. With his return from injury, Lyon did the same to Monaco in the league.

Race for the Championship

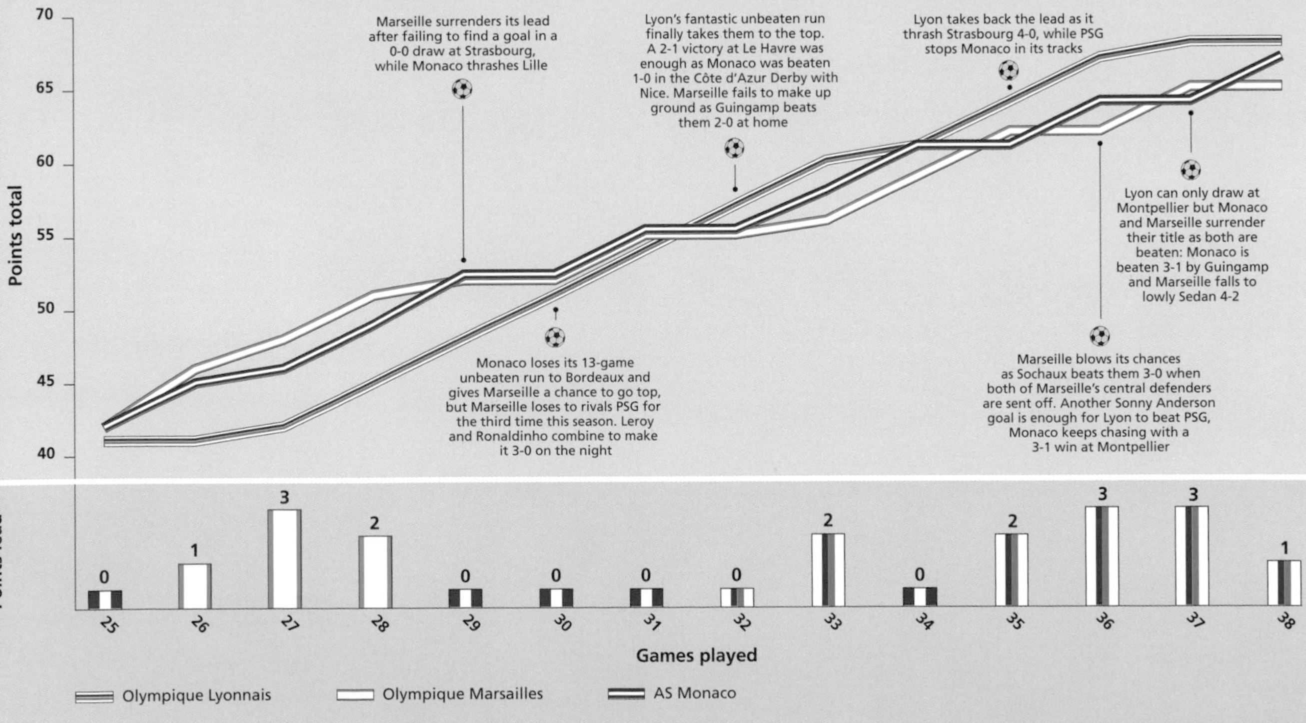

Marseille surrenders its lead after failing to find a goal in a 0-0 draw at Strasbourg, while Monaco thrashes Lille

Lyon's fantastic unbeaten run finally takes them to the top. A 2-1 victory at Le Havre was enough as Monaco was beaten 1-0 in the Côte d'Azur Derby with Nice. Marseille fails to make up ground as Guingamp beats them 2-0 at home

Lyon takes back the lead as it thrash Strasbourg 4-0, while PSG stops Monaco in its tracks

Monaco loses its 13-game unbeaten run to Bordeaux and gives Marseille a chance to go top, but Marseille loses to rivals PSG for the third time this season. Leroy and Ronaldinho combine to make it 3-0 on the night

Lyon can only draw at Montpellier but Monaco and Marseille surrender their title as both are beaten: Monaco is beaten 3-1 by Guingamp and Marseille falls to lowly Sedan 4-2

Marseille blows its chances as Sochaux beats them 3-0 when both of Marseille's central defenders are sent off. Another Sonny Anderson goal is enough for Lyon to beat PSG, Monaco keeps chasing with a 3-1 win at Montpellier

Points total (y-axis: 40, 45, 50, 55, 60, 65, 70)

Points lead

Games played	25	26	27	28	29	30	31	32	33	34	35	36	37	38
Points lead	0	1	3	2	0	0	0	0	2	0	2	3	3	1

Olympique Lyonnais Olympique Marsailles AS Monaco

FRANCE

courts of fraud. Troyes and Sedan, however, could not find the inspiration that would take them out of the danger zone and they, together with Le Havre, took the drop.

Three-way race for the title

In the second half of the season the championship race focused on three clubs: Monaco, Marseilles and Olympique Lyonnais. Most unlikely contender was Monaco who had flirted with relegation last season, was well known to be carrying crippling levels of debt and was sufficiently desperate to contemplate investment from some very dubious Russian utilities companies. Add to this a new manager in Didier Deschamps and the usual kinds of backstairs intrigue that a club connected to a royal family and a tax haven should expect, and the prospects did not look particularly good. However, under Deschamps the club was transformed, and was unbeaten in the league from November to March. Playmaker Ludovic Giuly and striker Shabani Nonda impressed.

Marseille kept Monaco company at the top through most of the spring. Although it occasionally struggled to score, the defence was miserly. But some terrible home defeats against PSG and Guingamp in the spring put them on the back foot. Its bid for the title finally collapsed in an ill-tempered 3-0 defeat by Sochaux, in which both Marseilles central defenders, Lebeouf and van Buyten, were sent off.

Lyon began the season by sticking to the script, as last year's champion was bundled out of both French cups and its league form through the winter left them some way off the top. Fans were angry enough to storm the club's training camp. It also departed the Champions League, but not before taking four points from Internazionale, including a scintillating 2-1 victory at the San Siro. Relieved of cup distractions, Lyon set about its domestic task with renewed concentration. Perhaps most important was the return of the inspirational Sonny Anderson from injury, which took them through a spell of 11 games unbeaten. As the season came to its conclusion, Lyon seemed to get stronger, with strikers Sidney Govou and Pegguy Luyindula on form. Lyon put its seal on the title with a 4-0 win over Strasbourg in May with a game to go.

Above: Monaco's Ludovic Giuly lifts the ball over Sochaux goalkeeper Teddy Richert in the League Cup Final. Giuly's two goals helped Monaco to its first League Cup as it convincingly beat Sochaux 4-1 after a second-half flood of goals.

Right: Didier Drogba led the line for tiny Breton club En Avant Guingamp this season. His 16 goals were the centrepiece of the club's success.

French League Cup

2003 FINAL

May 17 – Stade de France, Paris
AS Monaco **4-1** FC Sochaux
(Giuly 57, 77,   (Saveljic 88 pen)
Squillaci 61,
Prso 67)
h/t: 0-0 **Att:** 75,379
Ref: Ledentu

French Cup

2003 FINAL

May 31 – Stade de France, Paris
AJ Auxerre **2-1** Paris Saint-
(Cisse 77,   Germain
Boumsong 89)   (Leal 21)
h/t: 0-1 **Att:** 75,000
Ref: Layec

Top Goalscorers 2002–03

PLAYER	CLUB	NATIONALITY	GOALS
Shabani Nonda	AS Monaco	Congolese	26
Pedro Pauleta	Bordeaux	Portuguese	23
Didier Drogba	Guingamp	French	16

International Club Performances 2002–03

CLUB	COMPETITION	PROGRESS
AJ Auxerre	Champions League	1st Group Stage
	UEFA Cup	4th Round
RC Lens	Champions League	1st Group Stage
	UEFA Cup	3rd Round
Olympique Lyonnais	Champions League	1st Group Stage
	UEFA Cup	3rd Round
Bordeaux	UEFA Cup	3rd Round
Lorient	UEFA Cup	1st Round
PSG	UEFA Cup	3rd Round

Winning goalscorer Jean-Alain Boumsong and captain Yann Lachuer lift the French Cup after beating PSG 2-1 at the Stade de France; it was Auxerre's third victory in a French Cup Final.

Far left: *Monaco coach Didier Deschamps (left) shows PSG's Luiz Fernandez how to grip his raincoat in a statelier manner. Next season will begin without Fernandez as PSG's performances sent him on his way but Monaco secured a last-minute reprieve from its financial problems and will remain in the division.*

Left: *Sonny Anderson, Olympique Lyonnais' talismanic captain, lifts the extraordinary French league trophy. Despite going down 4-1 to Guingamp on the final day, Lyon had the league won already.*

Below: *Jean-Alain Boumsong leaves PSG's defence in his wake. In the French Cup Final Auxerre came back from 1-0 down and Boumsong grabbed the winner in the last minute of normal time.*

Association Football in France

1872: Le Havre Athletic Club formed (although first footballing section not formed until 1892)

1881: Girondins de Bordeaux formed; oldest independent French club

1904: Affiliation to FIFA. First international, v Belgium, drawn 3-3, venue: Brussels

1918: Formation of FA: Fédération Française de Football, (FFF). First French Cup Final

1922: First women's informal international v Dick Kerr's Ladies (England), drawn 1-1, venue: Paris

1932: National league established; professionalism legalized

1940–45: During war league championship played as play-offs between regions, cup continued

1954: Affiliation to UEFA

1992: Cup abandoned after Bastia disaster, a temporary stand collapsed in Cup semi-final, Bastia v Olympique Marseille, over 1,500 injured

1993: Olympique Marseille stripped of European Cup and French League title for match-fixing

FRANCE

Timeline: 1870, 1880, 1890, 1900, 1910, 1920, 1930, 1940, 1950, 1960, 1970, 1980, 1990, 2000, 2010

Jules Rimet (left) – lawyer, first President of FIFA and pioneer of the World Cup – hands its first-ever trophy to Dr Paul Jude, President of the Uruguayan FA. Uruguay beat Argentina 4-2 in the Final in Montevideo on 30 July 1930.

Key

- International football
- Affiliation to FIFA
- Affiliation to UEFA
- Women's football
- War
- Disaster
- World Cup host
- World Cup winner
- ■ European Championships host
- ● European Championships winner
- ○ Competition winner
- △ Competition runner-up

Bas - Bastia
Bor - Bordeaux
Mon - Monaco
OM - Olympique Marseille
PSG - Paris Saint-Germain
St-E - St-Etienne
St R - Stade de Reims

International Competitions

1938: ■

European Cup

1956: △ St R
1959: △ St R
1960: ■

1976: △ St-E
1978: △ Bas

UEFA Cup

European Cup-Winners' Cup

1984: ● ■

1991: △ OM
1992: ○ OM
1993: △ Mon

1996: △ Bor ○ PSG
1997: △ PSG
1998: ■ ■
1999: △ OM
2000: ●

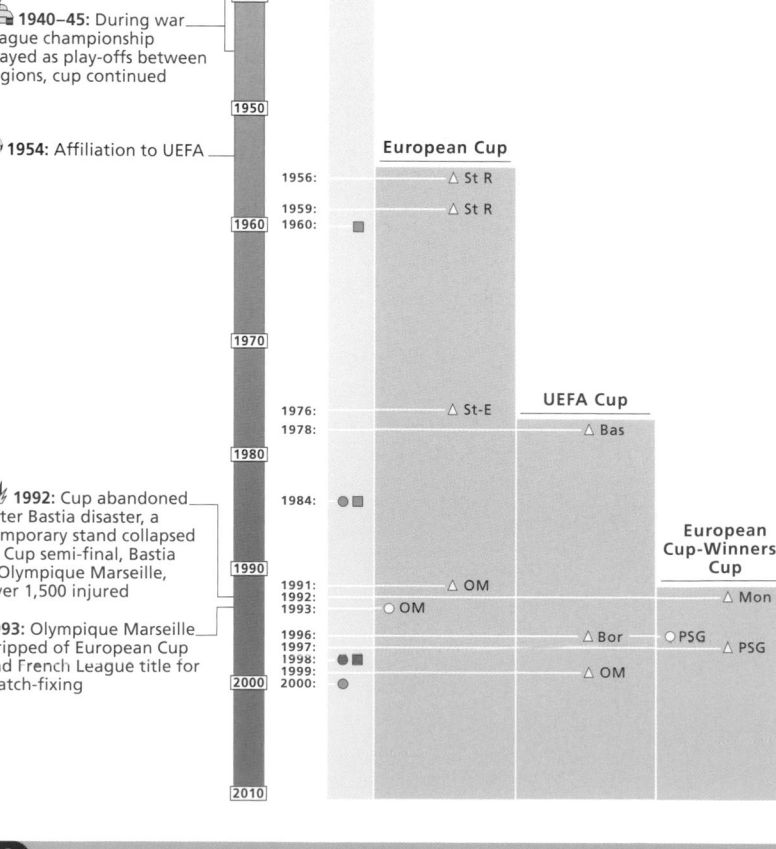

Stade Français 1883
Stade Red Star (1948–50).
Dissolved 1985

★ **CA Charenton** 1891

★ **Club Français Paris** 1892

★ **Red Star 93** 1897
Merged with Olympique de Paris to form Red Star Olympique, (1926–46)
Merged with Stade Français to form Stade Red Star, (1948–50)
Red Star Olympique Audonien, (1950–67)
Merged with Tolouse to form Red Star Tolouse, (1967–70)
Red Star 93, (1970–present)

Paris Saint-Germain FC 1970
Merger of Paris FC and St-Germain En Laye

★ **Racing Club de Paris** 1932
(Folded 1965)

CAS Généraux

Caen SM Caen 1913

Le Havre Le Havre A 1872

Guingamp ● En Avant Guingamp 1912

Brest Brest-Armorique FC 1912

Rennes Stade Rennais FC 1901

Laval Stade Lavallois MFC 1902

Lorient FC Lorient 1926

Le M Le Ma UC 72

Angers SCO Angers 1919

Tours FC Tours 1951

Nantes

FC Nantes Atlantique 1943
Merger of St Pierre, Mellenet, Loire, ASO Nantes and Stade Nantes (1943)

Niort ● Chamois Niortais FC 1925

Angoulême ● AS Angoulême 1925

FC Girondins de Bordeaux 1881

Bordeaux
F R

★ **Nîmes OSC** 1901
SC Nîmes (1901–1937)

Toulouse Toulouse FC 1970

★ **FC Sète** 1914

★ **Montpellier HSC** 1919/1974
Founded as Sports Olympique Montpellier, dissolved 1969

FC Martigues 1921

France

ORIGINS AND GROWTH OF FOOTBALL

THE DEVELOPMENT OF French domestic football was slow. Rugby was significantly more popular than football in 19th-century France, and early football clubs often grew up out of rugby clubs or other sport and athletic associations. For example, Le Havre was founded in 1872, but did not play football until 1892. Prior to the First World War, five different organizations claimed the mantle of the national FA before the creation of single institution, the FFF, in 1918. Though a national cup competition began almost immediately, it was only after considerable resistance that professionalism was accepted and a national league was not contested until 1932.

Rimet and Hunot

However, domestic disorganization and weakness was paralleled by international inventiveness. France was a founder member of FIFA and supplied its first president, Jules Rimet. Rimet was instrumental in establishing the World Cup, and Gabriel Hunot, editor of sports paper *L'Équipe*, was the inspiration behind the European Cup. However, it is only since the 1950s that French football has seen signs of sporting rather than organizational life. Stade de Reims' European adventures in the 1950s, Platini and the national team in the 1980s, Olympique Marseille and Monaco in the 1990s have been the high points in an era of otherwise mediocre performances and small crowds.

Exceeding all of these, however, is the extraordinary recent success of the national team and the massive financial and organizational investment in football's infrastructure by the French government. So far, this has delivered the World Cup in 1998 and the European Championships in 2000. In 2001, France finally displaced Brazil as the world's number one team in the FIFA rankings. But it was short-lived as a depleted French team crashed out in the first round of the 2002 World Cup.

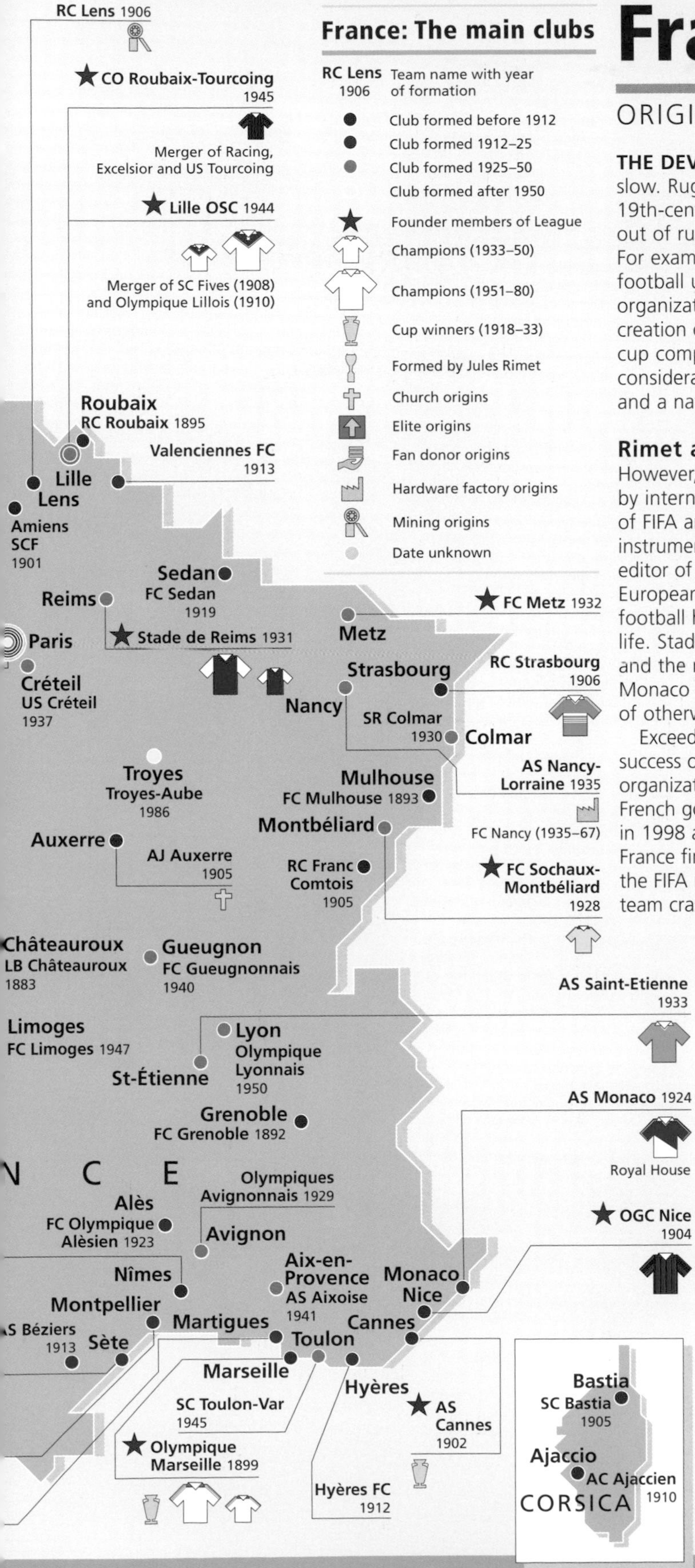

FRANCE

France: The main clubs

RC Lens 1906	Team name with year of formation
●	Club formed before 1912
●	Club formed 1912–25
●	Club formed 1925–50
●	Club formed after 1950
★	Founder members of League
	Champions (1933–50)
	Champions (1951–80)
	Cup winners (1918–33)
	Formed by Jules Rimet
†	Church origins
⬆	Elite origins
	Fan donor origins
	Hardware factory origins
	Mining origins
○	Date unknown

RC Lens 1906

CO Roubaix-Tourcoing 1945

Merger of Racing, Excelsior and US Tourcoing

Lille OSC 1944

Merger of SC Fives (1908) and Olympique Lillois (1910)

Roubaix
RC Roubaix 1895

Valenciennes FC 1913

Lille

Lens

Amiens SCF 1901

Sedan
FC Sedan 1919

FC Metz 1932

Reims

Stade de Reims 1931

Metz

Paris

Strasbourg
RC Strasbourg 1906

Créteil
US Créteil 1937

Nancy

SR Colmar 1930

Colmar

AS Nancy-Lorraine 1935

Troyes
Troyes-Aube 1986

Mulhouse
FC Mulhouse 1893

Auxerre

Montbéliard

FC Nancy (1935–67)

AJ Auxerre 1905

RC Franc Comtois 1905

FC Sochaux-Montbéliard 1928

Châteauroux
LB Châteauroux 1883

Gueugnon
FC Gueugnonnais 1940

AS Saint-Etienne 1933

Limoges
FC Limoges 1947

Lyon
Olympique Lyonnais 1950

St-Étienne

Grenoble
FC Grenoble 1892

AS Monaco 1924

Royal House

N C E

Alès
FC Olympique Alèsien 1923

Olympiques Avignonnais 1929

Avignon

Nîmes

Aix-en-Provence
AS Aixoise 1941

Monaco

Nice

OGC Nice 1904

Montpellier

AS Béziers 1913

Sète

Martigues

Cannes

Toulon

Marseille

SC Toulon-Var 1945

Hyères

Bastia
SC Bastia 1905

AS Cannes 1902

Olympique Marseille 1899

Hyères FC 1912

Ajaccio
AC Ajaccien 1910

CORSICA

Just Fontaine *challenges Real Madrid's goalkeeper in the 1959 European Cup Final. Fontaine's Stade de Reims was the brightest star in French football between the war and the rise of Tapie's Olympique Marseille in the early 1990s.*

France

FOOTBALL CITIES

THE GEOGRAPHY OF FRANCE'S football teams reflects the peculiar geography of French urbanization: late to develop, slow in coming and massively concentrated on Paris. No French city outside of Paris has been able to sustain two top-flight clubs for very long and even in Paris, where this has happened for a short period, no sustainable derby of the intensity of the Italian or English cities has been created. Paris produced two major clubs in the amateur era: Red Star 93, founded in 1897 by Jules Rimet and based in the Bauer district of the city, and Racing Club, which occupied the exclusive and stylish Colombes ground in the north-west of the city.

The professional era has been unkind to both, and Red Star has been forced to leave its Bauer heartland for the peripheral wastelands of Marville, while the Colombes ground may have hosted the 1938 World Cup but cannot currently sustain even Second Division football. This vacuum in Parisian football was finally filled by the creation of Paris Saint-Germain from FC Paris and Saint-Germain-en-Laye in the early 70s. Basing itself in Racing's old ground, the newly renovated Parc des Princes, PSG has climbed into the upper echelon of French football without ever dominating it.

One city, one team

Outside of Paris, it is one city, one team – Saint-Etienne, Stade Rennais, Girondins de Bordeaux, Olympique Marseille, Nice, Lyon, Nantes, Lens and Auxerre, although in the case of Monaco, it is one principality, one team. That said, in all of these cities, the connection with the football club is intimate: in Marseille, different districts of the town have their own *ultra* (fan group), each with its own space in the Stade Vélodrome, while in Bordeaux, Nantes and other provincial towns the city and regional governments have taken special care of their football clubs.

PARIS SAINT-GERMAIN 1970	
League	**1986,** *89,* **93, 94,** *96, 97,* **2000**
Cup	**1982,** *83, 85,* **93,** *95, 98, 2003*
European Cup-Winners' Cup	**1996,** *97*

RACING CLUB PARIS 1932	
League	**1936,** *61, 62*
Cup	**1936,** *39, 40, 45, 49, 50, 90*

RED STAR 93 1897	
Cup	*1921–23, 28, 42, 46*

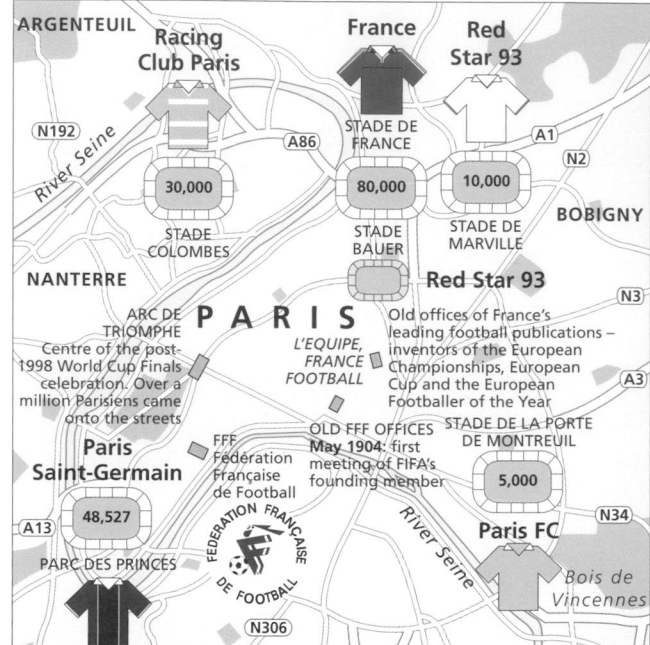

PARIS

FRANCE

PARC DES PRINCES

48,527

Club: Paris Saint-Germain
Built: 1897
Original Capacity: 50,000
Rebuilt: 1932, 1972
Significant Matches: 1938 World Cup: three matches; 1998 World Cup: six matches; 1984 European Championships: Final; European Cup Finals: 1956, 75, 81; European Cup-Winners' Cup Final: 1978, 95; UEFA Cup Final: 1998; French Cup Final: 1919, 38, 43, 44, 65–97

STADE DE FRANCE

80,000

Club: National team
Built: 1998
Significant Matches: 1998 World Cup: nine matches including quarter-final, semi-final and Final; French Cup Final 1998–present

STADE COLOMBES (Yves de Manoir)

30,000

Club: Racing Club Paris
Built: 1907
Original Capacity: 45,000
Rebuilt:
Record Attendance: 62,145 France v Soviet Union, 21 Oct 1965
Significant Matches: 1924 Paris Olympics; 1983 World Cup: three matches including quarter-final and Final; French Cup Final: 1925–39, 42–64

STADE RENNAIS 1901	
Cup	*1922, 35*, **65, 71**

FC NANTES 1943	
League	**1965, 66, 67, 73, 74, 77,** *78, 79,* **80, 81, 83,** *85,* **86, 95, 2001**
Cup	*1966, 70, 73,* **79,** *83, 93,* **99, 2000**

GIRONDINS DE BORDEAUX 1881	
League	**1950,** *52,* **65, 66,** *69, 83,* **84, 85, 87, 88, 90, 99**
Cup	**1941,** *43, 52, 55, 64, 68, 69,* **86, 87**
League Cup	*1997, 98,* **2002**
UEFA Cup	*1996*

RC LENS 1906	
League	*1956, 57, 77,* **98,** *2002*
Cup	*1948, 75,* **98**
League Cup	**1999**

AJ AUXERRE 1905	
League	**1996**
Cup	*1979,* **94, 96, 2003**

LILLE OSC 1944	
League	**1946,** *48–51,* **54**
Cup	*1945,* **46–48,** *49* **53, 55**

STADE DE REIMS 1931	
League	*1947,* **49, 53, 54, 55, 58, 60, 62,** *63*
Cup	**1950, 58,** *77*
European Cup	*1956, 59*

AS SAINT-ETIENNE 1933	
League	*1946, 57,* **64, 67–70,** *71,* **74–76, 81,** *82*
Cup	*1960, 62,* **68,** *70,* **74, 75, 77,** *81, 82*
European Cup	*1976*

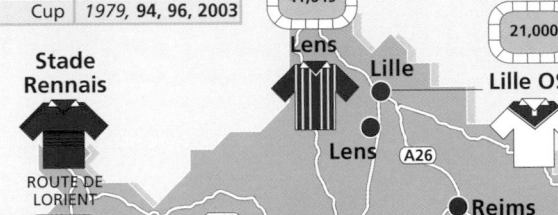

FÉLIX-BOLLAERT
41,649
Lens

GRIMONPREZ-JOORIS
21,000
Lille OSC

Lille

A26

Lens

Stade Rennais

ROUTE DE LORIENT
19,555
Rennes

A13

Paris

Reims

STADE DE REIMS CHAMPAGNE
18,000
Stade de Reims

A31 A4

A11 A10

Auxerre

ABBÉ-DES-CHAMPS
21,000
AJ Auxerre

F R A N C E

A6

Olympique Lyonnais

GERLAND
42,000

St-Étienne

A83
38,373
LA BEAUJOIRE-LOUIS-FONTENEAU
FC Nantes

A62

Nantes

Lyon

A7

AS Monaco

LOUIS II
16,000

PARC LESCURE
Bordeaux
34,088
Girondins de Bordeaux

AS Saint-Étienne

GEOFFROY-GUICHARD
A61
35,600

A9

Marseille

Olympique Marseille

VÉLODROME
60,000

Monaco
Nice

OGC Nice

MUNICIPAL DU RAY
15,750

FRANCE

Marseille's last league title was 1992, but it remains the best supported club in France. No other stadium can match the flags and flares of the Stade Vélodrome.

OLYMPIQUE MARSEILLE 1899	
League	**1937,** *38, 39,* **48,** *70,* **71, 72,** *75,* **87, 89–92, 94, 99**
Cup	*1924, 26, 27,* **34, 35, 38,** *40,* **43,** *54,* **69,** *72, 76,* **86,** *87,* **89, 91**
European Cup	*1991,* **93**
UEFA Cup	*1999*

OGC NICE 1904	
League	**1951, 52, 56, 59,** *68,* **73,** *76*
Cup	**1952, 54,** *78,* **97**

OLYMPIQUE LYONNAIS 1950	
League	*1995, 2001,* **02, 03**
Cup	*1963,* **64, 67,** *71, 73, 76*
League Cup	*1996,* **2001**

AS MONACO 1924	
League	**1961,** *63,* **64, 78, 82,** *84,* **88,** *91, 92,* **97,** *2000, 03*
Cup	*1960, 63,* **74,** *80,* **84, 85,** *89, 91*
League Cup	*2001,* **03**
European Cup-Winners' Cup	*1992*

France

FRANCE

FANS AND OWNERS

DESPITE HAVING BEEN World and European champions, France is less financially strong than the other big nations in Europe in terms of domestic football. Attendances and TV revenues have been lower, and the game is generally less commercialized. French clubs also face much larger tax bills, and the big clubs continue to subsidize smaller and amateur clubs. Little wonder that almost the entire French national squad plays overseas, and France's challenge at club level in Europe has been so limited in the last decade.

Rising income, rising debts

French club owners have been lobbying for some time to be allowed to raise more money. The FFF and the government have refused to allow them to float on the stock market but have introduced two categories of ownership: SAOS (*Société Anonyme à Objet Sportif*) and SASP (*Société Anonyme Sportive Professionelle*). The SAOS model is the status quo, leaving the clubs in the hands of private investors and the supporters' association. The SASP allows the clubs to distribute dividends to shareholders, pay salaries to elected officials and reduce the supporters' association share of the club below one-third. This second option is being pursued by the bigger clubs and big companies are beginning to take stakes in some of them. However, it is still risky; the clubs in the top division in 2002 were collectively in debt to the tune of £82.2 million

Although France has little of the *ultra* culture of Italy or Spain, in Marseille, Lens, Bastia and Metz the marginal status of the cities, geographically and socially, gives support a peculiar intensity. Marseille's many *ultra* groups, who come from different parts of the city, have their places in the stands clearly marked. There is very little violence in French football, but OM's fans can and do get pretty terse with their club. At the other end of the scale, the executive boxes built during the stadium refurbishment programme for the 1998 World Cup seem full as football acquires an elite glamour it has lacked in France for a long time.

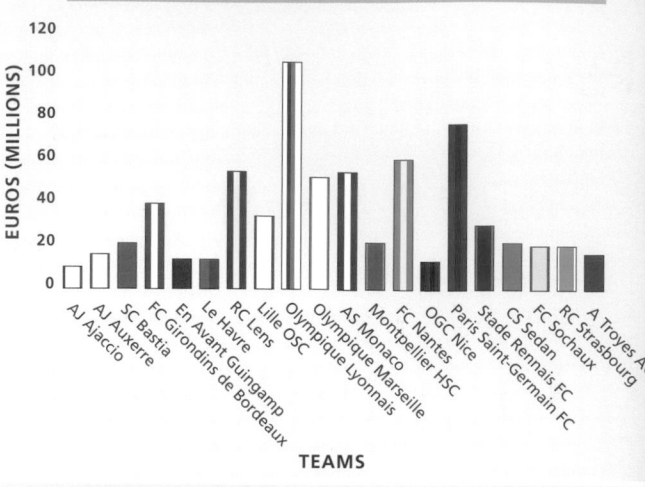

Club Budgets 2002–03

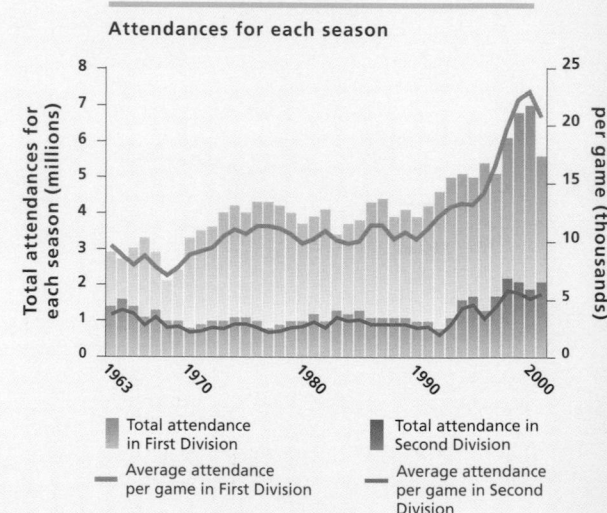

French Attendances

Attendances for each season

Total attendance in First Division
Total attendance in Second Division
Average attendance per game in First Division
Average attendance per game in Second Division

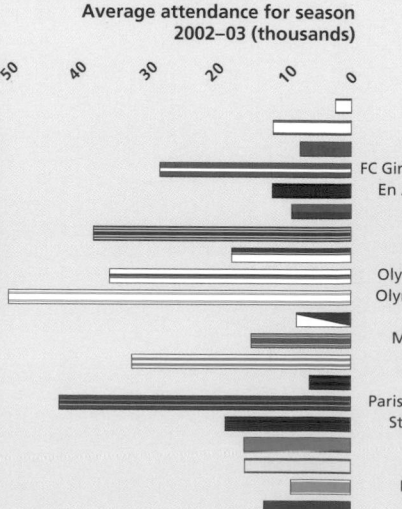

Prince Rainier of Monaco's money took the club to the first division in 1953. Since then the Grimaldi family's subventions have been augmented by a FF50 million subsidy from Monaco's national council. However, the club's debts continue to grow.

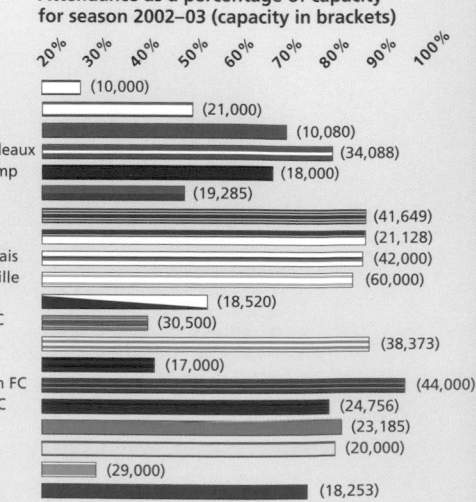

Average Attendance

Average attendance for season 2002–03 (thousands)

Capacity

Attendance as a percentage of capacity for season 2002–03 (capacity in brackets)

TEAMS	Capacity
AJ Ajaccio	(10,000)
AJ Auxerre	(21,000)
SC Bastia	(10,080)
FC Girondins de Bordeaux	(34,088)
En Avant Guingamp	(18,000)
Le Havre	(19,285)
RC Lens	(41,649)
Lille OSC	(21,128)
Olympique Lyonnais	(42,000)
Olympique Marseille	(60,000)
AS Monaco	(18,520)
Montpellier HSC	(30,500)
FC Nantes	(38,373)
OGC Nice	(17,000)
Paris Saint-Germain FC	(44,000)
Stade Rennais FC	(24,756)
CS Sedan	(23,185)
FC Sochaux	(20,000)
RC Strasbourg	(29,000)
A Troyes AC	(18,253)

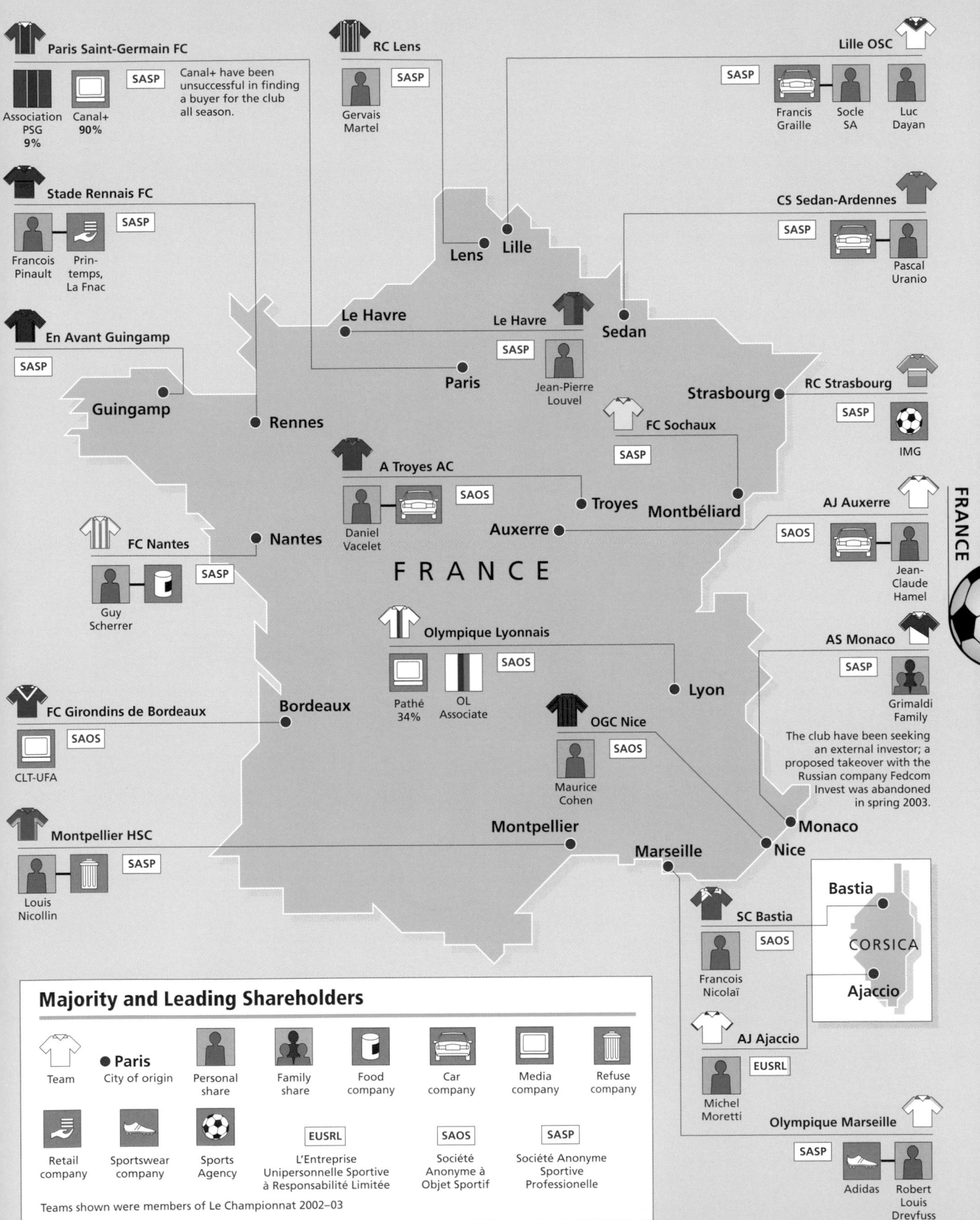

Paris Saint-Germain FC

Association PSG 9%

Canal+ 90%

SASP

Canal+ have been unsuccessful in finding a buyer for the club all season.

RC Lens

Gervais Martel

SASP

Lille OSC

SASP

Francis Graille

Socle SA

Luc Dayan

Stade Rennais FC

Francois Pinault

Prin-temps, La Fnac

SASP

CS Sedan-Ardennes

SASP

Pascal Uranio

En Avant Guingamp

SASP

Guingamp

Lens

Lille

RC Strasbourg

SASP

IMG

Le Havre

Le Havre

Sedan

Paris

SASP

Jean-Pierre Louvel

FC Sochaux

SASP

Strasbourg

Rennes

A Troyes AC

Daniel Vacelet

SAOS

Troyes

Montbéliard

AJ Auxerre

SAOS

Jean-Claude Hamel

FC Nantes

Guy Scherrer

SASP

Nantes

Auxerre

FRANCE

FC Girondins de Bordeaux

SAOS

CLT-UFA

Bordeaux

Olympique Lyonnais

Pathé 34%

OL Associate

SAOS

Lyon

AS Monaco

SASP

Grimaldi Family

The club have been seeking an external investor; a proposed takeover with the Russian company Fedcom Invest was abandoned in spring 2003.

OGC Nice

Maurice Cohen

SAOS

Montpellier HSC

Louis Nicollin

SASP

Montpellier

Marseille

Nice

Monaco

SC Bastia

Francois Nicolaï

SAOS

Bastia

CORSICA

Ajaccio

AJ Ajaccio

Michel Moretti

EUSRL

Olympique Marseille

SASP

Adidas

Robert Louis Dreyfuss

Majority and Leading Shareholders

Team

● **Paris** City of origin

Personal share

Family share

Food company

Car company

Media company

Refuse company

Retail company

Sportswear company

Sports Agency

EUSRL L'Entreprise Unipersonnelle Sportive à Responsabilité Limitée

SAOS Société Anonyme à Objet Sportif

SASP Société Anonyme Sportive Professionelle

Teams shown were members of Le Championnat 2002–03

France

FRANCE

PLAYERS AND MANAGERS

FRENCH FOOTBALL WENT PROFESSIONAL in the 1930s, but it was not until the postwar era that the first generation of international stars began to emerge. Just Fontaine (who holds the record for the most goals at a single World Cup Finals tournament) was among the first and like many to follow was born in French colonial North Africa – Morocco in his case. Playing alongside Fontaine at Reims was Raymond Kopa. Born of a Polish immigrant family, Raymond Kopaszeweski was the leading centre-forward of the era. France's next wave of great players emerged in the 1980s, built around the prodigious talent of Michel Platini, France's greatest-ever player. Platini's midfield colleagues Alain Giresse and Jean Tigana also stand out from this era and both have gone on to successful managerial careers. This era also saw the beginning of a transformation in the organization of training, management and scouting in France, with massive investment from government and clubs in talent and education.

However, France's coaching philosophy has older roots. Albert Batteux, generally acknowledged to be the father of the profession in France, coached the most successful clubs of the 1950s and 60s – Reims and St Etienne – as well as the national team at the 1958 World Cup. Nantes has also continued to provide players who become leading coaches – in the 2001–02 season one quarter of all top-flight clubs were coached by Nantes graduates.

Fantastic success

The leading players of the early 21st century are a product of this earlier era and again they reflect France's internal diversity and the continuing waves of African and Arabic immigration: Zidane, the outstanding player of his generation, was born of Algerian parents; Patrick Viera transferred from Senegalese to French citizenship. The fantastic success of the French team in recent years has seen the leading players head for Italy, Spain and, increasingly, England. French managers have followed them, with Arsène Wenger, Jean Tigana and Gérard Houllier all employed in the English Premiership. Simultaneously, there has been a huge influx of Africans in particular to the leading French clubs.

Top 20 International Caps

PLAYER	CAPS	GOALS	FIRST MATCH	LAST MATCH
Marcel Desailly*	104	3	1993	2003
Didier Deschamps	103	4	1989	2000
Laurent Blanc	97	16	1989	2000
Lilian Thuram*	85	2	1994	2003
Manuel Amoros	82	1	1982	1992
Youri Djorkaeff*	82	28	1993	2002
Bixente Lizarazu*	82	2	1992	2003
Zinedine Zidane*	82	22	1994	2003
Maxime Bossis	76	1	1976	1986
Michel Platini	72	41	1976	1987
Marius Trésor	65	4	1971	1983
Roger Marche	63	1	1947	1959
Emmanuel Petit*	63	6	1991	2003
Patrick Vieira*	62	4	1997	2003
Luis Fernandez	60	6	1982	1992
Robert Jonquet	58	0	1948	1960
Henri Michel	58	4	1967	1980
Fabien Barthez*	57	0	1994	2003
Patrick Battiston	56	3	1977	1989
Robert Pires*	56	11	1996	2003

Top 10 International Goalscorers

PLAYER	GOALS	CAPS	FIRST MATCH	LAST MATCH
Michel Platini	41	72	1976	1987
Just Fontaine	30	21	1953	1960
Jean-Pierre Papin	30	54	1986	1995
Youri Djorkaeff*	28	82	1993	2002
David Trezeguet*	22	43	1998	2003
Jean Vincent	22	46	1953	1961
Zinedine Zidane*	22	82	1994	2003
Jean Nicolas	21	25	1933	1938
Paul Nicolas	20	35	1920	1931
Eric Cantona	20	45	1987	1995

* Indicates players still playing at least at club level.

French International Managers

DATES	NAME	GAMES	WON	DRAWN	LOST
1960–64	Georges Verniet, Henri Guerin	24	4	6	14
1964–65	Henri Guerin	15	5	4	6
1966	Jean Snella, Jose Arribas	4	2	0	2
1967	Just Fontaine	9	2	3	4
1967–68	Louis Dugauquez	31	15	5	11
1969–73	Georges Boulogne	15	6	4	5
1973–75	Stefan Kovacs	15	6	4	5
1976–84	Michel Hidalgo	75	41	16	18
1984–88	Henri Michel	36	16	12	8
1988–92	Michel Platini	29	16	8	5
1992–93	Gérard Houllier	12	7	1	4
1994–98	Aime Jacquet	53	34	16	3
1998–2002	Roger Lemerre	53	34	11	8
2002–	Jacques Santini	9	7	1	1

All figures correct as of 30 April 2003.

Foreign Players in France (in top division squads)

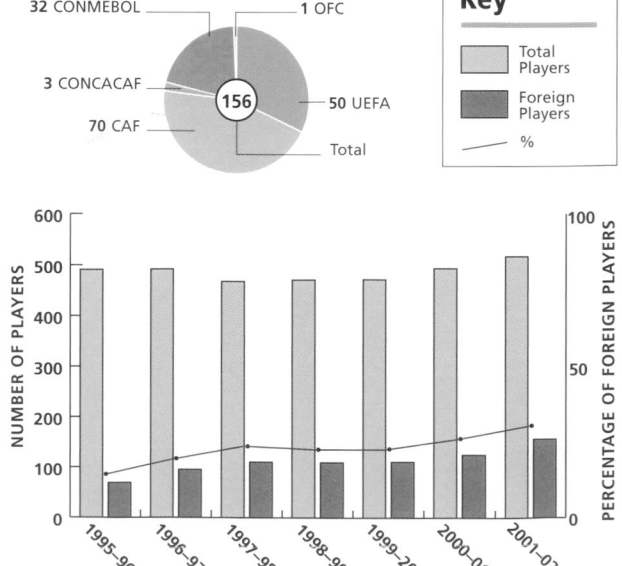

2002–03

32 CONMEBOL
1 OFC
3 CONCACAF
50 UEFA
70 CAF
156
Total

Key
▢ Total Players
▢ Foreign Players
— %

Player of the Year*

YEAR	PLAYER	CLUB
1963	Douis	AS Monaco
1964	Artelesa	AS Monaco
1965	Gondet	FC Nantes
1966	Gondet	FC Nantes
1967	Bosquier	AS Saint-Etienne
1968	Bosquier	AS Saint-Etienne
1969	Revelli	AS Saint-Etienne
1970	Carnus	AS Saint-Etienne
1971	Carnus	AS Saint-Etienne/ Olympique Marseille
1972	Trésor	Ajaccio/ Olympique Marseille
1973	Bereta	AS Saint-Etienne
1974	Bereta	AS Saint-Etienne
1975	Guillou	Angers/OGC Nice
1976	Platini	FC Nancy
1977	Platini	FC Nancy
1978	Petit	AS Monaco
1979	Bossis	FC Nantes
1980	Larios	AS Saint-Etienne
1981	Bossis	FC Nantes
1982	Giresse	Girondins de Bordeaux
1983	Giresse	Girondins de Bordeaux
1984	Tigana	Girondins de Bordeaux
1985	Fernandez	Paris Saint-Germain
1986	Amoros	AS Monaco
1987	Giresse	Olympique Marseille
1988	Paille	FC Sochaux
1989	Papin	Olympique Marseille
1990	Blanc	Montpellier
1991	Papin	Olympique Marseille
1992	Roche	Paris Saint-Germain
1993	Ginola	Paris Saint-Germain
1994	Lama	Paris Saint-Germain
1995	Guérin	Paris Saint-Germain
1996	Deschamps	Juventus [Ita]
1997	Thuram	Parma [Ita]
1998	Zidane	Juventus [Ita]
1999	Wiltord	Girondins de Bordeaux
2000	Henry	Arsenal [Eng]
2001	Vieira	Arsenal [Eng]
2002	Zidane	Real Madrid [Spain]

Never a favourite of the French national team manager, Eric Cantona raised the profile of French football when he left France for England in 1992. Hugely successful, both at Leeds and Manchester United, Cantona remains one of the finest players of the 1990s.

Manager of the Year*

YEAR	MANAGER	CLUB
1970	Batteux	AS Saint-Etienne
1970	Zatelli	O Marseille
1971	Firoud	Nîmes Olympique
1971	Prouff	Stade Rennais
1972	Snella	OGC Nice
1973	Herbin	AS Saint-Etienne
1974	Cahuzac	SC Bastia
1975	Huart	FC Metz
1976	Herbin	AS Saint-Etienne
1977	Cahuzac	SC Bastia
1978	Gress	RC Strasbourg
1979	Le Milinaire	Laval
1980	Hauss	FC Sochaux
1980	Vincent	FC Nantes
1981	Jacquet	Girondins de Bordeaux
1982	Hidalgo	France
1983	Le Milinaire	Laval
1984	Jacquet	Girondins de Bordeaux
1985	Suaudeau	FC Nantes
1986	Roux	AJ Auxerre
1987	Fernandez	AS Cannes
1988	Roux	AJ Auxerre
1989	Gili	O Marseille
1990	Kasperczak	SCP Montpelier
1991	Jeandupeux	Caen
1992	Suaudeau	FC Nantes
1993	Fernandez	AS Cannes
1994	Suaudeau	FC Nantes
1995	Smerecki	Guingamp
1996	Roux	AJ Auxerre
1997	Tigana	AS Monaco
1998	Jacquet	France
1999	Baup	Girondins de Bordeaux
2000	Dupont	FC Sedan
2001	Halilhodzic	Lille OSC
2002	Santini	O Lyonnais

*Elected by France Football magazine.

Jean Tigana was an integral part of the legendary French midfield of the 1980s along with Michel Platini and Alain Giresse.

Top Goalscorers 1963–2003

SEASON	PLAYER	CLUB	GOALS
1962–63	Masnaghetti	Valenciennes	35
1963–64	Oudjani	RC Lens	30
1964–65	Simon	FC Nantes	24
1965–66	Gondet	FC Nantes	36
1966–67	Revelli	Saint-Etienne	31
1967–68	Sansonetti	Ajaccio	26
1968–69	Guy	FC Lyon	25
1969–70	Revelli	Saint-Etienne	28
1970–71	Skoblar	O Marseille	44
1971–72	Skoblar	O Marseille	30
1972–73	Skoblar	O Marseille	26
1973–74	Bianchi	Stade Reims	30
1974–75	Onnis	AS Monaco	30
1975–76	Bianchi	Stade Reims	34
1976–77	Bianchi	Stade Reims	28
1977–78	Bianchi	Paris SG	37
1978–79	Bianchi	Paris SG	27
1979–80	Onnis	AS Monaco	21
1979–80	Kostedde	Laval	21
1980–81	Onnis	Tours	24
1981–82	Onnis	Tours	29
1982–83	Halilhodzic	FC Nantes	27
1983–84	Garande	AJ Auxerre	21
1983–84	Onnis	Toulon	21
1984–85	Halilhodzic	FC Nantes	28
1985–86	Bocandé	FC Metz	23
1986–87	Zénier	FC Metz	18
1987–88	Papin	O Marseille	19
1988–89	Papin	O Marseille	22
1989–90	Papin	O Marseille	30
1990–91	Papin	O Marseille	23
1991–92	Papin	O Marseille	27
1992–93	Boksic	O Marseille	22
1993–94	Djorkaeff	AS Monaco	20
1993–94	Boli	RC Lens	20
1993–94	Ouédec	FC Nantes	20
1994–95	Loko	FC Nantes	22
1995–96	Anderson	AS Monaco	21
1996–97	Guivarc'h	Stade Rennais	22
1997–98	Guivarc'h	AJ Auxerre	21
1998–99	Wiltord	Girondins de Bordeaux	22
1999–2000	Anderson	AS Monaco	23
2000–01	Anderson	Lyon	22
2001–02	Cisse	AJ Auxerre	22
2001–02	Pauleta	Bordeaux	22
2002–03	Nonda	AS Monaco	26

FRANCE

France

LE CHAMPIONNAT 1982–2002

AT THE BEGINNING OF THE 1980s, the French championship was evenly distributed between clubs built with old money and clubs built with new money. The new money came in the shape of Claude Bez, Girondins de Bordeaux's ambitious president. Without a title since 1950 and with its Lescure stadium devoted mainly to rugby and cycling, Bordeaux was transformed by Bez's injection of money and energy. In the early 1980s a new stadium and training centre were constructed, a considerable deal done with the newly emergent cable TV company Canal Plus, and a stylish team assembled under future national team coach Aimé Jacquet, including Jean Tigana and Alain Giresse. Those years belonged to Bordeaux with three league titles and a top four place for seven seasons. But Bez was accused and convicted of fraud and mismanagement, and Bordeaux was relegated by the league in 1991. The new money at Paris Saint-Germain brought in Luis Fernandez and Osvaldo Ardiles and saw the team finally take its first title in 1986. The old money and old form came in the shape of titles for Monaco, under Arsène Wenger, and for Nantes.

Further south, Olympique Marseille began the decade bankrupt and in the second division. But the potential of the biggest and most fiercely supported club in the country was in no doubt. Enter Bernard Tapie, then boss of Adidas, who bought the club in 1985. Tapie brought money, energy and connections as well as players of the calibre of Jean-Pierre Papin, Chris Waddle, Didier Deschamps and Abedi Pele. Elected as a socialist MP, Tapie was described as the 'Red Berlusconi', and he drove the right-wingers mad as five league titles and three tilts at the European Cup followed. Finally, in 1993, Tapie's Marseille beat Berlusconi's Milan 1-0 to take Europe's top club prize. The day afterwards it was revealed in the French press that there was serious evidence of match-fixing in Marseille's league game against US Valenciennes that season. The floodgates opened, accusations turned to convictions for match-fixing and illegal payments in the transfer market. Tapie was imprisoned, the club relegated and eventually made insolvent. Since then, despite considerable investment from Adidas's new boss Robert Louis Dreyfuss, the team has yet to show the form of the Tapie years.

TV and its money

In the mid-1990s money began to pour into French football from new TV deals, and salaries and transfers began to rise. But given France's high employment taxes and the relatively lower percentage incomes from sponsorship and TV available to French clubs (in comparison with Spain, Italy and England), the leading French players of the era, including nearly all of the 1998 World Cup-winning squad, played outside France. In their wake, French clubs have drawn extensively on African and Eastern European players, and none have been able to establish any kind of dominance.

In the late 1990s there have been titles for PSG, AJ Auxerre, RC Lens, Monaco and Nantes. At Auxerre, long-standing coach Guy Roux finally hit the jackpot with the club's youth academy. Nantes rose on money from Guy Scherrer, a millionaire in the food industry. Monaco took the 2000 title by a length with an attacking side including David Trezeguet and Marco Simeone. But European success has eluded French clubs, and the struggle to survive at the rarefied level of European competition has left them seriously in debt. Their competitors at the bottom of the league are equally troubled. The only serious new challenger to have emerged from the era of TV money has been Olympique Lyonnais, while for many of the old guard times have been even harder; Saint-Etienne, Stade de Reims, Racing Club Paris, SM Caen and OGC Nice have all found themselves slipping out of the top flight.

FC Nantes may come from a small provincial city, but the team's impressive youth academy and Guy Scherrer's biscuit company millions have kept the club at the top of the French game since the mid-1990s. This is the team that won the 1994–95 championship.

With roots in the mines of north-eastern France, Lens has become a title contender in recent years.

*The irrepressible **Bernard Tapie** and friends celebrate. Despite his downfall in 1993, Tapie has clawed his way back into French football with a short spell behind the scenes at Marseille in 2002.*

French League Income (in euros)

SEASON	1996–97	1997–98	1998–99	1999–2000	2000–01	2001–02
Income	292,630	322,714	393,183	607,194	608,424	643,090
Costs	300,070	368,313	462,721	570,866	646,847	740,821
Gross profit	-7,440	-45,599	-69,537	36,328	-38,422	-97,731
Net profit	25,077	51,075	65,885	8,135	-19,341	-68,080

Total for all top division clubs

Sources of Income 2002

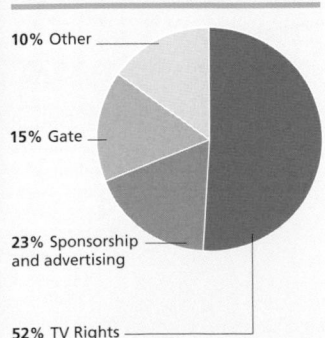

10% Other

15% Gate

23% Sponsorship and advertising

52% TV Rights

Income of French first division clubs in season 2001–02

Player Salaries 1996–2001

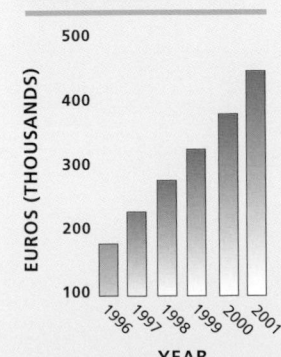

EUROS (THOUSANDS)

500
400
300
200
100

YEAR

1996 1997 1998 1999 2000 2001

Total wage bill of French first division clubs

Champions' Winning Margin 1992–2002

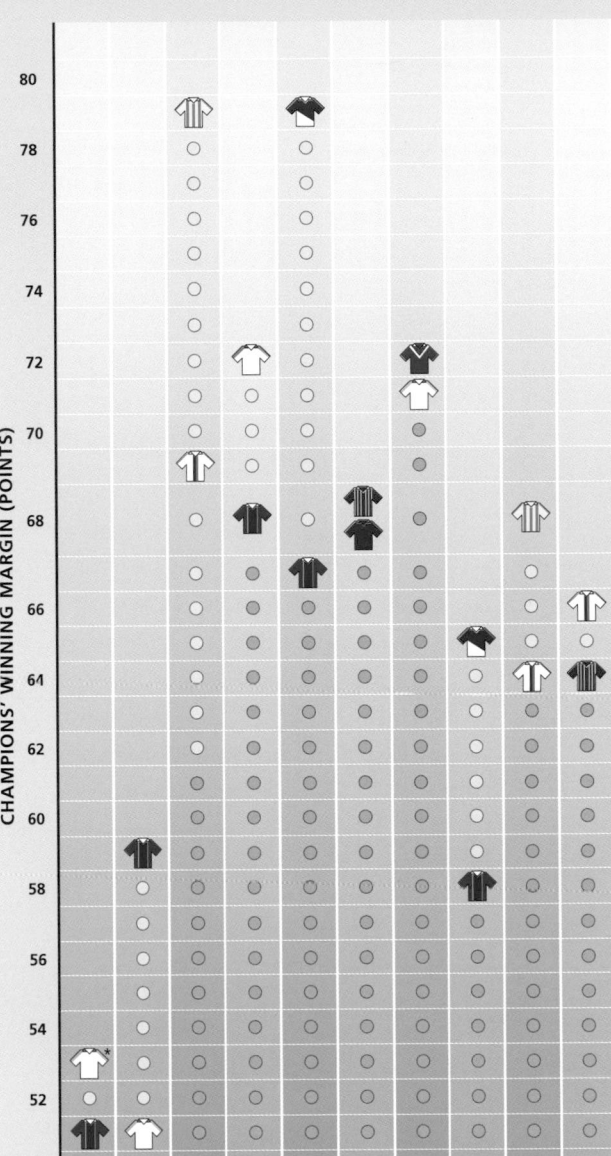

CHAMPIONS' WINNING MARGIN (POINTS)

80
78
76
74
72
70
68
66
64
62
60
58
56
54
52
50

SEASON

1992–93 1993–94 1994–95 1995–96 1996–97 1997–98 1998–99 1999–2000 2000–01 2001–02

38	38	38	38	38	34	34	34	34	34

Total games played by each team
(2 points awarded for a win until 1995, when 3 points awarded)

* Olympique Marseille finished with 53 points but were stripped of the title, which was not awarded

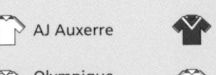 AJ Auxerre

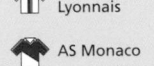 Girondins de Bordeaux

 RC Lens

 Olympique Lyonnais

Olympique Marseille

FC Metz

 AS Monaco

FC Nantes

 Paris Saint-Germain

FRANCE

215

Key to League Positions Table

- ▮ League champions
- ▯ Season of promotion to league
- ▯ Season of relegation from league
- ▯ Other teams playing in league
- 5 Final position in league

FRANCE

A young Thierry Henry provided the firepower to take Jean Tigana's AS Monaco to the French championship in 1997.

Guy Roux has been at Auxerre for almost four decades, nurturing talents like Eric Cantona. The club's scouting and youth network is second to none.

French League Positions 1982–2002

SEASON

TEAM	1982-83	1983-84	1984-85	1985-86	1986-87	1987-88	1988-89	1989-90	1990-91	1991-92	1992-93	1993-94	1994-95	1995-96	1996-97	1997-98	1998-99	1999-2000	2000-01	2001-02
AJ Ajaccio																				
SCO Angers											20									
AJ Auxerre	8	3	4	7	4	9	5	6	3	4	6	3	4	1	6	7	14	8	13	3
SC Bastia	17	11	14	20									15	15	7	9	13	10	8	11
Berrichonne Chat																17				
Girondins de Bordeaux	2	1	1	3	1	2	13	2	10†		4	4	7	16	4	5	1	4	4	6
Brest-Armorique FC	10	17	9	14	8	19		10	11†											
SM Caen						16	16	8	5	11	16	19		17						
AS Cannes						12	12	11	4	19			6	9	14	15	18			
FC Gueugnonnais													18							
En Avant Guingamp													10	12	16				10	16
Le Havre AC			17	17	20				7	15	17	12	13	14	10	15	17			
Stade Lavallois MFC	5	10	10	11	9	14	19													
RC Lens	4	13	7	5	10	17	20			8	9	10	5	5	13	1	6	5	14	2
Lille OSC	13	9	15	10	14	11	8	17	6	13	17	15	14	17	19				3	5
FC Lorient																16				18
Olympique Lyonnais	19							8	5	16	14	8	2	11	8	6	3	3	2	1
Olympique Marseille		17	12	2	6	1	1	1	1*	2**					11	4	2	15	15	9
FC Martigues											18	11	20							
FC Metz	9	12	5	6	6	8	15	14	12	12	12	12	8	4	5	2	10	11	12	17
AS Monaco	6	2	3	9	5	1	3	3	2	3	9	6	3		1	3	4	1	11	15
Montpellier HSC							3	9	13	7	6	10	7	17	6	10	12	8	18	13
FC Mulhouse	20						20													
AS Nancy-Lorraine	7	15	12	18	19				17	20						18	11	16		
FC Nantes	1	6	2	2	12	10	7	7	15	9	5	5	1	7	3	11	7	12	1	10
OGC Nice			8	11	16	6	18	14†					16	12	20					
Nîmes Olympique		19									15	20								
Chamois Niortais FC				18																
Paris Saint-Germain	3	4	13	1	7	15	2	5	9	3	2	1	3	2	2	8	9	2	9	4
Racing Club de Paris		20			13	7	17	19												
AS Saint-Etienne	14	18			16	4	14	15	13	10	7	11	18	19				6	17	
CS Sedan Ardennes																		7	5	14
Stade Rennais FC		20		13	20					20	18		13	8	16	14	5	13	6	12
FC Rouen	16	14	18																	
FC Sochaux	12	7	8	15	18		4	4	18	17	16	14	20			17				8
RC Strasbourg	15	8	16	19		18						8	13	10	9	9	13	12	9	18
SC Toulon-Var		16	6	16	15	5	11	12	16	14	19									
Toulouse FC	11	5	11	4	3	13	10	9	19	11	13	19				15	18		16	
FC Tours	18		19																	
A Troyes AC																		14	7	7
US Valenciennes											18									

Le Championnat

FC Nantes Atlantique	Team name
	League champions/ runners-up
1983, *85*	Champions in bold Runners-up in italics
	Other teams in Le Championnat
● Nantes	City of origin

Sonny Anderson, Olympique Lyonnais' Brazilian talisman, splits the Lens line of Fredrick Colly (left) and Jean Guy Wallemme as Lyon steals the title from under Lens' nose on the final day of the 2001–02 season.

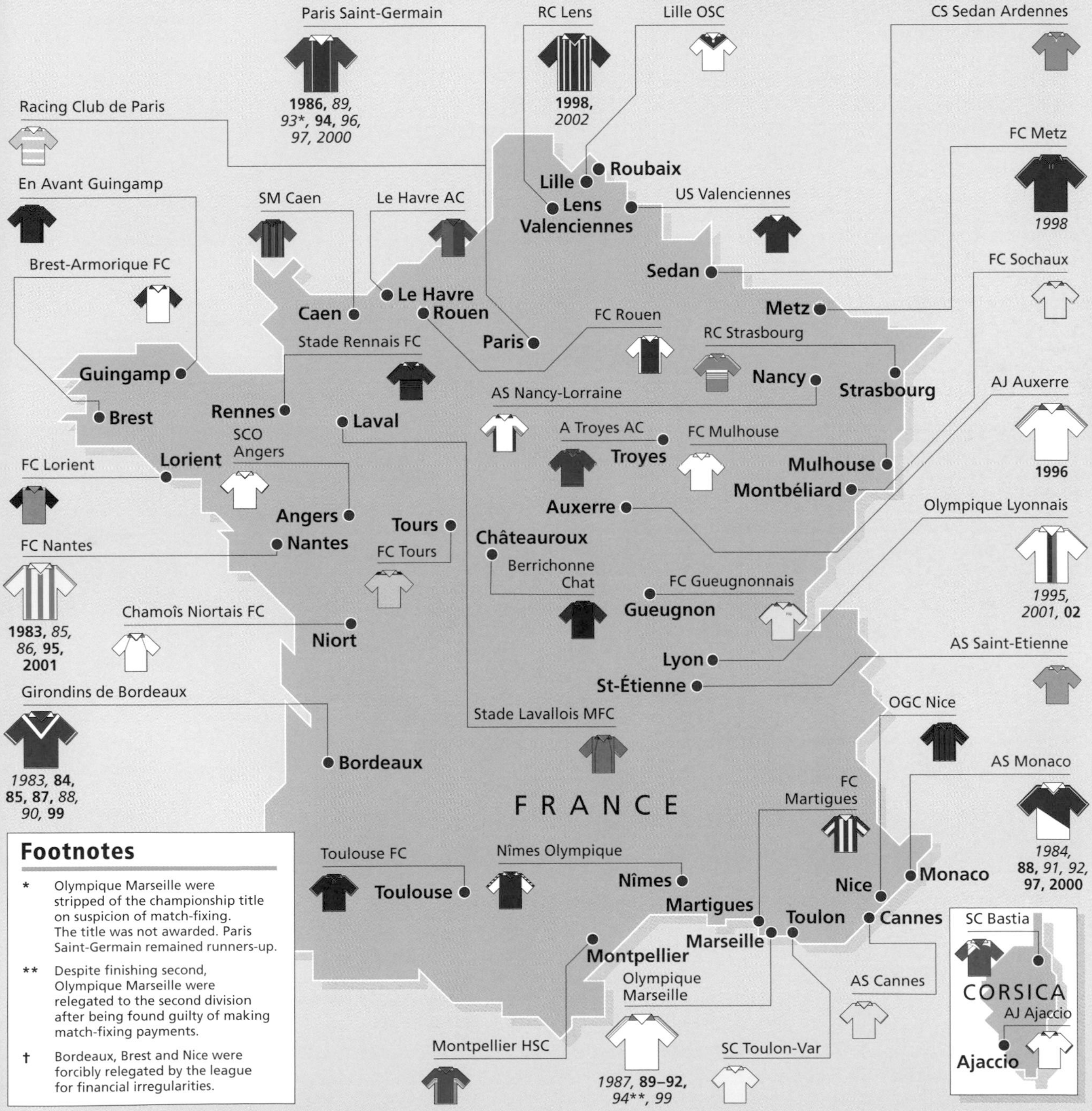

Paris Saint-Germain
1986, *89,* *93*,* **94,** *96,* *97,* **2000**

RC Lens
1998, *2002*

Lille OSC

CS Sedan Ardennes

Racing Club de Paris

FC Metz
1998

En Avant Guingamp

SM Caen

Le Havre AC

US Valenciennes

FC Sochaux

Brest-Armorique FC

RC Strasbourg

AJ Auxerre
1996

Stade Rennais FC

FC Rouen

AS Nancy-Lorraine

Olympique Lyonnais
1995, **2001,** *02*

SCO Angers

A Troyes AC

FC Mulhouse

FC Lorient

AS Saint-Etienne

FC Nantes
1983, *85,* *86,* **95,** **2001**

FC Tours

Berrichonne Chat

FC Gueugnonnais

Chamoîs Niortais FC

OGC Nice

Girondins de Bordeaux
1983, **84,** **85,** **87,** **88,** **90,** **99**

Stade Lavallois MFC

AS Monaco
1984, **88,** *91,* **92,** **97,** **2000**

Toulouse FC

Nîmes Olympique

FC Martigues

Footnotes

* Olympique Marseille were stripped of the championship title on suspicion of match-fixing. The title was not awarded. Paris Saint-Germain remained runners-up.

** Despite finishing second, Olympique Marseille were relegated to the second division after being found guilty of making match-fixing payments.

† Bordeaux, Brest and Nice were forcibly relegated by the league for financial irregularities.

Montpellier HSC
1987, **89–92,** *94**,* **99**

Olympique Marseille

AS Cannes

SC Toulon-Var

SC Bastia

CORSICA
AJ Ajaccio

Map labels

Lille · Roubaix · Lens · Valenciennes · Sedan · Metz · Caen · Le Havre · Rouen · Paris · FC Rouen · Nancy · Strasbourg · Guingamp · Brest · Rennes · Laval · Troyes · Mulhouse · Montbéliard · Lorient · Auxerre · Angers · Nantes · Tours · Châteauroux · Gueugnon · Niort · Lyon · St-Étienne · Bordeaux · Nice · Monaco · Toulouse · Nîmes · Nice · Cannes · Martigues · Toulon · Marseille · Montpellier · Ajaccio

F R A N C E

FRANCE

France

Fédération Française de Football
Founded: 1918
Joined FIFA: 1904
Joined UEFA: 1954

FRANCE

DESPITE BEING AT THE FOREFRONT of the global organization of football, French domestic football began in a chaotic manner. In the early part of the 20th century five different football federations vied to organize the national game and each established a separate national league.

With the creation of the Fédération Française de Football in 1918, the first national cup competition was established. The French Cup has been played for every year since, except for 1992, when tragic events overshadowed the French game. In a semi-final match between the Corsican club SC Bastia and Olympique Marseille, a temporary stand collapsed, leaving 15 dead and over 1,500 injured. The tournament was abandoned. In 2000, Calais, an amateur team from the fourth division, reached the Cup Final, only to lose 2-1 to FC Nantes, who scored the winner in the 90th minute.

A national league was formed in 1926, and was solidified by the advent of professionalism in 1932. The national championships acquired a different format during the Second World War with the champions of different zones (North [Occupied], South and Central) playing off against each other. In 1993 Olympique Marseille won the league, but was stripped of its title for alleged match fixing.

French League Record 1933–2003

SEASON	CHAMPIONS	RUNNERS-UP
1933	Olympique Lille	AS Cannes
1934	FC Sète	SC Fives
1935	FC Sochaux	RC Strasbourg
1936	Racing Club Paris	Olympique Lille
1937	Olympique Marseille	FC Sochaux
1938	FC Sochaux	Olympique Marseille
1939	FC Sète	Olympique Marseille
1940–45	*no championship*	
1946	Lille OSC	AS Saint-Etienne
1947	CO Roubaix	Stade de Reims
1948	Olympique Marseille	Lille OSC
1949	Stade de Reims	Lille OSC
1950	Girondins de Bordeaux	Lille OSC
1951	OGC Nice	Lille OSC
1952	OGC Nice	Girondins de Bordeaux
1953	Stade de Reims	FC Sochaux
1954	Lille OSC	Stade de Reims
1955	Stade de Reims	FC Toulouse
1956	OGC Nice	RC Lens
1957	AS Saint-Etienne	RC Lens
1958	Stade de Reims	Nîmes Olympique
1959	OGC Nice	Nîmes Olympique
1960	Stade de Reims	Nîmes Olympique
1961	AS Monaco	Racing Club Paris

One of France's greatest footballers was Michel Platini. His career started with Nancy, but he joined AS Saint-Etienne in 1979. Almost at the end of its golden era, having won the league title seven times in the previous ten years, Saint-Etienne's fortunes were reignited by Platini. The team won the title again in 1981, and finished second in 1982, before Platini moved to Juventus in Italy.

The legendary Raymond Kopa. He was born to a Polish immigrant family in inter-war France – similar origins to many French players of the era. His goals made Stade de Reims one of the most successful teams in France during the late 1950s. He moved to Real Madrid in 1956, but returned to Reims as European Footballer of the Year two years later.

French League Summary

TEAM	TOTALS	CHAMPIONS & RUNNERS-UP (BOLD) (ITALICS)
AS Saint-Etienne	10, 3	*1946,* **57, 64, 67–70, 71, 74–76, 81,** *82*
FC Nantes	8, 7	**1965, 66, 67, 73, 74, 77, 78, 79, 80, 81, 83, 85, 86, 95, 2001**
Olympique Marseille	8, 7	*1937, 38, 39,* **48,** *70,* **71, 72,** *75,* **87,** *89–92,* **94,** *99*
AS Monaco	7, 5	**1961, 63, 64, 78, 82, 84, 88, 91, 92, 97, 2000,** *03*
Stade de Reims	6, 3	*1947,* **49, 53,** *54, 55,* **58, 60, 62,** *63*
Girondins de Bordeaux	5, 7	*1950, 52,* **65, 66, 69,** *83,* **84, 85, 87,** *88,* **90,** *99*
OGC Nice	4, 3	**1951,** *52,* **56, 59,** *68, 73,* **76**
Paris Saint-Germain	2, 5	**1986,** *89,* **93,** *94, 96, 97,* **2000**
Lille OSC	2, 4	**1946,** *48–51,* **54**
FC Sochaux	2, 3	**1935,** *37,* **38,** *53, 80*
Olympique Lyonnais	2, 2	*1995, 2001,* **02, 03**
FC Sète	2, 0	**1934, 39**
RC Lens	1, 4	*1956, 57, 77,* **98,** *2002*
Racing Club Paris	1, 2	**1936,** *61, 62*
Olympique Lille	1, 1	**1933,** *36*
RC Strasbourg	1, 1	*1935,* **79**
AJ Auxerre	1, 0	**1996**
CO Roubaix	1, 0	**1947**
Nîmes Olympique	0, 4	*1958–60, 72*
AS Cannes	0, 1	*1933*
FC Metz	0, 1	*1998*
FC Toulouse	0, 1	*1955*
SC Fives	0, 1	*1934*

French League Record (*continued*)

SEASON	CHAMPIONS	RUNNERS-UP
1962	Stade de Reims	Racing Club Paris
1963	AS Monaco	Stade de Reims
1964	AS Saint-Etienne	AS Monaco
1965	FC Nantes	Girondins de Bordeaux
1966	FC Nantes	Girondins de Bordeaux
1967	AS Saint-Etienne	FC Nantes
1968	AS Saint-Etienne	OGC Nice
1969	AS Saint-Etienne	Girondins de Bordeaux
1970	AS Saint-Etienne	Olympique Marseille
1971	Olympique Marseille	AS Saint-Etienne
1972	Olympique Marseille	Nîmes Olympique
1973	FC Nantes	OGC Nice
1974	AS Saint-Etienne	FC Nantes
1975	AS Saint-Etienne	Olympique Marseille
1976	AS Saint-Etienne	OGC Nice
1977	FC Nantes	RC Lens
1978	AS Monaco	FC Nantes
1979	RC Strasbourg	FC Nantes
1980	FC Nantes	FC Sochaux
1981	AS Saint-Etienne	FC Nantes
1982	AS Monaco	AS Saint-Etienne
1983	FC Nantes	Girondins de Bordeaux
1984	Girondins de Bordeaux	AS Monaco
1985	Girondins de Bordeaux	FC Nantes
1986	Paris Saint-Germain	FC Nantes
1987	Girondins de Bordeaux	Olympique Marseille
1988	AS Monaco	Girondins de Bordeaux
1989	Olympique Marseille	Paris Saint-Germain
1990	Olympique Marseille	Girondins de Bordeaux
1991	Olympique Marseille	AS Monaco
1992	Olympique Marseille	AS Monaco
1993	Olympique Marseille*	Paris Saint-Germain
1994	Paris Saint-Germain	Olympique Marseille**
1995	FC Nantes	Olympique Lyonnais
1996	AJ Auxerre	Paris Saint-Germain
1997	AS Monaco	Paris Saint-Germain
1998	RC Lens	FC Metz
1999	Girondins de Bordeaux	Olympique Marseille
2000	AS Monaco	Paris Saint-Germain
2001	FC Nantes	Olympique Lyonnais
2002	Olympique Lyonnais	RC Lens
2003	Olympique Lyonnais	AS Monaco

Another brilliant striker rolls off the Auxerre production line. Djibril Cisse was a key member of Auxerre's 2003 cup winning team.

* Title won by Olympique Marseille but taken away from them for alleged match-fixing payments. Title not awarded.

** Despite finishing second Olympique Marseille was relegated to the Second Division after being found guilty of match-fixing payments.

FRANCE

George Weah signed for AS Monaco in 1988, bought from Tonnerre Yaoundé of Cameroon by manager Arsène Wenger. He went on to become one of the finest players in the world, also appearing for PSG, Milan, Chelsea, Manchester City and Olympique Marseille.

French Cup Record 1918–2003

YEAR	WINNERS	SCORE	RUNNERS-UP
1918	Olympique de Pantin	3-0	FC Lyon
1919	CAS Généraux	3-2 (aet)	Olympique Paris
1920	CA Paris	2-1	Le Havre AC
1921	Red Star Paris	2-1	Olympique Paris
1922	Red Star Paris	2-0	Stade Rennais
1923	Red Star Paris	4-2	FC Sète
1924	Olympique Marseille	3-2	FC Sète
1925	CAS Généraux	1-1 (aet), (replay) 3-2	FC Rouen
1926	Olympique Marseille	4-1	AS Valentigney
1927	Olympique Marseille	3-0	US Quevilly
1928	Red Star Paris	3-1	CA Paris
1929	SO Montpellier	2-0	FC Sète
1930	FC Sète	3-1	Racing Club France
1931	Club Français	3-0	SO Montpellier
1932	AS Cannes	1-0	Racing Club Roubaix
1933	Excelsior Roubaix	3-1	Racing Club Roubaix
1934	FC Sète	2-1	Olympique Marseille
1935	Olympique Marseille	3-0	Stade Rennais
1936	Racing Club Paris	1-0	US Charleville
1937	FC Sochaux	2-1	RC Strasbourg
1938	Olympique Marseille	2-1 (aet)	FC Metz

French Cup Record (*continued*)

YEAR	WINNERS	SCORE	RUNNERS-UP
1939	Racing Club Paris	3-1	Olympique Lille
1940	Racing Club Paris	2-1	Olympique Marseille
1941	Girondins de Bordeaux	2-0	SC Fives
1942	Red Star Paris	2-0	FC Sète
1943	Olympique Marseille	2-2 (aet), (replay) 4-0	Girondins de Bordeaux
1944	Nancy-Lorraine XI	4-0	Reims-Champagne XI
1945	Racing Club Paris	3-0	Lille OSC
1946	Lille OSC	4-2	Red Star Paris
1947	Lille OSC	2-0	RC Strasbourg
1948	Lille OSC	3-2	RC Lens
1949	Racing Club Paris	5-2	Lille OSC
1950	Stade de Reims	2-0	Racing Club Paris
1951	RC Strasbourg	3-0	US Valenciennes
1952	OGC Nice	5-3	Girondins de Bordeaux
1953	Lille OSC	2-1	FC Nancy
1954	OGC Nice	2-1	Olympique Marseille
1955	Lille OSC	5-2	Girondins de Bordeaux
1956	FC Sedan	3-1	FC Troyes-Aube
1957	FC Toulouse	6-3	SC Angers
1958	Stade de Reims	3-1	Nîmes Olympique
1959	Le Havre AC	2-2 (aet), (replay) 3-0	FC Sochaux
1960	AS Monaco	4-2 (aet)	AS Saint-Etienne
1961	FC Sedan	3-1	Nîmes Olympique
1962	AS Saint-Etienne	1-0	FC Nancy
1963	AS Monaco	0-0 (aet), (replay) 2-0	Olympique Lyonnais
1964	Olympique Lyonnais	2-0	Girondins de Bordeaux
1965	Stade Rennais	2-2 (aet), (replay) 3-1	FC Sedan
1966	RC Strasbourg	1-0	FC Nantes
1967	Olympique Lyonnais	3-1	FC Sochaux
1968	AS Saint-Etienne	2-1	Girondins de Bordeaux
1969	Olympique Marseille	2-0	Girondins de Bordeaux
1970	AS Saint-Etienne	5-0	FC Nantes
1971	Stade Rennais	1-0	Olympique Lyonnais
1972	Olympique Marseille	2-1	SC Bastia
1973	Olympique Lyonnais	2-1	FC Nantes
1974	AS Saint-Etienne	2-1	AS Monaco
1975	AS Saint-Etienne	2-0	RC Lens
1976	Olympique Marseille	2-0	Olympique Lyonnais
1977	AS Saint-Etienne	2-1	Stade de Reims
1978	AS Nancy	1-0	OGC Nice
1979	FC Nantes	4-1 (aet)	AJ Auxerre
1980	AS Monaco	3-1	US Orléans
1981	SC Bastia	2-1	AS Saint-Etienne
1982	Paris Saint-Germain	2-2 (aet)(6-5 pens)	AS Saint-Etienne
1983	Paris Saint-Germain	3-2	FC Nantes
1984	FC Metz	2-0 (aet)	AS Monaco
1985	AS Monaco	1-0	Paris Saint-Germain
1986	Girondins de Bordeaux	2-1 (aet)	Olympique Marseille
1987	Girondins de Bordeaux	2-0	Olympique Marseille
1988	FC Metz	1-1 (aet)(5-4 pens)	FC Sochaux
1989	Olympique Marseille	4-3	AS Monaco
1990	SCP Montpellier	2-1 (aet)	Racing Club Paris
1991	AS Monaco	1-0	Olympique Marseille
1992*		*no final*	
1993	Paris Saint-Germain	3-0	FC Nantes
1994	AJ Auxerre	3-0	SCP Montpellier
1995	Paris Saint-Germain	1-0	RC Strasbourg
1996	AJ Auxerre	1-0	Nîmes Olympique
1997	OGC Nice	1-1 (aet)(4-3 pens)	Guingamp
1998	Paris Saint-Germain	2-1	RC Lens
1999	FC Nantes	1-0	FC Sedan
2000	FC Nantes	2-1	Calais
2001	RC Strasbourg	0-0 (aet)(5-4 pens)	Amiens
2002	FC Lorient	1-0	SC Bastia
2003	AJ Auxerre	2-1	Paris Saint-Germain

* No final was held in 1992 following the collapse of a temporary stand at the SC Bastia v Olympique Marseille semi-final.

Victorious FC Nantes players celebrate in front of their fans after overcoming fourth division amateurs Calais 2-1 in the Final of the French Cup in 2000. Nantes won with a last-minute goal.

French Cup Summary (*continued*)

TEAM	TOTALS	WINNERS & RUNNERS-UP (BOLD) (*ITALICS*)
Calais	0, *1*	*2000*
FC Lyon	0, *1*	*1918*
FC Rouen	0, *1*	*1925*
FC Troyes-Aube	0, *1*	*1956*
Guingamp	0, *1*	*1997*
Olympique Lille	0, *1*	*1939*
Racing Club France	0, *1*	*1930*
Reims-Champagne XI	0, *1*	*1944*
SC Angers	0, *1*	*1957*
SC Fives	0, *1*	*1941*
US Charleville	0, *1*	*1936*
US Orléans	0, *1*	*1980*
US Quevilly	0, *1*	*1927*
US Valenciennes	0, *1*	*1951*

French League Cup Record 1995–2003

YEAR	WINNERS	SCORE	RUNNERS-UP
1995	Paris Saint-Germain	2-0	SC Bastia
1996	RC Metz	0-0 (aet)(5-4 pens)	Olympique Lyonnais
1997	RC Strasbourg	0-0 (aet)(6-5 pens)	Girondins de Bordeaux
1998	Paris Saint-Germain	2-2 (aet)(4-2 pens)	Girondins de Bordeaux
1999	RC Lens	1-0	FC Metz
2000	Gueugnon	2-0	Paris Saint-Germain
2001	Olympique Lyonnais	2-1 (aet)	AS Monaco
2002	Girondins de Bordeaux	3-0	FC Lorient
2003	AS Monaco	4-1	FC Sochaux

French League Cup Summary

TEAM	TOTALS	WINNERS & RUNNERS-UP (BOLD) (*ITALICS*)
Paris Saint-Germain	2, *1*	**1995, 98**, *2000*
Girondins de Bordeaux	1, *2*	*1997, 98*, **2002**
AS Monaco	1, *1*	*2001*, **03**
RC Metz	1, *1*	**1996**, *99*
Olympique Lyonnais	1, *1*	*1996*, **2001**
RC Lens	1, *0*	**1999**
Strasbourg	1, *0*	**1997**
Gueugnon	1, *0*	**2000**
FC Lorient	0, *1*	*2002*
SC Bastia	0, *1*	*1995*
FC Sochaux	0, *1*	*2003*

French Cup Summary

TEAM	TOTALS	WINNERS & RUNNERS-UP (BOLD) (*ITALICS*)
Olympique Marseille	10, *6*	**1924, 26, 27,** *34,* **35, 38, 40, 43, 54,** *69, 72, 76,* **86, 87, 89, 91**
AS Saint-Etienne	6, *3*	**1960,** *62,* **68, 70, 74, 75, 77,** *81, 82*
AS Monaco	5, *3*	**1960, 63,** *74,* **80,** *84,* **85,** *89,* **91**
Lille OSC	5, *2*	**1945,** *46–48,* **49,** *53,* **55**
Paris Saint-Germain	5, *2*	**1982, 83,** *85,* **93, 95, 98,** *2003*
Racing Club Paris	5, *2*	**1936, 39, 40, 45, 49,** *50, 90*
Red Star Paris	5, *1*	**1921–23, 28, 42,** *46*
Girondins de Bordeaux	3, *6*	**1941,** *43, 52, 55, 64, 68, 69,* **86, 87**
FC Nantes	3, *5*	*1966, 70, 73,* **79,** *83, 93,* **99, 2000**
Olympique Lyonnais	3, *3*	*1963,* **64, 67,** *71,* **73,** *76*
RC Strasbourg	3, *3*	*1937, 47,* **51, 66,** *95,* **2001**
AJ Auxerre	3, *1*	**1979, 94, 96,** *2003*
OGC Nice	3, *1*	**1952, 54,** *78,* **97**
FC Sète	2, *4*	*1923, 24, 29,* **1930,** *34, 42*
FC Sedan	2, *2*	**1956, 61,** *65, 99*
Stade Rennais	2, *2*	*1922, 35,* **65, 71**
FC Metz	2, *1*	*1938,* **84, 88**
Stade de Reims	2, *1*	**1950,** *58,* **77**
CAS Généraux	2, *0*	**1919, 25**
FC Sochaux	1, *3*	**1937,** *59, 67, 88*
SC Bastia	1, *2*	*1972,* **81,** *2002*
CA Paris	1, *1*	**1920,** *28*
Le Havre AC	1, *1*	**1920,** *59*
SCP Montpellier	1, *1*	**1990,** *94*
SO Montpellier	1, *1*	**1929,** *31*
AS Cannes	1, *0*	**1932**
AS Nancy	1, *0*	**1978**
Club Français	1, *0*	**1931**
Excelsior Roubaix	1, *0*	**1933**
FC Lorient	1, *0*	**2002**
FC Toulouse	1, *0*	**1957**
Nancy-Lorraine XI	1, *0*	**1944**
Olympique de Pantin	1, *0*	**1918**
Nîmes Olympique	0, *3*	*1958, 61, 96*
RC Lens	0, *3*	*1948, 75, 98*
FC Nancy	0, *2*	*1953, 62*
Olympique Paris	0, *2*	*1919, 21*
Racing Club Roubaix	0, *2*	*1932, 33*
Amiens	0, *1*	*2001*
AS Valentigney	0, *1*	*1926*

Andorra

Federació Andorrana de Futbol
Founded: 1994
Joined FIFA: 1996
Joined UEFA: 1996

SEASON	LEAGUE CHAMPIONS
1999	CE Principat
2000	Constelació Esportiva
2001	FC Santa Coloma
2002	Encamp Dicoansa
2003	Don Pernil Santa Coloma

YEAR	CUP WINNERS
1998	CE Principat
1999	CE Principat
2000	Constelació Esportiva
2001	FC Santa Coloma
2002	Lusitanos

Better late than never, tiny Andorra became UEFA's 51st member in 1996, equipped with a fledgling league and a national stadium that holds 1,000 people. Their first victory was 2-0 in a friendly against Belarus in April 2000.

Portugal

THE SEASON IN REVIEW 2002–03

THE 2002 WORLD CUP WAS A DISASTER for Portuguese football, as the national team was bundled out of the first round by those football giants South Korea and the USA. With the 2004 European Championships looming on the horizon, the Portuguese FA sought to redress its footballing problems by employing Phil Scolari, Brazil's World Cup-winning coach, as the new national team manager.

The actual task of hosting the championship is proving more difficult to secure. A massive programme of stadium rebuilding was finally begun this year. The new government has refused additional funds, and architectural and social critics have described the rebuilding as the 'apotheosis of the concrete lobby'. How many Portuguese clubs will remain solvent enough to go and play in these arenas is less clear. Portuguese football is broke; income has risen just three per cent in the last three years but costs have risen by over 40 per cent; four out every five clubs pay their players late or very late. Accusations and evidence of corruption are rife. Guimarães' president was arrested for embezzling funds from the club. The board of Acádemica stood down.

Porto rise above it

Rising above it all this year, Porto was back with a vengeance. Despite a miserable third in the league last year it led the league from start to finish and never for a moment did it look like the club would lose its hold. Under new coach, José Maurinho, a blend of youth and experience was fashioned. Vítor Baía in goal, Jorge Costa in defence, Alenichev up front and the fantastic Deco Souza – a gifted playmaker – at the heart of it all. Benfica, under Antonio Camacho, found a new and surprising discipline that was sufficient to earn them a Champions League spot. Last year's champions and runners-up, Sporting and Boavista, never looked like challengers at all. Sporting never seemed to replace the ailing Mario Jardel, whose emotional and psychological state was not good at the best of times this season; and apart from its UEFA Cup run, Boavista was dismal. Without the pressure of a tight domestic finish, Porto was able to give its best in a long UEFA Cup run that took them past sides of the quality of Lazio and Panathinaikos to win the trophy in Seville against Celtic. On this form the team will not be out of place in the Champions League.

The tip of the iceberg. Endemic gossip about corruption in Portuguese football finally saw someone arrested. Antonio Pimenta Machado, president of Vitoria Guimarães, is led away on charges of embezzlement from the club. Despite this, Guimarães did brilliantly to finish fourth in the league.

1 Divisão League Table 2002–03

CLUB	P	W	D	L	F	A	Pts	
FC Porto	34	27	5	2	73	26	86	Champions League
SL Benfica	34	23	6	5	74	27	75	Champions League
Sporting CP	34	17	8	9	52	38	59	UEFA Cup
Vitória Guimarães	34	14	8	12	47	46	50	
União Leiria	34	13	10	11	49	47	49	
Paços Ferreira	34	12	9	13	40	47	45	
CS Marítimo	34	13	5	16	36	48	44	
Gil Vicente FC	34	13	5	16	42	53	44	
CF Os Belenenses	34	11	10	13	47	48	43	
Boavista FC	34	10	13	11	32	31	43	
CD Nacional	34	9	13	12	40	46	40	
Moreirense FC	34	9	12	13	42	46	39	
SC Beira Mar	34	10	9	15	43	50	39	
SC Braga	34	8	14	12	34	47	38	
Acádemica de Coimbra	34	8	13	13	38	48	37	
Varzim SC	34	10	6	18	38	51	36	Relegated
CD Santa Clara	34	8	11	15	39	54	35	Relegated
Vitória Setúbal	34	6	13	15	40	53	31	Relegated

Promoted clubs: Rio Ave FC, FC Alverça, CF Estrela Amadora.

International Club Performances 2002–03

CLUB	COMPETITION	PROGRESS
Boavista FC	Champions League	3rd Qualifying Stage
	UEFA Cup	Semi-final
Sporting Lisbon	Champions League	3rd Qualifying Stage
	UEFA Cup	1st Round
Leixões	UEFA Cup	1st Round
FC Porto	UEFA Cup	Winners

Top Goalscorers 2002–03

PLAYER	CLUB	NATIONALITY	GOALS
Fary Faye	SC Beira Mar	Portuguese	18
Sabrosa Simao	Benfica	Portuguese	18
Adriano	Nacional	Portuguese	16
Gaucho (Eric Gomes)	CS Maritimo	Brazilian	15

Portuguese Cup

2003 FINAL

June 15 – National Stadium, Lisbon

FC Porto **1-0** União Leiria
(Derlei 63)

h/t: 0-0 **Att:** 38,000

Ref: Pedro Heriques

Below, left: Laslo Boloni, coach of Sporting Lisbon, finds no answers in his notebooks. Sporting finish 16 points off second-placed Benfica.

Below: Stability at Benfica, surely not? Coach Jose Antonio Comacho has signed for a second stint after taking Benfica back to the Champion's League.

Far left: *Jose Mourinho, Porto's new coach, watches sternly over his charges.*

Left: *Mario Jardel's early season absence from Sporting Lisbon, as his personal life disintegrated, saw last year's double winners take a terrible dip in form.*

Below, left: *Benfica's last game at the old Estadio da Luz was a 1-0 win over Santa Clara in late March. Eusebio claims to have wept on the occasion.*

Below: *The New Estadio da Luz towers over the remains of its predecessor.*

Below, middle: *Its handbags time as Porto and Boavista scuffle. Porto's defeat of its city and title rivals in January virtually wrapped up the championship.*

Below, bottom: *And that makes three: Porto celebrates its victory in the Portuguese cup to add to its League title and UEFA Cup triumphs.*

Porto's Capucho against Uniao Leiria's Manuel in the Portuguese Cup Final.

Association Football in Portugal

PORTUGAL

1900

1903: Boavista formed, Portugal's oldest major existing club

1910

1914: Formation of FA: Federação Portuguesa de Futebol

1920

1921: First international, v Spain, lost 1-3, venue: Madrid

1922: First Portuguese Cup Final

1923: Affiliation to FIFA

1930

1935: National league established

1940

1944: National stadium at Caxias, Lisbon inaugurated

1946: OS Belenenses win the Championship, the first time one of the big three did not win it

1950

1954: Affiliation to UEFA

1960

1961: Eusebio joins Benfica

1965: Eusebio given European Footballer of the Year award

1970

1974–76: Portuguese Revolution took place. Football continued, but stadiums were regularly used for political rallys

1980

1986–88: Saltillo affair: Portuguese internationals refused to play in conflict over appearance fees

1990

2000: Boavista win league championship, breaking 54-year domination of Benfica, Sporting and Porto

2000

2004: Portugal hosting European Championships

2010

In 1961, *a young player from Mozambique, named Eusebio, joined Benfica and started a golden era in Portuguese football.*

Key

🏴	International football	○	Competition winner
⚽	Affiliation to FIFA	△	Competition runner-up
⚽	Affiliation to UEFA		

Ben – Benfica
Porto – FC Porto
Sport – Sporting CP

International Competitions

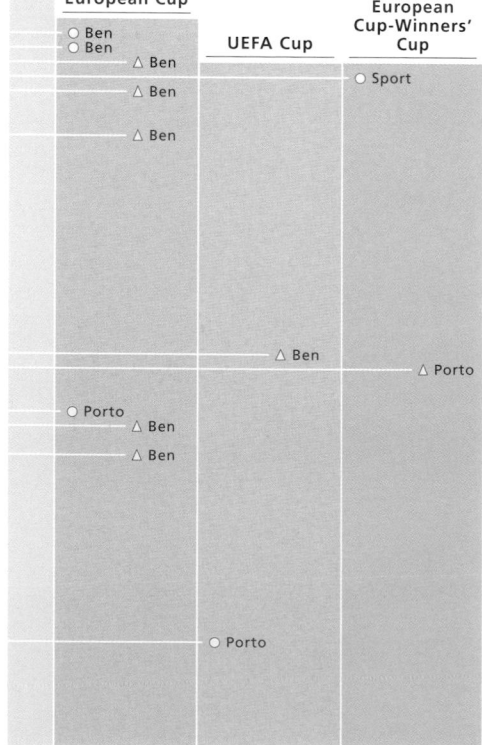

	European Cup	UEFA Cup	European Cup-Winners' Cup
1961:	○ Ben		
1962:	○ Ben		
1963:	△ Ben		
1964:	△ Ben		
1965:	△ Ben		
1968:	△ Ben		
1983:		△ Ben	
1984:			△ Porto
1987:	○ Porto		
1988:	△ Ben		
1990:	△ Ben		
2003:		○ Porto	

Portugal: The main clubs

Chaves 1949 Team name with year of formation

 ● Club formed before 1912

 ● Club formed 1912–25

 ● Club formed 1925–50

○ Club formed after 1950

● Date unknown

★ Founder members of National League 1934–35

👕 Champions (1935–80)

👕 Cup winners (1929–80)

Leça FC 1923

★ **Academico do Porto** 1911

★ **FC Porto** 1906

SC Salgueiros 1911

Boavista FC 1903

Leixões SC 1907

THE AZORES

Ponta Delgada ●
CD Santa Clara 1921

★ **Sporting CP** 1906

★ **CF Os Belenenses** 1919

Amadora

Cascais ●
GD Estoril Praia 1939

Lisbon

★ **Atletico CP** 1942

Merger of Carcavelinhos and União (founded league as União)

MADEIRA

Funchal

CS Marítimo 1910

Portugal

ORIGINS AND GROWTH OF FOOTBALL

IN THE LATE 19th century, Portugal was part of an informal British Empire, with extensive British communities trading and sailing from Lisbon and Porto. University students were recorded playing the game as early as 1866, and the first recorded club, Lisbon FC, was founded in 1875. By the 1890s Portuguese students returning from England started forming their own teams.

The popularity of the sport gathered pace and the country's four biggest clubs were formed in the first decade of the 20th century; in Lisbon, Benfica and Sporting Lisbon in 1904, and in Porto, Boavista in 1903 and Porto in 1906. By 1914, major teams were being established in the provinces and in the smaller cities. A national FA was set up in 1914 and professional league and cup competitions were running by the 1930s.

The golden era

After the Second World War, the Portuguese game was significantly boosted by the arrival of players from Portugal's African empire – Angola, Mozambique and Guinea-Bissau. Above all, the arrival of Eusebio from Mozambique to play for Benfica heralded a short golden era. Benfica, triumphant at home, also broke Real Madrid's monopoly on the European Cup, winning the tournament in 1961 and 1962. The following year, the Portuguese team made it to the semi-finals of the World Cup only to go out to the host and eventual winner, England.

Despite the talent at home, this period represents the country's peak international performance, having only qualified for two World Cups since 1934. The rather dormant Portuguese football scene of the 1970s was lifted by Porto's success in the European Cup in 1987, the arrival of many Brazilian players and the recent promise of the national team – semi-finalists at Euro 2000. However, their abject performance at the 2002 World Cup and the persistent accusations of corruption in the game overshadow the prospects of success.

PORTUGAL

Map labels

Barcelos
Gil Vicente FC
1924

SC Braga 1921

Chaves
1949

CD Aves 1930

Desportivo Aves 1930

Vitória Guimarães
1922

Felgueiras
1934

Varzim FC 1915

Rio Ave FC 1939

voa de rzim

Aves

Maia
1954

Penafiel
1951

FC Paços Ferreira 1950

SC Freamunde

Porto

São João da Madeira
Espinho
1944

Aviero
SC Beira Mar
1922

Covilhã
SC Covilhã
1923

Coimbra ★ Académica 1876

Figueira da Foz
Naval 1 de Maio
1893

União Lamas
1932

Leiria
União Leiria
1966

P O R T U G A L

CF Estrela Amadora 1932

FC Marco
1929

C Alverca
939

★ SL Benfica 1904

Campo Maior
SC Campomaiorense
1926

Barreiro

FC Barreirense

GD Quimigal

★ Vitória Setúbal 1910

Casa Pia 1920

Amora FC 1921

Oriental Lisboa

FC Seixal

SC Olhãnense 1912

Faro
SC Farense
1910

Albufeira
Imortal DC
1920

Olhão

Out of the frying pan into the fire. Having won the World Cup with Brazil, Phil Scolari explains his need for pressure from an irascible and unforgiving press. His appointment as Portugal's national team coach with a mission to win the 2004 European Championships on home soil should suit him well.

225

PORTUGAL

SL BENFICA 1904

League 1935–2003 (including Campionata de Portugal 1922–38)	**1930, 31, 35***, *36–38, 38**, **42, 43, 44, 45,** *46–49,* **50,** *52, 53,* **55, 56, 57,** *59,* **60, 61,** *63–65,* **66, 67–69,** *70,* **71–73,** *74,* **75–77,** *78, 79,* **81,** *82,* **83, 84,** *86,* **87, 88, 89,** *90,* **91,** *92, 93,* **94,** *96,* **98,** *03*
Cup	*1939,* **40, 43, 44,** *49,***51–53,** *55,* **57,** *58, 59,* **62, 64,** *65,* **69, 70, 71, 72,** *74, 75,* **80, 81, 83, 85–87,** *89,* **93,** *96, 97*
European Cup	**1961, 62,** *63, 65, 68,* **88,** *90*
UEFA Cup	*1983*
World Club Cup	*1961, 62*

SPORTING CP 1906

League 1935–2003 (including Campionata de Portugal 1922–38)	*1922,* **23,** *25, 28, 33,* **34,** *35,* **35*,** *36**, *37*,* **38*,** *39, 40, 41, 42, 43,* **44, 45,** *47–49,* **50,** *51–54,* **58,** *60, 61,* **62,** *66,* **68,** *70,* **71,** *74,* **77,** *80,* **82,** *85,* **95,** *97,* **2000,** *02*
Cup	*1941,* **45, 46,** *48,* **52,** *54, 55,* **60,** *63,* **70,** *71, 72,* **73, 74,** *78,* **79,** *82,* **87,** *94,* **95, 96,** *2000,* **02**
European Cup-Winners' Cup	**1964**

ESTADIO DA LUZ

77,844

Club:	SL Benfica
Built:	1954
Original Capacity:	60,000
Rebuilt:	1960 (at 120,000)
Significant Matches:	European Cup Final: 1967; European Cup-Winners' Cup Final: 1992

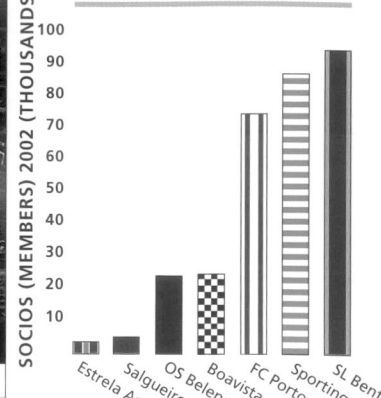

Lisbon and Porto Socios 2002

SOCIOS (MEMBERS) 2002 (THOUSANDS)

DOMESTIC CLUBS

(Estrela Amadora, Salgueiros, OS Belenenses, Boavista, FC Porto, Sporting CP, SL Benfica)

CF OS BELENENSES 1919

League 1935–2003 (including Campionata de Portugal 1922–38)	*1926,* **27, 29,** *32,* **33,** *36*, 37, 46, 55, 73*
Cup	*1940, 41,* **42,** *48, 60, 86,* **89**

Estrela Amadora
JOSÉ GOMES
25,000

PONTINHA

CAMPO DA FEITEIRA
Benfica played here (1908–12)

SL Benfica
(1954–)
ESTÁDIO DA LUZ
77,844

JOSÉ ALVALADE
52,411

Sporting CP
(1956–)

QUINTA DOS LILAZES

CAMPO GRANDE
Until the 1960s this was a large area of open ground where many of the city's teams had pitches or small stadiums

A1

BRANDOA

AVENIDA GOMES PEREIRA

BENFICA

SL Benfica
(1917–25)

BURACA

ESTASIO PINA MANIQUE

IC19

IC19

SETE RIOS

SL Benfica
(1941–54)

Sporting CP
(1917–45)

CIDADE UNIVERSITÁRIA

LISBON

SL Benfica
(1913–17)

ARCO CEGO

ALTO DO PINA

Oriental Lisboa

CAMPO CARLOS SALEMA

CHELAS

Rio Tejo

Casa Pia

Sporting CP
(1945–56)

EN117

A5

Parque

Florestal

de Monsanto

CAMPOLIDE

Parque Eduardo VII

ESTADIO AMOREIRAS

SÃO SEBASTIÃO

SL Benfica
(1915–40)

ESTEFÂNIA

FEDERAÇÃO PORTUGUESA DE FUTEBOL HEADQUARTERS

PORTUGUESE STOCK EXCHANGE
FC Porto and Sporting CP have both partially floated on the Portuguese Stock Exchange

CAMINHOS DE FERRO

Lisbon and Porto

40,000	Capacity of stadium
	Stadium no longer in use for top-flight football
	Team colours
	Semi-professional or amateur team colours
M1	Motorway
A82	Major road
1900	Champions
2000	Runners-up
*	Denotes honours in Campionata de Portugal

CARAMÃO

RESTELO
40,000

OS Belenenses

SANTO AMARO

TAPADINHA

E01

Atletico Lisbon

Sporting CP
(1945–56)

BELÉM

ALCÂNTARA

MADRAGOA

ESTADIO NACIONAL
Built in Caxias, 10km west of Lisbon, in 1944, this stadium hosted many of Benfica and Sporting CP's big games between 1945 and 1954

Rio Tejo

E01

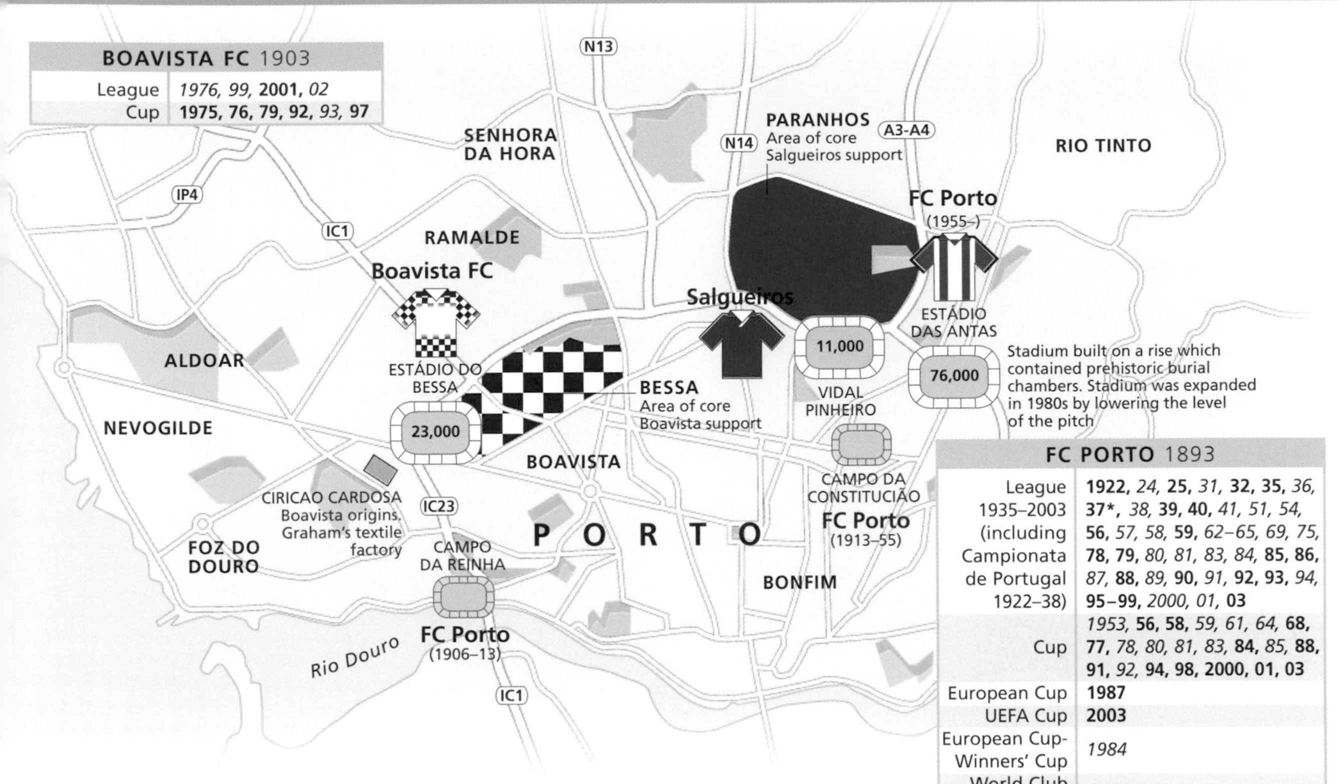

BOAVISTA FC 1903

League	1976, 99, **2001**, 02
Cup	**1975, 76, 79, 92**, 93, 97

N13

SENHORA
DA HORA

IP4

IC1

RAMALDE

Boavista FC

ALDOAR

NEVOGILDE

ESTÁDIO DO
BESSA

23,000

CIRICAO CARDOSA
Boavista origins,
Graham's textile
factory

FOZ DO
DOURO

IC23

CAMPO
DA REINHA

FC Porto
(1906–13)

Rio Douro

IC1

P O R T O

BOAVISTA

PARANHOS
Area of core
Salgueiros support

N14

A3-A4

RIO TINTO

FC Porto
(1955–)

Salgueiros

11,000

BESSA
Area of core
Boavista support

VIDAL
PINHEIRO

CAMPO DA
CONSTITUCIÃO
FC Porto
(1913–55)

BONFIM

ESTÁDIO
DAS ANTAS

76,000

Stadium built on a rise which
contained prehistoric burial
chambers. Stadium was expanded
in 1980s by lowering the level
of the pitch

FC PORTO 1893

League 1935–2003 (including Campionata de Portugal 1922–38)	**1922, 24, 25, 31, 32, 35,** 36, **37***, 38, **39, 40,** 41, 51, **54,** 56, **57,** 58, **59,** 62–65, 69, 75, **78, 79,** 80, 81, **83, 84, 85, 86,** 87, **88,** 89, **90, 91, 92, 93, 94, 95–99,** 2000, 01, **03**
Cup	1953, **56,** 58, **59,** 61, 64, **68,** 77, 78, **80,** 81, **83, 84,** 85, **88,** 91, 92, **94, 98, 2000, 01, 03**
European Cup	**1987**
UEFA Cup	**2003**
European Cup-Winners' Cup	1984
World Club Cup	**1987**

PORTUGAL

Lisbon and Porto

FOOTBALL CITIES

PORTUGUESE FOOTBALL IS CONCENTRATED in two cities – Lisbon and Porto – and although both have their local derbies (SL Benfica v Sporting CP and FC Porto v Boavista) neither can match the intensity of the clashes between teams from the two cities. Similar to the contrast between Rio and São Paulo or Amsterdam and Rotterdam, Lisbon is the city of glamour, of bohemian lifestyles and irresponsible hedonism; Porto is the city that gets up and goes to work. Porto makes things and sells them; Lisbon lives off its cut.

Lisbon has a scattering of small clubs who have on occasion made it to the top flight, like Casa Pia and Oriental, a medium-sized club in Os Belenenses, who sit in the historic suburb of Bélem to the west of the city, and a penumbra of teams in its distant suburbs. There are only two really big clubs in the city, however: Benfica and Sporting, who both roamed the city before settling on their current stadiums in the north. Benfica was founded in 1904 in Bélem with a nationalist, Portuguese-only policy – but this policy was bent to allow Portuguese colonial citizens from Africa into the squad. Led by Eusebio and accruing massive support, the team peaked in the 1960s and won two European Cups, famously breaking Real Madrid's stranglehold on the competition. Sporting drew on the land and finances of the Viscount of Alvalade and built the best team in postwar Portugal, though titles have been thinner on the ground in recent years.

Political rally at the Das Antas in 1975. During the Portuguese Revolution (1974–76) football stadiums all over the country hosted enormous political rallies.

The rise of Boavista

Porto's football has for a long time been dominated by FC Porto, who started off at the Campo da Constitucião before moving to the enormous Estádio das Antas in the 1950s. However, Porto's monopoly on the city's footballing triumphs and affections is being challenged. Boavista, the inner-city team from Bessa, is gaining ground. Founded by the English managers and Portuguese workers of Graham's textile factory, by 1905 the team had acquired a stadium, and in 1909 it changed its name from Boavista Footballers to Boavista Futebol Clube. After many years of obscurity, Boavista finally rose to take a well-deserved championship victory in 2001. The big Porto clubs are joined by tiny Salgueiros from the working-class Paranhos district of the city.

Portugal

1 DIVISÃO 1989–2002

IN 1982, SPORTING CP from Lisbon took the title under the eccentric English manager Malcolm Allison, after which the Portuguese championship was shared between SL Benfica and FC Porto for 19 seasons. Under Sven-Göran Eriksson, Benfica showed something of its old dominance, winning five titles and going to two European Cup Finals. Porto, revived under coach and former player José María Pedroto and striker Fernando Gomes, took three titles in the mid-1980s and two in the early 1990s. Benfica continued to challenge, but was progressively diminished by escalating debts and incredible inconsistency in managers and squads. By contrast, Porto was rock solid, taking a record-breaking five titles in a row in the 1990s, first under Bobby Robson, then Antonio Oliveira, and finally Fernando Santos. The club was unstoppable and in Brazilian Mario Jardel it had one of the greatest goalscorers of the time.

The Boavista surprise

A briefly revived Benfica, under manager Juup Heynckes, looked a threat to the Porto monopoly, but the swirling mists of corruption overtook the club and president João Vale e Azevedo was arrested and later tried and convicted on embezzlement charges. Instead, the challenge came first from Sporting, who, despite managerial changes and boardroom reshuffles, took the title in 2000 with talismanic Dane Peter Schmeichel in goal and again in 2002. In 2001, the real surprise package was Porto's Boavista FC. Gradually improving throughout the 1990s, the team took the lead early in the tournament and held it over Porto, showing outstanding discipline and tenacity across the whole season.

Beyond the charmed circle, who have held on to nearly all the money available from European qualification, the composition of the league has been very unstable. The only additional permanent members of the top flight are Vitória SC Guimarães, SC Braga and more recently CS Marítimo, SC Farense and SC Salgueiros. In order to survive, Farense has sold itself to a Spanish businessman, and Braga has floated on the stock exchange. However, the truth is that neither strategy looks likely to upset the *status quo* at the top of the Portuguese football ladder.

Boavista FC celebrates entry to the Champions League after its spectacular league championship in 2001. The club's budget is one tenth of that available to rivals FC Porto and Sporting CP.

Portuguese League Positions 1989–2002

TEAM	1989–90	1990–91	1991–92	1992–93	1993–94	1994–95	1995–96	1996–97	1997–98	1998–99	1999–2000	2000–01	2001–02
Academica									15	18			
FC Alverca										15	11	12	18
CD Aves											17		
SC Beira Mar	11	6	8	8	14	17			16			8	11
CF Os Belenenses	6	19		7	13	12	6	13	18		12	7	5
SL Benfica	2	1	2	2	1	3	2	3	2	3	3	6	4
Boavista FC	8	4	3	4	4	9	4	7	6	2	4	1	2
SC Braga	12	7	11	12	15	10	8	4	10	9	9	4	9
SC Campomaiorense								17	11	13	13	16	
GD Chaves	5	8	9	18		14	15	10	16	17			
Espinho			17				16						
GD Estoril Praia			10	13	18								
CF Estrela Amadora	13	18			9	15	11	9	7	8	8	18	
FC Famalicão		14	14	14	17								
SC Farense		11	6	6	8		13	11	14	11	14	13	17
CD Feirense	18												
FC Felgueiras							16						
FC Paços Ferreira			12	10	16							9	8
Gil Vicente FC		13	13	9	10	13	12	18			5	14	13
Vitória SC Guimarães	4	9	5	11	7	4	5	5	3	7	7	15	10
Leça FC							14	14	12				
União Leiria							6	7	17	6	10	5	7
CD Nacional Madeira	14	20											
CF União Madeira	16	12	18		12	16							
CS Marítimo	10	10	7	5	5	7	9	8	5	10	6	11	6
FC Moreirense													
FC Penafiel	15	15	17										
Portimonense SC	17												
FC Porto	1	2	1	1	2	1	1	1	1	1	2	2	3
Rio Ave FC									15	9	14	17	
SC Salgueiros		5	15	15	11	11	10	6	8	12	15	10	16
CD Santa Clara											18		14
Vitória Setúbal	7	17			6	18			12	13	5	16	12
Sporting CP	3	3	4	3	3	2	3	2	4	4	1	3	1
FC Tirsense	9	16		16	8	18							
SCU Torreense		16											
Varzim FC										17			15

Key to League Positions Table

League champions   Other teams playing in league   Season promoted to league   Season of relegation from league | 5 | Final position in league

PORTUGAL

PORTUGAL

1 Divisão

Boavista FC	Team name
	League champions/ runners-up
1999, *2001*	Champions in bold Runners-up in italics
	Other teams in the 1 Divisão
● **Porto**	City of origin

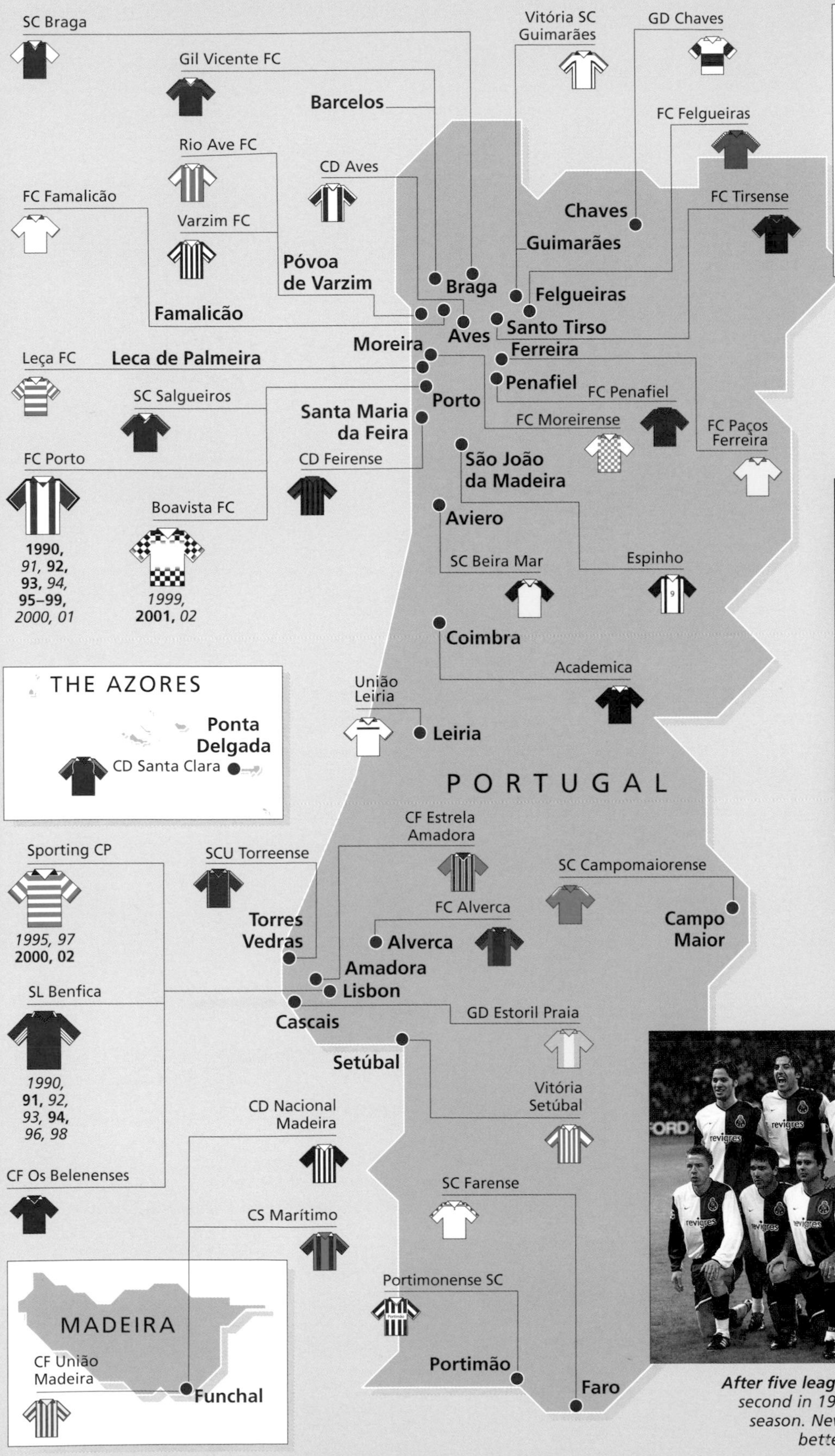

SC Braga

Gil Vicente FC

Barcelos

Vitória SC Guimarães

GD Chaves

FC Felgueiras

Rio Ave FC

CD Aves

FC Famalicão

Varzim FC

Póvoa de Varzim

Chaves

FC Tirsense

Guimarães

Braga

Felgueiras

Famalicão

Aves

Santo Tirso

Leça FC

Leça de Palmeira

Moreira

Ferreira

Penafiel

FC Penafiel

SC Salgueiros

Santa Maria da Feira

Porto

FC Moreirense

FC Paços Ferreira

FC Porto

CD Feirense

São João da Madeira

1990, 91, 92, 93, 94, 95–99, 2000, 01

Boavista FC

1999, **2001,** *02*

Aviero

SC Beira Mar

Espinho

Coimbra

Academica

THE AZORES

Ponta Delgada

CD Santa Clara

União Leiria

Leiria

PORTUGAL

João Vale e Azevado,
ex-president of Benfica,
leaving court where he spent
most of season 2001–02 in a
long-running case over
corruption and embezzlement.

Sporting CP

SCU Torreense

CF Estrela Amadora

SC Campomaiorense

1995, 97 **2000, 02**

Torres Vedras

FC Alverca

Campo Maior

SL Benfica

Alverca

Amadora

Lisbon

1990, *91, 92,* *93, 94,* *96, 98*

Cascais

GD Estoril Praia

CF Os Belenenses

CD Nacional Madeira

Setúbal

Vitória Setúbal

CS Marítimo

SC Farense

MADEIRA

CF União Madeira

Portimonense SC

Portimão

Funchal

Faro

After five league titles in five years, Porto came
second in 1999–2000 and again the following
season. New coach José Mourinho hopes for
better things from his talented squad.

Portugal

Federação Portuguesa de Futebol
Founded: 1914
Joined FIFA: 1923
Joined UEFA: 1954

PORTUGUESE FOOTBALL WAS ESTABLISHED in the early years of the 20th century, but no national league championship was properly organized until 1935. Prior to this, local tournaments centred on Lisbon and Oporto had been played and, in 1922, a national cup competition, the Campionata de Portugal, had been established. The winners of this cup were considered to be national champions.

Since 1935, the league championship has been dominated by three clubs – Benfica, FC Porto and Sporting CP from Lisbon – with only CF Os Belenenses and Boavista FC occasionally making waves. Unlike most of mainland Europe, Portuguese neutrality ensured that league football continued throughout the Second World War. The league currently consists of 18 teams with a standard three up, three down promotion and relegation system.

The entrance to the old Stadium of Light, home to SL Benfica of Lisbon until 2003. A new Stadium of Light has been constructed next door.

Campionata de Portugal 1922–38

YEAR	WINNERS	SCORE	RUNNERS-UP
1922	FC Porto	3-1	Sporting CP
1923	Sporting CP	3-0	Academica
1924	SC Olhãnense	4-2	FC Porto
1925	FC Porto	2-1	Sporting CP
1926	CS Marítimo	2-0	CF Os Belenenses
1927	CF Os Belenenses	3-0	Vitória Setúbal
1928	Carcavelinhos	3-1	Sporting CP
1929	CF Os Belenenses	2-1	União de Lisboa
1930	SL Benfica	3-1	FC Barreirense
1931	SL Benfica	3-0	FC Porto
1932	FC Porto	2-0	CF Os Belenenses
1933	CF Os Belenenses	3-1	Sporting CP
1934	Sporting CP	4-3	FC Barreirense
1935	SL Benfica	2-1	Sporting CP
1936	Sporting CP	3-1	CF Os Belenenses
1937	FC Porto	3-2	Sporting CP
1938	Sporting CP	3-1	SL Benfica

Portuguese League Record 1935–2003

SEASON	CHAMPIONS	RUNNERS-UP
1935	FC Porto	Sporting CP
1936	SL Benfica	FC Porto
1937	SL Benfica	CF Os Belenenses
1938	SL Benfica	FC Porto
1939	FC Porto	Sporting CP
1940	FC Porto	Sporting CP
1941	Sporting CP	FC Porto
1942	SL Benfica	Sporting CP
1943	SL Benfica	Sporting CP

Portuguese League Record (*continued*)

SEASON	CHAMPIONS	RUNNERS-UP
1944	Sporting CP	SL Benfica
1945	SL Benfica	Sporting CP
1946	CF Os Belenenses	SL Benfica
1947	Sporting CP	SL Benfica
1948	Sporting CP	SL Benfica
1949	Sporting CP	SL Benfica
1950	SL Benfica	Sporting CP
1951	Sporting CP	FC Porto
1952	Sporting CP	SL Benfica
1953	Sporting CP	SL Benfica
1954	Sporting CP	FC Porto
1955	SL Benfica	CF Os Belenenses
1956	FC Porto	SL Benfica
1957	SL Benfica	FC Porto
1958	Sporting CP	FC Porto
1959	FC Porto	SL Benfica
1960	SL Benfica	Sporting CP
1961	SL Benfica	Sporting CP
1962	Sporting CP	FC Porto
1963	SL Benfica	FC Porto
1964	SL Benfica	FC Porto
1965	SL Benfica	FC Porto
1966	Sporting CP	SL Benfica
1967	SL Benfica	Academica
1968	SL Benfica	Sporting CP
1969	SL Benfica	FC Porto
1970	Sporting CP	SL Benfica
1971	SL Benfica	Sporting CP
1972	SL Benfica	Vitória Setúbal
1973	SL Benfica	CF Os Belenenses
1974	Sporting CP	SL Benfica
1975	SL Benfica	FC Porto
1976	SL Benfica	Boavista FC
1977	SL Benfica	Sporting CP
1978	FC Porto	SL Benfica
1979	FC Porto	SL Benfica
1980	Sporting CP	FC Porto
1981	SL Benfica	FC Porto
1982	Sporting CP	SL Benfica
1983	SL Benfica	FC Porto
1984	SL Benfica	FC Porto
1985	FC Porto	Sporting CP
1986	FC Porto	SL Benfica
1987	SL Benfica	FC Porto
1988	FC Porto	SL Benfica
1989	SL Benfica	FC Porto
1990	FC Porto	SL Benfica
1991	SL Benfica	FC Porto
1992	FC Porto	SL Benfica
1993	FC Porto	SL Benfica
1994	SL Benfica	FC Porto
1995	FC Porto	Sporting CP
1996	FC Porto	SL Benfica
1997	FC Porto	Sporting CP
1998	FC Porto	SL Benfica
1999	FC Porto	Boavista FC
2000	Sporting CP	FC Porto
2001	Boavista FC	FC Porto
2002	Sporting CP	Boavista FC
2003	FC Porto	SL Benfica

PORTUGAL

Portuguese League Summary

TEAM	TOTALS	CHAMPIONS & RUNNERS-UP (BOLD) (ITALICS)
SL Benfica	33, 24	1930, 31, 35*, 36–38, 38*, 42, 43, 44, 45, 46–49, 50, 52, 53, 55, 56, 57, 59, 60, 61, 63–65, 66, 67–69, 70, 71–73, 74, 75–77, 78, 79, 81, 82, 83, 84, 86, 87, 88, 89, 90, 91, 92, 93, 94, 96, 98, 2003
FC Porto	23, 25	1922, 24, 25, 31, 32, 35, 36, 37*, 38, 39, 40, 41, 51, 54, 56, 57, 58, 59, 62–65, 69, 75, 78, 79, 80, 81, 83, 84, 85, 86, 87, 88, 89, 90, 91, 92, 93, 94, 95–99, 2000, 01, 03
Sporting CP	22, 21	1922, 23, 25, 28, 33, 34, 35*, 35, 36*, 37*, 38*, 39, 40, 41, 42, 43, 44, 45, 47–49, 50, 51–54, 58, 60, 61, 62, 66, 68, 70, 71, 74, 77, 80, 82, 85, 95, 97, 2000, 02
CF Os Belenenses	4, 6	1926, 27, 29, 32, 33, 36*, 37, 46, 55, 73
Boavista FC	1, 3	1976, 99, 2001, 02
Carcavelinhos	1, 0	1928
CS Marítimo	1, 0	1926
SC Olhãnense	1, 0	1924
Academica	0, 2	1923, 67
FC Barreirense	0, 2	1930, 34
Vitória Setúbal	0, 2	1927, 72
União de Lisboa	0, 1	1929

* denotes honours in Campionata de Portugal.

Portuguese Cup Record 1939–2003

YEAR	WINNERS	SCORE	RUNNERS-UP
1939	Academica	4-3	SL Benfica
1940	SL Benfica	3-1	CF Os Belenenses
1941	Sporting CP	4-1	CF Os Belenenses
1942	CF Os Belenenses	2-0	Vitória SC Guimarães
1943	SL Benfica	5-1	Vitória Setúbal
1944	SL Benfica	8-0	GD Estoril Praia
1945	Sporting CP	1-0	SC Olhãnense
1946	Sporting CP	4-2	Atletico CP
1947		no competition	
1948	Sporting CP	3-1	CF Os Belenenses
1949	SL Benfica	2-1	Atletico CP
1950		no competition	
1951	SL Benfica	5-1	Academica
1952	SL Benfica	5-4	Sporting CP
1953	SL Benfica	5-0	FC Porto
1954	Sporting CP	3-2	Vitória Setúbal
1955	SL Benfica	2-1	Sporting CP
1956	FC Porto	3-0	SCU Torreense
1957	SL Benfica	3-1	SC Covilhã
1958	FC Porto	1-0	SL Benfica
1959	SL Benfica	1-0	FC Porto
1960	CF Os Belenenses	2-1	Sporting CP
1961	Leixões SC	2-0	FC Porto
1962	SL Benfica	3-0	Vitória Setúbal
1963	Sporting CP	4-0	Vitória SC Guimarães
1964	SL Benfica	6-2	FC Porto
1965	Vitória Setúbal	3-1	SL Benfica
1966	SC Braga	1-0	Vitória Setúbal
1967	Vitória Setúbal	3-2	Academica
1968	FC Porto	2-1	Vitória Setúbal
1969	SL Benfica	2-1	Academica
1970	SL Benfica	3-1	Sporting CP
1971	Sporting CP	4-1	SL Benfica
1972	SL Benfica	3-2	Sporting CP
1973	Sporting CP	3-2	Vitória Setúbal
1974	Sporting CP	2-1	SL Benfica
1975	Boavista FC	2-1	SL Benfica
1976	Boavista FC	2-1	Vitória SC Guimarães
1977	FC Porto	2-1	SC Braga

Portuguese Cup Record (*continued*)

YEAR	WINNERS	SCORE	RUNNERS-UP
1978	Sporting CP	1-1, (replay) 2-1	FC Porto
1979	Boavista FC	1-1, (replay) 1-0	Sporting CP
1980	SL Benfica	1-0	FC Porto
1981	SL Benfica	3-1	FC Porto
1982	Sporting CP	4-0	SC Braga
1983	SL Benfica	1-0	FC Porto
1984	FC Porto	4-1	Rio Ave FC
1985	SL Benfica	3-1	FC Porto
1986	SL Benfica	2-0	CF Os Belenenses
1987	SL Benfica	2-1	Sporting CP
1988	FC Porto	1-0	Vitória SC Guimarães
1989	CF Os Belenenses	2-1	SL Benfica
1990	CF Estrela Amadora	3-1 (aet)	SC Farense
1991	FC Porto	3-1	SC Beira Mar
1992	Boavista FC	2-1	FC Porto
1993	SL Benfica	5-2	Boavista FC
1994	FC Porto	2-1 (aet)	Sporting CP
1995	Sporting CP	2-0	CS Marítimo
1996	SL Benfica	3-1	Sporting CP
1997	Boavista FC	3-2	SL Benfica
1998	FC Porto	3-1	SC Braga
1999	SC Beira Mar	1-0	SC Campomaiorense
2000	FC Porto	3-1 (aet)	Sporting CP
2001	FC Porto	2-0	CS Marítimo
2002	Sporting CP	1-0	Lexiões SC
2003	FC Porto	1-0	União Leiria

Portuguese Cup Summary

TEAM	TOTALS	WINNERS & RUNNERS-UP (BOLD) (ITALICS)
SL Benfica	23, 8	1939, 40, 43, 44, 49, 51–53, 55, 57, 58, 59, 62, 64, 65, 69, 70, 71, 72, 74, 75, 80, 81, 83, 85–87, 89, 93, 96, 97
Sporting CP	13, 10	1941, 45, 46, 48, 52, 54, 55, 60, 63, 70, 71, 72, 73, 74, 78, 79, 82, 87, 94, 95, 96, 2000, 02
FC Porto	12, 10	1953, 56, 58, 59, 61, 64, 68, 77, 78, 80, 81, 83, 84, 85, 88, 91, 92, 94, 98, 2000, 01, 03
Boavista FC	5, 1	1975, 76, 79, 92, 93, 97
CF Os Belenenses	3, 4	1940, 41, 42, 48, 60, 86, 89
Vitória Setúbal	2, 6	1943, 54, 62, 65, 66, 67, 68, 73
Academica	1, 3	1939, 51, 67, 69
SC Braga	1, 3	1966, 77, 82, 98
Leixões SC	1, 1	1961, 2002
SC Beira Mar	1, 1	1991, 99
CF Estrela Amadora	1, 0	1990
Vitória SC Guimarães	0, 4	1942, 63, 76, 88
Atletico CP	0, 2	1946, 49
CS Marítimo	0, 2	1995, 2001
GD Estoril Praia	0, 1	1944
Rio Ave FC	0, 1	1984
SC Campomaiorense	0, 1	1999
SC Covilhã	0, 1	1957
SC Farense	0, 1	1990
União Leiria	0, 1	2003
SC Olhãnense	0, 1	1945
SCU Torreense	0, 1	1956

PORTUGAL

Spain

THE SEASON IN REVIEW 2002–03

SPAIN, ONCE AGAIN, LEFT A WORLD CUP EARLIER than its talent promised, this time on penalties to South Korea in the quarter-finals. In European competition, despite taking three Champions League quarter-final spots, only Real Madrid could progress to the semi-finals and once there fell to the hunger, organization and defensive tenacity of Juventus. But is there a better, more competitive, more compelling league in Europe, in the world? England can boast more goals and bigger crowds. Serie A remains a fearsomely difficult league to win and had delivered a fine theatrical performance off the field. But neither compares with the taut competitiveness of La Liga and its bountiful, generous, attacking and expressive football this season.

It was this kind of play and £30 million that took Ronaldo from Internazionale to Real Madrid as President Florentine Perez and footballing director Jorge Valldano pursued their strategy of signing the best each season. Barcelona President Joan Gaspart, to everyone's amazement, brought Louis van Gaal back to the Nou Camp for a second stint as coach. Van Gaal remained so loathed by the city's fans and press that he returned to the club by car rather than face a noisy reception at the airport. But beyond the two richest clubs, money was tight, the transfer market quiet. No wonder, over the season, the level of accumulated debts on Spanish football trickled out; Deportivo and Valencia are said to be over 90 million euros in the red, Barca around 50 and the smaller clubs proportionally in debt. By the end of the season battle lines had been drawn between a consortium of the biggest clubs (informally the G-12) and the rest of the top two divisions, in the fierce struggle for shares of TV revenue.

But there was barely any need for reinforcements, for the existing squads fashioned a season of eventful and compelling football. For the leading sides, inconsistency was the theme for the beginning of the season. Ronaldo scored on his debut for Real and then stopped. As he struggled to adapt to his new surroundings, sections of the hypercritical crowd and press took a detailed interest in his weight and commitment, a censoriousness confirmed after Ronaldo renounced a trip to the Rio Carnival. *Marca*, the Madrid sports daily, ran the headline 'No to Carnival,

Primera Liga Table 2002–03

CLUB	P	W	D	L	F	A	Pts	
Real Madrid	38	22	12	4	86	42	**78**	Champions League
Real Sociedad	38	22	10	6	71	45	**76**	Champions League
RC Deportivo	38	22	6	10	67	47	**72**	Champions League
RC Celta	38	17	10	11	45	36	**61**	Champions League
Valencia CF	38	17	9	12	56	35	**60**	UEFA Cup
Barcelona	38	15	11	12	63	47	**56**	UEFA Cup
Athletic Bilbao	38	15	10	13	63	61	**55**	
Real Betis	38	14	12	12	56	53	**54**	
RCD Mallorca	38	14	10	14	49	56	**52**	UEFA Cup (cup winners)
Sevilla FC	38	13	11	14	38	39	**50**	
Atlético Madrid	38	12	11	15	51	56	**47**	
CA Osasuna	38	12	11	15	40	48	**47**	
Real Valladolid	38	12	10	16	37	40	**46**	
Málaga CF	38	11	13	14	44	49	**46**	
Villareal CF	38	11	12	15	44	53	**45**	
Racing Santander	38	13	5	20	54	64	**44**	
RCD Espanyol	38	10	13	15	48	54	**43**	
Recreativo Huelva	38	8	12	18	35	61	**36**	Relegated
Dep Alavés	38	8	11	19	38	68	**35**	Relegated
Rayo Vallecano	38	7	11	20	31	62	**32**	Relegated

Promoted clubs: Real Murcia, Real Zaragoza, Albacete Balompié.

Right: It's that serious? Luis Figo asks for calm as Real Madrid take on Barcelona at the Nou Camp in November 2002. Figo, lured from Barca to Real three seasons ago, was pelted with objects and had a pig's head thrown at him.

Below: The top and the bottom of football in Madrid. Real's Falvio Conceicao closes down on Rayo Vallecano's Luis Cembranos.

Another one for the collection. Ronaldo shows off his new club shirt while Real club President Florentine Perez and Honorary President, Alfredo di Stefano, look on.

SPAIN

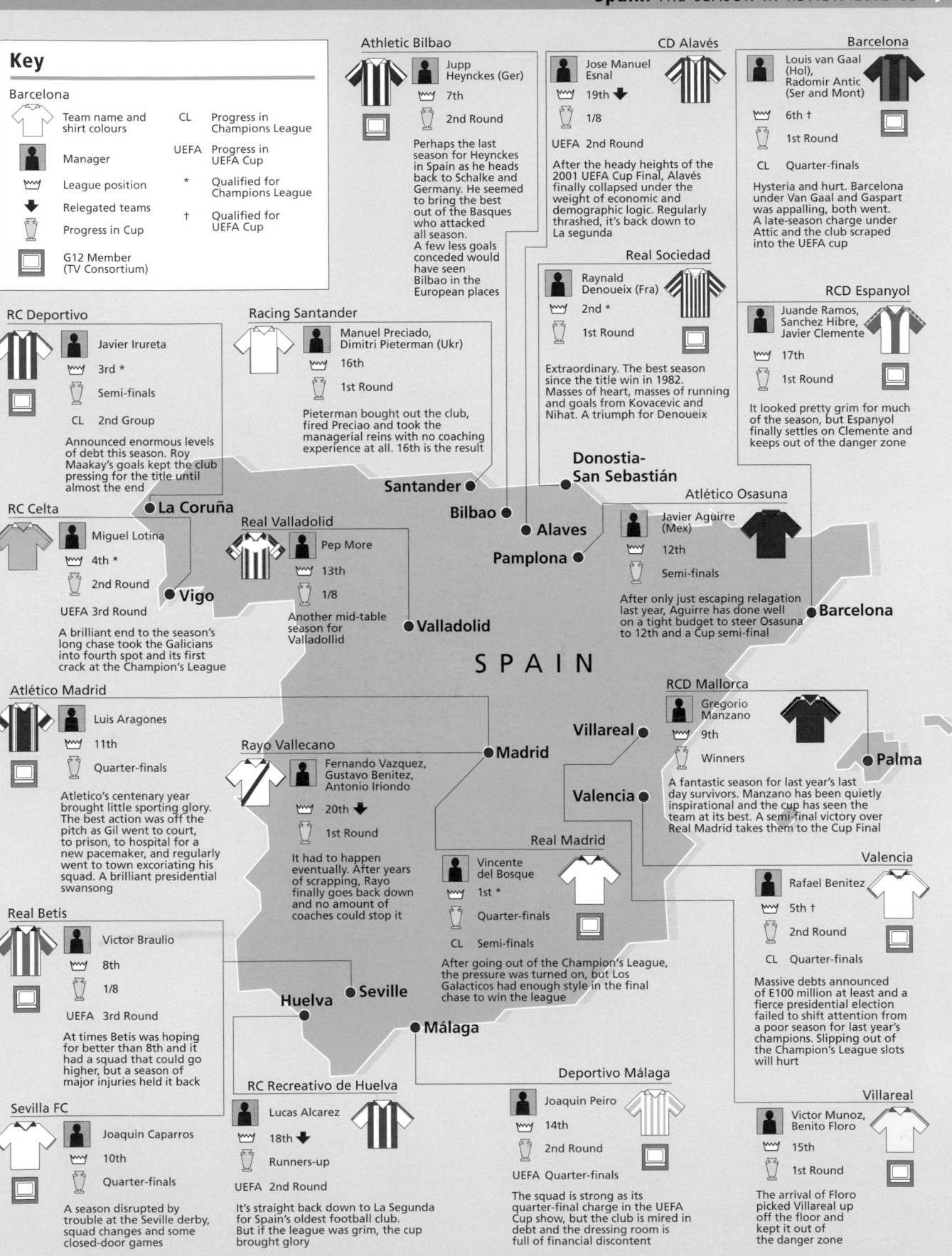

Key

Barcelona

Team name and shirt colours

Manager

League position

Relegated teams

Progress in Cup

G12 Member (TV Consortium)

CL — Progress in Champions League

UEFA — Progress in UEFA Cup

* — Qualified for Champions League

† — Qualified for UEFA Cup

Athletic Bilbao

Jupp Heynckes (Ger)

7th

2nd Round

Perhaps the last season for Heynckes in Spain as he heads back to Schalke and Germany. He seemed to bring the best out of the Basques who attacked all season. A few less goals conceded would have seen Bilbao in the European places

---

CD Alavés

Jose Manuel Esnal

19th ↓

1/8

UEFA 2nd Round

After the heady heights of the 2001 UEFA Cup Final, Alavés finally collapsed under the weight of economic and demographic logic. Regularly thrashed, it's back down to La segunda

---

Barcelona

Louis van Gaal (Hol), Radomir Antic (Ser and Mont)

6th †

1st Round

CL Quarter-finals

Hysteria and hurt. Barcelona under Van Gaal and Gaspart was appalling, both went. A late-season charge under Attic and the club scraped into the UEFA cup

---

Real Sociedad

Raynald Denoueix (Fra)

2nd *

1st Round

Extraordinary. The best season since the title win in 1982. Masses of heart, masses of running and goals from Kovacevic and Nihat. A triumph for Denoueix

---

RCD Espanyol

Juande Ramos, Sanchez Hibre, Javier Clemente

17th

1st Round

It looked pretty grim for much of the season, but Espanyol finally settles on Clemente and keeps out of the danger zone

---

RC Deportivo

Javier Irureta

3rd *

Semi-finals

CL 2nd Group

Announced enormous levels of debt this season. Roy Maakay's goals kept the club pressing for the title until almost the end

---

Racing Santander

Manuel Preciado, Dimitri Pieterman (Ukr)

16th

1st Round

Pieterman bought out the club, fired Preciao and took the managerial reins with no coaching experience at all. 16th is the result

---

RC Celta

Miguel Lotina

4th *

2nd Round

UEFA 3rd Round

A brilliant end to the season's long chase took the Galicians into fourth spot and its first crack at the Champion's League

---

Real Valladolid

Pep More

13th

1/8

Another mid-table season for Valladollid

Atlético Osasuna

Javier Aguirre (Mex)

12th

Semi-finals

After only just escaping relagation last year, Aguirre has done well on a tight budget to steer Osasuna to 12th and a Cup semi-final

---

Atlético Madrid

Luis Aragones

11th

Quarter-finals

Atletico's centenary year brought little sporting glory. The best action was off the pitch as Gil went to court, to prison, to hospital for a new pacemaker, and regularly went to town excoriating his squad. A brilliant presidential swansong

---

Rayo Vallecano

Fernando Vazquez, Gustavo Benitez, Antonio Iriondo

20th ↓

1st Round

It had to happen eventually. After years of scrapping, Rayo finally goes back down and no amount of coaches could stop it

---

Real Madrid

Vincente del Bosque

1st *

Quarter-finals

CL Semi-finals

After going out of the Champion's League, the pressure was turned on, but Los Galacticos had enough style in the final chase to win the league

---

RCD Mallorca

Gregorio Manzano

9th

Winners

A fantastic season for last year's last day survivors. Manzano has been quietly inspirational and the cup has seen the team at its best. A semi-final victory over Real Madrid takes them to the Cup Final

---

Real Betis

Victor Braulio

8th

1/8

UEFA 3rd Round

At times Betis was hoping for better than 8th and it had a squad that could go higher, but a season of major injuries held it back

---

Sevilla FC

Joaquin Caparros

10th

Quarter-finals

A season disrupted by trouble at the Seville derby, squad changes and some closed-door games

---

RC Recreativo de Huelva

Lucas Alcarez

18th ↓

Runners-up

UEFA 2nd Round

It's straight back down to La Segunda for Spain's oldest football club. But if the league was grim, the cup brought glory

---

Deportivo Málaga

Joaquin Peiro

14th

2nd Round

UEFA Quarter-finals

The squad is strong as its quarter-final charge in the UEFA Cup show, but the club is mired in debt and the dressing room is full of financial discontent

---

Valencia

Rafael Benitez

5th †

2nd Round

CL Quarter-finals

Massive debts announced of £100 million at least and a fierce presidential election failed to shift attention from a poor season for last year's champions. Slipping out of the Champion's League slots will hurt

---

Villareal

Victor Munoz, Benito Floro

15th

1st Round

The arrival of Floro picked Villareal up off the floor and kept it out of the danger zone

---

SPAIN

Santander • Donostia-San Sebastián

La Coruña • Bilbao • Alaves

Vigo • Pamplona

Valladolid

Madrid • Barcelona

Villareal • Palma

Valencia

Real Madrid

Huelva • Seville

Málaga

Yes to Hard Work'. Deportivo and Celta Vigo also struggled to find their form, while last year's champions Valencia continued with the same defensive solidity and climbed to second by Christmas. The big surprises were Real Sociedad, because the team was so good, and Barcelona, because it was so bad.

Real Sociedad last won La Liga in 1982 and the intervening years for the Basque side from San Sebastián have been harsh. This season, under ex-Nantes coach Reynald Denoueix, it was unrecognisable. As a unit it was irrepressible, spirited, committed and skilful. In Darko Kovacevic and main new signing Turkish striker Nihat Kahveci, it possessed two exemplary goalscorers in form. An unbeaten run of 19 games took them to the summit of La Liga in October and a five-point lead at the half-way stage.

By contrast, Barcelona was appalling. Despite bringing in 16 new players at a cost over £140 million during the Gaspart presidency, the squad was unbalanced. In the Champions League it found its form in a long run of unbeaten games, but at home it was a disaster. By Christmas it was two points off the relegation zone. The anger and bitterness spilt over into an unprecedented display of hostility towards Luis Figo in the Derby game with Real. When Sevilla beat them 3-0 at the Nou Camp an already embittered crowd booed Van Gaal's every move and assailed President Gaspart with a five-minute chorus of 'Resign!'. His head bowed, he soaked up the spleen, proud and alone for five minutes. By mid-February both he and Van Gaal had gone.

Enric Reyna, the club vice-president, stepped up as president prior to the May election of the post, and Radomir Antic was drafted in on a four-month contract to save the season. This he duly did: defensive solidity was established, Luis Enrique got fit, Saviola was allowed to play and Barca dragged themselves into sixth spot and a UEFA Cup place.

But below the top six there was plenty of football good enough to regularly upset the top teams – Mallorca's 5-0 thrashing of Real Madrid, Sevilla's 3-0 defeat of Barcelona and Recreativo Huelva's heroic goalless draw with Madrid. Atlético

SPAIN

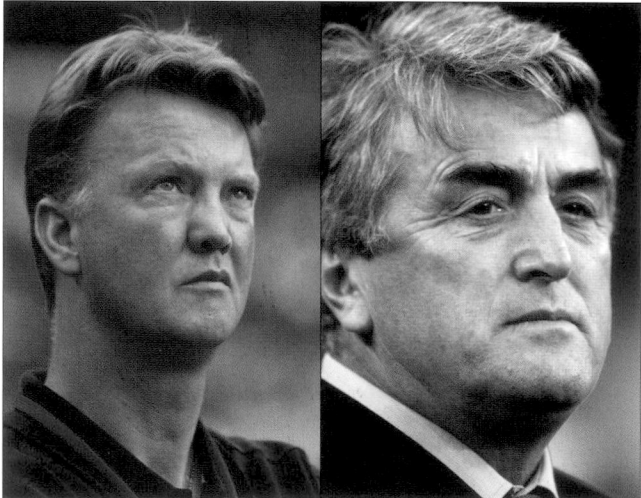

Above, left: Louis van Gaal watches the heavens for a sign. His second stint as Barca coach was an unmitigated disaster.

Above, right: Radomir Antic took over from Van Gaal, and managed to haul the side back up to sixth place as well as a Champion's League quarter-final. His reward, the sack and replacement by Frank Rijkaard.

Right: Roy Makaay, Deportivo La Coruña's Dutch striker and top scorer in La Liga this season. Here he celebrates a goal against Seville with Victor Sanchez.

Left: *Fernando Torres is the great young hope at Atlético Madrid.*

Far left: *Real Sociedad's Serbian striker Darko Kovacevic goes through the Recreativo de Huelva defence. Kovacevic's scoring record was brilliant and he was at his most deadly in the six-yard area.*

Below: *Rafael Benitez, Valencia manager, implores his side to actually score – something Valencia found hard this season.*

Race for the Championship

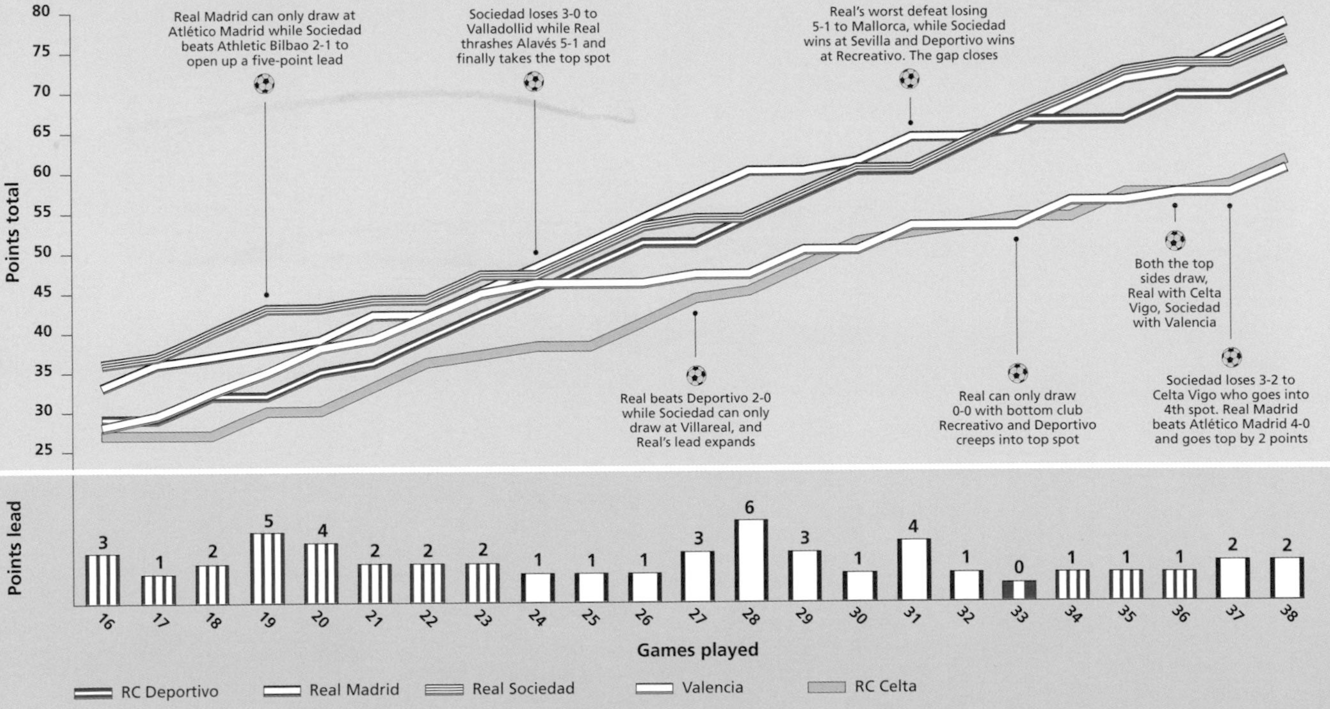

Real Madrid can only draw at Atlético Madrid while Sociedad beats Athletic Bilbao 2-1 to open up a five-point lead

Sociedad loses 3-0 to Valladollid while Real thrashes Alavés 5-1 and finally takes the top spot

Real's worst defeat losing 5-1 to Mallorca, while Sociedad wins at Sevilla and Deportivo wins at Recreativo. The gap closes

Both the top sides draw, Real with Celta Vigo, Sociedad with Valencia

Real beats Deportivo 2-0 while Sociedad can only draw at Villareal, and Real's lead expands

Real can only draw 0-0 with bottom club Recreativo and Deportivo creeps into top spot

Sociedad loses 3-2 to Celta Vigo who goes into 4th spot. Real Madrid beats Atlético Madrid 4-0 and goes top by 2 points

Points total (y-axis: 25, 30, 35, 40, 45, 50, 55, 60, 65, 70, 75, 80)

Points lead (bar values): 3, 1, 2, 5, 4, 2, 2, 2, 1, 1, 1, 3, 6, 3, 1, 4, 1, 0, 1, 1, 1, 2, 2

Games played: 16, 17, 18, 19, 20, 21, 22, 23, 24, 25, 26, 27, 28, 29, 30, 31, 32, 33, 34, 35, 36, 37, 38

— RC Deportivo   — Real Madrid   ≡ Real Sociedad   □ Valencia   ▨ RC Celta

235

SPAIN

Madrid, started well in its centenary year, briefly topping the table before dropping like a stone to mid-table.

By far the season's best performance came from President Jesus Gil y Gil. Another marathon court case, over charges of embezzlement and the false acquisitions of club shares, reached a judgement which would in normal circumstances have seen him go to prison. But appeals in higher courts await and his visit to hospital mid-season for a new pacemaker mean that he is certain not to serve any time. Commenting on Atlético's dismal performance from his hospital bed, Gil exploded 'Every time we play, we play with seven'. When his interviewer reminded Gil of the delicate state of his heart he replied 'I'm sick of people telling me to relax – they can stick my heart where the sun doesn't shine. Carreas, Santi and Otero are not good enough for this team.'

Racing Santander acquired a new owner, coach and official photographer in the shape of Dimtri Pieterman who bought a share in the debt-ridden club. He promptly demoted the coaches and installed himself in charge. When the Spanish League refused him access to the bench because of his lack of official qualifications he had himself registered as an official photographer and took up his coaching duties from the side of the dugout.

In the long run-in for the title, Sociedad was the first to falter, losing its unbeaten record in a 3-0 defeat in the Basque derby at Athletic Bilbao. Real and Deportivo took their chances. Ronaldo rediscovered his scoring form and Zidane began to orchestrate a long period of sensational Madrid performances, exemplified by the 4-1 defeat of Valencia. It has been a very long time since anyone has put four goals past the meanest defence in La Liga and Zidane was instrumental. His vision, subtlety, grace and speed were unmatched this year. Deportivo also found consistency and a fit Roy Makaay found the goals to keep them in touch with the lead all spring. An improving Celta Vigo and stagnant, bad tempered Valencia were left to battle it out for fourth and fifth and in the final weeks of the season they had a final say: Valencia beat Deportivo, Celta beat both Deportivo and Sociedad, but Real forced a draw from them and swept Atlético Madrid and Athletic Bilbao aside to win La Liga on the final day.

Above: Sneaking through. Real Madrid's striker Raúl nips through the Sevilla defence (Juan Navarro, right and Pablo Alfaro, left) in another brilliant season, especially in the Champions League where he is now the highest scorer of all time.

Right: Reynald Denoueix came from Nantes to coach Real Sociedad and second spot is a fantastic success for him.

International Club Performances 2002–03

CLUB	COMPETITION	PROGRESS
Barcelona	Champions League	Quarter-finals
RC Deportivo	Champions League	2nd Group Phase
Real Madrid	Champions League	Semi-finals
Valencia CF	Champions League	Quarter-finals
CD Alavés	UEFA Cup	2nd Round
Málaga CF	UEFA Cup	Quarter Finals
Real Betis	UEFA Cup	3rd Round
RC Celta	UEFA Cup	3rd Round

Top Goalscorers 2002–03

PLAYER	CLUB	NATIONALITY	GOALS
Roy Makaay	RC Deportivo	Dutch	28
Kahveci Nihat	Real Sociedad	Turkish	22
Ronaldo	Real Madrid	Brazilian	21
Darko Kovacevic	Real Sociedad	Serbian	20

Spanish Cup

2003 FINAL

June 28 – Martinez Valléro
Recreativo **0-3** RCD Mallorca
Huelva   *(Pandiani 21 pen, Eto'o 74, 84)*
h/t: 0-1   **Att:** 37,000
Ref: Iturralde Gonzalez

Atlético Madrid fans celebrate the club's centenary in central Madrid. The flag, it is claimed, is the longest ever made, stretching over a kilometre in length. It was carried through the streets of the city to the club's Vincente Calderon stadium.

Above: Deportivo's Fran goes past Valencia's Pablo Aimar, as Valencia slip down the table.

Left, top: Rearguard action. Barcelona's Carlos Puyol makes it difficult for Ronaldo in the derby in Madrid. Barcelona played it tight and got away with a draw, but it couldn't stop Real's progress to the title.

Below, left: Valencia's John Carew clashes with Real central defenders – Fernando Hierro and Ivan Helguera – who were the side's Achilles heel this season.

Left: Vincente Del Bosque. Four major titles in four seasons (two domestic leagues, two Champions Leagues) was not enough to save Vincente del Bosque. The day after Real won La Liga he got the sack.

Below: Los Galacticos after beating Athletic Bilbao on the final day of the season celebrates its 29th League Championship.

Association Football in Spain

SPAIN

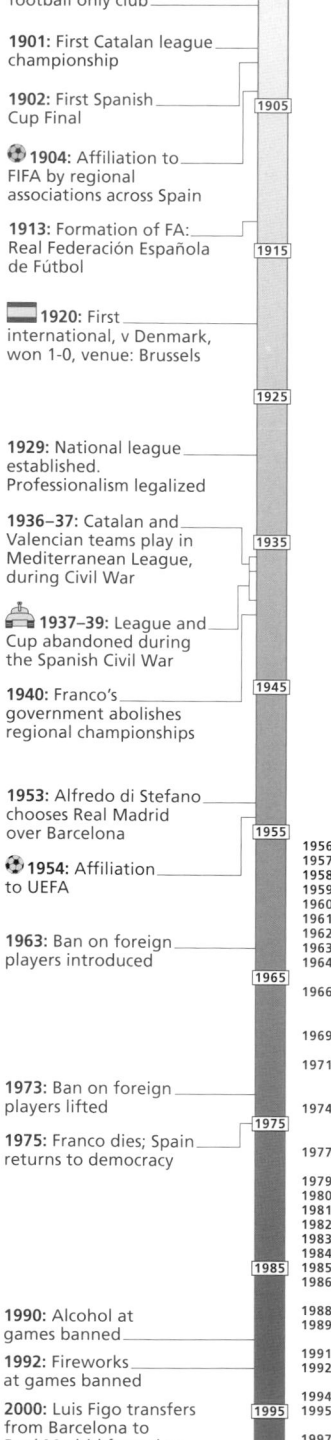

1898: Athletic Bilbao formed. Spain's oldest football only club — **1895**

1901: First Catalan league championship

1902: First Spanish Cup Final — **1905**

1904: Affiliation to FIFA by regional associations across Spain

1913: Formation of FA: Real Federación Española de Fútbol — **1915**

1920: First international, v Denmark, won 1-0, venue: Brussels — **1925**

1929: National league established. Professionalism legalized

1936–37: Catalan and Valencian teams play in Mediterranean League, during Civil War — **1935**

1937–39: League and Cup abandoned during the Spanish Civil War — **1945**

1940: Franco's government abolishes regional championships

1953: Alfredo di Stefano chooses Real Madrid over Barcelona — **1955**

1954: Affiliation to UEFA

1963: Ban on foreign players introduced — **1965**

1973: Ban on foreign players lifted

1975: Franco dies; Spain returns to democracy — **1975**

1990: Alcohol at games banned — **1985**

1992: Fireworks at games banned

2000: Luis Figo transfers from Barcelona to Real Madrid for a then record transfer fee — **1995**

2001: Real Madrid break world transfer fee again for Zinedine Zidane from Juventus — **2005**

Real Madrid, Spanish champions for the fourth consecutive year in 1964, included almost the entire Spanish national team: (back row left to right) Vicente, Isidro, Santamaria (from Uruguay), Casado, Muller (from France), Zoco; (front row) Amancio, Felo, di Stefano, Puskas (from Hungary) and Gento.

Key

International football		○	Competition winner
Affiliation to FIFA		△	Competition runner-up
Affiliation to UEFA		Alav	– CD Alavés
War		Atl B	– Athletic Bilbao
		Atl M	– Atlético Madrid
■ World Cup host		Barca	– Barcelona
● World Cup winner		Esp	– RCD Español
▲ World Cup runner-up		RCD	– RCD Mallorca
■ European Championships host		Real M	– Real Madrid
● European Championships winner		Val	– Valencia
▲ European Championships runner-up		Zara	– Real Zaragoza

International Competitions

Year	European Cup	UEFA Cup	European Cup-Winners' Cup
1956	○ Real M		
1957	○ Real M		
1958	○ Real M	○ Barca	
1959	○ Real M		
1960	○ Real M	○ Barca	
1961	△ Barca		
1962	△ Real M	○ Val △ Barca	○ Atl M
1963		○ Val	△ Atl M
1964	●■ △ Real M	○ Zara △ Val	
1966	○ Real M	○ Barca △ Zara	
1969			△ Barca
1971			△ Real M
1974	△ Atl M		
1977		△ Atl B	
1979			○ Barca
1980			○ Val
1981	△ Real M		○ Barca
1982	■		△ Real M
1983			
1984	▲		
1985		○ Real M	
1986	△ Barca	○ Real M	△ Atl M
1988		△ Esp	
1989			○ Barca
1991			△ Barca
1992	○ Barca		
1994	△ Barca		
1995		○ Zara	
1997		○ Barca	
1998	○ Real M		
1999			△ RCD
2000	○ Real M △ Val		
2001	△ Val	△ Alav	
2002	○ Real M		

The Royal House in Spain has played a big part in the nation's footballing history. Many of the big clubs bear the name 'Real' meaning 'royal', and the Copa del Rey (Cup of the King) is named after King Alfonso XIII (1886–1931).

★ **Athletic Bilbao** 1898

RC Deportivo 1904

Sporting Gijón 1905

La Coruña

Santiago
SD Compostela 1962

Pontevedra 1928

Celta Vigo 1923

Vigo

Merger of Fortuna and Sporting

Spain: The main clubs

Cadiz 1910	Team name with year of formation
●	Club formed before 1912
●	Club formed 1912–25
●	Club formed 1925–50
	Club formed after 1950
★	Founder members of National League (1929)
	Winners Copa del Rey 1902–29
	English origins
	Swiss origins
	Catalonian regional identity
	Galician regional identity
	Basque regional identity
	Foreign student origins
	Mining origins
	Originated from a cycling club
	Student origins
	Railway workers
	Royal house

Spain

ORIGINS AND GROWTH OF FOOTBALL

SPAIN'S OLDEST FOOTBALL CLUB, Real Club Recreativo de Huelva, was founded in 1889 as an informal sports club with a football team based around the British presence of railway and copper-mine workers. Over the next decade clubs formed in Madrid, the Basque Country, Barcelona and Seville. British influences through sailors, miners and expatriate traders were significant in Seville, Barcelona and Bilbao.

Modern Spanish history is dominated by the political and cultural struggles between the centre (especially Madrid and Castille) and the regions of Spain. This was immediately reflected in the organization of Spanish football. Strong regional leagues were established in the first years of the 20th century, the first in Catalonia in 1901. These continued despite the establishment

of a national professional league in 1929. The Spanish monarchy's concern with centralizing power extended to the establishment of the Copa del Rey in 1902 by King Alfonso XIII – a national championship among regional champions. The Royal House had also seen fit to bestow its patronage on clubs across the country.

The Spanish Civil War (1936–39) was a struggle between right and left but also between the centre and the regions. With the victory of Franco's centralizing nationalist forces, regional leagues were abolished, foreign influences in club origins played down and the Copa del Rey renamed the Copa del Generalisimo. Atlético Madrid was forced to change name – to Atlético Aviación – but received the crack Air Force football squad as part of the deal. Strict control of the press and most social and political institutions saw football clubs become an even more significant symbol of regional identities. With the death of Franco in 1975, Spain returned to democracy and a revived regionalism. Spanish club performances in European tournaments have been second only to Italy, but the national team continues to underperform in major tournaments.

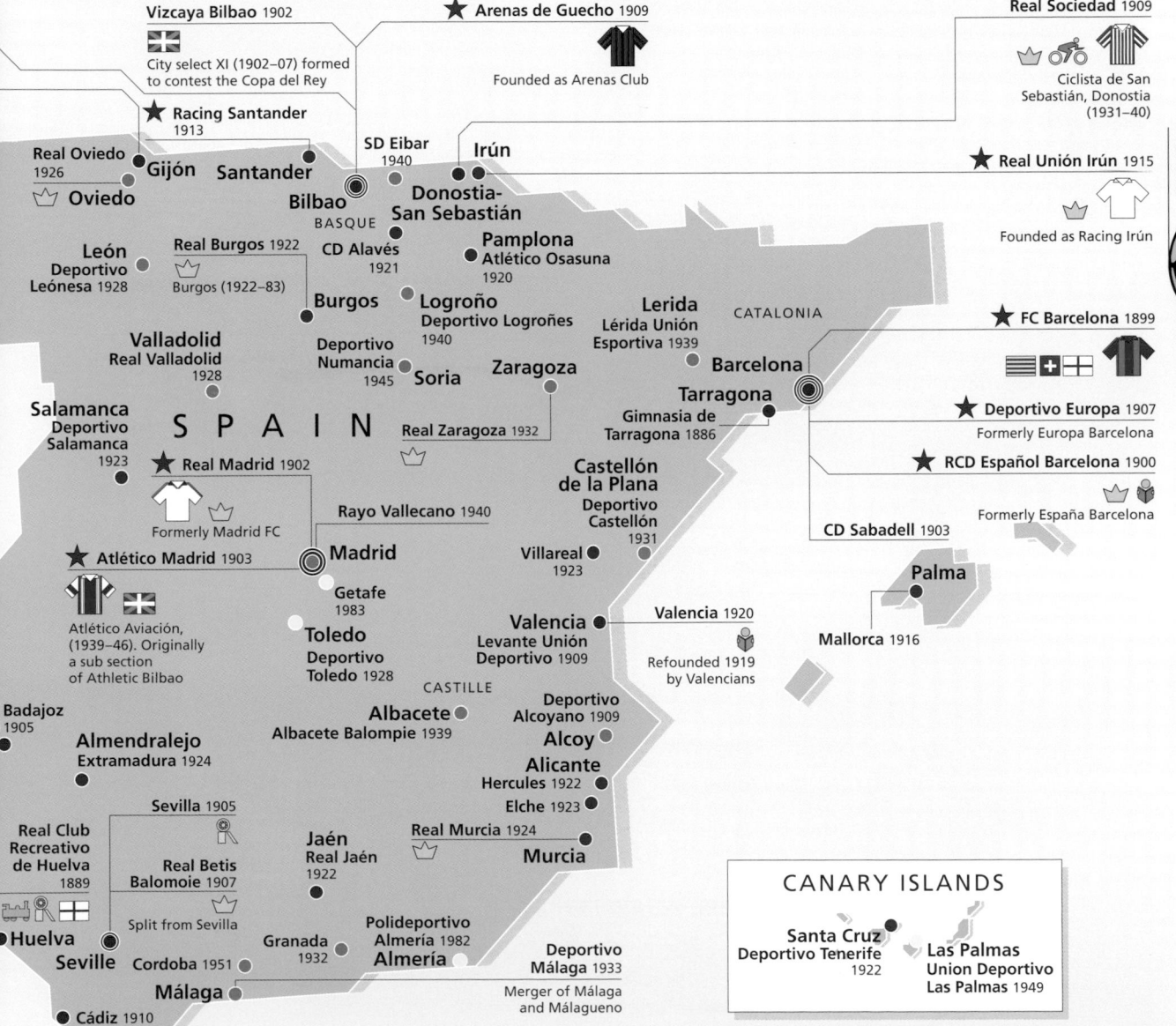

Barcelona

FOOTBALL CITY

ALTHOUGH FC BARCELONA was one of the key institutions in the creation of Catalan nationalism in the 20th century, it was founded and initially run by a Swiss, Hans Gamper, and an Englishman, Arthur Witty, both expatriate businessmen attracted by the city's dynamic economic growth. The team's first game was played on Christmas Eve 1899 at the racetrack in Bonanova against FC Catala and, while the team's opponents were Catalan, Barcelona's team was overwhelmingly foreign. But the Catalan nationalism that was growing rapidly at the turn of the century could absorb foreign influences: Barcelona was coached by foreigners throughout the 1920s and 1930s and had regularly fielded foreign players. On top of that, Andalusian immigrants, attracted to the booming industrial estates of the city in the 1950s, swelled its support. The club's cosmopolitanism was matched by success and, by the early 1930s, the club had acquired a major stadium in Les Corts, a series of national and regional titles, a massive following and a fierce, politically-charged rivalry with Real Madrid.

Barça and Catalan nationalism

The weight of these nationalist identities was given a massive boost by the outcome of the Spanish Civil War (1936–39). Centralist and right-wing forces under General Franco brutally suppressed the regional, left-wing forces that included most of Barcelona, Catalonia and FC Barcelona. In the 1940s and 1950s, Madrid's political domination of Catalonia, interference in the running of the club, and repression of nearly all forms of political opposition, made the connection between supporting FC Barcelona and Catalan nationalism even clearer, a connection that has remained in the years since Franco's death and the subsequent democratization and devolution of Spain.

In the long shadow cast by Barça sits the city's second club, RCD Espanyol. The club was founded by a group of students with the Castilian name Español – an attempt to wind up the Catalan nationalists down the road – and it traditionally attracts state employees and those migrant workers from Andalusia with Castilian sentiments. But with only two cup wins and some near misses in the late 1980s and early 1990s to its name, its challenge has been symbolic rather than sporting. Time and tastes have forced even this bastion of Royalism and Centralism to take the Catalan spelling for its name. To make matters worse, the club was forced to clear an enormous debt by selling its Sarria stadium and moving into the large but unatmospheric Olympic stadium on Montjuïc.

THE NATIONAL DERBY

| BARCELONA | REAL |

226 matches played

93 Barcelona wins
84 Real Madrid wins
49 draws

0   50   100   150   200   250
NUMBER OF MATCHES
(All matches up to May 2003)

Barcelona B

MINI ESTADI
15,000

SANT RAMON
NOU CAMP
98,600

Barcelona
(1957–)

LES TRES TORRES

Avinguda Diagonal

LES CORTS
LES CORTS

Barcelona
(1922–57)

Stadium was closed for 6 months in 1925 by General Primo de Rivera after Barca fans whistled during a royalist song played during half time

Carrer de Collblanc

Carrer de Sants

BADAL

SANTS

BARCELONA 1899

League	*1929*, **30**, **45**, **46**, *48*, **49**, **52**, **53**, **54–56**, **59**, **60**, **62**, **64**, **67**, *68*, **71**, **73**, **74**, **76–78**, **82**, **85**, **86**, **87**, **89**, **91–94**, *97*, **98**, **99**, *2000*
Cup	*1902*, **10**, **12**, **13**, *19*, **20**, **22**, **25**, **26**, **28**, *32*, **36**, **42**, **51–53**, *54*, **57**, **59**, **63**, **68**, **71**, *74*, **78**, **81**, **83**, **84**, **86**, **88**, **90**, *96*, **97**, **98**
European Cup	*1961*, **86**, *92*, *94*
European Cup-Winners' Cup	*1969*, **79**, **82**, **89**, *91*, **97**
UEFA Cup	**1958**, **60**, *62*, **66**
World Club Cup	*1992*

VIVENDES DE LA SEAT

Passeig de la Zona Franca

MONTJUÏC

ESTADI OLÍMPIC
56,000

Originally built for the International Expo of 1929 and rebuilt for 1992 Olympics

Parc de Montjuic

RCD Espanyol
(1997–)

Ronda del Litoral

NOU CAMP

98,600

Club:	Barcelona
Built:	1957
Original Capacity:	90,000
Rebuilt:	1982
Significant Matches:	1982 World Cup: five matches; 1992 Barcelona Olympics: opening ceremony, football Final; European Cup Final: 1989, 1999; European Cup-Winners' Cup Final: 1982

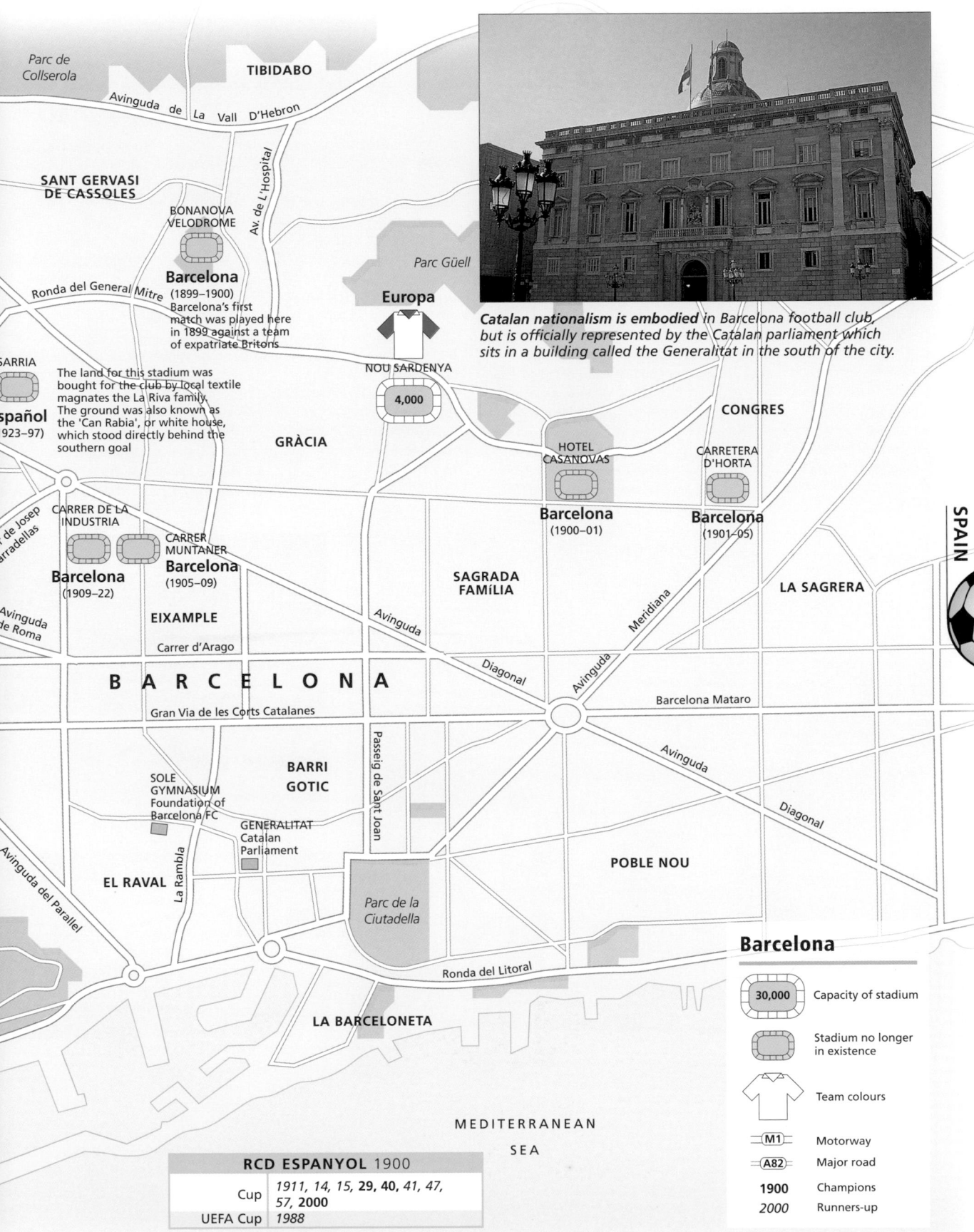

Parc de Collserola

TIBIDABO

Avinguda de La Vall D'Hebron

SANT GERVASI DE CASSOLES

BONANOVA VELODROME

Barcelona
(1899–1900)
Barcelona's first match was played here in 1899 against a team of expatriate Britons

Ronda del General Mitre

Av. de L'Hospital

Parc Güell

Europa

NOU SARDENYA

4,000

GRÀCIA

SARRIA

The land for this stadium was bought for the club by local textile magnates the La Riva family. The ground was also known as the 'Can Rabia', or white house, which stood directly behind the southern goal

spañol
(1923–97)

HOTEL CASANOVAS

Barcelona
(1900–01)

CONGRES

CARRETERA D'HORTA

Barcelona
(1901–05)

LA SAGRERA

Avinguda Meridiana

Carrer de Josep *arradellas*

CARRER DE LA INDUSTRIA

CARRER MUNTANER

Barcelona
(1905–09)

Barcelona
(1909–22)

EIXAMPLE

Carrer d'Arago

Avinguda de Roma

SAGRADA FAMÍLIA

Avinguda Diagonal

Avinguda

Barcelona Mataro

B A R C E L O N A

Gran Via de les Corts Catalanes

Avinguda

Diagonal

Passeig de Sant Joan

BARRI GOTIC

SOLE GYMNASIUM
Foundation of Barcelona FC

GENERALITAT
Catalan Parliament

POBLE NOU

Avinguda del Parallel

EL RAVAL

La Rambla

Parc de la Ciutadella

Ronda del Litoral

LA BARCELONETA

Catalan nationalism is embodied in Barcelona football club, but is officially represented by the Catalan parliament which sits in a building called the Generalitat in the south of the city.

SPAIN

MEDITERRANEAN SEA

Barcelona

30,000	Capacity of stadium
	Stadium no longer in existence
	Team colours
M1	Motorway
A82	Major road
1900	Champions
2000	Runners-up

Madrid

FOOTBALL CITY

REAL MADRID GREW OUT OF AN ELITE CLUB called Football Sky, which was founded in 1895. A team split in 1900 saw Español de Madrid emerge, which transmuted into Madrid FC in 1902. When King Alfonso XIII accepted the offer of royal patronage in 1920, the team became known as Real. Although Real Madrid was successful in the national championships in the first decade of the 20th century, it did not acquire a permanent home until the construction of the Campo O'Donnell in 1912, and a proper stadium had to await the construction of Chamartîn in 1924.

Located in the most exclusive financial and residential district of Madrid, Real was transformed by the arrival of Santiago Bernabéu as president and the Franco regime at the end of the Spanish Civil War. Although Franco was undoubtedly a Real fan, and his regime benefited hugely from the successful international exposure the great Real team of the 1950s brought, his real influence on the club is probably less than Bernabéu and the network of financiers and bankers he amassed. Constant access to funds has allowed Real to build one of the world's largest stadiums, fund record-breaking transfers, and return after two quiet decades to dominant ways, winning three European Cups (1998, 2000 and 2002). This has also allowed Real to accumulate the biggest debts in global football, only paid off by the sale of its training ground in 2001 for massive real estate development.

Hard-won success

Atlético was founded in 1903 by three Basques studying in Madrid as an offshoot of their home team, Athletic Bilbao. The team played in Athletic's blue and white stripes before switching to its current red and white stripes in 1911. The club performed poorly before the Civil War, only returning to the league afterwards because Oviedo's ground had been destroyed and they could no longer play in the league. It merged with the air force's brilliant side, Atlético Aviacion, which brought it two immediate titles. Although historically it is among the most successful teams in Spain, Atlético is better known for the fanaticism of its *ultras* (fans) and the erratic and financially dubious behaviour of the team's long term president, Jesus Gil. The club's recent poor fortunes have often left it behind the tiny Rayo Vallecano, which survives on a shoestring in the city's rough southern suburbs.

The Royal Palace in Madrid: the Spanish Royal House has played a big part in the history of Spanish football. Madrid FC became Real or 'Royal' Madrid in 1920, when King Alphonso XIII accepted the offer of royal patronage of the team. General Franco too was a Real fan, and with such supporters as this it is little wonder that Real has come to be associated with the elite elements of Spanish society.

VINCENTE CALDERÓN (Estadio Manzanares)

57,500

Club: Atlético Madrid
Built: 1966
Rebuilt: 1982
Significant Matches: 1982 World Cup: three group matches

SANTIAGO BERNABÉU

106,500

Club: Real Madrid
Built: 1947
Original Capacity: 75,000
Rebuilt: 1982, 1998
Significant Matches: 1964 European Championships: Final; 1982 World Cup: three group matches; European Cup Finals: 1957, 69, 80

SPAIN

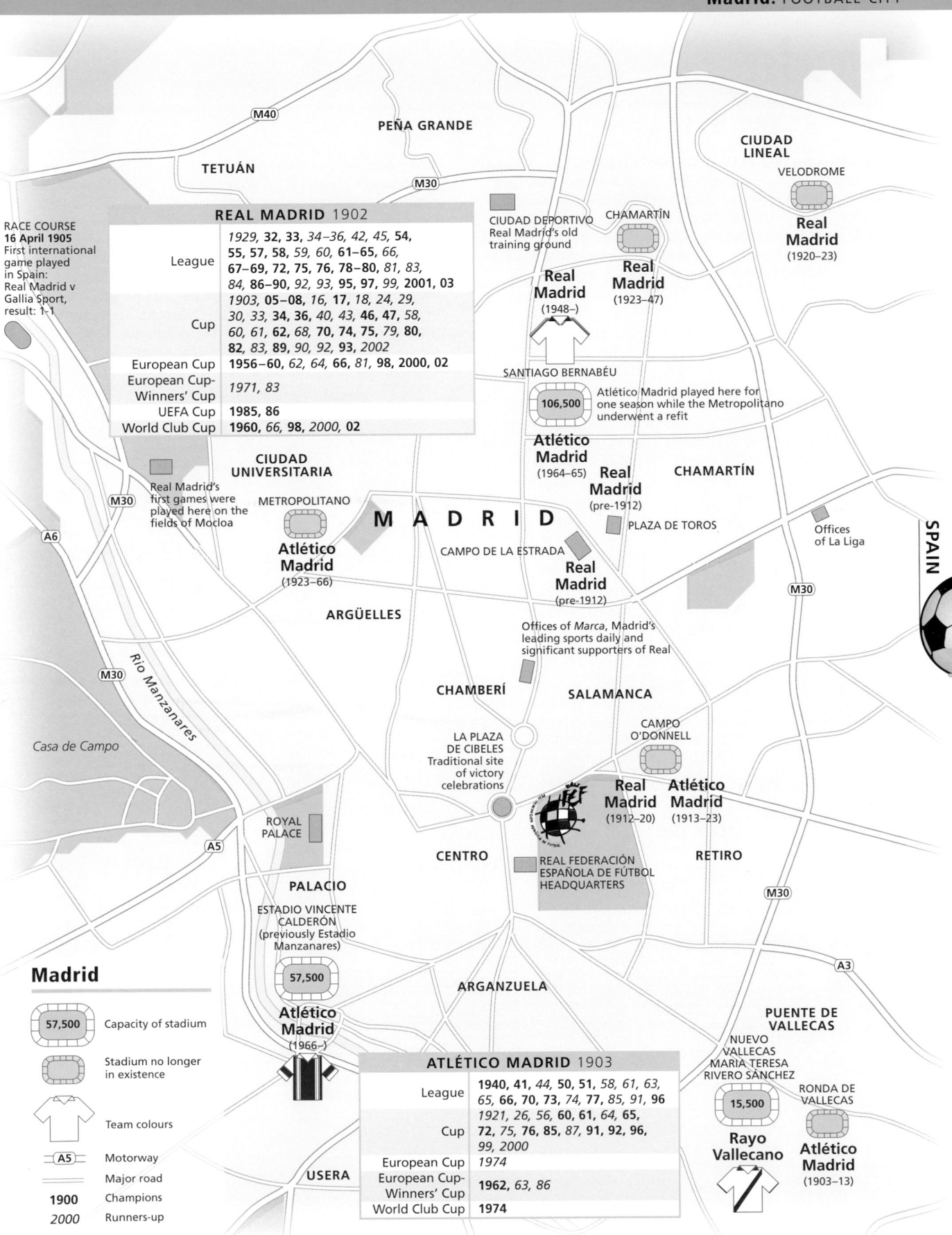

M40

PEÑA GRANDE

TETUÁN

M30

CIUDAD
LINEAL

VELODROME

**Real
Madrid**
(1920–23)

CIUDAD DEPORTIVO
Real Madrid's old
training ground

CHAMARTÍN

**Real
Madrid**
(1923–47)

**Real
Madrid**
(1948–)

SANTIAGO BERNABÉU

RACE COURSE
16 April 1905
First international
game played
in Spain:
Real Madrid v
Gallia Sport,
result: 1-1

REAL MADRID 1902

League	*1929*, **32**, **33**, *34–36*, **42**, **45**, **54**, **55**, **57**, **58**, *59*, *60*, **61–65**, *66*, **67–69**, **72**, **75**, **76**, **78–80**, **81**, *83*, **84**, **86–90**, **92**, *93*, **95**, *97*, *99*, **2001**, **03**
Cup	*1903*, **05–08**, **16**, *17*, *18*, *24*, *29*, *30*, **33**, **34**, *36*, **40**, **43**, **46**, *47*, *58*, *60*, *61*, **62**, *68*, **70**, **74**, **75**, *79*, **80**, **82**, *83*, **89**, *90*, **92**, *93*, **2002**
European Cup	**1956–60**, *62*, **64**, *66*, *81*, **98**, **2000**, **02**
European Cup-Winners' Cup	*1971*, *83*
UEFA Cup	**1985**, **86**
World Club Cup	**1960**, *66*, **98**, *2000*, **02**

M30

Real Madrid's
first games were
played here on the
fields of Mocloa

A6

CIUDAD
UNIVERSITARIA

METROPOLITANO

**Atlético
Madrid**
(1923–66)

ARGÜELLES

M30

Casa de Campo

Río Manzanares

106,500

Atlético Madrid played here for
one season while the Metropolitano
underwent a refit

**Atlético
Madrid**
(1964–65)

**Real
Madrid**
(pre-1912)

CHAMARTÍN

PLAZA DE TOROS

CAMPO DE LA ESTRADA

**Real
Madrid**
(pre-1912)

Offices
of La Liga

M30

SPAIN

Offices of *Marca*, Madrid's
leading sports daily and
significant supporters of Real

CHAMBERÍ

SALAMANCA

CAMPO
O'DONNELL

LA PLAZA
DE CIBELES
Traditional site
of victory
celebrations

**Real
Madrid**
(1912–20)

**Atlético
Madrid**
(1913–23)

RETIRO

M30

A3

REAL FEDERACIÓN
ESPAÑOLA DE FÚTBOL
HEADQUARTERS

CENTRO

ROYAL
PALACE

A5

PALACIO

ESTADIO VINCENTE
CALDERÓN
(previously Estadio
Manzanares)

57,500

**Atlético
Madrid**
(1966–)

ARGANZUELA

PUENTE DE
VALLECAS

NUEVO
VALLECAS
MARÍA TERESA
RIVERO SÁNCHEZ

RONDA DE
VALLECAS

15,500

**Rayo
Vallecano**

**Atlético
Madrid**
(1903–13)

USERA

Madrid

57,500	Capacity of stadium
	Stadium no longer in existence
	Team colours
A5	Motorway
	Major road
1900	Champions
2000	Runners-up

ATLÉTICO MADRID 1903

League	**1940**, **41**, *44*, **50**, **51**, *58*, **61**, *63*, **65**, **66**, **70**, **73**, *74*, **77**, *85*, **91**, **96**
Cup	*1921*, *26*, *56*, *60*, **61**, **64**, **65**, **72**, *75*, **76**, **85**, *87*, **91**, **92**, **96**, *99*, **2000**
European Cup	*1974*
European Cup-Winners' Cup	**1962**, *63*, **86**
World Club Cup	**1974**

Spain

FANS AND OWNERS

THERE IS A MIXED ECONOMY in the ownership of clubs in Spain; some are run as sporting and social clubs, others are private limited companies, some with a single dominant investor and others with multiple-share ownership. The two biggest clubs in the country, Real Madrid and Barcelona, are owned by their members, or *socios*, who select the paid officials that run the clubs in highly politicized and expensive elections. The biggest incomes and highest attendances of Spain's top teams are concentrated among the big five – Real, Barcelona, Valencia, Athletic Bilbao and RC Deportivo from La Coruña, although when Atlético Madrid is in the top flight, it joins that elite group.

The rising tide of debt

But despite huge TV income, other investments, and a lot of European success, Spanish clubs are heavily indebted. Real has recently escaped from a crippling debt of around $150 million by selling its city-centre training ground. In the last couple of seasons, smaller clubs with smaller assets have seen board resignations, unpaid creditors and a search for new investors (Las Palmas, for example, is over £30 million in debt). Worse still, the bankruptcy of Atlético Madrid in 2002 led to an investigation by the Spanish treasury which has revealed unpaid taxes among the top clubs for the years 1996–99 of £129 million. Clubs with debts of more than one third of their capital are technically bankrupt in Spain – and this would apply to about a third of the Primera Liga if the debts were immediately enforced.

Spanish fans were traditionally organized in *peñas* or supporters' clubs, often based around a particular bar, which arranged away trips and social events. With the passing of Franco's authoritarian regime and the development of a distinctive youth culture in Spain, it was inevitable that the

ultra model would be imported from Italy by a new generation of supporters. The first *ultra* groups emerged in Madrid in 1982 at both Real (*Ultras Sur*) and Atlético (*El Frente Atlético*) and they have more recently been joined by groups at Barcelona (*ICC – Inter City Cules*), Sevilla (*Peña Biri-Biri*) and Athletic Bilbao. Although there has been some violence between groups outside the stadiums, the phenomenon appears to have peaked since a Real Sociedad fan was stabbed outside Atlético Madrid's Vincente Calderón stadium in 1998. Barriers, fences and moats have become commonplace fixtures at Spanish stadiums.

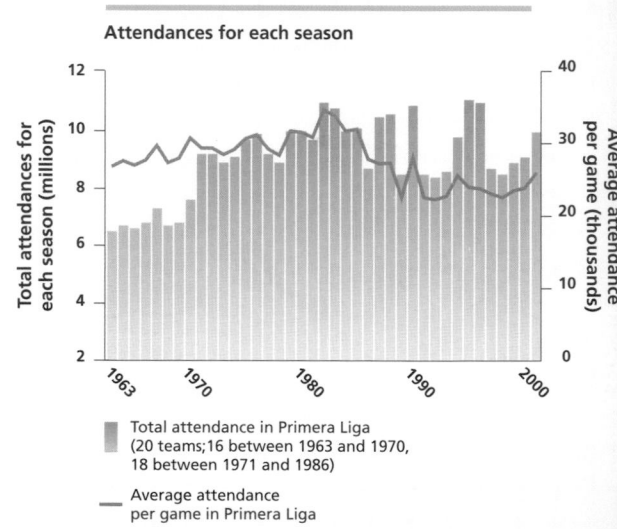

Spanish Attendances

Attendances for each season

Total attendance in Primera Liga
(20 teams; 16 between 1963 and 1970, 18 between 1971 and 1986)

Average attendance
per game in Primera Liga

Average Attendance

Average attendance for season 2002–03 (thousands)

Capacity

Attendance as a percentage of capacity for season 2002–03 (capacity in brackets)

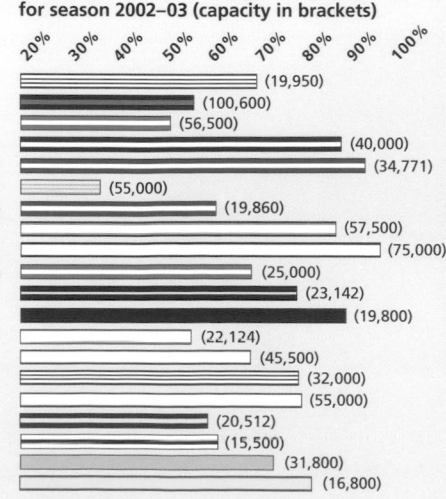

TEAMS	Capacity
CD Alavés	(19,950)
FC Barcelona	(100,600)
Real Betis	(56,500)
Athletic Bilbao	(40,000)
RC Deportivo	(34,771)
RCD Espanyol	(55,000)
Recreativo Huelva	(19,860)
Atlético Madrid	(57,500)
Real Madrid	(75,000)
Deportivo Málaga	(25,000)
RCD Mallorca	(23,142)
Atlético Osasuna	(19,800)
Racing Santander	(22,124)
Sevilla	(45,500)
Real Sociedad	(32,000)
Valencia	(55,000)
Real Valladolid	(20,512)
Rayo Vallecano	(15,500)
RC Celta	(31,800)
Villareal	(16,800)

Jesus Gil, owner of Atlético Madrid, was tried on charges of embezzling £16.4 million during his tenure as Mayor of Marbella.

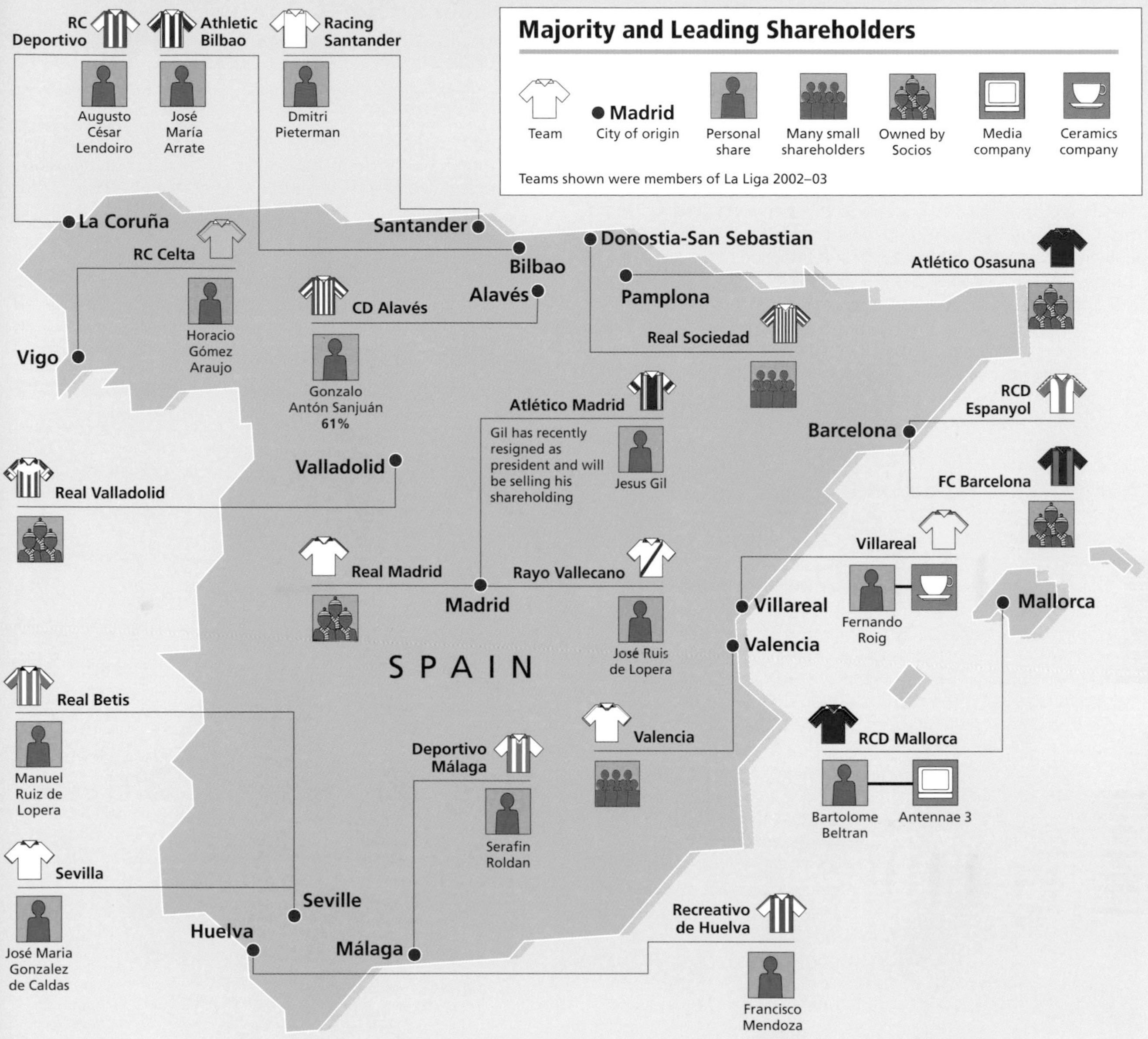

RC Deportivo

Augusto César Lendoiro

Athletic Bilbao

José María Arrate

Racing Santander

Dmitri Pieterman

Majority and Leading Shareholders

Team — ● **Madrid** City of origin — Personal share — Many small shareholders — Owned by Socios — Media company — Ceramics company

Teams shown were members of La Liga 2002–03

● La Coruña

Santander

● Donostia-San Sebastian

Atlético Osasuna

RC Celta

Horacio Gómez Araujo

Vigo

CD Alavés

Bilbao

Alavés

Pamplona

Real Sociedad

Barcelona

RCD Espanyol

Gonzalo Antón Sanjuán 61%

Valladolid

Atlético Madrid

Gil has recently resigned as president and will be selling his shareholding

Jesus Gil

FC Barcelona

Villareal

Real Valladolid

Real Madrid

Rayo Vallecano

Madrid

José Ruis de Lopera

SPAIN

● Villareal

Fernando Roig

● Mallorca

● Valencia

Real Betis

Manuel Ruiz de Lopera

Deportivo Málaga

Serafin Roldan

Valencia

RCD Mallorca

Bartolome Beltran — Antennae 3

Sevilla

José Maria Gonzalez de Caldas

Seville

Huelva

Málaga

Recreativo de Huelva

Francisco Mendoza

SPAIN

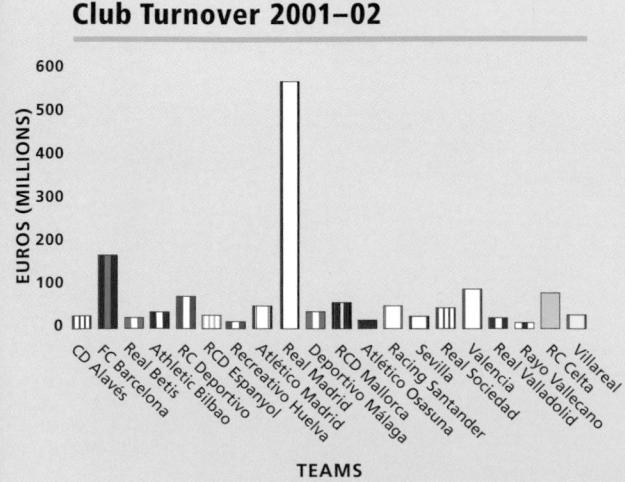

Club Turnover 2001–02

EUROS (MILLIONS)

600
500
400
300
200
100

TEAMS

CD Alavés, FC Barcelona, Real Betis, Athletic Bilbao, RC Deportivo, RCD Espanyol, Recreativo Huelva, Atlético Madrid, Real Madrid, Deportivo Málaga, RCD Mallorca, Atlético Osasuna, Racing Santander, Sevilla, Real Sociedad, Valencia, Real Valladolid, Rayo Vallecano, RC Celta, Villareal

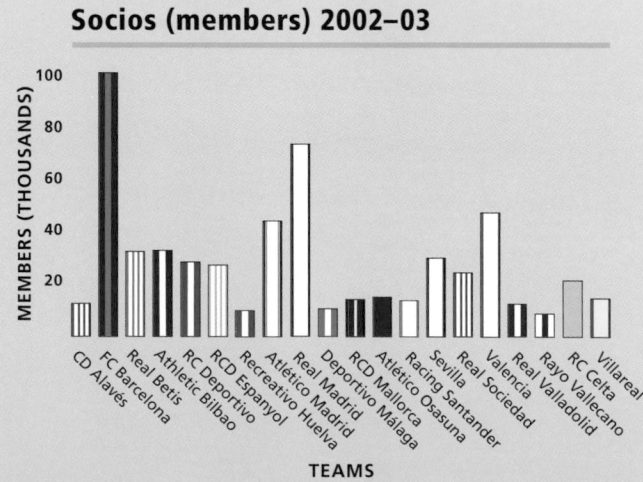

Socios (members) 2002–03

MEMBERS (THOUSANDS)

100
80
60
40
20

TEAMS

CD Alavés, FC Barcelona, Real Betis, Athletic Bilbao, RC Deportivo, RCD Espanyol, Recreativo Huelva, Atlético Madrid, Real Madrid, Deportivo Málaga, RCD Mallorca, Atlético Osasuna, Racing Santander, Sevilla, Real Sociedad, Valencia, Real Valladolid, Rayo Vallecano, RC Celta, Villareal

Spain

PLAYERS AND MANAGERS

WHILE FITNESS IS ASSUMED among Spanish footballers, a certain professional craftiness is required to be regarded as a real player, and the possession of *calidad* ('quality of technique') is a Spanish footballer's most prized asset. This style is exemplified by the magisterial Raúl at today's Real Madrid. Of course, you also need a good nickname to get on. The leading goalscorer in Spanish football is known as 'Pichichi', named in honour of Rafael Moreno Aranzadi, the great Basque centre-forward who played for Athletic Bilbao in the 1920s. In his wake, Spain's great strikers have included Emilio Butragueño, nicknamed 'the Vulture' for his capacity to pick up and devour chances in the box, and Francisco Gento, 'El Supersonico', the only man to win six European Cup winner's medals.

Nationalism v cosmopolitanism

The roster of great Spanish players and managers expresses both the country's inward-looking nationalism and its outward-looking cosmopolitanism. On the playing side (and recently on the managerial side as well), Spanish football has drawn widely and deeply on the pool of foreign talent. In the postwar era, Franco's Spain was pleased to accept Alfredo di Stefano from Argentina and Ferenc Puskas from Hungary, and award Spanish citizenship to both. In the 1960s, nationalist paranoia saw a decade-long ban on foreign players until a new wave of talent arrived in the shape of Johan Cruyff at Barcelona in the 1970s and then Diego Maradona in the early 1980s. However, at Athletic Bilbao the strict Basque-only policy on players remains in place. In recent years, the enormous amount of money in the Spanish game has seen a steady rise in the number of overseas players, especially from Latin America, with Brazilians, Argentinians and Uruguayans flooding the top division.

Born on the first day of the 20th century, legendary keeper Ricardo Zamora was known as 'El Divino'.

Top 14 International Caps

PLAYER	CAPS	GOALS	FIRST MATCH	LAST MATCH
Andoni Zubizarreta	129	0	1985	1998
Fernando Ruiz Hierro*	90	29	1989	2003
José Antonio Camacho	81	0	1975	1988
Rafael Gordillo	75	3	1978	1988
Emilio Butragueño	69	26	1984	1992
Luis Miguel Arconada	68	0	1977	1985
Miguel González 'Michel'	66	21	1985	1992
Raúl González Blanco*	64	32	1996	2003
Miguel Angel Nadal*	63	3	1991	2001
Luis Enrique*	62	12	1991	2002
Victor Muñoz	60	3	1981	1988
Julio Salinas Fernández	56	22	1986	1996
Carlos Alonso Santillana	56	15	1975	1985
Barjuan Sergi	56	1	1994	2003

Top 11 International Goalscorers

PLAYER	GOALS	CAPS	FIRST MATCH	LAST MATCH
Raúl González Blanco*	32	64	1996	2003
Fernando Ruiz Hierro*	29	90	1989	2003
Emilio Butragueño	26	69	1984	1992
Alfredo di Stefano	23	31	1957	1961
Julio Salinas Fernández	22	56	1986	1996
Miguel González 'Michel'	21	66	1985	1992
Telmo Zarraonandia 'Zarra'	20	20	1945	1951
Fernando Morientes*	20	31	1998	2003
Isidro Lángara	17	12	1932	1936
Luis Regueiro	16	25	1927	1936
José Martínez 'Pirri'	16	41	1966	1978

* Indicates players still playing at least at club level.
Nicknames are indicated between inverted commas.

Spanish International Managers

DATES	NAME	GAMES	WON	DRAWN	LOST
1955–56	Guillermo Eizaguirre	3	0	1	2
1957–59	Manuel Meana	12	7	3	2
1959–60	José Luis Costa, Ramón Gabilondo, José Luis Lasplazas	5	4	0	1
1961	Pedro Escartin	7	5	2	0
1962	Pablo Hernandez	3	1	0	2
1962–66	Jose Villalonga	22	9	5	8
1966–68	Domingo Balmanya	11	4	3	4
1968–69	Eduardo Toba	4	1	2	1
1969	Salvador Artigas, Luis Molowny, Miguel Munoz	4	2	1	1
1969–80	Ladislao Kubala	68	32	21	15
1980–82	José Santamaria	23	10	6	7
1982–88	Miguel Munoz	59	31	13	15
1988–91	Luis Suárez	27	15	4	8
1991–92	Vincente Miera	8	4	2	2
1992–98	Javier Clemente	62	36	19	7
1998–2002	José Antonio Camacho	44	28	9	7
2002–	Iñaki Saez	12	6	5	1

All figures correct as of 11 June 2003.

Foreign Players in Spain (in top division squads)

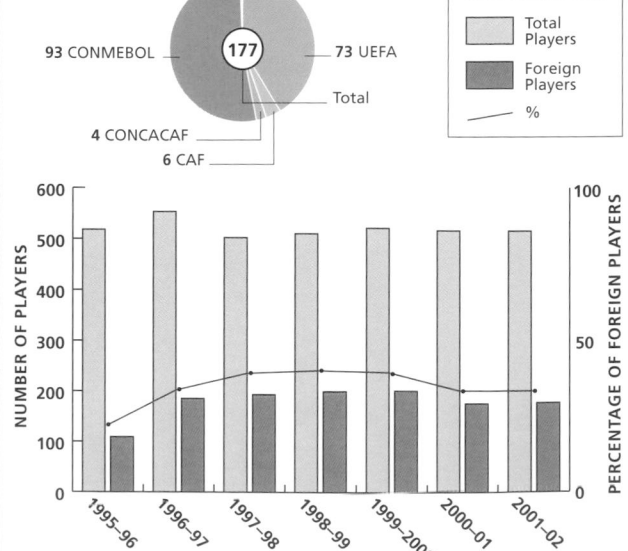

2002–03

1 OFC
93 CONMEBOL — 177 — 73 UEFA
Total
4 CONCACAF
6 CAF

Key
Total Players
Foreign Players
%

Player of the Year

YEAR	PLAYER	CLUB
1976	Ángel	Real Madrid
1977	'Juanito'	Real Burgos
1978	'Migueli'	Barcelona
1979	'Quini'	Sporting Gijón
1980	Gordillo	Real Madrid
1981	'Urruti'	RCD Español
1982	Tendillo	Valencia
1983	Señor	Real Zaragoza
1984	Cervantes	Real Murcia
1985	'Migueli'	Barcelona
1986	'Michel'	Real Madrid
1987	Zubizarreta	Barcelona
1988	Larrañaga	Real Sociedad
1989	Fernando	Valencia
1990	Martín Vázquez	Real Madrid
1991	Goikoetxea	Barcelona
1992	Elduayen	Real Burgos
1993	'Fran'	RC Deportivo
1994	Guerrero	Athletic Bilbao
1995	Amavisca	Real Madrid
1996	Caminero	Atlético Madrid
1997	Raúl	Real Madrid
1998	Alfonso	Real Betis
1999	Raúl	Real Madrid
2000	Raúl	Real Madrid
2001	Marino	Alavés
2002	Raúl	Real Madrid

Awarded by *Don Balon* magazine.

Foreign Player of the Year

PLAYER	CLUB	NATIONALITY
Neeskens	Barcelona	Dutch
Cruyff	Barcelona	Dutch
Cruyff	Barcelona	Dutch
Stielike	Real Madrid	German
Stielike	Real Madrid	German
Stielike	Real Madrid	German
Stielike	Real Madrid	German
Barbas	Real Zaragoza	Argentinian
Barbas	Real Zaragoza	Argentinian
Schuster	Barcelona	German
Valdano	Real Madrid	Argentinian
Hugo Sánchez	Real Madrid	Mexican
Alemão	Atlético Madrid	Brazilian
Ruggeri	CD Logroñés	Argentinian
Hugo Sánchez	Real Madrid	Mexican
Schuster	Atlético Madrid	German
Laudrup	Barcelona	Danish
Dujkic	RC Deportivo	Yugoslavian
Stoichkov	Barcelona	Bulgarian
Zamorano	Real Madrid	Chilean
Mijatovic	Valencia	Yugoslavian
Ronaldo	Barcelona	Brazilian
Rivaldo	Barcelona	Brazilian
Figo	Barcelona	Portuguese
Figo	Barcelona	Portuguese
R. Carlos	Real Madrid	Brazilian
Zidane	Real Madrid	French

Manager of the Year

MANAGER	CLUB	NATIONALITY
Miljanic	Real Madrid	Yugoslavian
Aragonés	Atlético Madrid	Spanish
Molowny	Real Madrid	Spanish
Molowny	Real Madrid	Spanish
Molowny	Real Madrid	Spanish
Ormachea	Real Sociedad	Spanish
Ormachea	Real Sociedad	Spanish
Clemente	Athletic Bilbao	Spanish
Clemente	Athletic Bilbao	Spanish
Venables	Barcelona	English
Molowny	Real Madrid	Spanish
Clemente	RCD Español	Spanish
Beenhakker	Real Madrid	Dutch
Toshack	Real Sociedad	Welsh
Toshack	Real Madrid	Welsh
Cruyff	Barcelona	Dutch
Cruyff	Barcelona	Dutch
Inglesias	RC Deportivo	Spanish
Fernandez	Real Zaragoza	Spanish
Inglesias	RC Deportivo	Spanish
Antic	Atlético Madrid	Yugoslavian
Cantatore	Real Valladolid	Uruguayan
'Irureta'	RC Celta	Spanish
Cúper	RCD Mallorca	Argentinian
'Irureta'	RC Deportivo	Spanish
Mane	Alavés	Spanish
Benitez	Valencia	Spanish

Top Goalscorers by Season 1975–2003

SEASON	PLAYER	CLUB	GOALS
1975–76	'Quini'	Real Sporting	18
1976–77	Kempes	Valencia	24
1977–78	Kempes	Valencia	28
1978–79	Krankl	Barcelona	26
1979–80	'Quini'	Real Sporting	24
1980–81	'Quini'	Barcelona	20
1981–82	'Quini'	Barcelona	26
1982–83	Rincón	Real Betis	20
1983–84	Da Silva	Real Valladolid	17
1983–84	'Juanito'	Real Madrid	17
1984–85	Sánchez	Atlético Madrid	19
1985–86	H. Sánchez	Real Madrid	22
1986–87	H. Sánchez	Real Madrid	34
1987–88	H. Sánchez	Real Madrid	29
1988–89	Baltazar	Atlético Madrid	35
1989–90	H. Sánchez	Real Madrid	38
1990–91	Butragueño	Real Madrid	19
1991–92	Manolo	Atlético Madrid	27
1992–93	Bebeto	RC Deportivo	29
1993–94	Romario	Barcelona	30
1994–95	Zamorano	Real Madrid	28
1995–96	Pizzi	Tenerife	31
1996–97	Ronaldo	Barcelona	34
1997–98	Vieri	Atlético Madrid	24
1998–99	Raúl	Real Madrid	25
1999–2000	Salva	Racing Santander	27
2000–01	Raúl	Real Madrid	24
2001–02	Tristan	RC Deportivo	21
2002–03	Makaay	Real Sociedad	28

Emilio Butragueño's 26 international goals included four in Spain's five-goal thrashing of Denmark in the second round of the 1986 World Cup Finals in Mexico.

Spain

PRIMERA LIGA 1982–2002

THE EARLY 1980s saw the Basque country rise to prominence in Spain, with titles for Real Sociedad and Athletic Bilbao. Both fielded Basque-only squads and in the relative freedom of the post-Franco years an intense Basque nationalism pervaded the mood of the crowds. At Bilbao, Javier Clemente built a tough, fiery team with Andoni Goikoetxea, the 'Butcher of Bilbao', leading a mean defensive line on Spain's wettest, slowest pitch. Although both teams have been permanent members of La Liga since then, neither has been able to sustain more than a season's serious challenge for the title. Most recently, Athletic, under Luis Fernandez, came second to Barcelona in 1998. Real Sociedad has abandoned its Basque-only policy and Athletic has been through a slew of foreign coaches including Howard Kendall, Guus Hiddink and Jupp Heynckes.

The 'Vulture Squad' v the 'Dream Team'

The Basque stranglehold on the title was broken by Barcelona in 1985 under English coach Terry Venables, only for the centre to reassert itself in the shape of Real Madrid and *La Quinta Del Buitre* – the 'Vulture Squad'. Despite an enormous turnover of managers and increasingly hysterical financial and administrative practices, Real had an inspired and disciplined spine in Emilio Butragueño (the 'Vulture'), Michel, Sanchis and Martín Vásquez. That was enough to take five straight titles in the 1980s.

At Barcelona, president José Luis Núñez lured ex-player and local hero Johan Cruyff back to the Bernabeu stadium as manager in 1988. Cruyff created a team made up of both homegrown players, like the young Pep Guardiola, and foreign internationals like Ronald Koeman, Hirsto Stoichkov and Michael Laudrup. The 'Dream Team', as it became known, took four titles in a row, though, rather ironically, two of them required lowly Tenerife to beat Real Madrid on the final day of the season to ensure the title went to Barça. The 1994 title came courtesy of Miroslav Djukic's last-minute penalty miss for the chasing RC Deportivo from La Coruña.

Despite the chaos and rising debts of Ramón Mendoza's Real Madrid, 1995 saw the club back at the top under Argentinian Jorge Valdano. Valdano was, of course, promptly fired, and in 1996 Atlético Madrid took its first title for over 20 years under its eccentric and improbable president Jesús Gil. Mayor of Marbella and inveterate dealer and fixer, Gil would eventually be convicted on a range of corruption charges in the late 1990s, and Atlético would plummet into the lower divisions, where it

After 31 years of waiting, Valencia won La Liga in 2001–02 with a final day victory over Málaga at home in the Mestalla. Major celebrations followed.

remained for several years. Over at Real, Mendoza was toppled by new president Lorenzo Sans. Sans brought in coach Fabio Capello, fresh from his success with Milan, and authorized a massive spend on the squad, bringing in Clarence Seedorf, Roberto Carlos and Davor Suker. It was enough to take the title in 1997 and the team went on to win the European Champions League the following season. However, a ridiculous turnover of managers once again saw the club unable to provide the consistency required to win the league title.

The arrival of the Dutchmen

That consistency was delivered by the new-look Barcelona who, having dispensed with both Bobby Robson and Ronaldo, brought in the architect of the new Ajax, Louis van Gaal. The core of the Dutch national squad, including the De Boers, Kluivert, Overmars, Cocu, Zenden and Reiziger, were purchased to play alongside Rivaldo and Luis Figo. Barcelona stormed the table in 1998 and 99. A triple was blocked by Deportivo La Coruña who finally made good on its promise throughout the 1990s and won in 2000. Real was back the following year, now augmented by Luis Figo, who'd been 'stolen' from Barcelona at the beginning of the season.

Competition in Spanish football has been fierce, with good sustainable sides built at RCD Mallorca under Hector Cuper in the mid-1990s, and Valencia (also led by Cuper) who contested two consecutive Champions League finals. The tiny Basque team CD Alavés, Galician RC Celta from Vigo and Real Zaragoza have also all proved tough regular competitors. The big southern clubs, Real Betis and Sevilla FC, have proved less successful, and both have tasted lower division football. However, despite the healthy competition, clubs in the lower reaches of the league are beset by debt, and demands from the Spanish treasury in 2002 for unpaid taxes threatened to bankrupt half the teams in La Liga.

Despite a few seasons in the second division Seville's two clubs, Real Betis (in stripes) and Sevilla, play out one of the most fearsome derbies in the Spanish league.

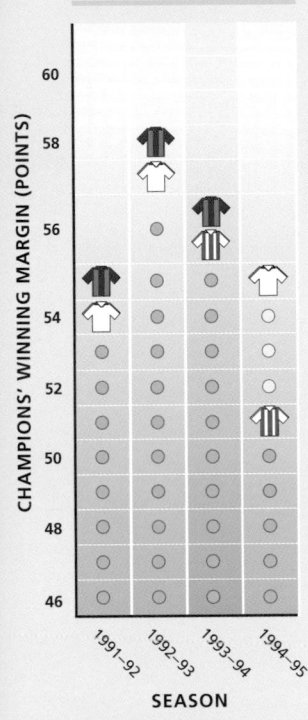

No one is bigger than Real Madrid. President Lorenzo Sanz saw his side win the Champions League in 2000 only to lose a snap election for the presidency to Florentine Pérez.

Above: Johan Cruyff returned to Barcelona as coach, winning four consecutive league titles between 1991 and 94.

Right: José Núñez was elected president of Barcelona in 1978 after a bruising campaign. He ruled the club as something close to a fiefdom before his shock defeat to Joan Gaspart in the 2001 presidential elections.

Champions' Winning Margin 1991–95

CHAMPIONS' WINNING MARGIN (POINTS)

SEASON

1991–92	1992–93	1993–94	1994–95
38	38	38	38

Total games played by each team (2 points awarded for a win)

Champions' Winning Margin 1995–2002

SEASON

1995–96	1996–97	1997–98	1998–99	1999–2000	2000–01	2001–02
42	42	38	38	38	38	38

Total games played by each team (3 points awarded for a win)

 Barcelona   Athletic Bilbao

 RC Deportivo   Atlético Madrid

 Real Madrid   Valencia

SPAIN

Key to League Positions Table

- ▨ League champions
- ▫ Season of promotion to league
- ▫ Season of relegation from league
- ▫ Other teams playing in league
- | 5 | Final position in league

SPAIN

Real Betis broke the world transfer record to buy Brazilian Denilson of São Paulo. Relegation followed, but the team has clawed its way back into La Liga's top flight.

The flying Ruben Baraja's goals from midfield were a major factor in Valencia's hugely successful 2001–02 season.

Spanish League Positions 1982–2002

SEASON

TEAM	82–83	83–84	84–85	85–86	86–87	87–88	88–89	89–90	90–91	91–92	92–93	93–94	94–95	95–96	96–97	97–98	98–99	99–2000	2000–01	2001–02
CD Alavés																	16	6	10	7
Albacete Balompié										7	17	13	17	20						
Barcelona	4	3	1	2	2	6	2	3	1	1	1	1	4	3	2	1	1	2	4	4
Real Betis	11	5	14	8	9	16	18		20			3	8	4	8	11	18			6
Athletic Bilbao	1	1	3	3	13	4	7	12	12	14	8	5	8	15	6	2	8	11	12	9
Real Burgos									11	9	20									
Cádiz		16		15	18	12	15		15	18	18	19								
Deportivo Castellón								14	19											
RC Celta	17		18			7	8	19			11	15	13	11	16	6	5	7	6	5
SD Compostela													16	10	11	17				
RC Deportivo										17	3	2	2	9	3	12	6	1	2	2
Elche CF		17			20															
RCD Espanyol	9	10	8	11	3	15	17		16	16	18		6	4	12	10	7	14	9	14
CF Extremadura															19		17			
Sporting Gijón	8	13	4	6	4	9	13	5		8	12	14	18	15	20					
Hércules			15	17												21				
RC Recreativo de Huelva																				
Unión Deportivo Las Palmas	16			13	14	20													11	18
Lérida Unión Esportiva												19								
Deportivo Logroñes							13	14	7	10	10	15	16	20		22				
Atlético Madrid	3	4	2	5	7	3	4	2	3	6	12	14	1	5	7	13	19			
Real Madrid	2	2	5	1	1	1	1	1	3	2	2	4	1	6	1	4	2	5	1	3
Deportivo Málaga	10	9	16		16	17												12	8	10
RCD Mallorca		17			6	18		10	15	20						5	3	10	3	16
CP Mérida																21		19		
Real Murcia		11	18			11	17	19												
CD Numancia																		17	20	
Atlético Osasuna	14	15	6	14	16	5	10	8	4	15	10	20							15	17
Real Oviedo								12	11	6	11	16	9	9	14	17	18	14	16	18
CD Sabadell				15	19															
Deportivo Salamanca	13	18														22		15	20	
Racing Santander	18		11	12	17								8	12	17	13	14	15	15	19
Sevilla FC	5	8	12	9	12	10	9	6	8	12	7	6	5	12	20			20		8
Real Sociedad	7	6	7	7	8	2	11	5	13	5	13	11	11	7	8	3	10	13	13	13
Deportivo Tenerife								18	14	13	5	10	15	5	9	16	19			19
Valencia	15	12	9	16		14	3	2	7	4	4	7	10	2	10	9	4	3	5	1
Real Valladolid	12	14	13	10	10	8	6	16	9	19		18	19	16	7	11	12	8	16	12
Rayo Vallecano									20			14	17			19	18	9	14	11
Villarreal																	18		7	15
Real Zaragoza	6	7	10	4	5	11	5	9	17	6	9	3	7	13	14	13	9	4	17	20

Primera Liga

Real Madrid — Team name

League champions/runners-up

1990, *92* — Champions in bold / Runners-up in italics

Other teams in the Primera Liga

● **Madrid** — City of origin

When RC Deportivo from La Coruña was promoted in 1991, club president Augusto César Lendorio announced 'Barcelona, Madrid, we are here'. With the 1999–2000 squad the team finally arrived, running away with the title under coach Javier Irureta.

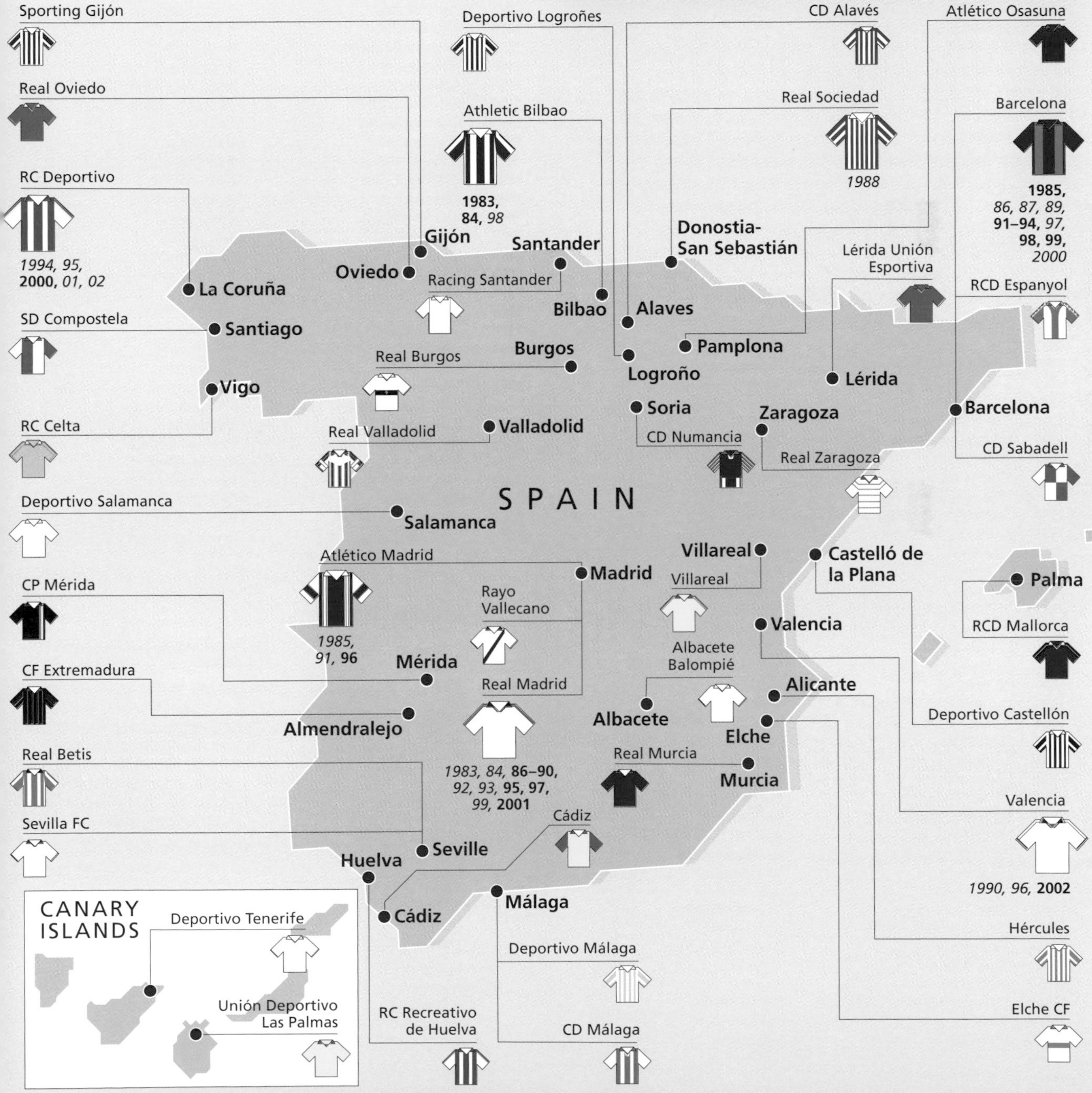

SPAIN

Sporting Gijón

Real Oviedo

RC Deportivo
1994, 95, **2000, 01, 02**

SD Compostela

RC Celta

Deportivo Salamanca

CP Mérida

CF Extremadura

Real Betis

Sevilla FC

Deportivo Logroñes

Athletic Bilbao
1983, 84, *98*

Racing Santander

Real Burgos

Real Valladolid

Atlético Madrid
1985, 91, **96**

Rayo Vallecano

Real Madrid
1983, 84, **86–90, 92, 93, 95, 97, 99, 2001**

CD Alavés

Real Sociedad
1988

Atlético Osasuna

Barcelona
1985, *86, 87, 89,* **91–94, 97, 98, 99,** *2000*

RCD Espanyol

Lérida Unión Esportiva

CD Numancia

Real Zaragoza

CD Sabadell

Villareal

Albacete Balompié

Real Murcia

Cádiz

Deportivo Málaga

CD Málaga

RC Recreativo de Huelva

Castelló de la Plana

RCD Mallorca

Deportivo Castellón

Valencia
1990, 96, **2002**

Hércules

Elche CF

SPAIN map labels

● Gijón
● Oviedo
● La Coruña
● Santiago
● Vigo
● Santander
● Bilbao
● Burgos
● Logroño
● Soria
● Valladolid
● Salamanca
● Madrid
● Mérida
● Almendralejo
● Seville
● Huelva
● Cádiz
● Málaga
● Donostia-San Sebastián
● Alaves
● Pamplona
● Zaragoza
● Lérida
● Barcelona
● Villareal
● Castelló de la Plana
● Valencia
● Albacete
● Alicante
● Elche
● Murcia
● Palma

S P A I N

CANARY ISLANDS

Deportivo Tenerife

Unión Deportivo Las Palmas

Spain

Real Federación Española de Fútbol
Founded: 1913
Joined FIFA: 1904
Joined UEFA: 1954

FROM ITS EARLIEST DAYS, SPANISH FOOTBALL had a strong regional character. A Catalonian league was up and running by 1901, and the first years of the 20th century saw the establishment of regional leagues all over the country. The first national league began in 1929 comprising ten clubs. It grew steadily to a peak of 22 clubs in the 1990s, but has now decreased in size to just 20.

The first national competition, the Copa del Rey, was created in 1902. Not surprisingly given its title, it was supported by the centralizing monarchy in the person of King Alfonso XIII. The name, if not the format, of the cup has shifted with Spain's constitution. In 1934 it became the short-lived Copa del Republica, but was halted by the civil war, and reinvented under Franco's regime as the Copa del Generalisimo. With the return of the monarchy after Franco's death, the name of the competition reverted to its original title, the Copa del Rey.

Spanish League Record 1929–2003

SEASON	CHAMPIONS	RUNNERS-UP
1929	Barcelona	Real Madrid
1930	Athletic Bilbao	Barcelona
1931	Athletic Bilbao	Racing Santander
1932	Real Madrid	Athletic Bilbao
1933	Real Madrid	Athletic Bilbao
1934	Athletic Bilbao	Real Madrid
1935	Real Betis	Real Madrid
1936	Athletic Bilbao	Real Madrid
1937–39	*no championship*	
1940	Atlético Aviación	Sevilla
1941	Atlético Aviación	Athletic Bilbao
1942	Valencia	Real Madrid
1943	Athletic Bilbao	Sevilla
1944	Valencia	Atlético Aviación
1945	Barcelona	Real Madrid
1946	Sevilla	Barcelona
1947	Valencia	Athletic Bilbao
1948	Barcelona	Valencia
1949	Barcelona	Valencia
1950	Atlético Madrid	RC Deportivo
1951	Atlético Madrid	Sevilla
1952	Barcelona	Athletic Bilbao
1953	Barcelona	Valencia
1954	Real Madrid	Barcelona
1955	Real Madrid	Barcelona
1956	Athletic Bilbao	Barcelona
1957	Real Madrid	Sevilla
1958	Real Madrid	Atlético Madrid
1959	Barcelona	Real Madrid
1960	Barcelona	Real Madrid
1961	Real Madrid	Atlético Madrid
1962	Real Madrid	Barcelona
1963	Real Madrid	Atlético Madrid
1964	Real Madrid	Barcelona
1965	Real Madrid	Atlético Madrid
1966	Atlético Madrid	Real Madrid
1967	Real Madrid	Barcelona
1968	Real Madrid	Barcelona
1969	Real Madrid	Las Palmas
1970	Atlético Madrid	Athletic Bilbao
1971	Valencia	Barcelona

Spanish League Record (*continued*)

SEASON	CHAMPIONS	RUNNERS-UP
1972	Real Madrid	Valencia
1973	Atlético Madrid	Barcelona
1974	Barcelona	Atlético Madrid
1975	Real Madrid	Real Zaragoza
1976	Real Madrid	Barcelona
1977	Atlético Madrid	Barcelona
1978	Real Madrid	Barcelona
1979	Real Madrid	Sporting Gijón
1980	Real Madrid	Real Sociedad
1981	Real Sociedad	Real Madrid
1982	Real Sociedad	Barcelona
1983	Athletic Bilbao	Real Madrid
1984	Athletic Bilbao	Real Madrid
1985	Barcelona	Atlético Madrid
1986	Real Madrid	Barcelona
1987	Real Madrid	Barcelona
1988	Real Madrid	Real Sociedad
1989	Real Madrid	Barcelona
1990	Real Madrid	Valencia
1991	Barcelona	Atlético Madrid
1992	Barcelona	Real Madrid
1993	Barcelona	Real Madrid
1994	Barcelona	RC Deportivo
1995	Real Madrid	RC Deportivo
1996	Atlético Madrid	Valencia
1997	Real Madrid	Barcelona
1998	Barcelona	Athletic Bilbao
1999	Barcelona	Real Madrid
2000	RC Deportivo	Barcelona
2001	Real Madrid	RC Deportivo
2002	Valencia	RC Deportivo
2003	Real Madrid	Real Sociedad

Spanish League Summary

TEAM	TOTALS	CHAMPIONS & RUNNERS-UP (BOLD) (*ITALICS*)
Real Madrid	29, 15	*1929*, **32**, **33**, *34–36*, *42*, *45*, **54**, **55**, **57**, **58**, **59**, **60**, **61–65**, *66*, **67–69**, **72**, **75**, **76**, **78–80**, *81*, **83**, *84*, **86–90**, *92*, *93*, **95**, **97**, *99*, **2001**, **03**
Barcelona	16, 20	**1929**, *30*, **45**, *46*, **48**, **49**, **52**, **53**, **54–56**, *59*, **60**, *62*, **64**, *67*, *68*, *71*, *73*, **74**, *76–78*, *82*, **85**, *86*, *87*, *89*, **91–94**, *97*, **98**, **99**, *2000*
Atlético Madrid (including Atlético Aviación)	9, 8	**1940**, **41**, **44**, **50**, **51**, *58*, **61**, **63**, *65*, *66*, **70**, **73**, *74*, **77**, *85*, *91*, *96*
Athletic Bilbao	8, 7	**1930**, **31**, *32*, *33*, **34**, **36**, **41**, *43*, *47*, *52*, *56*, *70*, **83**, **84**, *98*
Valencia	5, 6	**1942**, **44**, **47**, *48*, *49*, *53*, **71**, *72*, *90*, **96**, **2002**
Real Sociedad	2, 3	*1980*, **81**, **82**, *88*, *2003*
RC Deportivo	1, 5	*1950*, *94*, *95*, **2000**, *01*, *02*
Sevilla	1, 4	*1940*, *43*, **46**, *51*, *57*
Real Betis	1, 0	**1935**

This summary only features clubs that have won the Spanish League. For a full list of league champions and runners-up please see the League Record above.

Spanish Cup Record 1902–2003

YEAR	WINNERS	SCORE	RUNNERS-UP
1902	Vizcaya Bilbao	2-1	Barcelona
1903	Athletic Bilbao	3-2	Real Madrid
1904	Athletic Bilbao	w/o	
1905	Real Madrid	1-0	Athletic Bilbao
1906	Real Madrid	4-1	Athletic Bilbao
1907	Real Madrid	1-0	Vizcaya Bilbao
1908	Real Madrid	2-1	Vigo Sporting
1909	Ciclista San Sebastián	3-1	Español Madrid
1910	Athletic Bilbao	1-0*	Basconia
1910	Barcelona	3-2**	Español Madrid
1911	Athletic Bilbao	3-1	RCD Español
1912	Barcelona	2-0	Gimnastica Madrid
1913	Barcelona	2-2, (replay) 0-0, (replay) 2-1*	Real Sociedad
1913	Racing Irún	2-2, (replay) 1-0**	Athletic Bilbao
1914	Athletic Bilbao	2-1	España Barcelona
1915	Athletic Bilbao	5-0	RCD Español
1916	Athletic Bilbao	4-0	Real Madrid
1917	Real Madrid	0-0, (replay) 2-1	Arenas Guecho Bilbao
1918	Real Unión Irún	2-0	Real Madrid
1919	Arenas Guecho Bilbao	5-2 (aet)	Barcelona
1920	Barcelona	2-0	Athletic Bilbao
1921	Athletic Bilbao	4-1	Atlético Madrid
1922	Barcelona	5-1	Real Unión Irún
1923	Athletic Bilbao	1-0	Europa Barcelona
1924	Real Unión Irún	1-0	Real Madrid
1925	Barcelona	2-0	Arenas Guecho Bilbao
1926	Barcelona	3-2 (aet)	Atlético Madrid
1927	Real Unión Irún	1-0 (aet)	Arenas Guecho Bilbao
1928	Barcelona	1-1, (replay) 1-1, (replay) 3-1	Real Sociedad
1929	RCD Español	2-1	Real Madrid
1930	Athletic Bilbao	3-2 (aet)	Real Madrid
1931	Athletic Bilbao	3-1	Real Betis
1932	Athletic Bilbao	1-0	Barcelona
1933	Athletic Bilbao	2-1	Real Madrid
1934	Real Madrid	2-1	Valencia
1935	Sevilla	3-0	Sabadell
1936	Real Madrid	2-1	Barcelona
1937–38		no competition	
1939	Sevilla	6-2	Racing Ferrol
1940	RCD Español	3-2 (aet)	Real Madrid
1941	Valencia	3-1	RCD Español
1942	Barcelona	4-3 (aet)	Athletic Bilbao
1943	Athletic Bilbao	1-0 (aet)	Real Madrid
1944	Athletic Bilbao	2-0	Valencia
1945	Athletic Bilbao	3-2	Valencia
1946	Real Madrid	3-1	Valencia
1947	Real Madrid	2-0 (aet)	RCD Español
1948	Sevilla	4-1	RC Celta
1949	Valencia	1-0	Athletic Bilbao
1950	Athletic Bilbao	4-1 (aet)	Valladolid
1951	Barcelona	3-0	Real Sociedad
1952	Barcelona	4-2 (aet)	Valencia
1953	Barcelona	2-1	Athletic Bilbao
1954	Valencia	3-0	Barcelona
1955	Athletic Bilbao	1-0	Sevilla
1956	Athletic Bilbao	2-1	Atlético Madrid
1957	Barcelona	1-0	RCD Español
1958	Athletic Bilbao	2-0	Real Madrid
1959	Barcelona	4-1	Granada
1960	Atlético Madrid	3-1	Real Madrid
1961	Atlético Madrid	3-2	Real Madrid
1962	Real Madrid	2-1	Sevilla
1963	Barcelona	3-1	Real Zaragoza
1964	Real Zaragoza	2-1	Atlético Madrid
1965	Atlético Madrid	1-0	Real Zaragoza
1966	Real Zaragoza	2-0	Athletic Bilbao
1967	Valencia	2-1	Athletic Bilbao

Spanish Cup Record (*continued*)

YEAR	WINNERS	SCORE	RUNNERS-UP
1968	Barcelona	1-0	Real Madrid
1969	Athletic Bilbao	1-0	Elche
1970	Real Madrid	3-1	Valencia
1971	Barcelona	4-3	Valencia
1972	Atlético Madrid	2-1	Valencia
1973	Athletic Bilbao	2-0	Castellón
1974	Real Madrid	4-0	Barcelona
1975	Real Madrid	0-0 (aet)(4-3 pens)	Atlético Madrid
1976	Atlético Madrid	1-0	Real Zaragoza
1977	Real Betis	2-2 (aet)(8-7 pens)	Athletic Bilbao
1978	Barcelona	3-1	Las Palmas
1979	Valencia	2-0	Real Madrid
1980	Real Madrid	6-1	Castilla
1981	Barcelona	3-1	Sporting Gijón
1982	Real Madrid	2-1	Sporting Gijón
1983	Barcelona	2-1	Real Madrid
1984	Athletic Bilbao	1-0	Barcelona
1985	Atlético Madrid	2-1	Athletic Bilbao
1986	Real Zaragoza	1-0	Barcelona
1987	Real Sociedad	2-2 (aet)(4-2 pens)	Atlético Madrid
1988	Barcelona	1-0	Real Sociedad
1989	Real Madrid	1-0	Valladolid
1990	Barcelona	2-0	Real Madrid
1991	Atlético Madrid	1-0 (aet)	Mallorca
1992	Atlético Madrid	2-0	Real Madrid
1993	Real Madrid	2-0	Real Zaragoza
1994	Real Zaragoza	0-0 (aet)(5-4 pens)	RC Celta
1995	RC Deportivo	2-1†	Valencia
1996	Atlético Madrid	1-0 (aet)	Barcelona
1997	Barcelona	3-2 (aet)	Real Betis
1998	Barcelona	1-1 (aet)(5-4 pens)	Mallorca
1999	Valencia	3-0	Atlético Madrid
2000	RCD Espanyol	2-1	Atlético Madrid
2001	Real Zaragoza	3-1	RC Celta
2002	RC Deportivo	2-1	Real Madrid
2003	RCD Mallorca	3-0	Recreativo Huelva

w/o denotes walk over
* Copa de la Federación Española de Fútbol.
** Copa de la Unión Española de Clubs de Fútbol.
† Match was abandoned in the 80th minute due to torrential rain (at 1-1) and finished a few days later.

Spanish Cup Summary

TEAM	TOTALS	WINNERS & RUNNERS-UP	
		(BOLD)	(ITALICS)
Barcelona	24, 9	*1902,* **10, 12, 13,** *19,* **20, 22, 25, 26, 28, 32, 36, 42, 51–53,** *54,* **57,** *59,* **63, 68, 71, 74, 78, 81, 83,** *84,* **86,** *88,* **90, 96, 97, 98**	
Athletic Bilbao	23, 11	**1903, 04,** *05, 06,* **10, 11,** *13,* **14–16,** *20,* **21, 23, 30–33,** *42,* **43–45, 49, 50,** *53, 55, 56, 58,* **66, 67, 69, 73,** *77, 84, 85*	
Real Madrid	17, 18	*1903,* **05–08,** *16,* **17,** *18, 24, 29, 30, 33, 34, 36, 40, 43,* **46, 47,** *58, 60, 61,* **62, 68, 70, 74, 75,** *79,* **80, 82,** *83,* **89,** *90,* **92, 93,** *2002*	
Atlético Madrid	9, 8	*1921, 26, 56,* **60, 61,** *64,* **65, 72,** *75, 76,* **85,** *87,* **91, 92, 96,** *99, 2000*	
Valencia	6, 9	*1934,* **41,** *44–46,* **49,** *52,* **54,** *67, 70–72,* **79,** *95,* **99**	
Real Zaragoza	5, 4	*1963,* **64,** *65,* **66,** *76,* **86,** *93,* **94, 2001**	
Real Unión Irún (includes Racing Irún)	4, 1	**1913, 18, 22, 24, 27**	
RCD Espanyol (includes RCD Español, España Barcelona)	3, 6	*1911, 14, 15,* **29,** *40, 41, 47, 57,* **2000**	
Sevilla	3, 2	**1935, 39, 48,** *55, 62*	

This summary only features clubs that have won the Spanish Cup three or more times. For a full list of cup winners and runners-up please see the Cup Record above.

SPAIN

253

Italy

THE SEASON IN REVIEW 2002–03

WHEN, ONCE AGAIN, THE CONCLUDING stages of the 2002 Champions League were conducted without Italian interest, the fragile national sports psyche began another ritual fragmentation. As the once great Fiorentina was legally dissolved and the precarious economic state of many other clubs was revealed, a 'crisis of calico' was announced. The national team ignominiously departed the World Cup unacceptably early. After only scraping through its opening rounds, Italy was punished for its caution and defeated by South Korea. Worse still, it went out to a golden goal from Ahn Jung-hwan, who began the tournament on the books of Serie A club Perugia. Ahn was sacked by Perugia's president, FIFA was petitioned, conspiracies evoked and Byron Moreno – the Ecuadorian referee responsible for disallowing two Italian goals in the South Korea game – was the subject of particular invective. But Italy's bark is worse than its bite. Ahn was reinstated and sold and Moreno got a very tidy payday for comic turns on Italian TV chat shows.

Financial realities

Beyond the histrionics, the harsh economic reality of Italian football took centre stage in the pre-season. A protracted struggle over the value of TV rights was conducted between the smaller clubs in Serie A and the shrinking Italian cable and satellite TV industry. The stakes were sufficiently high for the start of the season to be delayed; an impasse only rescued by the bigger clubs donating some of their already secured TV money to the smaller ones; an act of generosity mobilized by the stark realization in the game's economic elite that the massive inequalities between the clubs were not sustainable if a meaningful domestic competition was to be conducted. A glance at the transfer market shows how sharp those divisions have become. Where only four or five seasons ago Parma, Roma, Lazio and Fiorentina would have been active in the market as buyers, they are now on balance all sellers. Only Juve, Inter and Milan could contemplate a significant strengthening of their squads. All three have cherry-picked from the second tier's best players: Di Viao and Cannavaro moving from Parma to Juventus and Inter, while Ronaldo's departure to Real Madrid funded the moves of Crespo and Nesta from Lazio to Inter.

When the season finally started it did so in Tripoli. The Italian Super Cup pitted champions Juventus against cup-winners Parma, Juve winning 2-1. But why in Tripoli? Joining the Juve celebrations was Juventus board member Al-Saadi Gaddafi. In addition to his directorships Gaddafi also runs the Tripoli club Al-Ittihad and the Libyan FA, and is running for the presidency of the CAF.

The Milan clubs pull ahead

The Super Cup aside, Juve started slowly; Lazio, Chievo and Bologna were pretty much permanent fixtures in the top six, but as the halfway mark approached Milan and Inter had pulled just ahead of the pack. After imploding at Lazio on the last day of last season, Inter was looking organized and winning games. Cuper's team looked sharp and resilient. The defence, built on Cordoba and Zanetti, was mean but skilled, and the team stole games on moments of brilliance from Vieri, Recoba or Crespo. Milan, by contrast, opened in free-flowing mood, the midfield of Pirlo, Gattuso, Rui Costa and Seedorf showing plenty of invention. Juve,

Serie A League Table 2002–03

CLUB	P	W	D	L	F	A	Pts	
Juventus	34	21	9	4	64	29	72	Champions League
Internazionale	34	19	8	7	64	38	65	Champions League
Milan	34	18	7	9	55	30	61	Champions League
Lazio	34	15	15	4	57	32	60	Champions League
Parma	34	15	11	8	55	36	56	UEFA Cup
Udinese	34	16	8	10	38	35	56	UEFA Cup
Chievo	34	16	7	11	51	39	55	
Roma	34	13	10	11	55	46	49	UEFA Cup (cup finalists)
Brescia	34	9	15	10	36	38	42	
Perugia	34	10	12	12	40	48	42	
Bologna	34	10	11	13	39	47	41	
Modena	34	9	11	14	30	48	38	
Empoli	34	9	11	14	36	46	38	
Atalanta	34	8	14	12	35	47	38	Relegated (play-off)
Reggina	34	10	8	16	38	53	38	
Piacenza	34	8	6	20	44	62	30	Relegated
Como	34	4	12	18	29	57	24	Relegated
Torino	34	4	9	21	23	58	21	Relegated

Promoted clubs: Sampdoria, Sienna, Genoa, Lecce.

Above: Back scratching all round. Al-Saadi Gaddafi and Italian league boss Adriano Galliani celebrate with Juventus in Tripoli after their victory in the Super Cup.

Below, left: Questions, questions. Inter president Massimo Moratti wonders why Inter just can't win the Scudetto.

Below, right: The second year is harder. Luigi Del Neri exhorts Chievo. But seventh is a step backwards after finishing in the European places last year.

ITALY

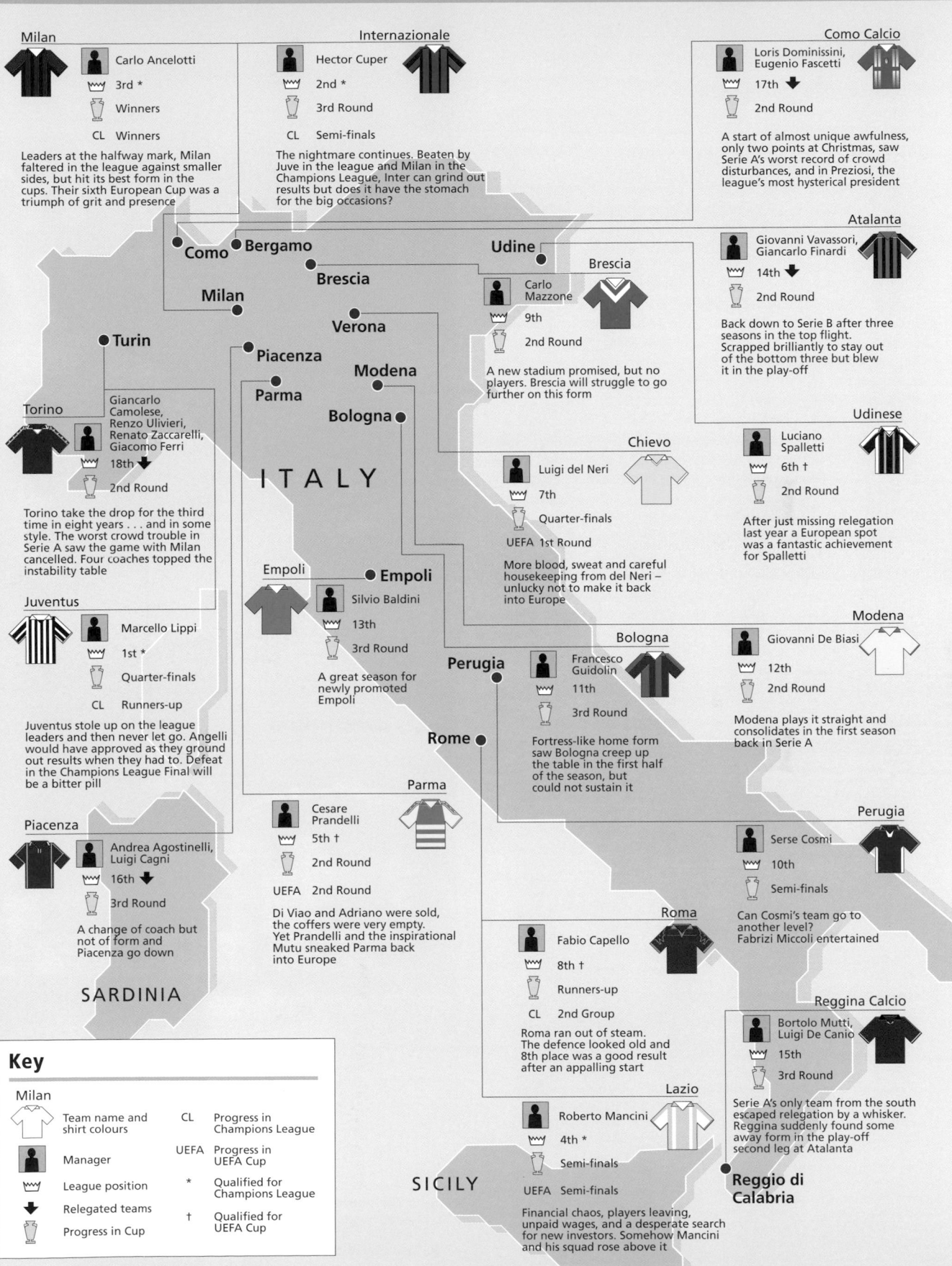

Milan
- Carlo Ancelotti
- 👑 3rd *
- 🏆 Winners
- CL Winners

Leaders at the halfway mark, Milan faltered in the league against smaller sides, but hit its best form in the cups. Their sixth European Cup was a triumph of grit and presence

Internazionale
- Hector Cuper
- 👑 2nd *
- 🏆 3rd Round
- CL Semi-finals

The nightmare continues. Beaten by Juve in the league and Milan in the Champions League, Inter can grind out results but does it have the stomach for the big occasions?

Como Calcio
- Loris Dominissini, Eugenio Fascetti
- 👑 17th ⬇
- 🏆 2nd Round

A start of almost unique awfulness, only two points at Christmas, saw Serie A's worst record of crowd disturbances, and in Preziosi, the league's most hysterical president

Atalanta
- Giovanni Vavassori, Giancarlo Finardi
- 👑 14th ⬇
- 🏆 2nd Round

Back down to Serie B after three seasons in the top flight. Scrapped brilliantly to stay out of the bottom three but blew it in the play-off

Brescia
- Carlo Mazzone
- 👑 9th
- 🏆 2nd Round

A new stadium promised, but no players. Brescia will struggle to go further on this form

Udinese
- Luciano Spalletti
- 👑 6th †
- 🏆 2nd Round

After just missing relegation last year a European spot was a fantastic achievement for Spalletti

Torino
- Giancarlo Camolese, Renzo Ulivieri, Renato Zaccarelli, Giacomo Ferri
- 👑 18th ⬇
- 🏆 2nd Round

Torino take the drop for the third time in eight years . . . and in some style. The worst crowd trouble in Serie A saw the game with Milan cancelled. Four coaches topped the instability table

Chievo
- Luigi del Neri
- 👑 7th
- 🏆 Quarter-finals
- UEFA 1st Round

More blood, sweat and careful housekeeping from del Neri – unlucky not to make it back into Europe

Juventus
- Marcello Lippi
- 👑 1st *
- 🏆 Quarter-finals
- CL Runners-up

Juventus stole up on the league leaders and then never let go. Angelli would have approved as they ground out results when they had to. Defeat in the Champions League Final will be a bitter pill

Empoli
- Silvio Baldini
- 👑 13th
- 🏆 3rd Round

A great season for newly promoted Empoli

Bologna
- Francesco Guidolin
- 👑 11th
- 🏆 3rd Round

Fortress-like home form saw Bologna creep up the table in the first half of the season, but could not sustain it

Modena
- Giovanni De Biasi
- 👑 12th
- 🏆 2nd Round

Modena plays it straight and consolidates in the first season back in Serie A

Piacenza
- Andrea Agostinelli, Luigi Cagni
- 👑 16th ⬇
- 🏆 3rd Round

A change of coach but not of form and Piacenza go down

Parma
- Cesare Prandelli
- 👑 5th †
- 🏆 2nd Round
- UEFA 2nd Round

Di Vaio and Adriano were sold, the coffers were very empty. Yet Prandelli and the inspirational Mutu sneaked Parma back into Europe

Perugia
- Serse Cosmi
- 👑 10th
- 🏆 Semi-finals

Can Cosmi's team go to another level? Fabrizi Miccoli entertained

Roma
- Fabio Capello
- 👑 8th †
- 🏆 Runners-up
- CL 2nd Group

Roma ran out of steam. The defence looked old and 8th place was a good result after an appalling start

Reggina Calcio
- Bortolo Mutti, Luigi De Canio
- 👑 15th
- 🏆 3rd Round

Serie A's only team from the south escaped relegation by a whisker. Reggina suddenly found some away form in the play-off second leg at Atalanta

Lazio
- Roberto Mancini
- 👑 4th *
- 🏆 Semi-finals
- UEFA Semi-finals

Financial chaos, players leaving, unpaid wages, and a desperate search for new investors. Somehow Mancini and his squad rose above it

Map labels: Como, Bergamo, Udine, Brescia, Milan, Verona, Piacenza, Modena, Parma, Bologna, Turin, ITALY, Empoli, Perugia, Rome, Parma, SARDINIA, SICILY, Reggio di Calabria

Key

Milan
- Team name and shirt colours
- Manager
- 👑 League position
- ⬇ Relegated teams
- 🏆 Progress in Cup
- CL Progress in Champions League
- UEFA Progress in UEFA Cup
- * Qualified for Champions League
- † Qualified for UEFA Cup

underperforming but never quite out of the race, steadily forged a fantastically compact and tenacious defence and midfield.

Violence goes unchecked

In the early weeks of the season Roma, last year's runners-up, seemed to have forgotten how to play, a state typified when it lost at home to lowly Modena in mid-September. The following week Roma Ultras gathered at the club's training ground and attacked defender Jonathan Zebina. It was just the first and most high-profile incident of violence in Italian football during the season. Indeed, the problems at Serie A games and clubs, although attracting the most coverage, were just the tip of the iceberg. On a single day in November, Emanuele Manitta – Messina's goalkeeper – was beaten unconscious by a fan at Cagliari, and police and fans clashed at Como after a disallowed goal, as well as in the streets of Turin before the Derby game. Violence at Como games continued unabated; its match with Udinese was abandoned with flares thrown on the pitch, and the away game at Atalanta was marked by trouble. Players at Cagliari and Napoli were attacked by fans. The situation peaked at the Torino-Milan game in February. With Torino 3-0 down and heading for relegation, fans attempted a pitch invasion, which though halted temporarily, descended into a gruesome terrace battle. The game was abandoned as tear gas was released in the Della Alpi. The inquest into these incidents was predictably brief and shallow. The issues of the incompetence of the police, the meanness of Italian football's dominant values, and the impossibility of legally addressing the problem in a legal system so cumbersome, inefficient and disregarded were all left undisturbed.

Italy's endemic contempt for authority was most publicly displayed by Como President Enrico Preziosi, who owns a leading Italian toy company. After complaining all season about biased refereeing, Preziosi's firm released a new toy boxing game called 'Hit the Ref', while his scurrilous attacks on another club president were replicated in the company's football board game.

ITALY

Italian Cup

2003 FINAL (2 legs)
May 20 – Olimpico, Rome
Roma 1-4 Milan
(Totti 28) (Serginho 62 pen, 73, Ambrosini 79, Shevchenko 89)
h/t: 1-0 **Att:** 60,000
Ref: Paparesta
May 31 – San Siro, Milan
Milan 2-2 Roma
(Rivaldo 65, Inzaghi 93) (Totti 56, 64)
h/t: 0-0 **Att:** 76,061
Ref: Rosetti
Milan won 6-3 on aggregate

Relegation play-off

2003 PLAY-OFF (2 legs)
May 29 – Oreste Granillo, Reggina
Reggina 0-0 Atalanta
h/t: 0-0 **Att:** 24,764
Ref: De Sanctis
June 2 – Atleti Azzuri d'Italia, Bergamo
Atalanta 1-2 Reggina
(Natale 18) (Cozza 33, Bonazzoli 85)
h/t: 1-1 **Att:** 23,500
Ref: Collina
Reggina won on 2-1 on aggregate
Atalanta relegated

International Club Performances 2002–03

CLUB	COMPETITION	PROGRESS
Internazionale	Champions League	Semi-finals
Juventus	Champions League	Runners-up
Milan	Champions League	Winners
Roma	Champions League	2nd Group Stage
Chievo	UEFA Cup	1st Round
Lazio	UEFA Cup	Semi-finals
Parma	UEFA Cup	2nd Round

Top Goalscorers 2002–03

PLAYER	CLUB	NATIONALITY	GOALS
Christian Vieri	Internazionale	Italian	24
Adrian Mutu	Parma	Romanian	18
Filippo Inzaghi	Milan	Italian	17

Above: Light touch policing, Italian style. Tear gas rains down on Torino supporters during the abandoned game with Milan in February.

Right: The world's most expensive goalkeeper behind Italy's meanest defence – Juventus's Gianluigi Buffon makes his feelings heard.

Christian Vieri heads home as Inter beat Udinese in November. Vieri's power in the air and bullish physical presence brought him 24 goals. His run at Serie A's goalscoring record was halted when he was injured in the spring.

Left: The dynasty continues. New Juventus president Umberto Agnelli and coach Marcello Lippi plot.

Below: 'They didn't like me at Barca, but at least I played'. Rivaldo muses as he and Jon Dahl Tomasson keep the Milan bench warm again.

Below, left: Parma's Emiliano Bonazzoli found his best form while on loan at Reggina. His goals kept the most southerly club in the top flight.

Race for the Championship

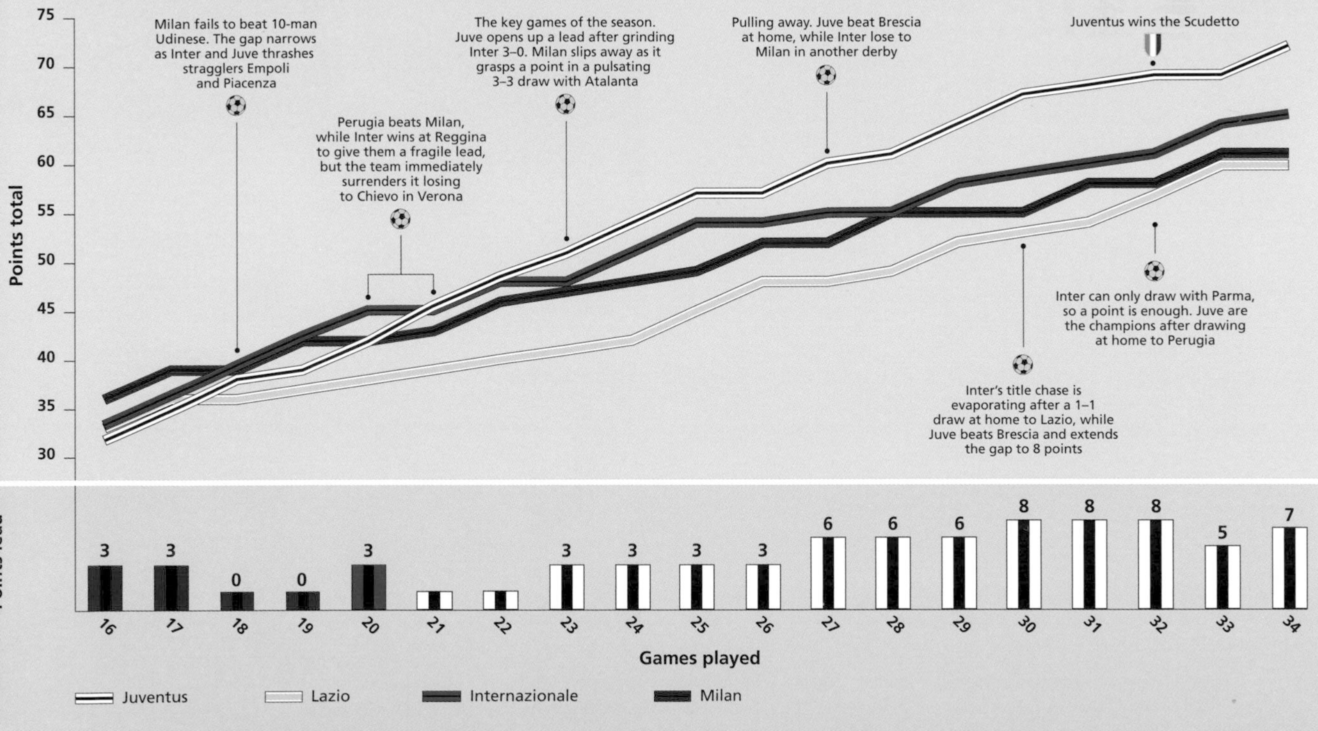

Milan fails to beat 10-man Udinese. The gap narrows as Inter and Juve thrashes stragglers Empoli and Piacenza

Perugia beats Milan, while Inter wins at Reggina to give them a fragile lead, but the team immediately surrenders it losing to Chievo in Verona

The key games of the season. Juve opens up a lead after grinding Inter 3–0. Milan slips away as it grasps a point in a pulsating 3–3 draw with Atalanta

Pulling away. Juve beat Brescia at home, while Inter lose to Milan in another derby

Juventus wins the Scudetto

Inter can only draw with Parma, so a point is enough. Juve are the champions after drawing at home to Perugia

Inter's title chase is evaporating after a 1–1 draw at home to Lazio, while Juve beats Brescia and extends the gap to 8 points

Points total: 75, 70, 65, 60, 55, 50, 45, 40, 35, 30

Points lead

Games played	16	17	18	19	20	21	22	23	24	25	26	27	28	29	30	31	32	33	34
Points lead	3	3	0	0	3			3	3	3	3	6	6	6	8	8	8	5	7

▭ Juventus   ▭ Lazio   ▬ Internazionale   ▬ Milan

ITALY

Grim at the bottom

The football made it back onto centre stage as the real balance of power in Serie A began to emerge in late spring. Chievo, Lazio, Parma and Bologna's connection to the top three eventually withered, leaving them scrapping for the last Champions League spot and UEFA Cup places. It had been a very grim season at the bottom. Torino and Como were relegated together at the beginning of May but they had been all but gone since Christmas, Como managing only two points by the turn of the year. Torino was barely any better, and though both clubs got through a few coaches, there was no hint of a reprieve. Piacenza lasted a little longer, but not much. On the final day of the season, Atalanta and Reggina couldn't be separated and the matter went to a play-off with Reggina squeezing through in the second leg.

Juve take the prize

The New Year began with the death of Juventus president Giovanni Agnelli – a towering figure in the political, economic and sporting life of postwar Italy. He had described Zidane at Juventus as 'more interesting to watch than useful' and it is fitting that Marcello Lippi had fashioned a Juventus side this season that was the reverse of Zidane. Milan seemed to scupper its chances of the title in the spring as Ancelotti abandoned the open play of the autumn and winter and had to be satisfied domestically with the Italian Cup. Inter hovered for a moment at the top of the table as Vieri's goalscoring disguised the side's limits. But in the 'Derby d'Italia' Inter met its nemesis. Juve's game of the season put Inter psychologically and physically through the wringer. It ended 3-0 to Juventus, and established a lead that the team never relinquished. Inter had its chances to catch up as Juventus dropped points, but its charge was epitomized by its game with Roma in which a 3-1 lead in the second half ended in a 3-3 draw.

Crisis, what crisis?

So what happened to the Italian football crisis? Issues of violence have been effectively ignored and the economic chaos of the league has been sidelined. Even the collapse of Sergio Cragnotti's Cirio food empire and Lazio's search for benefactors don't seem to be a problem. Better still for the stage managers, the final rounds of European competitions found three Italian clubs in the quarter-finals of the Champions League and Lazio in the semi-final of the UEFA Cup. Lazio went out, but Inter, Juve and Milan all progressed to the semi-finals with varying displays of defensive, calculating, steel-hard technical football. Valencia's coach Benitez claimed that 'Inter was the death of football'. Lippi and Juventus responded by trouncing Real Madrid. It wasn't pretty, but it demanded respect. With Milan squeezing Inter out of the other semi-final, the Italian season ended at Old Trafford with the Champions League Final. Milan's wafer-thin margin over Juve, after 120 taut goalless minutes, rewarded its slightly bolder play. The country's sporting ego may be in remission, but the crisis is far from over.

Right, top: Edgar Davids salutes the crowd at the Delle Alpi as Juventus draw 2-2 with Perugia but takes its 27th Scudetto with two games to spare. David's uncompromising play was at the heart of Juve's muscular and competitive midfield.

Right, middle: Unbelievable football. Atalanta and Milan coaches Giovanni Vavassori and Carlo Ancelotti have to smile as their teams finish a pulsating 3-3 draw.

Right, bottom: Milan's midfield celebrate their 1-0 victory over Inter – Rui Costa, Pirlo, Gattuso.

Never say never. After almost an entire season at the bottom, Reggina's battling squad stayed up in the play-offs.

After a disappointing season personally, David Trezeguet's crucial penalty against Perugia kept Juventus in the game. It finished 2-2 and Juve was eight points clear with three games to go.

Above: Roma coach Fabio Capello tries to fathom his team's disastrous form.

Right: And that makes it two. Milan's captain Paolo Maldini lifts the Italian Cup a few days after its Champions League triumph at Old Trafford.

Association Football in Italy

ITALY

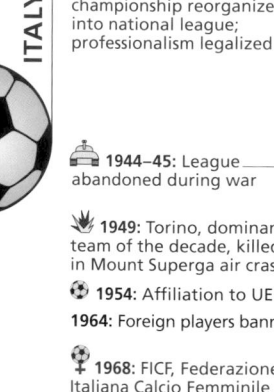

1887: Palestra Ginnastica Libertas, Italy's oldest club formed (later merged into Fiorentina) — 1885 / 1890

1898: Formation of FA: Federazione Italiana Giuoco Calcio. First national championship — 1895 / 1900

1905: Affiliation to FIFA — 1905

1910: First international, v France, won 6-2, venue: Milan — 1910

— 1915

1916–19: League abandoned during war — 1920

1922: First Italian Cup Final
1929: Mussolini de-anglicizes name changes for Genoa and Inter who become Genova and Ambrosiana Inter — 1925

1930: National championship reorganized into national league; professionalism legalized — 1930 / 1935

— 1940

1944–45: League abandoned during war — 1945

1949: Torino, dominant team of the decade, killed in Mount Superga air crash — 1950

1954: Affiliation to UEFA — 1955

1964: Foreign players banned

1968: FICF, Federazione Italiana Calcio Femminile founded. — 1960

First women's international, v Czechoslovakia, won 2-0, venue: Viareggio — 1965

1970: Breakaway Women's FA formed – FFIGC — 1970

1972: Reunification of women's association to form the FIGCF, Federazione Italiana Giuoco Calcio Femminile — 1975

1980: Ban on foreign players lifted. FIGCF becomes associate member of FIGC (national FA) — 1980 / 1985

1986: FIGCF fully incorporated into FIGC — 1990

1997: Clubs required to convert themselves into limited companies — 1995

1998: Lazio is first Italian club to float on the stock exchange — 2000

2002: Italian Supercup played in Libya for first time — 2005

Valentino Mazzola leads out *Il Grande Torino; four-time consecutive champions (1946–49), backbone of the national team, tragically killed in the Mount Superga air crash.*

Key

🇮🇹	International football
⚽	Affiliation to FIFA
⚽	Affiliation to UEFA
⚥	Women's football
🛡	War
🌿	Disaster
■	World Cup host
●	World Cup winner
▲	World Cup runner-up
■	European Championships host
●	European Championships winner
▲	European Championships runner-up
○	Competition winner
△	Competition runner-up

Fiore – Fiorentina
Inter – Internazionale
Juve – Juventus
Nap – Napoli
AC – Milan
Samp – Sampdoria

International Competitions

1934: ● ■
1938: ●

European Cup / UEFA Cup / European Cup-Winners' Cup

Year	European Cup	UEFA Cup	European Cup-Winners' Cup
1957:	△ Fiore		
1958:	△ AC		
1961:		○ Roma	○ Fiore
1962:			△ Fiore
1963:	○ AC		
1964:	○ Inter		
1965:	○ Inter		△ Juve
1967:	△ Inter		
1968:	●■		○ AC
1969:	■ ○ AC		
1970:	▲		△ Juve
1971:			
1972:	△ Inter		○ AC
1973:	△ Juve		
1974:			△ AC
1977:		○ Juve	
1980:	■		
1982:	●		
1983:	△ Juve		○ Juve
1984:	△ Roma		
1985:	○ Juve		
1989:	○ AC	○ Nap	
1990:	■ ○ AC	○ Juve △ Fiore	△ Samp
1991:		○ Inter ○ Roma	○ Samp
1992:			○ Torino
1993:	△ Samp △ AC	○ Juve	○ Parma
1994:	▲ ○ AC	○ Inter	△ Parma
1995:	○ AC	○ Parma △ Juve	
1996:	○ Juve		
1997:		△ Juve △ Inter	
1998:	△ Juve	○ Inter △ Lazio	
1999:		○ Parma	○ Lazio
2000:	△		
2003:	○ AC △ Juve		

Italy: The main clubs

Milan 1899
Milan Cricket and Football Club (1899–1905). Milan Football Club (1905–38)

Pro Vercelli 1892

Juventus 1897
Originated from the Massimo d'Azeglio Grammar School

Torino 1906
Merger FC Torinese and splinter group from Juventus (in 1901 FC Torinese founded 1887, merged with Internazionale Torino)

Casale 1909

Alessandria 1920
Merger of US Alessandria and Alessandria FC

Genoa 1893*
Genoa Football and Cricket Club (1893–99), Genoa FC (1899–1929), Genova (1893, 1929–45)

Sampierdarenese 1901
Merged with Andrea Doria to become Sampdoria in 1946

Milan 1899 ... **Com Calc** 19
Vare F 19
Gallaratese 1909
Novara Calcio 1908
Vercel
Turin — **Casal**
Alessandria
Novese 1908
Genoa
Vado 1908

Parma 1938
Began in 1913 as Verdi, then Parma. Bankru in 1968 and re-established

Cagliari 1920 Team name with year of formation
● Club formed before 1912
● Club formed 1912–25
● Club formed 1925–50
○ Club formed after 1950
👕 Winners of Amateur Championship (1899–1929)
👕 Runners-up in Amateur Championship
⊞ English origins
✛ Swiss origins
▥ Originated from a cricket club
⬡ Originated from a school or college
★ 10 Scudettos†
★★ 20 Scudettos

* Shirts shown are in teams' original colours

†*Scudetto = Italian Championship*
1 star awarded & worn for 10 Scudettos
2 stars awarded & worn for 20 Scudettos

SARDINI

Cagliari 1920

Italy

ORIGINS AND GROWTH OF FOOTBALL

UNLIKE MUCH OF CONTINENTAL EUROPE, Italy had its own traditions of folk football – the Florentine *Calcio* and the Roman *Harpastum* – to draw upon when association football first arrived in the late 19th century. British influences combined with domestic interests to produce a flourishing football scene in Northern Italy around Genoa, Turin and Milan. English expatriate cricket clubs started Genoa and AC Milan, while the first organized game of football is said to have been arranged by Edorado Bosio of Turin, a businessman with extensive connections in Britain.

The first leagues
The early organization of Italian football reflected the divided geographical loyalties of the nation and the weakness of national institutions. The national Football Association was set up in 1898; it changed location four times before settling in Rome in the 1920s. It also faced challenges to its authority from the clubs and rival organizations. Regional leagues and championships were early to form, and remained so strong that, despite the creation of a national championship as early as 1898, it was a rather low-key and disorganized affair. With the advent of professionalism the national league finally became the dominant competition in 1930. Football continued to be dominated by teams from the industrial cities of the north, with only Rome and Naples able to sustain teams of sufficient weight to challenge them.

The national game
The popularity of Italian football with the public, politicians and business exceeded that of almost any other nation in the first half of the 20th century. Industrialists, like Pirelli (tyres and AC Milan) and Agnelli (cars and Juventus), were very active participants in the game. Italy won two of its three World Cups in the 1930s. In the postwar era Italian domestic football's sophistication, politicization and wealth continued to develop and expand, delivering from the early 1960s onwards an extraordinary catalogue of European club success.

ITALY

Internazionale 1908

Splinter from Milan.
Merged with US Milanese (1928).
Renamed Ambrosiana Inter (1929–46)

Lecce Calcio
1908

Bergamo
Atalanta
1907 Brescia 1918
Monza
1912 Brescia
Calcio
1911
Milan Verona
Mantova 1911
icenza
9 Parma
Legnano
1913
Modena
1912 Ferrara
1907
Reggiana
1914
Lucchese-
Libertas
1905
Pistoia
Pistoiese 1921
Florence
Pisa
1909 Empoli 1921
Livorno
Siena
1904
Livorno
1915

Chievo 1929
Hellas Verona 1903

Vicenza 1902
Udinese 1896
Udine Tristina 1918
Treviso
1909 Trieste
Venice
Venezia 1907
Padua
Padova 1910
Citadella 1973
Ravenna Merger of US Citadellese
1913 and AS Olympia
Cesena
1940 Bologna 1909*
SAN MARINO
(see inset)
Fiorentina 1926
Merger of Palestra
Ginnastica Libertas,
Sportive and CS Firenze.
Club liquidated in 2002.
Refounded as
Fiorentina Viola

Ancona
1905
Ascoli Calcio
1898
Perugia Terni
1905 Ternana 1925
Pescara
1936

Roma 1927
Merger in 1927
of Fortitudo,
Pro Roma,
Roma FBC and Alba

Rome

ITALY

Lazio 1900
SP Lazio
(1900–25)

Napoli 1926
Merger of Internaples
and Naples

Savoia 1908 1908

Naples
Foggia
1920
Avellino
1912
Salerno
Salernitana
1919

Bari 1928
Merger of FC Bari
and US Ideale
as US Bari (1928–45)

Lecce
1908

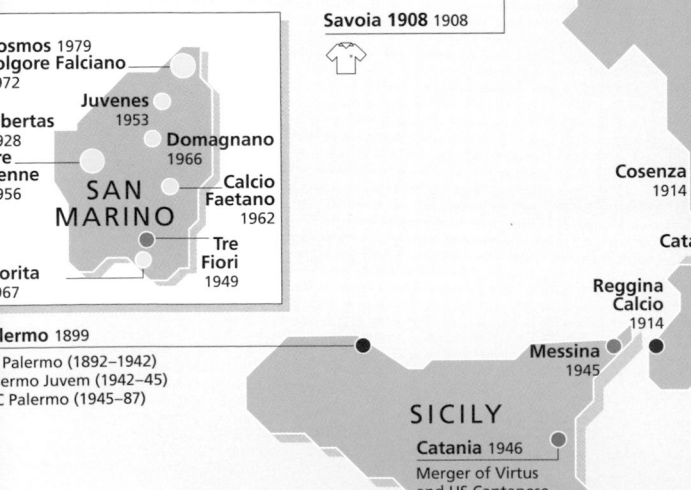

Cosmos 1979
olgore Falciano
972
Juvenes
1953
ibertas Domagnano
928 1966
re
enne Calcio
956 Faetano
1962
SAN
MARINO
Tre
Fiori
iorita 1949
967

alermo 1899
Palermo (1892–1942)
lermo Juvem (1942–45)
C Palermo (1945–87)

Cosenza
1914
Crotone
1923
Catanzaro
1929
Reggina
Calcio
1914

Messina
1945

SICILY

Catania 1946
Merger of Virtus
and US Cantanese

*Vittorio Pozzo
(1886–1968) was Italy's
first great coach. He was
active in the management
of Torino over two decades
and coach of the national
side that won the World
Cup in 1934 and 1938.*

Turin

FOOTBALL CITY

MILAN MAY HAVE GLAMOUR AND STYLE, but when it comes to the hard grit of winning, Turin has no equal. Between them the city's two clubs, Torino and Juventus, have won over 30 Scudetti. In 1887, Eduardo Bosio went back to Turin after a trip to England and took a football with him. Soon after, clubs began to form: Internazionale Torino and FC Torinese were up and running and competing in the fledgling national championships. They fused in 1906 as Torino. Juventus was founded by students in 1897, and took its first title in 1905. The teams settled in the south of the city, their stadiums separated by a single road. The amateur era was quiet for both sides, but with the coming of professionalism Turin's economic and demographic weight really began to count. Juventus has been tied to the Agnelli family and Fiat for over 50 years; its support is strong among southern Italian immigrants to the city and also has a national and international dimension. Torino, by contrast, has claimed deeper and wider roots in the city itself and in its people, not least among Fiat's workforce.

Success and tragedy

Juve, *la Vecchia Signora* (the 'Old Lady') as the club is known, has an extraordinary record. In every decade since the 1920s it has won the domestic championship; it has won every European competition going; and along with the glory, the club has earned the distaste and envy of every other team in the country. Torino, by contrast, has had only one truly great era, that of Il Grand Torino when the team won four successive *Scudetti* from 1946 to 1949. Under coach Vittorio Pozzo, Il Grand Torino was led by the charismatic striker Valentino Mazzola. In May 1949, following a friendly match, the entire squad was killed in the Superga air crash (see box). This tragedy saw the heart torn from Torino and two decades of mid-table football followed. Only in 1976 was the club able to lay a few ghosts to rest when it won the championship once more under Gigi Radice. Since then a cycle of relegation and promotion has been Torino's fate. Both clubs moved to the Stadio delle Alpi on the northern outskirts of town after the 1990 World Cup. Unloved and sterile, it is barely ever half full, even for big games. Juventus has finally bought the stadium from the city council and is planning a complete redevelopment.

The scene after the aircrash on the mountain of Superga, on the outskirts of Turin, which killed all 31 passengers when a plane came down in mist and torrential rain on 4 May 1949.

THE SUPERGA AIRCRASH

On 4 May 1949, a Fiat G212 airliner left Lisbon with the Torino squad on board. They had been playing a friendly match against Benfica in honour of the great Portuguese player Franciso Ferriera. The plane carried 31 passengers, including 18 Torino squad members, two club directors, four other club staff and three journalists. In mist and torrential rain, the plane, heading for the Aeritalia airfield, was seen emerging from a bank of cloud and crashing into an embankment below the Superga Basilica, a church and monastic complex set on the hills rising to the east of the city. There were no survivors. Two days later, funerals were held at the Palazzo Madama. Half a million people lined the streets of the city centre to pay their last respects, led by the youth teams of Torino and Juventus in full kit.

Cars being tested on the roof of the Fiat factory in Turin in 1929. Despite its sponsorship of Juventus, the company's workforce is split in its support of the city's two big clubs.

STADIO DELLE ALPI

69,041

Clubs:	Juventus, Torino
Built:	1990
Original Capacity:	71,000
Record Attendance:	71,010 Juventus v Internazionale, 28 Apr 1998
Significant Matches:	1990 World Cup: five matches including semi-final

STADIO COMMUNALE

Club:	Currently Juventus' training ground. Torino is likely to play here in 2003
Built:	1933
Original Capacity:	55,000
Significant Matches:	1934 World Cup: two matches

ITALY

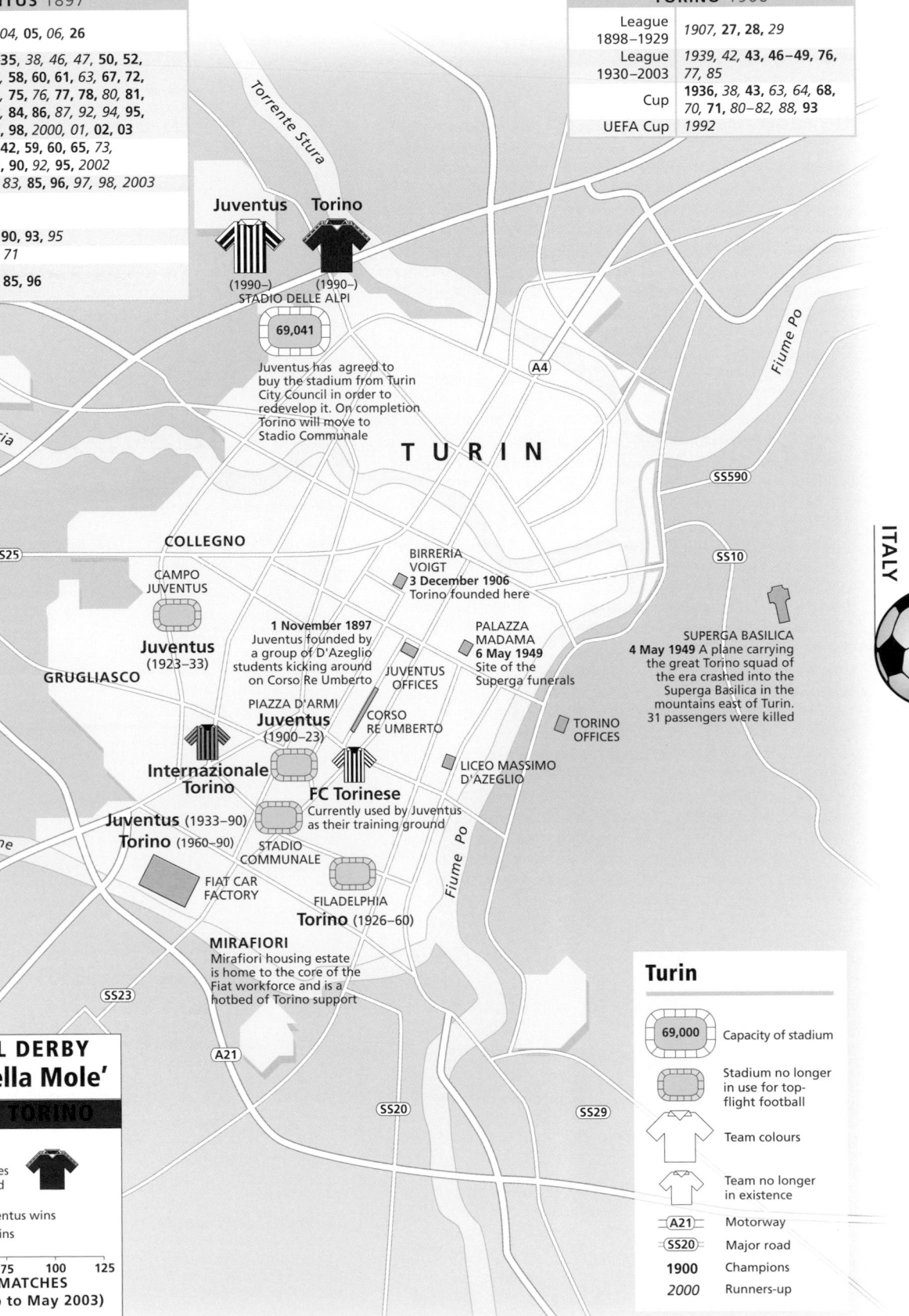

JUVENTUS 1897

League 1898–1929	*1903, 04,* **05, 06,** *26*
League 1930–2003	**1931–35,** *38,* **46, 47, 50, 52,** *53, 54,* **58, 60, 61,** *63,* **67,** *72,* **73, 74,** *75, 76,* **77, 78,** *80,* **81,** **82,** *83,* **84, 86,** *87,* **92,** *94,* **95,** **96,** *97,* **98, 2000,** *01,* **02, 03**
Cup	**1938, 42, 59, 60, 65,** *73,* *79,* **83, 90,** *92,* **95,** *2002*
European Cup	*1973,* **83, 85,** *96,* **97, 98, 2003**
European Cup-Winners' Cup	**1984**
UEFA Cup	**1977, 90, 93,** *95*
Fairs Cup	*1965, 71*
World Club Cup	*1973,* **85, 96**

TORINO 1906

League 1898–1929	*1907,* **27, 28,** *29*
League 1930–2003	*1939, 42,* **43,** *46–49,* **76,** *77,* **85**
Cup	**1936,** *38,* **43,** *63,* **64,** *68,* *70,* **71,** *80–82,* **88,** *93*
UEFA Cup	*1992*

Juventus (1990–)
Torino (1990–)
STADIO DELLE ALPI

69,041

Juventus has agreed to buy the stadium from Turin City Council in order to redevelop it. On completion Torino will move to Stadio Communale

Torrente Stura

A4

T U R I N

SS590

SS10

ITALY

Dora Riparia

COLLEGNO

BIRRERIA VOIGT
3 December 1906
Torino founded here

PALAZZA MADAMA
6 May 1949
Site of the Superga funerals

SUPERGA BASILICA
4 May 1949 A plane carrying the great Torino squad of the era crashed into the Superga Basilica in the mountains east of Turin. 31 passengers were killed

SS25

CAMPO JUVENTUS

Juventus (1923–33)

GRUGLIASCO

1 November 1897
Juventus founded by a group of D'Azeglio students kicking around on Corso Re Umberto

JUVENTUS OFFICES

TORINO OFFICES

PIAZZA D'ARMI

Juventus (1900–23)

CORSO RE UMBERTO

LICEO MASSIMO D'AZEGLIO

Internazionale Torino

Juventus (1933–90)
Torino (1960–90)

FC Torinese
Currently used by Juventus as their training ground

STADIO COMMUNALE

FIAT CAR FACTORY

FILADELFIA
Torino (1926–60)

Torrente Sangone

MIRAFIORI
Mirafiori housing estate is home to the core of the Fiat workforce and is a hotbed of Torino support

SS23

A21

SS20

SS29

Fiume Po

Turin

69,000	Capacity of stadium
	Stadium no longer in use for top-flight football
	Team colours
	Team no longer in existence
A21	Motorway
SS20	Major road
1900	Champions
2000	Runners-up

THE LOCAL DERBY
'Il derby della Mole'

JUVENTUS	TORINO

100 matches played

45 Juventus wins
28 Torino wins
27 draws

0   25   50   75   100   125
NUMBER OF MATCHES
(Serie A games up to May 2003)

Milan

FOOTBALL CITY

THE MILAN FOOTBALL AND CRICKET CLUB was founded in 1899 by a mixture of English and Swiss expatriate businessmen led by the Englishman Alfred Edwards. Milan FC achieved early success, winning three national championships before 1907. In 1908, disaffected members of the club, resenting its Anglo dominance, split to form a new club called Internazionale. Rivalry between the two clubs has consumed the city ever since, although the social meaning of the conflict has changed. At first Inter attracted the elite and middle class, and Milan the working class, though over time this relationship seems to have shifted.

Class divide

Milan moved to the San Siro in 1926, financed by the millions of tyre magnate Piero Pirelli. Internazionale played in the Arena in the centre of town. With the arrival of Fascism, Inter's cosmopolitan leanings looked suspect, and the club was forced to merge with US Milanese and change its name to Ambrosiana-Inter. Despite its name, the team proved brilliant, with a forward line led by the great Giuseppe Meazza. In 1946, it joined its city rival at the San Siro. Milan's English connections made the team even more suspicious to the Fascist authorities and it was only after the Second World War that the club really flourished: four *Scudetti* in the 1950s, followed by two in the 1960s as well as two great European Cup victories. Inter took the European Cup twice (1964 and 65) under the charismatic Helenio Herrera who brought the playing style of *catenaccio* (see page 471) and strict squad discipline to the city, and helped encourage the first organized fan clubs, or *tifosi*, who would travel to Inter's away games in Europe.

In the 1980s and 1990s it was Milan that prospered. Money flooded into the club from the Berlusconi fortune and, under Arrigo Sacchi and Fabio Capello, Milan became the dominant force in European football. Inter has countered with the oil-based fortunes of Massimo Moratti (whose father had owned the club in the 1950s). Inter's spending in the transfer market has been phenomenal (including the purchase of Christian Vieri and Ronaldo for almost £50 million), but so far only one UEFA Cup trophy sits in the cabinet under the Moratti regime.

ITALY

MILAN 1899	
League 1898–1929	**1901**, *02*, **06**, **07**
League 1930–2003	*1948*, *50*, **51**, **52**, **55**, **56**, **57**, *59*, *61*, **62**, *65*, **68**, *71–73*, **79**, **88**, *90*, *91*, **92–94**, *96*, *99*
Cup	*1942*, *67*, *68*, *71*, *72*, *73*, *75*, *77*, *85*, *90*, *98*, **2003**
European Cup	*1958*, *63*, **69**, **89**, **90**, *93*, **94**, *95*, **2003**
European Cup-Winners' Cup	**1968**, **73**, *74*
World Club Cup	*1963*, *69*, **89**, **90**, *93*, *94*

STADIO GIUSEPPE MEAZZA (SAN SIRO)

85,700

Clubs: Internazionale, Milan
Built: 1926
Original Capacity: 35,000
Rebuilt: 1955, 1990
Significant Matches: 1934 World Cup: three matches; 1990 World Cup: five matches; European Cup Finals: 1965, 70, 2001

INTERNAZIONALE 1908	
League 1898–1929	**1910**, **20**
League 1930–2003	**1930**, *33–35*, **38**, **40**, **41**, *49*, **51**, **53**, **54**, *62*, *63*, **64**, **65**, **66**, *67*, *70*, **71**, **80**, **89**, *93*, *98*, **2003**
Cup	**1939**, *59*, **65**, *77*, **78**, **82**, *2000*
European Cup	**1964**, **65**, *67*, *72*
UEFA Cup	**1991**, **94**, *97*, **98**
World Club Cup	**1964**, **65**

The Piazza del Duomo in the centre of the city is the traditional location of victory celebrations for fans of both Milan and Internazionale.

SS233

A8

SS33

A4

PERO

BAGGIO

CESANO BOSCONE

CÓRSICO

BUCCINASCO

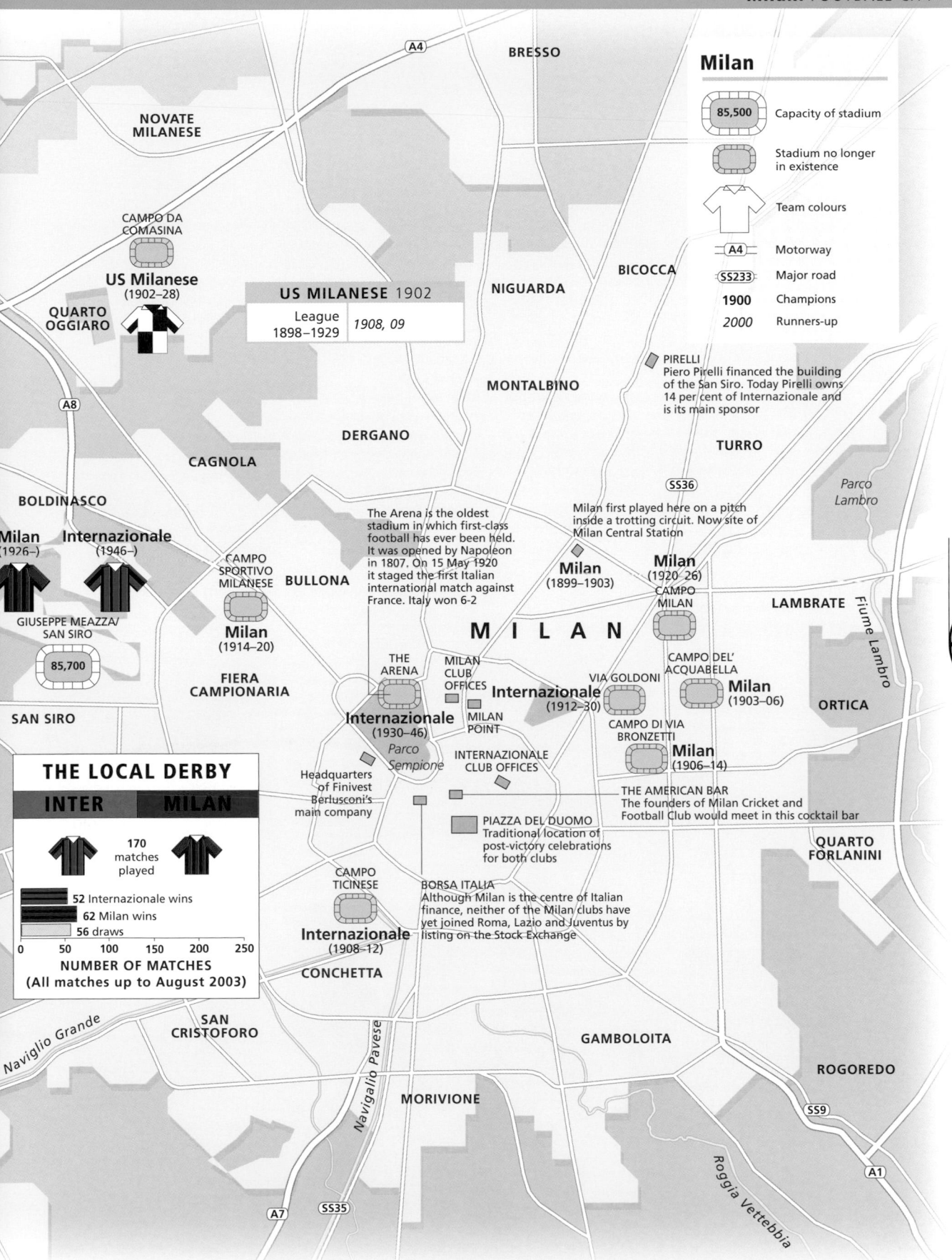

Milan

85,500	Capacity of stadium
	Stadium no longer in existence
	Team colours
A4	Motorway
SS233	Major road
1900	Champions
2000	Runners-up

CAMPO DA COMASINA

US Milanese
(1902–28)

QUARTO OGGIARO

NOVATE MILANESE

BRESSO

NIGUARDA

BICOCCA

MONTALBINO

TURRO

US MILANESE 1902

League 1898–1929	*1908, 09*

PIRELLI
Piero Pirelli financed the building of the San Siro. Today Pirelli owns 14 per cent of Internazionale and is its main sponsor

Parco Lambro

DERGANO

CAGNOLA

BOLDINASCO

Milan
(1926–)

Internazionale
(1946–)

GIUSEPPE MEAZZA/ SAN SIRO

85,700

SAN SIRO

CAMPO SPORTIVO MILANESE

Milan
(1914–20)

FIERA CAMPIONARIA

BULLONA

The Arena is the oldest stadium in which first-class football has ever been held. It was opened by Napoleon in 1807. On 15 May 1920 it staged the first Italian international match against France. Italy won 6-2

THE ARENA

MILAN CLUB OFFICES

Internazionale
(1930–46)

MILAN POINT

Parco Sempione

INTERNAZIONALE CLUB OFFICES

Headquarters of Finivest Berlusconi's main company

Milan first played here on a pitch inside a trotting circuit. Now site of Milan Central Station

Milan
(1899–1903)

Milan
(1920–26)

CAMPO MILAN

M I L A N

Internazionale
(1912–30)

VIA GOLDONI

CAMPO DI VIA BRONZETTI

Milan
(1906–14)

CAMPO DEL' ACQUABELLA

Milan
(1903–06)

LAMBRATE

Fiume Lambro

ORTICA

THE AMERICAN BAR
The founders of Milan Cricket and Football Club would meet in this cocktail bar

PIAZZA DEL DUOMO
Traditional location of post-victory celebrations for both clubs

QUARTO FORLANINI

THE LOCAL DERBY

INTER	MILAN

170 matches played

52 Internazionale wins
62 Milan wins
56 draws

0   50   100   150   200   250
NUMBER OF MATCHES
(All matches up to August 2003)

CAMPO TICINESE

Internazionale
(1908–12)

CONCHETTA

BORSA ITALIA
Although Milan is the centre of Italian finance, neither of the Milan clubs have yet joined Roma, Lazio and Juventus by listing on the Stock Exchange

Naviglio Grande

SAN CRISTOFORO

Naviglio Pavese

MORIVIONE

GAMBOLOITA

Roggia Vettabbia

ROGOREDO

A7   SS35

ITALY

Rome

FOOTBALL CITY

LAZIO WAS FOUNDED IN 1900 by an Italian army officer, Luigi Bigarelli, and adopted Greek colours and secluded itself in the wealthy northern suburbs of the city. The team soon acquired the well-appointed Rondinella stadium to play in and Benito Mussolini as a fan. But Il Duce's plans for the capital of the new Roman Empire extended to its football stadium, and he moved Lazio to his monumental and bombastic Fascist Party stadium (the PNF) in the 1930s, and strutted around the city when Italy hosted and won the 1934 World Cup.

Lazio acquired a proper rival with the creation of Roma in 1927 from the fusion of four small clubs (Alba, Fortitudo, ProRoma and Roma FBC). Roma settled in the working-class streets of Testaccio, where it built the extraordinary all-wooden Campo Testaccio. The area still remains the club's spiritual heartland. Roma too was shipped out to the PNF until after the war, and both clubs moved again to the new Olympic stadium built across the Tiber in the north-east of the city in the early 1950s.

Investment pays off

Although prosperity and geographical mobility have fractured the old core areas of club support, Roma's fans are more working-class, left-wing and urban in origin, while Lazio has drawn on middle-class support in the city along with fans from across the Lazio region. Recently it has attracted more vociferous, right-wing *ultras* from the city's southern housing projects. These new fans first made their presence felt when Lazio won its first *Scudetto* in 1974, with a rough, tough squad schooled in the Estudiantes sides of the 1960s and inspired by Argentinian coach Juan Carlos Lorenzo.

Since the late 1990s, Rome has at last become the country's footballing capital. Under the presidencies of Sensi and Cragnotti, Roma and Lazio became the first Italian clubs to float on the stock exchange, and both have spent hugely to create cosmopolitan and powerful squads. Lazio's double in 1999 (managed by Sven Goran Eriksson), and Roma's first *Scudetto* for almost 20 years in 2001 (managed by Fabio Capello), have been the pay-off.

However, Rome's fall from footballing grace has been as fast as its ascent. Sergio Cragnotti has been forced to put Lazio on the market after suffering financial difficulties at his Cirio food company. The club's unsustainable wage bill has seen many of its stars sold on. Roma's finances are in better shape but after running Juventus close for the 2001–02 championship, the club has plummeted into mid-table obscurity.

ITALY

This aerial shot of Rome was taken just before the 1960 Olympic Games and shows the Olimpico (centre left) and other smaller arenas which were also used for the Games.

OLIMPICO

 82,566

Club:	Lazio, Roma, Italy
Built:	1952
Original	
Capacity:	80,000
Rebuilt:	1989–90
Significant Matches:	1990 World Cup: six matches including Final; 1968 European Championships: Final and replay; 1980 European Championships: Final; European Cup Finals: 1977, 84, 96

LAZIO 1900

League 1898–1929	*1913, 14, 23*
League 1930–2003	*1937,* **74, 95, 99, 2000**
Cup	**1958,** *61,* **98, 2000**
European Cup- Winners' Cup	**1999**
UEFA Cup	*1998*

ROMA 1927

League 1930–2003	*1931, 36,* **42,** *81,* **83,** *84, 86,* **2001,** *02*
Cup	*1937, 41,* **64, 69, 80, 81, 84, 86, 91, 93,** *2003*
European Cup	*1984*
UEFA Cup	*1991*
Fairs Cup	**1961**

FLAMINIO

24,500

Club:	Lodigiani (major games; others are played at Tre Fontane in the southern suburbs). Roma and Lazio played here in 1989 during rebuilding of Olimpico
Built:	1953
Original Capacity:	55,000
Significant Matches:	1934 World Cup: Final (as PNF); 1960 Rome Olympics

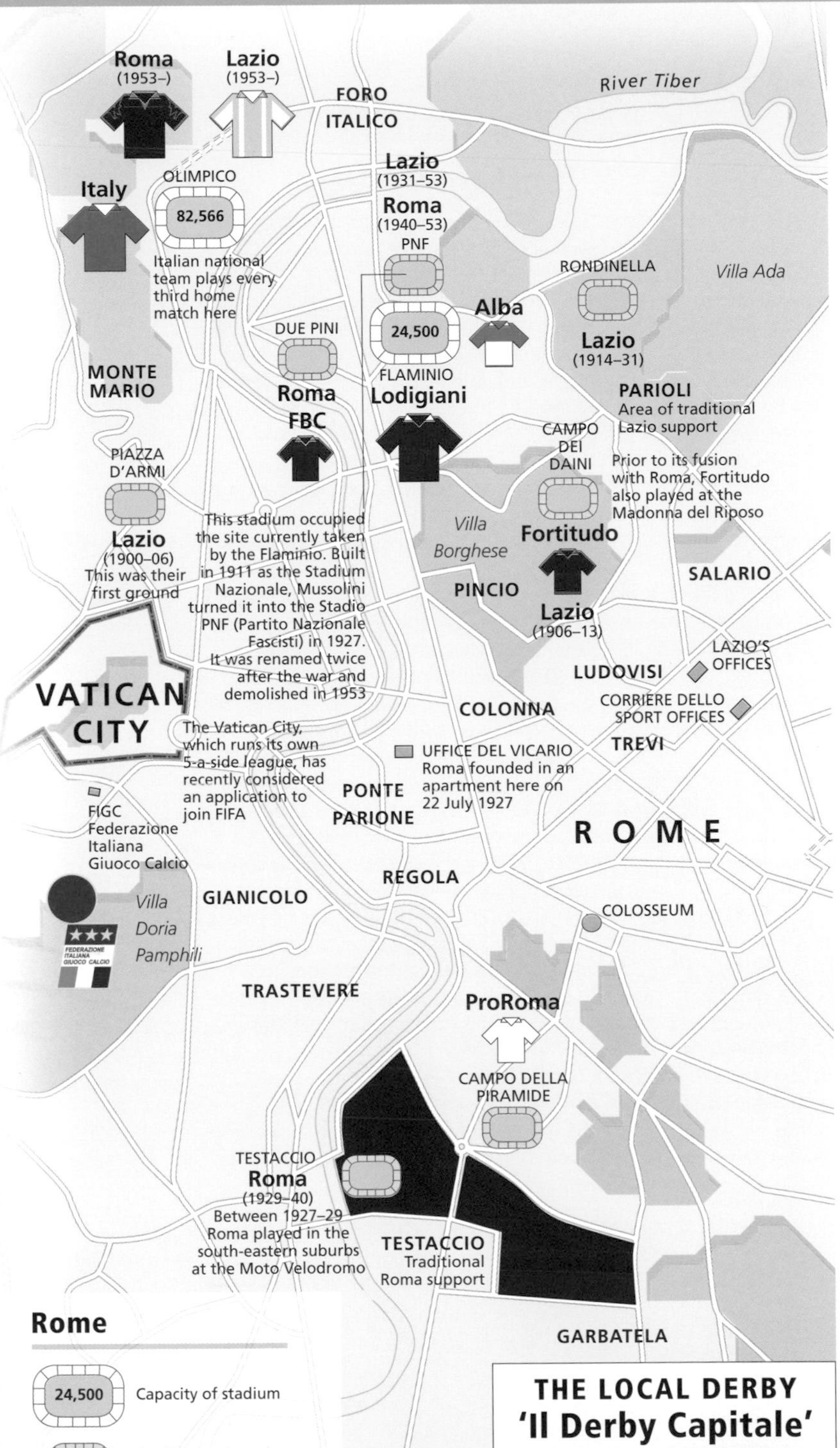

Roma (1953–)

Lazio (1953–)

FORO ITALICO

River Tiber

Italy

OLIMPICO 82,566

Italian national team plays every third match here

Lazio (1931–53)

Roma (1940–53) PNF

Alba

RONDINELLA

Villa Ada

Lazio (1914–31)

MONTE MARIO

DUE PINI

24,500 FLAMINIO

Roma FBC

Lodigiani

PARIOLI
Area of traditional Lazio support

CAMPO DEI DAINI

Prior to its fusion with Roma, Fortitudo also played at the Madonna del Riposo

PIAZZA D'ARMI

Lazio (1900–06)
This was their first ground

This stadium occupied the site currently taken by the Flaminio. Built in 1911 as the Stadium Nazionale, Mussolini turned it into the Stadio PNF (Partito Nazionale Fascisti) in 1927. It was renamed twice after the war and demolished in 1953

Villa Borghese

Fortitudo

Lazio (1906–13)

SALARIO

VATICAN CITY

The Vatican City, which runs its own 5-a-side league, has recently considered an application to join FIFA

PINCIO

LUDOVISI

COLONNA

LAZIO'S OFFICES

CORRIERE DELLO SPORT OFFICES

TREVI

UFFICE DEL VICARIO
Roma founded in an apartment here on 22 July 1927

FIGC Federazione Italiana Giuoco Calcio

PONTE PARIONE

R O M E

ITALY

Villa Doria Pamphili

FEDERAZIONE ITALIANA GIUOCO CALCIO

GIANICOLO

REGOLA

COLOSSEUM

TRASTEVERE

ProRoma

CAMPO DELLA PIRAMIDE

TESTACCIO

Roma (1929–40)
Between 1927–29 Roma played in the south-eastern suburbs at the Moto Velodromo

TESTACCIO
Traditional Roma support

GARBATELA

Rome

24,500	Capacity of stadium
	Stadium no longer in existence
	Team colours
	Teams fused to form Roma in 1927
––––	Vatican City border
=====	Major road
1900	Champions
2000	Runners-up

OSTIENSE

THE LOCAL DERBY 'Il Derby Capitale'

LAZIO	ROMA

136 matches played

35 Lazio wins	
47 Roma wins	
54 draws	

0   50   100   150   200   250
NUMBER OF MATCHES
(All Matches to May 2003)

Italy

FANS AND OWNERS

UNTIL RECENTLY, nearly every club in Italy was privately owned by a single dominant figure on the board and linked to a large company with which it had made its fortune. This is still the case at the Milan giants, Internazionale and Milan, and the clubs of the smaller northern cities. But in the last few years the enormous demand for capital that success in Italian football requires has led Roma, Lazio and Juventus to the stock market for partial flotation, although in each case, a majority shareholder remains in charge. Equally enormous wage bills have swallowed the astronomical income of Italian clubs. Attendances have stagnated or fallen, TV income is jeopardized by the pirating of satellite channels on a massive scale, and the recent merger of Italy's main pay-per-view TV companies. Not surprisingly, the debt of many clubs has risen substantially. The crisis in Italian football is biting hardest at the clubs that have failed to deliver on ambitious expenditures: Napoli, Sampdoria and Genoa have all changed hands as owners' finances and patience have run out. Fiorentina was declared bankrupt and dissolved in 2002 while Lazio's president, Sergio Cragnotti, has been seeking to unload his share holding and the club's expensive squad.

Italy's lay religion

The huge, working-class crowds that gathered on a Sunday afternoon for Italian football always had an element of ritual and religion to them. In the 1970s, young Italian fans organized themselves into groups called *ultras* which specialized in the construction of vast banners, choreographed displays of colours, drumming, singing and chanting. The fierce localism of these groups means that no similar following for the national team exists. By 1983, symbolic contest turned to organized violence and the earlier left-wing bent of some *ultra* groups was replaced by the presence of the far right. In the 1990s, a new generation of *ultras* have emerged, older groups have fragmented, and increased policing has subdued the scene. However, since 2000 there has been a renewed spate of violence outside grounds and attacks by fans on poorly performing players and coaches.

ITALY

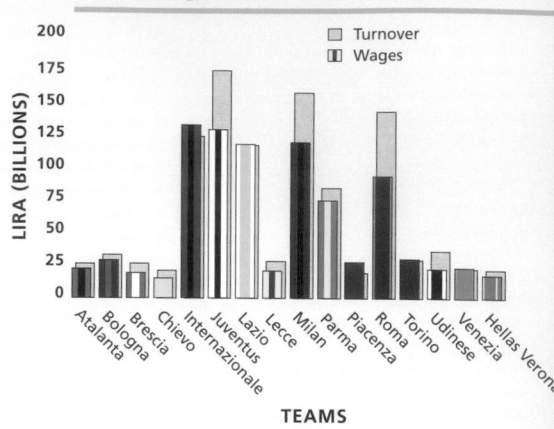

Club Wages and Turnover 2002

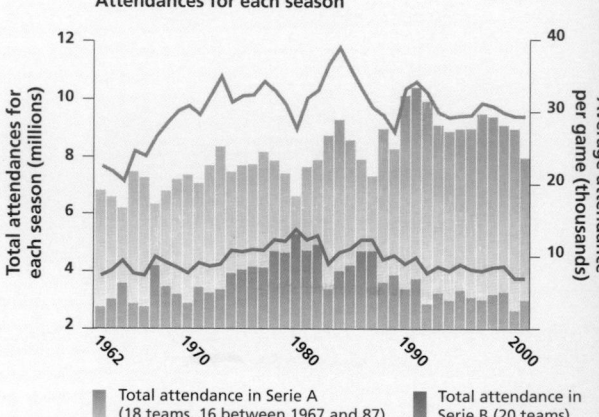

Italian Attendances

Attendances for each season

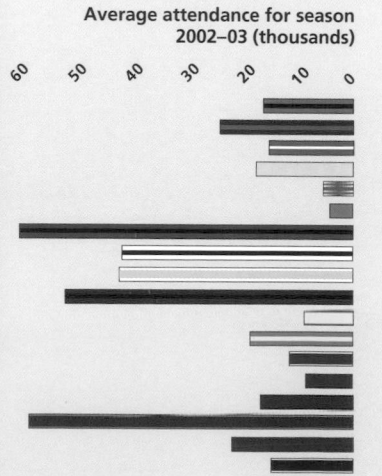

Average Attendance

Average attendance for season 2002–03 (thousands)

AS Roma's fans clash with police before its match against Juventus at Olympic stadium in Rome 1 December 2002.

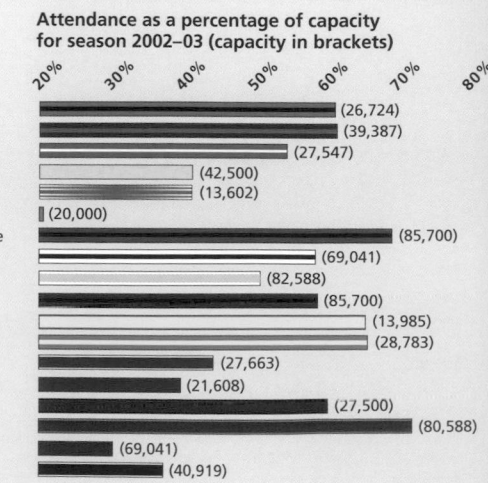

Capacity

Attendance as a percentage of capacity for season 2002–03 (capacity in brackets)

TEAMS	
Atalanta	(26,724)
Bologna	(39,387)
Brescia	(27,547)
Chievo	(42,500)
Como Calcio	(13,602)
Empoli	(20,000)
Internazionale	(85,700)
Juventus	(69,041)
Lazio	(82,588)
Milan	(85,700)
Modena	(13,985)
Parma	(28,783)
Perugia	(27,663)
Piacenza	(21,608)
Reggina	(27,500)
Roma	(80,588)
Torino	(69,041)
Udinese	(40,919)

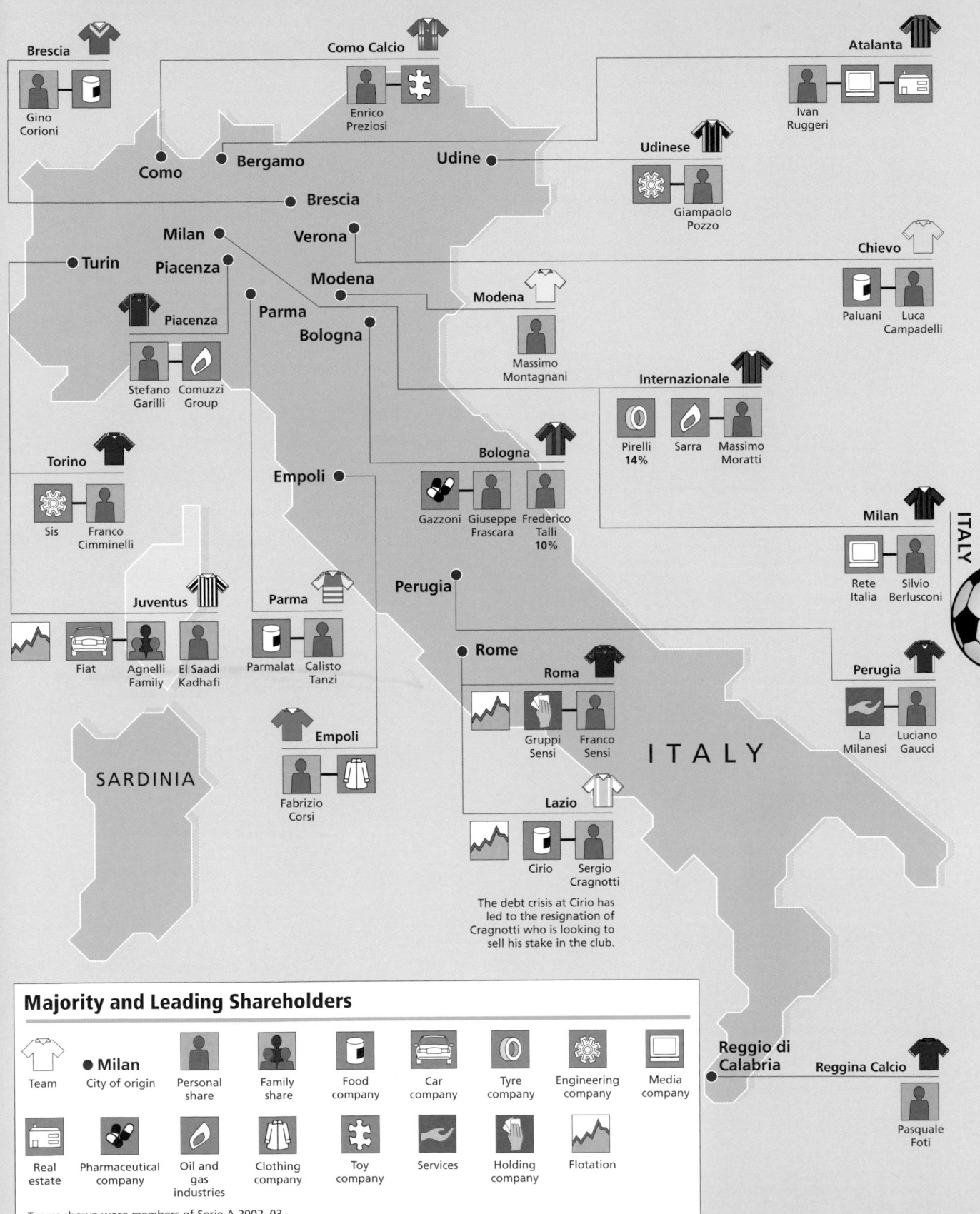

Brescia

Gino Corioni

Como Calcio

Enrico Preziosi

Atalanta

Ivan Ruggeri

Como

Bergamo

Udine

Udinese

Giampaolo Pozzo

Brescia

Milan

Verona

Chievo

Piacenza

Modena

Paluani — Luca Campadelli

Turin

Piacenza

Parma

Stefano Garilli — Comuzzi Group

Modena

Massimo Montagnani

Bologna

Internazionale

Pirelli 14% — Sarra — Massimo Moratti

Torino

Sis — Franco Cimminelli

Empoli

Bologna

Gazzoni — Giuseppe Frascara — Frederico Talli 10%

Milan

Rete Italia — Silvio Berlusconi

Juventus

Fiat — Agnelli Family — El Saadi Kadhafi

Parma

Parmalat — Calisto Tanzi

Perugia

Perugia

La Milanesi — Luciano Gaucci

Rome

Roma

Gruppi Sensi — Franco Sensi

Empoli

Fabrizio Corsi

SARDINIA

Lazio

Cirio — Sergio Cragnotti

The debt crisis at Cirio has led to the resignation of Cragnotti who is looking to sell his stake in the club.

ITALY

Majority and Leading Shareholders

Team	● Milan — City of origin
Personal share	Family share
Food company	Car company
Tyre company	Engineering company
Media company	

Real estate — Pharmaceutical company — Oil and gas industries — Clothing company — Toy company — Services — Holding company — Flotation

Teams shown were members of Serie A 2002–03

Reggio di Calabria

Reggina Calcio

Pasquale Foti

Italy

PLAYERS AND MANAGERS

ITALIAN PLAYERS AND MANAGERS HAVE perhaps the most intensely pressurized and scrutinized footballing careers in the world. Italy's extraordinarily voracious and dedicated sporting press leaves no stone unturned in analyzing performance, rumour, gossip and behaviour. Of course, there are salaries and adulation to match, tied to an obsessive culture of training, discipline and, in many cases, the prescription of pre-match sex. In the 1990s, foreigners have come in increasing numbers into the Italian game, with many of the very best Germans, Dutch, Yugoslavs, Argentinians and Brazilians finding their way to Serie A. Similarly, foreign coaches have begun to find their way at the top of the Italian game. As a consequence, the capacity of Italian teams to absorb and deal with pressure and grind out results has been formidable.

The art of defence

What marks out Italian football culture from many others is that it is perhaps the only nation where defenders are not only regarded with a respect usually reserved for strikers, but that defending is considered an art form full of technical virtuosity and perfect timing that has no superior. Gianni Facchetti redefined the role of the modern sweeper and full-back at Internazionale in the 1960s, where man-marking left him free to build and join attacks and score freely. His modern descendents include Claudio Gentile, Gaetano Scirea, Franco Baresi, Giuseppe Bergomi, Paolo Maldini, and more recently Alessandro Nesta. Scirea in particular was noted for the grace rather than the viciousness of his tackling. That said, Italian strikers have proved their enduring worth in the guise of Giuseppe Meazza, Gianni Rivera, Paolo Rossi and Roberto Baggio. Nicknamed 'il condino divino', or the divine ponytail, Baggio was the leading forward of his era, noted not only for his hair but also for his quiet Buddhism and ferocious goalscoring. Riots broke out in the streets of Florence when his transfer to Juventus was announced in 1990.

Top 17 International Goalscorers

PLAYER	GOALS	CAPS	FIRST MATCH	LAST MATCH
Luigi Riva	35	42	1965	1974
Giuseppe Meazza	33	53	1930	1939
Silvio Piola	30	34	1935	1952
Roberto Baggio*	27	55	1988	1999
Adolfo Baloncieri	25	47	1920	1930
Alessandro Altobelli	25	61	1980	1988
Francesco Graziani	23	64	1975	1983
Alessandro Del Piero*	22	57	1995	2003
Alessandro Mazzola	22	70	1963	1974
Paolo Rossi	20	48	1977	1986
Roberto Bettega	19	42	1975	1983
Christian Vieri*	17	31	1997	2003
Gianlucca Vialli	16	59	1985	1992
Fillipo Inzaghi*	15	36	1997	2002
Gino Colaussi	15	26	1935	1940
Julio Libonatti	15	17	1926	1931
Angelo Schiavio	15	21	1925	1934

* Indicates players still playing at least at club level.

Italian International Managers

DATES	NAME	GAMES	WON	DRAWN	LOST
1960	Gipo Viani	3	1	1	1
1960–62	Giovanni Ferrari	16	7	5	4
1962–66	Edmondo Fabbri	29	18	6	5
1966–67	Helenio Herrera	4	3	1	0
1967–74	Ferruccio Valcareggi	58	31	21	6
1974–77	Fulvio Bemardini	22	12	4	6
1977–86	Enzo Bearzot	104	51	28	25
1986–92	Azeglio Vicini	54	32	15	7
1992–96	Arrigo Sacchi	53	34	11	8
1996–98	Cesare Maldini	20	10	8	2
1998–2000	Dino Zoff	23	11	7	5
2000–	Giovanni Trapattoni	31	17	8	6

All figures correct as of 6 June 2003.

Top 20 International Caps

PLAYER	CAPS	GOALS	FIRST MATCH	LAST MATCH
Paolo Maldini*	126	7	1988	2003
Dino Zoff	112	0	1968	1983
Giacinto Fachetti	94	3	1963	1977
Franco Baresi	81	1	1982	1994
Giuseppe Bergomi	81	6	1982	1998
Marco Tardelli	81	6	1976	1985
Demitrio Albertini*	78	2	1991	2002
Gaetano Scirea	78	2	1975	1986
Giancarlo Antognoni	73	7	1974	1983
Antonio Cabrini	73	9	1978	1987
Claudio Gentile	71	1	1975	1984
Alessandro Mazzola	70	22	1963	1974
Fabio Cannavaro*	69	0	1997	2003
Tarcisio Burgnich	66	2	1963	1974
Francesco Graziani	64	23	1975	1983
Franco Causio	63	6	1972	1983
Roberto Donadoni	63	5	1986	1996
Alessandro Altobelli	61	25	1980	1988
Dino Baggio*	60	7	1991	1999
Gianni Rivera	60	14	1962	1974

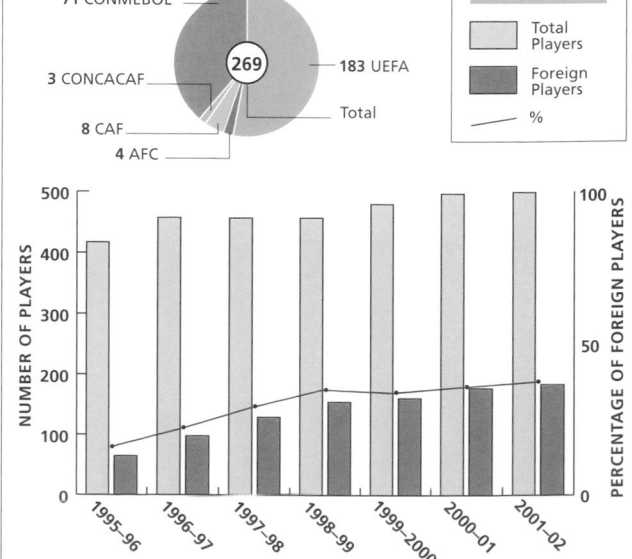

Foreign Players in Italy (in top division squads)

2002–03

71 CONMEBOL
3 CONCACAF
8 CAF
4 AFC
269
183 UEFA
Total

Key
- Total Players
- Foreign Players
- %

(Bar chart: NUMBER OF PLAYERS vs PERCENTAGE OF FOREIGN PLAYERS, seasons 1995–96, 1996–97, 1997–98, 1998–99, 1999–2000, 2000–01, 2001–02)

ITALY

Player of the Year

YEAR	PLAYER	CLUB
1976	Sala	Torino
1977	Sala	Torino
1978	Filippi	Vicenza
1979	Filippi	Napoli
1980	Castellini	Napoli
1981	Krol	Napoli
1982	Causio	Udinese
1983	Vierchowod	Roma
1984	Platini	Juventus
1985	Maradona	Napoli
1986	Renato	Torino
1987	Zenga	Internazionale
1988	Mancini	Sampdoria
1989	Brehme	Internazionale
1990	Baresi	Milan
1991	Mancini	Sampdoria
1992	Rijkaard	Milan
1993	Signori	Lazio
1994	Massaro	Milan
1995	Sousa	Juventus
1996	Chiesa	Sampdoria
1997	Pagliuca	Internazionale
1997	Peruzzi	Juventus
1997	Thuram	Parma
1998	Totti	Roma
1999	Almeyda	Lazio
2000	Frey	Verona
2001	R. Baggio	Brescia

Awarded by *Guerin Sportivo* magazine.

Championship Winning Managers

YEAR	MANAGER	CLUB
1976	Radice	Torino
1977	Trappatoni	Juventus
1978	Trappatoni	Juventus
1979	Liedholm [Swe]	Milan
1980	Bersellini	Internazionale
1981	Trappatoni	Juventus
1982	Trappatoni	Juventus
1983	Liedholm [Swe]	Roma
1984	Trappatoni	Juventus
1985	Bagnoli	Verona
1986	Trappatoni	Juventus
1987	Bianchi	Napoli
1988	Sacchi	Milan
1989	Trappatoni	Internazionale
1990	Bigon	Napoli
1991	Boskov [Yugo]	Sampdoria
1992	Capello	Milan
1993	Capello	Milan
1994	Capello	Milan
1995	Lippi	Juventus
1996	Capello	Milan
1997	Lippi	Juventus
1998	Lippi	Juventus
1999	Zaccheroni	Milan
2000	Ericksson [Swe]	Lazio
2001	Capello	Roma
2002	Lippi	Juventus
2003	Lippi	Juventus

Marco Tardelli turns in triumph after scoring for Italy in the 1982 World Cup Final against West Germany. Tardelli is one of only a select few players to have won every major domestic European honour, as well as a World Cup winner's medal.

Top Goalscorers 1929–2003

SEASON	PLAYER	CLUB	GOALS
1929–30	Meazza	Internazionale	31
1930–31	Volk	Roma	29
1931–32	Petrone	Fiorentina	25
1931–32	Schiavio	Bologna	25
1932–33	Borel II	Juventus	29
1933–34	Borel II	Juventus	32
1934–35	Guaita	Roma	28
1935–36	Meazza	Internazionale	25
1936–37	Piola	Lazio	21
1937–38	Meazza	Internazionale	20
1938–39	Boffi	Milan	19
1938–39	Puricelli	Bologna	19
1939–40	Boffi	Milan	24
1940–41	Puricelli	Bologna	22
1941–42	Boffi	Milan	22
1942–43	Piola	Lazio	21
1943–45	*no competition*		
1945–46	Castiglione	Torino	13
1946–47	V. Mazzola	Torino	29
1947–48	Boniperti	Juventus	27
1948–49	Nyers	Internazionale	26
1949–50	Nordahl	Milan	35
1950–51	Nordahl	Milan	34
1951–52	J. Hansen	Juventus	30
1952–53	Nordahl	Milan	26
1953–54	Nordahl	Milan	23
1954–55	Nordahl	Milan	27
1955–56	Pivatelli	Bologna	29
1956–57	Da Costa	Roma	22
1957–58	Charles	Juventus	28
1958–59	Angelillo	Internazionale	33
1959–60	Sivori	Juventus	27
1960–61	Brighenti	Sampdoria	27
1961–62	Altafini	Milan	22
1961–62	Milani	Fiorentina	22
1962–63	Manfredini	Roma	19
1962–63	Nielsen	Bologna	19
1963–64	Nielsen	Bologna	21
1964–65	A. Mazzola	Internazionale	17
1964–65	Orlando	Fiorentina	17
1965–66	Vinicio	Vicenza	25
1966–67	Riva	Cagliari	18
1967–68	Prati	Milan	15
1968–69	Riva	Cagliari	20
1969–70	Riva	Cagliari	21
1970–71	Boninsegna	Inter	24
1971–72	Boninsegna	Internazionale	22
1972–73	P. Pulici	Torino	17
1972–73	Rivera	Milan	17
1972–73	I. Savoldi	Bologna	17
1973–74	Chignaglia	Lazio	24
1974–75	P. Pulici	Torino	18

Top Goalscorers (*continued*)

SEASON	PLAYER	CLUB	GOALS
1975–76	P. Pulici	Torino	21
1976–77	Graziani	Torino	21
1977–78	P. Rossi	Vicenza	24
1978–79	Giordano	Lazio	19
1979–80	Bettega	Juventus	16
1980–81	Pruzzo	Roma	18
1981–82	Pruzzo	Roma	15
1982–83	Platini	Juventus	16
1983–84	Platini	Juventus	20
1984–85	Platini	Juventus	18
1985–86	Pruzzo	Roma	19
1986–87	Virdis	Milan	17
1987–88	Maradona	Napoli	15
1988–89	Serena	Internazionale	22
1989–90	van Basten	Milan	19
1990–91	Vialli	Sampdoria	17
1991–92	van Basten	Milan	25
1992–93	Signori	Lazio	26
1993–94	Signori	Lazio	23
1994–95	Batistuta	Fiorentina	26
1995–96	Signori	Lazio	24
1995–96	Protti	Bari	24
1996–97	Inzaghi	Atalanta	24
1997–98	Bierhoff	Udinese	27
1998–99	Amoroso	Udinese	22
1999–2000	Schevchenko	Milan	24
2000–01	Crespo	Lazio	26
2001–02	Hubner	Piacenza	24
2001–02	Trezuguet	Juventus	24
2002–03	Vieri	Internazionale	24

Five championships in Italy, and one in Spain with Real Madrid in 1997, have made Fabio Capello one of Europe's most sought-after managers.

Italy

SERIE A 1981–2002

THE 1980s BEGAN IN Serie A as the 1970s had ended: with Juventus, under Giovanni Trapattoni, fielding the core of the Italian national squads for the 1978 and 1982 World Cups, playing with an iron defence and spring-loaded counterattacks, and winning the *Scudetto*. As foreigners were allowed back into the Italian game, Juventus scooped up Liam Brady and the sublime Michel Platini, winning the *Scudetto* again in 1984 and 86. But between these triumphs the title went to smaller, battling sides. Roma won in 1983 under Swede Nils Liedholm and the inspirational Brazilian Falcão. Hellas Verona, under Osvaldo Bagnoli, was promoted from Serie B in 1982 with a core of good Italian players. The team added foreigners Elkjaer and Briegel, pushed hard and took its first and only *Scudetto* in 1985. A burst of money and stars followed, only to see the club disappear from Serie A for most of the 1990s.

Off the field, the legal and economic framework of Italian football was beginning to change, and 1981 saw the introduction of contract freedom for players and the first bidding war for TV rights between the state-owned RAI and Silvio Berlusconi's private channels. RAI won the first round but the steady ratcheting up of the value of TV rights had begun: simultaneously, transfer and wages costs began their inexorable rise.

When Trapattoni and Platini left Juventus in 1986, a power vacuum opened in Serie A and the next five years saw four clubs take the title. First off the mark was Napoli. Under president Ferlaino Corrado, Napoli signed Diego Maradona from Barcelona for a record-breaking fee of £5 million. When the club couldn't find the cash to pay, an appeal for donations saw fans queuing up at the San Paolo stadium to contribute. Coming off his extraordinary performance at the 1986 World Cup, Maradona and coach Ottavio Bianchi took Napoli to its first *Scudetto* (the most southerly in the league's history) and a second three years later in 1990, although accusations of playacting in a crucial game at Atalanta have tarnished the triumph. Maradona's departure saw the side in steady decline until its relegation in 1998.

Berlusconi arrives

Milan had been a shadow of the team's former self, relegated in 1981 after accusations of match-fixing against its president Felice Colombo; the club bounced back only to be relegated again in 1983. In 1986, TV and property magnate Silvio Berlusconi bought the club and its debts, and began turning Milan into a serious business. Installing Arrigo Sacchi as manager, Milan combined a skilled but tough back four (Baresi, Maldini, Tassoti and Costacurta) with Saachi's aggressive pressing game in midfield. The team took the title in 1988 and, adding the star quality of Dutch imports Gullit, van Basten and Rijkaard, went on to take two European Cups. Titles also went to the old money at Internazionale in 1989, and the new

Above: Referee Stefano Braschi refuses to hear Inter's protests as he rules out a goal in its match with Juventus in December 2002.

Right: From cruise ship crooner to media mogul, from president of Milan to Italian prime minister, Silvio Berlusconi has been the single most significant operator in Italian football for almost 20 years.

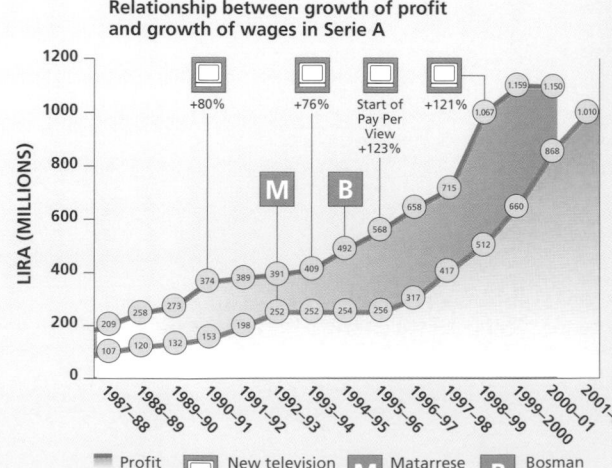

Growth of Profit and Wages

Relationship between growth of profit and growth of wages in Serie A

Profit values (circles along the profit line): 107, 209, 258, 273, 374, 389, 391, 409, 492, 568, 658, 715, 1.067, 1.159, 1.150, 1.010

Wages values (circles along the wages line): 120, 132, 153, 198, 252, 252, 254, 256, 317, 417, 512, 660, 868

Television contract markers: +80%, +76%, Start of Pay Per View +123%, +121%

Years (x-axis): 1987–88, 1988–89, 1989–90, 1990–91, 1991–92, 1992–93, 1993–94, 1994–95, 1995–96, 1996–97, 1997–98, 1998–99, 1999–2000, 2000–01, 2001–02

LIRA (MILLIONS) axis: 0, 200, 400, 600, 800, 1000, 1200

Legend:
- Profit
- Wages
- New television contract
- **M** Matarrese reform*
- **B** Bosman ruling

* Matarrese reform allowed clubs to sign as many players with EU passports as they wanted plus two non-EU passport holders

acquired some serious backing in the form of oil magnate Paolo Mantovani, who astutely built a team around Roberto Mancini and Gianluca Vialli.

The avalanche of TV money and increased attendances that followed the success of Italia '90 saw the old order reassert itself. At Milan, Sacchi had given way to his junior Fabio Capello and the Dutch masters to a new generation of foreign stars (Desailly, Weah, Boban and Savicevic). They duly delivered four out of the next five titles, including an amazing run of 58 unbeaten matches (1991–93) and an entire season 1991–92 undefeated in Serie A. Juventus ended almost a decade without titles, winning under Marcello Lippi in 1995 and again in 1997 and 98. Lippi's squad included Zidane, Davids and Del Piero.

Hysterical spending

Challenges to the big two came from Internazionale, whose hysterical spending in the transfer market, and its turnover of managers, has been second to none. Parma and Fiorentina have also spent big, but cup and European success have not been matched by success in the gruelling league battle. Atalanta, Udinese and Bologna have all established themselves as regular mid-table stayers. The presence of clubs from the south has steadily diminished and only Lecce and Bari have been able to sustain more than a season in the top flight.

The Milan-Juventus monopoly was finally broken by the capital's two big clubs, Lazio and Roma in 2000 and 2001. But the financial bubble burst in 2002 as clubs' income was eaten up by ever increasing salaries. Seasons 2001–02 and 2002–03 saw a return to form by the old guard of teams from the big northern clubs.

Italian League Income (in million lire)

SEASON	1997–98	1998–99	1999–2000	2000–01
Revenue	650	714	1059	1151
Costs	872	1049	1465	1861
Gross profit	-222	-335	-406	-710
Net profit	-38	-11	35	-133

Total for all Serie A clubs

La Vecchia Signora, the 'Old Lady': after a barren spell in the early 1990s, Juventus has come back and has finished in the top two in all but one season since 1994.

Champions' Winning Margin 1992–2002

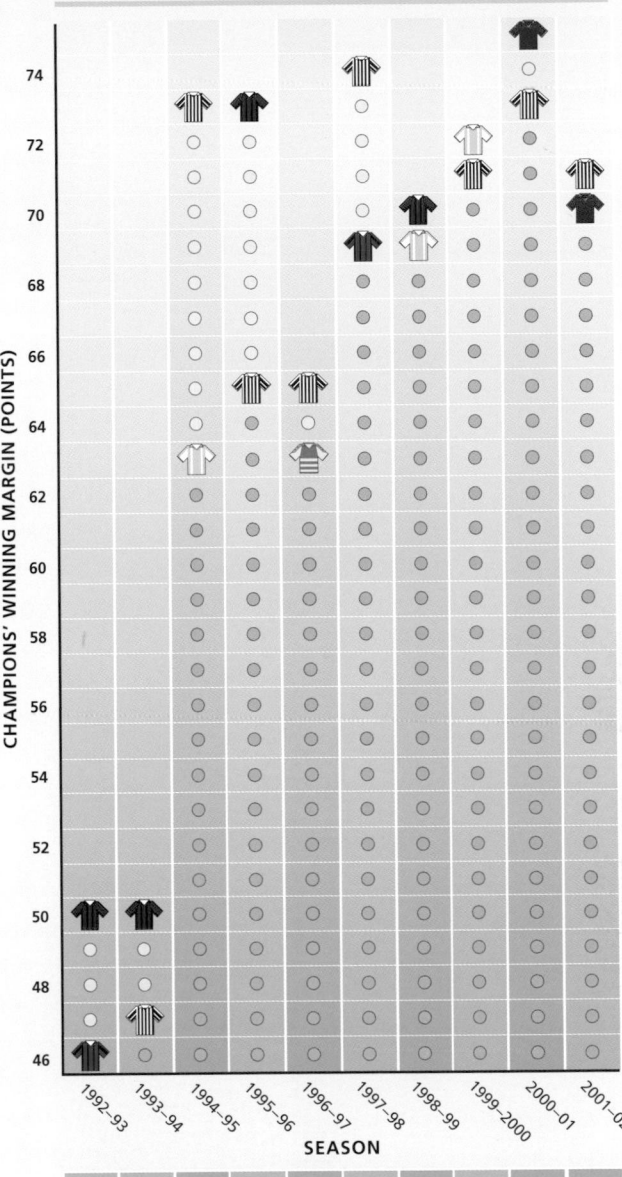

Total games played by each team
(2 points awarded for a win until 1995, when 3 points awarded)

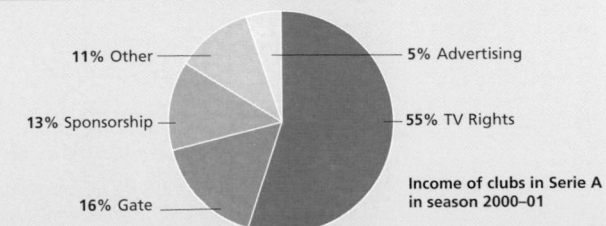

Sources of Income 2001

11% Other
5% Advertising
13% Sponsorship
55% TV Rights
16% Gate

Income of clubs in Serie A in season 2000–01

Italian League Positions 1981–2002

Key to League Positions Table

- ■ League champions
- ■ Season of promotion to league
- ■ Season of relegation from league
- ■ Other teams playing in league
- | 5 | Final position in league

ITALY

Gianluca Vialli helped Sampdoria to the very top of Italian football in the early 1990s. A decade later Vialli was sacked by Watford and Sampdoria have slumped to Serie B.

Fabio Capello, Scudetto *winner with both Milan and Roma, works on his worry lines.*

SEASON

TEAM	81–82	82–83	83–84	84–85	85–86	86–87	87–88	88–89	89–90	90–91	91–92	92–93	93–94	94–95	95–96	96–97	97–98	98–99	99–00	00–01	01–02
Ancona												17									
Ascoli Calcio	6	13	10	14		12	12	12	18		18										
Atalanta			10	8	15		6	7	10	11	7	17		13	10	16				7	9
Avellino	8	9	11	13	12	8	15														
Bari					15				10	13	15			12	15		11	10	14	18	
Bologna	15				14		14	8	18							7	8	9	11	10	7
Brescia											14		18			15				8	13
Cagliari										14	13	6	12	9	10	15		12	17		
Catania				16																	
Catanzaro	7	16																			
Cesena	10	15					9	13	14	17											
Chievo																					5
Como Calcio	16				11	9	9	11	18												
Cremonese			16		13			17		17				10	13	17					
Empoli							16									12	18				
Fiorentina	2	5	3	9	4	10	8	7	12	12	12	16		10	4	9	5	3	7	9	17
Foggia										9	11	9	16								
Genoa	13	12	14						11	4	14	13	11	14							
Internazionale	5	3	4	3	6	3	5	1	3	3	8	2	13	6	7	3	2	8	4	5	3
Juventus	1	2	1	6	1	2	6	4	4	7	2	4	2	1	2	1	1	6	2	2	1
Lazio		13	15					10	9	11	10	5	4	2	3	4	7	2	1	3	6
Lecce					16			9	13	15				18			17		13	13	16
Milan	14		8	5	7	5	1	3	2	2	1	1	1	4	1	11	10	1	3	6	4
Modena																					
Napoli	4	10	12	8	3	1	2	2	1	8	4	11	6	7	12	13	18		17		
Padova															15	18					
Parma										6	7	3	5	3	6	2	6	4	5	4	10
Perugia																16		14	10	11	8
Pescara						14	16				18										
Piacenza														15		14	14	13	13	18	12
Pisa		11	15		14		13	17	16												
Reggina Calcio														14	17		18			12	14
Roma	3	1	2	7	2	7	3	8	6	9	5	10	7	5	5	12	4	5	6	1	2
Salernitana																	15				
Sampdoria		7	7	4	11	6	4	5	5	1	6	7	3	8	8	6	9	16			
Torino	9	8	5	2	5	11	7	15		5	3	9	8	11	16				15		11
Udinese	11	6	9	12	13	16		15			14	16		11	5	3	7	8		12	14
Venezia																		11	16		18
Hellas Verona				4	6	1	10	4	10	11	16		16				17		9	15	15
Vicenza															9	8	14	17		16	

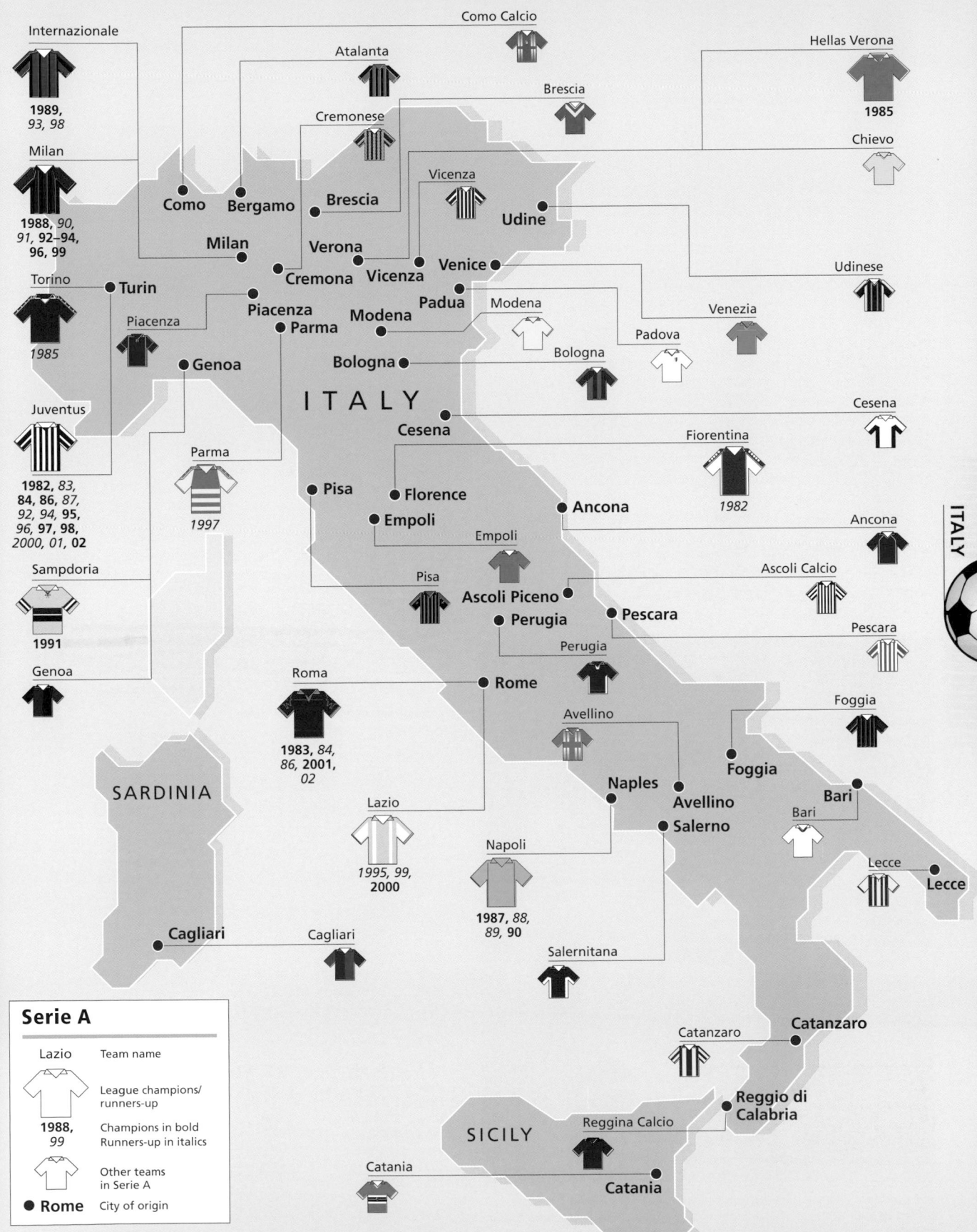

Internazionale
1989, *93, 98*

Milan
1988, *90, 91, 92–94,* **96, 99**

Torino
1985

Piacenza

Juventus
1982, *83,* **84, 86,** *87,* **92, 94, 95, 96, 97, 98,** *2000, 01,* **02**

Parma
1997

Sampdoria
1991

Genoa

Roma
1983, *84,* **86, 2001,** *02*

Lazio
1995, 99, **2000**

Napoli
1987, *88, 89,* **90**

Cagliari

Salernitana

Como Calcio

Atalanta

Cremonese

Brescia

Vicenza

Modena

Bologna

Padova

Empoli

Pisa

Avellino

Hellas Verona
1985

Chievo

Udinese

Venezia

Cesena

Fiorentina
1982

Ancona

Ascoli Calcio

Pescara

Foggia

Bari

Lecce

Catanzaro

Reggina Calcio

Catania

Como
Bergamo
Milan
Cremona
Brescia
Verona
Vicenza
Venice
Udine
Turin
Piacenza
Parma
Piacenza
Padua
Modena
Genoa
Bologna
ITALY
Cesena
Pisa
Florence
Empoli
Ascoli Piceno
Perugia
Pescara
Ancona
Rome
Naples
Avellino
Salerno
Foggia
Bari
Lecce
SARDINIA
Cagliari
Catanzaro
Reggio di Calabria
SICILY
Catania

ITALY

Italy

Federazione Italiana Giuoco Calcio
Founded: 1898
Joined FIFA: 1905
Joined UEFA: 1954

REGULAR COMPETITIVE FOOTBALL LEAGUES had been established in Italy in the 1890s, and the national championship was created in 1898. However, like most things national in Italy, it was in reality rather fragmented and regional. Until 1910 the national component of the championship consisted of various play-off rounds between champions from the north, centre and south of the country and it was only in 1910, and for one season, that a single national league format was used. Indeed, the regional component grew so large that there were 18 separate regional leagues of wildly different standards.

With the advent of professionalism, a single national league was re-established in 1930, and this formed the basis of today's Serie A, the top national division. The title is known as *Lo Scudetto*, and refers to the tricolor shield that the previous year's champions are entitled to wear on their shirts. During the 1980s and 90s Serie A was regarded by many as the most exciting league in Europe.

The Copa Italia, a national cup competition, is a rather more low-key affair, played first in 1922 and again for a few years in the 1930s before being re-established in 1958 to provide an Italian entrant for the Cup-Winners' Cup. The bottom clubs in Serie A do not join until the second round, and the top eight join in the third round.

Italian Amateur League Record 1898–1929

SEASON	CHAMPIONS	RUNNERS-UP
1898	Genoa	Internazionale Torino
1899	Genoa	Internazionale Torino
1900	Genoa	FC Torinese
1901	Milan	Genoa
1902	Genoa	Milan
1903	Genoa	Juventus
1904	Genoa	Juventus
1905	Juventus	Genoa
1906	Milan	Juventus
1907	Milan	Torino
1908	Pro Vercelli	US Milanese
1909	Pro Vercelli	US Milanese
1910	Internazionale	Pro Vercelli
1911	Pro Vercelli	Vicenza
1912	Pro Vercelli	Vicenza
1913	Pro Vercelli	Lazio
1914	Casale	Lazio
1915	Genoa*	
1916–19	*no championship*	
1920	Internazionale	Livorno
1921	Pro Vercelli	Pisa
1922	Novese	Sampierdarenese
1922	Pro Vercelli**	Fortitudo
1923	Genoa	Lazio
1924	Genoa	Savoia
1925	Bologna	Alba
1926	Juventus	Alba
1927	Torino†	Bologna
1928	Torino	Genoa
1929	Bologna	Torino

* Genoa awarded title after league suspended at start of First World War.
** CCI organized championship.
† Torino's title was revoked because of alleged payments to a Juventus player before its match which Torino won 2-1.

Italian Professional League Record 1930–2003

SEASON	CHAMPIONS	RUNNERS-UP
1930	Ambrosiana Inter	Genoa
1931	Juventus	Roma
1932	Juventus	Bologna
1933	Juventus	Ambrosiana Inter
1934	Juventus	Ambrosiana Inter
1935	Juventus	Ambrosiana Inter
1936	Bologna	Roma
1937	Bologna	Lazio
1938	Ambrosiana Inter	Juventus
1939	Bologna	Torino
1940	Ambrosiana Inter	Bologna
1941	Bologna	Ambrosiana Inter
1942	Roma	Torino
1943	Torino	Livorno
1944–45	*no championship*	
1946	Torino	Juventus
1947	Torino	Juventus
1948	Torino	Milan
1949	Torino	Internazionale
1950	Juventus	Milan
1951	Milan	Internazionale
1952	Juventus	Milan
1953	Internazionale	Juventus
1954	Internazionale	Juventus
1955	Milan	Udinese
1956	Fiorentina	Milan

Football is a team game and one player does not always make a difference. However, Diego Maradona inspired Napoli to two Italian championships and UEFA Cup glory during his seven-year stay.

ITALY

Italian Professional League Record (*continued*)

SEASON	CHAMPIONS	RUNNERS-UP
1957	Milan	Fiorentina
1958	Juventus	Fiorentina
1959	Milan	Fiorentina
1960	Juventus	Fiorentina
1961	Juventus	Milan
1962	Milan	Internazionale
1963	Internazionale	Juventus
1964	Bologna	Internazionale
1965	Internazionale	Milan
1966	Internazionale	Bologna
1967	Juventus	Internazionale
1968	Milan	Napoli
1969	Fiorentina	Cagliari
1970	Cagliari	Internazionale
1971	Internazionale	Milan
1972	Juventus	Milan
1973	Juventus	Milan
1974	Lazio	Juventus
1975	Juventus	Napoli
1976	Torino	Juventus
1977	Juventus	Torino
1978	Juventus	Vicenza
1979	Milan	Perugia
1980	Internazionale	Juventus
1981	Juventus	Roma
1982	Juventus	Fiorentina
1983	Roma	Juventus
1984	Juventus	Roma
1985	Verona	Torino
1986	Juventus	Roma
1987	Napoli	Juventus
1988	Milan	Napoli
1989	Internazionale	Napoli
1990	Napoli	Milan
1991	Sampdoria	Milan
1992	Milan	Juventus
1993	Milan	Internazionale
1994	Milan	Juventus
1995	Juventus	Lazio
1996	Milan	Juventus
1997	Juventus	Parma
1998	Juventus	Internazionale
1999	Milan	Lazio
2000	Lazio	Juventus
2001	Roma	Juventus
2002	Juventus	Roma
2003	Juventus	Internazionale

Italian League Summary

TEAM	TOTALS	CHAMPIONS & RUNNERS-UP (BOLD) (*ITALICS*)
Juventus	27, 19	1903, 04, **05**, 06, **26**, 31–35, 38, 46, 47, **50**, **52**, 53, 54, 58, 60, 61, 63, 67, **72**, 73, 74, 75, 76, **77**, **78**, 80, **81**, **82**, 83, **84**, **86**, 87, 92, 94, **95**, 96, **97**, **98**, 2000, 01, **02**, 03
Milan	16, 12	**1901**, 02, **06**, **07**, 48, 50, **51**, 52, **55**, 56, **57**, 59, **61**, **62**, **65**, 68, 71–73, **79**, 88, 90, 91, **92**–**94**, **96**, **99**
Internazionale (includes Ambrosiana Inter)	13, 13	**1910**, **20**, **30**, 33–35, **38**, **40**, 41, 49, 51, **53**, **54**, 62, **63**, **64**, **65**, 66, **67**, 70, **71**, 80, **89**, 93, 98, **2003**
Genoa	9, 4	**1898**–**1900**, **01**, **02**–**04**, **05**, 15, 23, 24, 28, 30
Torino	8, 6	1907, **27**, 28, 29, 39, **42**, **43**, **46**–**49**, 76, 77, **85**
Bologna	7, 4	**1925**, 27, **29**, **32**, **36**, **37**, 39, 40, 41, **64**, 66

Italian League Summary (*continued*)

TEAM	TOTALS	CHAMPIONS & RUNNERS-UP (BOLD) (*ITALICS*)
Pro Vercelli	7, 1	**1908**, **09**, **10**, **11**–**13**, **21**, 22
Roma	3, 6	1931, 36, 42, 81, **83**, 84, 86, **2001**, 02
Lazio	2, 6	1913, 14, 23, 37, **74**, 95, 99, **2000**
Fiorentina	2, 5	**1956**, 57–60, **69**, 82
Napoli	2, 4	1968, 75, **87**, 88, 89, **90**
Cagliari	1, 1	1969, **70**
Casale	1, 0	**1914**
Novese	1, 0	**1922**
Sampdoria	1, 0	**1991**
Verona	1, 0	**1985**
Vicenza	0, 3	1911, 12, 78
Alba	0, 2	1925, 26
Internazionale Torino	0, 2	1898, 99
Livorno	0, 2	1920, 43
US Milanese	0, 2	1908, 09
FC Torinese	0, 1	1900
Fortitudo	0, 1	1922
Parma	0, 1	1997
Perugia	0, 1	1979
Pisa	0, 1	1921
Sampierdarenese	0, 1	1922
Savoia	0, 1	1924
Udinese	0, 1	1955

Italian Cup Record 1922–2003

YEAR	WINNERS	SCORE	RUNNERS-UP
1922	Vado	1-0 (aet)	Udinese
1923–35		*no competition*	
1936	Torino	5-1	Alessandria
1937	Genoa	1-0	Roma
1938	Juventus	3-1, 2-1 (2 legs)	Torino
1939	Internazionale	2-1	Novara
1940	Fiorentina	1-0	Genoa
1941	Venezia	3-3 (aet), (replay) **1-0**	Roma
1942	Juventus	1-1 (aet), (replay) **4-1**	Milan
1943	Torino	4-0	Venezia
1944–57		*no competition*	
1958	Lazio	1-0	Fiorentina
1959	Juventus	4-1	Internazionale
1960	Juventus	3-2 (aet)	Fiorentina
1961	Fiorentina	2-0	Lazio
1962	Napoli	2-1	Spal
1963	Atalanta	3-1	Torino
1964	Roma	0-0 (aet), (replay) **1-0**	Torino
1965	Juventus	1-0	Internazionale
1966	Fiorentina	2-1 (aet)	Catanzaro
1967	Milan	1-0	Padova
1968	Torino	(mini-league format)	Milan
1969	Roma	(mini-league format)	Cagliari
1970	Bologna	(mini-league format)	Torino
1971	Torino	(mini-league format)	Milan
1972	Milan	2-0	Napoli
1973	Milan	1-1 (5-2 pens)	Juventus
1974	Bologna	0-0 (5-4 pens)	Palermo
1975	Fiorentina	3-2	Milan
1976	Napoli	4-0	Verona
1977	Milan	2-0	Internazionale
1978	Internazionale	2-1	Napoli
1979	Juventus	2-1 (aet)	Palermo
1980	Roma	0-0 (3-2 pens)	Torino
1981	Roma	1-1, (replay) 1-1 (5-3 pens)	Torino

Italian Cup Record (*continued*)

YEAR	WINNERS	SCORE	RUNNERS-UP
1982	Internazionale	1-0, 1-1 (2 legs)	Torino
1983	Juventus	0-2, 3-0 (aet) (2 legs)	Verona
1984	Roma	1-1, 1-0 (2 legs)	Verona
1985	Sampdoria	1-0, 2-1 (2 legs)	Milan
1986	Roma	1-2, 2-0 (2 legs)	Sampdoria
1987	Napoli	3-0, 1-0 (2 legs)	Atalanta
1988	Sampdoria	2-0, 1-2 (aet) (2 legs)	Torino
1989	Sampdoria	0-1, 4-0 (2 legs)	Napoli
1990	Juventus	0-0, 1-0 (2 legs)	Milan
1991	Roma	3-1, 1-1 (2 legs)	Sampdoria
1992	Parma	0-1, 2-0 (2 legs)	Juventus
1993	Torino	3-0, 2-5 (2 legs)	Roma
1994	Sampdoria	0-0, 6-1 (2 legs)	Ancona
1995	Juventus	2-0, 1-0 (2 legs)	Parma
1996	Fiorentina	1-0, 2-0 (2 legs)	Atalanta
1997	Vicenza	0-1, 3-0 (aet) (2 legs)	Napoli
1998	Lazio	0-1, 3-1 (2 legs)	Milan
1999	Parma	1-1, 2-2 (2 legs)	Fiorentina
2000	Lazio	2-1, 0-0 (2 legs)	Internazionale
2001	Fiorentina	1-0, 1-1 (2 legs)	Parma
2002	Parma*	1-2, 1-0 (2 legs)	Juventus
2003	Milan	4-1, 2-2 (2 legs)	Roma

* Denotes winners on away goals rule.

The San Siro plays host *to one of the most hotly-contested derbies in Italian football: Milan v Internazionale. The fans of both sides greet the teams with a show with flags, scarves and flares.*

Italian Cup Summary

TEAM	TOTALS	WINNERS & RUNNERS-UP (BOLD) (*ITALICS*)
Juventus	9, 3	**1938, 42, 59, 60, 65,** *73,* **79, 83, 90, 92, 95,** *2002*
Roma	7, 4	*1937, 41,* **64, 69, 80, 81, 84, 86,** *91, 93,* **2003**
Fiorentina	6, 3	**1940,** *58,* **60, 61, 66,** *75,* **96,** *99,* **2001**
Torino	5, 8	**1936,** *38,* **43,** *63, 64,* **68,** *70, 71, 80–82,* **88,** *93*
Milan	5, 7	*1942, 67, 68, 71,* **72, 73,** *75,* **77,** *85, 90, 98,* **2003**
Sampdoria	4, 2	**1985,** *86,* **88, 89,** *91,* **94**
Internazionale	3, 4	**1939,** *59,* **65,** *77,* **78,** *82, 2000*
Napoli	3, 4	**1962,** *72, 76, 78,* **87,** *89,* **97**
Parma	3, 2	**1992,** *95,* **99,** *2001,* **02**
Lazio	3, 1	**1958,** *61,* **98, 2000**
Bologna	2, 0	**1970, 74**
Atalanta	1, 2	**1963,** *87, 96*
Genoa	1, 1	**1937,** *40*
Venezia	1, 1	**1941,** *43*
Vado	1, 0	**1922**
Vicenza	1, 0	**1997**
Verona	0, 3	*1976, 83, 84*
Palermo	0, 2	*1974, 79*
Alessandria	0, 1	*1936*
Ancona	0, 1	*1994*
Cagliari	0, 1	*1969*
Catanzaro	0, 1	*1966*
Novara	0, 1	*1939*
Padova	0, 1	*1967*
Spal	0, 1	*1962*
Udinese	0, 1	*1922*

ITALY

Malta

Malta Football Association
Founded: 1900
Joined FIFA: 1959
Joined UEFA: 1960

THE MALTA FOOTBALL ASSOCIATION was formed in 1900, when the island was still under British rule. It was in turn affiliated to the FA in London, rather than FIFA, for the first half of the century. A league was first played in 1910, and in 1935 the Malta FA Trophy competition was inaugurated. Self-government of the country began in 1947, though membership of FIFA in 1959 (and UEFA in 1960) preceded Malta's full independence, gained in 1964. Despite this, the country played their first World Cup qualifying campaign in an African group in 1960.

League and cup competitions have been dominated by five teams – Floriana, Sliema Wanderers, Valletta, Hamrun Spartans and Hibernians. There are ten teams in the top flight playing each other three times a season (extended from twice in a season in 1996). All games are played in the Ta' Qali national stadium in Valletta. Promotion and relegation is a simple two up, two down system. In addition to the Maltese Trophy Cup (listed here) top teams also compete in the Löwenbrau Super Cup and the Löwenbrau Fives Cup.

Maltese League Record 1910–2003

SEASON	CHAMPIONS	SEASON	CHAMPIONS
1910	Floriana	1952	Floriana
1911	no championship	1953	Floriana
1912	Floriana	1954	Sliema Wanderers
1913	Floriana	1955	Floriana
1914	Hamrun Spartans	1956	Sliema Wanderers
1915	Valletta United	1957	Sliema Wanderers
1916	no championship	1958	Floriana
1917	St George's	1959	Valletta
1918	Hamrun Spartans	1960	Valletta
1919	KOMR Militia	1961	Hibernians
1920	Sliema Wanderers	1962	Floriana
1921	Floriana	1963	Valletta
1922	Floriana	1964	Sliema Wanderers
1923	Sliema Wanderers	1965	Sliema Wanderers
1924	Sliema Wanderers	1966	Sliema Wanderers
1925	Floriana	1967	Hibernians
1926	Sliema Wanderers	1968	Floriana
1927	Floriana	1969	Hibernians
1928	Floriana	1970	Floriana
1929	Floriana	1971	Sliema Wanderers
1930	Sliema Wanderers	1972	Sliema Wanderers
1931	Floriana	1973	Floriana
1932	Valletta United	1974	Valletta
1933	Sliema Wanderers	1975	Floriana
1934	Sliema Wanderers	1976	Sliema Wanderers
1935	Floriana	1977	Floriana
1936	Sliema Wanderers	1978	Valletta
1937	Floriana	1979	Hibernians
1938	Sliema Wanderers	1980	Valletta
1939	Sliema Wanderers	1981	Hibernians
1940	Sliema Wanderers	1982	Hibernians
1941–44	no championship	1983	Hamrun Spartans
1945	Valletta	1984	Valletta
1946	Valletta	1985	Rabat Ajax
1947	Hamrun Spartans	1986	Rabat Ajax
1948	Valletta	1987	Hamrun Spartans
1949	Sliema Wanderers	1988	Hamrun Spartans
1950	Floriana	1989	Sliema Wanderers
1951	Floriana	1990	Valletta

Maltese League Record (continued)

SEASON	CHAMPIONS	SEASON	CHAMPIONS
1991	Hamrun Spartans	1999	Valletta
1992	Valletta	2000	Birkirkara
1993	Floriana	2001	Valletta
1994	Hibernians	2002	Hibernians
1995	Hibernians	2003	Sliema Wanderers
1996	Sliema Wanderers		
1997	Valletta		
1998	Valletta		

Maltese Cup Record 1935–2003

YEAR	WINNERS	YEAR	WINNERS
1935	Sliema Wanderers	1972	Floriana
1936	Sliema Wanderers	1973	Gżira United
1937	Sliema Wanderers	1974	Sliema Wanderers
1938	Floriana	1975	Valletta
1939	Melita St Julians	1976	Floriana
1940	Sliema Wanderers	1977	Valletta
1941–44	no competition	1978	Valletta
1945	Floriana	1979	Sliema Wanderers
1946	Sliema Wanderers	1980	Hibernians
1947	Floriana	1981	Floriana
1948	Sliema Wanderers	1982	Hibernians
1949	Floriana	1983	Hamrun Spartans
1950	Floriana	1984	Hamrun Spartans
1951	Sliema Wanderers	1985	Żurrieq
1952	Sliema Wanderers	1986	Rabat Ajax
1953	Floriana	1987	Hamrun Spartans
1954	Floriana	1988	Hamrun Spartans
1955	Floriana	1989	Hamrun Spartans
1956	Sliema Wanderers	1990	Sliema Wanderers
1957	Floriana	1991	Valletta
1958	Floriana	1992	Hamrun Spartans
1959	Sliema Wanderers	1993	Floriana
1960	Valletta	1994	Floriana
1961	Floriana	1995	Valletta
1962	Hibernians	1996	Valletta
1963	Sliema Wanderers	1997	Valletta
1964	Valletta	1998	Hibernians
1965	Sliema Wanderers	1999	Valletta
1966	Floriana	2000	Sliema Wanderers
1967	Floriana	2001	Valletta
1968	Sliema Wanderers	2002	Birkirkara
1969	Sliema Wanderers	2003	Birkirkara
1970	Hibernians		
1971	Hibernians		

San Marino

Federazione Sammarinese Giuoco Calcio
Founded: 1931
Joined FIFA: 1988
Joined UEFA: 1988

San Marino is a tiny independent enclave in northern Italy. Organized football dates back to the 1930s, but it was only in 1988 that they joined UEFA and began to play internationals. The league has 16 teams in two groups of eight with the top three in each progressing to an end of season play-off for the championship.

SEASON	LEAGUE CHAMPIONS
1999	Faetano
2000	Folgore
2001	Cosmos
2002	Domagnano
2003	Domagnano

YEAR	CUP WINNERS
1998	Faetano
1999	Cosmos
2000	Tre Penne
2001	Domagnano
2002	Domagnano

MALTA, SAN MARINO

Central Europe

THE SEASONS IN REVIEW 2002–03

THE BIGGEST RESULT IN CENTRAL EUROPEAN football this year was the successful bid by Switzerland and Austria to host the 2008 European Championships, beating off admittedly weak bids from, among other places, Scotland and Ireland, the Nordic countries, Russia and Hungary. Results in European football were not as good. FC Basel's progress to the second round of the Champions League was by far and away the strongest showing; it was the only central European club to make it out of the qualifying stages, though Zalaegerszegi's home win in a losing tie against Manchester United in the qualifying stages was a memorable triumph. Things were hardly better in the UEFA Cup where only Slavia Praha made it as far as the fourth round.

In Austria there was never anyone in the title chase except Austria Wien. Under new German coach Christoph Daum, the club went straight to the top of the table and never looked like losing its place. Its domestic dominance was sealed when it won the Cup as well. Vladamir Janocko, its Slovak midfielder, was the heart of the team. The biggest surprise was that newly promoted SV Pasching made a decent start and stayed up, though Grazer's rise from the bottom of the table to second spot under coach Walter Schachner was pretty unlikely.

In the Czech Republic Sparta and Slavia slugged it out for the top spot. The decisive moment came in April when Sparta beat Slavia in the Prague Derby 2-0 at home. Sparta went into the penultimate game of the season needing a win to be sure of the title. Ahead and cruising to victory against the small Prague club Bohemians, the game was abandoned after Bohemians fans attacked an assistant referee who had allowed a Sparta goal they considered to be offside. The game was awarded to Sparta and with it the title. Bohemians was relegated.

In Hungary, MTK squeezed into the top spot after chasing Ferencváros through the spring Wisła Kraków won the first half of its double in May. Despite losing the first leg of the Cup Final to Wisła Płock, it roared back in the second away leg to win 3-1 on aggregate. In Slovakia, Slovan Bratislava was the league leader for most of the season, but was caught by the eventual

Austrian Bundesliga Table 2002–03

CLUB	P	W	D	L	F	A	Pts	
FK Austria Wien	36	21	7	8	59	28	70	Champions League
Grazer AK	36	15	12	9	56	39	57	Champions League
SV Salzburg	36	15	11	10	51	46	56	UEFA Cup
SK Rapid Wien	36	13	12	11	40	38	51	
SV Pasching	36	13	10	13	41	37	49	
SK Sturm Graz	36	14	5	17	50	62	47	
VfB Admira Wacker Mödling	36	11	11	14	36	46	44	
FC Kärnten	36	11	8	17	45	57	41	UEFA Cup (cup finalists)
SW Bregenz	36	9	12	15	48	58	39	
SV Ried	36	10	8	18	41	56	38	Relegated

Promoted club: SV Mattersburg.

Austrian International Club Performances 2002–03

CLUB	COMPETITION	PROGRESS
Grazer AK	Champions League	3rd Qualifying Stage
	UEFA Cup	1st Round
SK Sturm Graz	Champions League	3rd Qualifying Stage
	UEFA Cup	3rd Round
FC Kärnten	UEFA Cup	1st Round
Austria Wien	UEFA Cup	2nd Round

Austrian Top Goalscorers 2002–03

PLAYER	CLUB	NATIONALITY	GOALS
Axel Lawaree	SW Bregenz	Belgian	21
Eduard Glieder	SV Salzburg	Austrian	16
Marijo Maric	FC Kärnten	Croatian	16
Vladimir Janocko	FK Austria Wien	Slovakian	12

Austrian Cup

2003 FINAL

June 1 – Schwarzenegger Stadion, Graz

FK Austria 3-0 FC Kärnten Wien

(Janacko 15,
Rushfeldt 47, 87)

h/t: 1-0   **Att:** 6,000
Ref: Steiner

Austria Vienna celebrates its cup win over FC Kärnten and the Austrian double under German coach Christoph Daum.

Friedrich Stickler (left), president of Austria's soccer association, prays and Ralph Zloczower (right), president of Switzerland's soccer association, makes a call on his mobile phone while waiting for the decision by UEFA on the hosts for the 2008 European football Championship in Geneva.

Czech Republic League Table 2002–03

CLUB	P	W	D	L	F	A	Pts	
Sparta Praha	30	20	5	5	51	17	65	Champions League
Slavia Praha	30	18	10	2	65	19	64	Champions League
Slovan Liberec	30	14	8	8	43	36	50	
Viktoria Žižkov	30	14	8	8	38	33	50	UEFA Cup
Baník Ostrava	30	13	6	11	41	38	45	
FK Teplice	30	13	6	11	33	32	45	UEFA Cup (cup winners)
FC Zlín	30	11	9	10	34	41	42	
1. FC Synot	30	11	7	12	39	40	40	
FC Stavo Artikel Brno	30	10	9	11	35	31	39	
Marila Příbram	30	9	12	9	34	30	39	
Sigma Olomouc	30	8	10	12	29	33	34	
FK Jablonec 97	30	7	13	10	29	39	34	
Ceske Budéjovice	30	8	6	16	36	54	30	
Chmel Blšany	30	7	7	16	28	39	28	
Bohemians Praha	30	5	9	16	34	56	24	Relegated
SK Hradec Králové	30	3	13	14	23	54	22	Relegated

Promoted clubs: FC Viktoria Plzen, Slezsky FC Opava.

Czech Rep International Club Performances 2002–03

CLUB	COMPETITION	PROGRESS
Sparta Praha	Champions League	3rd Qualifying Stage
	UEFA Cup	2nd Round
Slovan Liberec	Champions League	3rd Qualifying Stage
	UEFA Cup	3rd Round
Sigma Olomouc	UEFA Cup	Qualification Round
Slavia Praha	UEFA Cup	4th Round
Viktoria Žižkov	UEFA Cup	2nd Round

Czech Republic Top Goalscorers 2002–03

PLAYER	CLUB	NATIONALITY	GOALS
Jiri Kowalik	1. FC Synot	Czech	16
Vaclav Sverkos	Baník Ostrava	Czech	14
Ales Piki	Viktoria Žižkov	Czech	11
Libor Dosek	FC Stavo Artikel Brno	Czech	10
Tomas Dosek	Slavia Praha	Czech	10

The Prague Derby.
Slavia's Patrik Gedeon charges past Sparta's Martin Petras. Sparta won 2-0 in mid April and effectively won the championship.

Czech Republic Cup

2003 FINAL

May 27 – Strahov Stadium, Prague
FK Teplice 1-0 FK Jablonec 97
(Hunal 32)
h/t: 1-0 **Att:** 5,833
Ref: Gulajev

Hungarian Champions League Table 2002–03

CLUB	P	W	D	L	F	A	Pts	
MTK Hungária FC	32	20	6	6	59	34	66	Champions League
Ferencváros	32	19	7	6	50	24	64	UEFA Cup
Debreceni VSC	32	13	14	5	57	38	53	UEFA Cup (cup finalists)
Újpestl FC	32	15	7	10	54	41	52	
Siófok	32	12	11	9	46	44	47	
Győri ETO FC	32	9	9	14	41	50	36	

Hungarian Relegation League Table 2002–03

CLUB	P	W	D	L	F	A	Pts	
Zalahús ZTE FC	32	15	8	9	62	49	53	
Videoton	32	11	7	14	46	41	40	
Matáv Sopron	32	9	9	14	47	54	36	
Békéscsaba	32	9	5	18	42	71	32	
Kispest-Honvéd FC	32	8	5	19	43	66	29	Relegated
Dunaferr SE	32	4	8	20	37	72	20	Relegated

Promoted clubs: Pécs, Haladas (Szombathely).
The Hungarian season is divided into two. In the first half of the season 12 clubs play each other three times. The top six go into a final championship league taking the points with them and play each other once. The bottom six go into a similar relegation league.

Hungarian International Club Performances 2002–03

CLUB	COMPETITION	PROGRESS
Zalahús ZTE FC	Champions League	3rd Qualifying Stage
	UEFA Cup	1st Round
Ferencváros	UEFA Cup	2nd Round
Újpesti FC	UEFA Cup	1st Round

Hungarian Top Goalscorers 2002–03

PLAYER	CLUB	NATIONALITY	GOALS
Krisztián Kenesei	Zalahús ZTE FC	Hungarian	22
Béla Illés	MTK Hungária FC	Hungarian	21
Sumudica	Debreceni VSC	Hungarian	16
Atilla Tököli	Ferencváros	Hungarian	15

Hungarian Cup

2003 FINAL

May 6 – Ferenc Puskás Stadium, Budapest
Ferencváros 2-1 Debreceni VSC
(Tölköi 68, 78)   (Szücs o.g. 43)
h/t: 0-1 **Att:** 10,000
Ref: Megybírí

Top of Page: Last season's top scorer in Hungary, Ferencváros' Atilla Tököli, celebrates another goal, but it's not enough to take the title which went to Budapest arch-rivals MTK.

CENTRAL EUROPE

champions MSK Zilina. To make matters worse, Slovan lost the Cup in extra time to lowly Matador Púchov. Slovenia, by contrast saw the usual suspect, NK Maribor, take the title in a late run of form, overtaking the earlier leaders and cup finalists Publikum and Olimpija Ljubljana.

In Switzerland, football was played, uncharacteristically for the country, against a backdrop of financial problems and low level crowd trouble. A number of second division clubs looked like going out of business and things weren't much healthier at the top. FC Basel's crowd proved particularly feisty, and the club suffered a number of fines and was forced to play home games without the crowd. In the league, Grasshoppers and FC Basel were just in a different class, over 20 points ahead of the third place side – Neuchatel Xamax. The difference in quality was cruelly exposed in the Cup Final when Basel beat Neuchatel 6-0. But in the League it was Grasshoppers who took the title – FC Basel's Champions League adventure proving too onerous a task on top of domestic duties as well.

Polish Champions League Table 2002–03

CLUB	P	W	D	L	F	A	Pts	
Wisła Kraków	30	21	5	4	75	28	**68**	Champions League
Groclin Dysko-bolia Grodzisk	30	18	8	4	56	26	**62**	UEFA Cup
GKS Katowice	30	19	4	7	39	21	**61**	UEFA Cup
Legia Warszawa	30	17	9	4	61	29	**60**	
Odra Wadzisław	30	17	5	8	55	42	**56**	
Amica Wronki	30	11	10	9	43	34	**43**	
Górnik Zabrze	30	10	11	9	46	32	**41**	
Polonia Warszawa	30	11	8	11	37	45	**41**	

Polish Relegation League Table 2002–03

CLUB	P	W	D	L	F	A	Pts	
Orlen Plock	30	10	7	13	29	38	**37**	UEFA Cup (cup winners)
Widzew Łódź	30	10	7	13	29	39	**37**	
Lech Poznan	30	8	11	11	41	38	**35**	
Zagłębie Lublin	30	8	8	14	34	44	**32**	
Garbarnia SJ	30	8	8	14	40	54	**32**	
Ruch Chorzów	30	7	11	12	29	39	**32**	Relegated
KSZO Ostrowiec	30	4	3	23	21	63	**15**	Relegated
Pogoń Szczecin	30	2	3	25	14	77	**9**	Relegated

Promoted clubs: KS Górnik Polkowice, MKS Swit Nowy Dwor Mazowiecki, GKS Górnik Leczna.
The Polish season is divided into two. In the first half of the season two leagues of eight clubs play each other twice. The top four from each group go into a final championship league taking their points with them and play each other twice. The bottom four from each group go into a similar relegation league.

Polish International Club Performances 2002–03

CLUB	COMPETITION	PROGRESS
Legia Warszawa	Champions League UEFA Cup	3rd Qualifying Stage 2nd Round
Wisła Kraków	UEFA Cup	4th Round
Polonia Warszawa	UEFA Cup	1st Round
Amica Wronki	UEFA Cup	2nd Round

Polish Top Goalscorers 2002–03

PLAYER	CLUB	NATIONALITY	GOALS
Stanko Svitlica	Legia Warszawa	Polish	24
Maciej Zurawski	Wisła Kraków	Polish	22
Marcin Kuzba	Wisła Kraków	Polish	21
Andrzej Niedzielan	Górnik Zabrze	Polish	15

Slovakian Mars Superliga Table 2002–03

CLUB	P	W	D	L	F	A	Pts	
MSK Žilina	34	20	6	8	65	28	**66**	Champions League
Slovan Bratislava	34	19	6	9	57	35	**63**	UEFA Cup
Artmedia Petrzalka	34	18	7	9	46	31	**61**	
Spartak Trnava	34	13	11	10	48	46	**50**	
Matador Púchov	34	13	8	13	43	42	**47**	UEFA Cup (cup winners)
ZTS Dubnica	34	12	6	16	39	49	**42**	
SCP Ružomberok	34	12	5	17	42	55	**41**	
Inter Bratislava	34	11	7	16	42	54	**40**	
Ozeta Dukla Trenčin	34	11	3	20	43	64	**36**	
1. FC Košice	34	6	11	17	37	58	**29**	Relegated

Promoted club: FC Dukla Banská Bystrica.

Slovakian International Club Performances 2002–03

CLUB	COMPETITION	PROGRESS
MSK Žilina	Champions League	2nd Qualifying Stage
Matador Púchov	UEFA Cup	1st Round
Koba Senec	UEFA Cup	Qualifying Round

Slovakian Top Goalscorers 2002–03

PLAYER	CLUB	NATIONALITY	GOALS
Marek Mintál	MSK Žilina	Slovakian	21
Lubos Pernis	Matador Púchov	Slovakian	15
Robert Vittek	Slovan Bratislava	Slovakian	14
Henrick Bencik	Artmedia Petrzalka	Slovakian	11

Left: Wisła Kraków celebrates its Polish League triumph and a memorable double having won the Polish Cup beforehand.

Below: The Slovakian Cup Final – Slovan Bratislava in blue and Matador Púchov in red slug it out; a dismal 12,000 showed up.

Polish Cup

2003 FINAL (2 legs)

May 7 – Wisła Stadium, Kraków
Wisła Kraków 0-1 Wisła Plock
(Jelen 15)
h/t: 0-1 **Att:** 5,500
Ref: Malek

May 10 – Orlen Stadium, Plock
Wisła Plock 0-3 Wisła Kraków
(Zurawski 27, Kuzba 59, 60)
h/t: 0-1 **Att:** 8,000
Ref: Ryzska

Wisła Kraków won 3-1 on aggregate

Slovakian Cup

2003 FINAL

May 8 – Topol Stadium, Topolcany
Matador 2-1 Slovan
Púchov   Bratislava
*(Pernis 111,   (Hornyák 114)
Breska 116)*
(after extra time)
h/t: 0-0 **90 mins:** 0-0
Att: 12,000 **Ref:** Gadosi

Slovenian Premier League Table 2002–03

CLUB	P	W	D	L	F	A	Pts	
NK Maribor	31	18	8	5	57	32	**62**	Champions League
NK Publikum	31	15	10	6	57	38	**55**	UEFA Cup
SCT Olimpija Ljubljana	31	14	12	5	54	32	**54**	UEFA Cup (cup winners)
Esotec Smartno	31	12	10	9	46	42	**46**	
NK Koper	31	12	9	10	41	41	**45**	
Primorje Ajdovščina	31	13	5	13	47	44	**44**	
NK Dravograd	31	9	9	13	40	43	**36**	
HIT Gorica	31	7	13	11	34	43	**34**	
Mura Murska Sobota	31	9	7	15	38	48	**34**	
Ljubljana	31	9	6	16	41	66	**30**	
NK Rudar Velenje*	31	6	7	18	32	51	**25**	Relegated
Korotan Prevalje†	11	2	4	5	7	14	**3**	Relegated

Promoted clubs: NK Domzale, Drava Ptuj.
* Ljubljana was deducted three points for a no-show.
† Prevalje was excluded after two no-shows and only the team's matches from rounds 1–11 count. It was also deducted seven points.

Slovenian International Club Performances 2002–03

CLUB	COMPETITION	PROGRESS
NK Maribor	Champions League	2nd Qualifying Stage
Primorje Ajdovščina	UEFA Cup	1st Round
HIT Gorica	UEFA Cup	Qualifying Round

Slovenian Top Goalscorers 2002–03

PLAYER	CLUB	NATIONALITY	GOALS
Marko Kmetic	Olimpija Ljubljana	Slovenian	23
Marko Vogric	Primorje	Slovenian	17
Ramiz Smajlovic	Smartno	Slovenian	16

Slovenian Cup

2003 FINAL (2 legs)

May 14 – Bezigrad Stadium, Ljubljana
Olimpija 1-1 Publikum Celje
Ljubljana
(Puc 89)   (Kvas 38 pen)
h/t: 0-1   **Att:** 4,000
Ref: Ceferin

May 21 – Celje Skalna Klet, Celje
Publikum 2-2 Olimpija
Celje   **Ljubljana**
(Koren 15,   (Zlogar 59,
Kvas 72)   Prosinecki 65)
h/t: 1-0   **Att:** 3,000
Ref: Krajnc

Olimpija Ljubljana won on away goals rule

Below, right: Christian Gross, FC Basel's boss, points the way. Under Gross, Basel made it to the second group stage of the Champions League, where it was hardly outclassed – a major achievement.

Below: Slovenian football's best European performance this season was Primorje's charge to the first round of the UEFA Cup, seen here against Wisła Kraków to whom the team lost.

Swiss Championship Play-off Table 2002–03

CLUB	P	W	D	L	F	A	Pts	
Grasshopper-Club	14	9	5	0	37	15	**57**	Champions League
FC Basel	14	10	2	2	38	17	**56**	UEFA Cup
Neuchatel Xamax FC	14	5	4	5	18	17	**35**	UEFA Cup
BSC Young Boys Berne	14	6	1	7	21	29	**34**	UEFA Cup
FC Zürich	14	4	3	7	20	23	**31**	
Servette FC	14	4	4	6	16	26	**31**	
FC Thun	14	3	3	8	18	30	**28**	
FC Wil 1900	14	2	4	8	19	30	**26**	

Promoted clubs: FC Aarau, FC St.-Gallen.
The Swiss season is divided into two. The first half of the season is a regular 12-club league with each team playing each other twice. For the second half of the season, the top eight teams go into a final championship league (taking half their points with them) where they play each other twice. The bottom four teams join the top four from the second division in a promotion/relegation league.

Swiss International Club Performances 2002–03

CLUB	COMPETITION	PROGRESS
FC Basel	Champions League	2nd Group Stage
Grasshopper-Club	UEFA Cup	2nd Round
Servette FC	UEFA Cup	1st Round

Swiss Top Goalscorers 2002–03

PLAYER	CLUB	NATIONALITY	GOALS
Richard Nuñez	Grasshopper-Club	Uruguayan	26
Christian Giminez	FC Basel	Argentinian	23
Julio Rossi	FC Lugano	Argentinian	20
Alexander Frei	Servette FC	Swiss	16

Swiss Cup

2003 FINAL

May 11 – Sankt Jakob-Park, Basel
FC Basel 6-0 Neuchatel
(Hugel 13,   **Xamax FC**
Gimenez 35, 43,
Murat Yakin 64,
Smiljanic 77,
Barberis 83)
h/t: 3-0   **Att:** 31,500
Ref: Rogalla

FC Basel's Bernt Haas up against Patrick Eseosa of Young Boys in a Swiss league game – but 20 points and a gulf in class separate the teams.

Association Football in Central Europe

CENTRAL EUROPE

1896: Prague-based Czech league established

1893: Czechoslovakia's oldest clubs, Sparta Praha and Slavia Praha, formed

1901: Formation of Czech FA, Českomoravský Fotbalový Svaz

1906: Poland's oldest club, KS Cracovia, formed

1906: Czech affiliation to FIFA

1915: Czech Stredocesky league established

1918: Polish independent republic formed

1919: Formation of Polish FA: Polski Związek Piłki Nóżnej

1920: Czechoslovakia's first international, v Yugoslavia, won 7-0, venue: Antwerp

1921: Poland's first international, v Hungary, lost 0-1, venue: Budapest. First national league

1922: Formation of Czechoslovak FA

1923: Polish affiliation to FIFA. Czechoslovakian affiliation to FIFA

1926: First Polish Cup Final

1925: National Czechoslovak league established and professionalism introduced

1934: Czechoslovakia runners-up in World Cup in Italy

1939–44: During war and occupation, Czechoslovak football divided into separate leagues and cups

1939–45: No football in Poland during the war

1945–46: Polish borders radically redrawn, many Polish clubs transferred to Soviet leagues and some German clubs to the Polish league. Communist reorganization of clubs. League re-established

1946–48: Communist takeover and reorganization of Czechoslovak football

1949: League and Cup reorganized on a national basis

1951: Polish Cup re-established

1954: Czechoslovakian affiliation to UEFA. Polish affiliation to UEFA

1961: Czechoslovak Cup established

1962: Czechoslovakia reach World Cup Final in Chile

1968: Czech Uprising

1976: Czechoslovakia win European Championships

1993: Czechoslovakia separates into Czech Republic and Slovakia. Independent leagues, cups and FAs created. Separate affiliation to UEFA and FIFA. Legia Warszawa stripped of league title after match-fixing scandal

1996: Czech Republic runners-up in European Championships. Widzew Łódź and Legia Warszawa have their grounds closed for a season after worst incidents of football violence in Poland

Key

International football (Czech Republic)

International football (Poland)

Affiliation to FIFA

Affiliation to UEFA

War

Warta Poznań 1945
Zwiakowiec (1949–55)

Olimpia Poznań 1922

Lech Poznań 1947
Kolejarz (1947–56)

SK Hradec Králové 1905

Slovan Liberec 1958

Teplice 1945

Jablonec 97 1964

SK Kladno 1903

Viktoria Plzeň 1911

1. FC Union Cheb 1951

Dukla Příbram 1948

ATK Praha (1948–52)
UDA Praha (1952–56)
Dukla Praha (1956–98)

SK Pardubice 1911

České Budějovice 1899

Boby Brno 1913
Moravian Nationalism

Sigma Olomouc 1919

Petra Drnovice 1932

SK Líbeň (Folded)

DFC Praha (Folded)

Sparta Praha 1893

AC Sparta (1893–1949), Sparta Bratrstvi, (1949–51), Sparta Sokolovo (1951–53), Spartak Sokolovo (1953–64), Sparta CKD (1964–90)

Olympia

Bohemians Praha 1903

AFK Vršovice (1903–27), Bohemians (1927–39), AFK Bohemia (1939–49), Železničář (1949–51), Spartak Stalingrad (1951–61), Bohemians CKD (1961–90)

Slavia Praha 1893

SK Slavia (1893–1949)
Dynamo Slavia (1949–51)
TJ Slavia (1951–90)

Gdańsk
Lechia Gdańsk 1945
Budowlany (1949–56)

Zawisza Bydgoszcz 1946
Bydgoszcz

TKS Toruń

Szczecin
Pogon Szczecin 1906

Wronki
Amica Wronki 1992

Poznań

Grodzisk
Groclin Dyskobolia Grodzisk 1922

Wrocław

Slask Wrocław 1947
1948–56 Ogniwo

FC Banik Ostrava OKD 192

TJ Vítkovice 1922

Slezský Opava 1907

Teplice   Liberec

Jablonec nad Nisou

Hradec Králové

Cheb

Kladno

Plzeň

PRAGUE (see inset)

Příbram

CZECH REPUBLIC

Opava

Pardubice   Ostrav

Olomouc

Žlín   Žil

Drnovice   Dubni

Brno

Trenčín Prievid

Budějovice

Trnava

Nitra

Bratislav

Svit Žlín 1919

Dunajská Streda
Artme
Petrzalka 1

In
Bratislava 1

Slov
Bratislava 1

Spartak Trnava 1

Elbe

Vltava

PRAGUE

Central Europe

ORIGINS AND GROWTH OF FOOTBALL

IN BOHEMIA, PRAGUE PRODUCED the first football clubs, Sparta and Slavia, in 1893. A Prague league was running by 1896, followed by the Charity Cup in 1906. With the collapse of the Austro-Hungarian Empire, Czech and Slovak football were brought together and with the coming of professionalism in 1925 a new fully national league was established. Under Communist rule Dukla Praha (now Dukla Příbram) broke the Slavia–Sparta stranglehold with support from the Czech army. Slovan Bratislava also rose to challenge the Prague duopoly. With the separation of the Czech Republic and Slovakia, football in the region divided once again into separate leagues and cup competitions.

Like Czechoslovakia, Poland's football organizations preceded independence. KS Cracovia was formed in 1906 and Wisław (who wore the white star of Polish independence) in 1908, and clubs formed in Warsaw and Katowice before the formation of modern Poland in 1919. The national league was dominated by these three cities until the Second World War. After the war, Polish football was given the usual Communist treatment with name changes, and clubs were allocated to, or taken over by, a variety of state institutions. Under this order Polish football had its golden era, qualifying for every World Cup between 1974 and 1986, reaching the semi-finals in 1974 and 1982.

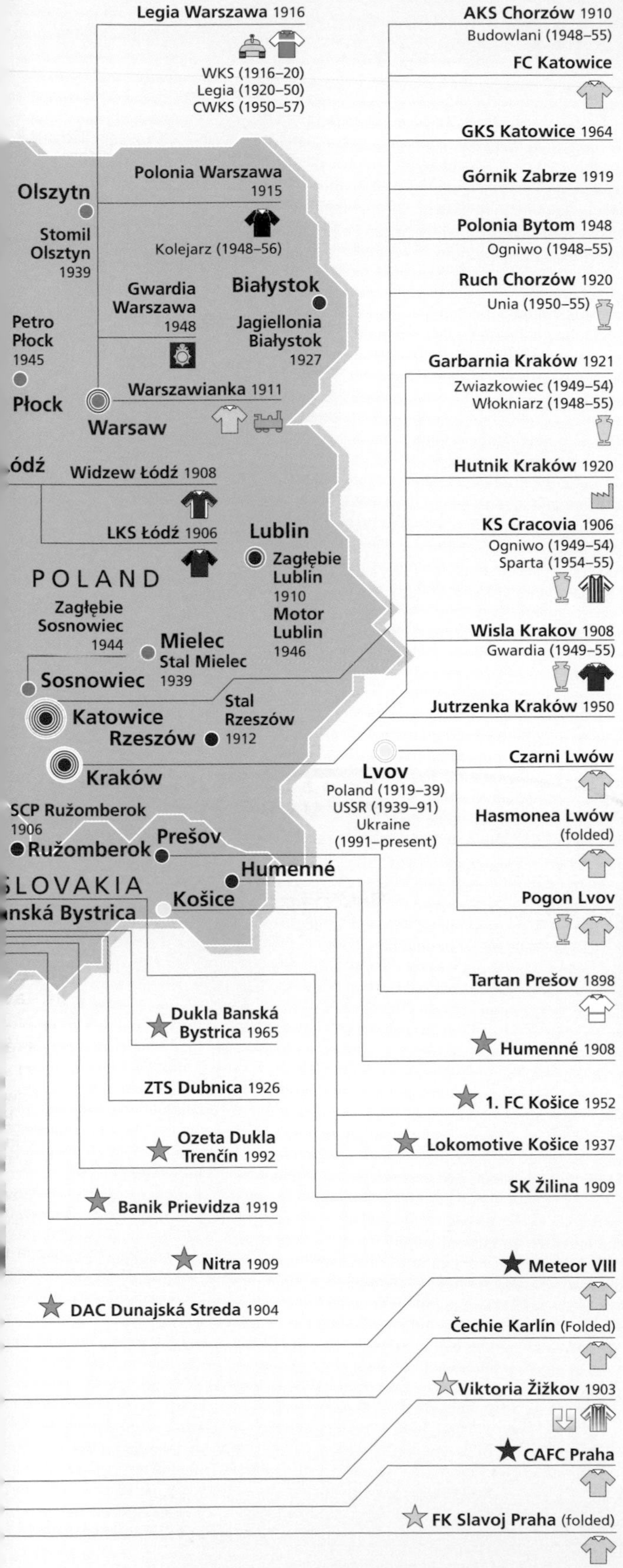

Legia Warszawa 1916
WKS (1916–20)
Legia (1920–50)
CWKS (1950–57)

Olsztyn
Stomil Olsztyn 1939

Polonia Warszawa 1915
Kolejarz (1948–56)

Gwardia Warszawa 1948

Białystok
Jagiellonia Białystok 1927

Petro Płock 1945

Warszawianka 1911
Płock
Warsaw

łódź
Widzew Łódź 1908
LKS Łódź 1906

Lublin
Zagłębie Lublin 1910
Motor Lublin 1946

POLAND
Zagłębie Sosnowiec 1944

Mielec
Stal Mielec 1939
Sosnowiec

Katowice
Stal Rzeszów 1912
Rzeszów

Kraków

SCP Ružomberok 1906
Ružomberok
Prešov
Humenné
SLOVAKIA
anská Bystrica
Košice

Dukla Banská Bystrica 1965
ZTS Dubnica 1926
Ozeta Dukla Trenčín 1992
Banik Prievidza 1919
Nitra 1909
DAC Dunajská Streda 1904

AKS Chorzów 1910
Budowlani (1948–55)
FC Katowice

GKS Katowice 1964

Górnik Zabrze 1919

Polonia Bytom 1948
Ogniwo (1948–55)

Ruch Chorzów 1920
Unia (1950–55)

Garbarnia Kraków 1921
Zwiazkowiec (1949–54)
Włokniarz (1948–55)

Hutnik Kraków 1920

KS Cracovia 1906
Ogniwo (1949–54)
Sparta (1954–55)

Wisla Krakov 1908
Gwardia (1949–55)

Jutrzenka Kraków 1950

Lvov
Poland (1919–39)
USSR (1939–91)
Ukraine (1991–present)

Czarni Lwów
Hasmonea Lwów (folded)
Pogon Lvov

Tartan Prešov 1898
Humenné 1908
1. FC Košice 1952
Lokomotive Košice 1937
SK Žilina 1909

Meteor VIII
Čechie Karlín (Folded)
Viktoria Žižkov 1903
CAFC Praha
FK Slavoj Praha (folded)

Dukla Praha is one of Central Europe's most successful teams. Here the team celebrates a goal against Real Madrid in the 1964 European Cup. However, Dukla lost the tie 6-2 on aggregate.

Central Europe: The main clubs

Teplice 1945	Team name with year of formation	
●	Club formed before 1912	
●	Club formed 1912–25	
●	Club formed 1925–50	
●	Club formed after 1950	
★	Founder members of Prague League 1912	
	Founder members of 1925/27 Czech/Polish League	
	Polish champions 1921–39	
☆	Founder members of Czech League 1994	

★	Founder members of Slovakian League 1994
	Intellectuals/Universities
	Linked to Skoda car company
	Originated from army
	Railway workers
	Steel workers
	Warsaw police
	Working class
	Colours and date unknown

Czech Republic (including former Czechoslovakia)

Českomoravský Fotbalový Svaz
Founded: 1901
Joined FIFA: 1906
Joined UEFA: 1954

FOOTBALL PROSPERED EARLY in the 20th century in this Bohemian province of the Austro-Hungarian Empire; the Prague-based Středočeský League and Czech Charity Cup were up and running before the First World War. With the postwar creation of Czechoslovakia, Bohemian, Moravian and Slovakian football were fused to create a professional Czech league in 1925.

During the Second World War, Germany absorbed part of Czechoslovakia, and created a newly independent, but German, satellite: Slovakia. Separate Slovak and Czech leagues and cups were played during the war. The Czechoslovak league was recreated under the Communists in 1946 and remained until the separation of the Czech Republic and Slovakia in 1993, after which two separate national leagues have operated.

Separate cups for the two nations were established under the Communists with a play-off to decide the Czechoslovakian Cup.

Czech League Record 1925–93

SEASON	CHAMPIONS	RUNNERS-UP
1925	SK Slavia Praha	AC Sparta Praha
1926	AC Sparta Praha	SK Slavia Praha
1927	AC Sparta Praha	SK Slavia Praha
1928	Victoria Žižkov	SK Slavia Praha
1929	SK Slavia Praha	Victoria Žižkov
1930	SK Slavia Praha	AC Sparta Praha
1931	SK Slavia Praha	AC Sparta Praha
1932	AC Sparta Praha	SK Slavia Praha
1933	SK Slavia Praha	AC Sparta Praha
1934	SK Slavia Praha	AC Sparta Praha
1935	SK Slavia Praha	AC Sparta Praha
1936	AC Sparta Praha	SK Slavia Praha
1937	SK Slavia Praha	AC Sparta Praha
1938	AC Sparta Praha	SK Slavia Praha
1939	AC Sparta Praha	SK Slavia Praha
1940	SK Slavia Praha	AC Sparta Praha
1941	SK Slavia Praha	SK Plzeň
1942	SK Slavia Praha	SK Prostějov
1943	SK Slavia Praha	AC Sparta Praha
1944	AC Sparta Praha	SK Slavia Praha
1945	*no championship*	
1946	AC Sparta Praha	SK Slavia Praha
1947	SK Slavia Praha	AC Sparta Praha
1948	AC Sparta Praha	SK Slavia Praha
1948*	Dynamo Slavia Praha	Škoda Plzeň
1949	NV Bratislava	Bratrstvi Sparta Praha
1950	NV Bratislava	Bratrstvi Sparta Praha
1951	NV Bratislava	Sparta CKD Praha
1952	Sparta CKD Sokolovo	NV Bratislava
1953	ÚDA Praha	Spartak Sokolovo Praha
1954	Spartak Sokolovo Praha	Baník Ostrava
1955	Slovan Bratislava	ÚDA Praha
1956	Dukla Praha	Slovan Bratislava
1957*		
1958	Dukla Praha	Spartak Sokolovo Praha
1959	RH Bratislava	Dukla Praha
1960	Spartak Hradec Králové	Slovan Bratislava
1961	Dukla Praha	RH Bratislava
1962	Dukla Praha	Slovan Nitra
1963	Dukla Praha	Jednota Trenčín
1964	Dukla Praha	Slovan Bratislava
1965	Sparta Praha	Tatran Prešov
1966	Dukla Praha	Sparta Praha

Czech League Record (continued)

SEASON	CHAMPIONS	RUNNERS-UP
1967	Sparta Praha	Slovan Bratislava
1968	Spartak Trnava	Slovan Bratislava
1969	Spartak Trnava	Slovan Bratislava
1970	Slovan Bratislava	Spartak Trnava
1971	Spartak Trnava	VSS Košice
1972	Spartak Trnava	Slovan Bratislava
1973	Spartak Trnava	Tatran Prešov
1974	Slovan Bratislava	Dukla Praha
1975	Slovan Bratislava	Inter Bratislava
1976	Baník Ostrava	Slovan Bratislava
1977	Dukla Praha	Inter Bratislava
1978	ZJS Brno	Dukla Praha
1979	Dukla Praha	Baník Ostrava
1980	Baník Ostrava	ZJS Brno
1981	Baník Ostrava	Dukla Praha
1982	Dukla Praha	Baník Ostrava
1983	Bohemians Praha	Baník Ostrava
1984	Sparta Praha	Dukla Praha
1985	Sparta Praha	Bohemians Praha
1986	FC Vítkovice	Sparta Praha
1987	Sparta Praha	FC Vítkovice
1988	Sparta Praha	Dukla Praha
1989	Sparta Praha	Baník Ostrava
1990	Sparta Praha	Baník Ostrava
1991	Sparta Praha	Slovan Bratislava
1992	Slovan Bratislava	Sparta Praha
1993	Sparta Praha	Slavia Praha

* Between 1948 and 1956 the Czech League was played during the summer months. The 1957–58 season result is therefore given as 1958.

Czech Republic League Record 1994–2003

SEASON	CHAMPIONS	RUNNERS-UP
1994	Sparta Praha	Slavia Praha
1995	Sparta Praha	Slavia Praha
1996	Slavia Praha	Sigma Olomouc
1997	Sparta Praha	Slavia Praha
1998	Sparta Praha	Slavia Praha
1999	Sparta Praha	FK Teplice
2000	Sparta Praha	Slavia Praha
2001	Sparta Praha	Slavia Praha
2002	Slovan Liberec	Sparta Praha
2003	Sparta Praha	Slavia Praha

Czech League Summary

TEAM	TOTALS	CHAMPIONS & RUNNERS-UP (BOLD) (*ITALICS*)
Sparta Praha (includes AC Sparta Praha, Bratrstvi Sparta Praha, Sparta CKD Praha, Sparta CKD Sokolovo and Spartak Sokolovo)	29, 19	*1925*, **26, 27**, *30, 31, 32, 33–35*, **36, 37, 38, 39, 40, 43, 44, 46, 47, 48**, *49–51*, **52, 53, 54, 58, 65, 66, 67, 84, 85**, *86*, **87–91**, *92*, **93–95, 97–2001**, *02*, **03**
Slavia Praha (includes SK Slavia Praha and Dynamo Slavia Praha)	15, 18	**1925**, *26–28*, **29–31**, *32*, **33–35, 36, 37, 38, 39, 40–43**, *44, 46, 47, 48, 48**, **93–95, 96**, *97, 98*, **2000**, *01*, **03**
Marila Příbram (includes ÚDA Praha and Dukla Praha)	11, 7	**1953**, *55*, **56**, *58, 59*, **61–64**, *66*, **74**, *77*, **78, 79**, *81*, **82**, *84*, **88**

This summary only features the top three clubs in the Czech League. For a full list of league champions and runners-up please see the League Records opposite.

CZECH REPUBLIC

Czech Cup Record 1918–93

YEAR	WINNERS	SCORE	RUNNERS-UP
1918	Sparta Praha	4-1	Slavia Praha
1919	Sparta Praha	2-0	Viktoria Žižkov
1920	Sparta Praha	5-1	Viktoria Žižkov
1921	Viktoria Žižkov	3-0	Sparta Praha
1922	Slavia Praha	3-2	Chechie Karlín
1923	Slavia Praha	3-1	Slavia Praha
1924	Sparta Praha	5-1	AFK Vršovice
1925	Sparta Praha	7-0	CAFC Vinohrady
1926	Slavia Praha	10-0	CAFC Vinohrady
1927	Slavia Praha	1-0	Sparta Praha
1928	Slavia Praha	1-1, (replay) 1-1, (replay) 3-2	Sparta Praha
1929	Viktoria Žižkov	3-1	SK Libeň
1930	Slavia Praha	4-2	SK Kladno
1931	Sparta Praha	3-1	Slavia Praha
1932	Slavia Praha	2-1	Sparta Praha
1933	Viktoria Žižkov	2-1	Sparta Praha
1934	Sparta Praha	6-0	SK Kladno
1935	Slavia Praha	4-1	Bohemians Praha
1936	Sparta Praha	1-1, (replay) 1-0	Slavia Praha
1937–39		no competition	
1940	Viktoria Žižkov	5-3	Sparta Praha
1940*	ASO Olomouc	3-1, 2-1 (2 legs)	SK Prostějov
1941	Slavia Praha	13-2	SS Plincner
1941*	Slavia Praha	2-3, 6-3 (2 legs)	Sparta Praha
1942	Bohemians Praha	8-6	Sparta Praha
1942*	Slavia Praha	5-2, 5-5 (2 legs)	Bohemians Praha
1943*	Sparta Praha	3-1, 7-1 (2 legs)	Viktoria Plzeň
1944*	Sparta Praha	4-2, 4-3 (2 legs)	Viktoria Plzeň
1945	Slavia Praha	1-1, 5-2 (2 legs)	SK Rakovník
1946	Sparta Praha	6-0, 3-0 (2 legs)	Slezská Ostrava
1947–50		no competition	
1951	Kovosmalt Trnava	1-0	Armaturka Ústi
1952	ATK Praha	4-3	Sokol Hradec Králové
1953–54		no competition	
1955	Slovan Bratislava	2-0	ÚDA Praha
1956–59		no competition	
1960	RH Brno	3-1	Dynamo Praha
1961	Dukla Praha	3-0	Dynamo Žilina
1962	Slovan Bratislava	1-1, 4-1 (2 legs)	Dukla Praha
1963	Slovan Bratislava	0-0, 9-0 (2 legs)	Dynamo Praha
1964	Spartak Praha Solokovo	4-1	VSS Košice
1965	Dukla Praha	0-0 (aet)(5-3 pens)	Slovan Bratislava
1966	Dukla Praha	2-1, 4-0	Tatran Prešov
1967	Spartak Trnava	2-4, 2-0 (5-4 pens)	Sparta Praha
1968	Slovan Bratislava	0-1, 2-0	Dukla Praha
1969	Dukla Praha	1-1, 1-0	VCHZ Pardubice
1970	TJ Gottwaldov	3-3, 0-0 (4-3 pens)	Slovan Bratislava
1971	Spartak Trnava	2-1, 5-1	Škoda Plzeň
1972	Sparta Praha	0-1, 4-3 (aet)(4-3 pens)	Slovan Bratislava
1973	Baník Ostrava	1-2, 3-1	VSS Košice
1974	Slovan Bratislava	0-1, 1-0 (aet)(4-3 pens)	Slavia Praha
1975	Spartak Trnava	3-1, 1-0	Sparta Praha
1976	Sparta Praha	3-2, 1-0	Slovan Bratislava
1977	Lokomotíva Košice	2-1	Sklo Union Teplice
1978	Baník Ostrava	1-0	Jednota Trenčín
1979	Lokomotíva Košice	2-1	Baník Ostrava
1980	Sparta Praha	2-0	ZTS Košice
1981	Dukla Praha	4-1	Dukla Banská Bystrica
1982	Slovan Bratislava	0-0 (aet)(4-2 pens)	Bohemians Praha
1983	Dukla Praha	2-1	Slovan Bratislava
1984	Sparta Praha	4-2	Inter Bratislava
1985	Dukla Praha	3-2	Lokomotíva Košice
1986	Spartak Trnava	1-1 (aet)(4-3 pens)	Sparta Praha
1987	DAC Dunajská Streda	0-0 (aet)(3-2 pens)	Sparta Praha
1988	Sparta Praha	2-0	Inter Bratislava
1989	Sparta Praha	3-0	Slovan Bratislava
1990	Dukla Praha	1-1 (aet)(5-4 pens)	Inter Bratislava
1991	Baník Ostrava	6-1	Spartak Trnava

Czech Cup Record (*continued*)

YEAR	WINNERS	SCORE	RUNNERS-UP
1992	Sparta Praha	2-1	Tatran Prešov
1993	1. FC Košice	5-1	Sparta Praha

* Denotes results in the short-lived Cesky' Pohár (Czech Cup).

Czech Republic Cup Record 1994–2003

YEAR	WINNERS	SCORE	RUNNERS-UP
1994	Viktoria Žižkov	2-2 (aet)(6-5 pens)	Sparta Praha
1995	SK Hradec Králové	0-0 (aet)(3-1 pens)	Viktoria Žižkov
1996	Sparta Praha	4-0	FC Petra Drnovice
1997	Slavia Praha	1-0 (aet)	FK Dukla Praha
1998	FK Jablonec	2-1 (asdet)	FC Petra Drnovice
1999	Slavia Praha	1-0 (asdet)	FC Slovan Liberec
2000	FC Slovan Liberec	2-1	Baník Ratíškovice
2001	Viktoria Žižkov	2-1 (aet)	Sparta Praha
2002	Slavia Praha	2-1	Sparta Praha
2003	FK Teplice	1-0	FK Jablonec 97

Czech Cup Summary

TEAM	TOTALS	WINNERS & RUNNERS-UP (BOLD) (ITALICS)
Sparta Praha (includes Spartak Praha Sokolovo)	21, 16	**1918–20, 21, 23–25, 27, 28, 31, 32, 33, 34, 36, 40, 41*, 42, 43*, 44*, 46, 64, 67, 72, 75, 76, 80, 84, 86, 87, 88, 89, 92, 93, 94, 96, 2001, 02**
Slavia Praha (includes Dynamo Praha)	14, 7	**1918, 22, 23, 26–28, 30, 31, 32, 35, 36, 41, 41*, 42*, 45, 60, 63, 74, 97, 99, 2002**
Marila Příbram (includes ÚDA Praha, and Dukla Praha)	8, 3	**1955, 61, 62, 65, 66, 68, 69, 81, 83, 85, 90**
Slovan Bratislava (includes Internacional Bratislava)	6, 9	**1955, 62, 63, 65, 68, 70, 72, 74, 76, 82, 83, 84, 88–90**
Viktoria Žižkov	6, 3	**1919, 20, 21, 29, 33, 40, 94, 95, 2001**
Spartak Trnava	4, 1	**1967, 71, 75, 86, 91**
Baník Ostrava	3, 1	**1973, 78, 79, 91**
Lokomotíva Košice	2, 1	**1977, 79, 85**

This summary only features clubs that have won the Czech Cup two or more times. For a full list of league champions and runners-up please see the Cup Record left.

Slovakia

Slovensky Futbalovy Zvaz
Founded: 1938
Joined FIFA: 1994
Joined UEFA: 1993

SEASON	LEAGUE CHAMPIONS
1999	Slovan Bratislava
2000	Internacional Bratislava
2001	Internacional Bratislava
2002	MSK Zilina
2003	MSK Zilina

YEAR	CUP WINNERS
1999	Slovan Bratislava
2000	Internacional Bratislava
2001	Internacional Bratislava
2002	Koba Senec
2003	Matador Púchov

Though football has been played in Slovakia since the late 19th century, it has mostly been part of Czechoslovakian football. When Slovakia gained political independence from Czechoslovakia in 1993, a national 'Superliga' was formed. A Slovakian Cup started in 1970.

Poland

Polski Związek Piłki Nóżnej
Founded: 1919
Joined FIFA: 1923
Joined UEFA: 1954

FOOTBALL ARRIVED IN POLAND before it became a nation state. While the game took off in the cities of Łódź, Kraków and Warsaw in the early 20th century, the modern Polish state did not emerge until after the First World War. Carved out of parts of the German, Russian and Austrian empires, the new Poland quickly acquired a football association in 1919, and a national league followed two years later. However, Poland's borders have not stayed still since then, and the Polish league is littered with clubs that are now located in other states. Pogoń Lwów – who won four championships in the 1920s – comes from what was once the Soviet Union and is now the Ukraine. The city of Gdańsk (previously Danzig), home to several top teams, was once part of Germany as were Szczecin and Wrocław (previously Stettin and Breslau).

Cup football was slower in coming to Poland, with a single tournament held in 1926 and then nothing until the Communist-initiated Puchar Polski began in 1951. Alongside the new cup competition, Poland's new Communist rulers reorganized football at every level with extensive changes of clubs' names and control. The collapse of the Communist regime saw a further swathe of name changes and increasing problems of crowd violence. The latter culminated in October 1996, with a riot between fans of Widzew Łódź and Legia Warszawa, which resulted in each team's stadium being closed for the rest of the season.

The current league consists of an 18-club top flight and two 18-club second divisions, one based in the east of the country and one in the west. Four teams are relegated from the first division, replaced by promotions for the winners and runners-up from the regional leagues. There are currently plans to radically reduce the number of teams in the top flight.

Polish League Record 1921–2003

SEASON	CHAMPIONS	RUNNERS-UP
1921	Cracovia Kraków	Polonia Warszawa
1922	Pogoń Lwów	Warta Poznań
1923	Pogoń Lwów	Wisła Kraków
1924	*no championship*	
1925	Pogoń Lwów	Warta Poznań
1926	Pogoń Lwów	Polonia Warszawa
1927	Wisła Kraków	I.FC Katowice
1928	Wisła Kraków	Warta Poznań
1929	Warta Poznań	Garbarnia Kraków
1930	Cracovia Kraków	Wisła Kraków
1931	Garbarnia Kraków	Wisła Kraków
1932	Cracovia Kraków	Pogoń Lwów
1933	Ruch Chorzów	Pogoń Lwów
1934	Ruch Chorzów	Cracovia Kraków
1935	Ruch Chorzów	Pogoń Lwów
1936	Ruch Chorzów	Wisła Kraków
1937	Cracovia Kraków	AKS Chorzów
1938	Ruch Chorzów	Warta Poznań
1939–45	*no championship*	
1946	Polonia Warszawa	Warta Poznań
1947	Warta Poznań	Wisła Kraków
1948	Cracovia Kraków	Wisła Kraków
1949	Wisła Kraków	Ogniwo Kraków
1950	Wisła Kraków	Ruch Chorzów
1951	Ruch Chorzów*	

Polish League Record (*continued*)

SEASON	CHAMPIONS	RUNNERS-UP
1952	Ruch Chorzów	Ogniwo Kraków
1953	Ruch Chorzów	Wawel Kraków
1954	Polonia Bytom	LKS Łódź
1955	Legia Warszawa	Stal Sosnowiec
1956	Legia Warszawa	Ruch Chorzów
1957	Górnik Zabrze	Gwardia Warsawa
1958	LKS Łódź	Polonia Bytom
1959	Górnik Zabrze	Polonia Bytom
1960	Ruch Chorzów	Legia Warszawa
1961	Górnik Zabrze	Polonia Bytom
1962	Polonia Bytom	Górnik Zabrze
1963	Górnik Zabrze	Ruch Chorzów
1964	Górnik Zabrze	Zagłębie Sosnowiec
1965	Górnik Zabrze	Szombierkj Bytom
1966	Górnik Zabrze	Wisła Kraków
1967	Górnik Zabrze	Zagłębie Sosnowiec
1968	Ruch Chorzów	Legia Warszawa
1969	Legia Warszawa	Górnik Zabrze
1970	Legia Warszawa	Ruch Chorzów
1971	Górnik Zabrze	Legia Warszawa
1972	Górnik Zabrze	Zagłębie Sosnowiec
1973	Stal Mielec	Ruch Chorzów
1974	Ruch Chorzów	Górnik Zabrze
1975	Ruch Chorzów	Stal Mielec
1976	Stal Mielec	GKS Tychy
1977	Śląsk Wrocław	Widzew Łódź
1978	Wisła Kraków	Śląsk Wrocław
1979	Ruch Chorzów	Widzew Łódź
1980	Szombierkj Bytom	Widzew Łódź
1981	Widzew Łódź	Wisła Kraków
1982	Widzew Łódź	Śląsk Wrocław
1983	Lech Poznań	Widzew Łódź
1984	Lech Poznań	Widzew Łódź
1985	Górnik Zabrze	Legia Warszawa
1986	Górnik Zabrze	Legia Warszawa
1987	Górnik Zabrze	Pogoń Szczecin
1988	Górnik Zabrze	GKS Katowice
1989	Ruch Chorzów	GKS Katowice
1990	Lech Poznań	Zagłębie Lubin
1991	Zagłębie Lubin	Górnik Zabrze
1992	Lech Poznań	GKS Katowice
1993	Lech Poznań**	
1994	Legia Warszawa	GKS Katowice
1995	Legia Warszawa	Widzew Łódź
1996	Widzew Łódź	Legia Warszawa
1997	Widzew Łódź	Legia Warszawa
1998	LKS-PTAK Łódź	Polonia Warszawa
1999	Wisła Kraków	Widzew Łódź
2000	Polonia Warszawa	Wisła Kraków
2001	Wisła Kraków	Pogoń Szczecin
2002	Legia Warszawa	Wisła Kraków
2003	Wisła Kraków	Groclin-Dyskobolia Grodzisk

* Ruch Chorzów finished sixth, but as the league programme was not completed it was awarded the title because of its cup win.

** Lech Poznań was awarded the title after Legia Warszawa and LKS Łódź (who finished first and second) were penalized for match-fixing allegations.

Polish League Summary

TEAM	TOTALS	CHAMPIONS & RUNNERS-UP (BOLD) (*ITALICS*)
Ruch Chorzów	14, *5*	1933–36, 38, *50*, 51–53, *56*, 60, *63*, 68, *70*, 73, 74, 75, 79, 89
Górnik Zabrze	14, *4*	1957, 59, 61, *62*, 63–67, *69*, 71, 72, *74*, 85–88, *91*

POLAND

Polish League Summary (*continued*)

TEAM	TOTALS	CHAMPIONS & RUNNERS-UP (BOLD) (*ITALICS*)
Wisła Kraków	**8**, *10*	*1923*, **27, 28**, *30, 31, 36, 47, 48*, **49**, *50, 66*, **78**, *81*, **99, 2000, 01, 02, 03**
Legia Warszawa	**7**, *7*	**1955, 56**, *60*, **68, 69, 70**, *71*, **85, 86, 94, 95, 96, 97, 2002**
Cracovia Kraków	**5**, *1*	**1921, 30, 32**, *34*, **37, 48**
Lech Poznań	**5**, *0*	**1983, 84, 90, 92, 93**
Widzew Łódź	**4**, *7*	*1977, 79, 80*, **81, 82**, *83, 84*, **95**, *96, 97, 99*
Pogoń Lwów	**4**, *3*	**1922**, *23*, **25, 26**, *32, 33, 35*
Warta Poznań	**2**, *5*	*1922*, **25**, *28*, **29**, *38, 46*, **47**
Polonia Warszawa	**2**, *3*	*1921, 26*, **46, 98, 2000**
LKS Łódź	**2**, *1*	*1954*, **58, 98**
Stal Mielec	**2**, *1*	**1973**, *75*, **76**
Polonia Bytom	**2**, *3*	*1954, 58, 59*, **61, 62**
Śląsk Wrocław	**1**, *2*	**1977**, *78*, **82**
Garbarnia Kraków	**1**, *1*	*1929*, **1931**
Szombierkj Bytom	**1**, *1*	*1965*, **80**
Zagłębie Lubin	**1**, *1*	*1990*, **91**
GKS Katowice	**0**, *4*	*1988, 89, 92, 94*
Zagłębie Sosnowiec	**0**, *3*	*1964, 67, 72*
Ogniwo Kraków	**0**, *2*	*1949, 52*
AKS Chorzów	**0**, *1*	*1937*
Groclin-Dyskobolia Grodzisk	**0**, *1*	*2003*
GKS Tychy	**0**, *1*	*1976*
Gwardia Warszawa	**0**, *1*	*1957*
I.FC Katowice	**0**, *1*	*1927*
Pogoń Szczecin	**0**, *1*	*1987*
Stal Sosnowiec	**0**, *1*	*1955*
Wawel Kraków	**0**, *1*	*1953*

Polish Cup Record 1926–2003

YEAR	WINNERS	SCORE	RUNNERS-UP
1926	Wisła Kraków	2-1	Sparta Lwów
1927–50		no competition	
1951	Ruch Chorzów	2-0	Wisła Kraków
1952	Polonia Warszawa	1-0	Legia Warszawa
1953		no competition	
1954	Gwardia Warszawa	0-0 (aet)(replay)3-1	Wisła Kraków
1955	Legia Warszawa	5-0	Lechia Gdańsk
1956	Legia Warszawa	3-0	Górnik Zabrze
1957	LKS Łódź	2-1	Górnik Zabrze
1958–61		no competition	
1962	Zagłębie Sosnowiec	2-1	Górnik Zabrze
1963	Zagłębie Sosnowiec	2-0	Ruch Chorzów
1964	Legia Warszawa	2-1 (aet)	Polonia Bytom
1965	Górnik Zabrze	4-0	Czarni Zagań
1966	Legia Warszawa	2-1 (aet)	Górnik Zabrze
1967	Wisła Kraków	2-0 (aet)	Raków Częstochowa
1968	Górnik Zabrze	3-0	Ruch Chorzów
1969	Górnik Zabrze	2-0	Legia Warszawa
1970	Górnik Zabrze	3-1	Ruch Chorzów
1971	Górnik Zabrze	3-1	Zagłębie Sosnowiec
1972	Górnik Zabrze	5-2	Legia Warszawa
1973	Legia Warszawa	0-0 (aet)(4-2 pens)	Polonia Bytom
1974	Ruch Chorzów	2-0	Gwardia Warszawa
1975	Stal Rzeszów	0-0 (aet)(3-2 pens)	ROW II Rybnik
1976	Śląsk Wrocław	2-0	Stal Mielec
1977	Zagłębie Sosnowiec	1-0	Polonia Bytom
1978	Zagłębie Sosnowiec	2-0	Piast Gliwice
1979	Arka Gdynia	2-1	Wisła Kraków
1980	Legia Warszawa	5-0	Lech Poznań
1981	Legia Warszawa	1-0 (aet)	Pogoń Szczecin
1982	Lech Poznań	1-0	Pogoń Szczecin
1983	Lechia Gdańsk	2-1	Piast Gliwice
1984	Lech Poznań	3-0	Wisła Kraków
1985	Widzew Łódź	0-0 (aet)(3-1 pens)	GKS Katowice
1986	GKS Katowice	4-1	Górnik Zabrze
1987	Śląsk Wrocław	0-0 (aet)(4-3 pens)	GKS Katowice
1988	Lech Poznań	1-1 (aet)(3-2 pens)	Legia Warszawa

Polish Cup Record (*continued*)

YEAR	WINNERS	SCORE	RUNNERS-UP
1989	Legia Warszawa	5-2	Jagiellonia Białystok
1990	Legia Warszawa	2-0	GKS Katowice
1991	GKS Katowice	1-0	Legia Warszawa
1992	Miedz Legnica	1-1 (aet)(4-3 pens)	Górnik Zabrze
1993	GKS Katowice	1-1 (aet)(5-4 pens)	Ruch Chorzów
1994	Legia Warszawa	2-0	LKS Łódź
1995	Legia Warszawa	2-0	GKS Katowice
1996	Ruch Chorzów	1-0	GKS Bełchatów
1997	Legia Warszawa	2-0	GKS Katowice
1998	Amica Wronki	5-3 (aet)	Aluminium Konin
1999	Amica Wronki	1-0	GKS Bełchatów
2000	Amica Wronki	2-2, 3-0 (2 legs)	Wisła Kraków
2001	Polonia Warszawa	2-1, 2-2 (2 legs)	Górnik Zabrze
2002	Wisła Kraków	4-2, 4-0 (2 legs)	Amica Wronki
2003	Wisła Kraków	0-1, 3-0 (2 legs)	Wisła Plock

Polish Cup Summary

TEAM	TOTALS	WINNERS & RUNNERS-UP (BOLD) (*ITALICS*)
Legia Warszawa	**12**, *5*	*1952*, **55, 56, 64, 66**, *69*, **72, 73, 80, 81**, *88, 89, 90*, **91, 94, 95**, *97*
Górnik Zabrze	**6**, *7*	*1956, 57, 62*, **65**, *66*, **68–72**, *86, 92*, **2001**
Wisła Kraków	**4**, *5*	**1926**, *51, 54*, **67**, *79, 84*, **2000, 02, 03**
Zagłębie Sosnowiec	**4**, *1*	**1962, 63, 71, 77, 78**
GKS Katowice	**3**, *5*	*1985*, **86**, *87, 90*, **91**, *93*, **95**, *97*
Ruch Chorzów	**3**, *4*	**1951**, *63, 68, 70*, **74**, *93*, **96**
Amica Wronki	**3**, *1*	**1998–2000**, *02*
Lech Poznań	**3**, *1*	*1980*, **82, 84, 88**
Polonia Warszawa	**2**, *0*	**1952, 2001**
Śląsk Wrocław	**2**, *0*	**1976, 87**
Gwardia Warszawa	**1**, *1*	**1954**, *74*
Lechia Gdańsk	**1**, *1*	*1955*, **83**
LKS Łódź	**1**, *1*	*1957*, **94**
Arka Gdynia	**1**, *0*	**1979**
Miedz Legnica	**1**, *0*	**1992**
Stal Rzeszów	**1**, *0*	**1975**
Widzew Łódź	**1**, *0*	**1985**
Polonia Bytom	**0**, *3*	*1964, 73, 77*
GKS Bełchatów	**0**, *2*	*1996, 99*
Piast Gliwice	**0**, *2*	*1978, 83*
Pogoń Szczecin	**0**, *2*	*1981, 82*
Aluminium Konin	**0**, *1*	*1998*
Czarni Zagań	**0**, *1*	*1965*
Jagiellonia Białystok	**0**, *1*	*1989*
Raków Częstochowa	**0**, *1*	*1967*
ROW II Rybnik	**0**, *1*	*1975*
Sparta Lwów	**0**, *1*	*1926*
Stal Mielec	**0**, *1*	*1976*
Wisła Plock	**0**, *1*	*2003*

Zbigniew Boniek is widely regarded as the greatest ever Polish footballer. He made his name with Widzew Łódz, Polish League Champions in 1981 and 82, but it was his performances for the national team in the 1982 World Cup that persuaded Juventus of Italy to pay £1.1 million for him – then a record for a Polish player.

POLAND

SOUTHEAST EUROPE

Association Football in Southeast Europe

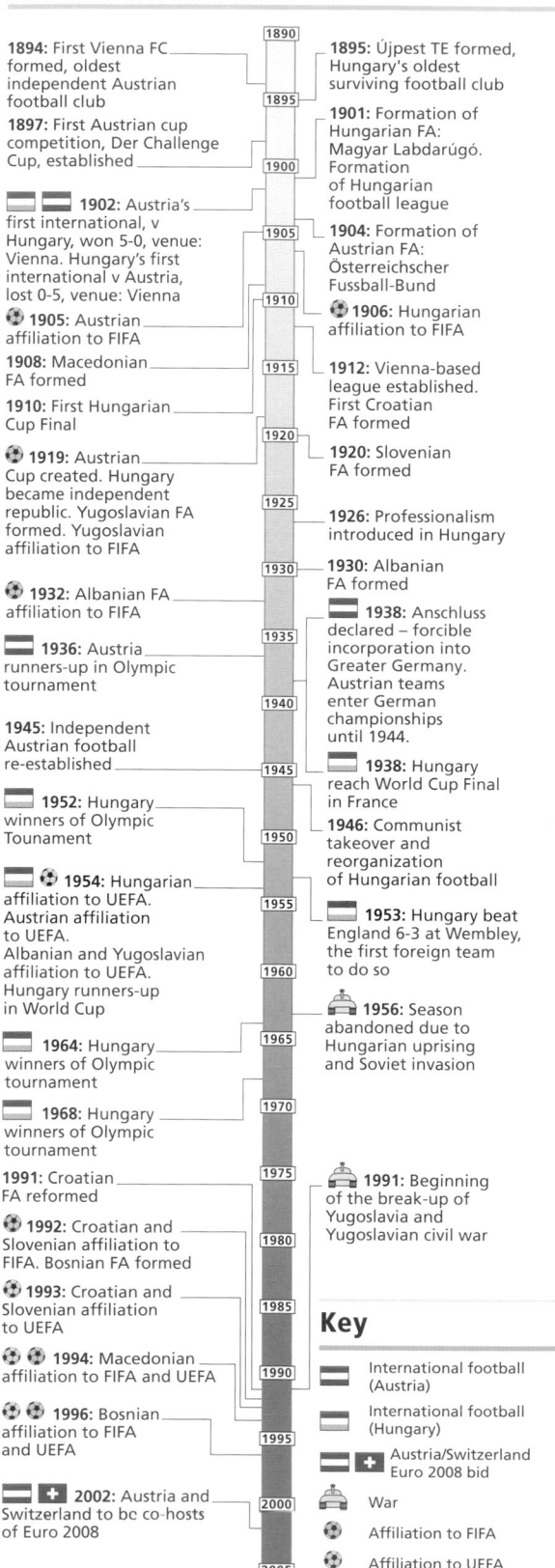

1894: First Vienna FC formed, oldest independent Austrian football club

1897: First Austrian cup competition, Der Challenge Cup, established

1902: Austria's first international, v Hungary, won 5-0, venue: Vienna. Hungary's first international v Austria, lost 0-5, venue: Vienna

1905: Austrian affiliation to FIFA

1908: Macedonian FA formed

1910: First Hungarian Cup Final

1919: Austrian Cup created. Hungary became independent republic. Yugoslavian FA formed. Yugoslavian affiliation to FIFA

1932: Albanian FA affiliation to FIFA

1936: Austria runners-up in Olympic tournament

1945: Independent Austrian football re-established

1952: Hungary winners of Olympic Tournament

1954: Hungarian affiliation to UEFA. Austrian affiliation to UEFA. Albanian and Yugoslavian affiliation to UEFA. Hungary runners-up in World Cup

1964: Hungary winners of Olympic tournament

1968: Hungary winners of Olympic tournament

1991: Croatian FA reformed

1992: Croatian and Slovenian affiliation to FIFA. Bosnian FA formed

1993: Croatian and Slovenian affiliation to UEFA

1994: Macedonian affiliation to FIFA and UEFA

1996: Bosnian affiliation to FIFA and UEFA

2002: Austria and Switzerland to be co-hosts of Euro 2008

Timeline: 1890, 1895, 1900, 1905, 1910, 1915, 1920, 1925, 1930, 1935, 1940, 1945, 1950, 1955, 1960, 1965, 1970, 1975, 1980, 1985, 1990, 1995, 2000, 2005

1895: Újpest TE formed, Hungary's oldest surviving football club

1901: Formation of Hungarian FA: Magyar Labdarúgó. Formation of Hungarian football league

1904: Formation of Austrian FA: Österreichscher Fussball-Bund

1906: Hungarian affiliation to FIFA

1912: Vienna-based league established. First Croatian FA formed

1920: Slovenian FA formed

1926: Professionalism introduced in Hungary

1930: Albanian FA formed

1938: Anschluss declared – forcible incorporation into Greater Germany. Austrian teams enter German championships until 1944.

1938: Hungary reach World Cup Final in France

1946: Communist takeover and reorganization of Hungarian football

1953: Hungary beat England 6-3 at Wembley, the first foreign team to do so

1956: Season abandoned due to Hungarian uprising and Soviet invasion

1991: Beginning of the break-up of Yugoslavia and Yugoslavian civil war

Key

- International football (Austria)
- International football (Hungary)
- Austria/Switzerland Euro 2008 bid
- War
- Affiliation to FIFA
- Affiliation to UEFA

First Vienna FC 1894

Wiener SC 1893

Cricket FV 1894

Wiener AC 1900

Wiener AF 1912

Rapid Wien 1898
Founded as Wiener Arbeiter-Fussballklub till 1899

Hat factory team
FC Wien 1918
Nicholson (1918–32)

FK Austria 1911
Amateure (1911–26), 1973 absorbed Wiener Athletik

SW Bregenz 1920
Bregenz
Lustenau
Austria Lustenau 1914

Kremser FC 1919

Vorwärts Steyr 1919

FC Stahl Linz 1949

Linzer ASK 1908

SV Ried 1912

Sturm Graz 1909

Innsbruck
FC Tirol 1914

Ried Im Innkreis

Salzburg
Austria Salzberg 1933

SK Austria 1920
Klagenfurt

Hertha 1
Rudolfshü
1. Simmerin SC Wien 1
Hakoah 1

FC Admira Mödling 1971
Merger of Admira Wien 1905 and Wacker Wien, 1908. Moved from Florisdorf to Maria Enzersdorf as FC Admira Wacker then merged with VfB Mödling 1997

VIENNA

VIEN (see inset)

Krems
Maria Enzersdorf
VfB Mödling 1911

Steyr

SV Gloggnitz 1922

Graz
Grazer AK 1902

AUSTRIA

Danube

SLOVENIA (see inset)

NK Maribor 1958

SLOVENIA

Feroterm Pohorje 1956

Rudar Velenje 1948

Ruse

Nova Gorica
Celje
Publikum Celje 1946

Ljubljana

Primorje Ajdovščina 1924

Sct Olimpija Ljubljana 1911

Hit Gorica 1938

Dinamo Zagreb 1945

Zagreb 1949

Varteks Varaždin 1931

Slaven Belupo Koprivnica 1912

Osijek 1946

Ciballia Vinkovci 1947

Marsonia Slavonski Brod 1909

OFK Beograd 1911

Obilic Beograd 1924

Partizan Beograd 1945

Crvena Zvezda Beograd 1945

Cukaricki Beograd 1926

Rad Beograd 1958

Varazdin
Zagreb

Istra Pula 1961
Pula

Rijeka 1946

Sibenik 1932

Split

Hajduk Split 1911

Buducnost Banovici

Rudar Kakanj

Boksit Milici

Zeljeznicar Sarajevo 1921

Sarajevo 1946

Lushnja 1927

Danube

BELGRADE

Zeleznik Beograd 1930

Southeast Europe

ORIGINS AND GROWTH OF FOOTBALL

FOOTBALL ARRIVED EARLY in Central and Eastern Europe and rose in popularity quickly with stylish, innovative play. The first football association in Vienna was founded by M.D. Nicholson, a Thomas Cook travel agent, in 1904. In Hungary, clubs emerged in the 1880s and 90s, often from gym clubs. MTK was made up of liberal Jewish defectors from a pro-Hapsburg national gym club. A league was founded in 1901 and a cup competition in 1910.

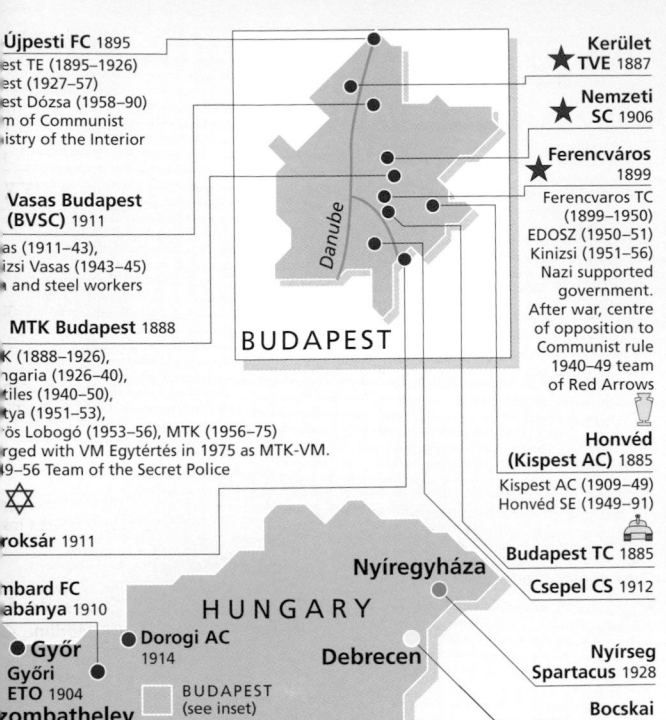

BUDAPEST

Újpesti FC 1895
est TE (1895–1926)
est (1927–57)
est Dózsa (1958–90)
m of Communist
istry of the Interior

Vasas Budapest
(BVSC) 1911
as (1911–43),
izsi Vasas (1943–45)
and steel workers

MTK Budapest 1888
K (1888–1926),
ngaria (1926–40),
tiles (1940–50),
tya (1951–53),
ös Lobogó (1953–56), MTK (1956–75)
rged with VM Egyetértés in 1975 as MTK-VM.
9–56 Team of the Secret Police

roksár 1911

Kerület
★ TVE 1887

Nemzeti
★ SC 1906

Ferencváros
★ 1899
Ferencvaros TC
(1899–1950)
EDOSZ (1950–51)
Kinizsi (1951–56)
Nazi supported
government.
After war, centre
of opposition to
Communist rule
1940–49 team
of Red Arrows

Honvéd
(Kispest AC) 1885
Kispest AC (1909–49)
Honvéd SE (1949–91)

Budapest TC 1885

Csepel CS 1912

Danube

HUNGARY

mbard FC
abánya 1910

● Győr
Győri
ETO 1904

zombatheley
Haladas
Milos 1919

Zalaegerszeg
Zalahus ZTE 1920

Nagykanizsa
1945

privnica

Osijek

ROATIA

Vinkovci
boda Novi Grad
Banovici

OSNIA
HERZE.

Posusje
Posusje

Citluk
Brotnjo
Citluk

● Dorogi AC
1914

Debrecen

BUDAPEST
(see inset)

Székesfehérvár
Videoton SC 1941

Dunaújváros
Dunaferr
SE 1951

Kula
Hajduk
Kula 1925

Novi Sad
Vojvodina Novi
Sad 1914

FK Zemun
1946

BELGRADE
(see inset)

Nyíregyháza

Nyírség
Spartacus 1928

Bocskai
Debrecen 1924

Debreceni
VSC 1979

Békéscsaba

Békéscsaba ESSC 1912

Sloga Jugomagnat
Skopje 1927

Rabotnicki Kometal
Skopje 1937

Cementarnica
55 Skopje 1955

Makedonija
GP Skopje 1932

Vardar
Skopje 1947

YUGOSLAVIA

● Kakanj

● Milici

Sarajevo

Čačak
Borac Čačak
1926

Kragujevac
Radnicki
Kragujevac 1924

Niš
Radnicki
Niš 1923

Nikšič
Sutjeska Nikšič 1944

udnocnost
odgorica 1925

Podgorica

Skopje

Kratovo

MACEDONIA

Veles

Prilep

Kavadarci

Bitola

Sileks Kratovo 1965

Borec MHK
Veles 1926

Tikves
Kavadarci 1926

Probeda Prilep 1941

Pelister Bitola 1945

ALBANIA

euta Durrës 1920

inamo Tirana 1950

artizani Tirana 1946

K Tirana 1920

nkumbini Peqin 1924

yliss Ballsh 1972

omori Berat 1923

kenderbeu Korçë 1909

hqiponja Gjirokastër 1930

Durrës

Tirana

Lushnjë

Ballsh

Peqin

Berat

● Korçë

Gjirokastër

Southeast Europe: The main clubs

Hakoah 1901	Team name with year of formation	Champions 1912–44
●	Club formed before 1912	Originated from English football
●	Club formed 1912–25	Jewish origins
●	Club formed 1925–50	Croatian
●	Club formed after 1950	Muslim
★	Founder members of League 1912	Serbian
👕	Founder members of League 1949	Colours and date unknown

International Competitions

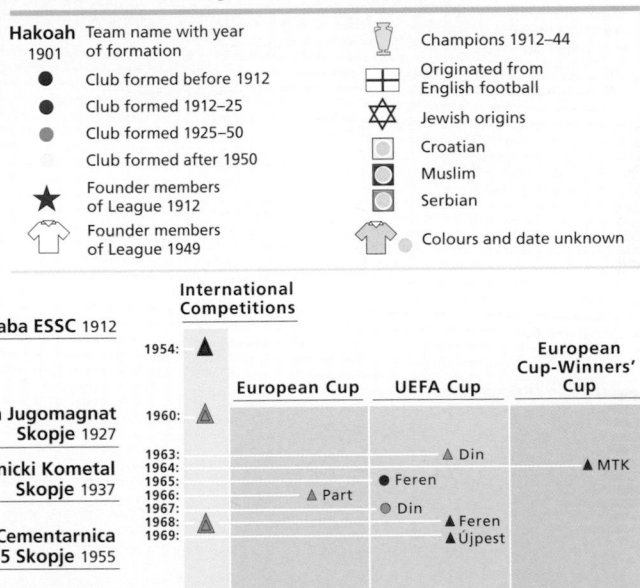

	European Cup	UEFA Cup	European Cup-Winners' Cup
1954: ▲			
1960: ▲▲			
1963:		▲ Din	
1964:			▲ MTK
1965:		● Feren	
1966:	▲ Part		
1967:		● Din	
1968: ▲		▲ Feren	
1969:		▲ Újpest	
1975: ■			▲ Feren
1976:			
1978:			△ FK
1979:		▲ Red	
1985:		▲ Video	△ Rapid
1991:	● Red		
1994:			△ Salz
1996:			△ Rapid

Key

▲ World Cup runner-up
▲ European Championships runner-up
■ European Championship host
○ Austrian competition winner
△ Austrian competition runner-up
● Hungarian competition winner
▲ Hungarian competition runner-up
● Yugoslavian competition winner
▲ Yugoslavian competition runner-up

Din – Dinamo Zagreb
Feren – Ferencváros
FK – FK Austria Wien
MTK – MTK Budapest
Part – Partizan Beograd
Rapid – Rapid Wien
Red – Crvena Zvezda Beograd
(Red Star Belgrade)
Salz – Austria Salzburg
Újpest – Újpest Dózsa
Video – Videoton

Austria

Österreichischer Fussball-Bund
Founded: 1904
Joined FIFA: 1905
Joined UEFA: 1954

IN AUSTRIA, EARLY COMPETITIVE FOOTBALL was firmly centred on the capital, Vienna. A local cup competition – Der Challenge Cup – ran from 1897 to 1911, and included teams invited from Hungary. It was superseded by a Vienna-based league. After the 1938 *Anschluss* with Germany, Austria's top clubs competed in a greater German league as well as their own, and indeed won that competition a number of times. After the Second World War the league was re-established on a national basis, the top flight consisting of ten teams playing each other four times a season.

The Austrian Cup was first played in 1919, and although it lapsed during the Second World War and for nearly a decade afterwards, it has been running annually again since 1959.

Austrian League Record 1911–2003

SEASON	CHAMPIONS	RUNNERS-UP
1911	SK Rapid Wien	Wiener Sport-Club
1912	SK Rapid Wien	Wiener Sport-Club
1913	SK Rapid Wien	Wiener Association FC
1914	Wiener Association FC	SK Rapid Wien
1915	Wiener AC	Wiener Association FC
1916	SK Rapid Wien	FAC Wien
1917	SK Rapid Wien	FAC Wien
1918	FAC Wien	SK Rapid Wien
1919	SK Rapid Wien	SC Rudolfshügel Wien
1920	SK Rapid Wien	SV Amateure Wien
1921	SK Rapid Wien	SV Amateure Wien
1922	Wiener Sport-Club	SC Hakoah Wien
1923	SK Rapid Wien	SV Amateure Wien
1924	SV Amateure Wien	First Vienna FC
1925	SC Hakoah Wien	SV Amateure Wien
1926	SV Amateure Wien	First Vienna FC
1927	Admira Wien	Brigittenauer AC Wien
1928	Admira Wien	SK Rapid Wien
1929	SK Rapid Wien	Admira Wien
1930	SK Rapid Wien	Admira Wien
1931	First Vienna FC	Admira Wien
1932	Admira Wien	First Vienna FC
1933	First Vienna FC	SK Rapid Wien
1934	Admira Wien	SK Rapid Wien
1935	SK Rapid Wien	Admira Wien
1936	Admira Wien	First Vienna FC
1937	Admira Wien	FK Austria Wien
1938	SK Rapid Wien	Wiener Sport-Club
1939	Admira Wien	SC Wacker Wien
1940	SK Rapid Wien	SC Wacker Wien
1941	SK Rapid Wien	SC Wacker Wien
1942	First Vienna FC	FC Wien
1943	First Vienna FC	Wiener AC
1944	First Vienna FC	FAC Wien
1945	SK Rapid Wien	SC Wacker Wien
1946	SK Rapid Wien	FK Austria Wien
1947	SC Wacker Wien	SK Rapid Wien
1948	SK Rapid Wien	SC Wacker Wien
1949	FK Austria Wien	SK Rapid Wien
1950	FK Austria Wien	SK Rapid Wien
1951	SK Rapid Wien	SC Wacker Wien
1952	SK Rapid Wien	FK Austria Wien
1953	FK Austria Wien	SC Wacker Wien
1954	SK Rapid Wien	FK Austria Wien
1955	First Vienna FC	Wiener Sport-Club
1956	SK Rapid Wien	SC Wacker Wien

Austrian League Record (*continued*)

SEASON	CHAMPIONS	RUNNERS-UP
1957	SK Rapid Wien	First Vienna FC
1958	Wiener Sport-Club	SK Rapid Wien
1959	Wiener Sport-Club	SK Rapid Wien
1960	SK Rapid Wien	Wiener Sport-Club
1961	FK Austria Wien	First Vienna FC
1962	FK Austria Wien	Linzer ASK
1963	FK Austria Wien	Admira Energie
1964	SK Rapid Wien	FK Austria Wien
1965	Linzer ASK	SK Rapid Wien
1966	Admira Energie	SK Rapid Wien
1967	SK Rapid Wien	Wacker Innsbruck
1968	SK Rapid Wien	Wacker Innsbruck
1969	FK Austria Wien	Wiener Sport-Club
1970	FK Austria Wien	Wiener Sport-Club
1971	Wacker Innsbruck	Austria Salzburg
1972	Wacker Innsbruck	FK Austria Wien
1973	Wacker Innsbruck	SK Rapid Wien
1974	VÖEST Linz	Wacker Innsbruck
1975	Wacker Innsbruck	VÖEST Linz
1976	FK Austria/WAC	Wacker Innsbruck
1977	Wacker Innsbruck	SK Rapid Wien
1978	FK Austria/WAC	SK Rapid Wien
1979	FK Austria Wien	Wiener Sport-Club
1980	FK Austria Wien	VÖEST Linz
1981	FK Austria Wien	SK Sturm Graz
1982	SK Rapid Wien	FK Austria Wien
1983	SK Rapid Wien	FK Austria Wien
1984	FK Austria Wien	SK Rapid Wien
1985	FK Austria Wien	SK Rapid Wien
1986	FK Austria Wien	SK Rapid Wien
1987	SK Rapid Wien	FK Austria Wien
1988	SK Rapid Wien	FK Austria Wien
1989	FC Tirol Innsbruck	FC Admira Wacker
1990	FC Tirol Innsbruck	FK Austria Wien
1991	FC Tirol Innsbruck	FK Austria Wien
1992	FK Austria Wien	SV Austria Salzburg
1993	FK Austria Wien	SV Austria Salzburg
1994	SV Austria Salzburg	FK Austria Wien
1995	SV Austria Salzburg	SK Sturm Graz
1996	SK Rapid Wien	SK Sturm Graz
1997	SV Austria Salzburg	SK Rapid Wien
1998	SK Sturm Graz	SK Rapid Wien
1999	SK Sturm Graz	FC Tirol Innsbruck
2000	FC Tirol Innsbruck	SK Sturm Graz
2001	FC Tirol Innsbruck	SK Rapid Wien
2002	FC Tirol Innsbruck	SK Sturm Graz
2003	FK Austria Wien	Grazer AK

Liechtenstein

Liechtensteiner Fussballverband
Founded: 1934
Joined FIFA: 1974
Joined UEFA: 1992

YEAR	CUP WINNERS
1999	FC Vaduz
2000	FC Vaduz
2001	FC Vaduz
2002	FC Vaduz
2003	FC Vaduz

It's hard to run a league with only 35,000 inhabitants, and the handful of registered club sides in the Fussballverband play in the lower reaches of the Swiss league. However, Liechtenstein's annual cup has been running since 1946, during which time the trophy has been won 30 times by FC Vaduz.

AUSTRIA, LIECHTENSTEIN

Austrian League Summary

TEAM	TOTALS	CHAMPIONS & RUNNERS-UP (BOLD) (*ITALICS*)
SK Rapid Wien	32, *21*	**1911–13**, *14*, **16**, **17**, *18*, **19–21**, **23**, *28*, **29**, **30**, *33*, *34*, **35**, **38**, **40**, **41**, **45**, **46**, *47*, **48**, **49**, **50**, **51**, **52**, **54**, **56**, **57**, *58*, *59*, **60**, **64**, **65**, **66**, **67**, **68**, **73**, **77**, **78**, *82*, *83*, *84–86*, **87**, **88**, **96**, *97*, *98*, *2001*
FK Austria Wien (Includes SV Amateure Wien)	19, *17*	*1920*, *21*, *23*, **24**, **25**, **26**, *37*, *46*, *49*, **50**, *52*, **53**, *54*, **61–63**, **64**, *69*, *70*, *72*, **79–81**, *82*, *83*, **84–86**, **87**, *88*, *90*, *91*, **92**, **93**, **94**, **2003**

This summary only features the top two clubs in the Austrian League. For a full list of league champions and runners-up please see the League Record opposite.

Austrian Cup Record 1919–2003

YEAR	WINNERS	SCORE	RUNNERS-UP
1919	SK Rapid Wien	3-0	Wiener Sport-Club
1920	SK Rapid Wien	5-2	SV Amateure Wien
1921	SV Amateure Wien	2-1	Wiener Sport-Club
1922	Wiener Association FC	2-1	SV Amateure Wien
1923	Wiener Sport-Club	3-1	SC Wacker Wien
1924	SV Amateure Wien	8-6 (aet)	SK Slovan Wien
1925	SV Amateure Wien	3-1	First Vienna FC
1926	SV Amateure Wien	4-3	First Vienna FC
1927	SK Rapid Wien	3-0	FK Austria Wien
1928	Admira Wien	2-1	Wiener AC
1929	First Vienna FC	3-2	SK Rapid Wien
1930	First Vienna FC	1-0	FK Austria Wien
1931	Wiener AC	16 pts-15 pts (league system)	FK Austria Wien
1932	Admira Wien	6-1	Wiener AC
1933	FK Austria Wien	1-0	Brigittenauer AC Wien
1934	Admira Wien	8-0	SK Rapid Wien
1935	FK Austria Wien	5-1	Wiener AC
1936	FK Austria Wien	3-0	First Vienna FC
1937	First Vienna FC	2-0	Wiener SC
1938	WAC Schwarz-Rot	1-0	Wiener SC
1939–45	no competition		
1946	SK Rapid Wien	2-1	First Vienna FC
1947	Wacker Wien	4-3	FK Austria Wien
1948	FK Austria Wien	2-0	SK Sturm Graz
1949	FK Austria Wien	5-2	Vorwärts Steyr
1950–58	no competition		
1959	Wiener AC	2-0	SK Rapid Wien
1960	FK Austria Wien	4-2	SK Rapid Wien
1961	SK Rapid Wien	3-1	First Vienna FC
1962	FK Austria Wien	4-1	Grazer AK
1963	FK Austria Wien	1-0	Linzer ASK
1964	Admira Energie	1-0	FK Austria Wien
1965	Linzer ASK	1-1, 1-0	Wiener Neustadt
1966	Admira Energie	1-0	SK Rapid Wien
1967	FK Austria Wien	1-2,1-0 (aet)(2 legs)	Linzer ASK
1968	SK Rapid Wien	2-0	Grazer AK
1969	SK Rapid Wien	2-1	Wiener Sport-Club

Austrian Cup Record (*continued*)

YEAR	WINNERS	SCORE	RUNNERS-UP
1970	Wacker Innsbruck	1-0	Linzer ASK
1971	FK Austria Wien	2-1 (aet)	SK Rapid Wien
1972	SK Rapid Wien	1-2, 3-1	Wiener Sport-Club
1973	Wacker Innsbruck*	1-0, 1-2	SK Rapid Wien
1974	FK Austria Wien	2-1, 1-1	Austria Salzburg
1975	Wacker Innsbruck	3-0, 0-2	Sturm Graz
1976	SK Rapid Wien*	1-0, 1-2	Wacker Innsbruck
1977	FK Austria Wien	1-0, 3-0	Wiener Sport-Club
1978	Wacker Innsbruck	1-1, 2-1	VÖEST Linz
1979	Wacker Innsbruck	1-0, 1-1	FC Admira/Wacker
1980	FK Austria Wien	0-1, 2-0	Austria Salzburg
1981	Grazer AK	0-1, 2-0 (aet)(2 legs)	Austria Salzburg
1982	FK Austria Wien	1-0, 3-1	Wacker Innsbruck
1983	SK Rapid Wien	3-0, 5-0	Wacker Innsbruck
1984	SK Rapid Wien*	1-3, 2-0	FK Austria Wien
1985	SK Rapid Wien	3-3 (aet) (4-3 pens)	FK Austria Wien
1986	FK Austria Wien	6-4 (aet)	SK Rapid Wien
1987	SK Rapid Wien	2-0, 2-2	FC Tirol Innsbruck
1988	Kremser SC*	2-0, 1-3	FC Tirol Innsbruck
1989	FC Tirol Innsbruck	0-2, 6-2	FC Admira/Wacker
1990	FK Austria Wien	3-1 (aet)	SK Rapid Wien
1991	SV Stockerau	2-1	SK Rapid Wien
1992	FK Austria Wien	1-0	FC Admira/Wacker
1993	Wacker Innsbruck	3-1	SK Rapid Wien
1994	FK Austria Wien	4-0	FC Linz
1995	SK Rapid Wien	1-0	DSV Leoben
1996	SK Sturm Graz	3-1	FC Admira/Wacker
1997	SK Sturm Graz	2-1	First Vienna FC
1998	SV Ried im Innkreis	3-1	SK Sturm Graz
1999	SK Sturm Graz	1-1 (aet) (4-2 pens)	Linzer ASK
2000	Grazer AK	2-2 (aet) (4-3 pens)	Austria Salzburg
2001	FC Kärnten	2-1 (aet)	FC Tirol Innsbruck
2002	Grazer AK	3-2	SK Sturm Graz
2003	FK Austria Wien	3-0	FC Kärnten

* Denotes winners on away goals rule.

Austrian Cup Summary

TEAM	TOTALS	WINNERS & RUNNERS-UP (BOLD) (*ITALICS*)
FK Austria Wien (includes SV Amateure Wien)	23, *9*	*1920*, **21**, **22**, **24–26**, **27**, *30*, *31*, **33**, **35**, *36*, *47*, **48**, **49**, **60**, **62**, **63**, *64*, **67**, **71**, **74**, **77**, **80**, **82**, *84*, *85*, **86**, **90**, **92**, **94**, **2003**
SK Rapid Wien	14, *11*	**1919**, *20*, **27**, *29*, *34*, **46**, *59*, *60*, **61**, **66**, *68*, **69**, *71*, **72**, **73**, *76*, **83–85**, *86*, **87**, *90*, *91*, **93**, *95*

This summary only features the top two clubs in the Austrian Cup. For a full list of league champions and runners-up please see the Cup Record above.

Slovenia

Nogometna Zveza Slovenije
Founded: 1920
Joined FIFA: 1992
Joined UEFA: 1993

A separate national league and cup competition have been running in Slovenia since the country's independence in 1991.

SEASON	LEAGUE CHAMPIONS
1999	NK Maribor
2000	NK Maribor
2001	NK Maribor
2002	NK Maribor
2003	NK Maribor

YEAR	CUP WINNERS
1999	NK Maribor
2000	SCT Olimpija Ljubljana
2001	HIT Gorica
2002	HIT Gorica
2003	SCT Olimpija Ljubljana

Switzerland

Schweizerischer Fussballverband
Founded: 1895
Joined FIFA: 1904
Joined UEFA: 1954

A national championship began in Switzerland in 1898, contested by regional league winners. A national cup followed in 1926 and a national league in 1934.

SEASON	LEAGUE CHAMPIONS
1999	Servette FC Genève
2000	FC St. Gallen
2001	Grasshopper-Club
2002	FC Basel
2003	Grasshopper-Club

YEAR	CUP WINNERS
1999	Lausanne-Sports
2000	FC Zurich
2001	Servette FC Genève
2002	FC Basel
2003	FC Basel

AUSTRIA, SLOVENIA, SWITZERLAND

Hungary

Magyar Labdarúgó Szövetség
Founded: 1901
Joined FIFA: 1906
Joined UEFA: 1954

THE HUNGARIAN FOOTBALL ASSOCIATION and the league championship were both established in 1901, but drew on a decade's competitive football firmly established in Budapest. Hungarian football was always quite separate from any other part of the Austro-Hungarian Empire, which disintegrated in 1918. The amateur years (1901–26) were dominated by the Budapest teams MTK Budapest and Ferencváros, and saw the establishment of a national cup competition in 1910. During the Second World War, the league carried on until 1944, with teams from outside Hungary. The 1944 champion, Nagyváradi AC, was from north-western Romania.

After the war, domestic football was treated to the usual Communist takeover and reorganization. Not surprisingly, the army-backed team Honvéd dominated the era. The 1956 uprising against both Soviet occupiers and homegrown Communists saw the league abandoned and the rapid departure of star players Puskas, Kocis and Czibor for Spain. The final decades of Communist rule saw Honvéd and Ujpesti in the forefront of the Hungarian league.

The post-Communist era has seen a return of MTK (now called MTK Hungária FC) and Ferencváros to prominence, though woeful finances, betting scandals and stadium violence have left all in the league struggling.

Hungarian Amateur League Record 1901–26

SEASON	CHAMPIONS	RUNNERS-UP
1901	BTC	MUE
1902	BTC	FTC
1903	FTC	BTC
1904	MTK	FTC
1905	FTC	Postas
1906	no championship	
1907	FTC	MAC
1908	MTK	FTC
1909	FTC	MAC
1910	FTC	MTK
1911	FTC	MTK
1912	FTC	MTK
1913	FTC	MTK
1914	MTK	FTC
1915–16	no championship	
1917	MTK	Törekvés
1918	MTK	FTC
1919	MTK	FTC
1920	MTK	KAC
1921	MTK	ÚTE
1922	MTK	FTC
1923	MTK	ÚTE
1924	MTK	FTC
1925	MTK	FTC
1926	FTC	MTK

Hungarian Professional League Record 1927–2003

SEASON	CHAMPIONS	RUNNERS-UP
1927	Ferencváros	Újpest
1928	Ferencváros	Hungária
1929	Hungária	Ferencváros
1930	Újpest	Ferencváros

Hungarian League Record (*continued*)

SEASON	CHAMPIONS	RUNNERS-UP
1931	Újpest	Hungária
1932	Ferencváros	Újpest
1933	Újpest	Hungária
1934	Ferencváros	Újpest
1935	Ujpest	Ferencváros
1936	Hungária	Újpest
1937	Hungária	Ferencváros
1938	Ferencváros	Újpest
1939	Újpest	Ferencváros
1940	Ferencváros	Hungária
1941	Ferencváros	Újpest
1942	Csepeli WMFC	Újpest
1943	Csepeli WMFC	Nagyváradi AC
1944	Nagyváradi AC	Ferencváros
1945	no championship	
1946	Újpest	Vasas
1947	Újpest	Kispest
1948	Csepel	Vasas
1949	Ferencváros	Hungária
1950	Honvéd	EDOSZ
1950*	Honvéd	Textiles
1951	Bástya	Honvéd
1952	Honvéd	Bástya
1953	Vörös Lobogó	Honvéd
1954	Honvéd	Vörös Lobogó
1955	Honvéd	Vörös Lobogó
1956	no championship**	
1957	Vasas SC	Hungária
1958	MTK	Honvéd
1959	Csepel	MTK
1960	Újpest Dozsa	Ferencváros
1961	Vasas SC	Újpest Dozsa
1962	Vasas SC	Újpest Dozsa
1963	Ferencváros	MTK
1963*	Győri V. ETO	Honvéd
1964	Ferencváros	Honvéd
1965	Vasas SC	Ferencváros
1966	Vasas SC	Ferencváros
1967	Ferencváros	Újpest Dozsa
1968	Ferencváros	Újpest Dozsa
1969	Újpest Dozsa	Honvéd
1970	Újpest Dozsa	Ferencváros
1971	Újpest Dozsa	Ferencváros
1972	Újpest Dozsa	Honvéd
1973	Újpest Dozsa	Ferencváros
1974	Újpest Dozsa	Ferencváros
1975	Újpest Dozsa	Honvéd
1976	Ferencváros	Videoton
1977	Vasas SC	Újpest Dozsa
1978	Újpest Dozsa	Honvéd
1979	Újpest Dozsa	Ferencváros
1980	Honvéd	Újpest Dozsa
1981	Ferencváros	Tatabánya
1982	Rába ETO Győr	Ferencváros
1983	Rába ETO Győr	Ferencváros
1984	Honvéd	Rába ETO Győr
1985	Honvéd	Rába ETO Győr
1986	Honvéd	PMSC
1987	MTK-VM	Újpest Dozsa
1988	Honvéd	Tatabánya
1989	Honvéd	Ferencváros
1990	Újpest Dozsa	MTK-VM
1991	Honvéd	Ferencváros
1992	Ferencváros	Vác FC Samsung
1993	Kispest-Honvéd	Vác FC Samsung
1994	Vác FC Samsung	Kispest HFC
1995	Ferencváros	ÚTE
1996	Ferencváros	BVSC

Hungarian League Record (*continued*)

SEASON	CHAMPIONS	RUNNERS-UP
1997	MTK	ÚTE
1998	Újpesti FC	Ferencváros
1999	MTK Hungária FC	Ferencváros
2000	Dunaferr FC	MTK Hungária FC
2001	Ferencváros	Dunaferr FC
2002	Zalahús Zte FC	Ferencváros
2003	MTK Hungária FC	Ferencváros

* Extra autumn leagues played during these years.

** League championship was abandoned following the Soviet invasion.

Hungarian League Summary

TEAM	TOTALS	CHAMPIONS & RUNNERS-UP (BOLD) (*ITALICS*)
Ferencváros (includes FTC and EDOSZ)	27, 32	*1902*, **03**, *04*, **05**, **07**, *08*, **09–13**, *14*, *18*, *19*, *22*, *24*, *25*, **26–28**, *29*, *30*, **32**, **34**, *35*, *37*, **38**, *39*, **40**, **41**, *44*, **49**, *50*, *60*, **63**, **64**, *65*, *66*, **67**, **68**, *70*, *71*, *73*, *74*, **76**, *79*, **81**, *82*, *83*, *89*, *91*, **92**, **95**, *96*, *98*, *99*, **2001**, *02*, **03**
MTK Hungária FC (includes MTK, Hungária, Vörös Lobogó, Bástya, MTK-VM and Textiles)	22, 18	**1904**, **08**, **10–13**, **14**, **17–25**, **26**, **28**, **29**, **31**, **33**, **36**, **37**, **40**, **49**, **50***, **51**, **52**, **53**, **54**, **55**, **57**, **58**, **59**, **63**, **87**, **90**, **97**, **99**, **2000**, **03**
Újpesti FC (includes ÚTE, Újpest and Újpest Dozsa)	19, 18	*1921*, *23*, *27*, **30**, **31**, **32**, **33**, **34**, **35**, **36**, *38*, *39*, *41*, *42*, **46**, **47**, **60**, *61*, *62*, *67*, *68*, **69–75**, **77**, **78**, **79**, *80*, *87*, **90**, *95*, *97*, *98*
Kispest-Honvéd FC (includes Kispest, Kispest HFC and Honvéd)	13, 11	*1947*, **50**, **50***, *51*, **52**, *53*, **54**, **55**, *58*, *63**, **64**, **69**, *72*, *75*, *78*, **80**, **84–86**, **88**, **89**, **91**, **93**, **94**

* Denotes honours in extra autumn leagues.

This summary only features the top four clubs in the Hungarian League. For a full list of league champions and runners-up please see the League Record above.

Hungarian Cup Record 1910–2003

YEAR	WINNERS	SCORE	RUNNERS-UP
1910	MTK	1-1, (replay) 3-1	BTC
1911	MTK	1-0	MAC
1912	MTK	w/o	FTC
1913	FTC	2-1	BAK
1914	MTK	4-0	MAC
1915–21		*no competition*	
1922	FTC	2-2, (replay) 1-0	ÚTE
1923	MTK	4-1	ÚTE
1924		*no competition*	
1925	MTK	4-0	ÚTE
1926	Kispest AC	1-1, (replay) 3-2 (aet)	Budapest EAC
1927	Ferencváros	3-0	Újpest
1928	Ferencváros	5-1	Attila Miskolc
1929		*no competition*	
1930	Bocskai Debrecen	5-1	Bástya Szeged
1931	Kerület TVE	4-1	Ferencváros
1932	Hungária	1-1, (replay) 4-3	Ferencváros
1933	Ferencváros	1-1	Újpest
1934	Soroksar	2-2, (replay) 1-1, (replay) 2-0	BSZKRT
1935	Ferencváros	2-1	Hungária
1936–40		*no competition*	
1941	Szolnoki MAV	3-0	Salgótarján BTC
1942	Ferencváros	6-2	DIMAVAG
1943	Ferencváros	3-0	Salgótarján BTC
1944	Ferencváros	2-2, (replay) 3-1	Kolozsvári AC

Hungarian Cup Record (*continued*)

YEAR	WINNERS	SCORE	RUNNERS-UP
1945–51		*no competition*	
1952	Bástya	3-2	Dorogi AC
1953–54		*no competition*	
1955	Vasas	3-2	Honvéd
1956	Ferencváros	2-1	Salgótarján BTC
1957–63		*no competition*	
1964	Honvéd	1-0	Győri V. ETO
1965	Győri V. ETO	4-0	Diósgyőri VTK
1966	Győri V. ETO	1-1, (replay) 3-2	Ferencváros
1967	Győri V. ETO	1-0	Salgótarján BTC
1968	MTK	2-1	Honvéd
1969	Újpest Dozsa	3-1	Honvéd
1970	Újpest Dozsa	3-2	Komio Bányász
1971		*no competition*	
1972	Ferencváros	2-1	Tatabánya Bányász
1973	Vasas	4-3	Honvéd
1974	Ferencváros	3-1	Komio Bányász
1975	Újpest Dozsa	3-2	Haladás VSE
1976	Ferencváros	1-0	MTK-VM
1977	Diósgyőri VTK	*	Ferencváros
1978	Ferencváros	4-2	Pécsi MSC
1979	Rába ETO Győr	1-0	Ferencváros
1980	Diósgyőri VTK	3-1	Vasas
1981	Vasas	1-0	Diósgyőri VTK
1982	Újpest Dozsa	2-0	Videoton
1983	Újpest Dozsa	3-2	Honvéd
1984	Siófoki Bányász	2-1	Rába ETO Győr
1985	Honvéd	5-0	Tatabánya Bányász
1986	Vasas	0-0 (5-4 pens)	Ferencváros
1987	Újpest Dozsa	3-2	Pécsi MSC
1988	Békéscsaba ESSC	3-2	Honvéd
1989	Honvéd	1-0	Ferencváros
1990	Pécsi MSC	2-0	Honvéd
1991	Ferencváros	1-0	Vác Izzo FC
1992	Újpest Dozsa	1-0	Vác FC Samsung
1993	Ferencváros	1-1, (replay) 1-1 (5-3 pens)	Szombathely Haladás VSE
1994	Ferencváros	3-0, 2-1 (2 legs)	Honvéd
1995	Ferencváros	2-0, 4-3 (2 legs)	Vác FC Samsung
1996	Honvéd	1-0, 2-0 (2 legs)	BVSC Dreher
1997	MTK Hungária FC	6-0, 2-0 (2 legs)	BVSC Budapest
1998	MTK Hungária FC	1-0	Újpesti FC
1999	Debreceni VSC	2-1	Lombard FC Tatabánya
2000	MTK Hungária FC	3-1	Vasas DH
2001	Debreceni VSC	5-2	Videoton
2002	Újpesti FC	2-1	Szombathely Haladás VSE
2003	Ferencváros	2-1	Debreceni VSC

w/o denotes walk over

* A league format was used to determine the winner of the 1977 cup.

Hungarian Cup Summary

TEAM	TOTALS	WINNERS & RUNNERS-UP (BOLD) (*ITALICS*)
Ferencváros (includes FTC)	19, 8	*1912*, **13**, *22*, **27**, *28*, *31*, *32*, *33*, **35**, **42–44**, **56**, *66*, **72**, **74**, **76**, **77**, **78**, *79*, *86*, *89*, **91**, **93–95**, **2003**
MTK Hungária FC (includes MTK, Hungária, Bástya and MTK-VM)	12, 2	**1910–12**, **14**, **23**, **25**, **32**, **35**, *52*, **68**, *76*, **97**, **98**, **2000**
Újpesti FC (includes ÚTE, Újpest and Újpest Dozsa)	8, 6	*1922*, *23*, *25*, *27*, *33*, **69**, **70**, **75**, **82**, **83**, **87**, **92**, *98*, **2002**

This summary only features the top three clubs in the Hungarian Cup. For a full list of cup winners and runners-up please see the Cup Record above.

HUNGARY

Serbia & Montenegro

Fooball Association of Serbia & Montenegro
Founded: 1919
Joined FIFA: 1919
Joined UEFA: 1993

BEFORE THE FIRST WORLD WAR, clubs existed in Belgrade, Split, Zagreb and elsewhere. After the postwar dismemberment of the Ottoman and Austro-Hungarian Empires, the new state of Yugoslavia was formed. With it, in 1919, came a national FA. A national league was established in 1923 but, like Yugoslavia, it was fragmented by the Second World War. Croatia's alliance with Germany saw the creation of an independent Croatian league which lasted for the duration of the war.

With the end of the war and the triumph of General Tito's Communist partisans, Yugoslavian football was reorganized and a national league re-created. It has run continuously ever since, despite war in the 1990s and the departure of Croatian, Bosnian, Slovenian and Macedonian states and clubs. The Yugoslavian FA was renamed the FA of Serbia & Montenegro in 2002.

Yugoslavian League Record 1923–91

SEASON	CHAMPIONS	RUNNERS-UP
1923	Gradanski Zagreb	SASK Sarajevo
1924	Yugoslavia Beograd	Hajduk Split
1925	Yugoslavia Beograd	Gradanski Beograd
1926	Gradanski Zagreb	Yugoslav Beograd
1927	Hajduk Split	BSK Beograd
1928	Concordia Zagreb	Hajduk Split
1929	Hajduk Split	BSK Beograd
1930	Concordia Zagreb	Yugoslav Beograd
1931	BSK Beograd	Concordia Zagreb
1932	Concordia Zagreb	Hajduk Split
1933	BSK Beograd	Hajduk Split
1934	*no championship*	
1935	BSK Beograd	Yugoslav Beograd
1936	BSK Beograd	Slavia Sarajevo
1937	Gradanski Zagreb	Hajduk Split
1938	HASK Zagreb	BSK Beograd
1939	BSK Beograd	Gradanski Beograd
1940	Gradanski Zagreb	BSK Beograd
1941–46	*no championship*	
1947	Partizan Beograd	Dinamo Zagreb
1948	Dinamo Zagreb	Hajduk Split
1949	Partizan Beograd	Crvena Zvezda
1950	Hajduk Split	Crvena Zvezda
1951	Crvena Zvezda	Dinamo Zagreb
1952	Hajduk Split	Crvena Zvezda
1953	Crvena Zvezda	Hajduk Split
1954	Dinamo Zagreb	Partizan Beograd
1955	Hajduk Split	BSK Beograd
1956	Crvena Zvezda	Partizan Beograd
1957	Crvena Zvezda	Vojvodina Novi Sad
1958	Dinamo Zagreb	Partizan Beograd
1959	Crvena Zvezda	Partizan Beograd
1960	Crvena Zvezda	Dinamo Zagreb
1961	Partizan Beograd	Crvena Zvezda
1962	Partizan Beograd	Vojvodina Novi Sad
1963	Partizan Beograd	Dinamo Zagreb
1964	Crvena Zvezda	OFK Beograd
1965	Partizan Beograd	FK Sarajevo
1966	Vojvodina Novi Sad	Dinamo Zagreb
1967	FK Sarajevo	Dinamo Zagreb
1968	Crvena Zvezda	Dinamo Zagreb
1969	Crvena Zvezda	Dinamo Zagreb
1970	Crvena Zvezda	Partizan Beograd
1971	Hajduk Split	Željeznicar Sarajevo
1972	Željeznicar Sarajevo	Crvena Zvezda

Yugoslavian League Record (*continued*)

SEASON	CHAMPIONS	RUNNERS-UP
1973	Crvena Zvezda	Velez Mostar
1974	Hajduk Split	Velez Mostar
1975	Hajduk Split	Vojvodina Novi Sad
1976	Partizan Beograd	Hajduk Split
1977	Crvena Zvezda	Dinamo Zagreb
1978	Partizan Beograd	Crvena Zvezda
1979	Hajduk Split	Dinamo Zagreb
1980	Crvena Zvezda	FK Sarajevo
1981	Crvena Zvezda	Hajduk Split
1982	Dinamo Zagreb	Crvena Zvezda
1983	Partizan Beograd	Dinamo Zagreb
1984	Crvena Zvezda	Partizan Beograd
1985	FK Sarajevo	Hajduk Split
1986	Partizan Beograd	Crvena Zvezda
1987	Partizan Beograd	Velez Mostar
1988	Crvena Zvezda	Partizan Beograd
1989	Vojvodina Novi Sad	Crvena Zvezda
1990	Crvena Zvezda	Dinamo Zagreb
1991	Crvena Zvezda	Dinamo Zagreb

Serbia & Montenegro League Record 1992–2003

SEASON	CHAMPIONS	RUNNERS-UP
1992	Crvena Zvezda	Partizan Beograd
1993	Partizan Beograd	Crvena Zvezda
1994	Partizan Beograd	Crvena Zvezda
1995	Vojvodina Novi Sad	Crvena Zvezda
1996	Partizan Beograd	Crvena Zvezda
1997	Partizan Beograd	Crvena Zvezda
1998	FK Obilić	Crvena Zvezda
1999	Partizan Beograd	FK Obilić
2000	Crvena Zvezda	Partizan Beograd
2001	Crvena Zvezda	Partizan Beograd
2002	Partizan Beograd	Crvena Zvezda
2003	Partizan Beograd	Crvena Zvezda

Serbia & Montenegro League Summary

TEAM	TOTALS	CHAMPIONS & RUNNERS-UP (BOLD) (*ITALICS*)
Crvena Zvezda	21, 17	*1949, 50,* **51,** *52,* **53,** *56,* **57,** *59,* **60, 61, 64, 68–70,** *72,* **73, 77,** *78,* **80, 81,** *82,* **84,** *86,* **88, 89, 90–92,** *93–98,* **2000, 01,** *02, 03*
Partizan Beograd	18, 10	**1947, 49,** *54,* **56,** *58,* **59, 61–63, 65,** *70,* **76, 78, 83,** *84,* **86, 87,** *88,* **92, 93, 94, 96, 97,** *99,* **2000, 01, 02, 03**
Hajduk Split	9, 10	*1924,* **27,** *28,* **29,** *32, 33,* **37,** *48,* **50,** *52, 53, 55,* **71,** *74,* **75,** *76,* **79,** *81, 85*
BSK Beograd	5, 5	*1927, 29,* **31,** *33,* **35, 36,** *38, 39, 40,* **55**

This summary only features the top four clubs in the Serbia & Montenegro League. For a full list of league champions and runners-up please see the League Record above.

Yugoslavian Cup Record 1947–91

YEAR	WINNERS	SCORE	RUNNERS-UP
1947	Partizan Beograd	2-0	Naša Krila Zemun
1948	Crvena Zvezda	3-0	Partizan Beograd
1949	Crvena Zvezda	3-2	Naša Krila Zemun
1950	Crvena Zvezda	1-1, (replay) 3-0	Dinamo Zagreb
1951	Dinamo Zagreb	2-0, 2-0 (2 legs)	Vojvodina Novi Sad
1952	Partizan Beograd	6-0	Crvena Zvezda
1953	BSK Beograd	2-0	Hajduk Split
1954	Partizan Beograd	4-1	Crvena Zvezda
1955	BSK Beograd	2-0	Hajduk Split

SERBIA& MONTENEGRO

Yugoslavian Cup Record (*continued*)

YEAR	WINNERS	SCORE	RUNNERS-UP
1956		*no competition*	
1957	Partizan Beograd	5-3	Radnicki Beograd
1958	Crvena Zvezda	4-0	Velez Mostar
1959	Crvena Zvezda	3-1	Partizan Beograd
1960	Dinamo Zagreb	3-2	Partizan Beograd
1961	Vardar Skopje	2-1	Varteks Varaždin
1962	OFK Beograd	4-1	Spartak Subotica
1963	Dinamo Zagreb	4-1	Hajduk Split
1964	Crvena Zvezda	3-0	Dinamo Zagreb
1965	Dinamo Zagreb	2-1	Budučnost Titograd
1966	OFK Beograd	6-2 (aet)	Dinamo Zagreb
1967	Hajduk Split	2-1	FK Sarajevo
1968	Crvena Zvezda	7-0	FK Bor
1969	Dinamo Zagreb	3-3, (replay) 3-0	Hajduk Split
1970	Crvena Zvezda	2-2, (replay) 1-0 (aet)	Olimpia Ljubljana
1971	Crvena Zvezda	4-0	Sloboda Turzia
1972	Hajduk Split	2-1	Dinamo Zagreb
1973	Dinamo Zagreb	2-1	Crvena Zvezda
1974	Hajduk Split	1-1, (replay) 2-1	Crvena Zvezda
1975	Hajduk Split	1-0	Borac Banja Luka
1976	Hajduk Split	1-0 (aet)	Dinamo Zagreb
1977	Hajduk Split	2-0 (aet)	Budučnost Titograd
1978	NK Rijeka	1-0 (aet)	Trepca Mitrovica
1979	NK Rijeka	0-0, (replay) 2-1	Partizan Beograd
1980	Dinamo Zagreb	1-1, (replay) 1-0	Crvena Zvezda
1981	Velez Mostar	3-2	Željeznicar Sarajevo
1982	Crvena Zvezda	2-2, (replay) 4-2	Dinamo Zagreb
1983	Dinamo Zagreb	3-2	FK Sarajevo
1984	Hajduk Split	0-0, (replay) 2-1	Crvena Zvezda
1985	Crvena Zvezda	1-1, (replay) 2-1	Dinamo Zagreb
1986	Velez Mostar	3-1	Dinamo Zagreb
1987	Hajduk Split	1-1 (aet)(9-8 pens)	NK Rijeka
1988	Borac Banja Luka	1-0	Crvena Zvezda
1989	Partizan Beograd	6-1	Velez Mostar
1990	Crvena Zvezda	1-0	Hajduk Split
1991	Hajduk Split	1-0	Crvena Zvezda

Serbia & Montenegro Cup Record 1992–2003

YEAR	WINNERS	SCORE	RUNNERS-UP
1992	Partizan Beograd	1-0, 2-2 (2 legs)	Crvena Zvezda
1993	Crvena Zvezda	0-1, 1-0 (5-4 pens)(2 legs)	Partizan Beograd
1994	Partizan Beograd	3-2, 6-1 (2 legs)	Spartak Subotica
1995	Crvena Zvezda	4-0, 0-0 (2 legs)	FK Obilić
1996	Crvena Zvezda	3-0, 3-1 (2 legs)	Partizan Beograd
1997	Crvena Zvezda	0-0, 1-0 (2 legs)	Vojvodina Novi Sad
1998	Partizan Beograd	0-0, 2-0 (2 legs)	FK Obilić
1999	Crvena Zvezda	4-2, 4-0 (2 legs)	Partizan Beograd
2000	Crvena Zvezda	4-0	Napradak Kruševac
2001	Partizan Beograd	1-0	Crvena Zvezda
2002	Crvena Zvezda	1-0	Sartid Smederovo
2003	Sartid Smederovo	1-0	Crvena Zvezda

Serbia & Montenegro Cup Summary

TEAM	TOTALS	WINNERS & RUNNERS-UP (BOLD) (*ITALICS*)
Crvena Zvezda	**19**, *11*	1948–50, *52, 54,* **58, 59, 64, 68, 70, 71, 73, 74, 80, 82, 84, 85,** *88,* **90,** *91, 92, 93,* **95–97, 99, 2000,** *01,* **02,** *03*
Partizan Beograd	**9**, *7*	**1947,** *48,* **52, 54, 57, 59, 60,** *79,* **89,** *92, 93,* **94,** *96,* **98,** *99,* **2001**
Hajduk Split	**9**, *5*	*1953, 55, 63,* **67,** *69,* **72, 74–77, 84,** *87,* **90,** *91*
Dinamo Zagreb	**8**, *8*	*1950,* **51,** *60,* **63,** *64, 65, 66,* **69,** *72, 73, 76,* **80,** *82, 83, 85, 86*

This summary only features the top four clubs in the Serbia & Montenegro Cup. For a full list of cup winners and runners-up please see the Cup Record above.

Albania

Federata Shqiptarë e Futbollit
Founded: 1930
Joined FIFA: 1932
Joined UEFA: 1954

Albania's national league began in 1929 (prior to the formation of the national FA), and the cup competition in 1947. Both tournaments have been dominated by teams from the capital city, Tirana.

SEASON	LEAGUE CHAMPIONS
1999	SK Tirana
2000	SK Tirana
2001	Vllaznia Shkodër
2002	Dinamo Tiranë
2003	SK Tirana

YEAR	CUP WINNERS
1999	SK Tirana
2000	Teuta Durrës
2001	SK Tirana
2002	SK Tirana
2003	Dinamo Tiranë

Bosnia-Herzegovina

Nogometni Savez Bosne i Hercegovine
Founded: 1992
Joined FIFA: 1996
Joined UEFA: 1996

A Bosnian FA was established in 1992 and league football in separate Serbian, Muslim and Croat leagues in 1996. In the 2002–03 season all three leagues were integrated into a single national league.

SEASON	LEAGUE CHAMPIONS
1999	*Play-offs cancelled*
2000	Brotnjo Citluk
2001	Željeznicar Sarajevo
2002	Željeznicar Sarajevo
2003	FK Leotar

YEAR	CUP WINNERS
1999	Sarajevo
2000	Željeznicar Sarajevo
2001	Željeznicar Sarajevo
2002	Sarajevo
2003	Željeznicar Sarajevo

Croatia

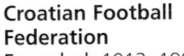

Croatian Football Federation
Founded: 1912, 1991
Joined FIFA: 1992
Joined UEFA: 1993

Croatia's FA was formed in 1912, when still part of Austro-Hungary, but was incorporated into Yugoslavia in 1918. With the break-up of Yugoslavia in 1991, Croatian football regained its independence.

SEASON	LEAGUE CHAMPIONS
1999	Dinamo Zagreb
2000	Dinamo Zagreb
2001	Hajduk Split
2002	NK Zagreb
2003	Dinamo Zagreb

YEAR	CUP WINNERS
1999	Osijek
2000	Hajduk Split
2001	Dinamo Zagreb
2002	Dinamo Zagreb
2003	Hajduk Split

Macedonia

Macedonian Football Union
Founded: 1908
Joined FIFA: 1994
Joined UEFA: 1994

Contemporary Macedonia emerged from the break-up of the former Yugoslavia in 1991. National football competitions, cup and league, rapidly followed independence, starting in the 1992–93 season.

SEASON	LEAGUE CHAMPIONS
1999	Sloga Jugomagnat Skopje
2000	Sloga Jugomagnat Skopje
2001	Sloga Jugomagnat Skopje
2002	Vardar Skopje
2003	Vardar Skopje

YEAR	CUP WINNERS
1999	Vardar Skopje
2000	Sloga Jugomagnat Skopje
2001	Pelister Bitola
2002	Pobeda Prilep
2003	Cementarnica Skopje

Romania

Federaţia Româna de Fotbal
Founded: 1908
Joined FIFA: 1930
Joined UEFA: 1954

ROMANIANS took to football earlier and more enthusiastically than any other Balkan nation, and despite war, revolution and penury, football remains an enduring passion in the country. The national FA was set up in 1908, with the considerable support of Prince Carol, heir to the Romanian throne. The first national league was set up in 1910, with play-offs to contest the title until 1934. In 1935, a formal national league and cup competition were established.

The Communist re-creation of Romanian football after the Second World War involved considerable change. Cities were generally restricted to a single team; many clubs that had explicitly regional and ethnic connections (Hungarian, Jewish and German teams) were transformed or wound down. The league was cancelled in 1957 to allow the new season to start in the autumn of that year and finish in spring the following year.

Romanian League Record 1910–2003

SEASON	CHAMPIONS	RUNNERS-UP
1910	Olimpia Bucureşti	*not known*
1911	Olimpia Bucureşti	*not known*
1912	United FC Ploieşti	*not known*
1913	Colentina Bucureşti	*not known*
1914	Colentina Bucureşti	*not known*
1915	România-Americana	*not known*
1916	Prahova Ploiesti	*not known*
1917–19	*no championship*	
1920	Venus Bucureşti	*not known*
1921	Venus Bucureşti	*not known*
1922	Chinezul Timişoara	Victoria Cluj
1923	Chinezul Timişoara	Victoria Cluj
1924	Chinezul Timişoara	CAO Oradea
1925	Chinezul Timişoara	UCAS Petroşani
1926	Chinezul Timişoara	Juventus Bucureşti
1927	Chinezul Timişoara	Coltea Braşov
1928	Coltea Braşov	Jiul Lupeni
1929	Venus Bucureşti	România Cluj
1930	Juventus Bucureşti	Gloria CFR Arad
1931	UDR Reşiţa	SG Sibiu
1932	Venus Bucureşti	UDR Reşiţa
1933	Ripensia Timişoara	Universitatea Cluj
1934	Venus Bucureşti	Ripensia Timişoara
1935	Ripensia Timişoara	CAO Oradea
1936	Ripensia Timişoara	AMEFA Arad
1937	Venus Bucureşti	Rapid Bucureşti
1938	Ripensia Timişoara	Rapid Bucureşti
1939	Venus Bucureşti	Ripensia Timişoara
1940	Venus Bucureşti	Rapid Bucureşti
1941	Unirea Tricolor	Rapid Bucureşti
1942–46	*no championship*	
1947	IT Arad	Carmen Bucureşti
1948	IT Arad	CFR Timişoara
1949	ICO Oradea	CFR Bucureşti
1950	Flamura Roşie	Lokomotiva Buch
1951	CCA Bucureşti	Dinamo Bucureşti
1952	CCA Bucureşti	Dinamo Bucureşti
1953	CCA Bucureşti	Dinamo Bucureşti
1954	Flamura Roşie	CCA Bucureşti
1955	Dinamo Bucureşti	Flacără Ploieşti
1956	CCA Bucureşti	Dinamo Bucureşti
1957*		
1958	Petrolul Ploieşti	CCA Bucureşti

Romanian League Record (*continued*)

SEASON	CHAMPIONS	RUNNERS-UP
1960	CCA Bucureşti	Steagul Rosu Braşov
1961	CCA Bucureşti	Dinamo Bucureşti
1962	Dinamo Bucureşti	Petrolul Ploieşti
1963	Dinamo Bucureşti	Steaua Bucureşti
1964	Dinamo Bucureşti	Rapid Bucureşti
1965	Dinamo Bucureşti	Rapid Bucureşti
1966	Petrolul Ploieşti	Rapid Bucureşti
1967	Rapid Bucureşti	Dinamo Bucureşti
1968	Steaua Bucureşti	FC Argeş Piteşti
1969	UT Arad	Dinamo Bucureşti
1970	UT Arad	Rapid Bucureşti
1971	Dinamo Bucureşti	Rapid Bucureşti
1972	FC Argeş Piteşti	UT Arad
1973	Dinamo Bucureşti	Universitatea Craiova
1974	Universitatea Craiova	Dinamo Bucureşti
1975	Universitatea Craiova	ASA Tirgu Mureş
1976	Steaua Bucureşti	Dinamo Bucureşti
1977	Dinamo Bucureşti	Steaua Bucureşti
1978	Steaua Bucureşti	FC Argeş Piteşti
1979	FC Argeş Piteşti	Dinamo Bucureşti
1980	Universitatea Craiova	Steaua Bucureşti
1981	Universitatea Craiova	Dinamo Bucureşti
1982	Dinamo Bucureşti	Universitatea Craiova
1983	Dinamo Bucureşti	Universitatea Craiova
1984	Dinamo Bucureşti	Steaua Bucureşti
1985	Steaua Bucureşti	Dinamo Bucureşti
1986	Steaua Bucureşti	Sportul Studentesc
1987	Steaua Bucureşti	Dinamo Bucureşti
1988	Steaua Bucureşti	Dinamo Bucureşti
1989	Steaua Bucureşti	Dinamo Bucureşti
1990	Dinamo Bucureşti	Steaua Bucureşti
1991	Universitatea Craiova	Steaua Bucureşti
1992	Dinamo Bucureşti	Steaua Bucureşti
1993	Steaua Bucureşti	Dinamo Bucureşti
1994	Steaua Bucureşti	Universitatea Craiova
1995	Steaua Bucureşti	Universitatea Craiova
1996	Steaua Bucureşti	National Bucureşti
1997	Steaua Bucureşti	National Bucureşti
1998	Steaua Bucureşti	Rapid Bucureşti
1999	Rapid Bucureşti	Dinamo Bucureşti
2000	Dinamo Bucureşti	Rapid Bucureşti
2001	Steaua Bucureşti	Dinamo Bucureşti
2002	Dinamo Bucureşti	National Bucureşti
2003	Rapid Bucureşti	Steaua Bucureşti

* There were no recorded league champions for 1957 as Romania's football league changed from a winter-to-winter season to an autumn-to-spring season.

Romanian League Summary

TEAM	TOTALS	CHAMPIONS & RUNNERS-UP (BOLD) (*ITALICS*)
Steaua Bucureşti (includes CCA Bucureşti)	21, 10	**1951–53**, *54*, **56**, *58*, **60**, **61**, *63*, **68**, **76**, *77*, **78**, *80*, **84**, **85–89**, *90–92*, **93–98**, **2001**, *03*
Dinamo Bucureşti	15, 19	*1951–53*, **55**, *56*, **59**, *61*, **62–65**, *67*, **69**, *71*, **73**, **74**, *76*, **77**, *79*, **81**, *82–84*, *85*, *87–89*, **90**, *92*, **93**, *99*, **2000**, *01*, *02*
Venus Bucureşti	8, 0	**1920**, **21**, **29**, **32**, **34**, **37**, **39**, **40**
Chinezul Timişoara	6, 0	**1922–27**
Universitatea Craiova	5, 5	*1973*, **74**, **75**, **80**, **81**, *82*, *83*, **91**, *94*, *95*
Ripensia Timişoara	4, 2	**1933**, *34*, **35**, **36**, *38*, **39**
UT Arad (includes IT Arad)	4, 1	**1947**, **48**, **69**, **70**, *72*
Rapid Bucureşti	3, 11	*1937*, *38*, *40*, *41*, *64–66*, **67**, *70*, *71*, *98*, *99*, *2000*, **03**
Petrolul Ploieşti	3, 1	**1958**, *59*, **62**, **66**
FC Argeş Piteşti	2, 2	*1968*, **72**, **78**, *79*
Colentina Bucureşti	2, 0	**1913**, **14**
Flamura Roşie	2, 0	**1950**, **54**

Romanian League Summary (*continued*)

TEAM	TOTALS	CHAMPIONS & RUNNERS-UP (BOLD) (*ITALICS*)
Olimpia Bucureşti	2, 0	**1910, 11**
Coltea Braşov	1, 1	*1927,* **28**
Juventus Bucureşti	1, 1	*1926,* **30**
UDR Reşiţa	1, 1	**1931,** *32*
ICO Oradea	1, 0	**1949**
Prahova Ploieşti	1, 0	**1916**
România-Americana	1, 0	**1915**
Unirea Tricolor	1, 0	**1941**
United Ploieşti	1, 0	**1912**
National Bucureşti	0, 3	*1996, 97, 2002*
CAO Oradea	0, 2	*1924, 35*
Victoria Cluj	0, 2	*1922, 23*
AMEFA Arad	0, 1	*1936*
ASA Tîrgu Mureş	0, 1	*1975*
Carmen Bucureşti	0, 1	*1947*
CFR Bucureşti	0, 1	*1949*
CFR Timişoara	0, 1	*1948*
Flacără Ploieşti	0, 1	*1955*
Gloria CFR Arad	0, 1	*1930*
Jiul Lupeni	0, 1	*1928*
Lokomotiva Buch	0, 1	*1950*
România Cluj	0, 1	*1929*
SG Sibiu	0, 1	*1931*
Sportul Studentesc	0, 1	*1986*
Steagul Rosu Braşov	0, 1	*1960*
UCAS Petroşani	0, 1	*1925*
Universitatea Cluj	0, 1	*1933*

Romanian Cup Record 1934–2003

YEAR	WINNERS	SCORE	RUNNERS-UP
1934	Ripensia Timişoara	5-0	Universitatea Cluj
1935	CFR Bucureşti	6-5 (aet)	Ripensia Timişoara
1936	Ripensia Timişoara	5-1	Unirea Tricolor
1937	Rapid Bucureşti	5-1	Ripensia Timişoara
1938	Rapid Bucureşti	3-2	CAMT Timişoara
1939	Rapid Bucureşti	2-0	Sportul Studentesc
1940	Rapid Bucureşti	2-2 (aet), (replay) 4-4 (aet), (replay) 2-2 (aet), (replay) 2-1	Venus Bucureşti
1941	Rapid Bucureşti	4-3	Unirea Tricolor
1942	Rapid Bucureşti	7-1	Universitatea Cluj
1943	Tirnu Severin	4-0	Sportul Studentesc
1944–47		*no competition*	
1948	IT Arad	3-2	CFR Timişoara
1949	CSCA Bucureşti	2-1	CSU Cluj
1950	CCA Bucureşti	3-1	Flamura Roşie
1951	CCA Bucureşti	3-1 (aet)	Flacără Medias
1952	CCA Bucureşti	2-0	Flacără Roşie
1953	Flamura Roşie	1-0 (aet)	CCA Bucureşti
1954	Metalul Reşiţa	2-0	Dinamo Bucureşti
1955	CCA Bucureşti	6-3	Progresul Oradea
1956	Progresul Oradea	2-0	Metalul Turzil
1957		*no competition*	
1958	Ştiinţa Timişoara	1-0	Progresul Bucureşti
1959	Dinamo Bucureşti	4-0	Minerul Baia Mare
1960	Progresul Bucureşti	2-0	Dinamo Bucureşti
1961	Arieşul Turda	2-1	Rapid Bucureşti
1962	Steaua Bucureşti	5-1	Rapid Bucureşti
1963	Petrolul Ploieşti	6-1	Siderurgistul Galaţi
1964	Dinamo Bucureşti	5-3	Steaua Bucureşti
1965	Ştiinţa Cluj	2-1	Dinamo Piteşti
1966	Steaua Bucureşti	4-0	IT Arad
1967	Steaua Bucureşti	6-0	Foresta Fălticeni
1968	Dinamo Bucureşti	3-1 (aet)	Rapid Bucureşti
1969	Steaua Bucureşti	2-1	Dinamo Bucureşti
1970	Steaua Bucureşti	2-1	Dinamo Bucureşti
1971	Steaua Bucureşti	3-2	Dinamo Bucureşti

Romanian Cup Record (*continued*)

YEAR	WINNERS	SCORE	RUNNERS-UP
1972	Rapid Bucureşti	2-0	Jiul Petroşani
1973	Chimia Vîlcea	1-1 (aet), (replay) 3-0	Constructorul Galatizi
1974	Jiul Petroşani	4-2	Politehnica Timişoara
1975	Rapid Bucureşti	2-1 (aet)	Universitatea Craiova
1976	Steaua Bucureşti	1-0	CSU Galaţi
1977	Universitatea Craiova	2-1	Steaua Bucureşti
1978	Universitatea Craiova	3-1	Olimpia Satu Mare
1979	Steaua Bucureşti	3-0	Sportul Studentesc
1980	Politehnica Timişoara	2-1 (aet)	Steaua Bucureşti
1981	Universitatea Craiova	6-0	Politehnica Timişoara
1982	Dinamo Bucureşti	3-2	FC Baia Mare
1983	Universitatea Craiova	2-1	Politehnica Timişoara
1984	Dinamo Bucureşti	2-1	Steaua Bucureşti
1985	Steaua Bucureşti	2-1	Universitatea Craiova
1986	Dinamo Bucureşti	1-0	Steaua Bucureşti
1987	Steaua Bucureşti	1-0	Dinamo Bucureşti
1988	Steaua Bucureşti	2-1*	Dinamo Bucureşti
1989	Steaua Bucureşti	1-0	Dinamo Bucureşti
1990	Dinamo Bucureşti	6-4	Steaua Bucureşti
1991	Universitatea Craiova	2-1	FC Bacău
1992	Steaua Bucureşti	1-1 (aet)(3-2 pens)	Politehnica Timişoara
1993	Universitatea Craiova	2-0	Dacia Unirrea Brăila
1994	Gloria Bistraţi	1-0	Universitatea Craiova
1995	Petrolul Ploieşti	1-1 (aet)(5-3 pens)	Rapid Bucureşti
1996	Steaua Bucureşti	3-1	Gloria Bistraţi
1997	Steaua Bucureşti	4-2	National Bucureşti
1998	Rapid Bucureşti	1-0	Universitatea Craiova
1999	Steaua Bucureşti	2-2 (aet)(4-2 pens)	Rapid Bucureşti
2000	Dinamo Bucureşti	2-0	Universitatea Craiova
2001	Dinamo Bucureşti	4-2	Rocar Bucureşti
2002	Rapid Bucureşti	2-1	Dinamo Bucureşti
2003	Dinamo Bucureşti	1-0	National Bucureşti

* Match abandoned at 1-1. However, Romanian FA awarded the match to Steaua as 2-1 victory.

Romanian Cup Summary

TEAM	TOTALS	WINNERS & RUNNERS-UP (BOLD) (*ITALICS*)
Steaua Bucureşti (includes CCA Bucureşti)	20, 7	**1950–52,** *53,* **55, 62,** *64,* **66, 67, 69–71, 76,** *77,* **79,** *80, 84, 85,* **86, 87–89, 90,** *92,* **96, 97, 99**
Dinamo Bucureşti	10, 9	*1954,* **59, 60,** *64,* **68,** *69–71,* **82,** *84, 86, 87–89,* **90, 2000, 01,** *02,* **03**
Rapid Bucureşti	10, 5	**1937–42,** *61, 62,* **68,** *72,* **75,** *95, 98, 99,* **2002**
Universitatea Craiova	6, 5	**1975,** *77,* **78, 81, 83,** *85,* **91, 93,** *94, 98, 2000*
Ripensia Timişoara	2, 2	**1934,** *35,* **36,** *37*
Petrolul Ploieşti	2, 0	**1963, 95**
Politehnica Timişoara	1, 4	*1974,* **80,** *81, 83, 92*
Flamura Roşie	1, 1	**1950,** *53*
Gloria Bistraţi	1, 1	**1994,** *96*
IT Arad	1, 1	**1948,** *66*
Jiul Petroşani	1, 1	**1972,** *74*
Progresul Bucureşti	1, 1	**1958,** *60*
Progresul Oradea	1, 1	**1955,** *56*
Arieşul Turda	1, 0	**1961**
CFR Bucureşti	1, 0	**1935**
Chimia Vîlcea	1, 0	**1973**
CSCA Bucureşti	1, 0	**1949**
Metalul Reşiţa	1, 0	**1954**
Ştiinţa Cluj	1, 0	**1965**
Ştiinţa Timişoara	1, 0	**1958**
Tirnu Severin	1, 0	**1943**

This summary only features the clubs who have won the Romanian Cup. For a full list of runners-up please see the Cup Record above.

Greece

THE SEASON IN REVIEW 2002–03

IT WAS A SATISFYING AND PREDICTABLE season in Greece: Olympiakos winning its seventh straight title, economic meltdown, chaotic and often violent crowds, ill-disciplined managers and presidents and Machiavellian politics of the highest order. The whole tone of the season was set by the collapse of the digital pay-per-view channel Alpha Digital, whose unfeasible generosity had deluded both its own management and that of many of Greece's biggest clubs. The collapse of the company was sufficiently threatening to the Greek league's survival that the clubs declared a strike in an effort to get the government to part with more of its own money, or the football pools' money, or frankly anyone's money but their own. For once, sanity prevailed; the government held firm and the league resumed after a month's absence.

Title chase

The title proved to be a chase between Olympiakos and Panathinaikos, decisively settled in the penultimate game of the season as Olympiakos beat its Athenian rival. Pana fans were sufficiently incensed to mount an attack on the team's training ground after the game, which was only dispersed by police tear gas. Similarly unpleasant outbursts of violence accompanied the Olympiakos v AEK match, with Olympiakos fans attacking AEK officials, while AEK hosted Panathinaikos and treated it to the sight of bonfires in the stands. Matters were no better outside of Athens; in Salonika PAOK and Aris hosted some unpleasant fights, and regularly failed to pay the wage bill, but at least shared the Cup Final. Struggling Giannina was docked an incredible 90 points for being broke and unable to service its debts.

But the prize for best off-the-field entertainment was won at AEK by a head. Club president Makis Psomiadis, sentenced to 12 years in jail for forgery, avoided incarceration by claiming he was suffering from tuberculosis. The strength of his argument was not reinforced by his cigar smoking and whisky drinking in the directors' box at Nikos Goumas. But such shameless flouting of the law was trumped by his intimidation of the club's leading striker Demis Nikolaidis and the coach Dusan Bajevic. Only then did the Greek government effectively force him from his post.

International Club Performances 2002–03

CLUB	COMPETITION	PROGRESS
AEK Athens	Champions League	1st Group Stage
	UEFA Cup	4th Round
Olympiakos	Champions League	1st Group Stage
Iraklis	UEFA Cup	1st Round
Panathinaikos	UEFA Cup	Quarter-finals
PAOK	UEFA Cup	3rd Round
Xanthi	UEFA Cup	1st Round

Top Goalscorers 2002–03

PLAYER	CLUB	NATIONALITY	GOALS
Nikos Liberopoulos	Panathinaikos	Greek	16
Stelios Giannkopoulos	Olympiakos	Greek	15
Predrag Djordjevic	Olympiakos	Greek	14
Giorgias Georgiadis	Olympiakos	Greek	14

Greek League Table 2002–03

CLUB	P	W	D	L	F	A	Pts	
Olympiakos	30	21	7	2	75	21	70	Champions League
Panathinaikos	30	22	4	4	50	19	70	Champions League
AEK Athens	30	21	5	4	74	29	68	UEFA Cup
PAOK	30	16	5	9	59	38	53	UEFA Cup
Panionios	30	15	8	7	35	25	53	UEFA Cup
Aris	30	15	6	9	37	34	51	UEFA Cup
Iraklis	30	15	4	11	44	37	49	
OFI Crete	30	12	8	10	39	34	44	
Xanthi	30	8	11	11	31	33	35	
Aegaleo	30	7	10	13	28	44	31	
Proodeftiki Piraeus	30	7	9	14	25	38	30	
Akratitos	30	7	5	18	33	62	26	
Kallithea Athens	30	6	8	16	29	46	26	
Ionikos	30	5	9	16	22	42	24	
Panahaiki	30	1	6	23	11	71	9	Relegated
Giannina*	30	6	7	17	25	44	-59	Relegated

* Giannina deducted 90 points for long-standing debts.
Promoted clubs: Paniliakos Pyrgos, Halkidona Peiraia.

***Above:** PAOK celebrates its victory over local rivals Aris in the Greek Cup Final.*

Greek Cup

2003 FINAL

May 17 – Gipedo Tournbas, Salonica
PAOK Salonica 1-0 Aris Salonica
(Giorgiadis 24)
h/t: 1-0

***Below:** How do they keep going? Action from PAS Giannina (in white) v Akratitos. Giannina was deducted three points per game this season as a punishment for long-standing debts – it finished the campaign with -59 points.*

Left: *Aris's Demba Nyreen hopes to control the ball while Aegaleo's Alexopoulos looks on. The commitment of the Aris fans is clear from the banner behind.*

Below, left: *AEK fans express their disapproval, lighting fires in the stands in the game against Panathinaikos.*

Below, middle: *Olympiakos fans mount an assault on AEK officials in its league clash.*

Below: *'Big Mac', as he is known: AEK president Makis Psomiadis was forced out of office this season after revelations of massive embezzlement from the club.*

Bottom, left: *Olympiakos fans celebrate their seventh consecutive league title in the usual manner – by ripping the stadium up. Siemens must be delighted with the publicity.*

Bottom, right: *Christian Karembeu shields the ball from Panathinaikos' Jan Michaelsen. The gap between the two teams was just goal difference.*

Association Football in Greece

GREECE

1895: FA rules first translated into Greek — 1895

1896: Football played as exhibition sport at Athens Olympics — 1900

1899: The Athletics Federation of Greece recognises and takes control of football — 1905

1906: First Athens v Salonika match at the Intermediate Olympics. Game abandoned due to fighting — 1910

— 1915

1920: First international, v Sweden, lost 0-9, venue: Antwerp — 1920

1926: Formation of FA — 1925

1927: Affiliation to FIFA

1928: National championship established — 1930

1932: First Greek Cup Final — 1935

1934: Enter World Cup

1941–45: League abandoned during the war. Cup abandoned until 1947 — 1940 / 1945

1950: League abandoned due to civil war — 1950

1952: League abandoned due to disagreement between top clubs — 1955

1954: Affiliation to UEFA

1960: Reorganization of National League — 1960

1962: Cup Final abandoned due to violence between Olympiakos and Panathinaikos fans — 1965

1963: Second division created

1967: Greek Colonels take power. First live televised football. Wave of forced club mergers — 1970

1967–74: Champions of Cyprus play in Greek first division — 1975

1971: Panathinaikos runners-up in European Cup — 1980

1979: Full-time professionalism introduced — 1985

1980: First appearance in European Championships Finals — 1990

1981: Karaiskakis Stadium disaster. 21 spectators crushed to death after Olympiakos beat AEK Athens 6-0 — 1995

1994: First appearance in World Cup finals — 2000

2002: Collapse of Alpha Digital. Economic crisis leads to players' strike — 2005

Despite football's enormous popularity in Greece, the national team has only managed a single qualification for the World Cup Finals, in the USA in 1994. However, losses against Argentina (above), Bulgaria and Nigeria meant that the team went out at the group stage.

The last time anyone other than Olympiakos or Panathinaikos, the two giants of Greek domestic football, won the Greek league was in 1994 when AEK from Athens finished seven points clear of Panathinaikos. However, Athens' rival Panathinaikos got its revenge by beating AEK 4-2 on penalties to claim the 1994 Greek Cup.

International Competitions

European Cup

1971: △ Pan

UEFA Cup

European Cup-Winners' Cup

Key

🇬🇷	International football
⚽	Affiliation to FIFA
⚽	Affiliation to UEFA
⚔	War
🌿	Disaster
△	Competition runner-up
Pan	– Panathinaikos

SALONIKA

Makedonikos Thessaloniki 1928

Thermaikos Thessaloniki 1925

Kastoría 1963

AS Ioánnina Panipirotikos 1966

Yannina 1966

GS Niki Vólos 1924

Olympiakos Vólos 1934

Panahaiki GS 1891/1923

AO Paniliakos 1958

⭐ Panaigialeios 1927

GAS Véroia 1958

Kastoría Véria

Kateri

Yannina

AO Tríkala Lá

G R E E C E

Agrínion
Panaitolikos 1926

Levádhiakos

Patras Aigi

Pírgos Cori

Arg

Kalamáta

Greece: The main clubs

Pierikos 1961	Team name with year of formation
●	Club formed before 1912
●	Club formed 1912–25
●	Club formed 1925–50
○	Club formed after 1950
⭐	Founder members of National League 1960
👕	League winners 1960–2002
🏆	Cup winners 1932–2002
⊞	English origins
△	Refugees
⬆	Elite
⬇	Working class
●	Date unknown

Greece

ORIGINS AND GROWTH OF FOOTBALL

FOOTBALL ARRIVED IN GREECE via British sailors and traders who played quayside games in the big commercial ports in the late 19th century. The key point of entry was Salonika in the north, which was part of the Ottoman Empire until 1912. The early development of the game suffered from official disapproval; nonetheless it was popular enough for a match to be played between Salonika and Athens at the 1906 Intermediate Olympics – a match that ended in fighting between players and fans and set the tone for subsequent Greek football culture.

The growth of football and the birth of many clubs was shaped by the turbulent years before and after the First World War, during which the modern Greek nation state emerged. The Ottoman Empire gave up its hold on northern Greece and a massive wave of refugees arrived there from the Turkish mainland. AEK Athens and PAOK Salonica were founded by refugees from Istanbul, and Panionios by refugees from Izmir.

Organization arrives

It was only in 1926 that a national FA was finally formed and a championship was established in which the leading clubs from Athens and Salonika took part. A cup was added in 1932 and the national championship was expanded to include champions from other regions. In 1959, a single national league was created and full-time professionalism finally arrived in 1979.

Both competitions have been dominated by the big teams from Athens with rare successes for provincial teams. Despite enormous domestic support and a great deal of money, the international returns for clubs and the national team have been minimal. A single qualification for the World Cup, in 1994, and Panathinaikos' defeat in the 1971 European Cup Final to Ajax are the highlights. In the last decade progress at club level has been marred by crowd violence and what appears to be extensive corruption and tax dodging in the game.

GREECE

★ AS Apollon Kalamarias 1891
★ PAOK Salonica 1926
★ AS Thessaloniki 1914
Formed by Greek refugees from Istanbul
★ Iraklis Salonica 1980
Dráma
Xánthi
Sérrai
Pansérraikos 1964
Kavála
SALONIKA (see inset)
AS Xánthi Skoda 1967
AO Kavála 1965
★ Doxa Dráma 1918
Larisa 1964
★ Megas Alexandros Kateríni 1922
'ólos
Pierikos Kateríni 1961
Olympiakos Chalkidos
Chalkida
ádhia
AO Chalkida 1931
Elefsina
AO Panelefsiniakos 1931
Aégara
ATHENS/ PIRAEUS (see inset)
Vyzas Mégaron 1928
★ Pankorinthiakos 1931
PAE FC Korinthos 1963
Panargiakos 1926
AO Kalamáta 1967
Iráklion
OFI Crete 1925

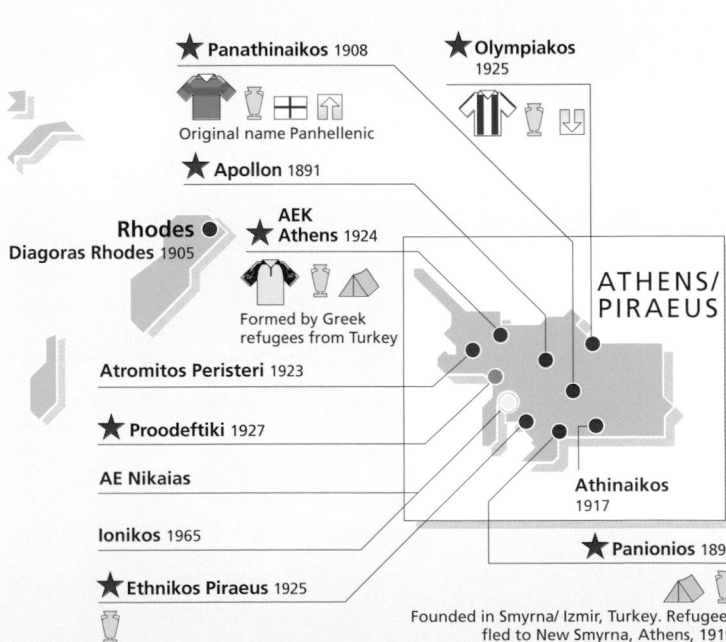

★ Panathinaikos 1908
★ Olympiakos 1925
Original name Panhellenic
★ Apollon 1891
Rhodes
Diagoras Rhodes 1905
★ AEK Athens 1924
Formed by Greek refugees from Turkey
ATHENS/ PIRAEUS
Atromitos Peristeri 1923
★ Proodeftiki 1927
Athinaikos 1917
AE Nikaias
Ionikos 1965
★ Panionios 1890
★ Ethnikos Piraeus 1925
Founded in Smyrna/ Izmir, Turkey. Refugees fled to New Smyrna, Athens, 1919

Athens

FOOTBALL CITY

ATHENS MAY BE THE SPIRITUAL HOME of the Olympics, but in the material world football is king. Although Athens is home to a dozen pro and semi-pro teams, the crown is really contested by the big three: Panathinaikos, AEK Athens and Olympiakos. Panathinaikos was originally founded by English bankers and merchants as Panhellenic, and only adopted its Greek name in 1908. Since then Pana has retained an elite following and demeanour. It rose in the 1960s, peaking in 1971 as defeated European Cup finalists (losing 2-0 to Ajax), and also contesting the World Club Cup (losing 3-2 on aggregate to Nacional from Uruguay). Pana is a club with tradition and its older fans gathered around the team's old city centre stadium, Apostolos Nikolaidis, abandoned when the team moved north to the Spiyros Louis. The club has since returned.

Pana acquired proper opposition with the foundation of Olympiakos in 1925, led by the five Andrianopoulos brothers. Lying at the heart of the working-class port district of Piraeus, the club converted the old Olympic velodrome into the Karaiskakis Stadium. Plans to redevelop the stadium after Olympiakos left for the OAKA stadium have been abandoned after protracted bureaucratic and political struggles and the club has announced it will be building a new stadium from scratch in 2003.

The city's third club, AEK Athens (Athlitiki Enosii Konstantinopolous), was founded in 1924 by Greek refugees who had fled from Turkish Constantinople (now Istanbul) and who built the team's original Nea Filadelphia stadium, now called Nikos Goumas. Panionios, to the south-east of the city centre, was actually founded by a community of Greek refugees in 1890 in what was Smyrna and is now Turkish Izmir.

OAKA 'SPIYROS LOUIS'

74,443	**Club:** Olympiakos **Built:** 1982 **Original Capacity:** 75,000 **Rebuilt:** 2002–04 **Record Attendance:** 73,537 Olympiakos v Ajax, 1983 **Significant Matches:** European Cup Finals: 1983, 1994; European Cup-Winners' Cup Final: 1987

Ethniko Astir
(2001–)

PERISTERI

PERISTERIC

12,500

Atromit

HAIDARI

Proodeftiki

KORIDALOS

DIMOTIK AIGALEC

3,500

Halkidona

DIMOTIKO NEAPOLIS

Aigale

Ionikos Nikea

4,360

KORIDALOS

8,500

NIKEA

MOSCHATO

DRAPETSONA

YORGOS KARAISKAKIS

A reconstruction of the stadium is currently stalled by economic and political difficulties. Its completion date is uncertain.

Olympiakos
(1925–97)
Ethnikos Piraeus
(1925–98)

PIRAEUS

SARONIC GULF

Like rivals Olympiakos, Panathinaikos has a fanatical following. Violence on the terraces has been a problem since the 1960s. Local Athens derbies and matches between the top clubs in Athens and Salonika have proved the most troublesome.

GREECE

AEK ATHENS 1924

League	1939, 40, 46, 58–60, 63, 65, 67, 68, 70, 71, 75, 76, 78, 79, 81, 88, 89, 90, 92–94, 96, 97, 99, 2002
Cup	1932, 39, 48, 49, 50, 53, 56, 64, 66, 78, 79, 83, 94, 95, 96, 97, 2000, 02

OLYMPIAKOS 1925

League	1931, 33, 34, 36–38, 47, 48, 49, 51, 53, 54–59, 61, 62, 64, 66, 67, 68, 69, 72, 73–75, 77, 79, 80–83, 84, 87, 89, 91, 92, 95, 97–2003
Cup	1947, 51–54, 55, 57–61, 63, 65, 66, 68, 69, 71, 73, 74, 75, 76, 81, 86, 88, 90, 92, 93, 99, 2001, 02

E75

Olympiakos
(1997–2003)

AEK Athens

Panathinaikos
(1984–2000)

PEFKI

STADIO OAKA
'SPIYROS LOUIS'
(NATIONAL STADIUM)

KAMATERO

NIKOS GOUMAS

MAROUSI

22,014

74,443

IRAKLIO

Greece

N. LIOSIA

GIPEDO RIZOUPOLIS

VRILISIA

16,500

Apollon Athinon

FILOTHEI

PANATHINAIKOS 1908

League	1930, 31, 32, 36, 49, 53, 54, 55, 57, 60–62, 63, 64, 65, 66, 69, 70, 72, 74, 77, 82, 84, 85, 86, 87, 90, 91, 93, 94, 95-96, 98, 2000, 01, 03
Cup	1940, 48, 49, 55, 60, 65, 67, 68, 69, 72, 75, 77, 82, 84, 86, 88, 89, 91, 93–95, 97–99
European Cup	1971
World Club Cup	1971

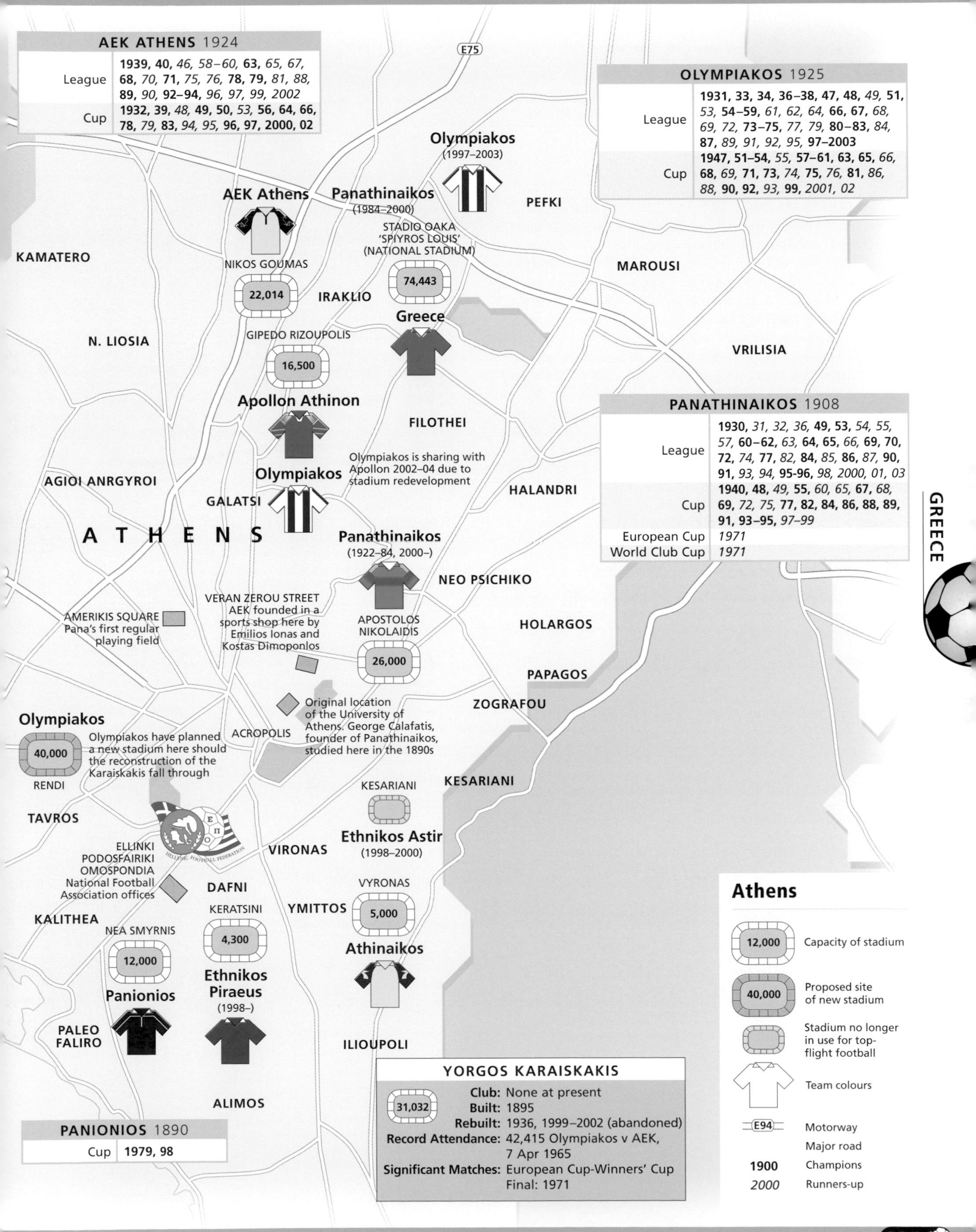

Olympiakos

AGIOI ANRGYROI

HALANDRI

GALATSI

Olympiakos is sharing with
Apollon 2002–04 due to
stadium redevelopment

A T H E N S

Panathinaikos
(1922–84, 2000–)

NEO PSICHIKO

VERAN ZEROU STREET
AEK founded in a
sports shop here by
Emilios Ionas and
Kostas Dimoponlos

HOLARGOS

AMERIKIS SQUARE
Pana's first regular
playing field

**APOSTOLOS
NIKOLAIDIS**

26,000

PAPAGOS

Original location
of the University of
Athens. George Calafatis,
founder of Panathinaikos,
studied here in the 1890s

ACROPOLIS

ZOGRAFOU

Olympiakos

Olympiakos have planned
a new stadium here should
the reconstruction of the
Karaiskakis fall through

KESARIANI

KESARIANI

40,000

RENDI

TAVROS

Ethnikos Astir
(1998–2000)

ELLINKI
PODOSFAIRIKI
OMOSPONDIA
National Football
Association offices

VIRONAS

VYRONAS

DAFNI

KALITHEA

KERATSINI

YMITTOS

5,000

NEA SMYRNIS

Athinaikos

12,000

Panionios

**Ethnikos
Piraeus**
(1998–)

4,300

PALEO
FALIRO

ILIOUPOLI

ALIMOS

PANIONIOS 1890

Cup	1979, 98

YORGOS KARAISKAKIS

31,032	**Club:**	None at present
	Built:	1895
	Rebuilt:	1936, 1999–2002 (abandoned)
	Record Attendance:	42,415 Olympiakos v AEK, 7 Apr 1965
	Significant Matches:	European Cup-Winners' Cup Final: 1971

GREECE

Athens

12,000	Capacity of stadium
40,000	Proposed site of new stadium
	Stadium no longer in use for top-flight football
	Team colours
E94	Motorway
	Major road
1900	Champions
2000	Runners-up

Greece

Hellenic Football Federation
Founded: 1926
Joined FIFA: 1927
Joined UEFA: 1954

GREEK FOOTBALL WAS ORGANIZED AND PLAYED at a regional level before the national level. Local leagues were operating in Athens and Salonika long before a national Greek FA was set up in 1926. In 1928 an Athens-Salonika league was set up, but the national championships were decided by play-offs with regional league champions. In 1960, a fully-fledged national league was created. It became full-time professional in 1979. There are 18 clubs in the top division with a standard three up, three down promotion and relegation system.

The Greek Cup was established in 1932 and now consists of four two-legged rounds followed by a Final. Over the years tournaments have either not been held due to war or have been cancelled due to extensive crowd trouble at Olympiakos v Panathinaikos derbies. In 1962 the Final between these two teams was abandoned by the referee as violence spilled over onto the pitch. In 1964, the two teams met in a semi-final and again the game could not be completed. The tournament was consequently abandoned and the cup was awarded to AEK Athens, winners of the other semi-final.

Greek League Record 1928–2003

SEASON	CHAMPIONS	RUNNERS-UP
1928	Aris Salonica	Ethnikos Piraeus
1929	no championship	
1930	Panathinaikos	Aris Salonica
1931	Olympiakos	Panathinaikos
1932	Aris Salonica	Panathinaikos
1933	Olympiakos	Aris Salonica
1934	Olympiakos	Iraklis Salonica
1935	no championship	
1936	Olympiakos	Panathinaikos
1937	Olympiakos	PAOK Salonica
1938	Olympiakos	Apollon Athens
1939	AEK Athens	Iraklis Salonica
1940	AEK Athens	PAOK Salonica
1941–45	no championship	
1946	Aris Salonica	AEK Athens
1947	Olympiakos	Iraklis Salonica
1948	Olympiakos	Apollon Athens
1949	Panathinaikos	Olympiakos
1950	no championship	
1951	Olympiakos	Panionios
1952	no championship	
1953	Panathinaikos	Olympiakos
1954	Olympiakos	Panathinaikos
1955	Olympiakos	Panathinaikos
1956	Olympiakos	Ethnikos Piraeus
1957	Olympiakos	Panathinaikos
1958	Olympiakos	AEK Athens
1959	Olympiakos	AEK Athens
1960	Panathinaikos	AEK Athens
1961	Panathinaikos	Olympiakos
1962	Panathinaikos	Olympiakos
1963	AEK Athens	Panathinaikos
1964	Panathinaikos	Olympiakos
1965	Panathinaikos	AEK Athens
1966	Olympiakos	Panathinaikos
1967	Olympiakos	AEK Athens
1968	AEK Athens	Olympiakos
1969	Panathinaikos	Olympiakos
1970	Panathinaikos	AEK Athens

Greek League Record (*continued*)

SEASON	CHAMPIONS	RUNNERS-UP
1971	AEK Athens	Panionios
1972	Panathinaikos	Olympiakos
1973	Olympiakos	PAOK Salonica
1974	Olympiakos	Panathinaikos
1975	Olympiakos	AEK Athens
1976	PAOK Salonica	AEK Athens
1977	Panathinaikos	Olympiakos
1978	AEK Athens	PAOK Salonica
1979	AEK Athens	Olympiakos
1980	Olympiakos	Aris Salonica
1981	Olympiakos	AEK Athens
1982	Olympiakos	Panathinaikos
1983	Olympiakos	Larisa
1984	Panathinaikos	Olympiakos
1985	PAOK Salonica	Panathinaikos
1986	Panathinaikos	OFI Crete
1987	Olympiakos	Panathinaikos
1988	Larisa	AEK Athens
1989	AEK Athens	Olympiakos
1990	Panathinaikos	AEK Athens
1991	Panathinaikos	Olympiakos
1992	AEK Athens	Olympiakos
1993	AEK Athens	Panathinaikos
1994	AEK Athens	Panathinaikos
1995	Panathinaikos	Olympiakos
1996	Panathinaikos	AEK Athens
1997	Olympiakos	AEK Athens
1998	Olympiakos	Panathinaikos
1999	Olympiakos	AEK Athens
2000	Olympiakos	Panathinaikos
2001	Olympiakos	Panathinaikos
2002	Olympiakos	AEK Athens
2003	Olympiakos	Panathinaikos

Greek League Summary

TEAM	TOTALS	CHAMPIONS & RUNNERS-UP (BOLD) (*ITALICS*)
Olympiakos	**32**, *15*	**1931, 33, 34, 36–38, 47, 48, 49,** *51, 53,* **54–59,** *61, 62,* **64, 66, 67, 68, 69,** *72,* **73–75,** *77, 79,* **80–83,** *84,* **87,** *89,* *91, 92,* **95, 97–2003**
Panathinaikos	**18**, *18*	**1930,** *31, 32, 36,* **49,** *53, 54, 55, 57,* **60–62,** *63,* **64, 65, 66, 69, 70,** *72, 74,* **77,** *82,* **84, 85, 86, 87, 90, 91,** *93, 94,* **95, 96,** *98,* **2000,** *01, 03*
AEK Athens	**11**, *16*	**1939,** *40,* **46,** *58–60,* **63,** *65,* **67, 68,** *70,* **71,** *75, 76,* **78, 79,** *81,* **88, 89,** *90,* **92–94,** *96, 97, 99,* **2002**
Aris Salonica	**3**, *3*	**1928,** *32,* **30,** *33,* **46,** *80*
PAOK Salonica	**2**, *4*	*1937, 40, 73,* **76,** *78,* **85**
Larisa	**1**, *1*	*1983,* **88**
Iraklis Salonica	**0**, *3*	*1934, 39, 47*
Apollon Athens	**0**, *2*	*1938, 48*
Ethnikos Piraeus	**0**, *2*	*1928, 56*
Panionios	**0**, *2*	*1951, 71*
OFI Crete	**0**, *1*	*1986*

Greek Cup Record 1932–2003

YEAR	WINNERS	SCORE	RUNNERS-UP
1932	AEK Athens	5-3	Aris Salonica
1933	Ethnikos Piraeus	2-2, (replay) 2-1	Aris Salonica
1934–38		*no competition*	
1939	AEK Athens	2-1	PAOK Salonica
1940	Panathinaikos	3-1	Aris Salonica
1941–46		*no competition*	
1947	Olympiakos	5-0	Iraklis Salonica
1948	Panathinaikos	2-1	AEK Athens
1949	AEK Athens	0-0, (replay) 2-1 (aet)	Panathinaikos
1950	AEK Athens	4-0	Aris Salonica
1951	Olympiakos	4-0	PAOK Salonica
1952	Olympiakos	2-2, (replay) 2-0	Panionios
1953	Olympiakos	3-2	AEK Athens
1954	Olympiakos	2-0	Doxa Drama
1955	Panathinaikos	2-0	PAOK Salonica
1956	AEK Athens	2-1	Olympiakos
1957	Olympiakos	2-0	Iraklis Salonica
1958	Olympiakos	5-1	Doxa Drama
1959	Olympiakos	2-1	Doxa Drama
1960	Olympiakos	1-1, (replay) 3-0	Panathinaikos
1961	Olympiakos	3-0	Panionios
1962		*not awarded**	
1963	Olympiakos	3-0	Pierikos Katerini
1964	AEK Athens	**	
1965	Olympiakos	1-0	Panathinaikos
1966	AEK Athens	w/o	Olympiakos
1967	Panathinaikos	1-0	Panionios
1968	Olympiakos	1-0	Panathinaikos
1969	Panathinaikos	1-1†	Olympiakos
1970	Aris Salonica	1-0	PAOK Salonica
1971	Olympiakos	3-1	PAOK Salonica
1972	PAOK Salonica	2-1	Panathinaikos
1973	Olympiakos	1-0	PAOK Salonica
1974	PAOK Salonica	2-2 (4-3 pens)	Olympiakos
1975	Olympiakos	1-0	Panathinaikos
1976	Iraklis Salonica	4-4 (6-5 pens)	Olympiakos
1977	Panathinaikos	2-1	PAOK Salonica
1978	AEK Athens	2-0	PAOK Salonica
1979	Panionios	3-1	AEK Athens
1980	Kastoria	5-2	Iraklis Salonica
1981	Olympiakos	3-1	PAOK Salonica
1982	Panathinaikos	1-0	Larisa
1983	AEK Athens	2-0	PAOK Salonica
1984	Panathinaikos	2-0	Larisa
1985	Larisa	4-1	PAOK Salonica
1986	Panathinaikos	4-0	Olympiakos
1987	OFI Crete	1-1 (3-1 pens)	Iraklis Salonica
1988	Panathinaikos	2-2 (4-3 pens)	Olympiakos
1989	Panathinaikos	3-1	Panionios
1990	Olympiakos	4-2	OFI Crete
1991	Panathinaikos	3-0, 2-1 (2 legs)	Athinaikos
1992	Olympiakos	1-1, 2-0 (2 legs)	PAOK Salonica
1993	Panathinaikos	1-0	Olympiakos
1994	Panathinaikos	3-3 (aet)(4-2 pens)	AEK Athens
1995	Panathinaikos	1-0 (aet)	AEK Athens
1996	AEK Athens	7-1	Apollon
1997	AEK Athens	0-0 (5-3 pens)	Panathinaikos
1998	Panionios	1-0	Panathinaikos
1999	Olympiakos	2-0	Panathinaikos
2000	AEK Athens	2-0	Ionikos
2001	PAOK Salonica	4-2	Olympiakos
2002	AEK Athens	2-1	Olympiakos
2003	PAOK Salonica	1-0	Aris Salonica

w/o denotes walk over

* Final between Olympiakos and Panathinaikos abandoned at 0-0, cup not awarded.

** AEK Athens awarded cup by Greek FA.

† Panathinaikos won on toss of a coin.

Greek Cup Summary

TEAM	TOTALS	WINNERS & RUNNERS-UP (BOLD) (*ITALICS*)
Olympiakos	**20**, *10*	**1947**, *51–54*, **55**, *57–61*, **63**, **65**, *66*, **68**, *69*, **71**, **73**, **74**, **75**, **76**, **81**, *86*, **88**, **90**, **92**, *93*, **99**, *2001*, **02**
Panathinaikos	**15**, *9*	**1940**, *48*, **49**, **55**, *60*, **65**, **67**, *68*, **69**, *72*, *75*, **77**, **82**, *84*, **86**, **88**, **89**, *91*, *93–95*, *97–99*
AEK Athens	**13**, *5*	**1932**, **39**, *48*, **49**, **50**, *53*, **56**, *64*, **66**, **78**, *79*, **83**, *94*, *95*, **96**, *97*, **2000**, **02**
PAOK Salonica	**4**, *12*	*1939*, *51*, *55*, *70*, *71*, **72**, *73*, **74**, *77*, *78*, *81*, *83*, *85*, *92*, **2001**, **03**
Panionios	**2**, *4*	*1952*, *61*, **67**, *79*, **89**, **98**
Aris Salonica	**1**, *5*	*1932*, *33*, *40*, *50*, **70**, *2003*
Iraklis Salonica	**1**, *4*	*1947*, *57*, **76**, *80*, *87*
Larisa	**1**, *2*	*1982*, *84*, **85**
OFI Crete	**1**, *1*	**1987**, *90*
Ethnikos Piraeus	**1**, *0*	**1933**
Kastoria	**1**, *0*	**1980**
Doxa Drama	**0**, *3*	*1954*, *58*, *59*
Apollon	**0**, *1*	*1996*
Athinaikos	**0**, *1*	*1991*
Ionikos	**0**, *1*	*2000*
Pierikos Katerini	**0**, *1*	*1963*

***Olympiakos and Panathinaikos** (in green) have dominated Greek football since its early days. Their rivalry is geographical, social and sporting, and often boils over on derby day, resulting in violence and injury.*

Turkey

THE SEASON IN REVIEW 2002–03

THE NEXUS OF FOOTBALL, money and politics in Turkish life was neatly encapsulated at the start of this season when prime minister Bulent Ecevit rewarded Turkey's World Cup 2002 squad with £500,000 worth of republican gold coins. But the limits of football's political utility were starkly revealed by the failure of the laughable joint Turkish-Greek bid to host the European Championships in 2008. The bid's pious hopes of peacemaking were publicly shattered by the violence that surrounded Fenerbahçe's UEFA Cup ties with Panathinaikos and the simmering Cyprus dispute that fuelled it.

Tempers were equally frayed in the league. In August, a Fenerbahçe fan hid in Galatasary's stadium the night before their Derby match. He emerged just before kick-off to plant a Fener flag in the pitch. It was the high point of Fenerbahçe's season. Galatasaray won the derby 4-1, and Fener never looked like challenging them. Radical action in the New Year saw Werner Lorant sacked and Oguz Cetin installed. New signings followed, the club conducted a massive crackdown on internal dissent and installed another new coach, Tamer Guny. But it was all to no avail.

Personal twist

The early form was with the small Ankara club Gençlerbirligi who prospered from the goals of Egyptian striker Ahmed Hassan Kamel and Souleymane Youla. Though it lost the lead to Galatasaray in the late autumn, Gençlerbirligi looked set for Europe next season along with unfancied Gaziantepspor. The battle at the top between Beşiktaş and Galatasaray was given a personal twist. Beşiktaş' Romanian coach Mircea Lucescu had won the title with Gala last year; his reward was the sack and replacement by the club's prodigal son, Faith Terim. However, Galatasaray announced debts of $33 million and its Champions League performance was abject. Beşiktaş, celebrating its centenary year, was better. Its defence was tight leading to a season-long whine by their opponents, alleging official corruption. But the matter was settled with two games still to play as Beşiktaş beat Galatasaray with a 90th-minute goal from Timur Metin in front of a packed Inonu.

Turkish League Table 2002–03

CLUB	P	W	D	L	F	A	Pts	
Beşiktaş	34	26	7	1	63	21	85	Champions League
Galatasaray SK	34	24	5	5	61	27	77	Champions League
Gençlerbirligi	34	19	9	6	76	40	66	UEFA Cup
Gaziantepspor	34	16	9	9	61	41	57	UEFA Cup
Malatyaspor	34	14	10	10	56	45	52	UEFA Cup
Fenerbahçe SK	34	13	12	9	55	42	51	
Trabzonspor K	34	13	12	9	44	33	51	UEFA Cup (cup winners)
MKE Ankaragücü	34	15	4	15	44	42	49	
Istanbulspor	34	12	7	15	42	47	43	
Denizlispor	34	10	10	14	37	42	40	
Adanaspor	34	10	10	14	44	54	40	
Samsunspor	34	10	9	15	42	59	39	
Elazigspor	34	10	7	17	40	59	37	
Diyarbakirspor	34	9	9	16	34	47	36	
Bursaspor K	34	9	9	16	42	62	36	
Altay	34	9	8	17	46	69	35	Relegated
Göztepe SC	34	5	11	18	32	57	26	Relegated
Kocaelispor	34	6	4	24	32	64	22	Relegated

Promoted clubs: Kombassan Konyaspor K, Çaykur Rizespor K, Akçaabat Sebatspor K.

International Club Performances 2002–03

CLUB	COMPETITION	PROGRESS
Fenerbahçe SK	Champions League	3rd Qualifying Round
	UEFA Cup	2nd Round
Galatasaray SK	Champions League	1st Group Stage
MKE Ankaragücü	UEFA Cup	1st Round
Beşiktaş	UEFA Cup	Quarter-finals
Denizlispor	UEFA Cup	4th Round
Kocaelispor	UEFA Cup	1st Round

Top Goalscorers 2002–03

PLAYER	CLUB	NATIONALITY	GOALS
Okan Vilmaz	Bursaspor K	Turkish	24
Necati Ates	Adanaspor	Turkish	19
Umit Karan	Galatasaray SK	Turkish	16

Right: Fenerbahçe coach Oguz Cetin has balls but no players – he soon had no job as well.

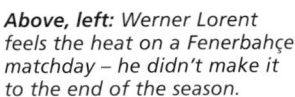

Above, left: Werner Lorent feels the heat on a Fenerbahçe matchday – he didn't make it to the end of the season.

Above: Beşiktaş' Sergin Yalcin and Galatasaray's Haspolati clash in the end-of-season Derby. Yalcin's goal gave Beşiktaş its first championship in eight years.

Left, above: Turkish FA chief Haluk Ulusoy (right) gives a Turkish national team shirt to prime minister Bulent Ecevit (left). The smiling man has just counted his Republican gold. Kemal Atatürk looks sternly down from the picture behind.

Left, below: Beşiktaş fans celebrate winning the league after the last-minute win over Galatasaray.

Below: Trabzonspor lifts the Turkish Cup – the club's first cup triumph for 19 years.

Turkish Cup

2003 FINAL
April 23 – Atatürk Stadium, Antalya
Trabzonspor 3-1 Gençlerbirligi
(Yilmaz 9,   (Kamel 44)
Karadenyz 31, 70)
h/t: 2-1 **Att:** 12,000
Ref: Çulcu

Fenerbahçe's Serhat Akin tries to squeeze round Galatasaray's Bulent Korkma – but neither side could win any silverware this year.

Serdar Bilgili, president of Beşiktaş (second right), celebrates with other officials and the Turkish championship trophy.

TURKEY

Association Football in Turkey

1895: First recorded football game played in Izmir

1903: Beşiktaş, Turkey's oldest club, founded

1905: First Istanbul League started

1923: Formation of FA: Türkiye Futbol Federasyono. Affiliation to FIFA. First international, v Romania, drawn 2-2, venue: Istanbul

1924: New Istanbul League established

1937: National championship by play-off introduced

1951: Professionalism introduced

1954: First appearance in World Cup

1959: National League established

1962: Affiliation to UEFA

1963: First Turkish Cup Final

1971: Kayseri Stadium disaster, stand collapses at Kayserispor v Siwas, 44 killed

1996: First appearance in European Championships finals

2000: Galatasaray win UEFA Cup

2002: Turkey reach World Cup semi-final, its best-ever international performance

1895 · 1900 · 1905 · 1910 · 1915 · 1920 · 1925 · 1930 · 1935 · 1940 · 1945 · 1950 · 1955 · 1960 · 1965 · 1970 · 1975 · 1980 · 1985 · 1990 · 1995 · 2000 · 2005

Hasan Sas of Galatasaray was one of the national team's biggest successes in its brilliant performance at the 2002 World Cup. Sas's superb technique, directness, energy and sinuous running are indicative of the strength and quality of modern Turkish football.

Galatasaray's victory against Arsenal in the 2000 UEFA Cup Final was the first major triumph for a Turkish football club.

Key

International football		Disaster	
Affiliation to FIFA		○ Competition winner	
Affiliation to UEFA		Galat - Galatasaray	

International Competitions

	European Cup	UEFA Cup	European Cup-Winners' Cup
2000:		○ Galat	

Turkey: The main clubs

Altay GK 1914	Team name with year of formation
●	Club formed before 1912
●	Club formed 1912–25
●	Club formed 1925–50
○	Club formed after 1950
★	Founder members of National League (1959)
👕	Champions (1959–2001)
🏆	Cup winners
	Originated from a school or college

★ **Istanbulspor AS** 1926

★ **Vefa Simtel SK** 1908

★ **Adalet SK** 1946

★ **Kasimpaşa SK** 1921

★ **Feriköy SK** 1927

Sariyer Gençlik SK 1940

★ **Beykoz SK** 1908

ISTANBUL

Izmir

Yeşildirek SK 1951

Bakirköyspor K 1949

Zeytinburnu SK 1953

★ **Karagümrük SK** 1926

Beyoğluspor 1914

★ **Galatasaray SK** 1905

Turkey

ORIGINS AND GROWTH OF FOOTBALL

WHEN FOOTBALL FIRST APPEARED on the playing fields of Istanbul in the late 19th century, it was met with suspicion by the ruling authorities. The last Sultan of the Ottoman Empire, already in terminal decline and fearful of Western political and cultural influences, banned his subjects from playing. Not surprisingly, football was initially concentrated in the Jewish, Christian and Greek communities of Istanbul. But the game was unstoppable. Beşiktaş was established in 1903 with the support of Osman Pasha, a member of the Sultan's government, Turkish high school students formed Galatasaray in 1905, and Fenerbahçe – the last of Turkey's big three – grew out of St. Joseph's, a French college in the city, in 1907. An Istanbul Sunday amateur league was created in 1905, but the development of organized football was held back by the First World War, the subsequent collapse of the Ottoman Empire and the creation of the Turkish Republic. The new republic, declared by Kemal Atatürk in 1923, was led by a diehard Fenerbahçe fan and the formation of a national FA and official regional and Istanbul leagues quickly followed. As transport improved and the quality of the provincial game rose, a national championship was created in 1937, with play-offs between top Istanbul clubs and regional champions.

The game's growing popularity saw professionalism introduced in 1951 and the creation of a fully-fledged national league in 1959. However, it is only in the 1990s that these factors have begun to generate international success with the national team performing well at the 1996 and 2000 European Championships, Galatasaray's victory in the UEFA Cup 2000 and the national team's amazing run to the semi-finals of the 2002 World Cup.

TURKEY

★ Karşiyaka SK 1912

★ Altay GK 1914

★ Altinordu SK 1923

★ Göztepe SK 1925

★ Izmirspor K 1923

Trabzonspor K 1967

Caykur Rizespor 1968

Rizespor K 1953

Samsunspor K 1965

ISTANBUL (see inset)

Zonguldak
Zonguldakspor K 1966

Samsun

Orduspor K 1967

Rize

Adapazari
Sakaryaspor K 1965

Karabük
DC Karabukspor 1969

Trabzon

Izmit
Kocaelispor K 1966

Bolu
Boluspor K 1965

Ordu

Giresun
Giresunspor K 1967

Erzurum

ursa
Bursaspor K 1963

ANKARA (see inset)

Erzurumspor K 1968

Yozgat
Yimpas Yozgatspor 1959

ikesir
ikesirspor 1966

Kirikkale
MKE Kirikkalespor K 1967

T U R K E Y

Eskişehir
Eskişehirspor K 1965

Van
Vanspor K 1974

Kayseri
Kayserispor K 1966

Aydin
Aydinspor K 1966

Siirt
Siirt Jet PA 1969

Denizli
Denizlispor K 1966

Konya
Konyaspor K 1981

Kahramanmaraş
Kahramanmaraşspor K 1969

Diyarbakir

Antalya
Antalyaspor K 1966

Mersin
Mersin Idmanyurdu SK 1925

Gaziantep
Gaziantepspor K 1969

Adana

Diyarbakirspor K 1968

Adanaspor AS SK 1954

Adana Demirspor K 1940

★ Beşiktaş JK 1903

★ Hacettepe SK 1945

ANKARA

★ Ankara Dermispor 1932

★ Gençlerbirligi SK 1923

★ MKE Ankaragücü SK 1910

sman Pasha, a member of Sultan's Court, was the club's first patron

★ Fenerbahçe SK 1907

★ Sekerspor KD 1947

PTT SK 1954

★ Seker Hilal SK Ankara 1958

Istanbul

FOOTBALL CITY

TURKEY

ISTANBUL, IN ITS FORMER LIFE as Constantinople, was the seat of the Byzantine and Ottoman Empires for more than 1,500 years. In 1923, when the Turkish Revolution swept the Ottoman sultanate away, political power migrated to Ankara, but footballing power and the national FA have always remained in Istanbul. It is a power that rests on the presence of Turkey's three leading clubs: Galatasaray and Beşiktaş in the old European centre of the city, and Fenerbahçe across the Bosporus in Asian Turkey. Between them, they have completely dominated Turkish football.

English merchants first played football in Istanbul in the late 19th century, and by 1904 had set up the first Istanbul league schedule. The Ottoman sultan, Abdülhamid III, banned this pernicious British game from Istanbul as contrary to Islamic law. However, non-Muslims were exempt from the ruling, and clubs began to form across the city, starting in foreign schools and Christian and Jewish areas.

The big three

The social and political allegiances of the big three are not entirely clear cut. Fenerbahçe considers itself the people's team, drawing on the populism of its greatest fan – the leader of the Turkish revolution himself – Kemal Ataturk. While Fenerbahçe is the best-supported club, Galatasaray is the richest, and has made the most of the recent boom in European football with success in the UEFA Cup (2000) and flotation on the Turkish stock exchange (2002). Beşiktaş, despite considerable domestic success, is stuck as the city's 'third team'. All three can muster ferocious support at home, which has spilled into violence at both Fener-Gala derbies and at big European games. Visits by Manchester United (1993) and Leeds United (2000), whose teams have been greeted at Istanbul airport with signs reading 'Welcome to Hell', have seen violence and some have ended with fans' deaths.

Beyond the big three, other Istanbul teams have had a presence in the top Turkish division. In the south-west, Zeytinburnu has risen out of the concrete and neglect of one of Istanbul's poorest districts. In the far west of the city, Istanbulspor has won the city league and rose for a time on the money of Istanbul media magnate Cem Uzan. North of the city centre on the banks of the Bosporus, Sariyer GK held onto a mid-table position throughout the 1990s.

For more than 1,500 years the seat of the Ottoman and Byzantine Empires, Istanbul is also the home city of Turkish football. A mosque towers over Beşiktaş's İnönü stadium.

BJK İNÖNÜ

35,000	**Club:** Besiktas JK
	Built: 1947
	Original Capacity: 39,000
	Record Attendance: 39,000 Besiktas v Malmö, 1994

IKITELLI
BAYRAMPASA STADI

11,000

Istanbulspor AS

E80

ISTANBULSPOR AS 1926

Istanbul League 1924–58	1932

VEFA SIMTEL SK 1908

Istanbul League 1924–58	1925, 47
League 1959–2003	1959

Istanbul

45,000	Capacity of stadium
	Minor clubs
	Team colours
	Minor clubs that are ground sharing
100	Motorway
	Major road
1900	Champions
2000	Runners-up

ISTANBUL AIRPORT

100

Yeşildirek SK

BAKIRKÖY

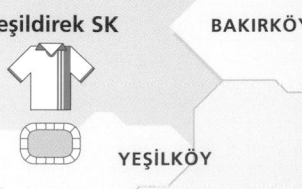

YEŞILKÖY

ALI SAMI YEN

Club: Galatasaray SK
Built: 1953
Original Capacity: 30,000
Rebuilding planned: 2003–05 (provisional capacity of 41,000)

`20,000`

SÜKRÜ SARACOGLU

Club: Fenerbahçe SK
Built: 1948
Original Capacity: 25,000
Rebuilt: 1960–81, 1999–2001, 2002–03 (provisional capacity of 63,000)

`54,000`

BOSPORUS CLUBS

Sariyer Gençlik SK	Beykoz SK
YUSUF ZIYA ÖNIS STADI	
`12,000`	

GALATASARAY SK 1905

Istanbul League 1924–58	*1924*, **25–27**, **29**, *30*, **31**, *35*, *36*, *42*, *49*, *51*, *52*, *54*, **55**, **56**, **57**, *58*
League 1959–2003	*1961*, *62*, *63*, *66*, *69*, *71–73*, *75*, *79*, *86*, **87**, **88**, *91*, **93**, **94**, **97–2000**, *01*, **02**, *03*
Cup	**1963–66**, *69*, **73**, **76**, *80*, **82**, **85**, **91**, *93*, **94**, *95*, **96**, *98*, *99*, **2000**
UEFA Cup	**2000**

Galatasaray SK

ALI SAMI YEN

`20,000`

BEŞIKTAŞ JK 1903

Istanbul League 1924–58	**1924**, *33*, **34**, *39–43*, **44**, **45**, **46**, *48*, *49*, *50–52*, *53*, **54**, *55*
League 1959–2003	*1960*, *63–65*, **66**, **67**, *68*, *74*, **82**, *85*, **86**, *87–89*, **90–92**, *93*, **95**, *97*, *99*, **2000**, **03**
Cup	*1966*, **75**, *77*, *84*, *89*, *90*, *93*, **94**, *98*, *99*, *2002*

T U R K E Y

I S T A N B U L

GAZIOSMANPAŞA

BALAT
Centre of Istanbul's Jewish community and enthusiastic footballers at the turn of the century

Kasimpaşa SK

EYÜP

FERER
Centre of Istanbul's Greek community before the Greco-Turkish war (1920–23) and hotbed of football

GALATASARAY HIGH SCHOOL
Galatasaray SK founded by students from the school

ORTAKÖY

BJK INÖNÜ
`35,000`

Beşiktaş JK

Karadeniz Boğazı

GALATASARAY ISLAND
Owned by Galatasaray, the club has built a swimming pool and restaurant on the island

BAYRAMPAŞA

FATİH

ZEYTINBURNU
`10,000`

ZEYTINBURNU

BEYOĞLU

DOLMABAHÇE MOSQUE AND PALACE
Housed the Sultan's last harem

Kasimpaşa SK

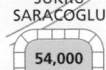

BEYLERBEYI

Vefa Simtel SK

Vefa Simtel SK

Haliç

EMINÖNÜ

SULTAN'S PALACE

Fenerbahçe SK
(1960–81)

ÜSKÜDAR

ÜMRANIYE

Zeytinburnu SK

MARMARA DENIZI (SEA OF MARMARA)

KADIKÖY

SÜKRÜ SARACOGLU
`54,000`

E80

...kirköyspor K

FENERBAHÇE SK 1907

Istanbul League 1924–58	*1926*, *27*, *29*, **30**, **31**, *33*, **34**, *35–37*, *38–41*, *43*, **44**, *45*, *46*, **47**, **48**, *50*, **53**, *56*, **57**, *58*
League 1959–2003	**1959**, *60*, *61*, *62*, *64*, *65*, *67*, **68**, *70*, *71*, *73*, **74**, **75**, *76*, *77*, *78*, *80*, **83**, *84*, **85**, *89*, *90*, *92*, *94*, **96**, *98*, **2001**, *02*
Cup	*1963*, *65*, **68**, *74*, *79*, *83*, *89*, *96*, *2001*

Fenerbahçe SK

Fenerbahçe has played in this area since before the First World War when its ground was known as the Priest's Marsh. The ground was used as part of a chain, smuggling weapons to Atatürk's republican army during the Allied occupation 1918–20. Shortly after the declaration of the Turkish Republic in1923 Fenerbahçe symbolically defeated a British Army XI 2-1

FENERBAHÇE

ERENKÖY

`100`

Turkey

Türkiye Futbol Federasyonu
Founded: 1923
Joined FIFA: 1923
Joined UEFA: 1962

THE ORIGINS OF ORGANIZED football in Turkey are very much centred on Istanbul with a regular Istanbul league created in 1905. However, a combination of disapproval by the ruling Ottoman authorities and the First World War led to two decades of decline. In the immediate aftermath of the Turkish Revolution, a national football association was created in 1923, and a new Istanbul league followed a year later.

Between 1937 and 1950 a national championship was contested in play-offs between the top Istanbul clubs and regional champions. Professionalism arrived in 1951, but it took until 1959 to create a single national league. A national cup competition was set up in 1963.

Turkish League Summary

TEAM	TOTALS	CHAMPIONS & RUNNERS-UP (BOLD) (ITALICS)
Galatasaray SK	**15**, *8*	***1961, 62, 63, 66, 69, 71–73, 75, 79, 86, 87, 88, 91, 93, 94, 97–2000, 01, 02, 03***
Fenerbahçe SK	**14**, *14*	***1959**, 60, 61, 62, **64**, **65**, 67, **68**, 70, 71, 73, **74**, **75**, 76, 77, **78**, 80, **83**, 84, 85, **89**, 90, 92, **94**, **96**, **98**, **2001**, 02*
Beşiktaş JK	**10**, *13*	***1960**, 63–65, **66**, **67**, 68, 74, **82**, **85**, 86, 87–89, **90–92**, 93, **95**, 97, 99, 2000, 03*
Trabzonspor K	**6**, *5*	***1976, 77, 78, 79–81**, 82, 83, **84**, 95, 96*
Eskişehirspor K	**0**, *3*	*1969, 70, 72*
Adanaspor K	**0**, *1*	*1981*
Vefa SK	**0**, *1*	*1959*

Turkish League Record 1959–2003

SEASON	CHAMPIONS	RUNNERS-UP
1959	Fenerbahçe SK	Vefa SK
1960	Beşiktaş JK	Fenerbahçe SK
1961	Fenerbahçe SK	Galatasaray SK
1962	Galatasaray SK	Fenerbahçe SK
1963	Galatasaray SK	Beşiktaş JK
1964	Fenerbahçe SK	Beşiktaş JK
1965	Fenerbahçe SK	Beşiktaş JK
1966	Beşiktaş JK	Galatasaray SK
1967	Beşiktaş JK	Fenerbahçe SK
1968	Fenerbahçe SK	Beşiktaş JK
1969	Galatasaray SK	Eskişehirspor K
1970	Fenerbahçe SK	Eskişehirspor K
1971	Galatasaray SK	Fenerbahçe SK
1972	Galatasaray SK	Eskişehirspor K
1973	Galatasaray SK	Fenerbahçe SK
1974	Fenerbahçe SK	Beşiktaş JK
1975	Fenerbahçe SK	Galatasaray SK
1976	Trabzonspor K	Fenerbahçe SK
1977	Trabzonspor K	Fenerbahçe SK
1978	Fenerbahçe SK	Trabzonspor K
1979	Trabzonspor K	Galatasaray SK
1980	Trabzonspor K	Fenerbahçe SK
1981	Trabzonspor K	Adanaspor K
1982	Beşiktaş JK	Trabzonspor K
1983	Fenerbahçe SK	Trabzonspor K
1984	Trabzonspor K	Fenerbahçe SK
1985	Fenerbahçe SK	Beşiktaş JK
1986	Beşiktaş JK	Galatasaray SK
1987	Galatasaray SK	Beşiktaş JK
1988	Galatasaray SK	Beşiktaş JK
1989	Fenerbahçe SK	Beşiktaş JK
1990	Beşiktaş JK	Fenerbahçe SK
1991	Beşiktaş JK	Galatasaray SK
1992	Beşiktaş JK	Fenerbahçe SK
1993	Galatasaray SK	Beşiktaş JK
1994	Galatasaray SK	Fenerbahçe SK
1995	Beşiktaş JK	Trabzonspor K
1996	Fenerbahçe SK	Trabzonspor K
1997	Galatasaray SK	Beşiktaş JK
1998	Galatasaray SK	Fenerbahçe SK
1999	Galatasaray SK	Beşiktaş JK
2000	Galatasaray SK	Beşiktaş JK
2001	Fenerbahçe SK	Galatasaray SK
2002	Galatasaray SK	Fenerbahçe SK
2003	Beşiktaş JK	Galatasaray SK

Turkish Cup Record 1963–2003

YEAR	WINNERS	SCORE	RUNNERS-UP
1963	Galatasaray SK	2-1, 2-1 (2 legs)	Fenerbahçe SK
1964	Galatasaray SK	0-0, w/o (2 legs)	Altay GK
1965	Galatasaray SK	0-0, 1-0 (2 legs)	Fenerbahçe SK
1966	Galatasaray SK	1-0	Beşiktaş JK
1967	Altay GK	2-2*	Göztepe SK
1968	Fenerbahçe SK	2-0, 0-1 (2 legs)	Altay GK
1969	Göztepe SK	1-0, 1-1 (2 legs)	Galatasaray SK
1970	Göztepe SK	1-2, 3-1 (2 legs)	Eskişehirspor K
1971	Eskişehirspor K	0-1, 2-0 (2 legs)	Bursaspor K
1972	MKE Ankaragücü SK	0-0, 3-0 (2 legs)	Altay GK
1973	Galatasaray SK	3-1, 1-1 (2 legs)	MKE Ankaragücü SK
1974	Fenerbahçe SK	0-1, 3-0 (2 legs)	Bursaspor K
1975	Beşiktaş JK	0-1, 2-0 (2 legs)	Trabzonspor K
1976	Galatasaray SK	1-1, 1-1 (5-4 pens) (2 legs)	Trabzonspor K
1977	Trabzonspor K	1-0, 0-0 (2 legs)	Beşiktaş JK
1978	Trabzonspor K	3-0, 0-0 (2 legs)	Demirspor K
1979	Fenerbahçe SK	1-2, 2-0 (2 legs)	Altay GK
1980	Altay GK	1-0, 1-1 (2 legs)	Galatasaray SK
1981	MKE Ankaragücü SK	2-1, 0-0 (2 legs)	Boluspor K
1982	Galatasaray SK	3-0, 1-2 (2 legs)	MKE Ankaragücü SK
1983	Fenerbahçe SK	2-0, 2-1 (2 legs)	Mersin Idmanyurdu SK
1984	Trabzonspor K	2-0	Beşiktaş JK
1985	Galatasaray SK	2-1, 0-0 (2 legs)	Trabzonspor K
1986	Bursaspor K	2-0	Altay GK
1987	Gençlerbirligi SK	5-0, 1-2 (2 legs)	Eskişehirspor K
1988	Sakaryaspor K	2-0, 0-1 (2 legs)	Samsunspor K
1989	Beşiktaş JK	1-0, 2-1 (2 legs)	Fenerbahçe SK
1990	Beşiktaş JK	2-0	Trabzonspor K
1991	Galatasaray SK	3-1	MKE Ankaragücü SK
1992	Trabzonspor K	0-3, 5-1 (2 legs)	Bursaspor K
1993	Galatasaray SK	1-0, 2-2 (2 legs)	Beşiktaş JK
1994	Beşiktaş JK	3-2, 0-0 (2 legs)	Galatasaray SK
1995	Trabzonspor K	3-2, 1-0 (2 legs)	Galatasaray SK
1996	Galatasaray SK	1-0, 1-1 (2 legs)	Fenerbahçe SK
1997	Kocaelispor K	1-0, 1-1 (2 legs)	Trabzonspor K
1998	Beşiktaş JK	1-1, 1-1 (4-2 pens)	Galatasaray SK
1999	Galatasaray SK	0-0, 2-0 (2 legs)	Beşiktaş JK
2000	Galatasaray SK	5-3 (aet)	Antalyaspor
2001	Gençlerbirligi SK	2-2 (aet)(4-1 pens)	Fenerbahçe SK
2002	Kocaelispor	4-0	Beşiktaş JK
2003	Trabzonspor K	3-1	Gençlerbirligi SK

w/o denotes walk over
* Altay GK won on toss of a coin.

Turkish Cup Summary

TEAM	TOTALS	WINNERS & RUNNERS-UP (BOLD) (*ITALICS*)
Galatasaray SK	13, *5*	**1963–66**, *69*, **73**, **76**, *80*, **82**, **85**, **91**, **93**, *94*, *95*, **96**, **98**, **99**, **2000**
Trabzonspor K	6, *5*	*1975*, *76*, **77**, **78**, **84**, *85*, *90*, *92*, *95*, *97*, **2003**
Beşiktaş JK	5, *6*	*1966*, *75*, **77**, **84**, **89**, **90**, *93*, *94*, **98**, *99*, **2002**
Fenerbahçe SK	4, *5*	**1963**, *65*, **68**, **74**, *79*, **83**, *89*, **96**, *2001*

This summary only features clubs that have won the Turkish Cup four or more times. For a full list of cup winners and runners-up please see the Cup Record left.

Armenia

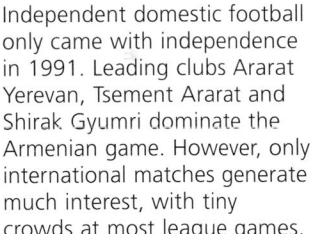

Football Federation of Armenia
Founded: 1992
Joined FIFA: 1992
Joined UEFA: 1993

Independent domestic football only came with independence in 1991. Leading clubs Ararat Yerevan, Tsement Ararat and Shirak Gyumri dominate the Armenian game. However, only international matches generate much interest, with tiny crowds at most league games.

SEASON	LEAGUE CHAMPIONS
1997*	FK Yerevan
1998	Tsement Ararat
1999	Shirak Gyumri
2000	Araks Ararat
2001	Pyunik Yerevan
2002	Pyunik Yerevan

YEAR	CUP WINNERS
1998	Tsement Ararat
1999	Tsement Ararat
2000	MIKA Ashtarak
2001	MIKA Ashtarak
2002	Pyunik Yerevan

* Transitional season.

Azerbaijan

Association of Football Federations of Azerbaijan
Founded: 1992
Joined FIFA: 1994
Joined UEFA: 1994

The championship was originally decided through mini-leagues. Today, a more conventional system is used. However, a bitter conflict between the clubs and the FA has led to the abandonment of the league.

SEASON	LEAGUE CHAMPIONS
1999	Kapaz Gäncä
2000	Şämkir
2001	Şämkir
2002	Şämkir
2003	Şämkir

YEAR	CUP WINNERS
1999	Neftçi Baku
2000	Kapaz Gäncä
2001	Şafa Baku
2002	*abandoned*
2003	*abandoned*

Bulgaria

Bŭlgarski Futbolen Sŭyuz
Founded: 1923
Joined FIFA: 1924
Joined UEFA: 1954

A national league started in 1937, but was reconstituted in 1946 by the Communists. The Bulgarian Cup, which began in 1938, was known as the Soviet Army Cup between 1946 and 1991.

SEASON	LEAGUE CHAMPIONS
1999	Lovech
2000	Levski Sofia
2001	Levski Sofia
2002	Levski Sofia
2003	CSKA Sofia

YEAR	CUP WINNERS
1999	CSKA Sofia
2000	Levski Sofia
2001	Lovech
2002	Levski Sofia
2003	Levski Sofia

Cyprus

Kipriaki Omospondia Podosferu
Founded: 1934
Joined FIFA: 1948
Joined UEFA: 1962

The division of the island in 1974 between Greek and Turkish areas also divided the league. Turkish Northern Cyprus has its own organization but is not recognized by FIFA.

SEASON	LEAGUE CHAMPIONS
1999	Anorthosis Famagusta
2000	Anorthosis Famagusta
2001	Omonia Nicosia
2002	APOEL Nicosia
2003	Omonia Nicosia

YEAR	CUP WINNERS
1999	APOEL Nicosia
2000	Omonia Nicosia
2001	Apollon Limassol
2002	Anorthosis Famagusta
2003	Anorthosis Famagusta

Georgia

Georgian Football Federation
Founded: 1990
Joined FIFA: 1992
Joined UEFA: 1992

Uniquely among ex-Soviet republics, Georgia managed to establish a separate national league and cup before formal political independence in 1991. Georgian football has been dominated by Dinamo Tbilisi.

SEASON	LEAGUE CHAMPIONS
1999	Dinamo Tbilisi
2000	Torpedo Kutaisi
2001	Torpedo Kutaisi
2002	Torpedo Kutaisi
2003	Dinamo Tbilisi

YEAR	CUP WINNERS
1999	Torpedo Kutaisi
2000	Lokomotivi Tbilisi
2001	Torpedo Kutaisi
2002	Lokomotivi Tbilisi
2003	Dinamo Tbilisi

Israel

Israel Football Association
Founded: 1928
Joined FIFA: 1929
Joined UEFA: 1992

An FA was affiliated to the Asian Football Confederation before the creation of Israel in 1948. Political upheavals have affected Israeli football since then, but membership of UEFA in 1992 has stabilized the situation.

SEASON	LEAGUE CHAMPIONS
1999	Hapoel Haifa
2000	Hapoel Tel-Aviv
2001	Maccabi Haifa
2002	Maccabi Haifa
2003	Maccabi Tel-Aviv

YEAR	CUP WINNERS
1999	Hapoel Tel-Aviv
2000	Hapoel Tel-Aviv
2001	Maccabi Tel-Aviv
2002	Maccabi Tel-Aviv
2003	Hapoel Ramat Gan

Moldova

Federaţia Moldoveneasca de Fotbal
Founded: 1990
Joined FIFA: 1994
Joined UEFA: 1992

Moldova was formed from the break up of the Soviet Union in 1991, with the formation of a national FA and national league and cup competitions preceding a formal state of independence.

SEASON	LEAGUE CHAMPIONS
1999	Zimbru Chişinău
2000	Zimbru Chişinău
2001	Serif Tiraspol
2002	Serif Tiraspol
2003	Serif Tiraspol

YEAR	CUP WINNERS
1999	Serif Tiraspol
2000	Constructorul Chişinău
2001	Serif Tiraspol
2002	Serif Tiraspol
2003	Zimbru Chişinău

Belarus

Football Federation of the Republic of Belarus
Founded: 1989
Joined FIFA: 1992
Joined UEFA: 1993

Estonia

Eesti Jalgpalli Liit
Founded: 1921
Joined FIFA: 1923–43, 1992
Joined UEFA: 1992

BELARUS IS NOW AN INDEPENDENT NATION sandwiched between the western border of Russia and the eastern border of Poland. For nearly all of its history it has been a province of Imperial Russia or a republic of the Soviet Union. Speaking a variant of the Russian language, the Belarusians (or White Russians) imported football from Moscow and the Ukraine in the early years of the 20th century. The top Belarusian team – Dinamo Minsk – played in the top Soviet league while most clubs of the region languished in obscure regional leagues.

Independence was established in 1992, and the Belarusians set up their own independent FA and organized a national

league and cup competition. Dinamo Minsk has continued to prosper, but other teams are now on the scene as a wave of new post-Communist clubs have emerged and old Soviet-era backers have receded. The top league has 16 teams playing home and away. The league, like many in the region, has switched from having a split season with a winter break to a single season starting in the spring.

Without doubt the best Belarusian player these days is Vasily Baranov. Captain of the national team, he plays his club football in Russia for Spartak Moskva.

FOOTBALL ARRIVED IN ESTONIA via English merchant seamen, having dockside kickabouts with the locals. The earliest converts appear to have been boys' gangs in the capital and port city of Tallinn. It rapidly spread to other Estonian cities before the First World War. In Narva, Russian textile workers adopted the game and played by the newly-imported Russian rules. In the university town of Tartu, German-speaking students and German rules predominated. In Tallinn itself, English coaches and English rules were followed.

Despite the chaos of the First World War and the arrival of formal independence from the Russian Empire in 1918, a national league was up and running (under a single set of rules) by 1920. A national cup competition was first played in 1938, just in time for all football to stop for the war. Like its neighbours the same fate befell Estonian society and football: German invasion, Soviet recapture, and absorption as a region into the Soviet Union; Estonia left FIFA in 1943. Independence, a national FA and a new national league and national cup competition were established in 1991. The season was played with a winter break in two phases, but has now switched to a single phase starting in the spring.

Estonian League Record 1921–2002

SEASON	CHAMPIONS	SEASON	CHAMPIONS
1921	Sport Tallinn	1940	Olümpia Tartu
1922	Sport Tallinn	1941–90	*no national championship*
1923	Kalev Tallinn		
1924	Sport Tallinn	1991	TVMK Tallinn
1925	Sport Tallinn	1992	FC Norma Tallinn
1926	TJK Tallinn	1993	FC Norma Tallinn
1927	Sport Tallinn	1994	FC Norma Tallinn
1928	TJK Tallinn	1995	FC Flora Tallinn
1929	Sport Tallinn	1996	FC Lantana Tallinn
1930	Kalev Tallinn	1997	FC Lantana Tallinn
1931	Sport Tallinn	1998	FC Flora Tallinn
1932	Sport Tallinn	1998*	FC Flora Tallinn
1933	Sport Tallinn	1999	FC Levadia Maardu
1934	Estonia Tallinn	2000	FC Levadia Maardu
1935	Estonia Tallinn	2001	FC Flora Tallinn
1936	Estonia Tallinn	2002	FC Flora Tallinn
1937	*no championship*		
1938	Estonia Tallinn		
1939	Estonia Tallinn		

* Extra transitional autumn league – played in order to allow a season to start in spring and end in autumn.

Belarus League Record 1992–2002

SEASON	CHAMPIONS	SEASON	CHAMPIONS
1992	Dinamo Minsk	1999	FC BATE Borisov
1993	Dinamo Minsk	2000	Slavia Mazyr
1994	Dinamo Minsk	2001	Belshyna Babruisk
1995	Dinamo Minsk	2002	FC BATE Borisov
1995*	Dinamo Minsk		
1996	MPKC Mozyr		
1997	Dinamo Minsk		
1998	Dnepr-Transmash Mogilev		

* Extra transitional autumn league – played in order to allow a season to start in spring and end in autumn.

Belarus Cup Record 1992–2003

YEAR	CUP WINNERS	YEAR	CUP WINNERS
1992	Dinamo Minsk	1999	Belshyna Babruisk
1993	Neman-Belkard Grodno	2000	Slavia Mazyr
1994	Dinamo Minsk	2001	Belshyna Babruisk
1995	Dynamo '93	2002	FK Homel
1996	MPKC Mozyr	2003	Dinamo Minsk
1997	Belshyna Babruisk		
1998	Lokomotiv-96 Vitebsk		

Estonian Cup Record 1938–2003

YEAR	CUP WINNERS	YEAR	CUP WINNERS
1938	Sport Tallinn	1996	Tallinna Sadam
1939	TJK Tallinn	1997	Tallinna Sadam
1940	TJK Tallinn	1998	FC Flora Tallinn
1941–90	*no national competition*	1999	FC Levadia Maardu
		2000	FC Levadia Maardu
1991	TVMK Tallinn	2001	Trans Narva
1992	*no competition*	2002	FC Levadia Tallinn
1993	Nikol Tallinn	2003	TVMK Tallinn
1994	FC Norma Tallinn		
1995	FC Flora Tallinn		

Latvia

Football Association of Latvia
Founded: 1921
Joined FIFA: 1923–43, 1991
Joined UEFA: 1992

LATVIAN FOOTBALL HAS FOLLOWED a similar course to that of its Baltic neighbours: early stirrings before the First World War, a national FA arriving with political independence after the war, and national cup and league competitions beginning soon afterwards. As usual, everything stopped for the Second World War, which saw German invasion and occupation (1940–43) and then occupation by the Red Army. The Soviet Union absorbed Latvia, and Latvian football was reduced to a rather poor local league for 50 years.

Independence in 1991 brought a truly national league and cup competition and a whole swathe of new clubs that now occupy the top division. The new league was played in two phases to accommodate a winter break. In 1999 Latvia switched to a single phase season starting in the spring and ending before winter conditions become too harsh. Ten teams play in the top league, playing home and away twice during the course of the year. Whatever the format, contemporary Latvian football has been completely dominated by Skonto Riga.

Latvian League Record 1910–2002

SEASON	CHAMPIONS	SEASON	CHAMPIONS
1910	RV Union (Riga)*	1937	*no championship*
1911	Britannia FC (Riga)	1938	Olimpija Liepāja
1912	RV Union (Riga)	1939	Olimpija Liepāja
1913	SV Kaiserwood (Riga)	1940	RFK Riga
1914	Britannia FC (Riga)	1941–90	*no national championship*
1915	Britannia FC (Riga)		
1916–21	*no championship*	1991	Skonto Riga
1922	Kaiserwood Riga	1992	Skonto Riga
1923	Kaiserwood Riga	1993	Skonto Riga
1924	RFK Riga	1994	Skonto Riga
1925	RFK Riga	1995	Skonto Riga
1926	RFK Riga	1996	Skonto Riga
1927	Olimpija Liepāja	1997	Skonto Riga
1928	Olimpija Liepāja	1998	Skonto Riga
1929	Olimpija Liepāja	1999	Skonto Riga
1930	RFK Riga	2000	Skonto Riga
1931	RFK Riga	2001	Skonto Riga
1932	SKA Riga	2002	Skonto Riga
1933	Olimpija Riga		
1934	RFK Riga		
1935	RFK Riga		
1936	Olimpija Liepāja		

* Awarded to RV Union after disqualification of British FC (Riga) later renamed Britannia FC.

Latvian Cup Record 1937–2002

YEAR	CUP WINNERS	YEAR	CUP WINNERS
1937	RFK Riga	1996	RAF Jelgava
1938	Rigas Vilki Riga	1997	Skonto Riga
1939	RFK Riga	1998	Liepāja
1940–90	*no national competition*	1999	FK Riga
		2000	Skonto Riga
1991	Celtnieks Daugavpils	2001	Skonto Riga
1992	Skonto Riga	2002	Skonto Riga
1993	RAF Jelgava		
1994	Olimpija Riga		
1995	Skonto Riga		

Lithuania

Lietuvos Futbolo Federacija
Founded: 1922
Joined FIFA: 1923–43, 1992
Joined UEFA: 1992

LITHUANIA IS THE LARGEST and most southerly of the three Baltic States. Like the others, it has spent most of the modern era as part of either the Tsarist Russian Empire or the Communist Soviet Union. Independence came after the First World War in 1918, but it would take another four years of postwar chaos to achieve a national football association (affiliated to FIFA in 1923) and a national league competition. The league ran from 1922 to 1939, after which war intervened. Initially occupied by the Germans, Lithuania was recaptured by the Soviets and absorbed into the Soviet Union; a mere region now rather than a nation, Lithuania left FIFA in 1943.

As everywhere, the Communists reorganized Lithuanian football in their own image, and most of today's clubs can date their origins to the postwar decades. Although Lithuanian clubs could play in the top Soviet division, very few managed the transition, and a local regional league was played. Lithuania declared independence from the Soviet Union in 1990, which was formally settled in 1991. With independence came a new football association, league and cup competition. For all but one season this has been a standard 16-team league format, with the top eight and bottom eight forming mini-leagues in the second half of the season. In the 1996–97 season a two-phase league was tried, but the experiment was not successful.

Lithuanian League Record 1922–2002

SEASON	CHAMPIONS	SEASON	CHAMPIONS
1922	LFLS Kaunas	1940–90	*no national championship*
1923	LFLS Kaunas		
1924	Kovas Kaunas	1991	Zalgiris Vilnius
1925	Kovas Kaunas	1992	Zalgiris Vilnius
1926	Kovas Kaunas	1993	Ekranas Panevėžys
1927	LFLS Kaunas	1994	ROMAR Mažeikiai
1928	KSS Klaipėda	1995	Inkaras Kaunas
1929	KSS Klaipėda	1996	Inkaras Kaunas
1930	KSS Klaipėda	1997	Kareda Šiauliai
1931	KSS Klaipėda	1998	Kareda Šiauliai
1932	LFLS Kaunas	1999	Zalgiris Vilnius
1933	Kovas Kaunas	1999*	Zalgiris Kaunas
1934	MSK Kaunas	2000	FBK Kaunas
1935	Kovas Kaunas	2001	FBK Kaunas
1936	Kovas Kaunas	2002	FBK Kaunas
1937	KSS Klaipėda		
1938	KSS Klaipėda		
1939	LGSF Kaunas		

* Extra transitional autumn league – played in order to allow a season to start in spring and end in autumn.

Lithuanian Cup Record 1991–2003

YEAR	CUP WINNERS	YEAR	CUP WINNERS
1992	Lietuvos Vilnius	1999	Kareda Šiauliai
1993	Zalgiris Vilnius	2000	Ekranas Panevėžys
1994	Zalgiris Vilnius	2001	Atlantas Klaipėda
1995	Inkaras Kaunas	2002	FBK Kaunas
1996	Kareda Šiauliai	2003	Atlantas Klaipėda
1997	Zalgiris Vilnius		
1998	Ekranas Panevėžys		

LATVIA, LITHUANIA

Russia

THE SEASON IN REVIEW 2002

THE RENAMING OF RUSSIA'S top division as the Premiere League and the introduction of payment for referees seemed to announce a minor reform of the nation's football, but as the season started Spartak remained the favourites to take a seventh consecutive title. However, the relentless transfers of its best players west and their replacement with untested reserves and second-rate imports made the squad look a little threadbare. Challenging the champions in the closest fought season for years was Moscow rival CSKA and Lokomotiv.

Trouble and strife

Oleg Romantsev, in his dual role as national team and Spartak coach, kept his club in touch with the leaders until a disastrous summer and autumn saw Russia crash out of the group stages of the World Cup and Spartak lose all six of its Champions League games. When CSKA beat them 2-1 in the teeth of a Muscovite snowstorm in November, its season was over. CSKA had already picked up the Russian Cup and, looking for the double, chased Lokomotiv to the wire – both teams finishing the season on 66 points. The season seemed set to end with a bang as CSKA's fans invaded the pitch at Saturn in Ramenske after their side's final day 3-0 victory ensured the top of the table tie. Russian riot police responded accordingly. On the same day, two bombs went off at the Alania Vladikavaz v Rotor Volgograd match in the strife-torn capital of North Ossetia.

Rather than settling matters on goal difference or won and lost records – both of which favoured CSKA – the title went down to a 'Golden Match' played before a sell-out crowd at Dinamo's stadium in Moscow. As the team had for much of the season, CSKA controlled the game, but there was no way past the meanest defence in modern Russian football. Lokomotiv had conceded a mere 14 goals in 30 games. Stealing an early goal against the run of play, Lokomotiv held on to win the first league title in its 67-year history.

Top: Beaten by Japan, Russia's dismal World Cup campaign came to an early end, triggering riots in central Moscow. Drunken brawls around giant screens in the city centre saw one man killed, 30 injured and mass arrests.

Above: *Not a good year: Oleg Romantsev takes a wander round training at Spartak. After resigning as Russian national team coach he led Spartak to its poorest season for a decade.*

Russian League Table 2002 – First Level

CLUB	P	W	D	L	F	A	Pts	
CSKA Moskva	30	21	3	6	60	26	66	Championship Play-off
Lokomotiv Moskva	30	19	9	2	46	14	66	Championship Play-off
Spartak Moskva	30	16	7	7	49	36	55	UEFA Cup
Torpedo Moskva	30	14	8	8	47	32	50	
Krylya Sovetov Samara	30	15	4	11	39	32	49	
Saturn Moscow Region	30	13	8	9	41	37	47	
Shinnik Yaroslavl	30	13	8	9	42	37	47	
Dinamo Moskva	30	12	6	12	38	33	42	
Rotor Volgograd	30	11	5	14	27	34	38	
Zenit Sankt-Peterburg	30	8	9	13	36	42	33	
Rostselmash Rostov-na-Donu	30	7	10	13	29	49	31	
Alania Vladikavkaz	30	8	6	16	31	42	30	
Uralan Elista	30	6	11	13	32	42	29	
Torpedo-ZIL Moskva	30	6	10	14	20	39	28	
Anzhi Makhachkala	30	5	10	15	22	43	25	Relegated
Sokol Saratov	30	5	8	17	24	45	23	Relegated

Promoted clubs: Rubin Kazan, Chernomorets Novorossiysk.

Championship Play-off

2002 GOLDEN MATCH
November 21 – Dinamo Stadium, Moscow
CSKA Moskva 0-1 Lokomotiv Moskva
(Loskov 6)
h/t: 0-1   **Att:** 34,000
Ref: Ivanov

Russian Cup

2002 FINAL
May 12 – Luzhniki Stadium, Moscow
CSKA Moskva 2-0 Zenit Sankt-Peterburg
(Solomatin 30, Yanovskiy 52)
h/t: 1-0   **Att:** 48,000
Ref: Chebotaryov

Top Goalscorers 2002

PLAYER	CLUB	NATIONALITY	GOALS
Roland Gusev	CSKA Moskva	Russian	15
Dmitriy Kirichenko	CSKA Moskva	Russian	15
Aleksandr Kerzhakov	Zenit Sankt-Peterburg	Russian	14
Vladimir Beschastnykh	Spartak Moskva	Russian	12
Andrei Karyaka	Krylya Sovetov Samara	Russian	12

International Club Performances 2002–03

CLUB	COMPETITION	PROGRESS
Lokomotiv Moskva	Champions League	2nd Group Stage
Spartak Moskva	Champions League	1st Group Stage
CSKA Moskva	UEFA Cup	1st Round
Zenit Sankt-Peterburg	UEFA Cup	1st Round

RUSSIA

The Golden Match.
Inseparable in the league,
a single goal decided the
Russian championship.
Andrei Solomatin (CSKA)
and Dmitri Loskov
(Lokomotiv) clash in the
one-off decider held at
Dinamo's Moscow stadium.

Top left: The revival is for real.
CSKA close down another Zenit
Sankt-Peterburg attack and take
the Russian Cup.

Top right: The CSKA squad celebrates
its win in the Russian Cup. Coach
Valeri Gazzayev enjoys the moment.

Above: Dmitri Loskov scored the goal
that gave Lokomotiv its first Russian
league championship.

Ukraine

THE SEASON IN REVIEW 2002–03

THIS SEASON THE OLD ORDER HAS RETURNED to Ukrainian football. Last season it appeared to be passing with the death of Valeriy Lobanovsky – national team and Dynamo Kyiv coach and the central figure in Ukrainian football for two decades. The obituaries were being written when Dynamo Kyiv's unbroken run of nine championships was smashed and Shaktar Donetsk took its first Ukrainian title. But on the final day of this season, Dynamo cruised to victory, beating Metalist Kharkov 4-2, acquiring its tenth national title.

It hadn't looked a likely outcome for much of the season. Shaktar opened the season powerfully at home. The scale of the club's ambitions were signalled when Nevio Scala, its victorious Italian coach last season, was sacked for another poor showing in European competition: Shaktar was eliminated from the first round of the UEFA Cup losing 5-1 to Austria Wien. With new signings and plenty of goals from striker Olexly Belik, Shaktar took a five-point lead at the winter break, while Dynamo struggled to find form, made an early and undignified exit from the Champions League and even moved out of the top two on occasion. Matters seemed to worsen as its attempts to strengthen the squad in the new year were thwarted: Vladyslav Vaschuk and Dimtri Sychev, both of Spartak Moscow, ended up staying home and going to Marseilles respectively. But under new coach Alexei Mikhailichenko Dynamo found its form, and the goals were rolling in from Uzbek striker Maxim Shatskikh, who ended up the league's top scorer with 22 goals. Shaktar, meanwhile, began to leak points. After losing 2-0 to the bottom club Chernomorets, Shaktar's new coach Valeriy Yaremchenko cried foul play – accusing the referee of giving the game to Chernomerets and being in the pay of an unnamed third party. Worse was to come when the newly promoted Volyn-1 beat Shaktar at home 2-0 in the final run-in, while Dynamo racked up the points.

When Dynamo beat Shaktar in the Ukrainian Cup, the writing was on the wall, a fact confirmed by a further victory for Dynamo over its rivals in the newly inaugurated Valeriy Lobanovsky Cup (top Ukrainian and Russian teams play). Yaremchenko commented on Shaktar's form 'My players… were constantly undisciplined and tried to show their fans their artistic tricks. But we are not in the circus. We have to play football'. As Shaktar is owned by the richest man in the Ukraine, Rinat Akhmetov, it is inconceivable that the circus will cease, though whether Shaktar can remember

Top Goalscorers 2002–03

PLAYER	CLUB	NATIONALITY	GOALS
Maxim Shatskikh	Dynamo Kyiv	Uzbekistanian	22
Olexi Belik	Shakhtar Donetsk	Ukrainian	21
Oleh Venhlinsky	Dnipro Dnipropetrovsk	Ukrainian	19
Shalva Apkhazava	Arsenal Kyiv	Ukrainian	14
Olexandr Haidash	Tavriya Simferopol	Ukrainian	12

International Club Performances 2002–03

CLUB	COMPETITION	PROGRESS
Dynamo Kyiv	Champions League	1st Group Stage
	UEFA Cup	3rd Round
Shakhtar Donetsk	Champions League	3rd Qualifying Round
	UEFA Cup	1st Round
Metalurg Donetsk	UEFA Cup	1st Round
Metalurg Zaporizhzhya	UEFA Cup	1st Round

Ukrainian Premier League Table 2002–03

CLUB	P	W	D	L	F	A	Pts	
Dynamo Kyiv	30	23	4	3	66	20	73	Champions League
Shakhtar Donetsk	30	22	4	4	61	24	70	Champions League
Metalurg Donetsk	30	18	6	6	44	26	60	UEFA Cup
Dnipro Dnipropetrovsk	30	18	5	7	48	27	59	UEFA Cup
Arsenal Kyiv	30	16	8	6	49	24	56	
SC Volyn-1 Lutsk	30	12	5	13	37	44	41	
Karpaty Lviv	30	9	9	12	29	37	36	
Chornomorets Odesa	30	10	4	16	31	45	34	
Tavriya Simferopol	30	9	7	14	36	50	34	
Illichivets Mariupol*	30	8	10	12	34	38	34	
Vorskla Poltava	30	8	8	14	26	41	32	
Kryvbas Kryvyi Rih	30	8	7	15	25	37	31	
FC Olexandriya**	30	7	9	14	26	43	30	
Obolon Kyiv	30	7	7	16	32	45	28	
Metalurg Zaporizhzhya	30	6	8	16	22	41	26	Relegated
Metalist Kharkiv	30	6	5	19	19	43	23	Relegated

Promoted clubs: Zirka Kirovohrad, Borysfen.
* Metalurg Mariupol changed name to Illichivets during the winter break.
**Polihraftechnika changed name to FC Olexandriya during the winter break.

Restoring the old order. Dynamo's new coach Alexei Mikhailichenko has revived the club after a poor season last year.

Ukrainian Cup

2003 FINAL

May 25 – Olympic Stadium, Kyiv
Dynamo **2-1** Shakhtar
Kyiv   Donetsk
(Khatskevich 58,   (Vrobey 18)
Rincó 89)
h-t: 0-1 **Att:** 70,000

Right, top: Dynamo Kyiv's captain Valentine Belkevich lifts the Lobanovsky Cup.

Right, middle: Dynamo Kyiv's Vladislav Vaschuk watches the ball – he spent a great deal of the season looking at his contracts.

Paying their respects. Tens of thousands queue at Dynamo's stadium in Kiev to pay their respects to Valeriy Lobanovsky who died last May.

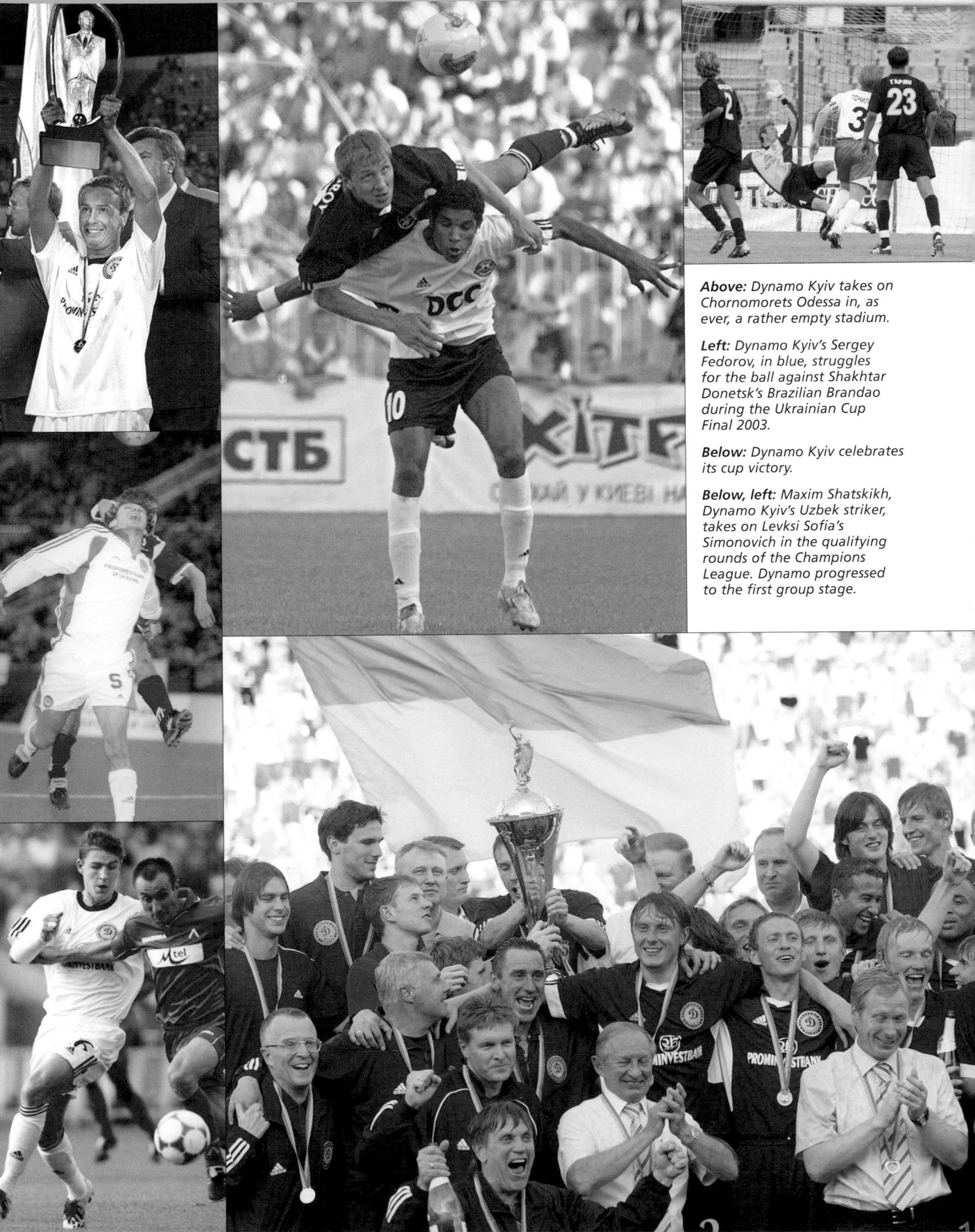

Above: Dynamo Kyiv takes on Chornomorets Odessa in, as ever, a rather empty stadium.

Left: Dynamo Kyiv's Sergey Fedorov, in blue, struggles for the ball against Shakhtar Donetsk's Brazilian Brandao during the Ukrainian Cup Final 2003.

Below: Dynamo Kyiv celebrates its cup victory.

Below, left: Maxim Shatskikh, Dynamo Kyiv's Uzbek striker, takes on Levksi Sofia's Simonovich in the qualifying rounds of the Champions League. Dynamo progressed to the first group stage.

Association Football in Russia

RUSSIA

1887: Football first introduced into Russia

1898: Football Association and league established in St Petersburg

1912: Formation of FA: All-Russia Football Union. Affiliated to FIFA as Russia. First Russian international, v Finland, lost 1-2, venue: Stockholm

1922–24: Key Moscow clubs all established: Spartak, Lokomotiv, Dinamo, CSKA, Torpedo

1936: National league championship established

1941–44: League abandoned, Cup not played 1940–43 due to war

1952: First international as Soviet Union, v Bulgaria, won 2-1, venue: Kotka, Finland

1960: Soviet Union win inaugural European Championships in Paris

1974: Withdrew from World Cup after refusing to play-off with Chile

1982: Disaster at Luzhniki Stadium, 340 crushed to death at Spartak Moskva v Haarlem in UEFA Cup 2nd Round match

1992: Secession of central Asian FAs, re-establishment of Russian league and cup. Establishment of Russian Football Federation

2002: Top division renamed Premiere League. Squad names and numbers introduced for first time. Riots in central Moscow after dismal World Cup showing

1924: First Soviet international, v Turkey, won 3-0, venue: Moscow

1945: Dinamo Moscow visit Britain, the first foreign tour by a Soviet team

1946: Affiliation to FIFA as Soviet Union

1954: Affiliation to UEFA

1961: Dinamo Kiev become first non-Muscovite club to win the league

1985: Sokolniki Sports Palace disaster. Twenty killed in stampede at World Football Youth Championships

1991: Last Soviet League, secession of Ukrainian, Caucasian and Baltic FAs. Last Soviet international. Played as CIS until 1994, then as Russia

Key

	International football
	Affiliation to FIFA
	Affiliation to UEFA
	War
	Disaster

(Timeline years: 1885, 1890, 1895, 1900, 1905, 1910, 1915, 1920, 1925, 1930, 1935, 1940, 1945, 1950, 1955, 1960, 1965, 1970, 1975, 1980, 1985, 1990, 1995, 2000, 2005)

Russia: The main clubs

Dinamo Minsk 1928 — Team name with year of formation

● Club formed 1912–25
● Club formed 1925–50
○ Club formed after 1950

LITHUANIA (1922) Ind. 1991 — Country, formation of national FA, and independence from USSR

★ Founder members of National League, 1936

👕 Soviet era champions

🏆 Soviet era Cup winners

🚗 Army

🚙 Car factory

⚡ Electrical workers

KGB

🚂 Railway workers

✈ Aviation industry origins

⬇ Working class origins

Metalist Kharkov 1944
Lokomotiv (1944–56)
Avangard (1956–66)

Dnipro Dnipropetrovsk 1936
Stal (1936–48), Metallurg (1948–62)

Zarja Lugansk 1938
Jerjinec (1938–64)
Zarja Voroschilovgrad (1964–90)

Shakhtar Donetsk 1936
Stachanovec Stalino (1935–47)
Shachter Stalino (1947–61)

★ **Zenit Sankt-Peterburg 1931**
Stalin Leningrad (1931–40)
Zenit Leningrad (1940–91)

★ **Elektrik Leningrad 1931**

★ **Dinamo Sankt Petersburg 1925**
Dinamo Leningrad (1925–40)

★ **Lokomotiv Moskva 1923**
Korthen Kazanska (1923–36)

ESTONIA (1921) Ind. 1991
LATVIA (1921) Ind. 1991
LITHUANIA (1922) Ind. 1991

Dinamo Minsk 1928

● Mins

BELARUS (1991) Ind. 1992

SKA Karpati Lvov 1963

Kiev

Lvov

UKRAINE (1991) Ind. 1991

MOLDOVA (1991) Ind. 1991

CENTRAL ASIAN REPUBLICS

UZBEKISTAN (1946) Ind. 1991

KAZAKHSTAN (1914) Ind. 1992

KYRGYZSTAN (1992) Ind. 1992

TURKMENISTAN (1992) Ind. 1991

TAJIKISTAN (1991) Ind. 1991

Russia (including the former Soviet Union)

ORIGINS AND GROWTH OF FOOTBALL

THE EARLIEST REPORTS OF FOOTBALL IN RUSSIA are of games played by British traders and bankers, gradually joined by Russian students, cadets and clerks. In 1894, Harry Charnock, general manager of the Morozov Mill, east of Moscow, introduced the game to his workers who played as Orekhovoclub Sport. In 1896, a set of rules was first translated into Russian and the following year, Sport, the first Russian club, was established in St. Petersburg. The popularity of football rose rapidly in the years before the First World War with leagues formed in St. Petersburg (1901), Moscow (1912), and finally an all-Russian FA in 1912.

In the chaotic years of revolution and civil war after 1917, the military initially took over all football clubs, and began a drive to bring the game to Central Asia. During the 1920s, however, under the New Economic Policy, competitive sport was officially frowned upon and the game remained disorganized. But under Stalin it was revived, new clubs were established, each explicitly linked to a state institution (the secret police, the army, railway unions, cooperatives etc.) and a seven-team league began in 1936. Moscow remained the centre of the Soviet game but new teams and powers emerged after the Second World War in Kiev, Tbilisi and Leningrad. Crowds remained huge in the 1950s and 60s, and though political interference was rife, football provided a peculiarly depoliticized space in Soviet life. With the break up of the Soviet Union football associations, leagues and cups have all fragmented. The economic decline of Russia has left the game in deep trouble.

RUSSIA

Spartak Moskva 1922
Moskovski Klub Sporta (1922–35)

Torpedo Moskva 1924
Proletarskkaja Kuznica (1924–36)
Zil Motors factory team

Dinamo Moskva 1923
Roots of club in Orekhovoclub Sport

CSKA Moskva 1923
Previously Society of Ski Enthusiasts, (1901–23). Offical formation as football club, Olls (1923), OPVV (1923–28), CDKA (1928–50), CDSA (1950–58), CSK-MO (1958–59)

Arctic Circle

Petersburg
ningrad (1924–91)

Novgorod
komotiv
zhniy
ovgorod
87

Yaroslavl
Shinnik Yaroslavl 1957

R U S S I A

Moscow
Ramenske
Saturn Ramenske 1958

Krylya Sovetov Samara 1943
Krylya Sovetov Kuybyshev (1943–52), Zenit Sovetov Kuybyshev (1952–53), Krylya Sovetov Kuybyshev (1953–91)

Dynamo Kyiv 1927

Samara (Kubeyshev till 1991)

Voronezh
Fakel Voronezh 1954

Kharkiv

Dnipropetrovs'k

Volgograd
Stalingrad (1925–45)

Luhans'k

Donets'k

Rostov na Donu

Elista
Uralan Elista 1958

Novorossiysk

Sochi

Vladikavkaz

Makhachkala

GEORGIA (1990) Ind. 1991

Tbilisi

AZERBAIJAN (1991) Ind. 1991

Yerevan

ARMENIA (1934) Ind. 1991

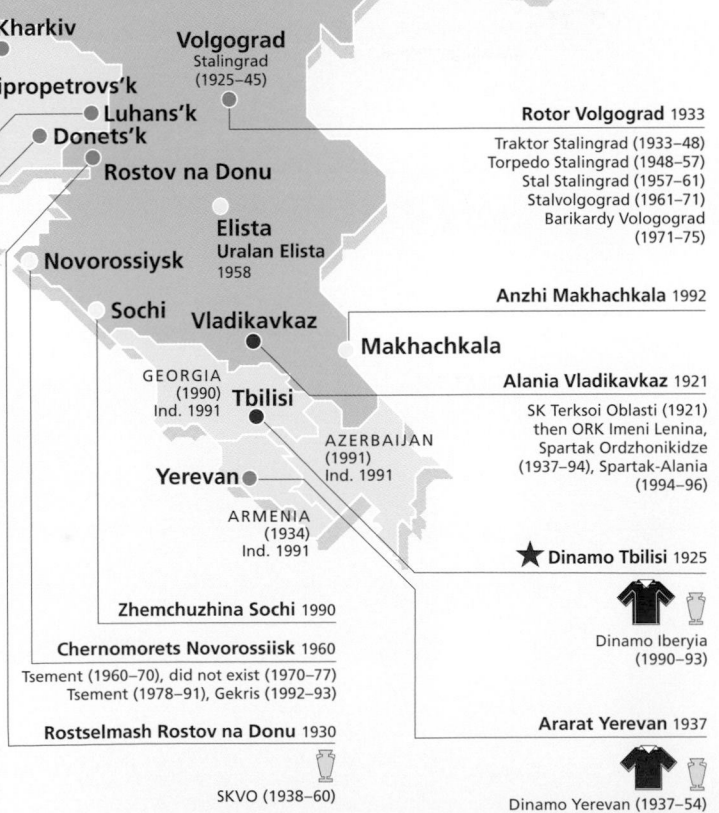

Rotor Volgograd 1933
Traktor Stalingrad (1933–48)
Torpedo Stalingrad (1948–57)
Stal Stalingrad (1957–61)
Stalvolgograd (1961–71)
Barikardy Vologograd (1971–75)

Anzhi Makhachkala 1992

Alania Vladikavkaz 1921
SK Terksoi Oblasti (1921) then ORK Imeni Lenina, Spartak Ordzhonikidze (1937–94), Spartak-Alania (1994–96)

Dinamo Tbilisi 1925
Dinamo Iberyia (1990–93)

Zhemchuzhina Sochi 1990

Chernomorets Novorossiisk 1960
Tsement (1960–70), did not exist (1970–77)
Tsement (1978–91), Gekris (1992–93)

Rostselmash Rostov na Donu 1930
SKVO (1938–60)

Ararat Yerevan 1937
Dinamo Yerevan (1937–54)
Spartak Yerevan (1954–62)

Key

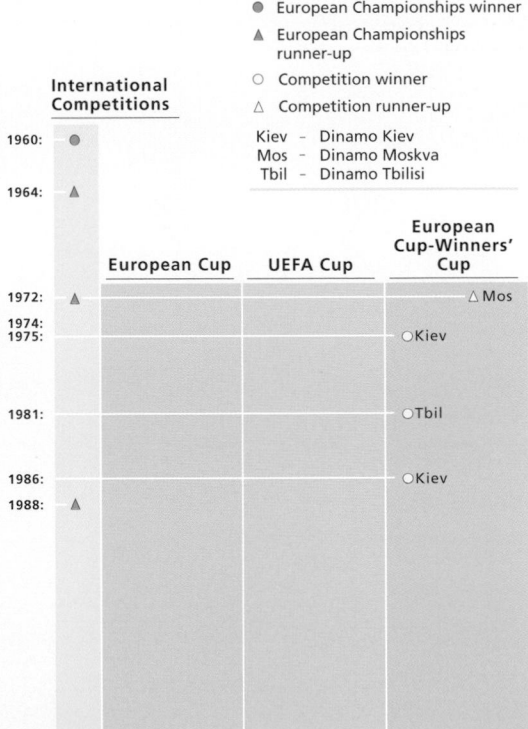

● European Championships winner
▲ European Championships runner-up
○ Competition winner
△ Competition runner-up

Kiev – Dinamo Kiev
Mos – Dinamo Moskva
Tbil – Dinamo Tbilisi

International Competitions	European Cup	UEFA Cup	European Cup-Winners' Cup
1960: ●			
1964: ▲			
1972: ▲			△ Mos
1974:			
1975:			○ Kiev
1981:			○ Tbil
1986:			○ Kiev
1988: ▲			

Moscow

FOOTBALL CITY

MOSCOW'S FOOTBALLING HISTORY began in 1894 when Harry Charnock, the English manager of the Morozov mill, arranged for a company football pitch to be created and a team established. Though Charnock failed to break the link between his Russian workers' leisure time and their consumption of vodka (as he had hoped), he certainly established football in the wider culture. Before the First World War, a Moscow league was up and running, and indigenous Russian teams began to outnumber the English and other foreign teams in the capital. However, the political upheavals of the time pretty much stopped football in its tracks. By the mid-1920s, the Bolsheviks had come to recognize the power and popularity of the game, and with their usual unpleasant thoroughness began its nationwide reorganization. All of Moscow's five main clubs date from this era, and all have been linked to one arm of the Soviet state or another.

The influence of state institutions

Dinamo Moskva, in the north-west of the city, had its roots in Charnock's Orekhovo Club, but when Felix Dzerzhinsky – future leader of the KGB – took charge in 1923, it became a team sponsored by the secret police. CSKA, further to the west, was the Red Army's side; Lokomotiv was tied to the railway workers' union; and Torpedo in the south was for many years part of the great Zil automobile empire. The collapse of Zil in the face of Mercedes and BMW has seen only a shadow outfit continue as Torpedo Zil, while the main team has tried to reinvent itself at the Luzhiniki stadium.

Spartak was notionally attached to a food producers' co-operative, and was the only team to achieve any kind of autonomy from state institutions. Led by Nikolai Starostin, who spent three years in prison camps for his temerity in challenging CSKA and Dinamo at the height of Stalin's rule, Spartak has not surprisingly been the people's choice. In post-Communist Moscow, Spartak has been the only side to regularly attract significant crowds, and dominated the new Russian league until Lokomotiv's breakthrough in 2002.

RUSSIA

Felix Dzerzhinsky, leader of the Russian secret police, took charge of Dinamo Moskva in 1923. His statue, which stood in Red Square, was torn down during the political unrest of 1991.

MOSCOW STADIUM DISASTERS

Moscow is second only to Glasgow in the number of tragedies and disasters endured by the footballing public. In October 1982, Spartak Moskva was playing at the then Lenin (now Luzhniki) stadium, in a second-round UEFA Cup match against Haarlem of the Netherlands. With the score at 1-0, Spartak scored a late second goal to make the tie safe, sparking a surge in one very cramped section of open and icy terracing. How many were killed and injured in the ensuing crush is uncertain, as the Soviet authorities banned any domestic reporting. Initial reports suggested 70 dead and 100 injured but plausible claims of 340 dead have been made. In August 1985, at a World Youth Championship match between the Soviet Union and Canada at the Sokolniki Sports Palace, at least 20 people were killed in a panic-stricken stampede after the lights failed. In the late 1980s, persistent and regular rioting and fighting between CSKA and Spartak fans at the Luzhniki saw a number of deaths and injuries.

After years of being Moscow's fourth of fifth team, Lokomotiv's 2002 championship triumph has finally brought glory to its compact Lokomotiv Stadium. Once the railway workers' team, Lokomotiv's stadium is embellished with a neon engine and classical Soviet era script.

Nikolai Starostin, revered founder, star player and 'club leader' of Spartak Moskva, was associated with the club from its foundation in 1922 to his death in 1996. He was arrested by Stalin in 1942 and spent three years in the gulag prison camps for his association with the club.

Moscow

29,300	Capacity of stadium	
	Team colours	
M1	Motorway	
A82	Major road	
1900	Champions	
2000	Runners-up	

CSKA MOSKVA 1923

CSKA Moskva (1936–)

PESCHANOJE

League	*1938, 45,* **46–48,** *49,* **50, 51, 70, 90, 91, 98, 2002**
Cup	*1944,* **45,** *48,* **51, 55,** *67,* **91,** *92, 93, 94,* **2000, 02**

10,500
RUSSIAN ARMY SPORTS COMPLEX
FRUNZE

DINAMO
36,850

Dinamo Moskva (1936–)
M9

LOKOMOTIV MOSKVA 1923

League	*1959, 95, 99–2001,* **02**
Cup	**1936,** *57,* **90,** *96, 97, 98,* **2000, 01**

DZERZHINSKY

SOKOLNIKI

DINAMO MOSKVA 1923

League	**1936, 37, 40, 45,** *46–48,* **49,** *50,* **54, 55,** *56,* **57,** *58,* **59,** *62,* **63,** *67, 70, 76, 86, 94*
Cup	**1937,** *45,* **49,** *50,* **53,** *54, 55,* **67,** *70, 77, 79,* **84,** *95, 97, 99*
European Cup-Winners' Cup	*1972*

SPARTAK MOSKVA OFFICES

RUSSIAN MINISTRY OF DEFENCE

SOKOLNIKI SPORTS PALACE
Contains Europe's largest indoor football stadium

LOKOMOTIV
29,300

Lokomotiv Moskva (1936–)

Spartak Moskva (1995–)

KRASNAYA

M O S C O W

E95

A103

9 June 2002, around 5,000 fans gathered to watch the Russian national team beaten 1-0 by Japan in the World Cup. In the riot that followed two people were killed and many injured

STATUE OF FELIX DZERZHINSKY
M8

LUBYANKA HEADQUARTERS OF KGB

BAUMAN

MANEZH SQUARE

M1

KREMLIN

RED SQUARE
A game was staged here on May Day 1936 between two Spartak teams. The fixture was repeated in 1942 and 1943 at the height of the Second World War

KALININ

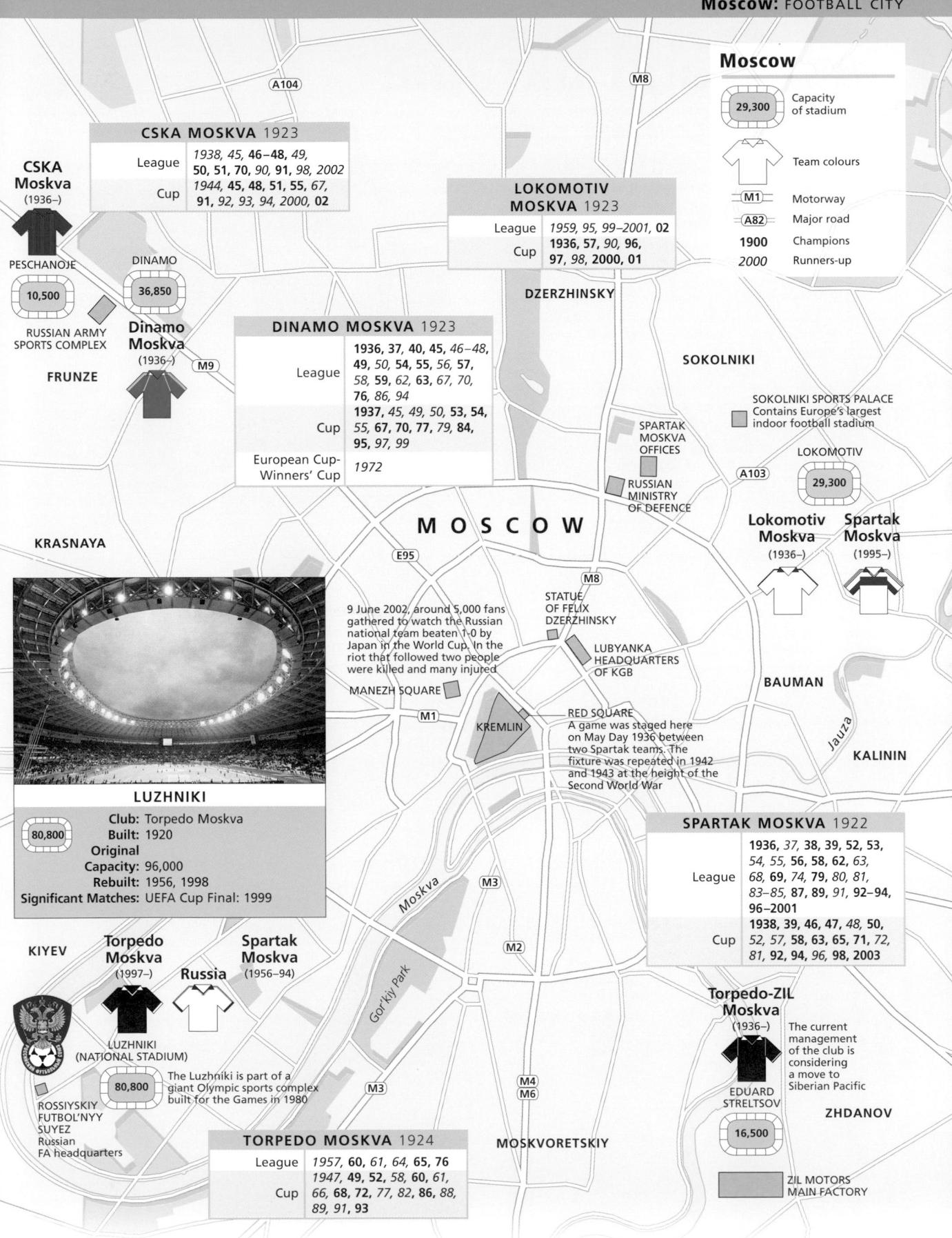

LUZHNIKI

80,800

Club: Torpedo Moskva
Built: 1920
Original Capacity: 96,000
Rebuilt: 1956, 1998
Significant Matches: UEFA Cup Final: 1999

SPARTAK MOSKVA 1922

League	**1936,** *37, 38, 39,* **52, 53,** *54, 55,* **56, 58, 62,** *63,* **68, 69,** *74,* **79,** *80,* **81,** *83–85,* **87,** *89,* **91,** *92–94, 96–2001*
Cup	**1938,** *39,* **46, 47,** *48,* **50,** *52,* **57, 58,** *63,* **65,** *71,* **72,** *81,* **92,** *94, 96,* **98, 2003**

KIYEV

Torpedo Moskva (1997–)

Russia

Spartak Moskva (1956–94)

LUZHNIKI (NATIONAL STADIUM)

80,800

The Luzhniki is part of a giant Olympic sports complex built for the Games in 1980

ROSSIYSKIY FUTBOL'NYY SUYEZ
Russian FA headquarters

Gor'kiy Park

Moskva

M3

M2

M4
M6

M3

TORPEDO MOSKVA 1924

League	*1957,* **60, 61,** *64, 65,* **76**
Cup	*1947, 49, 52, 58,* **60,** *61, 66,* **68, 72,** *77, 82,* **86,** *88, 89, 91,* **93**

MOSKVORETSKIY

Torpedo-ZIL Moskva (1936–)

The current management of the club is considering a move to Siberian Pacific

EDUARD STRELTSOV
16,500

ZHDANOV

ZIL MOTORS MAIN FACTORY

Russia and Ukraine

THE VYSSHAYA LIGA AND THE VISCHCHA LIGA 1992–2002

WITH THE BREAK-UP OF the Soviet Union in 1991, Soviet football also broke into separate national leagues. Out of the chaos emerged the Vysshaya Liga in Russia and the Vischcha Liga in the Ukraine. In the new Russia, teams dependent for funding and support on the old order – especially Dinamo and CSKA from Moscow – found the post-Communist going hard. Spartak Moskva, always the outsider, quickly aligned itself with sponsors Gazprom – the oil and gas giant spirited away from the wreckage of the Soviet state by ruthless carpetbaggers – and has comprehensively dominated the league under chain-smoking coach Oleg Romantsev, winning the league nine times in ten years. Challengers have arisen in the provinces, where ambitious local officials and politicians have backed Alania Vladikavkaz and Rotor Volgograd. In Moscow, Torpedo and Lokomotiv have nurtured local talent and crept their way into contention. Rotor has boasted Russia's finest striker of the era in Oleg Veretennikov, who has refused to move to a bigger club and who was the victim of an unprovoked acid attack in 1997.

Dominance of Dynamo

Post-Communist Ukraine has proved to be an even tighter footballing monopoly than that found in Russia, with the first nine championship going to Dynamo Kyiv, many with barely a threat to the leaders during the whole season. Under Soviet-era boss Valeri Lobanovsky, Dynamo proved fantastically connected to money and power in the new Ukraine, and has such resources that its reserves regularly win the Second Division championship but are barred from promotion.

By contrast, many smaller teams are in such terrible financial circumstances that they have refused promotion (like Torpedo Zaporizhya in 1999). CSKA Kyiv has left the army and been bought up by the city council.

The old order finally passed when Shakhtar Donetsk from the Ukraine's coal mining region pipped Dynamo to the 2002 title. Dynamo's season was undercut by the death of manager Valeri Lobanovsky while Shakhtar thrived under the leadership of new manager Nevio Scala.

'I always get my man'. Shakhtar Donetsk president Rinat Akhmetov (left) unveils his secret weapon: Italian coach Nevio Scala.

CSKA Moskva
1998, 2002

Dinamo Moskva
1994

Lokomotiv Moskva
1995, 99–2001, 02

Spartak Moskva
1992–94, 96–2001

RUSSIA

Moscow

Dynamo Kyiv
1993 –2001, 02

Shakhtar Donetsk
1994, 97–2001, **02**

UKRAINE

Kiev

Volgograd

Rotor Volgograd
1993, 97

Dnipropetrovsk
Odesa

Donetsk

Chornomorets Odesa
1995, 96

Alania Vladikavkaz
1992, *95, 96*

Vladikavkaz

Dnipro Dnipropetrovsk
1993

Vysshaya Liga and Vischcha Liga

Dynamo Kyiv — Team name

1982, *83* — League champions/ runners-up. Champions in bold. Runners-up in italics

● Moscow — City of origin

RUSSIA AND UKRAINE

Veteran Oleg Veretennikov celebrates another goal for Rotor Volgograd on his way to a record 141 goals in the Vysshaya Liga.

Key to League Positions Tables

- League champions
- Other teams playing in league
- Season promoted to league
- Season of relegation from league
- 5 Final position in league

Russian League Positions 1992–2002

TEAM	1992	1993	1994	1995	1996	1997	1998	1999	2000	2001	2002
Kamaz-Chally Nab. Chelny		10	6	9	14	18					
Baltika Kaliningrad				7	9	15					
Textilschik Kamyshin	10	4	7	10	17						
Rubin Kazan											
Kuban Krasnodar	18										
Lada Togliatti			16		18						
Anzhi Makhachkala									4	13	15
Asmaral Moskva	7	18									
CSKA Moskva	5	9	10	6	5	12	2	3	8	7	2
Dinamo Moskva	3	3	2	4	3	9	5	5	5	9	8
Lokomotiv Moskva	4	5	3	2	6	5	3	2	2	2	1
Spartak Moskva	1	1	1	3	1	1	1	1	1	1	3
Torpedo Moskva	11	7	11	5	12	11	11	4	3	4	4
Torpedo ZIL-Moskva										14	14
Okean Nakhodka	13	16									
Lokomotiv Nizhniy Novgorod	6	11	8	12	8	17		11	15		
Chernomorets Novorossiisk				11	13	6	10	14	6	16	
Rostselmash Rostov-Na-Donu	8	17		14	11	13	6	7	12	12	11
Zenit Sankt-Peterburg	16				10	8	5	8	7	3	10
Krylya Sovetov Samara	14	14	13	15	9	7	12	12	14	5	5
Sokol Saratov										8	16
Zhemchuzhina Sochi		13	9	13	15	14	13	15			
Dinamo Stravropol	15	12	15								
Saturn Ramonsko								10	9	6	7
Dinamo-Gazovik Tyumen	20		12	16							
FK Tyumen					15	16					
Uralan Elista						7	9	16			13
Alania Vladikavkaz	2	6	5	1	2	10	8	6	10	11	12
Luch Vladivostok		15									
Rotor Volgograd	12	2	4	7	3	2	4	13	11	10	9
Fakel Voronezh	17					16			13	15	
Shinnik Yaroslavl	19				4	14	16				6
Uralmash Yekaterinburg	9	8	14	8	16						

Ukrainian League Positions 1992–2002

TEAM	1992–93	1993–94	1994–95	1995–96	1996–97	1997–98	1998–99	1999–2000	2000–01	2001–02
Stal' Alchevsk									13	
Bukovyna Cherivtsi	12	17								
Dnipro Dnipropetrovsk	2	4	3	3	4	4	12	11	3	6
Metalurg Donetsk						6	14	7	5	3
Shakhtar Donetsk	4	2	4	10	2	2	2	2	2	1
Prikarpattya Ivano-Frankivsk		11	11	13	10	15	14			
Metalist Kharkov	5	18					6	5	9	5
Kremin Kremenchuk	9	15	10	9	15					
Kryvbas Kryvi-Rih	8	6	6	14	12	8	3	3	11	9
CSCA Kyiv/Arsenal Kyiv			4	11	13	7	10	6	12	
Dynamo Kyiv	1	1	1	1	1	1	1	1	1	2
Obolon Kyiv										
Zirka Kyrovohrad				6	10	11	11	16		
Zarja Lugans'k	15	14	16	18						
Volun-1 Luts'k	11	11	15	17						
SKA Karpati Lvov	6	5	8	8	5	3	4	9	10	8
Metalurg Mariupol						12	5	8	4	10
SK Mykolajv		13	16				16			
Chornomorets Odesa	3	3	2	2	7	15		15		
Naftovyk Okhtyrka										
Polihraftechnika Oleksandriya										13
Vorskla Poltava				3	5	10	4	12	11	
Veres Rivne	16	12	18							
Temp Shepetivka		9	17							
Tavriya Simferopol	10	8	5	12	6	14	9	13	7	7
Nyva Ternopil		7	12	13	9	7	13	12	14	
Zakarpattya Uzhgorod										14
Nyva Vynnytsya	14	10	14	15	16					
Metalurg Zaporizhzhya	7	16	9	5	8	9	8	6	8	4
Torpedo Zaporizhzhya	13	13	7	7	14	16				

Russia (including the former Soviet Union)

Rossiyskiy Futbol'nyy Soyuz
Founded: 1912, 1991
Joined FIFA: 1912, 1992
Joined UEFA: 1954

ALTHOUGH FOOTBALL HAD arrived in Moscow by the turn of the 19th century, it was slow to spread beyond the major Russian cities. A national football association, founded in 1912, was unable to create a national league from the small-scale affairs in Moscow and St. Petersburg. The re-creation of a domestic football programme under the Communists was slow, as they found it hard to arrange and play national league football in a country so geographically huge, so bereft of functioning transportation and in a state of social upheaval. But, by 1936, the trains were reliable enough and the clubs settled enough for an all-Soviet league and cup to be established.

With a break for the war, these competitions continued until 1991, but the 1991–92 season saw both state and league fragment with the emergence of independent Baltic (Lithuania, Latvia, Estonia) and Caucasian (Georgia, Armenia, Azerbaijan) states, as well as the Ukraine, Moldova and Belarus (for details of these leagues see pages 314–17). The Central Asian republics of the former Soviet Union soon followed (Turkmenistan, Kazakhstan, Kyrgyzstan, Tajikistan and Uzbekistan). Details of these leagues can be found on pages 450–51.

Soviet Union League Record 1936–91

SEASON	CHAMPIONS	RUNNERS-UP
1936	Dinamo Moskva	Dinamo Kiev
1936*	Spartak Moskva	Dinamo Moskva
1937	Dinamo Moskva	Spartak Moskva
1938	Spartak Moskva	CDKA Moskva
1939	Spartak Moskva	Dinamo Tbilisi
1940	Dinamo Moskva	Dinamo Tbilisi
1941–44	no championship	
1945	Dinamo Moskva	CDKA Moskva
1946	CDKA Moskva	Dinamo Moskva
1947	CDKA Moskva	Dinamo Moskva
1948	CDKA Moskva	Dinamo Moskva
1949	Dinamo Moskva	CDKA Moskva
1950	CDKA Moskva	Dinamo Moskva
1951	CDKA Moskva	Dinamo Tbilisi
1952	Spartak Moskva	Dinamo Kiev
1953	Spartak Moskva	Dinamo Tbilisi
1954	Dinamo Moskva	Spartak Moskva
1955	Dinamo Moskva	Spartak Moskva
1956	Spartak Moskva	Dinamo Moskva
1957	Dinamo Moskva	Torpedo Moskva
1958	Spartak Moskva	Dinamo Moskva
1959	Dinamo Moskva	Lokomotiv Moskva
1960	Torpedo Moskva	Dinamo Kiev
1961	Dinamo Kiev	Torpedo Moskva
1962	Spartak Moskva	Dinamo Moskva
1963	Dinamo Moskva	Spartak Moskva
1964	Dinamo Tbilisi	Torpedo Moskva
1965	Torpedo Moskva	Dinamo Kiev
1966	Dinamo Kiev	SKA Rostov-na-Donu
1967	Dinamo Kiev	Dinamo Moskva
1968	Dinamo Kiev	Spartak Moskva
1969	Spartak Moskva	Dinamo Kiev
1970	CSKA Moskva	Dinamo Moskva
1971	Dinamo Kiev	Ararat Yerevan
1972	Zarja Vorosch'grad	Dinamo Kiev
1973	Ararat Yerevan	Dinamo Kiev
1974	Dinamo Kiev	Spartak Moskva

Soviet Union League Record (*continued*)

SEASON	CHAMPIONS	RUNNERS-UP
1975	Dinamo Kiev	Shakhtar Donetsk
1976	Dinamo Moskva	Ararat Yerevan
1976*	Torpedo Moskva	Dinamo Kiev
1977	Dinamo Kiev	Dinamo Tbilisi
1978	Dinamo Tbilisi	Dinamo Kiev
1979	Spartak Moskva	Shakhtar Donetsk
1980	Dinamo Kiev	Spartak Moskva
1981	Dinamo Kiev	Spartak Moskva
1982	Dinamo Minsk	Dinamo Kiev
1983	Dnipro Dnipropetrovsk	Spartak Moskva
1984	Zenit Leningrad	Spartak Moskva
1985	Dinamo Kiev	Spartak Moskva
1986	Dinamo Kiev	Dinamo Moskva
1987	Spartak Moskva	Dnipro Dnipropetrovsk
1988	Dnipro Dnipropetrovsk	Dinamo Kiev
1989	Spartak Moskva	Dnipro Dnipropetrovsk
1990	Dinamo Kiev	CSKA Moskva
1991	CSKA Moskva	Spartak Moskva

* Extra transitional autumn league – played in order to allow a season to start in spring and end in autumn.

Soviet Union League Summary

TEAM	TOTALS	CHAMPIONS & RUNNERS-UP (BOLD) (*ITALICS*)
Dinamo Kiev	**13**, *11*	*1936, 52, 60,* **61,** *65,* **66–68,** *69,* **71,** *72, 73,* **74, 75,** *76,* **77,** *78,* **80, 81,** *82,* **85, 86,** *88,* **90**
Spartak Moskva	**12**, *12*	**1936,** *37,* **38, 39,** *52, 53,* **54,** *55,* **56,** *58,* **62,** *63,* **68,** *69,* **74,** *79,* **80,** *81, 83–85,* **87,** *89,* **91**
Dinamo Moskva	**11**, *11*	**1936,** *36,* **37,** *40,* **45,** *46–48,* **49,** *50,* **54, 55,** *56,* **57,** *58, 59,* **62,** *63,* **67,** *70,* **76,** *86*

This summary only features the top three clubs in the Soviet Union League. For a full list of league champions and runners-up please see the League Record above.

Soviet Union Cup Record 1936–92

YEAR	WINNERS	SCORE	RUNNERS-UP
1936	Lokomotiv Moskva	2-0	Dinamo Tbilisi
1937	Dinamo Moskva	5-2	Dinamo Tbilisi
1938	Spartak Moskva	3-2	Elektrik Leningrad
1939	Spartak Moskva	3-1	Stalinets Leningrad
1940–43		no competition	
1944	Zenit Leningrad	2-1	CDKA Moskva
1945	CDKA Moskva	2-1	Dinamo Moskva
1946	Spartak Moskva	3-2	Dinamo Tbilisi
1947	Spartak Moskva	2-0	Torpedo Moskva
1948	CDKA Moskva	3-0	Spartak Moskva
1949	Torpedo Moskva	2-1	Dinamo Moskva
1950	Spartak Moskva	3-0	Dinamo Moskva
1951	CDSA Moskva	2-1	Komanda Kalinin
1952	Torpedo Moskva	1-0	Spartak Moskva
1953	Dinamo Moskva	1-0	Kriliya Kuybyshev
1954	Dinamo Moskva	2-1	Spartak Yerevan
1955	CDSA Moskva	2-1	Dinamo Moskva
1956		no competition	
1957	Lokomotiv Moskva	1-0	Spartak Moskva
1958	Spartak Moskva	1-0	Torpedo Moskva

RUSSIA

Soviet Union Cup Record (*continued*)

YEAR	WINNERS	SCORE	RUNNERS-UP
1959		*no competition*	
1960	Torpedo Moskva	4-3	Dinamo Tbilisi
1961	Shakhtar Donetsk	3-1	Torpedo Moskva
1962	Shakhtar Donetsk	2-0	Znarnia Truda O-Z
1963	Spartak Moskva	2-1	Shakhtar Donetsk
1964	Dinamo Kiev	1-0	Kriliya Kuybyshev
1965	Spartak Moskva	0-0, (replay) 2-1	Dinamo Minsk
1966	Dinamo Kiev	2-0	Torpedo Moskva
1967	Dinamo Moskva	3-0	CSKA Moskva
1968	Torpedo Moskva	1-0	Pakhtakor Tashkent
1969	SKA Karpati Lvov	2-1	SKA Rostov-na-Donu
1970	Dinamo Moskva	2-1	Dinamo Tbilisi
1971	Spartak Moskva	2-2, (replay) 1-0	SKA Rostov-na-Donu
1972	Torpedo Moskva	0-0, (replay) 1-1 (aet)(5-1 pens)	Spartak Moskva
1973	Ararat Yerevan	2-1	Dinamo Kiev
1974	Dinamo Kiev	3-0	Zarja Voroshilovgrad
1975	Ararat Yerevan	2-1	Zarja Voroshilovgrad
1976	Dinamo Tbilisi	3-0	Ararat Yerevan
1977	Dinamo Moskva	1-0	Torpedo Moskva
1978	Dinamo Kiev	2-1	Shakhtar Donetsk
1979	Dinamo Tbilisi	0-0 (aet)(5-4 pens)	Dinamo Moskva
1980	Shakhtar Donetsk	2-1	Dinamo Tbilisi
1981	SKA Rostov-na-Donu	1-0	Spartak Moskva
1982	Dinamo Kiev	1-0	Torpedo Moskva
1983	Shakhtar Donetsk	1-0	Metalist Kharkov
1984	Dinamo Moskva	2-0	Zenit Leningrad
1985	Dinamo Kiev	2-1	Shakhtar Donetsk
1986	Torpedo Moskva	1-0	Shakhtar Donetsk
1987	Dinamo Kiev	3-3 (aet)(4-2 pens)	Dinamo Minsk
1988	Metalist Kharkov	2-0	Torpedo Moskva
1989	Dnipro Dnipropetrovsk	1-0	Torpedo Moskva
1990	Dinamo Moskva	6-1	Lokomotiv Moskva
1991	CSKA Moskva	3-2	Torpedo Moskva
1992	Spartak Moskva	2-0	CSKA Moskva

Soviet Union Cup Summary

TEAM	TOTALS	WINNERS & RUNNERS-UP (BOLD) (*ITALICS*)
Spartak Moskva	10, 5	**1938, 39, 46, 47,** *48,* **50,** *52,* **57, 58,** **63, 65, 71,** *72,* **81, 92**
Dinamo Kiev	8, 1	**1964, 66,** *73,* **74, 78, 82, 85, 87, 90**
Dinamo Moskva	7, 5	**1937,** *45, 49,* **50,** *53, 54, 55,* **67,** *70, 77, 79, 84*
Torpedo Moskva	6, 9	*1947,* **49,** *52,* **58,** *60, 61,* **66, 68,** *72, 77, 82,* **86,** *88, 89, 91*
CSKA Moskva (includes CDKA Moskva, CDSA Moskva)	5, 3	*1944,* **45, 48, 51, 55,** *67,* **91,** *92*

This summary only features the clubs that have won the Soviet Union Cup five times or more. For a full list of cup winners and runners-up please see the Cup Record above.

Russian League Record 1992–2002

SEASON	CHAMPIONS	RUNNERS-UP
1992	Spartak Moskva	Alania Vladikavkaz
1993	Spartak Moskva	Rotor Volgograd
1994	Spartak Moskva	Dinamo Moskva
1995	Alania Vladikavkaz	Lokomotiv Moskva
1996	Spartak Moskva	Alania Vladikavkaz
1997	Spartak Moskva	Rotor Volgograd
1998	Spartak Moskva	CSKA Moskva
1999	Spartak Moskva	Lokomotiv Moskva
2000	Spartak Moskva	Lokomotiv Moskva
2001	Spartak Moskva	Lokomotiv Moskva
2002	Lokomotiv Moskva	CSKA Moskva

Russian League Summary

TEAM	TOTALS	CHAMPIONS & RUNNERS-UP (BOLD) (*ITALICS*)
Spartak Moskva	9, 0	**1992–94, 96–2001**
Lokomotiv Moskva	1, 4	*1995, 99–2001,* **02**
Alania Vladikavkaz	1, 2	**1992,** *95, 96,*
CSKA Moskva	0, 2	*1998, 2002*
Rotor Volgograd	0, 2	*1993, 97*
Dinamo Moskva	0, 1	*1994*

Russian Cup Record 1993–2003

YEAR	WINNERS	SCORE	RUNNERS-UP
1993	Torpedo Moskva	1-1 (aet)(5-3 pens)	CSKA Moskva
1994	Spartak Moskva	2-2 (aet)(4-2 pens)	CSKA Moskva
1995	Dinamo Moskva	0-0 (aet)(8-7 pens)	Rotor Volgograd
1996	Lokomotiv Moskva	3-2	Spartak Moskva
1997	Lokomotiv Moskva	2-0	Dinamo Moskva
1998	Spartak Moskva	1-0	Lokomotiv Moskva
1999	Zenit Sankt-Peterburg	3-1	Dinamo Moskva
2000	Lokomotiv Moskva	3-2 (aet)	CSKA Moskva
2001	Lokomotiv Moskva	1-1 (aet)(4-3 pens)	Anzhi Makhachkala
2002	CSKA Moskva	2-0	Zenit Sankt-Peterburg
2003	Spartak Moskva	1-0	FK Rostov

Russian Cup Summary

TEAM	TOTALS	WINNERS & RUNNERS-UP (BOLD) (*ITALICS*)
Lokomotiv Moskva	4, 1	**1996, 97, 98,** *2000,* **01**
Spartak Moskva	3, 1	**1994,** *96,* **98, 2003**
CSKA Moskva	1, 3	*1993, 94,* **2000,** *02*
Dinamo Moskva	1, 2	**1995,** *97, 99*
Zenit Sankt-Peterburg	1, 1	**1999,** *2002*
Torpedo Moskva	1, 0	**1993**
Anzhi Makhachkala	0, 1	*2001*
FK Rostov	0, 1	*2003*
Rotor Volgograd	0, 1	*1995*

Ukraine

Football Federation of Ukraine
Founded: 1991
Joined FIFA: 1992
Joined UEFA: 1992

Ukrainian football has until recently been played in the shadow of the institutions and competitions of the Soviet Union. A separate national league and cup were established after independence was gained from the USSR in 1991. The league has since been dominated by Dynamo Kyiv.

SEASON	LEAGUE CHAMPIONS
1998	Dynamo Kyiv
1999	Dynamo Kyiv
2000	Dynamo Kyiv
2001	Dynamo Kyiv
2002	Shakhtar Donetsk
2003	Dynamo Kyiv

YEAR	CUP WINNERS
1998	Dynamo Kyiv
1999	Dynamo Kyiv
2000	Dynamo Kyiv
2001	Shakhtar Donetsk
2002	Shakhtar Donetsk
2003	Dynamo Kyiv

RUSSIA, UKRAINE

THE CONMEBOL NATIONS

COLOMBIA
1924, 1938, 1971
Federación
Colombiana
de Fútbol
1940
(1936–50,
1954)

1975, **2001**

VENEZUELA
1926
Federación
Venezolana
de Fútbol
1952 (1952)

GUYANA
(affiliated to
CONCACAF)

SURINAM
(affiliated to
CONCACAF)

**FRENCH
GUIANA**
(affiliated to the
French FA)

ATLANTIC
OCEAN

ECUADOR
1925
Asociación
Ecuatoriana
de Fútbol
1930 (1926)

BRAZIL
1914
Confederação
Brasileira
de Futebol
1916 (1923)

1950, **58, 62,
70, 94**, *98*, **2002**

1919, *21*, **22**,
37, **49**, *53, 57,
59, 83, 89, 91,
95, 97, 99*

PERU
1922
Federación
Peruana
de Fútbol
1926 (1924)

1939, 75

BOLIVIA
1925
Federación
Boliviana
de Fútbol
1926 (1926)

1963, *97*

PACIFIC
OCEAN

ASUNCIÓN
CONMEBOL
Headquarters

PARAGUAY
1906
Asociación
Paraguaya
de Fútbol
1921 (1921)

*1922, 29, 47,
49, 53, 63, 79*

ARGENTINA
1893
Asociación
del Fútbol
Argentino
**1916
(1912)**

1930, **78,
86, 90**

1917, 20, **21**,
23, **24, 25, 26,
27**, *29, 37, 42,
47*, **55, 57, 59**,
67, **91, 93**

CHILE
1895
Federación
de Fútbol de Chile
1916 (1912)

*1955, 56,
79, 87*

URUGUAY
1900
Asociación
Uruguaya
de Fútbol
1916 (1923)

1930, 50

1917, *19*, **20**,
23, **24, 26**, *27,
39*, **42**, *67*, **83**,
87, 89, **95**, *99*

CONMEBOL

C.S.F.

**South American
Tournaments
and Cup Competitions:**
Copa América
Copa Libertadores
Copa Sudamericana
Campeonato Sudamericano
Femenino

The Development of South American Football

1910 First unoffical
Copa América

1960 Copa Libertadores
established

1910   1920   1950   1960

1916
CONMEBOL
founded

1917 First offical
Copa América

1954 South
American Youth
Cup established

1968 Copa
Interamericana
established

The CONMEBOL Nations

Date of affiliation to CONMEBOL

- Founder member
- 1917–29
- 1930–49
- 1950–present

Formation of National FA — **1916**

COUNTRY 1916
Name of Football Association

Date of affiliation to CONMEBOL — **1916 (1912)** — Date of affiliation to FIFA

Team colours

World Cup — **1990** — Winners in bold

Copa América — *2000* — Runners-up in italic

(Official tournaments only)

Above: *Fallen giants: Colo Colo (right), Chile's leading club, went bankrupt in 2002. This is just the tip of an iceberg of debt and financial irregularities in South American football.*
Below: *Ecuador qualified for the World Cup finals in 2002 for the first time in its history. After decades of discrimination, it was the national team's first predominantly black squad.*

1971 Unofficial South American Footballer of the Year award established

1991 Teams from CONCACAF first invited to Copa América. South American Women's Championship established

2002 Copa Sudamericana replaced Copa Mercosur and Merconorte

1996 Last Copa de Oro

1980
1990
2000

1986 CONMEBOL South American Footballer of the Year Award established

1992 Copa CONMEBOL established

1993 Copa de Oro established

1998 Copa Mercosur and Copa Merconorte established

2003 Copa América postponed until 2005

The CONMEBOL Nations

CONMEBOL (CONFEDERACIÓN SUDAMERICANA DE FÚTBOL) was founded in 1916 and is the first and oldest of the world's regional football confederations. In July 1916, an informal international football tournament was held in Buenos Aires, Argentina, between the hosts, Chile, Uruguay and Brazil, part of a festival celebrating 100 years of independence from Spain. Recognizing the growing power and influence of the European-based and controlled FIFA (founded 1904), Héctor Gomez, a Uruguayan educationalist, took the opportunity to gather representatives of the four football associations and created CONMEBOL.

Since then CONMEBOL has grown to represent all of the South American nations minus Surinam and Guyana (members of CONCACAF) and French Guiana (which remains affiliated to the French FA). Its headquarters is in the Paraguayan capital, Asunción, from where it exerts considerable influence over FIFA as well as more local footballing matters. Its major international tournament, the Copa América, had been played on a varying but approximately biennial basis since 1916. Since then other international club tournaments have been established, including the prestigious Copa Libertadores in 1960, and a variety of less successful, made-for-television tournaments. Most recently CONMEBOL has dissolved the Copas Mercosur and Merconorte to create a single continental club tournament, the Copa Sudamericana. Although launched without Brazilian participation in 2001–02, it has been a success. Brazilian teams are set to participate in the next tournament.

Ronaldo celebrates Brazil's fifth World Cup victory in 2002. Brazil now looks set to host the tournament in 2014.

Calendar of Events

Club Tournaments	Copa Libertadores 2003–04
	Copa Sudamericana 2003–04
International Tournaments	Qualifying Tournament for 2004
	Olympic Games (Under–23s)

SOUTH AMERICA

South America

THE SEASONS IN REVIEW 2002, 2002–03

'FOOTBALL IS DYING,' SAID MAURICO MENDEZ, president of the Bolivian football league, announcing the imposition of a maximum wage in Bolivian football and a raft of cost-cutting measures. 'We can only carry on if we have an austerity programme.' It could have been almost any one of the continents' political leaders speaking. Where an austerity programme has not or cannot be implemented, football, like the wider economy, has seen non-payment of wages, labour disputes and strikes and the bankruptcy of venerable institutions. Violence and conflict has been particularly widespread in Argentina this year. Corruption and short cuts to wealth and power remain rife.

In Chile, Colo Colo was declared bankrupt mid season, in Peru, champions Universitario were forced to disband the squad they could not pay. At Bolivar and Nacional in Uruguay players conducted strikes, go slows and refused to train. Brazil may have won the World Cup, but like all of South America, nearly everyone is playing in Europe. The gap between European and South American club football was revealed at the World Club Cup where Real Madrid effortlessly outclassed Olimpia of Paraguay.

But there is just perhaps a hint of a different football future. The Copa Libertadores's popularity grows and the Copa Sudamericana is a surprise success. But most alluring of all, 30 years on from the club's Pele-inspired heyday, Santos is back playing fantastic football. In the shape of its young striker Robinho it has, perhaps, a player of rare charisma and calibre. The election of Lula as Brazil's president has seen the first meaningful legislation enacted to regulate the corruption and injustices of the game; and if Brazilian football can be sorted out then it can be done anywhere.

Copa Sudamericana

2002 FINAL (2 legs)

Nov 27 – Estadio Atanasio Girardot, Medellin
Atlético 0-4 San Lorenzo
Nacional   (Argentina)
(Colombia)   *(Saja 2 pen, Michelini 25, Romagnoli 51, Astudillo 67)*
h/t: 0-2 **Att:** 45,000
Ref: Rezende (Brazil)

Dec 11 – Estadio Nuevo Gasómetro, Buenos Aires
Atlético 0-0 San Lorenzo
Nacional
Att: 40,000
Ref: González (Paraguay)

San Lorenzo won 4-0 on aggregate

Right, top: Nicholas Leoz, president to CONMEBOL tries to surpress a snigger after suggesting that the World Cup in 2006 should be expanded to 36 teams at short notice.

Right: Universidad Catolica had a great season in Chile, winning the Apertura and coming second in the Clausura. Here defender Andres Bayas takes the ball from the feet of Carlos Zegarra of Peru's Sporting Cristal in the Copa Libertadores.

Below: Defying gravity, Colo Colo is bankrupt but champions. (Left to right) Huaquipan, Espina and Zunga celebrate as the team beats Apertura champions Universidad Catolica 3-2. Perhaps they will now be paid.

Top 10 South American Leagues

COUNTRY	CHAMPIONS	RUNNERS-UP
Argentina – Apertura	Independiente	Boca Juniors
Argentina – Clausura	River Plate	(see page 378)
Bolivia – Apertura	Bolívar	The Strongest
Bolivia – Clausura	Bolívar	Oriente Petrolero
Bolivia – National Championship	Bolívar	
Brazil – National Championship	Santos	Corinthians
Chile – Apertura	Universidad Católica	Rangers
Chile – Clausura	Colo Colo	Universidad Católica
Colombia – Apertura	América de Cali	Atlético Nacional
Colombia – Clausura	Independiente Medellín	Deportivo Pasto
Ecuador – Apertura	Barcelona	Aucas
Ecuador – Clausura	Deportivo Quito	El Nacional
Ecuador – National Championship	Emelec	Barcelona
Paraguay – Apertura	Libertad	Cerro Porteño
Paraguay – Clausura	12 de Octubre	Libertad
Paraguay – National Championship	Libertad	12 de Octubre
Peru – Apertura	Universitario	Alianza Lima
Peru – Clausura	Sporting Cristal	Alianza Lima
Peru – National Championship	Sporting Cristal	
Uruguay – Apertura	Nacional	Peñarol
Uruguay – Clausura	Danubio	Peñarol
Uruguay – National Championship	Nacional	Danubio
Venezuela – Apertura	Caracas FC	Ital-Chacao
Venezuela – Clausura	Unión Atlético Maracaibo	Ital-Chacao
Venezuela – National Championship	Caracas FC	Unión Atlético Maracaibo

San Lorenzo players Acosta, Paredes and Saja celebrate their victory in the Copa Sudamericana. The squad had feared that the crowd would strip them naked if they won and appealed for them not to. The tournament proved a surprising success with audiences.

Above: Byron Moreno, the controversial Ecuadorian referee, finally returns to work after a long suspension. Accused of favouring his home team in a vital Ecuadorian league match, Moreno took off for Italy and its chat show circuit. His notoriety after refereeing Italy's World Cup defeat to South Korea meant he was top billing.

Below: Bolivar made a clean sweep of Bolivia's titles this season. Striker Chiorazo shoots past Olmeda's Mina.

Bottom: Robinho of Santos, the most sensational player of the year in South America, takes the ball away from Jiminez of Cruz Azul in a Copa Libertadores game.

Bottom, left: Universidad Catolica's goalkeeper, Johnnie Walker, gets down for the ball in the team's final championship clash with Colo Colo at the National Stadium, Santiago.

Copa América

TOURNAMENT OVERVIEW

INTERNATIONAL FOOTBALL started early in South America with Argentina and Uruguay contesting the Lipton Cup (donated by Sir Thomas Lipton, the English tea merchant) beginning in 1905, and the Newton Cup from 1906. With regular international football across the River Plate and the opening of a rail link to Chile, the Argentine FA invited Uruguay, Chile and Brazil to Buenos Aires for a four-way tournament in 1910 (this is now thought of as the first 'unofficial' Copa América, as CONMEBOL was not formed until 1916). The Brazilians decided not to show, but the tournament went ahead with victories for Uruguay and Argentina over Chile. For the deciding match, 40,000 fans gathered at Gimnasia's stadium – and promptly burnt down a stand. The game was abandoned. The next day, a heavily policed rematch at Racing Club's ground saw Argentina win 4-1.

The second tournament was held in 1916 to celebrate the centenary of Argentinian independence. This time the Brazilians did show, but Uruguay won the title. In 1917, the holders hosted and won the first official championships in Montevideo. Two years later it was the turn of Brazil, and Rio aristocrats Fluminense built a new stadium to stage the matches. In a final play-off with Uruguay, Freidenreich, the Brazilian striker, ended the match with a goal after 43 minutes of extra time. Brazil won again in 1922, but the 1920s really belonged to Uruguay and Argentina. After a six-year gap (1929–35), while domestic struggles over professionalism were worked out, the tournament resumed appropriately with Uruguayan (1935) and Argentinian (1937) victories.

Argentina and Brazil dominant

A protracted players' strike in Argentina saw the team withdraw from both the 1949 and 1953 tournaments, but over the era as a whole it was the dominant side. Peru's victory in 1939, and Bolivia's in 1963, gave the continent's minnows a look-in. By the early 1960s the popularity of the tournament was declining as the Copa Libertadores took off and club versus country disputes over player availability sharpened. With Argentina and Brazil fielding consistently weak teams, the tournament took an eight-year break (1967–75) before recommencing as a finals-only event.

The tournament was relaunched in 1987 with all matches held in a single host country during the European close season to maximize player availability and TV and sponsorship money. The perennial problem of creating a tournament format with ten teams was solved in 1993 by inviting two outside nations – Mexico and the USA. This format has been replicated since with appearances for South Korea, Costa Rica and Japan as well. In the modern era, Argentina and Brazil have won when they have fielded their strongest sides, but their weaker teams have let the Uruguayans and the Colombians in.

Unofficial tournaments

YEAR	WINNERS	RUNNERS-UP	THIRD PLACE
1910	Argentina	Uruguay	Chile
1916	Uruguay	Argentina	Brazil
1935	Uruguay	Argentina	Brazil
1941	Argentina	Uruguay	Chile
1945	Argentina	Brazil	Chile
1946	Argentina	Brazil	Paraguay
1956	Uruguay	Chile	Argentina
1959	Uruguay	Argentina	Brazil

Copa América: winners and runners-up

TEAM COLOURS	COUNTRY	TOTAL WINS, YEARS	TOTAL RUNNERS-UP, YEARS
15	Argentina	**15:** 1910*, 21, 25, 27, 29, 37, 41*, 45*, 46*, 47, 55, 57, 59, 91, 93	**10:** 1916*, 17, 20, 23, 24, 26, 35*, 42, 59*, 67
14	Uruguay	**14:** 1916*, 17, 20, 23, 24, 26, 35*, 42, 56*, 59*, 67, 83, 87, 95	**7:** 1910*, 19, 27, 39, 41*, 89, 99
6	Brazil	**6:** 1919, 22, 49, 89, 97, 99	**11:** 1921, 25, 37, 45*, 46*, 53, 57, 59, 83, 91, 95
2	Paraguay	**2:** 1953, 79	**5:** 1922, 29, 47, 49, 63
	Peru	**2:** 1939, 75	0
1	Bolivia	**1:** 1963	**1:** 1997
1	Colombia	**1:** 2001	**1:** 1975
0	Chile	0	**4:** 1955, 56*, 79, 87
0	Mexico	0	**2:** 1993, 2001

* honours in unofficial tournaments

COPA AMÉRICA

VENEZUELA

COLOMBIA

ECUADOR

BRAZIL

PERU

1939 **1927**

1927 1939

BOLIVIA

1919, **1921,** **1917,**
22 **25, 37** **20, 42**

1919 1922

PARAGUAY

1922, **1923,**
29 **24, 25,**
39

CHILE

1926

1920

1926

PACIFIC
OCEAN

URUGUAY

1917, **1919,** **1921,**
20, 23, **27, 39** **22, 29,**
24, 26, **37**
42

1917 1923 1924 1942

ARGENTINA

1921, **1917,** **1919**
25, 27, **20, 23,**
29, 37 **24, 26,**
42

1921 1925

1929 1937

ATLANTIC
OCEAN

*Artur Freidenreich was the first
great black Brazilian footballer.
He scored the winner for Brazil
against Uruguay in the 1919
Copa América Final in Rio.*

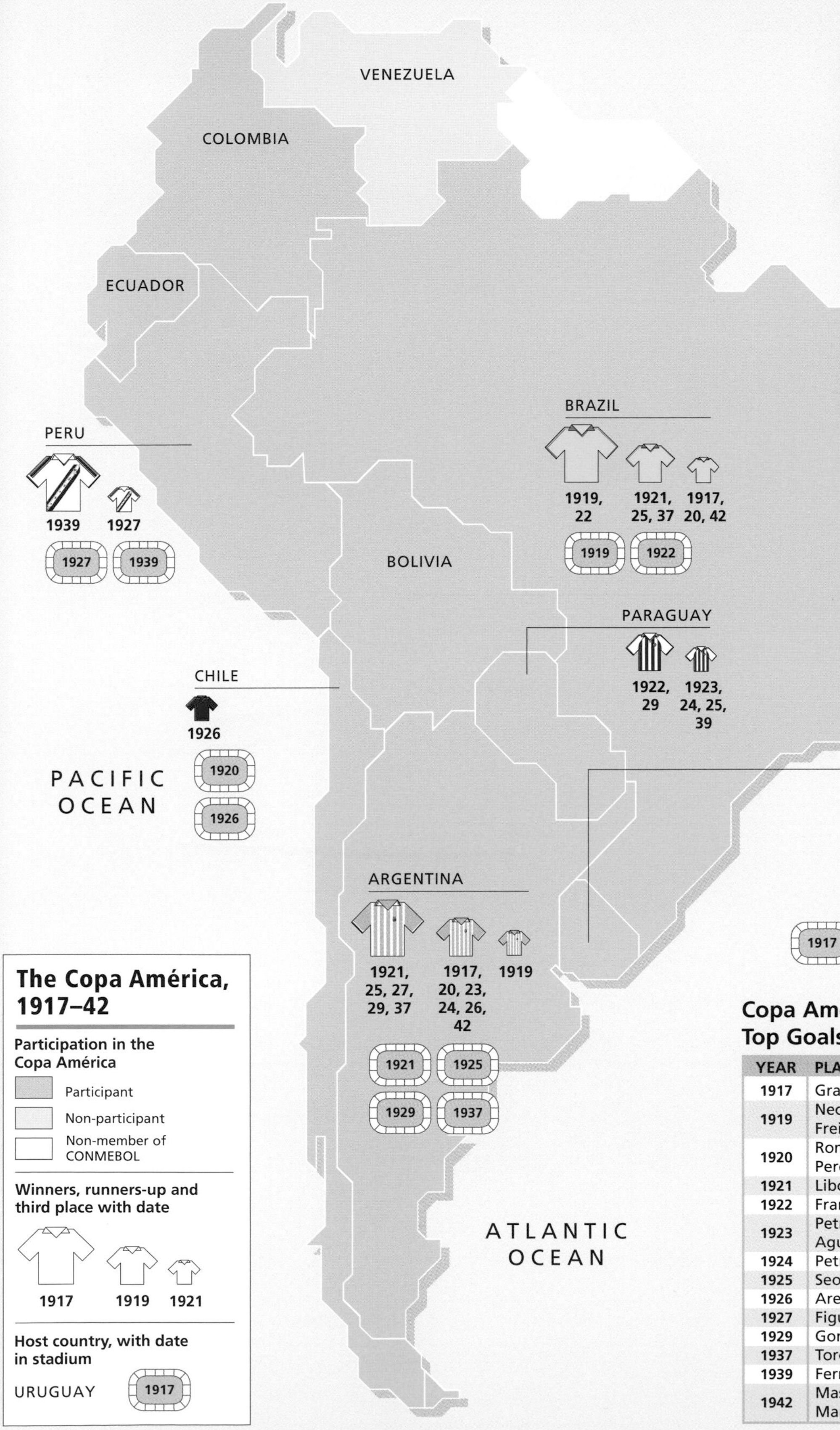

COPA AMÉRICA

The Copa América, 1917–42

**Participation in the
Copa América**

Participant

Non-participant

Non-member of
CONMEBOL

**Winners, runners-up and
third place with date**

1917 1919 1921

**Host country, with date
in stadium**

URUGUAY 1917

Copa América Top Goalscorers (1917–42)

YEAR	PLAYER	NATIONALITY	GOALS
1917	Gradin	Uruguayan	3
1919	Neco	Brazilian	4
	Freidenreich	Brazilian	
1920	Romano	Uruguayan	3
	Perez	Uruguayan	
1921	Libonatti	Argentinian	3
1922	Francia	Argentinian	4
1923	Petrone	Uruguayan	3
	Aguirre	Argentinian	
1924	Petrone	Uruguayan	4
1925	Seoane	Argentinian	6
1926	Arellano	Chilean	7
1927	Figueroa	Uruguayan	4
1929	Gonzalez	Paraguayan	5
1937	Toro	Chilean	7
1939	Fernandez	Peruvian	7
1942	Masantonio	Argentinian	7
	Marino	Argentinian	

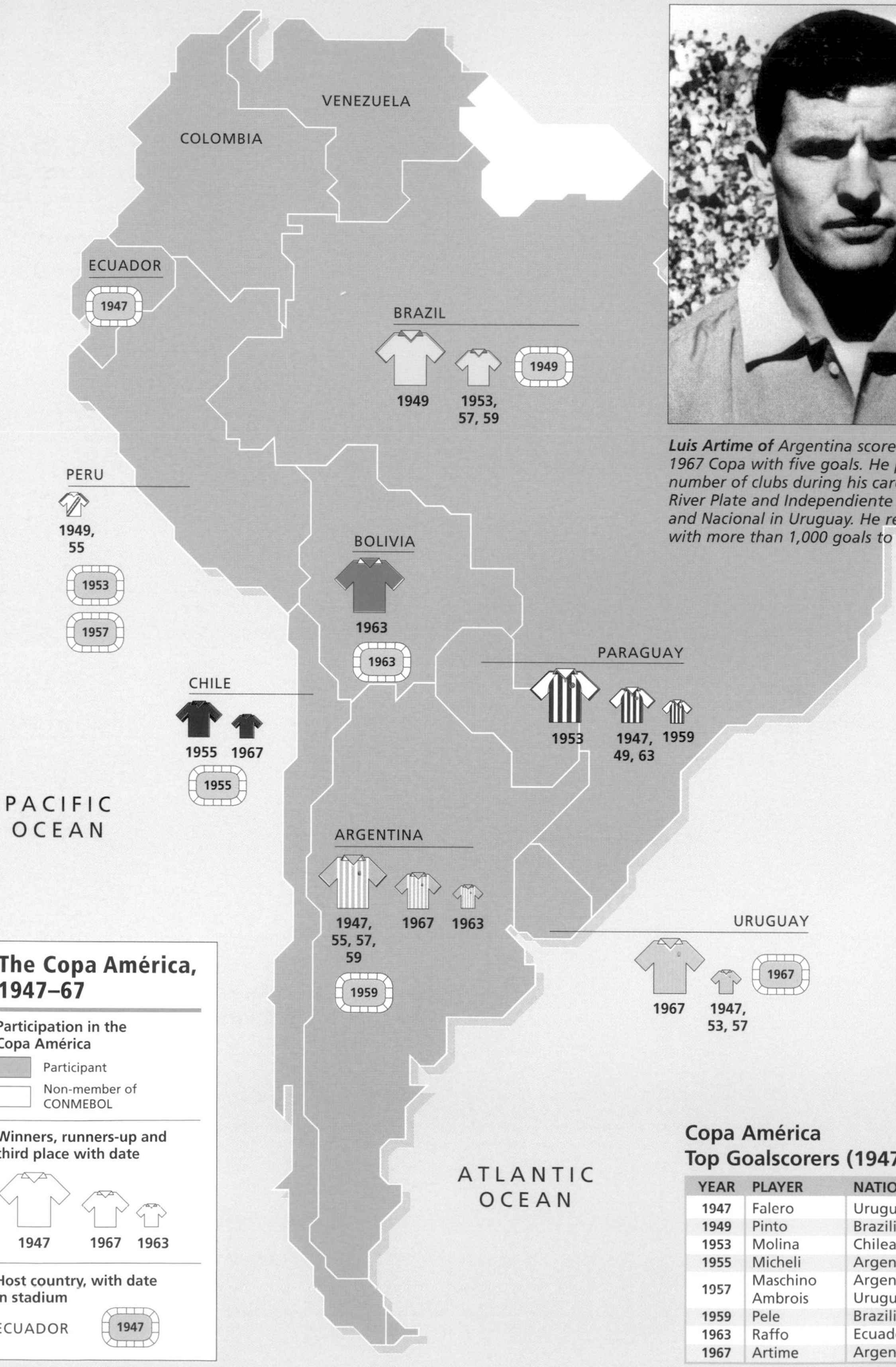

COPA AMÉRICA

VENEZUELA

COLOMBIA

ECUADOR

| 1947 |

BRAZIL

1949   1953,
        57, 59

| 1949 |

*Luis Artime of Argentina scored most in the
1967 Copa with five goals. He played for a
number of clubs during his career including
River Plate and Independiente in Argentina
and Nacional in Uruguay. He retired in 1974
with more than 1,000 goals to his name.*

PERU

1949,
55

| 1953 |

| 1957 |

BOLIVIA

1963

| 1963 |

PARAGUAY

1953   1947,   1959
        49, 63

CHILE

1955   1967

| 1955 |

PACIFIC
OCEAN

ARGENTINA

1947,   1967   1963
55, 57,
59

| 1959 |

URUGUAY

1967   1947,
        53, 57

| 1967 |

ATLANTIC
OCEAN

The Copa América, 1947–67

Participation in the Copa América

Participant

Non-member of CONMEBOL

Winners, runners-up and third place with date

1947   1967   1963

Host country, with date in stadium

ECUADOR | 1947 |

Copa América
Top Goalscorers (1947–67)

YEAR	PLAYER	NATIONALITY	GOALS
1947	Falero	Uruguayan	7
1949	Pinto	Brazilian	9
1953	Molina	Chilean	7
1955	Micheli	Argentinian	8
1957	Maschino Ambrois	Argentinian Uruguayan	9
1959	Pele	Brazilian	8
1963	Raffo	Ecuadorian	6
1967	Artime	Argentinian	5

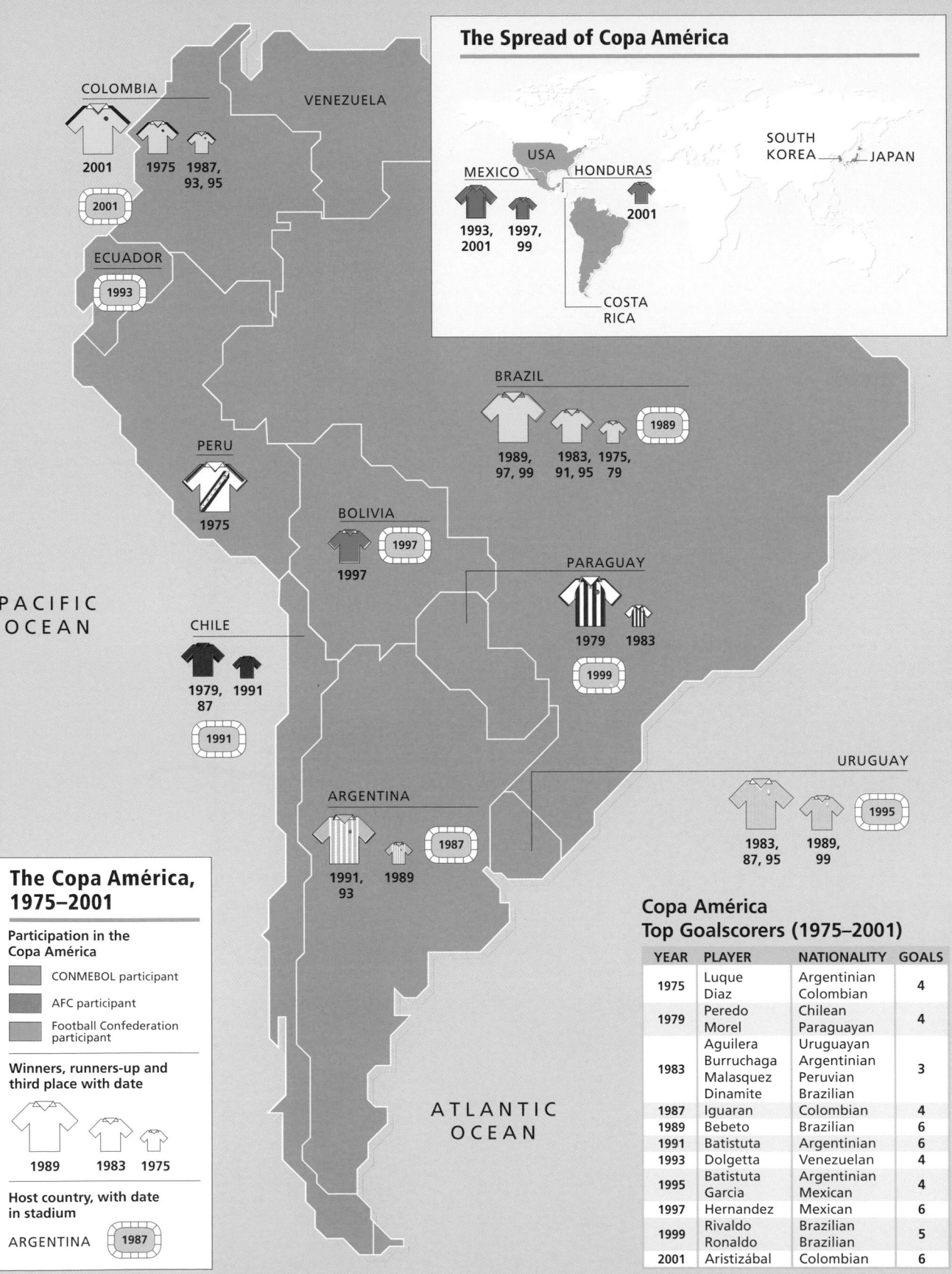

COLOMBIA
2001   1975   1987, 93, 95
2001

ECUADOR
1993

VENEZUELA

The Spread of Copa América

MEXICO   USA   HONDURAS
1993,   1997,   2001
2001   99

SOUTH KOREA → JAPAN

COSTA RICA

BRAZIL
1989,   1983,   1975,   1989
97, 99   91, 95 79

PERU
1975

BOLIVIA
1997   1997

PARAGUAY
1979   1983
1999

CHILE
1979,   1991
87
1991

URUGUAY
1983,   1989,   1995
87, 95   99

PACIFIC OCEAN

ARGENTINA
1991,   1989   1987
93

ATLANTIC OCEAN

COPA AMÉRICA

The Copa América, 1975–2001

Participation in the Copa América

- CONMEBOL participant
- AFC participant
- Football Confederation participant

Winners, runners-up and third place with date

1989   1983   1975

Host country, with date in stadium

ARGENTINA   1987

Copa América Top Goalscorers (1975–2001)

YEAR	PLAYER	NATIONALITY	GOALS
1975	Luque	Argentinian	4
	Diaz	Colombian	
1979	Peredo	Chilean	4
	Morel	Paraguayan	
1983	Aguilera	Uruguayan	3
	Burruchaga	Argentinian	
	Malasquez	Peruvian	
	Dinamite	Brazilian	
1987	Iguaran	Colombian	4
1989	Bebeto	Brazilian	6
1991	Batistuta	Argentinian	6
1993	Dolgetta	Venezuelan	4
1995	Batistuta	Argentinian	4
	Garcia	Mexican	
1997	Hernandez	Mexican	6
1999	Rivaldo	Brazilian	5
	Ronaldo	Brazilian	
2001	Aristizábal	Colombian	6

Copa América

TOURNAMENT REVIEW 2001

COLOMBIA LOST THE right to host the 1986 World Cup because of fears of disruption and chaos created by the endemic violence born of a massive narcotics industry. It went on to almost lose the 2001 Copa América to a wave of bombings and shootings that heralded yet another breakdown of the country's fragile peace process. Throughout May and early June, the civil war between the government, left-wing paramilitaries FARC and right-wing paramilitaries erupted with bombings in Bogotá, Cali and Medellín. Twelve people were killed and over 200 injured in the cities due to host two groups and the Final. However, the CSF (South American Football Confederation) repeatedly confirmed Colombia as hosts as president Andrés Pastrana promised massive troop deployments during the tournament.

In late June, Hernán Mejía Campuzano, vice-president of the Colombian Football Federation, was kidnapped by FARC paramilitaries. The CSF, panicked, announced that the Copa would now take place with an alternative host. Campuzano was promptly released, and headed straight for a meeting of the CSF executive in Buenos Aires. There, on 30 June, the Copa was returned to Colombia, but was to be played in 2002. Finally, on 5 July, under pressure from both Colombian president Andrés Pastrana and Brazilian TV company Traffic, the CSF announced that the Copa would go ahead as planned in Colombia, kicking off just six days later. Pastrana had gone on national TV declaring that the cup was essential to the maintenance of national pride and solidarity. Traffic threatened lawsuits resulting from loss of return on the $7 million it had invested in the TV rights.

COPA AMÉRICA

COLOMBIA
1995 Third place
1997 Quarter-finalists
1999 Quarter-finalists
Deportivo Cali 4

VENEZUELA
1995 Group stage
1997 Group stage
1999 Group stage
Caracas FC 5
7

ECUADOR
1995 Group stage
1997 Quarter-finalists
1999 Group stage
El Nacional 7
3

PERU
1995 Group stage
1997 Semi-finalists
1999 Quarter-finalists
Alianza Lima 4
Sporting Cristal 4
3

BOLIVIA
1995 Quarter-finalists
1997 Runners-up
1999 Group stage
Oriente Petrolero 5
3

CHILE
1995 Group stage
1997 Group stage
1999 Semi-finalists
Santiago Wanderers 4
7

URUGUAY
1995 Champions
1997 Group stage
1999 Runners-up
Defensor Sporting 4
Danubio 4
Wanderers 4
1

BRAZIL
1995 Runners-up
1997 Champions
1999 Champions
Barcelona 2
Cruzeiro 2
Milan 2
Palmeiras 2
9

ARGENTINA
1995 Quarter-finalists
1997 Quarter-finalists
1999 Quarter-finalists

PARAGUAY
1995 Quarter-finalists
1997 Quarter-finalists
1999 Quarter-finalists
Sportivo Luqueño 6
3

Copa América 2001 Qualification

Means by which the national team qualified
- Host
- Participant
- Withdrew
- Did not enter

National squads
COLOMBIA — Team name
Team shirt
1995 Third place — Performance in last 3 tournaments
Oriente Petrolo 5 — Number of players from club team in national squad
12 — Number of squad members (out of 22) that play abroad

Foreign participants in Copa América 2001

- Participant
- Withdrew
- Late replacement

CANADA

MEXICO
1995 Quarter-finalists
1997 Third place
1999 Third place
3

COSTA RICA
1997 Group stage
5

HONDURAS
2

Not everyone was convinced by the CSF and by Pastrana's assurances. Argentina and Canada, who were due to play group games in Medellín, thought better of it and withdrew. Costa Rica and Honduras agreed to make up the numbers.

If the political prospects for the tournament looked poor, the sporting prospects were not that much better. The long South American World Cup qualification tournament had already stolen much of the Copa's thunder. Argentina, the strongest of the South American sides, was not present, Uruguay sent a reserve squad, and no settled Brazilian squad existed to be sent. Barranquilla, a humid port on the coast, and Bogotá, high up in the Andes, both presented serious problems of acclimatization for the players.

A massive police presence was promised by President Pastrana in order to persuade the CSF to allow Colombia to host the tournament.

Copa América 2001: The Venues

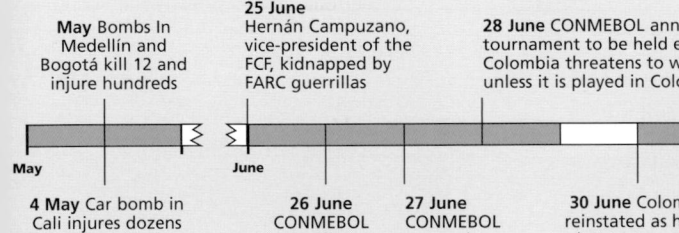

- **45,600** Tournament stadium with capacity and name **PASCUAL GUERRERO**
- **Cali** Location of stadium
- Scene of bomb attacks

Barranquilla — **50,220** METROPOLITANO
52,800 ATANASIO GIRARDOT
Medellín
34,000 HERNÁN RAMÍREZ VILLEGAS
Manizales
Pereira
Arm;énia — **46,310** EL CAMPÍN
Bogotá
29,000 CENTENARIO
Cali
45,600 PASCUAL GUERRERO
35,000 PALOGRANDE
COLOMBIA

The Development of Copa América 2001

May Bombs In Medellín and Bogotá kill 12 and injure hundreds

25 June Hernán Campuzano, vice-president of the FCF, kidnapped by FARC guerrillas

28 June CONMEBOL announces tournament to be held elsewhere; Colombia threatens to withdraw unless it is played in Colombia

5 July CONMEBOL announce tournament to take place on original dates

9 July Costa Rica agrees to participate

11 July Tournament begins

May
June
July

4 May Car bomb in Cali injures dozens including Colombian players and coaches

26 June CONMEBOL ratifies Colombia as hosts for Copa América

27 June CONMEBOL suspends decision, Campuzano released

30 June Colombia reinstated as hosts, but tournament postponed to 2002

6 July Argentina withdraws

7 July Canada withdraws

10 July Honduras agrees to participate

THE GROUP STAGES

In Group A, Colombia and Chile outclassed Ecuador and Venezuela. Colombia, under Francisco Maturana, fielded a young team with an experienced defence, including Mario Yepes and Ivan Córdoba. In Group B, the poor form of Brazil continued, beaten by Mexico and threatened for much of the game by an experimental Paraguayan side. In Group C, late arrivals Costa Rica and Honduras hit form and qualified along with Uruguay.

COLOMBIA — CHILE · A · ECUADOR — VENEZUELA

BRAZIL — MEXICO · B · PERU — PARAGUAY

COSTA RICA — HONDURAS · C · URUGUAY — BOLIVIA

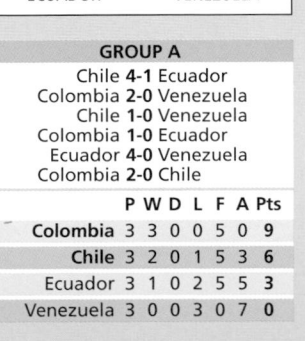

GROUP A

Chile 4-1 Ecuador
Colombia 2-0 Venezuela
Chile 1-0 Venezuela
Colombia 1-0 Ecuador
Ecuador 4-0 Venezuela
Colombia 2-0 Chile

	P	W	D	L	F	A	Pts
Colombia	3	3	0	0	5	0	9
Chile	3	2	0	1	5	3	6
Ecuador	3	1	0	2	5	5	3
Venezuela	3	0	0	3	0	7	0

GROUP B

Peru 3-3 Paraguay
Mexico 1-0 Brazil
Brazil 2-0 Peru
Paraguay 0-0 Mexico
Peru 1-0 Mexico
Brazil 3-1 Paraguay

	P	W	D	L	F	A	Pts
Brazil	3	2	0	1	5	2	6
Mexico	3	1	1	1	1	1	4
Peru	3	1	1	1	4	5	4
Paraguay	3	0	2	1	4	6	2

GROUP C

Uruguay 1-0 Bolivia
Costa Rica 1-0 Honduras
Uruguay 1-1 Costa Rica
Honduras 2-0 Bolivia
Costa Rica 0-0 Bolivia
Honduras 1-0 Uruguay

	P	W	D	L	F	A	Pts
Costa Rica	3	2	1	0	6	1	7
Honduras	3	2	0	1	3	1	6
Uruguay	3	1	1	1	2	2	4
Bolivia	3	0	0	3	0	7	0

COPA AMÉRICA

THE QUARTER-FINALS

Chile and Peru gave Mexico and Colombia easy quarter-final victories, though the Peruvians held out against a rampant Colombian attack for the first 50 minutes. It required an inspired shot from Aristizábal to break the deadlock and a header ten minutes later to seal it. Costa Rica and Uruguay met again after drawing 1-1 in the group stage – Uruguay went through to the last four winning 2-1. The big upset came in the Brazil v Honduras tie. The Hondurans were expected to play for a draw and penalties, but their passing and movement were too much for a lethargic, leaden Brazil, and they triumphed 2-0.

22 July – Pereira
Attendance 20,000

0-2

Chile — Mexico

h/t: 0-1

Scorers	Arellano 17, Osorno 78
☐☐ Yellow cards	☐☐☐
Red cards	

22 July – Armênia
Attendance 29,000

1-2

Costa Rica — Uruguay

h/t: 0-0

Wanchope 52	Scorers	Lemos 60 (pen) Lima 87
☐☐☐☐ Yellow cards		☐☐☐
Red cards		

23 July – Armênia
Attendance 30,000

3-0

Colombia — Peru

h/t: 0-0

Aristizábal 50, 69 Hernández 66	Scorers	
☐ Yellow cards		☐☐
Red cards		

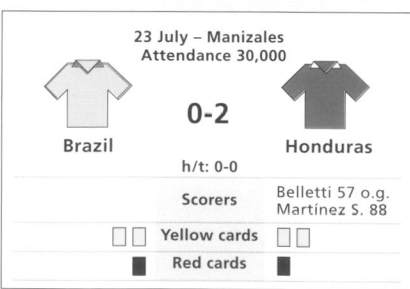

23 July – Manizales
Attendance 30,000

0-2

Brazil — Honduras

h/t: 0-0

Scorers	Belletti 57 o.g. Martínez S. 88
☐☐ Yellow cards	☐☐
■ Red cards	■

THE SEMI-FINALS

Colombia proved too strong for Honduras with the team's stars Freddy Grisales and Victor Hugo Aristizábal combining to put the hosts 2-0 ahead and so progress to the Final. Throughout the tournament Grisales gave Colombia's midfield energy and purpose while Aristizábal scored six goals – the biggest tally in a Copa América since Pele in 1959. Mexico was compact and composed in the victory over Uruguay, but picked up injuries and suspensions to key players, late red cards for García Aspe and Vidrio proving costly in the Final.

25 July – Pereira
Attendance 20,000

2-1

Mexico — Uruguay

h/t: 1-1

Borgetti 14 García Aspe 67 (pen)	Scorers	Morales R. 32
☐☐☐☐ Yellow cards		☐☐☐☐
■■ Red cards		■■

26 July - Manizales
Attendance 40,000

2-0

Colombia — Honduras

h/t: 1-0

Bedoya 6 Aristizábal 63	Scorers	
☐☐ Yellow cards		☐☐☐☐
Red cards		

THIRD PLACE PLAY-OFF

Honduras continued to show great form in the third-fourth play-off match, and the team's teenage winger, Fabian Estoyanoff, ran the Uruguayan right-wing ragged. But Uruguay dug in and found equalizers to both the Honduran strikes. However, when it came to penalties, the Honduran players held their nerve.

July 29 - Bogotá
Attendance 47,000

2-2
(after extra time)
Honduras won
5-4 on pens

Uruguay — Honduras

h/t: 2-2 f/t: 2-2

Bizera 21 Martínez 44	Scorers	Martínez S. 14 Izaguirre 41
☐☐☐☐ Yellow cards		☐☐
Red cards		

THE FINAL

Without captain Aspe and centre-backs Vidrio and Márquez, Mexico barely troubled Colombia in the Final. Cue a short burst of national celebration that the tournament had been peaceful and well supported and had ended in a home victory. It is a shame but no surprise that since the tournament Colombian politics and peace negotiations have shown no sign of following a similar path.

The Colombian squad celebrates its victory by holding up the Copa América trophy in a shower of red, yellow and blue ticker tape. A peaceful tournament and a home victory more than justified the decision to award the Copa to Colombia.

The Winning Goal

With 64 minutes on the clock, Colombia was awarded a free kick on the right-hand side of the pitch. Ivan López curled in a cross and Colombian captain Ivan Córdoba leapt over the Mexican defence to head powerfully into the net past keeper Oscar Pérez.

The Starting Line-Up

July 29 - El Campín, Bogotá
Attendance 46,310

MEXICO	Referee	COLOMBIA
Formation: 3-5-2	⦿	Formation: 4-4-2
Manager	Ubaldo Aquino	**Manager**
Javier Aguirre	(Paraguay)	Francisco Maturana

Substitutes		Substitutes	
Sánchez	1	8	Ferriera
Victorino	10	11	Arriaga
Osorno	11	12	Calero
Reyes	16	16	González
Hierro	17	18	Castillo
Zepeda	19	21	Diaz
Martinez	22	23	Molina

Highlights of the Game

KEY

Player booked	▯	Substitution
Player sent off	▮	Goal

MEXICO — KICK OFF **0 mins** — **COLOMBIA**

1 min: Play interrupted briefly as a parachutist drifted onto the pitch crashing into the sideline advertising placards

5 min: Victor Aristizábal hits the post

20 min: Bedoya

28 min: Vargas

31 min: Castillo on, Aristizábal off after a collision with goalie Oscar Pérez almost draws a penalty

35 min: Coach Javier Aguirre refused to leave the bench after being sent off for stepping out of coach's area

45 mins

HALF-TIME: **0-0**

54 min: Victorino on, Arellano off

65 min: Ivan Córdoba puts Colombia ahead

67 min: Osorno on, Johan Rodríguez off

70 min: Ramón Carlos Morales

74 min: Zepeda on, Alberto Rodríguez off

79 min: Juan Rodríguez sent off for a violent tackle

87 min: Molina on, Hernández off

90 min: Gerardo Torrado sent off for violent conduct

90 mins

+ *3 mins injury time*

93 min: Molina

FULL-TIME: **0-1**

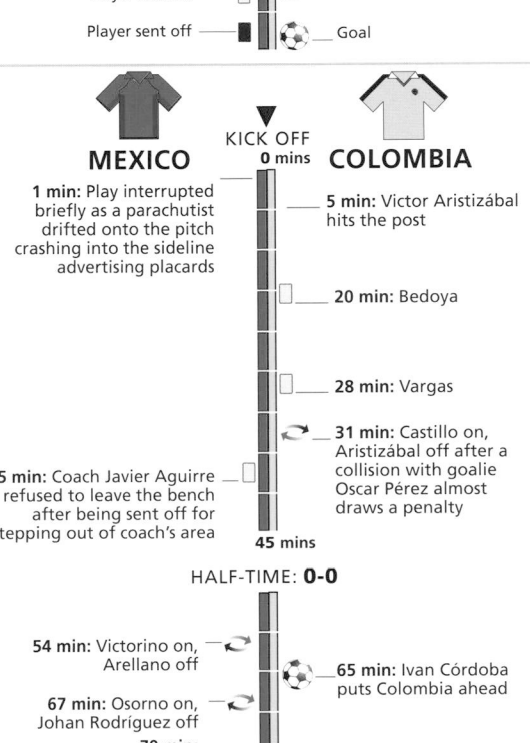

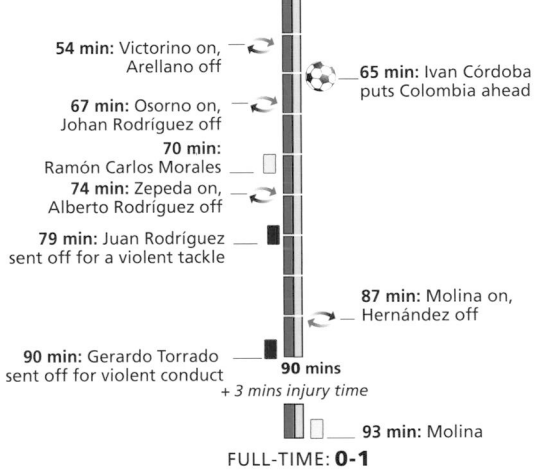

2: Ivan Córdoba rises above the Mexican defenders to power his header past Oscar Pérez

1: Ivan López crosses from a free-kick into a packed penalty area

Colombian full-back *Ivan Córdoba rises to meet Ivan López's free kick and heads the only goal of the Final of Copa América 2001.*

Copa América

THE COPA AMÉRICA is the oldest continental football tournament. Unofficial tournaments were played as far back as 1910 and 1916, with the first official tournament held in 1917. The small number of South American nations and the vast differences in the strength of teams across the continent have produced an ever-changing range of tournament formats.

Most of the early tournaments were based on a mini-league format with play-offs in the event of ties. In 1975 CONMEBOL radically changed the format by playing the first rounds of the competition all over South America. Three groups of three played for three semi-final places, the fourth slot going to the reigning champions. Public interest, already at a low level, dipped even further with this bizarre elongated format, and in 1987 the tournament was re-established in a single host nation over two or three weeks.

In 1989 and 1991 two leagues of five were played to produce four semi-finalists, and from 1993 the tournament was enlarged, with two places being given to teams invited from the rest of the Americas and Asia: the USA, Costa Rica, Mexico and Japan have all participated. Twelve teams allow for a model based on three groups of four with winner, runners-up and the two best-placed third teams going on to knockout quarter-finals. Due to fixture congestion and the complexities of holding a bi-annual tournament, CONMEBOL have cancelled the 2003 tournament and the next Copa América will be played in Peru in 2005.

1910 ARGENTINA*
1 Argentina
2 Uruguay
3 Chile

1916 ARGENTINA*
1 Uruguay
2 Argentina
3 Brazil

1917 URUGUAY
1 Uruguay
2 Argentina
3 Brazil

1919 BRAZIL
1 Brazil (after play-off)
2 Uruguay
3 Argentina

PLAY-OFF
May 29 – das Laranjeiras, Rio de Janeiro
Brazil 1-0 Uruguay
(Friedenreich 122)
(after extra time)
h/t: 0-0 **90 mins:** 0-0
Att: 28,000 **Ref:** Barbera (Argentina)

1920 CHILE
1 Uruguay
2 Argentina
3 Brazil

1921 ARGENTINA
1 Argentina
2 Brazil
3 Uruguay

1922 BRAZIL
1 Brazil (after play-off)
2 Paraguay
3 Uruguay

PLAY-OFF
October 22 – das Laranjeiras, Rio de Janeiro
Brazil 3-1 Paraguay
(Neco 11,   (G. Rivas 60)
Formiga 48, 89)
h/t: 1-0 **Att:** 20,000
Ref: Guevara (Chile)

1923 URUGUAY
1 Uruguay
2 Argentina
3 Paraguay

1924 URUGUAY
1 Uruguay
2 Argentina
3 Paraguay

1925 ARGENTINA
1 Argentina
2 Brazil
3 Paraguay

1926 CHILE
1 Uruguay
2 Argentina
3 Chile

1927 PERU
1 Argentina
2 Uruguay
3 Peru

1929 ARGENTINA
1 Argentina
2 Paraguay
3 Uruguay

1935 PERU*
1 Uruguay
2 Argentina
3 Peru

1937 ARGENTINA
1 Argentina (after play-off)
2 Brazil
3 Uruguay

PLAY-OFF
February 1 – Gasómetro, Buenos Aires
Argentina 2-0 Brazil
(De la Mata 109, 122)
(after extra time)
h/t: 0-0 **90 mins:** 0-0
Att: 80,000 **Ref:** Macias (Argentina)

1939 PERU
1 Peru
2 Uruguay
3 Paraguay

1941 CHILE*
1 Argentina
2 Uruguay
3 Chile

1942 URUGUAY
1 Uruguay
2 Argentina
3 Brazil

1945 CHILE*
1 Argentina
2 Brazil
3 Chile

1946 ARGENTINA*
1 Argentina
2 Brazil
3 Paraguay

1947 ECUADOR
1 Argentina
2 Paraguay
3 Uruguay

1949 BRAZIL
1 Brazil (after play-off)
2 Paraguay
3 Peru

PLAY-OFF
May 11 – São Januario, Rio de Janeiro
Brazil 7-0 Paraguay
(Ademir 17, 27, 48,
Tesourinha 43, 70,
Jair 72, 89)
h/t: 3-0 **Att:** 55,000
Ref: Berrick (England)

1953 PERU
1 Paraguay (after play-off)
2 Brazil
3 Uruguay

PLAY-OFF
April 1 – Nacional, Lima
Paraguay 3-2 Brazil
(A. Lopez 14,   (Baltazar 56, 65)
Gavilan 17,
R. Fernández 41)
h/t: 3-0 **Att:** 35,000
Ref: Dean (England)

1955 CHILE
1 Argentina
2 Chile
3 Peru

1956 URUGUAY*
1 Uruguay
2 Chile
3 Argentina

1957 PERU
1 Argentina
2 Brazil
3 Uruguay

1959 ARGENTINA
1 Argentina
2 Brazil
3 Paraguay

1959 ECUADOR*
1 Uruguay
2 Argentina
3 Brazil

1963 BOLIVIA
1 Bolivia
2 Paraguay
3 Argentina

1967 URUGUAY
1 Uruguay
2 Argentina
3 Chile

1975 FINAL** (2 legs)
October 16 – El Campín, Bogotá
Colombia 1-0 Peru
(P. Castro)
Att: 50,000 **Ref:** Comesaña (Argentina)

October 22 – Nacional, Lima
Peru 2-0 Colombia
(Zárate,
Ramírez)
Att: 50,000 **Ref:** Silvagno (Chile)

PLAY-OFF
October 28 – Olímpico, Caracas
Peru 1-0 Colombia
(Sotil 25)
h/t: 1-0 **Att:** 30,000
Ref: Barreto (Uruguay)

Copa América Winners

Argentina
1910, 21, 25, 27, 29, 37, 41*, 45*, 46* 47, 55, 57, 59, 91, 93

Uruguay
1916*, 17, 20, 23, 24, 26, 35*, 42, 56*, 59*, 67, 83, 87, 95

Brazil
1919, 22, 49, 89, 97, 99

Peru
1939, 75

Paraguay
1953, 79

Bolivia
1963

Colombia
2001

1979 FINAL** (2 legs)

November 28 – Defensores del Chaco, Asunción
Paraguay 3-0 Chile
(C. Romero 12, 65,
M. Morel 36)
h/t: 2-0 **Att:** 40,000
Ref: Da Rosa (Uruguay)

December 5 – Nacional, Santiago
Chile 1-0 Paraguay
(Rivas 10)
h/t: 1-0 **Att:** 55,000
Ref: Barreto (Uruguay)

PLAY-OFF

December 11 – José Amalfitani, Buenos Aires
Paraguay 0-0 Chile
h/t: 0-0 **Att:** 6,000
Ref: Coelho (Brazil)
Paraguay won on goal difference

1983 FINAL**(2 legs)

October 27 – Centenario, Montevideo
Uruguay 2-0 Brazil
(Francescoli
41 pen, Diogo 80)
h/t: 1-0 **Att:** 65,000
Ref: Ortiz (Paraguay)

November 4 – Fonte Nova, Salvador
Brazil 1-1 Uruguay
(Jorginho 23) *(Aguilera 77)*
h/t: 1-0 **Att:** 95,000
Ref: Perez (Peru)
Uruguay won 3-1 on aggregate

1987 ARGENTINA

THIRD PLACE PLAY-OFF

July 11 – Monumental, Buenos Aires
Colombia 2-1 Argentina
(G. Gomez 8, *(Caniggia 86)*
Galeano 27)
h/t: 2-0 **Att:** 15,000
Ref: Corujo (Venezuela)

FINAL

July 12 – Monumental, Buenos Aires
Uruguay 1-0 Chile
(Bengochea 56)
h/t: 0-0 **Att:** 35,000
Ref: Romualdo Arppi (Brazil)

1989 BRAZIL

1 Brazil
2 Uruguay
3 Argentina

1991 CHILE

1 Argentina
2 Brazil
3 Chile

1993 ECUADOR

THIRD PLACE PLAY-OFF

July 3 – Reales Tamarindos, Portoviejo
Colombia 1-0 Ecuador
(Valencia 84)
h/t: 0-0 **Att:** 18,000
Ref: Arbolda (Venezuela)

FINAL

July 4 – Monumental, Guayaquil
Argentina 2-1 Mexico
(Batistuta 65, 84) *(Galindo 76 pen)*
h/t: 0-0 **Att:** 40,000
Ref: Marcio Rezende (Brazil)

1995 URUGUAY

THIRD PLACE PLAY-OFF

July 22 – Campus Municipal, Maldonado
Colombia 4-1 United States
(Quinones 31, *(Moore 53 pen)*
Valderrama 38,
Asprilla 50,
Rincon 76)
h/t: 2-0 **Att:** 2,500
Ref: Imperatore (Chile)

FINAL

July 23 – Centenario, Montevideo
Uruguay 1-1 Brazil
(Bengoechea 48) *(Tulio 30)*
(after extra time)
90 mins: 0-0 **Att:** 58,000
Ref: Brizio Carter (Mexico)
Uruguay won 5-3 on pens

1997 BOLIVIA

THIRD PLACE PLAY-OFF

June 28 – Jesús Bermúdez, Oruro
Mexico 1-0 Peru
(Hernández 82)
Ref: Borgesano (Venezuela)

FINAL

June 29 – Hernando Siles, La Paz
Brazil 3-1 Bolivia
(Edmundo 40, *(E. Sanchez 44)*
Ronaldo 79,
Ze Roberto 90)
h/t: 1-1 **Att:** 50,000
Ref: Nieves (Uruguay)

1999 PARAGUAY

THIRD PLACE PLAY-OFF

July 17 – Defensores del Chaco, Asunción
Mexico 2-1 Chile
(Palencia 26, *(Palacios 81)*
Zepeda 86)
Att: 4,000 **Ref:** Elizondo (Argentina)

* Unofficial.
** No fixed venues for these tournaments; matches were played home and away.

FINAL

July 18 – Defensores del Chaco, Asunción
Brazil 3-0 Uruguay
(Rivaldo 20, 27,
Ronaldo 46)
h/t: 2-0 **Att:** 40,000
Ref: Ruiz (Colombia)

2001 COLOMBIA

THIRD PLACE PLAY-OFF

28 July – El Campín, Bogotá
Honduras 2-2 Uruguay
(Martínez 14, 45) *(Bizera 22,*
Izaguirre 42)
h/t: 2-2 **Att:** 47,000
Ref: Hidalgo (Peru)
Honduras won 5-4 on pens

FINAL

29 July – El Campín, Bogotá
Colombia 1-0 Mexico
(I. Cordoba 65)
h/t: 0-0 **Att:** 47,000
Ref: Aquino (Paraguay)

The 1999 Copa América Final *between Brazil and Uruguay took place in the Defensores del Chaco stadium in Asunción, Paraguay. Brazil won 3-0 with two goals from Rivaldo and one from Ronaldo. Mexico beat Chile 2-1 in the same stadium to claim third place.*

Copa Libertadores

TOURNAMENT REVIEW 2002

AFTER 11 YEARS OF Brazilian and Argentinian domination of South America's top club tournament, previous winners Olimpia of Paraguay finally broke their stranglehold. The tournament got off to an inauspicious start when rights owners, the TV network PSN, went bankrupt and Fox Sports picked up the TV rights. This was great unless you lived in Brazil, where half the continent lives and Fox does not broadcast.

The four semi-finalists reflected the range of Latin American football. At one end of the scale, Mexico's América, generously funded by Televisa, boasted a large squad and quality foreign imports. Brazil's Grêmio and Paraguay's Olimpia, both financially troubled big clubs, continue to survive on a mixture of debt, patronage and well-connected individuals. São Caetano, runners-up in the last two Brazilian National Championships, is a tiny provincial São Paulo team driven by its charismatic and parsimonious coach Jair Picerni. In the first contest, São Caetano played its best passing and moving game over two legs to beat the Mexican giants. In the other game, Olimpia, with what appeared to be considerable help from the referee, beat Grêmio on penalties. In the opening leg of the Final São Caetano stunned everyone by winning 1-0. Olimpia's president, Oswaldo Dominguez Dibbs, was incandescent at the team's lacklustre performance. With many of his team found in an Asunción nightclub after the game, he resigned in a fit of pique. He was back, of course, for the second leg, but with Olimpia 1-0 down at half time, he might have been forgiven for resigning again. However, in the second half a revived Olimpia scored twice and, despite going down to ten men, hung on for penalties. São Caetano lost it in the cauldron of the Pacaembu, with Marlon and Serginho blasting their spot-kicks over the crossbar.

GROUP STAGES

GROUP 1

CLUB	P	W	D	L	F	A	Pts	
São Caetano (Brazil)	6	4	0	2	14	4	12	Second Round
Cobreloa (Chile)	6	4	0	2	12	8	12	Second Round
Cerro Porteño (Paraguay)	6	3	1	2	7	6	10	
Alianza Lima (Peru)	6	0	1	5	1	16	1	

GROUP 2

CLUB	P	W	D	L	F	A	Pts	
Grêmio (Brazil)	6	4	0	2	11	7	12	Second Round
Cienciano (Peru)	6	3	0	3	8	7	9	Second Round
12 de Octubre (Paraguay)	6	3	0	3	5	7	9	
Oriente Petrolero (Bolivia)	6	2	0	4	10	13	6	

GROUP 3

CLUB	P	W	D	L	F	A	Pts	
Peñarol (Uruguay)	6	4	0	2	11	7	12	Second Round
El Nacional (Ecuador)	6	4	0	2	10	6	12	Second Round
San Lorenzo (Argentina)	6	2	0	4	6	8	6	
Real Potosí (Bolivia)	6	2	0	4	10	16	6	

GROUP 4

CLUB	P	W	D	L	F	A	Pts	
América de Cali (Colombia)	6	3	2	1	10	3	11	Second Round
Olmedo (Ecuador)	6	3	0	3	7	7	9	Second Round
Bolívar (Bolivia)	6	2	2	2	11	13	8	
Atlético Paranaense (Brazil)	6	1	2	3	10	15	5	

GROUP 5

CLUB	P	W	D	L	F	A	Pts	
Morelia (Mexico)	6	4	2	0	15	7	14	Second Round
Nacional (Uruguay)	6	3	2	1	13	12	11	Second Round
Vélez Sarsfield (Argentina)	6	2	2	2	8	8	8	
Sporting Cristal (Peru)	6	0	0	6	5	14	0	

GROUP 6

CLUB	P	W	D	L	F	A	Pts	
Boca Juniors (Argentina)	6	4	1	1	7	2	13	Second Round
Montevideo Wanderers (Uruguay)	6	3	1	2	8	7	10	Second Round
Santiago Wanderers (Chile)	6	2	3	1	6	6	9	
Emelec (Ecuador)	6	0	1	5	4	10	1	

GROUP 7

CLUB	P	W	D	L	F	A	Pts	
América (Mexico)	6	5	1	0	9	2	16	Second Round
River Plate (Argentina)	6	2	3	1	8	4	9	Second Round
Talleres (Argentina)	6	1	2	3	5	9	5	
Corporación Tuluá (Colombia)	6	1	0	5	9	16	3	

GROUP 8

CLUB	P	W	D	L	F	A	Pts	
Olimpia (Paraguay)	6	3	2	1	8	5	11	Second Round
Universidad Católica (Chile)	6	3	1	2	9	8	10	Second Round
Once Caldas (Colombia)	6	3	0	3	10	11	9	
Flamengo (Brazil)	6	1	1	4	6	9	4	

Ivan Zamorano of América keeps the ball from River Plate's Sarabia. América cruised past River in its opening group.

SECOND ROUND (2 legs)

Universidad 1-1 São Caetano
Católica
São Caetano 1-1 Universidad
Católica
São Caetano won 4-2 on pens

River Plate 1-2 Grêmio
Grêmio 4-0 River Plate
Grêmio won 6-1 on aggregate

Montevideo 2-2 Peñarol
Wanderers
Peñarol 2-2 Montevideo
Wanderers
Peñarol won 3-0 on pens

Nacional 1-0 América
de Cali
América 0-0 Nacional
de Cali
Nacional won 1-0 on aggregate

Olmedo 0-5 Morelia
Morelia 3-2 Olmedo
Morelia won 8-2 on aggregate

El Nacional 0-0 Boca Juniors
Boca Juniors 2-0 El Nacional
Boca Juniors won 2-0 on aggregate

Cienciano 0-1 América
América 4-1 Cienciano
América won 5-1 on aggregate

Cobreloa 1-1 Olimpia
match abandoned at half time, but awarded as 2-0 to Olimpia
Olimpia 2-1 Cobreloa
Olimpia won 4-1 on aggregate

Left: Argentinian referee Daniel Giminez protected by riot police. Two controversial calls in the second leg of the Grêmio v Olimpia semi-final saw the Paraguayans slip through to the Final. The police try to calm down irate Grêmio players as Giminez leaves the field.

Left, below: São Caetano celebrates its semi-final triumph over Mexico's América. CONMEBOL officials breathe a sigh of relief that a Mexican club will not be in the Final again.

Below: Olimpia's Uruguayan midfielder Sergio Orteman tussles for the ball in the Final – Orteman's dynamism saw him made Player of the Tournament.

QUARTER-FINALS (2 legs)

Peñarol **1-0** São Caetano
São Caetano **2-1** Peñarol

São Caetano won 3-1 on pens

Grêmio **1-0** Nacional
Nacional **1-1** Grêmio

Grêmio won 2-1 on aggregate

Morelia **1-2** América
América **2-1** Morelia

América won 4-2 on aggregate

Boca Juniors **1-1** Olimpia
Olimpia **1-0** Boca Juniors

Olimpia won 2-1 on aggregate

SEMI-FINALS (2 legs)

São Caetano **2-0** América
América **1-1** São Caetano

São Caetano won 3-1 on aggregate

Olimpia **3-2** Grêmio
Grêmio **1-0** Olimpia

Olimpia won 5-4 on pens

2002 FINAL (2 legs)

July 24 – Defensores, Asunción
Olimpia **0-1** São Caetano
(Ailton 61)
h/t: 0-0 Att: 40,000
Ref: Elizondo (Argentina)

July 31 – Pacaembú, São Paulo
São Caetano **1-2** Olimpia
(Ailton 31)   (Córodoba 49,
                 Báez 58)
h/t: 1-0 Att: 55,000
Ref: Ruiz (Colombia)

Olimpia won 4-2 on pens

Olimpia celebrates winning the Copa Libertadores. Some squad members will soon be looking out for lucrative European deals.

Copa Libertadores

TOURNAMENT OVERVIEW

SOUTH AMERICA'S first international club competition was held in 1948 in Chile, staged by Santiago's leading club Colo Colo. The winners were Brazil's Vasco da Gama, but the event proved a financial disaster and was not repeated. But by the late 1950s the success of UEFA's European Cup and the offer of a World Club Cup between European and South American champions spurred clubs and federations into action. The Copa Libertadores was launched at a meeting in Montevideo in 1960.

The opening match was played in April 1960 between San Lorenzo and Bahia ending in a 3-0 win for the home side. San Lorenzo went on to meet the eventual winners, Peñarol, of Montevideo. The format was so popular with the Uruguayan crowds that San Lorenzo played both legs of the tie in Montevideo. Peñarol beat Olimpia of Paraguay to take the title and then beat Palmeiras to win again in 1961. Peñarol were the Real Madrid of the Copa Libertadores – the team that recognized and reaped the massive commercial potential of the new tournament.

Shifting power base

But when Peñarol's reign was terminated in 1962 by Pele's Santos, the tournament suddenly acquired glamour. In the Final, Santos had won 2-1 at Peñarol. But just after half-time in the return leg, Peñarol led 3-2. A stone thrown from the crowd knocked the referee unconscious and the game was suspended for an hour. At the restart what appeared to be a Santos equalizer was ruled out when the linesman was also knocked unconscious. The game finally finished after almost three and a half hours, and after much wrangling the score was left 3-2 to Peñarol. In a play-off at the Monumental in Buenos Aires Santos won 3-0.

The shifting power base of South American club football can be traced through the Copa Libertadores results. Following Santos' second win (1963), the cup stayed with Uruguayan and Argentinian teams until Cruzeiro's victory in 1976. Argentinian teams dominated the 1980s, but in the 1990s Brazilian clubs regained their prowess. However, Boca Juniors' double in 2000 and 2001 and Olimpia's victory in 2002 have broken the pattern again.

Racing Club of Argentina won its only Copa Libertadores in 1967, beating Nacional of Uruguay in the Final. Its line-up featured Raffo (front row, far right) whose 14 goals made him the tournament's leading scorer that year.

Copa Libertadores
Top Goalscorers (1960–2002)

YEAR	SCORER	TEAM	COUNTRY	GOALS
1960	Spencer	Peñarol	Uruguay	7
1961	Panzutto	Independiente Santa Fé	Colombia	4
1962	Spencer	Peñarol	Uruguay	6
	Coutinho	Santos	Brazil	
	Raymondi	Emelec	Ecuador	
1963	Sanfillipo	Boca Juniors	Argentina	7
1964	Rodríguez	Independiente	Argentina	6
1965	Pelé	Santos	Brazil	8
1966	Onega	River Plate	Argentina	17
1967	Raffo	Racing Club	Argentina	14
1968	Tupãzinho	Palmeiras	Brazil	11
1969	Ferrero	Santiago Wanderers	Chile	8
1970	Bertocchi	Liga Universitaria Quito	Ecuador	9
	Mas	River Plate	Argentina	
1971	Castronovo	Peñarol	Uruguay	10
	Artime	Nacional	Uruguay	
1972	Toninho	São Paulo	Brazil	6
	Cubillas	Alianza Lima	Peru	
	Rojas	Alianza Lima	Peru	
	Ramírez	Universitario de Deportes	Peru	
1973	Caszely	Colo Colo	Chile	9
1974	Morena	Peñarol	Uruguay	7
	Terto	São Paulo	Brazil	
	Rocha	São Paulo	Brazil	
1975	Morena	Peñarol	Uruguay	8
	Ramírez	Universitario de Deportes	Peru	
1976	Palhinha*	Cruzeiro	Brazil	13
1977	Scotta	Deportivo Cali	Colombia	5
	Silva	Portuguesa FC	Venezuela	
1978	Scotta	Deportivo Cali	Colombia	8
	La Rosa	Alianza Lima	Peru	
1979	Miltão	Guaraní	Brazil	6
	Oré	Universitario de Deportes	Peru	
1980	Victorino	Nacional	Uruguay	6
1981	Zico	Flamengo	Brazil	11
1982	Morena	Peñarol	Uruguay	7
1983	Luzardo	Nacional	Uruguay	8
1984	Tita	Flamengo	Brazil	8
1985	Sánchez	Blooming	Bolivia	11
1986	De Lima	Deportivo	Ecuador	9
1987	Gareca	América de Cali	Colombia	7
1988	Iguarán	Millonarios	Colombia	5
1989	Aguillera	Peñarol	Uruguay	10
	Amarilla	Olimpia	Paraguay	
1990	Samaniego	Olimpia	Paraguay	7
1991	Gaúcho	Flamengo	Brazil	8
1992	Palhinha**	São Paulo	Brazil	7
1993	Almada	Universidad Católica	Chile	9
1994	Rivas	Minervén	Venezuela	7
1995	Jardel	Grêmio	Brazil	12
1996	De Ávila	América de Cali	Colombia	11
1997	Acosta	Universidad Católica	Chile	11
1998	Sergio João	Bolívar	Bolivia	10
1999	Bonilla	Deportivo Cali	Colombia	6
	Baiano	Corinthians	Brazil	
	Gauchinho	Cerro Porteño	Paraguay	
	Morán	Estudiantes de Mérida	Venezuela	
	Sosa	Nacional	Uruguay	
	Zapata	Deportivo Cali	Colombia	
2000	Luizão	Corinthians	Brazil	14
2001	Lopes	Palmeiras	Brazil	9
2002	Mendes	Grêmio	Brazil	10

* Wanderlei Eustáquio de Oliveira
** Jorge Ferreira da Silva

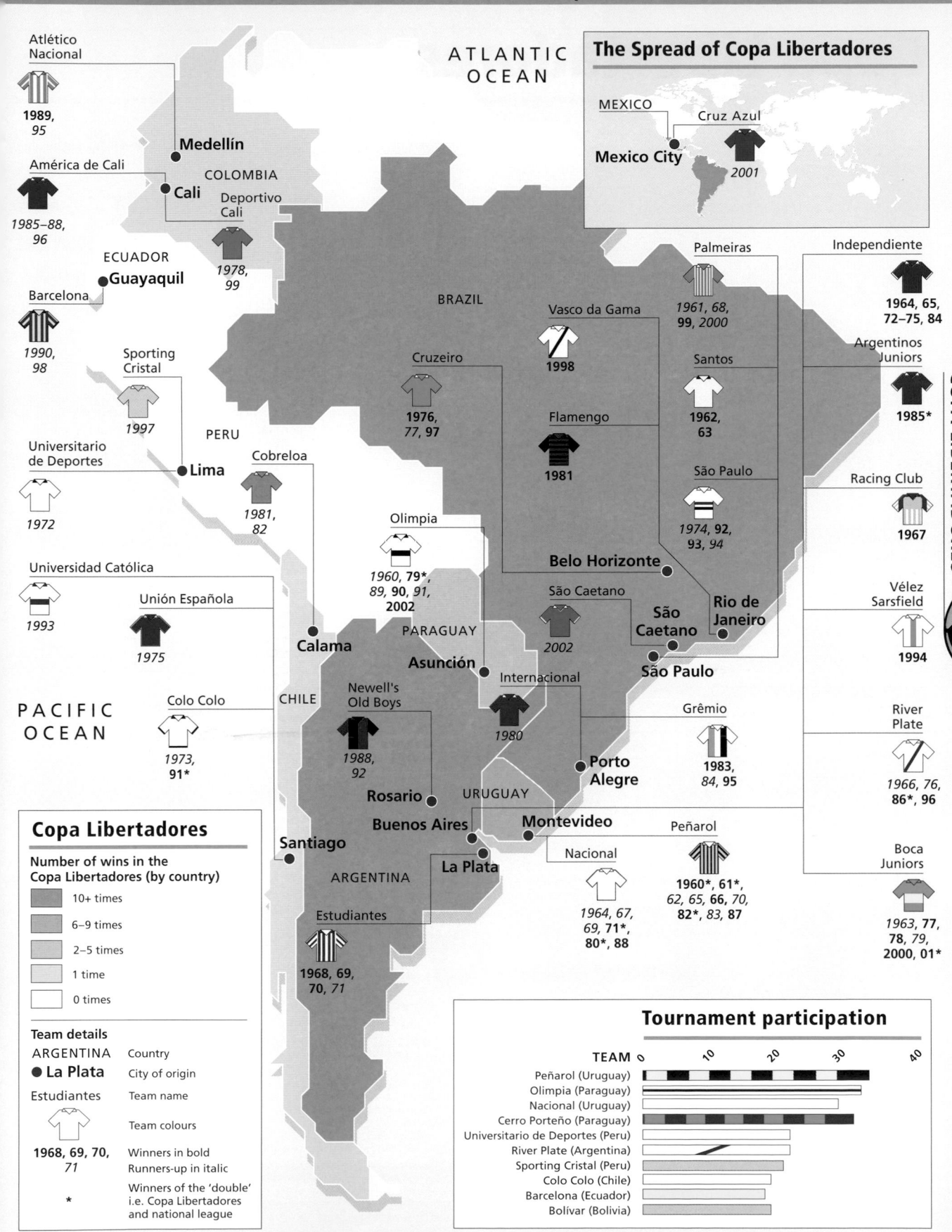

Copa Libertadores

THE COPA LIBERTADORES is the oldest and most prestigious South American international club championship. When first played, in 1960, it was contested by national champions in a knockout competition with matches played over two legs. From 1962, it consisted of three mini-leagues of three to decide three semi-finalists to meet the previous year's champions. In 1968, it expanded to 20 teams with two places allocated to each member of CONMEBOL. Five leagues of four produced eight quarter-finalists who met the previous year's champion in three further mini-leagues of three. In 1988, the format switched to two-leg knockouts for the quarter-finals, semi-finals and Final. The Final is now determined by aggregate scores, but had, until 1988, been determined by aggregate points over the final matches. Extra time and penalties are used to decide tied fixtures.

Each nation chooses its own method of filling its two places in the competition; for example, in Uruguay, the top six clubs play an end-of-season mini-league, while in Chile one place goes to the national champion and a second to the winner of a play-off among the next four teams in the league.

1960 FINAL (2 legs)
June 12 – Centenario, Montevideo
Peñarol 1-0 Olimpia
(Uruguay)   (Paraguay)
(Spencer 79)

June 19 – Sajonia, Asunción
Olimpia 1-1 Peñarol
(Recalde 28)   (Cubilla 83)
Peñarol won on points aggregate

1961 FINAL (2 legs)
June 9 – Centenario, Montevideo
Peñarol 1-0 Palmeiras
(Uruguay)   (Brazil)
(Spencer 89)

June 11 – Pacaembú, São Paulo
Palmeiras 1-1 Peñarol
(Nardo 77)   (Sasia 2)
Peñarol won on points aggregate

1962 FINAL (2 legs)
July 28 – Centenario, Montevideo
Peñarol 1-2 Santos
(Uruguay)   (Brazil)
(Spencer 18)   (Coutinho 29, 70)

Aug 2 – Villa Belmiro, Santos
Santos 2-3 Peñarol
(Dorval 27,   (Spencer 73,
Mengalvio 50)   Sasia 18, 48)

PLAY-OFF
Aug 30 – Monumental, Buenos Aires
Santos 3-0 Peñarol
(Coutinho 11
Pele 48, 89)

1963 FINAL (2 legs)
September 3 – Maracaná, Rio de Janeiro
Santos 3-2 Boca Juniors
(Brazil)   (Argentina)
(Coutinho 2, 21,   (Sanfilippo
Lima 28)   43, 89)

September 11 – La Bombonera, Buenos Aires
Boca Juniors 1-2 Santos
(Sanfilippo 46)   (Coutinho 50,
Pele 82)
Santos won on points aggregate

1964 FINAL (2 legs)
Aug 6 – Centenario, Montevideo
Nacional 0-0 Independiente
(Uruguay)   (Argentina)

Aug 12 – La Doble Visera, Avellaneda
Independiente 1-0 Nacional
(Rodriguez 35)
Independiente won on points aggregate

1965 FINAL (2 legs)
April 9 – La Doble Visera, Avellaneda
Independiente 1-0 Peñarol
(Argentina)   (Uruguay)
(Bernao 83)

April 12 – Centenario, Montevideo
Peñarol 3-1 Independiente
(Goncalves 14,   (De la Mata 88)
Reznik 43,
Rocha 46)

PLAY-OFF
April 15 – Estadio Nacional, Santiago
Independiente 4-1 Peñarol
(Acevedo 10,   (De la Mata 88)
Bernao 27,
Avallay 33,
Mura 82)

1966 FINAL (2 legs)
May 12 – Centenario, Montevideo
Peñarol 2-0 River Plate
(Uruguay)   (Argentina)
(Abaddie 75,
Joya 85)

May 18 – Monumental, Buenos Aires
River Plate 3-2 Peñarol
(D. Onega 38,   (Rocha 32,
Sarnari 52,   Spencer 50)
E. Onega 73)

PLAY-OFF
May 20 – Estadio Nacional, Santiago
Peñarol 4-2 River Plate
(Spencer 57, 101,   (D. Onega 37,
Abbadie 72,   Solari 42)
Rocha 109)

(after extra time)

1967 FINAL (2 legs)
August 15 – Mozart Y Cuyo, Avellaneda
Racing Club 0-0 Nacional
(Argentina)   (Uruguay)

August 25 – Centenario, Montevideo
Nacional 0-0 Racing Club

PLAY-OFF
August 29 – Estadio Nacional, Santiago
Racing Club 2-1 Nacional
(Cardozo 14,   (Esparrago 79)
Raffo 43)

1968 FINAL (2 legs)
May 2 – La Plata, La Plata
Estudiantes 2-1 Palmeiras
(Argentina)   (Brazil)
(Veron 83,   (Servillio 50)
Flores 87)

May 7 – Pacaembú, São Paulo
Palmeiras 3-1 Estudiantes
(Tupazinho 10, 68,   (Veron 72)
Reinaldo 54)

PLAY-OFF
May 15 – Centenario, Montevideo
Estudiantes 2-0 Palmeiras
(Ribaudo 13,
Veron 82)

1969 FINAL (2 legs)
May 15 – Centenario, Montevideo
Nacional 0-1 Estudiantes
(Uruguay)   (Argentina)
(Flores 66)

May 22 – La Plata, La Plata
Estudiantes 2-0 Nacional
(Flores 31,   (Veron 72),
Conigliaro 37)
Estudiantes won on points aggregate

1970 FINAL (2 legs)
May 21 – La Plata, La Plata
Estudiantes 1-0 Peñarol
(Uruguay)   (Argentina)
(Togneri 87)

June 2 – Centenario, Montevideo
Peñarol 0-0 Estudiantes
Estudiantes won on points aggregate

1971 FINAL (2 legs)
May 26 – La Plata, La Plata
Estudiantes 1-0 Nacional
(Uruguay)   (Argentina)
(Romeo 60)

June 2 – Centenario, Montevideo
Nacional 1-0 Estudiantes
(Masnik 17)

PLAY-OFF
June 9 – Estadio Nacional, Lima
Nacional 2-0 Estudiantes
(Esparrago 22,
Artime 65)

1972 FINAL (2 legs)
May 17 – Estadio Nacional, Lima
**Universitario 0-0 Independiente
de Deportes**   (Argentina)
(Peru)

May 24 – Cordero, Avellaneda
Independiente 2-1 Universitario
(Maglioni 6, 60)   de Deportes
(Rojas 79)
Independiente won on points aggregate

1973 FINAL (2 legs)
May 22 – Cordero, Avellaneda
Independiente 1-1 Colo Colo
(Argentina)   (Chile)
(Mendoza 75)   (Caszely 71)

May 29 – Estadio Nacional, Santiago
Colo Colo 0-0 Independiente

PLAY-OFF
June 6 – Centenario, Montevideo
Independiente 2-1 Colo Colo
(Mendoza 25,   (Caszely 39)
Giachello 107)

1974 FINAL (2 legs)
October 12 – Pacaembú, São Paulo
São Paulo 2-1 Independiente
(Brazil)   (Argentina)
(Rocha 48,   (Saggioratto 28)
Mirandinha 50)

October 16 – Cordero, Avellaneda
Independiente 2-0 São Paulo
(Bochini 34,
Balbuena 48)

PLAY-OFF
October 19 – Estadio Nacional, Santiago
Independiente 1-0 São Paulo
(Pavoni 37)

1975 FINAL (2 legs)
June 18 – Estadio Nacional, Santiago
Unión Española 1-0 Independiente
(Chile)   (Argentina)
(Ahumada 87)

June 25 – Cordero, Avellaneda
Independiente 3-1 Unión Española
(Rojas 1,   (Las Heras 56)
Pavoni 58,
Bertoni 83)

PLAY-OFF
June 29 – Defensores del Chaco, Asunción
Independiente 2-0 Unión Española
(Ruiz Moreno 29,
Bertoni 65)

1976 FINAL (2 legs)
July 21 – Mineirão, Belo Horizonte
Cruzeiro 4-1 River Plate
(Brazil)   (Argentina)
(Nelinho 22,   (Mas 62)
Palinha 29, 40,
Waldo 80)

July 28 – Monumental, Buenos Aires
River Plate 2-1 Cruzeiro
(J.J. Lopez 10,   (Palinha 48)
Gonzalez 76)

PLAY-OFF
July 30 – Estadio Nacional, Santiago
Cruzeiro 3-2 River Plate
(Nelinho 24,   (Mas 59,
Ronaldo 55,   Urquiza 64)
Joazinho 88)

1977 FINAL (2 legs)

September 6 – La Bombonera, Buenos Aires
Boca Juniors **1-0** Cruzeiro
(Argentina)   (Brazil)
(Veglio 3)

September 11 – Mineirão, Belo Horizonte
Cruzeiro **1-0** Boca Juniors
(Nelinho 76)

PLAY-OFF

September 14 – Centenario, Montevideo
Cruzeiro **0-0** Boca Juniors
Boca Juniors won 5-4 on pens

1978 FINAL (2 legs)

November 23 – Pascual Guerrero, Cali
Deportivo Cali **0-0** Boca Juniors
(Colombia)   (Argentina)

November 28 – La Bombonera, Buenos Aires
Boca Juniors **4-0** Deportivo Cali
(Perotti 15, 85
Mastrangelo 60
Salinas 71)
Boca Juniors won on points aggregate

1979 FINAL (2 legs)

July 22 – Defensores del Chaco, Asunción
Olimpia **2-0** Boca Juniors
(Paraguay)   (Argentina)
(Aquino 3
Piazza 27)

July 27 – La Bombonera, Buenos Aires
Boca Juniors **0-0** Olimpia
Olimpia won on points aggregate

1980 FINAL (2 legs)

July 30 – Biera Rio, Porto Alegre
Internacional **0-0** Nacional
(Brazil)   (Uruguay)

August 6 – Centenario, Montevideo
Nacional **1-0** Internacional
(Victorino 35)
Nacional won on points aggregate

1981 FINAL (2 legs)

November 13 – Maracanã, Rio de Janeiro
Flamengo **2-1** Cobreloa
(Brazil)   (Chile)
(Zico 12, 30)   *(Merello 65)*

November 20 – Estadio Nacional, Santiago
Cobreloa **1-0** Flamengo
(Merello 79)

PLAY-OFF

November 23 – Centenario, Montevideo
Flamengo **2-0** Cobreloa
(Zico 18, 79)

1982 FINAL (2 legs)

November 26 – Centenario, Montevideo
Peñarol **0-0** Cobreloa
(Uruguay)   (Chile)

November 30 – Estadio Nacional, Santiago
Cobreloa **0-1** Peñarol
(Morena 89)
Peñarol won on points aggregate

1983 FINAL (2 legs)

July 22 – Centenario, Montevideo
Peñarol **1-1** Grêmio
(Uruguay)   (Brazil)
(Morena 35)   *(Tita 12)*

July 28 – Olimpico, Porto Alegre
Grêmio **2-1** Peñarol
(Caio 9,   (Morena 70)
Cesar 87)
Grêmio won on points aggregate

1984 FINAL (2 legs)

July 24 – Olimpico, Porto Alegre
Grêmio **0-1** Independiente
(Brazil)   (Argentina)
(Burruchaga 24)

July 27 – Cordero, Avellaneda
Independiente **0-0** Grêmio
Independiente won on points aggregate

1985 FINAL (2 legs)

October 17 – La Bombonera, Buenos Aires
Argentinos **1-0** América de Cali
Juniors   (Colombia)
(Argentina)
(Comisso 40)

October 22 – Pascual Guerrero, Cali
América de Cali **1-0** Argentinos
(Ortiz 3)   Juniors

PLAY-OFF

October 24 – Defensores del Chaco, Asunción
Argentinos **1-1** América de Cali
Juniors   *(Gareca 42)*
(Comisso 37)
Argentinos Juniors won 5-4 on pens

1986 FINAL (2 legs)

October 22 – Pascual Guerrero, Cali
América de Cali **1-2** River Plate
(Colombia)   (Argentina)
(Cabanas 47)   *(Funes 22,*
Alonso 25)

October 29 – Monumental, Buenos Aires
River Plate **1-0** América de Cali
(Funes 70)
River Plate won on points aggregate

1987 FINAL (2 legs)

October 21 – Pascual Guerrero, Cali
América de Cali **2-0** Peñarol
(Colombia)   (Uruguay)
(Battaglia 21,
Cabanas 35)

October 28 – Centenario, Montevideo
Peñarol **2-1** América de Cali
(Aguirre 58,   (Cabanas 19)
Villar 86)

PLAY-OFF

October 31 – Estadio Nacional, Santiago
Peñarol **1-0** América de Cali
(Aguirre 119)

1988 FINAL (2 legs)

October 19 – Parque de la Independencia, Rosario
Newell's **1-0** Nacional
Old Boys   (Uruguay)
(Argentina)
(Gabrich 60)

October 26 – Centenario, Montevideo
Nacional **3-0** Newell's
*(Vargas 10,   Old Boys
Ostolaza 30,*
De Leon 81)
Nacional won 3-1 on aggregate

1989 FINAL (2 legs)

May 24 – El Bosque, Asunción
Olimpia **2-0** Atlético
(Paraguay)   Nacional
(Bobadilla 36,   (Colombia)
Sanabria 60)

May 31 – El Campin, Bogotá
Atlético **2-0** Olimpia
Nacional
(Amarilla 46,
Usurriaga 64)
Atlético Nacional won 5-4 on pens

1990 FINAL (2 legs)

October 3 – El Bosque, Asunción
Olimpia **2-0** Barcelona
(Paraguay)   (Ecuador)
(Amarilla 47,
Samaniego 65)

October 10 – Modelo, Guayaquil
Barcelona **1-1** Olimpia
(Trobbiani 61)   *(Amarilla 80)*
Olimpia won 3-1 on aggregate

1991 FINAL (2 legs)

May 29 – Defensores del Chaco, Asunción
Olimpia **0-0** Colo Colo
(Paraguay)   (Chile)

June 5 – Estadio Nacional, Santiago
Colo Colo **3-0** Olimpia
(Perez 13, 18,
Herrera 85)
Colo Colo won 3-0 on aggregate

1992 FINAL (2 legs)

June 10 – Parque de la Independencia, Rosario
Newell's **1-0** São Paulo
Old Boys   (Brazil)
(Argentina)
(Berizzo 38)

June 17 – Pacaembú, São Paulo
São Paulo **1-0** Newell's
(Rai 65)   Old Boys
São Paulo won 3-2 on pens

1993 FINAL (2 legs)

May 19 – Pacaembú, São Paulo
São Paulo **5-1** Universidad
(Brazil)   Católica
(Lopez o.g. 31,   (Chile)
Dinho 41,   (Almada 85 pen)
Gilmar 55,
Rai 61,
Muller 65)

May 26 – San Carlos de Aponquindo, Santiago
Universidad **2-0** São Paulo
Católica
(Lunari 9,
Almada 16 pen)
São Paulo won 5-3 on aggregate

1994 FINAL (2 legs)

August 24 – José Amalfitani, Buenos Aires
Vélez Sarsfield **1-0** São Paulo
(Argentina)   (Brazil)
(Asad 35)

August 31 – Pacaembú, São Paulo
São Paulo **1-0** Vélez Sarsfield
(Muller 32 pen)
Vélez Sarsfield won 5-3 on pens

1995 FINAL (2 legs)

August 24 – Olimpico, Porto Alegre
Grêmio **3-1** Atlético
(Brazil)   Nacional
(Marulanda o.g.   (Colombia)
36, Jardel 40,   (Angel 71)
Paulo Nunes 56)

August 30 – Atanasio Girardot, Medellin
Atlético **1-1** Grêmio
Nacional   *(Dinho 85)*
(Aristizabal 13)
Grêmio won 4-2 on aggregate

1996 FINAL (2 legs)

June 19 – Pascual Guerrero, Cali
América de Cali **1-0** River Plate
(Colombia)   (Argentina)
(De Avila 72)

June 26 – Monumental, Buenos Aires
River Plate **2-0** América de Cali
(Crespo 7, 14)
River Plate won 2-1 on aggregate

1997 FINAL (2 legs)

August 6 – San Martin de Porres, Lima
Sporting Cristal **0-0** Cruzeiro
(Peru)   (Brazil)

August 13 – Mineirão, Belo Horizonte
Cruzeiro **1-0** Sporting Cristal
(Elivelton 75)
Cruzeiro won 1-0 on aggregate

1998 FINAL (2 legs)

August 12 – São Januario, Rio de Janeiro
Vasco da Gama **2-0** Barcelona
(Brazil)   (Ecuador)
(Donizete 7,
Luizao 33)

August 26 – Monumental Isidro Romero,
Guayaquil
Barcelona **1-2** Vasco da Gama
(De Avila 79)   *(Luizao 24,*
Donizete 45)
Vasco da Gama won 4-1 on aggregate

1999 FINAL (2 legs)

June 2 – Pascual Guerrero, Cali
Deportivo Cali **1-0** Palmeiras
(Colombia)   (Brazil)
(Bonilla 42)

June 16 – Morumbi, São Paulo
Palmeiras **2-0** Deportivo Cali
(Evair 63 pen,   (Zapata 69 pen)
Oseas 75)
Palmeiras won 2-1 on aggregate

2000 FINAL (2 legs)

June 14 – La Bombonera, Buenos Aires
Boca Juniors **2-2** Palmeiras
(Argentina)   (Brazil)
(Arruabarrena   (Pena 43,
22, 61)   *Euller 63)*

June 21 – Parque Antarctica, São Paulo
Palmeiras **0-0** Boca Juniors
Boca Juniors won 4-2 on pens

2001 FINAL (2 legs)

June 20 – Azteca, Mexico City
Cruz Azul **0-1** Boca Juniors
(Mexico)   (Argentina)
(Delgado 79)

June 28 – La Bombonera, Buenos Aires
Boca Juniors **0-1** Cruz Azul
(Palencia 45)
Boca Juniors won 3-1 on pens

2002 FINAL (2 legs)

July 24 – Defensores del Chaco, Asunción
Olimpia **0-1** São Caetano
(Paraguay)   (Brazil)
(Ailton 61)

July 31 – Pacaembú, São Paulo
São Caetano **1-2** Olimpia
(Ailton 31)   *(Córdoba 49,*
Báez 58)
Olimpia won 4-2 on pens

Colombia

THE SEASON IN REVIEW 2002

THEY SAY LIGHTNING doesn't strike twice, but Colombia's football season had a very familiar ring about it. The country's ever-present civil war and its accompanying climate of violence threw a nasty shadow over the game. The tragic death of two Deportivo Cali players struck by lightning at the club's training ground joined the list of football directors, players and coaches, shot or kidnapped this season. Rene Higuita, Colombia's favourite goalkeeper, made another comeback with Deportivo Periera, but two games later he was banned for six months after testing positive for cocaine.

Other familiar features of the season included crowd violence at the Medellín derby, sufficiently bad to see games in the city cancelled. At the once dominant Bogotá club Millonarios, players' wages went unpaid, coaches came and went and the team tumbled to the bottom of the table. At Atlético Huila, wages were so late that the players went on strike during the Clausura. Real Cartagena was relegated by the authorities for playing Ivan Valenciano; his failure to pay damages after losing a court case had seen him banned by the FA. On the pitch, the injustices of the play-off system saw Deportivo Cali, who won both the Apertura and the Clausura, go out in the Second Phases and saw the Apertura pass to one of the usual contenders, América de Cali. But the Clausura went to Independiente Medellín for the first time since 1957.

Colombian Apertura League Table 2002

CLUB	P	W	D	L	F	A	Pts	
Deportivo Cali	22	11	6	5	44	24	39	Qualified for Second Phase
Independiente Santa Fé	22	10	8	4	26	13	38	Qualified for Second Phase
Atlético Nacional	22	10	8	4	24	18	38	Qualified for Second Phase
Envigado FC	22	10	6	6	21	18	36	Qualified for Second Phase
Deportivo Pasto	22	9	7	6	29	27	34	Qualified for Second Phase
Atlético Bucaramanga	22	9	6	7	24	22	33	Qualified for Second Phase
Unión Magdalena	22	9	6	7	27	27	33	Qualified for Second Phase
América de Cali	22	8	9	5	27	22	33	Qualified for Second Phase
Once Caldas	22	9	5	8	36	29	32	
Deportivo Pereira	22	8	8	6	20	16	32	
Deportes Quindío	22	7	9	6	24	30	30	
Atlético Júnior	22	7	5	10	19	25	26	
CD Millonarios	22	5	8	9	17	21	23	
Atlético Huila	22	5	7	10	21	32	22	
Corporación Tuluá	22	5	6	11	16	25	21	
Independiente Medellín	22	4	9	9	26	32	21	
Real Cartagena	22	4	8	10	17	25	20	
Deportes Tolima	22	3	9	10	18	30	18	

Second Phase – Group A

CLUB	P	W	D	L	F	A	Pts	
Atlético Nacional	6	5	1	0	12	4	16	Qualified for Final
Unión Magdalena	6	3	0	3	12	9	9	
Deportivo Cali	6	2	2	2	11	13	8	
Deportivo Pasto	6	0	1	5	4	13	1	

Second Phase – Group B

CLUB	P	W	D	L	F	A	Pts	
América de Cali	6	4	0	2	6	6	12	Qualified for Final
Independiente Santa Fé	6	3	2	1	9	5	11	
Envigado FC	6	2	2	2	6	4	8	
Atlético Bucaramanga	6	0	2	4	4	10	2	

Apertura Championship Play-off

2002 FINAL (2 legs)

June 16 – Pascual Guerrero, Cali

América 2-1 Atlético
de Cali   Nacional
(Castillo 48, 84)   *(Velásquez 41)*
h/t: 0-1 **Att:** 36,609
Ref: Ramirez

June 19 – Atanasio Giradot, Medellín

Atlético 0-1 América
Nacional   de Cali
              (Castillo 71)
h/t: 0-0 **Att:** 52,750
Ref: Hoyos

América de Cali won 3-1 on aggregate

Below, left: Jairo Castillo on target again. América's striker scored all its goals in the Apertura Play-offs.

Below: The killings continue. Cesar Villegas, main shareholder of Bogotá club Independiente Santa Fe, was shot dead leaving his office this year.

Below, bottom: Despite finishing seven places behind winners Deportivo Cali in the Apertura league, América de Cali went on to win the Play-offs.

Colombian Clausura League Table 2002

CLUB	P	W	D	L	F	A	Pts	
Deportivo Cali	22	14	5	3	38	15	**47**	Qualified for Second Phase
Deportivo Pasto	22	11	3	8	32	33	**36**	Qualified for Second Phase
Independiente Medellín	22	9	8	5	25	16	**35**	Qualified for Second Phase
América de Cali	22	10	4	8	26	24	**34**	Qualified for Second Phase
Atlético Bucaramanga	22	9	6	7	34	29	**33**	Qualified for Second Phase
Unión Magdalena	22	9	6	7	25	26	**33**	Qualified for Second Phase
Deportes Tolima	22	8	9	5	30	26	**33**	Qualified for Second Phase
Atlético Nacional	22	8	8	6	28	21	**32**	Qualified for Second Phase
Independiente Santa Fé	22	8	8	6	35	30	**32**	
Once Caldas	22	7	11	4	23	17	**32**	
Deportes Quindio	22	8	4	10	18	23	**28**	
Corporación Tuluá	22	8	4	10	21	27	**28**	
Deportivo Pereira	22	7	5	10	27	34	**26**	
Real Cartagena	22	7	4	11	20	30	**25**	
Atlético Huila	22	6	7	9	21	29	**25**	
CD Millonarios	22	6	5	11	25	31	**23**	
Atlético Júnior	22	4	9	9	27	33	**21**	
Envigado FC	22	3	6	13	16	27	**15**	

Second Phase – Group A

CLUB	P	W	D	L	F	A	Pts	
Independiente Medellín	6	3	2	1	7	4	**11**	Qualified for Final
Deportivo Cali	6	3	1	2	8	5	**10**	
Atlético Bucaramanga	6	2	1	3	5	8	**7**	
Deportes Tolima	6	1	2	3	5	8	**5**	

Right: A seven-tonne statue of Carlos Valderrama, Colombia's greatest-ever player, was unveiled in his home city of Santa Marta.

Below: Lightning strikes twice: Deportivo Cali fans swamp the hearse carrying Giovanny Cordoba at the club's Pascal Guerrero stadium. Cordoba and teammate Herman Gaviria were killed by lightning strikes at the club's training ground in October.

Second Phase – Group B

CLUB	P	W	D	L	F	A	Pts	
Deportivo Pasto	6	3	2	1	7	5	**11**	Qualified for Final
América de Cali	6	3	1	2	8	6	**10**	
Unión Magdelena	6	2	1	3	6	8	**7**	
Atlético Nacional	6	1	2	3	4	6	**5**	

Relegated club: Real Cartagena.
Promoted club: Centauros Vellavicencio.

Top Goalscorers 2002

NAME	CLUB	GOALS
APERTURA		
Luis Fernando Zuelta	Unión Magdelena	13
CLAUSURA		
Orlando Ballesteros	Atlético Bucaramanga	13
Milton Rodríguez	Deportivo Pereira	13

International Club Performances 2002

CLUB	COMPETITION	PROGRESS
América di Cali	Copa Libertadores	2nd Round
	Copa Sudamericana	1st Round
Corporación Tuluá	Copa Libertadores	Group Stage
Once Caldas	Copa Libertadores	Group Stage
Atlético Nacional	Copa Sudamericana	Runners-up

Clausura Championship Play-off

2002 FINAL (2 legs)

December 18 – Atanasio Giradot, Medellín
Independiente 2-0 Deportivo
Medellín   Pasto
(Muñoz 7,
Valencia 66 og)
h/t: 1-0 **Att:** 49,590
Ref: Cervantez

December 22 – Estadio Liberdad, Pasto
Deportivo 1-1 Independiente
Pasto   Medellín
(Escobar 57)   (Molina 28)
h/t: 0-1 **Att:** 14,000
Ref: Ruiz

Independiente Medellín won 3-1
on aggregate

COLOMBIA

Independiente Medellín celebrates victory in the Clausura Play-off.

Association Football in Colombia

Early 1880s: Football introduced to Colombia, mainly on Atlantic coast — 1880

1890

1900

1910

1924: First federation formed. Liga de Football del Atlántico started in Barranquilla — 1920

1936: Affiliation to FIFA

1938: Formation of national FA: Associación Colombiana de Fútbol. First international, v Mexico, lost 1-3, venue: Mexico City — 1930

1940: Affiliation to CONMEBOL — 1940

1948: National professional league, the *DiMayor*, established — 1950

1948–53: El Dorado. National federation suspended from FIFA, massive import of foreign players — 1960

1968: League format shifts to Apertura and Clausura Championships with a mini-league for the top teams at the end of the year

1971: National FA reformed — 1970

1981: 18 die and 45 injured in crush at match between Deportes Tolima and Deportivo Cali in Ibagúe

1982: 22 die and 200 injured in crush at derby between Deportivo and América in Cali — 1980

1984: Colombia withdraws from hosting World Cup

1989: League season abandoned after the assassination of a referee — 1990

1993: Colombia qualify for World Cup, beating Argentina 5-0 in Buenos Aires, 30 die in celebrations in Bogotá

1994: The national team's Andres Escobar shot dead in Medellín — 2000

2001: Colombia beat Mexico to win the Copa América — 2010

COLOMBIA

Carlos Valderrama, Colombia's finest player.

Key

	International football	Amér	- América de Cali
	Affiliation to FIFA	Atl N	- Atlético Nacional
	Affiliation to CONMEBOL	D Cali	- Deportivo Cali
	Disaster	Indep	- Independiente Santa Fé
■	Copa América host	Mill	- Millonarios
●	Copa América winner		
▲	Copa América runner-up		
○	Competition winner		
△	Competition runner-up		

International Competitions

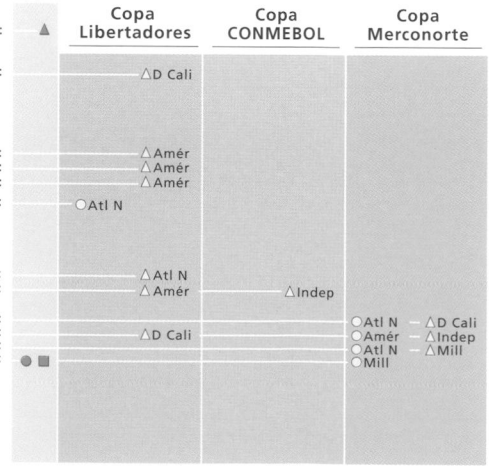

	Copa Libertadores	Copa CONMEBOL	Copa Merconorte
1975:	▲		
1978:	△D Cali		
1985:	△Amér		
1986:	△Amér		
1987:	△Amér		
1989:	○Atl N		
1995:	△Atl N		
1996:	△Amér	△Indep	
1998:			○Atl N △D Cali
1999:	△D Cali		○Amér △Indep
2000:			○Atl N △Mill
2001:	● ■		○Mill

★ Atlético Júnior 1924/1948

(1948)

Sporting Barranquilla 1950

★ Deportivo Barranquilla 1949

Deportivo 'Unicosta' 1995

Barranquilla
Cartagena
Real Cartagena 1971

★ Once Caldas 1948

(1950)

German Gómez García, club president, shot 1990. Guillermo Gómez Melgarejo, club vice-president, shot 1992

★ Deportivo Caldas 1947

Atlético Manizales 1954

Deportes Quindío 1947

(1953)

Corporación Tuluá 1967

Escuela Sarimento Lora 1984

Medellín
Envigado
Manizales
Armenia **Pereira**
Tuluá
Cali **Ibagué**
Deportes Tolima 1955
Neiva
Atlético Huila 1990

Pasto
● **Deportivo Pasto** 1949

Asociación 1962

Boca Júniors 1939

(1951, 52)

★ Deportivo Cali 1928

(1949)

★ América de Cali 1924

Controlled by Miguel Rodríguez Orejuelas, Cali cartel

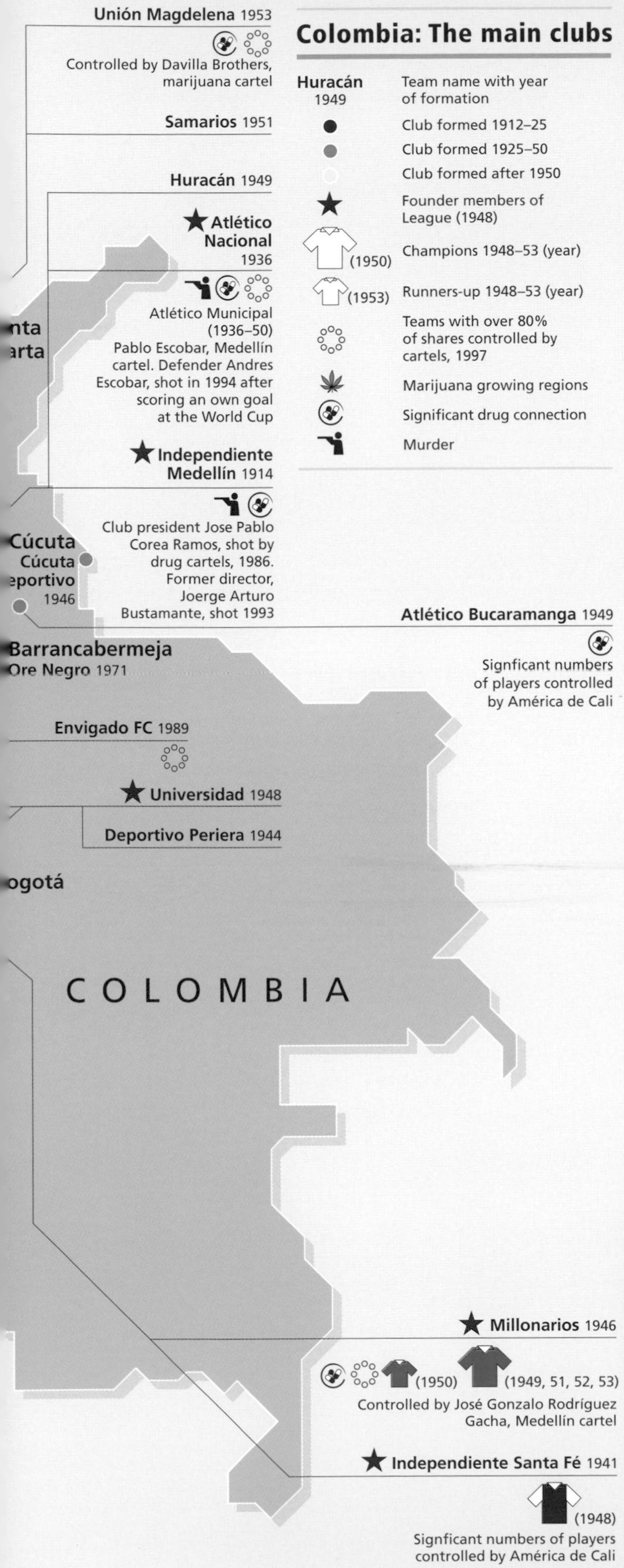

Colombia: The main clubs

Union Magdelena 1953

⚽ ⚬⚬⚬ Controlled by Davilla Brothers, marijuana cartel

Samarios 1951

Huracán 1949

★ **Atlético Nacional** 1936

🕴 ⚽ ⚬⚬⚬ Atlético Municipal (1936–50). Pablo Escobar, Medellín cartel. Defender Andres Escobar, shot in 1994 after scoring an own goal at the World Cup

★ **Independiente Medellín** 1914

🔫 🕴 ⚽ Club president Jose Pablo Corea Ramos, shot by drug cartels, 1986. Former director, Joerge Arturo Bustamante, shot 1993

Cúcuta Deportivo 1946

Barrancabermeja Ore Negro 1971

Envigado FC 1989

⚬⚬⚬

★ **Universidad** 1948

Deportivo Periera 1944

Bogotá

COLOMBIA

Atlético Bucaramanga 1949

⚽ Signficant numbers of players controlled by América de Cali

★ **Millonarios** 1946

⚽ ⚬⚬⚬ 👕 (1950) 👕 (1949, 51, 52, 53)
Controlled by José Gonzalo Rodríguez Gacha, Medellín cartel

★ **Independiente Santa Fé** 1941

👕 (1948)
Signficant numbers of players controlled by América de Cali

Key

Huracán 1949	Team name with year of formation
●	Club formed 1912–25
●	Club formed 1925–50
○	Club formed after 1950
★	Founder members of League (1948)
👕 (1950)	Champions 1948–53 (year)
👕 (1953)	Runners-up 1948–53 (year)
⚬⚬⚬	Teams with over 80% of shares controlled by cartels, 1997
♆	Marijuana growing regions
⚽	Significant drug connection
🔫	Murder

Colombia

ORIGINS AND GROWTH OF FOOTBALL

FOOTBALL BEGAN IN COLOMBIA in the early 1880s and the first recorded game was played in 1888. The early areas of footballing strength were in the country's northern ports and the first regular league, the Liga de Football del Atlántico, started in Barranquilla in 1924. FIFA membership followed in 1936, a national FA was set up in 1938, CONMEBOL membership in 1940 (after initially flirting with membership of the Central American Federation) and, in 1948, a new national professional league, the *DiMayor*, was established.

Almost immediately, conflict broke out between the FA and the big clubs, Millonarios and Independiente Santa Fé from Bogotá, who refused to pay transfer fees to foreign clubs. The struggle resulted in the formation of a rebel league. The extra money meant that Colombian clubs could offer massive wages and signing-on fees. They attracted star players from across the world, in particular a huge contingent from Argentina, including Alfredo di Stefano, who moved north as their long-running dispute with the Argentinian FA over the formation of a player's union remained deadlocked. The era from 1948–53, known as *El Dorado*, saw massive crowds and huge interest in football. But FIFA suspended Colombia from all international club competitions in 1949 and forced the Colombians to accept the global rules on transfers in 1954.

Drug money

In the 1970s, as Colombia's export-based industries collapsed during the global recession, the Colombian drug industry began its explosive growth and became the most powerful economic and political force in the country. Colombian clubs' finances were in disarray and their purchase provided both social status and an instrument for money laundering for the different drug cartels. The Cali cartel took over América, Pablo Escobar's Medellín cartel bought Atlético Nacional and took control of Millonarios in Bogotá. Despite repeated efforts to normalize the game in Colombia, the role of cartels and drug money in football is unresolved. The 1989 season was cancelled after the shooting of referee, Alvaro Ortega, on cartel orders, while assassinations, kidnapping, match-fixing and money laundering appear to be endemic. Colombia was forced to pull out of hosting the 1986 World Cup and the 2001 Copa América almost collapsed after a spate of bombings and shootings.

COLOMBIA

Colombian fans remember full-back Andres Escobar, who was shot dead in Medellín after returning from the 1994 World Cup. He had scored an own goal in a shock 2-1 defeat by the United States.

Colombia

APERTURA AND CLAUSURA 1993–2002

IN 1989, THREE PRESIDENTIAL CANDIDATES were assassinated in Colombia; Gonzalo Rodriguez-Gacha, a hit man for the Medellín drugs cartel and effective owner of Bogotá's Millonarios, was killed in a shootout with police; Miguel Rodriguez Orejuela, leader of the Cali drugs cartel and owner of América de Cali, was in prison; and the football season was cancelled at the play-off stage after referee Alvaro Ortega was shot in Medellín. Ortega, it was said, had failed to ensure the right result in the Medellín derby that season. In 1991, the Colombian FA appeared to be overhauling football's connections to what Colombians call *el narcotráfico*. Reform arrived in the shape of a new national league incorporating promotion and relegation, but the chaos continued. Pablo Escobar, leader of the Medellín cartel and owner of Atlético Nacional, was finally arrested by police in 1992. He escaped, only to be shot a year later. Juan José Bellini, former president of the Colombian FA and director of América, was imprisoned in 1997 on drug trafficking and corruption charges. A similar fate befell directors at Unión Magdelena and Millonarios.

Matters are no different today, and the last decade has seen Colombian football played under conditions of civil war and endemic violence. The country has been divided between the drug cartels, the left-wing paramilitaries FARC, an assortment of right-wing paramilitary groups, the military, the government and, most recently, the US government and army. Money laundering through football clubs continues, and the combination of drugs money, narcotics and gambling has ensured that players, club directors and referees are regularly threatened and even killed. Most recently, the Copa América 2001 was almost lost by Colombia after a spate of bombings and shootings in the big cities.

Colombian League Positions Table 1993–2002

SEASON

TEAM	1993 A	1993 C	Play-Offs	1994 A	1994 C	Play-Offs	1995	1995-96 A	1995-96 C	Play-Offs	1996-97 A	1996-97 C	Play-Offs	1998 A	1998 C	Play-Offs	1999 A	1999 C	Play-Offs	2000 A	2000 C	Play-Offs	2001 A	2001 C	Play-Offs	2002 A	Play-Offs	2002 C	Play-Offs
Atlético Júnior	1(B)	2	C	10	4	QF	C	3(B)	8		7	4(A)		7	7(A)		4	4		6	3	RU	8	12		12		17	
Atlético Nacional	2(B)	9	SF	1	1	C	3	1(B)	3	SF	2	4(B)		2	1(B)	QF	2	6	C	5	7		12	3		3	RU	8	Q
Atlético Bucaramanga	3(B)	8	QF	14	15			6(A)	13		8	2(A)	RU	14	4(B)		9	9		15	10		15	16		6	Q	5	Q
América de Cali	6(A)	4	SF	2	10	SF	2	2(B)	2	SF	1	6(A)	C	8	5(B)	QF	1	10	RU	2	1	C	7	5	C	8	C	4	Q
Deportivo Cali	5(A)	3	QF	6	6	QF	4	1(A)	1	C	3	1(B)		5	2(A)	C	7	5		1	15		2	4	QF	1	Q	1	Q
Real Cartagena																				10	13		13	14		17		14	
Cúcuta Deportivo	8(B)	11		7	9		16				16																		
Deportivo 'Unicosta'												8(B)			8(B)														
Envigado FC	5(B)	6		4	8	QF	12	6(B)	7		12	5(B)		13	4(A)		14	12		8	12		10	7		4	Q	18	
Atlético Huila	2(A)	15		8	7		15	4(B)	16					8	7(B)		16	16		11	11		14	15		14		15	
Independiente Medellín	4(B)	1	RU	9	3	SF	7	8(A)	12		5	8(A)		4	2(B)	QF	8	3		13	9		5	10	RU	16		3	C
Millonarios	3(A)	7	QF	5	2	RU	14	4(A)	6	RU	15	2(B)		9	5(A)	QF	11	1		4	4		9	2	QF	13		16	
Once Caldas	1(A)	5	QF	3	5	QF	8	5(A)	5		10	5(A)		1	1(A)	RU	3	7		12	6		3	1	QF	9		10	
Deportivo Pasto														12	8		14	8		16	6					5	Q	2	RU
Deportivo Pereira	4(A)	10		16	13		6	7(B)	11		14	7(B)											11	11		10		13	
Deportes Quindío	7(B)	13		15	11		10	7(A)	14		12	1(A)		11	3(A)	QF	13	15		16	14			11				11	
Independiente Santa Fé	7(A)	14		12	14		5	5(B)	15		11	7(A)		3	8(A)	QF	10	1		9	2	SF	6	9	QF	2	Q	9	
Deportes Tolima	8(A)	16					9	2(A)	4		4	3(A)		10	6(A)		5	11		3	5	SF	4	8	QF	18		7	Q
Corporación Tuluá				13	16		11	8(B)	9		9	6(B)		12	3(B)		6	2		7	16		1	13	QF	15		12	
Unión Magdalena	6(B)	12		11	12		13	3(A)	10		6	3(B)		15	6(A)		15	14								7	Q	6	Q
Centauros Villavicencio																													

(A) = Group A   (B) = Group B

Except for 1995, the season is divided into two leagues, Apertura and Clausura (marked A and C on the table). Also called Torneo Mustang I and II. The winners played off to decide the championship. In 2002, a new system was devised in which both the Apertura and Clausura had two phases. The first is a regular league, the top eight clubs (marked Q) qualifying for a second phase in which two groups of four play each other. The winners of each group meet in a Play-off for the championship.

Once Caldas were one of the surprises of the 2001 season, winning the Clausura – but once again the play-off system let the big teams back into the Championship.

Atlético Júnior

1993, 95, 2000

Deportivo 'Unicosta'

Pablo Escobar, leader of the Medellín drug cartel and lifelong Atlético Nacional fan, combined ruthless violence in the narcotics trade with philanthropic housing and playing field programmes in the city, while extensively bankrolling his favourite team.

COLOMBIA

Key to League Positions Table

	League champions
	Season of promotion to league
	Season of relegation from league
	Other teams playing in league
	Qualified for championship play-off
5	Final position in league

Barranquilla
Cartagena
Santa Marta

Real Cartagena

Unión Magdelena

Cúcuta Deportivo
Cúcuta

Atlético Bucaramanga

Bucaramanga

1997

Medellín

Envigado FC

Envigado

Manizales

Deportivo Pereira

Atlético Nacional

Pereira

Armenia

Deportes Quindío

1994, 99, 2002A

Tuluá

Ibagué

Independiente Medellín

Cali

Bogotá

Once Caldas

Neiva

Villavicencio

1998

C O L O M B I A

1993, 2001, 02C

América de Cali

Corporación Tuluá

Centauros Villavicencio

Deportivo Cali

1995, 97, 99, 2000, 01, 02A

1996, 98

Pasto

Atlético Huila

Independiente Santa Fé

Colombian League

América de Cali	Team name
	League champions/runners-up
1992, *95*	Champions in bold Runners-up in italics
	Other teams in the league
● Cali	City of origin

Deportes Tolima

Millonarios

Deportivo Pasto

1994, 96

2002C

Colombia

Federación Colombiana de Fútbol
Founded: 1924, reformed 1938, 1971
Joined FIFA: 1936–1950, 1954
Joined CONMEBOL: 1940

FOOTBALL WAS A LATE DEVELOPER in Colombia, with the first regular competition only established in the city of Barranquilla in 1924, and a national organization only created in 1938. But it would take until 1948 for the first professional national league to be set up: the *DiMayor*. The league broke away from the Colombian FA in 1950, before rejoining it and FIFA (which it had been a member of between 1936 and 1950) in 1954. It retained a simple format until 1968 when it switched to a season consisting of Apertura (opening), Clausura (closing) and play-off championships. The 1989 national championship has no recorded victor as the season was abandoned following the assassination of a referee and widespread allegations of drug-money handling, illegal gambling and match fixing throughout the game. Colombia has no significant national cup competition. In 2002 the league went back to an Apertura and Clausura format with no play-offs.

Colombian League Record 1948–2002

SEASON	CHAMPIONS	RUNNERS-UP
1948	Independiente Santa Fé	Atlético Júnior
1949	Millonarios	Deportivo Cali
1950	Once Caldas	Millonarios
1951	Millonarios	Boca Júniors
1952	Millonarios	Boca Júniors
1953	Millonarios	Atlético Quindio
1954	Atlético Nacional	Atlético Quindio
1955	Independiente Medellín	Atlético Nacional
1956	Atlético Quindio	Millonarios
1957	Independiente Medellín	Deportes Tolima
1958	Independiente Santa Fé	Millonarios
1959	Millonarios	Independiente Medellín
1960	Independiente Santa Fé	América de Cali
1961	Millonarios	Independiente Medellín
1962	Millonarios	Deportivo Cali
1963	Millonarios	Independiente Santa Fé
1964	Millonarios	Cucuta Deportivo
1965	Deportivo Cali	Atlético Nacional
1966	Independiente Santa Fé	Independiente Medellín
1967	Deportivo Cali	Millonarios
1968	Unión Magdalena	Deportivo Cali
1969	Deportivo Cali	América de Cali
1970	Deportivo Cali	Atlético Júnior
1971	Independiente Santa Fé	Atlético Nacional
1972	Millonarios	Deportivo Cali
1973	Atlético Nacional	Millonarios
1974	Deportivo Cali	Atlético Nacional
1975	Independiente Santa Fé	Millonarios
1976	Atlético Nacional	Deportivo Cali
1977	Atlético Júnior	Deportivo Cali
1978	Millonarios	Deportivo Cali
1979	América de Cali	Independiente Santa Fé
1980	Atlético Júnior	Deportivo Cali
1981	Atlético Nacional	Deportes Tolima
1982	América de Cali	Deportes Tolima
1983	América de Cali	Atlético Júnior
1984	América de Cali	Millonarios
1985	América de Cali	Deportivo Cali
1986	América de Cali	Deportivo Cali
1987	Millonarios	América de Cali
1988	Millonarios	Atlético Nacional
1989	*not awarded**	
1990	América de Cali	Atlético Nacional

Colombian League Record (*continued*)

SEASON	CHAMPIONS	RUNNERS-UP
1991	Atlético Nacional	América de Cali
1992	América de Cali	Atlético Nacional
1993	Atlético Júnior	Independiente Medellín
1994	Atlético Nacional	Millonarios
1995	Atlético Júnior	América de Cali
1996	Deportivo Cali	Millonarios
1997	América de Cali	Atlético Bucaramanga
1998	Deportivo Cali	Once Caldas
1999	Atlético Nacional	América de Cali
2000	América de Cali	Atlético Júnior
2001	América de Cali	Independiente Medellín
2002A	América de Cali	Atlético Nacional
2002C	Independiente Medellín	Deportivo Pasto

* The 1989 season was abandoned due to alleged criminal activities and the killing of a referee.

Colombian League Summary

TEAM	TOTALS	CHAMPIONS & RUNNERS-UP (BOLD) (*ITALICS*)
Millonarios	13, 9	**1949**, *50*, **51–53**, *56*, **58**, *59*, **61–64**, *67*, *72*, *73*, *75*, **78**, *84*, **87**, **88**, *94*, *96*
América de Cali	12, 6	*1960*, *69*, **79**, **82–86**, *87*, **90**, *91*, **92**, *95*, **97**, *99*, **2000**, **01**, **02A**
Deportivo Cali	7, 10	*1949*, *62*, **65**, *67*, *68*, **69**, *70*, *72*, **74**, *76–78*, *80*, *85*, *86*, **96**, **98**
Atlético Nacional	7, 8	**1954**, *55*, *65*, *71*, **73**, *74*, **76**, **81**, *88*, *90*, **91**, **92**, **94**, **99**, **2002A**
Independiente Santa Fé	6, 2	**1948**, **58**, **60**, *63*, **66**, **71**, **75**, *79*
Atlético Júnior	4, 4	*1948*, *70*, **77**, **80**, *83*, **93**, **95**, *2000*
Independiente Medellín	3, 5	**1955**, **57**, *59*, *61*, *66*, *93*, *2001*, **02C**
Atlético Quindio	1, 2	*1953*, *54*, **56**
Once Caldas	1, 1	**1950**, *98*
Unión Magdalena	1, 0	**1968**
Deportes Tolima	0, 3	*1957*, *81*, *82*
Boca Júniors	0, 2	*1951*, *52*
Atlético Bucaramanga	0, 1	*1997*
Cúcuta Deportivo	0, 1	*1964*
Deportivo Pasto	0, 1	*2002C*

Millonarios from Bogotá is the most successful club in Colombia. The team poses for the cameras after winning the 1952 league title.

COLOMBIA

Venezuela

Federación Venezolana de Fútbol
Founded: 1926
Joined FIFA: 1952
Joined CONMEBOL: 1952

AN ORGANIZED NATIONAL LEAGUE was set up in Caracas in 1921. However, the game has failed to take off, given the popularity of the national sport of baseball, and this has left Venezuela as the weakest of the ten footballing nations in South America. League teams turned professional in 1955 but have had very little success in the Copa Libertadores. The national team has also failed to make an impact in the Copa América.

Venezuelan Amateur League Record 1921–54

SEASON	CHAMPIONS	RUNNERS-UP
1921	América	Centro Atlético
1922	Centro Atlético	América
1923	América	Centro Atlético
1924	Centro Atlético	Vargas (La Guaira)
1925	Loyola SC	Venzóleo
1926	Centro Atlético	Venzóleo
1927	Venzóleo	Centro Atlético
1928	Deportivo Venezuela	Centro Atlético
1929	Deportivo Venezuela	Unión SC
1930	Centro Atlético	Unión SC
1931	Deportivo Venezuela	Centro Atlético
1932	Unión SC	Dos Caminos SC
1933	Deportivo Venezuela	Dos Caminos SC
1934	Unión SC	Dos Caminos SC
1935	Unión SC	Dos Caminos SC
1936	Dos Caminos SC	Centro Atlético
1937	Dos Caminos SC	Litoral SC
1938	Dos Caminos SC	Litoral SC
1939	Unión SC	Litoral SC
1940	Unión SC	Dos Caminos SC
1941	Litoral SC	Dos Caminos SC
1942	Dos Caminos SC	Loyola SC
1943	Loyola SC	Litoral SC
1944	Loyola SC	Dos Caminos SC
1945	Dos Caminos SC	Loyola SC
1946	Deportivo Español	Centro Atlético
1947	Unión SC	Universidad Central
1948	Loyola SC	Unión SC
1949	Dos Caminos SC	Universidad Central
1950	Unión SC	La Salle FC
1951	Universidad Central	Loyola SC
1952	La Salle FC	Loyola SC
1953	Universidad Central	La Salle FC
1954	Deportivo Vasco	Loyola SC

Venezuelan Professional League Record 1955–2003

SEASON	CHAMPIONS	RUNNERS-UP
1955	La Salle FC	Deportivo Español
1956	Banco Obrero	La Salle FC
1957	Universidad Central	La Salle FC
1958	Deportivo Portugués	Deportivo Español
1959	Deportivo Español	Deportivo Portugués
1960	Deportivo Portugués	Deportivo Español
1961	Deportivo Italia	Banco Agrícola y Pecuario
1962	Deportivo Portugués	Universidad Central
1963	Deportivo Italia	Deportivo Portugués
1964	Deportivo Galicia	Tiquire Flores
1965	Lara FC	Deportivo Italia
1966	Deportivo Italia	Deportivo Galicia
1967	Deportivo Portugués	Deportivo Galicia
1968	Unión Deportivo Canarias	Deportivo Italia
1969	Deportivo Galicia	Valencia FC

Venezuelan League Record (*continued*)

SEASON	CHAMPIONS	RUNNERS-UP
1970	Deportivo Galicia	Deportivo Italia
1971	Valencia FC	Deportivo Italia
1972	Deportivo Italia	Deportivo Galicia
1973	Portuguesa FC	Valencia FC
1974	Deportivo Galicia	Portuguesa FC
1975	Portuguesa FC	Deportivo Galicia
1976	Portuguesa FC	Estudiantes de Mérida
1977	Portuguesa FC	Estudiantes de Mérida
1978	Portuguesa FC	Deportivo Galicia
1979	Deportivo Táchira	Deportivo Galicia
1980	Estudiantes de Mérida	Portuguesa FC
1981	Deportivo Táchira	Estudiantes de Mérida
1982	Atlético San Cristóbal	Deportivo Táchira
1983	Universidad de Los Andes	Portuguesa FC
1984	Deportivo Táchira	Deportivo Italia
1985	Estudiantes de Mérida	Deportivo Táchira
1986	Unión Atlético Táchira	Estudiantes de Mérida
1987	CS Maritimo	Unión Atlético Táchira
1988	CS Maritimo	Unión Atlético Táchira
1989	Mineros de Guayana	Pepeganga Margarita
1990	CS Maritimo	Unión Atlético Táchira
1991	Universidad de Los Andes	CS Maritimo
1992	Caracas FC	Minervén
1993	CS Maritimo	Minervén
1994	Caracas FC	Trujillanos
1995	Caracas FC	Minervén
1996	Minervén	Mineros de Guayana
1997	Caracas FC	Atlético Zulia
1998	Atlético Zulia	Estudiantes de Mérida
1999	ItalChacoa	Unión Atlético Táchira
2000	Deportivo Táchira	ItalChacao
2001	Caracas FC	Trujillanos
2002	Nacional Táchira	Estudiantes de Mérida
2003	Caracas FC	Unión Atlético Maracaibo

Venezuelan League Summary

TEAM	TOTALS	CHAMPIONS & RUNNERS-UP (BOLD) (*ITALICS*)
Unión SC	7, 3	*1929, 30,* **32, 34, 35,** *39,* **40,** *47,* **48,** *50*
Dos Caminos SC	6, 7	*1932–35,* **36–38,** *40, 41,* **42,** *44,* **45,** *49*
Caracas FC	6, 0	**1992, 94, 95, 97, 2001, 03**
Portuguesa FC	5, 3	**1973,** *74,* **75–78,** *80,* **83**
Centro Atlético	4, 7	*1921,* **22, 23,** *24,* **26,** *27, 28,* **30, 31,** *36, 46*
Deportivo Galicia	4, 6	**1964,** *66, 67,* **69, 70,** *72,* **74,** *75, 78, 79*
Deportivo Italia	4, 5	**1961, 63,** *65,* **66,** *68,* **70, 71,** *72,* **84**
Loyola SC	4, 5	**1925,** *42,* **43, 44,** *45,* **48,** *51, 52, 54*
Deportivo Portugués	4, 2	**1958,** *59,* **60, 62,** *63,* **67**
Deportivo Táchira	4, 2	**1979, 81,** *82,* **84, 85, 2000**
CS Maritimo	4, 1	**1987, 88, 90,** *91,* **93**
Deportivo Venezuela	4, 0	**1928, 29, 31, 33**
Universidad Central	3, 3	*1947, 49,* **51,** *53,* **57,** *62*

This summary only features clubs that have won the Venezuelan League three or more times. For a full list of league champions and runners-up please see the league Records above.

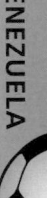

VENEZUELA

Bolivia

Federación Boliviana de Fútbol
Founded: 1925
Joined FIFA: 1926
Joined CONMEBOL: 1926

BOLIVIAN FOOTBALL CAN BE TRACED back to the formation of the first team, Oruro Royal Club, in 1896. Its first matches were against the clubs Nimbles Sports and Northern, formed by workers on the La Paz to Antofagasta railway. Football spread to the major cities high in the Andes over the next decade. Local leagues were formed and early national competitions between local league champions ran from 1914 to 1925. An official national tournament was held in 1926 after the creation of a national football federation. Teams from the capital La Paz, like Bolivar, The Strongest and Littoral, dominated the early years of Bolivian football. They have been challenged more recently by the Cochabamba team, Jorge Wilstermann and the Santa Cruz teams, Oriente Petrolero and Blooming.

Professionalism arrived in 1951 and between 1954 and 1957 a *Torneo Integrado* was held between the champions of the three major leagues in La Paz, Cochabamba and Oruro. In 1958 a national league was finally established. In 1977 this structure was replaced with the one in use today.

The season is split into two with an Apertura (opening) championship played at the beginning of the year, and a Clausura (closing) championship played at the end. The Apertura is a regular league with teams playing each other home and away. The Clausura consists of two groups of six teams playing each other home and away with the addition of two inter-group derbies. The national champions are the winners of a two-leg play-off between the Apertura and Clausura winners. Relegation is decided on a points average over the previous two seasons.

A cup competition – La Copa Simón Bolívar – has also run intermittently in Bolivia. Between 1960 and 1976 the winners became the Bolivian entrant to the Copa Libertadores. It was revived in 1989 as a way of organizing promotion from the regional to the national leagues.

Bolivian Cup Record 1960–76

YEAR	WINNERS	YEAR	WINNERS
1960	Jorge Wilstermann	1969	CD Universitario
1961	Deportivo Municipal	1970	Chaco Petrolero
1962–63	*no competition*	1971	Oriente Petrolero
1964	The Strongest	1972	Jorge Wilstermann
1965	Deportivo Municipal	1973	Jorge Wilstermann
1966	Bolívar	1974	The Strongest
1967	Jorge Wilstermann	1975	Guabirá
1968	Bolívar	1976	Bolívar

Bolivian Cup Record 1989–2002

YEAR	WINNERS	YEAR	WINNERS
1989	Enrique Happ	1998	Unión Central
1990	Universidad	1999	Atlético Pompeya
1991	Enrique Happ	2000	Iberoamericano
1992	Enrique Happ	2001	San José
1993	Real Santa Cruz	2002	Aurora
1994	Stormers		
1995	Municipal		
1996	Blooming		
1997	Real Potosí		

Ecuador

Asociación Ecuatoriana de Fútbol
Founded: 1925
Joined FIFA: 1926
Joined CONMEBOL: 1930

THE FIRST ECUADORIAN CLUB, CS Pastria, was formed in the port city of Guayaquil in 1908, around a decade after visiting sailors had first played football in Ecuador. Local tournaments were organized in Guayaquil before and after the First World War, culminating in a short-lived city league which existed between 1922 and 1929.

Football spread slowly to the interior of the country and it was only in 1957 that the national football federation was reconstituted and a national league established. The league has been dominated by teams from Guayaquil (Barcelona and Emelec) and Quito (Deportivo, El Nacional and Liga Deportivo Universitaria).

In previous years the league had an awesomely complex structure. In the top division, Primera A, 12 teams competed home and away for the Apertura championship: the winners qualifying for the Copa Libertadores. In the Clausura championship the teams were first divided into three groups of four playing home and away. The winners and runners-up of each group then went into a group of six and the third and fourth placed teams went into a second group of six. The winners of the first mini-league then played-off against the winners of the Apertura to determine the overall national champions. The bottom two teams from the second mini-league were relegated. However, the league has now been simplified with the top six clubs from the Apertura and the Clausura playing-off in a final mini-league to decide the national champions.

Bolivian League Record 1958–2002

SEASON	CHAMPIONS	SEASON	CHAMPIONS
1958	Jorge Wilstermann	1982	Bolívar
1959	Jorge Wilstermann	1983	Bolívar
1960	Jorge Wilstermann	1984	Blooming
1961	Deportivo Municipal	1985	Bolívar
1962	Chaco Petrolero	1986	The Strongest
1963	The Strongest/Aurora	1987	Bolívar
1964	The Strongest	1988	Bolívar
1965	Deportivo Municipal	1989	The Strongest
1966	Bolívar	1990	Oriente Petrolero
1967	Jorge Wilstermann	1991	Bolívar
1968	Bolívar	1992	Bolívar
1969	CD Universitario	1993	The Strongest
1970	CD Chaco Petrolero	1994	Bolívar
1971	Oriente Petrolero	1995	CS San José
1972	Jorge Wilstermann	1996	Bolívar
1973	Jorge Wilstermann	1997	Bolívar
1974	The Strongest	1998	Blooming
1975	Guabirá	1999	Blooming
1976	Bolívar	2000	Jorge Wilstermann
1977	The Strongest	2001	Oriente Petrolero
1978	Bolívar	2002	Bolívar
1979	Oriente Petrolero		
1980	Jorge Wilstermann		
1981	Jorge Wilstermann		

Ecuadorian League Record 1957–2002

SEASON	CHAMPIONS	SEASON	CHAMPIONS
1957	Emelec	1964	Deportivo
1958	*no championship*	1965	9 du Octubre
1959	*no championship*	1966	Barcelona
1960	Barcelona	1967	El Nacional
1961	Emelec	1968	Deportivo
1962	Everest	1969	LDU
1963	Barcelona	1970	Barcelona

BOLIVIA, ECUADOR

Ecuadorian League Record (*continued*)

SEASON	CHAMPIONS	SEASON	CHAMPIONS
1971	Barcelona	1989	Barcelona
1972	Emelec	1990	Barcelona
1973	El Nacional	1991	Valdez
1974	El Nacional	1992	El Nacional
1975	LDU	1993	Barcelona
1976	Deportivo	1994	Emelec
1977	El Nacional	1995	Barcelona
1978	El Nacional	1996	El Nacional
1979	Emelec	1997	Barcelona
1980	Barcelona	1998	LDU
1981	LDU	1999	LDU
1982	El Nacional	2000	Olmedo
1983	El Nacional	2001	Emelec
1984	El Nacional	2002	Emelec
1985	Barcelona		
1986	El Nacional		
1987	Barcelona		
1988	Emelec		

Peru

Federación Peruana de Fútbol
Founded: 1922
Joined FIFA: 1924
Joined CONMEBOL: 1926

FOOTBALL WAS INTRODUCED TO PERU at the turn of the 19th century by British residents in the capital Lima. Many teams grew out of expatriate tennis and cricket clubs. A local league was formed in 1912, but it was only in 1922 that a national football federation was established.

A formalized Lima-based league was set up in 1926 and in 1931 Peruvian football went professional. In 1966 the league was expanded to encompass the strongest teams from the regional competitions. In 1972 the league changed again with a Lima-based metropolitan league and a network of regional leagues producing qualifiers for a national championship tournament. Lima teams have consistently led Peruvian football: Universitario de Deportes, Sporting Cristal, Alianza Lima, Sport Boys and Deportivo Municipal, all come from the capital.

In 1976 a single national league was established but with a fantastically complex structure. Again split into two leagues – Apertura and Clausura – the championship is decided via a play-off between the two champions, unless one club has won both. The winners claim a place in the Copa Libertadores. The six teams with the highest points total across the season (excluding the champions) then compete in an end-of-season play-off league to determine Peru's second spot in the competition. The two clubs with the overall lowest points total are relegated. The winners of the Lima regional league and the winners of the Copa Perú (a tournament between regional champions) are promoted to the top division.

Peruvian League Record 1926–2002

SEASON	CHAMPIONS	SEASON	CHAMPIONS
1926	Sport Progreso	1933	Alianza Lima
1927	Alianza Lima	1934	Universitario de Deportes
1928	Alianza Lima	1935	Sport Boys
1929	Universitario de Deportes	1936	*no championship*
1930	Atlético Chalaco	1937	Sport Boys
1931	Alianza Lima	1938	Deportivo Municipal
1932	Alianza Lima	1939	Universitario de Deportes

Peruvian League Record (*continued*)

SEASON	CHAMPIONS	SEASON	CHAMPIONS
1940	Deportivo Municipal	1973	Desensor Lima
1941	Universitario de Deportes	1974	Universitario de Deportes
1942	Sport Boys	1975	Alianza Lima
1943	Deportivo Municipal	1976	Unión Huaral
1944	FC Sucre	1977	Alianza Lima
1945	Universitario de Deportes	1978	Alianza Lima
1946	Universitario de Deportes	1979	Sporting Cristal
1947	Atlético Chalaco	1980	Sporting Cristal
1948	Alianza Lima	1981	Melgar FBC
1949	Universitario de Deportes	1982	Universitario de Deportes
1950	Deportivo Municipal	1983	Sporting Cristal
1951	Sport Boys	1984	Sport Boys
1952	Alianza Lima	1985	Universitario de Deportes
1953	FC Sucre	1986	Colegio San Agustín
1954	Alianza Lima	1987	Universitario de Deportes
1955	Alianza Lima	1988	Sporting Cristal
1956	Sporting Cristal	1989	Unión Huaral
1957	Centro Iqueño	1990	Universitario de Deportes
1958	Sport Boys	1991	Sporting Cristal
1959	Universitario de Deportes	1992	Universitario de Deportes
1960	Universitario de Deportes	1993	Universitario de Deportes
1961	Sporting Cristal	1994	Sporting Cristal
1962	Alianza Lima	1995	Sporting Cristal
1963	Alianza Lima	1996	Sporting Cristal
1964	Universitario de Deportes	1997	Alianza Lima
1965	Alianza Lima	1998	Universitario de Deportes
1966	Universitario de Deportes	1999	Universitario de Deportes
1967	Universitario de Deportes	2000	Universitario de Deportes
1968	Sporting Cristal	2001	Alianza Lima
1969	Universitario de Deportes	2002	Sporting Cristal
1970	Sporting Cristal		
1971	Universitario de Deportes		
1972	Sporting Cristal		

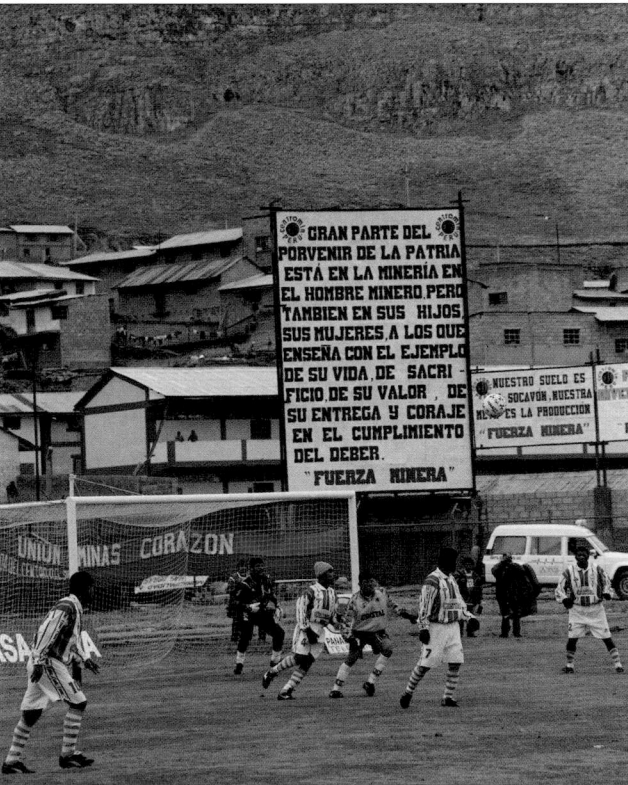

Peruvian football club Union Minas, which plays at 4,380m in the Andes near the border with Bolivia, holds the record for the professional team which plays at the highest altitude in the world. Half-time refreshment for the players comes in the form of oxygen.

PERU

Brazil

BRAZIL

THE SEASON IN REVIEW 2002

THE BEST AND THE WORST OF Brazilian football remained on show throughout 2002. A fifth World Cup victory, for clearly the most stylish team in the tournament, was balanced by the grinding chaos of the domestic game. Of the 17 senior football figures recommended for criminal prosecution by last year's senatorial report into the game, nearly all remain in their posts. Richard Teixeira, head of the CBF, has retreated to an impregnable office with sealed underground parking in an anonymous Rio suburb, but remains in charge and was available for glad-handing during the country's presidential elections.

The season opened with the usual mix of state and inter-state championships, and an early show of form from São Paulo, Fluminense and Corinthians. In an effort to get away from penalty shootouts and negative play, drawn matches in the Rio-São Paulo tournament were decided this year on who had the least red and yellow cards. São Paulo drew in the semi-finals with Palmeiras, but with only four yellow cards to Palmeiras' seven, São Paulo went to the Final; losing to Corinthians on goals rather than cards. Overall, the numbers of fouls and bookings significantly dropped.

Parreira's reward
The Final of the Copa do Brasil saw Corinthians meet Brasiliense, a third division team from the capital. Corinthians won the opening leg 2-1. The president of Brasiliense, Luiz Estevão, a man already removed from public office over alleged misuse

Romario scores on his debut for Fluminense against Cruzeiro. Despite slapping teammates, travelling alone and with special privileges and perks, including regular excusal from training, Romario helped the Rio club to the National Championship semi-finals.

Brazilian National Championship 2002 – First Phase

CLUB	P	W	D	L	F	A	Pts	
São Paulo	25	16	4	5	57	35	52	Qualified for Second Phase
São Caetano	25	14	5	6	42	28	47	Qualified for Second Phase
Corinthians	25	12	7	6	37	35	43	Qualified for Second Phase
Juventude	25	12	5	8	34	30	41	Qualified for Second Phase
Grêmio	25	11	8	6	39	29	41	Qualified for Second Phase
Atlético Mineiro	25	12	4	9	49	43	40	Qualified for Second Phase
Fluminense	25	12	4	9	43	46	40	Qualified for Second Phase
Santos	25	11	6	8	46	36	39	Qualified for Second Phase
Cruzeiro	25	11	6	8	40	39	39	
Vitória	25	11	4	10	46	42	37	
Coritiba	25	11	3	11	34	34	36	
Goiás	25	10	6	9	42	39	36	
Ponte Preta	25	10	4	11	35	34	34	
Atlético Paranaense	25	9	7	9	39	33	34	
Vasco da Gama	25	10	3	12	37	38	33	
Guarani	25	9	6	10	32	35	33	
Figueirense	25	9	4	12	34	43	31	
Flamengo	25	8	6	11	38	39	30	
Bahia	25	8	6	11	35	37	30	
Paysandu	25	9	2	14	35	46	29	
Internacional	25	7	8	10	36	37	29	
Paraná	25	8	4	13	37	42	28	
Portuguesa	25	7	6	12	26	40	27	Relegated
Palmeiras	25	6	9	10	37	46	27	Relegated
Gama	25	7	4	14	30	39	25	Relegated
Botafogo-RJ	25	6	7	12	24	39	25	Relegated

Promoted clubs: Criciúma, Fortaleza.

Brazilian State Championships 2002

STATE	CHAMPIONS
Bahia	Vitória
Ceará	Ceará
Goiás	Goiás
Minas Gerias	Cruzeiro
Paraná	Atlético Paranaense
Rio de Janeiro	Fluminense
Rio Grande do Sul	Internacional
Rio-São Paulo*	Corinthians
São Paulo	São Paulo

* Inter-State tournament

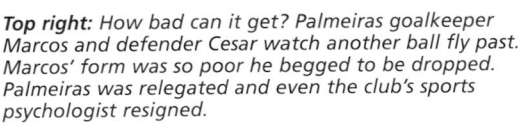

Top right: *How bad can it get? Palmeiras goalkeeper Marcos and defender Cesar watch another ball fly past. Marcos' form was so poor he begged to be dropped. Palmeiras was relegated and even the club's sports psychologist resigned.*

Middle right: *Kaka, São Paulo's attacking midfielder, enjoying the acclaim that came with his team's great early season form. Despite topping the National Championship league stage, the club crashed out in the first round of the play-offs.*

Bottom right: *São Caetano continue to defy the odds, as the tiny São Paulo state team reached the National Championship Play-off quarter-finals and the Final of the Copa Libertadores.*

of public funds, issued a fusillade of protest over key decisions in the game. Referee Carlos Eugenio Simon was suspended by the CBF's refereeing commission president Edson Resende – who comes from Brasilia. But all to no avail; Corinthians held on for a draw in the second leg and took the cup; reward for the transformation wrought by coach Carlos Alberto Parreira who took over a club in total disarray only six months before.

Other coaches were not so fortunate, as clubs chopped and changed managers with increasing and desperate velocity. Botafogo tried four, but was still relegated. Palmeiras, Copa Libertadores champions only four years ago, took the drop after three coaches. The gloom at the big club grew so great that World Cup keeper Marcos begged to be dropped and even the club's sports psychologist resigned. Flamengo, in financial crisis, is still paying the last six coaches that it sacked.

Better things to come?

The National Championship saw Corinthians, Santos, Grêmio and Fluminense in the semi-finals, but it was Santos above all that caught the eye. Without a title for nearly 20 years, the fans at Pele's former club had taken to holding their banners upside down and refusing to turn them until a title had been achieved. This year they were turned as Emerson Leao's amazingly young, effervescent, even cheeky squad stormed to the title.

With the election of Lula – Brazil's first left-wing president – the reform of Brazilian society might finally begin. The new sports minister is making noises about really cleaning up the game, and both Santos and the national team spent the year playing football like it's meant to be played in Brazil. Is this a hint of better things to come?

Brazilian National Championship – Second Phase

QUARTER-FINALS (2 legs)

FIRST LEG

November 24

Fluminense **3-0** São Caetano
(Magno Alves 70, 88, Roni 75)

Atlético **2-6** Corinthians
Mineiro   Gil 13, 54,
(Mancini 40,   Deivid 29, 52,
Michel 41)   73, 86)

Grêmio **0-0** Juventude

Santos **3-1** São Paulo
(Alberto 30,   (Kaká 45)
Robinho 51,
Diego Ribas 66)

SECOND LEG

November 27

São Caetano **2-0** Fluminense
(Daniel 15,
Magrão 46 pen)

Fluminense won 3-2 on aggregate

Corinthians **2-1** Atlético
(Marcinho 57,   Mineiro
Guilherme 85)   (Mancini 59)

Corinthians won 8-3 on aggregate

Juventude **0-1** Grêmio
(César Santin 55)

Grêmio won 1-0 on aggregate

São Paulo **2-1** Santos
(Léo 58,   (Luis Fabiano 4)
Diego Ribas 90)

Santos won 4-3 on aggregate

SEMI-FINALS (2 legs)

FIRST LEG

December 1

Fluminense **1-0** Corinthians
(Romario 76)

Santos **3-0** Grêmio
(Alberto 37, 68,
Robinho 79)

SECOND LEG

December 4

Corinthians **3-2** Fluminense
(Gil 35,   (Roni 20, 83)
Guilherme 58, 75)

Aggregate 3-3

Corinthians won on higher league placing

Grêmio **1-0** Santos
(Rodrigo
Fabri 68)

Santos won 3-1 on aggregate

FINAL (2 legs)

December 8 - Morumbi, São Paulo

Santos **2-0** Corinthians
(Alberto 15,
Renato 88)
h/t: 1-0   **Att:** 58,534
Ref: Pereira da Silva

December 15 - Morumbi, São Paulo

Corinthians **2-3** Santos
(Deivid 75,   (Robinho 37,
Anderson 84)   Elano 88, Léo 92)
h/t: 0-1   **Att:** 74,592
Ref: Simon

Santos won 5-2 on aggregate

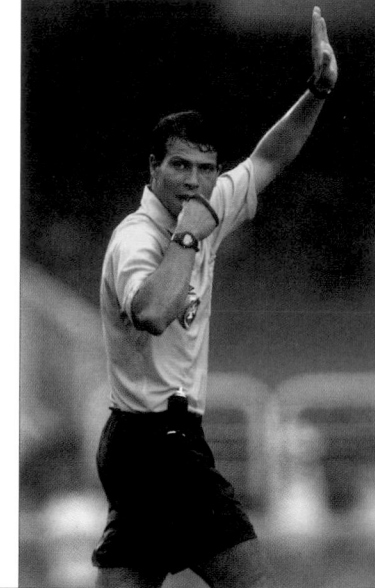

Below right: Near the end of a championship match in September between Coritiba and Santos, Coritiba striker Jaba received the ball near the touchline and looked to dribble the ball. Referee Leonardo Gaciba Junior booked him, arguing that this was a provocative action and a danger to him and others. Ludicrous as it sounds, there is some historical precedent. Brazilian midfielder Edilson was attacked in a match three years ago after playing keepy-uppy.

Below: Carlos Alberto Parreira performed miracles this season with a Corinthians team upset by the departure of Wanderley Luxemburgo, and only the running and brio of a rejuvenated Santos stopped them taking the National Championship. His dubious reward is to succeed Phil Scolari as national team coach with the evergreen Mario Zagallo as his technical director.

Above: Master of futebol moleque – literally 'cheeky schoolboy football'. Robinho, Santos' teenage striking sensation, takes the ball past Rogerio of Corinthians.

Above, far right: Santos players (r-l) Paulo Almeida, Elano and Preto lift the trophy after defeating Corinthians 3-2 in the Final of the Brazilian Championship.

Bottom right: Deivid (Corinthians) and Aldo (Brasiliense) jump for the ball during the Copa do Brasil Final.

Copa do Brasil

2002 FINAL (2 legs)

May 8 – Morumbi, São Paulo
Corinthians 2-1 Brasiliense
(Deivid 53, 69)   (Mauricio 60)
h/t: 0-0   **Att:** 65,627
Ref: Simon

May 15 – Estadio Elma Serejão, Taguatinga
Brasiliense 1-1 Corinthians
(Wellington   (Deivid 65)
Diaz 41)
h/t: 1-0   **Att:** 25,000
Ref: Mendonça

Corinthians won 3-2 on aggregate

International Club Performances 2002

CLUB	COMPETITION	PROGRESS
São Caetano	Copa Libertadores	Runners-up
Grêmio	Copa Libertadores	Semi-finals
Atlético Paranaense	Copa Libertadores	Group Stage
Flamengo	Copa Libertadores	Group Stage

Association Football in Brazil

BRAZIL

1894: Charles Miller returns to Brazil from England with first imported football equipment. First recorded match, São Paulo — **1890 / 1895**

1898: First club, Associacao Atletica of Mackenzie College, São Paulo founded — **1900**

1901: São Paulo League, Campeonata Paulista de Futebol, established — **1905**

1905: Bahia State League (first provincial league) established — **1910**

1906: Rio League established — **1915**

 1914: CBD founded: Confederação Brasileira de Desportos. First international v Argentina, lost 3-0, venue: Buenos Aires — **1920**

1916: Affiliation to CONMEBOL — **1925**

1923: Affiliation to FIFA — **1930**

1933: Professionalism legalized — **1935**

1940 / 1945

1950: Rio–São Paulo Tournament established — **1950 / 1955**

1959: Brazilian Cup established — **1960**

1967: Rio–São Paulo Tournament replaced by Taca de Prata — **1965**

1968: Brazilian Cup discontinued — **1970**
1971: Fully-fledged National League established, replaces Taca de Prata — **1975**

1980: CBF (Confederação Brasileira de Futbol) replaces CBD — **1980**

1982: First women's international, v Spain — **1985**

1989: Brazilian Cup re-established — **1990**

1993: Pele, Minister of Sport, fails to reform the game

2000: Massive judicial investigation launched into the finances of Brazilian football. National championship replaced by one-off João Havelange Tournament — **1995 / 2000**

2003: National Championships reformed, Play-offs abandoned — **2005**

International Competitions

1919:	● ■
1921:	▲
1922:	● ■
1925:	▲
1937:	▲
1945:	▲
1946:	▲
1949:	● ■
1950:	▲ ■
1953:	▲
1957:	▲
1958:	●
1959:	▲

Copa Libertadores

Year	Winner	Runner-up
1961:		△ Palm
1962:	○ Santos	
1963:	○ Santos	
1968:		△ Palm
1970:	●	
1974:		△ São P
1976:	○ Cruz	
1977:		△ Cruz
1980:		△ Inter
1981:	○ Flam	
1983:	○ Grêm	
1984:		△ Grêm

Copa CONMEBOL / Copa Mercosur

Year	Int'l	Copa Libertadores	Copa CONMEBOL	Copa Mercosur
1989:	● ■			
1991:	▲			
1992:		○ São P	○ Atl M	
1993:		○ São P	○ Bota	
1994:			○ São P	
1995:	▲	○ Grêm	△ São P	△ Atl M
1997:	●	○ Cruz	○ Atl M	
1998:	▲	○ Vasco	○ Santos	○ Palm / △ Cruz
1999:	●	○ Palm		○ Flam / △ Palm
2000:		△ Palm		○ Vasco / △ Palm
2001:				△ Flam
2002:	●	△ São C		

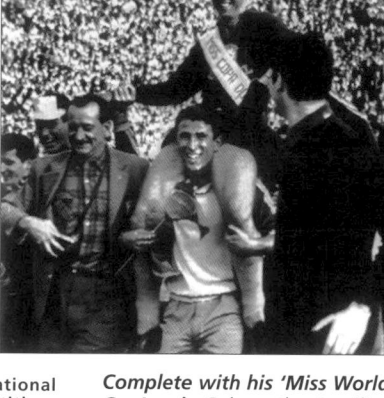

Complete with his 'Miss World Cup' sash, Gylmar the Brazilian goalkeeper is held up in triumph after victory in the 1962 World Cup Final against Czechoslovakia in Chile.

Key

	International football
	Affiliation to FIFA
	Affiliation to CONMEBOL
	Women's football
■	World Cup host
●	World Cup winner
▲	World Cup runner-up
■	Copa América host
●	Copa América winner
▲	Copa América runner-up
○	Competition winner
△	Competition runner-up

Atl M	Atlético Mineiro
Bota	Botafogo
Cruz	Cruzeiro
Flam	Flamengo
Grêm	Grêmio
Inter	Internacional
Palm	Palmeiras
São C	São Caetano
São P	São Paulo
Vasco	Vasco da Gama

Atlética Ponte Preta 1900

Guarani FC 1911

RORAIMA (1995)

AMAZONAS (1914)

ACRE (1989)

RONDÔNIA (1945)

Coritiba 1909

Paraná Clube 1989
Merger of Colorado and Pinheiros

Atlético Paranaense 1924

Criciúma EC 1947

Comerciaro (1978)

Brazil: The main clubs

Santos 1912	Team name with year of formation
●	Club formed before 1912
●	Club formed 1912–25
○	Club formed 1925–50
	Club formed after 1950
PARÁ (1913)	State (year of championship foundation)
	Founded 1900–10
	Founded 1910–20
	Founded 1920–50
	Founded 1950–80
	Founded 1980–95
	Team colours
	English origins
	German origins
	Italian origins
	Portuguese origins
	Lower class
	Upper class
	Originated from a cricket club
	Originated from a rowing club
	Railway company origins

Uniõn São João 1981

EC Vitória 1899

Club de Cricket Victoria
(1899–1946)

EC Bahia 1931

Merger of Atlética de
Bahia and Club
Bahiano de Tenis

AMAPÁ
(1944)

América FC 1915

SC Recife 1905

RIO GRANDE
DO NORTE
(1920)

PARÁ
(1913)

MARANHÃO
(1918)

Araras

CEARÁ
(1920)

Natal

PIAUÍ
(1918)

PARAÍBA
(1917)

Recife

B R A Z I L

PERNAMBUCO
(1915)

ALAGOAS
(1927)

TOCANTINS
(1993)

SERGIPE
(1918)

Salvador

MATO GROSSO
(1974)

DISTRITO
FEDERAL
(1973)

BAHIA
(1905)

Goiás EC 1943 Goiânia

Brasília
SE Gama
1975

MINAS
GERAIS

GOIAS
(1944)

ESPÍRITO
SANTO
(1940)

Atlético
Bragantino
1928

Belo
Horizonte

Bragança
Paulista

Campinas

Rio de
Janeiro

RIO DE
JANEIRO
(1906)

São
Caetano

São Caetano

Atlético
Mineiro 1908

MATO GROSSO DO SUL
(1979)

São
Paulo

SÃO PAULO
(1902)

Caetano
1989

Curitiba

Cruzeiro EC 1921

Santos 1912

PARANÁ
(1915)

Palestra Italia
(1921–42)

SANTA CATARINA
(1927)

SC Corinthians 1910

Criciúma

RIO GRANDE DO SUL
(1919)

Botafogo SP 1918

Flamengo 1895

Caxias du Sul

Porto
Alegre

Portuguesa de Desportos 1920

CR Vasco da
Gama 1898

Atlética das Palmeiras 1914

EC Juventude 1913

Societa Palestra Italia (1914–42)

Fluminense 1902

São Paulo FC 1935

SC Internacional 1909

Grêmio 1903

Botafogo 1914

Brazil

ORIGINS AND GROWTH OF FOOTBALL

THE EARLIEST REPORTS OF FOOTBALL in Brazil are of British and Dutch sailors playing on the Rio dockside in the 1870s and of British and Brazilian railway workers in São Paulo in 1882. But the written record begins with Charles Miller. Brazilian-born of English coffee-merchant parentage, Miller was educated in England. With a game for Hampshire against the Corinthians under his belt, he returned to Brazil in 1894 with a collection of footballs and a raging enthusiasm. Collecting together Englishmen from the São Paulo Railway, the local gas company and the London and Brazilian bank, he organized the first 'official' football match in São Paulo in 1895. Within five years teams had sprung up in São Paulo and Rio, drawing on German colleges and gym clubs, Portuguese immigrants, English companies, as well as members of elite cricket and rowing clubs.

The race issue

São Paulo's Campeonata Paulista de Futebol was the first organized tournament which started in 1901, followed by leagues in Bahia (1904) and Rio de Janeiro (1905). A national association running all sports, the CBD, was set up in 1914 with a football section. The elite and predominantly white origins of Brazilian football soon came into conflict with the mass popularity of the game on the issue of race. Carlos Alberto, a mulatto of mixed race, played for Fluminense in 1916 with rice flour on his face to lighten his complexion. In 1921, President Pesoa called for an all-white team to represent Brazil in the Copa América.

But in 1923, Vasco da Gama won the Rio Championship with a team dominated by black and mixed-race players. Rio's big teams, flushed with fear for their sporting and social status, organized an alternative league and sought to exclude black players by making the signing of a team sheet a pre-condition of participation. But the sporting and economic logic was against exclusion, and as players of all races began moving to Italy and elsewhere, professionalism was introduced into the Rio Championships in 1933 and quickly spread.

BRAZIL

The 1970 World Cup-winning Brazilian team is regarded by many as the finest football team ever. The side that faced Italy in the Final included: (back row left to right) Carlos Alberto, Brito, Piazza, Felix, Clodoaldo, Everaldo, Gerson; (front row) Jairzinho, Rivelino, Tostão, Pele and Paulo Cesar.

São Paulo

FOOTBALL CITY

SÃO PAULO IS THE INDUSTRIAL and commercial heart of Brazil. After an English public school education, Charles Miller (son of a coffee merchant family) returned to São Paulo in 1894 with some footballs. In 1895, he organized a game among British workers at the São Paulo Railway Company, the London and Brazilian Bank and the Gas Company on the Varzea do Carmo. More games were organized between football sections formed by the British at São Paulo Athletic Club and Mackenzie College. The word spread and Germans from the city's gymnastic clubs created SC Germania. Together with another club, CA Paulistino, these teams formed the city's first league in 1901. Within a year, São Paulo had over 60 clubs and the game began to spread beyond its European elite circles.

The five big teams of the professional era emerged a decade or so after this initial explosion. In 1910, Corinthians was founded by railway workers in Bom Retiro, and named after the English amateurs who had recently toured the city. In 1912, the Rio team América relocated to the port area of the city. After considering various names, like 'Africa' and 'Concordia', it settled on the area's name, Santos, for its new club. In 1914, the city's Italian immigrant population created Club Sociedada Esportivo Palestra Italia. During the Second World War, anti-Italian sentiment saw the side change its name to Palmeiras. The Portuguese community followed with the creation of Portuguesa from the merger of five clubs (Lusiadas, Portugal Marinhense, 5 de Outobro, Luzitano and Marques de Pombal).

Professionalism and disaster

These four clubs were among those teams which were paying their players and pushing for the development of a professional game in the 1920s. The last of the big five, São Paulo, rose out of the ashes of an earlier team of the same name. São Paulo 'I' was formed in 1930, when CA Paulistino stopped playing football in protest over the adoption of professionalism, and the club's players joined AA de Palmeiras. The venture folded in 1935 and São Paulo 'II' drew on what was left of the team to start again. By then a professional city league had been created.

The decades that followed were a peak for São Paulo football – a rash of stadium building, including the city government's funding of the Pacaembu, and the arrival of Pele at Santos. The club's victories in the Copa Libertadores in the early 1960s at last allowed the city to eclipse Rio. Forty years on, Corinthians and Santos are the city's leading clubs, but their financial situation is dire; gate takings are low, and all the clubs are mired in debt. The once mighty Palmeiras have been relegated to the Second Division.

São Paulo, Brazil's industrial and commercial heartland, has witnessed decades of explosive economic and demographic growth that has created extremes of wealth (in the central business district featured here) and poverty in the sprawling shanty towns of the city's periphery: perfect conditions for the creation of massive fan bases.

CÍCERO POMPEU DE TOLEDO – MORUMBI

Club:	São Paulo
Built:	1960
Original Capacity:	120, 000
Record Attendance:	138,032 Corinthians v Ponte Preta, 1977
Significant Matches:	2000 Club World Championship: six group matches

80,000

SÃO PAULO
SEE ENLARGEMENT FOR MORE DETAIL

Santos

AA Portuguesa Santos

URBANO CALDEIRA 'VILA BELMIRO'
18,500

ULRICO MURSA
15,000

SANTOS

ATLANTIC OCEAN

SANTOS 1912

National Championship	*1983, 95,* **2002**
São Paulo League	*1927–29,* **35,** *48,* **55, 56, 57, 58,** *59,* **60–62, 64, 65, 67–69,** *73, 78, 80, 84, 2000*
Rio-São Paulo Tournament	**1959, 63, 64, 66, 97,** *99*
Taca do Brasil (1959–68)	*1959,* **61–65,** *66*
Copa Libertadores	**1962, 63**
Copa CONMEBOL	**1998**
World Club Cup	**1962, 63**

CORINTHIANS 1910

National Championship	*1976,* **90, 94, 98, 99,** *2002*
São Paulo League	**1914,** *18,* **22–24,** *25,* **28–30,** *36,* **37–39, 41,** *42, 43,* **45–47, 51, 52, 54, 55, 62, 66, 68, 74, 77, 79, 82, 83, 84, 87, 88,** *91, 93,* **95, 97,** *98,* **99, 2001, 02, 03**
Rio-São Paulo Tournament	**1950, 53, 54,** *63,* **66,** *93,* **2002, 03**
Copa do Brasil (1989–2002)	**1995,** *2001,* **02**
FIFA Club World Championship	**2000**

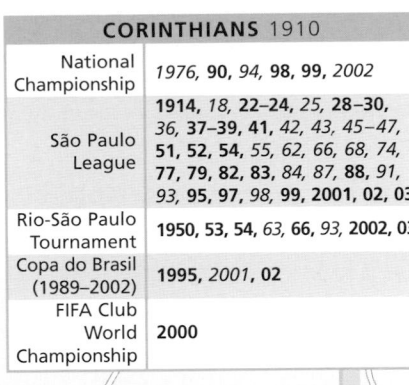

LIMAO

CASA VERDE

Palmeiras

Rio Tiete

PALESTRA ITÁLIA 'PARQUE ANTÁRCTICA'
32,000

BOM RETIRO

VILA GUILHERME

VILA MARIA

Via Presidente Dutra

OSWALDO TEIXEIRA DUARTE 'CANDIDÉ'
22,000

PARI

ALFREDO SCHURING 'PARQUE SÃO JORGE'
15,000

LAPA

PERDIZES

'PACAEMBU' Paulo Machado de Carvalho. This municipal stadium is used for big games by all the city's leading clubs
40,000

SANTA CECILIA

Portuguesa

CONDO RODOLFO CRESPI
9,000

Corinthians

BRAZIL

VILA MADALENA

REPUBLICA

BRAS

Juventus

CONSOLACAO

BELA VISTA

São Paulo AC

SÃO PAULO

ALTO DA MOOCA

Avenida Rebouças

PINHEIROS

Avenida Brasil

CAMBUCI

São Paulo

JARDIM AMERICA

JARDIM PAULISTA

IPIRANGA

Avenida Paulista

BUTANTA

CÍCERO POMPEU DE TOLEDO 'MORUMBI'
80,000

SC Germania

FEDERAÇÂO PAULISTA DE FUTEBOL STATE FA HEADQUARTERS

Rio Tiete

BROOKLIN PAULISTANA Birth place of Rivellino

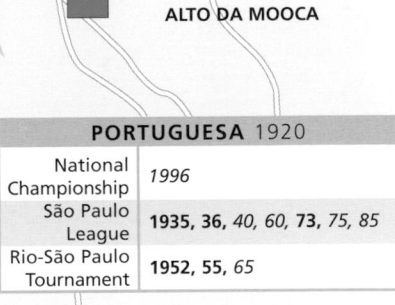

PORTUGUESA 1920

National Championship	*1996*
São Paulo League	**1935, 36,** *40,* **60,** *73, 75,* **85**
Rio-São Paulo Tournament	**1952, 55,** *65*

SÃO PAULO 1935

National Championship	*1971, 73, 77, 81, 86, 89, 90,* **91**
São Paulo League	*1930,* **31,** *32–34,* **38, 41,** *43,* **44, 45, 46, 48, 49, 50, 52, 53, 56, 57, 58,** *63,* **67,** *70,* **71,** *72,* **75,** *78,* **80, 81,** *82, 83,* **85, 87, 89, 91, 92,** *94, 96,* **97, 98, 2000,** *03*
Rio-São Paulo Tournament	*1965, 98,* **2001,** *02, 03*
Copa do Brasil (1989–2002)	*2000*
Copa Libertadores	*1974,* **92, 93,** *94*
Copa CONMEBOL	**1994**
Supercopa	**1993,** *97*
World Club Cup	**1992, 93**

PALMEIRAS 1914

National Championship	**1972, 73,** *78,* **93, 94,** *97*
São Paulo League	**1920,** *21, –23,* **26, 27, 31,** *32–34,* **35, 36, 37, 39, 40,** *42,* **44,** *47,* **49, 50, 51, 53, 54,** *59,* **61, 63, 64, 65, 66,** *69–71,* **72, 74, 76,** *86,* **92,** *93,* **94, 95, 96,** *99*
Rio-São Paulo Tournament	*1931,* **51,** *55, 61, 62,* **65,** *93,* **2000**
Taca do Brasil (1959–68)	**1960, 67**
Copa do Brasil (1989–2002)	*1996,* **98**
Copa Libertadores	*1961, 68,* **99,** *2000*
Copa Mercosur	**1998,** *99,* **2000**
World Club Cup	*1999*

São Paulo

32,000	Capacity of stadium
	Minor clubs
	Stadium no longer in use for top-flight football
	Team colours
	Early São Paulo teams
	Major road
1900	Champions
2000	Runners-up

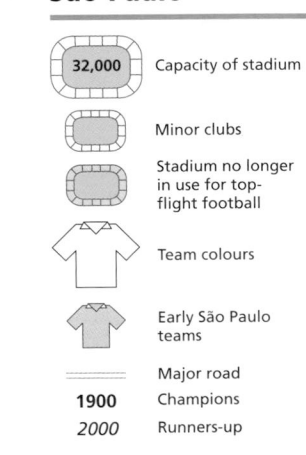

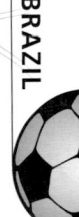

Rio de Janeiro

FOOTBALL CITY

BRAZIL

UNCONFIRMED REPORTS TELL OF British sailors playing football in Rio's docks throughout the late 19th century. The expatriate British elite played cricket (in Paissandu and Rio Cricket Sud in Niteroi) and formed rowing clubs. After a match between São Paulo and Rio in 1901, a rash of football clubs were set up among the expatriates: Fluminense in 1902, América and Botafogo in 1904. Fluminense attracted the pinnacle of society, students from the Alfredo Gomez College formed Botafogo, and Bangu were in effect the works' team of the British managers at a textile firm in the suburbs. In 1906 a local tournament, the Carioca, was established. In 1911, defectors from Fluminense joined Flamengo rowing club to create a Flamengo football section.

The literacy test

At first, elite control of Rio football was more absolute than in São Paulo, and the white expatriates, professionals and students of these clubs dominated the game. But in 1923, Vasco da Gama, a team formed by Portuguese immigrants, came into the top division, fielding four black players among poor white players. The key difference was that they were professionals, and the team was unstoppable. The big elite clubs left the

league and formed their own (LMDT), which ran the following year without Vasco. But the crowds went to Vasco, and the club – along with two others – was eventually asked to join the LMDT. However, pre-match paperwork in the league required literacy of all players, and Vasco's advantage was eradicated until the literacy test was abolished in 1929. By the early 1930s, all the clubs were paying players in an intense competitive struggle, and inevitably a professional league was established in 1933.

Although Vasco is a perennial challenger, and often the victor, the Flamengo-Fluminense rivalry is the key to football in Rio. In a single game, this local derby condenses the divisions of class and race in the city; Fluminense (the aristocracy) versus Flamengo (the people). It is this intensity for football, reflected citywide, that saw the creation of the world's largest football stadium – the Maracana – and the national disaster of defeat in the 1950 World Cup. Today, the clubs share power in Rio with the Confederação Brasileira de Futebol, who chose to locate here rather than in the capital Brasília, and the nation's gigantic TV company – Globo. The rising tide of accusations of corruption, match fixing and interference are now lapping at the doors of the presidents of the major Rio clubs and the Rio FA.

MARIO FILHO – MARACANA

95,095	**Clubs:** Botafogo, Flamengo, Fluminense
	Built: 1950
	Original Capacity: 180,000
	Rebuilt: 1993–98
	Record Attendance: 183,341 1969 Brazil v Paraguay, World Cup
	Significant Matches: 1950 World Cup: seven matches including final pool match; Copa América: 1989 final pool matches

Football in Rio reflects the divisions of class and race in the city. This is embodied in the Fla-Flu derby which pits the people (in the shape of Flamengo) against the aristocracy (in the shape of Fluminense).

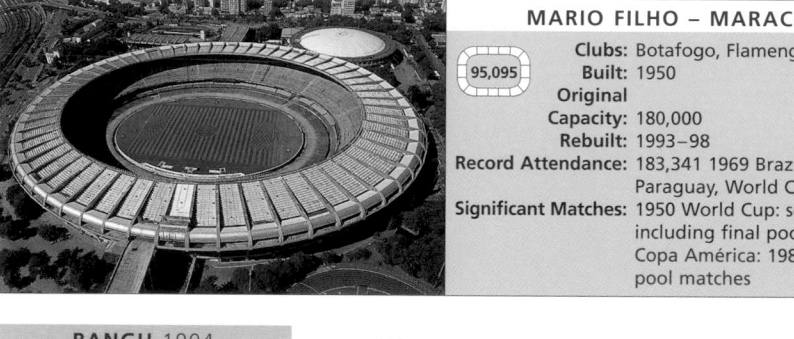

BANGU 1904

National Championship	1985
Rio League	1916, **33**, **51**, **59**, **64**, **65**, **66**, **67**, **85**

116
DUQUE DE CAXIAS Birthplace of Jairzinho
040
Olaria AC
RUA BARIRI
18,000
ANICETO MOSCOSO
MADUREIRA
10,000
RAMOS
Baia de Gunabara
210
101
MENDHANHA
465
MOCA BONITA
15,000
PILARES
EDSON PASSOS
NITEROI Birthplace of Gerson
ÍTALO DEL CIMA
BANGU
Bangu
Madureira
15,000
CENTRO
25,000
CAMPO GRANDE
RIO DE JANEIRO
América
108
Campo Grande
JACAREPAGUA
COPACABANA
SEE CENTRAL RIO FOR MORE DETAIL

AMÉRICA 1904

Rio League	1911, **13**, 14, 16, 17, 21, **22**, 28, 29, 31, 35, 50, 54, 55, **60**

101
071
ATLANTIC OCEAN

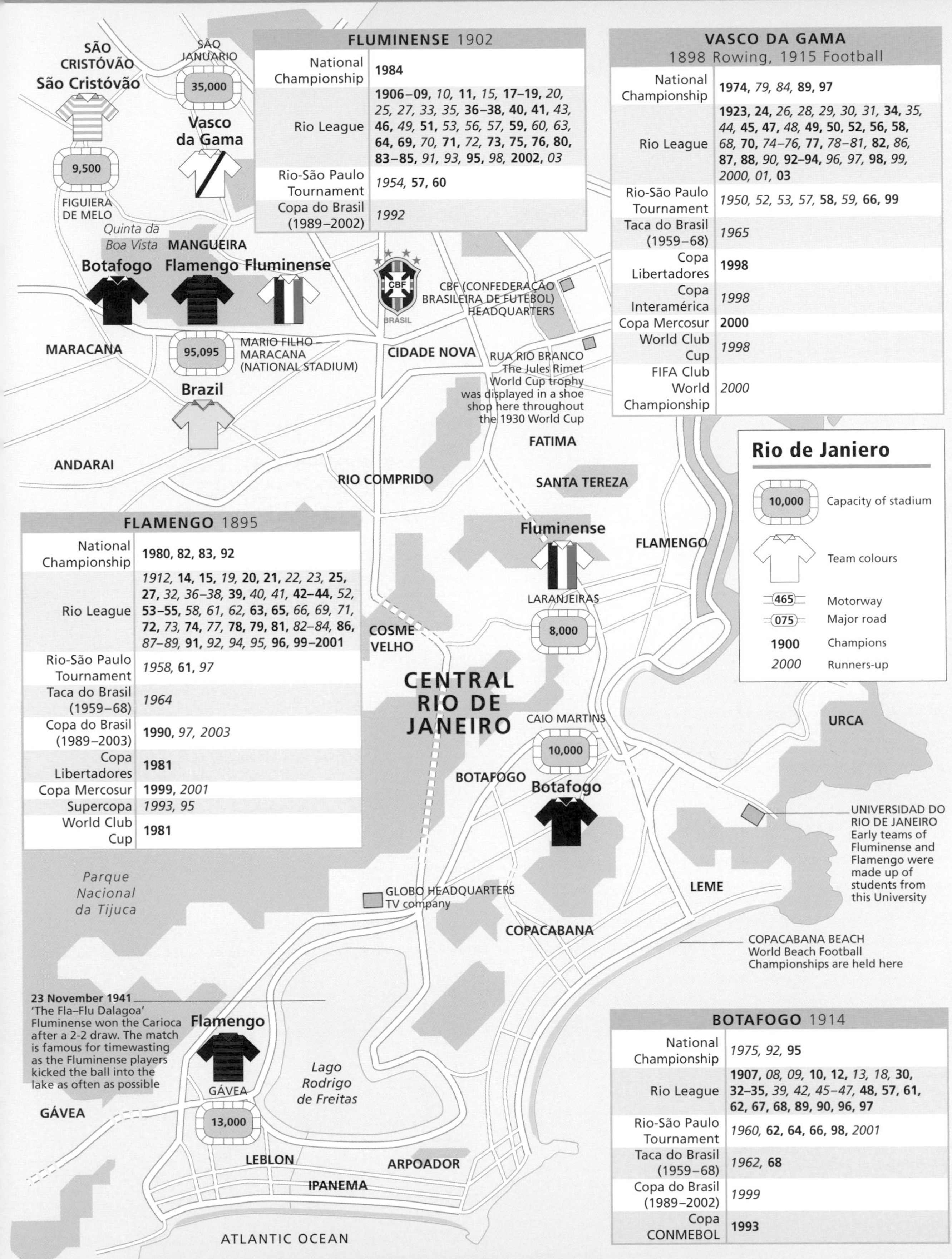

SÃO CRISTÓVÃO
São Cristóvão

9,500

FIGUIERA DE MELO

Quinta da Boa Vista

SÃO JANUARIO

35,000

Vasco da Gama

MANGUEIRA

Botafogo **Flamengo** **Fluminense**

MARACANA

95,095

MARIO FILHO – MARACANA (NATIONAL STADIUM)

Brazil

ANDARAI

CIDADE NOVA

CBF (CONFEDERAÇÃO BRASILEIRA DE FUTÉBOL) HEADQUARTERS

RUA RIO BRANCO
The Jules Rimet World Cup trophy was displayed in a shoe shop here throughout the 1930 World Cup

FATIMA

RIO COMPRIDO

SANTA TEREZA

Fluminense

LARANJEIRAS

8,000

FLAMENGO

COSME VELHO

CENTRAL RIO DE JANEIRO

CAIO MARTINS

10,000

BOTAFOGO

Botafogo

URCA

UNIVERSIDAD DO RIO DE JANEIRO
Early teams of Fluminense and Flamengo were made up of students from this University

GLOBO HEADQUARTERS
TV company

LEME

COPACABANA

COPACABANA BEACH
World Beach Football Championships are held here

Parque Nacional da Tijuca

23 November 1941
'The Fla–Flu Dalagoa'
Fluminense won the Carioca after a 2-2 draw. The match is famous for timewasting as the Fluminense players kicked the ball into the lake as often as possible

Flamengo

GÁVEA

13,000

Lago Rodrigo de Freitas

GÁVEA

LEBLON

ARPOADOR

IPANEMA

ATLANTIC OCEAN

FLUMINENSE 1902

National Championship	**1984**
Rio League	1906–09, 10, **11**, 15, **17–19**, 20, 25, 27, 33, 35, **36–38**, 40, 41, 43, **46**, 49, **51**, 53, **56**, **57**, **59**, **60**, **63**, **64**, **69**, **70**, **71**, 72, **73**, **75**, **76**, **80**, **83–85**, 91, 93, **95**, 98, **2002**, 03
Rio-São Paulo Tournament	1954, **57**, **60**
Copa do Brasil (1989–2002)	1992

VASCO DA GAMA
1898 Rowing, 1915 Football

National Championship	**1974**, 79, 84, 89, 97
Rio League	**1923**, 24, **26**, **28**, **29**, **30**, **31**, **34**, **35**, **44**, **45**, **47**, **48**, **49**, **50**, **52**, **56**, **58**, **68**, **70**, 74–76, **77**, 78–81, **82**, 86, **87**, **88**, **90**, 92–94, **96**, 97, **98**, 99, 2000, 01, **03**
Rio-São Paulo Tournament	1950, 52, 53, 57, **58**, **59**, 66, 99
Taca do Brasil (1959–68)	1965
Copa Libertadores	**1998**
Copa Interamérica	1998
Copa Mercosur	**2000**
World Club Cup	1998
FIFA Club World Championship	2000

Rio de Janiero

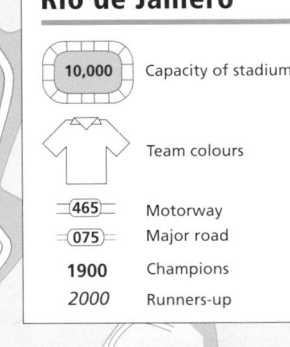

10,000	Capacity of stadium
	Team colours
465	Motorway
075	Major road
1900	Champions
2000	Runners-up

FLAMENGO 1895

National Championship	**1980**, **82**, **83**, **92**
Rio League	1912, **14**, **15**, **19**, **20**, **21**, **22**, **23**, **25**, **27**, 32, 36–38, **39**, **40**, **41**, 42–44, **52**, **53–55**, 58, **61**, **62**, **63**, **65**, **66**, **69**, **71**, **72**, 73, **74**, **77**, **78**, **79**, **81**, 82–84, **86**, 87–89, **91**, **92**, **94**, **95**, **96**, 99–2001
Rio-São Paulo Tournament	1958, **61**, 97
Taca do Brasil (1959–68)	1964
Copa do Brasil (1989–2003)	**1990**, 97, 2003
Copa Libertadores	**1981**
Copa Mercosur	**1999**, 2001
Supercopa	1993, 95
World Club Cup	**1981**

BOTAFOGO 1914

National Championship	1975, **92**, **95**
Rio League	**1907**, **08**, **09**, **10**, 12, **13**, **18**, **30**, **32–35**, 39, **42**, 45–47, **48**, **57**, **61**, **62**, **67**, **68**, 89, 90, 96, 97
Rio-São Paulo Tournament	1960, **62**, **64**, **66**, 98, 2001
Taca do Brasil (1959–68)	1962, **68**
Copa do Brasil (1989–2002)	1999
Copa CONMEBOL	**1993**

Brazil

FANS AND OWNERS

FOR MOST OF THEIR EXISTENCE Brazilian football clubs have operated in the legal twilight zone. As they have grown and their income has risen, they have become the perfect vehicles for those seeking influence, prestige and money. The chaotic, corrupt and opaque character of these clubs was supposed to be resolved by the Pele Law, passed in 1998 by the then Minister of Sport. The new law stated that Brazilian clubs were to become either civil or commercial companies regulated by law or, alternatively, they could spin off their professional arms as separate entities and outside investors could buy into them, bringing in modern management and much needed investment. The Pele Law also sought to modernize the archaic and inequitable player-club contracts and was therefore fiercely opposed by the leading teams or the Clube dos Treze, as they are better known. The 'Club of 13' was formed in 1997 to squeeze a better TV deal out of Globo, which they did. However, this being Brazil, the 13 are really 17.

Financial partners

Since the Pele Law came into force only a few clubs have explored the possibility of recruiting financial partners, and many of the schemes have ended in disaster. The American bank Hicks Muse, Tate and First (HMTF), operating as Pan-American Sports Teams, bought into Cruzeiro and Corinthians, while ISL, FIFA's marketing agents until their spectacular bankruptcy in mid-2001, bought into Grêmio and Flamengo. Nations Bank investment in Vasco da Gama has already been dissolved, while Parmalat has pulled out of its long-standing relationship with Palmeiras. But investors have rightly been cautious, as the Dias-Althoff report into Brazilian football in 2002 revealed that corruption and waste are endemic and numerous leading figures in the clubs, state football authorities and the CBF have been recommended for criminal prosecution, though as yet none have been brought to trial.

Violence on and off the pitch

The anarchy and viciousness of Brazil's clubs is paralleled by many of their fans. The big clubs have all acquired organized and often violent supporters' groups called *Torcida Organizada*. Equipped with firecrackers, noise bombs and, increasingly, with guns, these groups have ensured that violence inside and outside the grounds has been on the rise. In 2000, Vagner Jose Lima was killed when armed São Paulo fans attacked a small group of Corinthians supporters in the Bexiga district. São Paulo fans standing by their broken-down bus were shot at by a passing bus full of Santos fans. In 2001, Santos fans broke into the squad's training camp, attacking and berating the players for their poor performances. Four shootings were reported at the Bahia v Vitória derby in Salvador and shootings at Flamengo matches are common. Television coverage of, and judicial intervention in the violence is minimal as Globo seeks to protect its investments. But, whatever they show, the viciousness of the contemporary Brazilian game, dominated by fouling and diving, is mirrored in the stands. The concentration of power and money in the leading clubs is paralleled by the level of support for the big clubs. As the *Placar* survey shows, Flamengo, Corinthians, São Paulo, Vasco and Palmeiras are way out in front, with fans not only in their home towns but in other major cities.

Top: Can Lula clean up Brazilian football? Brazil's new president Luiz Inacio Lula da Silva has set himself some difficult tasks: abolishing hunger, equalizing incomes and cleaning up Brazilian football finances. No guesses for which will be the easiest.

Above: Vasco's president, Eurico Miranda, threatened to boycott the National Championship in retaliation to a fixture ban after violence at the stadium. Vasco's face-saving return to the championship began with this Miranda financed banner: 'Vasco is only playing in defence of its fans'.

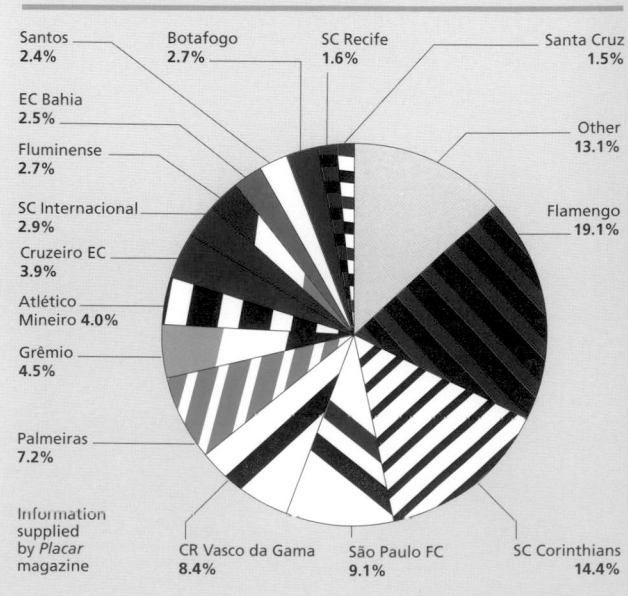

Club Support in Brazil 2001

Santos 2.4%
Botafogo 2.7%
SC Recife 1.6%
Santa Cruz 1.5%
EC Bahia 2.5%
Fluminense 2.7%
SC Internacional 2.9%
Cruzeiro EC 3.9%
Atlético Mineiro 4.0%
Grêmio 4.5%
Palmeiras 7.2%
Other 13.1%
Flamengo 19.1%
SC Corinthians 14.4%
São Paulo FC 9.1%
CR Vasco da Gama 8.4%

Information supplied by *Placar* magazine

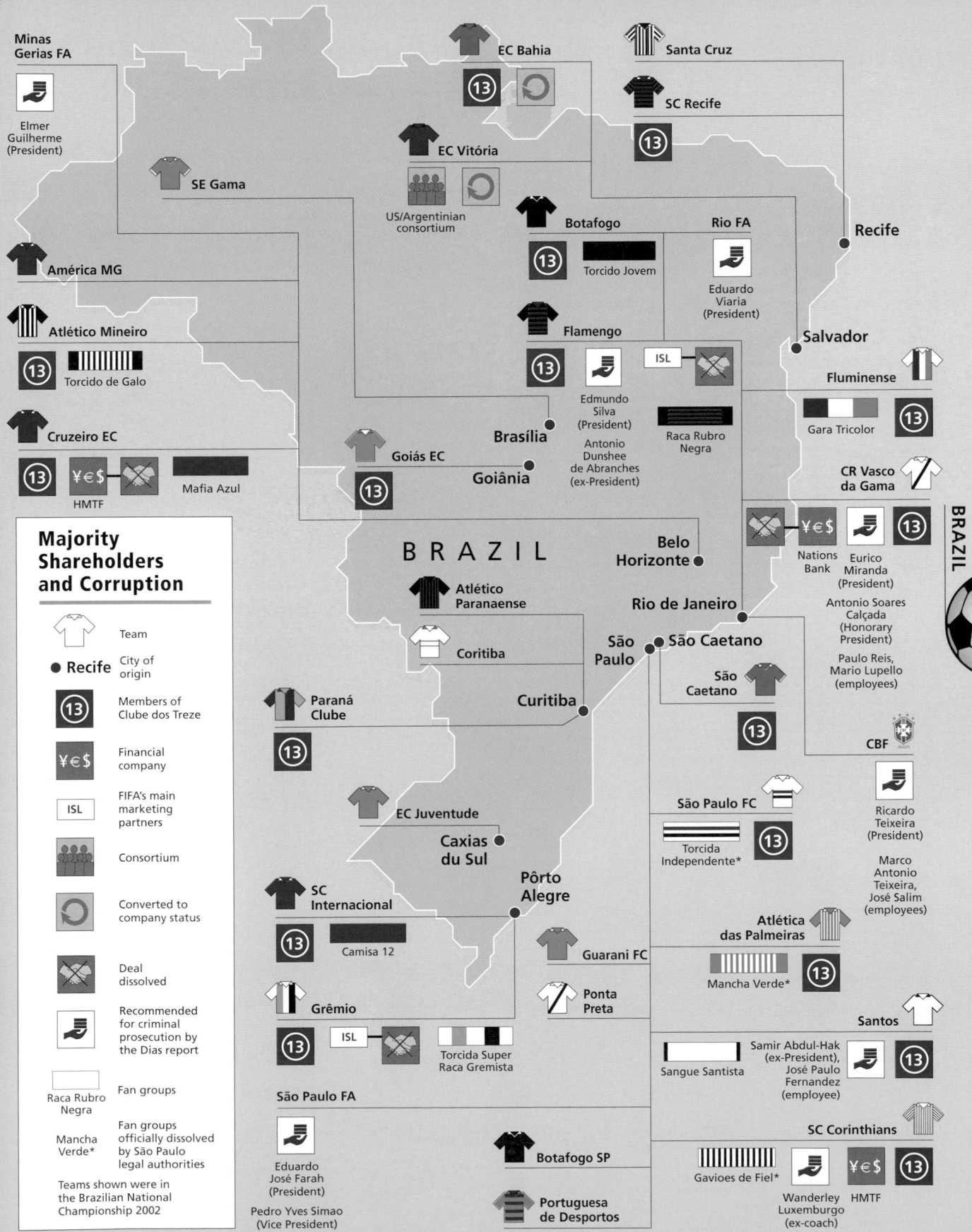

Minas
Gerias FA

Elmer
Guilherme
(President)

EC Bahia

Santa Cruz

SC Recife

13

13

SE Gama

EC Vitória

US/Argentinian
consortium

Recife

América MG

Botafogo

13

Torcido Jovem

Rio FA

Eduardo
Viaria
(President)

Atlético Mineiro

13 Torcido de Galo

Flamengo

13

Edmundo
Silva
(President)

Antonio
Dunshee
de Abranches
(ex-President)

ISL

Raca Rubro
Negra

Salvador

Fluminense

Gara Tricolor

13

Cruzeiro EC

13 ¥€$

HMTF Mafia Azul

Goiás EC

Goiânia

13

Brasília

B R A Z I L

Belo
Horizonte

Rio de Janeiro

CR Vasco
da Gama

13

Nations
Bank

¥€$

Eurico
Miranda
(President)

13

Antonio Soares
Calçada
(Honorary
President)

Paulo Reis,
Mario Lupello
(employees)

BRAZIL

Atlético
Paranaense

Coritiba

São
Paulo

São Caetano

São
Caetano

13

CBF

Paraná
Clube

13

Curitiba

São Paulo FC

Torcida
Independente*

13

Ricardo
Teixeira
(President)

Marco
Antonio
Teixeira,
José Salim
(employees)

EC Juventude

Caxias
du Sul

Pôrto
Alegre

Atlética
das Palmeiras

Mancha Verde*

13

SC
Internacional

13 Camisa 12

Guarani FC

Ponta
Preta

Santos

Grêmio

13 ISL ✕

Torcida Super
Raca Gremista

Sangue Santista

Samir Abdul-Hak
(ex-President),
José Paulo
Fernandez
(employee)

13

São Paulo FA

Eduardo
José Farah
(President)

Pedro Yves Simao
(Vice President)

Botafogo SP

Portuguesa
de Desportos

SC Corinthians

Gavioes de Fiel*

✋

Wanderley
Luxemburgo
(ex-coach)

¥€$

HMTF

13

Brazil

PLAYERS AND MANAGERS

FOOTBALL BEGAN IN BRAZIL as a game of the rich, white elite; black and mixed-race players were dissuaded, banned or disguised with make-up by the leading clubs until the rise of the predominantly black and very successful Vasco da Gama from Rio de Janeiro in the 1930s. Since the advent of professionalism, black players have dominated the game and the popular archetype on which their style of play is based is described as the *Malandro*: the wide boy from the *favellas*, who waltzes through life on a stream of trickery and cunning, guile and style, and who moves with the grace of the *capoeira* master (a black Brazilian version of *t'ai chi*). From the heady mix of black Brazilian urban culture sprang two generations of extraordinarily gifted, stylish players: Garrincha, Gerson, Pele, Jairzhino, Rivelino and Carlos Alberto, and with them came the 'Beautiful Game' as well as three World Cups.

Exodus

The great Brazilian teams of this golden era played their club football almost exclusively in Brazil, but with the steady decline of the Brazilian economy, an exodus of talent to Europe and Japan has become a tidal wave (see South American Exodus, pages 508–509). Today's leading Brazilian players (Cafu, Ronaldo, Roberto Carlos and Rivaldo) all play their football in Spain and Italy.

It is not only the Brazilian economy that has been in decline. The World Cup of 1970 represented the high point of Brazilian football. Despite a flickering renaissance in the early 1980s around players like Zico, Socrates and old-style manager Tele Santana, there has been a steady erosion of the *Malandro* as international and club managers have insisted on aggression, defence, persistent fouling and winning at any cost, exemplified by the dour, mechanical Brazilian team under Phil Scolari who only just scraped into the 2002 World Cup Finals – winning the tournament will have brought a welcome check to this despondent outlook. Brazilian managers have also been caught in the web of corruption that has engulfed Brazilian football, including ex-national coach Wanderley Luxemburgo, who was sacked in 2000 and is currently under investigation by the police.

Mario Zagallo brought a semblance of order to the Brazilian manager's job between 1995 and 1998. He is the longest-lasting manager of a national team that has had 125 managers since it first played an international match.

Top 11 International Caps

PLAYER	CAPS	GOALS	FIRST MATCH	LAST MATCH
Marcos Evangelista de Moeis **'Cafu'***	115	5	1990	2003
Claudio **Taffarel**	101	0	1987	1998
Djalma **do Santos**	98	3	1952	1968
Roberto Carlos da Silva*	95	7	1992	2003
Gylmar dos Santos Neves **'Gilmar'**	94	0	1953	1969
Carlos Caetano Beldorn Verri **'Dunga'**	91	6	1982	1998
Edson Arantes do Nascimento **'Pele'**	91	77	1957	1971
Roberto **Rivelino**	91	25	1965	1978
Nascimento dos Santos **Aldair***	81	3	1989	2001
Jair Ventura Filho **'Jairzinho'**	81	33	1963	1982
Emerson Leao	80	0	1970	1986

Top 10 International Goalscorers

PLAYER	GOALS	CAPS	FIRST MATCH	LAST MATCH
Edson Arantes do Nascimento **'Pele'**	77	91	1957	1971
Romario da Souza Faria*	54	68	1987	2001
Artur Antunes Coimbra **'Zico'**	48	71	1971	1989
Jose Roberto Gama de Oliveira **'Bebeto'**	38	75	1985	1998
Ronaldo Luis Nazario da Lima*	47	69	1994	2003
Rivaldo Vito Borba Ferreira	33	69	1993	2003
Jair Ventura Filho **'Jairzinho'**	33	81	1963	1982
Ademir Marques de Menezes	32	39	1945	1953
Eduardo Goncalves de Andrade **'Tostao'**	31	53	1966	1972
Thomaz Soaras da Silva **'Zizinho'**	30	55	1942	1957

* Indicates players still playing at least at club level.
Bold indicates players recognized by either their first name, last name or nickname. Nicknames are indicated between inverted commas.

Brazilian International Managers*

DATES	NAME	GAMES	WON	DRAWN	LOST
1979–80	Jaime Valente	12	7	2	3
1980–82	Tele Santana and	38	29	6	3
	Carlos Alberto Parreira	6	3	3	0
1983	Gilson Nunes,	3	2	0	1
	Carlos Alberto Parreira	7	1	4	2
	and Cleber Camerino	9	7	2	0
1984	Edu Antunes	3	1	1	1
	and Cleber Camerino	6	4	1	1
1985	Evaristo de Macedo	6	3	0	3
1985–86	Tele Santana	17	11	3	3
1986	Jair Pereira	4	2	2	0
1987–88	Carlos Alberto Silva	45	29	11	5
1989–90	Sebastiao Lazaroni	35	21	7	7
1990–91	Falcão	17	6	7	4
1991–92	Ernesto Paulo	8	4	1	3
1992–94	Carlos Alberto Parreira	45	26	14	4
1994–95	Mario Zagallo	3	3	0	0
1995	Pupo Giminez	5	3	2	0
1995–98	Mario Zagallo	90	65	17	8
1998–2000	Wanderley Luxemburgo	34	22	7	5
2000–01	Emerson Leao	10	3	4	3
2001–02	Luis Filipe Scolari	26	19	1	6
2002–03	Carlos Alberto Parreira	3	1	1	1

* Only includes managers who have been in charge on a regular basis.
All figures correct as of 30 April 2003.

Player of the Year

YEAR	PLAYER	CLUB
1973	Ancheta	Grêmio
1973	Cejas	Santos
1974	Zico	Flamengo
1975	Waldir Peres	São Paulo
1976	Elias Figueroa	Internacional
1977	Toninho Cerezo	Atlético Mineiro
1978	Falcão	Internacional
1979	Falcão	Internacional
1980	Toninho Cerezo	Atlético Mineiro
1981	Jesus	Grêmio
1982	Zico	Flamengo
1983	Costa	Atlético Paranaense
1984	Costa	Vasco da Gama
1985	Mahrino	Bangu Atlético
1986	Careca	São Paulo
1987	Renato Gaucho	Flamengo
1988	Taffarel	Internacional
1989	Rocha	São Paulo
1990	Sampaio	Santos
1991	Mauro da Silva	Bragantino
1992	Junior	Flamengo
1993	Sampaio	Palmeiras
1994	Marcio Amoroso	Guarani
1995	Giovanni	Santos
1996	Djalminha	Palmeiras
1997	Edmundo	Vasco da Gama
1998	Edilson	Corinthians
1999	Marcelinho	Corinthians
2000	Romario	Vasco da Gama
2001	Alex Mineiro	Atlético Paranaense
2002	Kaka	São Paulo

Awarded by *Placar* magazine as the Bola de Ouro.

Jairzinho was the first player ever to have scored in every round of the World Cup Finals on the way to victory. Here he celebrates the last goal of his record-breaking feat in the Final of the 1970 tournament against Italy in Mexico City.

Championship-Winning Managers

YEAR	MANAGER	CLUB
1971	Santana	Atlético Mineiro
1972	Brandao	Palmeiras
1973	Brandao	Palmeiras
1974	Travaglini	Vasco da Gama
1975	Minelli	Internacional
1976	Minelli	Internacional
1977	Minelli	São Paulo
1978	Silva	Guarani
1979	Andrade	Internacional
1980	Coutinho	Flamengo
1981	Andrade	Grêmio
1982	Torres	Flamengo
1983	Parriera	Flamengo
1984	Andrade	Coritiba
1985	Pepe	São Paulo
1986	Carlinhos	Flamengo
1987	Picerni	Sport Club Recife
1988	Macedo	Bahia
1989	Rosa	Vasco da Gama
1990	Batista	Corinthians
1991	Santana	São Paulo
1992	Carlinhos	Flamengo
1993	Luxemburgo	Palmeiras
1994	Luxemburgo	Palmeiras
1995	Autuori	Botafogo
1996	Scolari	Grêmio
1997	Lopes	Vasco da Gama
1998	Luxemburgo	Corinthians
1999	Oliveira	Corinthians
2000	Santana	Vasco da Gama
2001	Geninho	Atlético Paranaense
2002	Leao	Santos

BRAZIL

Top Goalscorers 1971–2002

SEASON	PLAYER	CLUB	GOALS
1971	Dario	Atlético Mineiro	15
1972	Dario	Atlético Mineiro	17
1972	Pedro Rocha	São Paulo	17
1973	Ramon	Santa Cruz	21
1974	Roberto Dinamite	Vasco da Gama	16
1975	Flávio	Internacional	16
1976	Dario	Internacional	16
1977	Reinaldo	Atlético Mineiro	28
1978	Paulinho	Vasco da Gama	19
1979	Roberto Cesar	Cruzeiro	12
1980	Zico	Flamengo	21
1981	Nunes	Flamengo	16
1982	Zico	Flamengo	20
1983	Serginho	Santos	22
1984	Roberto Dinamite	Vasco da Gama	16
1985	Edmar	Guarani	20
1986	Careca	São Paulo	25
1987	Muller	São Paulo	10
1988	Nilson	Internacional	15
1989	Túlio	Goiás	11
1990	Charles	Bahia	11

SEASON	PLAYER	CLUB	GOALS
1991	Paulinho	Santos	15
1992	Bebeto	Vasco da Gama	18
1993	Guga	Santos	15
1994	Túlio	Botafogo	19
1994	Amoroso	Guarani	19
1995	Túlio	Botafogo	23
1996	Nunes	Grêmio	16
1997	Edmundo	Vasco da Gama	29
1998	Viola	Santos	21
1999	Guilherme	Atlético Mineiro	28
2000	Adhemar	São Cãetano	22
2001	Alex Mineiro	Atlético Paranaense	21
2002	Fabiano	São Paulo	19
2002	Fabri	Grêmio	19

Romario da Souza Faria has been one of Brazil's leading goalscorers since the late 1980s. He began his career with Vasco da Gama, moved to Europe to play for PSV and Barcelona, before returning home to Vasco via Flamengo. His continued success was underlined when he was voted Brazilian Player of the Year in 2000.

Brazil

THE CAMPEONATO BRASILEIRO 1971–2002

BRAZIL WAS THE LAST major footballing nation to organize a national club tournament – the enormous size of the country, poor transport links and the huge inequalities in wealth and footballing prowess were major obstacles to overcome. However, in 1967, the Torneio Rio-São Paulo (between the leading clubs of the leading football cities) was expanded to include other state champions and renamed the Taça Roberto Gomes Pedrosa. In line with the then military dictatorship's desire for all things national, the Campeonato Brasileiro was first organized by the CBD in 1971. It began as a 20-team league with the top clubs going into a play-off round. Since then its format has changed every single year for almost three decades. Numbers of divisions, methods of qualification and classification, relegation and promotion have wildly fluctuated. Ticket sales were included in the classifications system in 1974, and in 1975 an extra point was awarded for winning matches by more than two goals. A struggle over TV money in 1987 saw two national tournaments – the big clubs' Copa União and the CBF's yellow module – played side-by-side.

In 1996, leading Rio club Fluminense was relegated but managed to maintain its position in the top flight by having the following year's league expanded by four clubs. However, this just delayed the inevitable as big clubs kept playing badly, so a two-season averaging system for relegation was introduced to try and bypass any awkward seasons. Nevertheless, Botafogo still managed to be relegated in 1999. The club went straight to the football authorities and won back two points from a game earlier in the season against São Paulo who had fielded an ineligible player. That meant that the small club Gama had to take the drop. Gama headed for the courts and was reinstated only to see FIFA ban the club from CBF leagues for having the temerity to resort to national courts rather than FIFA itself.

The deadlock was broken by the big clubs who organized a national championship – the monstrously complex 116-team Copa João Havelange – that began in 2000 with Gama and Botafogo both playing in the top division. Emblematic of the state of Brazilian football, a dreary, poorly attended championship culminated in a chaotic Final between Vasco and São Cāetano. Massive overcrowding in Vasco's stadium for the second leg led to a huge terrace crush, the game was abandoned and hundreds were injured.

Vasco's victory may have been the high point for Brazil's old guard. The escalating crisis of Brazilian football has opened the way for championship victories for smaller clubs (Atlético Paranaense and Santos).

While the emergency services attempted to deal with chaos at Vasco's São Januário stadium in the final play-off of the 2000 Brazilian championships, Eurico Miranda, Vasco president, tried to order ambulances and helicopters away, and demanded that the match be concluded. In a display of unabashed cynicism, he claimed the trophy as Vasco was leading when play was abandoned.

For all the fervour of Rio's big derby, neither Flamengo nor Fluminense have made a serious challenge on the Brazilian national championship for almost a decade, and both teams continue to disappoint their massive fan base.

BRAZIL

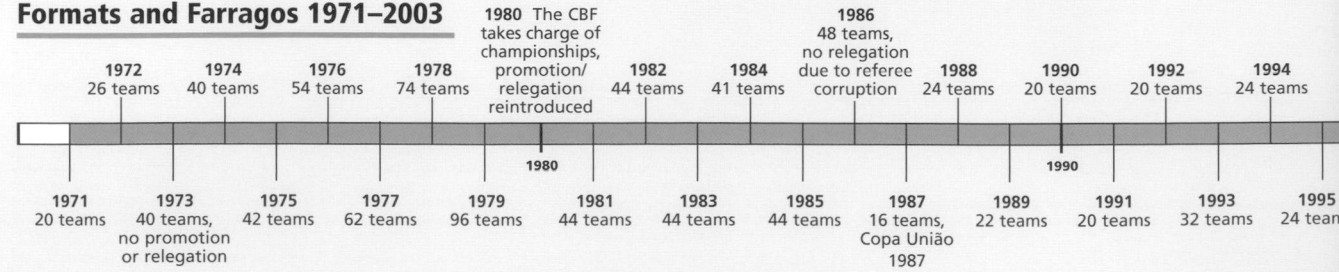

Formats and Farragos 1971–2003

1972 26 teams	

1980 The CBF takes charge of championships, promotion/relegation reintroduced

1986 48 teams, no relegation due to referee corruption

1972 26 teams
1974 40 teams
1976 54 teams
1978 74 teams
1982 44 teams
1984 41 teams
1988 24 teams
1990 20 teams
1992 20 teams
1994 24 teams

1980

1990

1971 20 teams
1973 40 teams, no promotion or relegation
1975 42 teams
1977 62 teams
1979 96 teams
1981 44 teams
1983 44 teams
1985 44 teams
1987 16 teams, Copa União 1987
1989 22 teams
1991 20 teams
1993 32 teams
1995 24 team

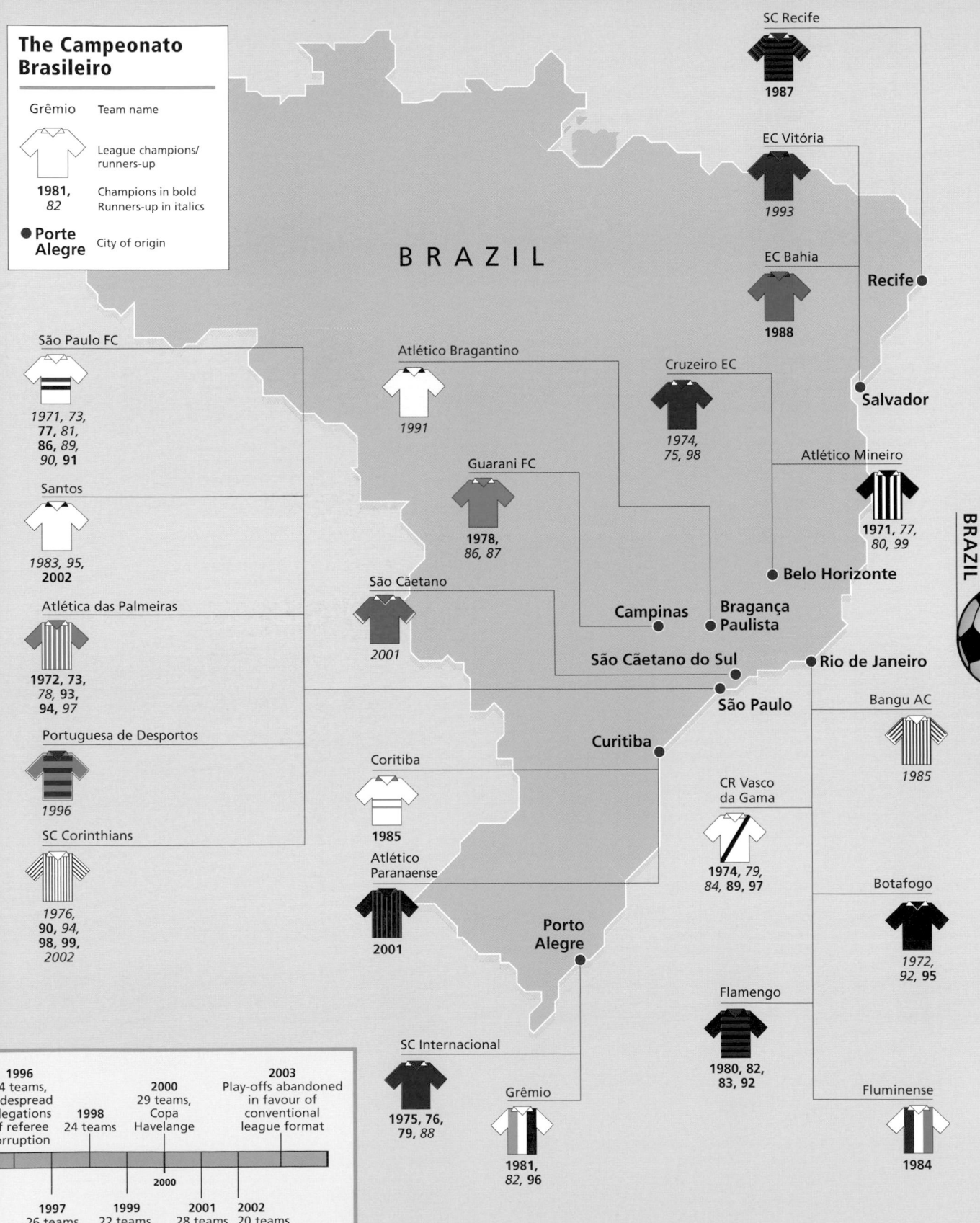

The Campeonato Brasileiro

Grêmio — Team name

League champions/ runners-up

1981, — Champions in bold
82 — Runners-up in italics

● **Porte Alegre** — City of origin

BRAZIL

BRAZIL

SC Recife
1987

EC Vitória
1993

EC Bahia
1988

● **Recife**

● **Salvador**

Atlético Mineiro
1971, *77,* *80,* **99**

Cruzeiro EC
1974, *75,* **98**

● **Belo Horizonte**

São Paulo FC
1971, 73, **77,** *81,* **86,** *89,* *90,* **91**

Santos
1983, 95, **2002**

Atlética das Palmeiras
1972, 73, *78,* **93,** **94,** **97**

Portuguesa de Desportos
1996

SC Corinthians
1976, **90,** **94,** **98,** **99,** *2002*

Atlético Bragantino
1991

Guarani FC
1978, *86, 87*

São Cãetano
2001

● **Campinas**

● **Bragança Paulista**

● **São Cãetano do Sul**

● **São Paulo**

● **Curitiba**

Coritiba
1985

Atlético Paranaense
2001

Porto Alegre

SC Internacional
1975, 76, *79, 88*

Grêmio
1981, *82,* **96**

CR Vasco da Gama
1974, *79,* **84,** **89,** **97**

● **Rio de Janeiro**

Bangu AC
1985

Botafogo
1972, *92,* **95**

Flamengo
1980, 82, **83,** **92**

Fluminense
1984

1996
24 teams, widespread allegations of referee corruption

1997
26 teams

1998
24 teams

1999
22 teams, the Gama scandal

2000
29 teams, Copa Havelange

2000

2001
28 teams

2002
20 teams

2003
Play-offs abandoned in favour of conventional league format

Brazil

BRASIL

Confederação Brasileira de Futebol
Founded: 1914
Joined FIFA: 1923
Joined CONMEBOL: 1916

THE ORGANIZATION OF Brazilian football parallels the uneven geography of this enormous nation. League football began at state rather than national level. The Campeonata Paulista de Futebol began in São Paulo in 1901. Rio's league, the Liga Metropolitan de Football, followed in 1905. For the first half of the 20th century Brazilian football was dominated by these two leagues, and a series of inter-city cups established the effective national champions. Simultaneously, state leagues were established all over the country, with significant areas of footballing strength developing beyond Rio and São Paulo.

With the creation of the Copa Libertadores de América, the Taca do Brasil was established as a national cup competition to determine Brazil's entrants. It was discontinued in 1968, replaced first by the Taca de Prata (or Roberto Gomes Pedrosa Cup) and then by a fully-fledged national league in 1971. The formats of the latter have changed in a complex and Byzantine fashion to ensure, irrespective of performance, regular pay days for the biggest clubs. Finally, in 2003, a conventional league format – with no play-offs – has been agreed for the National Championship. In 1989 a new national cup competition, the Copa do Brasil, was established with equally shifting formats and the winners also enter the Copa Libertadores alongside the national champions.

State leagues continue to run in the early part of the season ensuring an unrelenting schedule of football all year round.

São Paulo Championship Record 1902–2003

SEASON	CHAMPIONS	SEASON	CHAMPIONS
1902	São Paulo Athletic	1935	Santos/Portuguesa
1903	São Paulo Athletic	1936	Palestra Itália/Portuguesa
1904	São Paulo Athletic	1937	Corinthians
1905	Atlético Paulistano	1938	Corinthians
1906	Germania	1939	Corinthians
1907	Internacional	1940	Palestra Itália
1908	Atlético Paulistano	1941	Corinthians
1909	Atlética das Palmeiras	1942	Palmeiras
1910	Atlética das Palmeiras	1943	São Paulo
1911	São Paulo Athletic	1944	Palmeiras
1912	Americano	1945	São Paulo
1913	Americano/Atlético Paulista	1946	São Paulo
1914	Corinthians/Atlética São Bento	1947	Palmeiras
1915	Germania/Atlética das Palmeiras	1948	São Paulo
1916	Corinthians/Atlético Paulista	1949	São Paulo
1917	Atlético Paulistano	1950	Palmeiras
1918	Atlético Paulistano	1951	Corinthians
1919	Atlético Paulistano	1952	Corinthians
1920	Palestra Itália	1953	São Paulo
1921	Atlético Paulistano	1954	Corinthians
1922	Corinthians	1955	Santos
1923	Corinthians	1956	Santos
1924	Corinthians	1957	São Paulo
1925	Atlética São Bento	1958	Santos
1926	Palestra Itália/Atlético Paulista	1959	Palmeiras
1927	Palestra Itália/Atlético Paulista	1960	Santos
1928	Corinthians/Internacional	1961	Santos
1929	Corinthians/Atlético Paulista	1962	Santos
1930	Corinthians	1963	Palmeiras
1931	São Paulo	1964	Santos
1932	Palestra Itália	1965	Santos
1933	Palestra Itália	1966	Palmeiras
1934	Palestra Itália	1967	Santos

São Paulo Championship Record (*continued*)

SEASON	CHAMPIONS	SEASON	CHAMPIONS
1968	Santos	1987	São Paulo
1969	Santos	1988	Corinthians
1970	São Paulo	1989	São Paulo
1971	São Paulo	1990	Atlético Bragantino
1972	Palmeiras	1991	São Paulo
1973	Santos/Portuguesa	1992	São Paulo
1974	Palmeiras	1993	Palmeiras
1975	São Paulo	1994	Palmeiras
1976	Palmeiras	1995	Corinthians
1977	Corinthians	1996	Palmeiras
1978	Santos	1997	Corinthians
1979	Corinthians	1998	São Paulo
1980	São Paulo	1999	Corinthians
1981	São Paulo	2000	São Paulo
1982	Corinthians	2001	Corinthians
1983	Corinthians	2002	Ituano
1984	Santos	2003	Corinthians
1985	São Paulo		
1986	Atlética Internacional		

Rio Championship Record 1906–2003

SEASON	CHAMPIONS	SEASON	CHAMPIONS
1906	Fluminense	1950	Vasco da Gama
1907	Fluminense/Botafogo	1951	Fluminense
1908	Fluminense	1952	Vasco da Gama
1909	Fluminense	1953	Flamengo
1910	Botafogo	1954	Flamengo
1911	Fluminense	1955	Flamengo
1912	Botafogo/Paissandu	1956	Vasco da Gama
1913	América	1957	Botafogo
1914	Flamengo	1958	Vasco da Gama
1915	Flamengo	1959	Fluminense
1916	América	1960	América
1917	Fluminense	1961	Botafogo
1918	Fluminense	1962	Botafogo
1919	Fluminense	1963	Flamengo
1920	Flamengo	1964	Fluminense
1921	Flamengo	1965	Flamengo
1922	América	1966	Bangu Atlético
1923	Vasco da Gama	1967	Botafogo
1924	Vasco da Gama	1968	Botafogo
1925	Flamengo	1969	Fluminense
1926	São Cristovoa	1970	Vasco da Gama
1927	Flamengo	1971	Fluminense
1928	América	1972	Flamengo
1929	Vasco da Gama	1973	Fluminense
1930	Botafogo	1974	Flamengo
1931	América	1975	Fluminense
1932	Botafogo	1976	Fluminense
1933	Botafogo/Bangu Atlético	1977	Vasco da Gama
1934	Botafogo/Vasco da Gama	1978	Flamengo
1935	Botafogo/America	1979	Flamengo
1936	Fluminense	1979*	Flamengo
1937	Fluminense	1980	Fluminense
1938	Fluminense	1981	Flamengo
1939	Flamengo	1982	Vasco da Gama
1940	Fluminense	1983	Fluminense
1941	Fluminense	1984	Fluminense
1942	Flamengo	1985	Fluminense
1943	Flamengo	1986	Flamengo
1944	Flamengo	1987	Vasco da Gama
1945	Vasco da Gama	1988	Vasco da Gama
1946	Fluminense	1989	Botafogo
1947	Vasco da Gama	1990	Botafogo
1948	Botafogo	1991	Flamengo
1949	Vasco da Gama	1992	Vasco da Gama

BRAZIL

Rio Championship Record (*continued*)

SEASON	CHAMPIONS	SEASON	CHAMPIONS
1993	Vasco da Gama	1999	Flamengo
1994	Vasco da Gama	2000	Flamengo
1995	Fluminense	2001	Flamengo
1996	Flamengo	2002	Fluminense
1996*	Botafogo	2003	Vasco da Gama
1997	Botafogo		
1998	Vasco da Gama		

* Extra tournament.

Rio-São Paulo Tournament Record 1933–2003

SEASON	CHAMPIONS	RUNNERS-UP
1933	Palestra Itália	
1934–49	*no competition*	
1950	Corinthians	Vasco da Gama
1951	Palmeiras	Corinthians
1952	Portuguesa	Vasco da Gama
1953	Corinthians	Vasco da Gama
1954	Corinthians	Fluminense
1955	Portuguesa	Palmeiras
1956	*no competition*	
1957	Fluminense	Vasco da Gama
1958	Vasco da Gama	Flamengo
1959	Santos	Vasco da Gama
1960	Fluminense	Botafogo
1961	Flamengo	Palmeiras
1962	Botafogo	Palmeiras
1963	Santos	Corinthians
1964	Santos/Botafogo	
1965	Palmeiras	Portuguesa/São Paulo
1966	Corinthians/Santos/ Vasco da Gama/Botafogo	
1967–92	*no competition*	
1993	Palmeiras	Corinthians
1994–96	*no competition*	
1997	Santos	Flamengo
1998	Botafogo	São Paulo
1999	Vasco da Gama	Santos
2000	Palmeiras	Atlético Mineiro
2001	São Paulo	Botafogo
2002	Corinthians	São Paulo
2003	Corinthians	São Paulo

Brazilian National Championship Record 1971–2002

SEASON	CHAMPIONS	RUNNERS-UP
1971	Atlético Mineiro	São Paulo
1972	Palmeiras	Botafogo
1973	Palmeiras	São Paulo
1974	Vasco da Gama	Cruzeiro
1975	Internacional	Cruzeiro
1976	Internacional	Corinthians
1977	São Paulo	Atlético Mineiro
1978	Guarani	Palmeiras
1979	Internacional	Vasco da Gama
1980	Flamengo	Atlético Mineiro
1981	Grêmio	São Paulo
1982	Flamengo	Grêmio
1983	Flamengo	Santos
1984	Fluminense	Vasco da Gama
1985	Coritiba	Bangu Atlético
1986	São Paulo	Guarani
1987	Sport Club Recife	Guarani
1988	Bahia	Internacional
1989	Vasco da Gama	São Paulo
1990	Corinthians	São Paulo
1991	São Paulo	Atlético Bragantino
1992	Flamengo	Botafogo
1993	Palmeiras	Vitória
1994	Palmeiras	Corinthians
1995	Botafogo	Santos

Brazilian National Championship Record (*continued*)

SEASON	CHAMPIONS	RUNNERS-UP
1996	Grêmio	Portuguesa
1997	Vasco da Gama	Palmeiras
1998	Corinthians	Cruzeiro
1999	Corinthians	Atlético Mineiro
2000	Vasco da Gama	São Cãetano
2001	Atlético Paranaense	São Cãetano
2002	Santos	Corinthians

Brazilian National Championship Summary

TEAM	TOTALS	CHAMPIONS & RUNNERS-UP (BOLD) (*ITALICS*)
Palmeiras	4, 2	**1972, 73, 78, 93, 94,** *97*
Vasco da Gama	4, 2	**1974,** *79, 84,* **89, 97,** *2000*
Flamengo	4, 0	**1980, 82, 83, 92**
São Paulo	3, 5	*1971, 73,* **77,** *81,* **86,** *89, 90,* **91**
Corinthians	3, 3	*1976,* **90, 94, 98, 99,** *2002*
Internacional	3, 1	**1975, 76, 79,** *88*
Grêmio	2, 1	**1981,** *82,* **96**
Atlético Mineiro	1, 3	**1971,** *77, 80, 99*
Botafogo	1, 2	**1972,** *92,* **95**
Guarani	1, 2	**1978,** *86, 87*
Santos	1, 2	*1983, 95,* **2002**
Atlético Paranaense	1, 0	**2001**
Bahia	1, 0	**1988**
Coritiba	1, 0	**1985**
Fluminense	1, 0	**1984**
Sport Club Recife	1, 0	**1987**

This summary only features clubs that have won the Brazilian National Championship. For a full list of league champions and runners-up please see the League Record above.

Copa do Brasil Record 1989–2003

YEAR	WINNERS	SCORE	RUNNERS-UP
1989	Grêmio	0-0, 2-1 (2 legs)	Sport Club Recife
1990	Flamengo	1-0, 0-0 (2 legs)	Goias
1991	Criciuma	1-1, 0-0 (2 legs)	Grêmio
1992	Internacional	1-2, 1-0 (2 legs)	Fluminense
1993	Cruzeiro	0-0, 2-1 (2 legs)	Grêmio
1994	Grêmio	0-0, 1-0 (2 legs)	Ceara
1995	Corinthians	2-1, 1-0 (2 legs)	Grêmio
1996	Cruzeiro	1-1, 2-1 (2 legs)	Palmeiras
1997	Grêmio	0-0, 2-2 (2 legs)	Flamengo
1998	Palmeiras	0-1, 2-0 (2 legs)	Cruzeiro
1999	Juventude	2-1, 0-0 (2 legs)	Botafogo
2000	Cruzeiro	0-0, 2-1 (2 legs)	São Paulo
2001	Grêmio	2-2, 3-1 (2 legs)	Corinthians
2002	Corinthians	2-1, 1-1 (2 legs)	Brasiliense
2003	Cruzeiro	1-1, 3-1 (2 legs)	Flamengo

Copa do Brasil Summary

TEAM	TOTALS	WINNERS & RUNNERS-UP (BOLD) (*ITALICS*)
Grêmio	4, 3	**1989,** *91,* **93, 94,** *95,* **97, 2001**
Cruzeiro	4, 1	**1993, 96,** *98,* **2000, 03**
Corinthians	2, 1	**1995,** *2001,* **02**
Flamengo	1, 2	**1990,** *97,* **2003**
Palmeiras	1, 1	*1996,* **98**
Criciuma	1, 0	**1991**
Internacional	1, 0	**1992**
Juventude	1, 0	**1999**
Botafogo	0, 1	*1999*
Brasiliense	0, 1	*2002*
Ceara	0, 1	*1994*
Fluminense	0, 1	*1992*
Goias	0, 1	*1990*
São Paulo	0, 1	*2000*
Sport Club Recife	0, 1	*1989*

BRAZIL

Argentina

THE SEASON IN REVIEW 2002–03

ARGENTINIAN FOOTBALL OPERATED IN THE SHADOW of a disastrous World Cup performance in Japan in 2002 – made all the worse for the burden of expectation that the national team carried into the tournament. In the wake of a severe economic downturn, political chaos and street protest, the national team's ignominious exit from the first round was particularly hard to swallow. Worse still, the collapse of the European transfer market has meant that a vital financial lifeline to the heavily indebted clubs had dried up. At the bottom of the league, Talleres Cordoba failed to pay its electricity bills and found the lights turned off.

Worse, the persistent problem of violence and intimidation inside and outside football grounds will not go away. Matters peaked in May when coaches carrying supporters from River Plate and Newell's Old Boys crossed each other on the motorway. A massive roadway fight ensued in which two fans were killed. Although the police arrested over 900 supporters, no one was charged. This is the tip of the iceberg of an inability and perhaps unwillingness of the police to control disorder and the pervasive culture of corruption, violence and drug dealing among core sections of the fans. Police Chief Eduardo Capuchetti said of his officers' relationship with the barra bravas, 'If we don't accept their conditions, like allowing them to enter with drugs, they promise outrage on the terraces. Sometimes the police must consider the safety of the event and let them in.' Kidnappings again abounded in the desperate search for easy money that pervades urban Argentina. Independiente star Gabriel Militio paid for his father's release. Banfield midfielder Jorge Cevera was also captured.

In this context it is amazing what an injection of cash can do. Daniel Grinbank, a music entrepreneur and long-time fan of struggling Independiente, gathered together a business consortium to invest in the club. With new coach America Gallego and a new squad, Independiente, who began the season as the most likely

Right, top: Marcelo Delgado of Boca Juniors eludes River Plate's Celso Ayala. Delgado scored twice as Boca won the big Derby 2-1 and ended River's title run. After the game, fighting raged between fans and police inside and outside the stadium.

Right: Nestor Silvera and Frederico Insua of Independiente celebrate Silvera's goal against San Lorenzo. Silvera was the championship's top scorer while he ran the 'red devils' midfield.

Right: Manuel Pellegrini, Chilean coach of River Plate. Despite finishing third in the championship, River's fans were very unhappy with the team's performance: two matches had to be abandoned after crowd disturbances.

Apertura League Table 2002–03

CLUB	P	W	D	L	F	A	Pts
Independiente	19	13	4	2	48	19	43
Boca Juniors	19	12	4	3	32	15	40
River Plate	19	11	3	5	35	23	36
Chacarita Juniors	19	9	3	7	19	21	30
Vélez Sarsfield	19	8	4	7	23	19	28
Racing Club	19	8	4	7	28	28	28
Colón	19	7	7	5	26	26	28
Arsenal	19	7	6	6	29	25	27
San Lorenzo	19	7	6	6	28	25	27
Newell's Old Boys	19	7	6	6	23	22	27
Lanús	19	6	8	5	21	24	26
Banfield	19	6	7	6	21	17	25
Rosario Central	19	7	4	8	36	34	25
Unión	19	6	5	8	26	28	23
Talleres	19	5	8	6	23	27	23
Gimnasia LP	19	4	8	7	18	24	20
Olimpo	19	5	5	9	20	30	20
Nueva Chicago	19	3	6	10	20	29	15
Estudiantes	19	4	3	12	21	36	15
Huracán	19	2	5	12	17	42	11

Apertura Top Goalscorers

PLAYER	CLUB	GOALS
Andres Silvera	Independiente	16
Cesar Carignano	Colón	11
Luciano Figueroa	Rosario Central	10
Marcelo Delgado	Boca Juniors	9
Silvio González	Arsenal	9

Ten years of waiting is over: Gabriel Milito and the Independiente fans celebrate winning the opening championship after beating San Lorenzo 3-0 to clinch the title.

Small is Beautiful. Newly-promoted Arsenal (in blue and red), one of the only solvent clubs in Argentinian football, dug in and stayed up this season, finishing in eighth place in the Apertura.

ARGENTINA

candidates for relegation, stormed to the Apertura title. Gallego's team was built on the spine of defender Gabrille Milito – easily the best player of the tournament, who had played most of last season in the reserves – midfielder Frederico Insua and striker Andres Silva. Boca chased them all the way, but will rue dropping points in the 1-1 draw with Independiente, conceding a last-minute goal. It was not enough to save Boca's Uruguayan coach Oscar Tabarez, who made way for Boca favourite Carlos Biannchi. The season also saw the return of another old favourite – Carlos Bilardo, World Cup-winning manager in 1986, who returned to his old club Estudiantes La Plata promising to rescue them from endless mid-table mediocrity.

The strongest opening in the Clausura was made by Racing Club winning its three opening games. Alone among the Argentinian coaches in the Copa Libertadores 2003, Racing coach Osvaldo Ardilles fielded his strongest sides in both international and domestic competition. Boca and River played virtually different teams. The strain was too much for Racing, who had struggled all season to match the demands of fitness that Ardilles's pressing game had placed upon them. The team went out of the second round of the Libertadores, tumbled down the table and Ardilles, against the wishes of fans and management, resigned. The field was open for three contenders: River and the front two for most of the tournament – Boca and Vélez Sarsfield.

Vélez has fielded the youngest squad in the league under coach Carlos Ischia, and without the distraction of the Libertadores has played with élan. River started badly and continues to miss Ariel Ortega, now at Fenerbaçhe, and European transfer money to buy him or anyone else back. Nonetheless, Pelligrini's squad has shaped up and climbed back to the top of the table. Fernando Cavenaghi and Andres D'Allessandro continue to impress. Boca, preoccupied with its progress to the final of the 2003 Copa Libertadores, lost key matches, beaten at Velez 2-0. On the penultimate weekend of the championship Vélez lost to Estudiantes and River Plate won the Clausura after beating Olimpo 2-0.

Clausura League Table 2002–03 – matches played up to 30 June

CLUB	P	W	D	L	F	A	Pts
River Plate	18	13	4	1	42	15	43
Boca Juniors	18	12	3	3	34	16	39
Vélez Sarsfield	18	12	2	4	27	11	38
Rosario Central	18	9	7	2	33	16	34
Olimpo (Bahía Blanca)	18	8	4	6	21	17	28
Colón	18	6	8	4	18	14	26
Nueva Chicago	18	7	5	6	29	30	26
San Lorenzo	18	7	5	6	26	28	26
Estudiantes LP	18	6	7	5	22	18	25
Gimnasia LP	18	7	4	7	21	26	25
Lanús	18	7	3	8	26	28	24
Racing Club	18	5	7	6	23	23	22
Arsenal	18	4	9	5	12	13	21
Talleres	18	5	5	8	22	25	20
Banfield	18	5	5	8	15	20	20
Newell's Old Boys	18	4	7	7	19	25	19
Independiente	18	4	6	8	13	24	18
Unión	18	4	5	9	18	27	17
Chacarita Juniors	18	2	5	11	10	22	11
Huracán	18	1	3	14	12	45	6

Promoted teams: Union relegated after 18 games. One relegation and two promotion spots still undecided as of 30 June 2003.

Right, top: River Plate recapture some form, beating Racing Club.

Right, middle: Hurucán fans protest their undying faith, but they will probably be doing so in the Second Division next year. Hurucán's appalling season continues.

Right: The young Vélez squad celebrates a last minute goal over title rivals Boca Juniors.

International Club Performances 2002

CLUB	COMPETITION	PROGRESS
Boca Juniors	Copa Libertadores	Quarter-finals
	Copa Sudamericana	1st Round
River Plate	Copa Libertadores	2nd Round
	Copa Sudamericana	1st Round
San Lorenzo	Copa Libertadores	Group Stage
	Copa Sudamericana	Winners
Talleres	Copa Libertadores	Group Stage
Racing Club	Copa Sudamericana	Quarter-finals
Gimnasia LP	Copa Sudamericana	Quarter-finals

Right: Marcello Delgado of Boca Juniors takes the ball past Andres Anguilo of Independiente Medellín. Boca went to Colombia for the second leg of its Copa Libertadores semi-final and came away with another Libertadores final place.

Above: Osvaldo Ardilles in pensive mood. After fighting and losing on international and domestic fronts he resigned.

Left, above: The 172nd Superclassico ends 2-2 as River and Boca trade blows.

Below: Carlos Bianchi – wooed by Barcelona – chose to return to Boca Juniors for the Clausura and another crack at the Copa Libertadores, which he won with the club in 2000 and 2001.

ARGENTINA

Association Football in Argentina

1860s: British sailors bring football to Buenos Aires — 1860

1865

1865: Buenos Aires Football Club (now defunct) founded

1870

1882: Alexander Watson Hutton arrives in Buenos Aires — 1875

1880

1887: Quilmes and Gimnasia y Esgrima (La Plata) (oldest surviving clubs) founded — 1885

1890

1891: First championship played in Buenos Aires

1893: Argentine Association Football League first played — 1895

1900

1901: First international, v Uruguay, won 3-2, venue: Montevideo — 1905

1906: First provincial league formed: Liga Santiaguena de Futbol — 1910

1912: Rival Federacion Argentina de Football League set up — 1915

Affiliation to FIFA

1914: Federacion Argentina de Football League disbanded — 1920

1925

1916: Affiliation to CONMEBOL

1919: Associacion Amateurs founded as separate league in Buenos Aires — 1930

1935

1926: Last season of Associacion Amateurs

1931: Professionalism introduced and professional league established — 1940

1945

1948: Players' strike: mass exodus of professionals to Colombia — 1950

1955

1950 and 1954: President Peron bans national team from World Cup — 1960

1967: National and Metropolitan (Buenos Aires) championships run in same season — 1965

1970

1968: Buenos Aires: 74 died, 150 injured in crush and stand collapse at River v Boca match — 1975

1978: Argentina win World Cup in Buenos Aires — 1980

1986: Single national championship established — 1985

1990

1992: National championship shifts to Apertura and Clausura format — 1995

2000

2005

Argentina celebrates as Mario Kempes scores to give Argentina the lead during extra time in the 1978 World Cup Final in Buenos Aires.

International Competitions

1910:	●	■
1916:	▲	■
1917:	▲	
1920:	●	■
1921:	●	■
1923:	▲	
1924:	▲	
1925:	●	■
1926:	●	
1927:	●	
1929:	●	
1930:	▲	
1935:	▲	
1937:	●	■
1941:	●	
1942:	▲	
1945:	●	
1946:	●	■
1947:	●	
1955:	●	
1957:	●	
1959*:	●▲	■

Key

▦	International football
⚽	Affiliation to FIFA
⚽	Affiliation to CONMEBOL
✿	Disaster
■	World Cup host
●	World Cup winner
▲	World Cup runner-up
■	Copa América host
●	Copa América winner
▲	Copa América runner-up
○	Competition winner
△	Competition runner-up

* An extra unofficial tournament was held in 1959. See pages 370–71

Argen	–	Argentinos Juniors
Boca	–	CA Boca Juniors
Estud	–	CA Estudiantes
Indep	–	CA Independiente
Newell	–	CA Newell's Old Boys
River	–	CA River Plate
Rosario	–	CA Rosario Central
Racing	–	Racing Club
San L	–	San Lorenzo
Vélez	–	Vélez Sarsfield
Lanús	–	CA Lanús

Copa Libertadores

1963:			△Boca
1964:	○Indep		
1965:	○Indep		
1966:			△River
1967:	▲	○Racing	
1968:		○Estud	
1969:		○Estud	
1970:		○Estud	
1971:			△Estud
1972:	○Indep		
1973:	○Indep		
1974:	○Indep		
1975:	○Indep		
1976:			△River
1977:	○Boca		
1978:	● ■ ○Boca		
1979:			△Boca
1984:	○Indep		
1985:	○Argen		
1986:	●	○River	
1987:			
1988:			△Newell
1990:	▲		
1991:	●		
1992:			△Newell
1993:	●		
1994:	○Vélez		
1995:	○River		
1996:			
1997:			
1998:			
2000:	○Boca		
2001:	○Boca		
2002:			

Copa CONMEBOL

1993:	○Rosario
1995:	○Lanús
1996:	△Lanús
1997:	△Rosario

Copa Sudamericana

2002:	○San L

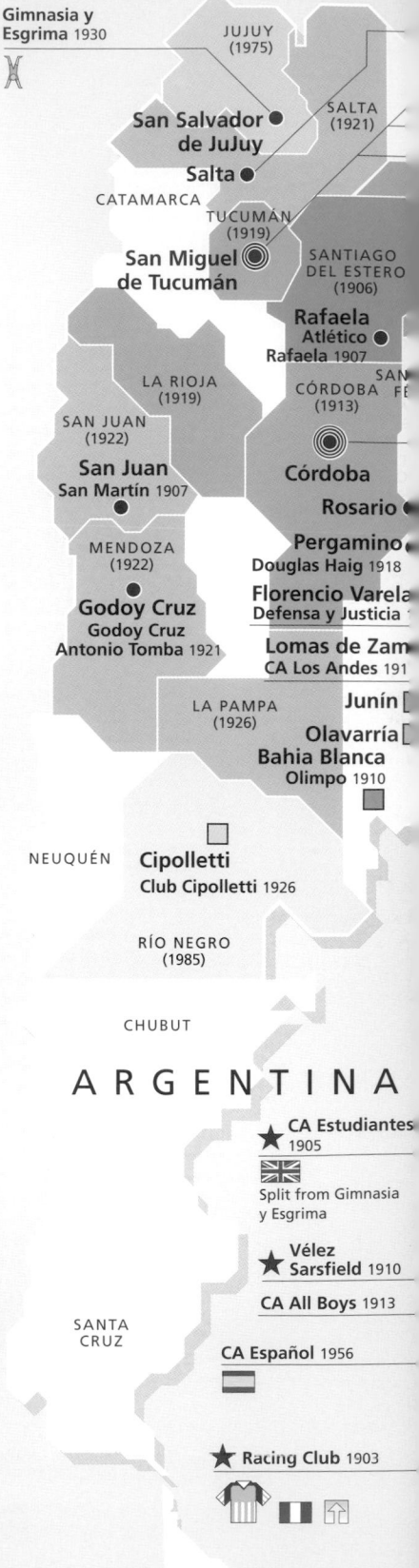

Gimnasia y Esgrima 1930

JUJUY (1975)

San Salvador de JuJuy

SALTA (1921)

Salta

CATAMARCA

TUCUMÁN (1919)

San Miguel de Tucumán

SANTIAGO DEL ESTERO (1906)

Rafaela
Atlético
Rafaela 1907

LA RIOJA (1919)

CÓRDOBA (1913)

SAN FE

SAN JUAN (1922)

San Juan
San Martín 1907

Córdoba

Rosario

Pergamino
Douglas Haig 1918

MENDOZA (1922)

Florencio Varela
Defensa y Justicia

Godoy Cruz
Godoy Cruz
Antonio Tomba 1921

Lomas de Zam
CA Los Andes 191

LA PAMPA (1926)

Junín

Olavarría

Bahia Blanca
Olimpo 1910

NEUQUÉN

Cipolletti
Club Cipolletti 1926

RÍO NEGRO (1985)

CHUBUT

ARGENTINA

CA Estudiantes 1905

Split from Gimnasia y Esgrima

Vélez Sarsfield 1910

CA All Boys 1913

SANTA CRUZ

CA Español 1956

Racing Club 1903

Argentina

ORIGINS AND GROWTH OF FOOTBALL

IN THE LAST QUARTER of the 19th century, Buenos Aires had a vibrant British community of around 40,000 people, with their own network of banks, schools and social events. It was in this outpost of Britain's informal empire that Buenos Aires Football Club was founded in 1867. In 1882, Alexander Watson Hutton arrived to teach at St Andrew's Scottish School. In 1884, he founded his own English high school, hired a games master and started football both there and at other schools in the city. A championship was first played between these teams in 1891. In 1893, under Hutton's leadership, five clubs founded the Argentine Association Football League, a championship which has continued unbroken to the present day.

The growth of the sport was rapid. By 1901, the AAFL were organizing four divisions in Buenos Aires alone. Outside the capital the first club was Lobos Athletic (1892), while Newell's Old Boys (1903) and Rosario Central (1905) established football in Rosario, Argentina's second city. Regular internationals with Uruguay across the River Plate began in 1901. In the first decade of the 20th century football became progressively less British and more Argentinian. The biggest clubs (Racing, Boca and River Plate) emerged from immigrant and indigenous groups. The AFA began to publish rules in Spanish. The transition of power and influence became clear when the annual match between Argentinos and Británicos saw Británicos lose 5-1, a defeat from which it never recovered.

The national organization of football was bedevilled by successive splits (1912–14, 1919–27) and the formation of alternative national organizations and rival leagues. Matters were settled due to pressure from the onset of professionalism, the need to stop the best players going to play in Italy, and the need to rationalize impossibly large leagues and uneven competition between clubs. In 1931, a national professional league of 18 big clubs was established.

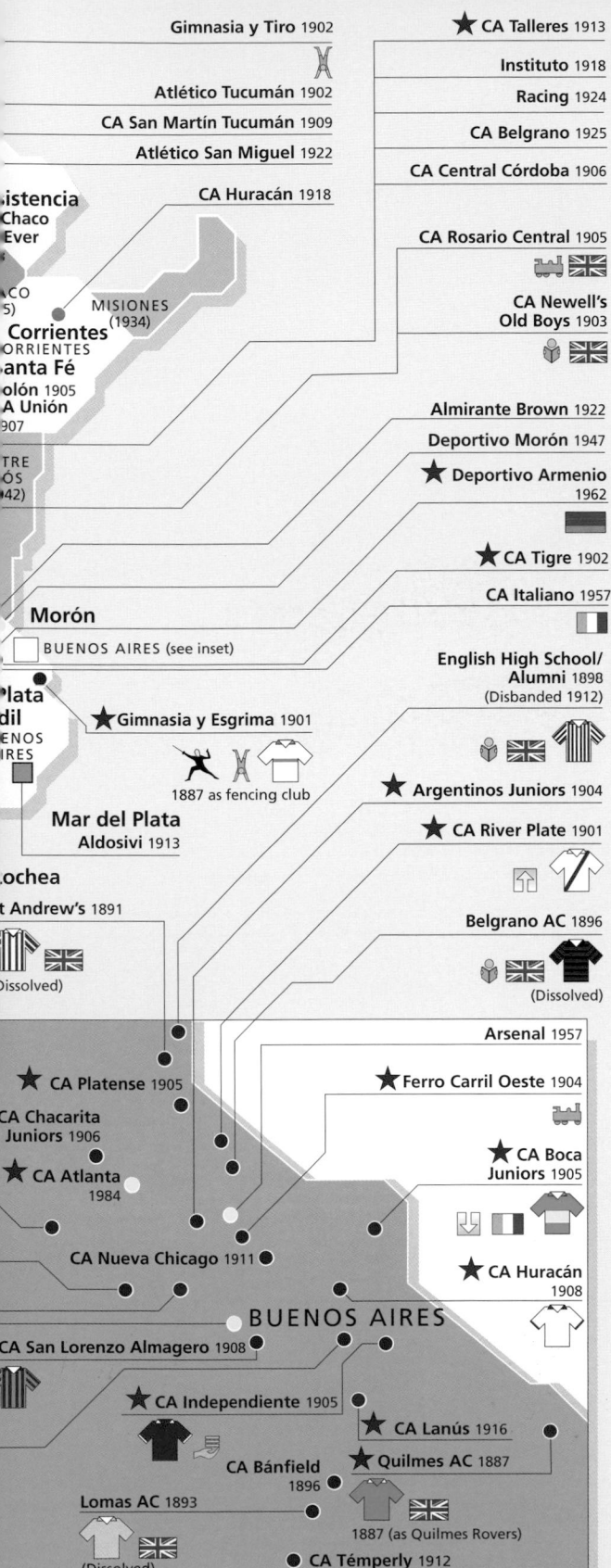

Argentina: The main clubs

Colón 1905	Team name with year of formation		Pre-professional champions
●	Club formed before 1912		Armenian origins
●	Club formed 1912–25		British origins
●	Club formed 1925–50		French origins
○	Club formed after 1950		Italian origins
JUJUY (1975)	State (year of Championship foundation)		Spanish origins
			Railway workers
	Founded 1900–10		Originated from a fencing club
	Founded 1901–20		Originated from a gymnastics club
	Founded 1920–50		Originated from a school
	Founded 1950–80		Shop workers
	Founded 1980–95		
	No championship		Elite
☐	City with regional league (colour coded as above)		Working class
★	Founder members of pre-professional league		Colours unknown

ARGENTINA

Buenos Aires

FOOTBALL CITY

ARGENTINA

SOME OF THE HISTORY OF BUENOS AIRES can be seen in the pattern and density of the football clubs that stud this enormous city of over 11 million people. In the 1860s, Buenos Aires had a population of just 170,000, of whom maybe 40,000 were Britons organizing and servicing a massive wave of British investment in Argentina. Schools, colleges, social and athletics clubs sprung up. As early as 1867, a British Buenos Aires Football Club had been set up, only to switch to rugby in 1887. The arrival of Alexander Watson Hutton at St. Andrews Scottish School in 1882, and at the English High School in 1884, was a catalyst. Teams at his schools began to play old boys clubs, and in 1891 a local championship was held. It was repeated in 1893 and has been played ever since.

The decline of British influence

In the following decade, dozens of British clubs appeared all over the city, some beginning to attract spectators. But in 1901, an Argentinian fencing and gymnastic club in La Plata – Argentina's new administrative centre to the south of Buenos Aires – formed a football section. Although the league was still dominated by British teams like Alumni, Lomas Athletic and Belgrano, the shift to Spanish-speaking players and Argentinian teams gathered pace quickly. The city's biggest clubs were founded in a few short years: River Plate in 1901, Racing Club in 1903, Boca Juniors and Independiente in 1905. By 1912, the AFA was using Spanish, and Alumni, for one, had disbanded.

Simultaneously, Buenos Aires grew explosively. By 1914, it had grown almost ten-fold with 1.5 million inhabitants, and it has barely stopped since. Its regular, grid-like structure created a series of neighbourhoods with clear boundaries, which have often been populated with specific immigrant groups or social classes, and every neighbourhood has acquired its own football team. The names speak for themselves: Deportivo Italiano, Deportivo Armenio, Deportivo Español, the list goes on. Everything about Buenos Aires' development was accelerated. British teams, including Southampton, Nottingham Forest, Tottenham and Everton, were regularly touring the city before the First World War. International matches with Uruguay were played regularly, and the first informal South American championship was held in the city in 1910.

The big city teams

The 1920s were consumed by the struggle over payments and professionalism until, in 1931, a professional league was established and the biggest teams in the city came to define and dominate the game. River Plate and Boca Juniors were both founded in Boca, the poor docks area in the city centre. River, which was formed from the merger of Santa Rosa and Rosales, migrated north and settled in the Retiro district of the city, acquiring a mass following with a distinctly elite tone. Boca, founded by an Irishman and a group of Italian students, has stayed close to its roots in the district. Alternately the two strongest teams through this era, their derby matches remain the highpoint of the city's season. Further south in the industrial zone of Avellaneda, Racing Club and Independiente play the city's other major derby. Independiente was founded by employees of the City of London department store.

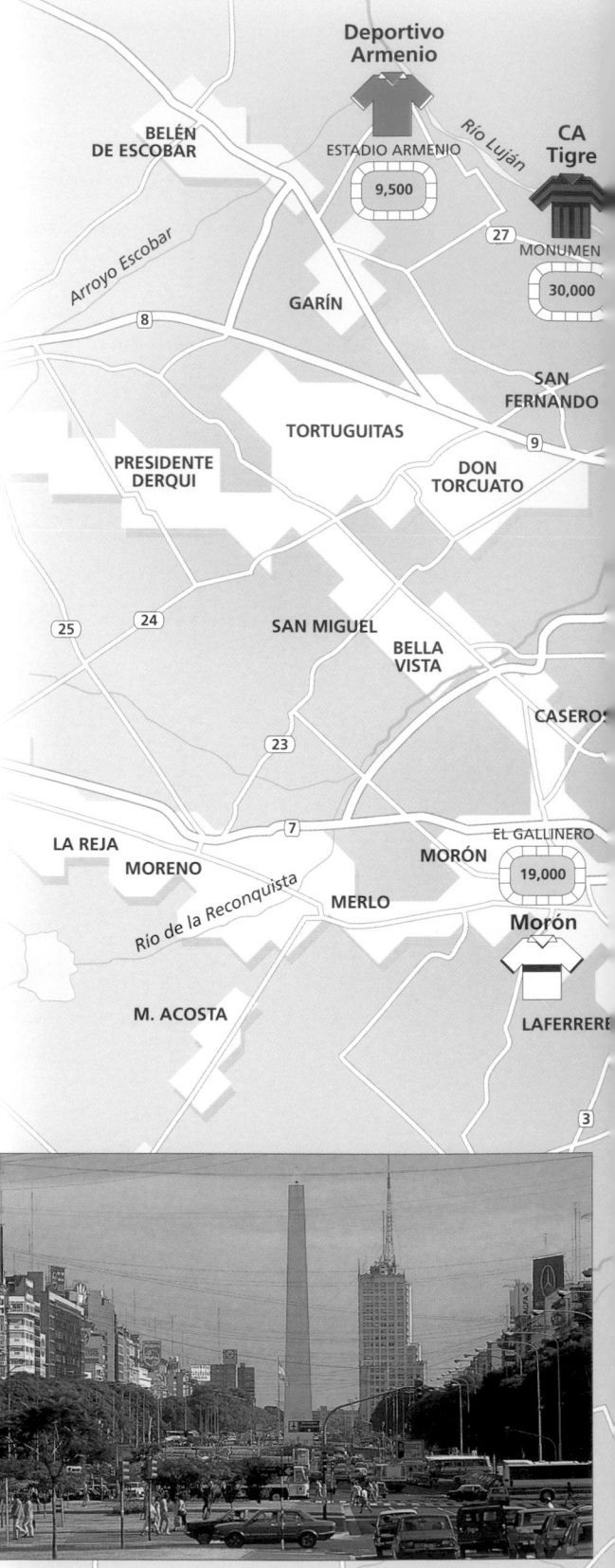

The Avenida 9 Julio is Buenos Aires' main thoroughfare. The spiritual home of Argentinian football since the 1860s, the city houses some 30 professional football teams.

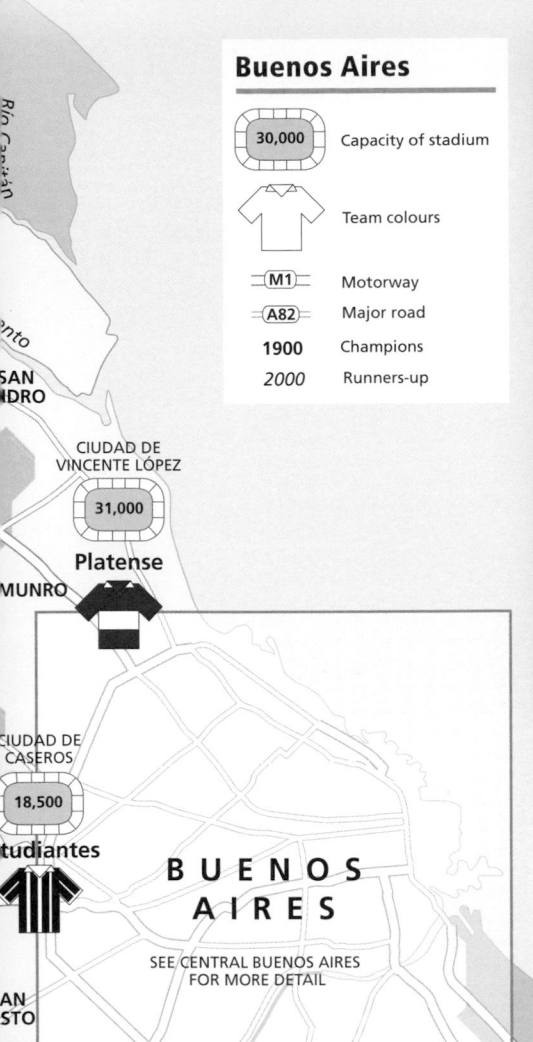

Buenos Aires

30,000	Capacity of stadium
	Team colours
M1	Motorway
A82	Major road
1900	Champions
2000	Runners-up

Rio Ceañán

ento

SAN DRO

CIUDAD DE VINCENTE LÓPEZ

31,000

Platense

MUNRO

CIUDAD DE CASEROS

18,500

tudiantes

BUENOS AIRES

SEE CENTRAL BUENOS AIRES FOR MORE DETAIL

AN STO

4

CA Banfield

FLORENCIO SOLÁ

30,000

TALLERES

16,500

Talleres

FRAGATA SARMIENTO

10,000

EDUARDO GALLARDÓN

35,000

MONTE GRANDE

Los Andes

CA Italiano

Almirante Brown

JOSÉ MARÍA EZEIZA

205

LONGCHAMPS

GLEW

TRISTÁN SUÁREZ

53

Buenos Aires, together with Montevideo across the mouth of the River Plate, is the cradle of football in South America. It was in these two great cities that the first South American international matches took place in the early years of the 20th century.

DON BOSCO

QUILMES

CENTENARIO

32,000

Quilmes

BERAZATEGUI

RIO DE LA PLATA

GIMNASIA Y ESGRIMA 1901

Amateur League (1891–1930)	**1929**
FAF League (1912–14)	*1913*
AAF League (1919–26)	*1924*
Apertura League (1992–2002)	*1999*
Clausura League (1992–2002)	*1995, 96, 2002*

ESTUDIANTES LA PLATA 1905

Amateur League (1891–1930)	*1919, 30*
FAF League (1912–14)	**1913**, *14*
Metropolitan League (1967–85)	*1967, 68,* **82**
National League (1967–85)	*1967, 75,* **83**
Copa Libertadores	**1968–70,** *71*
Copa Interamerica	**1969**
World Club Cup	**1968,** *69,* **70**

Gimnasia y Esgrima

JUAN CARLOS ZERILLO

11

20,401

VILLA ELISA

1

Estudiantes La Plata

LUIS JORGE HIRSCHI

26,000

ENSENADA

LA PLATA

2

QUILMES 1887

Amateur League (1891–1930)	*1895,* **1912**
Metropolitan League (1967–85)	**1978**
National League (1967–85)	*1982*

36

Racing, who took the name of a Parisian team of the time, was founded by French immigrants and attracted a well-heeled fan base that included the Peron family, a connection that took them all the way to the top, winning three championships in a row between 1949 and 1951.

Corruption rears its head

Argentina's long economic decline saw the city's leading clubs accumulate significant debts. In 1967, the government baled them out, but at the price of reorganizing the season and introducing provincial clubs from Rosario and Sante Fé into the competition. Under the Military Junta (1976–83), the city's clubs became more closely enmeshed with political factions in the government. On the bright side, a major clean up and stadium renovation programme was carried out in the run up to the 1978 World Cup. However, the economy has continued to falter, and the problem of massive corruption continues to plague the city's teams, while the spread of poverty fuels the criminal gangs that now run the clubs' *ultra* fan groups.

La Boca, once a poor area around the city's docks and the original home of both Boca Juniors and River Plate, is now an attractive and bohemian artists' quarter which attracts tourists by the thousand.

CENTRAL BUENOS AIRES

Chacarita Juniors
GUTIERREZ
23,000

Belgrano
DEFENSOR DE BELGRANO
8,500

Parque Sarmiento

CHACARITA JUNIORS 1906	
Metropolitan League (1967–85)	1969

ARGENTINOS JUNIORS 1904	
Amateur League (1891–1930)	1926
Metropolitan League (1967–85)	1980, 84
National League (1967–85)	1985
Copa Libertadores	1985
Copa Interamerica	1986
World Club Cup	1985

Atlant
HUMBOLE
12,000
BOYACA

Vélez Sarsfield

CA All Boys
12,000
ISLAS MALVINAS

JOSE AMALFITANI 'EL FORTIN'
49,806

Constructed on a lagoon filled with the rubble of the railway industry

Neuva Chicago

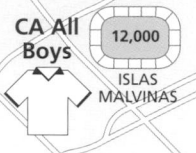

NUEVA CHICAGO
28,500

In the early 20th century, this area was home to Argentina's meat-packing industry, which rivalled that of Chicago. The area was quickly populated by immigrants

CA Españo
NUEVA ESPAÑA
32,500

Parque Almirar Guillermo Brov

ESTADIO DR CAMILO CICHERO, LA BOMBONERA	
58,750	**Club:** Boca Juniors **Built:** 1940 **Original Capacity:** 60,000 **Rebuilt:** 1949–53, 1995

VÉLEZ SARSFIELD 1910	
AAF League (1919–26)	*1919*
Argentine League (1931–66, 86–91)	*1953*
Metropolitan League (1967–85)	*1971, 79*
National League (1967–85)	**1968**, *85*
Apertura League (1992–2003)	*1994*, 96
Clausura League (1992–2003)	*1992, 93, 96, 98*
Copa Libertadores	**1994**
Copa Interamerica	**1996**
Supercopa	**1996**
World Club Cup	**1994**

ESTADIO ANTONIO VESPUCIO LIBERTI DE NUNEZ, 'MONUMENTAL'	
76,689	**Clubs:** River Plate, Argentina **Built:** 1938 **Original Capacity:** 100,000, Argentina v Brazil, Copa América, 4 April 1959 **Rebuilt:** 1973 **Significant Matches:** Copa América: 1959, 87; 1978 World Cup

SAN LORENZO 1908	
Amateur League (1891–1930)	**1927**
AAF League (1919–26)	**1923, 24, 25, 26**
Argentine League (1931–66, 86–91)	*1931, 33, 36, 41, 42,* **46**, *57, 59, 61, 88*
Metropolitan League (1967–85)	**1968, 72,** *83*
National League (1967–85)	*1971,* **72, 74**
Apertura League (1992–2003)	*1995*
Apertura League (1992–2003)	**1995, 2001**
Copa Sudamericana	**2002**

RIVER PLATE 1901

Amateur League (1891–1930)	*1909, 17, 18*
AAF League (1919–26)	**1920**, *21, 22*
Argentine League (1931–66, 86–91)	**1932, 36, 37**, *38, 39*, **41, 42, 43, 44, 45, 47**, *48, 49*, **52, 53, 55–57**, *60, 62, 63*, **65, 66**, *86, 90*
Metropolitan League (1967–85)	*1969, 70*, **75, 77, 79**, *80*
National League (1967–85)	*1968*, **69**, *72, 73*, **75, 76**, *78*, **79, 81**, *84*
Apertura League (1992–2003)	**1992**, *93*, **94, 95, 97, 98, 2000**, *01, 02*
Clausura League (1992–2003)	**1997**, *99*, **2000**, *01, 02*
Copa Libertadores	*1966, 76*, **86, 96**
Copa Interamerica	**1987**
Supercopa	**1991**, *97*
World Club Cup	**1986**, *96*

BOCA JUNIORS 1905

Amateur League (1891–1930)	**1919, 20, 23, 24, 26**, *27–29*, **30**
Argentine League (1931–66, 86–91)	**1931**, *33*, **34, 35, 40, 43, 44**, *45–47*, **50, 54, 58**, *62*, **64, 65**, *89, 91*
Metropolitan League (1967–85)	*1973*, **76**, *78*, **81**
National League (1967–85)	**1969, 70, 76**
Apertura League (1992–2003)	*1992*, **93, 98, 99**, *2001*, **03**
Clausura League (1992–2003)	**1999**
Copa Libertadores	*1963*, **77, 78**, *79*, **2000, 01**
Copa Interamerica	*1978*
Supercopa	**1989**, *94*
World Club Cup	**1977, 2000**, *01*

FERRO CARRIL OESTE 1904

Metropolitan League (1967–85)	*1981, 84*
National League (1967–85)	*1981*, **82, 84**

HURACÁN 1908

Amateur League (1891–1930)	**1921, 22**, *23*, **25, 28**
Metropolitan League (1967–85)	**1973**, *75, 76*
Clausura League (1992–2003)	*1994*

INDEPENDIENTE 1905

FAF League (1912–14)	*1912*
AAF League (1919–26)	**1922**, *23*, **26**
Argentine League (1931–66, 86–91)	*1932, 34, 35, 37*, **38, 39, 40, 48, 54, 60, 63, 64**, *89*, **90**
Metropolitan League (1967–85)	**1970, 71**, *77*, **82, 83**
National League (1967–85)	**1967, 77, 78**, *83*
Apertura League (1992–2003)	*1997*, **2003**
Clausura League (1992–2003)	*1993*, **94**, *2000*
Copa Libertadores	**1964, 65, 72–75, 84**
Copa Interamerica	**1973**, *74, 76*
Supercopa	**1989**, *94*, **95**
World Club Cup	*1964, 65*, **72**, *73*, **74, 84**

THE LOCAL DERBY

BOCA — RIVER

289 matches played

104 Boca Juniors wins
93 River Plate wins
92 draws

0   50   100   150   200   250

NUMBER OF MATCHES
(all first-class games up to May 2003)

Central Buenos Aires

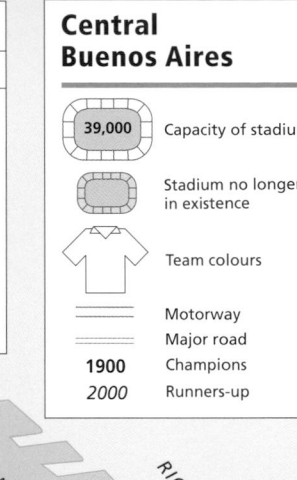

39,000	Capacity of stadium
	Stadium no longer in existence
	Team colours
	Motorway
	Major road
1900	Champions
2000	Runners-up

ESTADIO ANTONIO VESPUCIO LIBERTI DE NUNEZ, 'MONUMENTAL' (NATIONAL STADIUM)

76,689

River Plate

Argentina

Parque tres de Febrero

Atlanta bought the land for this stadium from Chacarita Juniors and evicted the team, creating an undying enmity between the clubs. The area around the stadium housed Buenos Aires' main Jewish community

Ferro Carril Oeste (1998–)

Argentinos Juniors

Q. RICARDO TCHEVERRY
24,812

San Lorenzo

PEDRO BIDEGAIN, 'EL NUEVO GASOMETRO'
39,000

TOMÁS ADOLFO DUCÓ
48,292

Huracán

Avenida Rivadavia

Avenida J. B. Alberdi

Avenida San Juan

Avenida Directorio

Autopista 25 Mayo

Avenida 9 De Julio

Avenida Saenz

Avenida Velez Sarsfield

27 De Febrero

Avenida Pte. F. Alcorta

Autopista A. Illia

RIO DE LA PLATA

PLAZA DEL MAYO
Relatives of 'the Disappeared' gathered here to protest and received significant press coverage during the 1978 World Cup Finals

Boca Juniors

ESTADIO DR CAMILO CICHERO, LA BOMBONERA
58,750

Racing Club

PRESIDENTE PERÓN
56,200

Independiente

DOBLE VISERA DE CEMENTE
57,901

ESTADIO DEL VIADUCTO
10,000

Arsenal di Sarandi

Lanús

LA FORTALEZA
46,519

ARGENTINA

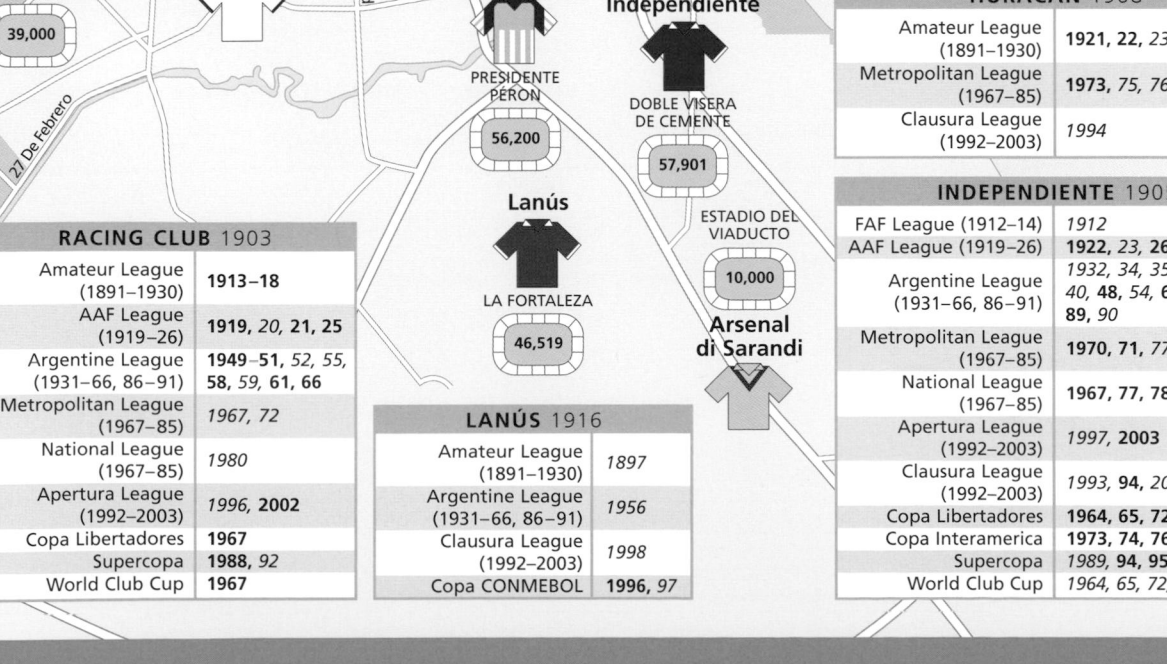

RACING CLUB 1903

Amateur League (1891–1930)	**1913–18**
AAF League (1919–26)	**1919, 20**, *21*, **25**
Argentine League (1931–66, 86–91)	**1949–51**, *52*, **55, 58**, *59*, **61**, *66*
Metropolitan League (1967–85)	*1967, 72*
National League (1967–85)	*1980*
Apertura League (1992–2003)	*1996*, **2002**
Copa Libertadores	**1967**
Supercopa	**1988**, *92*
World Club Cup	**1967**

LANÚS 1916

Amateur League (1891–1930)	*1897*
Argentine League (1931–66, 86–91)	*1956*
Clausura League (1992–2003)	*1998*
Copa CONMEBOL	**1996**, *97*

Argentina

FANS AND OWNERS

ARGENTINA'S CLUBS ARE IN CRISIS. With the exception of Colón from Santa Fé, every single club in the Argentinian first division (2001–02) is in debt. With the massive devaluation of the Peso and the emergency changes to banking in Argentina, these debts have become larger, though exactly how large nobody knows. Players and creditors go regularly unpaid, and at both national and club level players' strikes and lawsuits have been endemic. Yet money has still been flooding into the clubs. Player sales, overwhelmingly to Europe, have earned the clubs over half a billion dollars since 1975 ($360 million of which has been made in the last five years), television deals have improved massively, and although attendances have passed their peak, they are still significant.

So where has the money gone? Mostly it has been spent on massive, ludicrously paid squads, and been lost to corruption and skimming on all the transfers by club officials and agents. Racing Club was the first to collapse under the weight of debt, declaring bankruptcy in 2000, and allowed by government fiat to keep playing and trading until a private buyer could be found. Although still in debt, Racing, now owned by Fernando Marin and his company Blanquiceleste, is on an upward financial and footballing curve, while San Lorenzo, Boca and River Plate are all over $30 million in debt. These big clubs remain in the hands of small cliques of members and are constantly prey to internal feuding and struggles over elected officials. Some, like Boca, continue to count wealthy patrons among their boards, but most are administratively and financially crippled. The absence of transparent financial accounts from these murky institutions means that the data available on levels of debt is likely to underestimate the difficulties of Argentinian clubs.

The *barra bravas*

Another place that the money has gone is to the *barra bravas* – the organized supporters clubs attached to every team. The *barras* emerged in the 1950s as a combination of local street gangs and die-hard fans. Their fearsome and noisy displays at the stadiums and their small-scale criminal organization made them perfect vehicles for manipulation by club officials. An understanding between the two saw the *barras* at each club's disposal when it required its own players and coaches controlled, and when votes were required in the fierce politicking during elections for club boards. In return, the *barras* received match tickets (often resold) and cash. As a consequence, a lot of the data available on attendances needs to be scrutinized carefully. Free tickets are not recorded in the data, and indeed some of the sales of cheaper seats go unrecorded.

The older leadership of the *barras* began to disappear in the 1990s, when firearms, flares, noise bombs and drugs became standard equipment. *Barra* groups now have less to do with football and have become a network of career professionals, providing income for poor urban men with an interest in organized crime. The gangs regularly hijack buses to go to games, fleecing fans and food-sellers on the way, and shootings near grounds have become a regular feature of the weekend's fixtures. The clubs, police and judiciary have been slow to act and, while CCTV in the top division is bringing some change, the violence seems to be migrating to the lower divisions.

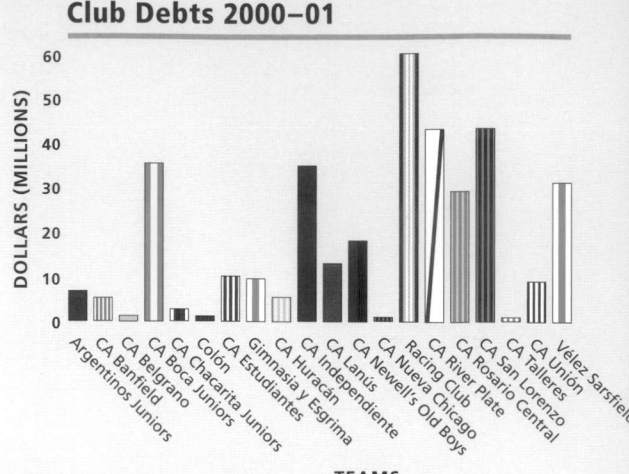

Club Debts 2000–01

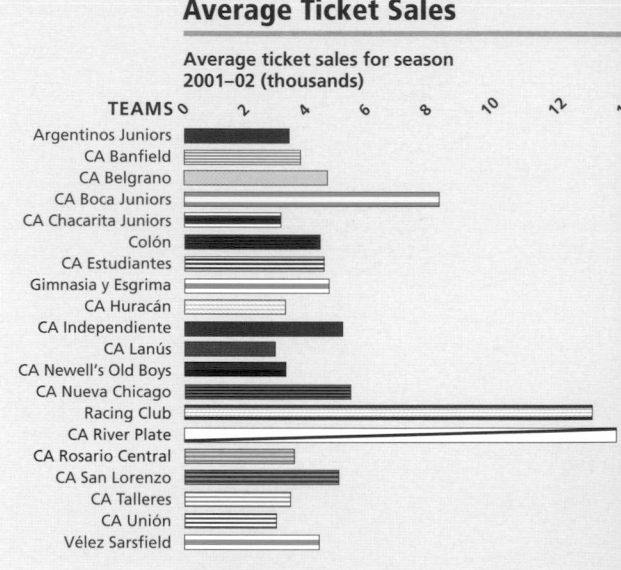

Average Ticket Sales

Average ticket sales for season 2001–02 (thousands)

Club members get in free at their own stadium and there are no conventional attendance records.

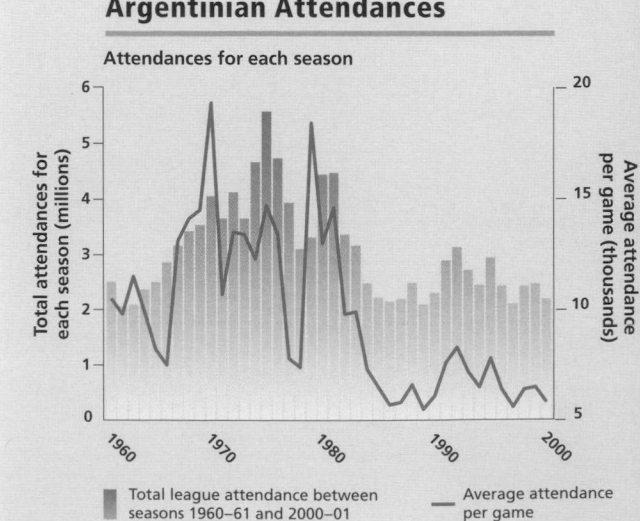

Argentinian Attendances

Attendances for each season

Total league attendance between seasons 1960–61 and 2000–01

Average attendance per game

Colón

La Banda de Rulo,
La Barra del Tablon,
La Banda del Santa Rosa

CA Unión

La Barra
de la Bombas

CA Talleres

Las Violetas, La Fiel,
Los Bulldogs,
La Barra de Juan

Santa Fé ●

CA Belgrano

Cordoba

Los Piratas,
La Banda del 2004,
La Banda del Jeton,
La Banda del Mosquito

Rosario ●

**Rosario
Central**

La Banda del Chapero,
La Banda de los Pillines

**Gimnasia
y Esgrima**

La 22

**CA
Newell's
Old Boys**

Cacho, Pimpi,
El Preso,
El Sapo, La Iata,
Los Anticannals,
La San Roque

BUENOS AIRES
(see inset)

La Plata ●

A R G E N T I N A

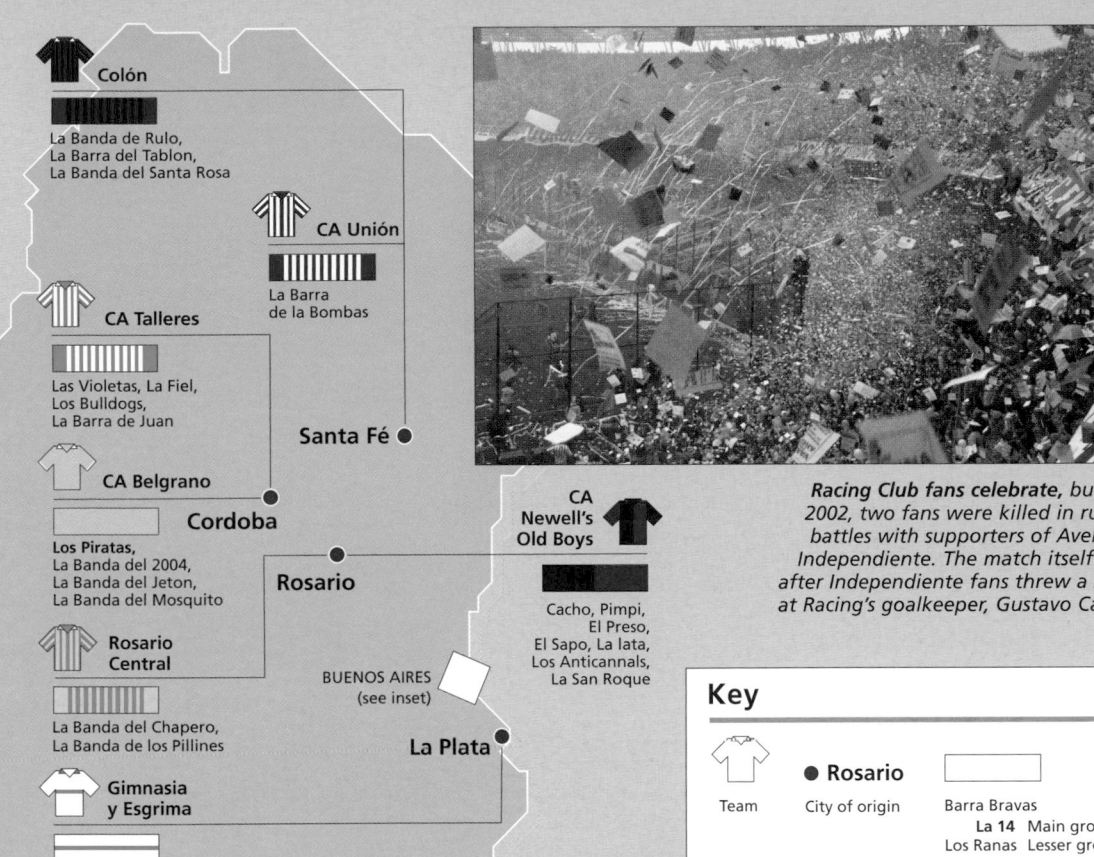

Racing Club fans celebrate, but in February 2002, two fans were killed in running street battles with supporters of Avellaneda rivals Independiente. The match itself was delayed after Independiente fans threw a smoke bomb at Racing's goalkeeper, Gustavo Campagnuolo.

ARGENTINA

Key

Team

● **Rosario**

City of origin

Barra Bravas
La 14 Main groups in bold
Los Ranas Lesser groups in roman

Teams shown were members
of the Primera Division 2001–02

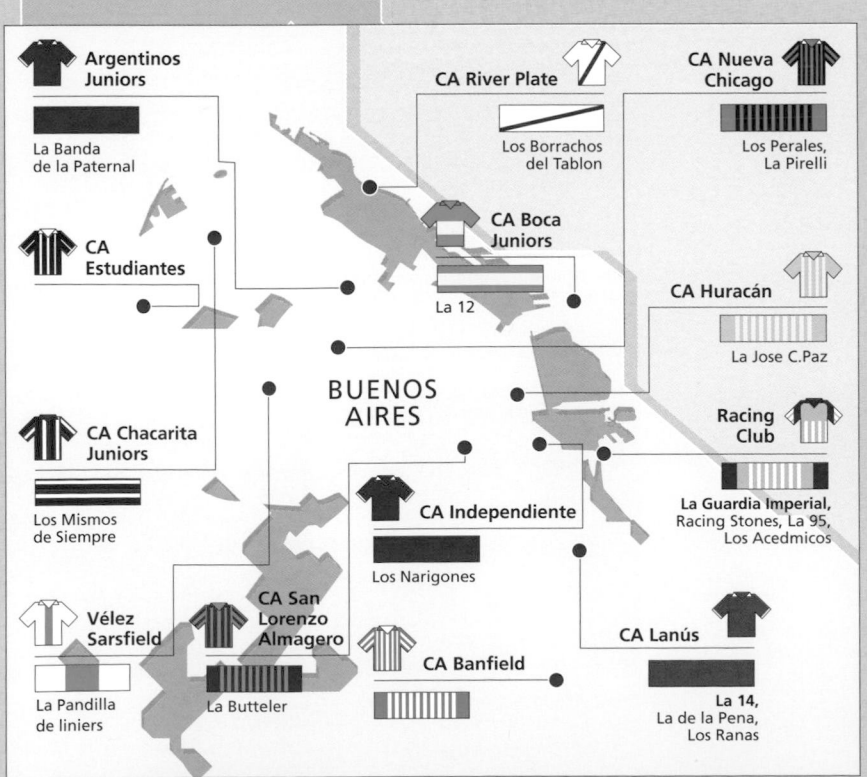

**Argentinos
Juniors**

La Banda
de la Paternal

CA River Plate

Los Borrachos
del Tablon

**CA Nueva
Chicago**

Los Perales,
La Pirelli

**CA Boca
Juniors**

La 12

CA Estudiantes

CA Huracán

La Jose C.Paz

**BUENOS
AIRES**

**CA Chacarita
Juniors**

Los Mismos
de Siempre

**Racing
Club**

La Guardia Imperial,
Racing Stones, La 95,
Los Acedmicos

CA Independiente

Los Narigones

**Vélez
Sarsfield**

La Pandilla
de liniers

**CA San
Lorenzo
Almagero**

La Butteler

CA Banfield

CA Lanús

La 14,
La de la Pena,
Los Ranas

Fernando Marin, owner of legal firm Blanquiceleste and now Racing Club, may be the first of a new generation of private owners of Argentinian clubs.

Argentina

PLAYERS AND MANAGERS

PLAYERS AND MANAGERS in Argentina appear to come from one of two schools of football: open, silky and stylish on the one hand; defensive, caustic and rough on the other. In the person of Maradona the two can be seen in an individual. These two sides of Argentinian football style are best expressed in the contrasting styles of the two managers that led Argentina to World Cup victories: César Menotti in 1978 and Carlos Bilardo in 1986. Menotti came from the city of Rosario and inherited its traditions of stylish football and radical politics. Although to some onlookers he was compromised by winning the 1978 cup for the Junta he despised, his claim that his team played in the old style of a lost Argentina was read as a coded condemnation of the generals. Bilardo, by contrast, built an altogether rougher, tougher team in the mould of the spiky and aggressive Estudiantes team of the 1960s in which he played and for whom gamesmanship and trickery were the essence of the game.

From a trickle to a flood

Although football's popularity in Argentina has never wavered, the smooth running of both football and the economy certainly have. Not surprisingly, Argentinian football is marked by waves of emigration and unrest among its players. In the late 1940s, a prolonged players' strike saw a mass exodus of stars to the newly reinvigorated Colombian professional league and subsequently many left for Spain and Italy, claiming citizenship there on the basis of their grandparents' origins. Alfredo di Stefano, the leading player of his age, played only a handful of games for Argentina before decamping to Real Madrid and the Spanish national team. By the 1990s, the steady flow had turned into a rush as almost the entire national squad earned their wages around the Mediterranean, while at the end of 2001 their compatriots at home were on strike again, chasing unpaid wages from bankrupt clubs.

Top 20 International Caps

PLAYER	CAPS	GOALS	FIRST MATCH	LAST MATCH
Diego Simeone*	106	11	1988	2003
Oscar Ruggeri	97	7	1983	1994
Diego Maradona	91	34	1977	1994
Ariel Ortega*	86	17	1993	2003
Gabriel Batistuta*	78	56	1991	2002
Roberto Ayala*	76	3	1994	2003
America Gallego	73	3	1975	1982
Javier Zanetti*	71	3	1994	2003
Daniel Passarella	70	22	1976	1986
Alberto Tarantini	61	1	1974	1982
Jorge Olguin	60	0	1976	1982
Roberto Sensini*	60	0	1987	2000
Jorge Burruchaga	59	13	1983	1990
Ubaldo Fillol	58	0	1974	1985
Rene Houseman	55	13	1973	1979
Claudio Javier Lopez*	54	10	1995	2003
Osvaldo Ardiles	53	8	1975	1982
Ricardo Giusti	53	0	1983	1990
Juan Sebastian Veron*	52	8	1996	2003
Claudio Caniggia*	50	16	1987	2002

Top 12 International Goalscorers

PLAYER	GOALS	CAPS	FIRST MATCH	LAST MATCH
Gabriel Batistuta*	56	78	1991	2002
Diego Maradona	34	91	1977	1994
Luis Artime	24	16	1961	1967
Leopoldo Luque	22	45	1975	1981
Daniel Passarella	22	70	1976	1986
Hermino Masantonio	21	19	1935	1942
Jose Sanfillipo	21	30	1956	1962
Mario Kempes	20	43	1973	1982
Rene Jenjaudro Pontoni	19	29	1942	1947
Norberto Mendez	19	31	1945	1956
Jose Moreno	19	34	1936	1950
Hernan Crespo	19	37	1995	2002

* Indicates players still playing at least at club level.

Argentinian International Managers

DATES	NAME	GAMES	WON	DRAWN	LOST
1940–58	Guillermo Stábile	110	74	18	18
1959	Victorio Luis Spinetto	6	5	1	0
1959	José Manuel Moreno	5	2	1	2
1960	Guillermo Stábile	10	6	1	3
1960–61	Victorio Luis Spinetto	10	5	3	2
1961	José D'Amico	2	1	0	1
1962	Juan Carlos Lorenzo*	5	2	2	1
1962	Jim López	2	1	1	0
1963	Horacio Amable Torres	8	4	1	3
1963	José D'Amico	2	1	0	1
1964–65	José Maria Minella*	15	9	5	1
1966	Juan Carlos Lorenzo	6	2	2	2
1967	Jim López	5	4	0	1
1967	Carmelo Faraone	2	0	0	2
1967–68	Renato Cesarini	5	1	1	3
1968	José Maria Minella	8	2	3	3
1969	Humberto Maschio	4	1	3	0
1969	Adolfo Alfredo Pedernera	4	1	1	2
1970–72	Juan José Pizzuti	23	10	8	5
1972–73	Omar Enrique Sivori	13	8	2	3
1974	Vladislao Wenceslao Cap	10	4	3	3
1974–82	César Luis Menotti	84	51	17	16
1983–90	Carlos Salvador Bilardo	70	36	23	11
1990–94	Alfio Oscar Basile	43	23	14	6
1994–98	Daniel Alberto Passarella	56	35	11	10
1999–	Marcelo Alberto Bielsa	50	31	11	8

* One match under different manager.
All figures correct as of 30 April 2003.

César Menotti's Argentina played some of the best football ever in the finals of its victorious 1978 World Cup campaign.

Carlos Bilardo led an aggressive and tricky Argentina, complete with Diego Maradona, to World Cup glory in Mexico in 1986.

ARGENTINA

Player of the Year

YEAR	PLAYER	CLUB
1970	Yazalde	Independiente
1971	Pastoriza	Independiente
1972	Bargas	Chacarita Juniors
1973	Brindisi	Huracán
1974	Raimondo	Independiente
1975	Scotta	San Lorenzo
1976	Passarella	River Plate
1977	Fillol	River Plate
1978	Kempes	Valencia [Sp]
1979	Maradona	Argentinos Juniors
1980	Maradona	Argentinos Juniors
1981	Maradona	Boca Juniors
1982	Gatti	Boca Juniors
1983	Bochini	Independiente
1984	Marcico	Ferro Carril Oeste
1985	Francescoli	River Plate
1986	Maradona	Napoli [Ita]
1987	Fabbri	Racing Club
1988	Paz	Racing Club
1989	Moreno	Independiente
1990	Goycochea	Racing Club/ Millonarios
1991	Ruggeri	Vélez Sarsfield
1992	Islas	Independiente
1993	Bello	River Plate
1994	Montoya	Boca Juniors
1995	Francescoli	River Plate
1996	Chilavert	Vélez Sarsfield
1997	Salas	River Plate
1998	Batistuta	Fiorentina [Ita]
1999	Saviola	River Plate
2000	Riquelme	Boca Juniors
2001	Riquelme	Boca Juniors
2002	Milito	Independiente

Awarded by the Argentinian Association of Sports Journalists.

Top Goalscorers 1931–2003

SEASON	PLAYER	CLUB	GOALS
1930–31	Zozaya	Estudiantes	33
1931–32	Ferreyra	River Plate	43
1932–33	Varallo	Boca Juniors	34
1933–34	Barrera	Racing Club	34
1934–35	Cosso	Vélez Sarsfield	33
1935–36	Barrera	Racing Club	32
1936–37	Erico	Independiente	47
1937–38	Erico	Independiente	43
1938–39	Erico	Independiente	40
1939–40	Langara	San Lorenzo	33
1939–40	Benitez Caceres	Racing Club	33
1940–41	Canteli	Newell's Old Boys	30
1941–42	Martino	San Lorenzo	25
1942–43	Arrieta	Lanús	23
1942–43	Labruna	River Plate	23
1942–43	Frutos	Platense	23
1943–44	Mellone	Huracán	26
1944–45	Labruna	River Plate	25
1945–46	Boye	Boca Juniors	24
1946–47	di Stefano	River Plate	27
1947–48	Santos	Rosario Central	21
1948–49	Simes	Racing Club	26
1948–49	Pizzuti	Banfield	26
1949–50	Papa	San Lorenzo	24
1950–51	Vernazza	River Plate	22
1951–52	Ricagni	Huracán	28
1952–53	Pizzuti	Racing Club	22
1952–53	Benavidez	San Lorenzo	22

Top Goalscorers (*continued*)

SEASON	PLAYER	CLUB	GOALS
1953–54	Berni	San Lorenzo	19
1953–54	Conde	Vélez Sarsfield	19
1953–54	Borello	Boca Juniors	19
1954–55	Massei	Rosario Central	21
1955–56	Castro	Rosario Central	17
1955–56	Grillo	Independiente	17
1956–57	Zarate	River Plate	22
1957–58	Sanfilippo	San Lorenzo	28
1958–59	Sanfilippo	San Lorenzo	31
1959–60	Sanfilippo	San Lorenzo	34
1960–61	Sanfilippo	San Lorenzo	26
1961–62	Artime	River Plate	25
1962–63	Artime	River Plate	25
1963–64	Veira	San Lorenzo	17
1964–65	Carone	Vélez Sarsfield	19
1965–66	Artime	Independiente	23
1967 M	Acosta	Lanús	18
1967 N	Artime	Independiente	11
1968 M	Obberti	Los Andes	13
1968 N	Wehbe	Vélez Sarsfield	13
1969 M	Machado da Silva	Racing Club	14
1969 N	Fischer	San Lorenzo	14
1969 N	Bulla	Platense	14
1970 M	Mas	River Plate	16
1970 N	Bianchi	Vélez Sarsfield	18
1971 M	Bianchi	Vélez Sarsfield	36
1971 N	Obberti	Newell's Old Boys	10
1971 N	Luniz	Juventud Antoniana	10
1972 M	Brindisi	Huracán	21
1972 N	Morete	River Plate	14
1973 M	Mas	River Plate	17
1973 M	Curioni	Boca Juniors	17
1973 M	Pena	Estudiantes	17
1973 N	Gomez Voglino	Atlanta	18
1974 M	Morete	River Plate	18
1974 N	Kempes	Rosario Central	25
1975 M	Scotta	San Lorenzo	32
1975 N	Scotta	San Lorenzo	28
1976 M	Kempes	Rosario Central	21
1976 N	Eresuma	San Lorenzo	12
1976 N	Luduena	Talleres	12
1976 N	Marchetti	Unión	12
1977 M	Alvarez	Argentinos Juniors	27
1977 N	Letanu	Estudiantes	13
1978 M	Andreuchi	Quilmes	22
1978 M	Maradona	Argentinos Juniors	22
1978 N	Reinaldi	Talleres	18
1979 M	Fortunato	Estudiantes	14
1979 M	Maradona	Argentinos Juniors	14
1979 N	Maradona	Argentinos Juniors	12
1980 M	Maradona	Argentinos Juniors	25
1980 N	Maradona	Argentinos Juniors	17
1981 M	Chaparro	Instituto	20
1981 N	Bianchi	Vélez Sarsfield	15
1982 N	Juarez	FC Oeste	22
1982 M	Morete	Independiente	20
1983 N	Husillos	Loma Negra	11
1983 M	Ramos	Newell's Old Boys	30

Top Goalscorers (*continued*)

SEASON	PLAYER	CLUB	GOALS
1984 N	Pasculli	Argentinos Juniors	9
1984 M	Francescoli	River Plate	24
1985 N	Comas	Vélez Sarsfield	12
1986†	Francescoli	River Plate	25
1986–87	Palma	Rosario Central	20
1987–88	Rodriguez	Deportivo Español	18
1988–89	Gorosito	San Lorenzo	20
1988–89	Dertycia	Argentinos Juniors	20
1989–90	Cozzoni	Newell's Old Boys	23
1990–91	Gonzalez	Vélez Sarsfield	18
1991–92 A	Diaz	River Plate	14
1991–92 C	Latorre	Boca Juniors	9
1992–93 A	Acosta AF	San Lorenzo	12
1992–93 C	Da Silva	River Plate	13
1993–94 A	Martinez	Boca Juniors	12
1993–94 C	Crespo	River Plate	11
1993–94 C	Espina	Platense	11
1994–95 A	Francescoli	River Plate	12
1994–95 C	Flores	Vélez Sarsfield	14
1995–96 A	Calderon	Estudiantes	13
1995–96 C	Lopez	Lanús	12
1996–97 A	Reggi	FC Oeste	11
1996–97 C	Martinez	Boca Juniors	15
1997–98 A	Da Silva	Rosario Central	15
1997–98 C	Sosa	Gimnasia	17
1998–99 A	Palermo	Boca Juniors	20
1998–99 C	Calderon	Independiente	17
1999–2000 A	Saviola	River Plate	15
1999–2000 C	Fuentes	Colón	17
2000–01 A	Angel	River Plate	13
2000–01 C	Romeo	San Lorenzo	15
2001–02 A	Cardetti	River Plate	17
2001–02 C	Cavenaghi	River Plate	15
2002–03 A	Silvera	Independiente	16

M Metropolitan League   **N** National League
† Reverted to a single league   **C** Clausura League
A Apertura League

Claudio Caniggia has remained playing at the top level for more than 15 years. His clubs have included River Plate, Boca Juniors, Verona and SL Benfica, and he currently plays for Rangers in Scotland.

ARGENTINA

Argentina

PRIMERA DIVISION 1985–2002

THE MID-1980s BEGAN with a reform of the old league system in which two separate tournaments – a Torneo Nacional and a Torneo Metropolitano – were played side-by-side. In 1985, a single national league kicked off. The increased representation of provincial sides (outside Buenos Aires) was confirmed with a series of titles for the two big Rosario teams, Rosario Central in 1987 and Newell's Old Boys in 1988 and 91. Newell's Old Boys built the club's success on an extensive scouting network and intensive youth policy, which produced strikers like Ariel Cozzoni. However, the big Buenos Aires clubs continued to win championships with one each for River Plate, Independiente and Boca Juniors, as well as victories for these teams plus Racing Club and San Lorenzo in the Liguilla – the qualifying tournament for the lucrative Copa Libertadores.

The financial screw

In 1992, another reorganization took place, with the national league being split into two separate 17-game leagues: the Apertura and Clausura. Competition has been open with championships going to River Plate, Boca Juniors, Independiente, San Lorenzo and Vélez Sarsfield. Although the financial screw has been on most clubs for the last decade, the big Buenos Aires clubs have pulled ahead of the others with bigger squads, more players imported from other Latin American countries and more lucrative sales of stars to top European clubs. During the 1990s, River Plate fielded Hernan Crespo, Oscar Ruggeri, Marcello Salas and Enzo Francescoli. Vélez Sarsfield, under coach Carlos Bianchi, starred Paraguayan goalkeeper José Luis Chilavert and striker José Flores and took back-to-back championships and a Copa Libertadores.

Most recently, Boca Juniors, also under Bianchi, has built a series of inspiring squads. Whenever the team has won a competition, however, the squad has been dismantled to pay the bills. Occasional challengers have included Gimnasia from La Plata, Racing Club and Lanús. Teams from Santa Fé and Córdoba have also reached the top flight and managed to hang in there. Nearly all clubs in Argentina are now in deep financial crisis, and almost every stadium is blighted by violence on match days.

Boca Juniors, 1997: another squad, another sales pitch. Boca Juniors' conveyor belt of talent keeps being sold on to Europe. The club has earnt over $100 million from transfers in the last 15 years.

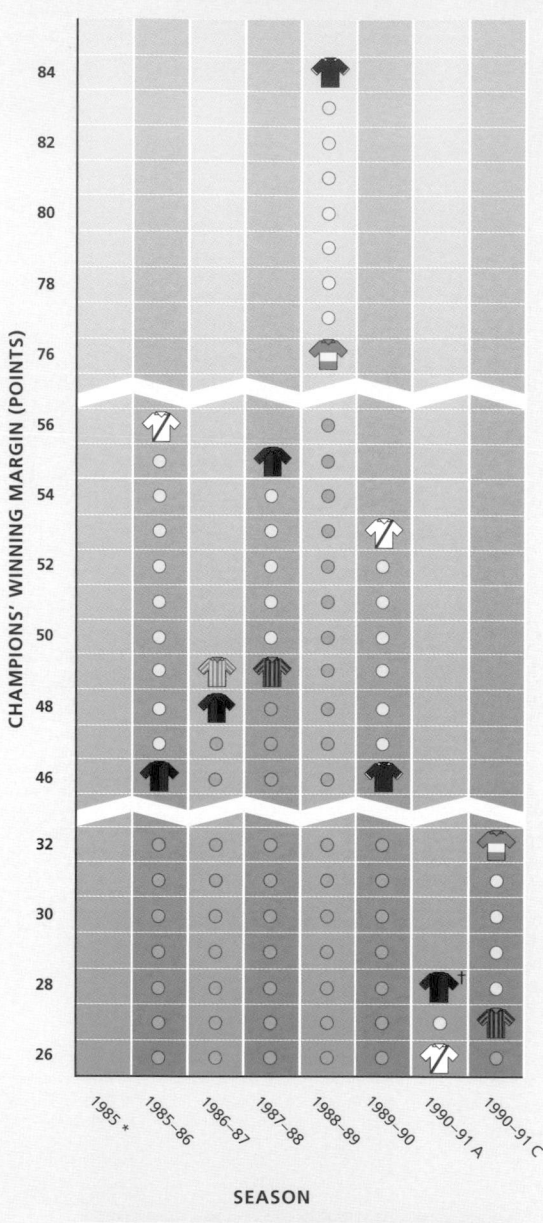

Champions' Winning Margin 1985–91

CHAMPIONS' WINNING MARGIN (POINTS)

SEASON: 1985 *, 1985–86, 1986–87, 1987–88, 1988–89, 1989–90, 1990–91 A, 1990–91 C

| 36 | 36 | 38 | 38 | 38 | 38 | 19 | 19 |

Total games played by each team
(2 points awarded for a win except in 1989–90, when 3 points were awarded for a win and 2 points for a win on penalties)

* Championship decided by play-off
† Newell's Old Boys won national title by play-off for 1991

Boca Juniors   Independiente   Newell's Old Boys

River Plate   Rosario Central   San Lorenzo

ARGENTINA

Argentinian Players Transferred Abroad 1985–2001

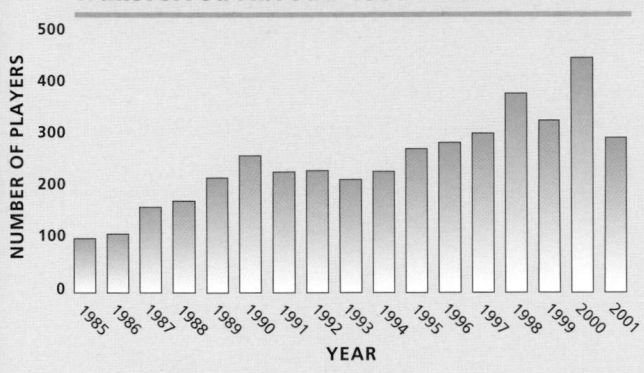

Bar chart — NUMBER OF PLAYERS (0–500) by YEAR (1985–2001).

Income from Foreign Transfers 1985–2001

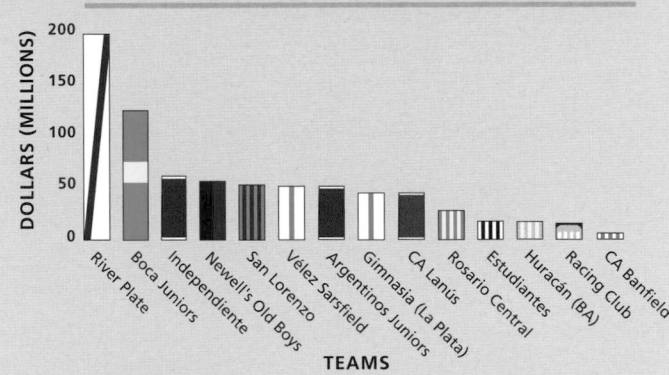

Bar chart — DOLLARS (MILLIONS) (0–200) by TEAMS: River Plate, Boca Juniors, Independiente, Newell's Old Boys, San Lorenzo, Vélez Sarsfield, Argentinos Juniors, Gimnasia (La Plata), CA Lanús, Rosario Central, Estudiantes, Huracán (BA), Racing Club, CA Banfield.

Argentinian League Positions 1985–1991

Key to League Positions Table

- ◼ League champions
- ◻ Season of promotion to league
- ◼ Season of relegation from league
- ◼ Other teams playing in league
- ◼ Qualified for championship play-off
- | 5 | Final position in league

* In the 1990–91 season the winners of the Apertura, Newell's Old Boys, and the winners of the Clausura, Boca Juniors, played-off for the national title. Newell's Old Boys won the title after a penalty shootout.

Newell's Old Boys

1986, 87, 88, 91 A, 91*

Rosario Central

1987

Argentinos Juniors

Boca Juniors

1989, 91 C, 91*   *1986, 90*

Independiente

1989, 90   *1987*

Racing Club

1988

River Plate

1986, 90, 91 A   *1989*

San Lorenzo

1988, 91 C   *1991*

ARGENTINA

● **Rosario**

● **Buenos Aires**

Primera Division 1986–91

Independiente — Team name

League champions/runners-up — Champions in bold, Runners-up in italics

1989, 90

Winners of Copa Libertadores Liguilla

● **Buenos Aires** — City of origin

TEAM	1985	1985–86	1986–87	1987–88	1988–89	1989–90	1990–91 A	1990–91 C
Argentinos Juniors	1	4	17	7	7	9	4	18
Deportivo Armenio				13	19			
CA Banfield					18			
CA Belgrano								
Boca Juniors	5	4	12	2	3	8		1
CA Chacarita Juniors	19							
CA Chaco For Ever						17	14	19
Deportivo Español	2	14	7	3	19	18	17	
CA Estudiantes	16	12	16	7	16	7	9	
Ferro Carril Oeste	6	5	14	18	6	4	16	
Gimnasia y Esgrima (La Plata)	9	12	5	10	6	4	14	
Huracán (Buenos Aires)	13						8	6
Independiente	9	3	11	1	2	10	5	
Instituto	11	8	14	20	20			
CA Italiano		20						
CA Lanús							20	12
Deportivo Mandiyú				12	10	17	3	
Newell's Old Boys	2	2	1	12	10		1*	8
CA Quilmes								
CA Platense	16	18	10	15	10	14	9	
Racing	18	15	17	15	17			
Racing Club		5	3	9	6	13	3	
River Plate		1	10	4	4	1	2	9
Rosario Central			1	7	12	3	4	15
San Lorenzo	6	5	2	5	15	10	2	
CA San Martín					17			
CA Unión Santa Fé	14	16	18		10	18	12	
CA Talleres	8	11	20	6	10	10	20	
CA Témperley	15	18						
Vélez Sarsfield	2	12	8	6	11	5	3	6

SEASON

ARGENTINA

ARGENTINA

River Plate and the club's fans remain the most powerful force in Argentinian soccer. However, despite big crowds and big transfers, the club remains mired in an ever deepening pit of debt.

Carlos Bianchi finally returned Boca Juniors to winning ways in the late 1990s after a lean era. Since his appointment, the club has won three championships and two Copa Libertadores.

The flamboyant José Luis Chilavert has helped San Lorenzo take two championships and the Copa Libertadores in the last few years.

Key to League Positions Table

▉ League champions	▉ Season of relegation from league
▉ Season of promotion to league	▉ Other teams playing in league
`5` Final position in league	
A Apertura	C Clausura

Argentinian League Positions 1992–2002

TEAM	1992-93 A	1992-93 C	1993-94 A	1993-94 C	1994-95 A	1994-95 C	1995-96 A	1995-96 C	1996-97 A	1996-97 C	1997-98 A	1997-98 C	1998-99 A	1998-99 C	1999-2000 A	1999-2000 C	2000-01 A	2000-01 C	2001-02 A	2001-02 C
Almagro																	18	10		
Argentinos Juniors	18	10	11	13	5	20	16	20			8	8	6	11	12	16	17	4	11	16
Arsenal																				
CA Banfield			9	7	8	13	19	18	20	19									18	7
CA Belgrano	7	13	16	9	6	15	20	13					19	9	18	14	16	16	9	18
Boca Juniors	1	6	4	7	13	4	2	5	10	9	2	6	1	1	3	7	1	3	3	3
CA Chacarita Juniors															8	15	9	6	8	17
Colón							13	9	8	2	14	16	5	12	16	3	10	13	4	11
Deportivo Español	11	4	18	14	18	4	17	11	18	16	17	19								
CA Estudiantes	7	13	20	15			9	3	10	16	10	11	11	15	10	17	7	9	6	9
Ferro Carril Oeste	4	16	10	15	14	13	17	9	14	10	12	11	17	19	19	20				
Gimnasia y Esgrima (Jujuy)			17	12	8	14	10	20	14	4	19	9	19	19						
Gimnasia y Esgrima (La Plata)	16	10	10	15	8	2	13	2	6	13	4	3	8	3	9	3		18	7	2
Gimnasia y Tiro		16	19								19	17								
Huracán (Buenos Aires)	4	6	11	2	14	19	5	7	18	14	19	18	16	20			8	7	19	4
CA Huracán (Corrientes)									17	15										
Independiente	15	2	4	1	11	9	13	12	2	4	7	10	14	5	8	2	14	17	10	20
Instituto															16	11				
CA Lanús	7	15	4	9	6	9	2	3	2	10	11	2	4	16	10	11	15	14	12	12
CA Los Andes																	19	19		
Deportivo Mandiyú	12	10	13	20	19	18														
Newell's Old Boys	20	17	13	9	4	15	11	17	8	2	18	8	6	7	12	5	13	12	14	6
CA Nueva Chicago																			13	13
Olimpo																				
CA Platense	18	18	13	5	14	7	11	14	15	8	9	14	20	18						
Racing Club	16	6	2	9	11	6	2	7	4	7	13	15	3	13	6	18	20	5	1	5
River Plate	2	3	1	5	1	9	7	14	1	1	1	6	14	2	1	1	2	2	2	1
Rosario Central	12	6	18	3	8	7	10	6	5	18	3	13	6	4	2	13	12	20	16	14
San Lorenzo	2	4	7	3	2	1	5	19	6	6	4	5	6	3	4	3	5	1	5	8
CA San Martín	12	19																		
CA Unión Santa Fé									16	10	14	19	6	5	12	8	11	15	17	15
CA Talleres	7	20		20	15										5	10	4	11	20	19
Vélez Sarsfield	6	1	2	18	3	3	1	1	13	5	4	1	11	13	7	5	6	8	15	10

Relegation is determined by averaging out points over three seasons rather than a points total over a single season.

ARGENTINA

Gimnasia y Esgrima (Jujuy)

Gimnasia y Tiro

CA Belgrano

Instituto

CA Talleres

CA San Martin

San Salvador de JuJuy

Salta

Colón

1997 C

CA Unión Santa Fé

San Juan

Rosario

Rosario Central

2000 A

Newell's Old Boys

Bahia Blanca

Olimpo

A R G E N T I N A

Santa Fé

Córdoba

CA Los Andes

Lomas de Zamora

La Plata

Gimnasia y Esgrima

1995 C, 96 C, 99 A, 2002 C

Racing Club

1996 A, **2002 A**

River Plate

1993 A, 94 A, 95 A, 97 A, 97 C, 98 A, 99 C, 2000 A, 00 C, 01 A, 01 C, 02 A, 02 C

Arsenal

CA Huracán

Deportivo Mandiyú

Corrientes

CA Chacarita Juniors

CA Platense

Buenos Aires

San Lorenzo

1995 A, 95 C, 2001 C

Vélez Sarsfield

1993 C, 94 A, 96 A, 96 C, 98 C

Primera Division 1992–2002

Independiente   Team name

League champions/ runners-up

1989, *90*   Champions in bold Runners-up in italics

Other teams in the Primera Division

● **Buenos Aires**   City of origin

Almagro

CA Banfield

Deportivo Español

Ferro Carril Oeste

CA Nueva Chicago

Argentinos Juniors

Boca Juniors

1993 A, 98 A, 99 A, 99 C, 2001 A

CA Estudiantes

Huracán

1994 C

CA Lanús

1998 C

Independiente

1993 C, 94 C, 97 A, 2000 C

The 'Super Classico' 1998: Boca Juniors v River Plate is one of the few games for which attendances have not fallen in recent years.

Argentina

Asociación del Fútbol Argentino
Founded: 1893
Joined FIFA: 1912
Joined CONMEBOL: 1916

THE ARGENTINE LEAGUE championship is, outside of the UK, the world's oldest league. It was established in 1891 by expatriate Briton Alexander Hutton under the auspices of the Argentine Association Football League (AAFL). English teams and colleges (Alumni, Lomas Athletic and English High School) dominated the early years of the league until Racing Club's victory in 1913 signalled a shift of power to Argentinian clubs. This division in Argentine football was reflected in two splits that created parallel football associations and league championships in the years 1912–14 and 1919–26.

Professionalism and a professional league were established in 1931. For the next four decades, Argentine football was dominated by the big five from Buenos Aires (Boca Juniors, Independiente, Racing Club, River Plate and San Lorenzo). From 1967 to 1985 the championship was divided into two consecutive leagues, the Metropolitan and National. A single league was re-established in the mid-1980s and an extra tournament for the top teams was created – the Pre-Libertadores Liguilla – with a place in the lucrative Copa Libertadores at stake. Both tournaments were replaced in the early 1990s by the division of the season into two short leagues – the Apertura (opening) and Clausura (closing) championships.

Cup football has never proved popular in Argentina and, despite cups being donated by government ministers and Swedish ambassadors, no tournament has ever lasted very long.

Argentine Amateur League Record 1891–1930

SEASON	CHAMPIONS	SEASON	CHAMPIONS
1891	St Andrew's	1922	Huracán
1892	no championship	1923	Boca Juniors
1893	Lomas Athletic	1924	Boca Juniors
1894	Lomas Athletic	1925	Huracán
1895	Lomas Athletic	1926	Boca Juniors
1896	Lomas Athletic	1927	San Lorenzo
1897	Lomas Athletic	1928	Huracán
1898	Lomas Athletic	1929	Gimnasia Y Esgrima
1899	Belgrano Athletic	1930	Boca Juniors
1900	English High School		
1901	Alumni		
1902	Alumni		
1903	Alumni	**FAF League Record 1912–14**	
1904	Belgrano Athletic	SEASON	CHAMPIONS
1905	Alumni	1912	Estudianil Porteno
1906	Alumni	1913	Estudiantes LP
1907	Alumni	1914	Estudianil Porteno
1908	Belgrano		
1909	Alumni		
1910	Alumni		
1911	Alumni		
1912	Quilmes	**AAF League Record 1919–26**	
1913	Racing Club	SEASON	CHAMPIONS
1914	Racing Club	1919	Racing Club
1915	Racing Club	1920	River Plate
1916	Racing Club	1921	Racing Club
1917	Racing Club	1922	Independiente
1918	Racing Club	1923	San Lorenzo
1919	Boca Juniors	1924	San Lorenzo
1920	Boca Juniors	1925	Racing Club
1921	Huracán	1926	Independiente

Argentine Professional League Record 1931–66

SEASON	CHAMPIONS	RUNNERS-UP
1931	Boca Juniors	San Lorenzo
1932	River Plate	Independiente
1933	San Lorenzo	Boca Juniors
1934	Boca Juniors	Independiente
1935	Boca Juniors	Independiente
1936	River Plate	San Lorenzo
1937	River Plate	Independiente
1938	Independiente	River Plate
1939	Independiente	River Plate
1940	Boca Juniors	Independiente
1941	River Plate	San Lorenzo
1942	River Plate	San Lorenzo
1943	Boca Juniors	River Plate
1944	Boca Juniors	River Plate
1945	River Plate	Boca Juniors
1946	San Lorenzo	Boca Juniors
1947	River Plate	Boca Juniors
1948	Independiente	River Plate
1949	Racing Club	River Plate
1950	Racing Club	Boca Juniors
1951	Racing Club	Banfield
1952	River Plate	Racing Club
1953	River Plate	Vélez Sarsfield
1954	Boca Juniors	Independiente
1955	River Plate	Racing Club
1956	River Plate	Lanús
1957	River Plate	San Lorenzo
1958	Racing Club	Boca Juniors
1959	San Lorenzo	Racing Club
1960	Independiente	River Plate
1961	Racing Club	San Lorenzo
1962	Boca Juniors	River Plate
1963	Independiente	River Plate
1964	Boca Juniors	Independiente
1965	Boca Juniors	River Plate
1966	Racing Club	River Plate

Metropolitan League Record 1967–85

SEASON	CHAMPIONS	RUNNERS-UP
1967	Estudiantes	Racing Club
1968	San Lorenzo	Estudiantes
1969	Chacarita Juniors	River Plate
1970	Independiente	River Plate
1971	Independiente	Vélez Sarsfield
1972	San Lorenzo	Racing Club
1973	Huracán	Boca Juniors
1974	Newell's Old Boys	Rosario Central
1975	River Plate	Huracán
1976	Boca Juniors	Huracán
1977	River Plate	Independiente
1978	Quilmes	Boca Juniors
1979	River Plate	Vélez Sarsfield
1980	River Plate	Argentinos Juniors
1981	Boca Juniors	Ferro Carril Oeste
1982	Estudiantes	Independiente
1983	Independiente	San Lorenzo
1984	Argentinos Juniors	Ferro Carril Oeste
1985	no championship	

National League Record 1967–85

SEASON	CHAMPIONS	RUNNERS-UP
1967	Independiente	Estudiantes
1968	Vélez Sarsfield	River Plate
1969	Boca Juniors	River Plate
1970	Boca Juniors	Rosario Central
1971	Rosario Central	San Lorenzo
1972	San Lorenzo	River Plate
1973	Rosario Central	River Plate
1974	San Lorenzo	Rosario Central
1975	River Plate	Estudiantes
1976	Boca Juniors	River Plate
1977	Independiente	Talleres
1978	Independiente	River Plate
1979	River Plate	Unión Santa Fé
1980	Rosario Central	Racing Club
1981	River Plate	Ferro Carril Oeste
1982	Ferro Carril Oeste	Quilmes
1983	Estudiantes	Independiente
1984	Ferro Carril Oeste	River Plate
1985	Argentinos Juniors	Vélez Sarsfield

Argentine League Record 1986–91

SEASON	CHAMPIONS	RUNNERS-UP
1986	River Plate	Newell's Old Boys
1987	Rosario Central	Newell's Old Boys
1988	Newell's Old Boys	San Lorenzo
1989	Independiente	Boca Juniors
1990	River Plate	Independiente
1991*	Newell's Old Boys	Boca Juniors

Apertura League Record 1992–2003

SEASON	CHAMPIONS	RUNNERS-UP
1992	River Plate	Boca Juniors
1993	Boca Juniors	River Plate
1994	River Plate	Vélez Sarsfield
1995	River Plate	San Lorenzo
1996	Vélez Sarsfield	Racing Club
1997	River Plate	Independiente
1998	River Plate	Boca Juniors
1999	Boca Juniors	Gimnasia y Esgrima LP
2000	River Plate	Rosario Central
2001	Boca Juniors	River Plate
2002	Racing Club	River Plate
2003	Independiente	Boca Juniors

Clausura League Record 1992–2003

SEASON	CHAMPIONS	RUNNERS-UP
1992	Newell's Old Boys	Vélez Sarsfield
1993	Vélez Sarsfield	Independiente
1994	Independiente	Huracán
1995	San Lorenzo	Gimnasia y Esgrima LP
1996	Vélez Sarsfield	Gimnasia y Esgrima LP
1997	River Plate	Colón
1998	Vélez Sarsfield	Lanús
1999	Boca Juniors	River Plate
2000	River Plate	Independiente
2001	San Lorenzo	River Plate
2002	River Plate	Gimnasia y Esgrima LP
2003	River Plate	†

* In the 1990–91 season the winners of the Apertura, Newell's Old Boys, and the winners of the Clausura, Boca Juniors, played-off for the national title. Newell's Old Boys won the title after a penalty shoot-out.
† Runner-up undecided at 30 June 2003

Argentine League Summary 1931–2003

TEAM	TOTALS	CHAMPIONS & RUNNERS-UP (BOLD) (ITALICS)
River Plate	31, 25	**1932**, **36**, **37**, *38*, *39*, **41**, **42**, **43**, **44**, **45**, **47**, *48*, *49*, **52**, **53**, **55–57**, *60*, *62*, *63*, *65*, *66*, *68†*, *69†*, *69**, *70**, *72†*, *73†*, **75***, **75†**, **76†**, **77***, *78†*, *79†*, *79**, *80**, *81†*, *84†*, **86**, **90**, **92§**, *93§*, *94§*, *95§*, **97†**, *97§*, **98§**, *99#*, **2000§**, *2000#*, **01§**, *01#*, *02§*, **02#**, *03#*
Boca Juniors	19, 13	**1931**, *33*, **34**, **35**, **40**, **43**, **44**, *45–47*, *50*, **54**, *58*, **62**, **64**, **65**, *69†*, **70†**, *73**, *76**, **76†**, *78**, **81***, **89**, **91**, *92§*, **93§**, **98§**, **99§**, *99#*, **2001§**, *03§*
Independiente	14, 14	*1932*, **34**, **35**, *37*, **38**, **39**, **40**, **48**, **54**, **60**, **63**, **64**, *67†*, **70***, **71***, *77**, **77†**, *78†*, *82**, **83***, *83†*, **89**, **90**, *93#*, *94#*, *97§*, *2000#*, **03§**
San Lorenzo	9, 10	*1931*, *33*, *36*, **41**, **42**, *46*, *57*, *59*, *61*, *68**, **71†**, **72***, *72†*, **74†**, *83**, *88*, **95#**, *95§*, **2001#**
Racing Club	7, 7	**1949–51**, **52**, **55**, **58**, **59**, **61**, **66**, *67**, *72**, *80†*, *96§*, **2002§**
Vélez Sarsfield	5, 6	*1953*, *68†*, **71***, *79**, *85†*, *92#*, *93#*, *94§*, *96§*, **96#**, **98#**
Rosario Central	4, 4	*1970**, **71†**, **73†**, *74†*, *74**, *80†*, **87**, *2000§*
Newell's Old Boys	4, 2	**1974***, *86*, *87*, **88**, **91**, *92#*
Estudiantes	3, 3	**1967***, *67†*, *68**, *75†*, *82**, *83†*
Ferro Carril Oeste	2, 3	*1981**, **81†**, *82†*, **84†**, *84**
Argentinos Juniors	2, 1	**1980***, **84***, *85†*
Huracán	1, 3	**1973***, *75**, *76**, *94#*
Quilmes	1, 1	**1978***, *82†*
Chacarita Juniors	1, 0	**1969***
Gimnasia y Esgrima (La Plata)	0, 4	*1995#*, *96#*, *99§*, *2002#*
Lanús	0, 2	*1956*, *98#*
Banfield	0, 1	*1951*
Colón	0, 1	*1997#*
Talleres	0, 1	*1977†*
Unión Santa Fé	0, 1	*1979†*

* denotes winners/runners-up of Metropolitan League
† denotes winners/runners-up of National League
§ denotes winners/runners-up of Apertura League
# denotes winners/runners-up of Clausura League

Pre-Libertadores Liguilla Record 1986–91

SEASON	CHAMPIONS
1986	Boca Juniors
1987	Independiente
1988	Racing Club
1989	River Plate
1990	Boca Juniors
1991	San Lorenzo

Pre-Libertadores Liguilla Summary

TEAM	TOTAL	WINNERS
Boca Juniors	2	1986, 90
River Plate	1	1989
Independiente	1	1987
Racing Club	1	1988
San Lorenzo	1	1991

Uruguay

THE SEASON IN REVIEW 2002

THE POOR STATE OF Uruguayan football's finances was made even worse when the most powerful man in Uruguayan football, Francisco Casal, announced his retirement at the start of the season. Through his company Tenfield, Casal has controlled the movements of almost every top Uruguayan player for 20 years. Paying desperately needed up-front money to the clubs in return for a controlling interest in their up and coming players, Casal has more than recouped his money when the best players have been sold on to European clubs. In addition, Tenfield owns the TV rights to domestic football. With Latin America's battered economies continuing to struggle and with advertising revenues falling, Tenfield took the opportunity to cut its payments to the Uruguayan FA. The extent of the country's economic decline was made clear when the visiting South Korean national squad had their belongings stolen from a dressing room during a friendly in Montevideo in February. In the early part of the season Peñarol looked the best side and in its newly acquired Argentinian striker – Daniel Jimenez – it had both a bargain and a steady supply of goals. However, it could not sustain it early season form, while rivals Nacional found its stride. Nacional beat Peñarol in the penultimate game to take the Apertura title. Worse was to follow for Peñarol as three points were docked from its Clausura tally as a punishment for crowd violence earlier in the season and the dispirited squad made an early exit from international competitions as well.

Nacional looked set for victory in the Clausura too, but financial problems mounted at the clubs and with wages arriving very late or not at all the squad began a go-slow, refusing to train more than once a day and refusing to attend the secluded *concentración* before games. As Nacional slowed, Danubio's spirited side scampered to the Clausura title, setting up a Championship Play-off with Nacional. With money coming in from successful runs in the Copa Libertadores and Copa Sudamericana, Nacional rediscovered its form again, winning both legs of the Final to take the overall title.

Apertura Torneo – Final Table

CLUB	P	W	D	L	F	A	Pts	
Nacional	9	8	1	0	20	6	25	Apertura winners
Peñarol	9	7	0	2	25	12	21	
Fénix	9	6	0	3	22	11	18	
Club Deportivo Maldonado	9	4	2	3	10	17	14	
Montevideo Wanderers	9	3	3	3	8	9	12	
Defensor Sporting	9	4	0	5	15	17	12	
Danubio	9	3	2	4	12	14	11	
CA Plaza	9	2	2	5	10	13	8	
Central Español	9	2	1	6	13	21	7	
Villa Española	9	0	1	8	8	23	1	

Clausura Torneo – Final Table

CLUB	P	W	D	L	F	A	Pts	
Danubio	9	6	2	1	16	8	20	Clausura winners
Peñarol	9	7	1	1	25	16	19*	
Fénix	9	4	3	2	24	18	15	
Defensor Sporting	9	4	3	2	16	12	15	
Nacional	9	4	2	3	20	16	14	
CA Plaza	9	4	2	3	16	12	14	
Villa Española	9	1	4	4	10	21	7	
Montevideo Wanderers	9	1	3	5	8	12	6	
Club Deportivo Maldonado	9	2	0	7	8	21	6	
Central Español	9	1	2	6	9	16	5	

* Peñarol had 3 points deducted due to incidents in a match against Danubio during Apertura 2002.

Relegated clubs: Racing Club, CA Progreso, Bella Vista (Paysandú).
Promoted clubs: Liverpool FC, Miramar Misiones, Deportivo Colonia.

Championship Play-off

2002 FINAL (2 legs)

December 4 – Jardines del Hipódromo, Danubio
Danubio 1-2 Nacional
(Biaggio 48)   (Vanzini 51, Peralta 90)
h/t: 0-0 **Att:** 10,000
Ref: Vázquez

December 6 – Centenario, Montevideo
Nacional 2-1 Danubio
(Scotti 16,   (Perrone 63)
Morales 88)
h/t: 1-0 **Att:** 60,000
Ref: Méndez
Nacional won 4-2 on aggregate

The structure of the season
The Uruguayan season acquired a new structure for 2001. It now opens with an 18-team first division, with teams playing each other once (17 games), but organized into three groups of six. This is collectively known as the Torneo Clasificatorio. The top two from each group together with the four next best teams go into a ten-team championship competition; the bottom eight go into a relegation competition. The championship competition involves two nine-game leagues: the Apertura and the Clausura. The winners of these two leagues play-off in a two-leg National Championship Final. The bottom eight play-off to avoid three relegation places.

Alejandro Lembo lifts the Apertura trophy after Nacional had beaten Peñarol in the penultimate game of the championship. Peñarol's already poor season was further diminished when three points were docked from the side in the Clausura standings after persistent crowd trouble during Apertura matches.

Top Goalscorers 2002

PLAYER	CLUB	NATIONALITY	GOALS
Germán Hornos	Fénix	Uruguayan	25
Richard Morales	Nacional	Uruguayan	23
Daniel Jiménez	Peñarol	Argentinian	21

International Club Performances 2002

CLUB	COMPETITION	PROGRESS
Peñarol	Copa Libertadores	Quarter-finals
Nacional	Copa Libertadores	Quarter-finals
	Copa Sudamericana	Semi-finals
Montevideo Wanderers	Copa Libertadores	2nd Round
Danubio	Copa Sudamericana	1st Round

Copa Libertadores Qualifiers 2002

TEAM AND QUALIFICATION
Nacional as winners of Apertura
Peñarol as winners of Torneo Clasificatorio
Fénix as winners of Pre-Libertadores Liguilla

URUGUAY

Above, left: *Peñarol's Fabian Estoyanoff fights for the ball with Nacional players Alejandro Lembo (front) and Oscar Morales (behind). Peñarol won this match 4-0 but it was little consolation in a very poor season for Uruguay's most decorated club.*

Above: *Small is beautiful. Danubio's players and fans celebrate after the team's tie against Fenix, making them champions of the Clausura tournament and qualifying them for the finals of the Uruguayan championship in Montevideo.*

Nacional and *Uruguayan national team striker Richard Morales enjoys the players' go-slow.*

Nacional players *Marce Vanzini, Fabian Coelho, Richard Morales and Alejandro Lembo (left to right) hold the Championship trophy aloft after beating Danubio in the final.*

Montevideo

FOOTBALL CITY

AT THE HEART OF MONTEVIDEO'S football landscape is the Centenario stadium, built for the first World Cup in 1930. Described by Jules Rimet as a 'temple of football', it is shared by the city's two biggest clubs: Peñarol and Nacional (who retain smaller grounds as well). It sits in the centre of a city that saw some of the earliest club championships and international matches in Latin America, and which hosts almost every team in the Uruguayan top division (and almost half the population of the country). Together with Buenos Aires, across the mouth of the River Plate, Montevideo is the cradle of football in Latin America.

The substantial expatriate British community, mostly involved in shipping and banking, was playing football informally in the 1880s and setting up schools and sports clubs across the city. Albion Cricket Club, formed in 1891, created a football section in 1893. British railway engineers set up CURCC (Central Uruguayan Railways Cricket Club) in 1891 and took to football soon after. The team first split from the company and then transformed itself into Peñarol in 1913. Peñarol is one half of the most successful double act in world football. Together with its rival, Nacional, they have won over 80 per cent of the Uruguayan championships ever played.

Nacional v Peñarol

Nacional was set up in 1899 by local students in self-conscious opposition to the foreigners running CURCC. Since this time, the team's social and political affiliations have always remained with the nationalist elite. In 1903, the Uruguayan FA put the Nacional squad in the national colours in a representative match against Argentinian Buenos Aires. Nacional still celebrates the occasion annually. Peñarol continues to be associated with the poorest, immigrant strands of Montevideo society. The annual derby matches are keenly contested. A similar derby is played out in a smaller way in the western suburb of Cerro, which has been absorbed into the city in the last few decades. Older, more middle-class residents have remained true to the area's original team, Rampla Juniors, while the new working-class immigrants tend to favour the recently-arrived Cerro.

Beyond the big two, Montevideo spawned an enormous number of clubs encouraged by the opening of Grand Central Park in 1900 by a tramway company who wanted people to use the park for football. Although over a hundred years of footballing history have passed, British influences linger on in many of the clubs' names – Liverpool, Racing, Wanderers and River Plate. The only significant recent challenge to the big two has come from Danubio and Defensor Sporting.

URUGUAY

BELLA VISTA 1920

| Amateur League (1900–1931) | 1924 |
| National League (1932–2002) | 1990 |

CERRO 1922

| National League (1932–2002) | 1960 |

RAMPLA JUNIORS 1914

| Amateur League (1900–1931) | 1923, 27, 28 |
| National League (1932–2002) | 1932, 40, 64 |

CA PROGRESO 1917

| National League (1932–2002) | 1989 |

Montevideo docks: River Plate was originally founded in the Customs House in the docks area of the city at the beginning of the 20th century.

Arroyo de Miguelete

MANGA

Rentistas

PARQUE
RENTISTAS
10,000

CASAVALLE

PIEDRAS
BLANCAS

Danubio

JARDINES DEL
HIPODROMO
16,000

PUNTA
DE RIELES

*Banado de
Carrasco*

THE LOCAL DERBY

NACIONAL	PEÑAROL

470
matches
played

149 Nacional wins
172 Peñarol wins
149 draws

0	50	100	150	200	250

NUMBER OF MATCHES
(all matches up to May 2003)

Montevideo

73,600	Capacity of stadium
16,000	Club's second stadium
	Team colours
	Second teams
M1	Motorway
A82	Major road
1900	Champions
2000	Runners-up

MONTEVIDEO WANDERERS 1902	
Amateur League (1900–1931)	**1906**, *07*, **09**, *11*, *22*, *26*, **31**
National League (1932–2002)	*1980, 85*

Sud América

CERRITO

ITUZAINGO

VILLA
ESPAÑOLA

CARLOS ANGEL
FOSSA
6,000

DANUBIO 1932	
National League (1932–2002)	*1954, 83*, **88**, *2001, 02*

**Villa
Española**

PLAY AT
VARIETY OF
STADIUMS

**El Tanque
Sisley**

VICTOR
DELLA VALLE
6,000

PASO
CARRASCO

**Miramar
Misiones**

MENDEZ PIANA

ITAHUALPA

BELLA
VISTA

UNION

M O N T E V I D E O

Nacional   **Uruguay**

PARQUE
CENTRAL
16,000

MAROÑAS

Basáñez

LA BOMBONERA
6,000

MALVIN
NORTE

CARRASCO
4,000

REDUCTO

Nacional   **Peñarol**

CENTENARIO
(NATIONAL STADIUM)
73,609

Huracán

MALVIN
NUEVO

PARQUE
HURACÁN
8,000

PUNTA
GORDA

RIVER
PLATE

LA BLANQUEADA

PARQUE
FEDERICO
SAROLDI
12,000

RETIRO

PARQUE
PALERMO
6,500

TRES
CRUCES

PARQUE
BATLLE

LAS ACASIAS
12,000

**Central
Español**

Peñarol

LUIS
FRANZINI

ATLANTIC
OCEAN

URUGUAY

PUNTA
CARRETAS
18,000

**Defensor
Sporting**

CENTENARIO

73,609	**Clubs:** Nacional, Peñarol, Uruguay
	Built: 1930
	Original Capacity: 80,000
	Significant Matches: 1930 World Cup: nine matches, including semi-final and Final; Copa América: 1942, 56, 67, and Finals 83, 95

NACIONAL 1899	
Amateur League (1900–1931)	*1901*, **02, 03**, *05, 06, 08*, **12, 13, 15–17**, *18*, **19, 20, 21, 22–24**, *29, 31*
National League (1932–2002)	**1933, 34**, *35–38*, **39–43, 44, 45, 46, 47, 49, 50, 51, 52, 53, 55–57**, *58, 59, 61, 62*, **63, 65, 66, 67, 68, 69–72**, *73–75*, **77, 78, 79, 80, 81, 83, 86, 87, 89–91, 92**, *94–96*, **98, 99, 2000–02**
Copa Libertadores	*1964, 67, 69*, **71**, *80*, **88**
Copa Interamérica	**1972**, *81*, **89**
Supercopa	*1990*
World Club Cup	**1971**, *80*, **88**

PEÑAROL 1899	
Amateur League (1900–1931)	**1900, 01**, *02, 03*, **05, 07**, *09, 10*, **11**, *12*, **14–17**, *18*, **20, 21, 26**, *27*, **28, 29**
National League (1932–2002)	**1932**, *33, 34*, **35–38**, *39*, **41–43, 44, 45, 46, 47, 49, 50, 51, 52**, *53, 54*, **55–57**, *58–62*, **63, 64**, *65, 66*, **67, 68**, *69–72*, **73–75, 76, 77**, *78, 79*, **81, 82**, *84*, **85**, *86*, **88**, *93–97*, **98, 99**, *2000*
Copa Libertadores	**1960, 61**, *62*, **65, 66**, *70*, **82**, *83*, **87**
Copa CONMEBOL	*1993, 94*
World Club Cup	*1960*, **61, 66, 82**, *87*

DEFENSOR SPORTING 1913	
National League (1932–2002)	**1976**, *82*, **87, 91**, *93, 97*

CENTRAL ESPAÑOL 1905	
National League (1932–2002)	**1984**

Uruguay

PRIMERA DIVISIÓN PROFESIONAL 1982–2001

THE 1980s BEGAN chaotically in Uruguay, with a brutal military government presiding over economic decline and urban disorder. With very strict controls and limits placed on conventional politics, many leading political figures migrated into the administration of football, including Julio Maria Sanguinetti, future Uruguayan president and then-president of Peñarol. Similarly, Tabaré Vázquez, future leader of the leftist Encuentro Progresista party, was president of Progreso. The *junta*, recognizing the popular appeal of the sport, were prepared to bale out clubs as the economic squeeze destroyed their balance sheets.

Military rule ended and democratic elections were held in 1984, and for a time it seemed that the old order of Peñarol and Nacional championship victories had been swept aside. That year the title went unexpectedly to the tiny Montevideo club Central Español, led by the top-scoring striker José Villareal. Indeed, the country's lesser lights won a whole string of championships in the late 1980s. Defensor took two, aided by the free-scoring Gerardo Miranda, followed by Danubio and Bella Vista.

The 1990s saw Peñarol and Nacional take back their stranglehold on the league, though Defensor amalgamated with a popular basketball club to become Defensor Sporting and won the Clausura in 1997. The club has maintained its challenge to the big two by shrewd spending, an active youth policy and lucrative forays into the Copa Libertadores. However, nearly all other clubs, big and small, struggled financially throughout the 1990s, and only the sale of players overseas (some 400 in the late 1990s) and the sale of bonds to long-suffering fans kept clubs afloat. In 1998, Frontera Riviera became the first side from outside Montevideo to be promoted to the top flight. The growing strength of provincial football was recognized by changes in the structure of the Uruguayan league. Places were guaranteed to clubs from outside Montevideo, and relegation systems changed to ensure a Montevideo-provincial balance.

Primera División Profesional

Peñarol	Team name
	League champions/runners-up
1985, *88*	Champions in bold Runners-up in italics
	Other teams in the Primera División Profesional
● Rocha	City of origin

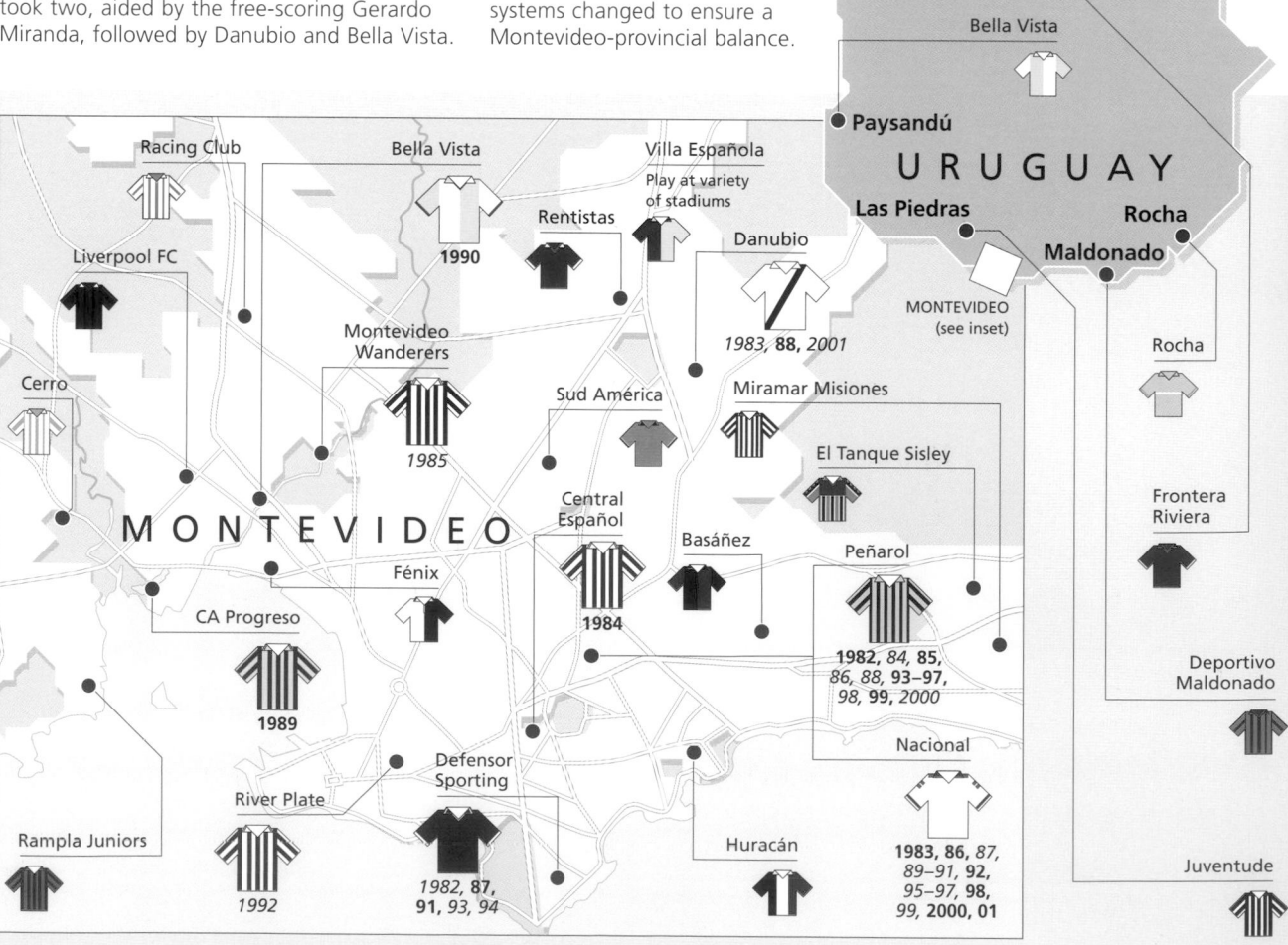

Nacional v Peñarol 2001: Most of Uruguay's social divisions continue to be played out in this derby – Colorados v Blancos, Italians v Spanish, working-class v middle-class. Although the match still attracts immense crowds and may even determine the Uruguayan championships, the big two have failed to make their mark in the big continental competitions, and both are perilously in debt.

Key to League Positions Table

- League champions
- Season of promotion to league
- Season of relegation from league
- Other teams playing in league
- Teams in relegation league (Clasificatorio)
- 5 — Final position in league

Uruguayan League Positions 1982–2001

TEAM	1982	1983	1984	1985	1986	1987	1988	1989	1990	1991	1992	1993	1994A	1994C	1995A	1995C	1996A	1996C	1997A	1997C	1998A	1998C	1999A	1999C	2000A	2000C	2001A	2001C
Basáñez												3	12	13	8													
Bella Vista (Montevideo)	4	4	5	13	5	3	11	5	1	9	5	11	13	11							2	6	4	8	7	9	8	10
Bella Vista (Paysandú)																							13	11	15	12	9	9
Central Español			1	8	3	10	9	12	4	6	13			12	5	5	12	12	7									
Cerro	10	8	12	4	10	9	8	4	12	7	11	6	4	3	7	11	10	11	11	5				6	10	5	7	
Danubio	7	2	4	11	9	6	1	7	6	5	3	3	11	10	10	5	4	5	9	12	11	5	3	3	2	4	1	2
Defensor Sporting	2	3	8	12	8	1	3	6	8	1	6	2	1	6	4	6	2	4	4	1	4	7	2	4	3	2	5	4
El Tanque Sisley									14																			
Fénix					12																						6	8
Frontera Riviera																						11	9	16	15			
Huracán	14	11	9	10	7	12	4	10	14	11	12					5	3	8	7	10	9	8	5	18	13			
Juventude																									12	11	10	6
Liverpool FC	11			5	11	7	8	10	9	9	7	2	7	9	10	5	4	12	8	15	6	14	17					
Deportivo Maldonado																							9	13	9	14		
Miramar Misiones	12	10	13			11	12																					
Nacional	3	1	3	5	1	2	7	2	2	2	1	4	6	2	3	1	3	1	1	6	1	1*	1	2	1	3*	3*	1*
Peñarol	1	7	2	1	2	8	2	3	3	4	1	2	1*	1	2*	1	6*	3	2*	3	4	5	1*	4	1	2	3	
CA Progreso	8	6	10	6	6	7	13		11	12	9	5	8	13	11	10												
Racing Club						5	10	8	13								12	10							11	8		
Rampla Juniors	9	12	7	7	11	13			8	10	9	12	3	6	2	6	11	7	10	14	12							
Rentistas							9	9	13	12									10	8	8	2	7	15	6	10		
River Plate	13	13		3	13	4	10	13	13		2	10	7	8	9	4	7	8	2	3	5	3	10	7	10	6		
Rocha																									13	16		
Sud América	6	9	11	9								8	13	11	12													
Deportivo Tacuarembó																							12	14	8	5	7	7
Villa Española																			9	11					17			
Montevideo Wanderers	5	5	6	2	4	5	6	8	10	3	7	7	5	4	6	9	8	9	7	9	6	12					4	5

*Denotes championship play-off winners.

Since 1993 the season has been divided into two leagues, Apertura and Clausura (marked A and C on the table), the winners of which play off to decide the championship.

In 1997 Nacional (winners of the Apertura) and Peñarol (the team with the most points overall) played off for the championship.

As of season 2001 the championship begins with Torneo Clasificatorio. The top 10 teams then play the Apertura and Clausura for the national championship. The remainder play in a relegation league.

Uruguay

Asociación Uruguaya de Fútbol
Founded: 1900
Joined FIFA: 1923
Joined CONMEBOL: 1916

THE FIRST RECORDED FOOTBALL MATCHES IN URUGUAY
took place in autumn 1878 in Montevideo between teams made up of British residents and visiting British sailors. The first club, Albion FC, was set up in 1886 by an Englishman, William Pool. A national football association was founded in 1900 and an amateur league soon followed, although it was initially restricted to only four clubs from Montevideo – Albion FC, Central Uruguayan Railways Cricket Club (later to become Peñarol), Uruguay Athletic Club and Deutsche Fussball Klub. Club numbers steadily expanded and though again restricted to the capital city the first three decades of the 20th century were a golden era for Uruguayan football. Enormous domestic interest was sustained and enhanced by amazing international successes: victory at the 1924 and 1928 Olympic Games – both held in Europe – and hosting and winning the 1930 World Cup. On the back of this wave of economic and sporting success, professionalism and a reconstituted national league were established in 1932.

Since then Uruguayan football has been dominated by two teams – Nacional and Peñarol, both from the capital Montevideo – more completely than any other significant footballing nation. Between them they have won the national championship over 80 times, ceding the title to only eight other clubs in over a century. In fact, all the country's major clubs are based in Montevideo and concern has often been aired about its metropolitan bias. To counter the effect of this bias a regional league system run by the Organization del Futbol del Interior has been established to ensure continued interest in the sport outside the capital.

The league is currently split into two halves – the Apertura (opening) and Clausura (closing) championships. A play-off between the two champions for the national title is held at the end of the season, unless the same team wins both championships. The national champions get a place in the Copa Libertadores. The next eight clubs from an aggregate table (across both championships) play in a post-season liguilla (mini-league) to decide the other entrants for the Copa Libertadores and the Copa Sudamericana. The two worst teams from Montevideo and the worst team from the interior (again from the aggregate table) are relegated.

Uruguayan League Record 1900–2002

SEASON	CHAMPIONS	SEASON	CHAMPIONS
1900	Peñarol	1915	Nacional
1901	Peñarol	1916	Nacional
1902	Nacional	1917	Nacional
1903	Nacional	1918	Peñarol
1904	no championship	1919	Nacional
1905	Peñarol	1920	Nacional
1906	Wanderers	1921	Peñarol
1907	Peñarol	1922	Nacional
1908	River Plate	1923	Nacional
1909	Wanderers	1924	Nacional
1910	River Plate	1925	no championship
1911	Peñarol	1926	Peñarol
1912	Nacional	1927	Rampla Juniors
1913	River Plate	1928	Peñarol
1914	River Plate	1929	Peñarol

Uruguayan League Record (*continued*)

SEASON	CHAMPIONS	SEASON	CHAMPIONS
1930	no championship	1968	Peñarol
1931	Wanderers	1969	Nacional
1932	Peñarol	1970	Nacional
1933	Nacional	1971	Nacional
1934	Nacional	1972	Nacional
1935	Nacional	1973	Peñarol
1936	Peñarol	1974	Peñarol
1937	Peñarol	1975	Peñarol
1938	Peñarol	1976	Defensor
1939	Nacional	1977	Nacional
1940	Nacional	1978	Peñarol
1941	Nacional	1979	Peñarol
1942	Nacional	1980	Nacional
1943	Nacional	1981	Peñarol
1944	Peñarol	1982	Peñarol
1945	Peñarol	1983	Nacional
1946	Nacional	1984	Central Español
1947	Nacional	1985	Peñarol
1948	no championship	1986	Nacional
1949	Peñarol	1987	Defensor
1950	Nacional	1988	Danubio
1951	Peñarol	1989	Progreso
1952	Nacional	1990	Bella Vista
1953	Peñarol	1991	Defensor
1954	Peñarol	1992	Nacional
1955	Nacional	1993	Peñarol
1956	Nacional	1994	Peñarol
1957	Nacional	1995	Peñarol
1958	Peñarol	1996	Peñarol
1959	Peñarol	1997	Peñarol
1960	Peñarol	1998	Nacional
1961	Peñarol	1999	Peñarol
1962	Peñarol	2000	Nacional
1963	Nacional	2001	Nacional
1964	Peñarol	2002	Nacional
1965	Peñarol		
1966	Nacional		
1967	Peñarol		

Chile

Federación de Fútbol de Chile
Founded: 1895
Joined FIFA: 1912
Joined CONMEBOL: 1916

FOOTBALL ARRIVED IN CHILE in the late 19th century via visiting British sailors in the coastal ports of Valparaíso and Viña del Mar. The first clubs were formed in the early 1890s, the earliest being Santiago Wanderers formed in Valparaíso in 1892. It was soon joined by others, especially in the capital Santiago, and in 1895 a national FA was founded.

The geography of Chile – very long, very thin – militated against the formation of a regular national tournament and regional leagues quickly developed instead.

At the prompting of the most successful clubs, a national league was established in 1933 and professionalism legalized. However, it was not until the 1950s that teams from outside Santiago entered the league, and not until 1971 that Unión San Felipe won the title for a provincial city.

The national league ran as a conventional single league until 1997 when the season was split into two championships – Apertura and Clausura. In 1998, the league reverted to a single championship format, with the top four behind the champions playing-off for Chile's second slot in the Copa Libertadores. In 2002 the league reverted to separate Apertura and Clausura tournaments. It was not until 1991 that a Chilean club, Colo Colo, won the Copa Libertadores. A national cup competition – the Copa Chile – was established in 1958 (but was not played between 1962–73).

Paraguay

Asociación Paraguaya de Fútbol
Founded: 1906
Joined FIFA: 1921
Joined CONMEBOL: 1921

THE TOP DIVISION IN PARAGUAY has 13 clubs playing an Apertura and a Clausura championship each year. The Apertura consists of a short league with each team playing the others once. Until 1997 draws were not allowed and penalty shootouts took place if the scores were level at the end of 90 minutes (victory by this method was only worth two points as against three for a normal time win). Out of this league, the top six teams form two mini-leagues which produce the contestants for a two-leg play-off Final. The Clausura is a normal league with clubs playing each other home and away. The national championship is decided by a two-leg play-off between Apertura and Clausura champions.

Chilean League Record 1933–2002

SEASON	CHAMPIONS	SEASON	CHAMPIONS
1933	Magallanes	1970	Colo Colo
1934	Magallanes	1971	Unión San Felipe
1935	Magallanes	1972	Colo Colo
1936	Audax Italiano	1973	Unión Española
1937	Colo Colo	1974	Huachipato
1938	Magallanes	1975	Unión Española
1939	Colo Colo	1976	Everton
1940	Universidad de Chile	1977	Unión Española
1941	Colo Colo	1978	Palestino
1942	Santiago Morning	1979	Colo Colo
1943	Unión Española	1980	Cobreloa
1944	Colo Colo	1981	Colo Colo
1945	Green Cross	1982	Cobreloa
1946	Audax italiano	1983	Colo Colo
1947	Colo Colo	1984	Universidad Católica
1948	Audax italiano	1985	Cobreloa
1949	Universidad Católica	1986	Colo Colo
1950	Everton	1987	Universidad Católica
1951	Unión Española	1988	Cobreloa
1952	Everton	1989	Colo Colo
1953	Colo Colo	1990	Colo Colo
1954	Universidad Católica	1991	Colo Colo
1955	Palestino	1992	Cobreloa
1956	Colo Colo	1993	Colo Colo
1957	Audax italiano	1994	Universidad de Chile
1958	Santiago Wanderers	1995	Universidad de Chile
1959	Universidad de Chile	1996	Colo Colo
1960	Colo Colo	1997A	Universidad Católica
1961	Universidad Católica	1997C	Colo Colo
1962	Universidad de Chile	1998	Colo Colo
1963	Colo Colo	1999	Universidad de Chile
1964	Universidad de Chile	2000	Universidad de Chile
1965	Universidad de Chile	2001	Santiago Wanderers
1966	Universidad Católica	2002A	Universidad de Chile
1967	Universidad de Chile	2002C	Colo Colo
1968	Santiago Wanderers		
1969	Universidad de Chile		

Chilean Cup Record 1958–2002

YEAR	WINNERS	YEAR	WINNERS
1958	Colo Colo	1988	Colo Colo
1959	Santiago Wanderers	1989	Colo Colo
1960	no competition	1990	Colo Colo
1961	Santiago Wanderers	1991	Universidad Católica
1962–73	no competition	1992	Unión Española
1974	Colo Colo	1993	Unión Española
1975	Palestino	1994	Colo Colo
1976	no competition	1995	Universidad Católica
1977	Palestino	1996	Colo Colo
1978	no competition	1997	no competition
1979	Universidad de Chile	1998	Universidad de Chile
1980	Deportes Iquique	1999	no competition
1981	Colo Colo	2000	Universidad de Chile
1982	Colo Colo	2001	Universidad de Chile
1983	Universidad Católica	2002	not known
1984	Everton		
1985	Colo Colo		
1986	Cobreloa		
1987	Cobresal		

Paraguayan League Record 1906–2002

SEASON	CHAMPIONS	SEASON	CHAMPIONS
1906	Guaraní	1957	Olimpia
1907	Guaraní	1958	Olimpia
1908	no championship	1959	Olimpia
1909	Nacional	1960	Olimpia
1910	Libertad	1961	Cerro Porteño
1911	Nacional	1962	Olimpia
1912	Olimpia	1963	Cerro Porteño
1913	Cerro Porteño	1964	Guaraní
1914	Olimpia	1965	Olimpia
1915	Cerro Porteño	1966	Cerro Porteño
1916	Olimpia	1967	Guaraní
1917	Libertad	1968	Olimpia
1918	Cerro Porteño	1969	Guaraní
1919	Cerro Porteño	1970	Cerro Porteño
1920	Libertad	1971	Olimpia
1921	Guaraní	1972	Cerro Porteño
1922	no championship	1973	Cerro Porteño
1923	Guaraní	1974	Cerro Porteño
1924	Nacional	1975	Olimpia
1925	Olimpia	1976	Libertad
1926	Nacional	1977	Cerro Porteño
1927	Olimpia	1978	Olimpia
1928	Olimpia	1979	Olimpia
1929	Olimpia	1980	Olimpia
1930	Libertad	1981	Olimpia
1931	Olimpia	1982	Olimpia
1932–34	no championship	1983	Olimpia
1935	Cerro Porteño	1984	Guaraní
1936	Olimpia	1985	Olimpia
1937	Olimpia	1986	Sol de América
1938	Olimpia	1987	Cerro Porteño
1939	Cerro Porteño	1988	Olimpia
1940	Cerro Porteño	1989	Olimpia
1941	Cerro Porteño	1990	Cerro Porteño
1942	Nacional	1991	Sol de América
1943	Libertad	1992	Cerro Porteño
1944	Cerro Porteño	1993	Olimpia
1945	Libertad	1994	Cerro Porteño
1946	Nacional	1995	Olimpia
1947	Olimpia	1996	Cerro Porteño
1948	Olimpia	1997	Olimpia
1949	Guaraní	1998	Olimpia
1950	Cerro Porteño	1999	Olimpia
1951	Sportivo Luqueño	2000	Olimpia
1952	Presidente Hayes	2001	Cerro Porteño
1953	Sportivo Luqueño	2002	Libertad
1954	Cerro Porteño		
1955	Cerro Porteño		
1956	Olimpia		

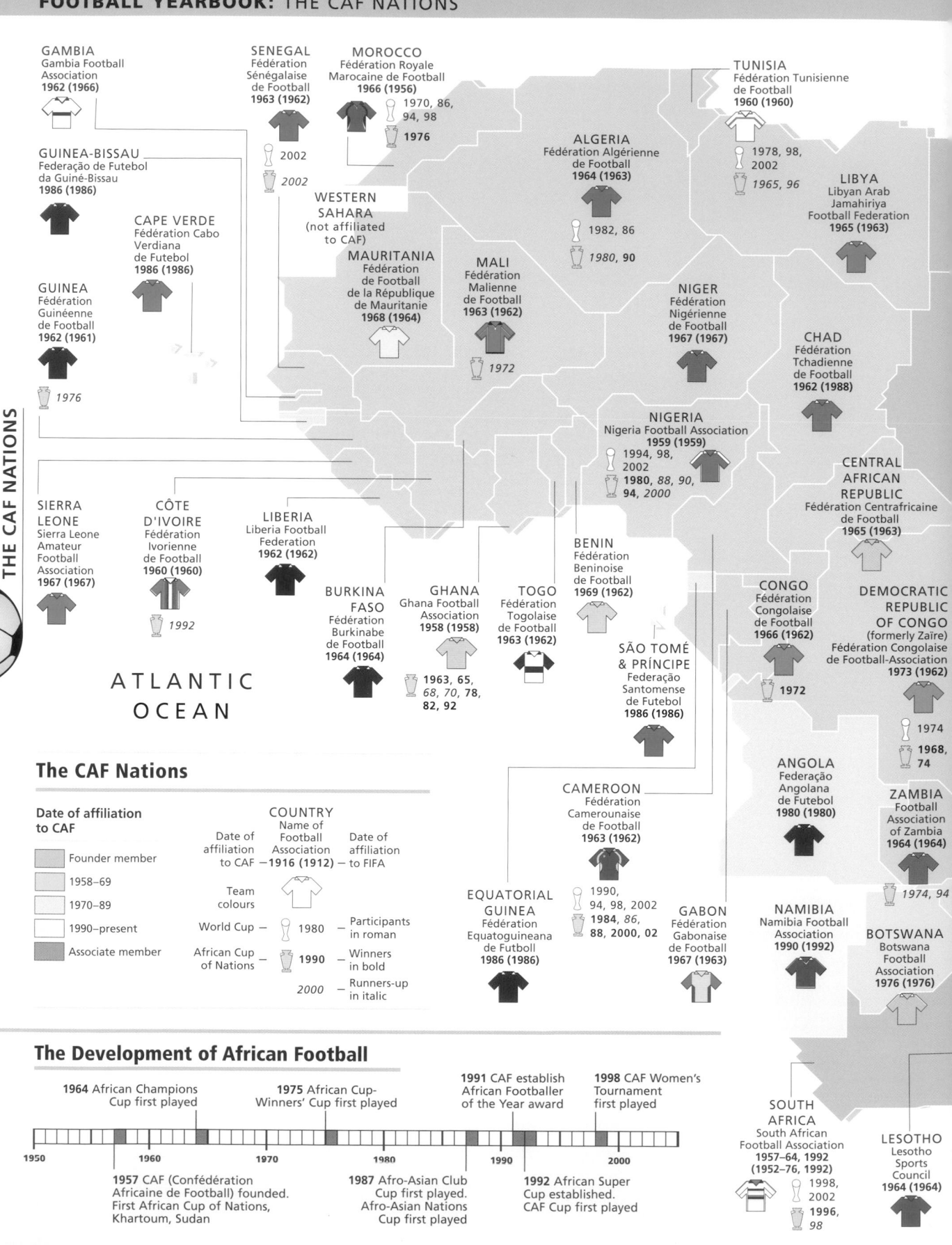

THE CAF NATIONS

GAMBIA
Gambia Football Association
1962 (1966)

GUINEA-BISSAU
Federação de Futebol da Guiné-Bissau
1986 (1986)

CAPE VERDE
Fédération Cabo Verdiana de Futebol
1986 (1986)

GUINEA
Fédération Guinéenne de Football
1962 (1961)
1976

SENEGAL
Fédération Sénégalaise de Football
1963 (1962)
2002
2002

MOROCCO
Fédération Royale Marocaine de Football
1966 (1956)
1970, 86, 94, 98
1976

WESTERN SAHARA
(not affiliated to CAF)

MAURITANIA
Fédération de Football de la République de Mauritanie
1968 (1964)

MALI
Fédération Malienne de Football
1963 (1962)
1972

ALGERIA
Fédération Algérienne de Football
1964 (1963)
1982, 86
1980, 90

NIGER
Fédération Nigérienne de Football
1967 (1967)

TUNISIA
Fédération Tunisienne de Football
1960 (1960)
1978, 98, 2002
1965, 96

LIBYA
Libyan Arab Jamahiriya Football Federation
1965 (1963)

CHAD
Fédération Tchadienne de Football
1962 (1988)

NIGERIA
Nigeria Football Association
1959 (1959)
1994, 98, 2002
1980, 88, *90, 94, 2000*

CENTRAL AFRICAN REPUBLIC
Fédération Centrafricaine de Football
1965 (1963)

SIERRA LEONE
Sierra Leone Amateur Football Association
1967 (1967)

CÔTE D'IVOIRE
Fédération Ivoirienne de Football
1960 (1960)
1992

LIBERIA
Liberia Football Federation
1962 (1962)

BURKINA FASO
Fédération Burkinabe de Football
1964 (1964)

GHANA
Ghana Football Association
1958 (1958)
1963, 65, 68, 70, *78, 82, 92*

TOGO
Fédération Togolaise de Football
1963 (1962)

BENIN
Fédération Beninoise de Football
1969 (1962)

SÃO TOMÉ & PRÍNCIPE
Federação Santomense de Futebol
1986 (1986)

CONGO
Fédération Congolaise de Football
1966 (1962)
1972

DEMOCRATIC REPUBLIC OF CONGO
(formerly Zaïre)
Fédération Congolaise de Football-Association
1973 (1962)
1974
1968, *74*

ATLANTIC OCEAN

CAMEROON
Fédération Camerounaise de Football
1963 (1962)
1990, 94, 98, 2002
1984, *86*, **88**, *2000, 02*

EQUATORIAL GUINEA
Fédération Equatoguineana de Futbol
1986 (1986)

GABON
Fédération Gabonaise de Football
1967 (1963)

ANGOLA
Federação Angolana de Futebol
1980 (1980)

ZAMBIA
Football Association of Zambia
1964 (1964)
1974, 94

NAMIBIA
Namibia Football Association
1990 (1992)

BOTSWANA
Botswana Football Association
1976 (1976)

The CAF Nations

Date of affiliation to CAF

- Founder member
- 1958–69
- 1970–89
- 1990–present
- Associate member

Date of affiliation to CAF — **1916 (1912)** — Date of affiliation to FIFA

COUNTRY
Name of Football Association

Team colours

World Cup — *1980* — Participants in roman
African Cup of Nations — **1990** — Winners in bold
2000 — Runners-up in italic

The Development of African Football

1964 African Champions Cup first played

1975 African Cup-Winners' Cup first played

1991 CAF establish African Footballer of the Year award

1998 CAF Women's Tournament first played

1950　1960　1970　1980　1990　2000

1957 CAF (Confédération Africaine de Football) founded. First African Cup of Nations, Khartoum, Sudan

1987 Afro-Asian Club Cup first played. Afro-Asian Nations Cup first played

1992 African Super Cup established. CAF Cup first played

SOUTH AFRICA
South African Football Association
1957–64, 1992
(1952–76, 1992)
1998, 2002
1996, *98*

LESOTHO
Lesotho Sports Council
1964 (1964)

The CAF Nations

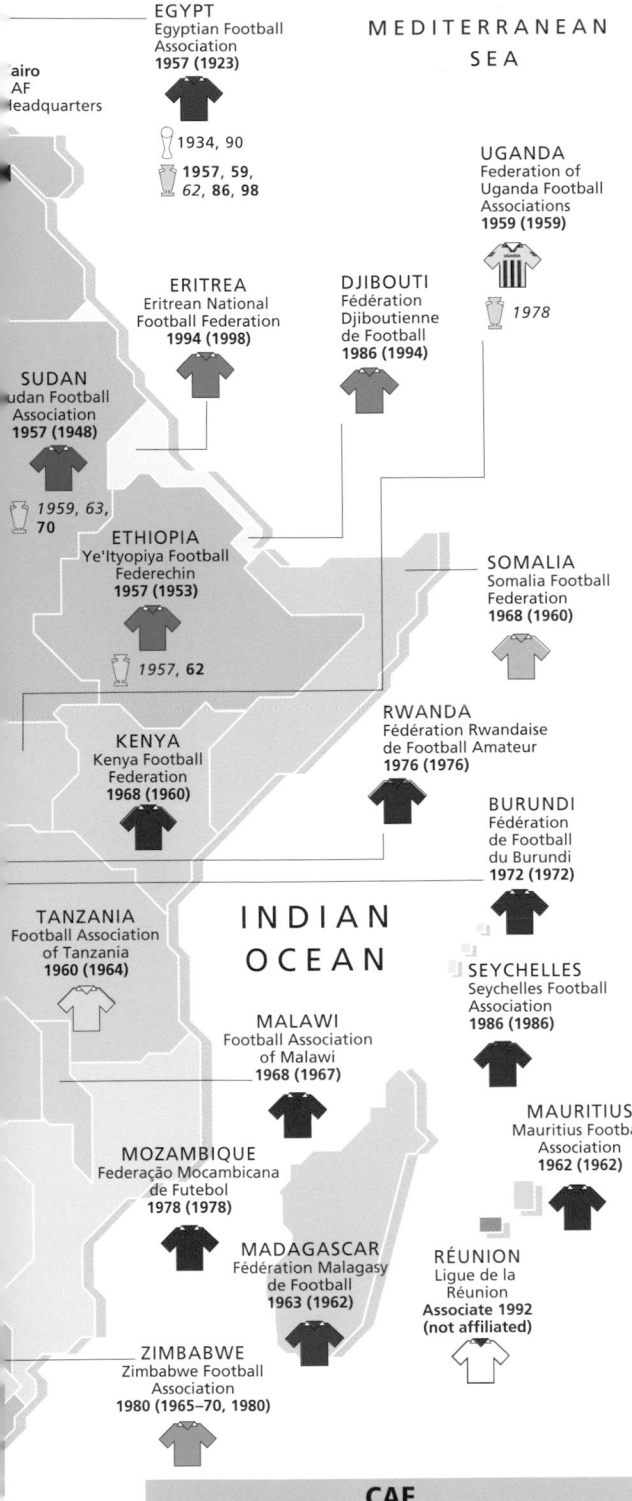

EGYPT
Egyptian Football
Association
1957 (1923)

airo
AF
Headquarters

🏆 1934, 90

🏆 **1957, 59,
62, 86, 98**

MEDITERRANEAN
SEA

UGANDA
Federation of
Uganda Football
Associations
1959 (1959)

🏆 *1978*

ERITREA
Eritrean National
Football Federation
1994 (1998)

DJIBOUTI
Fédération
Djiboutienne
de Football
1986 (1994)

SUDAN
udan Football
Association
1957 (1948)

🏆 *1959, 63,
70*

ETHIOPIA
Ye'Ityopiya Football
Federechin
1957 (1953)

🏆 *1957*, **62**

SOMALIA
Somalia Football
Federation
1968 (1960)

KENYA
Kenya Football
Federation
1968 (1960)

RWANDA
Fédération Rwandaise
de Football Amateur
1976 (1976)

BURUNDI
Fédération
de Football
du Burundi
1972 (1972)

TANZANIA
Football Association
of Tanzania
1960 (1964)

INDIAN
OCEAN

SEYCHELLES
Seychelles Football
Association
1986 (1986)

MALAWI
Football Association
of Malawi
1968 (1967)

MAURITIUS
Mauritius Football
Association
1962 (1962)

MOZAMBIQUE
Federação Mocambicana
de Futebol
1978 (1978)

MADAGASCAR
Fédération Malagasy
de Football
1963 (1962)

RÉUNION
Ligue de la
Réunion
**Associate 1992
(not affiliated)**

ZIMBABWE
Zimbabwe Football
Association
1980 (1965–70, 1980)

SWAZILAND
ational Football
Association of
Swaziland
1976 (1976)

CAF

African Tournaments
and Cup Competitions:
African Cup of Nations
CAF Cup
African Champions League
African Cup-Winners' Cup
CAF Super Cup

CAF (CONFEDERATION AFRICAINE DE FOOTBALL) was first proposed in 1956 by representatives of the only independent nations then in Africa: Egypt, Ethiopia, Sudan and South Africa. With FIFA support the organization was inaugurated in Khartoum in 1957 and then based in Cairo, Egypt. Politics intervened in CAF's development immediately when the South Africans proposed sending either an all-black or all-white team to the first African Cup of Nations in Sudan. South Africa was then suspended and remained outside the CAF until 1992.

With only three members CAF's global and continental influence was small but the wave of decolonization that swept Africa from the late 1950s rapidly increased its membership, while the quality and popularity of African football has steadily enhanced CAF's status and power at the FIFA table. CAF votes and influence were central to the success of João Havelange in winning the FIFA presidency in 1974 and African representation at the World Cup has climbed to five places.

Despite the size of the continent, the expense of travel and the often-shaky finances of local football associations, CAF has now established three international club tournaments and the biennial African Cup of Nations. Within CAF there are also five regional federations: the Arab Football Union, Confederation of East and Central African Football Associations, Confederation of Southern African Football Federations, Union of Football Associations of Central Africa and West African Football Union, each of which organizes its own cup competition.

Chaotic scenes like this one, as people jostle for a good view before a league match between Hearts of Oak and Asante Kotoko in Accra Stadium in Ghana, are commonplace at African football matches.

Calendar of Events	
Club Tournaments	African Champions League 2004
	African Cup-Winners' Cup 2004
	CAF Cup 2004
	CAF Super Cup 2004
International Tournaments	African Cup of Nations 2004
	Qualifying Tournament for 2004 Olympic Games (Under–23s)

Africa

THE SEASONS IN REVIEW 2001–02, 2002–03

AS IF WE NEEDED REMINDING OF THE quality of African football, the 2002 World Cup opened with Senegal's sensational defeat of reigning champions France and saw them progress to the quarter-finals. Striker El Hadji Diouf, despite a mediocre season at Liverpool, received his second African Player of the Year award as the most public figurehead of the Senegalese effort.

The administrative and political weakness of African football had been highlighted prior to the World Cup as Issa Hayatou, president of CAF, was decisively beaten in the contest for the FIFA presidency by incumbent Sepp Blatter, probably receiving less than half of Africa's vote. On returning to his new Cairo Offices, Hayatou has purged the organization, initiated a reformation of the Champions League with more money and games concentrated in the biggest clubs and countries, and merged the two other competitions into a single African Confederations Cup. Nonetheless, a number of candidates have already announced their intention to contest the presidency in 2004; his leading challenger will be Ismail Bhamjee, president of the Botswana FA.

The high football politics has been intense this year as contenders for the right to host African 2010 World Cup were forced to declare their hand. Nigeria did so at the last minute, but no one believes that FIFA will let the World Cup anywhere near Lagos. The competition is between runaway favourites South Africa and four North African states. South Africa came within a vote of winning it in 2006 and has the established infrastructure required. Tunisia is considered too small, Egypt too violent. Libya, despite or perhaps because of the furious manoeuvring of football supremo Saad Gaddaffi, is too unpredictable. That leaves Morocco, which is relatively calm and near to Europe.

The low politics of African football has seen players and coaches lose their lives in transport disasters in Mozambique and Sudan, while the usual catalogue of fights and scuffles have accompanied the South African Cup Final, Zamalek v Al-Ahly clashes and most of the North African home games in the African club competitions.

In these competitions, it was a clean sweep for North Africa. Zamalek won its fifth Champions League against Raja Casablanca. The finale descended into a particularly unpleasant on-field brawl between players, coaches, police and officials. An equally rough occasion saw JS Kabylie effectively wrap up its third consecutive CAF Cup, beating Tonnerre Yaoundé 4-0. WAC Casablanca made it three when it won the Cup-Winners' Cup, beating Asante Kotoko. But the biggest prize, the World Cup, is probably going south.

Tonnerre Yaoundé outjumps the JS Kabylie defence but to no avail, as Kabylie win 4-1 on aggregate.

Top 16 African Leagues

COUNTRY	CHAMPIONS	RUNNERS-UP	CUP WINNERS
Algeria	USM Alger	USm Blida	WA Telemen
Angola*	AS Aviaçaõ	Primeiro de Agosto	Petro Atlético
Cameroon*	Canon Yaoundé	Cotonsport	Mount Cameroon
Cote d'ivoire*	ASEC Abidjan	JC Abidjan	Africa Sports
DR Congo	no national league in 2002		DC Motema Pembe
Egypt	Zamalek	Al Ahly	Al Ahly
Ghana*	Hearts of Oak	Asante Kotoko	
Kenya	Nzoia Sugar	Tusker	Kenya Pipeline
Morocco			
Nigeria*	Enyimba	Enugu Rangers	Julius Berger
Senegal*			
South Africa	Orlando Pirates	Supersport United	Santos
Tanzania*	Simba FC	Police	JKT Ruvu Stars
Tunisia	Espérance Sportive	Étoile du Sahel	CS Sfaxien
Zambia*	Zanaco	Power Dynamos	Power Dynamos
Zimbabwe	Zimbabwe Highlanders	Black Rhinos	Masvingo United

* Data for season 2001–02, the rest correct to summer 2003.

Champions League

2002 FINAL (2 legs)

November 30 – Casablanca, Morocco
Raja 0-0 Zamalek
Casablanca   (Egypt)
(South Africa)
h/t: 0-0 **Att :** 75,000
Ref: Ndoye (Senegal)

December 13 – Cairo, Egypt
Zamalek 1-0 Raja
(Abdel Hamid 45)   Casablanca
h/t: 1-0 **Att:** 70,000
Ref: Shelmani (Libya)
Zamelek won 1-0 on aggregate

CAF Cup

2002 FINAL (2 legs)

November 8 – Algiers, Algeria
JS Kabylie 4-0 Tonnerre
(Algeria)   Yaoundé
(Amaouche 3,   (Cameroon)
Berguiga 45, 85,
Zafour 61)
h/t: 2-0 **Att:** 80,000
Ref: Codjia (Benin)

November 24 – Yaoundé, Cameroon
Tonnerre 1-0 JS Kabylie
Yaoundé
(Eyoum 11)
h/t: 1-0 **Att:** 5,000
Ref: Guirat (Tunisia)
JS Kabylie won 4-1 on aggregate

Cup-Winners' Cup

2002 FINAL (2 legs)

November 16 – Casablanca, Morocco
WAC 1-0 Asante
Casablanca   Kotoko
(Morocco)   (Ghana)
(Madihi 50)
h/t: 0-0 **Att:** 30,000
Ref: Divine (Cameroon)

December 8 – Kumasi, Ghana
Asante 2-1 WAC
Kotoko   Casablanca
(Ansah 54,   *(Talha 73)*
Osei 86)
h/t: 0-0 **Att:** 80,000
Ref: Al Ghandour (Egypt)
WAC Casablanca won on away goals rule

Super Cup

2003 FINAL

February 7 – Cairo, Egypt
Zamalek 3-1 WAC
(Egypt)   Casablanca
(Wahid 28,   (Morocco)
Emam 61, Ali 64)   *(Zadi 79)*
h/t: 1-0 **Att:** 60,000

Right: Jean Jacques of WAC Casablanca tries to find his way through Zamalek's defence in the African Super Cup.

WAC Casablanca grabs an away goal in Ghana to win the African Cup-Winners' Cup from Asante Kotoko.

Above: The Hassan Twins, Hossam on the left and Ibrahim on the right, clasp the African Champion's Cup 15 years since they won the Cup together with Zamalek's arch rivals Al Ahly.

Left: Zamalek celebrates its African Super Cup victory over WAC Casablanca.

Below: El Hadji Diouf, African Player of the Year for a second year running, the first double since George Weah.

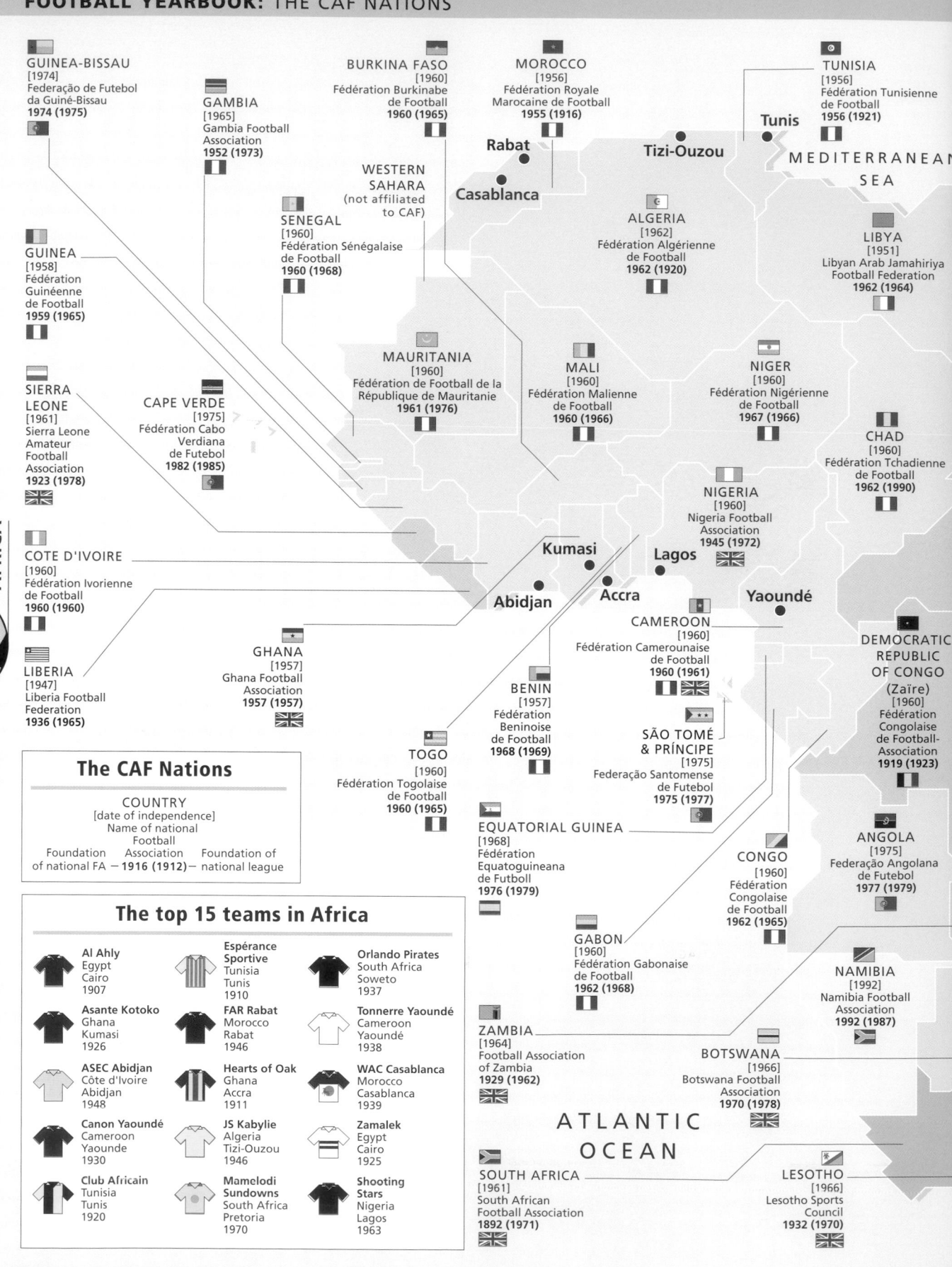

GUINEA-BISSAU
[1974]
Federação de Futebol
da Guiné-Bissau
1974 (1975)

GAMBIA
[1965]
Gambia Football
Association
1952 (1973)

BURKINA FASO
[1960]
Fédération Burkinabe
de Football
1960 (1965)

MOROCCO
[1956]
Fédération Royale
Marocaine de Football
1955 (1916)

TUNISIA
[1956]
Fédération Tunisienne
de Football
1956 (1921)

**WESTERN
SAHARA**
(not affiliated
to CAF)

SENEGAL
[1960]
Fédération Sénégalaise
de Football
1960 (1968)

GUINEA
[1958]
Fédération
Guinéenne
de Football
1959 (1965)

ALGERIA
[1962]
Fédération Algérienne
de Football
1962 (1920)

LIBYA
[1951]
Libyan Arab Jamahiriya
Football Federation
1962 (1964)

**SIERRA
LEONE**
[1961]
Sierra Leone
Amateur
Football
Association
1923 (1978)

CAPE VERDE
[1975]
Fédération Cabo
Verdiana
de Futebol
1982 (1985)

MAURITANIA
[1960]
Fédération de Football de la
République de Mauritanie
1961 (1976)

MALI
[1960]
Fédération Malienne
de Football
1960 (1966)

NIGER
[1960]
Fédération Nigérienne
de Football
1967 (1966)

CHAD
[1960]
Fédération Tchadienne
de Football
1962 (1990)

AFRICA

COTE D'IVOIRE
[1960]
Fédération Ivorienne
de Football
1960 (1960)

NIGERIA
[1960]
Nigeria Football
Association
1945 (1972)

Kumasi

Lagos

Yaoundé

Abidjan

Accra

GHANA
[1957]
Ghana Football
Association
1957 (1957)

CAMEROON
[1960]
Fédération Camerounaise
de Football
1960 (1961)

**DEMOCRATIC
REPUBLIC
OF CONGO**
(Zaïre)
[1960]
Fédération
Congolaise
de Football-
Association
1919 (1923)

LIBERIA
[1947]
Liberia Football
Federation
1936 (1965)

BENIN
[1957]
Fédération
Beninoise
de Football
1968 (1969)

**SÃO TOMÉ
& PRÍNCIPE**
[1975]
Federação Santomense
de Futebol
1975 (1977)

TOGO
[1960]
Fédération Togolaise
de Football
1960 (1965)

EQUATORIAL GUINEA
[1968]
Fédération
Equatoguineana
de Futboll
1976 (1979)

CONGO
[1960]
Fédération
Congolaise
de Football
1962 (1965)

ANGOLA
[1975]
Federação Angolana
de Futebol
1977 (1979)

GABON
[1960]
Fédération Gabonaise
de Football
1962 (1968)

NAMIBIA
[1992]
Namibia Football
Association
1992 (1987)

ZAMBIA
[1964]
Football Association
of Zambia
1929 (1962)

BOTSWANA
[1966]
Botswana Football
Association
1970 (1978)

SOUTH AFRICA
[1961]
South African
Football Association
1892 (1971)

LESOTHO
[1966]
Lesotho Sports
Council
1932 (1970)

MEDITERRANEAN
SEA

ATLANTIC
OCEAN

Tunis

Tizi-Ouzou

Rabat

Casablanca

The CAF Nations

COUNTRY
[date of independence]
Name of national
Football
Foundation   Association   Foundation of
of national FA — **1916 (1912)** — national league

The top 15 teams in Africa

Al Ahly
Egypt
Cairo
1907

**Espérance
Sportive**
Tunisia
Tunis
1910

Orlando Pirates
South Africa
Soweto
1937

Asante Kotoko
Ghana
Kumasi
1926

FAR Rabat
Morocco
Rabat
1946

Tonnerre Yaoundé
Cameroon
Yaoundé
1938

ASEC Abidjan
Côte d'Ivoire
Abidjan
1948

Hearts of Oak
Ghana
Accra
1911

WAC Casablanca
Morocco
Casablanca
1939

Canon Yaoundé
Cameroon
Yaounde
1930

JS Kabylie
Algeria
Tizi-Ouzou
1946

Zamalek
Egypt
Cairo
1925

Club Africain
Tunisia
Tunis
1920

**Mamelodi
Sundowns**
South Africa
Pretoria
1970

**Shooting
Stars**
Nigeria
Lagos
1963

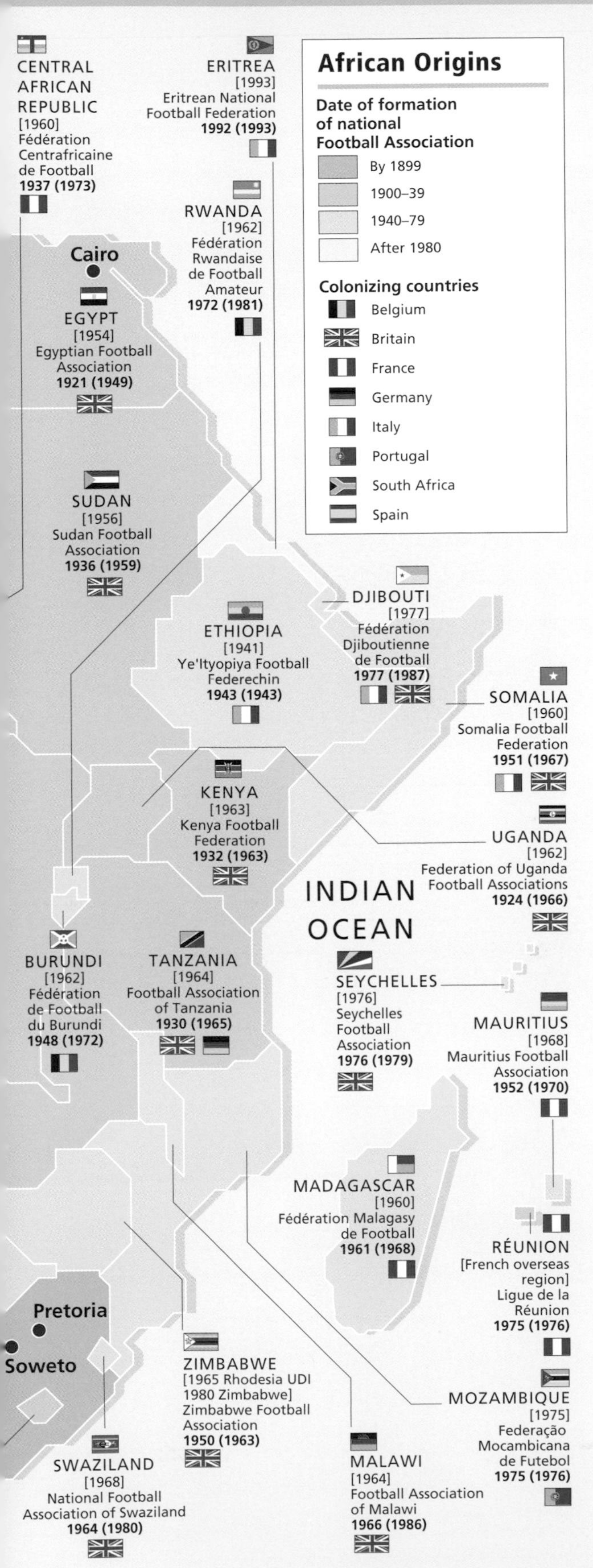

Africa

ORIGINS AND GROWTH OF FOOTBALL

FOOTBALL ARRIVED IN AFRICA via the usual routes – British sailors, missionaries, traders and administrators – but it was, of course, filtered through the various colonial establishments that ran the continent at the turn of 19th century. French, Belgian and Portuguese colonialists also imported football into the continent in the early years of the 20th century. As a consequence, organized football remained in schools and colleges for the most part, and independent national football associations and teams did not exist in most of the continent. The exception was the creation of the South African FA in 1892.

During the inter-war years, football began to gain a substantial following among Africans. By the 1920s, leagues had developed across North Africa (Egypt, Tunisia, Algeria and Morocco) and matches were played between French colonies. Egypt, the strongest footballing nation, played at the 1920 Olympics and the first World Cup in 1930. In the 1930s, Nigerian football acquired organized leagues and inter-colony matches were played in British West Africa. Belgian Congo (later Zaïre, or Democratic Republic of Congo) and Ghana also acquired formal football leagues in this era, but in these countries it was the European colonists that retained administrative control.

Not surprisingly, the development of African football in the postwar years is intimately connected to the process of decolonization and the establishment of new states. CAF, formed from the only independent African nations in 1957 (Egypt, Ethiopia, Sudan and South Africa), held its first tournament that year to celebrate Sudanese independence, and almost immediately expelled South Africa for its continuing racial segregation of football teams and players.

The enormous popularity and domestic political significance of football in Africa since independence can be seen from politicians' desire to be associated with the game (the Zambian national team was known as the 'Kenneth Kaunda XI'), the political reorganization of clubs and leagues (in Algeria, all teams were allocated to nationalized industrial groupings in the1970s) and political battles over the control of national FAs. Football has continued to be strong in North Africa, but has more recently been challenged by the rise of Nigeria, Ghana, DR Congo, Cameroon and South Africa as significant footballing nations.

AFRICA

Hugely successful domestically, Al Ahly from Cairo was voted CAF Club of the Century in 2000, having attained three victories in the African Champions League and four in the African Cup-Winners' Cup.

African Origins

Date of formation of national Football Association

- By 1899
- 1900–39
- 1940–79
- After 1980

Colonizing countries

- Belgium
- Britain
- France
- Germany
- Italy
- Portugal
- South Africa
- Spain

CENTRAL AFRICAN REPUBLIC
[1960]
Fédération Centrafricaine de Football
1937 (1973)

ERITREA
[1993]
Eritrean National Football Federation
1992 (1993)

RWANDA
[1962]
Fédération Rwandaise de Football Amateur
1972 (1981)

Cairo

EGYPT
[1954]
Egyptian Football Association
1921 (1949)

SUDAN
[1956]
Sudan Football Association
1936 (1959)

DJIBOUTI
[1977]
Fédération Djiboutienne de Football
1977 (1987)

ETHIOPIA
[1941]
Ye'Ityopiya Football Federechin
1943 (1943)

SOMALIA
[1960]
Somalia Football Federation
1951 (1967)

KENYA
[1963]
Kenya Football Federation
1932 (1963)

UGANDA
[1962]
Federation of Uganda Football Associations
1924 (1966)

INDIAN OCEAN

BURUNDI
[1962]
Fédération de Football du Burundi
1948 (1972)

TANZANIA
[1964]
Football Association of Tanzania
1930 (1965)

SEYCHELLES
[1976]
Seychelles Football Association
1976 (1979)

MAURITIUS
[1968]
Mauritius Football Association
1952 (1970)

MADAGASCAR
[1960]
Fédération Malagasy de Football
1961 (1968)

RÉUNION
[French overseas region]
Ligue de la Réunion
1975 (1976)

Pretoria

Soweto

ZIMBABWE
[1965 Rhodesia UDI 1980 Zimbabwe]
Zimbabwe Football Association
1950 (1963)

MOZAMBIQUE
[1975]
Federação Moçambicana de Futebol
1975 (1976)

SWAZILAND
[1968]
National Football Association of Swaziland
1964 (1980)

MALAWI
[1964]
Football Association of Malawi
1966 (1986)

The African Cup of Nations

TOURNAMENT OVERVIEW

THE COURSE OF THE AFRICAN CUP OF NATIONS inevitably parallels many aspects of Africa's postwar history. Prior to the massive wave of decolonization that swept the continent in the 1960s, only four nations were entered in the first tournament, in Sudan in 1957: Ethiopia, Egypt, South Africa and Sudan. South Africa was forced to withdraw by CAF because it refused to send a mixed-race team, and Egypt won the trophy easily, beating Ethiopia 4-0 in the Final.

In 1963 and 1965, Ghana, the first new nation to achieve independence in this era, announced West Africa's footballing prowess by winning both Finals against North African opposition. From Ghana, the baton passed to Central Africa, with the two Congos winning three of the next four tournaments.

In 1965, CAF ruled that each squad could only play two overseas-based players and the rule remained in force until 1982. By then, the rapidly increasing African presence in European leagues left the tournament without many of the leading stars of African football. The tournament further accommodated the power of European football by switching the finals to January, taking advantage of player availability during European football's mid-season break. Across this period, the growing strength of African football saw the tournament acquire a qualifying round and expand from four to eight participants in the finals. In 1992, it expanded again to 12 teams and in 1996 to 16.

With access to European-based players, the championships have been dominated by West Africa since the 1980s, with Ghana, Nigeria and Cameroon all taking the prize with an occasional look in for North African states and a resurgent post-apartheid South African victory in 1996.

The African Cup of Nations (1956–2002)

YEAR	WINNERS	SCORE	RUNNERS-UP
1957	Egypt	4-0	Ethiopia
1959	Egypt	*final tournament*	Sudan
1962	Ethiopia	4-2	Egypt
1963	Ghana	3-0	Sudan
1965	Ghana	3-2	Tunisia
1968	Congo-Kinshasa	1-0	Ghana
1970	Sudan	1-0	Ghana
1972	Congo	3-2	Mali
1974	Zaïre	2-2, replay 2-0	Zambia
1976	Morocco	*final tournament*	Guinea
1978	Ghana	2-0	Uganda
1980	Nigeria	3-0	Algeria
1982	Ghana	1-1 (7-6 pens)	Libya
1984	Cameroon	3-1	Nigeria
1986	Egypt	0-0 (5-4 pens)	Cameroon
1988	Cameroon	1-0	Nigeria
1990	Algeria	1-0	Nigeria
1992	Ghana	0-0 (11-10 pens)	Côte d'Ivoire
1994	Nigeria	2-1	Zambia
1996	South Africa	2-0	Tunisia
1998	Egypt	2-0	South Africa
2000	Cameroon	2-2 (4-3 pens)	Nigeria
2002	Cameroon	0-0 (3-2 pens)	Senegal

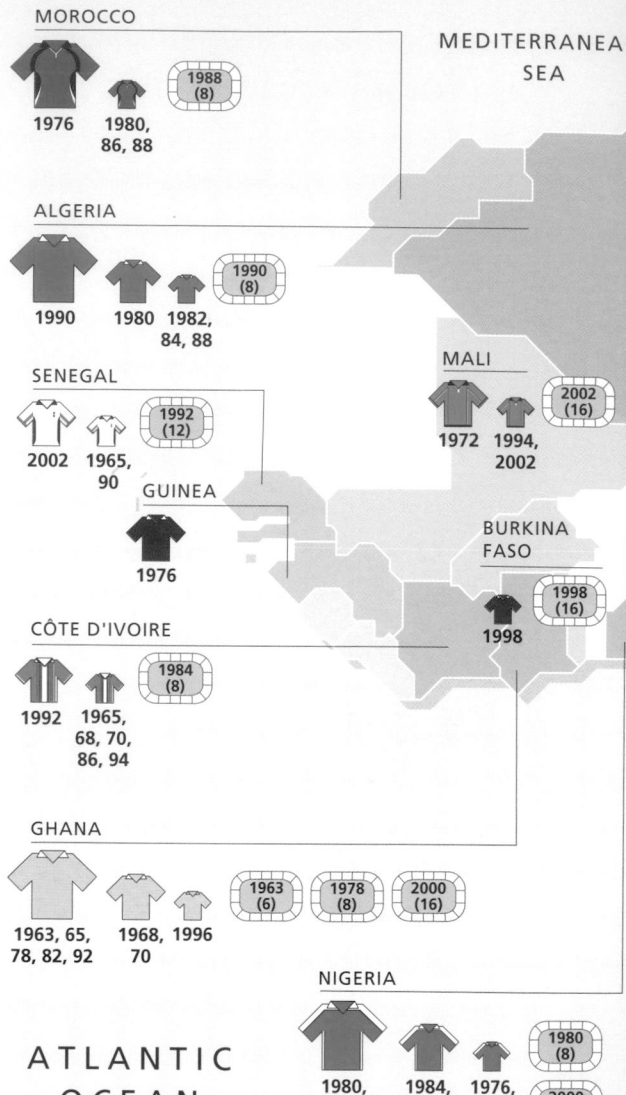

MOROCCO
1976 | 1980, 86, 88 | 1988 (8)

ALGERIA
1990 | 1980 | 1982, 84, 88 | 1990 (8)

SENEGAL
2002 | 1965, 90 | 1992 (12)

GUINEA
1976

CÔTE D'IVOIRE
1992 | 1965, 68, 70, 86, 94 | 1984 (8)

GHANA
1963, 65, 78, 82, 92 | 1968, 70 | 1996 | 1963 (6) | 1978 (8) | 2000 (16)

NIGERIA
1980, 94 | 1984, 88, 90, 2000 | 1976, 78, 92, 2002 | 1980 (8) | 2000 (16)

MALI
1972 | 1994, 2002 | 2002 (16)

BURKINA FASO
1998 | 1998 (16)

MEDITERRANEAN SEA

ATLANTIC OCEAN

The African Cup of Nations has been contested since 1957, but in recent years its colourful spectacle and top quality football has raised the tournament's profile.

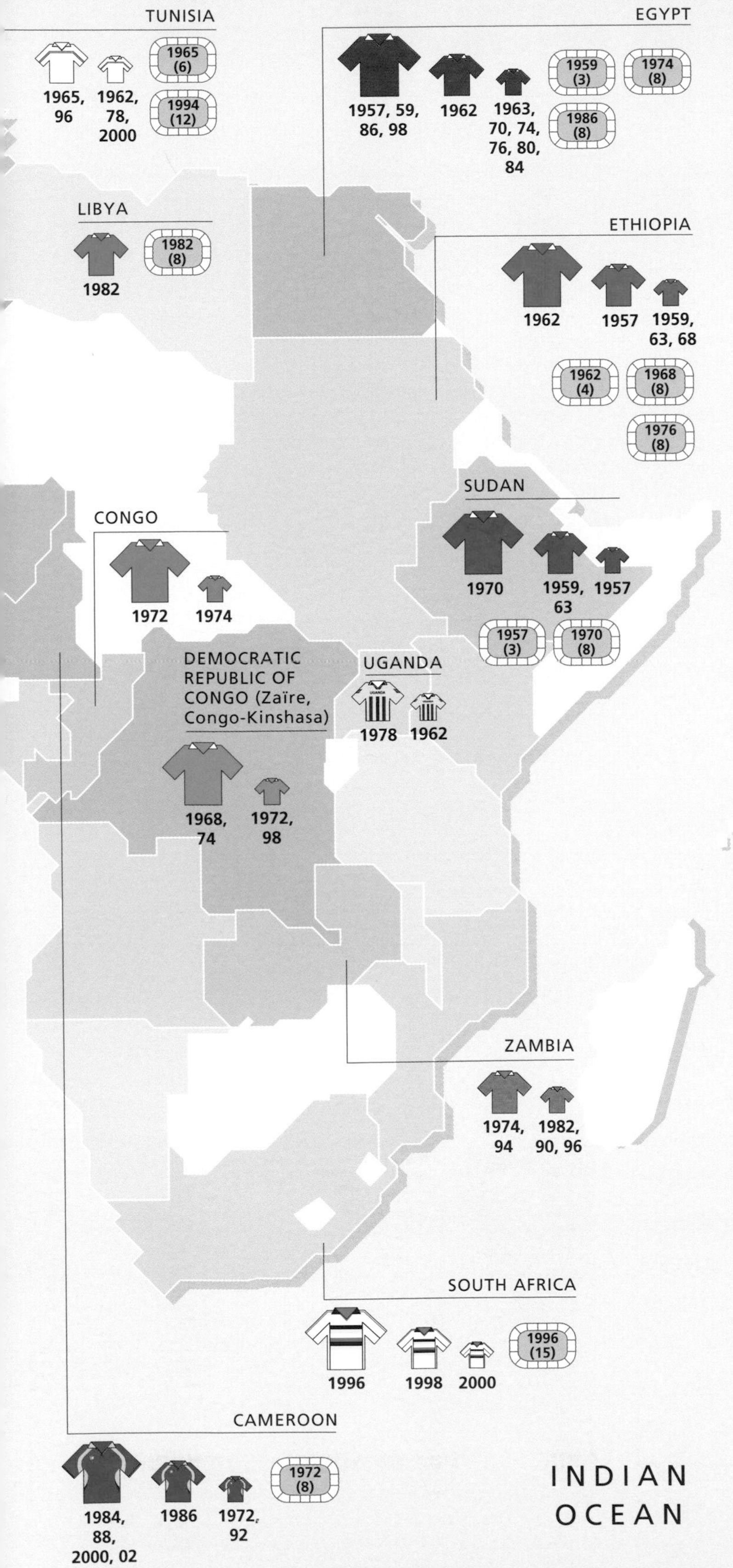

TUNISIA

1965, 96   1962, 78, 2000

1965 (6)
1994 (12)

EGYPT

1957, 59, 86, 98   1962   1963, 70, 74, 76, 80, 84

1959 (3)
1974 (8)
1986 (8)

LIBYA

1982

1982 (8)

ETHIOPIA

1962   1957   1959, 63, 68

1962 (4)
1968 (8)
1976 (8)

CONGO

1972   1974

SUDAN

1970   1959, 63   1957

1957 (3)
1970 (8)

DEMOCRATIC REPUBLIC OF CONGO (Zaïre, Congo-Kinshasa)

1968, 74   1972, 98

UGANDA

1978   1962

ZAMBIA

1974, 94   1982, 90, 96

SOUTH AFRICA

1996   1998   2000

1996 (15)

CAMEROON

1984, 88, 2000, 02   1986   1972, 92

1972 (8)

INDIAN OCEAN

The African Cup of Nations

Participation in the African Nations Cup

- 10+ times
- 6–9 times
- 2–5 times
- 1 time
- 0 times

Winners, runners-up and semi-finalists with date

1980   1980   1980

Host country, with date of tournament and number of participants in brackets

CAMEROON   1976 (4)

Football and the TV nation: Mali's unexpected but glorious run to the semi-finals in 2002 captivated the whole country.

The African Cup of Nations Top Goalscorers

YEAR	SCORER	NATIONALITY	GOALS
1957	El Attar	Egyptian	5
1959	Al-Gohari	Egyptian	3
1962	Badawi	Egyptian	3
	Worku	Ethiopian	
1963	Chazli	Egyptian	6
1965	Acheampong	Ghanaian	3
	Kofi	Ghanaian	
	Mangle	Côte d'Ivoire	
1968	Pokou	Côte d'Ivoire	6
1970	Pokou	Côte d'Ivoire	8
1972	Keita	Malian	5
1974	Ndaye	Zairean	9
1976	Mamadou	Guinean	4
1978	Omondi	Ugandan	4
1980	Labied	Moroccan	3
	Odegbami	Nigerian	
1982	Alhassan	Ghanaian	4
1984	Zeid	Egyptian	4
1986	Milla	Cameroon	4
1988	Abdelhamid	Egyptian	2
	Belloumi	Algerian	
	Milla	Cameroon	
	Traore	Côte d'Ivoire	
1990	Menad	Algerian	4
1992	Yekini	Nigerian	4
1994	Yekini	Nigerian	5
1996	Bwalya	Zambian	5
1998	Hassan	Egyptian	7
	McCarthy	South African	
2000	Bartlett	South African	5
2002	Aghahowa	Nigerian	3
	Mboma	Cameroon	
	Olembe	Cameroon	

The African Cup of Nations

TOURNAMENT REVIEW 2002

CAF'S COMMITMENT TO smaller and poorer African nations paid off in Mali, who managed to host a 16-nation, six-stadium tournament effectively. However, despite a great run by the home team, good attendances and balanced, competitive matches, the tournament will be remembered for a single act of violence. Before the Mali v Cameroon semi-final, local police attacked Cameroon's goalkeeping coach Thomas Nkono in full view of the crowd. Claims by CAF that he was the aggressor and by the Malian authorities that he had an incorrect ID card simply do not wash.

The group phase of the tournament was marred by rock hard pitches, imprecise finishing and very few goals. Qualification generally went with form, with Cameroon, Nigeria, Senegal and South Africa all winning their groups. Tunisia and Morocco played well below their best and went out, while home nation

Mali raised its game to qualify for the second phase. Liberia's exit saw the end of George Weah's legendary international career.

The quarter-finals were brought alive by Mali's 2-0 victory over South Africa, while Cameroon, Nigeria and Senegal's victories made the semi-finals all West African. Senegal and Cameroon proved worthy finalists, but both victories were overshadowed. Senegal v Nigeria descended into an orgy of red cards in an ill-tempered 30 minutes of extra time. Cameroon, taking revenge for mistreatment by the Malian authorities, convincingly dispatched the hosts 3-0. The Final was tense, with Cameroon having the best of the play. There were missed chances for Cameroon's N'Diefi and a disallowed goal for Eto'o. The match came down to penalties, and Senegal's captain Aliou Cissé saw his spot kick saved by Cameroon's Boukar Alioum; 3-2 to Cameroon.

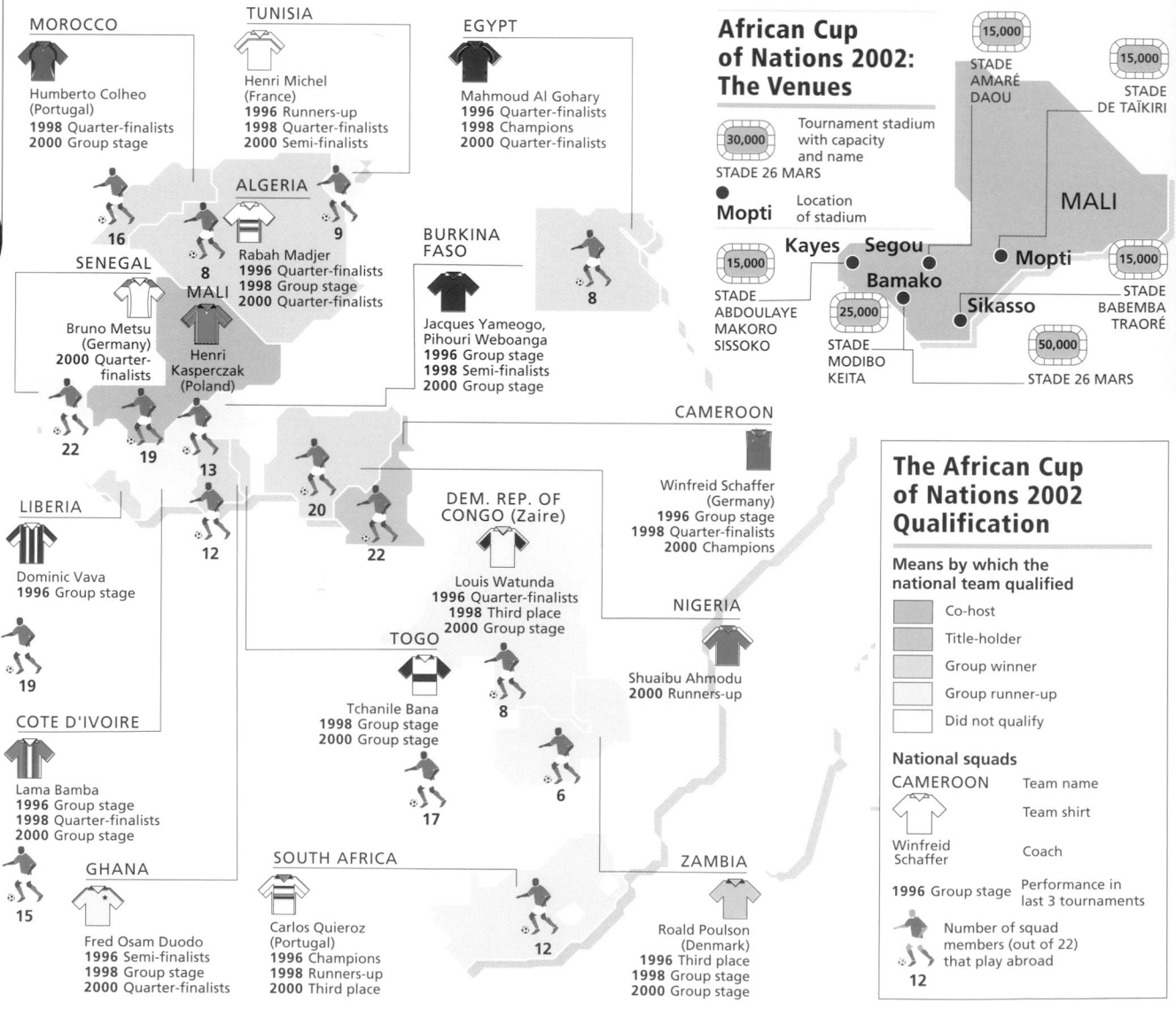

MOROCCO
Humberto Colheo (Portugal)
1998 Quarter-finalists
2000 Group stage

16

TUNISIA
Henri Michel (France)
1996 Runners-up
1998 Quarter-finalists
2000 Semi-finalists

EGYPT
Mahmoud Al Gohary
1996 Quarter-finalists
1998 Champions
2000 Quarter-finalists

ALGERIA
Rabah Madjer
1996 Quarter-finalists
1998 Group stage
2000 Quarter-finalists

9

8

SENEGAL
Bruno Metsu (Germany)
2000 Quarter-finalists

MALI
Henri Kasperczak (Poland)

BURKINA FASO
Jacques Yameogo, Pihouri Weboanga
1996 Group stage
1998 Semi-finalists
2000 Group stage

8

22

19

13

20

22

12

CAMEROON
Winfried Schaffer (Germany)
1996 Group stage
1998 Quarter-finalists
2000 Champions

LIBERIA
Dominic Vava
1996 Group stage

19

COTE D'IVOIRE
Lama Bamba
1996 Group stage
1998 Quarter-finalists
2000 Group stage

GHANA
Fred Osam Duodo
1996 Semi-finalists
1998 Group stage
2000 Quarter-finalists

15

DEM. REP. OF CONGO (Zaire)
Louis Watunda
1996 Quarter-finalists
1998 Third place
2000 Group stage

TOGO
Tchanile Bana
1998 Group stage
2000 Group stage

17

8

6

NIGERIA
Shuaibu Ahmodu
2000 Runners-up

SOUTH AFRICA
Carlos Quieroz (Portugal)
1996 Champions
1998 Runners-up
2000 Third place

12

ZAMBIA
Roald Poulson (Denmark)
1996 Third place
1998 Group stage
2000 Group stage

African Cup of Nations 2002: The Venues

30,000 Tournament stadium with capacity and name
STADE 26 MARS

● **Mopti** Location of stadium

15,000 STADE AMARÉ DAOU

15,000 STADE DE TAÏKIRI

MALI

Kayes   Segou   ● Mopti

Bamako

15,000 STADE ABDOULAYE MAKORO SISSOKO

25,000 STADE MODIBO KEITA

Sikasso

15,000 STADE BABEMBA TRAORÉ

50,000 STADE 26 MARS

The African Cup of Nations 2002 Qualification

Means by which the national team qualified

- Co-host
- Title-holder
- Group winner
- Group runner-up
- Did not qualify

National squads

CAMEROON — Team name

Team shirt

Winfried Schaffer — Coach

1996 Group stage — Performance in last 3 tournaments

12 — Number of squad members (out of 22) that play abroad

THE GROUP STAGES

GROUP A		
Mali **1-1** Liberia		
Nigeria **1-0** Algeria		
Mali **0-0** Nigeria		
Liberia **2-2** Algeria		
Mali **2-0** Algeria		
Nigeria **1-0** Liberia		

	P	W	D	L	F	A	Pts
Nigeria	3	2	1	0	2	0	7
Mali	3	1	2	0	3	1	5
Liberia	3	0	2	1	3	4	2
Algeria	3	0	1	2	2	5	1

GROUP B		
South Africa **0-0** Burkina Faso		
Morocco **0-0** Ghana		
South Africa **0-0** Ghana		
Morocco **2-1** Burkina Faso		
South Africa **3-1** Morocco		
Ghana **2-1** Burkina Faso		

	P	W	D	L	F	A	Pts
South Africa	3	1	2	0	3	1	5
Ghana	3	1	2	0	2	1	5
Morocco	3	1	1	1	3	4	4
Burkina Faso	3	0	1	2	2	4	1

GROUP C		
Cameroon **1-0** DR Congo		
Togo **0-0** Côte d'Ivoire		
Cameroon **1-0** Côte d'Ivoire		
DR Congo **0-0** Togo		
Cameroon **3-0** Togo		
DR Congo **3-1** Côte d'Ivoire		

	P	W	D	L	F	A	Pts
Cameroon	3	3	0	0	5	0	9
DR Congo	3	1	1	1	3	2	4
Togo	3	0	2	1	0	3	2
Côte d'Ivoire	3	0	1	2	1	4	1

GROUP D		
Senegal **1-0** Egypt		
Zambia **0-0** Tunisia		
Egypt **1-0** Tunisia		
Senegal **1-0** Zambia		
Egypt **2-1** Zambia		
Senegal **0-0** Tunisia		

	P	W	D	L	F	A	Pts
Senegal	3	2	1	0	2	0	7
Egypt	3	2	0	1	3	2	6
Tunisia	3	0	2	2	0	1	2
Zambia	3	0	1	2	1	3	1

THE QUARTER-FINALS

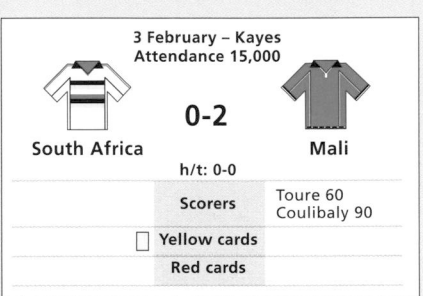

3 February – Kayes
Attendance 15,000

0-2

South Africa — Mali

h/t: 0-0

| Scorers | Toure 60 |
| | Coulibaly 90 |

☐ Yellow cards

Red cards

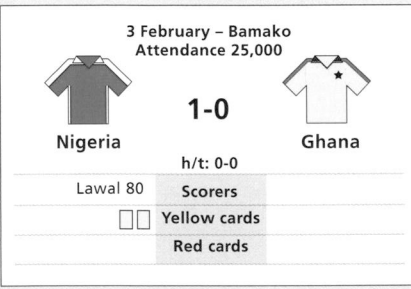

3 February – Bamako
Attendance 25,000

1-0

Nigeria — Ghana

h/t: 0-0

Lawal 80 | Scorers

☐☐ Yellow cards

Red cards

4 February – Sikasso
Attendance 15,000

1-0

Cameroon — Egypt

h/t: 0-0

Mboma 62 | Scorers

☐☐ Yellow cards ☐

Red cards

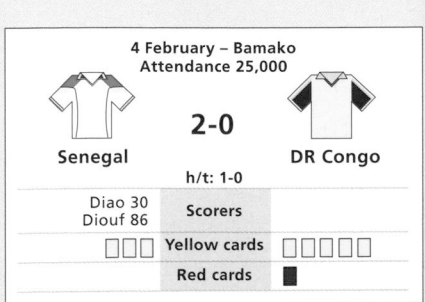

4 February – Bamako
Attendance 25,000

2-0

Senegal — DR Congo

h/t: 1-0

Diao 30 | Scorers
Diouf 86 |

☐☐☐ Yellow cards ☐☐☐☐☐

Red cards ■

THE SEMI-FINALS

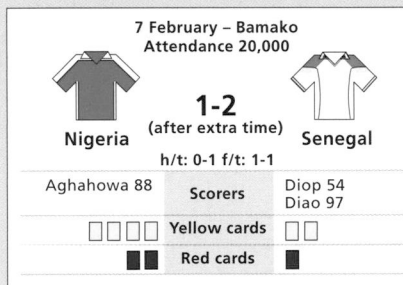

7 February – Bamako
Attendance 20,000

1-2
(after extra time)

Nigeria — Senegal

h/t: 0-1 f/t: 1-1

Aghahowa 88 | Scorers | Diop 54
| | Diao 97

☐☐☐☐ Yellow cards ☐☐

■■ Red cards ■

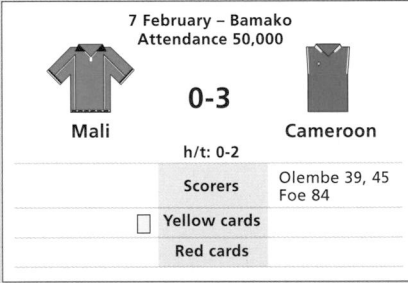

7 February – Bamako
Attendance 50,000

0-3

Mali — Cameroon

h/t: 0-2

| Scorers | Olembe 39, 45 |
| | Foe 84 |

☐ Yellow cards

Red cards

Cameroon celebrates after deservedly retaining the African Cup of Nations in Mali in 2002 after a tense Final against Senegal that ended in a penalty shootout.

THIRD PLACE PLAY-OFF

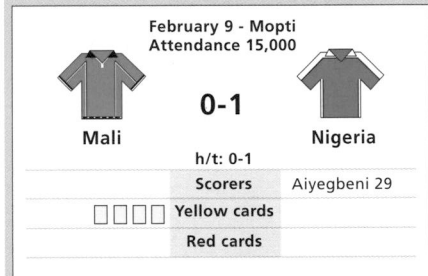

February 9 - Mopti
Attendance 15,000

0-1

Mali — Nigeria

h/t: 0-1

| Scorers | Aiyegbeni 29 |

☐☐☐☐ Yellow cards

Red cards

THE FINAL

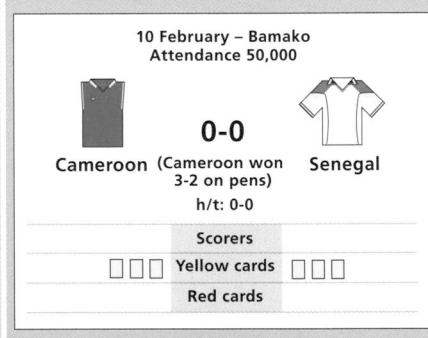

10 February – Bamako
Attendance 50,000

0-0

Cameroon (Cameroon won — Senegal
3-2 on pens)

h/t: 0-0

Scorers

☐☐☐ Yellow cards ☐☐☐

Red cards

The African Cup of Nations

ESTABLISHED ALONGSIDE the Confederation Africaine de Football (CAF) in 1957, the African Cup of Nations is the continent's main international tournament. Its timing has varied but has now been set for January to ensure that the increasingly large number of Africans who play in European leagues can attend during what is for many nations a midwinter break.

The early tournaments were small affairs with no qualifying rounds. Indeed, given the refusal of the CAF to accept an exclusively black or exclusively white South African team in 1957, the first tournament consisted of only two games. As the wave of decolonization crossed Africa in the late 1950s and 1960s the number of rounds, games and entrants steadily rose. Qualifying rounds were first introduced for the sixth tournament in 1968. By the early 1990s the final tournament had 12 entrants and this has now grown to 16.

1957 SUDAN

SEMI-FINALS

Ethiopia **w/o** South Africa
South Africa disqualified because of apartheid
Egypt **2-1** Sudan

FINAL

February 16 – Khartoum
Egypt **4-0** Ethiopia
(El Diba 4)
Att: 15,000 **Ref:** Youssef (Sudan)

1959 EGYPT

FINAL TOURNAMENT

May 22 – Cairo
Egypt **4-0** Ethiopia
(Gohri 29, 42, 73,
Cherbini 64)

May 22 – Cairo
Sudan **1-0** Ethiopia
(Drissa 40)

May 29 – Cairo
Egypt **2-1** Sudan
(Issam 12, 89)   (Manzual 65)

1 Egypt
2 Sudan
3 Ethiopia

1962 ETHIOPIA

SEMI-FINALS

Ethiopia **4-2** Tunisia
Egypt **2-1** Uganda

THIRD PLACE PLAY-OFF

January 20 – Addis Ababa
Tunisia **3-0** Uganda
(Djedidi,
Moncef Chérif,
Meddeb)

FINAL

January 21 – Addis Ababa
Ethiopia **4-2** Egypt
(Girma 74,   (Badawi 35, 75)
Menguitsou
84, 117,
Italo 101)
(after extra time)
h/t: 0-1 **90 mins:** 2-2
Att: 20,000 **Ref:** Brooks (Uganda)

1963 GHANA

THIRD PLACE PLAY-OFF

November 30 – Accra
Egypt **3-0** Ethiopia
(Raidh,
Taha,
Chazli)

FINAL

December 1 – Accra
Ghana **3-0** Sudan
(Aggrey-Fynn
62 pen,
Mfum 72, 82)
h/t: 0-0 **Att:** 50,000
Ref: Abdelkader (Tunisia)

1965 TUNISIA

THIRD PLACE PLAY-OFF

November 21 – Zouiten, Tunis
Côte d'Ivoire **1-0** Senegal
(Yobone 35)

FINAL

November 21 – Zouiten, Tunis
Ghana **3-2** Tunisia
(Odoi 37, 96,   (Chetali 47,
O. Kofi 79)   Chaibi 67)
(after extra time)
h/t: 1-0 **Att:** 30,000
Ref: Chekaimi (Algeria)

1968 ETHIOPIA

SEMI-FINALS

Congo- **3-2** Ethiopia
Kinshasa*
(after extra time)
Ghana **4-3** Côte d'Ivoire

THIRD PLACE PLAY-OFF

January 21 – Addis Ababa
Côte d'Ivoire **1-0** Ethiopia
(Pokou 28)

FINAL

January 21 – Addis Ababa
Congo- **1-0** Ghana
Kinshasa*
(Kalala 66)
h/t: 0-0 **Att:** 12,000
Ref: Al Diba (Egypt)

1970 SUDAN

SEMI-FINALS

Ghana **2-1** Côte d'Ivoire
(after extra time)
Sudan **2-1** Egypt
(after extra time)

THIRD PLACE PLAY-OFF

February 16 – Khartoum
Egypt **3-1** Côte d'Ivoire
(Chazli 3, 14, 15)   (Losseni 72)

FINAL

February 16 – Khartoum
Sudan **1-0** Ghana
(El Issed 12)
h/t: 1-0 **Att:** 35,000
Ref: Tesfaye (Ethiopia)

1972 CAMEROON

SEMI-FINALS

Congo **1-0** Cameroon
Mali **4-3** Zaïre
(after extra time)

THIRD PLACE PLAY-OFF

March 4 – Yaoundé
Cameroon **5-2** Zaïre
(Akono 4 pen,   (Kakoko 13,
Ndongo 31,   Majanga 17)
Owona 32,
Mouthé 34,
Ndoga 42)

FINAL

March 5 – Yaoundé
Congo **3-2** Mali
(M'bono 57, 59,   (Diakhité 42,
M'Pelé 63)   M. Traoré 75)
h/t: 0-1 **Att:** 5,000
Ref: Aoussi (Algeria)

1974 EGYPT

SEMI-FINALS

Zaïre **3-2** Egypt
Zambia **4-2** Congo
(after extra time)

THIRD PLACE PLAY-OFF

March 11 – Cairo
Egypt **4-0** Congo
(M. Abdou 5,
Chehata 18, 80,
Abngreisha 62)

FINAL

March 12 – Cairo
Zaïre **2-2** Zambia
(Ndaye 65, 117)   (Kaushi 40,
Sinyangwe 120)
(after extra time)
h/t: 0-1 **90 mins:** 1-1
Att: 5,000 **Ref:** Gamar (Libya)

REPLAY

March 14 – Cairo
Zaïre **2-0** Zambia
(Ndaye 30, 76)
h/t: 1-0 **Att:** 1,000
Ref: Gamar (Libya)

1976 ETHIOPIA

FINAL PHASE

March 9 – Addis Ababa
Guinea **1-1** Nigeria
(P. Camara 88)   (Lawal 52)

March 9 – Addis Ababa
Morocco **2-1** Egypt
(Faras 23,   (A. Rehab 34)
Zahraoui 88)

March 11 – Addis Ababa
Morocco **2-1** Egypt
(Faras 82,   (B. Otu 50)
Guezzar 87)

March 11 – Addis Ababa
Guinea **4-2** Egypt
(Léa 24, 65,   (Abdou 33,
Ghanem o.g. 53,   Siaguy 86)
Morciré 62)

March 14 – Addis Ababa
Nigeria **3-2** Egypt
(Ilerika 35, 62,   (Al-Khatib 7,
Lawal 82)   Ussama 41)

March 14 – Addis Ababa
Morocco **1-1** Guinea
(Baba 86)   (Chérif 33)

1 Morocco
2 Guinea
3 Nigeria

1978 GHANA

SEMI-FINALS

Ghana **1-0** Tunisia
Uganda **2-1** Nigeria

THIRD PLACE PLAY-OFF

March 16 – Accra
Nigeria **w/o** Tunisia
Tunisia withdrew at 1-1 after 30 mins.
Match awarded 2-0 to Nigeria

FINAL

March 18 – Accra
Ghana **2-0** Uganda
(Afriye 38, 64)
h/t: 1-0 **Att:** 40,000
Ref: El Ghoul (Libya)

1980 NIGERIA

SEMI-FINALS

Nigeria **1-0** Morocco
Egypt **2-2** Algeria
(after extra time)
Algeria won 4-2 on pens

THIRD PLACE PLAY-OFF

March 21 – Lagos
Morocco **2-0** Egypt
(Labied 9, 78)

FINAL

March 22 – Lagos
Nigeria **3-0** Algeria
(Odegbami 2, 42,
Lawal 50)
h/t: 2-0 **Att:** 80,000
Ref: Tesfaye (Ethiopia)

THE AFRICAN CUP OF NATIONS

The African Cup of Nations Winners

Egypt
1957, 59,
86, 98

Ethiopia
1962

Ghana
1963, 65, 78,
82, 92

Congo
1972

Sudan
1970

**Dem. Rep. of
Congo (Zaïre)**
1968, 74

Morocco
1976

Nigeria
1980, 94

Cameroon
1984, 88,
2000, 02

Algeria
1990

South Africa
1996

1982 LIBYA

SEMI-FINALS
Ghana **3-2** Algeria
(after extra time)
Libya **2-1** Zambia

THIRD PLACE PLAY-OFF
March 18 – Tripoli
Zambia **2-0** Algeria
*(Kamba 2,
Munshya 25)*

FINAL
March 19 – Tripoli
Ghana **1-1** Libya
(Al Hassan 35)   (Beshari 70)
(after extra time)
h/t: 0-1 **90 mins:** 1-1 **Att:** 50,000
Ref: Sohan Ramlochun (Mauritania)
Ghana won 7-6 on pens

1984 CÔTE D'IVOIRE

SEMI-FINALS
Nigeria **2-2** Egypt
(after extra time)
Nigeria won 8-7 on pens
Cameroon **0-0** Algeria
(after extra time)
Cameroon won 5-4 on pens

THIRD PLACE PLAY-OFF
March 17 – Abidjan
Algeria **3-1** Egypt
*(Madjer 67,   (Abdelghani
Belloumi 70,   74 pen)
Yahi 88)*

FINAL
March 17 – Abidjan
Cameroon **3-1** Nigeria
*(Ndjeya 32,   (Lawal 10))
Abega 79,
Ebongue 84)*
h/t: 1-1 **Att:** 50,000
Ref: Bennaceur (Tunisia)

1986 EGYPT

SEMI-FINALS
Egypt **1-0** Morocco
Cameroon **1-0** Côte d'Ivoire
(after extra time)

THIRD PLACE PLAY-OFF
March 20 – Cairo
Côte d'Ivoire **3-2** Morocco
*(Salah 8,   (Ghiati 44,
Kaondio   Sahil 85)
38 pen, 68)*

FINAL
March 21 – Cairo
Egypt **0-0** Cameroon
(after extra time)
h/t: 0-0 **90 mins:** 0-0
Att: 100,000 **Ref:** Bennaceur (Tunisia)
Egypt won 5-4 on pens

1988 MOROCCO

SEMI-FINALS
Cameroon **1-0** Morocco
Nigeria **1-1** Algeria
(after extra time)
Nigeria won 9-8 on pens

THIRD PLACE PLAY-OFF
March 26 – Casablanca
Algeria **1-1** Morocco
(Belloumi 87)   (Nader 67)
(after extra time)
Algeria won 4-3 on pens

FINAL
March 27 – Casablanca
Cameroon **1-0** Nigeria
(Kunde 55)
h/t: 1-0 **Att:** 50,000
Ref: Idrissa (Senegal)

1990 ALGERIA

SEMI-FINALS
Algeria **2-1** Senegal
Nigeria **2-0** Zambia

THIRD PLACE PLAY-OFF
March 15 – Algiers
Zambia **1-0** Senegal
(Chikabala 73)

FINAL
March 16 – Algiers
Algeria **1-0** Nigeria
(Oudjani 38)
h/t: 1-0 **Att:** 80,000
Ref: not known

1992 SENEGAL

SEMI-FINALS
Côte d'Ivoire **0-0** Cameroon
(after extra time)
Côte d'Ivoire won 3-1 on pens
Ghana **2-1** Nigeria

THIRD PLACE PLAY-OFF
January 21 – Dakar
Nigeria **2-1** Cameroon
*(Ekpo 75,   (Maboang 85)
Yekini 88)*
h/t: 2-1 **Att:** 2,000
Ref: Zeli (Côte d'Ivoire)

FINAL
January 26 – Dakar
Ghana **0-0** Côte d'Ivoire
(after extra time)
h/t: 0-0 **90 mins:** 0-0
Att: 60,000 **Ref:** Sene (Ghana)
Ghana won 11-10 on pens

*Cameroon's Salomon Olembe
celebrates after scoring the
winning penalty in the 2002 Final.*

1994 TUNISIA

SEMI-FINALS
Nigeria **2-2** Côte d'Ivoire
(after extra time)
Nigeria won 4-2 on pens
Zambia **4-0** Mali

THIRD PLACE PLAY-OFF
April 10 – Tunis
Côte d'Ivoire **3-1** Mali
*(Koné 2,   (Diallo 46)
Ouattara 68,
Sié 70)*

FINAL
April 10 – Tunis
Nigeria **2-1** Zambia
(Amunike 5, 46)   (Litana 3)
h/t: 1-1 **Att:** 25,000
Ref: Lim Kee Chong (Mauritania)

1996 SOUTH AFRICA

SEMI-FINALS
Tunisia **4-2** Zambia
South Africa **3-0** Ghana

THIRD PLACE PLAY-OFF
Zambia **1-0** Ghana

FINAL
Feb 3 – Johannesburg
South Africa **2-0** Tunisia
(Williams 73, 74)
h/t: 0-0 **Att:** 80,000
Ref: Massembe (Uganda)

1998 BURKINA FASO

SEMI-FINALS
South Africa **2-1** Congo-
Kinshasa*
(after extra time)
Egypt **2-0** Burkina Faso

THIRD PLACE PLAY-OFF
March 27 – Municipal, Ouagadougou
Congo- **4-4** Burkina Faso
Kinshasa*
Congo-Kinshasa won 4-1 on pens

FINAL
February 28 – 4 Août, Ouagadougou
Egypt **2-0** South Africa
*(A. Hassan 5,
T. Mostafa 13)*
h/t: 2-0 **Att:** 40,000
Ref: Belgola (Morocco)

2000 GHANA/NIGERIA

SEMI-FINALS
Nigeria **2-0** South Africa
Cameroon **3-0** Tunisia

THIRD PLACE PLAY-OFF
February 12 – Accra
South Africa **2-2** Tunisia
*(Bartlett 11,   (Zitouni 28, 90)
Novente 62)*
South Africa won 4-3 on pens

FINAL
February 13 – Lagos
Cameroon **2-2** Nigeria
*(Eto'o 26,   (Chukwu 44,
Mboma 31)   Okocha 47)*
h/t: 1-2 **90 mins:** 2-2
Att: 40,000 **Ref:** Daami (Tunisia)
Cameroon won 4-3 on pens

2002 MALI

SEMI-FINALS
Senegal **2-1** Nigeria
Mali **0-3** Cameroon

THIRD PLACE PLAY-OFF
February 9 – Mopti
Mali **0-1** Nigeria
(Aiyegbeni 29)

FINAL
February 10 – Bamako
Cameroon **0-0** Senegal
h/t: 0-0 **90 mins:** 0-0
Att: 50,000 **Ref:** Al Ghandour (Egypt)
Cameroon won 3-2 on pens

* Another name for Democratic Republic
of Congo/Zaïre

THE AFRICAN CHAMPIONS LEAGUE

The African Champions League

TOURNAMENT OVERVIEW

IN A REVERSE OF EUROPEAN FOOTBALL'S development, where continental club competitions preceded international tournaments, the African Champions Cup (as it was first known) followed the African Cup of Nations by seven years. It was first played in 1964, with the strongest support coming from Ghana, whose pan-Africanist president donated the tournament's Kwame Nkrumah trophy. Fourteen clubs played for the right to attend a finals tournament in Accra. The Ghanaian side, Real Republicans (closely associated with President Nkrumah and dissolved two years later after his fall), performed poorly, and the first champions were the Cameroonian side Oryx Douala. No tournament was played in 1965, and in 1966 it was played as a straight knockout over two legs.

For the first decade the cup belonged to Central and West African clubs. The Zaïrians Tout Puissant Englebert, Asante Kotoko of Ghana and Hafia Conakry from Guinea all won the title at least once during those early years, interspersed by Cameroonian and Congolese triumphs. TP Englebert's first victory came after two drawn legs against Asante Kotoko, who then refused a further play-off to decide the Final. After this incident, aggregate scores and then penalties were introduced to decide tied matches.

In the 1980s and 90s, the power base of African club football shifted north of the Sahara. Egyptian, Moroccan, Algerian and Tunisian teams have taken the title 17 times since 1981. Orlando Pirates' victory in 1995, after many years of South African exclusion, suggested the balance of power might tip again, but the recent victories of Hearts of Oak and Raja Casablanca suggests not. Following European developments, the tournament became the African Champions League in 1997 and acquired a mini-league format at the quarter-finals stage.

Asante Kotoko of Kumasi, Ghana, appeared in seven African Champions League finals between 1967 and 1993, winning the trophy in 1970 and 1983. The team is pictured here before the 1993 Final against the Egyptian side Zamalek.

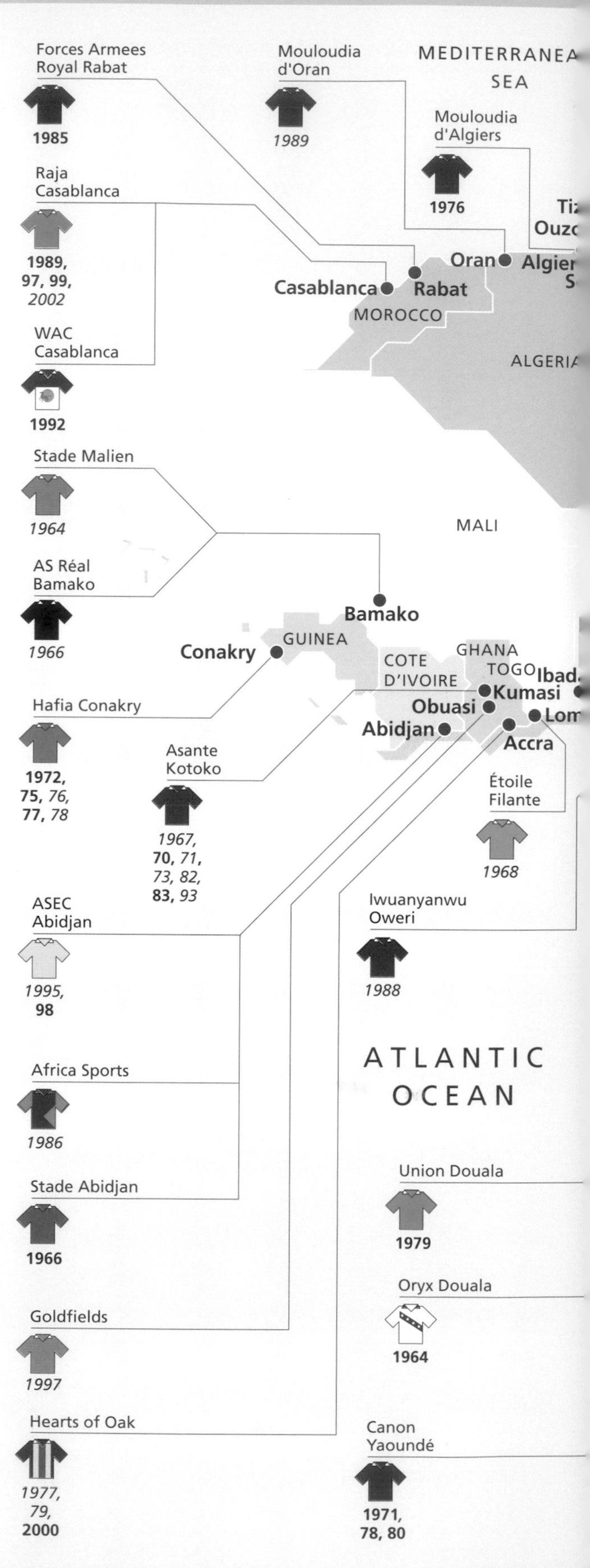

Forces Armees Royal Rabat
1985

Mouloudia d'Oran
1989

MEDITERRANEAN SEA

Mouloudia d'Algiers
1976

Raja Casablanca
1989, 97, 99, 2002

Tizi Ouzou

Oran • Algiers
S

Casablanca • Rabat
MOROCCO

WAC Casablanca
1992

ALGERIA

Stade Malien
1964

MALI

AS Réal Bamako
1966

Bamako

Conakry
GUINEA

GHANA
COTE D'IVOIRE
TOGO Ibad.
Kumasi
Obuasi Lom
Abidjan
Accra

Hafia Conakry
1972, 75, 76, 77, 78

Asante Kotoko
1967, 70, 71, 73, 82, 83, 93

Étoile Filante
1968

ASEC Abidjan
1995, 98

Iwuanyanwu Oweri
1988

ATLANTIC OCEAN

Africa Sports
1986

Stade Abidjan
1966

Union Douala
1979

Goldfields
1997

Oryx Douala
1964

Hearts of Oak
1977, 79, 2000

Canon Yaoundé
1971, 78, 80

418

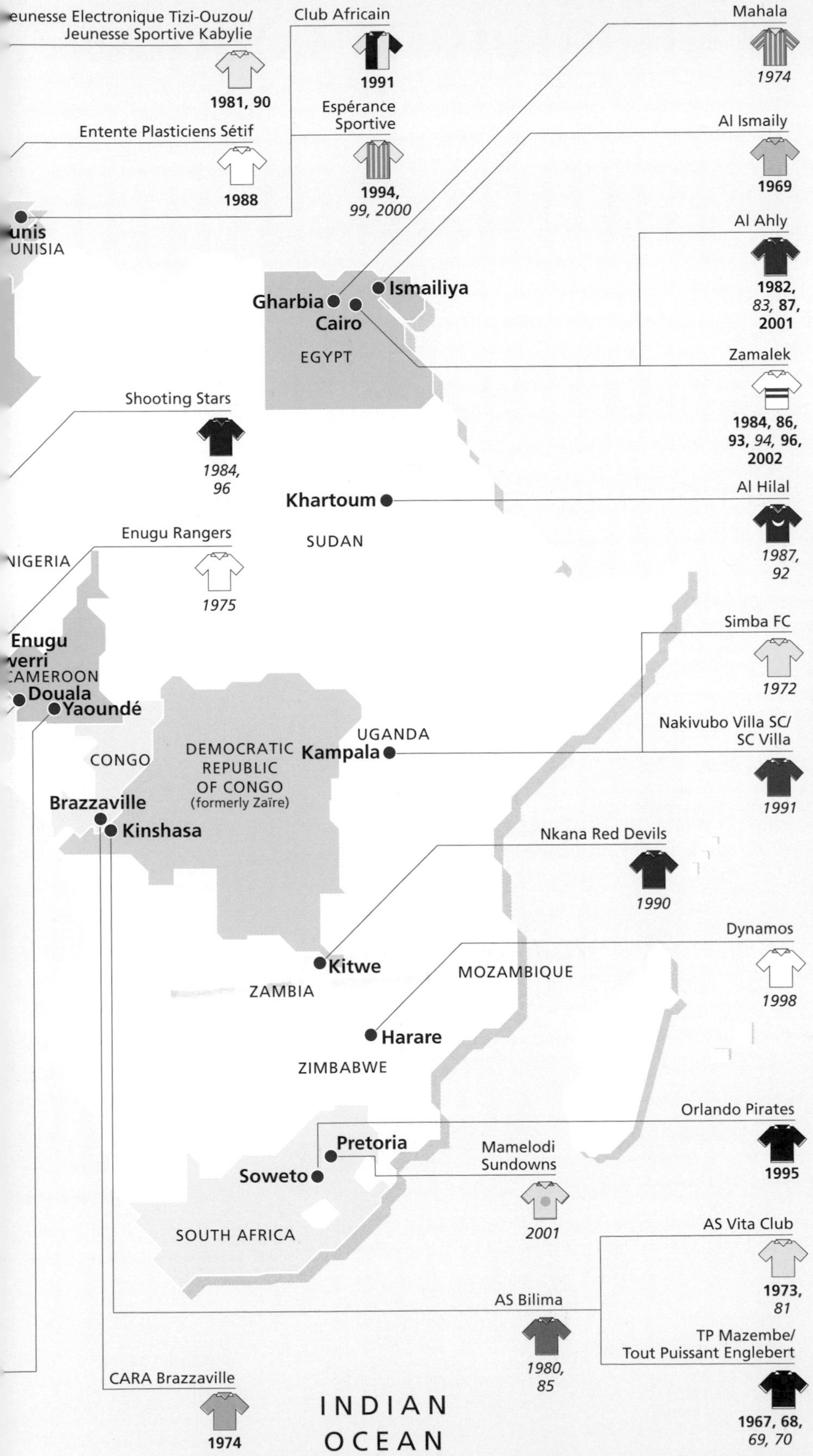

Jeunesse Electronique Tizi-Ouzou/
Jeunesse Sportive Kabylie

1981, 90

Entente Plasticiens Sétif

1988

Tunis
TUNISIA

Club Africain

1991

Espérance
Sportive

1994,
99, 2000

Mahala

1974

Al Ismaily

1969

Al Ahly

1982,
83, **87,**
2001

Zamalek

1984, 86,
93, *94,* **96,**
2002

Gharbia
Cairo
EGYPT

Ismailiya

Shooting Stars

1984,
96

Enugu Rangers

1975

NIGERIA

Enugu
verri
CAMEROON
Douala
Yaoundé

CONGO

Brazzaville
Kinshasa

DEMOCRATIC
REPUBLIC
OF CONGO
(formerly Zaïre)

Khartoum

SUDAN

Al Hilal

1987,
92

Simba FC

1972

Kampala

UGANDA

Nakivubo Villa SC/
SC Villa

1991

Nkana Red Devils

1990

Kitwe

ZAMBIA

MOZAMBIQUE

Harare

ZIMBABWE

Dynamos

1998

Orlando Pirates

1995

Pretoria

Soweto

Mamelodi
Sundowns

2001

SOUTH AFRICA

AS Vita Club

1973,
81

AS Bilima

1980,
85

TP Mazembe/
Tout Puissant Englebert

1967, 68,
69, 70

CARA Brazzaville

1974

INDIAN
OCEAN

The African Champions League

Number of wins in the African Champions League (by country)

- 4+ times
- 3 times
- 2 times
- 1 time
- 0 times

Team details

EGYPT — Country
● Cairo — City of origin
Al Ahly — Team name
 — Team colours
1982, *83,* — Winners in bold
87, 2001 — Runners-up in italic

Although naturally dominated by the continent's biggest clubs, the African Champions League is also a big stage for the little clubs. Here, ASEC from Adibjan (in yellow) take on FC 105 from Gabon in a qualifying match in 1999.

The African Champions League 1964–2002

COUNTRY	WINNERS	RUNNERS-UP
Egypt	9	3
Morocco	5	1
Cameroon	5	0
Algeria	4	1
Ghana	3	8
Democratic Republic of Congo	3	5
Guinea	3	2
Côte D'Ivoire	2	2
Tunisia	2	2
South Africa	1	1
Congo	1	0
Nigeria	0	4
Mali	0	2
Sudan	0	2
Uganda	0	2
Togo	0	1
Zambia	0	1
Zimbabwe	0	1

The African Champions League

THE OLDEST INTERNATIONAL African club competition is the African Champions League with its Sékou Touré Trophy. The competition was first played in 1964 with 14 participating clubs. The final four played in a three-day Final in Accra, Ghana. With a wave of decolonisation and state formation sweeping Africa in the 1960s, the tournament steadily expanded with all matches from the preliminary rounds being played over two legs. Aggregate points gave way to aggregate scores as a method of deciding draws. Replays were played for tied Finals, but in 1976 penalties were introduced. Since 1997, the quarter-finals have been played as two leagues of four teams, all playing each other home and away. The group winners progress to a two-leg Final.

The African Cup-Winners' Cup was started in 1975 for African domestic cup winners. If the cup winner is also in the African Champions League, the place goes to the defeated cup finalists. All matches are played over two legs; tied matches are decided on aggregate goals, away goals and, finally, penalties. Winners are awarded the Nelson Mandela Trophy. In 1992, a third African competition was created – the CAF Cup – for national league runners-up (or third- and fourth-placed teams, if clubs above them are involved in other international competitions). As with the Cup-Winners' Cup, all matches are played over two legs, and tied matches are decided on aggregate goals, away goals and, finally, penalties. The winners receive the Moshood Abiola Cup.

1964 FINAL
February 7 – Accra, Ghana
Oryx Douala **2-1** Stade Malien
(Cameroon)   (Mali)

1965 FINAL
no tournament

1966 FINAL (2 legs)
December 11 – Bamako, Mali
Réal Bamako **3-1** Stade Abidjan
(Mali)   (Côte d'Ivoire)

December 25 – Abidjan, Côte d'Ivoire
Stade Abidjan **4-1** Réal Bamako
Stade Abidjan won 5-4 on aggregate

1967 FINAL (2 legs)
November 19 – Kumasi, Ghana
Asante Kotoko **1-1** TP Englebert
(Ghana)   (Zaïre*)

November 26 – Kinshasa, Zaïre*
TP Englebert **2-2** Asante Kotoko
TP Englebert won after Asante Kotoko refused a play-off

1968 FINAL (2 legs)
March 16 – Kinshasa, Zaïre*
TP Englebert **5-0** Étoile Filante
(Zaïre*)   (Togo)

March 30 – Lomé, Togo
Étoile Filante **4-1** TP Englebert
TP Englebert won 6-4 on aggregate

1969 FINAL (2 legs)
December 22 – Kinshasa, Zaïre*
TP Englebert **2-2** Al Ismaily
(Zaïre*)   (Egypt)

January 9 – Cairo, Egypt
Al Ismaily **3-1** TP Englebert
Al Ismaily won 5-3 on aggregate

1970 FINAL (2 legs)
January 10 – Kumasi, Ghana
Asante Kotoko **1-1** TP Englebert
(Ghana)   (Zaïre*)

January 24 – Kinshasa, Zaïre*
TP Englebert **1-2** Asante Kotoko
Asante Kotoko won 3-2 on aggregate

1971 FINAL (2 legs)
December 5 – Kumasi, Ghana
Asante Kotoko **3-0** Canon Yaoundé
(Ghana)   (Cameroon)

December 19 – Yaoundé, Cameroon
Canon Yaoundé **2-0** Asante Kotoko
Result to be decided on points, not goal, aggregate so went to play-off

December 21 – Yaoundé, Cameroon
Canon Yaoundé **1-0** Asante Kotoko
Match abandoned at 1-0, result stood, Canon Yaoundé winners

1972 FINAL (2 legs)
December 10 – Conakry, Guinea
Hafia Conakry **4-2** Simba FC
(Guinea)   (Uganda)

December 22 – Kampala, Uganda
Simba FC **2-3** Hafia Conakry
Hafia Conakry won 7-4 on aggregate

1973 FINAL (2 legs)
November 25 – Kumasi, Ghana
Asante Kotoko **4-2** AS Vita Club
(Ghana)   (Zaïre*)

December 16 – Kinshasa, Zaïre*
AS Vita Club **3-0** Asante Kotoko
AS Vita Club won 5-4 on aggregate

1974 FINAL (2 legs)
November 29 – Brazzaville, Congo
CARA **4-2** Mahala
Brazzaville   (Egypt)
(Congo)

December 13 – Mahalla, Egypt
Mahala **1-2** CARA
Brazzaville
CARA Brazzaville won 6-3 on aggregate

1975 FINAL (2 legs)
December 7 – Conakry, Guinea
Hafia Conakry **2-1** Enugu Rangers
(Guinea)   (Nigeria)

December 20 – Lagos, Nigeria
Enugu Rangers **1-2** Hafia Conakry
Hafia Conakry won 4-1 on pens

1976 FINAL (2 legs)
December 5 – Conakry, Guinea
Hafia Conakry **3-0** Mouloudia
(Guinea)   d'Algiers
(Algeria)

December 12 – Algiers, Algeria
Mouloudia **3-0** Hafia Conakry
d'Algiers
Mouloudia d'Algiers won 4-1 on pens

1977 FINAL (2 legs)
December 4 – Accra, Ghana
Hearts of Oak **0-1** Hafia Conakry
(Ghana)   (Guinea)

December 18 – Conakry, Guinea
Hafia Conakry **3-2** Hearts of Oak
Hafia Conakry won 4-2 on aggregate

1978 FINAL (2 legs)
December 3 – Conakry, Guinea
Hafia Conakry **0-0** Canon Yaoundé
(Guinea)   (Cameroon)

December 17 – Yaoundé, Cameroon
Canon Yaoundé **2-0** Hafia Conakry
Canon Yaoundé won 2-0 on aggregate

1979 FINAL (2 legs)
December 2 – Accra, Ghana
Hearts of Oak **1-0** Union Douala
(Ghana)   (Cameroon)

December 16 – Yaoundé, Cameroon
Union Douala **1-0** Hearts of Oak
Union Douala won 5-3 on pens

1980 FINAL (2 legs)
November 30 – Yaoundé, Cameroon
Canon Yaoundé **2-2** AS Bilima
(Cameroon)   (Zaïre*)

December 14 – Kinshasa, Zaïre*
AS Bilima **0-3** Canon Yaoundé
Canon Yaoundé won 5-2 on aggregate

1981 FINAL (2 legs)
November 27 – Tizi-Ouzou, Algeria
JE Tizi-Ouzou **4-0** AS Vita Club
(Algeria)   (Zaïre*)

December 13 – Kinshasa, Zaïre*
AS Vita Club **0-1** JE Tizi-Ouzou
JE Tizi-Ouzou won 5-0 on aggregate

1982 FINAL (2 legs)
November 28 – Cairo, Egypt
Al Ahly **3-0** Asante Kotoko
(Egypt)   (Ghana)

December 12 – Kumasi, Ghana
Asante Kotoko **1-1** Al Ahly
Al Ahly won 4-1 on aggregate

1983 FINAL (2 legs)
November 27 – Cairo, Egypt
Al Ahly **0-0** Asante Kotoko
(Egypt)   (Ghana)

December 11 – Kumasi, Ghana
Asante Kotoko **1-0** Al Ahly
Asante Kotoko won 1-0 on aggregate

1984 FINAL (2 legs)
November 23 – Cairo, Egypt
Zamalek **2-0** Shooting Stars
(Egypt)   (Nigeria)

December 8 – Lagos, Nigeria
Shooting Stars **0-0** Zamalek
Zamalek won 2-0 on aggregate

1985 FINAL (2 legs)
November 30 – Rabat, Morocco
FAR Rabat **5-2** AS Bilima
(Morocco)   (Zaïre*)

December 22 – Lubumbashi, Zaïre*
AS Bilima **1-1** FAR Rabat
FAR Rabat won 6-3 on aggregate

1986 FINAL (2 legs)
November 28 – Cairo, Egypt
Zamalek **2-0** Africa Sports
(Egypt)   (Côte d'Ivoire)

December 21 – Abidjan, Côte d'Ivoire
Africa Sports **2-0** Zamalek
Zamalek won 4-2 on pens

1987 FINAL (2 legs)
November 29 – Khartoum, Sudan
Al Hilal **0-0** Al Ahly
(Sudan)   (Egypt)

December 18 – Cairo, Egypt
Al Ahly **2-0** Al Hilal
Al Ahly won 2-0 on aggregate

1988 FINAL (2 legs)

November 26 – Ibadan, Nigeria
Iwuanyanwu **1-0** Entente
Owerri   Sétif
(Nigeria)   (Algeria)

December 9 – Constantine, Algeria
Entente **4-0** Iwuanyanwu
Sétif   Owerri

Entente Sétif won 4-1 on aggregate

1989 FINAL (2 legs)

December 3 – Casablanca, Morocco
Raja **2-0** Mouloudia
Casablanca   d'Oran
(Morocco)   (Algeria)

December 15 – Oran, Algeria
Mouloudia **1-0** Raja
d'Oran   Casablanca

Raja Casablanca won 4-2 on pens

1990 FINAL (2 legs)

November 30 – Algiers, Algeria
JS Kabylie **1-0** Nkana Red
(Algeria)   Devils
                   (Zaïre*)

December 22 – Lusaka, Zambia
Nkana Red **1-0** JS Kabylie
Devils

JS Kabylie won 5-3 on pens

1991 FINAL (2 legs)

November 23 – Tunis, Tunisia
Club Africain **5-1** Nakivubo
(Tunisia)   Villa SC
                     (Zaïre*)

December 14 – Kampala, Uganda
Nakivubo **1-1** Club Africain
Villa SC

Club Africain won 6-2 on aggregate

1992 FINAL (2 legs)

November 29 – Casablanca, Morocco
WAC **2-0** Al Hilal
Casablanca   (Sudan)
(Morocco)

December 13 – Khartoum, Sudan
Al Hilal **0-0** WAC
                 Casablanca

WAC Casablanca won 2-0 on aggregate

1993 FINAL (2 legs)

November 26 – Kumasi, Ghana
Asante Kotoko **0-0** Zamalek
(Ghana)   (Egypt)

December 10 – Cairo, Egypt
Zamalek **0-0** Asante Kotoko

Zamalek won 7-6 on pens

1994 FINAL (2 legs)

December 4 – Cairo, Egypt
Zamalek **0-0** Espérance
(Egypt)   Sportive
                (Tunisia)

December 17 – Tunis, Tunisia
Espérance **3-1** Zamalek
Sportive

Espérance Sportive won 3-1 on aggregate

1995 FINAL (2 legs)

Johannesburg, South Africa
Orlando Pirates **2-2** ASEC Abidjan
(South Africa)   (Côte d'Ivoire)

Abidjan, Côte d'Ivoire
ASEC Abidjan **0-1** Orlando Pirates

Orlando Pirates won 3-2 on aggregate

1996 FINAL (2 legs)

Lagos, Nigeria
Shooting Stars **2-1** Zamalek
(Nigeria)   (Egypt)

Cairo, Egypt
Zamalek **2-1** Shooting Stars

Zamalek won 5-4 on pens

1997 FINAL (2 legs)

November 30 – Obuasi, Ghana
Goldfields **1-0** Raja
(Ghana)   Casablanca
                   (Morocco)

December 14 – Casablanca, Morocco
Raja **1-0** Goldfields
Casablanca

Raja Casablanca won 5-4 on pens

1998 FINAL (2 legs)

November 28 – Harare, Zimbabwe
Dynamos **0-0** ASEC Abidjan
(Zimbabwe)   (Côte d'Ivoire)

December 12 – Abidjan, Côte d'Ivoire
ASEC Abidjan **4-2** Dynamos

ASEC Abidjan won 4-2
on aggregate

1999 FINAL (2 legs)

November 27 – Casablanca, Morocco
Raja **0-0** Espérance
Casablanca   Sportive
(Morocco)   (Tunisia)

December 12 – Tunis, Tunisia
Espérance **0-0** Raja
Sportive   Casablanca

Raja Casablanca won 4-3 on pens

2000 FINAL (2 legs)

December 2 – Tunis, Tunisia
Espérance **1-2** Hearts of Oak
Sportive   (Ghana)
(Tunisia)

December 17 – Accra, Ghana
Hearts of Oak **3-1** Espérance
                      Sportive

Hearts of Oak won 5-2 on aggregate

2001 FINAL (2 legs)

December 8 – Pretoria, South Africa
Mamelodi **1-1** Al Ahly
Sundowns   (Egypt)
(South Africa)

December 21 – Cairo, Egypt
Al Ahly **3-0** Mamelodi
                Sundowns

Al Ahly won 4-1 on aggregate

2002 FINAL (2 legs)

November 30 – Casablanca, Morocco
Raja **0-0** Zamalek
Casablanca   (Egypt)
(Morocco)

December 13 – Cairo, Egypt
Zamalek **1-0** Raja
                Casablanca

Zamalek won 1-0 on aggregate

The African Cup-Winners' Cup and CAF Cup

The African Cup-Winners' Cup 1975–2002

YEAR	WINNERS	RUNNERS-UP
1975	Tonnerre Yaoundé (Cameroon)	Stella Club (Côte d'Ivoire)
1976	Shooting Stars (Nigeria)	Tonnerre Yaoundé (Cameroon)
1977	Enugu Rangers (Nigeria)	Canon Yaoundé (Cameroon)
1978	Horoya AC (Guinea)	Milaha Athletic (Algeria)
1979	Canon Yaoundé (Cameroon)	Gor Mahia (Kenya)
1980	TP Mazembe (Zaïre*)	Africa Sports (Côte d'Ivoire)
1981	Union Douala (Cameroon)	Stationery Stores (Nigeria)
1982	Al Mokaoulom (Egypt)	Power Dynamos (Zambia)
1983	Al Mokaoulom (Egypt)	Agaza Lomé (Togo)
1984	Al Ahly (Egypt)	Canon Yaoundé (Cameroon)
1985	Al Ahly (Egypt)	Leventis United (Nigeria)
1986	Al Ahly (Egypt)	AS Sogara (Gabon)
1987	Gor Mahia (Kenya)	Espérance Sportive (Tunisia)
1988	CA Bizerte (Tunisia)	Rancher Bees (Nigeria)
1989	Al Merreikh (Sudan)	Bendel United (Nigeria)
1990	BCC Lions (Nigeria)	Club Africain (Tunisia)
1991	Power Dynamos (Zambia)	BCC Lions (Nigeria)
1992	Africa Sports (Côte d'Ivoire)	Vital'O FC (Burundi)
1993	Al Ahly (Egypt)	Africa Sports (Côte d'Ivoire)
1994	DC Motema Pembe (Zaïre*)	Kenya Breweries (Kenya)
1995	JS Kabylie (Algeria)	Julius Berger (Nigeria)
1996	Arab Contractors (Egypt)	AC Sodigraf (Zaïre*)
1997	Étoile du Sahel (Tunisia)	FAR Rabat (Morocco)
1998	Espérance Sportive (Tunisia)	Primeiro de Agosto (Angola)
1999	Africa Sports (Côte d'Ivoire)	Club Africain (Tunisia)

The African Cup-Winners' Cup (continued)

YEAR	WINNERS	RUNNERS-UP
2000	Zamalek (Egypt)	Canon Yaoundé (Cameroon)
2001	Kaizer Chiefs (South Africa)	Inter Clube (Angola)
2002	WAC Casablanca (Morocco)	Asante Kotoko (Ghana)

The CAF Cup 1992–2002

YEAR	WINNERS	RUNNERS-UP
1992	Shooting Stars (Nigeria)	Nakivubo Villa SC (Uganda)
1993	Stella Club (Côte d'Ivoire)	Simba FC (Tanzania)
1994	Bendel Insurance (Nigeria)	Primeiro de Maio (Angola)
1995	Étoile du Sahel (Tunisia)	AS Kaloum Stars (Guinea)
1996	KAC Marrakech (Morocco)	Étoile du Sahel (Tunisia)
1997	Espérance Sportive (Tunisia)	Petro Atlético (Angola)
1998	CS Sfax (Tunisia)	ASC Jeanne d'Arc (Senegal)
1999	Étoile du Sahel (Tunisia)	WAC Casablanca (Morocco)
2000	JS Kabylie (Algeria)	Al Ismaily (Egypt)
2001	JS Kabylie (Algeria)	Étoile du Sahel (Tunisia)
2002	JS Kabylie (Algeria)	Tonnerre Yaoundé (Cameroon)

* Zaïre is now known as the Democratic Republic of Congo.

Egypt

Egyptian Football Asscoiation
Founded: 1921
Joined FIFA: 1923
Joined CAF: 1957

FOOTBALL ARRIVED IN Egypt during the British armed occupation at the turn of the 19th century. No British clubs from the era survive, but the dominant force in Egyptian football, the Cairo-based Al Ahly, was founded in 1907. The club has come to represent the republican strand of Egyptian nationalist politics, a fact confirmed when Nasser was made honorary president of the club in 1954. The team's eternal rival – Zamalek – was founded in 1911 as Kaser-el-nil, becoming Al Mukhtalat in 1925. Its allegiance became clear when the football fanatic King Farouk lent his support and name to the club in 1940. When Farouk was deposed in 1952, the club became Zamalek.

The prescience of Egyptian football can be seen from the early formation of the Egyptian FA (1921), preceding national independence by a year. A cup was donated that year by the king to create the first national competition. In 1920, Egypt played at the Olympic Games in Antwerp, the first African nation ever to do so. In 1924 in Amsterdam, Egypt made it to the quarter-finals, and in 1928, the semi-finals. Egypt was the first African side to play in the World Cup Finals (1934) and supplied the first African referee to the World Cup in 1966.

During the Second World War, Egyptian and Allied military teams played extensively, and in 1949, a national league was created alongside the cup. Politics has never been far from Egyptian football and in 1958 the army took over the national FA and professionalized the game through the back door. With the outbreak of the Arab-Israeli Six-Day War in 1967, Egyptian domestic football was regularly disrupted until after the Yom Kippur War in the 1970s. Enormous and fanatical support has tragically been accompanied by a series of disasters including a riot at the 1966 Cairo derby between Zamalek and Al Ahly that saw over 300 injured when the military took control of the stadium. In 1974, a wall collapsed at Zamalek during a friendly match against Dukla Praha killing 49 people.

Egyptian League Record (*continued*)

SEASON	CHAMPIONS		SEASON	CHAMPIONS
1995	Al Ahly		2001	Zamalek
1996	Al Ahly		2002	Al Ismaily
1997	Al Ahly		2003	Zamalek
1998	Al Ahly			
1999	Al Ahly			
2000	Al Ahly			

Cup of Egypt 1949–2003

YEAR	WINNERS		YEAR	WINNERS
1949	Al Ahly		1980	*no competition*
1950	Al Ahly		1981	Al Ahly
1951	Al Ahly		1982	*no competition*
1952	Zamalek		1983	Al Ahly
1953	Al Ahly		1984	Al Ahly
1954	Al Tersana		1985	Al Ahly
1955	Zamalek		1986	Al Tersana
1956	Al Ahly		1987	*no competition*
1957	Zamalek		1988	Zamalek
1958	Zamalek and Al Ahly*		1989	Al Ahly
1959	Zamalek		1990	Al Mokaoulom
1960	Zamalek		1991	Al Ahly
1961	Al Ahly		1992	Al Ahly
1962	Zamalek		1993	Al Ahly
1963	Al Ittihad		1994	*no competition*
1964	Quanah		1995	Al Mokaoulom
1965	Al Tersana		1996	Al Ahly
1966	Al Ahly		1997	Al Ismaily
1967	Al Tersana		1998	Al Masry
1968–72	*no competition*		1999	Zamalek
1973	Al Ittihad		2000	Al Ismaily
1974	*no competition*		2001	Al Ahly
1975	Zamalek		2002	Zamalek
1976	Al Ittihad		2003	Al Ahly
1977	Zamalek			
1978	Al Ahly			
1979	Zamalek			

* Cup shared.

Egyptian League Record 1949–2003

SEASON	CHAMPIONS		SEASON	CHAMPIONS
1949	Al Ahly		1974	*no championship*
1950	Al Ahly		1975	Al Ahly
1951	Al Ahly		1976	Al Ahly
1952	*no championship*		1977	Al Ahly
1953	Al Ahly		1978	Zamalek
1954	Al Ahly		1979	Al Ahly
1955	*no championship*		1980	Al Ahly
1956	Al Ahly		1981	Al Ahly
1957	Al Ahly		1982	Al Ahly
1958	Al Ahly		1983	Al Mokaoulom
1959	Al Ahly		1984	Zamalek
1960	Zamalek		1985	Al Ahly
1961	Al Ahly		1986	Al Ahly
1962	Al Ahly		1987	Al Ahly
1963	Al Tersana		1988	Zamalek
1964	Zamalek		1989	Al Ahly
1965	Zamalek		1990	*no championship*
1966	Olympia		1991	Al Ismaily
1967	Al Ismaily		1992	Zamalek
1968–72	*no championship*		1993	Zamalek
1973	Mahala		1994	Al Ahly

***Zamalek from Cairo** is the second best supported team in Egypt. The club enjoyed the support of King Farouk during the 1940s. It remains the most dangerous rival of neighbours Al Ahly.*

EGYPT

Football in Egypt

League champions
3 times or more
1966

League champions
1–2 times
1966

Other teams
1966

Cup of Egypt
winners
1966

● **Cairo**   City of origin

○ African Champions
League

⬤ African Cup-Winners' Cup

⬤ CAF Cup

1973   Winners in bold

1973   Runners-up in italics

*   Title shared

Al Ahly

(See box
bottom right)

Al Mokaoulom
(Arab Contractors)
1983   *1990,*   **1982,**
   95   *83, 96*

Al Tersana
(Arsenal)
1963   **1954,
65, 67, 86**

Zamalek
(See box
above top right)

Tanta

Mahala
1974   **1973**

Al
Mansurah

ZAMALEK SPORTING CLUB	
40,000	**City:** Cairo **Founded:** 1911 **Stadium:** Hassan Helmi

ZAMALEK	
League	*1951, 53, 54, 56–59,* **60,** *61–63,* **64,** **65,** *66,* **73,** *77,* **78,** *79–83,* **84,** *85–87,* **88,** *89,* **92, 93,** *95–99,* **2001, 03**
Cup of Egypt	*1949,* **52,** *53,* **55,** *57,* **58*,** *59,* **60,** *62, 63,* **75,** *77,* **78,** *79,* **88,** **92, 99,** *2002*
Farouk Cup	**1932, 35, 38, 41,** *43*,* **44,** *48*
African Champions League	**1984, 86, 93,** *94,* **96, 2002**
African Cup- Winners' Cup	**2000**
African Super Cup	**1993,** *96, 2000,* **03**

Alexandria ●

Olympia

1966

Al Ittihad
(Union Recreation)
**1963,
73, 76**

**El
Mahalla
el Kubra** ●

Tanta ●

**El
Mansûra** ●

**Port
Said** ●

*Suez
Canal*

Ismailiya ●

Cairo ●

Al Masry
1998

Quanah
1964

Al Ismaily
2000   ○ *1969*   **1997,
2000**   **1967,
91, 2002**

EGYPT

*Jubilant Al Ismaily
players* *celebrate after
their 4-0 victory over
Al Mokaoulom in the
2000 Cup of Egypt
Final. Four goals in
13 minutes of the
second half sealed
their triumph.*

Nile

*Lake
Nasser*

AL AHLY NATIONAL SPORTING CLUB	
20,000	**City:** Cairo **Founded:** 1907 **Stadium:** Mokhtar el Tetch

AL AHLY	
League	**1949–51, 53, 54, 56–59, 61, 62,** *67,* **75–77,** *78,* **79–82,** *84,* **85–87,** **88, 89,** *91,* **93,** *94–2000, 01–03*
Cup of Egypt	**1949–51,** *52,* **53, 56,** *58*,* **59,** **61, 66,** *73,* **76, 78, 81, 83–85, 89,** **91–93, 96, 97, 2001, 03**
Farouk Cup	**1924, 25,** *26,* **27, 28, 30, 31, 37,** **40,** *41,* **42,** *43*,* **44, 45–47**
African Champions League	*1982, 83,* **87, 2001**
African Cup- Winners' Cup	**1984–86, 93**
African Super Cup	*1993,* **2001, 02**

North Africa

APART FROM EGYPT (see pages 422-23) football arrived in North Africa at the turn of the 19th century via the colonial administration of French North Africa. Within a quarter of a century, leagues were up and running in Algeria (1920s), Morocco (1916) and Tunisia (1921). In the ex-Italian colony of Libya a league was finally established in 1964. Under French control a North African Club Championship was established (1919–49), and before independence internationals were played in the North African Cup (1919–30). In Algeria, separate regional leagues were played until independence (in Algiers, Constantine and Oran).

Successive club name changes indicate the degree of political involvement in football in Algeria; JS Kabylie was formally known as JE Tizi-Ouzou in an attempt to suppress the club's identification with regionalist sentiments. In Morocco royal and military patronage is evident in the leading clubs' names.

Algeria

Fédération Algérienne de Football
Founded: 1962
Joined FIFA: 1963
Joined CAF: 1964

Algerian League Record 1963–2003

SEASON	CHAMPIONS	SEASON	CHAMPIONS
1963	USM Algiers	1985	JE Tizi-Ouzou
1964	USM Annaba	1986	JE Tizi-Ouzou
1965	CR Belcourt	1987	Entente Sétif
1966	CR Belcourt	1988	Mouloudia d'Oran
1967	NA Hussein-Dey	1989	JE Tizi-Ouzou
1968	Entente Sétif	1990	KS Kabylie
1969	CR Belcourt	1991	MO Constantine
1970	CR Belcourt	1992	Mouloudia d'Oran
1971	Mouloudia d'Oran	1993	Mouloudia d'Oran
1972	Mouloudia d'Algiers	1994	US Chaouia
1973	JS Kabylie	1995	JS Kabylie
1974	JS Kabylie	1996	USM Alger
1975	Mouloudia d'Algiers	1997	CS Constantine
1976	Mouloudia d'Algiers	1998	USM El Harrach
1977	JS Kawkabi	1999	MC Alger
1978	Mouloudia d'Algiers	2000	CR Belouizdad
1979	Mouloudia d'Algiers	2001	CR Belouizdad
1980	JE Tizi-Ouzou	2002	USM Alger
1981	RS Kouba	2003	USM Alger
1982	JE Tizi-Ouzou		
1983	JE Tizi-Ouzou		
1984	GCR Mascara		

Algerian Cup Record 1963–2003

YEAR	WINNERS	YEAR	WINNERS
1963	Entente Sétif	1972	Hamra-Annaba
1964	Entente Sétif	1973	Mouloudia d'Algiers
1965	MC Saida	1974	USM Maison Carrée
1966	CR Belcourt	1975	Mouloudia d'Oran
1967	Entente Sétif	1976	Mouloudia d'Algiers
1968	Entente Sétif	1977	JS Kawkabi
1969	CR Belcourt	1978	CM Belcourt
1970	CR Belcourt	1979	MS Hussein-Dey
1971	Mouloudia d'Algiers	1980	Entente Sétif

Algerian Cup Record (*continued*)

YEAR	WINNERS	YEAR	WINNERS
1981	USK Algiers	1994	JS Kabylie
1982	DNC Algiers	1995	CR Belouizdad
1983	Mouloudia d'Algiers	1996	USM Alger
1984	Mouloudia d'Oran	1997	USM Alger
1985	Mouloudia d'Oran	1998	WA Tlemoen
1986	JE Tizi-Ouzou	1999	USM Alger
1987	USM El-Harrach	2000	MC Ouargla
1988	USK Algiers	2001	USM Alger
1989	*no competition*	2002	WA Tlemcen
1990	Entente Sétif	2003	USM Alger
1991	USM Bel Abbés		
1992	JS Kabylie		
1993	*no competition*		

Morocco

Fédération Royale Marocaine de Football
Founded: 1955
Joined FIFA: 1956
Joined CAF: 1966

Moroccan League Record 1916–2002

SEASON	CHAMPIONS	SEASON	CHAMPIONS
1916	CA Casablanca	1963	FAR Rabat
1917	US Marocaine	1964	FAR Rabat
1918	US Marocaine	1965	MAS Fès
1919	US Marocaine	1966	WAC Casablanca
1920	Olympique Marocaine	1967	FAR Rabat
1921	Olympique Marocaine	1968	FAR Rabat
1922	Olympique Marocaine	1969	WAC Casablanca
1923	US Fès	1970	FAR Rabat
1924	Olympique Marocaine	1971	RS Settat
1925	US Fès	1972	ADM Casablanca
1926	US Athletique	1973	KAC Kenitra
1927	Stade Marocaine	1974	RBM Beni Mellal
1928	*no championship*	1975	MC Oujda
1929	US Athletique	1976	WAC Casablanca
1930	Stade Marocaine	1977	WAC Casablanca
1931	US Marocaine	1978	WAC Casablanca
1932	US Marocaine	1979	MAS Fès
1933	US Marocaine	1980	Chebab Mohammedia
1934	US Marocaine	1981	KAC Kenitra
1935	US Marocaine	1982	KAC Kenitra
1936	Olympique Marocaine	1983	MAS Fès
1937	Olympique Marocaine	1984	FAR Rabat
1938	US Marocaine	1985	MAS Fès
1939	US Marocaine	1986	WAC Casablanca
1940	US Marocaine	1987	FAR Rabat
1941	US Marocaine	1988	Raja Casablanca
1942	US Marocaine	1989	FAR Rabat
1943	US Marocaine	1990	WAC Casablanca
1944	Stade Marocaine	1991	WAC Casablanca
1945	Racing Avant-Garde	1992	KAC Marrakech
1946	US Marocaine	1993	WAC Casablanca
1947	US Athletique	1994	Olympic Casablanca
1948	WAC Casablanca	1995	COD Meknes
1949	WAC Casablanca	1996	Raja Casablanca
1950	WAC Casablanca	1997	Raja Casablanca
1951	WAC Casablanca	1998	Raja Casablanca
1952–56	*no championship*	1999	Raja Casablanca
1957	WAC Casablanca	2000	Raja Casablanca
1958	KAC Marrakech	2001	Raja Casablanca
1959	EJS Casablanca	2002	Hassania US d'Agadir
1960	KAC Kenitra		
1961	FAR Rabat		
1962	FAR Rabat		

Moroccan Cup Record 1957–2002

YEAR	WINNERS	YEAR	WINNERS
1957	MC Oujda	1981	WAC Casablanca
1958	MC Oujda	1982	Raja Casablanca
1959	FAR Rabat	1983	CLAS Casablanca
1960	MC Oujda	1984	FAR Rabat
1961	KAC Kenitra	1985	FAR Rabat
1962	MC Oujda	1986	FAR Rabat
1963	KAC Marrakech	1987	KAC Marrakech
1964	KAC Marrakech	1988	*no competition*
1965	KAC Marrakech	1989	WAC Casablanca
1966	COD Meknes	1990–91	*no competition*
1967	FUS Rabat	1992	Olympic Casablanca
1968	Raja Casablanca	1993	KAC Marrakech
1969	RS Settat	1994	WAC Casablanca
1970	WAC Casablanca	1995	FAR Rabat
1971	FAR Rabat	1996	Raja Casablanca
1972	Chabab Mohammedia	1997	WAC Casablanca
1973	FUS Rabat	1998	WAC Casablanca
1974	Raja Casablanca	1999	FAR Rabat
1975	Chabab Mohammedia	2000	Majd Casablanca
1976	FUS Rabat	2001	WAC Casablanca
1977	Raja Casablanca	2002	Raja Casablanca
1978	WAC Casablanca		
1979	WAC Casablanca		
1980	MAS Fès		

Tunisia

Fédération Tunisienne de Football
Founded: 1956
Joined FIFA: 1960
Joined CAF: 1960

Tunisian League Record 1921–2003

SEASON	CHAMPIONS	SEASON	CHAMPIONS
1921	Racing Club	1956	CS Hammam-Lif
1922	Stade Gauloise	1957	Stade Tunisien
1923	Stade Gauloise	1958	Étoile du Sahel
1924	Racing Club	1959	Espérance Sportive
1925	Sporting Club	1960	Espérance Sportive
1926	Stade Gauloise	1961	Stade Tunisien
1927	Sporting Club	1962	Stade Tunisien
1928	Avant Garde	1963	Étoile du Sahel
1929	US Tunisienne	1964	Club Africain
1930	US Tunisienne	1965	Stade Tunisien
1931	Italia de Tunis	1966	Étoile du Sahel
1932	US Tunisienne	1967	Club Africain
1933	Sfax Railway	1968	Sfax Railway
1934	Italia de Tunis	1969	CS Sfax
1935	Italia de Tunis	1970	Espérance Sportive
1936	Italia de Tunis	1971	CS Sfax
1937	Savoia de la Goulette	1972	Étoile du Sahel
1938	CS Gabesien	1973	Club Africain
1939–40	*no championship*	1974	Club Africain
1941	Espérance Sportive	1975	Espérance Sportive
1942–43	*no championship*	1976	Espérance Sportive
1944	CA Bizerte	1977	JS Kairouan
1945	CA Bizerte	1978	CS Sfax
1946	Club Africain	1979	Club Africain
1947	Club Africain	1980	Club Africain
1948	CA Bizerte	1981	CS Sfax
1949	Étoile du Sahel	1982	Espérance Sportive
1950	CS Hammam-Lif	1983	CS Sfax
1951–55	*no championship*	1984	CA Bizerte

Tunisian League Record (*continued*)

SEASON	CHAMPIONS	SEASON	CHAMPIONS
1985	Espérance Sportive	1996	Club Africain
1986	Étoile du Sahel	1997	Espérance Sportive
1987	Étoile du Sahel	1998	Espérance Sportive
1988	Espérance Sportive	1999	Espérance Sportive
1989	Espérance Sportive	2000	Espérance Sportive
1990	Club Africain	2001	Espérance Sportive
1991	Espérance Sportive	2002	Espérance Sportive
1992	Club Africain	2003	Espérance Sportive
1993	Espérance Sportive		
1994	Espérance Sportive		
1995	CS Sfax		

Tunisian Cup Record 1922–2002

YEAR	WINNERS	YEAR	WINNERS
1922	Avant Garde	1968	Club Africain
1923	Racing Club	1969	Club Africain
1924	Stade Gauloise	1970	Club Africain
1925	Sporting Club	1971	CS Sfax
1926	Stade Gauloise	1972	Club Africain
1927-28	*no competition*	1973	Club Africain
1929	US Tunisienne	1974	Étoile du Sahel
1930	US Tunisienne	1975	Étoile du Sahel
1931	Racing Club	1976	Club Africain
1932	US Tunisienne	1977	AS Marsa
1933	US Tunisienne	1978	*no competition*
1934	US Tunisienne	1979	Espérance Sportive
1935	Italia de Tunis	1980	Espérance Sportive
1936	Stade Gauloise	1981	Étoile du Sahel
1937	Sporting Club	1982	CA Bizerte
1938	Espérance Sportive	1983	Étoile du Sahel
1939–40	*no competition*	1984	AS Marsa
1941	US Ferryville	1985	CS Hammam-Lif
1942–43	*no competition*	1986	Espérance Sportive
1944	Olympique Tunis	1987	CA Bizerte
1945	Patrie FC Bizerte	1988	COT Tunis
1946	CS Hammam-Lif	1989	Club Africain
1947	CS Hammam-Lif	1990	AS Marsa
1948	CS Hammam-Lif	1991	Étoile du Sahel
1949	CS Hammam-Lif	1992	Club Africain
1950	CS Hammam-Lif	1993	Olympique Beja
1951–55	*no competition*	1994	AS Marsa
1956	Stade Tunisien	1995	CS Sfaxien
1957	Étoile de Tunis	1996	Étoile du Sahel
1958	Stade Tunisien	1997	Espérance Sportive
1959	Étoile du Sahel	1998	Club Africain
1960	Stade Tunisien	1999	Espérance Sportive
1961	AS Marsa	2000	Club Africain
1962	Stade Tunisien	2001	CS Hammam-Lif
1963	Étoile du Sahel	2002	*abandoned*
1964	Espérance Sportive		
1965	Club Africain		
1966	Stade Tunisien		
1967	Club Africain		

Libya

Libyan Arab Jamahiriya Football Federation
Founded: 1962
Joined FIFA: 1963
Joined CAF: 1965

SEASON	LEAGUE CHAMPIONS
1999	Al Mahalah
2000	Al Ahly
2001	Al Medina
2002	Al Ittihad
2003	Al Ittihad

NORTH AFRICA

West Africa

WHILE NORTH AFRICA WAS SLIGHTLY earlier in its adoption of football and both Central and Southern Africa have significant league and cup competitions, African football has been most enduringly strong in West Africa. At the head of the pack have been Nigeria (see pages 428-29), Guinea, Côte d'Ivoire, Ghana and Senegal. In Ghana and Nigeria football arrived with British imperial administrations in the early 20th century. Ghana's oldest and most successful team, Hearts of Oak, was founded in 1911. City-based and regional tournaments began in the 1920s and, post-independence, a national league was established in 1957 and a cup in 1958.

In French West Africa (including what are now Guinea, Senegal and Côte d'Ivoire) many football clubs were established in the 1930s. Côte d'Ivoire's leading clubs, Africa Sports, Stella Abidjan and Stade Abidjan, were all founded in 1936. In Côte d'Ivoire and Senegal national league and cup competitions followed independence in 1960.

The Senegalese are coming

But while Côte d'Ivoire's clubs have won both the African Champions League and the CAF Cup, Senegalese teams have yet to take an African championship. The national team did, however, reach the Final of the 2002 African Nations Cup in Mali beating Nigeria in the semi-final. In the Final it lost to Cameroon on penalties. The team started the tournament in confident mood having qualified in sensational style for the 2002 World Cup Finals where many pundits rightly tipped it to perform well, and it certainly didn't disappoint, with a stunning overall performance. The 5-0 thrashing of Namibia in the last game of the qualifying tournament saw the team through to the Finals and hopes of a bright future.

Guinea's national league began in 1965 and is dominated by Hafia Conakry, three times winners of the African Champions League during the 1970s, but its fortunes have been on the wane in recent years.

Founded In 1911 Hearts of Oak, from Accra, is the most successful club in Ghana. Its greatest international success came in 2000 when it won the African Champions League, beating Espérance Sportive of Tunisia in the Final.

Ghana

Ghana Football Association
Founded: 1957
Joined FIFA: 1958
Joined CAF: 1958

Ghanaian League Record 1957–2002

SEASON	CHAMPIONS	SEASON	CHAMPIONS
1957	Hearts of Oak	1982	Asante Kotoko
1958	Hearts of Oak	1983	Asante Kotoko
1959	Asante Kotoko	1984	Hearts of Oak
1960	Eleven Wise FC	1985	Hearts of Oak
1961	Real Republicans	1986	Asante Kotoko
1962	Real Republicans	1987	Asante Kotoko
1963	Asante Kotoko	1988	Asante Kotoko
1964	Asante Kotoko	1989	Hearts of Oak
1965	Asante Kotoko	1990	Hearts of Oak
1966	BA United	1991	Asante Kotoko
1967	Asante Kotoko	1992	Asante Kotoko
1968	Asante Kotoko	1993	Asante Kotoko
1969	Asante Kotoko	1994	Goldfields
1970	Great Olympics	1995	Goldfields
1971	Hearts of Oak	1996	Goldfields
1972	Asante Kotoko	1997	Hearts of Oak
1973	Hearts of Oak	1998	Hearts of Oak
1974	Great Olympics	1999	Hearts of Oak
1975	Asante Kotoko	2000	Hearts of Oak
1976	Hearts of Oak	2001	Hearts of Oak
1977	Sekondi Hasaacas	2002	Hearts of Oak
1978	Hearts of Oak		
1979	Hearts of Oak		
1980	Asante Kotoko		
1981	Asante Kotoko		

Ghanaian Cup Record 1958–2001

YEAR	CUP WINNERS	YEAR	CUP WINNERS
1958	Asante Kotoko	1984	Asante Kotoko
1959	Cornerstones	1985	Sekondi Hasaacas
1960	Asante Kotoko	1986	Okwahu United
1961	*no competition*	1987	Hearts of Oak
1962	Real Republicans	1988	Hearts of Oak
1963	Real Republicans	1989	Hearts of Oak
1964	Real Republicans	1990	Asante Kotoko
1965	Real Republicans	1991	Asante Kotoko
1966–68	*no competition*	1992	Voradep
1969	Cape Coast Dwarfs	1993	Goldfields
1970–72	*no competition*	1994	Hearts of Oak
1973	Hearts of Oak	1995	Hearts of Oak
1974	Hearts of Oak	1996	Hearts of Oak
1975	Great Olympics	1997	Ghaphoa
1976	Asante Kotoko	1998	Asante Kotoko
1977	*no competition*	1999	Hearts of Oak
1978	Asante Kotoko	2000	Hearts of Oak
1979	Hearts of Oak	2001	Asante Kotoko
1980	Sekondi Hasaacas		
1981	Hearts of Oak		
1982	Eleven Wise FC		
1983	Great Olympics		

Benin

Fédération Beninoise de Football
Founded: 1962
Joined FIFA: 1962
Joined CAF: 1969

SEASON	LEAGUE CHAMPIONS
1998	Dragons de l'Ouémé
1999	Dragons de l'Ouémé
2000	*no official championship*
2001	*no official championship*
2002	Dragons de l'Ouémé

Benin *(continued)*

YEAR	CUP WINNERS
1998	Mogas 90
1999	Mogas 90
2000	Mogas 90
2001	Buffles de Borgou
2002	Jeunesse Sportive Pobé

Burkina Faso

Fédération Burkinabe de Football
Founded: 1960
Joined FIFA: 1964
Joined CAF: 1964

SEASON	LEAGUE CHAMPIONS
1999	ASFAY
2000	USFA
2001	Etoile Filante
2002	Etoile Filante
2003	ASFA Yennenga

YEAR	CUP WINNERS
1998	AS Fonctionnaires
1999	Etoile Filante
1999	Etoile Filante
2001	Etoile Filante
2002	USFA

Cape Verde

Fédération Cabo Verdiana de Futebol
Founded: 1982
Joined FIFA: 1986
Joined CAF: 1986

SEASON	LEAGUE CHAMPIONS
1998	CS Mindelense
1999	Amarante
2000	Derby FC
2001	Onze Unidos
2002	Sporting Clube da Praia

Côte d'Ivoire

Fédération Ivorienne de Football
Founded: 1960
Joined FIFA: 1960
Joined CAF: 1960

SEASON	LEAGUE CHAMPIONS
1998	ASEC Abidjan
1999	Africa Sports
2000	ASEC Abidjan
2001	ASEC Abidjan
2002	ASEC Abidjan

Côte d'Ivoire *(continued)*

YEAR	CUP WINNERS
1998	Africa Sports
1999	ASEC Abidjan
2000	Stade Abidjan
2001	Alliance Bouaké
2002	Africa Sports

Gambia

Gambia Football Association
Founded: 1952
Joined FIFA: 1966
Joined CAF: 1962

SEASON	LEAGUE CHAMPIONS
1998	Real Banjul
1999	Ports Authority
2000	Real Banjul
2001	Wallidan
2002	Wallidan

Guinea

Fédération Guinéenne de Football
Founded: 1959
Joined FIFA: 1961
Joined CAF: 1962

SEASON	LEAGUE CHAMPIONS
1998	AS Kaloum Stars
1999	*not held*
2000	Horoya AC
2001	Horoya AC
2002	Satellite FC

YEAR	CUP WINNERS
1998	AS Kaloum Stars
1999	Horoya AC
2000	Fello Stars Labé
2001	*unknown*
2002	Hafia Conakry

Guinea-Bissau

Federação de Futebol da Guiné-Bissau
Founded: 1974
Joined FIFA: 1986
Joined CAF: 1986

SEASON	LEAGUE CHAMPIONS
1999	*no championship*
2000	Sporting Clube de Bissau
2001	*no championship*
2002	Sporting Clube de Bissau
2003	UDIB

Liberia

Liberia Football Federation
Founded: 1936
Joined FIFA: 1962
Joined CAF: 1962

SEASON	LEAGUE CHAMPIONS
1998	Invincible XI
1999	LPRC Oilers
2000	Mighty Barolle
2001	Mighty Barolle
2002	LPRC Oilers

Mali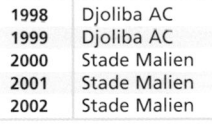

Fédération Malienne de Football
Founded: 1960
Joined FIFA: 1962
Joined CAF: 1963

SEASON	LEAGUE CHAMPIONS
1998	Djoliba AC
1999	Djoliba AC
2000	Stade Malien
2001	Stade Malien
2002	Stade Malien

YEAR	CUP WINNERS
1998	Djoliba AC
1999	Stade Malien
2000	Cercle Olympique
2001	Stade Malien
2002	Cercle Olympique

Mauritania

Fédération de Football de la République de Mauritanie
Founded: 1961
Joined FIFA: 1964
Joined CAF: 1968

SEASON	LEAGUE CHAMPIONS
1998	Garde Nationale
1999	SDPA Rosso
2000	Mauritel
2001	FC Nouadhibou
2002	FC Nouadhibou

Niger

Fédération Nigérienne de Football
Founded: 1967
Joined FIFA: 1967
Joined CAF: 1967

Niger *(continued)*

SEASON	LEAGUE CHAMPIONS
1998	*no championship*
1999	Olympic FC
2000	JS Ténéré
2001	JS Ténéré
2002	*no championship*

Senegal

Fédération Sénégalaise de Football
Founded: 1960
Joined FIFA: 1962
Joined CAF: 1963

SEASON	LEAGUE CHAMPIONS
1998	ASEC Ndiambour
1999	ASC Jeanne D'Arc
2000	ASC Diaraf
2001	ASC Jeanne D'Arc
2002	ASC Jeanne D'Arc

YEAR	CUP WINNERS
1999	ASEC Ndiambour
2000	Porte Autonome
2001	SONACOS
2002	AS Douanes
2003	ASEC Ndiambour

Sierra Leone

Sierra Leone Amateur Football Association
Founded: 1923
Joined FIFA: 1967
Joined CAF: 1967

SEASON	LEAGUE CHAMPIONS
1998	*not completed*
1999	East End Lions
2000	Mighty Blackpool
2001	Mighty Blackpool
2002	*no championship*

Togo

Fédération Togolaise de Football
Founded: 1960
Joined FIFA: 1962
Joined CAF: 1963

SEASON	LEAGUE CHAMPIONS
1998	*no competition*
1999	Semassi
2000	*not completed*
2001	Dynamic Togolais
2002	AS Douane

WEST AFRICA

Nigeria

Nigeria Football Association
Founded: 1945
Joined FIFA: 1959
Joined CAF: 1959

NIGERIA

THE FIRST RECORDED FOOTBALL IN NIGERIA dates from 1914 when matches between European players and King's College school were held in Lagos. Initially, teams were made up of white colonial administrators and soldiers, but by 1919 mixed European and African teams, such as Diamonds FC from Lagos, were competing for the War Memorial Cup. In 1931, the Lagos and District Amateur FA was created, followed by a national Nigerian football association and a national FA Cup in 1945.

The organization of Nigerian football was dominated almost exclusively by white Europeans, but on the field the best players were all Nigerian. In 1949, a Nigerian Select XI toured Britain and the first official Nigerian international match was played later that year against Sierra Leone. Membership of CAF and FIFA came in 1959, preceding independence from Britain by a year. For the first post-independence international, the national strip was changed and the Red Devils became the Green Eagles.

Biafran secession

Like everything else in Nigerian life, football was disrupted for the four years of the civil war (1967–70) and the secession of the state of Biafra. It was only in 1972 that a formal national league was created, won in its first year by the Mighty Jets from Jos. At the same time, from the ashes of Biafran independence, Enugu Rangers was founded, and politically and sportingly it has been the region's torchbearer. From its inception, Nigerian football has relied on public and private corporations to run football clubs; among the leading teams have been Lagos Railways, Bendel Insurance and Stationery Stores (all now defunct). Other once-powerful sides, such as Leventis United and Abiola Babes, have disappeared since their rich benefactors pulled out.

Nigerian football has proved increasingly successful on the international stage, with regular appearances at the World Cup, victories in the African Cup of Nations and a number of African club triumphs. However, problems with corruption, financial insecurity, the drain of talent to Europe and phenomenally dangerous stadiums have beset the game in recent years.

Stationery Stores from Lagos won the Nigerian Cup four times and the league title in 1992 before the company that sponsored it went out of business and the team folded.

Nigerian League Record 1972–2002

SEASON	CHAMPIONS	SEASON	CHAMPIONS
1972	Mighty Jets	1989	Iwuanyanwu Owerri
1973	Bendel Insurance	1990	Iwuanyanwu Owerri
1974	Rangers International	1991	Julius Berger
1975	Rangers International	1992	Stationery Stores
1976	Shooting Stars	1993	Iwuanyanwu Owerri
1977	Rangers International	1994	BCC Lions
1978	Racca Rovers	1995	Shooting Stars
1979	Bendel Insurance	1996	Udoji United
1980	Shooting Stars	1997	Eagle Cement
1981	Rangers International	1998	Shooting Stars
1982	Rangers International	1999	Lobi Stars
1983	Shooting Stars	2000	Julius Berger
1984	Rangers International	2001	Enyimba
1985	New Nigeria Bank	2002	Enyimba
1986	Leventis United		
1987	Iwuanyanwu Owerri		
1988	Iwuanyanwu Owerri		

Nigerian FA Challenge Cup 1945–2002

YEAR	WINNERS	YEAR	WINNERS
1945	Marine	1976	Rangers International
1946	Lagos Railways	1977	Shooting Stars
1947	Marine	1978	Bendel Insurance
1948	Lagos Railways	1979	Shooting Stars
1949	Lagos Railways	1980	Bendel Insurance
1950	GO Union	1981	Rangers International
1951	Lagos Railways	1982	Stationery Stores
1952	Lagos PAN Bank	1983	Rangers International
1953	Kano Pillars	1984	Leventis United
1954	Calabar Rovers	1985	Abiola Babes
1955	Port Harcourt	1986	Leventis United
1956	Lagos Railways	1987	Abiola Babes
1957	Lagos Railways	1988	Iwuanyanwu Owerri
1958	Port Harcourt	1989	BCC Lions
1959	Ibadan Lions	1990	Stationery Stores
1960	Lagos EDN	1991	El Kanemi Warriors
1961	Ibadan Lions	1992	El Kanemi Warriors
1962	Police	1993	BCC Lions
1963	Port Harcourt	1994	BCC Lions
1964	Lagos Railways	1995	Shooting Stars
1965	Lagos EDN	1996	Julius Berger
1966	Ibadan Lions	1997	BCC Lions
1967	Stationery Stores	1998	Wikki Tourists
1968	Stationery Stores	1999	Plateau United
1969	Ibadan Lions	2000	Niger Tornadoes
1970	Lagos EDN	2001	Dolphin FC
1971	Shooting Stars	2002	Julius Berger
1972	Bendel Insurance		
1973	*no winner*		
1974	Rangers International		
1975	Rangers International		

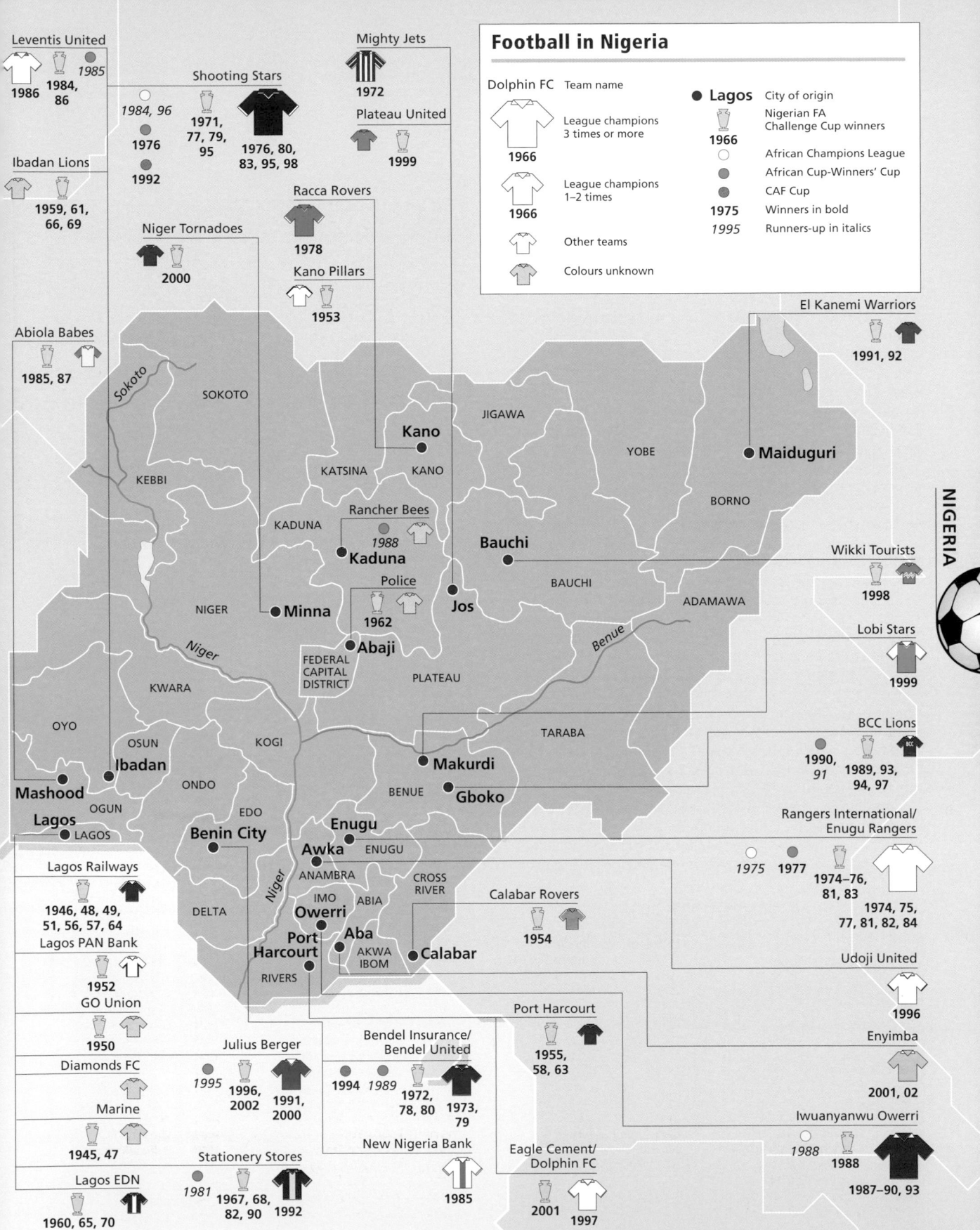

Football in Nigeria

Leventis United
1986   1984, 86   *1985*

Shooting Stars
1984, 96
1976
1992
1971, 77, 79, 95
1976, 80, 83, 95, 98

Mighty Jets
1972

Plateau United
1999

Ibadan Lions
1959, 61, 66, 69

Niger Tornadoes
2000

Racca Rovers
1978

Kano Pillars
1953

Abiola Babes
1985, 87

Dolphin FC — Team name
1966 — League champions 3 times or more
1966 — League champions 1–2 times
Other teams
Colours unknown

● **Lagos** — City of origin
1966 — Nigerian FA Challenge Cup winners
○ — African Champions League
● — African Cup-Winners' Cup
● — CAF Cup
1975 — Winners in bold
1995 — Runners-up in italics

El Kanemi Warriors
1991, 92

Wikki Tourists
1998

Rancher Bees
1988

Police
1962

Lobi Stars
1999

BCC Lions
1990, *91*   1989, 93, 94, 97

Rangers International/Enugu Rangers
1975   **1977**   1974–76, 81, 83   1974, 75, 77, 81, 82, 84

Calabar Rovers
1954

Udoji United
1996

Lagos Railways
1946, 48, 49, 51, 56, 57, 64

Lagos PAN Bank
1952

GO Union
1950

Port Harcourt
1955, 58, 63

Enyimba
2001, 02

Diamonds FC
1995   1996, 2002   1991, 2000

Julius Berger

Bendel Insurance/Bendel United
1994   *1989*   1972, 78, 80   1973, 79

Marine
1945, 47

Stationery Stores
1981   1967, 68, 82, 90   1992

New Nigeria Bank
1985

Iwuanyanwu Owerri
1988   1988   1987–90, 93

Lagos EDN
1960, 65, 70

Eagle Cement/Dolphin FC
2001   1997

SOKOTO
Sokoto
KEBBI
KATSINA
KADUNA
● Kano   KANO
JIGAWA
YOBE
● Maiduguri   BORNO
ADAMAWA
● Kaduna
● Bauchi
● Jos   BAUCHI
NIGER
● Minna
Niger
● Abaji
FEDERAL CAPITAL DISTRICT
PLATEAU
Benue
KWARA
OYO
OSUN
KOGI
● Makurdi
● Gboko   BENUE   TARABA
ONDO
OGUN
● Ibadan
● Mashood
Lagos   ● LAGOS
EDO
● Benin City
Niger
● Enugu   ENUGU
● Awka   ANAMBRA
CROSS RIVER
● Owerri   IMO   ABIA
DELTA
● Port Harcourt   RIVERS
● Aba   AKWA IBOM
● Calabar

NIGERIA

Cameroon

Fédération Camerounaise de Football
Founded: 1960
Joined FIFA: 1962
Joined CAF: 1963

CAMEROON WAS ORIGINALLY created and colonized by the Germans, from 1884 onwards. However, football did not follow until the expulsion of the Germans in 1916 by the British and French, who then received successive League of Nations and UN mandates to run the country. In the 1920s football developed among Africans in the colonial education system, and in the 1930s and 40s clubs and local competitions were established.

Political, sporting and social life in Cameroon is dictated by a series of linguistic and cultural divisions. Around a quarter of the population lives in the former British zone in the north-west – anglophone Cameroon. Its team is unquestionably PWD (Public Works Department) from Bamenda. The club's president in the late 1980s and early 90s was Ni John Frundi, founder and leader of the main opposition party, the SDF, and challenger in the bitter 1992 presidential elections. Rumours and accusations of corruption and match-fixing against the club abound among the politically and demographically dominant French-speaking parts of Cameroon.

Province and ethnicity

The rest of the country is formally francophone but is itself divided by province and ethnicity. The Bamileke from western Cameroon are allied with Racing Club Bafoussam at home and with Union Sportive and Diamant Yaoundé as migrants in the big cities. The Bassa and Douala from the Littoral province are tied to Dynamo Douala and the Beti from Centre province are concentrated in and around Yaoundé, supporting Canon and Tonnerre. In 1967, legislation was passed to disband ethnically-orientated organizations of all kinds, but football was exempted after huge public protest. Despite this, the national team is a multi-ethnic affair and a significant source of national unity, but, as ever, only when things are going well. The fantastic performance of the Cameroon national team at the 1990 World Cup, the best performance by an African team up to that time, was certainly used by President Biya in his bitter but successful campaign to retain the presidency in 1992.

Cameroon League 1961–2002

SEASON	CHAMPIONS	SEASON	CHAMPIONS
1961	Oryx Douala	1984	Tonnerre Yaoundé
1962	Caiman Douala	1985	Canon Yaoundé
1963	Oryx Douala	1986	Canon Yaoundé
1964	Oryx Douala	1987	Tonnerre Yaoundé
1965	Oryx Douala	1988	Tonnerre Yaoundé
1966	Diamant Yaoundé	1989	Racing Club Bafoussam
1967	Oryx Douala	1990	Union Sportive
1968	Caiman Douala	1991	Canon Yaoundé
1969	Union Sportive	1992	Racing Club Bafoussam
1970	Canon Yaoundé	1993	Racing Club Bafoussam
1971	Aigle Royale Nkongsamba	1994	Aigle Royale Nkongsamba
1972	Léopards Douala	1995	Racing Club Bafoussam
1973	Léopards Douala	1996	Unisport
1974	Canon Yaoundé	1997	Cotonsport
1975	Caiman Douala	1998	Cotonsport
1976	Union Sportive	1999	Sable Batié
1977	Canon Yaoundé	2000	Fovu Baham
1978	Union Sportive	2001	Cotonsport
1979	Canon Yaoundé	2002	Canon Yaoundé
1980	Canon Yaoundé		
1981	Tonnerre Yaoundé		
1982	Canon Yaoundé		
1983	Tonnerre Yaoundé		

Cameroon Cup 1956–2002

YEAR	WINNERS	YEAR	WINNERS
1956	Oryx Douala	1981	Dynamo Douala
1957	Canon Yaoundé	1982	Dragon Douala
1958	Tonnerre Yaoundé	1983	Canon Yaoundé
1959	Caiman Douala	1984	Dihep Nkam
1960	Lion Yaoundé	1985	Union Sportive
1961	Union Sportive	1986	Canon Yaoundé
1962	Lion Yaoundé	1987	Tonnerre Yaoundé
1963	Oryx Douala	1988	Panthère Sportive
1964	Diamant Yaoundé	1989	Tonnerre Yaoundé
1965	Lion Yaoundé	1990	Prévoyance Yaoundé
1966	Lion Yaoundé	1991	Tonnerre Yaoundé
1967	Canon Yaoundé	1992	Olympique Mvoylé
1968	Oryx Douala	1993	Canon Yaoundé
1969	Union Sportive	1994	Olympique Mvoylé
1970	Oryx Douala	1995	Canon Yaoundé
1971	Diamant Yaoundé	1996	Racing Club Bafoussam
1972	Diamant Yaoundé	1997	Union Sportive
1973	Canon Yaoundé	1998	Dynamo Douala
1974	Tonnerre Yaoundé	1999	Canon Yaoundé
1975	Canon Yaoundé	2000	Kumbo Strikers
1976	Canon Yaoundé	2001	Fovu Baham
1977	Canon Yaoundé	2002	Mount Cameroon
1978	Canon Yaoundé		
1979	Dynamo Douala		
1980	Union Sportive		

After its strong showing at Italia '90, Cameroon, shown here in 1992, has established itself as the strongest national team in Africa. Despite a convincing victory in the 2002 African Nations Cup, its World Cup campaign later in the year saw a disappointing first-round exit.

CAMEROON

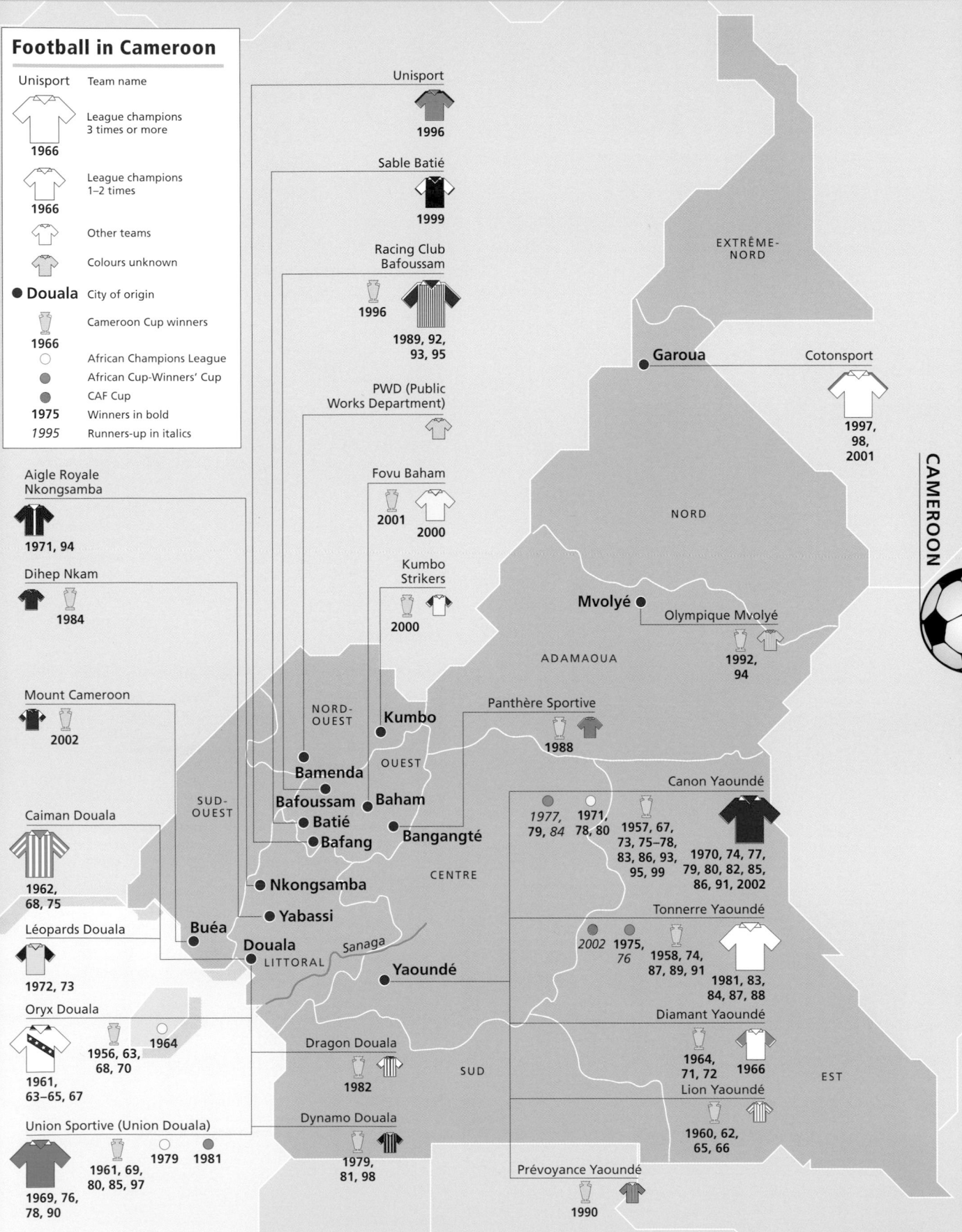

Football in Cameroon

Unisport · Team name

1966 — League champions 3 times or more

1966 — League champions 1–2 times

Other teams

Colours unknown

● **Douala** · City of origin

1966 — Cameroon Cup winners

○ African Champions League

◐ African Cup-Winners' Cup

● CAF Cup

1975 Winners in bold

1995 Runners-up in italics

Aigle Royale Nkongsamba
1971, 94

Dihep Nkam
1984

Mount Cameroon
2002

Caiman Douala
1962, 68, 75

Léopards Douala
1972, 73

Oryx Douala
1956, 63, 68, 70
1964
1961, 63–65, 67

Union Sportive (Union Douala)
1961, 69, 80, 85, 97
1979
1981
1969, 76, 78, 90

Unisport
1996

Sable Batié
1999

Racing Club Bafoussam
1996
1989, 92, 93, 95

PWD (Public Works Department)

Fovu Baham
2001
2000

Kumbo Strikers
2000

Panthère Sportive
1988

Dragon Douala
1982

Dynamo Douala
1979, 81, 98

Prévoyance Yaoundé
1990

EXTRÊME-NORD

● **Garoua** · **Cotonsport**
1997, 98, 2001

NORD

● **Mvolyé** · Olympique Mvolyé
1992, 94

ADAMAOUA

NORD-OUEST

● **Kumbo**

OUEST

● **Bamenda**
● **Bafoussam** ● **Baham**
● **Batié**
● **Bafang** ● **Bangangté**

SUD-OUEST

CENTRE

● **Buéa**
● **Nkongsamba**
● **Yabassi**
Douala ● *Sanaga*
LITTORAL
● **Yaoundé**

Canon Yaoundé
1977, 79, 84
1971, 78, 80
1957, 67, 73, 75–78, 83, 86, 93, 95, 99
1970, 74, 77, 79, 80, 82, 85, 86, 91, 2002

Tonnerre Yaoundé
2002
1975, 76
1958, 74, 87, 89, 91
1981, 83, 84, 87, 88

Diamant Yaoundé
1964, 71, 72
1966

Lion Yaoundé
1960, 62, 65, 66

SUD

EST

CAMEROON

Central and East Africa

ALTHOUGH EAST AND CENTRAL AFRICA are considered a single region by CAF, they are, in footballing terms, worlds apart. Central Africa has produced African club and national champions as well as World Cup qualifying national teams. East Africa's trophy cabinet is, by contrast, rather bare.

Central Africa's three key footballing nations are Cameroon (see pages 394–95), the Democratic Republic of Congo (or DRC, formerly known as Zaïre and the Belgian Congo) and Congo (formally known as Congo-Brazzaville and the French Congo). In the Belgian Congo, as it was then known, Africa's second oldest football association was established in the capital Léopoldville (now Kinshasa) in 1919, although a city league had been up and running since 1916. Zaïrian football's golden age lasted from independence in 1960 to the mid-1970s. The country's leading club, TP Englebert, won two and then lost two consecutive African Champions League Finals between 1967 and 1970, while the national side was the first sub-Saharan team to make it to the World Cup (1974). International matches were played between French and Belgian Congo between 1923 and 1950 in the Stanley Pool Championship (Stanley Pool is a lake that separates the capital cities of the two states).

Football first arrived in East Africa via British workers and colonists in Kenya, Uganda, Tanzania and Zanzibar. Kenya's oldest club, Mombassa FC, dates from 1906. The Gossage Cup, an international tournament between the four countries, was held between 1927 and 1972. Post-independence, national leagues were created. Kenya's Gor Mahia won the region's only African club championship – the Cup-Winners' Cup – in 1987, while two Ugandan teams have made it to the Final of the Champions League (Simba FC in 1972, and SC Villa in 1991). But otherwise, both at club and international level, the region's footballing record is weak. In Sudan, the 1930s saw the formation of leading Khartoum clubs Al Hilal and El Mourada. In Ethiopia a mixture of English and Italian influences introduced football during the 1930s, and a national league and football association accompanied independence in 1943.

SC Villa from Kampala (seen here in white) is one of Uganda's leading teams. Formerly known as Nakivubo Villa, the team has ten Ugandan league championships to its name.

Democratic Republic of Congo (formerly Zaïre)

Fédération Congolaise de Football-Association
Founded: 1919
Joined FIFA: 1962
Joined CAF: 1973

Democratic Republic of Congo League Record 1964–2002

SEASON	CHAMPIONS	SEASON	CHAMPIONS
1964	CS Imana	1985	US Tshinkunku
1965	Dragons	1986	FC Lupopo
1966	TP Englebert	1987	DC Motema Pembe
1967	TP Englebert	1988	AS Vita Club
1968	FC St. Eloi	1989	DC Motema Pembe
1969	TP Englebert	1990	FC Lupopo
1970	AS Vita Club	1991	Mikishi
1971	AS Vita Club	1992	US Bilombe
1972	AS Vita Club	1993	AS Vita Club
1973	AS Vita Club	1994	DC Motema Pembe
1974	CS Imana	1995	AS Bantous
1975	AS Vita Club	1996	*not known*
1976	TP Mazembe	1997	AS Vita Club
1977	AS Vita Club	1998	DC Motema Pembe
1978	CS Imana	1999	DC Motema Pembe
1979	AS Bilima	2000	TP Mazembe
1980	AS Vita Club	2001	TP Mazembe
1981	FC Lupopo	2002	FC Lupopo
1982	AS Bilima		
1983	Sanga Balende		
1984	AS Bilima		

Democratic Republic of Congo Cup Record 1964–2002

YEAR	WINNERS	YEAR	WINNERS
1964	DC Motema Pembe	1986	Kalamu
1965	AS Bilima	1987	Kalamu
1966	TP Mazembe	1988	Kalamu
1967	TP Mazembe	1989	Kalamu
1968	FC Lupopo	1990	DC Motema Pembe
1969–70	*no competition*	1991	DC Motema Pembe
1971	AS Vita Club	1992	US Bilombe
1972	AS Vita Club	1993	DC Motema Pembe
1973	AS Vita Club	1994	DC Motema Pembe
1974	DC Motema Pembe	1995	AC Sodigraf
1975	AS Vita Club	1996	AS Dragons
1976	TP Mazembe	1997	AS Dragons
1977	AS Vita Club	1998	AS Dragons
1978	DC Motema Pembe	1999	AS Dragons
1979	TP Mazembe	2000	TP Mazembe
1980	Lubumbashi Sport	2001	AS Vita Club
1981	AS Vita Club	2002	US Kenya
1982	AS Vita Club		
1983	AS Vita Club		
1984	DC Motema Pembe		
1985	DC Motema Pembe		

Burundi

Fédération de Football du Burundi
Founded: 1948
Joined FIFA: 1972
Joined CAF: 1972

SEASON	LEAGUE CHAMPIONS
1998	Vital'O FC
1999	Vital'O FC
2000	Vital'O FC
2001	Prince Louis FC
2002	*suspended*

Central African Republic

Fédération Centrafricaine de Football
Founded: 1937
Joined FIFA: 1963
Joined CAF: 1965

SEASON	LEAGUE CHAMPIONS
1998	*cancelled*
1999	*cancelled*
2000	Réal Olympique Castel
2001	*abandoned*
2002	*abandoned*

Chad

Fédération Tchadienne de Football
Founded: 1962
Joined FIFA: 1988
Joined CAF: 1962

SEASON	LEAGUE CHAMPIONS
1998	AS Coton Chad
1999	Renaissance
2000	FC Tourbillon
2001	*unknown*
2002	*unknown*

Congo

Fédération Congolaise de Football
Founded: 1962
Joined FIFA: 1962
Joined CAF: 1966

SEASON	LEAGUE CHAMPIONS
1998	Vita Club Mokanda
1999	Vita Club Mokanda
2000	Etoile du Congo
2001	Etoile du Congo
2002	AS Police

YEAR	CUP WINNERS
1998	Etoile du Congo
1999	TP Mystère
2000	Etoile du Congo
2001	AS Police
2002	Etoile du Congo

Djibouti

Fédération Djiboutienne de Football
Founded: 1977
Joined FIFA: 1994
Joined CAF: 1986

Djibouti *(continued)*

SEASON	LEAGUE CHAMPIONS
1999	Force Nationale de Police
2000	CDE
2001	Force Nationale de Police
2002	AS Borreh
2003	Gendarmerie Nationale

Equatorial Guinea

Fédération Equatoguineana de Futboll
Founded: 1976
Joined FIFA: 1986
Joined CAF: 1986

SEASON	LEAGUE CHAMPIONS
1998	CD Ela Nguema
1999	Cafe Band Sportif
2000	CD Ela Nguema
2001	Akonangui FC
2002	CD Ela Nguema

Ethiopia

Ye'Ityopiya Football Federechin
Founded: 1943
Joined FIFA: 1953
Joined CAF: 1957

SEASON	LEAGUE CHAMPIONS
1998	Mebrat Hail
1999	St. George
2000	St. George
2001	Mebrat Hail
2002	St. George

Gabon

Fédération Gabonaise de Football
Founded: 1962
Joined FIFA: 1963
Joined CAF: 1967

SEASON	LEAGUE CHAMPIONS
1998	FC 105
1999	Petrosport Port Gentil
2000	Mangasport
2001	FC 105
2002	US Nzambi

Kenya

Kenya Football Federation
Founded: 1932
Joined FIFA: 1960
Joined CAF: 1968

Kenya *(continued)*

SEASON	LEAGUE CHAMPIONS
1998	AFC Leopards
1999	Tusker FC
2000	Tusker FC
2001	Oserian Fastac
2002	Oserian Fastac

YEAR	CUP WINNERS
1998	Mumias Sugar
1999	Mumias Sugar
2000	Mathare United
2001	AFC Leopards
2002	Kenya Pipeline

Madagascar

Fédération Malagasy de Football
Founded: 1961
Joined FIFA: 1962
Joined CAF: 1963

SEASON	LEAGUE CHAMPIONS
1998	DAS Antanarivo
1999	AS Fortior
2000	AS Fortior
2001	Stade Olympique de l'Emyrne
2002	AS Adema

Rwanda

Fédération Rwandaise de Football Amateur
Founded: 1972
Joined FIFA: 1976
Joined CAF: 1976

SEASON	LEAGUE CHAMPIONS
1998	Rayon Sports
1999	FC APR
2000	FC APR
2001	FC APR
2002	Rayon Sports

São Tomé and Principe

Federação Santomense de Futebol
Founded: 1975
Joined FIFA: 1986
Joined CAF: 1986

SEASON	LEAGUE CHAMPIONS
1998	GD Os Operários
1999	Sporting Praia Cruz
2000	Inter Bom-Bom
2001	Bairros Unidos FC
2002	*cancelled*

Somalia

Somalia Football Federation
Founded: 1951
Joined FIFA: 1960
Joined CAF: 1968

SEASON	LEAGUE CHAMPIONS
1998	Ports Authority
1999	*no championship*
2000	Elman FC
2001	Elman FC
2002	Elman FC

Sudan

Sudan Football Association
Founded: 1936
Joined FIFA: 1948
Joined CAF: 1957

SEASON	LEAGUE CHAMPIONS
1998	Al Hilal
1999	Al Hilal
2000	Al Merreikh
2001	Al Merreikh
2002	Al Merreikh

Tanzania

Football Association of Tanzania
Founded: 1930
Joined FIFA: 1964
Joined CAF: 1960

SEASON	LEAGUE CHAMPIONS
1998	Maji Maji
1999	Prisons
2000	Young Africans
2001	Simba SC
2002	Simba SC

Uganda

Federation of Uganda Football Associations
Founded: 1924
Joined FIFA: 1959
Joined CAF: 1959

SEASON	LEAGUE CHAMPIONS
1998	SC Villa
1999	SC Villa
2000	SC Villa
2001	SC Villa
2002	SC Villa

Southern Africa

Zimbabwe

Zimbabwe Football Association
Founded: 1950
Joined FIFA: 1965–70, 1980
Joined CAF: 1980

IN ECONOMICS, POLITICS and in football, South Africa (see pages 436–437) is the giant of Southern Africa and the rest of the region has long lived in its shadow. The apartheid regime led to South Africa's exclusion from FIFA, CAF and global football in general until 1994, but throughout those years of exclusion, football retained a strong foothold in the country. So much so that the constant drain of players to their rich neighbour has limited the development of football in nearby Lesotho and Swaziland, while civil war has disrupted the game in Zimbabwe, Angola and Mozambique.

Railway workers

The most stable footballing nation in the region, Zambia, acquired a colonial FA in 1929 in the Northern Rhodesian FA. A national league and cup competition was set up following independence in 1962. In 1991, Zambian giants Power Dynamos won the Cup-Winners' Cup, the nation's only African championship victory. Like Zambia, football reached Zimbabwe with the arrival of British railway workers in the late 19th century, and a national league and cup were operating by the early 1960s. A Rhodesian FA was set up by Ian Smith's government in the wake of the declaration of independence in 1965, but was suspended by FIFA in 1970. The achievement of black majority rule in 1980 saw Zimbabwe's re-admission to FIFA, and a professional national league began in 1992.

Race politics also shamed football in Malawi. Before independence in 1966, a Nyasaland African FA (for black teams) and a Nyasaland FA (for white teams) ensured racially segregated football was played throughout the country.

Portuguese influence brought football to both Angola and Mozambique and in the shape of Mozambique's Eusebio created Africa's first global footballing star during the 1960s. But a chaotic process of Portuguese decolonization during 1975, as well as civil war, has left the region's societies and footballing cultures alike weak and disorganized.

Zimbabwean League Record 1962–2002

SEASON	CHAMPIONS	SEASON	CHAMPIONS
1962	Bulawayo Rovers	1984	Black Rhinos
1963	Dynamos	1985	Dynamos
1964	St. Pauls	1986	Dynamos
1965	Dynamos	1987	Black Rhinos
1966	St. Pauls	1988	Zimbabwe Saints
1967	Tornados	1989	Dynamos
1968	Sables	1990	Highlanders
1969	Sables	1991	Dynamos
1970	Dynamos	1992	Black Aces
1971	Arcadia United	1993	Zimbabwe Highlanders
1972	Sables	1994	Dynamos
1973	Metal Box	1995	Dynamos
1974	Sables	1996	CAPS United
1975	Chibuku	1997	Dynamos
1976	Dynamos	1998	*no championship*
1977	Zimbabwe Saints	1999	Zimbabwe Highlanders
1978	Dynamos	2000	Zimbabwe Highlanders
1979	CAPS United	2001	Zimbabwe Highlanders
1980	Dynamos	2002	Zimbabwe Highlanders
1981	Dynamos		
1982	Dynamos		
1983	Dynamos		

Zimbabwean Cup Record 1962–2002

YEAR	WINNERS	YEAR	WINNERS
1962	Bulawayo Rovers	1984	Black Rhinos
1963	Salisbury Callies	1985	Dynamos
1964	*no competition*	1986	Highlanders
1965	Salisbury City Wanderers	1987	Zimbabwe Saints
		1988	Dynamos
1966	Mangula	1989	Dynamos
1967	Salisbury Callies	1990	Highlanders
1968	Arcadia United	1991	Wankie FC
1969	Arcadia United	1992	CAPS United
1970	Wankie	1993	Tanganda
1971	Chibuku	1994	Blackpool
1972	Mangula	1995	Chapungu
1973	Wankie	1996	Dynamos
1974	Chibuku	1997	CAPS United
1975	Salisbury Callies	1998	CAPS United
1976	Dynamos	1999	*unknown*
1977	Zimbabwe Saints	2000	Dynamos
1978	Zisco Steel	2001	Zimbabwe Highlanders
1979	Zimbabwe Saints	2002	Masvingo United
1980	CAPS United		
1981	CAPS United		
1982	CAPS United		
1983	CAPS United		

Zimbabwean champions Dynamos, from Harare, took on ASEC Abidjan from Côte d'Ivoire in the 1998 African Champions League Final but lost 4-2 in the second leg after a 0-0 draw in the first leg.

Angola

Federação Angolana de Futebol
Founded: 1977
Joined FIFA: 1980
Joined CAF: 1980

SEASON	LEAGUE CHAMPIONS
1998	Primeiro de Agosto
1999	Primeiro de Agosto
2000	Petro Atlético
2001	Petro Atlético
2002	Atlético Sport Aviação

Angola *(continued)*

YEAR	CUP WINNERS
1999	Sagrada Esperança
2000	Petro Atlético
2001	Sonangol
2002	Petro Atlético
2003	*postponed*

Botswana

Botswana Football Association
Founded: 1970
Joined FIFA: 1976
Joined CAF: 1976

SEASON	LEAGUE CHAMPIONS
1999	Mogoditshane Fighters
2000	Mogoditshane Fighters
2001	Mogoditshane Fighters
2002	Botswana Defence Force
2003	Botswana Defence Force

YEAR	CUP WINNERS
1998	Botswana Defence Force
1999	Mogoditshane Fighters
2000	Mogoditshane Fighters
2001	TASC
2002	Tafic GF

Lesotho

Lesotho Sports Council
Founded: 1932
Joined FIFA: 1964
Joined CAF: 1964

SEASON	LEAGUE CHAMPIONS
1998	RL Defence Force
1999	RL Defence Force
2000	Lesotho Prison Service
2001	RL Defence Force
2002	Lesotho Prison Service

YEAR	CUP WINNERS
1998	Arsenal
1999	*not known*
2000	RL Defence Force
2001	*not known*
2002	*not known*

Malawi

Football Association of Malawi
Founded: 1966
Joined FIFA: 1967
Joined CAF: 1968

Malawi *(continued)*

SEASON	LEAGUE CHAMPIONS
1998	Telecom Wanderers
1999	Bata Bullets
2000	Bata Bullets
2001	Total Big Bullets
2002	Total Big Bullets

Mauritius

Mauritius Football Association
Founded: 1952
Joined FIFA: 1962
Joined CAF: 1962

SEASON	LEAGUE CHAMPIONS
1999	Fire Brigade FC
2000	*no championship*
2001	Olympique de Moka
2002	AS Port-Louis 2000
2003	AS Port-Louis 2000

YEAR	CUP WINNERS
1998	Fire Brigade FC
1999	*abandoned*
2000	*abandoned*
2001	USBBRH
2002	AS Port-Louis 2000

Mozambique

Federação Mocambicana de Futebol
Founded: 1975
Joined FIFA: 1978
Joined CAF: 1978

SEASON	LEAGUE CHAMPIONS
1998	*no official championship*
1999	Ferroviário
2000	Costa do Sol
2001	Costa do Sol
2002	Ferroviário

YEAR	CUP WINNERS
1998	Costa do Sol
1999	Costa do Sol
2000	Costa do Sol
2001	Maxaquene
2002	Costa do Sol

Namibia

Namibia Football Association
Founded: 1992
Joined FIFA: 1992
Joined CAF: 1990

The Zambian team which beat Mauritius 3-0 in Port Louis in a Nations Cup match on 25 April 1993. Two days later, en route to Senegal for a World Cup qualifier, the whole team was killed when their plane crashed off the coast of Gabon.

Namibia *(continued)*

SEASON	LEAGUE CHAMPIONS
1999	Black Africans Nashua
2000	Blue Waters
2001	*league format change*
2002	Liverpool
2003	Chief Santos

YEAR	CUP WINNERS
1999	Chief Santos
2000	Chief Santos
2001	*league format change*
2002	Orlando Pirates
2003	Civics FC

Swaziland

National Football Association of Swaziland
Founded: 1964
Joined FIFA: 1976
Joined CAF: 1976

SEASON	LEAGUE CHAMPIONS
1999	Manzini Wanderers
2000	Mbabane Highlanders
2001	Mbabane Highlanders
2002	Manzini Wanderers
2003	Manzini Wanderers

Swaziland *(continued)*

YEAR	CUP WINNERS
1997	Mbabane Highlanders
1998	Denver Sundowns
1999	*no official competition*
2000	*no official competition*
2001	Eleven Men in Flight

Zambia

Football Association of Zambia
Founded: 1929
Joined FIFA: 1964
Joined CAF: 1964

SEASON	LEAGUE CHAMPIONS
1998	Nchanga Rangers
1999	Nkana FC
2000	Power Dynamos
2001	Nkana FC
2002	Zanaco

YEAR	CUP WINNERS
1998	Konkola Blades
1999	Zamsure
2000	Nkana FC
2001	Power Dynamos
2002	Zanaco

Red Arrows from Lusaka (in red and black) was a fine cup team in the 1980s, winning the Zambian Cup in 1983 and 89. Today it is struggling in the Zambian Second Division.

South Africa

South African Football Association
Founded: 1892, 1991
Joined FIFA: 1952–76, 1992
Joined CAF: 1957–64, 1992

THE HISTORY OF FOOTBALL in South Africa is inevitably tied to the politics of race in the country. The first recorded game in South Africa took place in Natal in 1866 and the province also produced the first club – the white Pietermaritzburg Country – founded in 1879. Three further white clubs were quickly formed – Natal Wasps, Durban Alphas and Umgeni Stars – and in 1882 they formed the Natal FA. In 1891, a Cape Town FA was formed by four British military clubs, and a national organization, FASA (Football Association of South Africa), was formed in 1892. Western province joined in 1896 and Transvaal in 1899.

For all these organizational changes, football was always secondary to rugby in the affections of white South Africans, but among the black population, football was always the dominant sport. In 1898, the first black club – Orange Free State Bantu FC – was founded, and an Orange Free State FA was set up in 1930 in Bloemfontein, the centre of African national politics; a Natal Bantu FA followed in 1931. All of these associations provided a crucial training ground for black administrators and politicians, including the ANC leader Albert Luthili. However, the sporting heart of black football was

Johannesburg and the mining towns of the Rand where the Transvaal Pirates, Swallows and Evergreen Mighty Greens flourished. Subsequently, the region has provided the other dominant forces in South African football – the Orlando Pirates, Mamelodi Sundowns and Kaizer Chiefs.

With the imposition of strict apartheid in 1948, the racial and political divide in football solidified. The SASF was formed in 1952 representing African and coloured football and it formally declared itself a non-racial organization in 1963. The older FASA remained resolutely white and was eventually expelled from CAF and FIFA for refusing to field mixed-race international sides. Domestically, a whites-only national professional league (the NPFL) ran from 1959, while the black NPSL was formed in 1971. The two effectively merged in 1978, the economics of township crowds weighing more heavily than the politics of racial separation. During the state of emergency in the 1980s, football matches and grounds provided a location for political rallies of all kinds and the ANC celebrated the release of political prisoners in 1989 and 1990 at the FNB Stadium in Johannesburg. In 1992, South Africa was readmitted to FIFA and CAF.

*The **Kaizer Chiefs** from Johannesburg (in white) and the **Mamelodi Sundowns** from Pretoria are among the top teams in a strong South African football league.*

South African League and Cup Winners 1971–2003

YEAR	LEAGUE CHAMPIONS (NPSL till 1984 then NSL)	CUP WINNERS	TOP EIGHT CUP WINNERS (NPSL till 1984 then NSL)
1971	Orlando Pirates	Kaizer Chiefs	
1972	Amazulu	Kaizer Chiefs	Orlando Pirates
1973	Orlando Pirates	Orlando Pirates	Orlando Pirates
1974	Kaizer Chiefs	Orlando Pirates	Kaizer Chiefs
1975	Orlando Pirates	Orlando Pirates	Moroka Swallows
1976	Orlando Pirates	Kaizer Chiefs	Kaizer Chiefs
1977	Kaizer Chiefs	Orlando Pirates	Kaizer Chiefs
1978	Lusitano Club	Wits University	Orlando Pirates
1979	Kaizer Chiefs	Kaizer Chiefs	Moroka Swallows
1980	Highlands Park	Orlando Pirates	Witbank Black Aces
1981	Kaizer Chiefs	Kaizer Chiefs	Kaizer Chiefs
1982	Durban City	Kaizer Chiefs	Kaizer Chiefs
1983	Durban City	Moroka Swallows	Orlando Pirates
1984	Kaizer Chiefs	Kaizer Chiefs	Wits University
1985	Bush Bucks	Bloemfontein Celtic	Kaizer Chiefs
1986	Rangers FC	Mamelodi United	Arcadia
1987	Jomo Cosmos	Kaizer Chiefs	Kaizer Chiefs
1988	Mamelodi United	Orlando Pirates	Mamelodi United
1989	Kaizer Chiefs	Moroka Swallows	Kaizer Chiefs
1990	Mamelodi United	Jomo Cosmos	Mamelodi United
1991	Kaizer Chiefs	Moroka Swallows	Kaizer Chiefs
1992	Kaizer Chiefs	Kaizer Chiefs	Kaizer Chiefs
1993	Mamelodi United	Witbank Aces	Orlando Pirates
1994	Orlando Pirates	Vaal Professionals	Kaizer Chiefs
1995	Cape Town Spurs	Cape Town Spurs	Wits University
1996	Kaizer Chiefs	Orlando Pirates	Orlando Pirates
1997	Manning Rangers	*no competition*	*no competition*
1998	Mamelodi Sundowns	Mamelodi Sundowns	*no competition*
1999	Mamelodi Sundowns	Supersport United	*no competition*
2000	Mamelodi Sundowns	Kaizer Chiefs	Orlando Pirates
2001	Orlando Pirates	Santos	Kaizer Chiefs
2002	Santos	*no competition*	Santos
2003	Orlando Pirates		

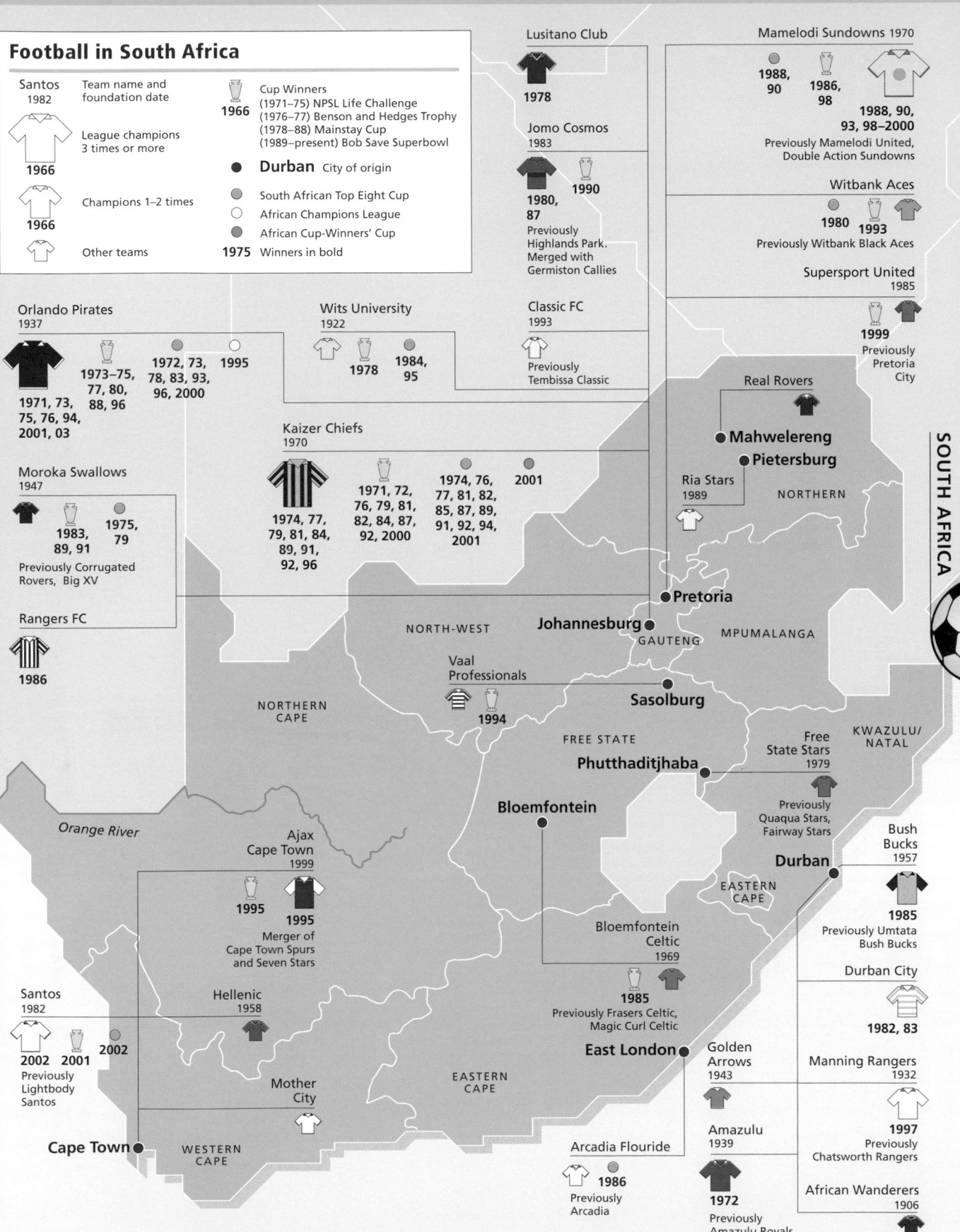

Football in South Africa

Santos 1982 — Team name and foundation date

1966 — Cup Winners
(1971–75) NPSL Life Challenge
(1976–77) Benson and Hedges Trophy
(1978–88) Mainstay Cup
(1989–present) Bob Save Superbowl

1966 — League champions 3 times or more

1966 — Champions 1–2 times

Durban City of origin

Other teams

1975 Winners in bold

South African Top Eight Cup
African Champions League
African Cup-Winners' Cup

Lusitano Club
1978

Jomo Cosmos 1983
1980, 87
1990
Previously Highlands Park. Merged with Germiston Callies

Mamelodi Sundowns 1970
1988, 90
1986, 98
1988, 90, 93, 98–2000
Previously Mamelodi United, Double Action Sundowns

Witbank Aces
1980
1993
Previously Witbank Black Aces

Supersport United 1985
1999
Previously Pretoria City

Orlando Pirates 1937
1973–75, 77, 80, 88, 96
1972, 73, 78, 83, 93, 96, 2000
1995
1971, 73, 75, 76, 94, 2001, 03

Wits University 1922
1978
1984, 95

Classic FC 1993
Previously Tembissa Classic

Real Rovers
Mahwelereng
Pietersburg
Ria Stars 1989
NORTHERN

Kaizer Chiefs 1970
1974, 77, 79, 81, 84, 89, 91, 92, 96
1971, 72, 76, 79, 81, 82, 84, 87, 92, 2000
1974, 76, 77, 81, 82, 85, 87, 89, 91, 92, 94, 2001
2001

Moroka Swallows 1947
1983, 89, 91
1975, 79
Previously Corrugated Rovers, Big XV

Rangers FC
1986

SOUTH AFRICA

Pretoria
Johannesburg
GAUTENG
NORTH-WEST
MPUMALANGA

Vaal Professionals
1994
Sasolburg

NORTHERN CAPE

FREE STATE

Free State Stars 1979
Previously Quaqua Stars, Fairway Stars

KWAZULU/ NATAL

Phutthaditjhaba

Bloemfontein

Orange River

Ajax Cape Town 1999
1995
1995
Merger of Cape Town Spurs and Seven Stars

Bloemfontein Celtic 1969
1985
Previously Frasers Celtic, Magic Curl Celtic

Durban
Bush Bucks 1957
1985
Previously Umtata Bush Bucks

Durban City
1982, 83

EASTERN CAPE

Hellenic 1958

Santos 1982
2002 **2001**
2002
Previously Lightbody Santos

Mother City

East London

Golden Arrows 1943

Amazulu 1939

EASTERN CAPE

Manning Rangers 1932

1997
Previously Chatsworth Rangers

Cape Town
WESTERN CAPE

Arcadia Flouride
1986
Previously Arcadia

1972
Previously Amazulu Royals

African Wanderers 1906

THE AFC NATIONS

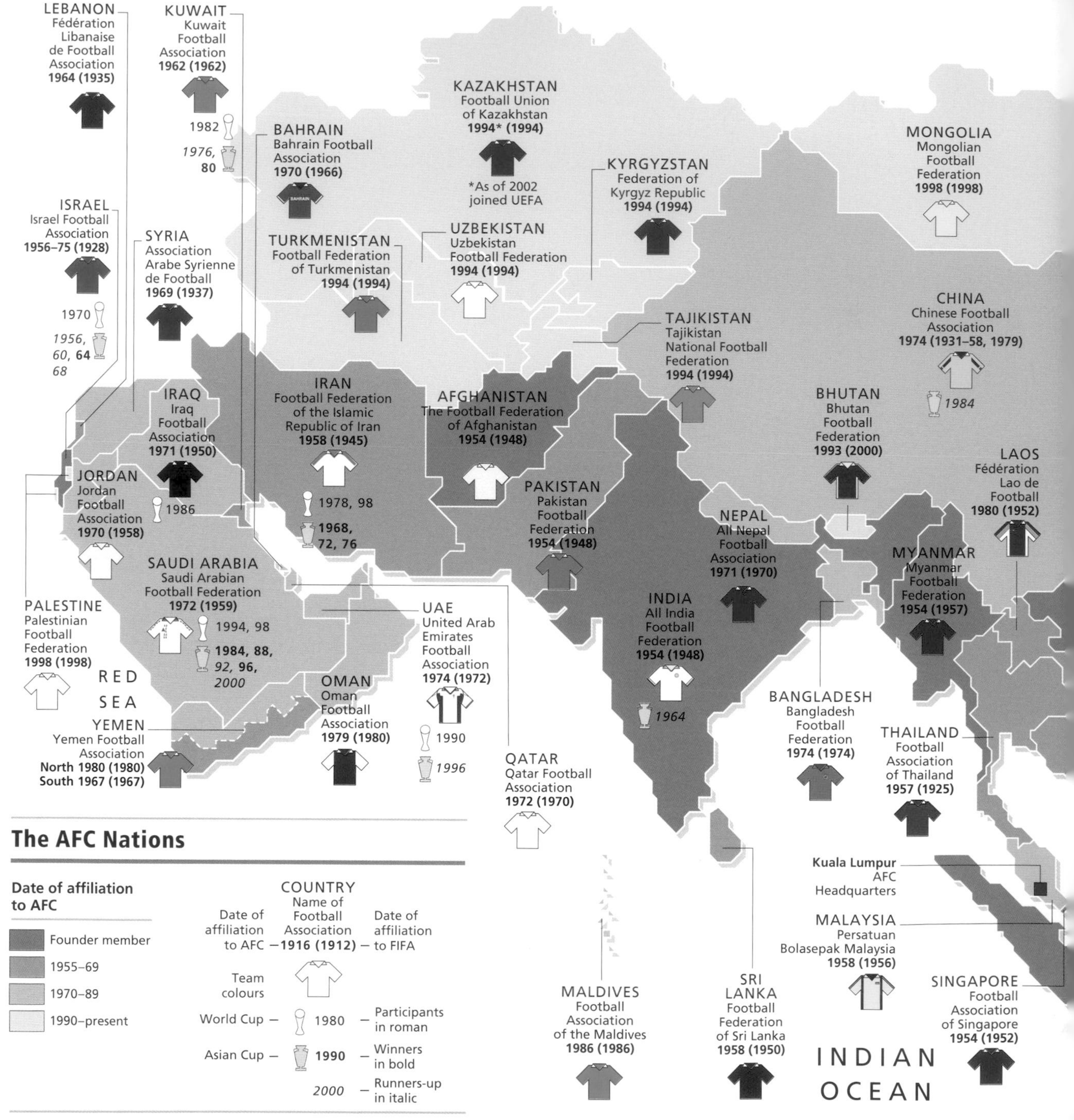

LEBANON
Fédération
Libanaise
de Football
Association
1964 (1935)

KUWAIT
Kuwait
Football
Association
1962 (1962)

1982
*1976,
80*

KAZAKHSTAN
Football Union
of Kazakhstan
1994* (1994)

*As of 2002
joined UEFA

MONGOLIA
Mongolian
Football
Federation
1998 (1998)

BAHRAIN
Bahrain Football
Association
1970 (1966)

KYRGYZSTAN
Federation of
Kyrgyz Republic
1994 (1994)

ISRAEL
Israel Football
Association
1956–75 (1928)

1970
*1956,
60,* **64**
68

SYRIA
Association
Arabe Syrienne
de Football
1969 (1937)

TURKMENISTAN
Football Federation
of Turkmenistan
1994 (1994)

UZBEKISTAN
Uzbekistan
Football Federation
1994 (1994)

TAJIKISTAN
Tajikistan
National Football
Federation
1994 (1994)

CHINA
Chinese Football
Association
1974 (1931–58, 1979)

1984

IRAQ
Iraq
Football
Association
1971 (1950)

IRAN
Football Federation
of the Islamic
Republic of Iran
1958 (1945)

1978, 98
**1968,
72, 76**

AFGHANISTAN
The Football Federation
of Afghanistan
1954 (1948)

BHUTAN
Bhutan
Football
Federation
1993 (2000)

LAOS
Fédération
Lao de
Football
1980 (1952)

JORDAN
Jordan
Football
Association
1970 (1958)

1986

PAKISTAN
Pakistan
Football
Federation
1954 (1948)

NEPAL
All Nepal
Football
Association
1971 (1970)

MYANMAR
Myanmar
Football
Federation
1954 (1957)

SAUDI ARABIA
Saudi Arabian
Football Federation
1972 (1959)

1994, 98
**1984, 88,
92, 96,
2000**

UAE
United Arab
Emirates
Football
Association
1974 (1972)

INDIA
All India
Football
Federation
1954 (1948)

1964

PALESTINE
Palestinian
Football
Federation
1998 (1998)

R E D
S E A

OMAN
Oman
Football
Association
1979 (1980)

1990

1996

BANGLADESH
Bangladesh
Football
Federation
1974 (1974)

THAILAND
Football
Association
of Thailand
1957 (1925)

YEMEN
Yemen Football
Association
North 1980 (1980)
South 1967 (1967)

QATAR
Qatar Football
Association
1972 (1970)

Kuala Lumpur
AFC
Headquarters

The AFC Nations

Date of affiliation to AFC

	Founder member
	1955–69
	1970–89
	1990–present

COUNTRY
Name of
Football
Association
Date of — **1916** (1912) — Date of
affiliation   affiliation
to AFC   to FIFA

Team
colours

World Cup — 1980 — Participants in roman

Asian Cup — **1990** — Winners in bold

2000 — Runners-up in italic

MALDIVES
Football
Association
of the Maldives
1986 (1986)

**SRI
LANKA**
Football
Federation
of Sri Lanka
1958 (1950)

MALAYSIA
Persatuan
Bolasepak Malaysia
1958 (1956)

SINGAPORE
Football
Association
of Singapore
1954 (1952)

I N D I A N
O C E A N

The Development of Asian Football

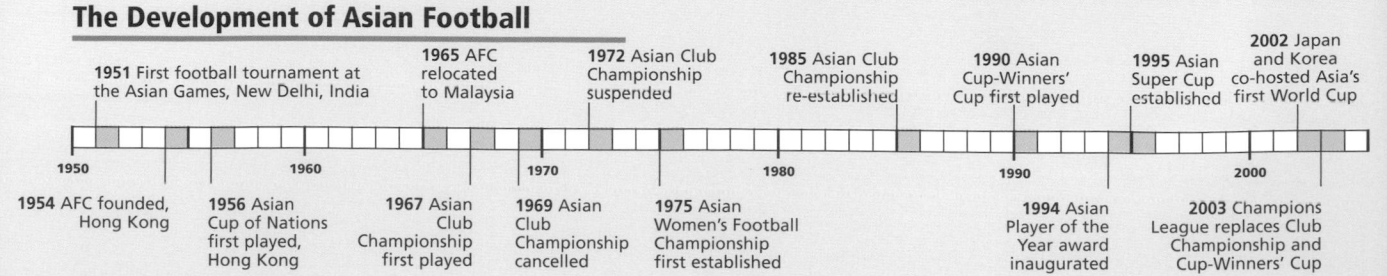

1951 First football tournament at
the Asian Games, New Delhi, India

1965 AFC
relocated
to Malaysia

1972 Asian Club
Championship
suspended

1985 Asian Club
Championship
re-established

1990 Asian
Cup-Winners'
Cup first played

1995 Asian
Super Cup
established

2002 Japan
and Korea
co-hosted Asia's
first World Cup

1950   1960   1970   1980   1990   2000

1954 AFC founded,
Hong Kong

1956 Asian
Cup of Nations
first played,
Hong Kong

1967 Asian
Club
Championship
first played

1969 Asian
Club
Championship
cancelled

1975 Asian
Women's Football
Championship
first established

1994 Asian
Player of the
Year award
inaugurated

2003 Champions
League replaces Club
Championship and
Cup-Winners' Cup

The AFC Nations

SOUTH KOREA
Korea Football
Association
1954 (1948)

1954 (as Korea), 86, 90, 94, 98

1956, 60, 72, 80, 88

NORTH KOREA
Football Association
of the Democratic
People's Republic
of Korea
1974 (1958)

1966

MACAO
Macau Football
Association
1976 (1976)

HONG KONG
Hong Kong
Football
Association
1954 (1954)

JAPAN
Japan Football
Association
1954 (1929–46, 1950)

1998

1992, 2000

TAIWAN
Chinese Taipei
Football
Association
1954–75, 1990 (1954)

PACIFIC OCEAN

VIETNAM
Vietnam
Football
Federation
1954 (1964)

PHILIPPINES
Philippines
Football
Federation
1954 (1928)

GUAM
Guam Soccer
Association
1996 (1996)

CAMBODIA
Cambodia
Football
Federation
1957 (1953)

BRUNEI
Football
Association of
Brunei Darussalam
1970 (1969)

INDONESIA
Persatuan
Sepakbola
Seluruh Indonesia
1954 (1952)

THE AFC (ASIAN FOOTBALL CONFEDERATION) is the ruling FIFA affiliated body for Asian football. Prior to the AFC's formation international football was played at the 1951 and 1954 Asian Games. The Manila Games of 1954 provided the opportunity for representatives of Asian football to form the AFC, based in Hong Kong until relocating to Malaysia in 1965. The AFC's Asian Cup, open to professionals and amateurs, has superseded the Asian Games as the continent's premier international tournament.

The enormous size and diversity of Asia has presented organizational dilemmas. International tournaments involve vast travelling distances for often poor clubs and leagues, and most competitions have used regionally-based qualifying rounds. Travel aside, the AFC (which included Israel and Taiwan among its members) has been beset by international politics. Indonesia refused travel visas for both nations' teams at the 1962 Asian Games and pressure continued over the next decade for both nations to be expelled. China protested Taiwan's presence and Middle Eastern nations objected to Israel. At the 1974 Asian Games North Korea and Iran refused to play Israel and the next year Israel and Taiwan were expelled. In the 1990s AFC has been busy with the modernization and commercialization of Asian football and the promotion of its international club tournaments.

The future of Asian football: *Ahn Jung-hwan's goal against Italy in the 2002 World Cup was one of the highpoints of the tournament. South Korea's fourth-place finish was the best ever by an Asian team.*

AFC

AFC
Asian Football Confederation

Asian Tournaments and Cup Competitions:
Asian Cup
Asian Games
Asian Super League
Asian Women's Championship

Calendar of Events

Club Tournaments	AFC Champions League 2004
	AFC Futsal Championship 2004
International Tournaments	Qualifying Tournament for Asian Cup 2004
	Asian Cup 2004
	Qualifying Tournament for 2004 Olympic Games (Under–23s)

Asia

THE SEASONS IN REVIEW 2002, 2002–03

THE 2002 KOREA/JAPAN WORLD CUP placed Asia at the very centre of global football. Japan's excellent showing and South Korea's miraculous progress to the semi-finals suggested that the continent might be about to become something more than an insatiable market for the merchandise of leading European clubs. It has certainly remained an insatiable market – David Beckham's extraordinary popularity in the Far East was an irresistible asset in his transfer to Real Madrid over the summer of 2003. Certainly a number of Asian players are trickling into European leagues – with Chinese internationals at both Everton and Manchester City, this unlikely English clash had over 300 million TV viewers in China this year. Shinji Ono – a cultured midfield player for Feyenoord and Japan – was named Asian player of 2002.

However, much of the season was played out under the stars of war and disease. Palestinian football was completely disrupted by the ongoing intifada against Israeli occupation, while the Iraqi season was sharply truncated by the war in spring 2003. The fall of Saddam Hussein's regime has allowed Iraq's return to international football and eased the perennial problem for the AFC that Kuwait would not meet any Iraqi team at any level.

War, or rather then threat of war, was the backdrop for the Asian Games held in South Korea. Although, amazingly, a North Korean side did attend and made it to the quarter-finals, the South Korean government was forced to give protracted assurances that no defections from the squad would be accepted. Mongolia withdrew from the games and was replaced by Afghanistan, playing its first tournament for 18 years. The team have some way to go as eventual champions Iran thrashed them 10-0 in their opening game.

The AFC's key plans for modernizing Asian football in the wake of the World Cup was the revamped Asian Champions League. The usual problems of the vast geography of Asia and the very different standards of national leagues was remedied by the extensive use of qualifying rounds, additional places for the strongest nations and the concentration of much of the tournament into two mini-leagues playing their games in one location to produce four quarter-finalists. Many of the most

fancied teams, including the Japanese and South Korean clubs, went out at this stage. Thai Champions BEC Tero Sasana was the first team from the country to make the Final since Thai Farmers Bank in 1985, after it beat Pakhator from Tashkent in Uzbekistan. In the other semi-final the UAE team Al-Ain, coached by Senegal's World Cup manager Bruno Metsu, looked poised to take the other spot after its first leg against Chinese champions Dalian Shide. But with the SARS virus epidemic in full swing, the tournament has been postponed until later this year.

Yes, I really did get a lot of votes in Asia. FIFA president Sepp Blatter chats with the Asian football confederation's new president, Mohammed Hammam.

Asian Champions League

2002–03
SEMI-FINALS (2 legs)

April 9 – Meesuwan Stadium, Bangkok
BEC Tero 3-1 Pachtakor
Sasana   Tashkent
(Thailand)   (Uzbekistan)
(Srimaka 41,   *(Soliev 80)*
Phuangprakob 69,
Chaiman 84)
h/t: 1-0 **Att** : 15,000
Ref: Jong-chul (South Korean)

April 22 – Pachtakor Stadium, Tashkent
Pachtakor 1-0 BEC Tero
Tashkent   Sasana
(Djeperov 86)
h/t: 0-0 **Att** : 50,000
Ref: Kamikawa (Japanese)
BEC Tero Sesana won 3-2 on aggregate

April 9 – Al Ain Stadium, Abu Dhabi
Al Ain 4-2 Dalian Shide
(UAE)   (China)
(Sango 62 pen, 83,   *(Haidong 17,*
Omar 64,   *Li Yao 88)*
Yaslam 75)
h/t: 0-1 **Att** : 20,000
Ref: Rahman (UAE)

Second leg postponed from April 23 due to SARS outbreak. Will be played 30 August 2003. The Final will be played in October 2003.

Top 16 Asian Leagues

COUNTRY	CHAMPIONS	RUNNERS-UP	CUP WINNERS
China*	Dalian Shide	Shenzhen Ping'an Insurance	Qingdao Hademen
India	East Bengal	Salgaocar SC	Mahindra United
Indonesia*	Petrokimia	Persita	*no cup*
Iran	Sepehan Isfahan	Paas Tehran	*no cup*
Japan*	Jubilo Iwata	*no league runner-up*	Kyoto Purple Sanga
Malaysia*	Perak	Selangor	Penang
Oman*	Rowi	Dhofar	Al Nasr
Qatar	Qatar SC	Al Sadd	Khor
Saudi Arabia	Al Ittihad	Al Ahly	Al Hilal
Singapore*	Singapore Armed Forces	Home United	Tampines Rovers
South Korea*	Seongnam Ilhwa Chunma	Ulsan Hyundai Horang-I	Suwon Samsung Bluewings
Syria	Al-Jaish	Al Ittihad	*no cup*
Thailand	Krung Thai Bank	BEC Tero Sasana	*no cup*
UAE	Al Ain	Al Wahda	Sharjah
Uzbekistan	Pachtakor Tashkent	Neftchi Ferghana	Pachtakor Tashkent*
Vietnam	Hoang Anh Gia Lai	Gach Dong Tam Long An	SLNA*

* Results for 2002 season.

ASIA

Right: *Iran celebrates after Mohsen's goal in its defeat of Japan in the Final of the Asian Games in South Korea.*

Far right, top: *Do you laugh or cry? Paul Gascoigne makes another come-back, but this time with the Chinese second division side Gansu Tianma. Top division clubs in China had rejected him on fitness grounds.*

Far right, upper middle: *Pachtakor Tashkent from Uzbekistan relax in the hotel lobby before the club's Champions League semi-final with BEC Tero Sasana of Thailand. The SARS epidemic was peaking in South East Asia at the time.*

Far right, lower middle: *Afghanistan makes a return to international competition with a scratch team, in training here for the 2002 Asian Games.*

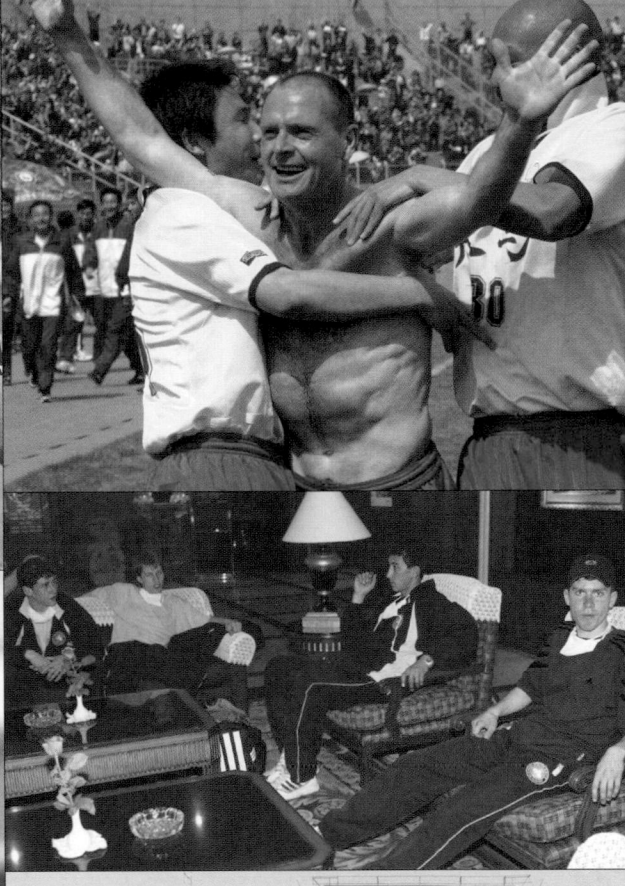

Dalian striker *Yan Song takes on the Al Ain defence.*

On the terraces in the UAE. *Al Ain fans watch their team demolish Dalian Shide in the first leg of its Champions League semi-final.*

Dalian Shide *(in blue) play Beijing Guo'an on the way to their seventh Chinese league title.*

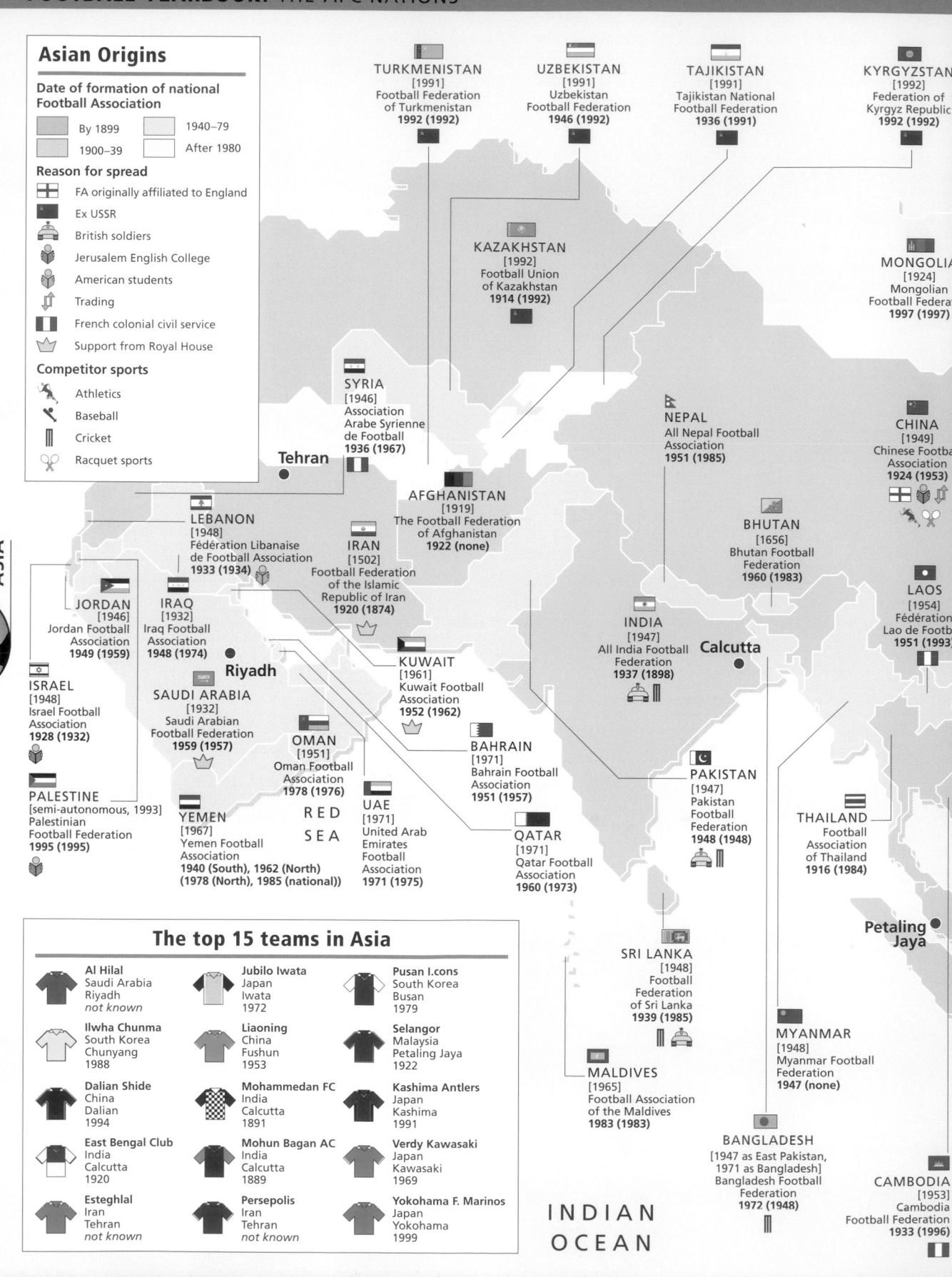

Asian Origins

Date of formation of national Football Association

- By 1899
- 1900–39
- 1940–79
- After 1980

Reason for spread

- FA originally affiliated to England
- Ex USSR
- British soldiers
- Jerusalem English College
- American students
- Trading
- French colonial civil service
- Support from Royal House

Competitor sports

- Athletics
- Baseball
- Cricket
- Racquet sports

ASIA

TURKMENISTAN
[1991]
Football Federation
of Turkmenistan
1992 (1992)

UZBEKISTAN
[1991]
Uzbekistan
Football Federation
1946 (1992)

TAJIKISTAN
[1991]
Tajikistan National
Football Federation
1936 (1991)

KYRGYZSTAN
[1992]
Federation of
Kyrgyz Republic
1992 (1992)

KAZAKHSTAN
[1992]
Football Union
of Kazakhstan
1914 (1992)

MONGOLIA
[1924]
Mongolian
Football Federation
1997 (1997)

SYRIA
[1946]
Association
Arabe Syrienne
de Football
1936 (1967)

Tehran

NEPAL
All Nepal Football
Association
1951 (1985)

CHINA
[1949]
Chinese Football
Association
1924 (1953)

AFGHANISTAN
[1919]
The Football Federation
of Afghanistan
1922 (none)

BHUTAN
[1656]
Bhutan Football
Federation
1960 (1983)

LEBANON
[1948]
Fédération Libanaise
de Football Association
1933 (1934)

IRAN
[1502]
Football Federation
of the Islamic
Republic of Iran
1920 (1874)

LAOS
[1954]
Fédération
Lao de Football
1951 (1993)

JORDAN
[1946]
Jordan Football
Association
1949 (1959)

IRAQ
[1932]
Iraq Football
Association
1948 (1974)

INDIA
[1947]
All India Football
Federation
1937 (1898)

Calcutta

KUWAIT
[1961]
Kuwait Football
Association
1952 (1962)

Riyadh

ISRAEL
[1948]
Israel Football
Association
1928 (1932)

SAUDI ARABIA
[1932]
Saudi Arabian
Football Federation
1959 (1957)

OMAN
[1951]
Oman Football
Association
1978 (1976)

BAHRAIN
[1971]
Bahrain Football
Association
1951 (1957)

PAKISTAN
[1947]
Pakistan
Football
Federation
1948 (1948)

PALESTINE
[semi-autonomous, 1993]
Palestinian
Football Federation
1995 (1995)

YEMEN
[1967]
Yemen Football
Association
**1940 (South), 1962 (North)
(1978 (North), 1985 (national))**

UAE
[1971]
United Arab
Emirates
Football
Association
1971 (1975)

QATAR
[1971]
Qatar Football
Association
1960 (1973)

THAILAND
Football
Association
of Thailand
1916 (1984)

RED
SEA

Petaling
Jaya

SRI LANKA
[1948]
Football
Federation
of Sri Lanka
1939 (1985)

MYANMAR
[1948]
Myanmar Football
Federation
1947 (none)

MALDIVES
[1965]
Football Association
of the Maldives
1983 (1983)

BANGLADESH
[1947 as East Pakistan,
1971 as Bangladesh]
Bangladesh Football
Federation
1972 (1948)

CAMBODIA
[1953]
Cambodia
Football Federation
1933 (1996)

INDIAN
OCEAN

The top 15 teams in Asia

Al Hilal
Saudi Arabia
Riyadh
not known

Jubilo Iwata
Japan
Iwata
1972

Pusan I.cons
South Korea
Busan
1979

Ilwha Chunma
South Korea
Chunyang
1988

Liaoning
China
Fushun
1953

Selangor
Malaysia
Petaling Jaya
1922

Dalian Shide
China
Dalian
1994

Mohammedan FC
India
Calcutta
1891

Kashima Antlers
Japan
Kashima
1991

East Bengal Club
India
Calcutta
1920

Mohun Bagan AC
India
Calcutta
1889

Verdy Kawasaki
Japan
Kawasaki
1969

Esteghlal
Iran
Tehran
not known

Persepolis
Iran
Tehran
not known

Yokohama F. Marinos
Japan
Yokohama
1999

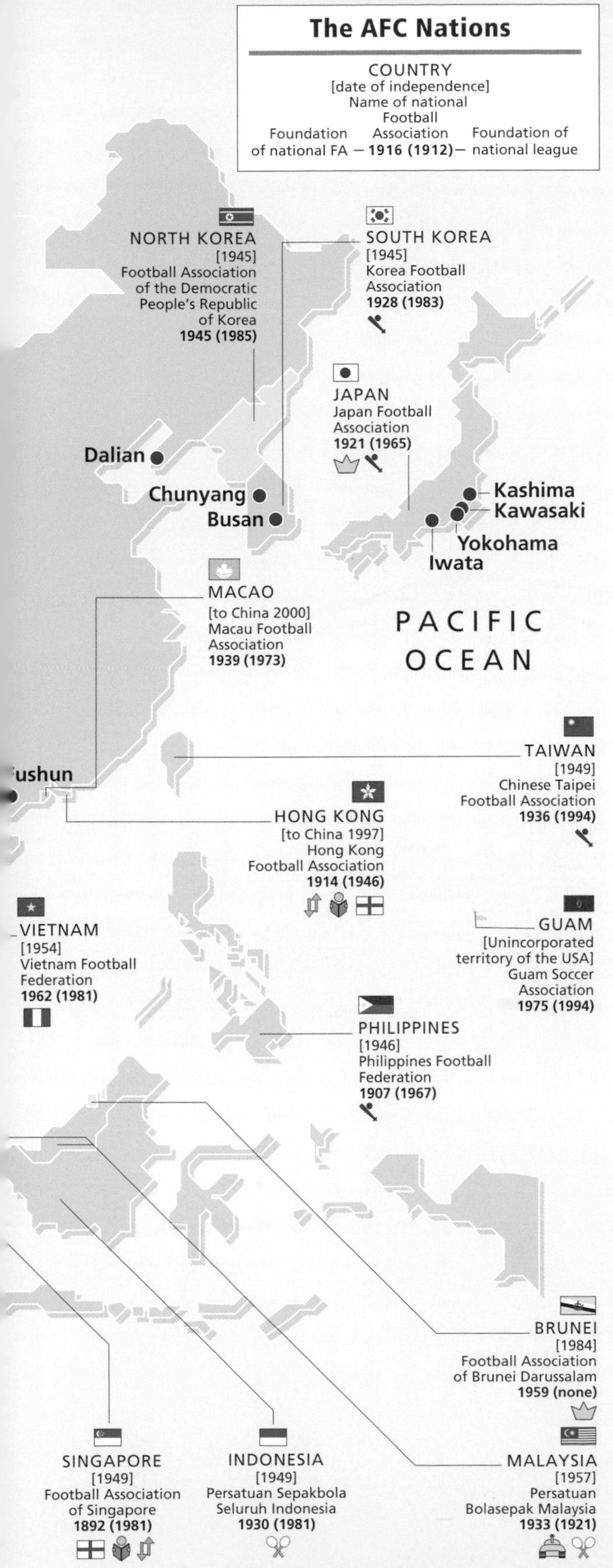

Asia

ORIGINS AND GROWTH OF FOOTBALL

FOOTBALL ARRIVED IN ASIA through the tentacles of the formal and informal British Empire as the nation's sailors, missionaries and teachers played football in the late 19th century in Japan and Korea. But these limited expatriate communities could not sustain formal clubs and leagues. The story in China and India, however, was different.

In Calcutta, clerks in Indian public service and teams from the British Army were playing regularly in the first decade of the 20th century and were soon joined by the locals, some of whom formed India's first indigenous club, Mohan Bagan, in 1889. The team was soon contesting the Indian Football Association Shield. British traders in Shanghai are on record as playing football as early as 1879, and in 1887 Shanghai Football Club was formed from the Shanghai Athletic Club. A Briton, John Prentice, set up another club – Engineers – and donated a cup contested by the various émigré teams in the city. Further south, Hong Kong FC was founded by Britons in 1886, and in 1896 the Hong Kong Shield was first contested in a tournament between civilian and military teams. Football was also played in Singapore in this era and by the early 20th century Shanghai had acquired its own FA (affiliated to London) and the Chinese themselves were beginning to play and form teams. Chinese football was represented in this era by the South China Athletic Association founded in 1904, which went on to represent China at the inaugural Far East Asian Olympic Games in 1913. Chinese resentment against European control of football culminated in 1931 when the nationalist Kuomintang government ordered all Chinese clubs to leave foreign leagues.

By the Second World War football had spread through the rest of Southeast Asia, though its popularity was limited. A more enthusiastic response came from Southwest Asia where both Iran and Iraq took up the game with royal and government patronage, a process that was repeated in the 1970s when oil wealth made the active promotion of football in the Gulf States possible. French colonists brought the game to Syria, while the British and Jewish emigrants brought the game to Palestine. In Central Asia, football primarily arrived via the Soviet occupiers who had taken control of the region in the 1930s.

The AFC Nations

COUNTRY
[date of independence]
Name of national
Football
Foundation   Association   Foundation of
of national FA — **1916 (1912)** — national league

NORTH KOREA
[1945]
Football Association
of the Democratic
People's Republic
of Korea
1945 (1985)

SOUTH KOREA
[1945]
Korea Football
Association
1928 (1983)

JAPAN
Japan Football
Association
1921 (1965)

Dalian

Chunyang

Busan

Kashima
Kawasaki
Yokohama
Iwata

MACAO
[to China 2000]
Macau Football
Association
1939 (1973)

PACIFIC
OCEAN

ushun

TAIWAN
[1949]
Chinese Taipei
Football Association
1936 (1994)

HONG KONG
[to China 1997]
Hong Kong
Football Association
1914 (1946)

GUAM
[Unincorporated
territory of the USA]
Guam Soccer
Association
1975 (1994)

VIETNAM
[1954]
Vietnam Football
Federation
1962 (1981)

PHILIPPINES
[1946]
Philippines Football
Federation
1907 (1967)

SINGAPORE
[1949]
Football Association
of Singapore
1892 (1981)

INDONESIA
[1949]
Persatuan Sepakbola
Seluruh Indonesia
1930 (1981)

BRUNEI
[1984]
Football Association
of Brunei Darussalam
1959 (none)

MALAYSIA
[1957]
Persatuan
Bolasepak Malaysia
1933 (1921)

The British Army was playing football regularly in India during the first decade of the 20th century. This picture shows action from an inter-regimental tournament played at Simla in 1907.

The Asian Cup & Asian Games

TOURNAMENT OVERVIEWS

THE ASIAN CUP & ASIAN GAMES (sidebar)

ALONE AMONG THE FOOTBALL REGIONS, Asia has two significant international competitions: the soccer tournament of the multi-sport, amateur-only Asian Games, first held in 1951, and the AFC-controlled Asian Cup, first held in 1956. The Asian Games have provided space for some of the older but perhaps weaker footballing nations to shine with early victories going to India, Burma (now Myanmar) and Taiwan, as well as the traditionally stronger countries of Israel and South Korea. Opportunities for the underdogs remain, with Uzbekistan winning the 1994 Games in Hiroshima. At the Tehran Games held in 1974, the host Iran beat Israel in its last appearance in Asian tournaments, as Israel was expelled from AFC the following year.

Shifting patterns

As football has become progressively richer and steadily more professionalized in Asia, the Asian Cup, open to professionals, has come to assume greater prestige in the region. Initially the final tournaments were held as mini-leagues, with the South Koreans and Israelis again dominating the early tournaments. Politics continued to haunt the tournament, with Pakistan and Afghanistan refusing to play Israel in the inaugural finals. From the 1970s, the football balance of power has steadily shifted, with victories going west – to Iran and Saudi Arabia (three-time winners in 1984, 88 and 96) and the UAE. More recently, the reinvigoration of Japanese football and the creation of the J.League has seen two Japanese victories (1992 and 2000).

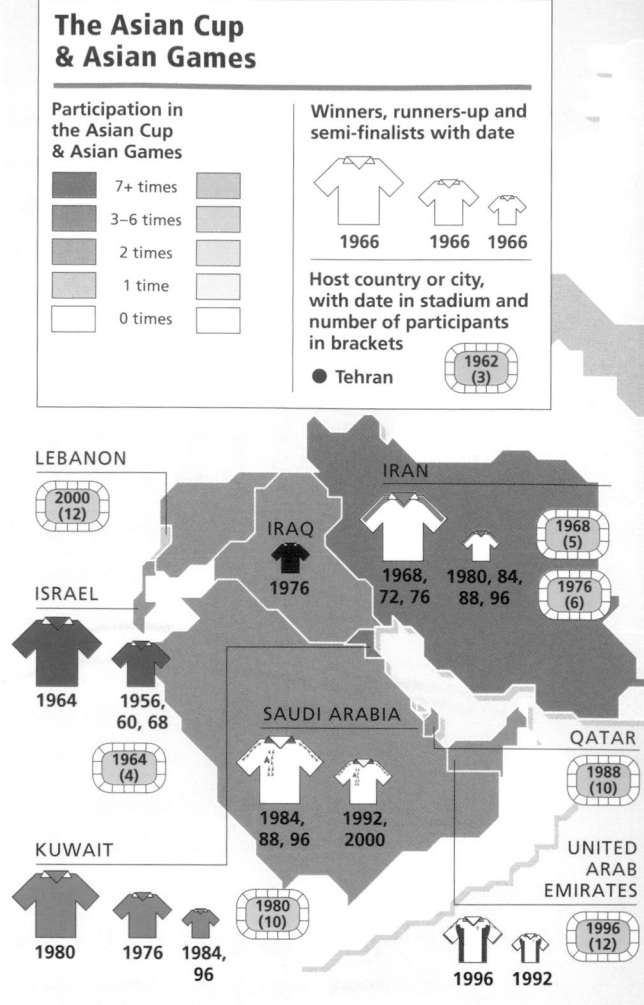

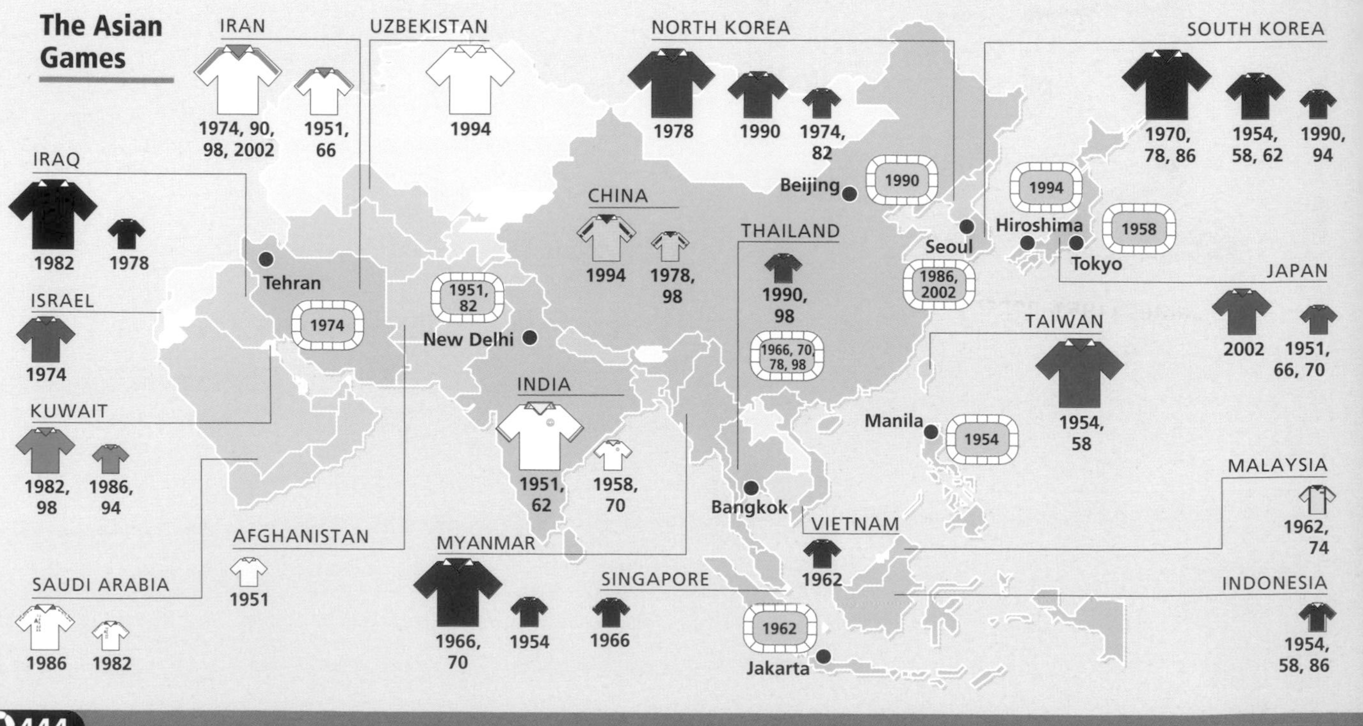

The Asian Cup & Asian Games

Participation in the Asian Cup & Asian Games
- 7+ times
- 3–6 times
- 2 times
- 1 time
- 0 times

Winners, runners-up and semi-finalists with date
1966 1966 1966

Host country or city, with date in stadium and number of participants in brackets
● Tehran
1962 (3)

LEBANON 2000 (12)

IRAN 1968, 72, 76 — 1980, 84, 88, 96 / 1968 (5) / 1976 (6)

IRAQ 1976

ISRAEL 1964 / 1956, 60, 68 / 1964 (4)

SAUDI ARABIA 1984, 88, 96 / 1992, 2000

QATAR 1988 (10)

UNITED ARAB EMIRATES 1996 (12) / 1996 / 1992

KUWAIT 1980 / 1976 / 1984, 96 / 1980 (10)

The Asian Games

IRAN 1974, 90, 98, 2002 / 1951, 66

UZBEKISTAN 1994

NORTH KOREA 1978 / 1990 / 1974, 82 / 1990

SOUTH KOREA 1970, 78, 86 / 1954, 58, 62 / 1990, 94

IRAQ 1982 / 1978

CHINA 1994 / 1978, 98 / Beijing

THAILAND 1990, 98 / Bangkok

Hiroshima 1994 / 1958

Tokyo / Seoul 1986, 2002

ISRAEL 1974 / Tehran 1974

New Delhi 1951, 82

TAIWAN 1954, 58 / Manila 1954

JAPAN 2002 / 1951, 66, 70

KUWAIT 1982, 98 / 1986, 94

INDIA 1951, 62 / 1958, 70

VIETNAM 1962

MALAYSIA 1962, 74

AFGHANISTAN 1951

MYANMAR 1966, 70 / 1954 / 1966

SINGAPORE

SAUDI ARABIA 1986 / 1982

Jakarta 1962

INDONESIA 1954, 58, 86

The Asian Cup

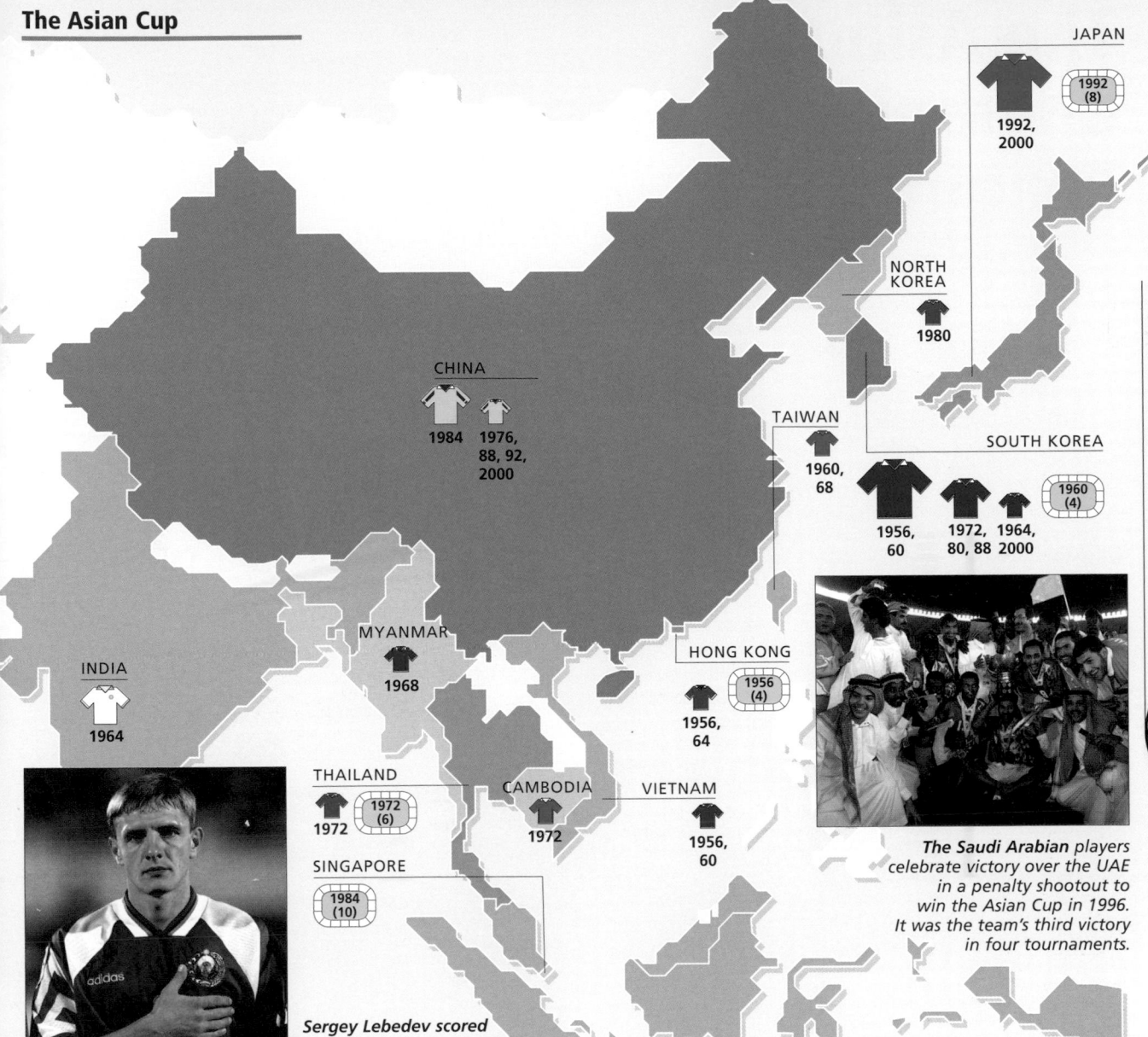

THE ASIAN CUP & ASIAN GAMES

JAPAN

1992 (8)

1992, 2000

NORTH KOREA

1980

CHINA

1984   1976, 88, 92, 2000

TAIWAN

1960, 68

SOUTH KOREA

1960 (4)

1956, 60   1972, 80, 88   1964 2000

MYANMAR

1968

INDIA

1964

HONG KONG

1956 (4)

1956, 64

THAILAND

1972 (6)

1972

CAMBODIA

1972

VIETNAM

1956, 60

SINGAPORE

1984 (10)

The Saudi Arabian players celebrate victory over the UAE in a penalty shootout to win the Asian Cup in 1996. It was the team's third victory in four tournaments.

Sergey Lebedev scored one of Uzbekistan's goals in the 4-2 win over China in the 1994 Asian Games Football Final.

The Asian Games (1951–2002)

YEAR	WINNERS	SCORE	RUNNERS-UP
1951	India	1-0	Iran
1954	Taiwan	5-2	South Korea
1958	Taiwan	3-2	South Korea
1962	India	2-1	South Korea
1966	Myanmar	1-0	Iran
1970	Myanmar	0-0 (title shared)	South Korea
1974	Iran	1-0	Israel
1978	South Korea	0-0 (title shared)	North Korea
1982	Iraq	1-0	Kuwait
1986	South Korea	2-0	Saudi Arabia
1990	Iran	0-0 (4-1 pens)	North Korea
1994	Uzbekistan	4-2	China
1998	Iran	2-0	Kuwait
2002	Iran	2-1	Japan

The Asian Cup (1956–2000)

YEAR	WINNERS	SCORE	RUNNERS-UP
1956	South Korea	*	Israel
1960	South Korea	*	Israel
1964	Israel	*	India
1968	Iran	*	Israel
1972	Iran	2-1	South Korea
1976	Iran	1-0	Kuwait
1980	Kuwait	3-0	South Korea
1984	Saudi Arabia	2-0	China
1988	Saudi Arabia	0-0 (4-3 pens)	South Korea
1992	Japan	1-0	Saudi Arabia
1996	Saudi Arabia	0-0 (asdet) (4-2 pens)	United Arab Emirates
2000	Japan	1-0	Saudi Arabia

* Tournament decided on league basis, no final match.

The Asian Champions League

TOURNAMENT OVERVIEW

THE ENORMOUS GEOGRAPHICAL SIZE OF ASIA and the relative weakness and unevenness of club football made the establishment of a regular international club tournament difficult. The AFC first decided to create a tournament modelled on the European Cup in 1962 called the Asian Club Championship, but it took five years to set up. In the event, only six clubs took part in a finals tournament held in Bangkok, Thailand, in 1967. Eventual champions, Hapoel Tel Aviv, only played a single match – the Final – after a series of byes, beating the Malaysian side Selangor 2-1. Ten teams competed in 1969, again in Bangkok, with Maccabi Tel Aviv beating the Korean side Yangzee 1-0 to claim the title.

Hapoel appeared in the Final again in 1970, but lost 2-1 to the Iranian army team, Taj Club. The following year Maccabi got to the Final and was set to meet Al Shorta from Iraq, but the Iraqis refused to play the match for political reasons and Maccabi was awarded the trophy. Israeli dominance of the competition ended in 1975 when the country's teams were expelled from AFC because of the war in the Middle East. Continuing political problems meant that the competition was abandoned until 1985, but then it was revamped with a proper geographically-based series of qualifying rounds and a six-team final tournament held that year in Jeddah in Saudi Arabia.

Since then the Asian football landscape has transformed. The competition has been dominated since 1985 by teams from Japan and South Korea. But there has also been success for the rapidly strengthening teams from the Gulf, like Al Sadd from Qatar in 1989, Al Hilal and Al Nassr from Saudi Arabia in the 1990s; for the revamped clubs of post-revolutionary Iran, like Esteghlal and Pas Club; for the back-to-back winners Thai Farmers Bank (in 1994 and 95); and for the Chinese, for whom Liaoning from Shenyang took the title in 1990.

In 2002, the AFC reorganised the tournament merging it with the now discontiued Asian Cup-Winners' Cup (see page 449), and have renamed it the Asian Champions League.

Thai Farmers Bank, from Bangkok, won the Asian Club Championship in 1994 and 95.

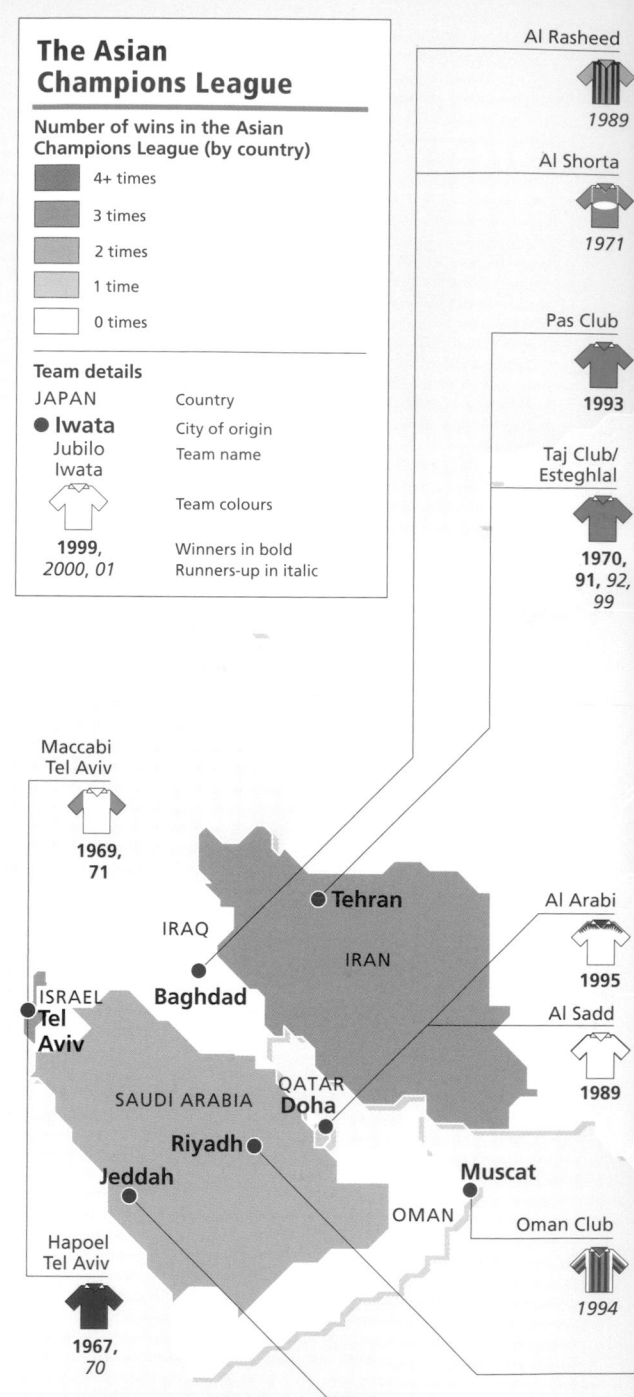

The Asian Champions League

Number of wins in the Asian Champions League (by country)

	4+ times
	3 times
	2 times
	1 time
	0 times

Team details

JAPAN	Country
● **Iwata**	City of origin
Jubilo Iwata	Team name
	Team colours
1999, *2000, 01*	Winners in bold Runners-up in italic

Al Rasheed — *1989*

Al Shorta — *1971*

Pas Club — **1993**

Taj Club/ Esteghlal — **1970**, *91, 92, 99*

Maccabi Tel Aviv — **1969**, *71*

Tehran

IRAQ

Baghdad

IRAN

ISRAEL
Tel Aviv

Al Arabi — *1995*

Al Sadd — **1989**

QATAR
Doha

SAUDI ARABIA

Riyadh

Jeddah

Muscat

OMAN

Oman Club — *1994*

Hapoel Tel Aviv — **1967**, *70*

The Asian Champions League

COUNTRY	WINNERS	RUNNERS-UP
South Korea	6	3
Japan	3	3
Iran	3	2
Israel	3	1
Saudi Arabia	2	5
Thailand	2	0
China	1	2
Qatar	1	1
Iraq	0	2
Malaysia	0	1
Oman	0	1

Al Ahly —  *1986*

*Sami Al Jaber (left) of Saudi
Arabian club Al Hilal kisses the
Asian Club Championship Cup
after the team's 3-2 victory over
Japan's Jubilo Iwata in the 2000
Final in Riyadh.*

The Asian Cup-Winners' Cup 1991–2002

YEAR	WINNERS	RUNNERS-UP
1991	Piroozi (Iran)	Muharraq (Bahrain)
1992	Nissan Motors (Japan)	Al Nassr (Saudi Arabia)
1993	Nissan Motors (Japan)	Piroozi (Iran)
1994	Al Qadisiya (Saudi Arabia)	South China (Hong Kong)
1995	Yokohama Flugels (Japan)	Al Shabab (Saudi Arabia)
1996	Bellmare Hiratsuka (Japan)	Talaba (Iraq)
1997	Al Hilal (Saudi Arabia)	Nagoya Grampus Eight (Japan)
1998	Al Nassr (Saudi Arabia)	Suwon Samsung Bluewings (Japan)
1999	Al Ittihad (Saudi Arabia)	Chunnam Dragons (South Korea)
2000	Shimizu S-Pulse (Japan)	Al Zawra (Iraq)
2001	Al Shabab (Saudi Arabia)	Dalian Shide (China)
2002	Al Hilal (Saudi Arabia)	Chonbuk Hyundai Motors (South Korea)

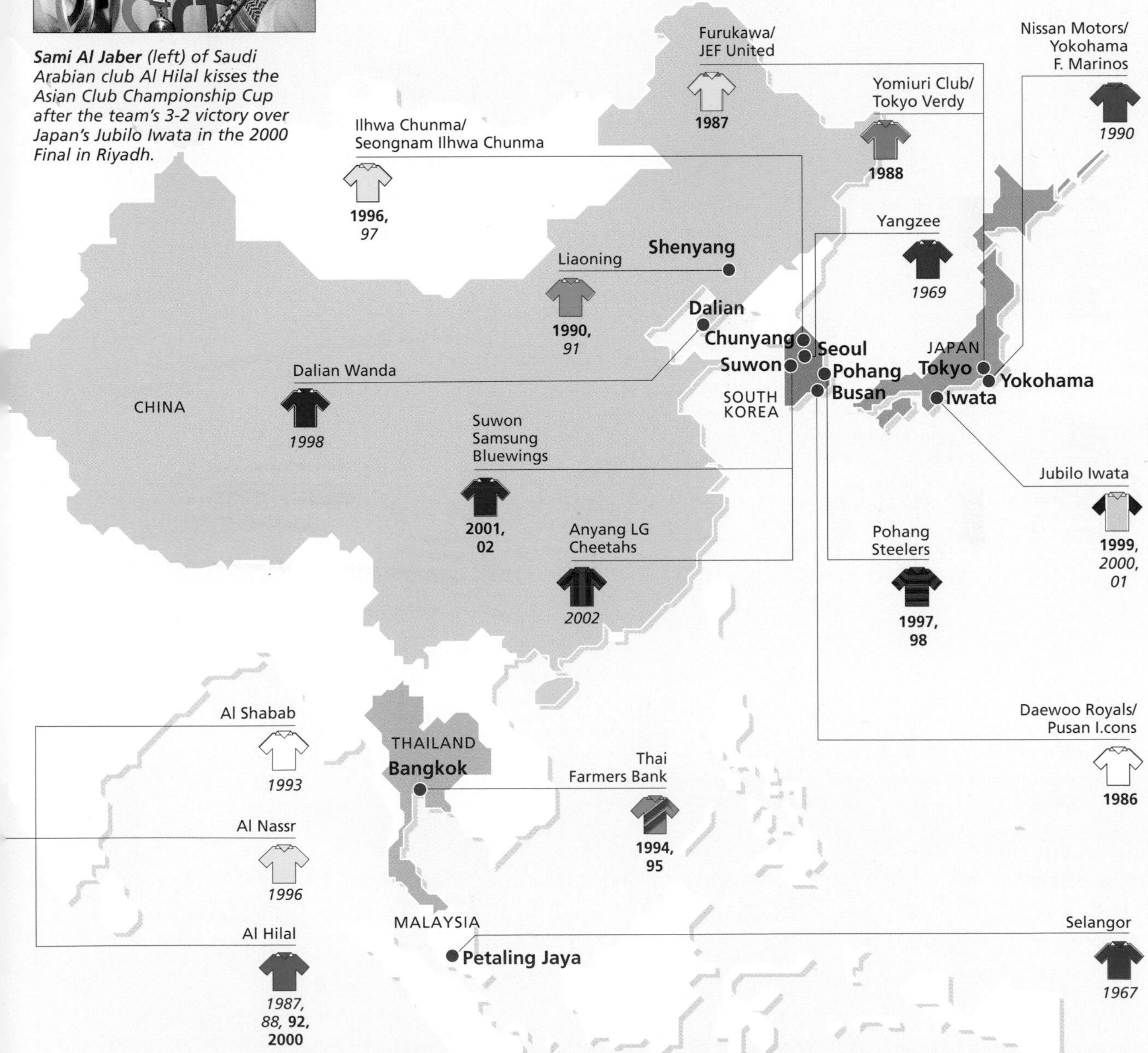

THE ASIAN CHAMPIONS LEAGUE

Furukawa/
JEF United
1987

Yomiuri Club/
Tokyo Verdy
1988

Nissan Motors/
Yokohama
F. Marinos
1990

Ilhwa Chunma/
Seongnam Ilhwa Chunma
**1996,
97**

Liaoning
**1990,
91**

Shenyang

Yangzee
1969

Dalian
Chunyang
Suwon

Seoul
Pohang
Busan

JAPAN
Tokyo
Yokohama
Iwata

**SOUTH
KOREA**

Dalian Wanda
CHINA
1998

Suwon
Samsung
Bluewings
**2001,
02**

Anyang LG
Cheetahs
2002

Pohang
Steelers
**1997,
98**

Jubilo Iwata
**1999,
2000,
01**

Daewoo Royals/
Pusan I.cons
1986

Al Shabab
1993

Al Nassr
1996

Al Hilal
*1987,
88, 92,
2000*

THAILAND
Bangkok

Thai
Farmers Bank
**1994,
95**

Selangor
1967

MALAYSIA
● **Petaling Jaya**

The Asian Cup

The Asian Cup Winners

South Korea
1956, 60

Israel
1964

Iran
1968, 72, 76

Kuwait
1980

Saudia Arabia
1984, 88, 96

Japan
1992, 2000

ASIA HAS TWO MAJOR international football competitions. The Asian Cup is the competition run by the FIFA affiliate AFC (Asian Football Confederation) while the other football tournament is played at the Asian Games, which is a multi-sports competition. The Asian Games were first held in 1951 and have continued every four years, without qualifying tournaments and a group/knockout stage format. The Asian Cup began in 1956 and is also played on a four-year cycle, but from 1960 it has had a pre-tournament qualifying round based on geographical zones. It has become the pre-eminent Asian football competition.

Decolonization and international politics have continued to influence the entrants and outcome of the tournaments. Taiwan's place in Asian football has been contested by China, and vice-versa, with both claiming to be the sole Chinese representative. Israel's place in Asian football has been equally problematic. Israel achieved a bye into the 1956 Asian Nations Cup as neither Pakistan or Afghanistan would play them. Again Israel reached the 1974 Asian Games Final in Tehran without touching a ball, after North Korea and Kuwait refused to play them. In the end both Taiwan and Israel were expelled from the AFC in 1975. Israel now plays within UEFA.

1956 HONG KONG*
1 South Korea
2 Israel
3 Hong Kong

1960 SOUTH KOREA*
1 South Korea
2 Israel
3 Taiwan

1964 ISRAEL*
1 Israel
2 India
3 South Korea

1968 IRAN*
1 Iran
2 Israel
3 Myanmar

1972 THAILAND**
SEMI-FINALS
Iran **2-1** Cambodia
South Korea **1-1** Thailand
South Korea won 2-1 on pens

THIRD PLACE PLAY-OFF
Thailand **2-2** Cambodia
Thailand won 5-3 on pens

FINAL
May 19 – Bangkok
Iran **2-1** South Korea
(Jabary 48,   (Lee Whae-taek 65)
Khalani 107)
(after extra time)
h/t: 0-0 **90 mins:** 1-1
Att: 8,000

1976 IRAN
SEMI-FINALS
Iran **2-0** China
Kuwait **3-2** Iraq

THIRD PLACE PLAY-OFF
China **1-0** Iraq

FINAL
June 13 – Tehran
Iran **1-0** Kuwait
Att: 40,000

1980 KUWAIT
SEMI-FINALS
Kuwait **2-1** Iran
South Korea **2-1** North Korea

THIRD PLACE PLAY-OFF
Iran **3-0** North Korea

FINAL
September 28 – Kuwait City
Kuwait **3-0** South Korea
Att: 35,000

1984 SINGAPORE
SEMI-FINALS
Saudi Arabia **1-1** Iran
Saudi Arabia won 5-4 on pens
China **1-0** Kuwait

THIRD PLACE PLAY-OFF
Kuwait **1-1** Iran
Kuwait won 5-3 on pens

FINAL
December 16 – Singapore
Saudi Arabia **2-0** China
(Shaye Nafisah 10,
Majed
Abdullah 47)
h/t: 1-0 **Att:** 40,000

1988 QATAR
SEMI-FINALS
Saudi Arabia **1-0** Iran
South Korea **2-1** China
(after extra time)

THIRD PLACE PLAY-OFF
Iran **0-0** China
Iran won 3-0 on pens

FINAL
December 19 – Doha
Saudi Arabia **0-0** South Korea
(after extra time)
h/t: 0-0 **90 mins:** 0-0
Att: 25,000
Saudi Arabia won 4-3 on pens

1992 JAPAN
SEMI-FINALS
Japan **3-2** China
Saudi Arabia **2-0** UAE

THIRD PLACE PLAY-OFF
China **1-1** UAE
China won 4-3 on pens

FINAL
November 8 – Hiroshima
Japan **1-0** Saudi Arabia
(Takagi 6)
h/t: 1-0 **Att:** 40,000
Ref: Al Sharif (Syria)

1996 UNITED ARAB EMIRATES
SEMI-FINALS
Iran **0-0** Saudi Arabia
Saudi Arabia won 4-3 on pens
UAE **1-0** Kuwait

THIRD PLACE PLAY-OFF
Iran **1-1** Kuwait
Iran won 3-2 on pens

FINAL
December 21 – Abu Dhabi
UAE **0-0** Saudi Arabia
(after extra time)
h/t: 0-0 **90 mins:** 0-0 **Att:** 60,000
Ref: Mohammed Nazri Abdullah
(Malaysia)
Saudi Arabia won 4-2 on pens

2000 LEBANON
SEMI-FINALS
Saudi Arabia **2-1** South Korea
Japan **3-2** China

THIRD PLACE PLAY-OFF
South Korea **1-0** China

FINAL
October 28 – Beirut
Japan **1-0** Saudi Arabia
(Mochizuki 29)
h/t: 1-0 **Att:** 57,600
Ref: Ali Bujsaim (UAE)

* League format.
** Finals tournament.

Ryuzo Morioka, the Japanese captain, celebrates victory in the 2000 Asian Nations Cup Final after Japan defeated Saudi Arabia 1-0 in Beirut.

THE ASIAN CUP

The Asian Champions League

THE ASIAN CLUB CHAMPIONSHIP, now rebranded as the Asian Champions League, is the leading international club competition in Asia. Originally conceived by the Asian Football Confederation in 1962, it took five years to launch the competition, which began as a six-team tournament played out in Bangkok. Geography has always dogged the competition, with Asia's enormous size making schedules difficult to arrange, and the inclusion of Israel in the AFC created significant conflicts with other members. In 1971, the Iraqi club Al Shorta, or Police Club, refused to play Maccabi Tel Aviv in the Final. The competition was only played again in 1985 by which time Israel had left the AFC.

The competition is open to national champions in all members of AFC. The early rounds are played on a geographical basis, dividing into East and West Asia. Semi-finals and a Final tournament are then staged in a single nation.

The other international club tournament in Asia has now been discontinued. From 2003, the Asian Cup-Winners' Cup will no longer be held, but for the last ten years it has been a significant event in the Asian football calendar. It was open to cup winners of all AFC member states, or losing finalists if the cup winner was entered for the Asian Club Championship. Early rounds were played over two legs with a small finals tournament (semi-finals, Final, third place play-off) in a single host city. The competition began in 1990 with 18 entrants, and by the mid-90s it was attracting more prize money and more teams. The last seven Finals were won by either Japanese or South Korean teams, except for the Saudi Al Hilal in 2000.

^1967 FINAL
December 19 – Bangkok, Thailand
Hapoel Tel Aviv 2-1 Selangor
(Israel) (Malaysia)

1968–69 FINAL
January 30 – Bangkok, Thailand
Maccabi Tel Aviv 1-0 Yangzee
(Israel) (South Korea)

1970 FINAL
April 10 – Tehran, Iran
Taj Club 2-1 Hapoel Tel Aviv
(Iran) (Israel)

1971 FINAL
April 2 – Bangkok, Thailand
Maccabi w/o Al Shorta Tel Aviv
(Israel) (Iraq)
Al Shorta withdrew from this match, awarded to Maccabi

1972 FINAL
tournament cancelled

1985–86 FINAL
January 24, 1986 – Jeddah, Saudi Arabia
Daewoo 3-1 Al Ahly Royals (Saudi Arabia)
(South Korea)

1986–87 TOURNAMENT
December, 1986 – Riyadh, Saudi Arabia
Al Talaba **2-2** Liaoning
Furukawa **4-3** Al Hilal
Furukawa **2-0** Al Talaba
Al Hilal **1-0** Liaoning
Furukawa **1-0** Liaoning
Al Hilal **2-1** Al Talaba

	P	W	D	L	F	A	Pts
1 Furukawa	3	3	0	0	7	3	6
2 Al Hilal	3	2	0	1	6	5	4
3 Liaoning	3	0	1	2	2	4	1
4 Al Talaba	3	0	1	2	3	6	1

1987–88 FINAL
Yomiuri Club w/o Al Hilal
(Japan) (Saudi Arabia)
Al Hilal withdrew before 1st leg

1988–89 FINAL (2 legs)
March 31
Al Rasheed 3-2 Al Sadd
(Iraq) (Qatar)

April 6
Al Sadd 1-0 Al Rasheed
Al Sadd won on away goals rule

1989–90 FINAL (2 legs)
April 22
Liaoning 2-1 Nissan Motors
(China) (Japan)

April 29
Nissan Motors 1-1 Liaoning

1990–91 FINAL
July 29 – Dhaka, Bangladesh
Esteghlal 2-1 Liaoning
(Iran) (China)

1991–92 FINAL
December 22, 1991 – Doha, Qatar
Al Hilal 1-1 Esteghlal
(Saudi Arabia) (Iran)
(Hussein *(Amir Abbas 58)*
Al Habashi 73)
(after extra time)
Al Hilal won 4-3 on pens

1992–93 FINAL
January 22 – Bahrain
Pas Club 1-0 Al Shabab
(Iran) (Saudi Arabia)

1993–94 FINAL
February 7 – Bangkok, Thailand
Thai Farmers 2-1 Oman Club Bank (Oman)
(Thailand) *(Zahir Salim 44)*
(Thawan Thamniyai 4, Sing Totavee 18)

1994–95 FINAL
January 29 – Bangkok, Thailand
Thai Farmers 1-0 Al Arabi Bank (Qatar)
(Thailand)
(Natipong Sritong-in 82)

1995–96 FINAL
December 29 – Riyadh, Saudi Arabia
Ilhwa 1-0 Al Nassr Chunma (Saudi Arabia)
(South Korea)
(Lee Tae Hong 110)
(after extra time)

Team Pakhtakor Toshkent from Uzbekistan taking no chances with the SARS virus on arrival in Thailand for an ACL semi-final. Opponents BEC Tero Sesana from Bangkok won 3-2 (agg).

1996–97 FINAL
March 9 – Kuala Lumpur, Malaysia
Pohang 2-1 Ilhwa Steelers Chunma
(South Korea) (South Korea)
(Park Tae-ha 77, (Park Ji-ho 79)
Hong Jong-kyong 118 pen)

1997–98 FINAL
April 5 – Hong Kong
Pohang 0-0 Dalian Wanda Steelers (China)
(South Korea)
Pohang Steelers won 6-5 on pens

1998–99 FINAL
April 30 – Tehran, Iran
Jubilo Iwata 2-1 Esteghlal
(Japan) (Iran)
(Suzuki 36, (Dinmohammadi Nakayama 45) 66)

1999–2000 FINAL
April 22 – Riyadh, Saudi Arabia
Al Hilal 3-2 Jubilo Iwata
(Saudi Arabia) (Japan)
(Ricardo (Nakayama 18, 3, 89, 102) Takahara 19)

2000–01 FINAL
May 26 – Suwon, South Korea
Suwon Samsung 1-0 Jubilo Iwata Bluewings (Japan)
(South Korea)
(Sandro dos Santos 15)

2001–02 FINAL
April 5 – Tehran, Iran
Suwon Samsung 0-0 Anyang LG Bluewings Cheetahs
(South Korea) (South Korea)
Suwon Samsung won 4-2 on pens

2002–03 FINAL
The 2003 Final has been re-scheduled for October 2003 because of the outbreak of SARS. It's between finalists BEC Tero Sesana from Thailand, and the winners of the semi-final between Al Ain (UAE) and Dalian Shide (China). The semi has also been postponed.

Southwest Asia

FOOTBALL BECAME POPULAR IN IRAN and Iraq well before the Second World War, with active royal support from the Shahs of Iran. Under the last Shah a programme of modernization and the importation of foreign coaches gave the game a huge boost. A national league was established in 1960, and became semi-professional in 1974. But football's development in Iran was stopped in its tracks by the Islamic revolution in 1978. The league only recommenced at the end of the Iran-Iraq War in 1988, and women were banned from matches until 1994. Nonetheless the depth of Iranian football saw them qualify for the 1998 World Cup. To their north, the states of Central Asia acquired football after their inclusion in the Soviet Union and all established independent FAs and national leagues in the wake of the break-up of the Soviet Union in 1991.

Football arrived in the Near East with French and British protectorate status and colonial administrations after the First World War. National leagues were established in Lebanon in 1934, Jordan in 1959 and Syria in 1981. The Gulf states, by contrast, have proved to be late starters and quick developers. With oil money to hand and active royal and state promotion, national leagues were established in Bahrain in 1957, Kuwait in 1962, Qatar in 1973, UAE in 1975 and Saudi Arabia in 1979, although the national King's Cup tournament has been running there since 1957. It has been virtually impossible to get information about football in Afghanistan in recent years. Since the fall of the regime Afghanistan has re-entered international football competitions. The Taleban discouraged competitiveness, so winners and losers alike were not recorded.

Although Saudi Arabia's Al Hilal has played second fiddle to Al Ittihad in the league in recent seasons, the Riyadh side has claimed two Asian Super Cups, two Asian Club Championships and has also won the Asian Cup-Winners' Cup twice.

Afghanistan

The Football Federation of Afghanistan
Founded: 1922
Joined FIFA: 1948
Joined AFC: 1954

SEASON	LEAGUE CHAMPIONS
1998	*unknown*
1999	*unknown*
2000	*unknown*
2001	*unknown*
2002	*disrupted*

Bahrain

Bahrain Football Association
Founded: 1951
Joined FIFA: 1966
Joined AFC: 1970

SEASON	LEAGUE CHAMPIONS
1999	Muharraq
2000	West Riffa
2001	Muharraq
2002	Muharraq
2003	West Riffa

YEAR	CUP WINNERS
1999	East Riffa
2000	East Riffa
2001	Al Ahli
2002	Muharraq
2003	Al Ahli

Iran

Football Federation of the Islamic Republic of Iran
Founded: 1920
Joined FIFA: 1945
Joined AFC: 1958

SEASON	LEAGUE CHAMPIONS
1999	Piroozi
2000	Piroozi
2001	Esteghlal
2002	Piroozi
2003	Sepehan Isfahan

YEAR	CUP WINNERS
1998	*no competition*
1999	Piroozi
2000	Esteghlal
2001	Fajr Sepasi
2002	Esteghlal

Iraq

Iraq Football Association
Founded: 1948
Joined FIFA: 1950
Joined AFC: 1971

SEASON	LEAGUE CHAMPIONS
1999	Al Shorta
2000	Al Zawra
2001	Al Zawra
2002	Al Talaba
2003	*abandoned*

YEAR	CUP WINNERS
1999	Al Zawra
2000	Al Zawra
2001	*no competition*
2002	Al Talaba
2003	*no competition*

Jordan

Jordan Football Association
Founded: 1949
Joined FIFA: 1958
Joined AFC: 1970

SEASON	LEAGUE CHAMPIONS
1999	Al Faysali
2000	Al Faysali
2001	Al Faysali
2002	*league format change*
2003	Al Faysali

YEAR	CUP WINNERS
1999	Al Faysali
2000	Al Wihdat
2001	Al Faysali
2002	*format change*
2003	Al Wihdat

Kazakhstan

Football Union of Kazakhstan
Founded: 1914
Joined FIFA: 1994
Joined AFC: 1994*

SEASON	LEAGUE CHAMPIONS
1998	Yelimay Semipalatinsk
1999	Irtysh Bastan Pavlodar
2000	Zhenis Astana
2001	Zhenis Astana
2002	Irtysh Bastan Pavlodar

* As of 2002 – joined UEFA.

Kuwait

**Kuwait Football
Association**
Founded: 1952
Joined FIFA: 1962
Joined AFC: 1962

SEASON	LEAGUE CHAMPIONS
1998	Al Salmiya
1999	Al Qadisiya
2000	Al Salmiya
2001	Al Kuwait
2002	Al Arabi

YEAR	CUP WINNERS
1998	Kazmah
1999	Al Arabi
2000	Al Arabi
2001	Al Salmiya
2002	Al Kuwait

Kyrgyzstan

**Federation
of Kyrgyz
Republic**
Founded: 1992
Joined FIFA: 1994
Joined AFC: 1994

SEASON	LEAGUE CHAMPIONS
1998	Dinamo Bishkek
1999	Dinamo Bishkek
2000	SKA-PVO Bishkek
2001	SKA-PVO Bishkek
2002	SKA-PVO Bishkek

YEAR	CUP WINNERS
1998	SKA-PVO Bishkek
1999	SKA-PVO Bishkek
2000	SKA-PVO Bishkek
2001	SKA-PVO Bishkek
2002	SKA-PVO Bishkek

Lebanon

**Fédération
Libanaise de
Football
Association**
Founded: 1933
Joined FIFA: 1935
Joined AFC: 1964

SEASON	LEAGUE CHAMPIONS
1999	Al Ansar
2000	Al Nejmeh
2001	abandoned
2002	Al Nejmeh
2003	Olympic Beirut

Oman

**Oman Football
Association**
Founded: 1978
Joined FIFA: 1980
Joined AFC: 1979

SEASON	LEAGUE CHAMPIONS
1999	Dhofar
2000	Al Arouba
2001	Dhofar
2002	Al Arouba
2003	Rowi

Palestine
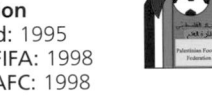

**Palestinian Football
Federation**
Founded: 1995
Joined FIFA: 1998
Joined AFC: 1998

SEASON	LEAGUE CHAMPIONS
1999	not known
2000	Khadamat Rafah
2001	abandoned
2002	no championship
2003	no championship

Qatar

**Qatar Football
Association**
Founded: 1960
Joined FIFA: 1970
Joined AFC: 1972

SEASON	LEAGUE CHAMPIONS
1999	Al Wakra
2000	Al Sadd
2001	Al Wakra
2002	Al Etehad
2003	Qatar FC

Saudi Arabia

**Saudi Arabian
Football Federation**
Founded: 1959
Joined FIFA: 1959
Joined AFC: 1972

SEASON	LEAGUE CHAMPIONS
1999	Al Ittihad
2000	Al Ittihad
2001	Al Ittihad
2002	Al Hilal
2003	Al Ittihad

Saudi Arabia (continued)

YEAR	CUP WINNERS
1999	Al Shabab
2000	Al Hilal
2001	Al Ittihad
2002	Al Ahly
2003	Al Hilal

Syria

**Association Arabe
Syrienne de
Football**
Founded: 1936
Joined FIFA: 1937
Joined AFC: 1969

SEASON	LEAGUE CHAMPIONS
1999	Al Jaish
2000	Jabla
2001	Al Jaish
2002	Al Jaish
2003	Al Jaish

YEAR	CUP WINNERS
1998	Al Jaish
1999	Jabla
2000	Al Jaish
2001	Hottin
2002	Al Jaish

Tajikistan

**National Football
Federation
Tajikistan**
Founded: 1936
Joined FIFA: 1994
Joined AFC: 1994

SEASON	LEAGUE CHAMPIONS
1998	Varzob Dushanbe
1999	Varzob Dushanbe
2000	Varzob Dushanbe
2001	Regar-TadAZ Tursunzade
2002	Regar-TadAZ Tursunzade

Turkmenistan

**Football
Federation of
Turkmenistan**
Founded: 1992
Joined FIFA: 1994
Joined AFC: 1994

SEASON	LEAGUE CHAMPIONS
1998	Kopétdag Ashkhabad
1999	Nisa Ashkhabad
2000	Kopétdag Ashkhabad
2001	Nisa Ashkhabad
2002	Shagadam Turkmenbashy

United Arab Emirates

**United Arab
Emirates Football
Association**
Founded: 1971
Joined FIFA: 1972
Joined AFC: 1974

SEASON	LEAGUE CHAMPIONS
1999	Al Wahda
2000	Al Ain
2001	Al Wahda
2002	Al Ain
2003	Al Ain

YEAR	CUP WINNERS
1999	Al Ain
2000	Al Wahda
2001	Al Ain
2002	Al Ahly
2003	Sharjah

Uzbekistan

**Uzbekistan
Football
Federation**
Founded: 1946
Joined FIFA: 1994
Joined AFC: 1994

SEASON	LEAGUE CHAMPIONS
1998	Pachtakor Tashkent
1999	Dustlik Tashkent
2000	Dustlik Tashkent
2001	Neftchi Ferghana
2002	Pachtakor Tashkent

YEAR	CUP WINNERS
1998	Navbakhor Namangan
1999	no competition
2000	Dustlik Tashkent
2001	Pachtakor Tashkent
2002	Pachtakor Tashkent

Yemen

**Yemen Football
Association**
Founded: 1940 (South),
1962 (North). 1990
Joined FIFA: 1967
(South), 1980 (North). 1990
Joined AFC: 1967 (South),
1980 (North). 1990

SEASON	LEAGUE CHAMPIONS
1999	Al Ahli
2000	Al Ahli
2001	Al Ahli
2002	Al Wahda
2003	Al Sha'ab Ibb

South and East Asia

FOOTBALL'S DEEPEST ROOTS in Asia are in India, where the game was extensively played by the British Army and the imperial administration. Calcutta is the home of Indian football and its local league championship has been running since 1898. More recently the spread of the game across the nation has seen the creation of the Santosh Trophy in 1971 (contested by state teams and the Indian Army) and the Federation Cup – a nationwide competition for clubs – in 1977. The National Football League was created in 1996. After the partition of British India in 1947, national FAs and leagues were established in what was West Pakistan (now Pakistan) and East Pakistan (now Bangladesh). In the case of Bangladesh the league was originally confined to Dhaka but went national in 2000.

Football in China began among English expatriates in Shanghai and Hong Kong at the turn of the 20th century. A separate national Chinese FA was founded in Beijing in 1924 and affiliated to FIFA in 1931. The Chinese FA left FIFA from 1958 to 1979 in protest at FIFA's recognition of Taiwan. A national league was founded in 1926 and disrupted by 30 years of invasion, civil war and revolution. Re-established in 1953, abandoned during the Cultural Revolution (1966–72), the league went professional in 1993. In contrast, Hong Kong's professional league dates from 1945 and is the oldest pro-league in Asia.

Football came to the Philippines via Spanish sailors in the late 19th century and an FA was set up in 1907. British soldiers brought football to Malaysia and, with Singaporean teams included, league and cup competitions have run since 1921. Thailand's league dates from 1916 and a pro-league from 1995. The Dutch brought football to Indonesia, and in 1930 seven regional associations and leagues were established which proved a basis strong enough for the country to appear as the Dutch East Indies in the 1938 World Cup Finals. A national league was created in 1979 and went professional in 1994. The French brought football to Vietnam, Cambodia and Laos. Cambodia's league dates from the 1950s, Vietnam's from 1981, after the conclusion of its wars of independence, and in Laos a national league was set up in 1997.

Mohun Bagan from Calcutta. The city rivalry with East Bengal is the most intense in Asian football. Mohun represents the indigenous West Bengalies of the city, and East Bengal Bangladesh's migrants.

Bangladesh

Bangladesh Football Federation
Founded: 1972
Joined FIFA: 1974
Joined AFC: 1974

SEASON	LEAGUE CHAMPIONS
1998	Muktijoddha SKC
1999	Mohammedan SC
2000	Muktijoddha SKC
2001	Abahani Ltd
2002	Mohammedan SC

Bhutan

Bhutan Football Federation
Founded: 1960
Joined FIFA: 2000
Joined AFC: 1993

SEASON	LEAGUE CHAMPIONS
1997	Royal Bhutan Police
1998	Royal Bhutan Police
1999	Kamglung
2000	Phuentsholing FC
2001	Druk Star FC

Brunei

Football Association of Brunei Darussalam
Founded: 1959
Joined FIFA: 1969
Joined AFC: 1970

BRUNEI HAS NO unified national championship – there are four district leagues. However, a Brunei team has played with some success in the Malaysian M-League.

Cambodia

Cambodia Football Federation
Founded: 1933
Joined FIFA: 1953
Joined AFC: 1957

SEASON	LEAGUE CHAMPIONS
1998	Royal Dolphins
1999	*no championship*
2000	National Police
2001	*unknown*
2002	Samart United

China

Chinese Football Association
Founded: 1924
Joined FIFA: 1931–58, 1979
Joined AFC: 1974

SEASON	LEAGUE CHAMPIONS
1998	Dalian Wanda
1999	Shandong Luneng Taishin
2000	Dalian Shide
2001	Dalian Shide
2002	Dalian Shide

YEAR	CUP WINNERS
1998	Shanghai Shenhua
1999	Shangdong Luneng Taishan
2000	Chongqing Lifan
2001	Dalian Shide
2002	Qingdao Hademen

Guam

Guam Soccer Association
Founded: 1975
Joined FIFA: 1996
Joined AFC: 1996

SEASON	LEAGUE CHAMPIONS
1998	Anderson Soccer Club
1999	Coors Light Silver Bullets
2000	Coors Light Silver Bullets
2001	Staywell Zoom S. Bullets
2002	Guam Shipyard

Hong Kong

Hong Kong Football Association
Founded: 1914
Joined FIFA: 1954
Joined AFC: 1954

SEASON	LEAGUE CHAMPIONS
1999	Happy Valley
2000	South China
2001	Happy Valley
2002	Happy Valley
2003	Happy Valley

YEAR	CUP WINNERS
1999	South China
2000	Happy Valley
2001	Instant-Dict
2002	South China
2003	Sun Hei

India

All India Football Federation
Founded: 1937
Joined FIFA: 1948
Joined AFC: 1954

SEASON	LEAGUE CHAMPIONS
1999	Salgoacar SC
2000	Mohun Bagan AC
2001	East Bengal Club
2002	Mohun Bagan AC
2003	East Bengal Club

YEAR	CUP WINNERS
1998	Mahindra and United Mahindra
1999	Salgoacar
2000	Mohun Bagan
2001	format change
2002	Mahindra

Indonesia

Persatuan Sepakbola Seluruh Indonesia
Founded: 1930
Joined FIFA: 1952
Joined AFC: 1954

SEASON	LEAGUE CHAMPIONS
1998	season not finished
1999	PSIS Semarang
2000	PSM Makassar
2001	Persija Jakarta
2002	Petrokimia Putra

YEAR	CUP WINNERS
1997	Bandung Raya
1998	abandoned
1999	Persebaya Surabaya
2000	Pupuk Kaldim
2001	PSM Makassar

Laos
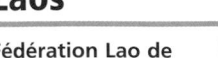

Fédération Lao de Football
Founded: 1951
Joined FIFA: 1952
Joined AFC: 1980

SEASON	LEAGUE CHAMPIONS
1998	Khammouan Province
1999	unknown
2000	Vientiane Municipality
2001	unknown
2002	Telecom & Transportation

Malaysia
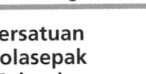

Persatuan Bolasepak Malaysia
Founded: 1933
Joined FIFA: 1956
Joined AFC: 1958

SEASON	LEAGUE CHAMPIONS
1998	Penang
1999	Penang
2000	Selangor
2001	Penang
2002	Perak

YEAR	CUP WINNERS
1998	Perak
1999	Brunei
2000	Perak
2001	Terengganu
2002	Penang

Maldives

Football Association of the Maldives
Founded: 1983
Joined FIFA: 1986
Joined AFC: 1986

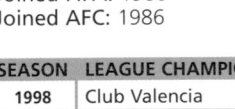

SEASON	LEAGUE CHAMPIONS
1998	Club Valencia
1999	Club Valencia
2000	Victory SC
2001	Victory SC
2002	IFC

YEAR	CUP WINNERS
1999	Club Valencia
2000	Victory SC
2001	New Radiant
2002	IFC
2003	IFC

Mongolia

Mongolian Football Federation
Founded: 1997
Joined FIFA: 1998
Joined AFC: 1998

SEASON	LEAGUE CHAMPIONS
1997	Delger
1998	Erchim
1999	ITI Bank Bars
2000	Erchim
2001	unknown

Myanmar
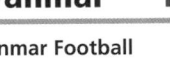

Myanmar Football Federation
Founded: 1947
Joined FIFA: 1957
Joined AFC: 1954

MYANMAR (FORMERLY BURMA) has no national championship but has a 12-team Premier League which is based in the city of Yangon (formerly Rangoon).

Nepal

All Nepal Football Association
Founded: 1951
Joined FIFA: 1970
Joined AFC: 1971

YEAR	CUP WINNERS
1998	Mahendra Police
1999	Mahendra Police
2000	no competition
2001	Eastern Region
2002	no competition

Pakistan

Pakistan Football Federation
Founded: 1948
Joined FIFA: 1948
Joined AFC: 1954

SEASON	LEAGUE CHAMPIONS
1999	Allied Bank Limited
2000	Allied Bank Limited
2001	WAPDA
2002	league format change
2003	WAPDA

Philippines

Philippines Football Federation
Founded: 1907
Joined FIFA: 1928
Joined AFC: 1954

YEAR	CUP WINNERS
1997	Air Force Hawks
1998	NCR South
1999	NCR B
2000	Navy
2001	no competition

Singapore

Football Association of Singapore
Founded: 1892
Joined FIFA: 1952
Joined AFC: 1954

SEASON	LEAGUE CHAMPIONS
1998	Singapore Armed Forces
1999	Home United
2000	Singapore Armed Forces
2001	Geyland United
2002	Singapore Armed Forces

Taiwan

Chinese Taipei Football Association
Founded: 1936
Joined FIFA: 1954
Joined AFC: 1954–75, 1990

SEASON	LEAGUE CHAMPIONS
1998	Tai-power
1999	Tai-power
2000	Tai-power
2001	Tai-power
2002	unknown

Thailand

Football Association of Thailand
Founded: 1916
Joined FIFA: 1925
Joined AFC: 1957

SEASON	LEAGUE CHAMPIONS
1999	Royal Thai Air Force
2000	BEC Tero Sasana
2001	BEC Tero Sasana
2002	league format change
2003	Krung Thai Bank

Vietnam

Vietnam Football Federation
Founded: 1962
Joined FIFA: 1964
Joined AFC: 1954

SEASON	LEAGUE CHAMPIONS
1999	no championship
2000	Song Lam Nghe An
2001	Song Lam Nghe An
2002	Cang Saigon
2003	Hoang Anh Gia Lai

SOUTH AND EAST ASIA

South Korea

THE SEASON IN REVIEW 2002

ALTHOUGH THE K-LEAGUE HAS BEEN in existence for almost two decades and the national team has made regular appearances at the World Cup finals and the Asian international tournaments, 2002 was a quantum leap in the country's footballing fortunes. Korea's co-hosting of the World Cup was a phenomenal success, even if the hoped-for reconciliation between Japan and North Korea did not materialize.

That success rested on the extraordinary performance of the national team during the World Cup. With the K-League and all other domestic football suspended for four months, Dutch coach Guus Hiddink was able to prepare his squad more fully than any other World Cup coach. It showed on the pitch where the South Koreans' style included not only organization and skill but also the most unyielding display of running, pressing and tackling. Sheer heart and the fantastic support pushed the national team all the way to the semi-finals, defeating Italy and Spain along the way, before finally losing to Germany.

Conduit for communication

Within hours of the World Cup finishing, South and North Korean naval forces clashed off the coast, leaving many dead. Despite this fragile state of affairs, football provided a significant conduit for North and South to speak to each other in 2002. In September a friendly game was held between the two nations in Seoul, and North Korea sent, along with many other athletes, a football squad to contest the Asian Games in South Korea. While crowds for the K-League rose substantially after the World Cup, the Asian Games proved a more dismal affair with a poor performance from the national team and low turnouts for many of the ties.

When domestic football did resume, Hiddink himself had departed for Holland as coach of PSV, and a number of the nation's star players had moved on to clubs in Europe and Japan. The league saw Seongnam Ilhwa Chunma lead from the front. Striker Kim Dae-ui provided and made goals all season and ended up as the league's MVP (Most Valued Player). The once-mighty Suwon Bluewings began poorly and, despite a strong surge at the end of the season, couldn't catch Seongnam. The Korean FA Cup was the team's compensation.

Above: Guus Hiddink receives the thanks of the nation once again. The Dutch coach of the South Korean national team returns from his new club PSV to watch South Korea take on North Korea.

Adidas K-Cup

2002 FINAL (2 legs)

May 8 – Ulsan Munsu Stadium
Ulsan Hyundai **1-3** Seongnam
Horang-i   Ilhwa Chunma
(Jeong   *(Sasa Drakulic*
Seong-hun 77)   *44, 75,*
     Kim Dae-ui 69)
h/t: 0-1 Att: 23,164
Ref: Kwon Jong-chul

May 12 – Seongnam Stadium
Seongnam **1-1** Ulsan Hyundai
Ilhwa Chunma   Horang-i
(Kim Sang-sik 57)   *(Kim*
     Hyeon-seok 33)
h/t: 0-1 Att: 24,728
Ref: Lee Sang-yong

Seongnam Ilhwa Chunma won 4-2
on aggregate

Korean FA Cup

2002 FINAL

December 15 – Jeju World Cup Stadium
Pohang **0-1** Suwon
Steelers   Samsung
   Bluewings
   (Sandro Cardoso
   Dos Santos 20)
h/t: 0-1 Att: 42,000
Ref: Lee Sang-yong

Top Goalscorers 2002

PLAYER	CLUB	NATIONALITY	GOALS
Edmilson Dias de Lucena	Chonbuk Hyundai Motors	Brazilian	13
Woo Seong-yong	Pusan I.cons	Korean	12
Moacir Bastos Tuta	Anyang LG Cheetahs	Brazilian	9
Goran Petreski	Pohang Steelers	Macedonian	9
Cheick Oumas Dabo	Bucheon SK	Malian	9
Kim Dae-ui	Seongnam Ilhwa Chunma	Korean	9

International Club Performances 2002

CLUB	COMPETITION	PROGRESS
Suwon Samsung Bluewings	Asian Club Championship	Winners
Anyang LG Cheetahs	Asian Club Championship	Runners-up
Chonbuk Hyundai Motors	Asian Cup-Winners' Cup	Runners-up
Suwon Samsung Bluewings	Asian Super Cup	Winners

South Korean K-League Table 2002

CLUB	P	W	D	L	F	A	Pts
Seongnam Ilhwa Chunma	27	14	7	6	43	32	49
Ulsan Hyundai Horang-i	27	13	8	6	37	27	47
Suwon Samsung Bluewings	27	12	9	6	40	26	45
Anyang LG Cheetahs	27	11	7	9	37	30	40
Chunnam Dragons	27	9	10	8	21	21	37
Pohang Steelers	27	9	9	9	31	34	36
Chonbuk Hyundai Motors	27	8	11	8	37	36	35
Bucheon SK	27	8	8	11	32	40	32
Pusan I.cons	27	6	8	13	36	45	26
Taejon Citizen	27	1	11	15	16	39	14

Daegu FC and Sangmu Phoenix joining league to make 12 teams next season.

Seongnam Ilhwa Chunma celebrates its second K-League Championship victory in a row.

SOUTH KOREA

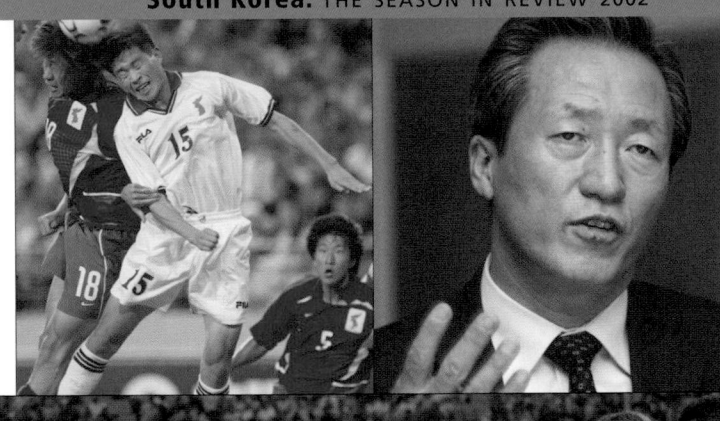

Right: *South Korea's Kim Eun-jung (L) battles for the ball with North Korea's Kim Yong-jun (C) as South Korea's Cho Sung-whan looks on.*

Far right: *Chung Mong-joon, President of the Korean FA and of the South Korean World Cup organizing committee, announced he might run for the nation's presidency in the glowing after-math of the tournament. But football will only take you so far: Chung abandoned his campaign in the autumn.*

Below: *Seo Jung-won, captain of Suwon Bluewings, lifts the Korean Cup; some compensation for a poor season for his team.*

In a year of escalating political tension between the two Koreas, a friendly match was played in Seoul between the two nations on 7 September 2002. A 60,000 sell out crowd saw an accurate representation of the peninsula's politics: a grinding 0-0 draw.

Shin Tae-yong, *captain of champions Seongnam, in action in the championship decider against Pusan I.cons.*

South Korea

Korea Football Association
Founded: 1928
Joined FIFA: 1948
Joined AFC: 1954

KFA

SOUTH KOREA

FOR MOST OF the first half of the 20th century the whole Korean peninsula was occupied and colonized by the Japanese but a national FA was established in Seoul in 1928 and amateur football flourished in the cities. After the Second World War, the peninsula was divided into North and South (Soviet and US occupation zones, respectively), a division solidified by the stalemate of the Korean War (1949–53). The Korea Football Association joined FIFA in 1948 and was a founder member of the AFC (Asian Football Confederation) in 1954. Football struggled as baseball was the dominant spectator sport. However, in the early 1980s, with the financial support of Chaebol (a number of large Korean companies), a professional league was established. Chaebol have not been the only investors in Korean clubs. The religious foundation of the Moonies own Songnam Ilhwa Chunma. Alongside the league a number of cup competitions have been held, some sporadically. A Korean FA Cup began in 1996 to ensure Korean representation in the AFC's Asian Cup-Winners' Cup. The league has ten clubs, with the top six going into a championship play-off at the end of the season.

Honours have been spread around the country since the inception of the professional league and South Korean clubs have proved very successful in international club competitions, with four victories in the Asian Club Championship – including an all-South Korean Final in 1997 when the reigning champions Ilhwa Chunma were beaten by the Pohang Steelers. Two South Korean teams also contested the 2002 Final: Suwon Samsung Bluewings and Anyang LG Cheetahs. The Bluewings won 4-2 on penalties.

South Korean K-League Record 1983–2002

SEASON	CHAMPIONS	RUNNERS-UP
1983	Hallelujah	Daewoo
1984	Daewoo Royals	Yukong Elephants
1985	LG Hwangso	POSCO Atoms
1986	POSCO Atoms	LG Hwangso
1987	Daewoo Royals	Yukong Elephants
1988	POSCO Atoms	Hyundai Horang-i
1989	Yukong Elephants	LG Hwangso
1990	LG Hwangso	Daewoo Royals
1991	Daewoo Royals	Hyundai Horang-i
1992	POSCO Atoms	Ilhwa Chunma
1993	Ilhwa Chunma	LG Cheetahs
1994	Ilhwa Chunma	Yukong Elephants
1995	Ilhwa Chunma	Pohang Atoms
1996	Ulsan Hyundai Horang-i	Suwon Samsung Bluewings
1997	Pusan Daewoo Royals	Chunnam Dragons
1998	Suwon Samsung Bluewings	Ulsan Hyundai Horang-i
1999	Suwon Samsung Bluewings	Pusan Daewoo Royals
2000	Anyang LG Cheetahs	Puchon SK
2001	Seongnam Ilhwa Chunma	Anyang LG Cheetahs
2002	Seongnam Ilhwa Chunma	Ulsan Hyundai Horang-i

South Korean FA Cup Record 1996–2002

YEAR	WINNERS	SCORE	RUNNERS-UP
1996	Pohang Atoms	0-0 (7-6 pens)	Suwon Samsung Bluewings
1997	Chunnam Dragons	1-0	Chonan Ilhwa Chunma
1998	Anyang LG Cheetahs	2-1	Ulsan Hyundai Horang-i
1999	Chonan Ilhwa Chunma	3-0	Chonbuk Hyundai Dinos
2000	Chonbuk Hyundai Motors	2-0	Songnam Ilhwa Chunma
2001	Taejon Citizen	1-0	Pohang Steelers
2002	Suwon Samsung Bluewings	1-0	Pohang Steelers

Adidas K-Cup Record 1992–2002

YEAR	WINNERS	YEAR	WINNERS
1992	Ilhwa Chunma	2000	Suwon Samsung Bluewings
1993	POSCO Atoms		
1994	Yukong Elephants	2001	Suwon Samsung Bluewings
1995	Hyundai Horang-i		
1996	Puchon Yukong	2002	Seongnam Ilhwa Chunma
1997	Pusan Daewoo Royals		
1998	*no competition*		
1999	Suwon Samsung Bluewings		

Top Goalscorers 1983–2002

YEAR	SCORER	TEAM	NATIONALITY	GOALS
1983	Park Yun-gi	Yukong Elephants	Korean	9
1984	Baek Jong-cheol	Hyundai Horang-i	Korean	16
1985	Piyapong Pue-on Kim Yong-se	LG Hwangso Yukong Elephants	Korean Korean	12
1986	Jeong Hae-won	Daewoo Royals	Korean	10
1987	Choi Sang-guk	POSCO Atoms	Korean	15
1988	Lee Gi-geun	POSCO Atoms	Korean	12
1989	Cho Gueng-yeon	POSCO Atoms	Korean	20
1990	Yun Sang-cheol	LG Cheetahs	Korean	12
1991	Lee Gi-geun	POSCO Atoms	Korean	16
1992	Im Geun-jae	LG Cheetahs	Korean	10
1993	Caha Sang-hae	POSCO Atoms	Korean	10
1994	Yun Sang-cheol	LG Cheetahs	Korean	21
1995	Roh Sang-rae	Chunnam Dragons	Korean	15
1996	Shin Tae-yong	Chonan Ilhwa Chunma	Korean	18
1997	Kim Hyun-seok	Ulsan Hyundai Horang-i	Korean	9
1998	Yoo Sang-chul	Ulsan Hyundai Horang-i	Korean	14
1999	Sasa Drakulic	Suwon Samsung Bluewings	Yugoslavian	14
2000	Kim Do-hoon	Chonbuk Hyundai Motors	Korean	12
2001	Sandro Dos Santos	Suwon Samsung Bluewings	Brazilian	13
2002	Edmilson dias de Lucera	Chonbuk Hyundai Motors	Brazilian	14

Ulsan's Kim Hyun-seok celebrates after scoring his record breaking 102nd K-League goal in a match against Taejon in October 2001.

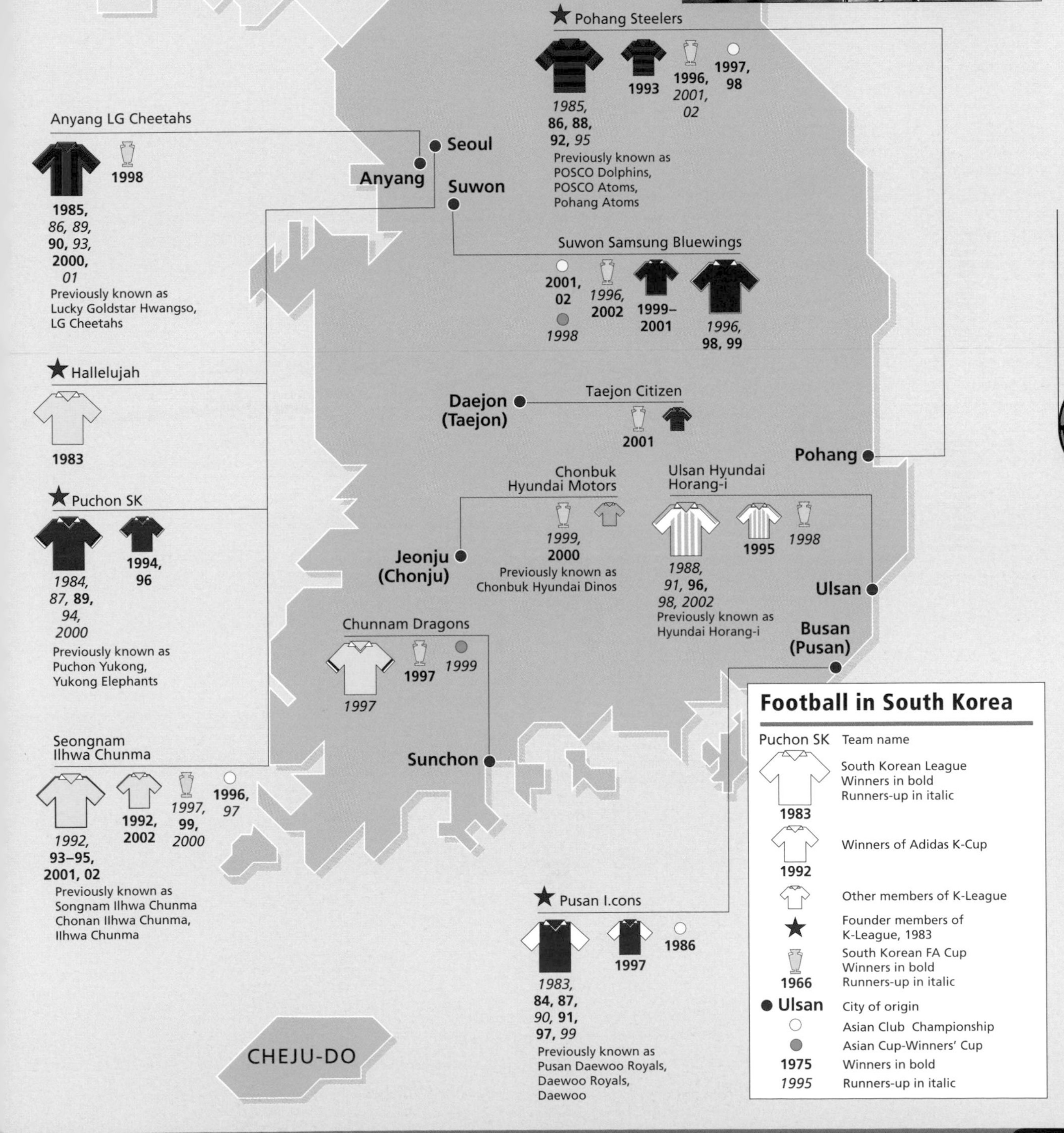

SOUTH KOREA

NORTH KOREA

★ Pohang Steelers

1985,
**86, 88,
92,** *95*

1993

1996,
*2001,
02*

**1997,
98**

Previously known as
POSCO Dolphins,
POSCO Atoms,
Pohang Atoms

Seoul

Anyang

Suwon

Anyang LG Cheetahs

1998

1985,
86, 89,
90, 93,
2000,
01

Previously known as
Lucky Goldstar Hwangso,
LG Cheetahs

Suwon Samsung Bluewings

**2001,
02**

1996,
2002

**1999–
2001**

*1996,
98, 99*

1998

★ Hallelujah

1983

Taejon Citizen

**Daejon
(Taejon)**

2001

Pohang

★ Puchon SK

*1984,
87,* **89,**
94,
2000

**1994,
96**

Previously known as
Puchon Yukong,
Yukong Elephants

Chonbuk
Hyundai Motors

Ulsan Hyundai
Horang-i

*1999,
2000*

Previously known as
Chonbuk Hyundai Dinos

*1988,
91, 96,
98, 2002*

Previously known as
Hyundai Horang-i

1995

1998

**Jeonju
(Chonju)**

Ulsan

**Busan
(Pusan)**

Chunnam Dragons

1997

1997

1999

Seongnam
Ilhwa Chunma

*1992,
93–95,*
2001, 02

**1992,
2002**

*1997,
99,
2000*

1996,
97

Previously known as
Songnam Ilhwa Chunma
Chonan Ilhwa Chunma,
Ilhwa Chunma

Sunchon

★ Pusan I.cons

1983,
**84, 87,
90, 91,
97,** *99*

1997

1986

Previously known as
Pusan Daewoo Royals,
Daewoo Royals,
Daewoo

CHEJU-DO

Football in South Korea

Puchon SK	Team name
1983	South Korean League Winners in bold Runners-up in italic
1992	Winners of Adidas K-Cup
	Other members of K-League
★	Founder members of K-League, 1983
1966	South Korean FA Cup Winners in bold Runners-up in italic
● **Ulsan**	City of origin
○	Asian Club Championship
●	Asian Cup-Winners' Cup
1975	Winners in bold
1995	Runners-up in italic

457

Japan

THE SEASON IN REVIEW 2002

JAPANESE FOOTBALL CAME OF AGE IN 2002: a successful co-hosting of the World Cup, a creditable performance from the national team and appropriate levels of mass hysteria and support for the team in the country's awesome new stadiums. In the last half of the season, attendance figures shot up and the J-League finally abandoned extra time and golden goals and embraced the complex drama of the draw.

Perhaps the oddities of a two-stage championship will be the next thing to go? In 2001 Jubilo Iwata managed 17 points more than eventual champions Kashima Antlers over the two stages of the J-League, only to be beaten in the play-offs. This year, there would be no mistake and no play-offs – for the first time since its inception, a single team won both stages of the tournament. That team was the unstoppable Jubilo Iwata, built around a solid defensive midfield, with the perennial Takashi Fukunishi at its heart. Fukunishi himself scored the golden goal that clinched the championship in extra time against Tokyo Verdy.

Yokohama F. Marinos pushed Jubilo Iwata hard in the first stage but fell away in the second after losing star Nakamura to Italian club Reggina. Brazilian striker Will was fired after kicking a teammate during a match and coach Sebastiao Lazaroni was shown the door. Steve Perryman suffered the same fate at Kashiwa Reysol when six straight defeats after the World Cup took them close to the relegation zone. Newly promoted Kyoto defied the sceptics, staying up with ease and as a bonus taking the Emperor's Cup. Consadole and Hiroshima, by contrast, played pitifully all season before mercifully taking the drop.

Above, top: *The Brazilian Connection: after Philippe Troussier's post World Cup departure, Zico was appointed coach of the national team.*

Above: *After helping South Korea to the World Cup semi-finals, Ahn Jung-hwan debuts for Shimizu S-Pulse against Urawa.*

Right: *The J-League gets cruel. Consadole Sapporo, already relegated, send fellow strugglers Sanfrecce Hiroshima down with this last minute winner in an epic 5-4 victory.*

J-League Division 1 Table 2002

FIRST STAGE

CLUB	P	W/OT*	D	L/OT*	F	A	Pts
Jubilo Iwata	15	9/4	1	1/0	39	17	36
Yokohama F. Marinos	15	8/3	3	1/0	28	11	33
Nagoya Grampus Eight	15	9/1	0	4/1	28	18	29
Gamba Osaka	15	8/1	1	3/2	35	19	27
Kashima Antlers	15	9/0	0	4/2	21	18	27
Kyoto Purple Sanga	15	5/4	1	5/0	26	18	24
Shimizu S-Pulse	15	5/3	3	4/0	17	19	24
JEF United	15	6/1	3	4/1	22	23	23
Vegalta Sendai	15	6/1	0	5/3	23	27	20
FC Tokyo	15	5/0	2	6/2	23	27	17
Urawa Red Diamonds	15	3/2	1	7/2	21	24	14
Tokyo Verdy	15	2/3	1	9/0	15	24	13
Vissel Kobe	15	3/1	1	5/5	12	22	12
Kashiwa Reysol	15	3/1	0	10/1	20	31	11
Sanfrecce Hiroshima	15	3/0	1	9/2	14	26	10
Consadole Sapporo	15	2/0	0	9/4	15	35	6

* 3 points for a win in 90 minutes;
2 points for a win in overtime.

SECOND STAGE

CLUB	P	W/OT*	D	L/OT*	F	A	Pts	
Jubilo Iwata	15	9/4	0	2/0	33	13	35	Asian Champions League/ Far East Club Championship
Gamba Osaka	15	7/3	0	4/1	24	13	27	
Kashima Antlers	15	8/1	0	6/0	25	21	26	Far East Club Championship
Tokyo Verdy	15	6/2	2	4/1	26	19	24	
FC Tokyo	15	6/2	0	6/1	20	19	22	
Yokohama F. Marinos	15	5/3	1	6/0	16	16	22	
Kyoto Purple Sanga	15	6/2	0	6/1	18	24	22	
Urawa Red Diamonds	15	4/4	1	4/2	20	14	21	
Kashiwa Reysol	15	6/0	3	4/2	18	17	21	
Vissel Kobe	15	5/1	2	4/3	21	22	19	
JEF United	15	6/0	0	8/1	16	19	18	
Shimizu S-Pulse	15	5/1	0	7/2	16	24	17	
Nagoya Grampus Eight	15	5/0	1	7/2	21	23	16	
Sanfrecce Hiroshima	15	4/1	2	4/4	18	21	16	Relegated
Vegalta Sendai	15	3/1	1	8/2	17	30	12	
Consadole Sapporo	15	2/1	1	7/4	15	29	9	Relegated

Promoted clubs: Oita Trinita, Cerezo Osaka.

Takashi Fukunishi scored Jubilo's winning goal in its second stage victory over Tokyo Verdy to seal its historic double.

Top Goalscorers 2002

PLAYER	CLUB	NATIONALITY	GOALS
Naohiro Takahara	Jubilo Iwata	Japanese	26
Magrao	Gamba Osaka	Brazilian	22
Ueslei	Nagoya Grampus Eight	Brazilian	20

International Club Performances 2002

CLUB	COMPETITION	PROGRESS
Kashima Antlers	Asian Club Championship	Quarter-finals
Shimizu S-Pulse	Asian Cup-Winners' Cup	Quarter-finals

Emperor's Cup

2002 FINAL

January 1, 2003 – Tokyo National Stadium

Kyoto Purple **2-1** Kashima
Sanga   Antlers
(Ji-sung 46,   (Euller 16)
Kurobe 85)*
h/t: 0-1 **Att:** 50,526
Ref: Masayoshi Okada

Below: Newly-promoted Kyoto Purple Sanga had a great season, finishing seventh in the league and winning the Emperor's Cup, beating Kashima Antlers 2-1.

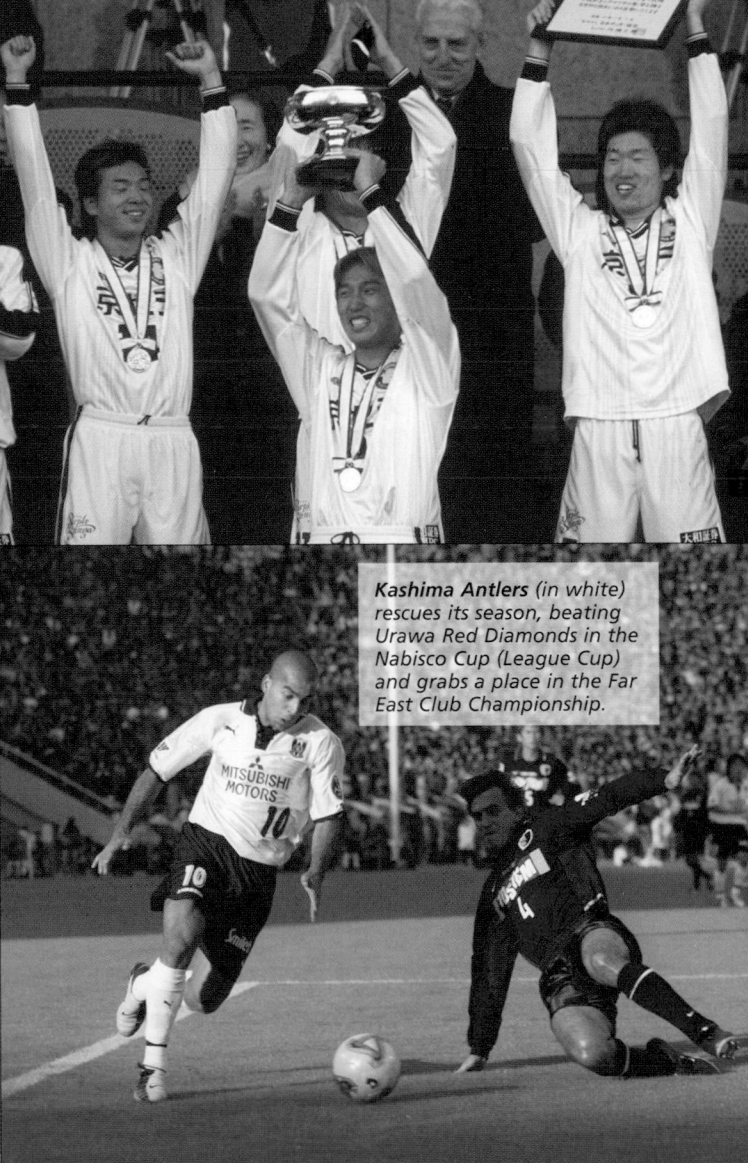

Kashima Antlers (in white) rescues its season, beating Urawa Red Diamonds in the Nabisco Cup (League Cup) and grabs a place in the Far East Club Championship.

Japan

THE J-LEAGUE 1992–2002

A NATIONAL FOOTBALL LEAGUE had been played in Japan since 1965, but the JSL was always a corporate amateur affair. Until the late 1980s there were no official professional contracts and teams were all sponsored by Japan's industrial giants as a combination of company welfare, advertising and philanthropy. With international club success in the 1980s coming to Japan (Furukawa Electric won the Asian Club Championship in 1987), the Japanese FA decided to organize a professional league.

The J-League was launched in 1993, with a capital injection of around $20 million. The top teams of the old JSL were revamped, corporate names were banned and hometown affiliations emphasized in clubs names and outlook. Riding the end of Japan's massive consumer binge of the early 1990s, the J-League proved enormously popular. Massive TV coverage, marketing and a slew of foreign players saw gate takings and income rise for four years. Brazilians, Italians and Eastern Europeans all made their way there towards the end of their careers, and more recently African players have followed in their footsteps.

Early years of the J-League

The early years of the J-League belonged to the leading teams of the JSL era: Yomiuri Club became Verdy Kawasaki and won the championship in 1993 and 94, and Nissan Motors became Yokohama Marinos and beat Verdy in the 1995 championship play-off. The late 90s saw a shift of power with titles alternating between two clubs with no pre-J-League pedigree, Kashima Antlers and Jubilo Iwata, before Kashima moved up a gear to take a treble of domestic trophies in 2000. Gamba Osaka, JEF United Ichihara, Nagoya Grampus Eight and Sanfrecce Hiroshima have proved the leagues underachievers.

Despite a dip in the late 1990s, as consumer indifference and economic stagnation set in, the quality of play and the size of crowds have risen again with the World Cup going to Japan in 2002. Distinctive fan cultures and solid gates have emerged at Shimizu S-Pulse, Uruwa Red Diamonds and Consadole Sapporo. Perhaps most importantly, a football gambling system – the Toto – was introduced in 2000 and has proved to be a massive commercial success.

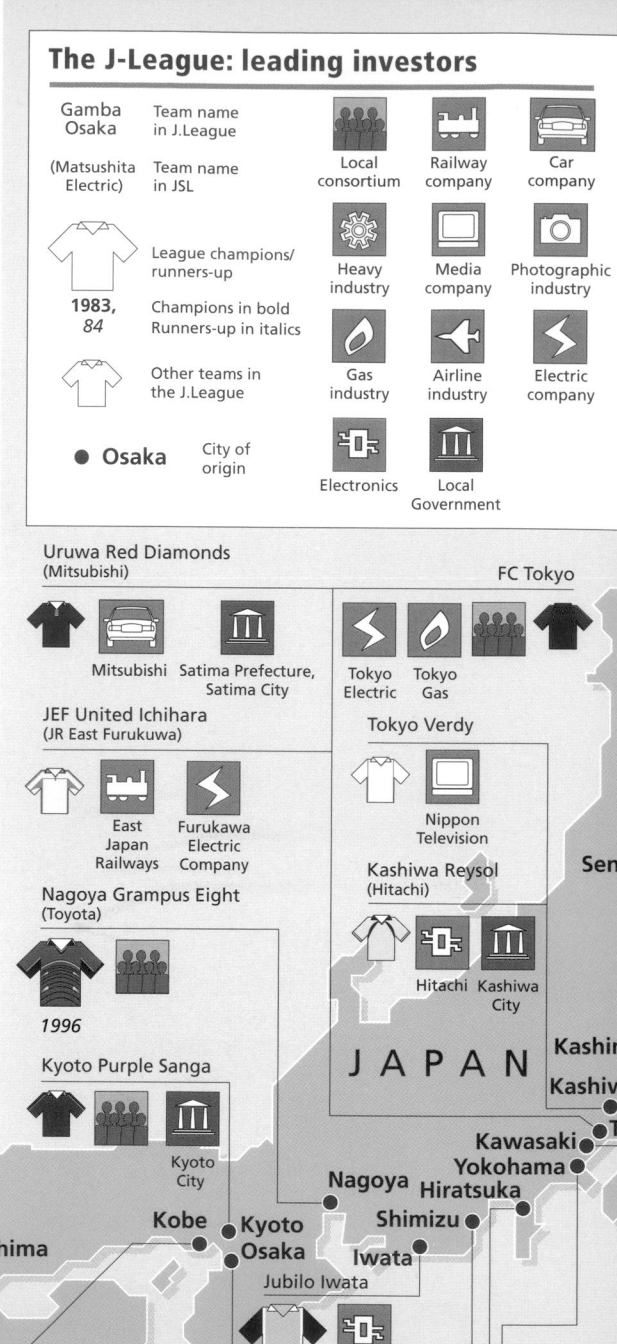

The J-League: leading investors

Gamba Osaka	Team name in J.League	Local consortium
(Matsushita Electric)	Team name in JSL	Railway company
	League champions/ runners-up	Car company
1983, *84*	Champions in bold Runners-up in italics	Heavy industry
	Other teams in the J.League	Media company
● Osaka	City of origin	Photographic industry
		Gas industry
		Airline industry
		Electric company
		Electronics
		Local Government

Uruwa Red Diamonds (Mitsubishi) — Mitsubishi — Satima Prefecture, Satima City

FC Tokyo — Tokyo Electric — Tokyo Gas

JEF United Ichihara (JR East Furukuwa) — East Japan Railways — Furukawa Electric Company

Tokyo Verdy — Nippon Television

Nagoya Grampus Eight (Toyota) — *1996*

Kashiwa Reysol (Hitachi) — Hitachi — Kashiwa City

Kyoto Purple Sanga — Kyoto City

J A P A N

Sendai
Kashima
Kashiwa
Kawasaki
Yokohama
Hiratsuka
Shimizu
Nagoya
Iwata
Kobe
Kyoto
Osaka
Toky[o]
Hiroshima
Fukuoka
Oita

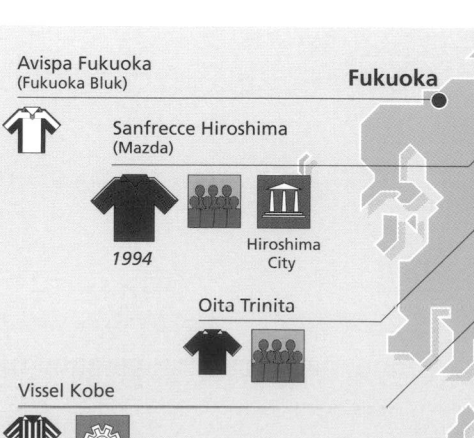

Avispa Fukuoka (Fukuoka Bluk)

Sanfrecce Hiroshima (Mazda) — *1994* — Hiroshima City

Oita Trinita

Vissel Kobe — Kawasaki Steel

Cerezo Osaka (Yanmar Diesel) — Osaka City

Gamba Osaka (Matsushita Electric) — Matsushita — West Japan Railway — Osaka Gas Company

Jubilo Iwata — *1997, 98, 99, 2001, 02* — Yamaha

Shimizu S-Pulse (Shimizu) — *1999*

Bellmare Hiratsuka (Fujita) — Hiratsuka City

Yokohama F Marinos (Yokohama Flugels merged with Yokohama Marinos in 1999 (previously All Nippon Airways))

1995, 2000

Nissan

Uruwa Red Diamond fans have created the most distinctive fan culture in the J-League, and the one most at odds with key elements of Japanese culture. Early fan groups were the first to boo their own players for poor performances and create an intimidating atmosphere for visiting teams.

The Brazilian connection: Zico in his playing days at Kashima Antlers. He was appointed Japanese national team coach in 2002.

Sapporo

Consadole Sapporo
(Toshiba)

Vegalta Sendai

Miyagi Prefecture, Sendai City

Kashima Antlers
(Sumitomo Honda)

 Sumitomo Metals   *1993, 96, 97, 98, 2000, 01*

Verdy Kawasaki
(Yomiuri Club)

Nippon Television   *1993, 94, 95*

Kawasaki Frontale

Fujitsu

Key to League Positions Table

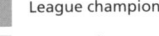 League champions

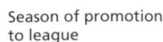 Season of promotion to league

Season of relegation from league

Other teams playing in league

| 5 | Final position in league |

JAPAN

Japanese League Positions 1992–2002

TEAM	1992–93	1992–93	1993–94	1993–94	1994–95	1994–95	1995–96	1996–97	1996–97	1997–98†	1997–98†	1998–99	1998–99	1999–2000	1999–2000	2000–01	2000–01	2001–02	2001–02
Avispa Fukuoka								15	17	15	18	15	11	15	14	6	12	15	
Bellmare Hiratsuka			7	2	7	14	11	4	9	12	12	16	16						
Sanfrecce Hiroshima	6	5	1	4	10	12	14	10	13	13	9	6	8	10	11	13	3	15	14
JEF United Ichihara	5	9	6	9	6	7	9	15	14	11	18	15	11	11	16	2	5	8	11
Jubilo Iwata			11	7	5	9	4	6	1*	1	2	1	12*	5	3	1	2	1	1**
Kashima Antlers	1	4	3	5	8	6	1	1	4	5	1*	9	6	8	1*	11	1*	5	3
Kashiwa Reysol					14	5	5	3	10	10	8	4	4	4	2	6	7	14	9
Kawasaki Frontale														15	15				
Verdy Kawasaki	2	1*	4	1*	2	1	7	16	12	6	17	2	10	9	10				
Vissel Kobe								14	17	17	14	12	7	7	14	10	13	13	10
Kyoto Purple Sanga								16	13	16	15	11	14	9	16	12		6	7
Nagoya Grampus Eight	9	8	8	12	4	2	2	12	5	3	6	8	2	12	7	3	6	3	13
Oita Trinita																			
Cerezo Osaka							9	10	13	11	8	9	13	5	5	2	9	14	16
Gamba Osaka	8	6	10	10	11	13	12	8	2	14	16	10	13	13	4	5	11	4	2
Consadole Sapporo												16	10			8	14	16	16
Vegalta Sendai																		9	15
Shimizu S-Pulse	4	2	2	6	12	4	10	7	6	2	5	3	1	3	13	4	4	7	12
Tokyo Verdy																16	9	12	4
FC Tokyo														6	8	9	8	10	5
Uruwa Red Diamonds	10	10	12	11	3	8	6	9	7	7	3	13	14			7	12	11	8
Yokohama Flugels	7	7	5	8	13	11	3	2	11	8	7								
Yokohama F Marinos	3	3	9	3	1	3*	8	5	3	4	4	7	3	1		15	10	2	6

*Denotes championship play-off winners.
Except 1995–96, season is divided into two stages with a play-off to decide the championship.

**Jubilo won both stages, so there was no play-off.

†First year of promotion and relegation.

Japan

Japan Football Association
Founded: 1921
Joined FIFA: 1929–46, 1950
Joined AFC: 1954

A RUDIMENTARY VERSION of football has been played in Japan for over 1,500 years. The rapid modernization of Japan on Western lines after the Meiji restoration (1868) saw modern football established in schools and universities in the early years of the 20th century. In 1921, the first national cup competition was established, modelled on the English FA Cup. Breaking for the war, it was replaced in 1946 by the Emperor's Cup. An additional cup competition, the Japan Soccer League Cup, was launched in 1976 and renamed the J-League Cup in 1992. Winners of this competition enter the Asian Cup-Winners' Cup.

National league football started in 1965, based on teams supported by industrial groups (Toyota, Hitachi, Nissan etc.). Although popular, the league was always second to baseball in Japan. In 1993, with enormous new commercial backing, the old structures were abandoned and Japanese league football was relaunched as the J-League in a ten-team premier league, later expanded to 16. A second division was added in 1999. Teams score three points for a win, two points for a win in extra time (drawn games always go to extra time) and one for a draw. Until 1998, drawn games after extra time were decided by a penalty shootout. The season was then divided into opening and closing championships with play-offs to decide the winners.

Japanese League Record 1965–2002

SEASON	CHAMPIONS	RUNNERS-UP
1965	Toyo Industrial	Yahata Steel
1966	Toyo Industrial	Yahata Steel
1967	Toyo Industrial	Furukawa Electric
1968	Toyo Industrial	Yanmar Diesel
1969	Mitsubishi Heavy Industrial	Toyo Industrial
1970	Toyo Industrial	Mitsubishi Heavy Industrial
1971	Yanmar Diesel	Mitsubishi Heavy Industrial
1972	Hitachi	Yanmar Diesel
1973	Mitsubishi Heavy Industrial	Hitachi
1974	Yanmar Diesel	Mitsubishi Heavy Industrial
1975	Yanmar Diesel	Mitsubishi Heavy Industrial
1976*		
1977	Furukawa Electric	Mitsubishi Heavy Industrial
1978	Fujita Industrial	Mitsubishi Heavy Industrial
1978†	Mitsubishi Heavy Industrial	Yanmar Diesel
1979	Fujita Industrial	Yomiuri Club
1980	Yanmar Diesel	Fujita Industrial
1981	Fujita Industrial	Yomiuri Club
1982	Mitsubishi Heavy Industrial	Yanmar Diesel
1983	Yomiuri Club	Nissan Motors
1984	Yomiuri Club	Nissan Motors
1985*		
1986	Furukawa Electric	Nippon Kokan
1987	Yomiuri Club	Nippon Kokan
1988	Yamaha Motors	Nippon Kokan
1989	Nissan Motors	All Nippon Airways
1990	Nissan Motors	Yomiuri Club
1991	Yomiuri Club	Nissan Motors
1992	Yomiuri Club	Nissan Motors
1993	Verdy Kawasaki	Kashima Antlers
1994	Verdy Kawasaki	Sanfrecce Hiroshima
1995	Yokohama Marinos	Verdy Kawasaki
1996	Kashima Antlers	Nagoya Grampus Eight
1997	Jubilo Iwata	Kashima Antlers
1998	Kashima Antlers	Jubilo Iwata

Japanese League Record (continued)

SEASON	CHAMPIONS	RUNNERS-UP
1999	Jubilo Iwata	Shimizu S-Pulse
2000	Kashima Antlers	Yokohama Marinos
2001	Kashima Antlers	Jubilo Iwata
2002	Jubilo Iwata**	Yokohama Marinos

* There is no result as the season changed its start and finish date.

† Two seasons were played in this year.

** No play-offs needed as Jubilo Iwata won both stages.

Japanese League Summary

TEAM	TOTALS	CHAMPIONS & RUNNERS-UP (BOLD) (ITALICS)
Verdy Kawasaki (includes Yomiuri Club)	7, 4	*1979*, **81, 83, 84, 87,** *90,* **91–94,** *95*
Sanfrecce Hiroshima (includes Toyo Industrial)	5, 2	**1965–68,** *69,* **70,** *94*
Mitsubishi Heavy Industrial	4, 6	**1969,** *70, 71,* **73, 74,** *75,* **77, 78, 78†,** *82*
Yanmar Diesel	4, 4	*1968,* **71,** *72,* **74, 75,** *78,* **80,** *82*
Jubilo Iwata (includes Yamaha Motors)	4, 2	**88,** *97,* **98, 99, 2001, 02**
Kashima Antlers	4, 2	**1993,** *96, 97,* **98, 2000, 01**
Yokohama Marinos (includes Nissan Motors)	3, 6	*1983, 84,* **89,** *90, 91, 92,* **95,** *2000, 02*
Fujita Industrial	3, 1	**1978, 79,** *80,* **81**
Furukawa Electric	2, 1	*1967,* **77, 86**
Hitachi	1, 1	**1972,** *73*
Nippon Kokan	0, 3	*1986–88*
Yahata Steel	0, 2	*1965, 66*
All Nippon Airways	0, 1	*1989*
Nagoya Grampus Eight	0, 1	*1996*
Shimizu S-Pulse	0, 1	*1999*

Japanese Cup Record 1921–2002

YEAR	WINNERS	SCORE	RUNNERS-UP
1921	Tokyo Shukyu-dan	1-0	Mikage Shukyu-dan
1922	Nagoya Shukyu-dan	1-0	Hiroshima Koto-shihan
1923	Astra Club	2-1	Nagoya Shukyu-dan
1924	Rijo FC	4-1	All Mikage Shihan Club
1925	Rijo FC	3-0	Tokyo University
1926		no competition	
1927	Kobe-Ichi Jr. Highschool Club	2-0	Rijo FC
1928	Waseda University WMW	6-1	Kyoto University
1929	Kwangaku Club	3-0	Housei University
1930	Kwangaku Club	3-0	Keio University BRB
1931	Tokyo University LB	5-1	Kobun Jr. Highschool
1932	Keio Club	5-1	Yoshino Club
1933	Tokyo University LB	4-1	Sendai Football Club
1934		no competition	
1935	All Keio Club	6-1	Tokyo Bunri University
1936	Keio University BRB	3-2	Fusei Senmon
1937	Keio University BRB	*	Kobe Commercial University
1938	Waseda University WMW	4-1	Keio University BRB
1939	Keio University BRB	3-2	Waseda University WMW

JAPAN

Japanese Cup Record (*continued*)

YEAR	WINNERS	SCORE	RUNNERS-UP
1940	Keio University BRB	1-0	Waseda University WMW
1941–45		no competition	
1946	Tokyo University LB	6-2	Kobe Keizai-dai Club
1947–48		no competition	
1949	Tokyo University LB	5-2	Kwangaku Club
1950	All Kwangaku	6-1	Keio University BRB
1951	Keio University BRB	3-2	Osaka Club
1952	All Keio University	6-2	Osaka Club
1953	All Kwangaku	5-4	Osaka Club
1954	Keio University BRB	5-3 (aet)	Toyo Industrial
1955	All Kwangaku	4-3	Chudai Club
1956	Keio University BRB	4-2	Yahata Steel
1957	Chuo University	2-1	Toyo Industrial
1958	Kwangaku Club	2-1	Yahata Steel
1959	Kwangaku Club	1-0	Chuo University
1960	Furukawa Electric	4-0	Keio University BRB
1961	Furukawa Electric	3-2	Chuo University
1962	Chuo University	2-1	Furukawa Electric
1963	Waseda University WMW	3-0	Hitachi
1964†	Yahata Steel	0-0 (aet)	Furukawa Electric
1965	Toyo Industrial	3-2	Yahata Steel
1966	Waseda University WMW	3-2 (aet)	Toyo Industrial
1967	Toyo Industrial	1-0	Mitsubishi Heavy Industrial
1968	Yanmar Diesel	1-0	Mitsubishi Heavy Industrial
1969	Toyo Industrial	4-1	Rikkyo University
1970	Yanmar Diesel	2-1 (aet)	Toyo Industrial
1971	Mitsubishi Heavy Industrial	3-1	Yanmar Diesel
1972	Hitachi	2-1	Yanmar Diesel
1973	Mitsubishi Heavy Industrial	2-1	Hitachi
1974	Yanmar Diesel	2-1	Eidai Industrial
1975	Hitachi	2-0	Fujita Industrial
1976	Furukawa Electric	4-1	Yanmar Diesel
1977	Fujita Industrial	4-1	Yanmar Diesel
1978	Mitsubishi Heavy Industrial	1-0	Toyo Industrial
1979	Fujita Industrial	2-1	Mitsubishi Heavy Industrial
1980	Mitsubishi Heavy Industrial	1-0	Tanabe Medecine
1981	NKK	2-0	Yomiuri Club
1982	Yamaha Motors	1-0 (aet)	Fujita Industrial
1983	Nissan Motors	2-0	Yanmar Diesel
1984	Yomiuri Club	2-0	Furukawa Electric
1985	Nissan Motors	2-0	Fujita Industrial
1986	Yomiuri Club	2-1	NKK
1987	Yomiuri Club	2-0	Mazda
1988	Nissan Motors	3-1 (aet)	Fujita Industrial
1989	Nissan Motors	3-2	Yamaha Motors
1990	Matsushita	0-0 (aet)(4-3 pens)	Nissan Motors
1991	Nissan Motors	4-1 (aet)	Yomiuri Club
1992	Yokohama Marinos	2-1 (aet)	Verdy Kawasaki
1993	Yokohama Flugels	6-2 (aet)	Kashima Antlers
1994	Bellmare Hiratsuka	2-0	Cerezo Osaka
1995	Nagoya Grampus Eight	3-0	Sanfrecce Hiroshima
1996	Verdy Kawasaki	3-0	Sanfrecce Hiroshima
1997	Kashima Antlers	3-0	Yokohama Flugels
1998	Yokohama Flugels	2-1	Shimizu S-Pulse
1999	Nagoya Grampus Eight	2-0	Sanfrecce Hiroshima
2000	Kashima Antlers	3-2 (asdet)	Shimizu S-Pulse
2001	Shimizu S-Pulse	3-2	Cerezo Osaka
2002	Kashima Antlers	1-0	Urawa Red Diamonds

Japanese Cup Summary

TEAM	TOTALS	WINNERS & RUNNERS-UP (BOLD) (ITALICS)
Keio University BRB (includes Tokyo Bunri)	7, 5	*1930*, **35, 36, 37**, *38, 39*, **40**, *50, 51*, **54, 56**, *60*
Yokohama Marinos (includes Nissan Motors)	6, 1	**1983, 85, 88, 89**, *90*, **91, 92**
Urawa Red Diamonds (includes Mitsubishi Heavy Industrial)	4, 4	*1967, 68*, **71**, *73*, **78**, *79*, **80, 2002**
Verdy Kawasaki (Includes Yomiuri Club)	4, 3	*1981*, **84**, *86*, **87**, *91*, **92, 96**
Furukawa Electric	4, 2	**1960, 61**, *62*, **64†**, *76*, **84**
Waseda University WMW	4, 2	*1928*, **38, 39, 40**, *63*, **66**
Kwangaku Club	4, 1	**1929**, *30*, **49**, *58, 59*
Tokyo University LB	4, 1	*1925*, **31, 33**, *46*, **49**
Sanfrecce Hiroshima (includes Toyo Industrial and Mazda)	3, 8	**1954**, *57*, **65**, *66*, **67**, *69, 70, 78, 87, 95, 96, 99*
Cerezo Osaka (includes Yanmar Diesel)	3, 7	**1968**, *70, 71, 72*, **74**, *76, 77, 83*, **94**, *2001*
Bellmare Hiratsuka (includes Fujita Industrial)	3, 4	*1975*, **77**, *79*, **82**, *85, 88*, **94**
Kashima Antlers	3, 1	*1993*, **97, 2000**, *02*
All Kwangaku	3, 0	**1950, 53, 55**
Chuo University	2, 2	**1957**, *59*, **61**, *62*
Hitachi	2, 2	*1963*, **72**, *73*, **75**
Rijo FC	2, 1	**1924**, *25*, **27**
Yokohama Flugels	2, 1	**1993**, *97*, **98**
Nagoya Grampus Eight	2, 0	**1995, 99**
Yahata Steel	1, 3	*1956, 58*, **64†**, *65*
Shimizu S-Pulse	1, 2	*1998, 2000*, **01**
Nagoya Shukyu-dan	1, 1	**1922**, *23*
NKK	1, 1	**1981**, *86*
Yamaha Motors	1, 1	**1982**, *89*
All Keio Club	1, 0	**1935**
All Keio University	1, 0	**1952**
Astra Club	1, 0	**1923**
Keio Club	1, 0	**1932**
Kobe-Ichi Jr. Highschool Club	1, 0	**1927**
Matsushita	1, 0	**1990**
Tokyo Shukyu-dan	1, 0	**1921**
Osaka Club	0, 3	*1951–53*
All Mikage Shihan Club	0, 1	*1924*
Chudai Club	0, 1	*1955*
Eidai Industrial	0, 1	*1974*
Fusei Senmon	0, 1	*1936*
Hiroshima Koto-shihan	0, 1	*1922*
Housei University	0, 1	*1929*
Kobe Commercial University	0, 1	*1937*
Kobe Keizai-dai Club	0, 1	*1946*
Kobun Jr Highschool	0, 1	*1931*
Kyoto University	0, 1	*1928*
Mikage Shukyu-dan	0, 1	*1921*
Rikkyo University	0, 1	*1969*
Sendai Football Club	0, 1	*1933*
Tanabe Medecine	0, 1	*1980*
Yoshino Club	0, 1	*1932*

* Final score unknown.
† This year the title was tied, as extra time did not produce a champion.

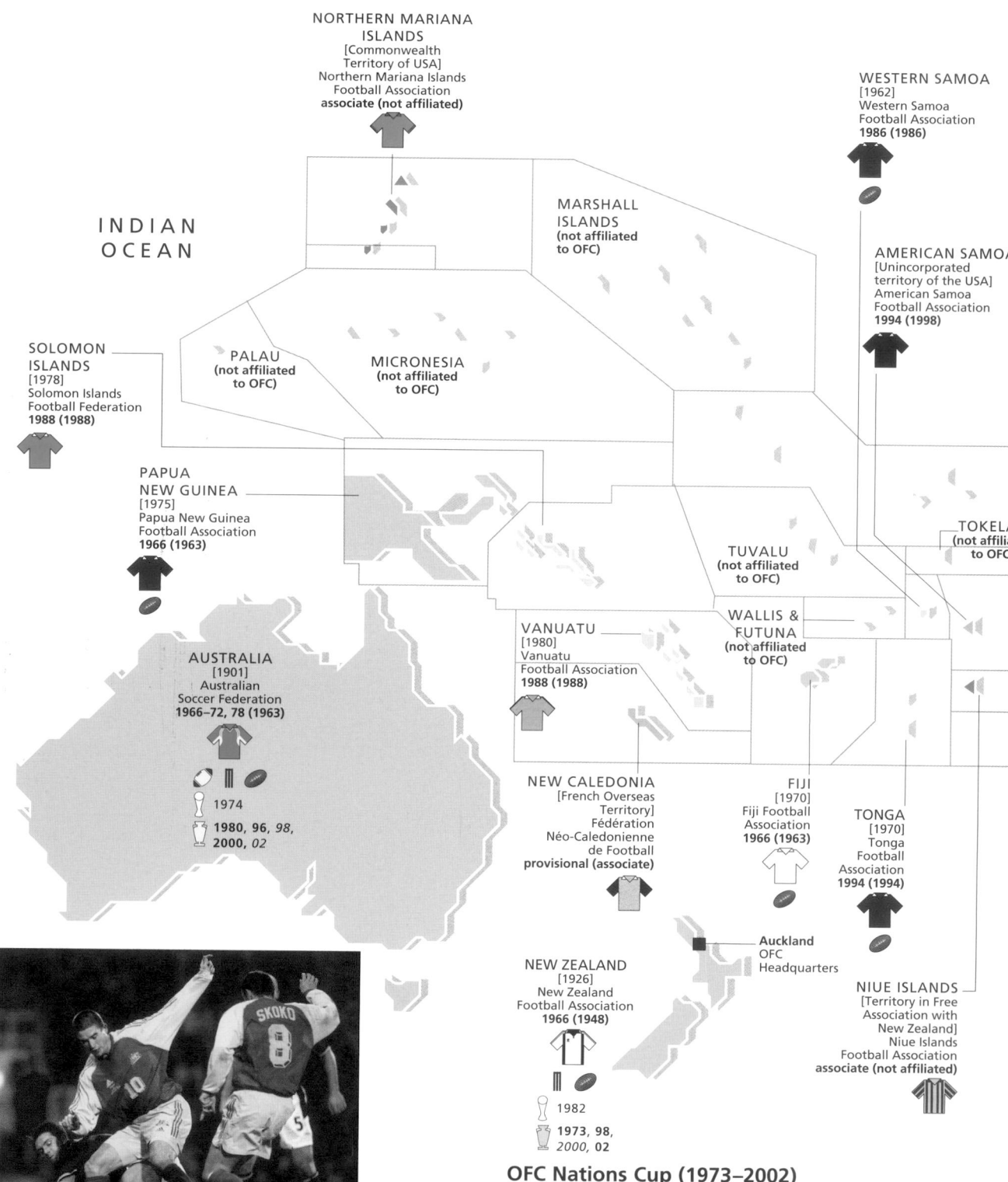

NORTHERN MARIANA ISLANDS
[Commonwealth Territory of USA]
Northern Mariana Islands Football Association
associate (not affiliated)

WESTERN SAMOA
[1962]
Western Samoa Football Association
1986 (1986)

INDIAN OCEAN

MARSHALL ISLANDS
(not affiliated to OFC)

AMERICAN SAMOA
[Unincorporated territory of the USA]
American Samoa Football Association
1994 (1998)

SOLOMON ISLANDS
[1978]
Solomon Islands Football Federation
1988 (1988)

PALAU
(not affiliated to OFC)

MICRONESIA
(not affiliated to OFC)

PAPUA NEW GUINEA
[1975]
Papua New Guinea Football Association
1966 (1963)

TOKELAU
(not affiliated to OFC)

TUVALU
(not affiliated to OFC)

WALLIS & FUTUNA
(not affiliated to OFC)

AUSTRALIA
[1901]
Australian Soccer Federation
1966–72, 78 (1963)

1974

1980, 96, 98, 2000, 02

VANUATU
[1980]
Vanuatu Football Association
1988 (1988)

NEW CALEDONIA
[French Overseas Territory]
Fédération Néo-Calédonienne de Football
provisional (associate)

FIJI
[1970]
Fiji Football Association
1966 (1963)

TONGA
[1970]
Tonga Football Association
1994 (1994)

Auckland
OFC Headquarters

NEW ZEALAND
[1926]
New Zealand Football Association
1966 (1948)

1982

1973, 98, 2000, 02

NIUE ISLANDS
[Territory in Free Association with New Zealand]
Niue Islands Football Association
associate (not affiliated)

1953 revisited: Australia defeated England for the first time ever at Upton Park in London in February 2003.

OFC Nations Cup (1973–2002)

YEAR	WINNERS	SCORE	RUNNERS-UP
1973	New Zealand	2-0	Tahiti
1980	Australia	4-2	Tahiti
1996	Australia	6-0, 5-0 (2 legs)	Tahiti
1998	New Zealand	1-0	Australia
2000	Australia	2-0	New Zealand
2002	New Zealand	1-0	Australia

The OFC Nations

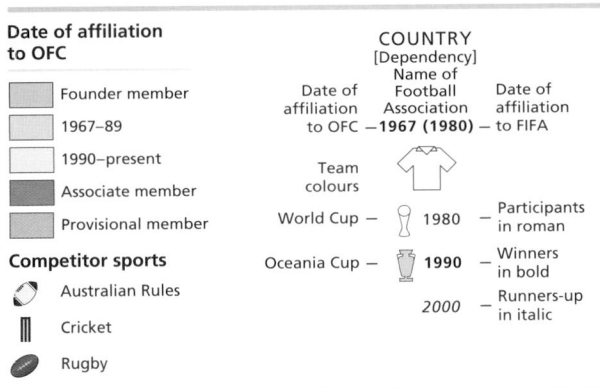

Date of affiliation to OFC

- Founder member
- 1967–89
- 1990–present
- Associate member
- Provisional member

Competitor sports

- Australian Rules
- Cricket
- Rugby

COUNTRY
[Dependency]
Name of
Football
Association

Date of
affiliation
to OFC — **1967 (1980)** — to FIFA

Date of
affiliation
to OFC

Team
colours

World Cup — 1980 — Participants in roman

Oceania Cup — **1990** — Winners in bold

2000 — Runners-up in italic

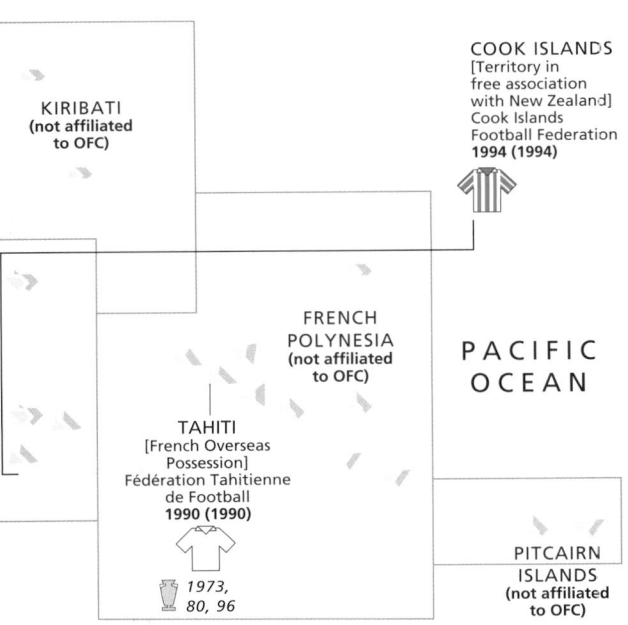

KIRIBATI
(not affiliated to OFC)

COOK ISLANDS
[Territory in free association with New Zealand]
Cook Islands Football Federation
1994 (1994)

FRENCH POLYNESIA
(not affiliated to OFC)

PACIFIC OCEAN

TAHITI
[French Overseas Possession]
Fédération Tahitienne de Football
1990 (1990)

1973, 80, 96

PITCAIRN ISLANDS
(not affiliated to OFC)

OFC

Oceania Tournaments and Cup Competitions:
Oceania Nations Cup
OFC Club Championship
Oceania Women's Tournament

The Development of Oceanian Football

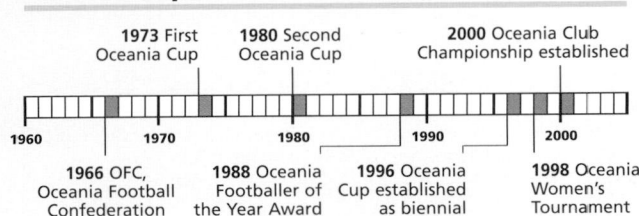

1973 First Oceania Cup

1980 Second Oceania Cup

2000 Oceania Club Championship established

1960   1970   1980   1990   2000

1966 OFC, Oceania Football Confederation founded

1988 Oceania Footballer of the Year Award established

1996 Oceania Cup established as biennial tournament

1998 Oceania Women's Tournament established

The OFC Nations

THE OFC (OCEANIA FOOTBALL CONFEDERATION) was the last of the world's football confederations to be formed. Hardly surprising given that in the major countries of the region rugby (union and league), Australian Rules and cricket have provided very stiff competition for football, as indeed they have in Fiji and the smaller Pacific societies. Prior to OFC's formation in 1966 Australia and others had played in Asian World Cup qualifiers.

OFC consists of Australia, New Zealand, Papua New Guinea and the island states, statelets, archipelagoes and dependencies of the vast Pacific Ocean. Football's organization and strengths in the region are very asymmetrical. The Oceania Games, the Oceania qualifying rounds of the World Cup, has been dominated by Australia, where postwar immigrant communities from Europe have given the game a huge boost. The relative weakness of the region's other clubs and leagues mean that no international club tournament is held. Australia sought to rejoin Asia in the 1970s given the paucity of local competition, but was refused. Since then Oceania's World Cup qualifiers have led to play-offs with UEFA and CONMEBOL sides.

Harry Kewell, Leeds and Australia striker, is just one of the many Australians playing in the English Premiership. Soccer Australia has established offices in London and is looking to play most national friendlies in England.

Calendar of Events	
Club Tournaments	OFC Club Championship 2004
International	OFC Nations Cup 2004
Tournaments	Qualifying Tournament for 2004 Olympic Games (Under–23s)

Oceania

FOOTBALL HAS ALWAYS STRUGGLED in Oceania, competing, especially in the most populated areas, with Australian Rules football and both rugby codes. Although a national FA was set up in Australia in 1882, football was only played at an amateur regional level. But its popularity was sustained and expanded by the new wave of European immigration to Australia in the mid-20th century – Italians, Hungarians, Croats and Greeks prominent among the soccer migrants and the names of the top clubs in the 1970s and 80s. In recent years the Australian Soccer Federation has encouraged more ethnically-neutral names in pursuit of the mainstream Australian sports dollar. A national league and a national cup competition were created in 1977. However, no team from Tasmania has ever been part of the league and it was nearly 23 years after starting that a team from Western Australia took part.

New Zealand's national league competition (although a split between leagues on each of the North and South Islands with a play-off between the winners for the national championship) dates from 1970s, and the main cup competition, the Chatham Cup (with a trophy donated by the Royal Navy ship HMS *Chatham*), has been played since 1923.

Australia

Australia Soccer Federation
Founded: 1961
Joined FIFA: 1963
Joined OFC: 1966–72, 1978

Australian League Record 1977–2002

SEASON	CHAMPIONS	RUNNERS-UP
1977	Sydney City	Marconi Fairfield
1978	West Adelaide	Sydney City
1979	Marconi Fairfield	Heidelberg United
1980	Sydney City	Heidelberg United
1981	Sydney City	South Melbourne
1982	Sydney City	Saint George
1983	Saint George	Sydney City
1984	South Melbourne	Sydney Olympic
1985	Brunswick	Sydney City
1986	Adelaide City	Sydney Olympic
1987	APIA Leichhardt	Preston
1988	Marconi Fairfield	Sydney Croatia
1989	Marconi Fairfield	Sydney Olympic
1990	Sydney Olympic	Marconi Fairfield
1991	South Melbourne	Melbourne Croatia
1992	Adelaide City	Melbourne Croatia
1993	Marconi Fairfield	Adelaide City
1994	Adelaide City	Melbourne Knights
1995	Melbourne Knights	Adelaide City
1996	Melbourne Knights	Marconi Fairfield
1997	Brisbane Strikers	Sydney United
1998	South Melbourne	Carlton
1999	South Melbourne	Sydney United
2000	Wollongong Wolves	Perth Glory
2001	Wollongong Wolves	South Melbourne
2002	Sydney Olympic Sharks	Perth Glory

Australian Cup Record 1977–1997

YEAR	WINNERS	SCORE	RUNNERS-UP
1977	Brisbane City	1-1 (aet)(5-3 pens)	Marconi Fairfield
1978	Brisbane City	2-1	Adelaide City
1979	Adelaide City	3-2	Saint George
1980	Marconi Fairfield	0-0, 3-0 (2 legs)	Heidelberg United
1981	Brisbane Lions	3-1	West Adelaide
1982	APIA Leichhardt	2-1	Heidelberg United
1983	Sydney Olympic	1-0, 1-0 (2 legs)	Heidelberg United
1984	Newcastle Rosebud	1-0	Melbourne Croatia
1985	Sydney Olympic	2-1	Preston
1986	Sydney City	3-2	West Adelaide
1987	Sydney Croatia	1-0, 1-0	South Melbourne
1988	APIA Leichhardt	0-0 (aet)(5-3 pens)	Brunswick
1989	Adelaide City	2-0	Sydney Olympic
1990	South Melbourne	4-1	Sydney Olympic
1991	Parramatta Eagles	1-0	Preston Macedonia
1992	Adelaide City	2-1	Marconi Fairfield
1993	Heidelberg United	2-1	Parramatta Eagles
1994	Parramatta Eagles	2-0	Sydney United
1995	Melbourne Knights	6-0	Heidelberg United
1996	South Melbourne	3-1	Newcastle Breakers
1997	Collingwood Warriors	1-0	Marconi Fairfield

New Zealand

NEW ZEALAND SOCCER

New Zealand Football Association
Founded: 1938
Joined FIFA: 1948
Joined OFC: 1966

New Zealand League Record 1970–2002

SEASON	CHAMPIONS	RUNNERS-UP
1970	Blockhouse Bay	Eastern Suburbs
1971	Eastern Suburbs	Mount Wellington
1972	Mount Wellington	Blockhouse Bay
1973	Christchurch United	Mount Wellington
1974	Mount Wellington	Christchurch United
1975	Christchurch United	North Shore United
1976	Wellington Diamond United	Mount Wellington
1977	North Shore United	Stop Out
1978	Christchurch United	Mount Wellington
1979	Mount Wellington	Christchurch United
1980	Mount Wellington	Gisborne City
1981	Wellington Diamond United	Dunedin City
1982	Mount Wellington	North Shore United
1983	Manurewa	North Shore United
1984	Gisborne City	Papatoetoe
1985	Wellington United	Gisborne City
1986	Mount Wellington	Miramar Rangers
1987	Christchurch United	Gisborne City
1988	Christchurch United	Mount Wellington
1989	Napier City Rovers	Mount Manganui
1990	Waitakere City	Mount Wellington
1991	Christchurch United	Miramar Rangers
1992	Waitakere City	Waikato United
1993	Napier City Rovers	Waitakere City
1994	North Shore United	Napier City Rovers
1995	Waitakere City	Waikato United
1996	Waitakere City	Miramar Rangers
1997	Waitakere City	Napier City Rovers
1998	Napier City Rovers	Central United
1999	Central United	Dunedin Technical
2000	Napier City Rovers	University Mount Wellington
2001	Central United	Miramar Rangers
2002	Miramar Rangers	Napier City Rovers

OCEANIA

New Zealand Cup Record 1986–2002

YEAR	WINNERS	SCORE	RUNNERS-UP
1986	North Shore United	0-1, 4-1 (2 legs)	Mount Manganui
1987	Gisborne City	5-1, 2-2 (2 legs)	Christchurch United
1988	Christchurch United	2-2, 1-1 (away goals)	Waikato United
1989	Christchurch United	7-1	Rotorua City
1990	Mount Wellington	3-3 (aet)(4-2 pens)	Christchurch United
1991	Christchurch United	2-1	Wellington United
1992	Miramar Rangers	3-1	Waikato United
1993	Napier City Rovers	6-0	Rangers
1994	Waitakere City	1-0	Wellington Olympic
1995	Waitakere City	4-0	North Shore United
1996	Waitakere City	3-1	Mount Wellington
1997	Central United	3-2 (aet)	Napier City Rovers
1998	Central United	5-0	Dunedin Technical
1999	Dunedin Technical	4-0	Waitakere City
2000	Napier City Rovers	4-1	Central United
2001	University Mount Wellington	3-3 (5-4 pens)	Central United
2002	Napier City Rovers	2-0	Tauranga City United

American Samoa

American Samoa Football Association
Founded: 1971
Joined FIFA: 1998
Joined OFC: 1994

SEASON	LEAGUE CHAMPIONS
1998	*unknown*
1999	Konika Machine FC
2000	Wild Wild West
2001	PanSa Soccer Club
2002	PanSa Soccer Club

Cook Islands

Cook Islands Football Federation
Founded: 1971
Joined FIFA: 1994
Joined OFC: 1994

SEASON	LEAGUE CHAMPIONS
1999	Tupapa FC
2000	Avatiu FC
2001	Sokattack Nikao
2002	Tupapa FC
2003	Tupapa FC

YEAR	CUP WINNERS
1999	Tupapa FC
2000	Tupapa FC
2001	Avatiu FC
2002	Tupapa FC
2003	Niaho

Fiji

Fiji Football Association
Founded: 1938
Joined FIFA: 1963
Joined OFC: 1966

SEASON	LEAGUE CHAMPIONS
1998	Nadi
1999	Ba
2000	Nadi
2001	Ba
2002	Ba

YEAR	CUP WINNERS
1998	Nadi
1999	Nadi
2000	Ba
2001	Rewa
2002	Nadi

New Caledonia

Fédération Néo-Caledonienne de Football
Founded: 1960
Joined FIFA: 1966
Provisional member only

SEASON	LEAGUE CHAMPIONS
1998	AS Poum
1999	FC Gaitcha
2000	JS Baco
2001	JS Baco
2002	JS Baco

New Caledonia *(continued)*

YEAR	CUP WINNERS
1998	JS Traput
1999	JS Traput
2000	AS Magenta
2001	AS Magenta
2002	AS Magenta

Papua New Guinea

Papua New Guinea Football Asociation
Founded: 1962
Joined FIFA: 1963
Joined OFC: 1966

SEASON	LEAGUE CHAMPIONS
1998	ICF University
1999	Guria
2000	Unitech
2001	Sobou Lae
2002	Sobou Lae

Solomon Islands

Solomon Islands Football Federation
Founded: 1988
Joined FIFA: 1988
Joined OFC: 1988

SEASON	LEAGUE CHAMPIONS
1998	Malaita Eagles FC
1999	*unknown*
2000	Lauga United
2001	Koloale
2002	*unknown*

Tahiti

Fédération Tahitienne de Football
Founded: 1938
Joined FIFA: 1990
Joined OFC: 1990

SEASON	LEAGUE CHAMPIONS
1998	AS Vénus
1999	AS Vénus
2000	AS Vénus
2001	AS Pirae
2002	AS Vénus

YEAR	CUP WINNERS
1998	AS Vénus
1999	AS Vénus
2000	AS Pirae
2001	AS Dragon
2002	AS Pirae

Tonga

Tonga Football Association
Founded: 1965
Joined FIFA: 1994
Joined OFC: 1994

SEASON	LEAGUE CHAMPIONS
1998	SC Lotoha'apai
1999	SC Lotoha'apai
2000	SC Lotoha'apai
2001	SC Lotoha'apai
2001	SC Lotoha'apai

Vanuatu

Vanuatu Football Association
Founded: 1934
Joined FIFA: 1988
Joined OFC: 1988

SEASON	LEAGUE CHAMPIONS
1998	Tafea FC
1999	Tafea FC
2000	Tafea FC
2001	Fara
2002	Tupuji Imere

Western Samoa

Western Samoa Football Association
Founded: 1968
Joined FIFA: 1986
Joined OFC: 1986

SEASON	LEAGUE CHAMPIONS
1998	Vaivase-tai
1999	Moata'a
2000	Titavi FC
2001	Gold Star
2002	Strickland Brothers

YEAR	CUP WINNERS
1998	Togafuafua
1999	Moaula
2000	Sogi
2001	Strickland Brothers
2002	Vaivase-tai

OCEANIA

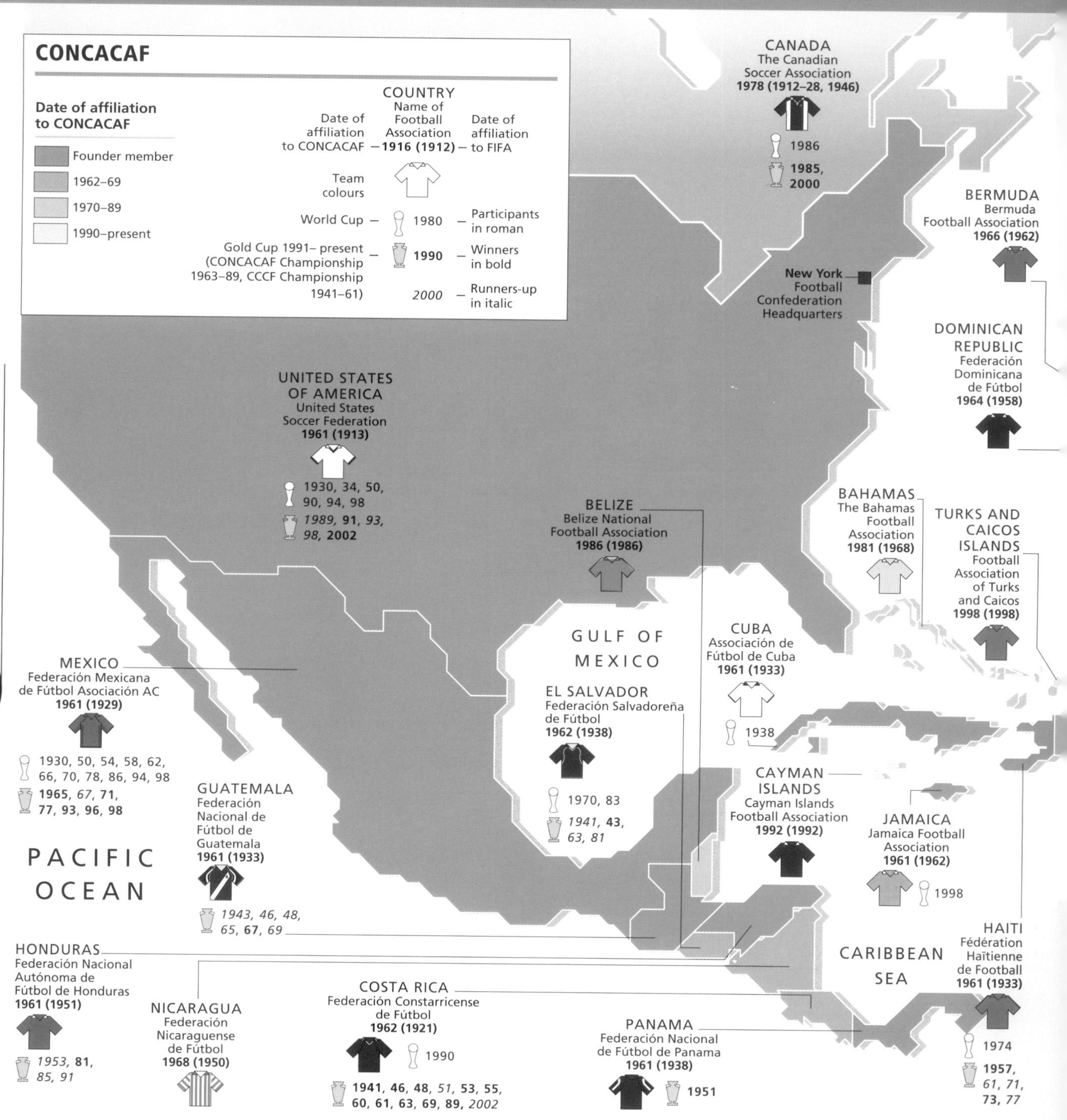

CONCACAF

Date of affiliation to CONCACAF

- Founder member
- 1962–69
- 1970–89
- 1990–present

COUNTRY
Name of
Football
Association
Date of
affiliation — **1916 (1912)** — Date of
to CONCACAF   affiliation
to FIFA

Team colours

World Cup — 1980 — Participants in roman

Gold Cup 1991– present
(CONCACAF Championship
1963–89, CCCF Championship
1941–61)

1990 — Winners in bold

2000 — Runners-up in italic

CANADA
The Canadian
Soccer Association
1978 (1912–28, 1946)

1986
1985, 2000

BERMUDA
Bermuda
Football Association
1966 (1962)

New York
Football
Confederation
Headquarters

DOMINICAN REPUBLIC
Federación
Dominicana
de Fútbol
1964 (1958)

UNITED STATES OF AMERICA
United States
Soccer Federation
1961 (1913)

1930, 34, 50, 90, 94, 98
1989, **91**, *93, 98*, **2002**

BELIZE
Belize National
Football Association
1986 (1986)

BAHAMAS
The Bahamas
Football
Association
1981 (1968)

TURKS AND CAICOS ISLANDS
Football
Association
of Turks
and Caicos
1998 (1998)

GULF OF MEXICO

CUBA
Asociación de
Fútbol de Cuba
1961 (1933)

1938

MEXICO
Federación Mexicana
de Fútbol Asociación AC
1961 (1929)

1930, 50, 54, 58, 62, 66, 70, 78, 86, 94, 98
1965, *67*, **71**, *77*, **93**, *96*, **98**

EL SALVADOR
Federación Salvadoreña
de Fútbol
1962 (1938)

1970, 83
1941, **43**, *63, 81*

CAYMAN ISLANDS
Cayman Islands
Football Association
1992 (1992)

JAMAICA
Jamaica Football
Association
1961 (1962)

1998

GUATEMALA
Federación
Nacional de
Fútbol de
Guatemala
1961 (1933)

1943, 46, 48, **65**, *67, 69*

PACIFIC OCEAN

HAITI
Fédération
Haïtienne
de Football
1961 (1933)

CARIBBEAN SEA

1974
1957, *61, 71, 73, 77*

HONDURAS
Federación Nacional
Autónoma de
Fútbol de Honduras
1961 (1951)

1953, **81**, *85, 91*

NICARAGUA
Federación
Nicaraguense
de Fútbol
1968 (1950)

COSTA RICA
Federación Constarricense
de Fútbol
1962 (1921)

1990

1941, 46, 48, **51**, *53, 55, 60, 61*, **63**, *69, 89, 2002*

PANAMA
Federación Nacional
de Fútbol de Panama
1961 (1938)

1951

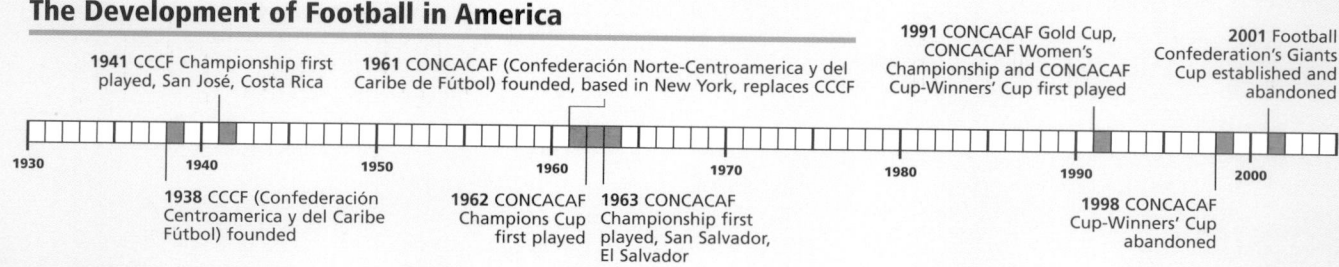

The Development of Football in America

1941 CCCF Championship first
played, San José, Costa Rica

1961 CONCACAF (Confederación Norte-Centroamerica y del
Caribe de Fútbol) founded, based in New York, replaces CCCF

1991 CONCACAF Gold Cup,
CONCACAF Women's
Championship and CONCACAF
Cup-Winners' Cup first played

2001 Football
Confederation's Giants
Cup established and
abandoned

1930   1940   1950   1960   1970   1980   1990   2000

1938 CCCF (Confederación
Centroamerica y del Caribe
Fútbol) founded

1962 CONCACAF
Champions Cup
first played

1963 CONCACAF
Championship first
played, San Salvador,
El Salvador

1998 CONCACAF
Cup-Winners' Cup
abandoned

The CONCACAF Nations

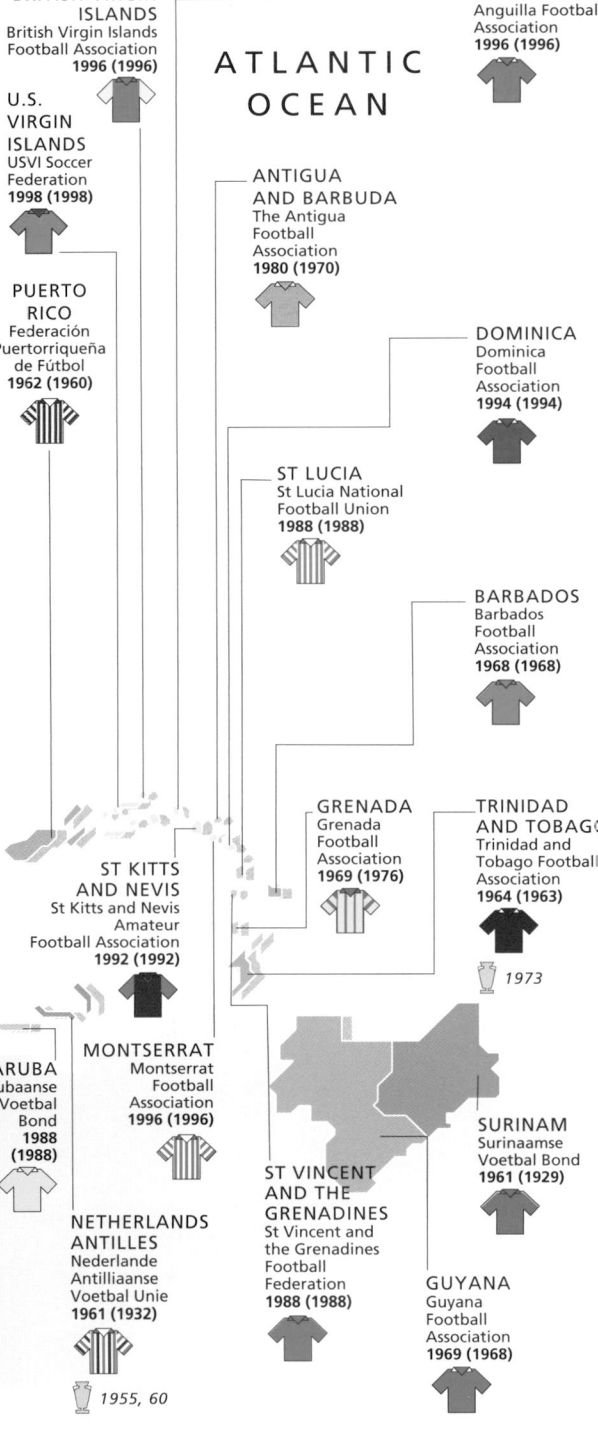

BRITISH VIRGIN ISLANDS
British Virgin Islands Football Association
1996 (1996)

ATLANTIC OCEAN

ANGUILLA
Anguilla Football Association
1996 (1996)

U.S. VIRGIN ISLANDS
USVI Soccer Federation
1998 (1998)

ANTIGUA AND BARBUDA
The Antigua Football Association
1980 (1970)

PUERTO RICO
Federación Puertorriqueña de Fútbol
1962 (1960)

DOMINICA
Dominica Football Association
1994 (1994)

ST LUCIA
St Lucia National Football Union
1988 (1988)

BARBADOS
Barbados Football Association
1968 (1968)

GRENADA
Grenada Football Association
1969 (1976)

TRINIDAD AND TOBAGO
Trinidad and Tobago Football Association
1964 (1963)

1973

ST KITTS AND NEVIS
St Kitts and Nevis Amateur Football Association
1992 (1992)

ARUBA
Arubaanse Voetbal Bond
1988 (1988)

MONTSERRAT
Montserrat Football Association
1996 (1996)

SURINAM
Surinaamse Voetbal Bond
1961 (1929)

NETHERLANDS ANTILLES
Nederlande Antilliaanse Voetbal Unie
1961 (1932)

ST VINCENT AND THE GRENADINES
St Vincent and the Grenadines Football Federation
1988 (1988)

GUYANA
Guyana Football Association
1969 (1968)

1955, 60

CONCACAF

North and Central American Tournaments and Cup Competitions:
CONCACAF Gold Cup
CONCACAF Women's Gold Cup
CONCACAF Champions Cup

THE ORGANIZATION OF FOOTBALL in North and Central America reflects the basic divisions and conflicts of the region. North America (USA and Canada) is on a different sporting and economic plane from the rest of the region. Mexico remains the singular dominant footballing power in the area, unsure whether to remain a big fish in a small pool or take a chance by joining the stronger footballing nations of South America.

Before the Second World War these divisions were reflected in the formation of both CCCF (Confederación Centroamerica y del Caribe de Fútbol) in 1938, made up of Central American and Caribbean nations, and NAFC (North American Football Confederation) in 1939, made up of Mexico, USA and Cuba. The NAFC held only two tournaments and its influence as a governing body dwindled. CCCF, without either Mexico or the USA, remained marginal.

In 1961 CONCACAF (Confederación Norte-Centroamerica y del Caribe de Fútbol) was created out of these former federations and was initially based in Guatemala City.

Over the last few decades one of CONCACAF's central missions has been to raise the profile of football in the USA in the hope of providing competition for Mexico and a steady flow of interest and money into the region's rather weak and one-sided international club competitions. As such CONCACAF was transformed into the more Anglo-sounding Football Confederation, its headquarters moved to New York and its regional tournament has been renamed the Gold Cup. It has now reverted to being called CONCACAF.

While the US has now both a stable professional league and held the 1994 World Cup, Mexican clubs have migrated south to CONMEBOL's Copa Libertadores. In response, the Football Confederation has abandoned some of its tournaments and joined with CONMEBOL to create the Copa Pan-Americana.

A member of the CONCACAF executive since 1990, Chuck Blazer, now General Secretary, has been the power behind the non-stop merry-go-round of ever-changing tournament formats.

Calendar of Events

Club Tournaments	CONCACAF Champions Cup 2004
International Tournaments	CONCACAF Gold Cup 2004
	Qualifying Tournament for 2004 Olympic Games (Under–23s)

CONCACAF

THE SEASONS IN REVIEW 2002, 2002–03

SO, AFTER THREE YEARS OF TRYING to convince the world to call them the Football Confederation, CONCACAF has gone back to its old name. Its not pretty, but it is a geographically accurate description of this sprawling football empire. The 2002 World Cup was a good one for the region – with the USA-Mexico clash in the second round seeing the Americans progress to a quarter-final match with Germany. Costa Rica, the region's third team, didn't make it out of the group stage but the team was good enough to give Brazil and Turkey a fright and played some very entertaining football. CONCACAF has been arguing incessantly ever since for an additional spot at the 2006 World Cup.

However, the organisation of football at a continental level remains beset by problems. The USA might have made it to the quarter-finals of the World Cup, but the standard of football in the MLS remains depressingly low, and the level of public interest in the professional game is not much higher. The Gold Cup – the region's international tournament – is to be held in the USA again this year, as is the rescheduled Women's World Cup Final – but it seems that no amount of exposure to international tournaments can make most Americans get it.

Mexican football dominates

The weakness of football in the US contrasts with the strength of Mexican football. Once again the main international club tournament – the CONCACAF Champions Cup – has been dominated by Mexican teams, who filled all four of the semi-final slots; none of their quarter-final opponents – Los Angeles Galaxy, Columbus Crew, Honduran team Municipal or Costa Rica's Alajuelense – looked like beating them. The Toluca-America game was the pick of the ties, with Toluca only sneaking through with a golden goal in extra time. Morelia, last year's losing finalists, held Necaxa to a goalless draw in Mexico City before demolishing them 6-0 at home. The Final, however, will have to await the conclusion of the Mexican season and the Gold Cup and is planned for some time in the autumn. More importantly for Mexican clubs is their continued participation in CONMEBOL's Copa Libertadores.

Away from the international stage, the season saw domestic victories for some regular suspects: Alajuelense in Costa Rica won its 29th national championship, Comunicaciones won in Guatemala and Villa Clara in Cuba, known as Naranja Mecanica or Clockwork Orange, won its ninth national title. Hazard United was the surprise winners in Jamaica, defeating the previously invincible Arnett Gardens, while Marathon won its first national title in Honduras for 18 years.

Top 12 CONCACAF Leagues

COUNTRY	CHAMPIONS	RUNNERS-UP
Belize*	Cayo Highlanders	New Site Erei
Costa Rica – Apertura	Alajuelense	Saprissa
Costa Rica – Clausura	Alajuelense	Cartagines
Costa Rica – National Championship	Alajuelense	
El Salvador – Apertura	CD Fas	San Salvador FC
EL Salvador – Clausura	San Salvador FC	Firpo
Guatemala – Apertura	Comunicaciones	Municipal
Guatemala – Clausura	Comunicaciones	Coban Imperial
Haiti – Ouverture	Roulado	Aigle Noir
Haiti – Clôture	Racing Club Haïtien	Aigle Noir
Honduras – Apertura	Olimpia	Platense
Honduras – Clausura	Marathon	Mantagua
Jamaica	Hazard United	Arnett Gardens
Mexico – Winter	Toluca	Atletico Morelia
Mexico – Summer	Monterrey	Morelia
Nicaragua	Esteli	Diriangen
Panama – Apertura	Deportivo Árabe Unido	San Francisco FC
Panama – Clausura	Plaza Amador	Tauro FC
Panama – National Championship	Plaza Amador	Deportivo Árabe Unido
Trinidad and Tobago	San Juan Jabloteh	W Communication
USA	Los Angeles Galaxy	New England Revolution

* Top teams have withdrawn from the Belize FA to form a pirate league but it is not recognised by CONCACAF.

Above: Cobi Jones of the Los Angeles Galaxy holds the MLS trophy after the team's narrow victory over New England Revolution.

Top: Bruce Arena, coach of the USA national team, wonders just how far he must get through a World Cup before the nation notices.

CONCACAF
Champions League

2002–03
SEMI-FINALS (2 legs)

April 30 – Estadio Mexico 70, Toluca
CD Toluca 1-4 América
(Mexico) (Mexico)
(Lozano 28) (Lipatin 34, 62,
Mariscal 56,
Blanco 83)
h/t: 1-1 **Att :** 8,000
Ref: Gasso (Mexico)

May 14 – Azteca, Mexico City
América 0-4 CD Toluca
(Espinoza 69,
Garcia 72, 88,
Ruiz 92 gg)
h/t: 0-0
Ref: Rodríguez (Mexico)

CD Toluca won on golden goal

April 30 – Estadio Municipale de
Aguascalientes, Necaxa
CD Necaxa 0-0 Monarcas
(Mexico) **Morelia**
(Mexico)
h/t: 0-0
Ref: Alcala (Mexico)

May 7 – Estadio Maria Morelos, Morelia
Monarcas 6-0 CD Necaxa
Morelia
(Navia 9, 21,
Palacios 28,
Hernandez 38,
Almiron 42,
Prieto 77)
h/t: 5-0
Ref: Archundia (Mexico)

Monarcas Morelia won
6-0 on aggregate

Final to be played Autumn 2003

The final day of the Honduran Apertura saw Platense (in white) beat leaders Olimpia (in red and blue). But 1-0 was not enough and Olimpia took the title.

Right: Sasha Victorine (LA Galaxy) and Steve Ralston (New England Revolution) collide in the MLS Final 2002.

Below: Alajuelense not only did the double in Costa Rica, but also celebrates here after winning the Central American Club Cup, thumping Honduras' Montagua 4-0.

Los Angeles Galaxy's Carlos Llamosa and New England Revolution Alejandro Moreno scrap for the ball in the MLS Final.

NORTH & CENTRAL AMERICA AND THE CARIBBEAN

Soccer is not new to North America having been played there since the 1870s. It thrived during the 1920s, especially in New England, with teams such as the Fall River Marksmen (in stripes) and Bethlehem Steel drawing big crowds and generating widespread interest in the game.

CANADA
[1867]
The Canadian
Soccer Association
1912 (1961)

**UNITED STATES
OF AMERICA**
[1776]
United States
Soccer Federation
1913 (1967/8)

Washington DC ●

**DOMINICAN
REPUBLIC**
[1865]
Federación
Dominicana
de Fútbol
1953 (1991)

BAHAMAS
[1973]
The Bahamas
Football Association
1967 (1996)

**CAYMAN
ISLANDS**
[British dependent
territory]
Cayman Islands
Football Association
1966 (1996)

GULF OF
MEXICO

CUBA
[1901]
Associación de
Fútbol de Cuba
1924 (1912)

MEXICO
[1836]
Federación Mexicana
de Fútbol Asociación AC
1927 (1941)

JAMAICA
[1962]
Jamaica Football
Association
1910 (1974)

PACIFIC
OCEAN

Guadalajara ●

CARIBBEAN
SEA

Kingston

**TURKS AND
CAICOS ISLANDS**
[British Crown Colony]
Football Association
of Turks and Caicos
1996 (1999)

● Mexico
City

Guatemala
City ●

Tegucigalpa ●

San ●
Salvador

Alajuela ●

● San
José

The top 15 teams in North & Central America and the Caribbean

 **Alajuelense**
Costa Rica
Alajuela
1919

 DC United
USA
Washington DC
1996

 Joe Public FC
Trinidad
Port of Spain
1996

Alianza FC
El Salvador
San Salvador
1959

 **Cruz Azul**
Mexico
Mexico City
1927

 Necaxa
Mexico
Mexico City
1923

América
Mexico
Mexico City
1916

Comunicaciones
Guatemala
Guatemala City
1939

Robin Hood
Surinam
Paramaribo
not known

 **Atlante**
Mexico
Mexico City
1916

 CSD Municipal
Guatemala
Guatemala City
1936

 Santos
Jamaica
Kingston
not known

Olimpia
Honduras
Tegucigalpa
1926

 Guadalajara
Mexico
Guadalajara
1906

 Saprissa
Costa Rica
San José
1935

 BELIZE
[1981]
Belize National
Football Association
1980 (1991)

GUATEMALA
[1838]
Federación Nacional de
Fútbol de Guatemala
1919 (1926)

EL SALVADOR
[1841]
Federación
Salvadoreña
de Fútbol
1935 (1972)

HONDURAS
[1838]
Federación Nacional
Autónoma de
Fútbol de Honduras
1951 (1965)

NICARAGUA
[1838]
Federación
Nicaraguense
de Fútbol
1931 (1963)

COSTA RICA
[1838]
Federación
Constarricense
de Fútbol
1921 (1921)

The CONCACAF Nations

COUNTRY
[date of independence]
Name of national
Football
Foundation   Association   Foundation of
of national FA — **1916 (1912)**— national league

North & Central America and the Caribbean

ORIGINS AND GROWTH OF FOOTBALL

IN NORTH AMERICA and the Caribbean the question remains: why has football developed in such a limited way? It was played in the USA through colleges and universities, in particular in the 1870s, but it soon fell behind in popularity to American football and baseball. The main areas of football strength were the New England industrial towns, New York, Los Angeles and St Louis.

However, for the most part football remained a game played by recent immigrants (Hispanic and European). Even when it did prosper (a professional national league ran through the 1920s and the USA made the semi-finals of the 1930 World Cup) the game was plagued by conflicts between professionals and amateurs, splits among the various leagues and, with the depression of the 1930s, the economic decimation of its main areas of support. The relative failure of men's football left open space in which American women's football could prosper in the 1970s. In Canada, Scottish immigrants led to the establishment of football in the 1880s, but again with little success.

The success of baseball within the USA was repeated all over the region. US military forces brought the game to Cuba, Nicaragua, Panama, Puerto Rico and the Dominican Republic. In Venezuela, baseball arrived with the US oil industry, which practically ran the country in the early years of the 20th century. In the Caribbean, cricket's popularity always restricted the growth of football (as the popularity of basketball does today). Only in Mexico (and later in Guatemala, Costa Rica, El Salvador and Honduras) has football truly prospered, introduced in the late 19th century by both British and Spanish expatriates.

ATLANTIC OCEAN

BERMUDA
[Self-governing British Crown colony]
Bermuda Football Association
1928 (1996)

ANTIGUA & BARBUDA
[1981]
The Antigua Football Association
1928 (1963)

BRITISH VIRGIN ISLANDS
[British dependent territory]
British Virgin Islands Football Association
1974 (1996)

ANGUILLA
[British dependent territory]
Anguilla Football Association
1990 (1996)

DOMINICA
[1973]
Dominica Football Association
1970 (1990)

U.S. VIRGIN ISLANDS
[Unincorporated territory of the USA]
USVI Soccer Federation
1998 (1999)

ST LUCIA
[1979]
St Lucia National Football Union
1979 (1980)

PUERTO RICO
[Commonwealth territory of the USA]
Federación Puertorriqueña de Fútbol
1940 (1990)

BARBADOS
[1966]
Barbados Football Association
1910 (1980)

ARUBA
[Dutch territory, self-governing 1986]
Arubaanse Voetbal Bond
1932 (1996)

GRENADA
[1974]
Grenada Football Association
1924 (1997)

TRINIDAD & TOBAGO
[1962]
Trinidad and Tobago Football Association
1908 (1990)

HAITI
[1804]
Féderation Haïtienne de Football
1904 (1937)

Port of Spain

Paramaribo

MONTSERRAT
[British dependent territory]
Montserrat Football Association
n/a (2000)

NETHERLANDS ANTILLES
[Autonomous part of the Netherlands]
Netherlands Antilaanse Voetbal Unie
1921 (1985)

ST KITTS & NEVIS
[1983]
St Kitts and Nevis Amateur Football Association
1932 (n\a)

ST VINCENT & THE GRENADINES
[1979]
St Vincent and Grenadines Football Federation
1979 (1997)

SURINAM
[1975]
Surinaamse Voetbal Bond
1920 (1950)

PANAMA
[1903]
Federación Nacional de Fútbol de Panamá
1937 (1988)

GUYANA
[1966]
Guyana Football Association
1902 (1990)

North & Central America and the Caribbean Origins

Date of formation of national Football Association

	By 1899
	1900–39
	1940–79
	After 1980

Competitor sports

American football
Baseball
Basketball
Cricket
Ice hockey

The CONCACAF and Gold Cups

TOURNAMENT OVERVIEW

THE FIRST INTERNATIONAL football tournament in the region was held as part of a local Olympic tournament in Havana in 1930. The organizing committee held two further games in 1935 and 1938 from which came the idea of an independent football tournament and organization. CCCF (Confederacion Centroamericano y del Caribe de Futbol) was set up in 1938 and held its first tournament in Costa Rica in 1941. The tournament's profile remained low for the next 30 years: the cost of participation was too high for most of the Caribbean teams, making it an exclusively Central American affair. The region's main football power, Mexico, did not participate, throwing its lot in with the US and Cuba in the North American Football Confederation.

This division was finally overcome with the formation of CONCACAF in 1963, which embraced the whole of the Americas outside CONMEBOL, and the first CONCACAF championship was held the same year. Low participation rates led to the 1973, 1977, 1981, 1985 and 1989 tournaments serving as qualifiers for the World Cups, but to no avail. With the accession of Trinidadian Chuck Blazer to the presidency of CONCACAF in 1991, the tournament was relaunched and rebranded as the Gold Cup. The name, designed to be more recognizable in the American market, was accompanied by increased sponsorship, invitations to Asian and South American teams and the promise of more tournaments hosted by the US.

THE CONCACAF AND GOLD CUPS

The CONCACAF Championships and the Gold Cup

Participation in the tournament 1963–2002

- 7+ times
- 5–6 times
- 3–4 times
- 1–2 times
- 0 times

Winners, runners-up and third place with date

1993   1993   1993

1993*   Third place tie

World Cup qualifiers 1973–89

1967   date

Host country, with date in stadium and number of participants in brackets

COSTA RICA

1969
(6)

The CONCACAF Championships 1963–89

MEXICO

1977   1967   1965, 71

Nations invited to the Gold Cup 1991–2002

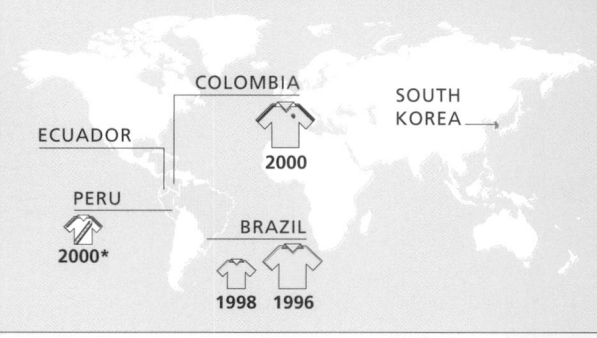

COLOMBIA
SOUTH KOREA
ECUADOR
2000
PERU
BRAZIL
2000*
1998   1996

The Gold Cup 1991–2002

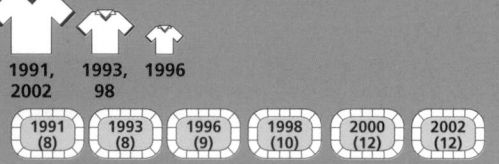

CANADA
2000   2002

UNITED STATES OF AMERICA

1991, 2002   1993, 98   1996

1991 (8)   1993 (8)   1996 (9)   1998 (10)   2000 (12)   2002 (12)

ATLANTIC OCEAN

PACIFIC OCEAN

MEXICO
1993, 96, 98   1991
1993 (8)

GULF OF MEXICO

GUATEMALA
EL SALVADOR
COSTA RICA
2002   1993*

HAITI
CUBA
JAMAICA
1993*
HONDURAS
1991
PANAMA

CARIBBEAN SEA

MARTINIQUE
ST VINCENT AND THE GRENADINES

TRINIDAD & TOBAGO
2000*

Cobi Jones (left) and Frankie Hejduk of the US men's national soccer team hold up the 2002 Gold Cup trophy after the 2-0 victory in the Final against Costa Rica at the Rose Bowl, Pasadena, California.

THE CONCACAF AND GOLD CUPS

CANADA
1985

UNITED STATES
OF AMERICA

ATLANTIC OCEAN

GUATEMALA

1967   **1965, 69**
1965 (6)

GULF OF MEXICO

CUBA

JAMAICA

HAITI
1971   **1973**

NETHERLANDS ANTILLES
1963, 69

1971 (6)
TRINIDAD & TOBAGO

HONDURAS
1981   **1967**
1967, 81 (6)

CARIBBEAN SEA

SURINAM

NICARAGUA

PANAMA

EL SALVADOR
1963   **1963 (9)**

COSTA RICA
1963, 69   **1965, 71**   **1989**
1969 (6)

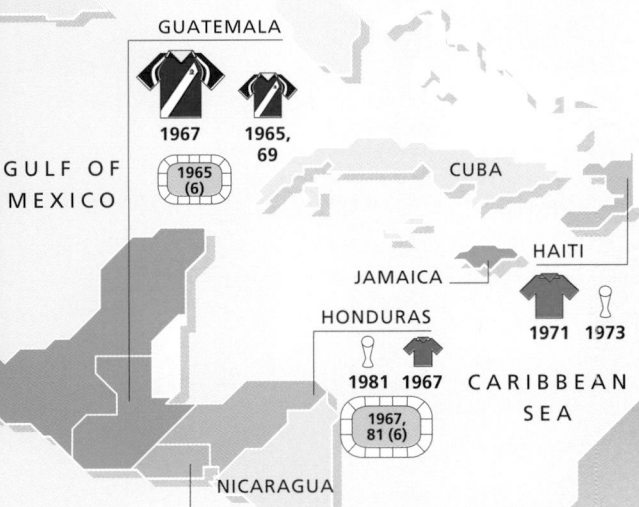

The Gold Cup 1991–2002

YEAR	WINNERS	SCORE	RUNNERS-UP
1991	USA	0-0 (4-3 pens)	Honduras
1993	Mexico	4-0	USA
1996	Mexico	2-0	Brazil
1998	Mexico	1-0	USA
2000	Canada	2-0	Colombia
2002	USA	2-0	Costa Rica

Mexico's three Gold Cup victories came in consecutive tournaments in the 1990s. In 1996, the Mexicans beat favourites Brazil, 2-0. Here, Villa and Davino combine to stop Caio's progress through midfield.

USA

THE SEASON IN REVIEW 2002

IN THE WAKE OF the national team's extraordinary progress to the World Cup quarter-finals, American soccer players finally made it to the David Letterman show. Admittedly they appeared more as curiosities than sporting heroes, but for a minor sport this was serious coverage. Domestic football, which continued throughout the World Cup, appeared in a state of retrenchment rather than expansion with the league shrinking from 12 teams to ten. MLS lost the disbanded Tampa Bay Mutiny and Miami Fusion, and three four-team divisions were converted into two five-team conferences. Perhaps more worryingly, the loss of two more rich and independent backers with the Florida franchises left telecom billionaire Phil Anschutz in control of six out of ten of the remaining clubs as well the company who owns the TV rights to MLS.

Ruiz grabs the winner

All ten were teams in contention for the eight play-off spots until almost the final matches. DC United didn't make the cut while the New York/New Jersey MetroStars contrived to lose their last three games and drop from the top to the bottom of the Eastern Conference. The championship decider pitched two Anschutz clubs against each other: Los Angeles Galaxy and New England Revolution, the latter revived by interim coach Steve Nicol. In a game billed as a clash between the MLS's top scorers, Galaxy's Carlos Ruiz and New England's Taylor Twellman, 61,000 fans saw almost 120 goalless minutes of tight organized defensive football saved from the ignominy of penalties by a sudden Galaxy counter-attack that saw Ruiz grab the winner.

Above: Another day, another franchise. Telecommunications billionaire Philip Anschutz increased his investment in MLS teams this season. Anschutz now owns half the clubs in the top flight.

Opposite, top left: El Pescaditio – the little fish – Guatemalan striker Carlos Ruiz leads the line for Los Angeles Galaxy, scoring 24 goals in the main season.

Opposite, top middle: Taylor Twellman (New England Revolution) (l) battles with Los Angeles Galaxy's Danny Califf (c) and Sasha Victorine (r).

Opposite, top right: Steve Nicol, ex-Liverpool and Scotland defender, became New England's coach early in the season and guided them to the Championship Final.

Major League Soccer 2002 – Final Table

CLUB	P	W	D	L	F	A	Pts	
Los Angeles Galaxy	28	13/3	3	6/3	44	33	51	Qualified for Play-offs
San Jose Earthquakes	28	13/1	3	11/0	45	35	45	Qualified for Play-offs
Dallas Burn	28	9/3	7	9/0	44	43	43	Qualified for Play-offs
Colorado Rapids	28	12/1	4	10/1	43	48	43	Qualified for Play-offs
New England Revolution	28	12/0	2	13/1	49	49	38	Qualified for Play-offs
Columbus Crew	28	10/1	5	9/3	44	43	38	Qualified for Play-offs
Chicago Fire	28	9/2	4	12/1	43	38	37	Qualified for Play-offs
Kansas City Wizards	28	9/0	9	8/2	37	45	36	Qualified for Play-offs
NY/NJ MetroStars	28	10/1	2	14/1	41	47	35	
DC United	28	7/2	5	12/2	31	40	32	

Top Goalscorers 2002

PLAYER	CLUB	GOALS
Carlos Ruiz	Los Angeles Galaxy	23
Taylor Twellman	New England Revolution	22
Jeff Cunningham	Columbus Crew	15

International Performances 2002

CLUB	COMPETITION	PROGRESS
DC United	FC Champions Cup	1st Round
Kansas City Wizards	FC Champions Cup	Semi-finals
San Jose Earthquakes	FC Champions Cup	Quarter-finals
Chicago Fire	FC Champions Cup	Quarter-finals

2002 Play-offs

QUARTER-FINALS (*3 legs)

* Three legs played unless one team wins both the first two legs

Dallas Burn **4-2** Colorado Rapids
San Jose Earthquakes **1-2** Columbus Crew
Los Angeles Galaxy **3-2** Kansas City Wizards (asdet)
New England Revolution **2-0** Chicago Fire
Columbus Crew **2-1** San Jose Earthquakes
Kansas City Wizards **4-1** Los Angeles Galaxy
Colorado Rapids **1-0** Dallas Burn
Chicago Fire **2-1** New England Revolution
New England Revolution **2-0** Chicago Fire
Dallas Burn **1-2** Colorado Rapids
Los Angeles Galaxy **5-2** Kansas City Wizards

SEMI-FINALS (*3 legs)

Los Angeles **4-0** Colorado Galaxy Rapids
New England **0-0** Columbus Crew Revolution
Columbus Crew **0-1** New England Revolution
Colorado **0-1** Los Angeles Rapids Galaxy
New England **2-0** Columbus Crew Revolution

MLS Championship

2002 FINAL

October 20 – Gillette Stadium, Foxboro
New England **0-1** Los Angeles
Revolution Galaxy
(Ruiz 113)
h/t: 0-0   90 mins: 0-0
Att: 61,316   Ref: Terry

At last: after losing three
MLS Finals Los Angles Galaxy
finally take the title.

USA

United States Soccer Federation
Founded: 1913
Joined FIFA: 1913
Joined CONCACAF: 1961

IT IS CLAIMED THAT the Pilgrim Fathers saw native Americans playing a rudimentary form of football, Passuckquakkohowog, in Massachusetts in 1620, and there was some kind of football played at American colleges as early as the 1820s. However, when the game split between handling and kicking codes, it was the handling game that prevailed and went on to dominate college and then professional sports. In competition with American football, baseball, basketball and ice hockey, soccer has always had a marginal place in American culture.

A series of amateur cups were created at the turn of the 19th century and a single season of professional league football was played in 1894. The first sustainable professional league was created in 1921, and lasted until the early 1930s. The majority of the teams in the league came from the East Coast and attracted newly arrived immigrant populations. With the ASL's demise, a national professional game had to wait for the 1968 merger of the United Soccer Association and the National Professional Soccer League for the formation of the NASL. The NASL survived until 1984 and indeed thrived in the mid-70s as a steady stream of exotic foreign players (at the end of their careers) took up the increasingly attractive financial rewards of US soccer.

The decline of audiences and sponsorship money in the early 1980s left the USA without a national professional league. However, football continued to grow, especially among women. By hosting the World Cup in 1994, the USA was committed to re-establishing a professional league, and MLS – Major League Soccer – was created in 1996, while pre-existing smaller leagues merged to create unified Second and Third Divisions.

The ASL Record 1922–32

SEASON	CHAMPIONS	RUNNERS-UP
1922	Philadelphia Field Club	New York Field Club
1923	J & P Coats	Bethlehem Steel
1924	Fall River Marksmen	Bethlehem Steel
1925	Fall River Marksmen	Bethlehem Steel
1926	Fall River Marksmen	New Bedford Whalers
1927	Bethlehem Steel	Boston Wonder Workers
1928	Boston Wonder Workers	New Bedford Whalers
1929	Fall River Marksmen*	
1929†	Fall River Marksmen	Providence Gold Bugs
1930	Fall River Marksmen	New Bedford Whalers
1930†	Fall River Marksmen	New Bedford Whalers
1931	New York Giants	New Bedford Whalers
1932	*incomplete*	

* No play-off.

† Autumn league played.

The NASL Record 1967–84

YEAR	WINNERS	PLAY-OFF	RUNNERS-UP
1967*	Los Angeles Wolves	5-4	Washington Whips
1967**	Oakland Clippers	0-1, 4-1	Baltimore Bays
1968†	Atlanta Chiefs	0-0, 3-0	San Diego Toros
1969††	Kansas City Spurs		Tampa Bay Rowdies
1970	Rochester Lancers	3-0, 3-1	Washington Darts
1971	Dallas Tornado	1-2, 4-1, 2-0	Atlanta Chiefs
1972	New York Cosmos	2-1	St. Louis Stars
1973	Philadelphia Atoms	2-0	Dallas Tornado
1974	Los Angeles Aztecs	4-3	Dallas Tornado
1975	Tampa Bay Rowdies	2-0	Portland Timbers
1976	Toronto Metros-Croatia	3-0	Minnesota Kicks
1977	New York Cosmos	2-1	Seattle Sounders
1978	New York Cosmos	3-1	Tampa Bay Rowdies
1979	Vancouver Whitecaps	2-1	Tampa Bay Rowdies
1980	New York Cosmos	3-0	Fort Lauderdale Strikers
1981	Chicago Sting	1-0	New York Cosmos
1982	New York Cosmos	1-0	Seattle Sounders
1983	Tulsa Roughnecks	2-0	Toronto Blizzard
1984	Chicago Sting	2-0	Toronto Blizzard

* USA   ** NPSL   † NASL   †† No play-off

Vancouver Royals
Vancouver Royal Canadians
Vancouver Whitecaps
Vancouver
Seattle
Seattle Sounders
1979
1977, 82
Golden Bay Earthquakes
Oakland Clippers
Portland Timbers
Portland
1967
1975
Oakland Stompers
San Francisco Gales
Los Angeles Galaxy
San Jose Earthquakes
1996, 99, 2001, **02**
San Francisco
2001
Las Vegas Quicksilver
California Surf
San Jose
Las Vegas
Los Angeles Aztecs
San Diego Sockers
1974
San Diego Toros
Los Angeles Wolves
Los Angeles
1967
San Diego
1968
Los Angeles Toros

PACIFIC OCEAN

The MLS Record 1996–2002

YEAR	WINNERS	PLAY-OFF	RUNNERS-UP
1996	DC United	3-2	Los Angeles Galaxy
1997	DC United	2-1	Colorado Rapids
1998	Chicago Fire	2-0	DC United
1999	DC United	2-0	Los Angeles Galaxy
2000	Kansas City Wizards	1-0	Chicago Fire
2001	San Jose Earthquakes	2-1 (aet)	Los Angeles Galaxy
2002	Los Angeles Galaxy	1-0 (asdet)	New England Revolution

THE USA

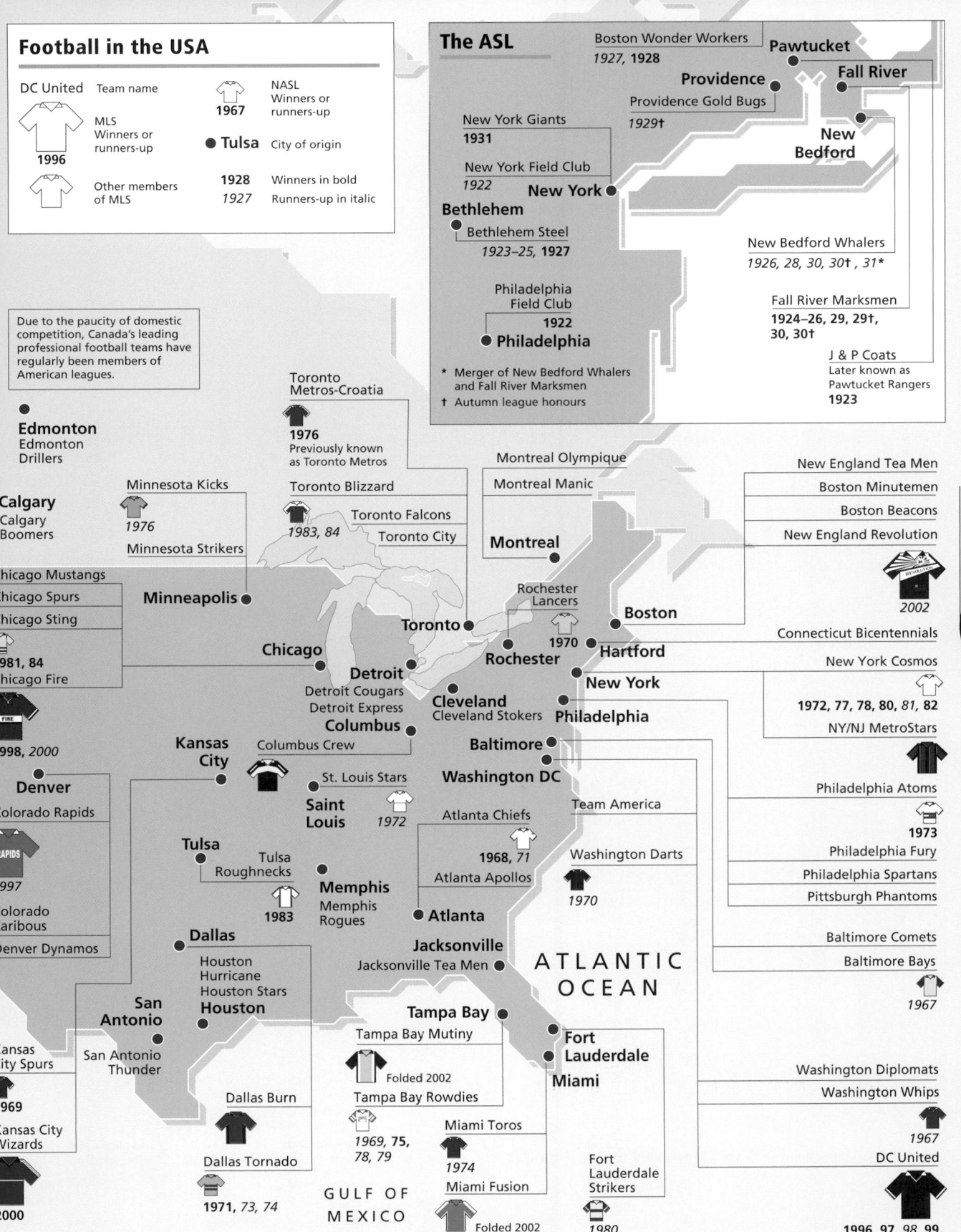

Football in the USA

DC United — Team name

MLS Winners or runners-up — **1996**

Other members of MLS

1967 — NASL Winners or runners-up

● **Tulsa** — City of origin

1928 — Winners in bold

1927 — Runners-up in italic

Due to the paucity of domestic competition, Canada's leading professional football teams have regularly been members of American leagues.

The ASL

Boston Wonder Workers
1927, **1928**

Pawtucket

Fall River

Providence

Providence Gold Bugs
1929†

New York Giants
1931

New York Field Club
1922

New York

New Bedford

Bethlehem Steel
1923–25, **1927**

Bethlehem

New Bedford Whalers
1926, 28, 30, 30†, *31**

Fall River Marksmen
1924–26, *29, 29*†, **30, 30*†

Philadelphia Field Club
1922

● **Philadelphia**

J & P Coats
Later known as Pawtucket Rangers
1923

* Merger of New Bedford Whalers and Fall River Marksmen
† Autumn league honours

● **Edmonton**
Edmonton Drillers

■ **Calgary**
Calgary Boomers

Toronto Metros-Croatia
1976
Previously known as Toronto Metros

Toronto Blizzard
1976

Toronto Falcons
1983, 84
Toronto City

Minnesota Kicks
1976
Minnesota Strikers

Chicago Mustangs
Chicago Spurs
Chicago Sting
1981, 84
Chicago Fire
1998, *2000*

Minneapolis ●

Chicago ●

Montreal Olympique
Montreal Manic
Montreal ●

Rochester Lancers
1970

New England Tea Men
Boston Minutemen
Boston Beacons
New England Revolution
2002

Toronto ●

Detroit ●
Detroit Cougars
Detroit Express

Columbus ●
Columbus Crew

Rochester ●

Boston ●

Hartford

Cleveland ●
Cleveland Stokers

New York ●

Connecticut Bicentennials

New York Cosmos
1972, 77, 78, *80*, **81**, *82*

NY/NJ MetroStars

Kansas City ●

St. Louis Stars

Baltimore ●

Washington DC ●

Team America

Denver
Colorado Rapids
1997
Colorado Caribous
Denver Dynamos

Saint Louis
1972

Atlanta Chiefs
1968, *71*
Atlanta Apollos

Washington Darts
1970

Philadelphia Atoms
1973
Philadelphia Fury
Philadelphia Spartans
Pittsburgh Phantoms

Tulsa ●
Tulsa Roughnecks
1983

Memphis
Memphis Rogues

Atlanta ●

Dallas ●
Houston Hurricane
Houston Stars
Houston

Jacksonville ●
Jacksonville Tea Men

ATLANTIC OCEAN

Baltimore Comets
Baltimore Bays
1967

San Antonio
San Antonio Thunder

Dallas Burn

Tampa Bay ●
Tampa Bay Mutiny
Folded 2002
Tampa Bay Rowdies
1969, **75**, *78, 79*

Fort Lauderdale ●

Miami

Kansas City Spurs
1969
Kansas City Wizards
2000

Dallas Tornado
1971, 73, 74

GULF OF MEXICO

Miami Toros
1974
Miami Fusion
Folded 2002

Fort Lauderdale Strikers
1980

Washington Diplomats
Washington Whips
1967

DC United
1996, 97, *98*, **99,**

THE USA

Mexico

THE SEASON IN REVIEW 2002–03

ALTHOUGH THE 2002 WORLD CUP was disappointing for Mexican football, the domestic season was engaging and closely fought. The Winter Championship saw impressive group stage performances from Toluca, whose freescoring Paraguayan striker, Jose Cardozo, continues to set Mexican footballing records. The team scored 70 goals in the championship, a record itself, while Cardozo netted 29 and was awarded the South American Footballer of the Year prize. The best points record went to Atletico Morelia, the defending champions, who showed more consistency than any other leading side. However, the championship goes to play-offs and then points count for nothing. Morelia made it to the Final taking a one-goal lead at home over Toluca and making it a two-goal lead in the opening minute of the return leg. But then the Toluca goal machine opened up and took the title.

The Summer Championship was equally close, and again Morelia dragged itself to the Final, facing Monterrey who had not won a title for 19 years. Under new coach, Argentinian Daniel Pasarella, Monterrey had enjoyed a torrid Winter Championship and Pasarella had promised he would resign if things did not improve. They did, and in the first leg, at home, Monterrey won 3-1 before eking out a goalless draw in Morelia. Back in Monterrey the city exploded; tens of thousands flooded the streets in a spontaneous celebration during which at least five people died and 300 were arrested.

MEXICO

Winter Championship 2002–03 Tables

GROUP 1								
CLUB	P	W	D	L	F	A	Pts	
América	19	13	4	2	34	14	**43**	Qualified for Play-offs
Toluca	19	12	5	2	55	25	**41**	Qualified for Play-offs
Atlas	19	7	1	11	28	31	**22**	
Puebla	19	6	4	9	23	29	**22**	
Celaya	19	5	6	8	24	32	**21**	

GROUP 2								
CLUB	P	W	D	L	F	A	Pts	
Pumas	19	10	3	6	39	35	**33**	Qualified for Play-offs
Tecos UAG	19	8	5	6	26	29	**29**	Qualified for Play-offs
Tigres	19	6	5	8	32	33	**23**	
Monterrey	19	5	7	7	18	20	**22**	
Pachuca	19	2	9	8	21	35	**15**	

GROUP 3								
CLUB	P	W	D	L	F	A	Pts	
Morelia	19	9	5	5	35	23	**32**	Qualified for Play-offs
Cruz Azul	19	7	7	5	30	26	**28**	Qualified for Play-offs
Necaxa	19	8	2	9	28	32	**26**	
San Luis	19	6	6	7	31	28	**24**	
Jaguares Chiapas	19	3	7	9	19	34	**16**	

GROUP 4								
CLUB	P	W	D	L	F	A	Pts	
Guadalajara	19	6	9	4	28	29	**27**	Qualified for Play-offs
Santos Laguna	19	7	5	7	30	28	**26**	Qualified for Play-offs
Atlante	19	6	7	6	31	33	**25**	
Gallos Blancos	19	6	5	8	28	34	**23**	
Veracruz	19	4	6	9	30	40	**18**	

Winter Top Goalscorers 2002–03

PLAYER	CLUB	NATIONALITY	GOALS
Jose Cardozo	Toluca	Paraguayan	29
Jared Borgetti	Santos	Mexican	13
Alex Fernandez	Morelia	Brazilian	13
Sebastian Gonzales	Atlante	Chilean	13

Winter Championship 2002–03 Play-offs

QUARTER-FINALS (2 legs)

Guadalajara **2-1** Toluca
Cruz Azul **0-0** Pumas
Tecos **1-3** Morelia
Santos **3-3** América

Toluca **3-0** Guadalajara
Morelia **4-1** Tecos
Pumas **3-2** Cruz Azul
América **1-2** Santos

SEMI-FINALS (2 legs)

Santos **3-5** Toluca
Morelia **4-0** Pumas

Toluca **2-1** Santos
Pumas **2-1** Morelia

FINAL (2 legs)

December 14 – Estadio Morelia, Morelia
Morelia **1-0** Toluca
(Saavedra 59)
Att: 40,000   Ref: Carter

December 21, Nemesio Diez, Toluca
Toluca **4-1** Morelia
(Carmona 33,   (Bautista 1)
Lopez 41,
Cardozo 50,
Garcia 65)
h/t: 2-1   Att: 26,000
Ref: Ramos Ruiz
Toluca won 4-2 on aggregate

Top right: Sebastian Abreu scores another for Cruz Azul, but his goals were not enough to take the side further than the quarter-finals.

Right: Toluca's Cardozo heads the ball over Banos of Atlante in their winter 2002 clash at the Azteca.

Summer Championship 2002–03 Tables

GROUP 1

CLUB	P	W	D	L	F	A	Pts	
Toluca	19	10	3	6	40	30	33	Qualified for Play-offs
Atlas	19	8	8	3	29	20	32	Qualified for Play-offs
América	19	8	5	6	29	20	29	
Colibríes*	19	6	5	8	24	27	23	Relegated
Puebla	19	4	4	11	15	31	16	

GROUP 2

CLUB	P	W	D	L	F	A	Pts	
Monterrey	19	9	7	3	31	22	34	Qualified for Play-offs
Tigres	19	10	4	5	25	22	34	Qualified for Play-offs
Pachuca	19	4	9	6	21	23	21	
Pumas	19	4	8	7	25	35	20	
Tecos UAG	19	1	4	14	15	37	7	

GROUP 3

CLUB	P	W	D	L	F	A	Pts	
Morelia	19	10	5	4	34	20	35	Qualified for Play-offs
Cruz Azul	19	5	9	5	24	24	24	Qualified for Play-offs
Necaxa	19	6	5	8	25	24	23	
San Luis	19	5	5	9	25	38	20	
Jaguares Chiapas	19	5	4	10	15	26	19	

GROUP 4

CLUB	P	W	D	L	F	A	Pts	
Atlante	19	10	4	5	39	26	34	Qualified for Play-offs
Veracruz	19	9	5	5	23	18	32	Qualified for Play-offs
Guadalajara	19	8	7	4	32	24	31	
Santos Laguna	19	9	3	7	30	24	30	
Gallos Blancos	19	3	8	8	13	23	17	

*Atlético Celaya changed name to Colibríes and moved to Xochitepec (near Cuernavaca) before the start of the Clausura.

Promoted club: Irapuato.

Summer Top Goalscorers 2002–03

PLAYER	CLUB	NATIONALITY	GOALS
José Cardozo	Toluca	Paraguayan	21
Sebastián González	Atlante	Chilean	16
Reinaldo Navia	Morelia	Chilean	13
Jared Borgetti	Santos	Mexican	11

International Performances 2002

CLUB	COMPETITION	PROGRESS
América	Copa Libertadores	Semi-finals
	FC Champions Cup	1st Round
Morelia	Copa Libertadores	Quarter-finals
	FC Champions Cup	Runners-up
Pachuca	FC Champions Cup	Winners
Santos Laguna	FC Champions Cup	Quarter-finals

Summer Championship 2002–03 Play-offs

PLAY-OFF FOR
QUARTER-FINAL (2 legs)

Cruz Azul **4-1** Guadalajara
Guadalajara **4-1** Cruz Azul

Guadalajara won on basis of better points total in League

QUARTER-FINALS (2 legs)

Atlas **1-1** Monterrey
Guadalajara **1-1** Morelia
Toluca **1-2** Tigres
Veracruz **1-1** Atlante

Monterrey **3-2** Atlas
Tigres **2-2** Toluca
Morelia **4-2** Guadalajara
Atlante **0-1** Veracruz

SEMI-FINALS (2 legs)

Veracruz **1-0** Morelia
Tigres **1-4** Monterrey

Morelia **2-0** Veracruz
Monterrey **1-2** Tigres

FINAL (2 legs)

June 11 – Estadio Technologico, Monterrey
Monterrey 3-1 Morelia
*(Walter Erviti 1,   (Adolfo
    Guillermo   Bautista 93)
    Franco 47,
Hector Castro 58)*

Att: ?   **Ref:** Rizo

June 14 – Estadio Morelia, Morelia
Morelia 0-0 Monterrey

Att: 90,000   **Ref:** Archundia

Monterrey won 3-1 on aggregate

Above: Monterrey's Brazilian striker Alesandro Fernadez takes the ball round Morelia's Carlos Gonzalez.

Left: The 12th man. Monterrey's fervent fans display their support in the second leg of the summer championships final.

Left: Toluca's Vicente Sanchez and Morelia's Heriberto Ramon Morales tussle during the first leg of their final championship match.

Right: Monterrey celebrates its first title in 19 years.

Association Football in Mexico

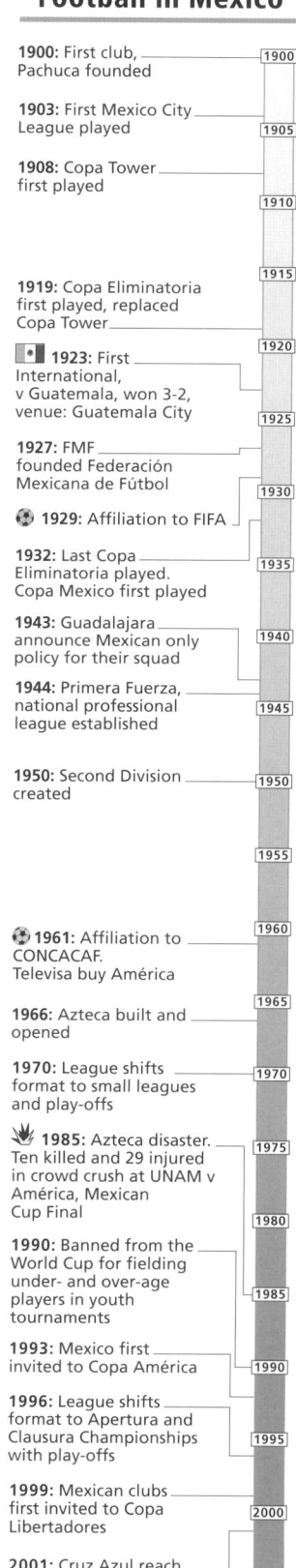

1900: First club, Pachuca founded — 1900

1903: First Mexico City League played — 1905

1908: Copa Tower first played — 1910

— 1915

1919: Copa Eliminatoria first played, replaced Copa Tower — 1920

1923: First International, v Guatemala, won 3-2, venue: Guatemala City — 1925

1927: FMF founded Federación Mexicana de Fútbol — 1930

1929: Affiliation to FIFA

1932: Last Copa Eliminatoria played. Copa Mexico first played — 1935

1943: Guadalajara announce Mexican only policy for their squad — 1940

1944: Primera Fuerza, national professional league established — 1945

1950: Second Division created — 1950

— 1955

1961: Affiliation to CONCACAF. Televisa buy América — 1960

1966: Azteca built and opened — 1965

1970: League shifts format to small leagues and play-offs — 1970

1985: Azteca disaster. Ten killed and 29 injured in crowd crush at UNAM v América, Mexican Cup Final — 1975

1990: Banned from the World Cup for fielding under- and over-age players in youth tournaments — 1980, 1985

1993: Mexico first invited to Copa América — 1990

1996: League shifts format to Apertura and Clausura Championships with play-offs — 1995

1999: Mexican clubs first invited to Copa Libertadores — 2000

2001: Cruz Azul reach Final of Copa Libertadores — 2005

The Azteca Stadium *(capacity 110,000) in Mexico City is home to several clubs including the country's most popular team, América, and has hosted two World Cup Finals, in 1970 and 1986.*

Key

🏳	International football	○	Competition winner
⚽	Affiliation to CONCACAF	△	Competition runner-up
⚽	Affiliation to FIFA	Amér –	América
🌿	Disaster	Atlan –	Atlante
■	World Cup host	Cruz –	Cruz Azul
●	CONCACAF Championship/ Gold Cup winner	Guad –	CD Guadalajara
		Monte –	Monterrey
▲	CONCACAF Championship/ Gold Cup runner-up	Nec* –	Necaxa (as Atlético Español)
		Tol –	CD Toluca
▲	Copa América runner-up	UAG –	UAG 'Los Tecos'
		Univ –	Universidad de Guadelajara

International Competitions

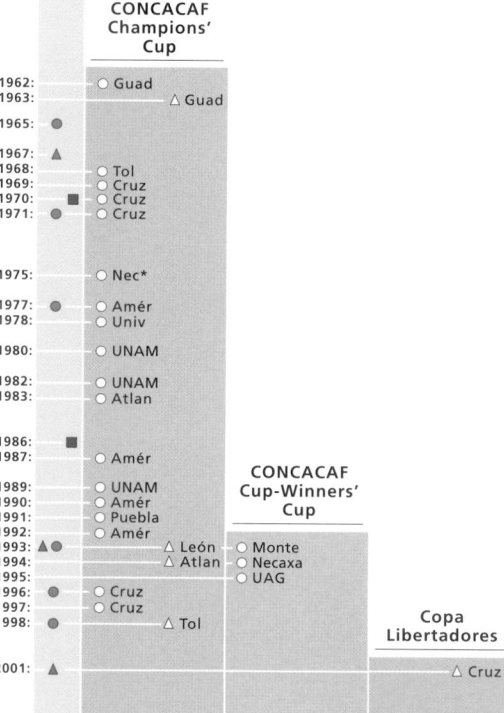

CONCACAF Champions' Cup

CONCACAF Cup-Winners' Cup

Copa Libertadores

Year	CONCACAF Champions' Cup	CONCACAF Cup-Winners' Cup	Copa Libertadores
1962: 1963:	○ Guad △ Guad		
1965:	●		
1967:	▲		
1968:	○ Tol		
1969:	○ Cruz		
1970:	● ○ Cruz		
1971:	● ○ Cruz		
1975:	○ Nec*		
1977:	● ○ Amér		
1978:	○ Univ		
1980:	○ UNAM		
1982:	○ UNAM		
1983:	○ Atlan		
1986:	■		
1987:	○ Amér		
1989:	○ UNAM		
1990:	○ Amér		
1991:	○ Puebla		
1992:	○ Amér		
1993:	▲● △ León	○ Monte	
1994:	△ Atlan	○ Necaxa	
1995:		○ UAG	
1996:	● ○ Cruz		
1997:	○ Cruz		
1998:	● △ Tol		
2001:	▲		△ Cruz

Mexico: The main clubs

CD Guadalajara 1906

Union FC (1906–08)

CD Atlas Guadalajara 1916

UAG, 'Los Tecos' 1971

Universidad de Guadalajara 1974

Purchased franchise from Torreón 1974. Withdrew from league football 1994

CF Puebla 1943 — Team name with year of formation

● Club formed before 1912

● Club formed 1912–25

● Club formed 1925–50

Club formed after 1950

★ Founder members Mexico City League 1902

👕 Founder members Professional League 1943

🏆 Amateur champions

 English origins

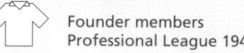 Spanish origins

 Scottish origins

Belgian founder

Franchise purchase

 Originated from a school or college

 Working class

Colours and date unknown

Mexico

ORIGINS AND GROWTH OF FOOTBALL

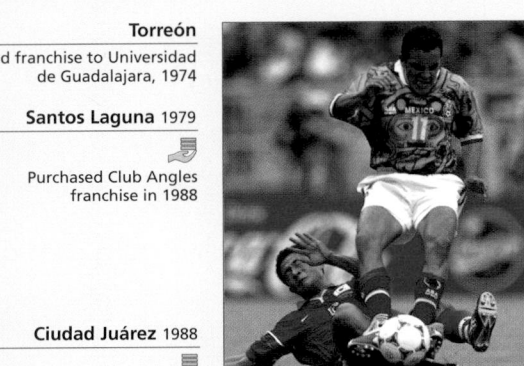

Mexico's Cuauhtemoc Blanco brought joy to millions with his 'rabbit' jump during the World Cup in France 1998.

FOOTBALL FIRST ARRIVED IN MEXICO CITY in the late 19th century via the expatriate British population and the French and Spanish immigrant communities. British mining engineers from the Compañía Real del Monte set up Pachuca Athletic Club, Mexico's first, in 1900. They contested the first championship with clubs of similar origins – Athletic, British Club, Reforma, Rovers, Mexico City Cricket Club and the Scottish-dominated champions Orizaba, all based in or near Mexico City.

Most of the British expatriate population left Mexico during the First World War and the game became dominated by Spanish speakers. A wave of Spanish clubs were formed at this time: Asturias, Real España, Cataluña and Aurora. Indigenous Mexican clubs were not far behind: Guadalajara was founded as Union FC in 1906, while América was formed as a merger of two clubs (Record FC and Colón FC) in 1916. At the same time, its eternal rival, Atlante, was founded as Sinaloa, changing its name to Lusitania and U-53, before settling on the current name in 1920. A national football association was founded in 1927 and affiliated to FIFA in 1929.

Cup and league established

The rapid growth of football in Mexico can be seen from the early development of national cup tournaments (the Copa Tower 1908–19, the Copa Eliminatoria 1920–32, and the Copa Mexico 1932–43) and the early arrival of professionalism in 1933. League football remained based on local and regional leagues until a single national league was established in 1944.

Mexico has been unable to translate these early strengths into enduring international success. It is easily the most powerful footballing nation in the CONCACAF region, but because of North American indifference and Central American and Caribbean weakness, neither its club teams nor its national team have been properly tested. Hosting two World Cups and regularly qualifying for others has not yielded a serious challenge for the trophy. The recent entry of Mexican clubs in the hitherto South American Copa Libertadores is the latest effort to break away from being a big fish in a small pond.

Torreón
Sold franchise to Universidad de Guadalajara, 1974

Santos Laguna 1979

Purchased Club Angles franchise in 1988

Ciudad Juárez 1988

Purchase of Cobra's franchise

Tampico FC

Merged in 1982 with Ciudad Madero and purchase of Atlas Campesionos franchise

Asturias (Folded)

RC España (Folded)

British Club 1901 (Folded)

UNAM, 'Los Pumas' 1954

CF Monterrey 1945

UANL, 'Los Tigres' 1967

Ciudad Juárez

Torreón
Monterrey

M E X I C O

Rayos del Necaxa 1923
merger of Luz y Fuerza and El Tranvias 1971, renamed Atlético Español. renamed Necaxa in 1982

San Luis Angeles

San Luis Potosí

CSD León 1920
León Atletico (1920-44)

Aguascalientes

León

Tampico

Atlético Pachuca 1900
Reformed 1950, 1960

Gallos Blancos 1949
Previously known as La Piedad

Guadalajara

Querétaro

Atlético Morelia 1947
Previously known as Oro

Mexico City

CD Cruz Azul 1927

CD Toluca 1917

Jasso

Nezahualcóyotl

Orizaba

Veracruz

Founded as Cruz Azul Jasso. Moved to Mexico City 1971

Cuernavaca
CD Zacatepec

CF Puebla 1943

Colibries 1994

Purchase of franchise Atlético Cuernavaca. Relocated 2002. Previously known as Atlético Celaya

Moctezuma (Folded)

Orizaba Charleston (Folded)

Tuxtla

CD Atlante 1916
Founded as Sinaloa. Changed to Lusitania in 1917 and U-53 in 1918, before CD Atlante in 1920

CD 'Toros Neza' 1981
Orignally known as Universidad Autónoma de Neza

CD Veracruz 1943
Folded 1983. Reformed in 1989 after purchasing Potros de Neza franchise

Jaguares de Chiapas 1915
Previously known as FD Irapuato. Relocated 2002

Marte FC (Folded)

CF América 1916
Merger of Record FC and Colón FC

Mexico CC 1901 (Folded)

Reforma AC 1901 (Folded)

Mexico City

FOOTBALL CITY

MEXICO

AT THE TURN OF THE CENTURY, Mexico City was host to a considerable mercantile and financial British community. Football clubs, like Reforma and Mexico Cricket Club, sprang up across the city and a city league began in 1902. The First World War and the Mexican Revolution saw most of the British drift away along with their teams, to be replaced by a mixture of Spanish immigrant and indigenous Mexican teams. It is only the latter that have survived the coming of professionalism.

The centralization of political power and the sharp social divisions of Mexican society are reflected in the city's football. The capital's clubs, particularly Cruz Azul, América and Necaxa – teams with national followings outside of Mexico City – all represent a specific strand of Mexican society. Cruz Azul, the solidly working-class team, was founded in Jasso in 1927, before being bought by a cement company and transferred to the south of Mexico City. UNAM, or Los Pumas as the team is more often known, sprang from the National Autonomous University of Mexico. The university no longer runs the team but it continues to field student players and is most widely known for giving youth its chance on the pitch. The club's supporters lean towards the younger, more intellectual, left-wing strands of Mexican life. América, by contrast, is the team of the ruling order and support for the club is often interpreted as an act of social climbing and aspiration. Atlante, originally from the poorest part of the inner city, is the people's team, representing the most marginalized members of Mexican society, while the ever-expanding suburbs have their team in Toros Neza to the west of the city.

The influence of Televisa

The concentration of power in Mexican football can be seen from the three clubs that have played at the Azteca Stadium. Televisa, the nation's biggest media company with business in every part of the Americas, owns the stadium and all the clubs. In 1961, the company bought the long-faded América, spent more money, (including the purchase of the first major wave of foreign players in Mexico) and, through relentless promotion, created a national following for the club. Televisa has since strengthened its grip on Mexican football by buying the Azteca itself, Necaxa in 1983 (which has now moved out of the city to the richer demographic fields of Aguascalientes) and Atlante in 1996. It has seen off all rivals to its pre-eminent position in TV coverage of Mexican football, helped gain host status for Mexico in two World Cups (1970 and 1986), and kept very close to the PRI – the political party that ruled Mexico uninterrupted from 1929 to 2000.

THE NATIONAL DERBY 'El Superclássico'

AMÉRICA	GUADALAJARA

 169 matches played

60 América wins
55 Guadalajara wins
54 draws

0   50   100   150   200   250

NUMBER OF MATCHES
(all matches up to May 2003)

Guadalajara is 360 miles/580 kms north-west of Mexico City

UNAM 'LOS PUMAS' 1954

National League (1944–2003)	*1968*, **77**, *78, 79*, **81**, *85, 88*, **91**
Cup	**1975**
CONCACAF Champions' Cup	**1980**, *82*, **89**
Interamerican Cup	**1981**, *90*

AZTECA

Clubs:	América, Necaxa, Mexico
Built:	1966
Original Capacity:	112,000
Rebuilt:	1986
Significant Matches:	1970 World Cup: ten matches including semi-final, 3rd place play-off, Final; 1986 World Cup: nine matches including semi-final and Final; 1993 Gold Cup

106,000

Televisa, Mexico's leading TV company, is based in Mexico City, from where it runs its footballing empire. It owns two of the city's big clubs, América and Atlante, as well as the Azteca Stadium.

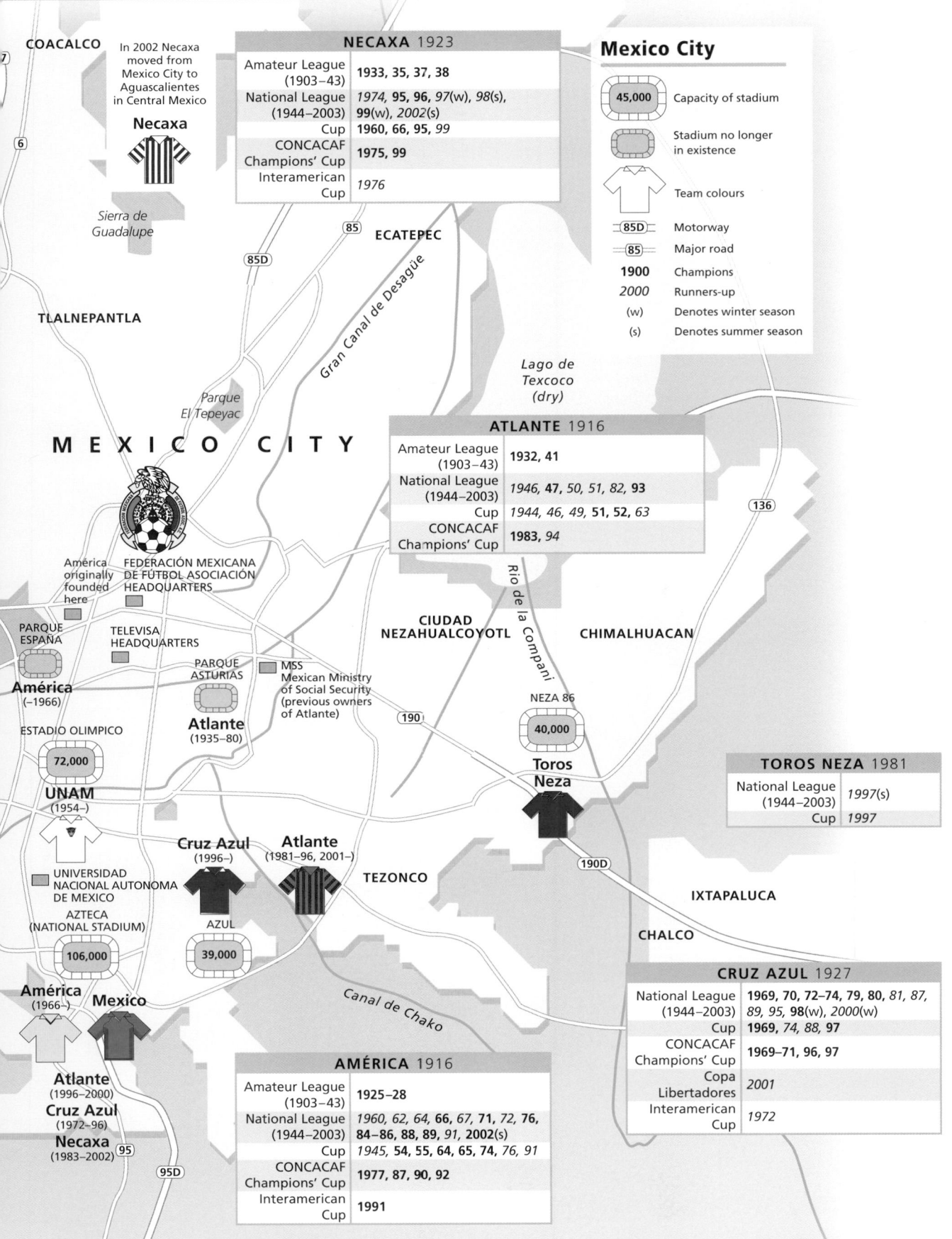

COACALCO

In 2002 Necaxa moved from Mexico City to Aguascalientes in Central Mexico

Necaxa

NECAXA 1923	
Amateur League (1903–43)	**1933, 35, 37, 38**
National League (1944–2003)	*1974,* **95, 96,** *97*(w), *98*(s), **99**(w), *2002*(s)
Cup	**1960, 66, 95,** *99*
CONCACAF Champions' Cup	**1975,** *99*
Interamerican Cup	*1976*

Mexico City

45,000	Capacity of stadium
	Stadium no longer in existence
	Team colours
85D	Motorway
85	Major road
1900	Champions
2000	Runners-up
(w)	Denotes winter season
(s)	Denotes summer season

MEXICO

Sierra de Guadalupe

85

85D

ECATEPEC

TLALNEPANTLA

Gran Canal de Desagüe

Lago de Texcoco (dry)

Parque El Tepeyac

M E X I C O   C I T Y

ATLANTE 1916	
Amateur League (1903–43)	**1932, 41**
National League (1944–2003)	*1946,* **47,** *50, 51, 82,* **93**
Cup	*1944, 46, 49,* **51, 52,** *63*
CONCACAF Champions' Cup	**1983,** *94*

136

América originally founded here

FEDERACIÓN MEXICANA DE FÚTBOL ASOCIACIÓN HEADQUARTERS

Río de la Compani

CIUDAD NEZAHUALCOYOTL

CHIMALHUACAN

PARQUE ESPAÑA

TELEVISA HEADQUARTERS

PARQUE ASTURIAS

MSS Mexican Ministry of Social Security (previous owners of Atlante)

América (–1966)

ESTADIO OLIMPICO

72,000

UNAM (1954–)

Atlante (1935–80)

NEZA 86

40,000

Toros Neza

190

TOROS NEZA 1981	
National League (1944–2003)	*1997*(s)
Cup	*1997*

Cruz Azul (1996–)

Atlante (1981–96, 2001–)

TEZONCO

190D

IXTAPALUCA

UNIVERSIDAD NACIONAL AUTONOMA DE MEXICO

AZTECA (NATIONAL STADIUM)

AZUL

39,000

CHALCO

106,000

América (1966–)

Mexico

Atlante (1996–2000)
Cruz Azul (1972–96)
Necaxa (1983–2002)

Canal de Chako

95

95D

CRUZ AZUL 1927	
National League (1944–2003)	**1969, 70,** *72–74,* **79, 80,** *81, 87,* **89, 95, 98**(w), *2000*(w)
Cup	**1969,** *74,* **88, 97**
CONCACAF Champions' Cup	**1969–71,** *96,* **97**
Copa Libertadores	*2001*
Interamerican Cup	*1972*

AMÉRICA 1916	
Amateur League (1903–43)	**1925–28**
National League (1944–2003)	*1960, 62, 64,* **66, 67,** *71, 72,* **76,** *84–86,* **88, 89,** *91, 2002*(s)
Cup	*1945,* **54, 55, 64, 65,** *74,* **76,** *91*
CONCACAF Champions' Cup	**1977, 87, 90, 92**
Interamerican Cup	**1991**

Mexico

PRIMERA DIVISIÓN 1981–2002

THE 1980s BEGAN with media giants Televisa determined to make CF América – its key footballing property – the best team in Mexico. A change of strip and an open chequebook did the trick and in 1984, under Carlos Reynos, América took the title, pipping long-standing rival CD Guadalajara to the post. Four out of the next six titles followed, CF Monterrey winning in 1986 and Guadalajara getting one back the following year.

The Mexican league has been through a variety of changes. It has always concluded with the top eight or ten teams playing off (over two legs) to determine the title, but leagues, mini-leagues and groups have all been used to determine the top teams, while relegation is decided on a Byzantine, multiple-season averaging system. In 1996, the league was split into two separate halves – a winter and a summer championship. But whatever system has been used, league football in Mexico has proved a very attractive business proposition. Since the 1980s

In recent years, smaller provincial teams like Atlético Morelia (in hoops), seen here in action against UAG (in checks), have risen to challenge the traditional giants of Mexican football. Morelia's finest moment came in 2001 when the team beat another small club, Toluca, to take the Winter Championship.

MEXICO

UAG
1994

CD Atlas
1999s

Universidad de Guadalajara
1990

CD Guadalajara
1983, 84, 87, 97s, 99w

Ciudad Juárez

MEXICO

Santos Laguna
1994, 97w, 2000s, 01s

Torreón

CSD Léon
1992, 98w

Union de Curtidores

CF Monterrey
Mexico 86, *93*

UANL
1982, *2002w*

UAT

Monterrey

Ciudad Victoria

Atlético Potosino

San Luis Potosí

FD Irapuato (formerly CD Veracruz, now called Jaguares de Chiapas)

León

Irapuato

Guadalajara

Celaya

Atlético Celaya (now called Colibries)
1996

La Piedad (now called Gallos Blancos)

La Piedad de Cavadas

Querétaro

Morelia

Atlético Morelia
2001w

CD Toluca
1998s, 99s, 2000s, *01w*

Toluca

Cuernavaca

CD Zacatepec

Mexico City

Jasso

Pachuca de Soto

Tampico

Nezahualcóyotl

CF Puebla
1983, 90, *92*

Veracruz

Tampico FC

Deportivo Neza

Querétaro (formerly Tampico-Madero)
Prode 85, Mexico 86

Atlético Pachuca
2000w, 01s, 02w

CD Toros Neza
1997s

CD Veracruz

UNAM
1985, 88, 91

CD Atlante
1982, *93*

Necaxa
1995, 96, 97w, 98s, 99w, *2002s*

CF América
1984, 85, Prode 85, 88, 89, 91, *2002s*

CD Cruz Azul
1987, 89, 95, 98w, *2000w*

Primera División

CF América — Team name

League champions/runners-up

1984, *91* — Champions in bold
Runners-up in italics

Other teams in the Primera División

● **Mexico City** — City of origin

w — winter season
s — summer season

Televisa has been joined by rival TV Azteca as multiple club proprietors, while cement, loan, brewing and petrochemical companies have all bought into Mexican clubs. Franchises (or membership of the league) can and have been bought and sold, enabling rich but relegated teams to buy their way back up.

América has continued to be a perennial contender and 2002 saw the team champions again at last. Honours have also been shared between outsiders CD Atlante and CSD Léon, who both took surprise titles in the early 1990s; Televisa's other key team, Necaxa, who won three titles in the 1990s; and Cruz Azul, who finally delivered on its promise, winning in 1998. In the late 1990s, the real surprises came from the smaller provincial teams: Toluca, Pachuca, Atlético Morelia and Santos Laguna.

Key to League Positions Table

- League champions
- Season of promotion to league
- Season of relegation from league
- Other teams playing in league
- Qualified for championship play-off

Mexican League Positions 1981–2002

SEASON

TEAM	1981–82	1982–93	1983–84	1984–85	Prode 85	Mexico 86	1986–87	1987–88	1988–89	1989–90	1990–91	1991–92	1992–93	1993–94	1994–95	1995–96	1996–97w	1996–97s	1997–98w	1997–98s	1998–99w	1998–99s	1999–2000w	1999–2000s	2000–01w	2000–01s	2001–02w	2001–02s
CF América	SF	SF	C	C	C	SF	QF	C	C	SF	RU		SF	SF	SF	SF		QF	SF	SF		QF	SF		QF	SF		C
CD Atlante	RU	QF	QF		SF	QF						QF	C	QF			QF	QF	SF	QF							QF	
CD Atlas			SF											QF		QF	QF		QF	SF	SF	RU	SF	QF	SF			QF
Atlético Celaya																RU												
CD Cruz Azul		SF	QF	QF	QF	RU		RU		QF	SF	QF	QF	RU	QF		C	QF	QF	SF	RU		QF				SF	
CD Guadalajara		RU	RU	QF	QF	SF	C	QF			SF	QF			SF		QF	C	QF		RU	QF	QF	SF			QF	
Universidad de Guadalajara	QF	SF		QF	QF			SF		RU	QF																	
FD Irapuato (now CD Veracruz)																												
Ciudad Juárez																												
La Piedad																												QF
CSD Léon				SF								C	SF						RU						QF			
CF Monterrey	QF		QF			C	QF				QF		RU			QF									QF			
Atlético Morelia						QF	QF	SF	SF			QF		QF			SF	QF		QF	QF				C			QF
Necaxa	QF									QF		SF	QF		C	C	RU	SF		RU	C	QF	QF	QF	QF		QF	RU
Deportivo Neza	SF																											
CD Toros Neza																	SF	RU	QF									
Atlético Pachuca																								C		QF	RU	C
Atlético Potosino		QF																										
CF Puebla		C		QF	SF	QF	SF	QF		C	SF	RU		QF		SF							QF		SF			
Querétaro (was Tampico-Madero)				RU	RU																							
Santos Laguna														RU	QF		C	QF		QF		SF	RU	SF	C	QF	SF	
Tampico FC																												
CD Toluca		QF					QF		QF				SF			QF		C	QF	C	QF	C	RU			SF		QF
UAG		QF	QF				QF	QF				QF	C	QF				QF	QF		QF				QF			
UANL	C		QF				QF			QF			QF			QF									QF	RU		
UAT										QF																		
UNAM			SF	RU				RU		SF	C	QF		QF			QF				SF			SF				SF
Union de Curtidores																												
CD Veracruz														QF				SF										
CD Zacatepec	QF																											

In Mexico, the championship is decided by play-offs, involving eight or ten teams.

In 1986, two shorter championships called Prode 85 and Mexico 86 were held before and after the World Cup. They are counted as official championships.

Since 1996–97 the season has been divided into two, with winter and summer championships.

MEXICO

Mexico

Federación Mexicana de Fútbol Asociación AC
Founded: 1927
Joined FIFA: 1929
Joined CONCACAF: 1961

MEXICO DOMINATES FOOTBALL in the Central American region. The national team has qualified for the finals of ten of the 15 World Cup tournaments, including Italia '90, when they were barred from the qualifying tournament by FIFA for having breached age regulations in a youth tournament. The country's unrivalled position has meant that the development of football has been hindered through lack of decent opposition.

Domestic competitions, however, have been hotly contested for a century. The first amateur league was established in 1903 by five clubs in Mexico City. The Primera Fuzera, based in Mexico City, ran alongside two provincial amateur leagues: Liga de Occidente and Liga Veracruzana. In 1943 the three competitions were fused to form a professional league and a second division was added in 1950. In 1970, the league format was changed to two then four groups, with a series of multi-leg play-off rounds to decide the championship.

Meanwhile, the Mexican Cup went through three incarnations during its amateur phase. These were the Copa Tower, which existed between 1908 and 1919; the Copa Eliminatoria between 1920 and 1932 (this tournament only accepted clubs that played in the Primera Fuerza); and the Copa Mexico between 1932 and 1943, a tournament that accepted clubs from all over the country. The Cup finally turned professional in 1944.

Mexican League Record 1944–2003

SEASON	CHAMPIONS	RUNNERS-UP
1944	Asturias	España
1945	España	Puebla
1946	Veracruz	Atlante
1947	Atlante	León
1948	León	Oro
1949	León	Atlas
1950	Veracruz	Atlante
1951	Atlas	Atlante
1952	León	Guadalajara
1953	Tampico	Zacatepec
1954	Marte	Oro
1955	Zacatepec	Guadalajara
1956	León	Oro
1957	Guadalajara	Toluca
1958	Zacatepec	Toluca
1959	Guadalajara	León
1960	Guadalajara	América
1961	Guadalajara	Oro
1962	Guadalajara	América
1963	Oro	Guadalajara
1964	Guadalajara	América
1965	Guadalajara	Oro
1966	América	Atlas
1967	Toluca	América
1968	Toluca	UNAM
1969	Cruz Azul	Guadalajara
1970	Guadalajara	Cruz Azul
1970*	Cruz Azul	Guadalajara
1971	América	Toluca
1972	Cruz Azul	América
1973	Cruz Azul	León
1974	Cruz Azul	Atlético Español

Mexican League Record (*continued*)

SEASON	CHAMPIONS	RUNNERS-UP
1975	Toluca	León
1976	América	Unión de Guadalajara
1977	UNAM	Unión de Guadalajara
1878	UANL	UNAM
1979	Cruz Azul	UNAM
1980	Cruz Azul	UANL
1981	UNAM	Cruz Azul
1982	UANL	Atlante
1983	Puebla	Guadalajara
1984	América	Guadalajara
1985	América	UNAM
1986†	América	Tampico-Madero
1986†	Monterrey	Tampico-Madero
1987	Guadalajara	Cruz Azul
1988	América	UNAM
1989	América	Cruz Azul
1990	Puebla	Unión de Guadalajara
1991	UNAM	América
1992	León	Puebla
1993	Atlante	Monterrey
1994	UAG	Santos Laguna
1995	Necaxa	Cruz Azul
1996	Necaxa	Atlético Celaya
1997 (w)§	Santos Laguna	Necaxa
1997 (s)	Guadalajara	Toros Neza
1998 (w)	Cruz Azul	León
1998 (s)	Toluca	Necaxa
1999 (w)	Necaxa	Guadalajara
1999 (s)	Toluca	Atlas
2000 (w)	Pachuca	Cruz Azul
2000 (s)	Toluca	Santos Laguna
2001 (w)	Morelia	Toluca
2001 (s)	Santos Laguna	Pachuca
2002 (w)	Pachuca	Tigres
2002 (s)	América	Necaxa
2003 (w)	Toluca	Morelia
2003 (s)	Monterrey	Morelia

* A short tournament was played before or after the 1970 World Cup in Mexico. It is counted as a championship.

† Due to the 1986 World Cup in Mexico, the 1985–86 season was cancelled and replaced by two short tournaments.

§ From 1997 a championship was played in both winter (**w**) and summer (**s**).

Mexican League Summary

TEAM	TOTALS	CHAMPIONS & RUNNERS-UP (BOLD) (*ITALICS*)
Guadalajara	10, 8	*1952*, **55**, **57**, **59–62**, *63*, **64**, **65**, **69**, **70**, *70*, **83**, **84**, **87**, *97 (s)*, *99 (w)*
América	9, 6	*1960*, *62*, *64*, **66**, *67*, **71**, *72*, **76**, **84–86†**, **88**, **89**, **91**, *2002 (s)*
Cruz Azul	8, 6	**1969**, *70*, *70*, **72–74**, *79*, **80**, *81*, **87**, *89*, *95*, **98 (w)**, **2000 (w)**
Toluca	7, 4	*1957*, *58*, **67**, **68**, *71*, **75**, **98 (s)**, *99 (s)*, **2000 (s)**, *01 (w)*, **03 (w)**
León	5, 5	**1947**, **48**, **49**, **52**, *56*, *59*, *73*, **75**, **92**, *98 (w)*
UNAM	3, 5	**1968**, **77**, *78*, *79*, **81**, *85*, *88*, *91*
Necaxa (includes Atlético Español)	3, 4	*1974*, **95**, **96**, **97 (w)**, *98 (s)*, **99 (w)**, *2002 (s)*
Atlante	2, 4	*1946*, **47**, *50*, *51*, **82**, **93**
Puebla	2, 2	*1945*, **83**, **90**, *92*
Santos Laguna	2, 2	*1994*, **97 (w)**, *2000 (s)*, **01 (s)**
Monterrey	2, 1	**1986†**, *93*, **2003 (s)**

Mexican League Summary (*continued*)

TEAM	TOTALS	CHAMPIONS & RUNNERS-UP (BOLD) (*ITALICS*)
Pachuca	2, 1	**2000 (w)**, *01 (s)*, **02 (w)**
UANL	2, 1	**1978**, *80*, **82**
Zacatepec	2, 1	*1953, 55*, **58**
Veracruz	2, 0	**1946, 50**
Oro	1, 5	*1948, 54, 56, 61,* **63**, *65*
Atlas	1, 3	*1949,* **51**, *66, 99 (s)*
Morelia	1, 2	**2001 (w)**, *03 (w)*, *03 (s)*
Tampico-Madero (includes Tampico)	1, 2	**1953**, *86†, 86†*
España	1, 1	**1944**, *45*
Asturias	1, 0	**1944**
Marte	1, 0	**1954**
UAG	1, 0	**1994**
Unión de Guadalajara	0, 3	*1976, 77, 90*
Atlético Celaya	0, 1	*1996*
Tigres	0, 1	*2002 (w)*
Toros Neza	0, 1	*1997 (s)*

(w) denotes winter season
(s) denotes summer season
† Due to the 1986 World Cup in Mexico, the league was replaced with two short tournaments. They both counted as championships.

Mexican Cup Record 1944–2002

YEAR	WINNERS	SCORE	RUNNERS-UP
1944	España	6-2	Atlante
1945	Puebla	6-4	América
1946	Atlas	5-4 (aet)	Atlante
1947	Moctezuma	4-3	Oro
1948	Veracruz	3-1	Guadalajara
1949	León	3-0	Atlante
1950	Atlas	3-1 (aet)	Veracruz
1951	Atlante	1-0	Guadalajara
1952	Atlante	2-0	Puebla
1953	Puebla	4-1	León
1954	América	1-1 (aet)(3-2 pens)	Guadalajara
1955	América	1-0	Guadalajara
1956	Toluca	2-1	Irapuato
1957	Zacatepec	2-1	León
1958	León	5-2 (aet)	Zacatepec
1959	Zacatepec	2-1	León
1960	Atlético Español	2-2 (aet)(10-9 pens)	Tampico
1961	Tampico	1-0	Toluca
1962	Atlas	3-3, (replay) 1-0	Tampico
1963	Guadalajara	2-1	Atlante
1964	América	1-1 (aet)(5-4 pens)	Monterrey
1965	América	4-0	Morelia
1966	Atlético Español	3-3, (replay) 1-0	León
1967	León	2-1	Guadalajara
1968	Atlas	2-1	Veracruz
1969	Cruz Azul	2-1 (aet)	Monterrey
1970	Guadalajara	3-2, 2-1 (2 legs)	Torreón
1971	León	0-0 (aet) (10-9 pens)	Zacatepec
1972	León	Final Group	Puebla
1973		no competition	
1974	América	2-1, 1-1 (2 legs)	Cruz Azul
1975	UNAM	Final Group	Unión de Guadalajara
1976	UANL	2-0, 1-2 (2 legs) won on away goals	América
1977–87		no competition	
1988	Puebla	0-0, 1-1 (2 legs)	Cruz Azul
1989	Toluca	2-1, 1-1 (2 legs)	Unión de Guadalajara
1990	Puebla	4-1, 0-2 (2 legs)	UANL
1991	Unión de Guadalajara	1-0, 0-0 (2 legs)	América

Mexican Cup Record (*continued*)

YEAR	WINNERS	SCORE	RUNNERS-UP
1992	Monterrey	4-2	Ciudad Juarez
1993–94		*no competition*	
1995	Necaxa	2-0	Veracruz
1996	UANL	1-1, 1-0 (2 legs)	Atlas
1997	Cruz Azul	2-0	Toros Neza
1998		*no competition*	
1999	Tigres	2-0	Necaxa
2000–		*tournament discontinued*	

Mexican Cup Summary

TEAM	TOTALS	WINNERS & RUNNERS-UP (BOLD) (*ITALICS*)
León	5, 4	**1949**, *53, 57,* **58, 59,** *66,* **67,** *71, 72*
América	5, 3	*1945,* **54, 55, 64, 65,** *74,* **76,** *91*
Puebla	4, 2	**1945,** *52,* **53,** *72,* **88,** *90*
Atlas	4, 1	**1946, 50, 62, 68,** *96*
Necaxa (includes Atlético Español)	3, 1	**1960,** *66,* **95,** *99*
Guadalajara	2, 5	*1948, 51, 54, 55,* **63,** *67,* **70**
Atlante	2, 4	*1944, 46, 49,* **51, 52,** *63*
Cruz Azul	2, 2	**1969,** *74, 88,* **97**
Zacatepec	2, 2	**1957,** *58,* **59,** *71*
Toluca	2, 1	**1956,** *61,* **89**
UANL	2, 1	**1976,** *90,* **96**
Veracruz	1, 3	**1948,** *50, 68, 95*
Monterrey	1, 2	**1964,** *69, 92*
Tampico	1, 2	*1960,* **61,** *62*
Unión de Guadalajara	1, 2	*1975, 89,* **91**
España	1, 0	**1944**
Moctezuma	1, 0	**1947**
Tigres	1, 0	**1999**
UNAM	1, 0	**1975**
Ciudad Juarez	0, 1	*1992*
Irapuato	0, 1	*1956*
Morelia	0, 1	*1965*
Oro	0, 1	*1947*
Toros Neza	0, 1	*1997*
Torreón	0, 1	*1970*

Necaxa 1999–2000: *four times Mexican champions, the team was founded in Mexico City in 1923. Bought by Spanish businessmen in 1971, it played as Atlético Español until TV giant, Televisa, bought it in 1982 and renamed it Necaxa. The team has recently relocated outside Mexico City to Aguascalientes, 150 miles northeast.*

Canada

The Canadian Soccer Association
Founded: 1912
Joined FIFA: 1912–28, 1946
Joined CONCACAF: 1978

DESPITE FOOTBALL'S EARLY ARRIVAL, Canada proved stony ground for the development of the game. Clubs were forming in the last quarter of the 19th century and national cup and league competitions were established in 1912 and 1922 respectively, but the transition to a regular national professional league has proved elusive.

The game's lacklustre progression may be attributed to three factors. Firstly, the country's vast size makes the administration of a single, national competition difficult. Secondly, football faces fierce competition from the major North American sports of ice hockey, gridiron, baseball and basketball. Thirdly, as the names of leading clubs suggest, football has been a game for recent, non-Anglo immigrants: Toronto Scots and Ulsters, Eintracht Vancouver, Vancouver Croatia and Scarborough Azzurri, and has yet to really enter the mainstream.

The first attempt to create a modern professional league was the Eastern Canada Professional Soccer League. It lasted only five years, 1961–65, forcing top Canadian teams to play in various US leagues in the 1970s and 80s. A further attempt to professionalize and commercialize the game came with the Canadian Soccer League in 1987. It was disbanded in 1992. Again leading clubs have been forced into American pro leagues. The semi-professional Canadian Professional Soccer League was re-established in Ontario in 1998 and has so far survived and expanded into Quebec. Currently, plans exist for the amalgamation of the CPSL and the top professional clubs playing in America to form a national league.

In 2000 Canada (in white) won the Gold Cup, beating Colombia 2-0 in the Final in Los Angeles. This was a major achievement for a team whose players almost all play outside their native country.

Canadian Soccer League Record 1987–1992

SEASON	CHAMPIONS	SEASON	CHAMPIONS
1987	Calgary Kickers	1990	Vancouver 86ers
1988	Vancouver 86ers	1991	Vancouver 86ers
1989	Vancouver 86ers	1992	Winnipeg Fury

Canadian Professional Soccer League Record 1998–2001

SEASON	CHAMPIONS	SEASON	CHAMPIONS
1998	St. Catharine's		
1999	Toronto Olympians		
2000	Toronto Croatia		
2001	St. Catharine's		

Canadian Challenge Cup Record 1913–2002

YEAR	WINNERS	YEAR	WINNERS
1913	Norwood Wanderers	1965	Vancouver Firefighters
1914	Norwood Wanderers	1966	British Columbia
1915	Winnipeg Scots	1967	Toronto
1916–18	*no competition*	1968	Toronto Royals
1919	Montreal Grand	1969	Columbus Vancouver
1920	Westinghouse Ontario	1970	*no competition*
1921	Toronto Scots	1971	Eintracht Vancouver
1922	Hillhurst Calgary	1972	New Westminster Blues
1923	Naniamo Wanderers	1973	Vancouver Firefighters
1924	Weston University	1974	Calgary Springer Kickers
1925	Toronto Ulsters		
1926	Weston University	1975	London Boxing Club Victoria
1927	Naniamo Wanderers		
1928	New Westminster Royals	1976	Victoria West SC
1929	CNR Montreal	1977	Columbus Vancouver
1930	New Westminster Royals	1978	Columbus Vancouver
1931	New Westminster Royals	1979	Victoria West SC
1932	Toronto Scots	1980	St. John Drydock
1933	Toronto Scots	1981	Toronto Ciociaro
1934	Verduns Montreal	1982	Victoria West SC
1935	Aldreds Montreal	1983	Vancouver Firefighters
1936	New Westminster Royals	1984	Victoria West SC
1937	Johnston Nationals	1985	Vancouver Croatia
1938	North Shore Vancouver	1986	Hamilton Steelers
1939	Radials Vancouver	1987	Lucania SC
1940–45	*no competition*	1988	Holy Cross
1946	Toronto Ulster United	1989	Scarborough Azzurri
1947	St. Andrews Vancouver	1990	Vancouver Firefighters
1948	Carsteel Montreal	1991	Norvan SC
1949	North Shore Vancouver	1992	Norvan SC
1950	Vancouver City	1993	West Side Rino
1951	Ulster United Toronto	1994	Edmonton Ital-Canadians
1952	Steelco Montreal		
1953	New Westminster Royals	1995	Mistral-Estrie
1954	Scottish Winnipeg	1996	Westside CIBC
1955	New Westminster Royals	1997	Edmonton Ital-Canadians
1956	Halecos Vancouver		
1957	Ukrainia SC Montreal	1998	RDP Condores
1958	New Westminster Royals	1999	Calgary CSFC
1959	Alouettes Montreal	2000	Luciana Winnipeg
1960	New Westminster Royals	2001	Halifax King of Donair
1961	Concordia Montreal	2002	Manifoba
1962	Scottish Winnipeg		
1963	*no competition*		
1964	Columbus Vancouver		

Central America

FOOTBALL IN CENTRAL AMERICA has had to compete with American sports, primarily baseball, for the affections and interest of fans and patrons. Where American influence (especially military influence) and occupation has been strongest, baseball has proved the winner, and football has been a minority sport in both Nicaragua and Panama. The region's strongest leagues have been traditionally in Costa Rica, Guatemala, Honduras and El Salvador. Football took off in the 1920s with leagues and clubs established in all of them. The Costa Rican league dates from 1921, the Salvadorian from 1926, and Guatemala began in 1919. Honduras has had formal tournaments since the 1920s but a properly constituted national league did not take off until 1965. All of these countries operate a complex national league system in which an opening championship (the Apertura) is followed by a closing (Clausura) championship. These are sometimes followed by a knockout competitions between the top six or eight teams in the league or with a final play-off between the winners of the two phases.

The centrality of football to popular culture and national identity in the region can be seen from an infamous event – the Futbal War. In 1969, El Salvador beat Honduras 3-2 in a World Cup qualifying match in Mexico City, following an unresolved two-leg play-off between the sides. This acted as the final trigger in a long-running border dispute between the states, and El Salvador invaded Honduras. Although little was resolved, over 2,000 people perished in the conflict.

Founded in 1935, Saprissa is one of the major teams in Costa Rica. Based in the capital, San José, it has won the Costa Rican League title over 20 times during its history.

El Salvador

Federación Salvadoreña de Fútbol
Founded: 1935
Joined FIFA: 1938
Joined CONCACAF: 1962

SEASON	LEAGUE CHAMPIONS
1998	Luis Angel Firpo
1999	Luis Angel Firpo
2000	Luis Angel Firpo
2001	CD Águila
2002	(Apertura) CD Fas
2002	(Clausura) San Salvador

Guatemala

Federación Nacional de Fútbol de Guatemala
Founded: 1919
Joined FIFA: 1933
Joined CONCACAF: 1961

SEASON	LEAGUE CHAMPIONS
2000	(Apertura) Comunicaciones
2000	(Clausura) Municipal
2001	(Apertura) Municipal
2001	(Clausura) Comunicaciones
2002	(Apertura) Municipal
2002	(Clausura) Municipal
2003	(Apertura) Comunicaciones
2003	(Clausura) Comunicaciones

YEAR	CUP WINNERS
1999	Municipal
2000	*unknown*
2001	*unknown*
2002	Jalapa
2003	Municipal

Guyana

Guyana Football Association
Founded: 1902
Joined FIFA: 1968
Joined CONCACAF: 1969

SEASON	LEAGUE CHAMPIONS
1998	Santos FC
1999	*unknown*
2000	*no championship*
2001	Fruta Conquerors
2002	*no championship*

YEAR	CUP WINNERS
1999	Doc's Khelwalnas
2000	Topp XX
2001	Topp XX
2002	Victoria Kings
2003	Fruta Conquerors

Honduras

Federación Nacional Autónoma de Fútbol de Honduras
Founded: 1951
Joined FIFA: 1951
Joined CONCACAF: 1961

SEASON	LEAGUE CHAMPIONS
2001	(Apertura) Olimpia
2001	(Clausura) Platense
2002	(Apertura) Motagua
2002	(Clausura) Marathon
2003	(Apertura) Olympia
2003	(Clausura) Marathon

Nicaragua

Federación Nicaraguense de Fútbol
Founded: 1931
Joined FIFA: 1950
Joined CONCACAF: 1968

SEASON	LEAGUE CHAMPIONS
1999	FC Real Estelí
2000	FC Diriangén
2001	Deportivo Walter Ferreti
2002	Jalapa
2003	FC Real Estelí

Panama

Federación Nacional de Fútbol de Panamá
Founded: 1937
Joined FIFA: 1938
Joined CONCACAF: 1961

SEASON	LEAGUE CHAMPIONS
1998	Tauro FC
1999	Deportivo Árabe Unido
2000	Tauro FC
2001	Panamá Viejo FC
2002	Plaza Amador

Surinam

Surinaamse Voetbal Bond
Founded: 1920
Joined FIFA: 1929
Joined CONCACAF: 1961

SEASON	LEAGUE CHAMPIONS
1998	Transvaal
1999	SNL
2000	Transvaal
2001	Voorwaarts
2002	Voorwaarts

Belize

Belize National Football Association
Founded: 1980
Joined FIFA: 1986
Joined CONCACAF: 1986

SEASON	LEAGUE CHAMPIONS
1999	Juventus
2000	Sagitún
2001	Kulture Yabra
2002	Kulture Yabra
2003	Cayo Highlanders

Costa Rica

Federación Costarricense de Fútbol
Founded: 1921
Joined FIFA: 1921
Joined CONCACAF: 1962

SEASON	LEAGUE CHAMPIONS
1999	Saprissa
2000	Alajuelense
2001	Alajuelense
2002	Alajuelense
2003	Alajuelense

The Caribbean

FOOTBALL IN THE CARIBBEAN has always been in fierce competition for players, fans and money with cricket, baseball and, increasingly, with basketball. Small populations and generally low incomes have made the competition fiercer and squeezed the space for football in the region. The strongest footballing traditions and leagues have been in Haiti, Cuba, Jamaica and Trinidad and Tobago.

Cuban football dates from the first decade of the 20th century, when it was played among Spaniards and Cubans educated in Britain. A league was established in the 1920s, and the first floodlit stadium in the region was built in Havana in 1928 – a subsequent wave of interest culminated in Cuba's appearance in the quarter-finals of the 1938 World Cup.

Football in Haiti dates from the same era with a national FA created in 1904, which became FIFA's first Caribbean member in 1933. Its most successful clubs, Violette Athlétique Club and Racing Club Haïtien, were founded in 1918 and 1923. Haiti was the first Caribbean nation to qualify for the World Cup Finals in 1974.

Jamaica's national FA was first established in 1910, joining FIFA after independence in 1962. Drawing on the increasingly large and dispersed global Jamaican diaspora, the national team qualified for the World Cup in 1998.

Trinidad and Tobago's national FA is even older (founded in 1908), though international success has eluded them both at club and national level.

Anguilla

Anguilla Football Association
Founded: 1990
Joined FIFA: 1996
Joined CONCACAF: 1996

SEASON	LEAGUE CHAMPIONS
1998	Coca Cola Spartans Int.
1999	Attackers
2000	no competition
2001	Roaring Lions
2002	Roaring Lions

Antigua and Barbuda

The Antigua Football Association
Founded: 1928
Joined FIFA: 1970
Joined CONCACAF: 1980

SEASON	LEAGUE CHAMPIONS
1998	Empire
1999	Empire
2000	Empire
2001	Empire
2002	Parham FC

Aruba

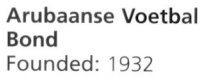

Arubaanse Voetbal Bond
Founded: 1932
Joined FIFA: 1988
Joined CONCACA: 1988

SEASON	LEAGUE CHAMPIONS
1998	SV Estrella
1999	SV Estrella
2000	Deportivo Nacional
2001	Deportivo Nacional
2002	RCA

Bahamas

The Bahamas Football Association
Founded: 1967
Joined FIFA: 1968
Joined CONCACAF: 1981

SEASON	LEAGUE CHAMPIONS
1999	Cavalier FC
2000	Abacom United FC
2001	Cavalier FC
2002	unfinished
2003	Bears FC

Barbados

Barbados Football Association
Founded: 1910
Joined FIFA: 1968
Joined CONCACAF: 1968

SEASON	LEAGUE CHAMPIONS
1999	Notre Dame SC
2000	Notre Dame SC
2001	Paradise
2002	Notre Dame SC
2003	Paradise

Bermuda

Bermuda Football Association
Founded: 1928
Joined FIFA: 1962
Joined CONCACAF: 1966

SEASON	LEAGUE CHAMPIONS
1999	Vasco da Gama FC
2000	PHC Zebras
2001	Dandy Town Hornets SC
2002	North Village
2003	North Village

British Virgin Islands

British Virgin Islands Football Association
Founded: 1974
Joined FIFA: 1996
Joined CONCACAF: 1996

SEASON	LEAGUE CHAMPIONS
1999	Veterans
2000	HBA Panthers
2000/01	HBA Panthers
2001	Future Stars United
2002	HBA Panthers

YEAR	CUP WINNERS
1998	United Kickers
1999	unknown
2000	Rangers
2001	Rangers
2002	unknown

Cayman Islands

Cayman Islands Football Association
Founded: 1966
Joined FIFA: 1992
Joined CONCACAF: 1992

SEASON	LEAGUE CHAMPIONS
1999	Georgetown SC
2000	Western Union FC
2001	Scholars International
2002	Georgetown SC
2003	Scholars International

Cuba

Associación de Fútbol de Cuba
Founded: 1924
Joined FIFA: 1933
Joined CONCACAF: 1961

SEASON	LEAGUE CHAMPIONS
1999	league format change
2000	FC Pinar del Río
2001	Ciudad de la Habana
2002	Ciego de Ávila
2003	FC Villa Clara

Dominica

Dominica Football Association
Founded: 1970
Joined FIFA: 1994
Joined CONCACAF: 1994

SEASON	LEAGUE CHAMPIONS
1999	Harlem Bombers
1999	Harlem Bombers
2000	Harlem Bombers
2002	Saint Joseph
2003	Harlem Bombers

Dominican Republic

Federación Dominicana de Fútbol
Founded: 1953
Joined FIFA: 1958
Joined CONCACAF: 1964

SEASON	LEAGUE CHAMPIONS
1999	FC Don Bosco
2000	unknown
2001	CD Pantoja
2002	Baninter
2003	Baninter

Grenada

Grenada Football Association
Founded: 1924
Joined FIFA: 1976
Joined CONCACAF: 1969

SEASON	LEAGUE CHAMPIONS
1998	Fontenoy United
1999	St. Andrews Football League Grenville
2000	DML Mutual Life Grenada Boys Secondary School St. George's
2001	Grenada Boys Secondary School St. George's
2002	QPR FC

Haiti

Féderation Haïtienne de Football
Founded: 1904
Joined FIFA: 1933
Joined CONCACAF: 1961

SEASON	LEAGUE CHAMPIONS
1999	Violette Athlétique Club
2000	Racing Club Haïtien
2001	FICA
2002	(Ouverture) Roulado
2002	(Clôture) Racing Club H
2003	(Ouverture) Don Bosco

Jamaica

Jamaica Football Association
Founded: 1910
Joined FIFA: 1962
Joined CONCACAF: 1961

SEASON	LEAGUE CHAMPIONS
1999	Tivoli Gardens
2000	Harbour View
2001	Arnett Gardens FC
2002	Arnett Gardens FC
2003	Hazard United

Montserrat

Montserrat Football Association
Founded: *unknown*
Joined FIFA: 1996
Joined CONCACAF: 1996

Montserrat *(continued)*

SEASON	LEAGUE CHAMPIONS
1998	*abandoned*
1999	*abandoned*
2000	Royal Montserrat Police Force
2001	Royal Montserrat Police Force
1999	*unknown*

Netherlands Antilles

Nederlande Antilliaanse Voetbal Unie
Founded: 1921
Joined FIFA: 1932
Joined CONCACAF: 1961

SEASON	LEAGUE CHAMPIONS
1998	Jong Colombia Boca Sami
1999	Jong Holland Willemstad
2000	Jong Colombia Boca Sami
2001	*unknown*
2002	*unknown*

Puerto Rico

Federación Puertorriqueña de Fútbol
Founded: 1940
Joined FIFA: 1960
Joined CONCACAF: 1962

SEASON	LEAGUE CHAMPIONS
1998	Académicos de Quintana
1999	CF Nacional
2000	Académicos de Quintana
2001	Académicos de Quintana
2002	Académicos de Quintana

St Kitts and Nevis

St Kitts and Nevis Amateur Football Association
Founded: 1932
Joined FIFA: 1992
Joined CONCACAF: 1992

SEASON	LEAGUE CHAMPIONS
1999	St. Paul's United
2000	*no championship*
2001	Garden Hotspurs FC
2002	Cayon Rockets
2003	Village Superstars

St Lucia

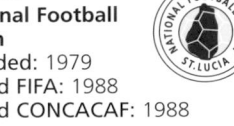

St Lucia National Football Union
Founded: 1979
Joined FIFA: 1988
Joined CONCACAF: 1988

SEASON	LEAGUE CHAMPIONS
1998	Mabouya Valley Rovers
1999	Roots Alley Ballers
2000	Roots Alley Ballers
2001	VSADC
2002	VSADC

St Vincent and the Grenadines

St Vincent and Grenadines Football Federation
Founded: 1979
Joined FIFA: 1988
Joined CONCACAF: 1988

SEASON	LEAGUE CHAMPIONS
1997	ASC Le Geldar
1998	AS Jahouvey Mana
1999	AJ Saint-Georges
2000	AJ Saint-Georges
2001	Conquering Lions

Trinidad and Tobago

Trinidad and Tobago Football Association
Founded: 1908
Joined FIFA: 1963
Joined CONCACAF: 1964

Trinidad and Tobago *(continued)*

SEASON	LEAGUE CHAMPIONS
1998	Joe Public FC
1999	Defence Force
2000	William's Connection FC
2001	William's Connection FC
2002	San Juan Jabloteh

Turks and Caicos Islands

Football Association of Turks and Caicos
Founded: 1996
Joined FIFA: 1998
Joined CONCACAF: 1998

SEASON	LEAGUE CHAMPIONS
1999	Tropic All-Stars
2000	Masters
2001	SWA Sharks
2002	Beaches FC
2003	Caribbean All Stars

U.S. Virgin Islands

USVI Soccer Federation
Founded: 1998
Joined FIFA: 1998
Joined CONCACAF: 1998

SEASON	LEAGUE CHAMPIONS
2000	UWS Upsetters
2001	UWS Upsetters
2002	Haitian Stars

Joe Public FC, based in Port of Spain, was runner-up in the Trinidad and Tobago League Championship in 1997, but the following year it took the title, and since then has remained one of the main teams on the island.

The Globalization of Football

NATIONS, CLUBS AND FANS

THE GLOBALIZATION OF football takes many forms. In the first place it is simply the world's most popular sport and the membership of FIFA parallels the steady increase in the number of nations on the planet, as empires have crumbled and new states emerged. FIFA now has more members than the United Nations. FIFA was established by eight Western European nations in 1904, and by 1920 it had temporarily acquired the four British football associations, and its first North and South American members. In the 1920s, it expanded to take in more Europeans and Latin Americans, but the European empires in Asia and Africa gave little scope for new recruits. With the end of the Second World War a long wave of decolonization began which saw FIFA triple its membership by the mid-1980s as African, Caribbean and Asian states flooded in. With the break-up of the Soviet empire and Yugoslavia in the 1990s, a further expansion has taken place, supplemented by the inclusion of many small islands and dependent territories. The entry of Palestine into FIFA in 1998 is indicative of the importance of national football institutions in the creation of modern nations.

Club ownership

The ownership of clubs has nearly always been local, but a change is coming. Colonel Gadaffi's son has bought into Juventus and ENIC, a sports management company, has snapped up a portfolio of clubs in England, Greece and the Czech Republic. Even more common is the establishment of cross-border feeder clubs by some of Europe's biggest sides. The big clubs gain access to talent and scouting networks and a place to send their reserves for first-team action, while the small clubs get fees, and better access to big clubs' transfer budgets. In Spain and Germany, the phenomenon has been limited because the big clubs play their reserve sides in the lower leagues, so player loans are less necessary. But in England, the Netherlands and Italy, this option is not available and controls exist on multiple-club ownership. The Dutch have been the leading force in creating international feeder clubs. Ajax, in particular, has bought directly into and transformed Ajax Cape Town (formed after two former Cape Town clubs were bought and merged) and Obuasi Goldfields. Feyenoord and PSV have followed suit, as have leading English and Italian clubs.

Today, the global reach of some football clubs is greater than ever. Clubs like Manchester United and Real Madrid have become global footballing brands, riding their waves of TV-transmitted glory. United in particular has capitalized on its fame, establishing massive support (and income streams) in South-East Asia and Scandinavia. Other clubs have similar ambitions. Football shirts of the world's leading clubs will soon be more commonly seen than advertisements for soft drinks in the world's more out-of-the-way places.

THE GLOBALIZATION OF FOOTBALL

FIFA Membership

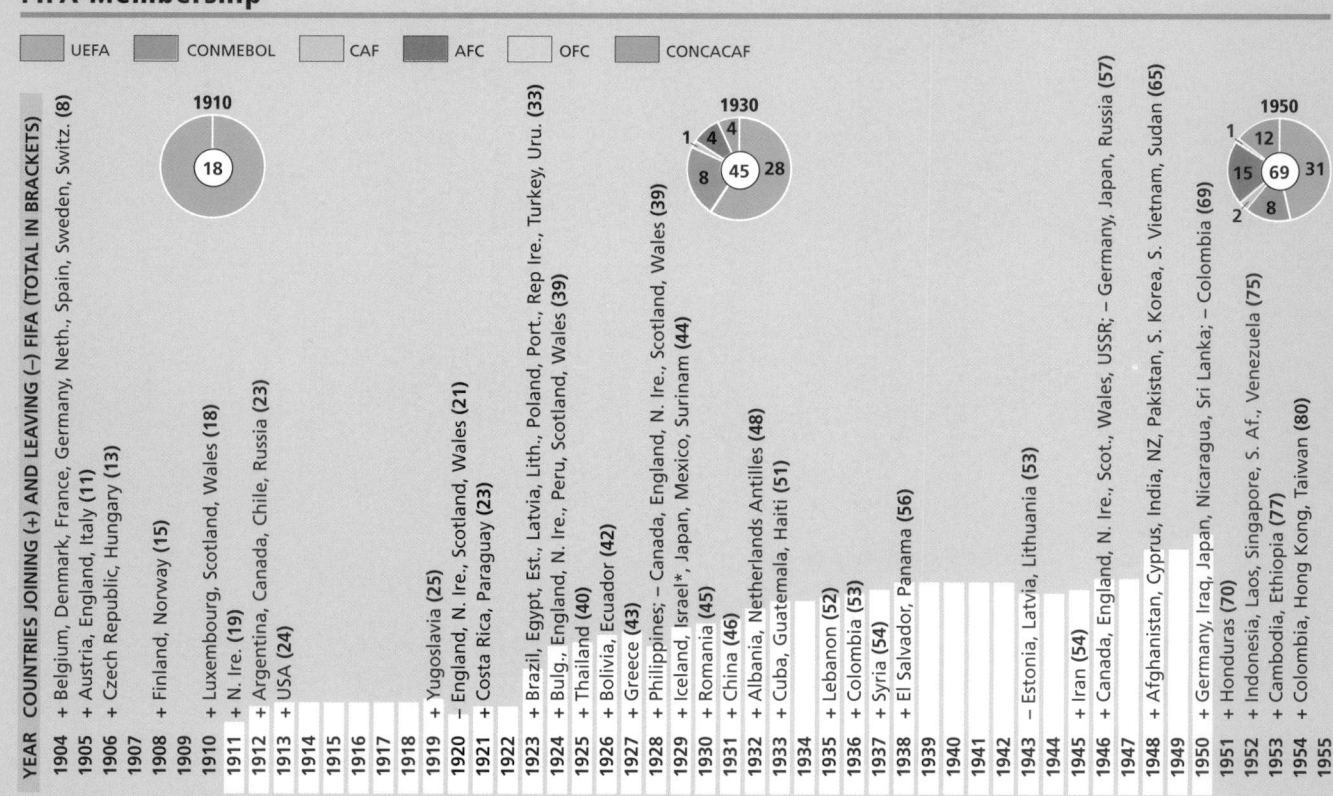

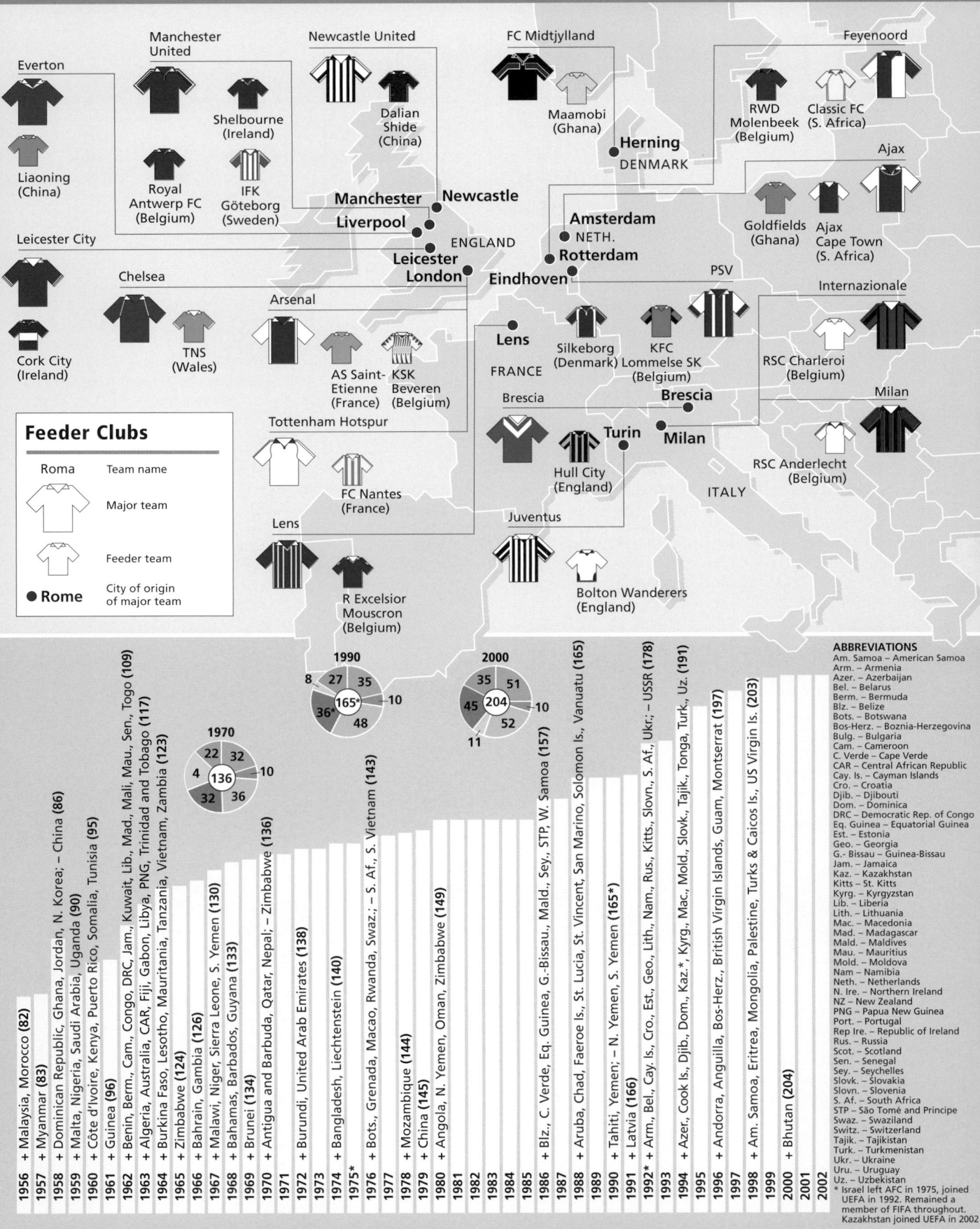

Everton — Liaoning (China)

Manchester United — Shelbourne (Ireland), Royal Antwerp FC (Belgium), IFK Göteborg (Sweden)

Newcastle United — Dalian Shide (China)

FC Midtjylland — Maamobi (Ghana)

Herning DENMARK

Feyenoord — RWD Molenbeek (Belgium), Classic FC (S. Africa)

Ajax — Goldfields (Ghana), Ajax Cape Town (S. Africa)

Leicester City — Cork City (Ireland)

Chelsea — TNS (Wales)

Arsenal — AS Saint-Etienne (France), KSK Beveren (Belgium)

Tottenham Hotspur — FC Nantes (France)

Lens — R Excelsior Mouscron (Belgium)

Manchester
Liverpool
Newcastle
ENGLAND
Leicester
London

Amsterdam NETH.
Rotterdam
Eindhoven PSV

Lens
FRANCE
Silkeborg (Denmark)
KFC Lommelse SK (Belgium)

Internazionale — RSC Charleroi (Belgium)

Milan — RSC Anderlecht (Belgium)

Brescia — Hull City (England)

Turin
Milan
Brescia
ITALY

Juventus — Bolton Wanderers (England)

Feeder Clubs

Roma — Team name
(major team)

Feeder team

● Rome — City of origin of major team

ABBREVIATIONS

Am. Samoa – American Samoa
Arm. – Armenia
Azer. – Azerbaijan
Bel. – Belarus
Berm. – Bermuda
Blz. – Belize
Bots. – Botswana
Bos-Herz. – Boznia-Herzegovina
Bulg. – Bulgaria
Cam. – Cameroon
C. Verde – Cape Verde
CAR – Central African Republic
Cay. Is. – Cayman Islands
Cro. – Croatia
Djib. – Djibouti
Dom. – Dominica
DRC – Democratic Rep. of Congo
Eq. Guinea – Equatorial Guinea
Est. – Estonia
Geo. – Georgia
G.-Bissau – Guinea-Bissau
Jam. – Jamaica
Kaz. – Kazakhstan
Kitts. – St. Kitts
Kyrg. – Kyrgyzstan
Lib. – Liberia
Lith. – Lithuania
Mac. – Macedonia
Mad. – Madagascar
Mau. – Mauritius
Mold. – Moldova
Nam – Namibia
Neth. – Netherlands
N. Ire. – Northern Ireland
NZ – New Zealand
PNG – Papua New Guinea
Port. – Portugal
Rep Ire. – Republic of Ireland
Rus. – Russia
Scot. – Scotland
Sen. – Senegal
Sey. – Seychelles
Slovk. – Slovakia
Slovn. – Slovenia
S. Af. – South Africa
STP – São Tomé and Principe
Swaz. – Swaziland
Switz. – Switzerland
Tajik. – Tajikistan
Turk. – Turkmenistan
Ukr. – Ukraine
Uru. – Uruguay
Uz. – Uzbekistan
* Israel left AFC in 1975, joined UEFA in 1992. Remained a member of FIFA throughout. Kazakhstan joined UEFA in 2002

1970 — 136: 22, 32, 10, 36, 32, 4

1990 — 165*: 8, 27, 35, 10, 48, 36*

2000 — 204: 35, 51, 10, 52, 11, 45

Bar chart (year + new members):
- 1956 + Malaysia, Morocco (82)
- 1957 + Myanmar (83)
- 1958 + Dominican Republic, Ghana, Jordan, N. Korea; – China (86)
- 1959 + Malta, Nigeria, Saudi Arabia, Uganda (90)
- 1960 + Côte d'Ivoire, Kenya, Puerto Rico, Somalia, Tunisia (95)
- 1961 + Guinea (96)
- 1962 + Benin, Berm., Cam., Congo, DRC, Jam., Kuwait, Lib., Mad., Mali, Mau., Sen., Togo (109)
- 1963 + Algeria, Australia, CAR, Fiji, Gabon, Libya, PNG, Trinidad and Tobago (117)
- 1964 + Burkina Faso, Lesotho, Mauritania, Tanzania, Vietnam, Zambia (123)
- 1965 + Zimbabwe (124)
- 1966 + Bahrain, Gambia (126)
- 1967 + Malawi, Niger, Sierra Leone, S. Yemen (130)
- 1968 + Bahamas, Barbados, Guyana (133)
- 1969 + Brunei (134)
- 1970 + Antigua and Barbuda, Qatar, Nepal; – Zimbabwe (136)
- 1972 + Burundi, United Arab Emirates (138)
- 1973 + Bangladesh, Liechtenstein (140)
- 1975* + Botz., Grenada, Macao, Rwanda, Swaz.; – S. Af., S. Vietnam (143)
- 1978 + Mozambique (144)
- 1979 + China (145)
- 1980 + Angola, N. Yemen, Oman, Zimbabwe (149)
- 1986 + Blz., C. Verde, Eq. Guinea, G.-Bissau, Mald., Sey., STP, W. Samoa (157)
- 1988 + Aruba, Chad, Faeroe Is., St. Lucia, St. Vincent, San Marino, Solomon Is., Vanuatu (165)
- 1990 + Tahiti, Yemen; – N. Yemen, S. Yemen (165*)
- 1991 + Latvia (166)
- 1992* + Arm., Bel., Cay. Is., Cro., Est., Geo., Lith., Nam., Rus., Kitts., Slovn., S. Af., Ukr.; – USSR (178)
- 1994 + Azer., Cook Is., Djib., Dom., Kaz.*, Kyrg., Mac., Mold., Slovk., Tajik., Tonga, Turk., Uz. (191)
- 1996 + Andorra, Anguilla, Bos-Herz., British Virgin Islands, Guam, Montserrat (197)
- 1998 + Am. Samoa, Eritrea, Mongolia, Palestine, Turks & Caicos Is., US Virgin Is. (203)
- 2000 + Bhutan (204)

The Transfer Market

BUYERS, SELLERS AND RECORD-BREAKERS

THE EXISTENCE OF THE TRANSFER MARKET arose from the introduction of player registration. Beginning in England with the establishment of professionalism, anyone who wanted to play professional football was required to register with the FA. However, the registration was held by the club, not by the player. If the player wanted to move to another club, that club would have to buy his registration; but selling clubs were under no obligation to release a player. Registration created a potential income stream for clubs and gave them enormous control over their players.

Transfer fees were regularly paid for players in England and Scotland in the early years of the 20th century. But the first escalation in the importance of transfers came in 1925 when Torino bought Julio Libonatti from Newell's Old Boys in Argentina.

At the end of the Second World War, it was clear that the biggest resources lay with Italian clubs who steadily increased the world record transfer fee to £500,000 when Juventus bought Pietro Anastasi from Varese in 1968. As more money has come into the global game, the fees have risen further and faster. Diego Maradona's transfers in the early 1980s were another step up, and the arrival of pay-per-view TV and contemporary commercialism has sent the record through the roof – and seen the mantle of biggest spending clubs shift from Italy to Spain.

The Bosman breakthrough

All through the 20th century, players' unions in Britain, Italy and Latin America have sought to challenge this system of contracts. There has been some shift in the balance of power between players and clubs, but it was only in 1995 that the almost medieval system of control was decisively broken. The European court ruled, in the case of Belgian player Jean-Marc Bosman, that a selling club could not demand a fee from the buyer if a player's contract has finished. In effect, this meant that contracted players were assets of declining value, as they became free agents when their contracts ended. The peculiarities of the football labour market and transfer system clearly became apparent to the European Union; in 1999, they embarked on negotiations with UEFA, the international players' union FIFpro and FIFA, to bring them into line with European labour law. The new contract system, hammered out in 2001, will have global scope, allowing some payments for transfers of under-23 players when a club has nurtured and developed them, but otherwise transfer fees for out-of-contract players will become a thing of the past.

A measure of economic reality returned to the transfer market in 2002. The collapsing value of TV rights and the demise of German media giant Kirch exposed the overstretched finances of European football's elite. The summer of 2002 proved the quietest market for years, and even Ronaldo's bitter transfer from Inter to Real Madrid fell outside the top five record transfers.

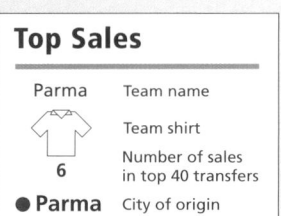

Top Sales

Parma — Team name

Team shirt

6 — Number of sales in top 40 transfers

● Parma — City of origin

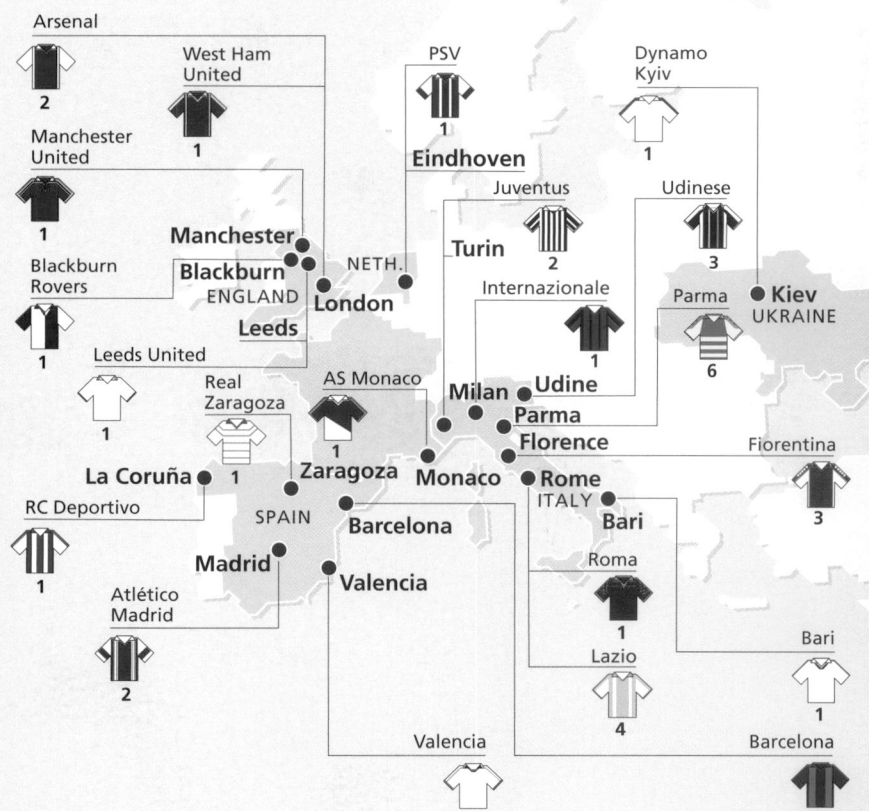

Top 40 Transfers*

FEE (millions)	NAME	FROM	TO	YEAR
£45.8	Zidane	Juventus	Real Madrid	2001
£37.5	Figo	Barcelona	Real Madrid	2000
£36	Crespo	Parma	Lazio	2000
£32.6	Buffon	Parma	Juventus	2001
£32	Vieri	Lazio	Internazionale	1999
£30	Ferdinand	Leeds United	Manchester United	2002
£30	Ronaldo	Internazionale	Real Madrid	2002
£28	Rui Costa	Fiorentina	Milan	2001
£28	Veron	Lazio	Manchester United	2001
£27	Mendieta	Valencia	Lazio	2001
£25.5	Nedved	Lazio	Juventus	2001
£23	Buffon	Parma	Juventus	2002
£22	Annelka	Arsenal	PSG	2000
£22	Batistuta	Fiorentina	Roma	2000
£22	Denilson	São Paulo	Real Betis	1998
£22	Thuram	Parma	Juventus	2001
£20	Lõpez	Valencia	Lazio	2000
£20	Overmars	Arsenal	Barcelona	2000
£20	Saviola	River Plate	Barcelona	2001
£19.1	Nakata	Roma	Parma	2001
£19	Cassano	Bari	Roma	2001

FEE (millions)	NAME	FROM	TO	YEAR
£19	van Nistelrooy	PSV	Manchester United	2001
£19	Vieri	Atlético Madrid	Lazio	1998
£18	Amoroso	Udinese	Parma	1999
£18	Ferdinand	West Ham United	Leeds United	2001
£18	Ronaldo	Barcelona	Internazionale	1997
£18	Toldo	Fiorentina	Internazionale	2001
£18	Veron	Parma	Lazio	1999
£17	Inzhagi	Juventus	Milan	2001
£17	Stam	Manchester United	Lazio	2001
£16.2	Shevchenko	Dynamo Kyiv	Milan	1999
£16	Milosevic	Real Zaragoza	Parma	2000
£16	Rivaldo	RC Deportivo	Barcelona	1997
£15.8	Amoroso	Parma	Borussia Dortmund	2001
£15	Hasselbaink	Atlético Madrid	Chelsea	2000
£15	Shearer	Blackburn Rovers	Newcastle United	1995
£14.9	Fiore	Udinese	Lazio	2001
£14.6	Almeyda	Lazio	Parma	2000
£14.6	Giannichedda	Udinese	Lazio	2001
£14	Trezeguet	AS Monaco	Juventus	2000

* Data correct up to March 2003

Inter president Massimo Moratti has spent more and more wildly over the past decade – more than any other club president in Europe – and still no Scudetto.

Record-breaking transfers

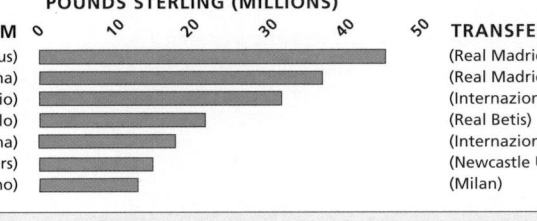

TRANSFERRED FROM	POUNDS STERLING (MILLIONS)	TRANSFERRED TO
2001 Zinedine Zidane (Juventus)		(Real Madrid)
2000 Luis Figo (Barcelona)		(Real Madrid)
1999 Christian Vieri (Lazio)		(Internazionale)
1998 Denilson (São Paulo)		(Real Betis)
1997 Ronaldo (Barcelona)		(Internazionale)
1995 Alan Shearer (Blackburn Rovers)		(Newcastle United)
1992 Gianluigi Lentini (Torino)		(Milan)

Top Buys

Lazio — Team name
— Team shirt
8 — Number of buys in top 40 transfers
● Rome — City of origin

Parma, UEFA Cup winners 1998: With little footballing tradition and a tiny support base Parma has survived in the top flight with the money from Parmalat. Funds have been used to buy and sell players like Lillian Thuram (back row, third from left) for significant profit.

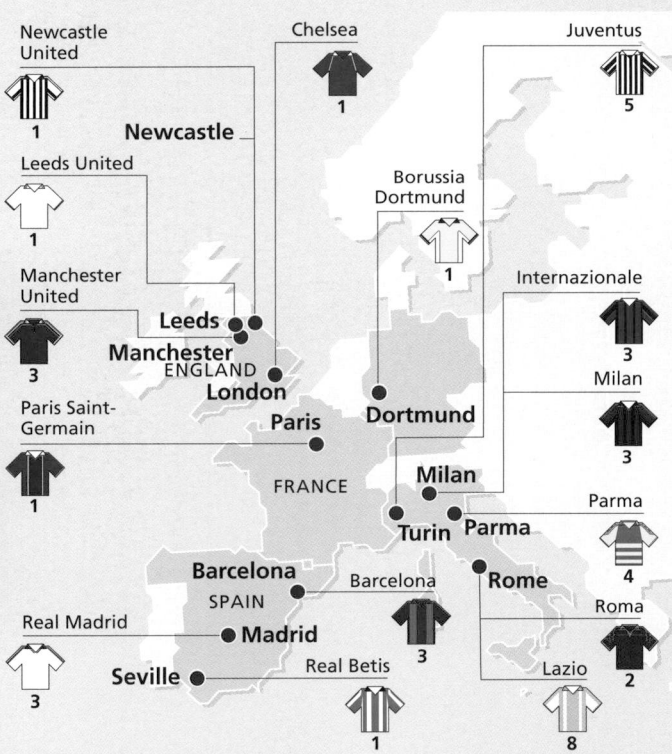

Financial Affairs

EUROPE'S RICHEST CLUBS

IN THE LAST 15 YEARS, since the arrival of satellite and pay-per-view television, money has flooded into European football – so much so that not a single Latin American club is represented in the top 30 richest clubs. Within Europe, the biggest leagues financially (in descending order) are in England, Italy, Spain, Germany and France. Italy and England have 14 of the top 20 clubs between them. Manchester United remains the richest club on the planet, but Real Madrid, Bayern München and the Italian giants are all chasing hard. Lower down the list, the bigger French and German clubs get a look in as well as the two big Glasgow clubs, Ajax of Amsterdam and the leading Turkish club, Galatasaray.

The financial and commercial pressures at the apex of European football have seen a transformation in the form of ownership and regulation of big clubs. In Italy, Scotland and England, leading clubs have been floated on the stock market (as well as partial flotations at Ajax, Galatasaray and Borussia Dortmund). The leading Portuguese and Danish clubs have followed suit, but without much hope of reaching even the lower end of the rich list. However, the very poor performance of most football stocks has dampened the enthusiasm of investors and clubs like Internazionale, Milan, Schalke 04 and Hertha Berlin have all abandoned proposed IPOs. In Spain, *socios* (fan-owner groups) continue to control the giants Barcelona and Real Madrid. In France, Germany and Turkey, clubs are changing their legal status to create commercial arms that can receive external investment and pay dividends. French clubs remain disadvantaged by the much higher employment and social security costs of star players.

The enormous amount of money at stake among the leading clubs saw the formation of the G-14 in 1998. This pressure group, made up of the leading European clubs, has lobbied hard for its member's interests with UEFA, FIFA and the European commission: limiting international call-ups for expensive players, mooting the formation of a European Super League, pushing for the expansion of the Champions League and the redistribution of income. The lower reaches of professional football are bogged down in actual or impending bankruptcy all across Europe. It is clear that the value of TV rights has peaked, and the collapse of a number of TV companies and deals looks set to make problems worse. Though most of the elite clubs will be relatively unscathed, no team is invulnerable. Fiorentina, a top 20 club in 2001, spent most of 2002 in and out of insolvency courts and was finally dissolved in spring 2002, reappearing as Fiorentina Viola in the Italian fourth division. Leeds and Lazio's debt crisis grew so large that both were forced to dismember their expensive squads.

Rising from the ashes? *Fiorentina Viola celebrates promotion to C1 (the Italian third division). Two years ago the team was in the top half of Serie A and the European Champions League.*

The World's Richest Clubs 2000

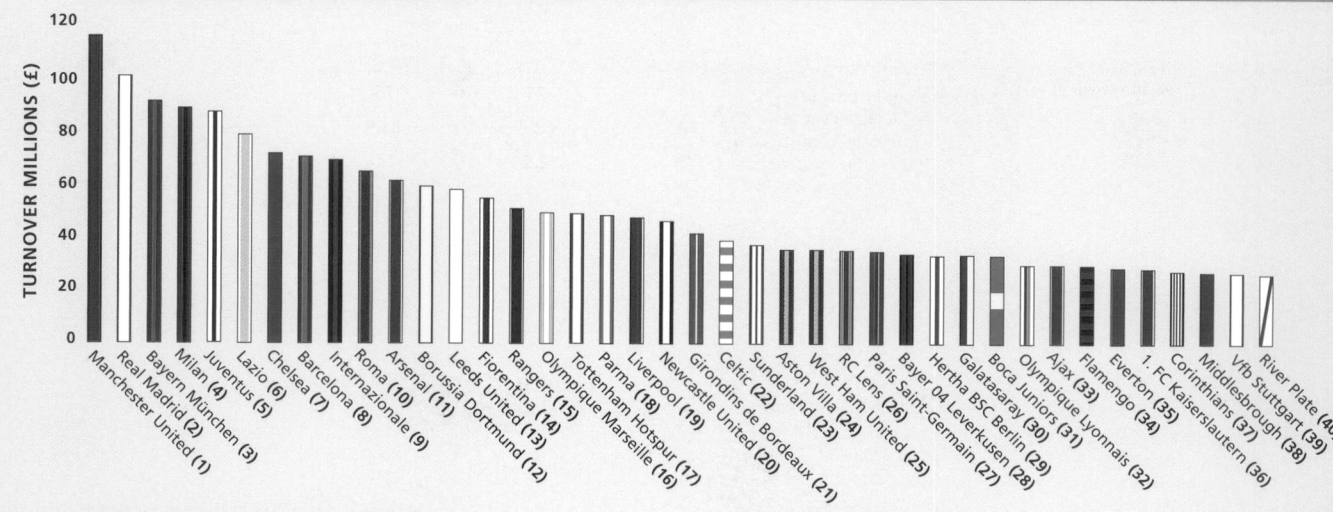

Source: Deloitte and Touche Rich List 2001

TEAM NAMES

FINANCIAL AFFAIRS

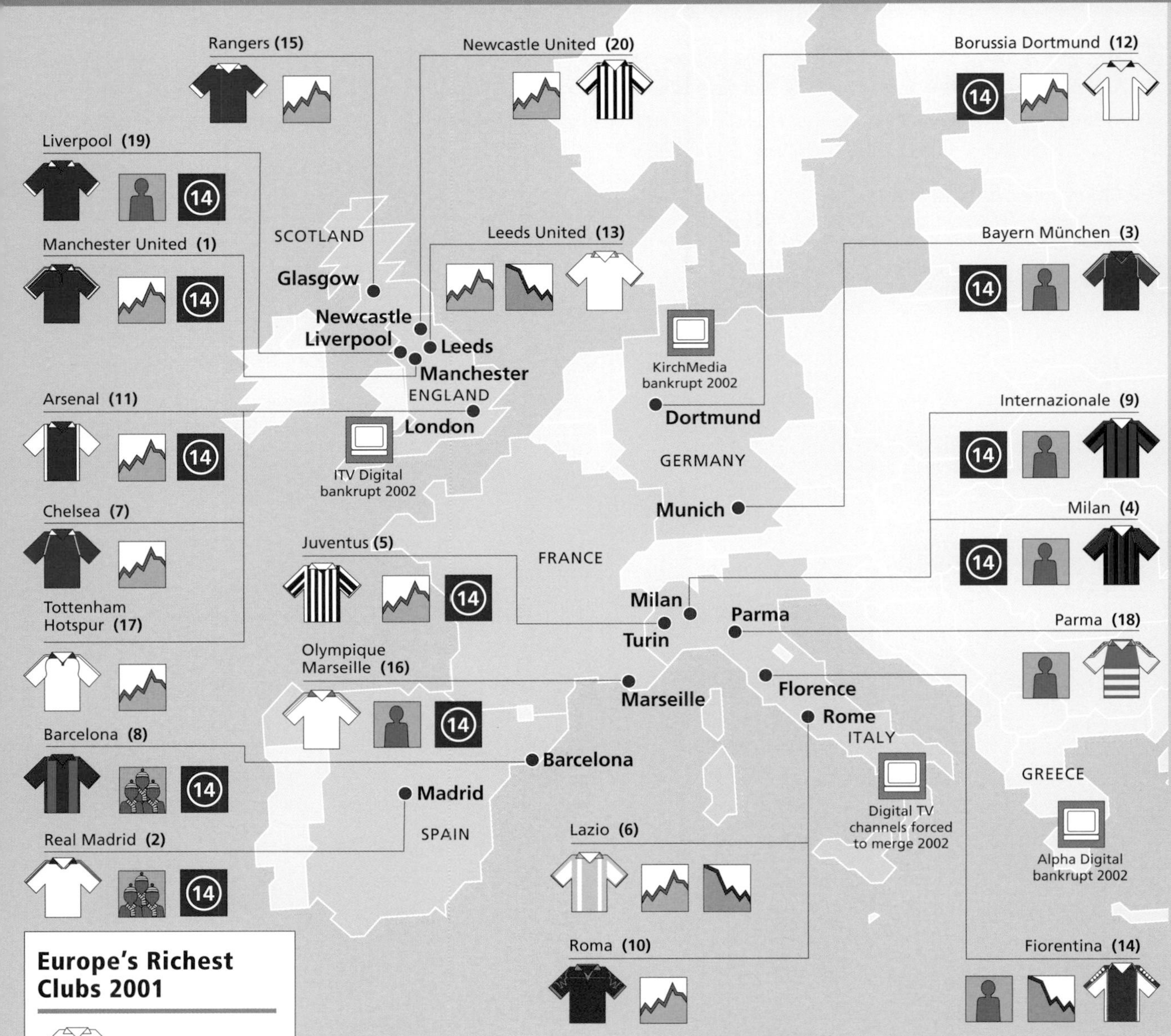

Rangers **(15)**

Newcastle United **(20)**

Borussia Dortmund **(12)**

Liverpool **(19)**

Bayern München **(3)**

Manchester United **(1)**

SCOTLAND

Glasgow

Newcastle

Leeds United **(13)**

Liverpool

Leeds

Manchester

ENGLAND

KirchMedia
bankrupt 2002

Internazionale **(9)**

Arsenal **(11)**

London

GERMANY

ITV Digital
bankrupt 2002

Dortmund

Milan **(4)**

Chelsea **(7)**

Juventus **(5)**

FRANCE

Munich

Tottenham
Hotspur **(17)**

Milan

Parma

Parma **(18)**

Turin

Olympique
Marseille **(16)**

Florence

Rome

Barcelona **(8)**

Marseille

ITALY

GREECE

Barcelona

Madrid

Digital TV
channels forced
to merge 2002

Real Madrid **(2)**

SPAIN

Lazio **(6)**

Alpha Digital
bankrupt 2002

Roma **(10)**

Fiorentina **(14)**

Europe's Richest Clubs 2001

Team Shirt	Manchester United **(1)** — Team name (and wealth ranking)
Privately Owned	Socios
Flotation	Group of 14 (**14**)
Failed TV Deal	Financial Crisis since 2001

Ajax, Bayer Leverkusen, Olympique Lyonnais, Porto, PSG, PSV and Valencia are also members of the Group of 14

Salary Comparison in Deutschmarks (Thousands)

	ENGLAND	ITALY	SPAIN	GERMANY	FRANCE
Player's net income (e.g.)	75	75	75	75	75
Player's taxes and social security	48	62.4	65.5	74	100.5
Club's social security	14.7	2.5	1.5	1.6	52.8
Gross cost to club	**137.7**	**139.9**	**142**	**150.6**	**228.3**

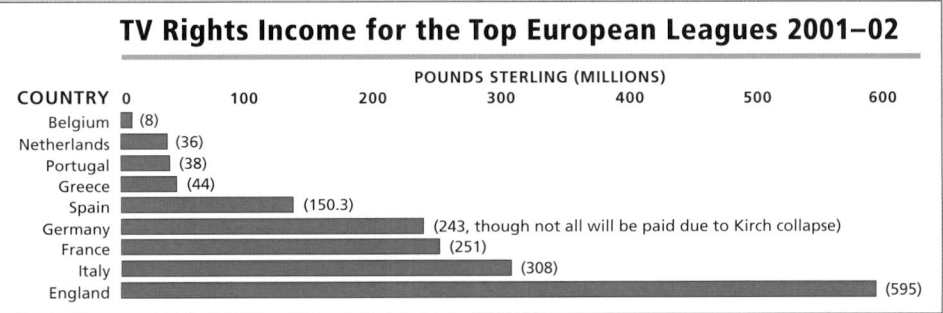

TV Rights Income for the Top European Leagues 2001–02

POUNDS STERLING (MILLIONS)

COUNTRY	
Belgium	(8)
Netherlands	(36)
Portugal	(38)
Greece	(44)
Spain	(150.3)
Germany	(243, though not all will be paid due to Kirch collapse)
France	(251)
Italy	(308)
England	(595)

Football Stadiums

THE LARGEST GROUNDS AND STADIUM DISASTERS

THE GREAT FOOTBALL STADIUMS OF THE WORLD are truly some of the most extraordinary structures of the 20th century. Enormous national stadiums have been built by governments hoping to benefit from the nationalism and grandeur generated by the international game. Modernist cathedrals have been created by the great clubs in pursuit of money and vanity. Yet although many stadiums are architectural triumphs, others are prime examples of appalling town planning.

While money has always been available for constructing stadiums to grand designs, the money and time necessary to make them safe has not. England and Scotland, the first countries to host truly enormous football crowds, have among the poorest stadium safety records of the Western nations. Outside of Europe, the precarious state of football's infrastructure compared to the size of crowds is most stark in Africa, where in 2000 alone four separate stadium disasters saw over 100 people killed. In Latin America persistent crowd trouble and undisciplined policing has added to this dangerous cocktail, making repeated disaster, death and injury at major football matches almost inevitable.

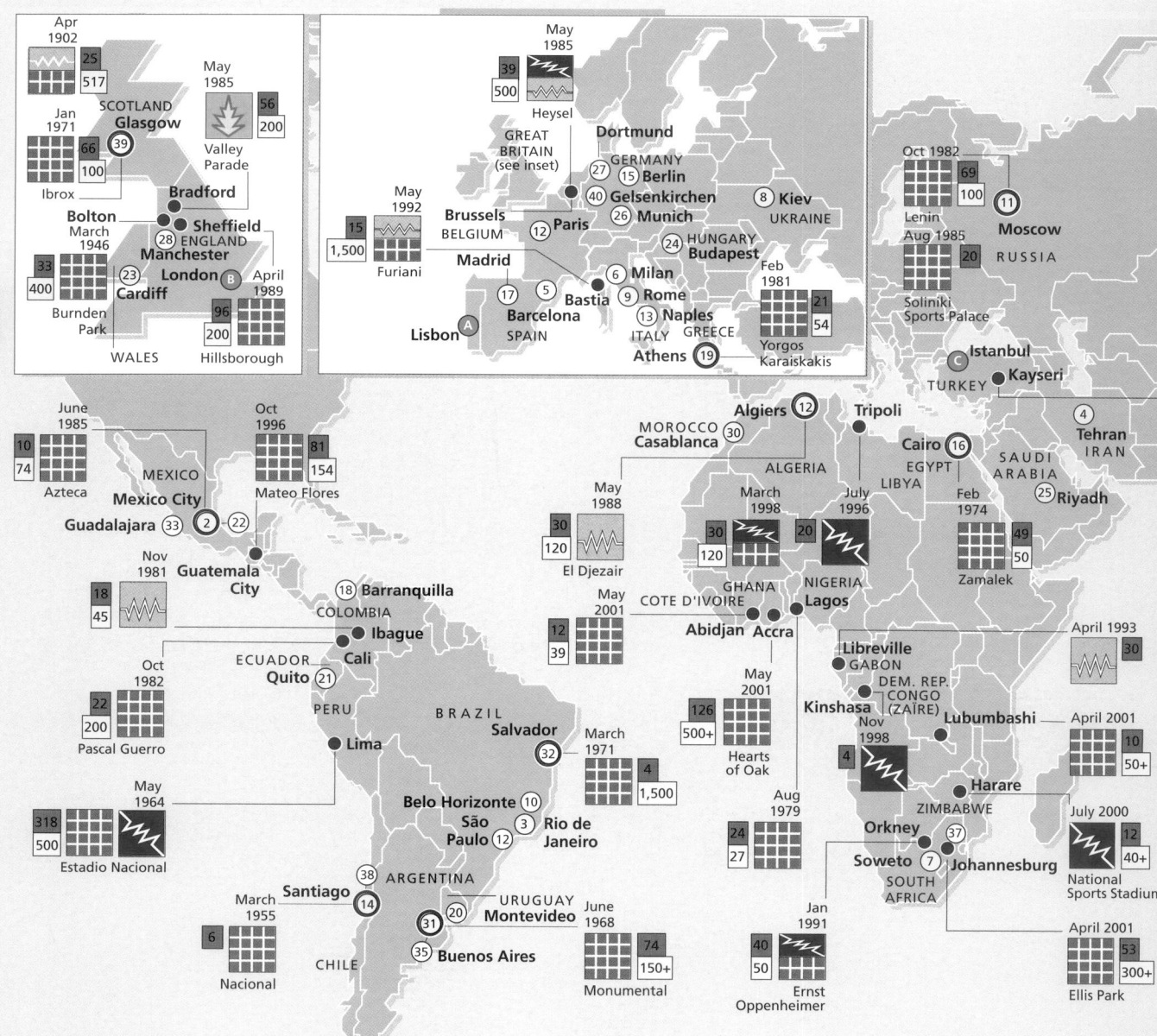

FOOTBALL STADIUMS

The Mario Filho stadium in Rio de Janeiro was opened in 1950 with 140,000 seats plus standing room for 40,000. Better known as the Maracana, it is the biggest stadium the world has ever seen, but a renovation in 1965 reduced its capacity to 103,000.

Key

Date
- Fire
- Stadium
- Police violence
- Crowd violence
- Building collapse
- Crowd crush

| 33 | Dead |
| 400 | Injured |

(1) Ranking by stadium capacity

○ National stadium

● **Lima** Location of disaster

● Major stadium currently under construction

A fire at Bradford City's Valley Parade ground, England, in 1985 claimed the lives of 56 supporters and injured hundreds of others. This disaster led to new legislation governing the safety of British sports grounds.

World's Largest Stadiums (by capacity)

RANK	STADIUM	CAPACITY	TEAMS
1	Saltlake, Calcutta, India	120,000	Mohammedan FC, Mohun Bagan AC, East Bengal
2	Azteca, Mexico City, Mexico	106,000	América
3	Journalista Mario Filho, Rio, Brazil (Maracana)	103,000	Flamengo, Fluminense
4	Azadi, Tehran, Iran	100,000	Piroozi, Esteghlal, Pas, Saypa, Bank Melli
5	Camp Nou, Barcelona, Spain	98,600	Barcelona
6	Giuseppe Meazza, Milan, Italy (San Siro)	85,700	Milan, Internazionale
7	FNB, Soweto, South Africa (Soccer City)	85,000	Orlando Pirates
8	Olimpiyskiy, Kiev, Ukraine	83,160	Dynamo Kyiv
9	Olimpico, Rome, Italy	82,556	Roma, Lazio
10	Mineiro, Belo Horizonte, Brazil	81,897	Cruzeiro, Atlético Mineiro
11	Luzhniki, Moscow, Russia	80,840	Spartak Moskva, Torpedo Moskva
12	5 Julliet 1962, Algiers, Algeria	80,000	MC Alger
12	Cicero Pompeu De Toldedo, São Paulo, Brazil	80,000	São Paulo
12	Shahalam, Kuala Lumpur, Malaysia	80,000	Selangor
12	Shanghai, Shanghai, China	80,000	Shanghai Shenhua
12	Stade de France, Paris	80,000	
13	San Paolo, Naples, Italy (Fuorigrotti)	78,000	Napoli
14	Nacional, Santiago, Chile	77,000	Universidad de Chile
15	Olympiastadion, Berlin, Germany	76,243	Hertha BSC Berlin
16	Cairo International Stadium, Cairo, Egypt	75,750	Al Ahly, Zamalek
17	Santiago Bernabeu, Madrid, Spain	75,500	Real Madrid
18	Metropolitano, Barranquilla, Colombia	75,000	Atlético Júnior
19	Spyros Louis, Athens, Greece	74,443	Panathinaikos, Olympiakos
20	Centenario, Montevideo, Uruguay	73,609	Nacional, Peñarol
21	Monumental, Quito, Ecuador	73,000	Barcelona
22	Olimpico Universitario, Mexico City, Mexico	72,449	UNAM
23	Millennium, Cardiff, Wales	72,000	
24	Ferenc Puskas, Budapest, Hungary	71,000	
25	King Fahd II, Riyadh, Saudi Arabia	70,000	
25	Worker's, Beijing, China	70,000	Beijing Hyundai Cars
25	Yokohama International, Yokohama, Japan	70,000	Yokohama F. Marinos
26	Olympiastadion, Munich, Germany	69,000	Bayern München, TSV 1860 München
27	Westfalenstadion, Dortmund, Germany	68,600	Borussia Dortmund
28	Old Trafford, Manchester, England	68,217	Manchester United
29	Daegu World Cup Stadium, Daegu, South Korea	68,014	Daegu FC
30	Mohammed V, Casablanca, Morocco	67,000	WAC Casablanca, Raja Casablanca
31	A.V. Liberti, Buenos Aires, Argentina (Monumental)	66,449	River Plate
32	Octavio Mangabeira, Salvador, Brazil	66,080	Bahia
33	Estadio Jalisco, Guadalajara, Mexico	66,000	Atlas
34	Seoul World Cup Stadium, Seoul, South Korea	64,667	
35	Presidente Peron, Buenos Aires, Argentina	64,161	Racing Club
36	Saitama Stadium, Saitama, Japan	63,700	
37	Ellis Park, Johannesburg, South Africa	63,000	Kaiser Chiefs
38	David Arellano, Santiago, Chile	62,500	Colo Colo
39	Celtic Park, Glasgow, Scotland (Parkhead)	60,823	Celtic
40	Arena Aufschalke, Gelsenkirchen, Germany	60,215	FC Schalke 04
A	Estadio Da Luz, Lisbon, Portugal	80,000	Under construction
B	Wembley, London, England	90,000	Under construction
C	Atatürk Olympic Stadium, Istanbul, Turkey	80,000	Under construction

FOOTBALL STADIUMS

Playing Styles

Key to Abbreviations

(GK) - Goalkeeper
(FB) - Full-back
(LB) - Left-back
(RB) - Right-back
(3/4B) - 3/4-back
(CB) - Centre-back
(LCB) - Left centre-back

(RCB) - Right centre-back
(HB) - Half-back
(WH) - Wing-half
(M) - Midfielder
(F) - Forward

(IF) - Inside-forward
(CF) - Centre-forward
(C) - Centre
(W) - Winger
(LW) - Left-winger
(RW) - Right-winger
opp. - Opposition

THE EARLIEST STYLES OF FOOTBALL were overwhelmingly attack oriented, with the emphasis on individuals dribbling with the ball while protected by their teammates. The introduction of the offside rule in 1867 limited this system and also prevented the problem of long balls and 'goal hanging'. Early innovations in England and Scotland shifted the emphasis from dribbling and hoofing the ball to quick, short passes and the increased use of space and movement on the pitch. Early pioneers of this style included the Royal Engineers and the 12 clubs who founded the English FA, as well as Scottish professionals and coaches in England and throughout Europe.

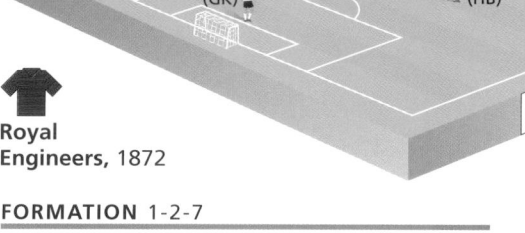

Royal Engineers, 1872

FORMATION 1-2-7

The Royal Engineers are often credited with the development of the first innovative football formations and tactics. The standard 1-2-7 formation was subtly adapted with the seven forwards split into four wingers and three centre-forwards, and the long ball and charge supplemented with short passes.

FORMATION 2-3-5

With the advent of short passing, two forwards were brought back to protect the defence, exemplified by Preston North End's league winning 2-3-5 formation. Defenders covered attacking forwards, the half-backs patrolled the wings and the centre-back in midfield was free to move from defence to attack as required.

Preston North End, 1888

Arsenal, 1926

FORMATION M-W

M-W, perfected by Herbert Chapman's Arsenal team in the 1920s, was a response to the change in the offside rule. Strict man-marking in the back three and withdrawn inside-forwards were complemented by passing through the midfield to the centre-forward, inside-forwards and wingers.

FORMATION M-U

The great Hungarian side retained the old M formation at the back but innovated at the front. A deep-lying centre-forward pulled the opposition markers out of position leaving space for the inside-forwards to raid the opposition box, helped by the fact that they were not required to track back in defence.

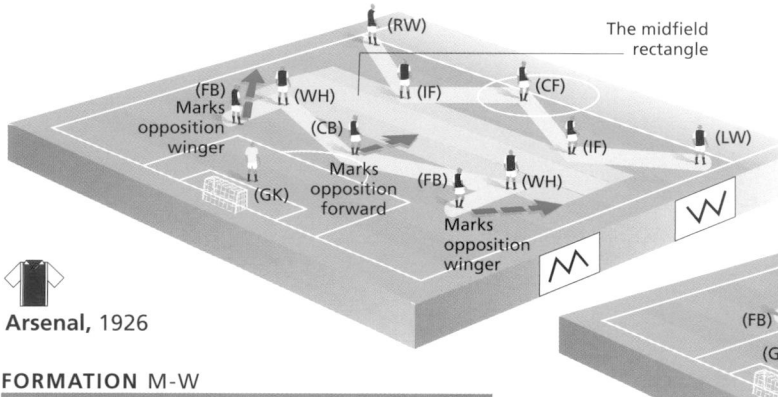

Hungary, 1953

The Development of Formations

1880s Passing game and wing play, developed particularly in Scotland, begin to transform the game and push more players into midfield

1925 Change in the offside rule

1860   1870   1880   1890   1920   1930   1940

Pre-1867 Pre-eminence of dribbling

1867 Offside rule first introduced

1870s First formations emerge – attributed to the Royal Engineers playing 1-2-7

1888–90 Preston North End (the Invincibles), win the first professional league with settled 2-3-5 formation

1934 Karl Rappan introduces the sweeper into the Swiss game

PLAYING STYLES

A new 2-3-5 formation was the mainstay of professional football at the start of the 20th century. However, its limits were soon discovered, and the offside rule gave ample opportunity for quick full-backs to exploit it. In response, play was often confined to a narrow strip near the halfway line. Revisions to the offside rule were capitalized on by Herbert Chapman's M-W formation, which became the standard formation for the next 30 years.

Outside Britain, tactical innovation continued in the inter-war era. Karl Rappan in Switzerland began to develop an early version of *catenaccio*, while the technical virtuosity of central Europeans encouraged a greater emphasis on midfield play and

accurate passing. The rise of the European game was confirmed by Hungary's historic 6-3 victory over England at Wembley in 1953.

In the 1960s and 1970s the flat back four was introduced. *Catenaccio* was perfected by Helenio Herrera's Internazionale, and the sweeper role was given an attacking edge by Franz Beckenbauer's Bayern München. Most exciting of all, Ajax and then Holland played total football, in which all players were required to take up whatever position and role the play of the game dictated. In the 1990s, the 4-4-2 system has come to dominate the global game, with only the occasional side braving the reintroduction of wing-backs in flexible 3-5-2/5-3-2 systems.

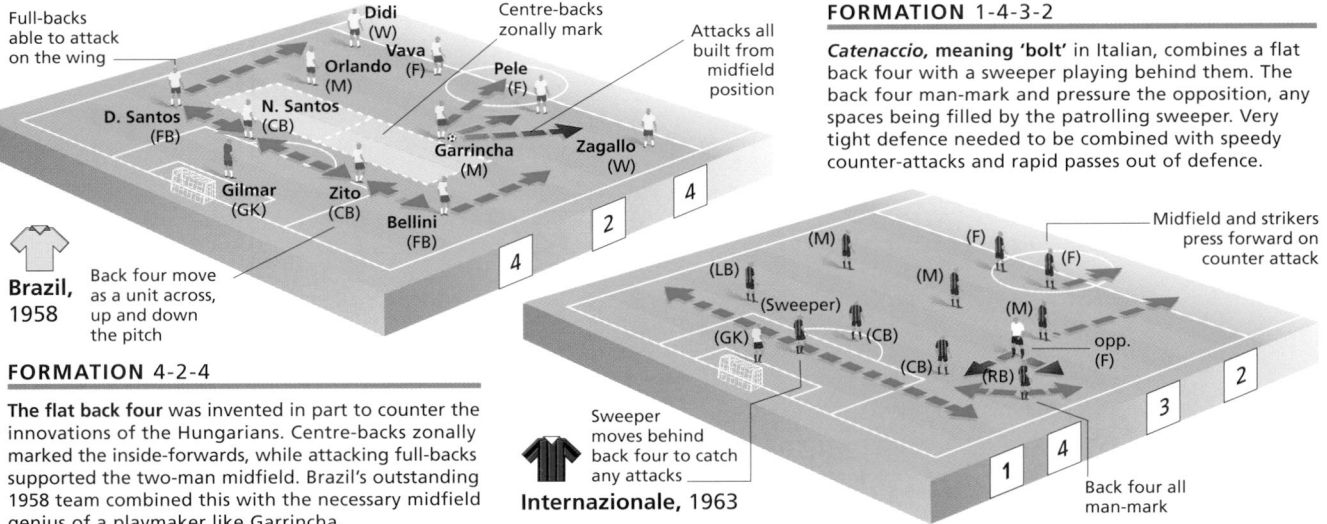

Brazil, 1958

FORMATION 4-2-4

The flat back four was invented in part to counter the innovations of the Hungarians. Centre-backs zonally marked the inside-forwards, while attacking full-backs supported the two-man midfield. Brazil's outstanding 1958 team combined this with the necessary midfield genius of a playmaker like Garrincha.

England, 1966

FORMATION 4-4-2

Although Ramsey's wingless wonders were labelled 4-3-3, the formation is really the first 4-4-2, with Bobby Charlton playing as an attacking midfielder, covered by the defensive solidity of Nobby Stiles alongside and behind him, converting the formation from 4-4-2 in defence to 4-3-3 in attack.

FORMATION 1-4-3-2

Catenaccio, meaning 'bolt' in Italian, combines a flat back four with a sweeper playing behind them. The back four man-mark and pressure the opposition, any spaces being filled by the patrolling sweeper. Very tight defence needed to be combined with speedy counter-attacks and rapid passes out of defence.

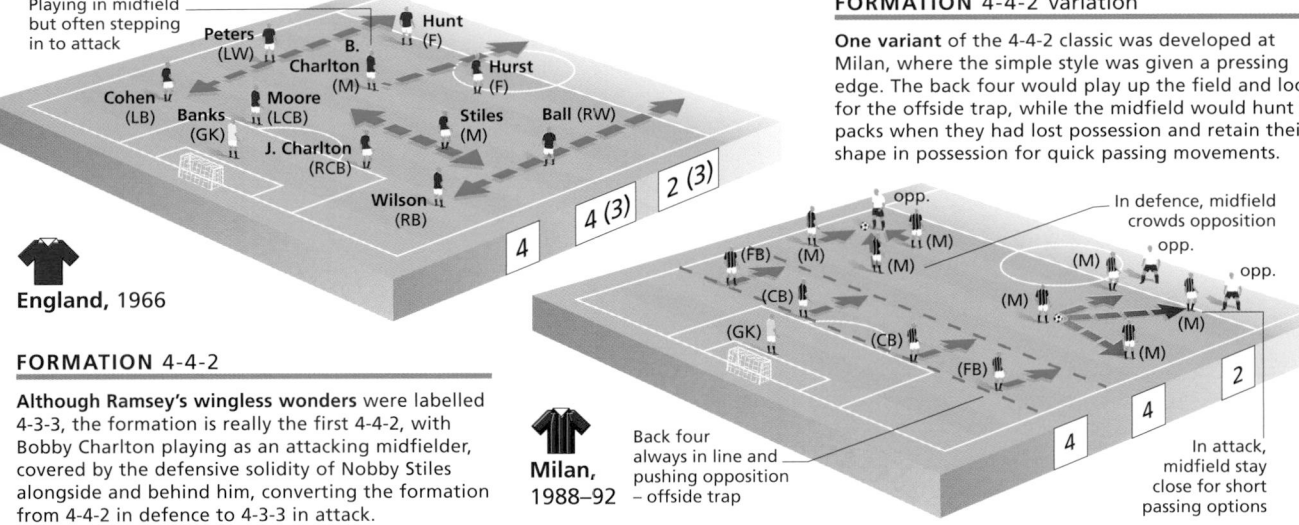

Internazionale, 1963

FORMATION 4-4-2 variation

One variant of the 4-4-2 classic was developed at Milan, where the simple style was given a pressing edge. The back four would play up the field and look for the offside trap, while the midfield would hunt in packs when they had lost possession and retain their shape in possession for quick passing movements.

Milan, 1988–92

| 1950–54 Honvéd and Hungary play W-M but transform attack with deep-lying centre-forwards | 1964–65 Helenio Herrera's Internazionale perfect *catenaccio* | 1970–74 Ajax and the Netherlands play total football | 1977–85 Paisley's Liverpool play classic 4-4-2 passing game | 1993 Wing-backs return to the English Premiership, 5-3-2 and 3-5-2 formations |

1950   1960   1970   1980   1990   2000

| 1958 Brazil win the World Cup with revolutionary flat back four and four strikers (4-2-4) | 1966 Alf Ramsey's England win the World Cup with a wingless 4-4-2 | 1972–76 Beckenbauer perfects the role of deep sweeper in Bayern München's three-person defence | 1988–92 Arrigo Sacchi's Milan play 4-4-2 variant with zonal marking and pressing |

CONCACAF

CONFEDERATION RANKING	WORLD RANKING	COUNTRY
1	9	Mexico
2	10	USA
3	22	Costa Rica
4	40	Honduras
5	49	Trinidad & Tobago

Data correct for March 2003

CONMEBOL

CONFEDERATION RANKING	WORLD RANKING	COUNTRY
1	1	Brazil
2	4	Argentina
3	18	Paraguay
4	28	Uruguay
5	31	Ecuador

Data correct for March 2003

CAF

CONFEDERATION RANKING	WORLD RANKING	COUNTRY
1	17	Cameroon
2	27	Senegal
3	29	Nigeria
4	30	South Africa
5	35	Morocco

Data correct for March 2003

AFC

CONFEDERATION RANKING	WORLD RANKING	COUNTRY
1	20	South Korea
2	24	Japan
3	32	Iran
4	38	Saudi Arabia
5	52	Iraq

Data correct for March 2003

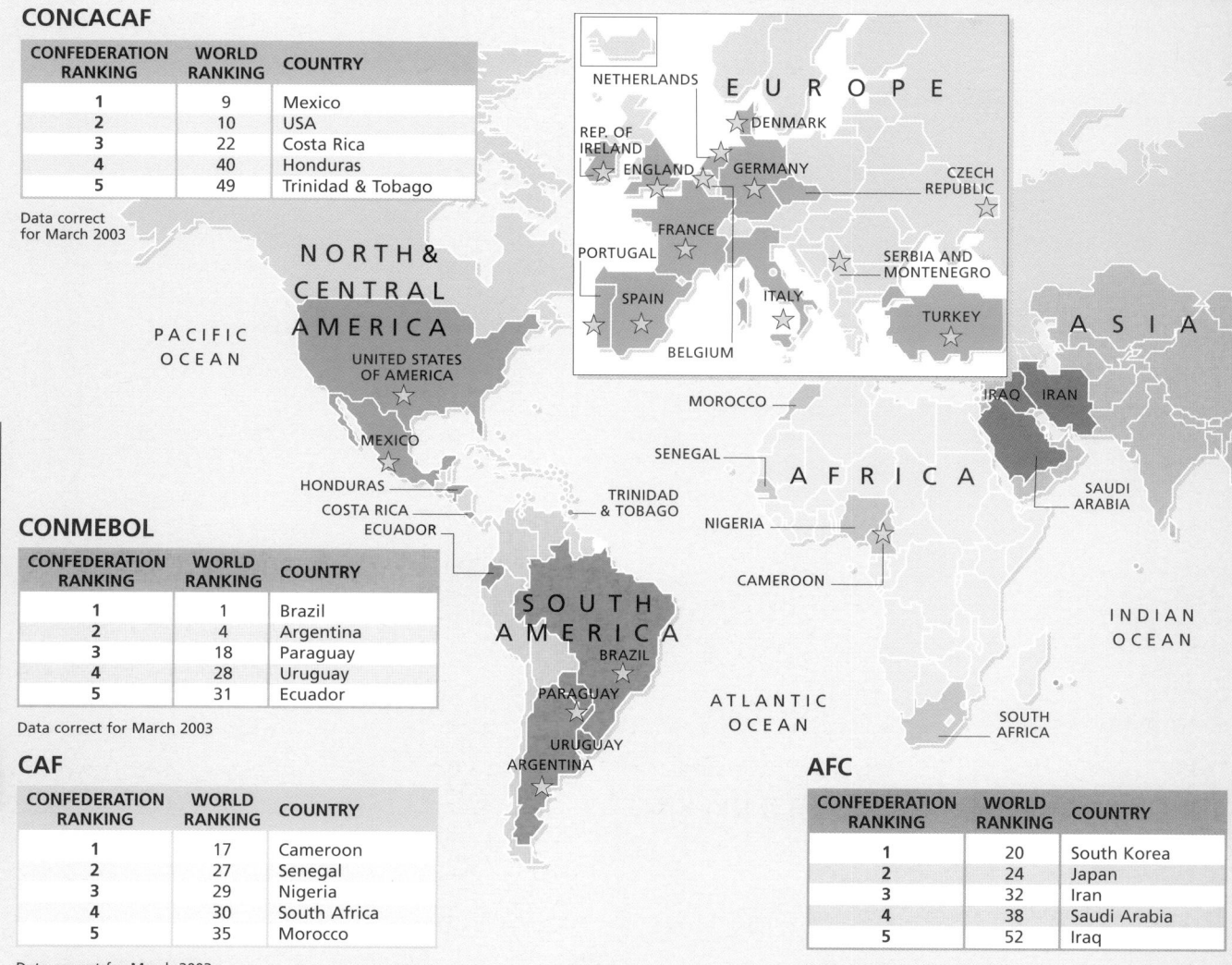

The Shifting Balance

POWER IN WORLD FOOTBALL

Just who is the best team in the world? Which nations are on the up and which are on the way down? Where is football's centre of gravity? A simple way of addressing this question is to look at World Cup results. Latin America and Europe are the only regional contenders, as no team from another continent had ever even made the semi-finals until the South Koreans' extraordinary progress in 2002. Given that South America has a fifth of the membership of UEFA, its performance at the World Cup is extraordinary, and almost wholly dependent on three nations: Argentina, Uruguay and Brazil. At club level, there are too few points of real comparison (apart from the World Club Cup), though on a financial level it is clear that Europe, and Western Europe in particular, stands head and shoulders above everyone.

But World Cup results tell just one strand, albeit an important one, of football's shifting balance of power. At a political and institutional level the make-up of FIFA, where every nation has one vote, is instructive. For the first 40 years of its existence, FIFA had a European majority and a major Latin American lobby group. Since the 1960s, the growth of African and Asian membership has made them the majority. Looking at results over time, FIFA's ranking system, first calculated in 1993, provides a rolling measure of national and continental strengths. Ratings are calculated by looking at results over the previous six years, factoring in the strength of the opposition and the importance of tournaments and competitive matches. At the turn of the century, Europe continues to dominate the top 20, Latin America takes three or four spots and occasional visitors include Mexico, Nigeria and Japan. However, FIFA's rankings give undue emphasis to a team's best performances, and allows many of its poor performances to be discounted. It also looks at the game over a very long period, and is often out of kilter with more contemporary form.

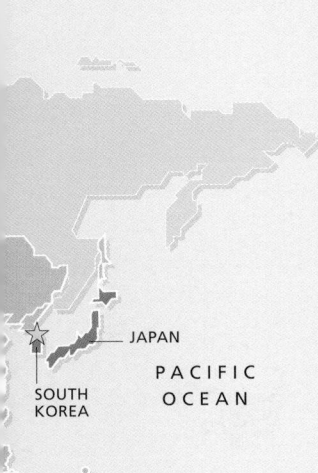

JAPAN

SOUTH KOREA

PACIFIC OCEAN

FIJI

AUSTRALIA

O C E A N I A

TAHITI

TONGA

NEW ZEALAND

FIFA's Top 20 Ranked Nations

RANK	1993	1997	2003
1	Germany	Brazil	Brazil
2	Italy	Germany	France
3	Brazil	Czech Republic	Spain
4	Norway	England	Argentina
5	Spain	Mexico	Germany
6	Denmark	France	Netherlands
7	Netherlands	Romania	Turkey
8	Argentina	Denmark	England
9	Sweden	Italy	Mexico
10	Rep. of Ireland	Colombia	USA
11	England	Spain	Denmark
12	Switzerland	Russia	Portugal
13	Romania	Norway	Italy
14	Russia	Japan	Rep. of Ireland
15	France	Morocco	Czech Republic
16	Mexico	Chile	Belgium
17	Uruguay	Argentina	Cameroon
18	Nigeria	Sweden	Paraguay
19	Czech Republic	Croatia	Serbia/Montenegro
20	Portugal	Yugoslavia	South Korea

UEFA

CONFEDERATION RANKING	WORLD RANKING	COUNTRY
1	2	France
2	3	Spain
3	5	Germany
4	6	Netherlands
5	7	Turkey
6	8	England
7=	11=	Denmark
7=	11=	Portugal
8	13	Italy
9	14	Rep. of Ireland
10	15	Czech Republic

Data correct for March 2003

OFC

CONFEDERATION RANKING	WORLD RANKING	COUNTRY
1	47	Australia
2	50	New Zealand
3	88	Tonga
4	115	Tahiti
5	140	Fiji

Data correct for March 2003

World Cup performance

Europe		South America
	Winners	
	Runners-up	
	Semi-finalists	

20
15
10
5
0
0
5
10

1930–54   1958–74   1978–2002

Back where they belong: Rivaldo (left) and Ronaldo celebrate Brazil's fifth World Cup triumph in Yokohama, Japan, in June 2002 – a victory that returned them to the top of the FIFA rankings.

Key to Confederation Rankings

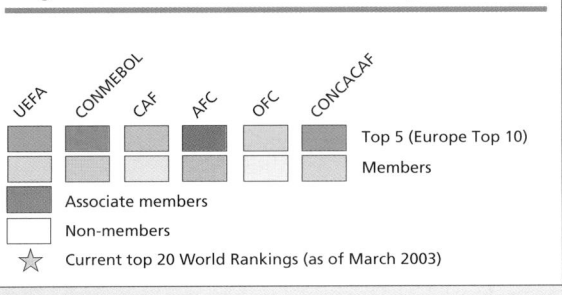

UEFA   CONMEBOL   CAF   AFC   OFC   CONCACAF

Top 5 (Europe Top 10)

Members

Associate members

Non-members

★ Current top 20 World Rankings (as of March 2003)

Make up of FIFA by Confederation

UEFA
CONMEBOL
CAF
AFC
OFC
CONCACAF

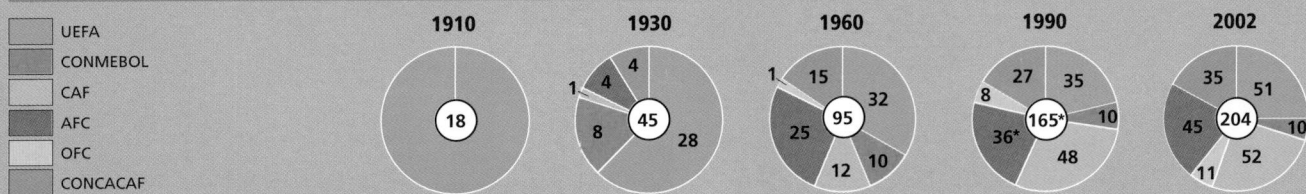

1910 — 18

1930 — 45 (1, 4, 4, 8, 28)

1960 — 95 (1, 15, 32, 25, 12, 10)

1990 — 165* (27, 35, 8, 36*, 48, 10)

2002 — 204 (35, 51, 45, 11, 52, 10)

* See page 494–495 for details on Israel

African Exodus

PLAYERS ON THE MOVE

THE EXTRAORDINARY RISE AND ENDURING PROBLEMS of African football are reflected in the migration of Africa's top players. Since Eusebio left Mozambique for Lisbon's SL Benfica in the early 1960s, Africans have been making their mark in European club football. However, as the locations of the African Player of the Year awards indicate, it is only since the 1980s that the northward migration of players has really begun.

The enormous pool of talent in African football, combined with desperate economic conditions at home and ever richer, more open European leagues, has seen a massive flow of talent to Europe. Nigeria, Cameroon, South Africa and the DRC are all key exporters of players. Their destinations remain concentrated in the richest leagues (Spain, Germany and Italy) and in countries with African imperial pasts (Portugal, Belgium, France and Britain), but such are the wage differentials between the continents that there are now Africans playing in almost every European league from the Caucasus to the Low Countries.

Indeed, many Africans are taking European citizenship and playing for European national teams as well as clubs. However, as is usual in the scramble for riches, there are plenty of casualties. Unscrupulous scouts and agents have shipped promising youngsters north only to leave them high and dry when clubs don't pick them up. And if they do eventually make it to the playing field, they must often endure the predictable and grotesque racism of certain elements of the European footballing public.

African players exported to Europe

Top divisions only

African Exodus 2002

	Players exported from CAF	Players imported into UEFA from CAF
	60+	40+
	40–60	20–40
	20–40	11–20
	1–20	1–10
	0	0

Top 10 exporters, with figure — 35
Top 10 importers, with figure — 35

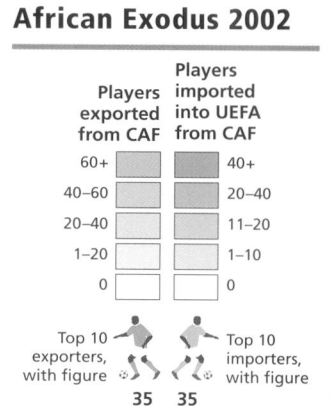

Albert Johanneson moved from South Africa to play for Leeds United in England in 1961.

MOROCCO 51
TUNISIA
MEDITERRANEAN SEA
ALGERIA
SENEGAL 38
EGYPT
CAPE VERDE
MALI
NIGER
GAMBIA
BURKINA FASO
NIGERIA 109
GUINEA
SIERRA LEONE
BENIN
CENTRAL AFRICAN REPUBLIC
LIBERIA 18
TOGO
KENYA
COTE D'IVOIRE
GHANA 37
SAO TOME & PRINCIPE
CONGO GABON
DEM.REP. OF CONGO (Zaire) 27
UGANDA
RWANDA
BURUNDI
CAMEROON 54
ANGOLA 15
TANZANIA
ATLANTIC OCEAN
ZAMBIA
MOZAMBIQUE
NAMIBIA
ZIMBABWE
SOUTH AFRICA 25
INDIAN OCEAN

African nations with African immigrant players

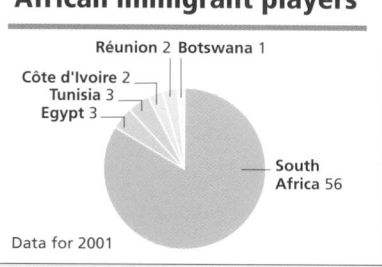

Réunion 2 Botswana 1
Côte d'Ivoire 2
Tunisia 3
Egypt 3
South Africa 56

Data for 2001

Ayew Abedi Pelé played for Olympique Marseille in France.

France Football: African Player of the Year

YEAR	PLAYER	NATIONALITY	CLUB	COUNTRY
1970	Keita	Malian	AS Saint-Etienne	France
1971	Sunday	Ghanaian	Asante Kotoko	Ghana
1972	Souleymane	Guinean	Hafia Conakry	Guinea
1973	Bwanga	Congolese	TP Mazembe	Zaire
1974	Moukila	Congolese	CARA Brazzaville	Congo
1975	Faras	Moroccan	Chebab Mohammedia	Morocco
1976	Milla	Cameroonian	Canon Yaoundé	Cameroon
1977	Dhiab	Tunisian	Espérance Sportive	Tunisia
1978	Razak	Ghanaian	Asante Kotoko	Ghana
1979	N'Kono	Cameroonian	Canon Yaoundé	Cameroon
1980	Manga-Onguene	Cameroonian	Canon Yaoundé	Cameroon
1981	Belloumi	Algerian	GCR Mascara	Algeria
1982	N'Kono	Cameroonian	RCD Español	Spain
1983	Al-Khatib	Egyptian	Al Ahly	Egypt
1984	Abega	Cameroonian	Toulouse FC	France
1985	Tomoumi	Moroccan	FAR Rabat	Morocco
1986	Zaki	Moroccan	RCD Mallorca	Spain
1987	Madjer	Algerian	FC Porto	Portugal
1988	Bwalya	Zambian	Club Brugge KV	Belgium
1989	Weah	Liberian	AS Monaco	France
1990	Milla	Cameroonian	Saint Denis	Réunion
1991	Abedi Pelé	Ghanaian	Olympique Marseille	France
1992	Abedi Pelé	Ghanaian	Olympique Marseille	France
1993	Abedi Pelé	Ghanaian	Olympique Marseille	France
1994	Weah	Liberian	Paris Saint-Germain	France
1995	Weah	Liberian	Milan	Italy
1996	Kanu	Nigerian	Internazionale	Italy

CAF African Player of the Year

YEAR	PLAYER	NATIONALITY	CLUB	COUNTRY
1992	Abedi Pelé	Ghanaian	Olympique Marseille	France
1993	Yekini	Nigerian	Vitória Setúbal	Portugal
1994	Amunike	Nigerian	Sporting CP	Portugal
1995	Weah	Liberian	Milan	Italy
1996	Kanu	Nigerian	Internazionale	Italy
1997	Ikpeba	Nigerian	AS Monaco	France
1998	Hadji	Moroccan	RC Deportivo	Spain
1999	Kanu	Nigerian	Arsenal	England
2000	Mboma	Cameroonian	Parma	Italy
2001	Diouf	Senegalese	Lens	France
2002	Diouf	Senegalese	Liverpool	England

Where African Players play 2001

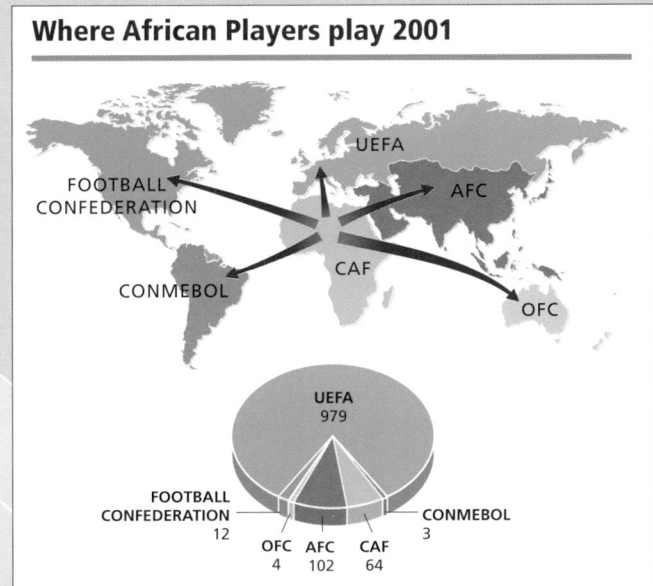

African players in Europe 2002

Top divisions only

His brilliant performances at the World Cup in Japan/Korea and his subsequent move to Liverpool helped El Hadji Diouf retain his CAF African Player of the Year award in 2002.

South American Exodus

PLAYERS ON THE MOVE

FOR MOST OF THE 19th AND 20th CENTURIES, South America has been a destination of European migration. But in the world of football the traffic has been in the opposite direction since the end of the First World War. Records show that some Argentinians were playing in Italy before 1914, but the earliest recorded transfer across the South Atlantic is probably Julio Libonatti from Newell's Old Boys to Torino in 1925.

The Olympic tournaments showcased American talent to the rich clubs of Europe. Leading striker Raimondo Orsi left Argentina for Juventus and as an *oriundi* (a descendant of Italian migrants) played for Italy in the 1934 World Cup. In 1931 Vasco da Gama's tour of Spain ended with their stars Fausto and Jaguare staying on in Barcelona. Only the coming of professionalism in Latin America slowed the flow to European clubs, though the exodus resumed after the Second World War especially during the players' strikes in Argentina and Uruguay in the late 1940s. The great Argentinian forward line of the 1950s – Sivori, Machio, Angellilio – all transferred to Italian clubs.

In a fit of footballing autarchy Spain, Portugal and Italy banned the further signing of foreigners in the 1970s and numbers dropped. With the removal of the ban in the 1980s and the steady disintegration of many Latin American economies, the flow increased, aided and abetted by the extensive use of false passports suggesting players have European grandparents. Today, some 400 Latin Americans play in Europe and not merely in their old Latin strongholds, but in every major and many minor leagues as well. More significantly, the leading players from recent World Cup squads almost all play their football in Europe.

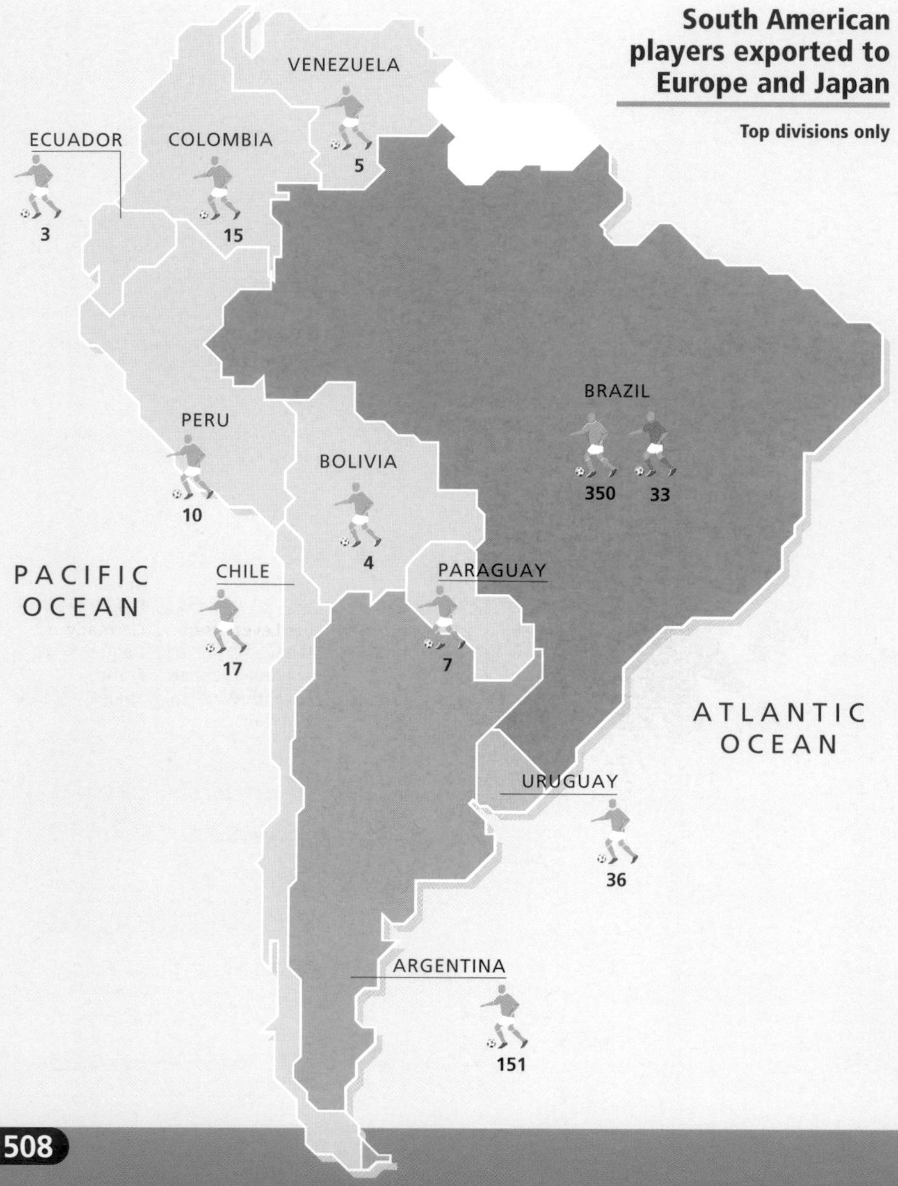

South American players exported to Europe and Japan

Top divisions only

VENEZUELA 5

ECUADOR 3

COLOMBIA 15

PERU 10

BOLIVIA 4

CHILE 17

PARAGUAY 7

BRAZIL 350 · 33

URUGUAY 36

ARGENTINA 151

PACIFIC OCEAN

ATLANTIC OCEAN

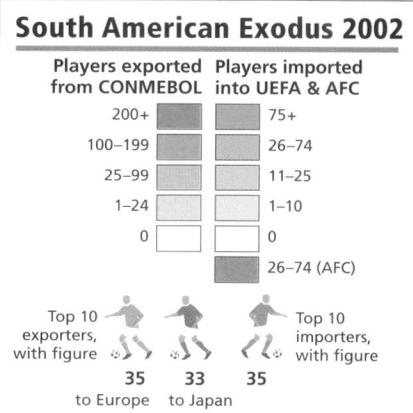

South American Exodus 2002

Players exported from CONMEBOL	Players imported into UEFA & AFC
200+	75+
100–199	26–74
25–99	11–25
1–24	1–10
0	0
	26–74 (AFC)

Top 10 exporters, with figure

Top 10 importers, with figure

35 to Europe 33 to Japan 35

Julio Libonatti left Newell's Old Boys of Rosario, Argentina, in 1925 to join Torino in Italy – the earliest recorded major football transfer across the South Atlantic.

South American players in Europe and Japan 2002

Top divisions only

ICELAND

FAEROE ISLANDS

ATLANTIC OCEAN

FINLAND
17

ENGLAND
17

SCOTLAND

SWEDEN

DENMARK

RUSSIA

NETHERLANDS

BELARUS

GERMANY
31

POLAND

BELGIUM

UKRAINE

CZECH. REP

SLOVAKIA

AUSTRIA

FRANCE
35

HUNGARY

SLOVENIA

ROMANIA

CROATIA

SERBIA & MONTENEGRO

BLACK SEA

LUXEMBOURG

ITALY
69

BULGARIA

MACEDONIA
ALBANIA

TURKEY
28

PORTUGAL
123

SPAIN
94

SWITZERLAND
38

GREECE
27

MALTA

MEDITERRANEAN SEA

ISRAEL

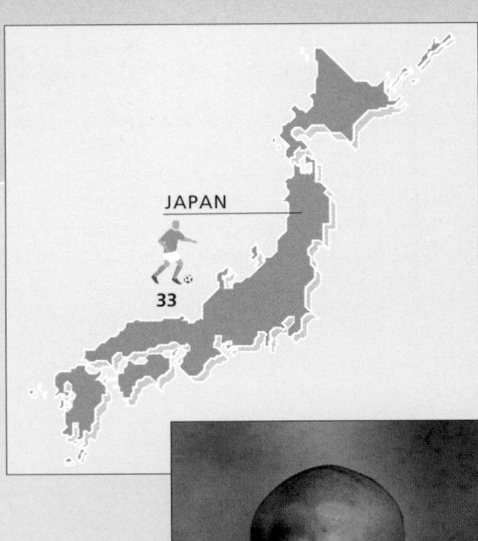

JAPAN
33

Juan Sebastian Veron played for several clubs in Italy before moving to Manchester United of England in 2001, a move thrown into doubt over the validity of his passport.

SOUTH AMERICAN EXODUS

Argentinian World Cup Squad 2002

NAME	CLUB	COUNTRY
Burgos	Atlético Madrid	Spain
Ayala	Valencia	Spain
Sorin	Cruzeiro	Brazil
Pochettino	PSG	France
Almeyda	Parma	Italy
Samuel	Roma	Italy
Lopez	Lazio	Italy
Zanetti	Internazionale	Italy
Batistuta	Roma	Italy
Ortega	River Plate	Argentina
Veron	Manchester United	England
Cavallero	RC Celta	Spain
Placente	Bayer Leverkusen	Germany
Simeone	Lazio	Italy
Husain	River Plate	Argentina
Aimar	Valencia	Spain
Lopez	RC Celta	Spain
Gonzalez	Valencia	Spain
Crespo	Lazio	Italy
Gallardo	AS Monaco	France
Caniggia	Rangers	Scotland
Chamot	Milan	Italy
Bonano	Barcelona	Spain

No way home: River Plate's parlous finances have made it difficult for them to re-sign Ariel Ortega after a mixed season with Fenerbahçe in Turkey.

Brazilian World Cup Squad 2002

NAME	CLUB	COUNTRY
Marcos	Palmeiras	Brazil
Cafu	Roma	Italy
Lucio	Bayer Leverkusen	Germany
Roque Junior	Milan	Italy
Edmilson	Olympique Lyonnais	France
Roberto Carlos	Real Madrid	Spain
Richardinho	Corinthians	Brazil
Gilberto Silva	Atlético Mineiro	Brazil
Ronaldo	Internazionale	Italy
Rivaldo	Barcelona	Spain
Ronaldinho	PSG	France
Dida	Corinthians	Brazil
Belletti	São Paulo	Brazil
Anderson Polga	Grêmio	Brazil
Kleberson	Atlético Paranaense	Brazil
Junior	Parma	Italy
Denilson	Real Betis	Spain
Vempeta	Corinthians	Brazil
Juninho	Flamengo	Brazil
Edilson	Cruzeiro	Brazil
Luizao	Grêmio	Brazil
Rogerio Ceni	São Paulo	Brazil
Kaka	São Paulo	Brazil

Top 20 Players

THE 20 GREATEST FOOTBALL PLAYERS – it's a list asking for trouble, inviting argument and fierce criticism. However, no book on the beautiful game would be complete without one. One category of players is automatic and uncontested – everyone's favourites: Pele, Maradona, Beckenbauer, Cruyff, Eusebio, di Stefano, van Basten, Puskas, Best, Yashin and Platini. But then it becomes more difficult. To simplify matters, this selection does not include any players from the amateur era. It was only in the early 1930s that all the major footballing nations ran professional leagues, so this list starts there. From the pre-war era comes Giuseppe Meazza; dominant at club level, he also won two World Cup winner's medals. Stanley Matthew's career spanned many eras, and he gets the nod for his longevity, his integrity and his popularity. From the postwar years come players from a spread of nations and eras. From Brazil comes Garrincha for speed and guile; from England, Bobby Moore fills out the defenders on the list; from Germany, the unstoppable goalscorer Gerd Müller; from Italy, the only football culture in which defenders are revered in the same way as strikers, the archetype Franco Baresi; and from Scotland comes Kenny Dalglish, the most successful player in British football. For a second goalkeeper it is Schmeichel over Banks and Zoff, and from the game now it has to be Zidane. Apologies to Nilton Santos, Daniel Passarella, Denis Law, Ruud Gullit and Raymond Kopa, who should all have been included, among others...

Marco **van Basten**

Born: October 31, 1964
Country: Netherlands
Position: Striker
Caps: 58
Goals: 24
Teams: Ajax
  ▲1987
  ●1982–84
  Milan
  ●1989, 90
  ●1988, 92, 93
Honours: World Footballer of the Year (WS): 1988, 92
World Player of the Year (FIFA): 1992
European Footballer of the Year (FF): 1988, 89, 92

Marco van Basten was the consummate modern goalscorer. He made his professional debut with Ajax in 1983, filling in for his mentor Johan Cruyff. He scored, and went on scoring, 128 goals in 133 games for Ajax in five years, including the winning goals in the 1987 European Cup-Winners' Cup Final. He won the European Golden Boot (top domestic scorer) in 1986. He moved to Milan in 1987 where the goals continued to come and alongside Milan's domestic and international trophies he won the European Footballer of the Year award three times. His international career began in 1983 and saw him score the amazing volley that won the Netherlands the 1988 European Championships Final against the Soviet Union. Persistent ankle injuries saw him retire from the game in 1993 after the European Cup Final against Marseille.

Franco **Baresi**

Born: May 8, 1960
Country: Italy
Position: Defender
Caps: 81
Goals: 1
Teams: Milan
  ●1989, 90
  ●1988, 92, 93, 94

Franco Baresi played his entire footballing career with a single club, Milan. He joined them as a teenager in 1977 (his elder brother Giuseppe joined rivals Internazionale). Baresi came to dominate and redefine the role of the modern sweeper through the 1980s and 90s. Always calm under pressure, his brilliant reading of the game, sharp intelligence and effortlessly timed tackling provided the defensive base onto which Milan could graft the attacking power of Dutchmen Ruud Gullit and Marco van Basten. But he was always more than a stopper; launching attacks for others and making powerful runs himself to give his side an extra attacking option. In the late 1980s, Baresi captained Milan and took them to two European Cup successes and four Serie A championships (suspension would deprive him of the chance to captain Milan in a third successful European Cup Final against Barcelona in 1994). Baresi's international career began in 1982 and culminated in his captaincy of the national team at the 1994 World Cup. The lynchpin of the team, he underwent knee surgery during the tournament, but returned to lead them in the Final against Brazil. A brilliant match and tournament was tragically capped when Baresi shot over the bar in the penalty shootout that decided the tournament in Brazil's favour.

Franz **Beckenbauer**

Born: September 11, 1945
Country: West Germany
  ■1974
  ■1967
Position: Defender
Caps: 103
Goals: 13
Teams: TSV 1860 München
  Bayern München
  ●1974–76
  ▲1967
  ●1969, 73, 74
  New York Cosmos
  Hamburger SV
Honours: European Footballer of the Year: 1972, 76

Franz Beckenbauer is a rarity – a footballer of intelligence and grace; a successful player and coach; and, as Germany's victory in the race to secure the World Cup in 2006 shows, a sharp political operator and administrator. Little wonder that his nickname is 'Der Kaiser'. He began his career with TSV 1860 München, but was quickly snapped up by big city rivals Bayern where he remained until 1976. He made his debut in 1964 and was chosen for the national squad a year later, a place he retained until 1977. He remains West Germany's most capped player. At Bayern, he matured from midfielder to an attacking sweeper, adept in defence, ruthless coming forward, always passing into space. After winning three European Cups with Bayern he played for New York Cosmos and Hamburger SV before retiring. He returned to the game as national team coach in 1984.

Key ■ World Cup ▲ World Club Cup ■ European Championships ● European Cup/Champions League ◆ UEFA Cup

George **Best**

Born: May 22, 1946
Country: Northern Ireland
Position: Striker
Caps: 37
Goals: 9
Teams: Manchester United
● 1968
● 1965, 67
Dunstable
Stockport County
Los Angeles Aztecs
Cork Celtic
Fulham
Fort Lauderdale
Strikers
Motherwell
Hibernian
San José Earthquakes
Honours: European Footballer
of the Year (FF): 1968

George Best arrived in Manchester from Belfast in 1963 to play for United at the age of 17. Ten years at Old Trafford yielded two league titles, the European Cup and the European Footballer of the Year award in 1968. More importantly, they saw some of the finest football ever seen in England. Best had speed, ferocity and extraordinary balance and grace on the ball. He played 361 league games for United, scoring 137 goals. Best was the first footballer to rise to the dizzy heights of global fame usually reserved for film and pop stars. Nicknamed 'El Beatle' in Spain, he lived a very public life of glamour, celebrity and heavy drinking. By 1973 he had begun to fall out with United and quit. A series of comebacks began at Stockport County, and while the grace remained, the speed and power were lost forever.

Kenny **Dalglish**

Born: March 4, 1951
Country: Scotland
Position: Striker
Caps: 102
Goals: 30
Teams: Celtic
(player) ● 1972–74, 77
Liverpool
● 1979, 80, 82, 83,
84
● 1978, 81, 84
(player/ Liverpool
manager) ● 1986, 88, 90

Kenny Dalglish is the most successful footballer Scotland has ever produced. He began his career at Celtic in 1967 where he played 204 league games, scoring a total of 112 goals. He was sold in 1977 for a transfer fee of £440,000 (then a UK record) to Liverpool, where he played 354 league games, scoring 118 goals. He progressed to player/manager of the team at Anfield in 1985 and in his first season became the first player/manager to win an English league and cup double. He retired suddenly from the game in 1991, only to return six months later as manager of Blackburn Rovers. Success again followed, with promotion to the top flight, followed in 1995 by the league title, Blackburn's first major trophy for 81 years. As a player he possessed pace, authority and clarity, and was the idol of the fans. In total, as a player and a manager he has won 26 major trophies, collected 102 caps and scored 30 international goals – a record he holds with Denis Law.

Johan **Cruyff**

Born: April 25, 1947
Country: Netherlands
Position: Striker
Caps: 48
Goals: 33
Teams: Ajax (twice)
● 1971–73
● 1966–68, 70, 72,
73, 83
Barcelona
● 1974
Los Angeles Aztecs
Washington Diplomats
Levante
Feyenoord
● 1984
Honours: European Footballer
of the Year (FF):
1971, 73, 74

Christened 'Pythagoras in boots', Johan Cruyff's brilliance lay in an ability to understand instantly the disposition of force on a football field, to see where space was available and to find the move, the pass, the feint that put the ball with the man who had the space – and all on 40 cigarettes a day. He was the pivot around which Ajax and manager Rinus Michels played total football – a style which the Dutch national squad would embrace in the 1970s. He also shook up the cosy patrician world of Dutch football, revolutionizing the treatment of players. After domestic and international success Cruyff moved on to Barcelona where he inspired the Catalans to win the championship in his first season. After quitting the game and the fags, he went on to coach Ajax and Barcelona, steering the latter to four consecutive league championships and the European Cup in 1992.

Alfredo **di Stefano**

Caps: 8 (Argentina),
31 (Spain)
Goals: 6 (Argentina),
23 (Spain)
Teams: Los Cardales
(youth team)
River Plate (twice)
● 1947
Huracán
Millonarios
● 1951, 52
Barcelona
Real Madrid
● 1956–60
● 1954, 55, 57, 58,
Honours: European Footballer
of the Year (FF):
1957, 59

Born: July 4, 1926
Country: Argentina, Spain
Position: Striker

Alfredo di Stefano was born in a Barracas, a working-class suburb of Buenos Aires. His father played for River Plate and both sons went on to play professional football. Alfredo began with River Plate in 1944, developed on loan at Huracán, and returned to River in 1947 as the finished article. An explosive centre-forward, he combined individual skills with team-organizing abilities. He first came to international notice in the Argentinian team, victors of the 1947 Copa América. When Argentina's players went on strike over pay in 1949, he was bought by Millonarios, the leading team in the non-FIFA Colombian league. On a tour with Millonarios in Spain in 1952 he was spotted by both Barcelona and Real Madrid. Barcelona tried to buy him from River Plate, Real from Millonarios. The Spanish state intervened saying he should play a season with each, but indifferent form at Barcelona saw him transfer to Real. Under di Stefano, Real won four Spanish championships and the first five consecutive European Cups.

▲ European Cup-Winners' Cup ■ Copa América ● Copa Libertadores ○ National League

Eusebio da Silva Ferreira

Born: January 25, 1942
Country: Portugal
Position: Striker
Caps: 64
Goals: 41
Teams: Gruppo Desportico de Maputo
SL Benfica
● 1961, 62
● 1963–65, 67–69, 71–73
Boston Minutemen
Toronto Metros
Croatia
Las Vegas Quicksilver
Monterrey
Honours: European Footballer of the Year (FF): 1965

Eusebio da Silva Ferreira was born in Mozambique, then a Portuguese colony, in 1942. He first travelled to Portugal in 1961 for a trial with Sporting CP. However, it is said that he was snatched off the aeroplane by officials of city rivals SL Benfica for whom he was to play for most of his career. In 13 seasons at SL Benfica, he won nine league championships, the European Cup twice (1961 and 62) and the European Golden Boot twice (1968 and 73). Prior to Mozambiquan independence Eusebio's international career lay with Portugal and he made his debut in 1961, scoring in a defeat against Luxembourg. He was the top scorer at the 1966 World Cup with nine goals, including four against the North Koreans in an amazing comeback – Portugal, 3-0 down after 22 minutes, won the match 5-3 and went on to take fourth place. Not always adequately rewarded for his play, Eusebio played out the twilight of his career in North America.

Diego Maradona

Born: October 30, 1960
Country: Argentina
■ 1986
Position: Striker
Caps: 90
Goals: 34
Teams: Argentinos Juniors
Boca Juniors (twice)
● 1981
Barcelona
Napoli
◆ 1989
● 1987, 1990
Sevilla
Newell's Old Boys
Quilmes
Honours: World Footballer of the Year (WS): 1986
South America,
El Mundo:
1979, 80, 86, 89, 90, 92

A teenage sensation in Argentina in the late 1970s and early 1980s, Diego Maradona was transferred for record-breaking fees to Barcelona (1983) and Napoli (1987). Short and stocky, Maradona possessed an explosive burst of pace, the most exquisite ball control under pressure of any footballer ever. He has also provided the game with some of its finest melodrama. He was sent off for dangerous play at the 1982 World Cup Final, almost single-handedly won the 1986 World Cup for Argentina, and scraped them into the 1990 finals before his ignominious dismissal and ban in 1994. He has been on the comeback trail ever since.

Garrincha (Manoel Francisco dos Santos)

Born: October 28, 1933
Died: January 20, 1983
Country: Brazil
■ 1958, 62
Position: Winger
Caps: 50
Goals: 12
Teams: Pao Grande
Botafogo
Corinthians
Athlético Junior
Flamengo
Red Star Paris

In the pantheon of Brazilian football Garrincha stands just below the hallowed figure of Pele. He was born Manoel Francisco dos Santos (his nickname means 'little bird'). As a child he required repeated corrective surgery on both legs, which were so twisted that it was thought likely that he would never walk. Despite this he proved to be an irresistibly fast, infectious and incisive right winger, making and scoring goals at the very highest levels. His club career was a little chaotic, with spells at many clubs in Brazil, Colombia and France, but at international level he was pivotal in Brazil's 1958 and 1962 World Cup victories. His reputation as a difficult character threatened his place in the 1958 World Cup squad and only a players' deputation led by Nilton Santos persuaded coach Vincente Feola to include him. On the day, he delivered both crosses for Brazil's goals in the 1958 Final, and after Pele's injury in Chile in 1962 he became the driving force of the side. Top scorer in the tournament, he scored twice in both the quarter- and semi-final victories. Injury eventually caught up with him and persistent knee problems forced him to quit the game. He tragically died of alcohol poisoning in 1983.

Stanley Matthews

Born: February 1, 1915
Died: February 23, 2000
Country: England
Position: Winger
Caps: 54
Teams: Stoke City
Blackpool
Honours: European Footballer of the Year (FF): 1956

Stanley Matthews never won a league championship, in a career as a professional footballer that spanned 33 years. Nor can he claim a single international honour from his 54 caps. Two second division titles with Stoke City and a single FA Cup triumph with Blackpool are his lot, yet it is unquestionable that he should be included in this company. Although he had a spell with Blackpool in mid-career, Matthews played most of his football at Stoke, making his professional debut in March 1932 and playing his final game in February 1965. His international career was similarly long; he played his last England game at the age of 42. He quickly acquired the nickname 'The Wizard of the Dribble' and was the leading English player of his era. Playing outside-right, his speed, ball control, capacity for moves, feints and changes of pace, opened up the tightest of defences. But Stoke simply could not mount a challenge on the league. His moment came with Blackpool in 1953 in what has since become known as the Matthews Final. Blackpool were 3-1 down to Bolton Wanderers until a blizzard of extraordinary wing play from Matthews successively carved the Bolton defence open – and Blackpool won it 4-3. Matthews was never booked and never sent off in his entire career.

Key ■ World Cup ▲ World Club Cup ■ European Championships ● European Cup/Champions League ◆ UEFA Cup

Giuseppe **Meazza**

Born: August 23, 1910
Died: August 21, 1979
Country: Italy
■ 1934, 38
Position: Striker
Caps: 53
Goals: 33
Teams: Internazionale
● 1930, 38
Milan
Juventus
Varese
Atalanta

Giuseppe Meazza was the leading striker of the first decade of Italian professional football and one of only two players who played in both of Italy's World Cup victories in 1934 and 1938 (the other was Giovanni Ferrari). Born in Milan, Meazza made his debut with Internazionale at the age of 17 and in his first full season with the club (1928–29) he was the top scorer with 33 goals. In his debut match with the national squad he scored twice as Italy beat Switzerland 4-2, the first of ten goals in his first year of international football and of the 33 goals in total he scored for Italy. During the late 1930s, Meazza found himself at odds with the hierarchy at Internazionale, which was by then run by Fascist Party representative Ferdinando Pozzani. After a decade with the club he crossed the city to rivals Milan where he stayed for four seasons before playing out the end of his career at Juventus, Varese and Atalanta. He was joint coach of the Italian national squad for couple of years in the 1950s. As one of the few players to have played for both Milanese giants, the San Siro was renamed in his honour after his death in 1979.

Gerd **Müller**

Born: November 3, 1945
Country: Germany
■ 1974
■ 1972
Position: Striker
Caps: 62
Goals: 68
Teams: TSV Nordlingen
Bayern München
● 1974–76
▲ 1967
● 1969, 72–74
Fort Lauderdale Strikers
Honours: European Footballer of the Year: 1970

Gerd Müller joined Bayern München in 1964. Coach Zlatko Cajkovski is reputed to have said 'I'm not putting that little elephant in among my string of thoroughbreds.' But his short, stocky centre-forward proved to be the most prolific goalscorer in German football history. Nicknamed 'Der Bomber', Müller was the most ruthless goal poacher in the penalty area, and especially the six-yard area, ever; Helmut Schon called him 'my little goalscorer'. With prods, pokes, balls stolen, flicked and dug out of the ground, Müller took every half chance that came his way. In his club career he racked up 365 goals and helped take Bayern from the regional leagues to three successive European Cup victories. At international level, a mere 62 caps yielded him an incredible 68 goals. Some have scored more international goals, but no one comes close to Muller's goals to games ratio. More than that, he could find goals for the very biggest occasion: ten at the 1970 Mexico World Cup, four more for the victorious West German team in 1974, including the winner in the Final against the Netherlands.

Bobby **Moore**

Born: April 21, 1941
Died: February 24, 1993
Country: England
■ 1966
Position: Defender
Caps: 108
Goals: 2
Teams: West Ham United
▲ 1965
Fulham
Herning
San Antonio Thunder
Seattle Sounders
Team America

Born in Barking in Essex, Bobby Moore joined east London's leading club, West Ham United, as an amateur, turning professional in 1958. He stayed at Upton Park for 16 years, playing 544 league matches before moving to Fulham. A long and distinguished club career only brought one FA Cup triumph in 1964 and a European Cup-Winners' Cup medal in 1965, both with West Ham. But it was in his international performances that Moore truly shone. He made his international debut against Peru just before the 1962 World Cup, the first of 108 caps, and missed only ten England games in the following ten years. In 1966, he led England to their greatest international triumph, winning the World Cup on home soil. Prior to the 1970 World Cup, while the England squad was training in Colombia, Moore was falsely accused of stealing jewellery from a shop in Bogotá; diplomatic intervention secured his release from custody. He displayed a characteristic icy calm and composure in the face of what was evidently a false charge. Moore went on to play in a similar fashion in Mexico, where he was acknowledged by no less an authority than Pele as the 'world's greatest defender'.

Pele (Edson Arantes do Nascimento)

Born: October 23, 1940
Country: Brazil
■ 1958, 62, 70
■ 1962, 63
Position: Striker
Caps: 92
Goals: 77
Teams: Bauru (youth team)
Santos
● 1963, 64
● 1959, 63, 64
New York Cosmos
● 1977

Pele is credited with 1,282 goals in 1,365 matches for his two clubs and the national Brazilian team. He was a member of three World Cup-winning squads – 1958, 1962 and 1970. His club career was mainly spent with the São Paulo team Santos, who he inspired to two victories in the Copa Libertadores and the World Club Cup. Yet none of this captures the indelible impression he has left on the game. Born Edson Arantes do Nascimento, he was teased at school with the moniker Pele and fought it, but it stuck. He joined Santos at the age of 15, was in the national squad at 16 and in the World Cup squad at 17. He was capable of scoring and making goals from any position in the final third of the field. His armoury included dipping free kicks, powerful twisting runs and dribbles, languid and deadly flicks and touches and unstoppable headers. Respected and honoured in every corner of the globe, Pele's three years in the US saw football reach its most popular point. In retirement, he has been drawn into the dangerous maw of Brazilian politics. His attempts to reform the cesspool of Brazilian football finances as Minister of Sport have barely scratched the surface of tax evasion and corruption that are eating away at the Brazilian game.

▲ European Cup-Winners' Cup   ■ Copa América   ● Copa Libertadores   ● National League

Michel **Platini**

Born: June 21, 1955
Country: France
■ 1984
Position: Striker
Caps: 72
Goals: 41
Teams: AS Nancy
AS Saint-Etienne
Juventus
● 1985
▲ 1984
◆ 1984, 86
Honours: World Footballer of
the Year (WS):
1984, 85
European Footballer
of the Year: 1983

Michel Platini played much of his career in France with Nancy and St-Etienne, but his greatest years were spent at Juventus (1983–87). Considered by the club to be its greatest player ever, he was top scorer in Italy for three seasons and helped Juventus to two Serie A titles, the European Cup and the European Cup-Winners' Cup. Internationally his influence on the previously weak French national squad was immense, inspiring fantastic performances at the 1982 and 86 World Cups (France made it to the semi-finals in both) as well as victory at the 1984 European Championships in which he was top scorer. After retiring from playing he coached the French national team (but stood down after the 1992 European Championships). He has proved more adept in the intensely political world of football administration, was the director and chief organizer of the 1998 World Cup in France and is set to succeed to the presidency of UEFA.

Peter **Schmeichel**

Born: November 18, 1963
Country: Denmark
■ 1992
Position: Goalkeeper
Teams: Hvidovre BK
Brøndby IF
● 1985, 87, 88, 90, 91
Manchester United
● 1999
● 1993, 94, 96, 97, 99
Sporting CP
● 2000
Aston Villa
Manchester City

Peter Schmeichel is the most accomplished and influential goalkeeper of his generation. In Sweden, 1991, he came to the attention of Manchester United, who bought him from Brøndby IF for a mere £750,000. During the next eight seasons he helped the club to win five English league championships, three FA Cups and a European Cup. Schmeichel marshals his defence with an uncommon ferocity and seems able to inspire his teams to victory. His shot-stopping has been brilliant, his capacity to make himself huge in a striker's eyes legendary and his power and bravery in the air without match. He also scores goals – most famously in a 1995 UEFA Cup tie for Manchester United against Rotor Volgograd. Schmeichel's charismatic power was also evident in inspiring the Danish team to victory in the 1992 European Championships and in his first seasons at Sporting CP in Lisbon, when the sleeping giants of Portuguese football finally regained its crown.

Ferenc **Puskas**

Born: April 2, 1927
Country: Hungary, Spain
Position: Striker
Caps: 84 (Hungary),
4 (Spain)
Goals: 83 (Hungary)
Teams: Kispest
Honvéd
● 1950, 52, 54, 55
Real Madrid
● 1959, 60, 66
● 1961–65

Ferenc Puskas remains the best remembered of the Magical Magyars – the revolutionary and scintillating Hungarian team of the early 1950s. Born into a footballing family, he joined Budapest club Kispest at the age of 16 and was a member of the international squad at 18. Puskas began as an immensely quick and agile inside-left, and then became the attacking edge of Hungary's innovative forward play – a deep-lying centre-forward. With Puskas, Hungary won the 1952 Olympics and thrashed England on home soil for the first time in the immortal 6-3 win at Wembley in 1953, only to lose to West Germany in the 1954 World Cup Final. In 1956, Honvéd were on tour in Western Europe when the Hungarian Uprising broke out. Puskas decided to stay in Western Europe and was welcomed at Real Madrid. Paired with di Stefano, Puskas' career blossomed; four-time top scorer in the Spanish league, and three-time European Cup winner, he eventually received Spanish citizenship and a place in the national squad at the 1962 World Cup. He retired in 1966 and took up coaching, peaking when he took unfancied Panathinaikos to the 1971 European Cup Final.

Lev **Yashin**

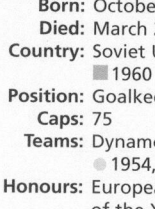

Born: October 22, 1929
Died: March 20, 1990
Country: Soviet Union
■ 1960
Position: Goalkeeper
Caps: 75
Teams: Dynamo Moskva
● 1954, 55, 57, 59, 63
Honours: European Footballer
of the Year (FF): 1963

Lev Yashin remains the only goalkeeper to receive the prestigious European Footballer of the Year award and is considered to be the greatest goalkeeper of the modern era. During his career he is reputed to have kept a clean sheet in 270 games and to have saved over 150 penalties. His sporting life began without a commitment to football; Yashin split his time between playing ice hockey and playing football for Dynamo Moskva, only choosing football as a full-time career in 1953 when Dynamo's first-team goalkeeper fell injured. A year later he made his international debut, and in 1956 he played in the Soviet side that won the Olympics tournament. Known as the 'Black Panther' because of his favoured black strip, he was renowned for his agility and the stunning speed of his reactions. A career of 22 seasons spent entirely with Dynamo Moskva brought five Soviet championship titles and appearances at three World Cup tournaments. In retirement, Yashin ran the Soviet Ministry of Sport's football department and was awarded the Order of Lenin by his country.

Key ■ World Cup ▲ World Club Cup ■ European Championships ● European Cup/Champions League ◆ UEFA Cup

Zinedine **Zidane**

Born: June 23,1972
Country: France
■ 1998
■ 2000
Position: Midfielder
Teams: Bordeaux
Juventus
● 1997, 98
Real Madrid
● 2002
▲ 2003
● 2003
Honours: World Footballer of the
Year (WS): 1998
World Footballer of the
Year (FIFA): 1998, 2000
European Footballer
of the Year: 1998

Zinedine Zidane was the midfield controller at the heart of France's fantastically successful team of the late 1990s and is probably the most technically accomplished player of his generation. Born of Algerian parents in Marseille, he began his career with Cannes before joining Bordeaux in 1992. In 1996, he was snapped up by Italian giants Juventus. Two Italian league championships followed before his decisive play in both the 1998 World Cup and Euro 2000. In 1998, he missed a game after receiving a red card in a match against Saudi Arabia. Returning for the quarter-finals, his playmaking was decisive in beating Italy and Croatia. Against Brazil in the Final, two headed goals won the cup for France. At Euro 2000, a dozen moments of the sublimest skill, flicks, pace and vision gave France the edge against increasingly tough opponents. In the summer of 2001, he transferred to Real Madrid for the world record sum of £45.8 million and helped them to success in the 2002 Champions League Final by scoring the winning goal.

Top 10 Managers

COMPILING A LIST of the ten greatest managers is an impossible task and, inevitably, omissions are many. For example, Brian Clough won two European Cups with a tiny budget at Nottingham Forest, Mario Zagallo has had a hand in multiple World Cup victories for Brazil, while Ottmar Hitzfeld's reign at Borussia Dortmund and Bayern München are reaping rewards that must place him close to the top. In the end, this list draws on a number of different reasons for its inclusions.

Several of them have delivered the goods in some of the toughest leagues in the world. Bela Guttman alone has won premier club tournaments in the two major footballing continents (Europe and Latin America). Herbert Chapman and Vittorio Pozzo invented the role of the modern football manager, while Herrera and Michels can all claim significant roles in the invention of new tactics and modes of play; and for sheer personality Bill Shankly is the unquestionable champion.

Herbert **Chapman**

Born: January 19, 1878
Died: January 6, 1934
Nationality: British (England)
Teams: Northampton Town
Leeds City
Huddersfield Town
● 1924, 25
Arsenal
● 1931, 33

Herbert Chapman was the first great football manager, the man who shaped and defined the role for a generation. A long playing career began at the turn of the 19th century. He turned professional in 1901 with Northampton Town before moving to Notts County and Tottenham. In 1907, he went into management with Northampton then moved north in 1912 to become club secretary at the now defunct Leeds City. Under Chapman, the team recorded its best-ever league performances. In 1919, the club was expelled from the Football League for making illegal wartime payments to players and Chapman was temporarily banned. He returned to management in 1921 with Huddersfield and stormed to two league titles. In 1925, he arrived at Arsenal where he fashioned the greatest English team of the inter-war era. On the field he innovated the game, creating the W-M formation of play, calling for floodlit games, white balls and numbered shirts. Off the field he took charge of coaching, tactics and local politics in a way no manager had combined before. He even persuaded the local council to rename the nearest tube stop Arsenal. He died mid-season in 1934 as Arsenal set course for a third league title under him.

Sir Alex **Ferguson**

Born: December 31, 1941
Nationality: British (Scotland)
Teams: Scotland
East Stirlingshire
St Mirren
Aberdeen
▲ 1983
● 1980, 84, 85
Manchester United
▲ 1999
● 1999
▲ 1991
● 1992, 94, 96,
97, 99–2001

Sir Alex Ferguson comes from the extraordinary seam of Scottish working-class culture that has yielded teams, players and managers of authority, grit and canniness. After a playing career with Dunfermline, Queen's Park and Glasgow Rangers he entered management with East Stirlingshire and St Mirren. But it was at Aberdeen that he made his mark. With minimal resources the Dons broke the hegemony of the Old Firm in Scottish football winning three league titles, three Scottish cups and the European Cup-Winners' Cup between 1980 and 1985. An unsuccessful stint as Scotland manager at the 1986 World Cup was followed by his appointment at Manchester United. After a slow start, Ferguson began to fashion the most comprehensive domination of the English league that any club has achieved — seven out of nine Premiership titles, including two doubles and a treble in 1999 with victory in the European Cup. Ferguson's teams have acquired an enormous psychological resilience and the capacity to win games from behind, while he is also the most successful British manager to elevate the manipulation of the sporting media to an art form.

▲ European Cup-Winners' Cup   ■ Copa América   ● Copa Libertadores   ○ National League

Bela **Guttman**

Born: 1900
Died: 1981
Nationality: Hungarian
Teams: Enschede
Újpest
● 1939
Dynamo Bucharest
Vasa Budapest
Honvéd
Padova, Triestina
Milan
● 1955
FC Porto
● 1959
SL Benfica
● 1961, 62
● 1960, 61, 63
Peñarol
▲ 1961
● 1961
● 1962, 64
Servette
Panathinaikos
FK Austria

Bela Guttman is the only manager to have won the top club trophy in both Europe and Latin America. He played as an amateur for MTK in Budapest and Hakoah in Vienna, as well as for the Hungarian Olympic team of 1924. Managerial posts and trophies followed at Enschede in Holland, Újpest Dosza in Hungary, Dinamo Bucharest in Romania and Honvéd in Hungary. His greatest successes include SL Benfica winning the 1961 European Cup, a Serie A title with Milan, and Peñarol, Uruguay, winning the national league and the Copa Libertadores.

Rinus **Michels**

Born: February 2, 1928
Nationality: Dutch
Teams: Netherlands
■ 1988
Ajax
● 1971
● 1966, 67, 68, 70
Barcelona
● 1974
Los Angeles Aztecs
1. FC Köln
Bayer Leverkusen

Rinus Michels began his career in the amateur era of Dutch football, playing as striker for the Netherlands national team. In 1965, he took control at Ajax, then struggling against relegation and turned the team around. 'Iron Rinus' was legendary for his insistence on discipline, rigour and constant improvement. He is known to have stood guard by hotel lifts to prevent late-night drinking by his players and his mind games in training could be cruel, but invariably effective. In the next six years Ajax won four Dutch league titles and three Dutch Cups, culminating in the first of Ajax's three European Cup victories in 1971. But his legacy is far greater than that. Under his lead, the career of Johan Cruyff was nurtured and developed and with it the notion of total football was elaborated at Ajax and intertwined with it. Michels proved himself equally adept at international level, taking the national team to the World Cup Final in 1974 and winning the 1988 European Championships. He has had the rare talents required to mould coherent fluid teams from the potentially explosive, unstable mix of talent, petulance and individualism that characterizes Dutch football.

Helenio **Herrera**

Born: April 17, 1917
Died: November 9, 1997
Nationality: Argentinian
Teams: Italy
Spain
Putuex
Red Star 93
Atlético Madrid
● 1950, 51
Malaga
Valladolid
Sevilla
Barcelona
◆ 1960
● 1959
Internazionale
▲ 1964, 65
● 1964, 65
● 1963, 65, 66
Roma

Helenio Herrera is among the most travelled and most successful of football coaches. Born in Argentina and raised in Morocco, he began a playing career in France. In the late 1940s, he coached a succession of top French teams before moving to Spain where four spells with both Atlético Madrid and Barcelona yielded league championships. Herrera's Spanish sides were aggressive and attacking but this style proved ineffective when he arrived at Internazionale in the early 1960s. Here, he reinvented and perfected the *catenaccio* (meaning a bolt or a padlock in Italian) system of defence – using a sweeper and man-to-man marking among the back four – combined with lethal counterattacking. Il Grande Inter won two European Cups and two World Club Cups under him as well as three league titles.

Bob **Paisley**

Born: January 21, 1919
Died: February 14, 1996
Nationality: British (England)
Teams: Liverpool
● 1977, 78, 81
◆ 1976
● 1976, 77,
79, 80, 82, 83

Bob Paisley's football career was almost entirely spent with Liverpool. A player with the club in the late 1940s, he joined the coaching team in 1954 and was a key member of Shankly's staff before taking over as manager in 1974. Under him, Liverpool played their greatest football and achieved the greatest triumphs: six English league titles and three European Cup wins. In contrast to his predecessor, Paisley appeared uncommunicative and unexcitable, and always cultivated an image of working-class understatement and simplicity. But as Graeme Souness, no shrinking violet himself, said of his time at Liverpool, '...let me tell you, he ruled Anfield with a rod of iron. He was a commanding man and there were few who dared mess around with him.' Anecdotal tales of his love of carpet slippers and a morning routine of tea at the local garage and picking horses from the paper have hidden the workings of the keenest of footballing brains. On the pitch he insisted that the short, swift passing game, the search for space and the application of intelligence were the route to victory. Off the pitch Paisley's attention to detail, accumulation of information and astonishingly accurate diagnosis of player injuries helped mould and sustain the club during its most successful period.

Key   ■ World Cup   ▲ World Club Cup   ■ European Championships   ● European Cup/Champions League   ◆ UEFA Cup

Vittorio **Pozzo**

Born: March 2, 1886
Died: December 21, 1968
Nationality: Italian
Teams: Torino
Italy
■ 1934, 38

Vittorio Pozzo brought the art of football management to Italy, defining the role for a generation. He learned his football in England where he had come to study before the First World War, though it seems he studied Manchester United more than anything else. On his return to Italy, he played a major part in the split between Juventus and a new club Torino. He became a regular part of the Torino set-up, as well as coaching the Italian team in the 1912 Olympic Games. But it was in the professional era of Italian football and at international level that Pozzo made his biggest mark. Appointed full-time national team coach in 1929, he took Italy to two successive World Cup victories in 1934 on home soil and in France in 1938. 'Il Vecchio Maestro', as he became known, was welcomed on his return to Turin with the victorious team as a national hero. To top this off, the Azzurri had also won the Olympic gold medal at the 1936 Olympics in Berlin with a team of students, and Pozzo was the coach. He remains the only European manager to win two World Cups and his record of 63 victories in 95 matches in 19 years makes him the most successful Italian international manager ever. He retired in 1948 to become a journalist on *La Stampa* for whom he reported on many Italian international matches.

Jock **Stein**

Born: October 5, 1923
Died: November 10, 1985
Nationality: British (Scotland)
Teams: Scotland
Dunfermline Athletic
Hibernian
Celtic
● 1967
● 1966–74, 77
Leeds United

Jock Stein began his football career with Scottish club Albion Rovers in the late 1940s. He soon transferred to Celtic, became captain, and led the team to a league and cup double in 1954, after which injury forced his early retirement from the game. He became Celtic's assistant coach and then moved to Dunfermline Athletic as manager in 1960, leading them to a surprise victory in the 1961 Scottish FA Cup. A short period at Hibernian followed, before his return to Celtic as manager in 1964. Stein's Celtic team won an extraordinary nine league championship titles between 1966 and 74, not to mention nine Scottish FA Cups and six League Cups. Moreover, he led Celtic to their greatest moment of all – victory in the 1967 European Cup Final against Internazionale in Lisbon. A brief and unhappy spell as manager of Leeds United was followed by his appointment as manager of the Scottish national squad, steering them successfully to both the 1982 and 1986 World Cup finals tournaments. He died in 1985, struck down by a heart attack in the closing minutes of the Scotland v Wales World Cup qualifying match.

Bill **Shankly**

Born: September 2, 1913
Died: September 29, 1981
Nationality: British (Scotland)
Teams: Grimsby Town
Workington
Huddersfield Town
Liverpool
◆ 1973
● 1964, 66, 73

Bill Shankly's playing career took him to Carlisle, Preston and five Scottish caps before beginning a long march through the lower echelons of English football league management. Spells with Grimsby, Workington and Huddersfield brought him to Liverpool in 1959 – a great club languishing in the Second Division. Shankly remained at Liverpool until 1974, winning three league titles, two FA Cups and the UEFA Cup. However, his legendary status derives from his extraordinary charisma, his dry wit, and the establishment of Liverpool FC as an institution that would reach the very heights of global football in the late 1970s and early 1980s. Shankly's powers of motivation drew on all these things – legend has him demanding the team throw their shirts on the floor before the match and ordering them to take a bath as they wouldn't be needed... 'I'll throw these shirts out on the field and the shirts will beat Ipswich themselves'; opponents were derided as having 'hearts as big as a caraway seed'; and his own team members were deliberately given the wrong meal before a match to put them in a suitably angry mood for the occasion. Shankly is honoured at Anfield, having the main gates named after him that bear the legend 'You'll never walk alone'.

Giovanni **Trapattoni**

Born: March 17, 1939
Nationality: Italian
Teams: Milan
▲ 1973
Juventus
▲ 1985
● 1985
◆ 1977
▲ 1984
● 1977, 78, 81, 82, 84, 86
Internazionale
◆ 1991
● 1989
Bayern München
● 1997
Cagliari
Fiorentina
Italy

Trapattoni's football career began in the late 1950s as wing-half for Milan with whom he won two European Cups (1963 and 69). After retiring from playing, he became Milan's youth coach and for a time was the caretaker manager of their first team, winning the 1973 Cup-Winners' Cup. In 1976, he moved to Juventus where a decade in charge brought six Italian championships, one each of the three European club competitions, the European Super Cup and the World Club Cup. Like all of his teams Juventus was characterized by unhurried, solid defence and lethal counter-attacking potential. His squad provided the steely backbone of the Italian World Cup winning side in 1982. In the excruciating hothouse pressure of Italian football, Trapattoni serenely reigns as the most successful coach. A spell at Internazionale in the 1980s saw another Serie A title as well as the UEFA Cup before a period at Bayern München in the mid-90s saw him become the first foreign coach to win a Bundesliga title. He coached Italy at the 2002 World Cup.

▲ European Cup-Winners' Cup　　■ Copa América　　● Copa Libertadores　　○ National League

TOP 10 MANAGERS

World Players of the Year

THE SEASON IN REVIEW 2002

RONALDO MAY HAVE SPENT most of the season recovering from injury and sitting on Inter's bench, but he finally stepped up to the plate in Korea/Japan. His performance at the 2002 World Cup, and above all his two goals in the Final, sealed the case for the voters as he won both the FIFA World Player of the Year and *France Football's* European Player of the Year awards. Competition was fierce however, as a case was made for Oliver Kahn, whose pugnacious and determined goalkeeping took Germany to the same Final; and for the surging play of Roberto Carlos who was central to both Brazil's World Cup run and to Real Madrid's European Champions League triumph. In the same Final, Zinedine Zidane could lay claim to the individual game and the goal of the season, but an awful injury-ridden World Cup put him out of the running. The consistency of Bayer Leverkusen's Michael Ballack was a tremendous achievement but yielded defeat in every domestic and international tournament in which he played.

In South America, a record-breaking tally of goals for the Paraguayan Jose Cardozo saw the first player from a Mexican side, Toluca, to be made Player of the Year. Mia Hamm confirmed her and America's dominance of women's football claiming the FIFA Women's World Player of the Year by some distance.

Redemption at last: Ronaldo finally consigns his bizarre trance-like performance at the 1998 World Cup Final to history, as Brazil triumph over Germany in Yokohama.

World Footballer of the Year (FIFA)

YEAR	PLAYER	CLUB	NATIONALITY
1991	Lothar Matthäus	Internazionale	German
1992	Marco van Basten	Milan	Dutch
1993	Roberto Baggio	Juventus	Italian
1994	Romario	Barcelona	Brazilian
1995	George Weah	Milan	Liberian
1996	Ronaldo	PSV/Barcelona	Brazilian
1997	Ronaldo	Barcelona/Inter	Brazilian
1998	Zinedine Zidane	Juventus	French
1999	Rivaldo	Barcelona	Brazilian
2000	Zinedine Zidane	Juventus	French
2001	Luis Figo	Real Madrid	Portuguese
2002	Ronaldo	Real Madrid	Brazilian

Elected by FIFA.

European Player of the Year

YEAR	PLAYER	CLUB	NATIONALITY
1956	Stanley Matthews	Stoke City	English
1957	Alfredo di Stefano	Real Madrid	Spanish
1958	Raymond Kopa	Real Madrid	French
1959	Alfredo di Stefano	Real Madrid	Spanish
1960	Luis Suárez	Barcelona	Spanish
1961	Omar Sivori	Juventus	Italian
1962	Josef Masopust	Dukla Praha	Czech
1963	Lev Yashin	Dinamo Moskva	Soviet
1964	Denis Law	Manchester United	Scottish
1965	Eusébio	SL Benfica	Portuguese
1966	Bobby Charlton	Manchester United	English
1967	Florian Albert	Ferencváros	Hungarian
1968	George Best	Manchester United	Northern Irish
1969	Gianni Rivera	Milan	Italian
1970	Gerd Müller	Bayern München	German
1971	Johan Cruyff	Ajax	Dutch
1972	Franz Beckenbauer	Bayern München	German
1973	Johan Cruyff	Ajax	Dutch
1974	Johan Cruyff	Ajax	Dutch
1975	Oleg Blokhin	Dynamo Kyiv	Soviet
1976	Franz Beckenbauer	Bayern München	German
1977	Allan Simonsen	Borussia Mönchengladbach	Danish
1978	Kevin Keegan	Hamburger SV	English
1979	Kevin Keegan	Hamburger SV	English
1980	Karl-Heinz Rummenigge	Bayern München	German
1981	Karl-Heinz Rummenigge	Bayern München	German
1982	Paolo Rossi	Juventus	Italian
1983	Michel Platini	Juventus	French
1984	Michel Platini	Juventus	French
1985	Michel Platini	Juventus	French
1986	Igor Belanov	Dynamo Kyiv	Soviet
1987	Ruud Gullit	Milan	Dutch
1988	Marco van Basten	Milan	Dutch
1989	Marco van Basten	Milan	Dutch
1990	Lothar Matthäus	Internazionale	German
1991	Jean-Pierre Papin	Olympique Marseille	French
1992	Marco van Basten	Milan	Dutch
1993	Roberto Baggio	Juventus	Italian
1994	Hristo Stoichkov	Barcelona	Bulgarian
1995	George Weah	Milan	Liberian
1996	Matthias Sammer	Borussia Dortmund	German
1997	Ronaldo	Barcelona	Brazilian
1998	Zinedine Zidane	Juventus	French
1999	Rivaldo	Barcelona	Brazilian
2000	Luis Figo	Barcelona	Portuguese
2001	Michael Owen	Liverpool	English
2002	Ronaldo	Real Madrid	Brazilian

Elected by *France Football* magazine.

South American Footballer of the Year

YEAR	PLAYER	CLUB	NATIONALITY
1971	Tostão*	Cruzeiro	Brazilian
1972	Teofilio Cubillas*	Alianza Lima	Peruvian
1973	Pele*	Santos	Brazilian
1974	Elias Figueroa*	Internacional	Chilean
1975	Elias Figueroa*	Internacional	Chilean
1976	Elias Figueroa*	Internacional	Chilean
1977	Zico*	Flamengo	Brazilian
1978	Mario Kempes*	Valencia	Argentinian
1979	Diego Maradona*	Argentinos Juniors	Argentinian
1980	Diego Maradona*	Boca Juniors	Argentinian
1981	Zico*	Flamengo	Brazilian
1982	Zico*	Flamengo	Brazilian
1983	Socrates*	Corinthians	Brazilian
1984	Enzo Francescoli*	River Plate	Uruguayan
1985	Romero*	Fluminense	Paraguayan
1986	Ruben Paz*	Racing Club	Uruguayan
1986	Antonio Alzamendi*	River Plate	Uruguayan
1987	Diego Maradona*	Napoli	Argentinian
1987	Carlos Valderrama	Deportivo Cali	Colombian
1988	Diego Maradona*	Napoli	Argentinian
1988	Ruben Paz	Racing Club	Uruguayan
1989	Bebeto*	Vasco da Gama	Brazilian
1989	Gabriel Batistuta	Boca Juniors/Fiorentina	Argentinian
1990	Diego Maradona*	Sevilla	Argentinian
1990	Raul Amarilla	Olimpia	Paraguayan
1991	Oscar Ruggeri	Vélez Sarsfield	Argentinian
1992	Rai	São Paulo	Brazilian
1993	Carlos Valderrama	Atlético Júnior	Colombian
1994	Cafu	São Paulo	Brazilian
1995	Enzo Francescoli	River Plate	Uruguayan
1996	Jose Luis Chilavert	Vélez Sarsfield	Paraguayan
1997	Marcelo Salas	River Plate	Chilean
1998	Martin Palermo	Boca Juniors	Argentinian
1999	Javier Saviola	River Plate	Argentinian
2000	Romario	Vasco da Gama	Brazilian
2001	Juan Román Riquelme	Boca Juniors	Argentinian
2002	Jose Cardozo	Toluca	Paraguayan

* Elected by *El Mundo*, Caracas; all others elected by *El Pais*, Montevideo.

Though he did not win the major prize, Oliver Kahn was voted Best European Goalkeeper by France Football *and* Top Goalkeeper at the World Cup by FIFA.

Jose Cardozo's goals took tiny provincial team Toluca to the top of the Mexican football tree in 2002.

Mia Hamm, striker for Washington Freedom and the USA national team, is without doubt the outstanding woman player of her generation.

Index

INDEX

INDEX

INDEX

INDEX

ACKNOWLEDGEMENTS

THANKS TO:
Sarah Bond for love, support and telling me to make it happen.
Andy Jones for inspiration. Johnny Acton, Barbara Wyllie and Sophie Woodward for research and Johnny for endless conversation and discussion.
Bob Bickerton for truly the most extraordinary knowledge of football colours one could imagine. Eric Weil for invaluable assistance with Latin America.
Soccer Investor for letting me wander through their library and illuminating me every Wednesday.
Historians, press officers, information officers, librarians, statisticians, archivists at national and regional FAs, leagues and clubs,
as well as hundreds and hundreds of fans' websites of so many clubs that I don't even know where to start.
Thanks also for help with pictures and facts to Agustín Beltrame, Patricia Quijano Dark, Svetlana N. Drazhnikova, David Litterer, Jen Little, Tim Maitland,
Emmanuel Maradas, Olexi Scherbak, Sergey Ukladov. For invaluable correspondence and corrections thanks to Ewen Anderson, Paul Craddock,
Matty of the West Hill Wasps, David Moore, Ted Ring, Jonnie Robinson and Iain Smith. Deepest apologies to our brilliant Greek correspondent
whose details we have mislaid – please get in touch again.

BIBLIOGRAPHY

WEBSITES
www.fifa.com
www.rsssf.com
www.transfermarkets.co.uk
www.uefa.com
www.worldstadiums.com

YEARBOOKS AND ENCYCLOPEDIAS
Football Asia, Kuala Lumpur, Asian Football Confederation, annual.
Ballard J. and Suff P., **The Dictionary of Football**, Boxtree, Basingstoke, 1999.
Creswell P. and Evans S., **European Football: A Fan's Handbook**, Rough Guide, London, 1998.
Deloitte and Touche Annual Review of Football Finance, Manchester, annual.
Il Calcio Italiano Analisi Economico, Deloitte and Touche, Milan, annual.
Hammond M. (ed.), **The European Football Yearbook**, Sports Projects, Birmingham, annual.
Jelinek R. and Tomes J., **Prvni Fotbalovy Atlas Sveta**, Inforkart, Prague, 2000.
Oliver G., **The Guinness Book of World Soccer**, 2nd Edition, Guinness, Enfield, 1995.
Presti S. (ed.), **Annuario del Calcio Mondiale**, SET, Torino, annual.
Radnedge K., **The Complete Encyclopedia of Football**, Carlton Books, London, 1999.
Ricci F. (ed.), **Pro-Sports African Football Yearbook**, Fillipo Maria Ricci, Rome, annual.
Rollin J., **The Rothmans Football Yearbook**, Headline Books, London, annual.

FA Premier League National Fan Survey, Sir Norman Chester Centre for Football Research, Leicester, annual survey.
Van Hoof S., Parr M., Yamenetti C., **The North and Latin American Football Guide**, Heart Books, Rijmenam, annual.

MAGAZINES AND NEWSPAPERS
African Football, AS, A Bola, Calcio 2000, Don Balon, L'Equipe, Football Asia, France Football, Gazetta dello Sport, Guido Sportivo, Kicker, Lance, Marca, Placar, Soccer Analyst, Soccer Investor, Voetbal International, When Saturday Comes, World Soccer. The Daily Telegraph, The Financial Times, The Independent.

OVERVIEWS, GLOBAL HISTORIES, COLLECTIONS
Armstrong G. and Giullianoti R. (eds.), **Entering the Field: New Perspectives on World Football**, Berg, Oxford, 1997.
Armstrong G. and Giullianoti R. (eds.), **Football Cultures and Indentities**, Macmillan, Basingstoke, 1998.
Armstrong G. and Giullianoti R. (eds.), **Fear and Loathing in World Football**, Berg, Oxford, 2001.
Finn G. and Giullianoti R. (eds.), **Football Cultures: Local Contest, Global Visions**, Cass, London, 2000.
Giulianotti R., **Football: A Sociology of the Global Game**, Polity Press, Cambridge, 1999.

Glanville B., **The Story of the World Cup**, Faber, London, 2001.
Inglis S., **The Football Grounds of England and Wales**, Willow, London, 1983.
Inglis S,. **The Football Grounds of Europe**, Willow, London, 1990.
Inglis S., **Sightlines: A Stadium Odyssey**, Yellow Jersey, London, 2000.
Kuper S., **Football Against the Enemy**, Orion, London, 1994.
Murray B., **The World's Game: A History of Soccer**, University of Illinois Press, Urbana, 1994.
Sugden J. and Tomlinson A., **Who Rules the People's Game? FIFA and the contest for World Football**, Polity Press, Cambridge, 1998.
Sugden J. and Tomlinson A., **Hosts and Champions: Soccer Cultures, National Identities and the USA World Cup**, Arena, Aldershot, 1994.
Walvin J., **The People's Game: The History of Football Revisited**, Mainstream, London, 1994.

BRAZIL
Bellos A., **Futbol: The Brazillian Way of Life**, Bloomsbury, London, 2002.
Lever J., **Soccer Madness**, University of Chicago Press, Chicago, 1983.

FRANCE
Ruhn C. (ed.), **Le Foot: The Legends of French Football**, Abacus, London, 2000.
Holt R., **Sport and Society in Modern France**, Macmillan, Basingstoke, 1981.

ITALY
Manna A. and Gibbs M., **The Day Italian Football Died**, Breedon Books, Derby, 2000.
Parks T., **A Season with Verona**, Secker and Warburg, London, 2002.

JAPAN
Birchall J., **Ultra Nippon: How Japan Reinvented Football**, Headline, London, 2000.
Moffet S., **Japanese Rules: Why Japan Needed Football and How it Got it**, Yellow Jersey, London, 2002.

LATIN AMERICA
Mason T., **Passion of the People? Football in South America**, Verso, London, 1995.
Taylor C., **The Beautiful Game: A Journey Through Latin American Football**, Phoenix, London, 1998.

NETHERLANDS
Winner D., **Brilliant Orange: The Neurotic Genius of Dutch Football**, Bloomsbury, London, 2000.

SPAIN
Burns J., **Barça, A People's Passion**, Bloomsbury, London, 1999.
Hall P., **Morbo: The Story of Spanish Football**, When Saturday Comes, London, 2001.

USSR
Edleman R., **Serious Fun: A History of Spectator Sports in the Soviet Union**, Oxford University Press, Oxford, 1993.

PICTURE CREDITS

(t=top, b=bottom, l=left, c=centre, m=middle, r=right)

All pictures supplied by **EMPICS**, except the following:
Action Images 35b, 57, 63, 95t, 112, 123c, 141, 276, 483, 501b, 510t, 512br; **African Soccer Magazine** 407, 411, 418, 419, 422, 423, 426, 428, 430, 432, 434, 435t & b, 436; **AFP** 408, 409cr & bl; **Agence Shot, Tokyo** 459 (all), 461r; **Ancient Art & Architecture Collection Ltd** 24bl; **Associated Press** 6t & b, 59cr, 140t, 187t, 210, 281tr, 318b, 320b, 321tm, 332c & b, 333bl, 345tl, 361tr & cr, 399tl & tr, 409tr, 471t, 476; **Bridgeman Art Library** 24t; **Clarín, Buenos Aires** 379br, 380 (all), 381tl & tr, 389 (both), 508; **Digital Sports Archive** (John Todd) 475t; **Edifice** (photo by Doroto Boisot) 241; **EPA** 162t, 186b,191, 280r, 281bl, 282 (both), 283r; **Mary Evans**

Picture Library 25t; **FIFA Football Museum** 24br, 25m, bl, bc & br; **Football Federation** 441; **Getty Images** 26, 27, 34tl, tc, tr, mr, bl & bc, 35tl & tc, 46, 55l, 97, 164, 184bl, 188b, 206, 224, 227, 238r, 242l, 262t & bl, 264b, 512tl, 513br, 517tl; **ITAR-TASS Photo Agency** 319tl, 320t, 321tl tr & cl, 324bl; **Paul Joannou** 105b; **Vikas Khot** 452; **Manchester Evening News** 103m; **Tony Matthews** 95b; **National Army Museum**, London 443; **National Soccer Hall of Fame** 472 (courtesy Colin Jose and David Litterer); **Offside** 359; **Pics United**, Eindhoven 155t, 161tl & br, 167b, 170, 171, 173; **Pitch Photos** 454b, 455cl & b, 457; **Danilo Pizarro**, El Tiempo, Bogotá 350cl, 351r & br, 355l; **Press Association** 409tr; **Reuters** 7tl & t, 51, 55r, 59br & bl, 67tr, 70bl, 77cl & cr, 99tr & b, 111tr, 160br, 181bl & br, 190, 202tr, 203tr, 204b, 205tr & b, 217, 232t, 234t & br, 236t, 237tl & br, 248r, 250b, 254t, 256t, 258t & b, 259cr

& b, 268, 280l, 283l, 301bl, 309tr & mb, 318t, 319tr, bl & br, 321bl & br, 331tl, 332t, 333tl, bm & br, 339, 340, 341, 344, 345cl, cr & b, 350cr, 381bl & br, 351bl, 360, 361br, 362b, 363 (all), 370 (both), 374 (both), 378 (both), 379t & bl, 398, 399 bl & br, 403, 440, 441tl, tr & cr, 454, 455tl, tr & cr, 458 (both), 471c, bl & br, 477tc, tr & b, 480 (all), 481t & br, 486, 519bl; **Rex Features** 167t, 324, 355r, 484; **South American Pictures** 366l, 368 (both), 384, 385, 386t, 400; **Sporting Pictures (UK) Ltd** 218, 246; **Derek Stewart** 128; **Juha Tamminen** 362c; **Topham Picturepoint** 336; **WSG Asia Ltd** 441cl, cr & bl, 446, 447, 449; **Xinhua News Agency, Beijing** 441br. Picture on page 162 taken from *Brilliant Orange*, David Winner, Bloomsbury, 2000. Pictures on pages 260 and 261 taken from *The Day Italian Football Died*, Alexandra Manna & Mike Gibbs, Breedon Books, 2000.